Solve with a Spreadsheet

Booth, Cleary, and Drake provide step-by-step instructions solving problems in spreadsheet software.

USING A SPREADSHEET TO SOLVE FOR THE FUTURE VALUE

We can use the FV function in Excel to calculate the future value:

$$= FV(RATE, NPER, PMT, PV, type)$$

where RATE = interest rate (expressed as a decimal)
  NPER = number of periods
  PMT = the payment amount, which is zero is in this case
  PV = present value
  type = 0 if it is an ordinary annuity, 1 if it is annuity due.[7]

Note the key difference between the financial calculator function and the spreadsheet function: The interest rate is in decimal form in the spreadsheet, but not with the financial calculator. If we want to determine the future value of $1,000 in five years with 10% interest, we would enter the following in the appropriate cell:

$$=FV(0.10, 5, 0, -1000, 0)$$

This yields 1,610.51.

Another difference between the spreadsheet and the calculator function is that you cannot leave out an element in the spreadsheet function unless it is the optional "type." For example, if the problem does not have a regular payment (that is PMT), and you do not type this in as the third argument in parentheses, the function will interpret the PV you entered as the PMT and the type as the PV, giving you an answer to a completely different problem.

Solve with a Calculator

Booth, Cleary, and Drake provide step-by-step key stroke instructions for various TI and HP calculators.

CALCULATOR TOOLS: COMPOUNDING WITH A FINANCIAL CALCULATOR

When calculating a future value, you have the present value, the interest rate, and the number of periods, and you need to determine the future value. In other words, you have three values, and your task is to solve for the one unknown value. Therefore:

  PV = 1000
  i = 10%
  n = 5

and you need to solve for FV.

The actual keystrokes for common financial calculators are the following:

HP10B	TI BAII	HP12C	TI83/84
1000 +/– PV	1000 +/– PV	1000 CHS PV	Using TVM Solver App:
10 I/YR	10 I/YR	10 i	N = 5
5 N	5 N	5 n	i = 10
FV	FV	FV	PV = –1000
			PMT = 0
			FV = Solve
			P/Y = 1
			C/Y = 1

WileyPLUS

WileyPLUS is a research-based online environment for effective teaching and learning.

WileyPLUS builds students' confidence because it takes the guesswork out of studying by providing students with a clear roadmap:

- what to do
- how to do it
- if they did it right

It offers interactive resources along with a complete digital textbook that help students learn more. With *WileyPLUS*, students take more initiative so you'll have greater impact on their achievement in the classroom and beyond.

WileyPLUS

ALL THE HELP, RESOURCES, AND PERSONAL SUPPORT YOU AND YOUR STUDENTS NEED!

www.wileyplus.com/resources

1st DAY OF CLASS ...AND BEYOND!

2-Minute Tutorials and all of the resources you and your students need to get started

WileyPLUS

Student Partner Program

Student support from an experienced student user

Wiley Faculty Network

Collaborate with your colleagues, find a mentor, attend virtual and live events, and view resources
www.WhereFacultyConnect.com

WileyPLUS

Quick Start

Pre-loaded, ready-to-use assignments and presentations created by subject matter experts

Technical Support 24/7
FAQs, online chat, and phone support
www.wileyplus.com/support

© Courtney Keating/iStockphoto

Your *WileyPLUS* Account Manager, providing personal training and support

CORPORATE FINANCE

FINANCIAL MANAGEMENT
IN A GLOBAL ENVIRONMENT

CORPORATE FINANCE

FINANCIAL MANAGEMENT IN A GLOBAL ENVIRONMENT

Laurence Booth, DBA
University of Toronto

W. Sean Cleary, PhD, CFA
Saint Mary's University

Pamela Peterson Drake, PhD, CFA
James Madison University

VICE PRESIDENT & EXECUTIVE PUBLISHER	George Hoffman
EXECUTIVE EDITOR	Joel Hollenbeck
SENIOR PRODUCT DESIGNER	Allison Morris
EDITORIAL OPERATIONS MANAGER	Yana Mermel
CONTENT EDITOR	Jennifer Manias
ASSISTANT EDITOR	Courtney Luzzi
ASSOCIATE DIRECTOR OF MARKETING	Amy Scholz
SENIOR MARKETING MANAGER	Jesse Cruz
SENIOR CONTENT MANAGER	Dorothy Sinclair
SENIOR PRODUCTION EDITOR	Erin Bascom
DESIGN DIRECTOR	Harry Nolan
PHOTO DEPARTMENT MANAGER	Hilary Newman
SENIOR EDITORIAL ASSISTANT	Erica Horowitz
MARKETING ASSISTANT	Justine Kay
SENIOR MEDIA SPECIALIST	Elena Santa Maria
PRODUCTION MANAGEMENT SERVICES	Bruce Hobart/Laserwords Maine
TEXT AND COVER DESIGNER	Madelyn Lesure
COVER PHOTO	© Stefan Siems/Getty Images, Inc.

Credit for author photos: Carole Booth, Sean Cleary, Katie Landis.
Repeated icon photos: (magnifying glass and spreadsheet) Joe Belanger/iStockphoto; (calculator) Jeremiah Thompson/iStockphoto

This book was set in Times Ten LT Std 10/12 by Laserwords and printed and bound by RRD/Jefferson City. The cover was printed by RRD/Jefferson City.

This book is printed on acid free paper. ∞

Founded in 1807, John Wiley & Sons, Inc. has been a valued source of knowledge and understanding for more than 200 years, helping people around the world meet their needs and fulfill their aspirations. Our company is built on a foundation of principles that include responsibility to the communities we serve and where we live and work. In 2008, we launched a Corporate Citizenship Initiative, a global effort to address the environmental, social, economic, and ethical challenges we face in our business. Among the issues we are addressing are carbon impact, paper specifications and procurement, ethical conduct within our business and among our vendors, and community and charitable support. For more information, please visit our website: www.wiley.com/go/citizenship.

Library of Congress Cataloging-in-Publication Data
Booth, Laurence D.
  Corporate finance / Laurence Booth, W. Sean Cleary, Pamela Peterson Drake.
    p. cm.
  Includes index.
  ISBN 978-0-470-44464-1 (cloth)
  1. Corporations—Finance. I. Cleary, W. Sean (William Sean), 1962- II. Peterson Drake, Pamela, 1954-
III. Title.
  HG4026.B646 2013
  658.15—dc23

2012026781

978-0-470-44464-1   (Main Book ISBN)
978-1-118-12936-4   (Binder-Ready Version ISBN)

Printed in the United States of America
10 9 8 7 6 5 4 3 2 1

Laurence Booth, D.B.A., M.B.A., M.A. (Indiana University); B.S. (London School of Economics) holds the CIT chair in structured finance at the Rotman School of Management at the University of Toronto. He has published over fifty articles in academic journals, as well as major textbooks for McGraw-Hill, *International Business*, with Alan Rugman and Don Lecraw, and John Wiley & Sons, *Introduction to Corporate Finance*, 2nd edition, with Sean Cleary.

At the University of Toronto since 1978, Laurence Booth has taught graduate courses in business finance, international financial management, corporate financing, mergers and acquisitions, financial management, and financial theory, as well as short executive programs on the money & foreign exchange markets, business valuation, mergers and acquisitions, and financial strategy. He is a frequent expert financial witness on financial management topics such as the cost of capital, financial structure and the importance of bond ratings.

W. Sean Cleary, Ph.D. (University of Toronto) M.B.A. (Saint Mary's University), B.Ed. (Saint Francis Xavier University), B.A. (Acadia University), CFA, is the BMO Professor of Finance and Director of the Master of Finance, Queen's School of Business, Queen's University.

In addition to numerous articles in various academic journals, he is coauthor of *Introduction to Corporate Finance*, John Wiley & Sons Canada Limited (2007, 2010). He is the Canadian author of the first three editions of the textbook, *Investments: Analysis and Management*, with Charles P. Jones, also published by John Wiley & Sons Canada Limited (1999, 2004, 2008). He coauthored the textbook, *Finance in a Canadian Setting* (6th edition), with Peter Lusztig and Bernard Schwab, published in 2001 by John Wiley & Sons Canada Limited. He is also the author of *The Canadian Securities Exam Fast Track Study Guide*, also published by John Wiley & Sons Canada Limited.

Sean Cleary has taught numerous university finance courses, including capital markets, financial institutions, investments, introductory finance, corporate finance, and mergers and acquisitions.

Pamela Peterson Drake, Ph.D. (University of North Carolina), B.S. (Miami University), CFA, is the J. Gray Ferguson Professor of Finance and Department Head, Department of Finance and Business Law in the College of Business at James Madison University.

In addition to authoring or coauthoring articles in academic journals, Pamela Peterson Drake has written a number of books with Frank Fabozzi, including *Analysis of Financial Statements*, *Basics of Finance*, *Capital Budgeting*, and *Financial Management and Analysis*, all published by John Wiley & Sons. She is also author or coauthor for numerous readings that are part of the CFA curriculum, as well as the monographs published by the CFA Institute, *Real Options*, with Don Chance, and *Company Performance and Measures of Value Added*, with David R. Peterson.

Pamela Peterson Drake has been at James Madison University since 2007 and teaches courses in financial management, financial analysis, analysis of financial policy, analytical methods, and spreadsheet skills. She taught financial management and quantitative methods previously at Florida State University (1981–2004) and Florida Atlantic University (2004–2007).

In this text, we have tried to address the basic question: What do students need to know about the principles of finance? Though not everyone who picks up this book is a finance major or is destined for a finance career, finance is ubiquitous; you can find it throughout any business enterprise.

What are the key ingredients to finance? Accounting, economics, and mathematics.

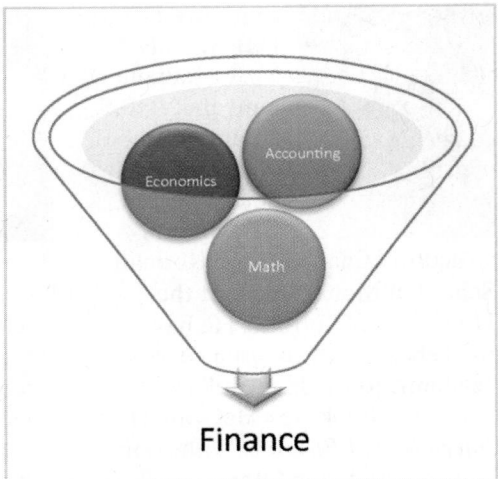

- Financial managers use accounting information, combined with market information, to make decisions.
- Financial decision making requires economic reasoning and the principles of both micro- and macroeconomics.
- Financial calculations at this level use algebra and well-disguised calculus.

The Structure of This Book

In a nutshell, this book begins with the building blocks of financial management:

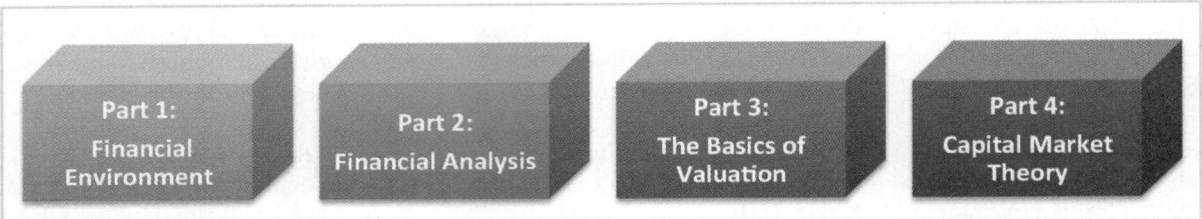

Setting the stage for the environment in which decisions are made, in Part 1 we introduce students to financial intermediation (Chapter 1) and financial markets (Chapter 2). We introduce students to financial analysis in Part 2 by first reviewing the financial statements (Chapter 3) and then focusing on how to use these financial statements to evaluate the financial performance and condition of a business enterprise (Chapter 4).

In part 3 we introduce the student to financial mathematics (Chapter 5) and then apply this to bonds (Chapter 6) and equity (Chapter 7). Recognizing that financial decision making of an enterprise is not made in a vacuum, but rather in the context of financial markets, in Part 4 we discuss the concepts and theories of the pricing of assets (Chapter 8), followed by a discussion of the theories of how assets are priced (Chapter 9).

We build on this foundation with applications that involve long-term investment and financing decisions:

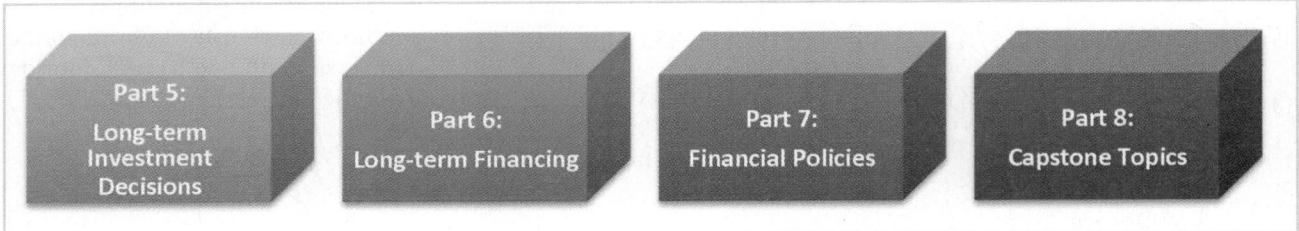

In Part 5 we detail the methods of evaluating long-term investments (a.k.a. capital budgeting; Chapter 10), followed by a discussion of and demonstration of the tools we use to make capital budgeting decisions (Chapter 11). Financial decisions involve not only the investment decisions—that is, what to do with funds to help the enterprise grow—but also how a company finances these investments, as we discuss in Part 6. In part 7 we discuss raising money using debt instruments (Chapter 12) and using equity securities (Chapter 13). We also detail the costs of financing (Chapter 14), which affect investment choices.

A discussion of financing instruments is not complete without a discussion of the factors that affect the company's choice of how to finance its investments (Chapter 15). Because any dividend paid to owners is a use of funds that could have been employed for investment purposes, we discuss the theories and reasons why companies pay dividends (Chapter 16).

We present a number of aspects of financial management decision making that affect both investments and financing in Part 8, including financial planning (Chapter 17), risk management (Chapter 18), working capital management (Chapter 19), leasing (Chapter 20), and mergers and acquisitions (Chapter 21). A module on Global Financial Management is also available online.

Focus

Our focus in this book is on decision making for a business enterprise, whether that enterprise is a small business, a publicly traded corporation, or a limited liability company. We also recognize that decisions of an enterprise are rarely restricted to a specific locale, so we have tried to take a global view of financial decision making. Though the original edition of this book was written for a Canadian readership, the present book is neither Canadian-centric nor U.S.-centric; rather, we attempt to explain decision making without regard to the country of the enterprise. Though a few topics are U.S. specific, such as taxes, these few topics can be viewed as representative of what an enterprise faces, regardless of whether the enterprise is located in India, Japan, China, the United States, or elsewhere.

Pedagogy

Throughout this book, we have tried to address different learning styles so that all students may be successful. To that end, we provide a number of pedagogical features:

Learning Outcomes correspond directly to the sections in the chapter and to specific end of chapter questions and problems.

Learning Outcomes

After reading this chapter, you should be able to:

LO 5.1 Describe and compare the principles of compound interest and simple interest, and apply these principles to solve present value and future value problems involving a single sum.

LO 5.2 Identify and apply the appropriate method of valuing different patterns of cash flows, including the ordinary annuity, annuity due, deferred annuity, and perpetuity.

A **running glossary** allows for a quick review of key terms. A comprehensive glossary with extended definitions is available at the back of the book.

simple interest interest paid or received on only the initial investment

principal amount loaned or the amount of the investment

Summary boxes to help put together the pieces.

SUMMARIZING

The equation for the future value, $FV_n = PV_0(1 + i)^n$, has four values, and if we know any three of them we can solve for the last one. We can solve four different types of finance problems using this equation:

1. *Future value problems*: How much will I have in w years at $x\%$ if I invest $\$y$?
2. *Present value problems*: What is the value today of receiving $\$z$ in w years if the interest rate is $x\%$?
3. *Determining the interest rate*: What rate of return will I earn if I invest $\$y$ today for w years and get $\$z$?
4. *Determining the number of periods*: How long do I have to wait to get $\$z$ if I invest $\$y$ today at $x\%$?

It's Greek to Me | FINANCE in the News

Sovereign debt is indebtedness issued by a national government. For example, the Treasury bills and bonds issued by the U.S. government are part of the sovereign debt of the U.S. One of the fallouts of the 2007–2008 crisis is the downgrading of sovereign debt. Greece, with its long history of budget problems, was the first to fall. Its debt was downgraded in 2009, in 2010, in 2011, and then again in 2012. The rating of Greece's debt from Moody's fell from A1 to C in this three-year period. To put this in perspective, the rating of Greece's debt went from "High economic, financial or institutional strength" to "One shock away from default, and/or material concerns about the willingness to pay."[28] The upshot of the downgrade is that the debt is considered riskier, and therefore, the cost of raising capital

increases. By 2012, the yield on 10-year Greek debt was over 3,300 basis points (that is, 33%) higher than other European sovereign debt, and the debt was, effectively, in default.[29] Other countries followed suit, with Portugal and Spain following close behind Greece.

Like any business, an economic slowdown such as the one that followed the global crisis affects the countries that have the weakest economies. Factors considered important in rating sovereign debt include gross domestic product, government policies in dealing with budgets, policies of the central bank, and unemployment.[30] The challenge is that once the debt is downgraded, the cost of raising new capital is greater, and the country will have difficulty raising capital to finance its operations.

Special topic boxes provide context, examples, and illustrations of the material in terms of Ethics (the good, the bad, and the ugly), Finance in the News (good and bad), Global Perspectives (it's a small world after all, isn't it?), and Lessons Learned (learning from the past).

Boxed examples that are illustrations of the calculations, both in terms of the math and with the use of calculators to solve the problems. We also provide additional examples on the book's web site in case the reader needs more.

PROBLEM   EXAMPLE 5.1

Suppose someone invests $10,000 today for a five-year term and receives 3% annual sim-   **Simple Interest**
ple interest on the investment. How much would the investor have after five years?

Solution

Annual interest = $10,000 × 0.03 = $300 per year.

Or

$$FV_5 = \$10,000 + [5 \times \$10,000 \times 0.03] = \$10,000 + 1,500 = \$11,500$$

Year	Beginning amount	Ending amount
1	$10,000	$10,300
2	10,300	10,600
3	10,600	10,900
4	10,900	11,200
5	11,200	11,500

The interest earned is $300 every year, regardless of the beginning amount, because interest is earned on only the original investment. Interest is *not* earned on any earned interest.

1. At what frequency of compounding is the effective annual rate equal to the annual   *Concept Review*
    percentage rate? Explain your answer.   *Questions*

2. The Truth-in-Lending law in the U.S. requires lenders to disclose the APR for any
    loan transaction. Does the APR overstate or understate the true cost of a loan?
    Explain.

Concept review questions at the end of each section, are designed to get the reader to think critically about the material in the section.

SUMMARY

Chapter summaries in bullet points, provide a quick review of the key concepts developed in the chapter.

- By applying the process of compounding or discount at an appropriate rate of return, we can calculate economically equivalent values through time. For example, we can calculate the future value five years from now of an amount today. We can also determine the equivalent present value or future value for a series of cash flows.

- Annuities represent a special type of cash flow stream that involve equal payments at the same interval, with the same interest rate being applied throughout the period. We see that these kinds of cash flow streams are commonplace in finance applications (e.g., loan payments) and that there are relatively simple formulas that enable us to determine the present value or future value of such cash flows.

- It is possible to convert a stated rate (that is, the annual percentage rate) into an effective rate, which is important because compounding often takes place at other than annual intervals and the annual percentage rate understates the true, effective rate.

- Time value of money principles may be applied to a number of situations, including the personal finance decisions related to saving for retirement and home mortgage problems.

End of Chapter Pedagogy

Multiple choice questions provide a quick test of the reader's comprehension of the chapter material. Answers are provided at the back of the book.

Multiple Choice

1. If you invest $1,000 today in an account that pays 5% interest, compounded annually, the balance in the account at the end of ten years, if you make no withdrawals, is *closest* to:
    A. $613.91   B. $1,000.00   C. $1,500.00   D. $1,628.89

2. Which of the following has the largest future value if € 1,000 is invested today?
    A. Ten years, with a simple annual interest rate of 8%
    B. Five years, with a simple annual interest rate of 12%
    C. Nine years, with a compound annual interest rate of 7%
    D. Eight years, with a compound annual interest rate of 8%

Practice Problems and Questions

5.1 Time Is Money

11. What is simple interest?

12. Explain how you would calculate the interest-on-interest on an investment.

Questions and Problems enable the reader to master the chapter material.

Cases provide in-depth analyses and application of the material in the chapter.

> **Case**
>
> **Case 5.1 Saving for retirement, considering different scenarios**
>
> Suppose you are advising a client, Arturo, who is planning for his retirement and wants to have $1 million by the time he retires at age sixty. And suppose you want to lay out alternative savings plans for different return scenarios:
>
> **Scenario 1:** *Steady state*
> Earns 8% on all funds invested.
> **Scenario 2:** *Declining returns*
> Earns 8% each year for the first five years, 6% for the next five years, and 4% thereafter.
> **Scenario 3:** *Increasing returns*
> Earns 8% each year for the first five years, 10% for the next five years, and 12% thereafter.
> **Scenario 4:** *Varying returns*
> Earns 8% each year for the first five years, 6% for the next five years, and 10% thereafter.

Robust Instructor and Student Resources

We have worked to develop myriad tools for teaching and learning corporate finance.

For the instructor

The book's *Companion Web Site*—www.wiley.com/college/booth—contains additional examples, explanations, and tools.

The *Instructors' Manual* includes teaching notes, solutions to end-of-chapter problems, solutions to concept questions, and discussion questions for the special topic boxes.

The *Test Bank* includes multiple choice, short answer, and practice problems, all with complete solutions. All these questions and problems are classified by the level of difficulty and the learning outcome. The *Computerized Test Bank* allows instructors to modify and add questions and customize exams.

PowerPoint Presentations provide highlights for each chapter. For chapters that include calculations, we provide worked out problems that are similar, but not identical, to those in the book.

For the student

We provide a number of resources on the book's *Companion Web Site*—www.wiley.com/college/booth—that supplement the book and the in-class experience, including:

Practice Quizzing: multiple-choice quizzes with instant feedback for additional practice;

Spreadsheet Templates for all worked-out examples in the book.

WileyPLUS

WileyPlus is an innovative, research-based online environment for effective teaching and learning.

WileyPlus builds students' confidence because it takes the guesswork out of studying by providing students with a clear road map: what to do, how to do it, if they did it right. This interactive approach focuses on:

Confidence Research shows that students experience a great deal of anxiety over studying. That's why we provide a structured learning environment that helps students focus on what to do, along with the support of immediate resources.

Motivation To increase and sustain motivation throughout the semester, *WileyPLUS* helps students learn how to do it at a pace that's right for them. Our integrated resources—available 24/7—function like a personal tutor, directly addressing each student's demonstrated needs with specific problem-solving techniques.

Success *WileyPLUS* helps to ensure that each study session has a positive outcome by putting students in control. Through instant feedback and study objective reports, students know if they did it right, and where to focus next, so they achieve the strongest results.

With *WileyPLUS*, our efficacy research shows that students improve their outcomes by as much as one letter grade. *WileyPLUS* helps students take more initiative, so you'll have greater impact on their achievement in the classroom and beyond.

What do students receive with *WileyPLUS*?

- The complete digital textbook, saving students up to 60% off the cost of a printed text.
- Question assistance, including links to relevant sections in the online digital textbook.
- Immediate feedback and proof of progress, 24/7.
- Integrated, multimedia resources—including animated problems, flash cards, prerequisite course reviews (accounting, economics, algebra, and statistics), problem-solving videos, and much more—that provide multiple study paths and encourage more active learning.

What do instructors receive with *WileyPLUS*?

- Reliable resources that reinforce course goals inside and outside the classroom.
- The ability to easily identify those students who are falling behind.
- Media-rich course materials and assessment content including—Instructor's Manual, Solutions Manual, Test Bank, Computerized Test Bank, PowerPoint®Slides, Pre- and Post-Lecture Quizzes, and much more.

www.wileyplus.com. Learn More.

Acknowledgments

A large-scale textbook project such as this one is not the work of just the authors; rather, it is a combined effort of many people whom we wish to acknowledge. We would first like to thank our many reviewers, listed here and several others who wish to remain anonymous, who took the time to read and evaluate the draft manuscripts. Without their many helpful comments, suggestions, and feedback, this textbook would not be what it is today.

Alexander Amati, *Rutgers University*; Alan Blaylock, *Murray State University*; Carol Boyer, *Long Island University*; Ed Boyer, *Temple University*; Susan J. Crain, *Missouri State University*; Julie Dahlquist, *University of Texas, San Antonio*; Michael Ferguson, *University of Cincinnati*; Eric Fricke, *California State University, East Bay*; Partha Gangopadhyay, *Saint Cloud State University*; Aparna Gupta, *Rensselaer Polytechnic Institute*; Eric Hayden, *University of Massachusetts, Boston*; Suzanne Hayes, *University of Nebraska, Kearney*; Michael B. Imerman, *Rutgers University*; Burhan Kawosa, *Wright State University*; Dongmin Ke, *Kean University*; Jiro Edouard Kondo, *Northwestern University*; Vladimir Kotomin, *University of Wisconsin–Eau Claire*; Gregory LaBlanc, *University of California, Berkeley*; Mark J. Laplante, *University of Georgia*; Malek K. Lashgari, *University of Hartford*; Richard L. B. LeCompte, *Wichita State University*; Bingxuan Lin, *University of Rhode Island*; Scott W. Lowe, CPA, CMA; William Mahnic, *Case Western Reserve University*; Stefano Mazzotta, *Kennesaw State University*; Hassan Moussawi, *Wayne State University*; David Offenberg, *Loyola Marymount University*; Hyuna Park, *Minnesota State University, Mankato*; Vedapuri Sunder Raghavan, *Embry-Riddle Aeronautical University*; Joshua Rauh, *Chicago Graduate School of Business*; Carolyn Reichert, *University of Texas, Dallas*; Manuel Chu Rubio, *UPC–Laureate International*; Harley E. Ryan, Jr., *Georgia State University*; Ronald F. Singer, *University of Houston*; Jan Strockis, *Santa Clara University*; John Strong, *College of William and Mary*; Dr. C. R. Krishna Swamy, *Western Michigan University*; James Teague, *University of Pittsburgh, Johnstown*; and Alan M. Weatherford, *California Polytechnic State University*.

In addition, several participated in Focus Groups:

Riza Emekter, *Robert Morris University*; Eric Fricke, *California State University, East Bay*; Suzanne Hayes, *University of Nebraska, Kearney*; Dongmin Ke, *Kean University*; and Carolyn Reichert, *University of Texas, Dallas*.

And, served on the Corporate Finance Advisory Board:

Francisca M. Beer, *California State University, San Bernardino*; Susan J. Crain, *Missouri State University*; Praveen Kumar Das, *University of Louisiana*; Amadeu DaSilva, *California State University, Fullerton*; Erik Devos, *The University of Texas at El Paso*; Tom G. Geurts, *The George Washington University*; Beverly Hadaway, *The University of Texas at Austin*; Karen L. Hamilton, *Georgia Southern University*; James D. Keys, *Florida International University*; Lan Liu, *California State University, Sacramento*; Suzan Puhl Murphy, *The University of Tennessee, Knoxville*; G. Michael Phillips, *California State University, Northridge*; Christopher R. Pope, *University of Georgia*; Helen Saar, *University of Hawaii, Manoa*; Mark Stohs, *California State University, Fullerton*; Devrim Yaman, *Western Michigan University*; Jasmine Yur-Austin, *California State University, Long Beach*; and Kermit C. Zieg, *Florida Institute of Technology*.

We have to acknowledge and thank Peg Monahan-Pashall for her assistance in developing the manuscript. We would also like to thank our team at Wiley, especially Joel Hollenbeck, Executive Editor, and Jennifer Manias, Content Editor, for their thoughtful direction. In addition, George Hoffman, Publisher; Erica Horowitz, Editorial Assistant; Madelyn Lesure, Senior Designer; Jesse Cruz, Senior Marketing Manager; Allison Morris, Senior Product Designer; Erin Bascom, Senior Production Editor; and Bruce Hobart at Laserwords were ever-helpful during the making of this book.

BRIEF CONTENTS

PART 1

THE FINANCIAL ENVIRONMENT

"Remember that time is money. He that can earn ten shillings a day by his labour and goes abroad or sits idle one-half of that day, though he spends but sixpence during his diversion or idleness, ought not to reckon that the only expense; he has really spent, or rather thrown away, five shillings besides.

Remember that credit is money. If a man lets his money lie in my hands after it is due, he gives me the interest, or so much as I can make of it during that time. This amounts to a considerable sum where a man has good and large credit and makes good use of it.

Remember that money is of the prolific, generating nature. Money can beget money, and its offspring can beget more, and so on. Five shillings turned is six; turned again it is seven and three pence, and so on till it becomes a hundred pounds. The more there is of it the more it produces every turning, so that the profits rise quicker and quicker. He that kills a breeding sow destroys all her offspring to the thousandth generation. He that murders a crown destroys all that might have produced even scores of pounds."

Benjamin Franklin, "Advice to a Young Tradesman," *Poor Richard's Almanack*, 1738

CHAPTER 1

AN INTRODUCTION TO FINANCE

© Kyu Oh/iStockphoto

From the letter to shareholders of Berkshire Hathaway, from Warren Buffett, accompanying the Berkshire Hathaway 2008 Annual Report which followed the U.S. Government's response to the financial crisis and problems in financial markets:

Whatever the downsides may be, strong and immediate action by government was essential last year if the financial system was to avoid a total breakdown. Had one occurred, the consequences for every area of our economy would have been cataclysmic. Like it or not, the inhabitants of Wall Street, Main Street and the various Side Streets of America were all in the same boat.

Amid this bad news, however, never forget that our country has faced far worse travails in the past. In the 20th Century alone, we dealt with two great wars (one of which we initially appeared to be losing); a dozen or so panics and recessions; virulent inflation that led to a 21½% prime rate in 1980; and the Great Depression of the 1930s, when unemployment ranged between 15% and 25% for many years. America has had no shortage of challenges.

Without fail, however, we've overcome them. In the face of those obstacles—and many others— the real standard of living for Americans improved nearly *seven*-fold during the 1900s, while the Dow Jones Industrials rose from 66 to 11,497. Compare the record of this period with the dozens of centuries during which humans secured only tiny gains, if any, in how they lived. Though the path has not been smooth, our economic system has worked extraordinarily well over time. It has unleashed human potential as no other system has, and it will continue to do so. America's best days lie ahead.

Learning Outcomes

After reading this chapter, you should be able to:

LO 1.1 Define finance and explain the types of decisions made in finance.

LO 1.2 Identify the basic types of financial instruments and explain how they are traded.

LO 1.3 Explain the significance of the global financial system and the global economy to business entities and a country's economy.

Chapter Preview Often, the first finance course that business students take is a finance principles course that focuses on financial management. Yet financial management cannot be taught in isolation; it is simply one part of finance, which includes securities and securities markets, financial institutions, and the economy. Moreover, events in 2007 and 2008 remind us that all these parts are inter-related and that finance is a truly global field.

1.1 WHAT IS FINANCE?

Finance, in its broadest terms, is the allocation of funds between those with more funds than they need and those who need the funds. More specifically, finance deals with the "how" and "under what terms" of this allocation.[1]

You may recognize in this definition a similarity between finance and economics. Economics deals with the allocation of scarce resources in an economy, whereas finance focuses on how resources are allocated and by what channels, as well as the terms of the allocation. In many ways, we can view finance as applied economics. For example, the scope of financial decision making within a business entity includes managing investments— whether these assets are production machinery, buildings, or inventory—and deciding how to finance the short-term and long-term needs of the business.

As you learn more about finance, you will notice that financial managers use accounting information in decision making. Accounting captures the company's financial condition and performance over a fiscal period (generally a year or a quarter), so it is capturing what has happened in the past. Finance is forward looking, and financial managers must make decisions about investments and financing now that may have consequences in both the short term and the long term. To formulate those projections, however, financial managers often look at historical financial statements to gauge past performance, growth rates in various accounts, relationships among different accounts, and so on. Therefore, financial managers must be able to read and interpret financial statements.

> **finance** study of how and under what terms funds are allocated between those with excess funds and those who need funds

The Three Primary Areas of Finance

Finance is a broad field, which we can break down into three areas, as we describe in Figure 1-1. **Business finance**, also referred to as **corporate finance** and **financial management**, deals with the financing decision making within a business entity, whether this be a sole proprietorship, a corporation, a partnership, or a limited liability company. The types of decisions that a financial manager faces in a business entity include decisions regarding long-term investments, how the business is financed, and where and when to borrow to meet seasonal needs. A **financial institution** is an entity that serves as an intermediary in the financial system and includes banks, credit unions, and financing companies. Financial managers in these entities manage financial products and services and operate in a highly regulated environment. **Investments** deals with financial markets and securities, including stocks, bonds, and options. Decision making in investment firms includes portfolio choices, making markets in securities, and analyzing alternative investments. Investment firms are regulated and operate in markets that are, for the most part, highly monitored.

> **business finance** or **corporate finance** or **financial management** financing decision making within a business entity
>
> **financial institution** entity that serves as an intermediary in the financial system, and includes banks, credit unions, and financing companies
>
> **investments** deals with financial markets and securities, including stocks, bonds, and options

FIGURE 1-1 **The Three Areas of Finance**

[1] In economics, providers of funds are often referred to as "surplus agents" or "lenders" and users of funds as "borrowers" or "deficit agents."

Our focus in this book is business finance. However, business finance shares the same foundation as the study of financial institutions and investments. Specifically, this foundation comprises:

- financial statements analysis;
- the time value of money and other valuation financial mathematics; and
- portfolio theory and asset pricing.

Along with the foundation material, an underlying theme in all areas is the global nature of financial decision making. We have long operated in an environment in which there are linkages among many countries, especially with respect to financial markets and the exporting and importing of goods and services. Financial managers in all three areas of finance face issues related to currency fluctuations, regulatory environments that differ among countries, different accounting standards, import and export fees and limitations, and a flow of funds that crosses borders with ease. Financial managers in the U.S. seldom operate solely in the U.S.; many businesses rely on outsourcing some of their production or services, import raw materials, and sell goods overseas. Therefore, financial managers must think globally in their decision making.

In this chapter, we review briefly financial instruments and markets, as well as the overall regulatory system for financial institutions and markets. By introducing you to financial markets and financial instruments, you will be able to follow the financial news during your study of financial management. We also introduce you to many of the players in the financial system, both in the U.S. and globally.

It is important that financial managers understand not only the role of business entities in the financial system, but also how the financial system affects their decisions. We also provide an overview of the 2007–2008 financial crisis and its reverberation for years that followed and discuss the lessons learned for the financial management of a business enterprise.

The Role of Financial Intermediaries

financial system environment in which households provide funds to businesses and government

financial intermediary entity that transforms the nature of securities in a market

market intermediary entity that facilitates the working of markets and helps provide direct intermediation but does not change the nature of the transaction; also called a *broker*

The **financial system** of any country provides an environment in which households provide funds to businesses and government, as we show in Figure 1-2. The basic financial flow is facilitated or intermediated through the financial system, which comprises financial intermediaries and market intermediaries. A **financial intermediary** transforms the nature of the securities they issue and invest in, whereas a **market intermediary** simply makes the markets work better.

Financial intermediaries include investment banks, commercial banks, insurance companies, and mutual funds, whereas market intermediaries include brokers, brokerage firms, and exchanges, such as the NYSE Euronext and the CME Group.[2] The whole package of institutions is the financial system.

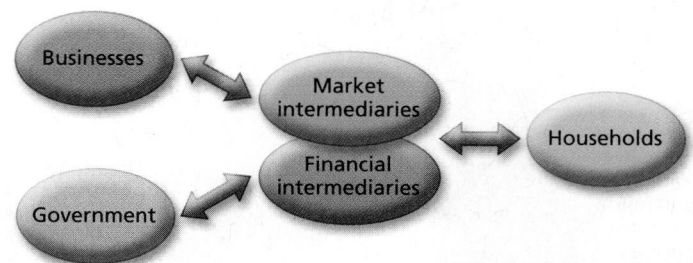

FIGURE 1-2 **The Financial System**

[2] The NYSE Euronext is the holding company that combined the New York Stock Exchange and Euronext to create a linkage between the world's largest equities exchanges. The CME Group is the world's largest futures and options exchange.

In a financial system, parties transfer money from those with a surplus to those who need it. This transfer occurs through **intermediation**, which is the process of bringing these parties together. If we think of how this intermediation may occur, one obvious way is for individuals to borrow directly from friends, relatives, and acquaintances.[3] Another is to borrow from a specialized financial institution, such as Bank of America or BB&T. These are two extremes in terms of the transfer of money from lenders to borrowers. In the first case, borrowers obtain funds directly from individuals, whereas in the second, they borrow indirectly from individuals who have first deposited their savings, which is lending their savings to a financial institution. The financial institution, in turn, lends funds to the ultimate borrowers, such as a homeowner who needs a mortgage.

We illustrate these two patterns of intermediation in Figure 1-3 using three basic channels. The first channel is intermediation, where the lender provides money directly to the ultimate borrower without any help from a specialist. This is a nonmarket transaction because the borrower and lender negotiate the exchange directly. An example would be a relative lending you money to buy a car.

The second channel also represents direct intermediation between the lender and borrower, but in this case, some help is needed because no one individual can lend the full amount needed or because the borrower is not aware of the available lenders. As a result, the borrower needs help to find suitable lenders, which is what market intermediaries do. A **market intermediary** or **intermediary** is simply an entity that facilitates the working of markets and helps the direct intermediation process.

Typically, we refer to market intermediary as a **broker**. The real estate market has real estate and mortgage brokers, who help with the sale and financing of houses. The insurance market has insurance brokers, who facilitate the sale of insurance, and the stock market has stockbrokers, who facilitate the sale of financial securities, particularly shares. In each case, market intermediaries help to make the market work; their responsibilities are to assist with the transaction and bring borrowers and lenders together, but they do not change the nature of the transaction itself. The most important financial markets in U.S. are the stock markets, including the New York Stock Exchange and the NASDAQ, which support a variety of market intermediaries, from stockbrokers who advise clients, through traders who buy and sell securities, to investment bankers who help companies raise capital. In each case, their raison d'être is to make markets work.

The third savings channel is completely different. It represents financial intermediation, in which the financial institution or financial intermediary lends the money to the ultimate borrowers, yet raises the money itself by borrowing directly from other individuals. In this case, the ultimate lenders have only an indirect claim on the ultimate borrowers; their direct claim is on the financial institution. The difference between a financial intermediary and a market intermediary is that a financial intermediary changes the nature of the transaction, whereas the market intermediary does not.

intermediation transfer of funds from lenders to borrowers

broker a market intermediary, who facilitates exchanges in a market

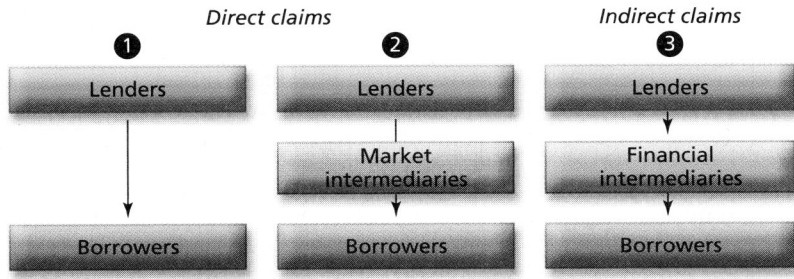

FIGURE 1-3 **Channels of Savings**

---

[3] In small business, this is often referred to as financing through the 3 Fs: family, friends, and fools.

1. What is finance?

2. What are the three areas of finance?

3. What differentiates market intermediaries from financial intermediaries?

1.2 FINANCIAL INSTRUMENTS AND MARKETS

Now that we have the big picture of how a financial system works, we can focus on the instruments and institutional arrangements that are used to transfer these funds in a financial system.

Financial Instruments

financial instrument legal agreement that represents an ownership interest, a debt obligation, or other claim on assets or income

security negotiable financial instrument that is evidence of indebtedness or ownership

A **financial instrument** is any legal agreement that represents an ownership interest, a debt obligation, or other claim on assets or income. A **security** is a negotiable financial instrument that is evidence of indebtedness or ownership. Securities include the following:

- Debt obligations, such as a bond or a note with a fixed term for repayment and interest to compensate the lender for the use of the funds

- Equity interests, such as common stock, which represent the ownership interest that the provider of funds has in the user of funds

- Hybrid securities, such as a convertible bond, that has characteristics of both equity and debt

Exchanging funds for securities opens up an opportunity to be creative in developing securities to facilitate the flow of funds, but additional risk may accompany this creativity and complexity. As a result, the study of finance requires an understanding of economics, securities, law, markets, and the institutions that facilitate and monitor the exchange of funds.

Financial assets are formal legal documents that set out the rights and obligations of all the parties involved. The two major categories of financial securities are debt and equity. A **debt instrument** represents legal obligations to repay borrowed funds at a specified maturity date and provide interim interest payments as specified in the agreement. The party lending the funds is the **creditor** of the borrower. Some of the most common examples of debt instruments are short-term borrowing, such as bank loans, commercial paper, bankers' acceptances, and U.S. Treasury bills (T-bills), and long-term borrowings, including mortgage loans, municipal bonds, and corporate bonds:[4]

debt instrument legal obligation to repay borrowed funds at a specified maturity date and to provide interim interest payments

creditor a party lending funds through a loan arrangement

Short-term debt

Bank loan	A loan made by a financial institution
Commercial paper	A loan issued by a business or governmental entity
Bankers' acceptance	A credit instrument that is issued by a business and guaranteed by a bank
U.S. Treasury bill	A short-term indebtedness of the U.S. government

---

[4] We will cover each of these later in this text. Bank loans are self-explanatory. Commercial paper is a promissory note with a maturity generally less than one year, usually used for short-term financing by large, creditworthy companies. Bankers' acceptances are short-term financing typically used in import/export transactions.

Long-term debt

Mortgage loan	A loan that is backed by specific collateral, such as a home in the case of a home mortgage
Municipal bond	An indebtedness issued by a state or local government
Corporate bond	An indebtedness issued by a corporation

The key is that debt instruments compensate the lender with interest, whether this interest is explicit or implicit.

A debt instrument may be backed or secured with collateral, or it may be unsecured. **Collateral** is the borrower's pledge of specific property, which may be a building, aircraft, or any other identifiable, tangible asset. If the borrower does not pay what is owed on the debt, the lender in a secured debt can take possession of the collateral or force its sale to recover funds. If debt is not secured, it is backed by the "full faith and credit" of the issuer.[5] We refer to this debt that is unsecured as a **debenture**.

A **bond** is a debt instrument that takes the form of a security that investors can buy and sell. The owner of the bond is the creditor of the bond issuer. A bond typically has a fixed maturity of more than ten years, pays interest (which is referred to as a coupon), and repays the loan at maturity. A **note** is similar to a bond, but with a maturity in the range of one to ten years. In common usage, however, the term "bond" is often used interchangeably with the term "note."

One type of municipal bond is the **general obligation bond**, which is backed by the full faith and credit of the issuer, much like U.S. Treasury bonds. Another type of municipal bond is the **revenue bond**, which is backed by a specific revenue stream of the issuing entity, such as the payments for electricity by customers of a city-owned electric utility. Still another type of municipal bond is the **assessment bond**, which is backed by the property taxes that are assessed by the local government. An advantage of investing in municipal debt is that the interest earned on this investment is exempt from federal income tax and, depending on the state, may be exempt from state income tax.

An **equity instrument** or **equity security** represents an ownership stake in a company. The most common form of equity is **common stock**. Common stock represents the residual ownership of a corporation; the common stock owners are last in line, in terms of seniority of claims on the company, but they also reap the benefits from the company's earnings and appreciation in value. Common stock owners generally also have voting rights, with the ability to elect members of the company's Board of Directors. Companies also issue another form of ownership, **preferred stock**, which usually entitles the owner to fixed dividend payments that must be made before any dividends are paid to common shareholders.

Aside from the debt versus equity distinction, financial instruments can be categorized in several additional ways. One way is to distinguish between nonmarketable and marketable financial assets. The most familiar forms of nonmarketable assets are savings accounts or demand deposits with financial institutions, such as commercial banks. These funds are available on demand, which guarantees the liquidity of these investments.

Marketable securities are those that can be traded among market participants. They are typically categorized not only according to whether they are debt or equity securities, but also by their "term to maturity," or time until the obligation must be repaid. A **money market security** is a short-term (i.e., maturity of less than one year) security; examples include debt instruments such as T-bills, commercial paper, and bankers' acceptances. A **capital market security** is a security with a maturity greater than one year and includes notes, bonds, and debentures, as well as equity securities, which represent ownership in a company and generally have no maturity date.

general obligation bond debt security backed by the general credit of the issuer

revenue bond debt obligation backed by a specific revenue stream

assessment bond security backed by the property taxes of a government entity

equity instrument or **equity security** ownership stake in a company

preferred stock equity security that usually entitles the owner to fixed dividend payments that must be made before any dividends are paid to common shareholders

money market security short-term debt instrument

capital market security debt security with a maturity of greater than one year

---

[5] Full faith and credit refers to the unconditional requirement to repay the borrowed funds and any interest owed.

As we mentioned earlier, governments raise new financing via the debt markets. They sell Treasury bills as a source of short-term financing, and they issue notes and bonds for long-term financing. Businesses raise short-term financing in the form of debt through loans, or by issuing commercial paper, bankers' acceptances, and so on. They raise long-term financing in the form of debt (i.e., through loans, by issuing bonds, or by using other long-term debt instruments) or in the form of equity (i.e., by issuing common shares or preferred shares).

Financial Markets

We now we provide a brief description of the financial markets that permit the issue and trading of financial instruments. It is important to recognize that financial markets play a critical role in any open economy by facilitating the transfer of funds from lenders or investors to borrowers. In addition, if markets are efficient, such funds will be allocated to those with the most productive use for them.

For discussion purposes we begin by distinguishing between primary and secondary markets. In a **primary market** issuers issue new securities in return for cash from investors. In the case of a debt obligation, the issuer is the borrower and the investor is the lender. For example, when the government sells new issues of T-bills or bonds, or when a company sells new common shares to the public, these are primary market transactions; new securities are created, and the borrowing entity raises monies it can spend. When a company goes public, selling equity interests to investors for the first time, we refer to the offering as an **initial public offering (IPO).** We show the initial public offering activity in the U.S. in Figure 1-4. The IPO activity tends to move along with the market, with more offerings in periods of strong economic activity and fewer during economic downturns.

Primary markets are the key to the wealth creation process because they enable money to be transferred to those who can make the best use of it in terms of developing new real assets like houses and factories. We provide a graph of the issuance of debt and equity by U.S. corporations from 1990 through 2010 in Figure 1-5. In this graph we show straight corporate debt (the typical notes and bonds) as well as convertible debt, which investors can exchange for the stock of the issuing company. We also include both the common and the preferred stock issuances in Figure 1-5.

> **primary market** market that involves the issue of new securities by the borrower in return for cash from investors (or lenders)
>
> **initial public offering (IPO)** first sale of equity interests to the public

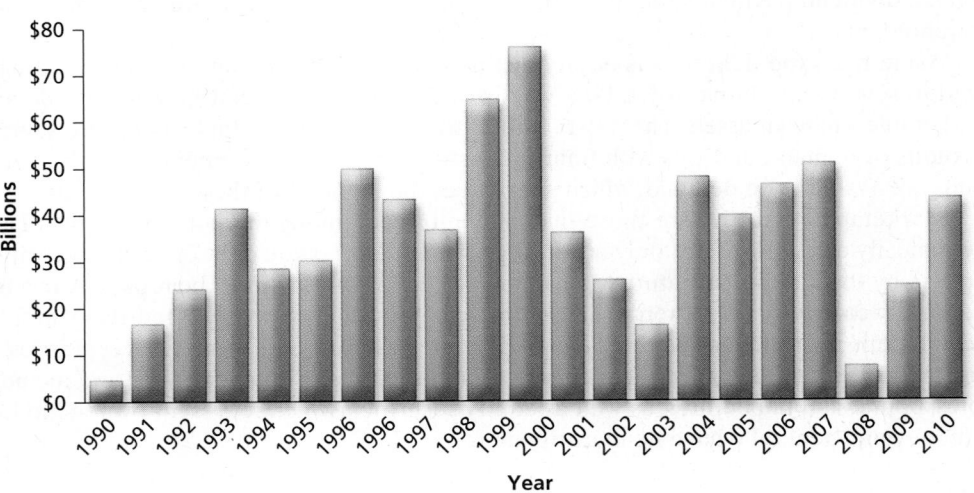

FIGURE 1-4 Initial Public Offerings by U.S. Corporations, 1990–2010
Source of data: *Securities Industry and Financial Markets Association*

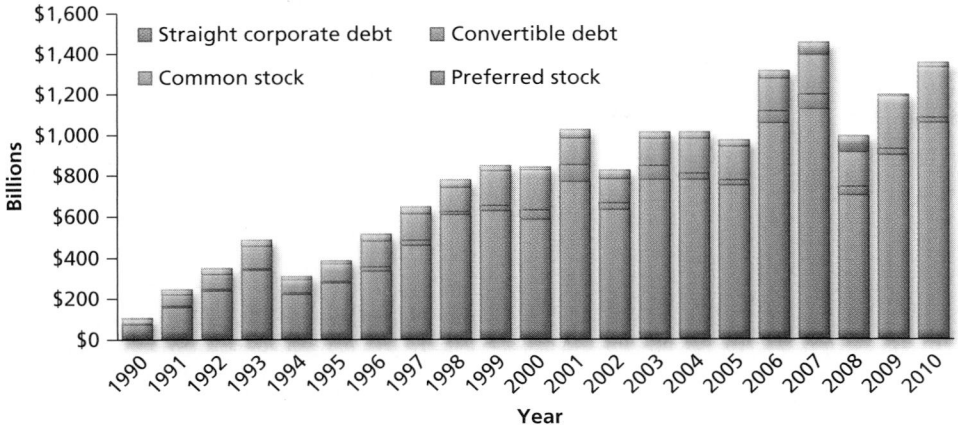

FIGURE 1-5 Debt and Equity Issuance by Corporations, 1990–2010
Source of data: *Securities Industry and Financial Markets Association*

Primary markets, however, will not work properly without a well-functioning **secondary market**. A secondary market provides trading (or market) environments that permit investors to buy and sell existing securities. This service is critical to the functioning of the primary markets because governments and companies would not be able to raise financing if investors were unable to sell their investments when necessary. Consider how reluctant an investor would be to buy a 20-year corporate bond worth $1,000 or $1,000 worth of a company's common shares if she was unable to sell the securities in the event she had to raise money in a hurry or because she became nervous about the company's future prospects.

There are two major types of secondary markets, although the distinction between them has becoming increasingly blurred over the past few years: (1) **exchange market** or **auction market**; and (2) **dealer market** or **over-the-counter (OTC) market**. Exchanges have been referred to as auction markets because they involve a bidding process that takes place in a specific location (i.e., similar to an auction). Investors (both buyers and sellers) are represented at these markets by brokers. In contrast, OTC or dealer markets do not have a physical location, but rather consist of a network of dealers who trade directly with one another. The distinction has become blurred in recent years because trading on most of the major exchanges in the world has become fully computerized, making the physical location of the exchanges of little consequence. At the same time, OTC markets have become increasingly automated, reducing the amount of direct haggling between dealers.

Money market instruments trade in dealer markets. They tend to be very large and are typically issued in sizes of $100,000 or more. As a result, money market trading is dominated by governments, financial institutions, and large corporations. Long-term debt instruments, such as bonds, are also traded primarily through dealer markets, though some are traded on exchanges.

Equity securities in general, and common shares in particular, represent the major financial security issued by corporations and comprise a proportionate ownership in a company. Unlike debt securities, which are normally paid back and result in constant refinancing activity, common shares are generally issued once and then stay outstanding indefinitely.[6] As a result, secondary market trading in equity securities is many times the size of the primary market, whereas for debt securities it is the opposite.

We often compare stocks by referring to their **market capitalization**. A company's market capitalization is the product of the market price of a share and the number of shares outstanding. For example, as of December 2010, the market capitalization of

secondary market trading (or market) environment that permits investors to buy and sell existing securities

exchange market or **auction market** secondary market that involves a bidding process that takes place in a specific location

dealer market or **over-the-counter (OTC) market** secondary market that does not have a physical location and consists of a network of dealers who trade directly with one another

---

[6] There are occasional share repurchases, but relative to the continuous retirement of debt, the amounts are generally insignificant.

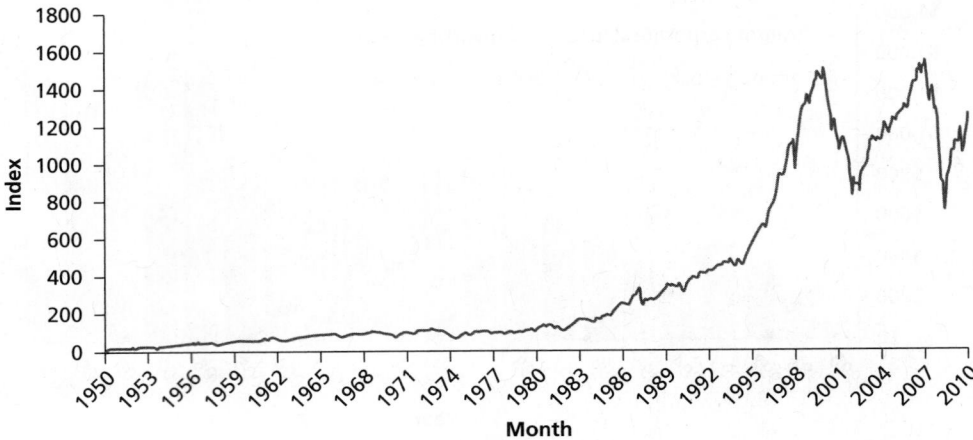

FIGURE 1-6 S&P 500 January 1950 Through March 2011
Source of data: *Yahoo! Finance*

General Electric was $17.50 × 10.65 million shares = $186 billion. In comparison, the market capitalization of Procter & Gamble Co. was $178 billion, Google was $189 billion, Motorola was $20 billion, and that of Yahoo! was $21 billion.

We can gauge the performance of stock markets by looking at specific indexes. For example, the S&P 500 is an index of 500 large, representative stocks. We plot this index over time in Figure 1-6. We can see the effect of the 2007–2008 financial crisis: The S&P 500 Index peaked in May 2007 and then got caught in the tailspin of the worldwide decline in equity markets as the U.S. banking system verged on collapse, recovering in 2009.

third market trading of securities that are listed on organized exchanges in the OTC market

fourth market trading of securities directly between investors without the involvement of brokers or dealers

In addition to the primary and secondary markets there are also the third and fourth markets. The **third market** refers to the trading of securities that are listed on organized exchanges in the OTC market. Historically, this market has been particularly important for "block trades," which are extremely large transactions involving at least 10,000 shares or $100,000. Finally, the **fourth market** refers to trades that are made directly between investors (usually large institutions), without the involvement of brokers or dealers. The fourth market operates through the use of privately owned automated systems, with one of the most widely recognized systems being Instinet.[7]

---

[7] Instinet is owned and operated by Instinet, LLC, which is owned by Nomura Holdings.

Equity Markets | GLOBAL PERSPECTIVE

The NYSE Euronext market in the U.S. is the world's largest equity market in terms of the value of the stocks listed with the exchange, as of November 2011:

Exchange	Market capitalization in billions of U.S. dollars
NYSE Euronext (US)	$11,233
NASDAQ OMX	3,855
London Stock Exchange	3,301
Tokyo Stock Exchange Group	3,287
NYSE Euronext (Europe)	2,509
Shanghai Stock Exchange	2,452
Hong Kong Exchanges	2,184
TMX Group	1,953
BM&FBOVESPA	1,256
Bombay SE	1,087

Source: World Federation of Exchanges, www.world-exchanges.org/statistics

The NYSE Euronext U.S. market's listings comprise 1790 domestic companies and 521 foreign companies. This contrasts with the Tokyo SE Group, which has 2,272 domestic listed companies and only twelve foreign listed companies, and with the Shanghai Stock Exchange, with 929 domestic but no foreign companies among its listings.

Regulation

Most economies operate with a central bank that oversees financial institutions and the economy's money supply. In the U.S., the central bank is the Federal Reserve System.[8] The **Federal Reserve System (the Fed)** consists of the Board of Governors and twelve districts banks, as we show in Figure 1-7. A financial institution may become a member of this system by becoming a nationally chartered bank or by being a state-chartered bank that voluntarily joins the system. As a member of the system, a financial institution can borrow from the Fed; the Fed becomes a lender of last resort.

The Board of Governors of the Federal Reserve System comprises seven members who are appointed by the president, and confirmed by the Senate, to 14-year terms. From these seven members, the chairman and the vice chairman of supervision are appointed

Federal Reserve System (the Fed) central bank of the U.S., consisting of the Board of Governors and twelve district banks

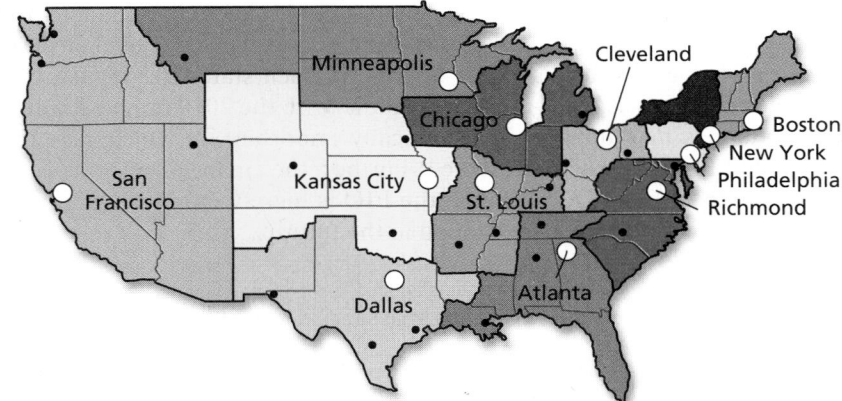

FIGURE 1-7 The Twelve Districts in the U.S. Federal Reserve System
Source: *www.federalreserveonline.org*

[8] The Federal Reserve System was established with the Federal Reserve Act of 1913.

by the president and confirmed by the Senate for four-year terms. The chairman of the Board of Governors, the most visible member of this board, reports to Congress on the board's monetary objectives and meets with the secretary of the treasury. The vice chairman of supervision position is relatively new, with this member charged with overseeing the supervision and regulation of entities within the Federal Reserve's jurisdiction, as well as making policy recommendations for the Federal Reserve.[9]

Federal Open Market Committee (FOMC) twelve-member committee that affects the monetary policy of the U.S.

The primary responsibility of the Board of Governors is to determine monetary policy, which it does through the **Federal Open Market Committee (FOMC)**. The FOMC consists of the seven members of the Board of Governors and the five Federal Reserve Bank presidents.

The Board of Governors establishes the reserve requirements of federally chartered banks, shares responsibility with the district banks regarding discount rate policy, sets margin requirements, participates in the payment system, and supervises and regulates the banks in the system.

The Banking Act of 1933, more familiarly known as the Glass-Steagall Act, gave the Fed the power to regulate the maximum interest rate that banks provide on deposits. The purpose of this power was to regulate competition among banks because it was believed that excessive competition led to the Great Depression of the 1930s. Over the years, the Fed has been given the power, among other things, to:

- establish margin requirements, which affect the extent that stock is purchased with borrowed funds;[10]
- require disclosures regarding consumer lending;[11] and
- assess reserve requirements of member banks and nondepository institutions.[12]

The responsibilities of the Fed in the financial industry are significant. Each time there is a financial crisis, the powers of the Fed are enhanced to deal with the new threat. For example, following the savings and loans crisis of the 1980s, in which 747 financial institutions failed, the Financial Institutions Reform, Recovery, and Enforcement Act of 1989 was passed. It created additional supervisory bodies (the Office of Thrift Supervision and the Federal Housing Finance Board) and regulations for the savings and loan industry. Following the 2007–2008 financial crisis, Congress gave the Board of Governors of the Federal Reserve greater responsibility to regulate nonbank financial companies that are deemed systematically important and to establish risk-based capital, liquidity, and leverage requirements.[13]

Historically, insurance was regulated at the state level. The National Association of Insurance Commissioners (NAIC) has worked with various state agencies to develop uniform evaluation standards of insurance companies, which has brought some degree of consistency in their regulation. For example, the NAIC developed the Insurance Regulatory Information System (IRIS) ratios, which are used to assess the financial solvency of an insurance company. Because insurance is regulated at the state level, insurance companies create state-based subsidiaries to operate in each state. The regulation of insurance companies, however, is changing. For example, with the 2010 financial reforms, some insurance companies may qualify as systemically important, in which case they would also be regulated by the Federal Reserve.[14] Further, the financial reforms establish the **Federal Insurance Office (FIO)**. Though the FIO is merely monitoring and advisory in nature at this time, its role may be expanded in the future.

Federal Insurance Office (FIO) federal agency responsible for monitoring and advising regulators about insurance companies' risk and solvency

[9] This position was created in 2010 by the Dodd-Frank Wall Street Reform and Consumer Protection Act.

[10] Regulations G, T, U and X.

[11] Regulation W, the Truth-in-Lending Act, Equal Credit Opportunity Act, the Fair Credit Billing Act, and the Community Reinvestment Act.

[12] Depository Institutions Deregulation and Monetary Control Act of 1980.

[13] In the most recent legislation, the Dodd-Frank Wall Street Reform and Consumer Protection Act, signed into law July 2010 [Public Law 111-203 H. R. 4173], systemically important nonbank companies are those with $50 billion or more in assets.

[14] A financial services company with $50 billion or more of assets may be deemed "systemically important."

The **Securities and Exchange Commission (SEC)** bears the responsibility of ensuring that financial markets are fair, orderly, and efficient. In addition, the SEC is tasked with encouraging capital flows from investors to businesses, but also with protecting investors. We list the major laws that regulate securities markets and securities transactions in Table 1-1, for which the SEC has primary responsibility. The first five laws in this table—Securities Act of 1933, the Securities Exchange Act of 1934, the Trust Indenture Act of 1939, the Investment Company Act of 1940, and the Investment Advisers Act of 1940—pertain to the regulation of securities, securities trading, investment managers, brokers, and dealers. The Sarbanes-Oxley (SOX) Act, passed into law in 2002 as a reaction to the scandal involving Enron, deals with financial management issues, including disclosures, corporate governance, and the accounting profession. The Dodd-Frank Wall Street Reform and Consumer Protection Act deals with wide-reaching changes in the structure of financial regulation.

The SEC has the responsibility of oversight of **self-regulatory organizations (SROs)**. The largest such SRO is the **Financial Industry Regulatory Authority (FINRA)**. FINRA was created in 2007 from the merger of the National Association of Security Dealers (NASD) and some functions of the New York Stock Exchange. FINRA registers brokers and brokerage firms, enforces securities laws among the registered brokers and firms, and regulates the NASDAQ stock market, the American Stock Exchange, the International Stock Exchange, and the Chicago Climate Exchange.

The regulatory power of the SEC was expanded in the 2010 financial reforms to include enhancing investor protections, regulating hedge funds, and expanding its regulation of credit rating agencies, among other things.

Securities and Exchange Commission (SEC) U.S. agency responsible for ensuring that financial markets are fair, orderly, and efficient

self-regulatory organization (SRO) organization that oversees and monitors its members and member organizations

Financial Industry Regulatory Authority (FINRA) self-regulatory organization that monitors and regulates brokerage firms, brokers, and market intermediaries

TABLE 1-1   Highlights of Selected U.S. Securities Laws

Law	*Purpose*
Securities Act of 1933	Requires disclosure of specific information about securities offered to the public, and prohibits misrepresentations and fraud in the sale of securities.
Securities Exchange Act of 1934	Created the Securities and Exchange Commission, giving the SEC the power and responsibility to regulate and oversee brokerage firms, agents, and self-regulatory organizations. Requires periodic reporting by companies with publicly traded securities.
Trust Indenture Act of 1939	Regulates the provisions of indentures for bonds, debentures, and notes sold to the public.
Investment Company Act of 1940	Regulates investment companies, such as mutual funds.
Investment Advisers Act of 1940	Regulates investment advisers, and specifies who must register with the SEC.
Sarbanes-Oxley Act of 2002	Increases disclosure requirements of publicly traded companies, creates oversight boards for independent public accountants, requires specific corporate governance provisions, and holds the chief executive officer and the chief financial officer accountable for a public company's disclosures.
Dodd-Frank Wall Street Reform and Consumer Protection Act of 2010	Increases oversight responsibility and regulation of hedge funds, credit-rating agencies, and brokers and dealers, among other things.

Deregulation of the Financial Services Industry

The Banking Act of 1933 and the Bank Holding Company Act of 1956 created barriers between different financial service businesses: banking, insurance, and securities.[15] The Financial Services Modernization (FSM) Act, more commonly referred to as the Gramm-Leach-Bliley (GLB) Act, was signed into law in 1999 and changed the shape of the financial services sector.[16] Many companies took advantage of the deregulation aspects of this act, entering into other financial services that were previously restricted because the changes permitted commercial banks, investment banks, and insurance companies to enter each other's markets.

One of the consequences of the Gramm-Leach-Bliley Act was the merging of companies within and across the different financial sectors. Large financial services mergers include J.P. Morgan & Co. and Chase Manhattan in 2000, Bank of America and Fleet Boston Financial in 2003, Travelers' Property Casualty and St. Paul Companies in 2003, JPMorgan Chase & Co. and Bank One in 2004, Wachovia and SouthTrust Corporation in 2004, and Bank of America Corporation and MBNA in 2006. The result? Fewer, but larger firms; the largest banking institutions became even more substantial, raising the issue of whether these institutions were too big to fail. In other words, if these institutions were so large that their failure would jeopardize the economy, then they were too big to be allowed to fail, necessitating some form of government or regulatory action to prevent or mitigate their failure.

The financial crisis of 2007–2008 resulted in a wave of mergers to avoid failures of certain institutions. Consider the institutions that we list in Table 1-2 as the largest financial institutions in terms of revenue in 2010. Bank of America grew from $113 billion in revenues in 2008 to $134 in 2010, mostly by virtue of its acquisition of Merrill Lynch in January 2010.[17] Other notable mergers resulting from the financial crisis include Wells Fargo's acquisition of Wachovia, PNC Bank's acquisition of National City, and JPMorgan Chase's acquisition of Washington Mutual.[18]

TABLE 1-2 Largest Financial Service Firms, 2010

United States

Rank	Company	2010 Revenues in billions of U.S. dollars
1	Fannie Mae	$154
2	General Electric	152
3	Berkshire Hathaway	136
4	Bank of America	134
5	JPMorgan Chase	115

Globally

Rank	Company	2010 Revenues in billions of U.S. dollars	Home country
1	Japan Post Holdings	$204	Japan
2	AXA	162	France
3	Fannie Mae	154	U.S.
4	General Electric	152	U.S.
5	ING Group	147	Netherlands

Source: *Insurance Information Institute Fact Book 2012*

[15] The Banking Act of 1933, commonly known as the Glass-Steagall Act [June 16, 1933, Ch 89 §20, 48 Stat. 188; Aug 23, 1935, Ch 614, Title III, § 302, 49 Stat. 707].

[16] U. S. Public Law No. 106-102, signed into law November 12, 1999.

[17] Bank of America acquired Countrywide Financial in mid-2008.

[18] Jonathan Rich and Thomas G. Scriven, "Bank Consolidation Caused by the Financial Crisis: How Should the Antitrust Division Review 'Shotgun Marriages,'" *The Antitrust Source*, www.antitrustsource.com, December 2008.

Concept Review Questions

1. What are the main differences between debt and equity securities?

2. What distinguishes primary and secondary markets?

3. What is the role of the Securities and Exchange Commission?

1.3 THE GLOBAL FINANCIAL CRISIS

The financial crisis of 2007–2008 was a significant event that affected businesses and economies around the world. To understand the crisis, it is important to first appreciate the linkages that exist among the global economies. After we emphasize the global linkages in the financial system, we explore the major events of this crisis and for a period following. After our overview of the events, we examine some of the challenges that this crisis presented to financial managers.

The Global Financial Community

In addition to domestic financial markets, global financial markets represent important sources of funds for borrowers and provide investors with significant alternatives. Indeed, U.S. debt and equity markets represent only a small proportion of the total global marketplace. Therefore, it makes sense for U.S. investors to borrow and invest abroad, which has become easier to do in today's global business environment as investment barriers are relaxed.

In Table 1-3 we illustrate the importance of global markets to U.S. investors and vice versa. As you can see in this table, the investment in the United States by non-U.S. investors exceeds the investment that U.S. investors have outside the United States in each year. More important, the extent that U.S. assets are owned outside the United States and foreign assets are owned by U.S. investors illustrates the interconnection of the economies. A **financial derivative** in this table is an investment whose value is based on some other investment, such as options (securities that give the investor the right to buy or sell a stock) and interest-rate swaps (agreements to exchange sets of cash flows, e.g., fixed interest for floating interest). We break out financial derivatives separately to give you an idea of the importance of these types of securities when compared to all other securities. The variations that we may see from year-to-year investments are likely caused by the performance of U.S. and non-U.S. markets, fluctuations in currency exchange rates, and

financial derivative investment whose value is based on some other investment

TABLE 1-3 U.S. Investors' International Investments, Second Quarter 2010 and 2011

Positive values indicate inflows to the U.S. and negative values indicate outflows from the U.S.

(in millions)	Second quarter 2010	Second quarter 2011
U.S.-owned assets abroad, excluding financial derivatives	–$175,174	–$343,848
Foreign-owned assets in the U.S., excluding financial derivatives	188,526	486,470
Net position	$13,352	$142,622
Financial derivatives, net	$9,980	$3,220

Source: *U.S. Bureau of Economic Analysis, Balance of Payments, Table 1, "U.S. International Transactions."*

changes in the economies throughout the world. The bottom line of this analysis is that there is substantial investment in the U.S. by non-U.S. investors, and there is also substantial investment outside the U.S. by U.S. investors.

The world's money markets and bond markets are very global in nature, with the U.S. markets representing the largest and most active debt markets in the world; global debt markets are primarily dealer markets. The United States also possesses the largest equity markets in the world. The **NYSE Euronext** is the world's largest stock market with a market capitalization at the end of January 2011 of $15.1 trillion. In total, as of January 2011, there were 7,803 companies listed on the NYSE Euronext, 2,452 of which were listed on the New York Stock Exchange (NYSE).[19]

NYSE Euronext world's largest stock market

The second-largest and most important stock market in the United States is the NASDAQ Stock Market, or, simply, the NASDAQ. The NASDAQ is the second-largest stock market in the world, based on its market capitalization of $3.6 trillion. In fact, the NASDAQ has more listed companies than the NYSE, with approximately 3,200; the average number of shares traded per day (2 billion) is close to the figure for the NYSE.[20] However, larger companies tend to list on the NYSE, which is why its market capitalization far exceeds that of the NASDAQ.

Securities exchanges around the world have been consolidating. In 2007, the NYSE and Euronext merged, creating the first truly global securities exchange. On January 16, 2009, the American Stock Exchange was phased out after its acquisition by the NYSE and became the NYSE's trading platform for options, closed-end funds, and exchange traded funds (ETFs).[21,22] Consequently, even though there are almost 200 stock exchanges around the world, the industry is rapidly consolidating.

The globalization of the equity markets means that linkages between the markets are getting tighter. Never has this been better demonstrated than by the events of 2007 and 2008, when a crisis in the U.S. banking sector turned into the first global financial meltdown and recession. The events also reinforce the fact that the financial decisions of a company are not made in a vacuum.

The Foundation for the Crisis

In addition to the globalization of financial investments and instruments, a number of other factors set the stage for the global crisis. But first we need to explain one of the simplest financial products, a mortgage, before we can understand the sources of problems in the financial crisis.

A **mortgage** is a debt obligation that is secured by specific property. The mortgages at the heart of the crisis are primarily home mortgages, where the collateral is the individual borrower's home. Normally, to qualify for a mortgage, the bank requires a down payment from the borrower and lends the balance with a loan secured on the value of the house. However, house prices in the U.S. started to increase quite dramatically as the U.S. recovered from a serious recession in 2002. The increase was fueled by economic expansion, low mortgage rates, and a series of financial innovations that in retrospect reduced the checks in the mortgage lending process.[23] These factors, combined with loose regulation by the U.S. banking authorities, meant that credit was easily available.

The increased activity in the real estate market, combined with real estate speculation, heated up some housing markets in the U.S., such as Las Vegas, Los Angeles, and Miami. As you can see in Figure 1-8, home prices began rising in the early 2000s, peaking in late 2006.

---

[19] Source: NYSE Euronext *Fact Book*, 2010–current.
[20] Source: NASDAQ website at www.nasdaq.com.
[21] An ETF is a security that tracks an index, a commodity, or a portfolio of assets that is traded just like common stock.
[22] And in 2011, the NYSE Euronext and Deutsche Börse plan to merge, though as of the end of 2011 this merger had not gone through because of antitrust concerns.
[23] The annual growth in gross domestic product was over 3% in both 2004 and 2005.

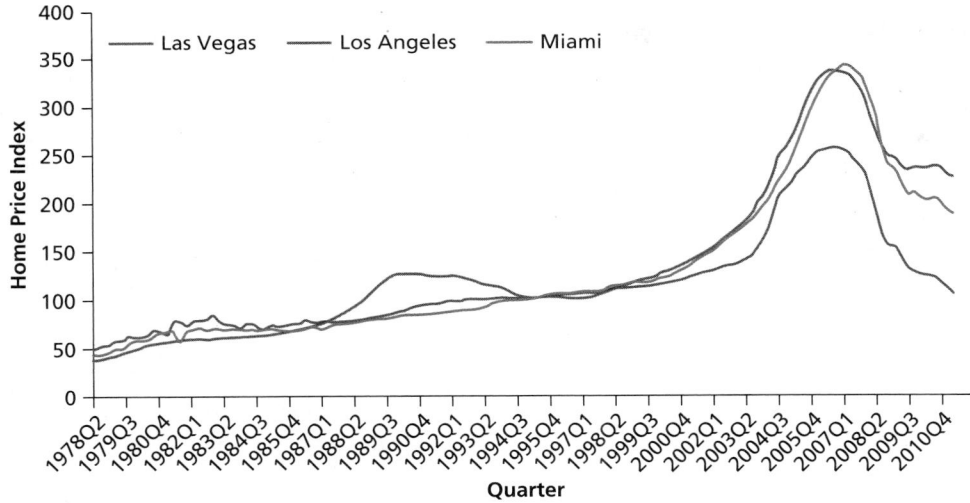

FIGURE 1-8 **Office of Federal Housing Enterprise Oversight Home Price Index, Second Quarter 1978 Through Third Quarter 2011 for Selected Metropolitan Statistical Areas**
Source: *Federal Housing Finance Agency (FHFA), HPI index.*

The annual rate of growth of home prices in these three markets during the period 2004–2006 averaged over 15% per year, much higher than the typical home value increase in a year. You can see the home-price bubble and the decline in values in these three markets after 2007.

The Financial Crisis

One of the challenges in understanding and dealing with the financial crisis of 2007–2008 is that there is no one single cause of the crisis, but rather many that occurred to create the perfect storm. One of the most visible causes of the crisis was the housing bubble, but others include lax lending standards, a push for the **government-sponsored entities (GSEs)** of Freddie Mac and Fannie Mae to purchase lower quality loans for resale as securities, the insatiable appetite of investors for high-return, high-risk securities that were backed by mortgages, and rampant fraud in mortgage origination.

In any discussion of the financial crisis, you will hear reference to securitization. **Securitization** is the process of converting loans into securities. In the case of mortgages, the mortgage originator (the party lending the funds to the borrower) sells mortgages to a party that pools them together and then sells securities that have rights to the cash flows of the mortgages. The party pooling the mortgages may be a GSE, such as Freddie Mac. This security is a **mortgage-backed security**, secured by the mortgages in the pool. Sounds simple? Not really, because predicting whether borrowers will default on a loan and predicting whether borrowers will pay off a loan early (e.g., refinancing) is not easy. And, as many learned, even the best prediction models did not consider the defaults in the magnitude that occurred.

government-sponsored entity (GSEs) financial service corporations that are created by the government to perform a service, such as buying mortgages

securitization pooling of loans, and then creating and selling securities that have rights to specific cash flows from this pool

mortgage-backed securities claims on the cash flows of a pool of mortgages

The beginning of the crisis: Early 2007

You would think that in an overheated housing market lenders would be more cautious in their lending. However, in the U.S. this did not happen as banks and other financial institutions often loaned in excess of 100% of the value of a house with very little documentation in NINJA loans: no income, no job, no assets.[24] Mortgages were originated for some borrowers who had poor credit histories and who could not otherwise qualify for

---

[24] Another nickname for these loans is "liar loans" because of the lack of information on the borrower's income or assets.

subprime mortgage home loan to a borrower with poor credit who would not otherwise qualify for a conventional mortgage

a conventional mortgage; we refer to this type of mortgage as a **subprime mortgage**. By 2006 the U.S. subprime market was exploding. Why would lenders lend money when documentation was deficient or when the borrower was a high credit risk? Because mortgage originators received fees based on the mortgages originated, not the quality of these mortgages. Further, there were ready buyers of these mortgages, which encouraged more production by originators. Loan originators sold these loans to dealers, who repackaged them into securities through securitization.

Everything might have been fine if home prices had continued to increase, but with the supply of homes outpacing demand, supply and demand principles dominated, and the housing market collapsed. Lenders started to catch on that credit was too generous, and financing started to contract. By summer 2007 U.S. house prices began to fall, as you can see in Figure 1-8. Loans made with a high ratio of loan to the value of the home—the **loan-to-value ratio**—were soon problematic, as the value of the home became much lower than the amount owed. In other words, these loans were "underwater," which provided the incentive for some homeowners to simply walk away from the home—and the loan.[25]

loan-to-value ratio ratio of the amount of a loan to the value of the collateral used as security on the loan

The crisis is heating up: Mid-2007

With U.S. house prices in hot markets off by an average of 40%, even prime U.S. mortgage loans were now greater than the value of the houses they were secured against. The result was an increase in late payments and defaults, followed by large losses for the banks that made the loans. These problems were magnified by the securitization of loans. Many loan originators went out of business, leaving behind mortgaged-backed securities with defaults and a declining value of the collateral. For example, New Century Financial Corporation, one of the largest originators of subprime mortgages, filed for bankruptcy in April 2007. Following this, Countrywide Financial Corporation, another large originator, became financially distressed, and American Home Mortgage Investment Corporation filed for bankruptcy in August 2007.

In addition to the mortgage originators, investment firms with significant investments in mortgage-backed securities began to disclose problems.[26] The first major sign of this involved Bear Stearns, an investment bank, and its liquidation in July of 2007 of two hedge funds that invested heavily in mortgage-backed securities. In addition, the major banking institutions of Citigroup, Bank of America, and JPMorgan Chase attempted to raise capital in October 2007 to support special-purpose vehicles that were used in securitizations.[27]

Early 2008

There were several acquisitions intended to stem the failures among financial institutions. For example, in January of 2008, Bank of America acquired Countrywide Financial, and JPMorgan Chase acquired Bear Stearns in March 2008. These acquisitions were problematic because the acquired firms had substantial stakes in mortgage-backed securities and, hence, large realized and unrealized losses in these securities.

The Economic Stimulus Act of 2008 was signed into law in February 2008 to help generate consumer spending, and the FOMC took actions to stabilize the economy. In addition, the Federal Reserve Board took several steps to provide liquidity to the markets, establishing the Term Securities Lending Facility (TSLF) and the Primary Dealer Credit Facility.

Mid-to-late 2008

systemic risk uncertainty that affects the larger economy

The problems related to lax lending standards and the securitization of subprime loans, accompanied by high default rates, led to systemic risk for the economy. **Systemic risk** is risk that affects the larger economy, and because the effects ripple throughout the

[25] Homeowners who walked away from their mortgages and home would mail the keys to the lender; hence the term "jingle mail" applied to these cases.

[26] Around this time, accounting rules went into effect that required valuation of these investments using some form of index rather than a company's own estimate of their value.

[27] In December 2007, these firms announced that this was not needed.

It's Greek to Me | FINANCE in the News

Sovereign debt is indebtedness issued by a national government. For example, the Treasury bills and bonds issued by the U.S. government are part of the sovereign debt of the U.S. One of the fallouts of the 2007–2008 crisis is the downgrading of sovereign debt. Greece, with its long history of budget problems, was the first to fall. Its debt was downgraded in 2009, in 2010, in 2011, and then again in 2012. The rating of Greece's debt from Moody's fell from A1 to C in this three-year period. To put this in perspective, the rating of Greece's debt went from "High economic, financial or institutional strength" to "One shock away from default, and/or material concerns about the willingness to pay."[28] The upshot of the downgrade is that the debt is considered riskier, and therefore, the cost of raising capital

increases. By 2012, the yield on 10-year Greek debt was over 3,300 basis points (that is, 33%) higher than other European sovereign debt, and the debt was, effectively, in default.[29] Other countries followed suit, with Portugal and Spain following close behind Greece.

Like any business, an economic slowdown such as the one that followed the global crisis affects the countries that have the weakest economies. Factors considered important in rating sovereign debt include gross domestic product, government policies in dealing with budgets, policies of the central bank, and unemployment.[30] The challenge is that once the debt is downgraded, the cost of raising new capital is greater, and the country will have difficulty raising capital to finance its operations.

---

economy, it cannot be diversified away. The systemic risk arising from the mortgage/housing crisis was pervasive in the financial system.

September 2008 marked the beginning of a credit crunch in the U.S. and other countries. A **credit crunch**, which we also refer to as a **credit squeeze**, is the lack of available loans for businesses; lenders stop or slow down lending and tighten credit standards, making it difficult for businesses to obtain funds, no matter the cost. A credit crunch is most significant for small businesses that cannot access capital markets to issue bonds or stock, but instead depend on bank lending to meet their liquidity needs.[31]

credit crunch or **credit squeeze** lack of available loans for businesses

The culmination of the severe liquidity crisis and the economic downturn resulted in restructuring in the financial system. Several large financial institutions failed in 2008, including IndyMac Bank in July, Integrity Bank in August, and Lehman Brothers Holdings Incorporated and Washington Mutual Bank in September. When Lehman Brothers was allowed to fail in the biggest ever bankruptcy at that time, it triggered a massive loss of confidence in the banking sector and desperate efforts by the U.S. government to shore up its banks.

To avoid failures, several acquisitions were arranged by the Federal Reserve, in which financially healthy institutions acquired unhealthy institutions. Examples include Bank of America's acquisition of Merrill Lynch, in a deal initiated in September, and Wells Fargo & Co.'s acquisition of Wachovia in October. In addition, Fannie Mae and Freddie Mac were placed in government conservatorship in September of 2008, and the U.S. Treasury put into place an agreement to purchase the preferred stock of the GSEs and to provide needed liquidity.

The stocks of several financial institutions, as well as nonfinancial firms, fell dramatically during the financial crisis, and it was believed that this was exaggerated by short selling pressure. Short selling, in a nutshell, is the sale of borrowed shares, with the expectation that the shares would be purchased at a later date at a lower price and the borrowed shares returned.[32] The Securities and Exchange Commission banned short selling the stock of GSEs in July 2008 and all financial stocks in September 2008.

---

[28] Moody's Investor Service, "Sovereign Bond Ratings," September, 2008, p. 4.

[29] Marcus Bensasson, "Greek debt rating cut three steps to B1 by Moody's on rising default risk," *Bloomberg*, March 7, 2011.

[30] Moody's Investors Service, "2010 in Perspective and Global Macro Risk Scenarios 2011–2012: Curbing Contagion," February 4, 2011.

[31] *Federal Reserve Bank of San Francisco Economic Letter*, Federal Reserve Bank of San Francisco, 2009–09; March 6, 2009.

[32] This uses the old adage "Buy low, sell high," but the selling is done first.

Troubled Asset Relief Program (TARP) U.S. government program to infuse capital in the financial system by purchasing assets and equity from troubled financial institutions

To address the lack of liquidity in the capital markets, several actions were taken. The most significant was the $700 billion **Troubled Asset Relief Program (TARP)**, created by Congress in October 2008.[33] A component of the TARP was the $250 billion Capital Repurchase Program, in which the U.S. Treasury acquired preferred stock of banks, providing needed funds. In addition, the Federal Reserve Board established several programs to inject funds into the financial system, including the Commercial Paper Funding Facility (CPFF) to purchase commercial paper from high-quality issuers. Actions were also taken to shore up individual companies, including providing $85 billion to American International Group (AIG) through certain transactions.[34] In addition to banks, the insurance companies Lincoln National, Hartford Financial Services, and Genworth Financial, as well as auto companies General Motors and Chrysler, received loans through the TARP program.

Early 2009

Term Asset-Backed Securities Loan Facility (TALF) U.S. government program to inject capital in the financial system by lending funds to investors of specific high-quality asset-backed securities

stress test scenario-based evaluation of a company's solvency, where the scenario is the worst-case scenario

The Federal Reserve Bank of New York began buying fixed-rate mortgage-backed securities guaranteed by Fannie Mae, Freddie Mac, and Ginnie Mae as a means of adding liquidity to the financial system.[35] In addition, Congress passed the American Recovery and Reinvestment Act of 2009 in February, with the intent of stimulating the economy with government spending and some tax cuts. Further, the U.S. Treasury and the Fed announced an additional program, the **Term Asset-Backed Securities Loan Facility (TALF)** to lend funds to owners of specific AAA-rated asset-backed securities, specifically to investors of high-quality loans backed by student loans, auto loans, credit card loans, and Small Business Administration–backed loans.

Federal regulators performed stress tests on large bank holding companies, addressing the issue of whether banks would have adequate capital under severe economic conditions. A **stress test** is a scenario-based evaluation of a company's solvency, where the scenario is the worst-case scenario of an economic depression. Of the nineteen companies examined, nine were found to have adequate capital; those not meeting the standards were required to develop a plan to enhance their capital.

Several banks began repaying TARP funds in June of 2009, including State Street Bank, Goldman Sachs, Morgan Stanley, Capital One Financial, American Express, and BB&T. Despite receiving TARP funds, however, General Motors filed for bankruptcy in June of 2009, and CIT Group Inc., a lender to small and medium-sized businesses, filed for bankruptcy in November 2009.

Developments in 2010 and 2011

Financial institutions continued to repay TARP funds in 2010, and most of the troubled financial institutions that were not acquired or liquidated began to show profitability. Of the $475 billion of funds authorized in the TARP program, $389 billion had been disbursed by November of 2010, and $122 billion was outstanding as of October 2011.[36] The U.S. had recouped $13.5 billion of its investment in General Motors (GM) when GM had an initial public offering in November of 2010.

The most important development from the financial crisis was the impetus for reform in the financial industry, which began with the Dodd-Frank Wall Street Reform and Consumer Protection Act of 2010. We discuss this act later in this chapter.

---

[33] October 3, 2008, Emergency Economic Stabilization Act of 2008 (Public Law 110–343).

[34] These transactions involved borrowing securities from AIG in exchange for cash. The total authorized assistance, in the form of debt and equity, was $123.948 billion, and the assistance outstanding in July 2011 was $85.011 billion. General Accounting Office, Troubled Asset Relief Program: *The Government's Exposure to AIG Following the Company's Recapitalization*, July 2011.

[35] Ginnie Mae is a "sister" of Freddie and Fannie. Ginnie Mae guarantees the principal and interest on Federal Housing Administration insured mortgages and Department of Veterans Affairs–guaranteed mortgages.

[36] Troubled Assets Relief Program (TARP), Month 105(a) Report, November 2010, U.S. Department of the Treasury. The TARP program ceased making new investments in October 2010.

Subprime Loans and More | ETHICS

It's a Bull Market for Financial Fraud

Imagine landing your dream home. Your credit is a bit shaky, but you manage to get a subprime loan with an adjustable rate mortgage. A few years later the interest rates jump, and you can no longer afford to pay. You see an ad for a business that's willing to help—it'll pay your mortgage for a modest monthly fee while you get back on your feet. But here's the heartbreak: it's a scam. The con artists just take your money and run . . .

It's just one of the latest schemes and frauds we're seeing these days across the financial services industry, our senior criminal investigators said during a briefing Tuesday with the news media in Washington.

These scams—which include plenty of shenanigans with mortgages and subprime loans—are costing the nation tens of billions of dollars a year.

"Greed is definitely not good for our economy right now," said our top criminal investigative exec Ken Kaiser following the briefing. "It's hurting homeowners. It's hurting honest businesses. And it's hurting investors and markets around the world."

All good reasons why we're squarely focused on cracking down on the largest of these financial crimes, launching proactive initiatives and shifting resources as trends emerge, all the while working hand-in-hand with a host of government and private sector partners.

Among the specifics discussed at the briefing:
Subprime mortgage loans:

- We're investigating 14 corporations involved in subprime lending as part of our Subprime Mortgage Industry Fraud Initiative launched last year.

- The companies come from across the financial services industry, from mortgage lenders to investment banks that bundle loans into securities sold to investors. We're also looking at insider trading by some executives.

Traditional mortgage fraud:

- We have more than 1,200 cases open today (up about 40% from last year), mostly involving fraud for profit, where groups of straw buyers, realtors, etc. rig schemes to buy properties that are flipped or allowed to go into foreclosure.

- Hotspots include California, Texas, Arizona, Florida, Ohio, Michigan, and Utah.

- Suspicious activity reports that we review for potential mortgage fraud have grown from 3,000 in fiscal year 2003 to 48,000 in fiscal year 2007. This year, we're on pace to receive more than 60,000 such reports.

- A recent case: In November, the owners of a long-time Minnesota homebuilder called Parish Marketing—along with a bank officer, a closing agent, and others—pled guilty to a $100 million mortgage scheme involving some 200 homes.

- Right now, we're seeing no links to organized crime syndicates, street gangs, or terrorist groups in our cases.

Source: Federal Bureau of Investigation, January 31, 2008, www.fbi.gov

What Is to Come

The U.S. financial markets and institutions are currently undergoing changes, with some of these changes yet to come. Until 2008 the U.S. was unique in having five very powerful investment banks that dominated the market intermediary function in the U.S. markets; no more. Lehman Brothers was allowed to fail in September of 2008, Merrill Lynch was acquired by Bank of America, Morgan Stanley required a capital injection from Asian investors and has become a bank so as to receive protection from the U.S. Federal Reserve Board, Bear Stearns was sold to J.P. Morgan in 2008, and Goldman Sachs converted to a bank holding company in September of 2008 to have access to the government's emergency lending facilities.

Among the elite U.S. commercial banks there is similar wreckage: Citibank received $65 billion in emergency funds from the U.S. government to stay solvent as well as getting special insurance to cover $306 billion in toxic subprime-related mortgages, and Bank of America has $109 billion in similar bad loan insurance with $45 billion in emergency funds. Almost every major U.S. bank accepted special financial support from the U.S. government through TARP, as the government realized that allowing more banks to fail would lead to the complete collapse of the U.S. financial system.

During and following the financial crisis of 2007–2008, many banks failed. However, we should put this in perspective. The number of banks failing during this recent financial crisis is far fewer than in prior economic downturns. As you can see in Figure 1-9, the consolidation of the industry due to deregulation in the 1990s has resulted in larger failures in terms of losses. Comparing 1989 with 2009, we see that even before we worry about adjusting for inflation, the losses during 1989 exceed those of 2009, though the average size of the loss per institution has increased significantly:[37]

	1989			*2009*		
	Number of failed institutions	**Losses in millions**	**Average loss per institution in millions**	**Number of failed institutions**	**Losses in millions**	**Average loss per institution in millions**
Commercial banks	206	$5,909	$29	126	$24,390	$203
Savings institutions	328	$47,514	$145	22	$12,967	$648

Source of data: *Federal Deposit Insurance Corporation, Failures and Assistance Transactions.*

In the banking crisis of the 1980s, Continental Illinois National Bank failed in May 1984. This failure raised two key issues: (1) Was regulatory oversight sufficient to evaluate and monitor a bank's risk, and (2) Was Continental Illinois National Bank, the seventh largest bank at the time, "too big to fail"?[38] A failure of a large financial institution could have significant effects on the rest of the economy. The Continental failure encouraged changes in the insurance program, but until the recent financial crisis, the changes had not been tested.[39] The failures of financial institutions in 2008 and 2009 raised, once again, the question of whether a financial institution could be "too big to fail."[40]

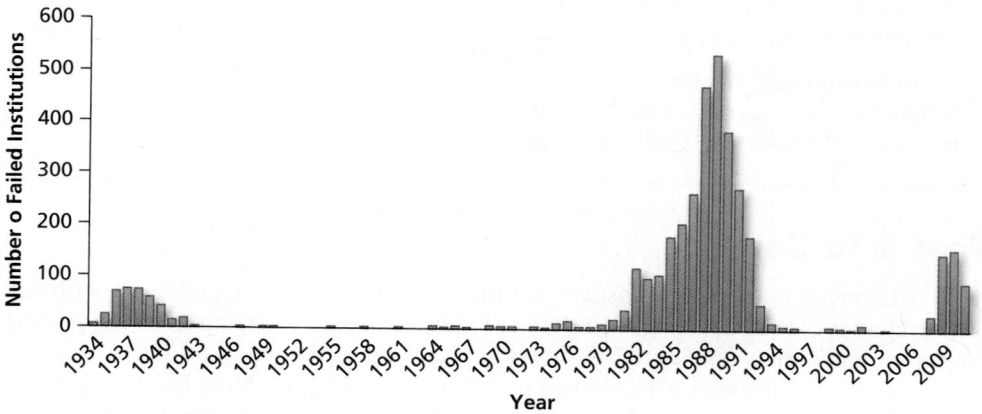

FIGURE 1-9 Bank and Savings Institution Failures 1934 Through 2011
Source: *Federal Deposit Insurance Corporation.*

[37] If we consider inflation, the $53.4 billion of losses in 1989 is equivalent, on an inflation-adjusted basis, to $92.4 billion in 2009 dollars, far exceeding the total losses in 2009 of $37.3 billion. The number of failures rose to 157 in 2010, but then fell to 92 in 2011. However, the failures in 2010 were of smaller institutions, with total losses of $19,931 million.

[38] "Continental Illinois and Too Big to Fail," Federal Deposit Insurance Corporation, *Histories of the Eighties—Lessons for the Future*, Chapter 7.

[39] Federal Deposit Insurance Corporation Improvement Act of 1991 (FDICIA).

[40] The Dodd-Frank Wall Street and Consumer Protection Act instituted a process of evaluating institutions that may be "too big to fail."

Stock markets reacted to the economic crisis, not just in the U.S., but throughout the world. For example, on September 15, 2008, the day Lehman Brothers filed for bankruptcy, all major world markets reacted, either in anticipation or as soon as the news was released, as we show in Table 1-4. On September 16, 2008, the U.S. Treasury and the Federal Open Market Committee took several actions, including a ban on short selling, to calm the markets, which helped the U.S. markets recover slightly.

Beginning in October 2008, the world moved into a serious recession. Recall that there is one big financial market, and all parts of it are interconnected to a greater or lesser degree. Events in the U.S. mortgage market have washed like a tsunami throughout the world and caused problems in corporate and government financing, as several countries from Iceland to Hungary have required emergency international loans to keep their economies afloat.

The regulatory structure in the U.S. financial system is undergoing changes to address the problems that created significant systemic risk. A major step in this reform was the passage of the Dodd-Frank Wall Street Reform and Consumer Protection Act of 2010, which was passed in mid-2010.[41] This is a wide-reaching act that altered the regulatory landscape in the U.S. financial system and set the stage for further changes. Among other things, the act:

- creates the Financial Stability Oversight Council, which provides a formal system of coordination among key regulators.
- creates criteria and standards for systemically important financial companies.
- provides for the orderly liquidation of financial companies that are insolvent.
- limits proprietary trading (Volcker Rule).

TABLE 1-4 Market Losses Around the World: September 15, 2008

Index or Average	Country	*Percentage change*	
		September 15, 2008	*September 16, 2008*
Sao Paulo Bovespa	Brazil	–7.59%	1.68%
S&P/TSX Composite	Canada	–4.04%	–0.22%
DAX	Germany	–2.74%	–1.63%
Hang Seng	Hong Kong	closed	–5.44%
Bombay Sensex	India	–3.35%	–0.09%
RTS Index	Russia	–4.78%	–11.47%
Johannesburg All Share	South Africa	–1.96%	–2.59%
Kospi	South Korea	closed	–6.10%
IBEX35	Spain	–4.50%	0.11%
FTSE 100	United Kingdom	–3.92%	–3.43%
Dow Jones Industrial Average	United States	–4.42%	1.30%
S&P 500 Index	United States	–4.71%	1.75%
Wilshire 500	United States	–4.55%	1.75%

Source of data: *Wall Street Journal Historical Data.*

[41] Dodd-Frank Wall Street Reform and Consumer Protection Act (H.R. 4173, Public Law No. 111-203, signed into law July 21, 2010).

- regulates derivatives, including swaps.
- regulates hedge funds, which previously operated without any required disclosures.
- enhances regulation of securities, including credit rating agencies and securitizations.
- creates the Bureau of Consumer Financial Protection, which deals with consumer financial products and services.

Consider the Financial Stability Oversight Council, which is responsible for monitoring the stability of the U.S. financial system. Under this act, the council comprises 15 members. The voting members of this council are:

- the U.S. Treasury Secretary
- the Chairman of the Federal Reserve Board
- the Chairman of the Office of the Comptroller of the Currency (OCC)
- the Chairman of the Bureau of Consumer Financial Protection
- the Chairman of the Securities Exchange Commission
- the Chairman of the Federal Depositor Insurance Commission
- the Chairman of the Commodity Futures Trading Commission
- the Director of the Federal Housing Finance Agency
- the Chairman of National Credit Union Administration
- an independent member with expertise in insurance

In addition to these members, there are five nonvoting members, two representing the Office of Financial Research and the Federal Insurance Office, one state insurance commissioner, one state banking supervisor, and one state securities commissioner. It is expected that by formally coordinating efforts, the council will be in a position to identify threats to the financial system, promote market discipline, and respond to risks that may arise.

Lessons for Financial Managers

The financial crisis presented many challenges and many lessons for financial managers. The economic downturn, coupled with a credit crunch, made the financial manager's job more difficult. Among these lessons:

1. *Financial risk management is important.* Financial managers need to identify, assess, and manage risks; companies must develop an assessment of how much risk they are willing to take (that is, their risk appetite), and risk management must be an essential part of a company's strategy.

2. *Companies that rely on securitizing their assets should be prepared for the associated risks.* Securitization of assets is performed by many companies, not just banks and, for example, has been a source of cash flow for companies that sell their receivables through these transactions. For instance, Harley-Davidson Financial Services securitized the loans made on the purchases of Harley-Davidson motorcycles; when the securitization market dried up and the company could no longer securitize the loans, it could not turn the loans into cash, but rather had to retain and maintain them.

3. *Reliance on bank financing for short-term needs is problematic during a credit crunch.* Many companies that relied on lines of credit from banks or issuing commercial paper to meet seasonal needs found that they could not get financing during severe times. For example, the commercial paper market was disrupted in September 2008 with Lehman Brothers' bankruptcy; in December 2008, the outstanding commercial paper was half of what is was at the end of 2007.[42]

---

[42] The U.S. Treasury and the Federal Reserve stepped in during October of 2008 to support the commercial paper market through the Money Market Investor Funding Facility, Richard G. Anderson and Charles S. Gascon, "The Commercial Paper Market, the Fed, and the 2007–2009 Financial Crisis," Federal Reserve Bank of St. Louis *Review*, November/December, 91, no. 6, 589–612.

4. *Executive compensation should be tied to some measure of risk, not just earnings*. Many financial institutions tied compensation to earnings, without regard to the risk associated with the expansion of the entity into other, riskier lines of business. The focus on earnings may have inadvertently encouraged excessive risk taking.

The financial management challenges that occurred during the financial crisis have reshaped financial decision making. For example, companies at the end of 2010 were sitting with a great deal of cash; interest rates in general were at historical lows, and capital markets had recovered, making it a great time to borrow. However, the uncertainties regarding the economic recovery and taxes, coupled with the recent experience with the credit crunch, have made many financial managers cautious and have, as a result, stifled the capital expenditures that are key to economic recovery.

The Benefit of Being Nimble | LESSONS LEARNED

The interest rates that companies pay on their borrowing fell during 2010 to record lows that hadn't been seen since the 1960s:

Interest rates of AAA rated corporate bonds: 1950 through 2010

Source of data: Board of Governors of the Federal Reserve System, Moody's Seasoned AAA Corporate Bond yield, Series, H.15.

These low rates encouraged many corporations to issue new debt, even those with lots of cash on hand. Why issue debt when you don't need to? The cost of debt capital is relatively cheap, and they can raise the new capital now instead of when their current debt matures, when interest rates are expected to rise.[43]

Case in point: Johnson & Johnson typically has around 15 percent of its assets in cash and marketable securities.

In its fiscal year 2010, Johnson had almost 27 percent of its assets in cash and marketable securities, thanks to its offering of $550 million in notes in August 2010. The vast majority of Johnson & Johnson's investment in cash and marketable securities is invested in government securities and obligations: $22.3 billion of its $27.7 billion in cash and marketable securities.[44]

1. Why are global financial markets so important to U.S. investors?

2. What was the role of subprime mortgages in the 2007–2008 financial crisis?

Concept Review Questions

---

[43] Robert McNatt, "Credit FAQ: Why Do Companies Issue Debt When They Don't Seem to Need the Money?," Standard & Poor's, October 20, 2010.
[44] Johnson & Johnson 2010 10-K filing with the Securities and Exchange Commission.

SUMMARY

- Finance as a subject area is the study of the flow of funds from those with funds to those who need funds. Financial decision making encompasses investment and financing decisions, which may be short-term or long-term decisions.

- A business may borrow funds, either through borrowing or selling equity interests in the business. Borrowing includes loans from banks, issuing commercial paper, or issuing notes or bonds. Borrowing requires repayment of the debt, as well as interest on the debt. Management may sell ownership stakes in the company, which are represented by shares of stock. These shares may be common stock or preferred stock.

- The financial system is global, with parties crossing borders to raise and invest funds. No better example of the globalization of the financial system is available than the 2007–2008 financial crisis, where linkages among the markets were evident as the U.S. economy faltered, along with economies around the world.

QUESTIONS AND PROBLEMS

Multiple Choice

1. An equity security represents:
   A. a debt obligation.   B. an ownership interest.

2. Which of the following transactions takes place in the primary market? An investor:
   A. selling a corporate bond.
   B. selling a U.S. Treasury bill.
   C. buying shares of stock through a broker.
   D. buying shares of an initial public offering.

3. Which of the following transactions takes place in the secondary market? An investor:
   A. selling a share of stock through a broker.
   B. buying shares of an initial public offering.
   C. buying a U.S. Treasury bill through the government auction.

4. Which of the following is considered a money market security?
   A. Common stock   B. Preferred stock   C. U.S. Treasury bills   D. U.S. Treasury notes

5. Regulators' stress tests on banks examine banks' capital adequacy under the:
   A. best-case economic scenario.   B. worst-case economic scenario.   C. most-likely economic scenario.

6. Which of the following is not a government program designed to assist financial institutions during the financial crisis of 2007–2008?
   A. Troubled Asset Relief Program
   B. Troubled Asset-Backed Securities Fund
   C. Term Asset-Backed Securities Loan Facility

7. The Financial Industry Regulatory Authority is best described as a:
   A. dealer market.
   B. government regulator.
   C. self-regulatory organization.
   D. government-sponsored entity.

8. Which of the following is not considered a debt obligation?
   A. Note   B. Debenture   C. Preferred stock   D. General obligation bond

9. A mortgage is best described as a:
   A. debenture.   B. secured debt.   C. equity instrument.

10. Systemic risk is best described as risk that:
    A. affects the entire economy.
    B. moves along with the risk of the market.
    C. is confined to one sector of the economy.
    D. affects only one geographical area of the country.

Practice Questions and Problems

1.1   What Is Finance?

11. List the primary areas of finance.

12. Why is it important for a financial manager to understand accounting and financial statements?

13. What is the role of a market intermediary?

14. What is an example of a financial intermediary?

1.2   Financial Instruments and Markets

15. What is meant by the description of a transaction as occurring in the primary market?

16. Provide three examples of a debt obligation.

17. What distinguishes a note from a bond?

18. Why are the owners of common stock referred to as the residual owners of a corporation?

19. What are secondary market transactions, and how do secondary markets facilitate the primary markets?

20. Who regulates the securities markets in the U.S.?

21. For each of the following companies, calculate the market capitalization:

		Number of shares outstanding	Market price per share
A.	Company A	1,000,000	$5
B.	Company B	10,000,000	$10
C.	Company C	5,000,000	$20
D.	Company D	3,500,000	$25
E.	Company E	300,000,000	$13

22. Classify each of the following transactions as occurring in either the primary market or the secondary market:

	Primary	Secondary
A. An investor buys 1,000 shares of Google through her broker at E-trade in November 2004.		
B. An investor sells 10,000 shares of General Motors common stock in December 2010 through his broker, Charles Schwab.		
C. Cirrus Logic, a publicly traded company, buys $20 million of its own shares in the open market from January 2009 through November 2010.		
D. General Motors goes public, offering 478 million shares in November 2010.		
E. Google goes public with an offering of 19.6 million shares in August 2004.		
F. Prudential Financial, which is already a publicly traded company, makes a public offering of 18 million shares in November 2010.		

23. Classify each of the following as either a money market security or a capital market security:

	Money market security	Capital market security
A. 90-day Treasury bill		
B. 20-year debenture		
C. 30-year bond		
D. Common stock of Microsoft		
E. Commercial paper		
F. 5-year Treasury note		
G. General obligation bond		

24. Consider the following information for a company:

Common shares outstanding	5 million shares
Book value per share of common stock	$3.50
Market value per share of common stock	$8.00
Total assets	$20 million

What is this company's market capitalization?

25. HCA Holdings had its first day as a publicly traded company on March 10, 2011. The stock closed at a price of $31.02, with 64.6 million shares traded on this day. There are 515 million shares of common stock outstanding after this offering.

A. What type of transaction took place on March 10, 2011?

B. What is the market capitalization of HCA, based on the price of a share at the end of trading March 10, 2011?

1.3 The Global Financial Crisis

26. What is meant by the term "subprime mortgage"?

27. Suppose a company has accounts receivable from its customers. Explain the process of securitizing these receivables by diagramming the process of converting them into securities.

28. What are the societal and ethical issues involved with originating mortgages for individuals with poor credit?

CAREERS IN FINANCE

Every manager should be a financial manager, in the sense that the concepts, principles, and analysis techniques discussed in this textbook are important for all managers within a company. However, when we think of finance jobs, we generally distinguish between jobs in corporate finance (i.e., working within the finance function of a nonfinancial company) and finance jobs within a financial service firm, such as JPMorgan Chase, Bank of America, Barclays, Goldman Sachs, and Manulife Financial Corporation.

1A.1 FINANCIAL OFFICERS

In Figure 1A-1 we provide the basic functional breakdown of the finance function within a nonfinancial corporation. The top person is generally designated as the **chief financial officer (CFO)**, or in more traditional companies, the **senior vice-president of finance**. Under the CFO are the two main finance jobs: the **treasurer** and the **controller**. Although the breakdown of responsibilities varies from company to company, typically the treasurer's responsibilities are primarily financial decision making, whereas the controller's responsibilities lie in accounting and financial reporting. Because accounting information is the primary information for financial decision making and reporting, anyone interested in working in a treasurer or controller capacity must have a strong accounting background.

The treasurer has the pure finance job in a company. The treasurer's basic function is to manage the company's funds. To do this, the treasurer has to manage the company's cash and decide whom to extend credit to: cash and credit management. The treasurer must then pay the bills and make sure that cash is available when needed. This means forecasting the company's future cash position, determining its capital expenditure plans, and arranging both debt and equity financing. If the company has a pension plan, the treasurer is also responsible for managing these financial assets the same way as a portfolio manager in a mutual fund would manage them. Finally, the treasurer is responsible for risk management. Traditionally, this has meant arranging adequate insurance and making

chief financial officer (CFO) top financial manager in a company

senior vice-president of finance in some companies functions as the CFO

treasurer one of the two main finance jobs in a nonfinancial company; focuses on the finance side: forecasting, pension management, capital budgeting, cash management, credit management, financing, risk management

controller one of the two main finance jobs in a nonfinancial company; focuses on the accounting side: compliance, tax management, systems/MIS, internal audit, accounting, and budgeting

FIGURE 1A-1 **Finance in a Nonfinancial Company**

sure the company was covered if a fire burned down the building. However, over the past 30 years, many new techniques have emerged to manage financial risks, such as the risk of serious exchange rate or interest rate movements. These new techniques of financial risk management are the responsibility of the treasurer.

The controller is responsible for compliance. This entails making sure that the company meets its statutory legal responsibilities with securities commissions and other regulatory bodies, makes its tax payments to the government, fulfills its responsibility to prepare and file financial statements, and ensures that its internal control systems eliminate fraud so that the financial statements fairly represent the company's financial position. As part of this financial system, the controller is normally responsible for the management information system (MIS) because its main purpose is to collect the data required for internal audits and to prepare the company's financial statements. Finally, the system that produces the financial statements is the same system that generates budgets and targets for the upcoming year.

From this brief description of the controller's functions, it follows that finance jobs in the controller's department require training in financial accounting, management accounting, taxes, MIS, and control systems. These are all regarded as "finance" in nonfinancial companies.

The important thing about finance jobs within a nonfinancial company is that the jobs are very broad and require a strong dose of accounting and knowledge developed in other courses in a business school as well as finance. This is still true, but to a lesser extent, for the finance jobs within a financial intermediary such as a bank or an insurance company.

1A.2 ENTRY-LEVEL AND MIDCAREER FINANCIAL POSITIONS

analyst entry-level job in a financial institution

associate second-level job in a financial institution; it requires an MBA or a professional designation (e.g., CFA)

account manager financial professional who manages a bank's relationships with companies, extending credit, helping to manage receivables and cash, and directing them to the bank's more specialized services

banking associate financial professional who generates reports on companies, prepares industry reports, and performs background checks on credit applicants

Generally, in the major financial institutions, a common entry-level position is as an **analyst**, who most often has an undergraduate degree.[45] The next step is **associate**, which normally requires an MBA or a professional designation, such as certified public accountant (CPA), certified management accountant (CMA), or chartered financial analyst (CFA), before being promoted to manager.

In the traditional commercial banking, or business lending side, positions include

| **account manager** | Manages the bank's relationships with companies by extending credit, helping to manage their receivables and cash, and directing them to the bank's more specialized services, such as foreign exchanges services, mergers and acquisitions, and specialized credit |
| **banking associate** | Generates reports on companies, prepares industry reports, and performs the background checks (due diligence) needed before extending credit. |

The investment banking side of the major bank holding companies has three major types of jobs, either in sales or trading, or in "pure" investment banking. The investment banking side of the business is structured as a separate business segment, which is referred to as an investment dealer or investment banks. The pure investment dealer activities reflect the division of the business into corporate financing and mergers and acquisitions (M&A). These are the advisory functions that mirror the corporate finance jobs in a nonfinancial company.

---

[45] Analysts are not unique to financial institutions, and you will find analyst positions in corporations, commercial banks, investment banks, and rating agencies, among others.

Corporate financing employees, whether analysts, associates, or managers, advise clients and help them access the capital markets to raise capital, either through borrowing or issuing new equity. Although a company may raise capital relatively infrequently, investment dealers constantly advise their clients on what is available in the capital market. In mergers and acquisitions, investment dealers advise their clients on suitable candidates for acquisition or on how to defend themselves against a hostile acquisition. This often involves restructuring operations, selling off divisions (divestitures), or changing the company's financial structure.

Investment dealers, whether in corporate financing or M&A, derive part of their expertise from their knowledge of what is happening in the financial markets. Positions with an investment dealer include

security analyst	monitors the valuations of the companies he or she follows and makes recommendations to buy and sell a company's shares.
sales and trading	executes trades on behalf of their clients and conducts proprietary trading for the dealer itself using the investment bank's own capital.
retail broker and **private banker**	helps their clients manage their personal wealth.

Insurance companies and pension funds have significant long-term investments. As a result, they employ buy side analysts to do research on which particular investments to buy or sell. Several positions support these decisions, including

financial analyst or **investment analyst**	conducts detailed analyses of individual investments and makes recommendations on overall financial strategy.
portfolio manager	manages an investment portfolio.
fixed income trader or **equity trader**	implements investment strategies involving the buying or selling of fixed income or equity securities.

The final major group with a significant number of finance jobs is the management consulting and accounting companies. In their consulting practices, these companies need to analyze the financial health of a company, and often their advice contains a corporate finance element. Many of the smaller deals that do not involve significant capital market access are structured by accounting and consulting companies. A finance professional in these organizations is typically referred to as a **corporate finance associate** or **consultant**, and he or she advises on restructuring, small-scale M&A, and corporate financing.

security analyst financial professional who monitors the valuations of the companies and makes recommendations to buy and sell a company's shares

sales and trading activity that involves executing trades on behalf of the clients and conducting proprietary trading for the dealer itself by using the bank's own capital

retail broker and **private banker** financial professional who helps clients, usually people who have small to medium-sized accounts, manage their personal wealth

financial analyst and **investment analyst** finance professional who performs research, conducts detailed analyses of individual investments, and makes recommendations on overall financial strategy

portfolio manager professional in charge of the overall management of a portfolio

fixed income or **equity trader** finance professional who implements investment strategies and either buys or sells the securities of companies

corporate finance associate or **consultant** finance professional who advises on restructuring, small-scale M&A, and corporate financing

1A.3 PROFESSIONAL DESIGNATIONS

There are numerous professional designations that someone in a finance career may want to obtain. Most of these designations require a great deal of self-study, testing, and demonstrated work experience in the field. Though there are too many to list here, we include the most common designations by field in Table 1A-1, along with the web site address if you wish to find additional information.

In addition to the professional designations that we list in Table 1A-2, financial professionals who are involved in the securities business must register with FINRA, the self-regulatory organization for the securities profession and markets, and qualify by passing exams appropriate for the type of securities involved. These exams are referred to as series, and they relate to specific product responsibilities.

TABLE 1A-1 Professional Designations in Finance Careers

Designation		Focus	Website
CFA	Chartered Financial Analyst	Investment management and research	www.cfainstitute.org
CFE	Certified Fraud Examiner	Fraud detection and prevention	www.acfe.com
CFP	Certified Financial Planner	Financial planning for individuals	www.cfp.net
ChFC	Chartered Financial Consultant	Financial planning	www.theamericancollege.edu
CIA	Certified Internal Auditor	Internal auditing of for-profit and non-profit entities	www.theiia.org
CMA	Certified Management Accountant	Financial management and accounting	www.imanet.org
CPA	Certified Public Accountant	Public accounting	www.aicpa.org
FRM	Financial Risk Manager	Risk management and analysis	www.garp.org

TABLE 1A-2 Registrations Required in the U.S. Securities Business

Series	Examination
4	Registered Options Principal
6	Investment Company Products/Variable Contracts Limited Representative
7	General Securities Representative
9 and 10	General Securities Sales Supervisor
11	Assistant Representative—Order Processing
14	Compliance Officer
22	Direct Participation Programs Limited Representative
23	General Securities Principal—Sales Supervisor Module
24	General Securities Principal
26	Investment Company Products/Variable Contracts Limited Principal
27	Financial and Operations Principal
28	Introducing Broker/Dealer Financial and Operations Principal
39	Direct Participation Programs Limited Principal
42	Registered Options Representative
51	Municipal Fund Securities Principal
52	Municipal Securities Representative
55	Equity Trader Limited Representative
53	Municipal Securities Principal
62	Corporate Securities Limited Representative
63	Uniform Securities Agent State Law Examination
65	Uniform Investment Adviser Law Examination
66	Uniform Combined State Law Examination
72	Government Securities Limited Representative
79	Limited Representative—Investment Banking
82	Limited Representative—Private Securities Offerings Representative
86 and 87	Research Analyst

Source: FINRA, www.finra.org.

CHAPTER 2

FINANCIAL MANAGEMENT

© malerapaso/iStockphoto

Social Responsibility? These days, businesses are being called upon more than ever to act in a manner that is socially, economically, and environmentally responsible.

Being a good corporate citizen, however, can put a company at odds with its fundamental obligation, which is to maximize the value of the entity for its owners. Consider Green Mountain Coffee Roasters, Inc., which was ranked as the number one company in the U.S. each year 2003 through 2007 by *Business Ethics*, and number 39 in 2010 in the Corporate Responsibility rankings of companies in the Russell 1000 index.* This ranking is an assessment of a company's business ethics, based on its community service, governance, diversity, employee relations, environment, product, and human rights. The company attributes its position as a leader in social and environmental responsibility to its view of "profit as a means to achieve a higher purpose."**

Learning Outcomes

After reading this chapter, you should be able to:

LO 2.1 List the advantages and disadvantages of the primary forms of a business organization.

LO 2.2 Describe the ultimate objective of a company and explain why this is a logical objective.

LO 2.3 List and describe agency costs and how they may affect owners' wealth.

LO 2.4 Discuss the primary types of decisions made by business entities regarding the financial management of assets, as well as the associated financing decisions.

Chapter Preview We discuss the role of the form of business in decision making in this chapter and provide the background necessary to analyze how a business's investment and financing decisions are made. In the process, we examine the goals of the corporation and how its internal affairs are organized.

Corporate Responsibility Magazine, www.thecro.com.
**Green Mountain Coffee, About Our Company, www.gmcr.com.

2.1 FORMS OF BUSINESS ORGANIZATIONS

The business sector makes investment decisions that are intended to increase its ability to produce goods and services in the future—that is, to generate future growth in consumption and wealth. But the business sector comprises different forms of business entities, including proprietorships, partnerships, and corporations. If you were to count the number of businesses in the U.S., you would find that sole proprietorships are the largest group. On the other hand, if you were to add up all the revenues generated by business entities, you would find that corporations contribute by far the largest share of revenues.

In the U.S., as in most countries, businesses can be organized in different ways. The major forms of business organizations are the:

1. sole proprietorship;
2. partnership;
3. limited liability company; and
4. corporation.

We discuss each of these next.

Sole Proprietorships

sole proprietorship business owned and operated by one person

A **sole proprietorship** is a business owned and operated by one person. Starting a proprietorship is as simple as drumming up business. Many important businesses have been started by someone trying to meet a market need, whether it's the neighbor's child who starts a lemonade stand one hot summer day or the teenager who cleans up yards to earn spending money. These people have both started sole proprietorships, in which one person begins working on his or her own rather than for someone else. If these examples seem trivial, think about Bill Gates and Paul Allen (Microsoft Corporation), who started out working on personal computers in their parents' garages.

The big advantage of a sole proprietorship is that setting one up is easy—no paperwork is involved, and the owner needs only to start doing business. Of course, if the business begins to grow, the owner might want to register a business name or web site, or even patent a particular business process to keep imitators away or at least make them pay a royalty. However, the critical thing is that the business is almost inseparable from the owner; if that lemonade turns out to be bad, or if part of that yard isn't cleaned up, the business owner is personally liable. This isn't a big factor for most very small businesses, but if that web page inadvertently damages a client by directing traffic elsewhere, the owner is personally liable. More to the point, the owner can be sued for damages. If the owner has other assets, he or she could lose them or, in extreme cases, be forced into bankruptcy and lose everything because of a bad decision made in the sole proprietorship. This accountability is **unlimited liability** because an owner is liable not only to the extent of what is invested in the business but also for any other assets owned.

unlimited liability responsibility for obligations of a business that extends beyond the original investment, including personal assets

Aside from the liability issue, there are financial implications to sole proprietorships. The sources of funds available for sole proprietorships are the same ones that are available to individuals. No complicated finance options are available—owners borrow from relatives and friends or, depending on their credit rating, from the bank, through either a loan or a credit card.[1] If businesses create some revenue, owners can use one of the many government programs designed to stimulate small businesses.

If a business grows and the owner wants to sell it, it can be problematic. All the contacts and relationships are personal and belong to the owner because legally the

---

[1] This is known as the three Fs: friends, fools, and family.

owner and the business are one in the same. Selling a profitable window-cleaning business may mean visiting every contact and explaining that someone new is taking over the business and will be serving them in the future. The fact is, there is no continuity in a sole proprietorship, which makes it difficult to sell and, of course, the business dies with the owner.

Because a sole proprietorship is legally inseparable from the individual, the owner has to report the income on his or her annual individual income tax return. Sole proprietors have to keep the same accounting records as big businesses do and report the income after deducting all reasonable expenses. However, the net income is simply added to any regular salary income and taxed at ordinary tax rates.

Advantages and Disadvantages to the Sole Proprietorship Form of Business

Advantages	*Disadvantages*
1. Easy to form.	1. Unlimited liability.
2. Business income is taxed once, at the individual's personal level.	2. Lack of continuity.
	3. Limited access to additional funds.

SUMMARIZING

Partnerships

Suppose you are designing a new web page and need some help from a friend. The two of you start working together. After a while, it becomes a solid relationship, and you always work together on jobs for clients. This relationship is a **partnership**, rather than a sole proprietorship. This partnership can be formalized by having a lawyer create a partnership agreement, which establishes how decisions are made, such as how each partner can buy out the other in the event that one wants to dissolve the partnership. If the partnership grows, then the owners also need to document how new partners enter and what their attendant obligations are, as well as how others can cash out.

partnership business owned and operated by two or more people

The partnership agreement further stipulates how the partnership's income is allocated among the partners. Individuals have to be careful with partnerships because a legal agreement is not required to be considered a partner. Sometimes a partnership can be implied by the actions of a group of people working together. This becomes a problem when a disaffected party sues everyone associated with a business, even people who are not formal partners.

Similar to sole proprietorships, the income of the partnership is taxed at the individual partner level. The partnership income is allocated according to the terms of the partnership agreement and included in the individual partners' taxable income, whether or not it is distributed.

Also similar to the sole proprietorship, continuity is a potential problem because if a partner no longer exists or if a partner wishes to exit the partnership, the partnership agreement must be rewritten. In a partnership with many partners, this may become quite burdensome to manage.

Partnerships' access to capital is somewhat easier to obtain than that of sole proprietorships, though instead of relying on one individual's personal assets the partnership relies on the personal assets of all the partners. The business's access to capital is limited, however, because raising capital beyond the partners' contributions and local banks may be challenging, especially in some economic environments. And because a partnership is owned 100% by its partners, bringing in additional owners would not be possible unless the partnership agreement is rewritten.

Nevertheless, some very big companies began operations as traditional partnerships, most of which were in the professional services area, such as accounting companies, investment banks, doctors' offices, engineering firms, and dentists' offices. Such companies needed more than one person to deliver a full range of services, yet "society" judged it important to hold each member individually responsible for his or her own actions and for those of his or her colleagues. But, over time, the increasing complexity of partnership operations—for example, in the accounting and investment banking areas—weakened this argument. With hundreds of partners in a company, imagine how difficult it would be to justify making all the partners responsible for the actions of one rogue partner. As a result, the importance of traditional partnerships has diminished.

Partnerships are still significant for smaller companies because they maintain the integration of partnership income with other income for each partner. However, newer partnership models have emerged that maintain this tax treatment while removing the unlimited personal liability. The two main partnership forms are the **general partnership** and the **limited liability partnership (LLP)**, which we often refer to as simply a **limited partnership**, though all partnerships have at least one general partner. In a general partnership, the partners share the management and income of the business. In an LLP, there is at least one general partner who manages the business, but there may be any number of limited partners, who are passive investors. These limited partners have limited liability in the event of a lawsuit against the company, yet each partner's income is still included as ordinary income and filed by using an individual tax return. As long as the limited partners are not active in the business, they have the advantage of **limited liability**; the most they can lose is their initial investment. The general partner, conversely, has unlimited liability as the operator of the business. In practice, however, many general partners are corporations (discussed later) and indirectly benefit from limited liability.[2]

We observe large partnerships in oil and gas exploration. In some countries, limited partnership interests can be traded publicly on the exchanges, in which case it is referred to as a **master limited partnership**. In the U.S., large master limited partnerships, such as Kinder Morgan Energy Partners (KMP) and Enterprise Products Partners (EPD), have ownership units that trade on the New York Stock Exchange, with market capitalizations of $22 billion and $34.7 billion, respectively, in 2011. The largest Canadian natural gas distribution company in Quebec is Gaz Métro Limited Partnership (GZM) with 2009 revenues of CAD $603 million and profit of CAD $222.6 million.[3]

general partnership form of business in which all partners share in the management and the profits of the business, and the income and losses from the business are reflected on the individual owners' tax returns

limited partnership or **limited liability partnership (LLP)** form of business in which there are both general and limited partners, with general partners making management decisions and having unlimited liability, and the limited partners being passive investors with limited liability

master limited partnership form of business in which there are general and limited partners, with limited partner interests traded in the public market

---

SUMMARIZING

Advantages and Disadvantages to the Partnership Form of Business

Advantages	*Disadvantages*
1. Easy to form.	1. Unlimited liability for general partners.
2. Business income is taxed once, at the individual partners' level.	2. Lack of continuity.
	3. Limited access to additional funds.

---

[2] Limited partnerships had been used as tax shelters and for this reason they are scrutinized by tax authorities to make sure they are not a vehicle for tax avoidance; however, there are legitimate reasons to set up a limited partnership.

[3] CAD indicates Canadian dollars. The CAD before the dollar sign lets you know that this is not U.S. dollars, which we would designate as USD.

Corporations

A **corporation** is easy to recognize because it has Inc. for incorporated, Ltd. for limited, or, in Europe, PLC for private limited corporation or AG for Aktiengesellschaft, after its name. In each case, the abbreviations or initials indicate that the owners have the benefit of **limited liability**: the maximum that owners can lose is their investment—that is, they cannot be forced to invest more in the company to make up for any losses the company incurs. Unlike a partnership or sole proprietorship, a business that operates as a corporation separates personal assets from any malfeasance or failure at the corporate level. Although the courts have occasionally "pierced the corporate veil" and extended that liability, it is very rare and happens only in cases involving significant public policy concerns.

A corporation is usually formed by filing articles of incorporation and receiving a certificate of incorporation from the state. The articles of incorporation indicate the most basic information about the company, such as its mailing address, name, line of business, number of shares issued, names and addresses of the officers of the company, and so on. The critical feature is that the corporation is a *distinct legal entity*. For this reason the corporation is entitled to sign contracts in its own name, file its own tax returns, borrow money, make investments, and sue and be sued—all in its own name.

As a distinct legal entity, the corporation has significant advantages over a partnership or a sole proprietorship. For one it is *immortal*. This indefinite life means that unlike people, corporations can borrow by using debt that will be paid off in 40, and even 100, years' time. Individuals, with finite lives, would have difficulty getting these terms from a bank. It also means that transferring and selling assets is relatively easy because all the contracts go with the company, and the share ownership is simply transferred. Therefore, there is no issue of continuity that we see with sole proprietorships and partnerships.

One of the most difficult aspects of corporations is the issue of control. In partnerships and sole proprietorships, the owners run the business. In corporations, the owners are the owners of the ownership interests—that is, the shareholders—who elect members of the board of directors, who in turn hire and monitor the company's management. For smaller companies, the separation of management and ownership isn't a problem, but for larger companies, it becomes a serious concern. This division is the fundamental problem of the governance structure of large companies. We will discuss governance in detail later because it is integral to the role of mergers and acquisitions and to understanding valuation.

Every company has a set of bylaws that indicate how it is to be run. Some of the content of the bylaws is determined by corporate law, but some is discretionary and up to the company. Some may be very broad, such as Berkshire Hathaway's bylaw 4.1:

> The Board of Directors shall consist of one or more members, the number thereof to be determined from time to time by resolution of the Board of Directors.[4]

or very specific, such as Ford Motor Company's Section 5, (2) power to determine working capital levels:

> (2) To fix, and from time to time to vary, the amount of working capital of the Company, and to set aside from time to time out of net profits, current or accumulated, or surplus of the Company such amount or amounts as they in their discretion may deem necessary and proper as, or as a safeguard to the maintenance of, working capital, as a reserve for contingencies, as a reserve for repairs, maintenance, or rehabilitation, or as a reserve for revaluation of profits of the Company or for such other proper purpose as may in the opinion of the directors be in the best interests of the Company; . . .[5]

corporation business organized as a separate legal entity under corporation law, with ownership divided into transferable shares

limited liability limit on the financial responsibility of owners of a business entity to the amount of their investment

---

[4] 4.1 *By-Laws of Berkshire Hathaway Inc*, as amended through April 29, 1991.

[5] *By-Laws of Ford Motor Company*, As Amended Through October 30, 2001, Article III, Section 5, subsection (2).

What is not discretionary is the requirement that the company have a board of directors whose responsibility is to represent the owners and manage the operating and financial affairs of the company. These directors are elected by the owners.[6]

In theory, the members of the board of directors are elected by the shareholders and act in shareholders' best interests. Their statutory responsibilities are determined by the law of the state in which the corporation is incorporated and, if the corporation's stock is publicly traded, the rules of the exchange on which it trades and the relevant securities law.

Essentially, this legal requirement means that members of the board of directors must exercise the normal standards of professionalism expected of people in their position. This standard is known as the "due diligence" standard, and as long as it is met, members of the board of directors cannot be sued for negligence. The scandal surrounding Enron Corporation inspired the passage of the Sarbanes-Oxley Act of 2002.[7] This act enhanced the responsibilities of the board of directors, holding the members of the board of directors responsible for attesting to the internal controls of the company, as well as the company's quarterly and annual reports.

Another challenge to the corporate form is the issue of taxation. Sole proprietorships and partnerships have **flow-through taxation**. This means that the income flows to the owners' tax return and is therefore taxed only once. Under Subchapter C of the Internal Revenue Code, corporations do not have the benefit of flow-through taxation; rather, corporate income may be taxed twice or more.[8] To see how this works, consider a corporation that has $10 million of income and pays this entire amount to shareholders in the form of dividends. If the corporation's income tax rate is 35% and the individual shareholders have a tax rate of 38%, what is the effective tax on this income after it passes through both layers of taxation?

> **flow-through taxation** income flows directly to the owners as taxable income and is not taxed at the business entity level

(in millions)

Corporate income before taxes	$10.000
Tax at 35%	3.500
Income after tax	$6.500
Dividend income of individuals	$6.500
Tax at 38%	2.470
Income after tax	$4.030

Total taxes paid are $3.50 + 2.47 = $5.97 million. This means that the effective tax on the $10 million of corporate income tax is $5.97 ÷ $10 = 59.7%. What if the corporation pays only half of its income in dividends? The effective rate would be 47.35%:

(in millions)

Corporate income before taxes	$10.000
Tax at 35%	3.500
Income after tax	$6.500
Dividend income of individuals	$3.250
Tax at 38%	1.235
Income after tax	$2.015

---

[6] In the United States, directors can only be removed for cause before the end of their term of appointment. This means that it is technically possible to own 51% of the company and yet not be able to immediately remove the board of directors and control the company. In Canada, in contrast, the owners may remove a director during his or her tenure.

[7] Public law 107–204, signed into law July 30, 2002. Enron Corporation met its demise in 2001 when accounting fraud was revealed, among other things.

[8] Title 26 U.S. Code, Subchapter C.

We can capture this in a formula, using t_c to represent the corporate tax rate, t_i to represent the individual tax rate, and *DPO* to represent the portion of dividends paid to owners:

$$\text{Effective tax rate on corporate income} = t_c + [(1 - t_c)\ DPO\ t_i] \qquad (2\text{-}1)$$

In the last example,

$$\text{Effective tax rate on corporate income} = 0.35 + [(1 - 0.35) \times 0.5 \times 0.38] = 0.4735 \text{ or } 47.35\%$$

Let's compare the taxation of a corporation with that of a partnership. Consider two companies, Company P, organized as a partnership, and Company C, organized as a corporation. Suppose that both companies have $100,000 of income and distribute all this income after tax to their owners. If corporate income is taxed at a rate of 35% and individual income is taxed at the rate of 30%, what is the difference in taxes paid on company income for each company?

	Company P	*Company C*
Taxable income	$100,000	$100,000
Taxes paid by the company	0	35,000
Income distributed to owners	$100,000	$65,000
Taxes paid by owners	30,000	19,500
Income to owners after taxes	$70,000	$45,500
Total taxes paid on company income	$30,000	$54,500
Effective tax rate on company income	30%	54.5%

The taxes paid on Company C's income are much higher than those of Company P: 54.5% compared to 30%. Taking this a step further, if any of Company C's shareholders are corporations, there may be additional layers of taxes paid on the income, depending on the relationship between the two corporations.[9] As you can see in this example, the flow-through taxation provides an advantage to the sole proprietorship and partnership forms of business when compared to the corporate form.

PROBLEM

ABC Corporation and DEF partnership are in the same line of business, and each has $1 million of income before taxes for the most recent fiscal year. Both companies pay out a quarter of income after tax to owners. ABC is subject to a corporation income tax of 40%, and all individuals are subject to a 30% tax on income. What is the effective rate of tax for each company's income, considering the taxes of the business and the owners?

Solution

For ABC, the effective rate of tax is $0.40 + [0.60 \times 0.30 \times 0.25] = 44.5\%$
For DEF, the effective rate of tax is 30%

EXAMPLE 2.1

The Benefit of Flow-Through Taxation

---

[9] We will discuss this in more detail in a later chapter, but basically if a corporation owns 100% of another corporation, the income will not be taxed again. However, if a corporation owns less than 100% of another corporation, some of the corporate income may be taxed.

SUMMARIZING

Advantages and Disadvantages to the Corporate Form of Business

Advantages	Disadvantages
1. Limited liability.	1. Income taxed at the corporate level and at the owners' level, when distributed.
2. Unlimited life.	
3. Access to capital.	2. Separation of owners and management.

Limited Liability Companies

limited liability company (LLC) business organized as a separate legal entity in which owners have limited liability, but the income is passed through to the owners for tax purposes

A **limited liability company (LLC)** is a company that embodies some of the best features of both the partnership and corporate forms of business. Similar to a corporation, the owners have limited liability. This means that creditors of the LLC cannot look to the owners of the LLC to pay off the company's debts. Like a corporation, the most that the owners of an LLC may lose is the amount of their investment.[10]

Similar to a partnership, the LLC has flow-through taxation.[11] That is, the owners report their share of the LLC's income on their individual tax return. If the owner is a corporation, then this income flows to the owner's own corporate tax return. The owners of an LLC are referred to as members, and there can be just one member or any number of members. And a member can be an individual, a partnership, a corporation, or even another LLC.

LLCs are regulated by state law, and these laws vary slightly among states. States restrict certain types of businesses from using the LLC form of business if viewed in the public interest. For example, insurance companies, banks, law offices, and nonprofit organizations are generally prohibited from becoming LLCs.

SUMMARIZING

Advantages and Disadvantages to the Limited Liability Company Form of Business

Advantages	Disadvantages
1. Limited liability for the owners.	1. Separation of owners and management.
2. Unlimited life.	2. Access to capital.
3. Income taxed only at the owners' level.	

Subchapter S Corporations

Sub S corporation corporation that elects to be taxed as a partnership

Corporations that meet specific requirements may elect annually to be treated as a partnership for tax purposes. A corporation electing such treatment is often referred to as a **Subchapter S corporation** or, simply, **Sub S corporation**, because the treatment is

[10] Of course, there are exceptions to this limited liability in the case where the individual owner commits fraud or directly injures someone. In addition, as in the case of a corporation, if the owners treat the business as an extension of their own personal affairs, instead of as a separate, legal entity, the limited liability protection may not apply.

[11] There is a limitation on the deductibility of losses, which can be a disadvantage to this form of business.

spelled out in Subchapter S of the Internal Revenue Code. Sub S is not a separate form of business, but rather is an annual election made by corporations on their tax returns. Even so, the term "Sub S" has crept into the nomenclature as equivalent to a form of business. We distinguish the Sub S corporation from a corporation that does not elect special treatment by referring to the later as a **C corporation**.

C corporation business taxed as a corporation according to Subsection C of the Internal Revenue Code

So how does a Sub S compare with an LLC? Let's consider their basic characteristics:

Characteristic	Sub S	LLC
Taxation	Pass-through	Pass-through
Ownership	Maximum of 75 shareholders	No maximum
Liability	Limited liability	Limited liability
Life	Perpetual	Limited

The Sub S status was once popular with small corporations, allowing them to avoid the double taxation that befalls corporations. However, with the widespread acceptance of limited liability companies, which accomplish this same tax treatment without such an election, the LLC is often viewed as a preferred form of business.

Forms of Business | GLOBAL PERSPECTIVE

The primary forms of business in the United States can be found in most other countries, as you can see in this table:

Form of business in the United States

Country	General partnership	Limited partnership	Corporation	Limited liability company
Germany	Offene Handelsgesellschaft (oHG)	Kommanditgesellschaft (KG)	Aktiengsellschaft (AG)	Gesellschaft mit beschränkter Haftung (GmbH)
Japan	Gomei Kaisha	Goshi Kaisha	Kabushiki Kaisha (KK)	Godo Kaisha (LLC)
France	Société en nom collectif	Société en commandite simple	Societe anonyme (SA)	Société à responsabilité limitée
United Kingdom	Unlimited company	Limited partnership	Public limited company (PLC)	Limited company (Ltd.)
Sweden	Handelsbolag (HB)	Kommanditbolag (KB)	Publikt aktiebolag (AB)	*no equivalent*

Prevalence

What are the most popular forms of business? Consider the statistics from the Internal Revenue Service, as we show in Figure 2-1. The most common form of business, in terms of number of businesses, is the sole proprietorship. However, if we consider the revenues, corporations have the largest share. In other words, although there are fewer corporations, the corporations are quite large relative to partnerships and sole proprietorships.

The IRS classifies limited liability companies as partnerships because the tax treatment is the same. The limited liability company form of business represents 59% of the number of partnerships and 54% of the revenues of partnerships.[12]

[12] This is in contrast to the proportions we observed in the 1980s, when LLCs were not an option, and the general partnership was the most prevalent form of partnerships in terms of both the number of businesses and the revenues.

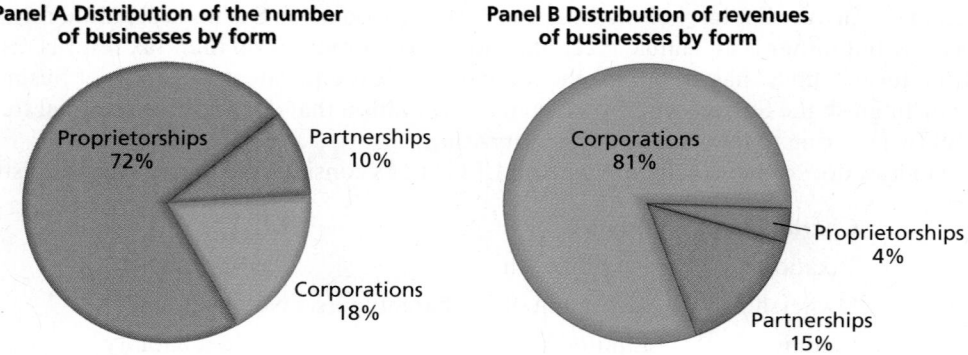

FIGURE 2-1 Distribution of Number of Businesses and Revenues of Business by Form
Source of data: *Statistics of Income, Internal Revenue Service, U.S. Department of the Treasury, using data from 2008 tax returns (the most recent data available).*

Concept Review Questions

1. Describe the main advantages and disadvantages of sole proprietorships and partnerships.

2. Explain why a business may be formed as an LLC instead of as a partnership.

3. What are the main advantages and disadvantages of the corporation structure?

2.2   THE GOALS OF THE BUSINESS ENTERPRISE

You might remember from your economics course that the goal of the company is to maximize its economic profits, where economic profits are the difference between revenues and expenses. These expenses are similar to the expenses we consider for accounting purposes, but also include the opportunity costs of the funds the business uses. Opportunity costs, basically, represent what could have been earned on funds if invested elsewhere.

Stakeholders

stakeholder any party affected by the decisions and actions of an entity

A **stakeholder** of a business is a party that is affected by the decisions and operations of the business entity. Stakeholders include not only the owners, but also the creditors, the employees, the suppliers, and the customers. We can also extend the concept of stakeholders to include the community in which the business operates. We illustrate the role of the business in relation to its stakeholders in Figure 2-2.

As you can see in Figure 2-2 the company is, essentially, an input–output mechanism. It takes inputs, such as raw materials, labor, and supplies, and transforms them into something more useful to society when it produces goods or services. For all companies, this activity is regulated both by implicit societal pressures to be "good" and by laws passed by government to prevent companies from doing things it regards as "bad." For example, minimum wage and employment laws prevent companies from using underage labor or paying wages that are too low. Similarly, laws on environmental protection, packaging of goods, and so on ensure that the company operates according to what is in consumers' interests.

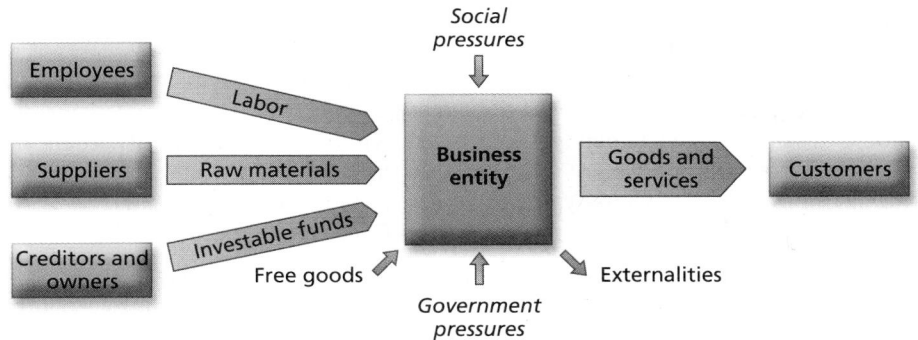

FIGURE 2-2 **The Business Entity and Its Stakeholders**

The Goal of the Business Enterprise

Recall that the goal of the management of a company is to enhance the owners' wealth. Apart from obeying the law, for sole proprietorships and partnerships, this is the end of the story; those companies are then run in the interests of their owners. Normally, this means that the management of companies enhances the owners' welfare by making decisions that maximize the value of the owners' interest. The value today of the owners' interest is the present value of all current and future cash flows to owners.[13]

Profit in this context refers to **economic profit**, not what is reported in a company's financial statements. The primary difference between economic profit and accounting profit is that the former includes a deduction of the opportunity cost of funds, whereas the latter does not. We discuss the relation between economic profits and wealth in more detail later in the context of valuation.

When the company's goal is applied to publicly traded companies, the goal of the company is to maximize the market value of the equity interest or, alternatively, *maximize shareholder value*: the company should take resources and create products that society values more highly than it values the inputs.

Note that there are two points in Figure 2-2 that we have not discussed: the existence of free goods and externalities. *Free goods* are goods or services that the company doesn't pay for. As a result, the company creates value without taking into account these other valuable resources and may make decisions that are not in the public's best interests. For example, consider the use of water. Should companies be allowed to use water without paying for it? Water is something that in some areas is in abundance, and it would be relatively easy to set up a plant to export water to, say, the U.S. southwest, which is largely a desert. In fact, it is possible to reverse the flow of water down the Mackenzie Valley, moving it down the Colorado River to Arizona and California, instead of having it go to the Arctic. This was an issue in the Free Trade Agreement (FTA) between the United States and Canada: Would the United States have the right to Canadian water, and would refusing a request be a violation of trade under the FTA? Clearly, large-scale diversion of water entails a cost not captured in the rates the public pays for water, and to charge this lower rate for large-scale water diversion is almost certainly not in the best interests of Canada, even though it may be in the best interests of people sponsoring the idea.

Externalities are costs or benefits from some decision to an entity or an individual who was not party to the decision. Examples of positive externalities (that is, those that create benefits) include a homeowner who paints his home and therefore enhances the value of other homes in the neighborhood, research that provides cures not originally intended, and education, which contributes to a more highly skilled workforce and hence a healthier economy. Examples of negative externalities (that is, those that create costs to

economic profit
difference between revenue and expenses, after considering the opportunity cost of funds

---

[13] The present value of the current and future profits is what someone would be willing to pay now to receive these future cash flows, considering the time value of money and the uncertainty of these future cash flows.

others) include air pollution, ground water contamination from fertilizer, and plastic bags that do not decay quickly in landfills.

The bottom line of both free goods and externalities is that these elements are generally not incorporated in decision making, even though there are benefits or costs arising from these. Why should this matter? When managers of a business maximize the value of owners' wealth, free goods and externalities are not considered in the decision making. Should they be?

The maximization of owners' value has been widely accepted, not just by academic theorists but also by regulators. Economist Milton Friedman argued that[14]

> there is one and only one social responsibility of business—to use its resources and engage in activities designed to increase its profits so long as it stays within the rules of the game, which is to say, engages in open and free competition without deception or fraud.

A company has a duty to do the right thing as enshrined in law and the contracts that it signs with employees, for example. The company should operate legally and in compliance with its contractual responsibilities, in the interests of its owners, by creating value for them. But is a company's management obligated to consider, for example, the social and environmental impact of each decision? Should financial managers of a corporation focus on shareholders or, more broadly, stakeholders? Milton Friedman would argue that as long as there is competition, the focus on the most efficient allocation of resources through owners' wealth maximization provides for the maximum benefit for all stakeholders. If, on the other hand, there were monopolies, the maximization of owners' wealth would not be consistent with an efficient allocation of resources because monopolistic owners would raise prices, and there would not necessarily be an incentive for the owners to produce the quantity of goods required by society.

LESSONS LEARNED | Economic Value Added

Economic value added, or simply economic profit, is the difference between revenues and expenses, where expenses include the cost of the capital used by the business. Stern Stewart & Co. trademarked the acronym EVA in the 1990s and promoted EVA as a tool to help nonfinance executives understand profitability in the economic sense.

Companies that focus on earnings-per-share tend to emphasize short-term gains and growth, rather than a long-term focus and value. For example, General Motors' bonus system, prior to its demise in 2009, was based on earnings per share. Although that alone was not the cause of GM's problems, it does illustrate a focus on the short term instead of the long term. As an example, GM exchanged lower wages for its unions for better retirement benefits, which resulted in lower operating costs, but higher debt obligations in terms of pension liabilities.

Economic value added is consistent with shareholder wealth maximization because it uses the cost of the company's capital as the hurdle in evaluating a company's or division's performance in a period. Calculating economic value added requires first calculating the net operating profits after taxes (NOPAT), and then subtracting the cost of capital in dollar terms. The cost of capital is the cost of using long-term sources of funds, whether they are debt or equity.

For example, if a company has a cost of capital of 7% and uses $10 million of capital (that is, interest-bearing debt plus equity), its cost of capital in dollar terms is 7% × $10 million = $0.7 million. If the company has NOPAT of $1 million, its economic profit or economic value added is $0.3 million.

Although economic value added is a useful tool for evaluating performance in a given period, it is not useful extended for multiple periods, such as when we evaluate a capital project. Another potential problem with using economic profit as a measure of performance is that it is short-sighted, which can tempt managers to make decisions that would affect this period's operating earnings, and hence economic profit, instead of taking the long view, which would maximize shareholder wealth.

Some companies promote the use of economic value added as a management tool that has improved the management of the company and enhanced shareholder wealth, but the use of economic value added is not a guarantee of success. Measuring economic value added is one of many tools that managers can use to evaluate performance.

---

[14] Milton Friedman, "The Social Responsibility of Business Is to Increase Profits," *New York Times Magazine*, September 13, 1970, p. 33.

Concept Review Questions

1. What is the primary goal of the corporation?

2. Who are the stakeholders for a company such as McDonald's?

2.3 THE ROLE OF MANAGEMENT AND AGENCY ISSUES

When making decisions within a business enterprise, it is necessary to have a goal in mind; otherwise, decision making would be quite random. But what should this goal be? If the managers and owners are the same people, as in small companies, the goal is most often to maximize the owners' wealth. Even some very large companies have a controlling shareholder to make certain that managers act in the shareholders' best interests.

For most large corporations, however, shareholders are widely dispersed, and there is most often a separation of the decision making of the company from the ownership of the company. And although managers have a responsibility to make decisions that will benefit shareholders, the interests of managers and shareholders do not necessarily coincide.

The Agency Relationship and Agency Costs

Managers are employees and as such are *agents* working on behalf of the shareholders. We refer to this relationship as **agency relationship**. And despite the fact that managers have a duty to shareholders, there is always the possibility that managers will act in their own self-interest. This is the classic **agency problem** associated with the separation of ownership from management.

The costs associated with the agency problem are referred to as **agency costs**. There are different types of agency costs: some direct, such as costs associated with producing financial statements and annual reports for investors and shareholders, and some indirect, such as the cost of making suboptimal investments and providing stock options to motivate managers.

Suppose you hire the son of a friend to clean up your yard. You could sit on the back porch and watch him to make sure he does a good job. However, this monitoring of his work is expensive for you; after all, you probably hired him because your time is valuable and you have other things to do. Monitoring him defeats the purpose. Instead, you can compensate him to try to meet your objectives. Suppose you pay him $10 an hour and think the job will take four hours. What might happen when you come back after four hours? If he does not expect repeat business (and therefore his reputation is not at stake), he'll probably be only partly finished because with a cost-plus contract, his incentive is to stretch out the job. Conversely, if you agree on a fixed fee, say $40, you'll probably come back after four hours and discover that he left two hours earlier. Then you'll have to check everything because he's probably taken shortcuts. In this case, his personal incentive is to finish early. What you want to do is align his interests with yours so you don't have to monitor and check his behavior.

Like your interests and those of your friend's son, the interests of managers and shareholders are usually fundamentally different. For example, shareholders tend to have a short-term interest in the company and hold the shares and other securities of many entities in a large investment portfolio. If they see the managers acting contrary to what they would like, rather than trying to remove management through a costly proxy fight at the annual general meeting, they will merely sell their shares and go elsewhere.[15] It is simply too costly for most shareholders to try to remove management in a large corporation; however, this is not to say that it doesn't happen. U.S. fund manager Tweedy Browne

agency relationship relationship that occurs when managers work on behalf of the shareholders

agency problem issue or conflict that arises due to potential divergence of interest between managers, shareholders, and creditors

---

[15] A proxy fight involves a party accumulating the votes of shareholders so as to be their representative when voting the shares on a particular issue, such as a takeover or obtaining seats on the board of directors.

Company LLC waged an expensive war to remove Conrad Black from Hollinger International Inc., a U.S. publishing company, and eventually succeeded. In this case the fund manager was angered by what was perceived as corporate wrongdoing: Conrad Black was found guilty of using company funds for his personal benefit, among other things.[16]

Aligning Managers' and Owners' Interests

Managers don't necessarily pursue the best interests of the shareholders because their investment in the corporation goes much deeper than that of a typical shareholder: Their careers are inextricably bound up with the company, and that goes beyond any stockholdings. For this very reason, managers tend to be more conservative in their decisions than would seem justified by the shareholder approach.

The different perspectives of managers and shareholders are evident in terms of performance measurement. For example, when being appraised, managers want to be judged relative to accounting numbers, such as profits and return on investment (ROI), because they can control these numbers to some extent.[17] In contrast, shareholders are interested in stock market performance because they want managers to create shareholder value. Similarly, in investment analysis, which involves selecting long-term projects, managers want to choose the internal rate of return (IRR) of the best project, relative to other divisions of the company or past performance, because, again, this is what they control.[18] In contrast, shareholders are interested in what they can do with the money, which can be measured by comparing the return on a project with the company's weighted average cost of capital. The **weighted average cost of capital (WACC)** is the marginal cost of funds, calculated as the weighted average of the marginal costs of the different sources of capital (that is, debt, preferred equity, and common equity).[19] If the company can't meet the shareholders' criteria, it should give the money to the shareholders so they can invest elsewhere.

FINANCE in the News | General Electric Sheds Light on Its Smooth Earnings

General Electric, a U.S.-based company with a market capitalization of over $175 billion, has reported smooth earnings growth to its shareholders from 1994 through 2004, meeting or exceeding analysts' expectations. However, this ability to smooth earnings and meet analysts' expectations has not come without a cost: In August of 2009, the Securities and Exchange Commission (SEC) fined General Electric $50 million for violating generally accepted accounting standards. Specifically, GE was able to manipulate its reported earnings by using several different accounting tricks during 2002 and 2003 fiscal years:

1. Reporting sales of locomotives that were not true sales.
2. Avoiding losses on some transactions by using unacceptable accounting (pertaining to its interest rate derivatives).

3. Improper application of accounting principles in accounting for a commercial paper funding program.
4. Improper changes for sales of aircraft engines' spare parts.

The pressure to meet or exceed analysts' forecasts—or to ensure making bonus targets—may encourage companies' management to manage or manipulate its reported financial statements. The reality is that companies most likely cannot always produce a pattern of smooth earnings over time and may not be able to meet or exceed analysts' forecasts each period.

Sources: U.S. Securities and Exchange Commission, Litigation Release No. 21166, August 4, 2009, and "Accounting Tricks Catch Up with GE," by Dan Fisher, *Forbes*, August 4, 2009.

---

[16] U.S. Securities and Exchange Commission v. Conrad M. Black, F. David Radler and Hollinger, Inc., Civil Action No. 04c7377.

[17] The return on investment is the ratio of the profit to the amount of the investment. We look closer at this and other performance metrics in later chapters.

[18] The internal rate of return is the return that a particular investment or set of investments is expected to provide. We discuss IRR in later chapters.

[19] We discuss WACC in detail later.

Shareholders and managers also differ in their approach to risk and financing. Shareholders take a portfolio approach because they hold many assets. This allows them to reduce risk by diversifying (that is, invest in assets whose returns are not perfectly in synch with one another), whereas managers may see their careers totally tied up with the company and tend to act more conservatively. This approach is carried over to financing, where many managers follow a "pecking order": They want to retain earnings first, rather than pay them out in dividends, then use bank debt, and finally issue new equity only as a last resort. In contrast, the shareholders want the company to use debt, then use retained earnings and new equity. Debt financing is attractive from a shareholders' perspective because the corporation can deduct the interest for tax purposes, making debt a much lower cost source of funds. But greater debt results in more risk.

The challenge is to design compensation schemes that encourage managers to act in the best interest of shareholders. The elements that are typically included are salary, bonus, and options. We list the five highest paid executives in the U.S. for fiscal year 2010 in Table 2-1, with a breakdown of their compensation by salary, bonus, shares of stock, options, and other. Notice that in all cases, the salary compensation is relatively low compared with the total package. This is likely the result of the limitation of $1 million per executive for the deductibility of compensation for tax purposes.[20] Annual bonuses are generally somewhat larger, but the largest component, by far, is share compensation. This comes in two forms: grants of restricted stock awarded under incentive plans, and stock options, for which if the company's stock price goes above a certain level, the executive gets the right to buy the stock at a fixed lower price, referred to as the exercise or strike price.

The idea behind share incentive plans is simply to affiliate the best interests of CEOs and senior managers with those of shareholders. Often, shares are granted based on reaching certain objectives, such as revenue targets or investment returns. In such cases, the manager has an incentive to get the share price up as high as possible. In the same way, if an executive is given the right to buy shares at a price of $50 when they are selling for $40, then the executive has incentive to get the share price over $50 to trigger the option. If the share price never reaches $50, the options are worthless. Grants of stock and stock options aim to achieve the basic objective of aligning the interests of shareholders and managers.

It is doubtful that share compensation schemes successfully meet their objectives, but sometimes it does happen. For example, Michael L. Bennett, CEO of Terra Industries, earned on average $3.5 million in compensation over the fiscal periods from 2003 through 2008, but shareholders earned an average of 64% per year. Similarly, the CEO of Amazon.com,

TABLE 2-1 CEO Compensation

		(in millions)				
CEO	*Company*	*Salary*	*Bonus*	*Shares/ Options*	*Other*	*Total*
Lawrence J. Ellison	Oracle	$1.00	10.78	$543.75	$1.45	$556.98
Ray R. Irani	Occidental Petroleum	1.30	3.63	184.39	33.32	222.64
John B. Hess	Hess	1.50	3.50	112.92	36.66	154.58
Michael D. Walford	Ultra Petroleum	0.60	1.75	113.48	1.1	116.93
Mark G. Papa	EOG Resources	0.94	1.00	69.67	18.86	90.47
William R. Berkley	WR Berkley	1.00	8.50	72.56	5.42	84.48
Matthew K. Rose	Burlington Santa Fe	1.18	1.68	45.06	20.70	68.62
Paul J. Evanson	Allegheny Energy	1.12	1.23	42.63	22.28	67.26
Hugh Grant	Monsanto	1.29	3.33	50.67	9.32	64.60
Robert W. Lane	Deere & Co.	1.44	3.59	41.04	15.24	61.30

Source: *"Special Report: CEO Compensation," Forbes.com, edited by Scott DeCarlo and Brian Zajac, April 22, 2009.*

[20] Anything over $1 million must be tied to performance to be tax deductible.

Jeffrey P. Bezos, earned an average annual compensation of $1 million, and the shareholders earned an annual return of 21%.[21]

Problems with aligning management's interests with shareholders' include the following:

1. Few companies require executives to own the stock after exercising an option, so often the shares obtained with an option exercise are sold immediately.

2. Some companies reprice the options if the stock's price is far under the original exercise price, setting the exercise price much below the original price.

3. It is challenging to establish a plan that compensates executives for making long-term strategy and investment decisions today that take the long-run view of maximizing owners' equity.

It would be nice to think that the senior management group would suffer losses along with their shareholders. But that is not always the case. For example, Kenneth D. Lewis, CEO of Bank of America, earned an average of $29.7 million for the six years 2003–2008, but the average annual stock return for the same period was –16%. As another example, Jeffrey R. Immelt, CEO of General Electric, enjoyed an average annual compensation of $14.4 million, but the shareholders of GE earned an average annual stock return during the same period of –11%.[22]

corporate governance
set of processes and procedures established to manage the organization in the best interests of its owners

Compensation structure is one component in the broader structure of corporate governance. **Corporate governance** is the set of processes and procedures established to manage the organization in the best interests of its owners. In addition to the compensation structure, corporate governance includes the composition and processes of the compensation committee of the company's board of directors, the composition of the committee that selects and oversees the work of the independent auditor, and the transparency of financial reporting.

The compensation committees of the board of directors that design compensation systems were not always completely independent of the CEOs who received the compensation, but this changed with the Sarbanes-Oxley Act of 2002 (SOX Act).[23] As a result of the SOX Act, publicly traded companies in the U.S. must now have compensation committees that comprise independent directors.

The important point to remember is that the interests of managers and shareholders are not aligned if, on the downside, managers do not suffer along with the shareholders. In fact, managers have an incentive to use short-sighted measures to pump up the share price so they can exercise their options or share grants. For the managers, this is a "heads they win, tails they don't lose" strategy.

One final wrinkle in the use of executive stock options is the fraud by management of many U.S. companies. The U.S. Securities and Exchange Commission investigated 74 companies for "backdating" executive stock options grants.[24] The fraud was that senior managers would get the compensation committee to award them stock options and then date them to an earlier period when the company's stock price was low.[25] Effectively, this meant that on the approval date (with the help of this backdating), the stock was already worth a large amount of money, so there was little incentive value to the grant. Companies charged by the SEC with backdating include Monster Worldwide, Converse Technology, Research in Motion, and UnitedHealth Group.

---

[21] "Special Report: CEO Compensation," Forbes.com, edited by Scott DeCarlo and Brian Zajac, April 22, 2009.
[22] "Special Report: CEO Compensation," Forbes.com, edited by Scott DeCarlo and Brian Zajac, April 22, 2009.
[23] Public Law 107-204, 116 Stat 745, enacted July 30, 2002. The compensation committees of the board of directors are supposed to be made up of outside directors to avoid this conflict of interest. Compensation committees must now comprise only independent members of the Board of Directors.
[24] David Henry, "How the Options Mess Got So Ugly and Expensive," *Business Week*, September 11, 2006.
[25] This type of fraud was more difficult in some other countries because the rules on reporting executive stock options are much tighter than in the United States.

Though companies are free to specify the exercise price of an option, the dating of the option has implications for tax purposes:

- If an option is granted when the stock's price is above the exercise price, there is no compensation for tax purposes at the time of the grant.
- If an option is granted when the stock's price is below the exercise price, there is a tax-deductible compensation for the company and taxable income to the employee.

One problem with backdating is that it involves altering official company documents, such as board of directors' meeting minutes. Another problem is a benefit to the employee at the expense of the employer: by backdating the option-grant date, the company is helping the employee who receives such an option to avoid taxes on the grant—while at the same time not getting a tax deduction for this compensation for the company. In March 2007, Research In Motion admitted to having backdated options, and Jim Balsillie resigned as chairman of the board of directors. This demonstrates some of the problems in designing incentive schemes where the people for whom incentives are provided are in charge of the program.

If compensation schemes have largely been used to reward management, rather than to provide managers with incentive to act like shareholders, where does this leave the goal of the company?[26] Luckily, it does not affect the goal of the company because of a more powerful control: the threat of acquisition. Poor management translates into poor stock market performance and a share price that is less than its intrinsic value. If a company owns assets with an intrinsic value of $50 a share and is selling them for $25 because management is incompetent, and $25 reflects the value of the profits they are generating, then more efficient managers can afford to bid for the company to turn it around for a profit. This is termed the *market for corporate control* because it is based on teams of managers competing for the right to manage corporate assets.

The most important task for regulators and governments is to ensure that the assets in the economy are managed as efficiently as possible so that the economy is as healthy as possible. This requires that the most successful managers be given the chance to manage assets. In turn, this means that hostile takeovers should be encouraged, and managers should be prevented from mounting defensive measures that simply entrench their ability to mismanage corporate assets. We examine mergers and acquisitions later, but for now, remember that this is the reason that finance people believe the best defense against a takeover is a high stock price. Ultimately, the market for corporate control, not managerial incentives, ascertains that shareholder value creation is the company's objective.

Concept Review Questions

1. Describe the nature of the basic owner–manager agency relationship.

2. Define agency costs and describe both types.

3. How have management compensation schemes been designed to better align owner–manager interests? How well have these schemes performed in this regard?

2.4 FINANCIAL MANAGEMENT

The combination of the real asset decisions and financial asset acquisition decisions represents acquisition or investment decisions. Generally, we talk about investment decisions in terms of financial management. **Financial management** is the management of the financial resources of a business or government entity, where financial resources include both the investments of the entity, but also how the entity finances these assets.

financial management
management of the financial resources of a business or government entity, where financial resources include both the investments of the entity, but also how the entity finances these assets

[26] Does $75 million really provide managers with that much more incentive than, say, $10 million? Or, alternatively, how many millions does it take to motivate management?

Investment Decisions

We refer to the framework for analyzing long-term investment or asset decisions as **capital budgeting** or **capital expenditure analysis**, and these decisions are some of the most important that a company can make. These long-term investments include building a new plant, introducing a new product, and acquiring another company. Without capital investments, the company will not continue as a going concern.

Evaluating capital budgets requires analyzing the future incremental cash flows that a project is expected to generate, considering the project's cost of capital. In most cases, a capital investment requires a substantial outlay at the beginning, but the investment is expected to generate incremental cash flows for a number of periods into the future. The incremental cash flows are how much the cash flows of the business are expected to change when the capital investment is made. The cost of capital is the return that providers of capital—that is, creditors and owners—require with their investment in the company. The project's cost of capital reflects the cost of funds, considering the risk of the project.

Long-term investments make up only 16% of total assets, on average, for U.S. business entities.[27] However, if we break this down by industry, we get a different picture: the investment of companies' assets varies by industry. For example, in the air, rail, and water transportation industry, 72% of the companies' assets are invested in plant, property, and equipment, whereas in the food manufacturing industry only 14% of the companies' assets are invested in plant assets.[28] In contrast, air, rail, and water transport companies have very little investment in operating assets, such as cash, inventory, and accounts receivable, compared to, say, gasoline retail stores, which have over 30% of their investments in these assets.

The investment in plant, property, and equipment is an investment in long-lived assets that are expected to provide benefits in the long term. The investments in **operating assets**, which are short-lived or current assets, support these long-term investments and are necessary for day-to-day operations of the business. We often refer to these operating assets as the company's **working capital** because they are put to work to support the long-term investments of the company and consist of cash, inventory, and accounts receivable. The amount of working capital a company needs is determined, in large part, by the company's line of business. For example, for the fiscal year ending January 31, 2011, Wal-Mart Stores had $51.9 billion of current assets, which is 29% of its total assets. As a retailer, Wal-Mart has substantial amount of inventory on hand at any point in time. In contrast, Darden Restaurants had only 13% of its assets in current assets, and CSX Corporation, a railway company, had only 11% of its assets in current assets. We compare the asset compositions of CSX, a railroad company, Wal-Mart Stores, and Darden Restaurants in Figure 2-3.

operating assets short-lived assets that support the company's long-term investments

working capital current, operating assets of a company; also known as operating assets

Financing Decisions

The financing decisions of a company involve the management of short-term obligations, such as bank loans, and long-term financing, which may be debt and/or equity. The management of short-term obligations requires understanding the needs of the company throughout the year for short-term borrowing and trade credit. There are many forms of short-term financing, and the financial manager must evaluate the cost of each available type.

An important decision of a company regards its capital structure. A company's **capital structure** is the mix of debt and equity that the company uses to finance its business. **Debt capital** consists of interest-bearing debt obligations, which may be notes or bonds, whereas **equity capital** consists of stock issues and retained earnings and is the ownership interest

debt capital interest-bearing obligations of an enterprise

equity capital ownership interest of an enterprise

[27] U.S. Internal Revenue Service, www.irs.gov
[28] Based on Statistics of Income, Internal Revenue Service, www.irs.gov, with the most recent available data for calendar year 2006.

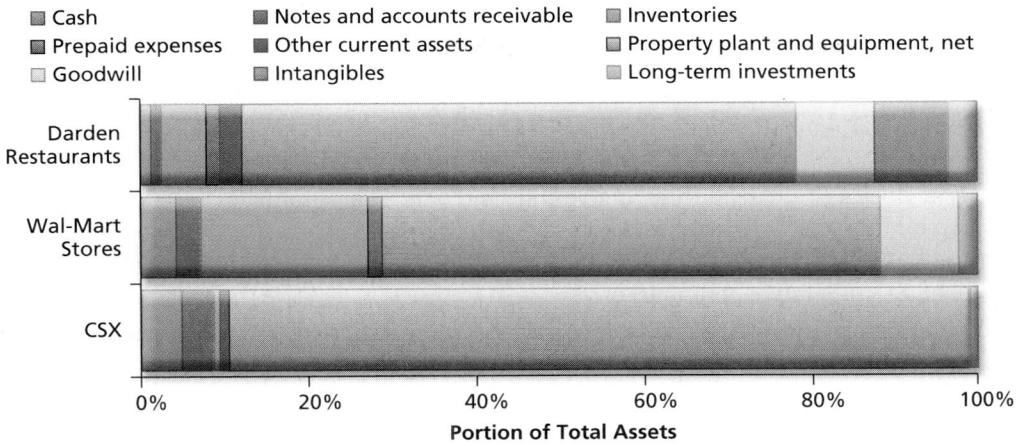

FIGURE 2-3 Asset Composition for CSX, Wal-Mart Stores, and Darden Restaurants

Source of data: *10-K filings of CSX (fiscal year ending 12/31/2011), Wal-Mart Stores (fiscal year ending 1/31/2011), and Darden Restaurants (fiscal year ending 5/29/2011).*

in a business enterprise. Because debt obligates the company to pay interest and repay the principal amount of the loan—whereas no such obligation exists with stock—using debt introduces some risk. Therefore, the capital structure decision affects the **financial risk** of a company: the more debt capital, relative to equity capital, the greater the company's financial risk.

So what do the liabilities and equity look like? We provide the composition of the capital of CSX, Wal-Mart Stores, and Darden Restaurants in Figure 2-4. Just as companies wait for others to pay them, they are also waiting to pay others, which gives rise to accounts payable (one of the major accounts included in short-term liabilities of Wal-Mart) for the customer side of the transaction.

The balance of short-term liabilities, long-term liabilities, and equity differs among industries. Some of this is due to customary practices, such as extending customers credit, and some is due to the business risk of the industry, which may permit a company to take on more risk in the form of larger long-term obligations relative to equity interests.

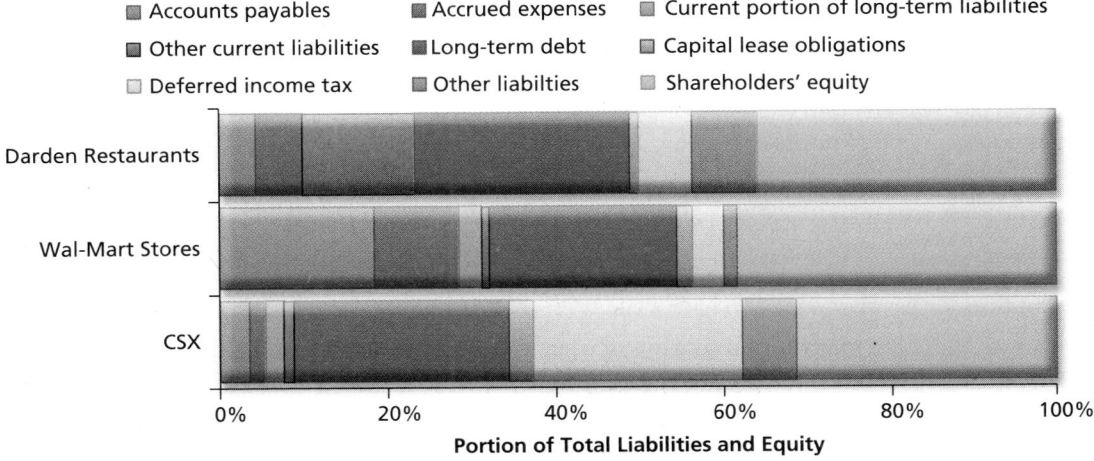

FIGURE 2-4 Capital Composition for CSX, Wal-Mart Stores, and Darden Restaurants

Source of data: *10-K filings of CSX (fiscal year ending 12/31/2011), Wal-Mart Stores (fiscal year ending 1/31/2011), and Darden Restaurants (fiscal year ending 5/29/2011).*

These relative amounts of liabilities and equity raise the following basic questions in corporate financing:

financing sources of
money for a company,
including using debt or
equity, retaining earnings
or issuing equity, going
public, using bank debt
or bonds, and using the
short-term money market
or borrowing from a bank

corporate finance
financial management
of assets and financing
decisions in a corporate
enterprise

1. How does a company decide between raising money through debt or through equity?
2. In terms of equity, how does a company raise the equity: through retaining earnings or through issuing new equity?
3. Why does a company decide to go public and issue shares to the general public versus remaining a nontraded private company?
4. If a company decides to issue debt, what determines whether it is bank debt or bonds issued to the public debt market?
5. What determines whether a company accesses the short-term money market versus borrowing from a bank?

These basic questions represent the core of liability management for corporations, which we refer to as their corporate **financing** decisions. Taken together, the financial management of assets and corporate financing decisions represent the area of **corporate finance**.

Concept Review Questions

1. Describe the two key decision areas with respect to the financial management of assets.

2. What are some of the key corporate financing decisions made by companies?

ETHICS | The Cost of Fraud

Under Section 304 of the Sarbanes-Oxley Act of 2002, when a company's management commits fraud, reporting greater profits than actually earned, any bonuses based on the exaggerated profits must be paid back to the company.[29] This is the case whether the manager conspired to commit the fraud or not. This "clawback" provision is designed to protect shareholders from paying bonuses that were not truly earned.

A case in point is Beazer Homes. The Securities and Exchange Commission (SEC) brought a case against Beazer Homes for their fiscal year 2006 financial statements. The company's senior vice-president and chief accounting officer, Michael Rand, was charged with violating Generally Accepted Accounting Principles in the scheme to exaggerate profits to meet analysts'

expectations. One of the techniques used was "cookie jar accounting," which is a scheme to save recognition of income or expenses for specific years rather than when they should be recognized based on generally accepted accounting principles (GAAP). Following charges by the SEC, Beazer Homes' financial statements for fiscal year 2006 (and other years) were restated in 2008.

Beazer Homes' CEO and president did not repay bonuses that he received in 2006, even though he had signed statements that attested to the financial reports' accuracy and was involved in the company's accounting. The CEO received a bonus of $7.1 million in 2006 and realized profits on the sale of his stock of $7.3 million. The SEC brought an action against the CEO in March of 2011 to compel repayment of the bonuses.[30]

SUMMARY

- There are many different ways of organizing businesses, including the sole proprietorship, partnership, corporate, and limited liability company forms of business.

- Considerations in evaluating the form of business enterprise include liability, taxation, control, and continuity.

[29] Public Law 107–204.

[30] Securities and Exchange Commission v. Ian J. McCarthy, United States District Court for the Northern District of Georgia Atlanta Division, Civil Action, March 3, 2011.

- The management of a company should make decisions that maximize owners' wealth, though this is not always the case. When the managers are also the owners, it is a simple situation. In large corporations, in which there is separation between management and owners, motivating management to act in the owners' best interest is challenging.

- Agency costs may arise because managers may not act in the best interests of shareholders or because they must be induced to act optimally.

- The primary decisions made by corporations involve the financial management of the company's real and financial assets, as well as the associated corporate financing decisions.

FORMULAS

(2-1)   Effective tax rate on corporate income $= t_c + [(1 - t_c)\, \mathrm{DPO}\, t_i]$

QUESTIONS AND PROBLEMS

Multiple Choice

1. Which of the following businesses is least likely to be operated as a partnership?

   A. Steel foundry   B. Dentist's office   C. Accounting firm   D. Physician's office

2. Which of the following statements is true?

   A. The ownership of limited liability partnerships cannot be traded publicly.

   B. In the limited and general partnership form, the general partner has limited liability.

   C. In the limited and general partnership form, the limited partners are passive investors.

3. Which of the following forms of business organization have owners with limited liability?

   A. Corporation   B. Sole proprietorship   C. General partnership

4. Income is taxed at only one level, the owners' individual income, for all but which of the following forms of business?

   A. Corporation   B. Partnership   C. Sole proprietorship   D. Limited liability company

5. Limited liability companies are specific to the United States.

   A. True   B. False

6. Which of the following are characteristics of a sole proprietorship?

	Liability	Life
A.	Limited	Limited
B.	Limited	Perpetual
C.	Unlimited	Limited
D.	Unlimited	Perpetual

7. Which of the following are characteristics of a corporation?

	Liability	Life
A.	Limited	Limited
B.	Limited	Perpetual
C.	Unlimited	Limited
D.	Unlimited	Perpetual

8. Which of the following best describes the taxation of corporations?
   A. Taxed once, as owners' income
   B. Taxed twice: once as corporate income, and again as owners' income
   C. Taxed twice: once as corporate income, and again as owners' income only if distributed

9. The interests of shareholders and managers are properly aligned if managers receive stock options.
   A. True   B. False

10. Which of the following is the primary concern from the point of view of a company's shareholders?
    A. Minimize risk
    B. Market value of equity
    C. Maximize earnings per share
    D. Maximize accounting return on investment

Practice Questions and Problems

2.1   Forms of Business Enterprise

11. List and describe briefly the four major forms of a business organization.

12. State the main differences between corporations and partnerships.

13. Describe what is meant by flow-through taxation.

14. What would be the advantage, if any, of forming a business as a corporation and electing Subchapter S status, rather than forming the business as a limited liability company?

15. Complete the following table, calculating the effective tax on corporate income:

	Dividend Payout	Corporate Tax Rate	Shareholders' Tax on Dividend Income	Effective Tax on Corporate Income
A.	40%	45%	15%	
B.	20%	40%	0%	
C.	25%	35%	15%	
D.	25%	40%	15%	

16. Consider a corporation that has $5 million of taxable income for the year and is subject to a 40% tax on corporate income. And suppose the corporation pays 25% of its income after tax to its shareholders.
    A. If its shareholders are taxed at a rate of 32%, what is the effective rate of tax on this corporation's income?
    B. If this corporation was a partnership instead, what would be the effective rate of tax on this income?

17. Consider a corporation that pays all its earnings to owners as dividends and has a tax rate of 36%.
    A. How much of the corporation's income is taxed at the corporate level?
    B. If the corporation's shareholders are taxed at a rate of 40% on dividend income, what is the effective tax rate on this corporation's income, considering the taxation at both the corporate and the individual levels?
    C. If the shareholders of this corporation have a tax rate of 20% on any dividends instead of 32%, what is the amount of tax at the individual owner level?

2.2   The Goals of the Business Enterprise

18. What is the goal of the management of a business entity?

19. What is a stakeholder?

20. Why does a company focus on the value of equity rather than earnings in making long-term decisions?

21. Is shareholder wealth maximization consistent with the efficient allocation of resources? Explain.

2.3 The Role of Management and Agency Issues

22. What are agency costs?

23. Provide an example of the conflicts of interest between shareholders and managers.

24. What measures can be taken to reduce agency costs?

25. Why would a bonus system that rewards managers based on earnings per share be problematic?

26. Why do corporations use stock options in executive compensation?

27. How do the owners of a corporation, which may have thousands of owners, monitor the management of the corporation?

2.4 Financial Management

28. What is meant by the term *capital structure*? How does capital structure relate to a company's financial risk?

29. What does a financial manager consider in evaluating an investment in a capital project?

30. Classify each of the following as either a financing decision or an investment decision:

Decision	Investment	Financing
Buying a new plant	☐	☐
Acquiring another company	☐	☐
Issuing a bond	☐	☐
A corporation buying back its own stock	☐	☐
Borrowing from a bank	☐	☐

31. Consider the information on three corporations for fiscal year 2010:

(in millions)	Hewlett-Packard	Boeing	Verizon
Line of business	Manufactures and sells computers and computer equipment	Manufactures and sells aircraft	Telecommunications provider
Current assets	$51,404	$40,572	$22,348
Total assets	$119,933	$68,565	$220,005

Calculate the proportion of assets that are invested in current assets for each company, and explain why these proportions differ from one another.

Cases

Case 2.1 The Tex Tech Company

When you hired Dan to manage your business, the Tex Tech Company, you agreed to pay him a bonus of 10% of profits at the end of each year. There are now two projects available for investment by Tex Tech, but it can only take on one of them: Project A will generate profits of $50,000 per year, and the detailed financial calculations show that it will increase the value of the company by $123,100. Project B will generate profits of $40,000 per year, but will increase the company's value by $125,500.

    A. Which project is Dan likely to choose, and why?

    B. Which project would you, the owner of the company, prefer?

    C. By what means can the owners of the company encourage Dan to focus on owners' wealth maximization?

Case 2.2 To Invest or Not to Invest

As the CFO of your company, it falls to you to make the final decision on large expenditures. Recently, your controller has proposed purchasing a new computer system at a cost of $50,000. He believes the system will deliver savings of $60,000 in the accounting department and could be useful to other departments as well. Your treasurer takes a decidedly different view of the proposal. She claims that the company will have to borrow money to buy the computer system, and this will cost $10,000 in interest. As well, she is concerned that the amount of savings promised by the controller won't materialize.

    A. What factors should you consider in this decision?

    B. Based on these facts, should you purchase the computer system? Justify your decision.

PART 2

FINANCIAL ANALYSIS

Accounting is the language of finance; if that is so, what is it saying to us when accounting scandals involving billions of dollars have led to the downfall of companies such as Lehman Brothers and HealthSouth? The tools of financial analysis have been developed so that external investors can better understand and interpret financial statements. Understanding how financial statements are prepared and what they mean to external investors is a key skill that is necessary for any student of finance. We develop and demonstrate these skills through a detailed analysis of an actual company.

CHAPTER 3

FINANCIAL STATEMENTS

How can a company generate a profit but not have cash flows from operations? Is it possible for a company to be profitable, yet not generate cash flows? Absolutely. For example, in 2010 a number of financial institutions reported a profit, but had negative cash flows from operations:

	Net Profit (in millions)	Operating Cash Flow (in millions)
JPMorgan Chase	$17,370	–$3,752
Deutsche Bank AG	$3,066	–$4,878
Piper Jaffray Co.	$24	–$27
Schwab (Charles) & Co.	$454	–$9

In each of these cases, the primary driver to the negative operating cash flows is the build-up in working capital, which reflects the improvement in their balance sheets as the economy recovered. Because these companies do not have inventory and do not sell goods on credit, the working capital increase is primarily attributed to the increased value of trading assets as financial markets improved over the year.

But we have a different interpretation when we look at other types of firms. Consider, for example, in 2010:

	Net Profit (in millions)	Operating Cash Flow (in millions)
Advanced Micro Devices	$471	–$412
Skechers U S A Inc.	$136	–$47
Sodastream International	$13	–$11
Swank Inc.	$4	–$2

In the case of Swank and Advanced Micro Devices, the difference is explained by a build-up in receivables, whereas with Skechers this difference is explained by a build-up in inventory. By identifying the source of the difference, an analyst has a starting point. For example, "Why did receivables increase from one year to the next, but inventory did not?" "Why did inventory increase, but this is not accompanied by an increase in sales and inventory?"

In the case of Sodastream International, maker of do-it-yourself soda-making devices, the difference is explained by the build-up in both receivables and inventory, which is characteristic of a high-growth company.

The comparison of net income and cash flows is one of the many useful approaches to analyzing the financial condition and performance of a company.

Source of data: *Annual report for fiscal year 2010 of each company.*

Learning Outcomes

After reading this chapter, you should be able to:

LO 3.1 Describe the importance of preparing financial statements in accordance with a given set of guidelines or principles, and explain how judgment enters into the preparation of accounting statements.

LO 3.2 Describe how the basic financial statements for a company are constructed, and identify the accounts that link these statements.

LO 3.3 Compare accounting income and income for tax purposes, identify the primary differences, and explain why these differences arise.

Chapter Preview Accounting is the language of business and one of the most important sources of corporate information. Gaining a good understanding of accounting is essential for any serious student of finance. In this chapter, we review the salient features of financial accounting, and although this chapter is no substitute for a course in financial accounting, it does deal with the issues that are vital to understanding finance.

3.1 ACCOUNTING PRINCIPLES

At its most basic level, accounting is simply an organized method of summarizing all of a company's transactions and presenting them in such a way that external users can understand the company's affairs. Clearly, problems arise when the company tries to present its accounting statements in a way that does *not* fairly represent its situation, either to creditors, like the bank, or to the common shareholders. Consequently, external users of the company's financial statements must become skilled in analyzing the statements and spotting signs that things may not be quite as management presents them.

Generally Accepted Accounting Principles

It is important to realize that management prepares the company's financial statements, not the company's auditors. Auditors, such as Deloitte & Touche LLP (Deloitte), attest to whether or not the financial statements fairly represent the company's financial position according to **generally accepted accounting principles (GAAP)**. GAAP are defined relative to the country in which the company reports its financial condition and performance. For example, companies reporting in the U.S. follow the principles promulgated by the **Financial Accounting Standards Board (FASB)**, whereas members of the European Economic Community, and other countries, follow the principles promulgated by the **International Accounting Standards Board (IASB)**.

The globalization of business activities has necessitated the use of standards that are common among many nations, leading to the establishment of the **International Financial Reporting Standards (IFRS)**, which are set forth by the IASB. Companies in the European Union countries adopted the IFRS in 2005; companies in Turkey adopted them in 2006; Canadian, Japanese, and Russian companies adopted the standards

generally accepted accounting principles (GAAP) set of basic principles and conventions that are applied in the preparation of financial statements

Financial Accounting Standards Board (FASB) organization that establishes the accounting principles for U.S. financial reporting

International Accounting Standards Board (IASB) organization that establishes the accounting principles for business entities in the European Economic Community

International Financial Reporting Standards (IFRS) accounting standards promulgated by the International Accounting Standards Board (IASB)

unqualified opinion audit opinion in which the auditors find that the financial statements are presented fairly in accordance with generally accepted accounting principles

qualified opinion audit opinion in which the auditors find that the financial statements are presented fairly in accordance with generally accepted accounting principles except for a matter of qualification

adverse opinion audit opinion when the financial statements do not represent fairly the financial position, results of operation, or the change in financial position in accordance with generally accepted accounting principles

disclaimer of opinion audit opinion in which the auditors cannot form an opinion on the business entity's financial statements

in 2011; and U.S. companies will convert from U.S. GAAP to IFRS by 2014. Other countries, such as Australia, have adopted or revised standards that are similar to, but not identical to, IFRS.

Independent auditors review the financial statements prepared by a company's management and provide a report, addressed to the company's board of directors and shareholders, that generally consists of the following:

1. A statement that the financial statements are the responsibility of the company, and that the auditor is providing an opinion on the financial statements, not the accounting records themselves.

2. A description of the scope of the audit, and that it was conducted according to generally accepted auditing standards.

3. The auditor's opinion, which is one of four types:

Unqualified opinion	The auditor applied generally accepted auditing standards and the financial statements present fairly and conform to GAAP.
Qualified opinion	The auditor's examination is limited in scope, or that there is an issue regarding the fairness of the financial statements according to GAAP.
Adverse opinion	The auditor concludes that the financial statements are not presented fairly according to GAAP.
Disclaimer of opinion	The auditor's examination is severely restricted or the auditor finds some condition is present that prevents the application of generally accepted auditing standards.

FINANCE in the News | Changing Auditors

When a publicly traded company's board of directors dismisses an auditor, they must explain the reason in disclosures to shareholders and the Securities and Exchange Commission. An example of a parting of ways with the auditor is Dave & Buster's dismissal of Ernst & Young in August of 2010:

> During the Company's most recent two fiscal years and through the subsequent interim period on or prior to August 25, 2010, (a) there were no disagreements between the Company and E&Y on any matter of accounting principles or practices, financial statement

disclosure, or auditing scope or procedure, which disagreements, if not resolved to the satisfaction of E&Y, would have caused E&Y to make reference to the subject matter of the disagreement in connection with its report; and (b) no reportable events as set forth in Item 304(a)(1)(v)(A) through (D) of Regulation S-K have occurred.[1]

Why state that there are no disagreements? Because if there are disagreements and dismissing an auditor was done to avoid a qualified or adverse opinion, this is important information that should be disclosed to investors.

Accounting Conventions: The Basic Principles

What is the difference between a bookkeeper and an accountant? In the most basic sense, the bookkeeper manages all the transactions in a company, whereas the accountant uses them to create the company's financial statements. Accountants do this by applying the GAAP that we described earlier so that other accountants and people interested in a business can understand and accept what was done. As noted earlier, GAAP are a set of basic

[1] Dave & Buster's Inc. Press release issued August 31, 2010.

principles and *conventions* applied in preparing financial statements. The principles are accepted by securities regulators, like the Securities and Exchange Commission (SEC), for use in preparing statements for securities offered to the general public.

The *Framework for the Preparation and Presentation of Financial Statements*, set forth by the IASB, details the objective, the qualitative characteristics, and elements of financial statements.[2] Based on this framework, the purpose of financial statements is to provide information, at least annually, to a wide range of external users, including investors, employees, lenders, governments, and the general public. The objective of the financial statements is to provide information about an entity's financial performance and changes in financial position, and the management of the entity has the primary responsibility for preparing and presenting the financial statements.

The underlying assumptions in the financial statements are that transactions are recorded on the accrual basis, and that the entity is a going concern, and hence will continue indefinitely. The **accrual basis** is the reporting convention in which revenues and expenses are recorded when a transaction occurs, regardless of when cash changes hands.[3] In addition, financial statements should possess the qualitative characteristics of understandability, relevancy, reliability, and comparability. The relevancy of financial statements includes consideration of the materiality of the information, the reliability of the information and related estimates, and prudence.

According to the framework of IFRS, a business entity measures and reports monetary amounts for the various elements in its financial statements. The different bases for measuring these elements include the following:

- **Historical cost**: what it cost the entity when it purchased the asset or took on the obligation.
- **Current cost**: what it would cost to replace the asset or settle the liability.
- **Net realizable value**: what the company would reasonably get for the asset if it had to dispose of it in an orderly sale, or the settlement value for a liability.
- **Present value**: the sum of the discounted expected future cash flows arising from the asset or expected to be paid in the case of a liability.
- **Fair value**: the amount reasonably expected to be received for an asset or settled in the case of a liability, between knowledgeable, willing parties to the transaction, which may be based on present value or market valuations.

Regarding when to recognize items, the basic criteria is that it is likely that the future benefit will flow to the entity, and the cost or value can be measured. In terms of the types of accounts:

Type	*When Recognized*	*Example*
Asset	Likely that the future economic benefit will flow to the entity and that the value can be measured reliably	Purchase of equipment
Liability	Likely that the outflow of resources will result and that the amount of the obligation can be measured reliably	Borrowing by issuing a debt obligation
Income	Increase in future economic benefit from an increase in an asset or a decrease in a liability can be measured reliably	Sale of goods or services, or waiver of a debt obligation
Expense	Decrease in future economic benefit from a decrease in an asset or an increase in a liability	Depreciation of equipment or accrual of wages to employees

accrual basis reporting convention in which revenues and expenses are recorded when a transaction occurs, regardless of when cash changes hands

historical cost amount paid for an asset when it is purchased

current cost what it would cost to replace the asset or settle the liability

net realizable value amount the company would reasonably get for the asset if it had to dispose of it in an orderly sale, or the settlement value for a liability

present value sum of the discounted expected future cash flows arising from the asset or expected to be paid in the case of a liability

fair value amount reasonably expected to be received for an asset, or settled in the case of a liability, between knowledgeable, willing parties to the transaction, which may be based on present value or market valuations

---

[2] International Accounting Standards Board, *Framework for the Preparation and Presentation of Financial Statements*, April 2001.

[3] This is different than the cash basis, which reflects revenues and expenses only at the time cash is exchanged.

Is there an opportunity to "manage" the financial statements? Accounting principles offer some flexibility because it is simply not possible to design a one-size-fits-all set of principles. The flexibility allows a company's management to select the accounting principles that best fit the company's situation. Such flexibility, however, can lead management to provide a more favorable view to shareholders and investors of the company's financial performance or condition than actually exists.

Consider the case of accounting for marketable securities. Marketable securities are short-term investments of companies and are accounted for at their fair value, which we also refer to as **mark-to-market**.[4] Mark-to-market involves writing an asset's value on the books either up or down, depending on its fair value relative to its current carrying or book value. When a company does write an asset's value up or down, there is an unrealized gain or loss (remember: when there is a debit or credit, there must be a balancing credit or debit). Recognizing this in net income on the income statement adds volatility to earnings as the market value of investments changes from year to year.

In U.S. GAAP, a company's management may choose the accounting principle and report the securities as:

- **available-for-sale**, in which case any unrealized gains or losses do not appear in the income statement, but rather appear in the accumulated other comprehensive income account in shareholders' equity in the balance sheet;

- **trading securities**, in which case any unrealized gains or losses are reported in the income statement and affect shareholders' equity through net income; or

- **held-to-maturity**, which applies to debt securities, in which case the securities are reported at cost on the balance sheet.

As you can imagine, if a company has losses in its marketable securities, it would most likely want to report the securities using available-for-sale accounting, and if a company has gains, it would most likely want to report the securities using trading securities accounting. This accounting choice, however, affects the company's reported net income and the company's balance sheet.

mark-to-market writing the value of an asset up or down, depending on its current market value

available-for-sale method of accounting for marketable securities in which unrealized gains or losses are reported as part of accumulated other comprehensive income

trading securities method of accounting for marketable securities in which unrealized gains or losses are reported in net income

held-to-maturity method of accounting used when marketable debt securities are reported at cost

---

LESSONS LEARNED | Marking to the Market

Mark-to-market accounting is valuing an asset or a liability at its current market value. Although this would be challenging if the assets were physical assets, such as equipment or a building, it is more straightforward when applied to financial assets and liabilities, for which traded values or some proxy can be determined.

Why do some say that mark-to-market accounting contributed to the financial crisis of 2007–08? It wasn't because there is a problem with market value, but rather with strict capital requirements—that is, minimum equity requirements for financial institutions. If the assets and liabilities are marked to the market, there is more volatility in the reported values, and because assets = liabilities + equity, there is more volatility in equity.

So, is mark-to-market accounting to blame for the demise of Lehman Brothers and others? Not necessarily. One of the related issues is that there are three types of

financial assets: Level 1 (those with observable market prices), Level 2 (those for which you could determine values based on models), and Level 3 (those that are difficult to value). The GAAP for accounting for Level 3 assets changed, providing specific guidance to how to value Level 3 assets for fiscal years beginning after November 15, 2007. Before this change, the company simply estimated the value of Level 3 assets.

What were these Level 3 assets? Many of these were mortgage-backed securities, whose value was dropping at the time of this accounting change. In its 10-Q filing with the Securities and Exchange Commission the quarter before filing for bankruptcy, Lehman Brothers had total assets of $613 billion and shareholders' equity of $26 billion. Lehman's Level 3 assets, the bulk of which were in mortgage-backed securities, were $38 billion. This meant that a substantial write-down of Lehman Brothers' holdings in mortgage-backed securities wiped out its equity.

---

[4] There are variations on the name for this concept, including marking-to-market and marked-to-market. No matter whether it is mark, marking, or marked, the idea is that assets are reported at their fair value.

The Effect of Recent Accounting Scandals

Whether or not a company's financial statements fairly represent its financial position became a major issue in the United States after the failure of Enron Corporation in 2001. At the time, Enron was a respected and widely admired U.S. company that had been ranked as high as seventh on the Fortune 500 list of U.S. companies. Enron's collapse triggered dozens of lawsuits and criminal charges:[5]

- Sixteen former Enron executives pleaded guilty to securities fraud, insider trading, and conspiracy.
- Four former Merrill Lynch & Co., Inc. executives and one midlevel Enron finance executive are in jail for misreporting loans.
- Merrill Lynch, J P Morgan & Co., Citigroup Inc., and the Canadian Imperial Bank of Commerce (CIBC) have paid US$400 million to settle allegations that they helped Enron "cook its books," and they have also paid US$6.6 billion to settle a variety of shareholder lawsuits against them.
- The last two CEOs of Enron, Kenneth Lay and Jeffrey Skilling, were found guilty on 25 counts of conspiracy, fraud, false statements, and insider trading between them. They were on trial for "misleading investors, analysts, auditor and employees through false and sanitized financial statements, empty hype and shady accounting maneuvers in financing broadband, trading, and retail energy units." Kenneth Lay died less than two months after being found guilty. Jeffrey Skilling is serving his sentence of 24 years and 4 months in a U.S. federal prison.[6]

The fallout from Enron's bankruptcy has had implications for accounting and finance. Quite simply, the financial collapse of Enron has changed the accounting landscape and what is expected of a company's financial statements. So many individuals were hurt by the collapse, and it happened so quickly to such a widely admired company, that the U.S. Congress had to act to restore public confidence in the U.S. financial system. As a direct consequence, the U.S. Congress in 2002 passed the **Sarbanes-Oxley Act (SOX)**.[7] The main provisions of this act are as follows:[8]

> **Sarbanes-Oxley Act (SOX)** law passed in 2002 in response to accounting scandals intended to restore confidence in corporate governance and public accounting

- The establishment of a Public Company Accounting Oversight Board to register and inspect public accounting firms and establish audit standards.
- The separation of audit functions from other services, such as consulting, provided by the big accounting firms, with the auditors rotating every 5 years so that they do not get too close to the companies they are auditing.
- The implementation of much stricter governance standards, including internal controls, with auditors reporting to the company's audit committee, which is to be composed of independent members of the board of directors with the power to engage independent consultants.
- The requirement that the company's annual report contain an internal control report that indicates the state of the company's internal controls and assesses their effectiveness.
- The requirement that both the chief executive officer (CEO) and the chief financial officer (CFO) "certify" that the company's financial statements "fairly present, in all material respects, the operations and financial condition of the issuer."

[5] This section is adapted from Kristen Hays, "Trial of Enron Founder Ken Lay and Ex CEO Jeffrey Skilling Starts January 30," *Associated Press*, January 22, 2006.

[6] However, part of his conviction was vacated by the U.S. Supreme Court in 2010, which sent the case to lower court for further proceedings regarding the "federal honest services law" under which he was convicted in 2004.

[7] Public Law 107-204, 107th Congress, signed into law July 30, 2002. We discussed this law in more detail in Chapters 1 and 2.

[8] See the summary on the web page of the American Institute of Certified Public Accountants (AICPA) at www .aicpa.org.

As the key provisions of SOX indicate, the main targets are the company and its auditors. There was widespread belief that Enron's auditor, Arthur Andersen LLP, was too tight with Enron, as many former Andersen people worked with Enron, and the local auditors overruled the head office in several key areas. Rotating the company's auditors every 5 years promotes their objectivity. Further, separating the nonauditing functions of the major accounting firms from their audit functions helps prevent a conflict of interest in accounting firms. Previously, many felt the accounting firms were treating auditing as a loss leader to secure consulting contracts. Consequently, they may not have been sufficiently objective in their audit responsibilities. This judgment is confirmed by the fact that the U.S. government set up an oversight body to regulate audit firms and take direct control of many accounting areas.

For U.S. companies, the major change is the requirement of stronger internal controls. One of the failures at Enron was apparently a weak audit committee that did not exercise proper oversight of the company's financial statements. Now, the audit committee must be composed of independent directors of the board of directors who have the power to engage external consultants and to have the external auditors report to them. **Independent directors** are not employees of the company. Further, management has to report on, and the auditors comment on, the company's internal controls, with the CEO and chief financial officer certifying that the statements are fair.

The SOX Act has had a major impact in the United States, improving public confidence in the objectivity of the financial statements of U.S. companies. It also affects a significant number of non-U.S. companies (especially the large ones) that issue securities in the United States and have to comply with U.S. securities laws. Indeed, although other countries have had fewer accounting scandals, and those that have occurred are on a smaller scale than those in the United States, concerns over such misrepresentations and their effect on the business environment have dictated that international regulatory authorities maintain strict controls over the auditing process, similar to those employed in the United States.

independent director member of the company's board of directors who is not employed by the company

Concept Review Questions

1. What is GAAP? What is IFRS?

2. What are the major provisions of SOX?

3.2 FINANCIAL STATEMENTS

Financial statements provide a summary of the transactions of a company. The balance sheet provides a snapshot of the company's assets, liabilities, and equity at a point in time, whereas the income statement and statement of cash flows summarize activity over the fiscal period, whether that be a quarter or a year. The statement of cash flows provides summaries of cash flows by operations, investing, and financing activities over a period of time. Key to understanding financial statements is appreciating that the balance sheet, income statement, and statement of cash flows are all interconnected.

International Business Machines (IBM) is a large global information technology company, based in the U.S. We present and discuss IBM's financial statements in this chapter; in the next chapter, we provide some tools that can be used to analyze these statements.

The Balance Sheet

balance sheet or **statement of financial condition** snapshot of the financial position of a company, listing assets on the left and liabilities and owner's equity on the right

accounting identity relationship resulting from double-entry bookkeeping such that assets are equal to the sum of liabilities and equity

The **balance sheet**, which we also refer to as the **statement of financial condition**, is a snapshot of the company's financial position, listing assets, liabilities, and equity. Because of double-entry bookkeeping, assets must be equal to the sum of liabilities and equity. We refer to this relationship as the **accounting identity**. In practice, the company's bookkeeper wouldn't make up a balance sheet after every transaction; he or she would record the transaction in a journal and ledger and then post all the transactions to the company's total balance sheet at the end of the fiscal period or year. Therefore, balance sheets are as of a particular date, such as the end of the fiscal year or fiscal quarter.

IBM's financial statements are very straightforward, which is one reason we chose them. We provide its balance sheet for its 2010 fiscal year in Table 3-1.[9] At the end of the 2010 fiscal year, IBM had total assets of $113.5 billion, liabilities of $90.4 billion, and equity of $23 billion.

IBM's assets include $48,116 million of current assets. **Current assets** are assets that can be converted into cash within a year as receivables are collected, inventories sold, and so on. These current assets represent the **working capital** of the company. **Current liabilities** are the short-term obligations of the company, including amounts owed the company's suppliers, which we refer to as **accounts payable** or **trade payables**, and any **accrued expenses**, which are amounts owned from transactions that have occurred but for which payments are not yet due. Accrued expenses includes what is owed employees (that is, **wages payable**), and what is owed in taxes (that is, **taxes payable**). If we subtract current liabilities from current assets, we arrive at IBM's **net working capital**: $48,116 million − 40,562 million = $7,554 million.

Whereas some companies report **gross property, plant, and equipment**, which is the sum total of the book value of long-lived, physical assets before any depreciation, some companies report **net property, plant, and equipment**, which is the difference between the gross property, plant, and equipment, and accumulated depreciation. In the case of IBM for fiscal year 2010, it had $40.289 billion of gross property, plant, and equipment and $14.096 billion of net property, plant, and equipment.

IBM reports $28.6 billion of intangible assets for fiscal year 2010. An **intangible asset** is an asset that has no physical presence, such as patents and trademarks. **Goodwill** is an intangible asset that is often broken out separately from intangibles on the balance sheet and arises when a company acquires another company but pays more for this acquired company than the fair market value of its identifiable assets.

For liabilities, IBM owed suppliers $7.8 billion at the end of 2010. In total, IBM had current liabilities of $40.562 billion. IBM's long-term liabilities consist of long-term debt and leases of $21.846 billion and other liabilities of $7.109 billion, which includes a $16.7 billion pension obligation. The book value, or carrying value, of equity was over $23 billion. You can see that IBM had a substantial Treasury Stock account of over $96 billion, which reflects repurchases of its own stock for the primary purpose of providing these shares to employees; when employees exercise the stock options, the shares become outstanding shares and increase shareholders' equity.

Companies may also have **capital leases**, which are long-term leases that are treated as debt, or **deferred income tax**, which are taxes the company expects to pay in the future. Further, a company may report a minority interest. If a company consolidates subsidiaries that are not 100% owned, the **minority interest** account reflects the assets of the subsidiary or subsidiaries that are not owned by the reporting company.[10] For example, suppose Company X owns 85% of Company Y. If Company Y has $100 million of assets and Company X consolidates Company Y into its financial statements, Company X will report 15% × $100 million = $15 million in minority interest. This is reported between the debt and the equity of a company.

current assets assets (cash and equivalents, short-term investments, accounts receivable, inventories, prepaid expenses) that are expected to be converted into cash within a year

current liabilities short-term obligations

accounts payable or **trade payables** amounts owed the suppliers of the business

accrued expenses amounts owed from transactions that have occurred but for which payment is not due

wages payable amounts that are owed the employees of the business

taxes payable amounts that are owed to federal, state, or local governments

net working capital current assets less current liabilities

gross property, plant, and equipment sum of book values of all physical long-lived assets

net property, plant, and equipment difference between the gross property, plant, and equipment and accumulated depreciation

intangible asset asset that does not have a physical presence

goodwill intangible asset that is the difference between what is paid for another business entity and the value of the acquired business entity's assets

capital leases long-term rental agreements that are considered liabilities

deferred income tax taxes that are anticipated to be paid in future years

minority interest represents the interest in a company that is not owned by the controlling parent company

[9] We have grouped a few accounts to keep things more manageable. For example, we have grouped the short-term receivables into one account and have done the same for the noncurrent receivable accounts as well.

[10] Consolidation is simply adding the two companies' accounts, removing any intercompany transactions to avoid double-counting.

TABLE 3-1   International Business Machines Balance Sheet for Fiscal Years Ending December 31, 2008, 2009 and 2010

	As of December 31		
(in millions)	*2010*	*2009*	*2008*
Cash & Equivalents	$10,661	$12,183	$12,741
Short Term Investments	990	1,791	166
Accounts Receivable - Trade, Net	28,225	26,793	27,555
Total Inventory	2,450	2,494	2,701
Prepaid Expenses	4,226	3,946	4,299
Other Current Assets	1,564	1,728	1,542
Total Current Assets	$48,116	$48,935	$49,004
Property/Plant/Equipment, Total - Gross	40,289	39,595	38,445
Accumulated Depreciation, Total	(26,193)	(25,431)	(24,140)
Long-term receivables	10,548	10,644	11,183
Long-term investments	5,778	5,379	5,058
Prepaid pension assets	3,068	3,001	1,601
Deferred taxes	3,220	4,195	7,270
Intangibles and Goodwill	28,624	22,704	21,104
Total Assets	$113,450	$109,022	$109,525
Accounts Payable	$7,804	$7,436	$7,014
Accrued Expenses	10,184	9,728	11,203
Taxes Payable	4,216	3,826	2,743
Notes Payable/Short Term Debt	2,761	1,945	2,295
Current Port. of LT Debt/Capital Leases	4,017	2,222	8,942
Deferred income	11,580	10,845	10,239
Total Current Liabilities	$40,562	$36,002	$42,436
Long Term Debt	21,846	21,932	22,689
Pension and Postretirement Benefit Obligation	15,978	15,953	19,452
Deferred Income	3,666	3,562	3,171
Other Liabilities	8,226	8,818	8,192
Total Liabilities	$90,278	$86,267	$95,940
Common Stock, Total	$45,418	$41,810	$39,129
Retained Earnings	92,532	80,900	70,353
Treasury Stock - Common	(96,161)	(81,243)	(74,171)
Accumulated Gains and Losses Not Affecting Retained Earnings	(18,743)	(18,830)	(21,845)
Total IBM Equity	$23,046	$22,637	$13,466
Non-controlling Interests	126	118	119
Total Equity	$23,172	$22,755	$13,585
Total Liabilities & Shareholders' Equity	$113,450	$109,022	$109,525

Source: *International Business Machines 10-K filing for fiscal year 2010.*

PROBLEM

Consider the balance sheet for Wal-Mart Stores, Inc. for the quarter ended October 31, 2011, in millions:

EXAMPLE 3.1

Identifying Elements in the Balance Sheet

Cash and short-term investments	$7,063	Accounts payable	$37,350
		Accrued expenses	16,890
Total receivables, net	4,757	Notes payable/short-term debt	9,594
Total inventory	44,135	Current portion of long-term debt	1,791
Prepaid expenses	3,227	Other current liabilities	1,714
Other current assets	89	Long-term debt	44,872
Property/Plant/Equipment, Gross	157,498	Capital lease obligations	2,979
		Deferred income tax	8,085
Accumulated depreciation	47,106	Minority interest	4,601
Goodwill	20,409	Total equity	67,163
Other long-term assets	4,927		
Total assets	195,039		

A. What is Wal-Mart's working capital at the end of this quarter?
B. What are the current liabilities for Wal-Mart at the end of this quarter?
C. What is Wal-Mart's net working capital at the end of this quarter?
D. What are the total liabilities for Wal-Mart at the end of this quarter?

Solution

A. Working capital = $7,063 + 4,757 + 44,135 + 3,227 + 89 = 59,271 million
B. Current liabilities = $37,350 + 16,890 + 9,594 + 1,791 + 1,714 = $67,339 million
C. Net working capital = $59,271 − 67,339 = −$8,068 million
D. Total liabilities = Total assets − Total equity = $195,039 − 67,163 = $127,876 million

The Structure of the Balance Sheet ‖ GLOBAL PERSPECTIVE

As you can see in looking at IBM's balance sheets, the order of the assets is by liquidity, with the most liquid listed first, and so on. This is different than what we see for companies reporting based on IFRS.

According to IFRS, unless there is a compelling reason to do otherwise, the asset accounts are listed in two groups: current and noncurrent.[11] For example SAP AG, a German computer company, reports the following in its 2010 balance sheet:

€ millions	
Cash and cash equivalents	3,518
Other financial assets	158
Trade and other receivables	3,099
Other nonfinancial assets	181
Tax assets	187
Total current assets	7,143
Goodwill	8431
Intangible assets	2,376
Property, plant, and equipment	1449
Other financial assets	475
Trade and other receivables	78
Other nonfinancial assets	31
Tax assets	122
Deferred tax assets	736
Total noncurrent assets	13,698
Total assets	20,841

Source: *SAP 2010 Annual Report*, p. 168.

[11] International Financial Reporting Standards, IAS 1 (2003).

The Income Statement

income statement or statement of earnings summary of the company's performance over a period of time, typically a fiscal quarter or a fiscal year

The **income statement**, which is also referred to as the **statement of earnings**, is a summary of the company's performance over a period of time, typically a fiscal quarter or a fiscal year. The structure of the income statement is simple: Begin with revenues and end with net income. In between, we subtract expenses, first operating expenses and then nonoperating expenses. The basic structure is the following:

	Revenues
Subtract	Cost of goods sold
Equals	Gross profit
Subtract	Selling, general, and administrative expenses
Equals	Earnings before interest, taxes, depreciation, and amortization (EBITDA)
Subtract	Depreciation and amortization
Equals	Earnings before interest and taxes (EBIT)
Subtract	Interest expense
Equals	Earnings before taxes (EBT)
Subtract	Taxes
Equals	Net income

You will find variations of this basic structure as you examine the income statements of actual companies. For example,

- revenues may be referred to as net revenues, sales, or net sales;[12]
- the cost of goods sold may be referred to as the cost of sales or direct costs;
- if the company mines or extracts minerals, gas, or oil, it may have depletion, which is similar to depreciation and amortization;
- the company may have research and development or other operating expenses that are deducted to arrive at EBITDA;
- the company may have other income or other expenses that may be added or deducted before or after EBIT, depending on the nature of the income or expense;
- if the company has preferred stock, net income may be presented before and after preferred stock dividends are subtracted, in which case the bottom-line net income may be referred to as net income available to common shareholders.

earnings before interest and taxes (EBIT) operating profit, calculated as gross profit, less operating expenses

earnings before interest, taxes, depreciation, and amortization (EBITDA) operating earnings before depreciation and amortization

How much money did IBM make in fiscal year 2010? To see this, we look at the income statement (also known as statement of earnings) in Table 3-2.

We can see from Table 3-2 that IBM Inc. had sales of almost $100 billion in 2010. Subtracting the cost of revenues, which is also referred to as the cost of sales or the cost of goods sold, IBM had gross profit of $46,014 million. Subtracting other operating expenses from gross profit provides $18,149 million in **earnings before interest and taxes (EBIT)**, or operating income. Some analysts prefer to analyze the **earnings before interest taxes, depreciation and amortization**, referred to often by its acronym, **EBITDA**. As the name implies, EBITDA is the sum of EBIT and depreciation and amortization. IBM does not provide depreciation and amortization as a separate account item in its income

---

[12] The "net" refers to returns and exchanges, most often used in retail businesses.

TABLE 3-2 International Business Machines Income Statement for Years Ended December 31, 2008, 2009, and 2010

	For the 12 months ending December 31,		
(in millions)	*2010*	*2009*	*2008*
Total Revenue	$99,870	$95,759	$103,630
Cost of Revenue, Total	53,857	51,972	57,969
Gross Profit	$46,013	$43,787	$45,661
Selling/General/Admin. Expenses, Total	20,904	20,047	22,068
Research & Development	6,026	5,820	6,337
Depreciation/Amortization	253	285	306
Unusual Expense (Income)	641	474	706
Other Operating Expenses, Total	40	147	306
Operating Income	$18,149	$17,014	$15,938
Other non-operating income	1,941	1,534	1,358
EBIT	$20,090	$18,548	$17,296
Interest expense	368	402	673
Income Before Tax	$19,722	$18,138	$16,715
Tax	4,890	4,713	4,381
Net income	$14,832	$13,425	$12,334

Source: *International Business Machines 10-K filing for fiscal year 2010.*

statements, but in footnotes to the statements (as well as the statement of cash flows, discussed later), we can locate the amount. IBM's EBITDA is $19,837 million:

		(in millions)
Start with	EBIT	$20,090
Add back	Depreciation	253
Equals	EBITDA	$19,837

Depreciation

"Wear and tear" has traditionally been referred to by accountants as **depreciation** because an asset is depreciating or reducing in value through time. The **depreciation expense** is the estimate of the loss of value of a long-lived tangible asset over a specified period of time, such as a year or a quarter. A similar concept is **amortization**, in which **amortization expense** is the loss of value of an intangible asset over time. For financial reporting purposes, the company is allowed to use any reasonable method for calculating depreciation or amortization.

The most common method of depreciation for financial reporting purposes is **straight-line depreciation**. Depreciation using the straight-line method is the same each year of the asset's life, calculated as the depreciable asset's cost, less an estimated salvage value, divided by its estimated useful life:

$$\text{Straight-line depreciation} = \frac{\text{Asset cost} - \text{salvage value}}{\text{Useful life}} \qquad (3\text{-}1)$$

depreciation reduction in value of a long-lived, tangible asset over a specified period of time

depreciation expense deduction from income that reflects the reduction in the value of tangible assets over a period of time

amortization expense deduction from income that reflects the reduction in the value of intangible assets over a period of time

straight-line depreciation allocation of an asset's cost, less salvage value, over the life of the asset, with an equal portion allocated to each period

EXAMPLE 3.2

Calculating Profits

PROBLEM

Consider the fiscal year ending May 31, 2011, income statement information for Nike, in millions

Revenues	$20,862
Cost of revenues	11,354
Selling/General/Administrative expenses	6,693
Other operating expenses	1
Other income	29
Tax	711

A. What is Nike's gross profit?
B. What is Nike's operating profit?
C. What is Nike's net income?

Solution

A. Gross profit = $20,862 − 11,354 = 9,508 million
B. Operating profit = $9,508 − 6,693 − 1 = $2,814
C. Net income = $2,814 + 29 − 711 = $2,132

The rate of depreciation is the same each year and is expensed that amount per year. Consider an asset that has a cost of $100,000 and a useful life of 5 years. If the asset's salvage value—that is, what the company expects to sell the asset for when the asset is at the end of its useful life—is $10,000, the depreciation each year is $18,000 per year:

$$\text{Depreciation} = \frac{\$100,000 - 10,000}{5} = \$18,000 \text{ per year}$$

In other words, 20% of the asset's cost (less salvage value) is depreciated each year.

Whereas straight-line depreciation results in the same depreciation expense each period, accelerated methods result in more depreciation in earlier years of the asset's life and less in the later years. One group of accelerated methods is the **declining balance methods of depreciation**. In the declining balance methods, we apply a fixed percentage against the carrying value of the asset, which declines each year with the depreciation.[13] The result is a declining depreciation expense through time. For example, applying the 150% declining method (which is known as 150 DB) in our example is 150% of the straight-line rate, or 1.5 × 20% = 30%. For the first year, the asset's depreciation is 30% × $90,000, or $27,000. In the second year, there is $90,000 − 27,000 = $63,000 remaining to be depreciated. Thirty percent applied against this value produces $18,900 for the second year's depreciation. Another declining balance method, the **double-declining balance (DDB)** method, follows a similar process, but the rate is twice that of straight-line. We often refer to the DDB method as the 200DB method because the rate is 200% of the straight-line rate.[14]

The choice of depreciation method affects both the income statement and the balance sheet of a company. We provide the detail of the depreciation expense (which affects the

declining balance depreciation allocation of an asset's cost, less salvage value, over the life of the asset, with a rate applied against the declining carrying value of the asset

carrying value book value of an asset, which for a depreciable asset is the cost less accumulated depreciation

double declining balance method allocation of an asset's cost, less salvage value, over the life of the asset, with a rate applied against the declining carrying value of the asset at twice the straight-line rate

[13] The carrying value is also referred to as the book value of the asset; that is, the value that is reported in financial statements.
[14] Still another accelerated method is the sum-of-the-years'-digits depreciation, in which the depreciation for a given year is the ratio of the remaining life to the sum of the digits in the life, applied against the original cost less the salvage value. In our example, the sum of the years is 1 + 2 + 3 + 4 + 5 = 15. Therefore, the depreciation in the first year, with four years remaining, is 5/15 = 33.33% of the $90,000, or $30,000. In the second year, the depreciation is 4/15 = 26.67% of the $60,000 carrying value, or $16,000.

income statement) and carrying value of the asset (which affects the balance sheet) for each year and method in Table 3-3. As you can see, the depreciation expense is lowest in the earlier years of the asset's life using the straight-line method, but highest in the later years. This means that the net income would be the highest in the early years and lowest in the later years using straight-line depreciation, compared to the other two methods of depreciation. Regarding how the asset is represented on the balance sheet, it would have a higher carrying value in the early years with the straight-line method. No matter the method chosen, however, $90,000 is the depreciation over the 5 years, and the carrying value at the end of 5 years is $10,000, as we show in Table 3-3.

SPREADSHEET TOOLS

Depreciation Method	Function
Declining balance	DB (cost, salvage, life, period, months)
Double-declining balance	DDB (cost, salvage, life, period, factor)
Straight-line	SLN (cost, salvage, life)

where

Cost   is the initial cost of asset;

Factor   is the rate of decline (that is, 150% or 200% or the straight-line rate);

Life   is the number of periods of depreciation;

Months   is the number of months in first year;

Period   is the year, indicated as 1, 2, 3; and

Salvage is the estimated salvage value.

Example

Consider an asset with a cost of $100,000, a salvage value of $10,000, and a useful life of 5 years. The depreciation for the first year is:

Straight-line   = SLN(100000,10000,5)

150 Declining balance   = DDB(100000,10000,5,1,1.5)

The depreciation for the second year is:

Straight-line   = SLN(100000,10000,5)

150 Declining balance   = DDB(100000,10000,5,2,1.5)

Comparing the specifications for the first and second years, you should notice that they are identical for the straight-line method, but differ with respect to the "period" argument for 150 declining balance methods.

Earnings per share

Overall, in 2010 IBM produced $14.833 billion in net income. We can restate profits in terms of the earning per share of stock. There are two types of earnings per share: basic and diluted. **Basic earnings per share (basic EPS)** are the earnings per share based on the weighted average of the number of common shares outstanding during the fiscal period:

$$\text{Basic earnings per share} = \frac{\text{Net income}}{\text{Weighted average shares}} \quad (3\text{-}2)$$

basic earnings per share (basic EPS) earnings per share of common stock based on the weighted average of the number of shares outstanding during the fiscal period

TABLE 3-3 **Depreciation Expense and Carrying Value of an Asset That Has a Cost of $100,000, a 5-Year Useful Life, and a Salvage Value of $10,000**

Year	Straight-line Depreciation		150% Declining Balance Depreciation	
	Depreciation Expense	*Carrying Value*	*Depreciation Expense*	*Carrying Value*
1	$18,000	$82,000	$30,000	$70,000
2	18,000	64,000	28,000	42,000
3	18,000	46,000	16,800	25,200
4	18,000	28,000	10,080	15,120
5	18,000	10,000	5,120	10,000
Sum	$90,000		$90,000	

diluted earnings per share (diluted EPS) net income divided by the total possible number of common shares that could be outstanding if all potentially dilutive securities outstanding were converted into common shares

Companies are also required to report **diluted earnings per share (diluted EPS)**, which is simply the adjusted net income divided by the total possible number of shares that could be outstanding if all potentially dilutive securities outstanding were converted into common shares:

$$\text{Diluted earnings per share} = \frac{\text{Adjusted net income}}{\text{Weighted average shares potentially outstanding}} \quad (3\text{-}3)$$

For example, a company might have some convertible bonds outstanding, which under certain circumstances could be converted into common shares, or executive stock options, which may be exercised and therefore exchanged for common shares.[15] What do we mean by adjusted net income? If a company has a convertible bond, we not only adjust the shares outstanding for the potential shares from conversion, but we also add back the interest that would have been deducted to arrive at the net income.

So when IBM's net income is divided by the weighted average number of shares outstanding of 1.269 billion, basic earnings per share (EPS) are $11.69 per share. IBM's diluted EPS takes into account all the potential shares that could dilute the EPS by spreading the net income over a greater number of shares. IBM has limited potential for equity dilution, so its diluted EPS is $11.52.

The Statement of Cash Flows

statement of cash flows or cash flow statement summary of a company's cash receipts and disbursements over a specified period

It should be obvious by now that judgment permeates a company's financial statements. How then can we assess the element of judgment in a company's financial statements, and how can we determine the amount of money IBM has *really* made? One answer is to look at the third major financial statement: the **statement of cash flows** or **cash flow statement**, which essentially undoes the effects of judgment as much as possible and tracks the actual flow of hard cash through a company. The statement of cash flows is a summary of the sources and uses of cash in the company over a period of time, such as a fiscal quarter or a fiscal year.

Let's examine IBM's statement of cash flows, which we present in Table 3-4. In terms of noncash items, the biggest item was depreciation. This "expense" is not actually paid out

---

[15] Convertible securities include convertible bonds, for which the investor has the option to convert or exchange the bond into shares of stock. In the case of executive stock options, this is more complicated (and outside the scope of this text) because assumptions must be made regarding whether the shares are newly issued or are bought by the company in the open market and, hence, do not involve any new shares.

TABLE 3-4 International Business Machines Cash Flow Statement for the years ending December 31, 2008, 2009, and 2010

	For the year ending December 31		
(in millions)	2010	2009	2008
Net income	$14,833	$13,425	$12,334
Depreciation	3,657	3,773	4,140
Amortization of intangibles	1,174	1,221	1,310
Stock-based compensation	629	558	659
Deferred taxes	1,294	1,773	1,900
Net loss (gain) on asset sales & other	(801)	(395)	(338)
Receivables (including financing receivables)	(489)	2,131	274
Retirement related	(1,963)	(2,465)	(1,773)
Inventories	92	263	(102)
Other assets/other liabilities	949	319	1,268
Accounts payable	174	170	(860)
Net cash flows from operating activities	$19,549	$20,773	$18,812
Payments for plant, rental machines, & other property	$(4,185)	$(3,447)	$(4,171)
Proceeds from disposition of plant, rental machines, & other property	770	330	350
Investment in software	(569)	(630)	(716)
Purchases of marketable securities & other investments	(6,129)	(5,604)	(4,590)
Proceeds from disposition of marketable securities & other investments	7,877	3,599	6,100
Nonoperating finance receivables – net	(405)	(184)	(16)
Divestiture of businesses, net of cash transferred	55	400	71
Acquisition of businesses, net of cash acquired	(5,922)	(1,194)	(6,313)
Net cash flows from investing activities	$(8,507)	$(6,729)	$(9,285)
Proceeds from new debt	$8,055	$6,683	$13,829
Payments to settle debt	(6,522)	(13,495)	(10,248)
Short-term borrows (repays)—less than 90 days—net	817	(651)	(6,025)
Common stock repurchases	(15,375)	(7,429)	(10,578)
Common stock transactions, other	3,774	3,052	3,774
Cash dividends paid	(3,177)	(2,860)	(2,585)
Net cash flows from financing activities	$(12,429)	$(14,700)	$(11,834)
Effect of exchange rate changes on cash & cash equivalents	$(135)	$98	$58
Net change in cash & cash equivalents	$(1,522)	$(558)	$(2,250)

Source: *International Business Machines 10-K filing for fiscal year 2010*

to anyone; rather, it represents the loss of value in plant and equipment during the period. The fact that it was positive conveys that the company was able to generate cash flows from operations—generally a sign of a healthy company.

The statement of cash flows begins with net income from the income statement and then makes adjustments for noncash items that affected net income, such as depreciation and amortization. Other adjustments include adding back compensation in the form of stock, write-offs, and deferred taxes, and subtracting non-cash income or gains, such as gains on sales of assets.

Another set of adjustments are for the changes in current assets and current liabilities accounts. These adjustments account for the fact that accrual accounting is used, but we are interested in cash flows. When a company sells its products, this sale results in an increase in the period's revenues. If the company extends credit to its customers and these customers use this credit, accounts receivable increases by the same amount as the revenue. If the company purchased the goods from a supplier and used trade credit, there was no cash outlay for the cost of goods. When a sale is made using accrual accounting, inventory decreases by the company's cost of the product, and cost of goods sold increases by this cost, even though the company may not have paid for the goods sold. Based on accrual accounting, the company's profit increases by the difference between the revenue and the cost of the goods sold in this transaction, even though no cash has exchanged hands. If the company uses cash basis accounting, there would be no profit until the accounts are collected and the company pays for the goods; if the company uses accrual accounting, there would be a profit. In the statement of cash flows, we adjust net income for the changes in the inventory, accounts receivable, and accounts payable accounts, which help transform the reported net income into a cash flow from operations.

So how do we adjust for the fact that we are using accrual accounting and not cash accounting in these transactions? We adjust for the changes in the working capital accounts.

Consider a simple example in which the company does not use trade credit, but does grant trade credit to its customers. And let's say that the company has the following accounts prior to the sale:

Accounts receivable	$75
Inventory	$50

If the company sells an item for $5 that costs $2, the profit is $3 and the accounts now have balances of:

Accounts receivable	$80
Inventory	$48

What is the cash flow from this transaction? We know that it is $0, but we can also determine this by starting with the net income of $3 and adjusting for the changes in accounts receivable and inventory:

	End of Period	Beginning of Period	Change
Accounts receivable	$80	$75	$5
Inventory	$48	$50	–2
Net change			$3

Therefore, working capital accounts increased by $3. If we start with the net income and then subtract the increase in working capital accounts, we arrive at net income: $0.

Working Capital Account	Adjustment in Net Income to Arrive at Cash Flow from Operations	
	from an Increase in the Working Capital Account	*from a Decrease in the Working Capital Account*
Accounts payable	Increase	Decrease
Accounts receivable	Decrease	Increase
Inventory	Decrease	Increase
Prepaid expenses	Decrease	Increase
Taxes payable	Increase	Decrease

SUMMARIZING: WORKING CAPITAL CHANGES AND CASH FLOWS

When we subtract the increase in net working capital of $2,186 million from the traditional cash flow of $20,786 million, we arrive at **cash flow for/from operations (CFO)** of $18,600 million. You will notice that we use "for/from" in referring to cash flows that appear in the statement of cash flows. This is because the cash flow may be negative (hence "for") or positive (and therefore "from"). As you become familiar with financial statements, you may observe some companies adopt a generic "from" or "for," to be used no matter the sign, or use the "for" or "from" as appropriate to indicate the sign. We will adopt the latter convention.

cash flow for/from operations (CFO) cash flow from the day-to-day operations of the business; the result of subtracting the increase in net working capital from traditional cash flow

Cash flow for/from operations is therefore:

$$\text{Cash flow for/from operations} = \frac{\text{Net}}{\text{income}} + \frac{\text{Noncash}}{\text{expenses}} - \frac{\text{Change in}}{\text{working capital}} \quad (3\text{-}4)$$

If working capital increases, we subtract the increase to arrive at CFO; if working capital decreases, we add this net decrease to determine CFO. In our example, working capital increased by $2,186 million; therefore, we subtract this amount from the traditional cash flow of $20,786 million.

The value of looking at CFO is that it takes into account changes in net working capital. It brings to light any increases in receivables and inventory, so the analyst can ask why people aren't paying for their purchases and why inventory is increasing. If sales are constant and yet the increase in net working capital is significant, it is one sign that the company's net income accounting may be aggressive.[16]

The next step in the cash flow statement is to consider the cash flow for/from investing. The **cash flow for/from investing (CFI)** reflects changes in long-term investments; if the company, on net, is investing in long-lived assets, cash flow for investing will be negative, and if the company is, on net, disposing of assets, cash flow from investing will be positive. IBM made investments in plant and property, software, and acquired business, and sold long-term securities and divested itself of a business. The net effect of these transactions that reflect investments is the cash flow for/from investing (CFI). For 2010, IBM had a cash flow for investment of $8,507 million.

cash flow for/from investing (CFI) cash flow, on net, from investing activities

The **cash flow for/from financing (CFF)** reflects whether the company is acquiring funds from outside the company. If the company is, on net, issuing new securities (bonds and/or stocks), the cash flow for financing will be positive; if the company is, on net, buying back securities, repaying debt, and paying dividends, CFF will be negative.

cash flow for/from financing (CFF) cash flow, on net, from financing activities

IBM had a cash flow for financing of $12,429 million. The largest cash flow in this category was IBM's $15,375 million repurchase of common stock, but IBM also issued new debt, retired debt, and paid cash dividends.

[16]However, net income would be down because of more reported and paid income tax.

Summarizing the cash flows on the statement of cash flows for IBM in 2010:

Cash flows from operations	$19,549
Cash flows for investing	–8,507
Cash flows for financing	–12,429
Net cash flow	–$1,387

The change in cash of –$1,387 reflects the change in the cash balance during this period, which we can trace to the balance sheet:

Ending balance of cash (end of fiscal year 2010)	$10,661
Beginning balance of cash (end of fiscal year 2009)	12,183
Change in cash	–$1,387

Whereas the net income that we started with ties this statement to the income statement, the change in cash is equal to the change in the cash account on the balance sheet from the prior fiscal year end to the current fiscal year end.

Most financial analysts focus on the cash flow statement. In general, a financially healthy company will have positive cash flows from operations and negative investing cash flows as it continues to invest in long-lived assets, but may have positive or negative financing cash flows. For example, if a company has negative cash flows from operations, positive investing cash flows, and positive financing cash flows, this paints a picture of a company that may not be sustainable: It is selling off assets and relying on outside funds to support itself.

A positive cash flow from investing would indicate that the company is selling more assets than it is buying, whereas a negative cash flow indicates that, on net, the company is making capital investments. In 2010, IBM's cash flow from investing (CFI) was negative, which means that, on net, the company was expending cash to invest in long-lived assets.

Regarding cash flow from financing activities, CFF, a positive value indicates that the company is raising funds from borrowing or selling new shares of stock. Cash outflows for financing occur when a company pays dividends or repays debt. The sign of CFF is not, in and of itself, indicative of any situation, but in conjunction with other elements can help paint a picture. For example, if a company has negative CFO, but positive CFF, this indicates that it is relying heavily on outside funds, rather than supporting itself through its operations. In the case of IBM in 2008, the cash flows are indicative of a healthy company: It was able to generate cash flows from its operations, make capital investments, pay dividends, repurchase its own stock, and repay debt obligations.

Other cash flow measures

In addition to the cash flows presented in the statement of cash flows, other measures of cash flow are used frequently to analyze a company's performance and cash flow generating ability. Other than the cash flows specific to the statement of cash flows, there is no standard definition or calculation of cash flow. We look at a few of these measures: simple cash flow, traditional cash flow, and free cash flow.

Simple cash flow   The most basic cash flow begins with net income and adds back depreciation, as well as any amortization or depletion expense that was used to arrive at net income. We refer to this measure as **simple cash flow** because it is the simplest to calculate:

simple cash flow net income plus depreciation, amortization, and depletion

$$\text{Simple cash flow} = \text{Net income} + \text{depreciation, amortization, and depletion} \quad (3\text{-}5)$$

Sirius XM, Inc. | LESSONS LEARNED

Sirius XM Inc. is the holding company for Sirius and XM Satellite Radio, which were separate, competing satellite broadcasting companies prior to the July 2008 merger.

Looking at the cash flows of Sirius XM, we can see that this company relied on external financing to support its operations for several of the years, as indicated by negative operating cash flows and positive financing cash flows:

This reliance on outside financing led to amassing debt, resulting in bond ratings that considered the debt to be "junk" (i.e., not investment grade). Following the 2008 merger, there were some economies in expenses, and the company was able to reduce some of its debt, though it continues to have a great deal of financial leverage, with long-term debt more than 81 times its book value of equity. Operations began to provide cash flows in 2009 and continued into 2010.

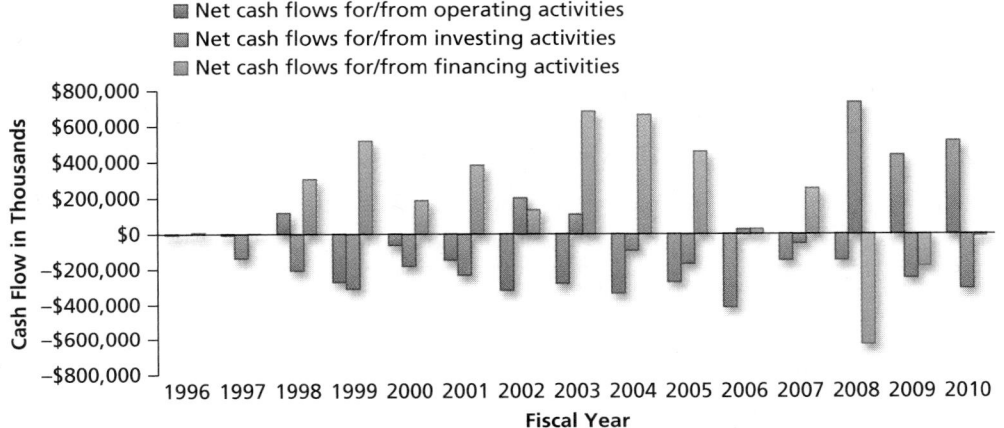

Source of data: Sirius XM Inc. and Sirius 10-K filings with the Securities and Exchange Commission, various years.

For IBM in 2010, the simple cash flow is $14,833 million + 4,831 million = $19,664 million.

This definition is very basic and does not consider all the other noncash entries that affect a company's cash flow, and it ignores the fact that the company needs to make capital expenditures to keep up to date and to grow.

Traditional cash flow Another cash flow measure considers depreciation, amortization, and depletion, but also considers other noncash expenses and income that affect net income. We often refer to this cash flow as **traditional cash flow**:[17]

$$\text{Traditional cash flow} = \frac{\text{Net}}{\text{income}} + \frac{\text{Noncash}}{\text{expenses or losses}} - \frac{\text{Noncash}}{\text{income or gains}} \quad (3\text{-}6)$$

> **traditional cash flow**
> cash flow measure that is equal to net income plus noncash expenses such as depreciation and deferred taxes

Historically, analysts have focused on traditional cash flow because for many manufacturing companies depreciation is a major noncash expense. Further, the traditional cash flow adjusts for any aggressive choice of depreciation by adding back whatever was subtracted in the income statement. Therefore, focusing on cash flow negates the effect of aggressive accounting for depreciation.

For IBM in 2010, the statement of cash flow begins with net income of $14,833 million. The adjustments for noncash income and expenses, which include depreciation, amortization, stock-based compensation, and deferred taxes, sum to $5,953 million. Therefore, IBM's traditional cash flow for 2010 is $14,833 + 5,953 = $20,786 million.

---

[17]If the company had noncash gains, such as an unrealized gain on its marketable securities, we would subtract this to arrive at the traditional cash flow.

free cash flow (FCF) funds available to the business, calculated as operating cash flows less capital expenditures

Free cash flow   A company's **free cash flow (FCF)** is the company's cash flow after its operating expenses and capital expenditures:

$$\text{Free cash flow} = \frac{\text{Cash flow}}{\text{from operations}} - \frac{\text{Capital}}{\text{expenditures}} \qquad (3\text{-}7)$$

Financial analysts focus on free cash flow to see whether a company is generating or using cash above and beyond the cash needed for investments necessary for the company to continue to grow. If we subtract capital expenditures from cash flow from operations for IBM in 2010, we estimate the free cash flow to be $19,549 million – 4,189 million = $15,360 million.

free cash flow to equity (FCFE) funds available to owners, calculated as cash flow from operations, less capital expenditures, plus net borrowing

Another version of the free cash flow concept is the **free cash flow to equity (FCFE)**. We calculate free cash flow to equity starting with the free cash flow of the company, but then adjust for the funds that are raised through borrowing—because it is this amount that is available—that is, free to be used—for the benefit of the owners. Therefore, we calculate free cash flow to equity by adding net borrowing to the free cash flow to the company, where net borrowing is the difference between funds raised by issuing debt and funds used to repay debts:[18]

$$\text{Free cash flow to equity} = \frac{\text{Cash flow}}{\text{for/from operations}} - \frac{\text{Capital}}{\text{expenditures}} + \text{Net borrowing} \quad (3\text{-}8)$$

In the case of IBM in 2010, the free cash flow to equity, in millions, is:

$$\text{Free cash flow to equity} = \$19,549 - 4,189 + 2,350 = \$17,710$$

SUMMARIZING: CASH FLOWS

	Net income		Net income
Plus	Depreciation, amortization, and depletion	*Plus*	Depreciation, amortization, and depletion
Equals	**Simple cash flow**	*Less*	Noncash income or gains
		Equals	**Traditional cash flow**
	Net income		Net income
Plus	Depreciation, amortization, and depletion	*Plus*	Depreciation, amortization, and depletion
Plus	Noncash income or gains	*Plus*	Noncash income or gains
Less	Change in working capital	*Less*	Change in working capital
Equals	**Cash flow for/from operations**	*Less*	Capital expenditures
		Equals	**Free cash flow**
	Net income		
Plus	Depreciation, amortization, and depletion		
Plus	Noncash income or gains		
Less	Change in working capital		
Less	Capital expenditures		
Plus	Net borrowing		
Equals	**Free cash flow to equity**		

[18]There is no generally accepted method of calculating free cash flow. A variation of free cash flow is to add back the interest paid on debt (less tax benefit from interest tax deductibility) because this represents the funds available to all providers of capital, that is, debt-holders and shareholders. This latter variation is often referred to as the *free cash flow to the firm*.

Sue an Auditor? | ETHICS

Auditors may be held responsible for errors in judgment. In late 2010, the attorney general of the State of New York filed a lawsuit against Ernst & Young, claiming that the auditor assisted Lehman Brothers in the accounting fraud related to removing obligations from Lehman's balance sheet. Using a device referred to as a "Repo 105" transaction, the Attorney General claims that the auditor knew that Lehman Brothers was transferring fixed income securities to European parties before the end of the fiscal quarter in exchange for cash, with the understanding that the exchange would be reversed after the fiscal quarter.

The People of the State of New York by Andrew M. Cuomo, Attorney General of the State of New York, Plaintiff, against Ernst & Young LLP, Defendant, December 21, 2010.

1. Who is responsible for the preparation of a company's financial statements?

2. What are the scope and purpose of the auditor's opinion?

3. How are the balance sheet and income statement linked?

4. What information does the statement of cash flows provide?

Concept Review Questions

3.3 THE TAX SYSTEM

Financial decision making focuses on cash flows, rather than account values, for financial reporting purposes. One of the most important cash flows is taxes, which may be federal, state, and local taxes or a combination of all three. In developed nations, taxes may be levied on both personal and corporate income. We begin by noting that the United States operates a classical system of double taxation, whereas Europe, by and large, operates a fully integrated system.[19] With a classical system of taxation, a corporation is taxed on its income and shareholders are taxed on any dividends that are paid out, hence encouraging companies to retain their earnings. With a fully integrated system, however, there is no double taxation; rather, corporate income is taxed at the corporate level only.

When there is potential for double taxation of income earned through a corporation, which is absorbed by shareholders, some consideration is generally given to somewhat reducing the burden of double taxation. How taxes are levied has implications for finance decision making, so it is important to realize from the outset that tax systems may differ among countries. As a result, corporate finance strategies that are based on the U.S. tax code are not directly applicable in Europe and Asia, and vice versa.

Corporations are distinct legal entities and are taxed as such. Corporations file income tax returns with the Internal Revenue Service (IRS) that are determined in much the same way as corporations prepare their income statements for investors. However, there are some differences. We will look at a few of these differences.

Interest and Dividends Received

The tax system may affect how companies invest their funds, whether short term or long term, and the type of financing that a company uses. For example, companies often make temporary investments while waiting to pay bills, and these assets generate investment

[19]European countries operate tax systems that are either partially or fully integrated. A good example of a fully integrated system is that used by China.

income. Similarly, companies may have both debt and common shares outstanding, so they pay interest on debt and may pay dividends on common shares. How investment income and expenses are treated for tax purposes is very important in finance.

The basic rule is that interest is fully taxable when received and fully deductible when paid. Looking at companies' financial statements, you may find that a company may combine these two items into one "net interest" amount.

Unlike interest, dividends are not tax deductible when paid; they are paid out of *after-tax income*. In the U.S. tax system, when a corporation receives dividends from another corporation, some or all the dividends are not included in the recipient company's taxable income by means of a deduction; in other words, the recipient corporation includes all of the dividends and then takes a deduction for a portion of these dividends. The proportion of dividends deducted, the **dividends received deduction**, depends on the ownership relationship between the two corporations:

dividends received deduction amount of the dividends a corporation receives from another corporation that may be deducted from income for tax purposes

Proportion of dividends deducted:	*Relationship*
100%	80% to 100% of the dividend-paying corporation owned by the dividend-receiving corporation
80%	20% to 80% of the dividend-paying corporation owned by the dividend-receiving corporation
70%	Less than 20% of the dividend-paying corporation owned by the dividend-receiving corporation

For example, suppose that Corporation A owns 5% of Corporation B. If Corporation B pays $10 million in dividends to Corporation A, these dividends appear in Corporation A's tax return as follows:

Dividend income		$10 million
Less: Dividends received deduction	70% of $10 million	7 million
Income included in taxable income		$3 million

If Corporation A's taxable income is taxed at the rate of 35%, the $3 million of included dividend income results in a tax of $1.05 million. Therefore, the effective tax on the $10 million of dividend income is $1.05 million ÷ $10 million = 10.5%, whereas without the dividends received deduction, this $10 million of income would be taxed at 35%. And so we see a difference between accounting income and income for tax purposes. In particular, for accounting purposes, any dividends received are added to income, whereas for tax purposes all the dividends are included in income, but then a portion of this income is deducted and, hence, is not taxed.

EXAMPLE 3.3

Dividends Received Deduction

PROBLEM

Suppose a corporation has $100 million of income before considering the $10 million in dividend income that it receives from its investments in other companies. If the corporation's dividends it receives are eligible for an 80% dividend received deduction, what is the taxable income of this corporation?

Solution

Taxable income = $100 million + 10 million − (0.8 × $10 million) = $102 million.

Depreciation

For U.S. tax purposes, the government requires a specific form of depreciation. In the U.S., this method is the **Modified Accelerated Cost Recovery System (MACRS)**, which is based on the following assumptions:[20]

- Using a 200% declining balance method (that is, the annual rate is 200% of what the straight-line rate would be for the same asset life);
- Ignoring salvage value for purposes of depreciation;
- Employing the **half-year convention** in the first year, which means that only one-half of the first year's depreciation is actually allowed the first year, resulting in an extra year of depreciation;[21] and
- Assigning prescribed lives, based on the type of asset. That is, an asset may be a 3-year MACRS asset or a 5-year MACRS asset (there is no 4-year MACRS asset). The taxpayer must look up the asset in the tax code to determine its MACRS life.

You do not have to worry about the details on MACRS depreciation, however, because the Internal Revenue Code specifies the rates to apply against the original cost of the asset, as we show in Table 3-5.

Suppose the lathe that the W Corporation bought for $30,000 qualifies as 7-year property under MACRS. This means that the depreciation for tax purposes in the first year is $30,000 \times 0.1429 = \$4,287$. The depreciation for the second year is $30,000 \times 0.2449 = \$7,347$, and so on.

Now suppose that the W Corporation uses straight-line depreciation over 8 years for financial reporting purposes and MACRS for tax purposes, and let's assume that there are no other differences in accounting between financial reporting and tax purposes. If the W Corporation has EBITDA of $10,000, no nonoperating expenses or income, and a tax rate of 40%,

Modified Accelerated Cost Recovery System (MACRS) system of depreciation prescribed in the U.S. tax code that requires first identifying the asset's MACRS life and then applying the appropriate rate of cost recovery

half-year convention use of half of a year's depreciation in the first year of depreciating an asset

TABLE 3-5 MACRS Rates for 3-, 5-, 7-, and 10-Year Assets

Year	3 Years	5 Years	7 Years	10 Years
1	33.33%	20.00%	14.29%	10.00%
2	44.45%	32.00%	24.49%	18.00%
3	14.81%	19.20%	17.49%	14.40%
4	7.41%	11.52%	12.49%	11.52%
5		11.52%	8.93%	9.22%
6		5.76%	8.92%	7.37%
7			8.93%	6.55%
8			4.46%	6.55%
9				6.56%
10				6.55%
11				3.28%

[20] A taxpayer may elect to use 150DB depreciation, but because the use of 200DB produces more depreciation sooner, 150DB would only be used in special circumstances.

[21] Other conventions are available, but the half-year is the most common.

The W Corporation

	Financial reporting	Tax reporting	Difference
EBITDA	$10,000	$10,000	$0
Depreciation	3,750	4,287	−537
Earnings before taxes	$6,250	$5,713	$537
Taxes @ 40%	2,500	2,285	215
Income after tax	$3,750	$3,428	$322

The only difference from W's original income statement is that the depreciation expense of $4,287 replaces the depreciation expense of $3,750. As a result, the actual tax bill for W is less than what is reported for financial statement purposes:

Taxes payable	$2,285
Plus: Deferred taxes	215
Tax expense	$2,500

So what are the deferred taxes of $2,500 − 2,285 = $215? The deferred taxes are what we estimate the company must pay sometime in the future. Another way of looking at these taxes is that this is the amount the W Corporation would pay if the government didn't allow accelerated depreciation for tax purposes. In other words, the $2,500 of taxes is composed of two parts: pay $2,285 now and $215 later; if the straight-line method was required for tax purposes instead of MACRS, W Corporation would have to pay $2,500 of taxes this period, not $2,285. The $215 deferred tax liability represents the difference in taxes when applying the depreciation for financial reporting purposes and for tax purposes. One way to look at **deferred tax liability** is that these are taxes that the company reasonably expects to pay in the future.

deferred tax liability
taxes that the company reasonably expects to pay in the future

EXAMPLE 3.4

Depreciation for Tax Purposes

PROBLEM

Suppose the Tonka Delivery Company acquired a new truck for its deliveries, for $200,000. The company expects to use the truck for 7 years, at which time the company expects the truck to be worthless. The truck is classified as a 5-year asset for tax purposes, and the rate of tax on the company's taxable income is 30%.

1. What is the depreciation expense and end-of-year book value for tax purposes for each year?
2. If the company uses straight-line depreciation over 7 years for financial reporting purposes, what is the amount of the deferred taxes in the first year?

Solution

1. Using a 5-year MACRS life requires depreciation over 6 years:

Year	MACRS rate	Depreciation	End-of-year book value
1	20.00%	$40,000	$160,000
2	32.00%	$64,000	$96,000
3	19.20%	$38,400	$57,600
4	11.52%	$23,040	$34,560
5	11.52%	$23,040	$11,520
6	5.76%	$11,520	$0
7	0.00%	$0	$0

2. Straight-line depreciation is $200,000 ÷ 7 = $28,571.43 per year. In the first year, the difference in depreciation is $40,000 − 28,571.43 = $11,428.57. The reported taxes payable amount is based on the MACRS rate, whereas the deferred taxes are based on the difference in taxes using these two depreciation expenses (that is, straight-line and MACRS) and is therefore $11,428.57 × 0.3 = $3,428.57.

Capital Gains

As we saw earlier in this chapter, depreciation for tax purposes is very specific with respect to the assets' lives and rates of depreciation in each year. The fact that the rate of depreciation is prescribed, rather than determined relative to actual deterioration or loss of value means that it is often the case that an asset is sold for an amount different than its book or carrying value for tax purposes. This gives rise to gains or losses at the time of the disposition of the asset, which must be dealt with.

capital gain taxable gain incurred when an asset is sold at a price greater than its original cost

First, if the selling price is greater than the original capital cost, a **capital gain** arises, which is taxable. However, the converse is not true; when a depreciable capital asset is sold below its original purchase price, this does not generate a tax deductible **capital loss** because this is expected (i.e., it is a depreciable asset and as such is expected to depreciate in value below its original cost). In fact, capital losses are generated only when a nondepreciable asset (such as land or financial assets) is sold at a price less than its original cost.

capital loss tax deductible loss generated when a nondepreciable asset is sold at a price lower than its original cost

Aside from capital gains, additional tax consequences may arise in the form of **depreciation recapture**. The amount by which the salvage value exceeds the asset's carrying value for tax purposes is the depreciation recapture and is fully taxable.[22] However, if the salvage value is less than the ending carrying value, the amount by which the book value exceeds the salvage value is a loss, which is fully tax deductible.

depreciation recapture amount by which the salvage value (sale price) of an asset exceeds the asset's book or carrying value

---

PROBLEM

Assume that a company sells equipment for $100,000 that it had purchased 3 years ago for $650,000. The asset was classified as a 5-year asset for MACRS purposes. What are the tax consequences of this transaction?

EXAMPLE 3.5

Sale of a Depreciable Asset at a Loss for Tax Purposes

---

[22] In other words, depreciation recapture is viewed as if the firm charged too much depreciation because the asset is sold for more than its depreciated book value for tax purposes. Therefore, the firm must pay back the amount of taxes it saved by charging too much depreciation.

Solution

First, check for capital gains. You notice that they do not occur in this example because the selling price of $200,000 is less than the original cost of $650,000.

Next, determine whether there is a recapture or a loss:

Year	Rate	Depreciation for tax purposes Rate × $650,000	End of year book value for tax purposes Beginning of year book value, less depreciation for year
1	20.00%	$130,000	$520,000
2	32.00%	$208,000	$312,000
3	19.20%	$124,800	$187,200
4	11.52%	$74,880	$112,320
5	11.52%	$74,880	$37,440
6	5.76%	$37,440	$0

At the end of three years, the asset has a carrying value for tax purposes of $187,200. Therefore, there is a loss of $100,000 – 187,200 = –$87,200, which is a capital loss.

EXAMPLE 3.6

Capital Gains and Depreciation Recapture

PROBLEM

Suppose a company purchases an asset for $650,000 that is classified as a 5-year asset for tax purposes. Assume that, after 2 years, the company sells the asset for $700,000. What are the tax consequences of this transaction?

Solution

First, check for capital gains. You see that they do occur in this example:

Capital gains = Selling price − Original cost = $700,000 − 650,000 = $50,000

Next, determine whether there is depreciation recapture. To do this, we must first determine the book value of the asset for tax purposes at the end of the second year. Using the rates for a 5-year asset, applied against the original cost of $650,000:

Year	Rate	Depreciation for tax purposes	End of year book value for tax purposes
1	20.00%	$130,000	$520,000
2	32.00%	$208,000	$312,000
3	19.20%	$124,800	$187,200
4	11.52%	$74,880	$112,320
5	11.52%	$74,880	$37,440
6	5.76%	$37,440	$0

At the end of the second year, the asset has a book value of $312,000.

The recapture will equal the excess amount of depreciation that the company charged, which can be determined as the difference between the lower of the selling price and the original cost, and the ending book value:

	Sales price	$700,000
Less	Original cost	650,000
Equals	Capital gain	$50,000 ⇦ taxed as a capital gain

	Original cost	$650,000
Less	Book value	312,000
Equals	Recapture of depreciation	$338,000 ⇦ taxed as ordinary income

This number is positive, so it represents a recapture of $338,000. The company must claim this taxable amount on its income tax return and include it as ordinary income.

Tax Rates

The tax rate system in the U.S. is progressive, with increasing amounts of income taxed at higher rates. Consider the tax rate schedule:

Taxable income		
over	**but not over**	**Tax rate**
$0	$50,000	15%
50,000	75,000	25%
75,000	100,000	34%
100,000	335,000	39%
335,000	10,000,000	34%
10,000,000	15,000,000	35%
15,000,000	18,333,333	38%
18,333,333		35%

A corporation with income of $11 million pays tax of:

Income layer	*Rate on layer*	*Tax*
First $50,000	15%	$7,500
Next $25,000	25%	6,250
Next $25,000	34%	8,500
Next $235,000	39%	91,650
Next $9,665,000	34%	3,286,100
Next $1,000,000	35%	350,000
		$3,750,000

This is a modified progressive system: The income in the bracket starting at $100,000 is taxed at a higher rate than the income in the bracket starting at $335,000. This "bubble" in the tax bracketing is designed to produce revenues for the government because that extra 5% (that is, 34% + 5% = 39%) is applied at a level that affects the largest number of corporations.

A corporation's average tax rate is the tax paid on the average dollar of income, or $3,750,000 ÷ $10,000,000 = 37.5%. The corporation's marginal tax rate (that is, the rate it pays on the next $1 of income) is 35%. In many countries, there are additional state or provincial taxes. For example, in the U.S., state tax on corporate income can be as high as 9.5% in Massachusetts, 9.99% in Pennsylvania, and 12% in Iowa.[23]

[23] Source: Tax Foundation, "State Corporate Income Tax Rates as of January 1, 2009," www.taxfoundation.org.

net operating loss (NOL)
loss generated when a company's tax deductions are greater than its taxable income

A **net operating loss (NOL)** may also be important for a corporation because it can be used to reduce taxable income. If a corporation has an operating loss, it can carry it back to prior years to restate prior tax returns and receive a refund on taxes that have been "overpaid." Any loss that cannot be used to offset prior years' taxable income may be carried forward to reduce future taxes payable.[24]

Concept Review Questions

1. Explain how to calculate the depreciation expense for tax purposes in a given year.

2. Why would companies prefer to receive dividend income and make interest payments rather than make dividend payments and receive interest payments?

GLOBAL PERSPECTIVE | Tax Burden for Companies, 2010

Tax rates differ significantly across countries, from a high of 80% in Bolivia to a low of 15.5% in Kuwait.

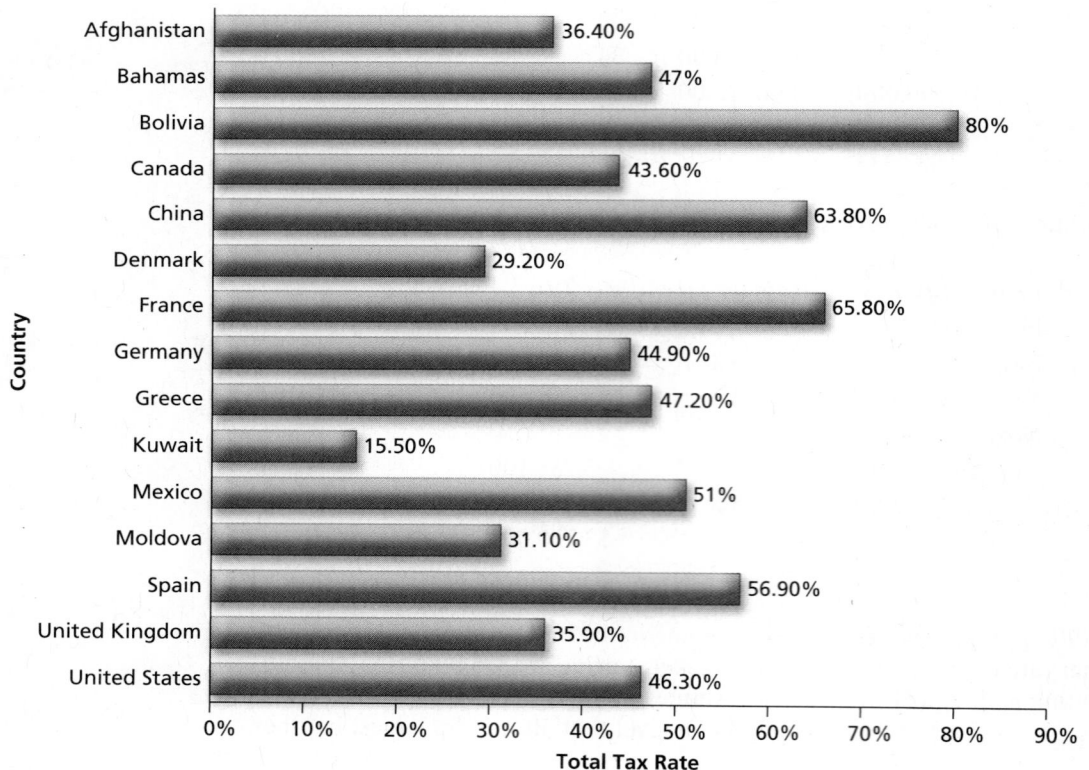

Total tax rates for limited liability companies and corporations, including labor taxes, for selected countries

Country	Total Tax Rate
Afghanistan	36.40%
Bahamas	47%
Bolivia	80%
Canada	43.60%
China	63.80%
Denmark	29.20%
France	65.80%
Germany	44.90%
Greece	47.20%
Kuwait	15.50%
Mexico	51%
Moldova	31.10%
Spain	56.90%
United Kingdom	35.90%
United States	46.30%

Source of data: Paying Taxes, 2010, The Global Picture, *PricewaterhouseCoopers*

---

[24] The number of years for the carryover in the U.S. varies by tax year, but the 2009 provisions allow a carry back in time to 2 years and a carry forward in time for 20 years. However, special provisions allow additional carryover years, such as the 5 years permitted for small businesses stipulated in the *American Recovery and Reinvestment Act of 2009.*

SUMMARY

- Financial statements are prepared in accordance with a given set of guidelines or principles, which allow comparability across time for a given company and across companies.

- Accounting principles allow some flexibility, which is important in having a uniform set of principles applied to companies in different industries and of different sizes. However, this flexibility puts a burden on those analyzing the financial statements to appreciate the degree of flexibility and the possible effect on the reported financial statements.

- The financial statements for a company are constructed based on entries throughout the period. Because statements are a result of transactions that involve debits and credits, there are linkages among these statements. Linkages include the period's retained earnings flowing in to the balance sheet retained earnings, the sum of the cash flows in the statement of cash flows equal to the change in cash balance on the balance sheet, and changes in balance sheet current assets and current liabilities accounts helping reconcile net income with cash flow on the statement of cash flows.

- The balance sheet provides the carrying value of assets, liabilities, and equity at a point in time, whereas the income statement is a summary of the revenues and expenses over the period. The statement of cash flows provides cash flows in terms of the three primary sources/uses: operations, investment, and financing.

- For financial reporting purposes, the management of the company may select among several different methods, including declining balance, sum-of-years'-digits, and straight-line. For tax purposes, companies in the U.S. must use the MACRS system for depreciation.

- Income for accounting purposes is not likely to be equal to taxable income because of differences in accounting for revenues and expenses. These differences may give rise to deferred assets (tax benefits to be received in the future) or deferred taxes (tax obligations to be paid in the future).

FORMULAS/EQUATIONS

(3-1) Straight-line depreciation $= \dfrac{\text{Asset cost} - \text{salvage value}}{\text{Useful life}}$

(3-2) Basic earnings per share $= \dfrac{\text{Net income}}{\text{Weighted average shares outstanding}}$

(3-3) Diluted earnings per share $= \dfrac{\text{Adjusted net income}}{\text{Weighted average shares potentially outstanding}}$

(3-4) Cash flow for/from operations $= \dfrac{\text{Net}}{\text{income}} + \dfrac{\text{Noncash}}{\text{expenses}} - \dfrac{\text{Change in}}{\text{working capital}}$

(3-5) Simple cash flow $=$ Net income $+$ depreciation, amortization, and depletion

(3-6) Traditional cash flow $= \dfrac{\text{Net}}{\text{income}} + \dfrac{\text{Noncash}}{\text{expenses or losses}} - \dfrac{\text{Noncash}}{\text{income or gains}}$

(3-7) Free cash flow $= \dfrac{\text{Cash flow}}{\text{from operations}} - \dfrac{\text{Capital}}{\text{expenditures}}$

(3-8) Free cash flow to equity $= \dfrac{\text{Cash flow}}{\text{for/from operations}} - \dfrac{\text{Capital}}{\text{expenditures}} + \text{Net borrowing}$

QUESTIONS AND PROBLEMS

Multiple Choice

1. Which of the following statements is correct?
    A. Shareholder's equity = Assets + Liabilities.
    B. The inventory account is debited when there is an increase in inventory.
    C. When a company pays a bill using cash, the only transaction is a credit to cash.
    D. A debit on the right side of the balance sheet may be an increase to accounts payable.

2. Which of the following is a source of cash inflows?
    A. Payment of dividends
    B. Decrease of inventories
    C. Decrease of accounts payable
    D. Increase of accounts receivable

3. Which of the following is a noncash item?
    A. Amortization
    B. Payment of interest
    C. Receipt of dividends
    D. Purchase of new equipment

4. Which of the following equations represents free cash flow to equity?
    A. Net income + Depreciation + Deferred income taxes
    B. Net income + Depreciation + Deferred income taxes +/– Change in working capital
    C. Net income + Depreciation + Deferred income taxes +/– Change in working capital – Capital expenditures
    D. Net income + Depreciation + Deferred income taxes +/– Change in working capital – Capital expenditures +/– Financing cash flows

5. Which of the following is *not* classified as cash flow for/from financing?
    A. Payment of dividends
    B. Purchase of equipment
    C. Issuance of long-term debt
    D. Repurchase of capital stock

6. Capital gains occur in which of the following cases?
    A. Selling price of the asset < Initial cost of the asset
    B. Selling price of the asset > Initial cost of the asset
    C. Selling price of the asset < Ending book value for tax purposes
    D. Selling price of the asset > Ending book value for tax purposes

7. An asset classified as a 3-year asset according to MACRS has a book value at the end of 3 years equal to:
    A. $0.
    B. 7.41% of the asset's cost.
    C. 7.41% of the asset's cost less salvage value.

8. Suppose a company buys a depreciable asset for $300,000. If this asset has a useful life of 10 years, a salvage value of $50,000, and is classified as a 5-year asset for tax purposes, the amount of depreciation for tax purposes in the first year is *closest* to:
    A. $25,000   B. $30,000   C. $50,000   D. $60,000.

9. Consider a company in its first year of operations has EBITDA of $10 million and a single depreciable asset that cost $12 million and has no salvage value. The company's management is intending to use straight-line depreciation over 20 years for financial reporting purposes. The asset qualifies as a 10-year asset for tax purposes. Based on the different depreciation methods alone, in this first year the company will report:

   A. a deferred tax asset.
   B. a deferred tax liability.
   C. neither a deferred tax liability nor a deferred tax asset.

10. The sum of the cash flow for/from operations, cash flow for/from investment, and cash flow for/from financing for an annual financial statement should be equal to:

   A. net income plus depreciation.
   B. net income, plus depreciation, amortization, and depletion.
   C. the ending cash balance on the current year's balance sheet.
   D. the change in the cash account balance from the previous year-end to the current year-end.

Practice Problems

3.1 Accounting Principles

11. Which of the auditor opinions is the most desirable from a shareholder's perspective? Why?

12. Property, plant, and equipment are generally reported at historical cost. Why do we not use fair market value to value these assets?

13. What is the accrual basis?

14. Considering mark-to-market, address each of the following questions:
   A. What is meant by "mark-to-market"?
   B. What is the advantage of reporting that is based on mark-to-market accounting from the perspective of the investor?
   C. What is the disadvantage of reporting that is based on mark-to-market accounting from the perspective of the investor?

15. Why is the audit committee of a board of directors comprised of independent directors? Explain.

16. Why is understanding the accounting principles that a company uses important from the perspective of a company's shareholders?

3.2 Financial Statements

17. Why would you likely observe positive cash flows from operations for a financially healthy company?

18. CVS Caremark Corporation, a retail drugstore company, reported the following cash flows in millions:[25]

| | *Fiscal Year End 12-31* | | |
	2010	*2009*	*2008*
Cash flow from operating activities	$4,779	$4,035	$3,947
Cash flow from investing activities	–1,640	–1,069	–4,581
Cash flow from financing activities	–2,798	–3,232	929

   A. Interpret the cash flow from operating activities for each year.
   B. What is the change in the cash balance for each year?

[25] Source of data: CVS Caremark 10-K filings with the Securities and Exchange Commission.

19. Consider the following account balances for a company:

	End of 20X1 Fiscal Year	End of 20X0 Fiscal Year
Inventory	$20,000	$15,000
Accounts receivable	$30,000	$28,000
Accounts payable	$30,000	$27,000

A. What is the adjustment for changes in working capital accounts for the statement of cash flows for fiscal year 20X1?

B. If the company's net income for the 20X1 fiscal year is $80,000 and depreciation of $10,000 is the only noncash expense, what is this company's cash flow for/from operations?

20. Google, an Internet company, reported the following information for fiscal year 2010:[26]

(in millions of dollars)

Property, plant, and equipment, gross	$11,771
Accumulated depreciation	$4,012
Current liabilities	$9,996
Shareholders' equity	$46,241
Total assets	$57,851
Other liabilities	$1,614
Total revenue	$8,440
Cost of revenue	$2,946
Cash flow from operations	$11,081
Cash flow from investing activities	–$10,680
Change in cash balance	$3,432

A. What is the amount of Google's long-term debt?

B. What is the amount of Google's net property, plant, and equipment?

C. What is the amount of Google's gross profit?

D. What is the amount of Google's cash flow for/from financing?

21. Complete the following based on basic accounting relationships:

Cash and cash equivalents	$100	Accounts payable		$50
Inventory	300	Wages payable		25
Accounts receivable	250	Current portion of long-term debt		100
Current assets	☐	Current liabilities		☐
Gross plant and equipment	4,000	Long-term debt		2,000
Accumulated depreciation	1,200			
Net plant and equipment	☐	Common stock		10
Intangibles	50	Paid-in capital in excess of par		190
Total assets	☐	Retained earnings		☐
		Treasury stock		100
		Total shareholders' equity		☐
		Total liabilities and shareholders' equity		☐

[26] Source: Google's 2010 10-K filing with the Securities and Exchange Commission.

22. The balance sheet for Austin Company shows total assets of $429,500 and total liabilities of $379,000.
    A. What is the value of the owners' equity?
    B. If the company had retained earnings of $5,000 at the beginning of the year, net income for the year was $7,500, and the company paid out $4,000 in dividends, what is the book value of its retained earnings at the end of the year?

23. Cordell Candies Inc. paid dividends of $2.5 million during 2012. However, the company needed extra cash to open new stores, so it issued $1.3 million in new stock. What was Cordell's cash flow for/from financing in 2012?

24. Complete the following balance sheet, calculating the values for total current assets, net property, plant, and equipment, total current liabilities, retained earnings, and shareholders' equity:

Assets		*Liabilities*	
Cash	$20	Accounts payable	$30
Accounts receivable	30	Current portion of long-term debt	10
Inventory	40	Total current liabilities	
Total current assets		Long-term debt	500
Net property, plant, and equipment		*Equity*	
Intangible assets	40	Common stock	10
Total assets	$1,000	Retained earnings	
		Shareholders' equity	
		Total liabilities and equity	$1,000

25. Estimate cash flow from operations for Lubbock Inc. using the following information:

Net income	$90,000
Depreciation	10,000
Deferred income taxes	5,000
Increase in inventories	20,000
Decrease in accounts receivable	1,000
Increase in accounts payable	2,000

26. Calculate the traditional cash flow, the cash flow from operations, free cash flow, and free cash flow to equity for Richmond Corporation, using the following information:

Net income	$101,000
Depreciation	20,000
Increase in inventories	10,000
Increase in accounts receivable	12,000
Increase in accounts payable	15,000
Increase in prepaid expenses	5,000
Debt repayment	50,000
Bonds issued	45,000
New equity issued	15,000
Dividends paid	20,000
Capital expenditures	40,000

27. Estimate the traditional cash flow, cash flow from operations, free cash flow, and free cash flow to equity for Norman Co., using the following information:

Net income	$1,000
Depreciation	500
Increase in inventories	100
Increase in accounts receivable	200
Decrease in accounts payable	250
Debt repayment	500
Bonds issued	600
Capital expenditures	300

3.3   The Tax System

28. What is MACRS?

29. We observe many companies with deferred income tax on their balance sheet. What are deferred income taxes, and why might we observe so many companies reporting this account?

30. Calculate the depreciation and carrying value each year of the useful life for equipment that cost $100,000, has a useful life of 7 years, and is classified as a 5-year MACRS asset.

31. Calculate the depreciation and carrying value each year of the useful life for equipment that cost $100,000, has a useful life of 5 years, and is classified as a 3-year MACRS asset.

32. Consider an asset that costs $100,000, has a useful life of 5 years, and an estimated salvage value of $10,000. The asset is considered a 3-year asset for tax purposes.

    A. What is the depreciation for financial reporting purposes if the company uses the straight-line method of depreciation?

    B. What is the depreciation for financial reporting purposes if the company uses the 150DB method of depreciation?

    C. What is the depreciation each year for tax purposes?

    D. Calculate and graph the difference in depreciation each year between each of the three methods of depreciation: straight-line, 150 DB, and MACRS.

33. Raleigh Rowboats Ltd. purchases and begins to use its first six rowboats for a total cost of $12,000. Raleigh's management believes the boats can be used for 5 years, providing the company with equal value each year. After 5 years, the boats will be worthless.

    A. Using your best judgment, what is reasonable amount to charge to depreciation expense each year?

    B. What is the book value of the boats for each of the 5 years they will be used?

    C. Assuming that the boats qualify as 3-year assets for purposes of MACRS, what is the depreciation expense and book value of the boats for tax purposes for each of the 5 years?

Cases

Case 3.1   Finns' Fridges

Twin brothers, David and Douglas Finn, started a small business from their college dormitory room. Finns' Fridges purchased several refrigerators to rent to other students for use in their rooms. At the end of their first year of operations, the brothers' records showed the following information.

Current assets (cash and accounts receivable)	$2,000
Interest payable	200
Other current liabilities	800
Property and equipment (net)	4,000
Long-term liabilities	3,200
Owners' equity	1,800
Revenues	2,000
Interest expense	200
Depreciation expense	1,000

A. Construct a balance sheet and income statement for the business.

B. Based on the balance sheet you created, how much working capital does Finns' Fridges have?

C. Suppose Finns' Fridges is subject to corporate income tax at a rate of 30%. What will the company's net income after tax be?

D. David and Douglas invested $500 each to capitalize Finns' Fridges. To allow for future flexibility (such as selling shares to other investors), they placed a par value of $10 on each share; thus each brother owns 50 shares. What were the basic earnings per share (EPS) of Finns' Fridges for its first year of operations?

E. David Finn notices that the local appliance store is now charging $210 for the same model of refrigerator his company bought for $200. Given that Finns' Fridges purchased 25 of these refrigerators, what should the company's balance sheet show as the value of property and equipment? Why?

Case 3.2   Charlotte Honey Bee Company

Charlotte Honey Bee Company (CHBC) is considering the acquisition of equipment that would cost $200,000 to acquire and set up. CHBC expects a useful life of six years from this equipment, at which time it estimates that it could sell the equipment for $20,000. CHBC expects to generate net income of $50,000 each year before depreciation.

A. If CHBC uses straight-line depreciation, what is its expected net income after depreciation but before tax for this equipment each year?

B. If this equipment is classified as a 5-year asset for tax purposes, what is CHBC's depreciation for tax purposes each year?

C. What, if any, is the gain or loss for tax purposes if CHBC sells the equipment at the end of six years for $20,000?

D. If CHBC's income before depreciation is the same for both financial reporting and tax purposes, what is the difference in income for reporting and tax purposes each year? [Caution: Remember to include your result from Part C, if appropriate.]

E. What method of depreciation for financial reporting purposes do you recommend? Explain your recommendation.

CHAPTER 4

FINANCIAL STATEMENT ANALYSIS

Analyzing Financial Statements It is important to be able to understand what financial information is being presented and how it should or should not be used to analyze a company's health. Recall from Chapter 3 that companies have some flexibility in terms of which accounting principles to apply, and analysts may adjust financial data in a manner not consistent with generally accepted accounting principles (GAAP). For example, during the Internet boom, when many companies were created to take advantage of online commerce, companies began to provide what they termed "pro forma" financial statements. These were not "pro forma" in the usual sense (that is, forecasting); rather, these were statements that were created with their own version of accounting—not consistent with GAAP.

When these were first provided, investors were faced with two sets of numbers, and this was quite confusing. However, following the Sarbanes-Oxley Act of 2002, the Securities and Exchange Commission adopted a rule that requires companies to provide a reconciliation of the amounts indicated as pro forma with amounts determined using GAAP.* Since this rule has been in place, the SEC has brought enforcement action against a number of companies, including Trump Hotels & Casino Resorts.

Learning Outcomes

After reading this chapter, you should be able to:

LO 4.1 Discuss the issues that arise in using accounting information in financial analysis.

LO 4.2 Calculate, interpret, and evaluate the key ratios related to leverage, efficiency, productivity, and liquidity.

LO 4.3 Explain and demonstrate why returns are "bottom-line" measures for assessing a company's performance, analyze return ratios using the DuPont system, and compare ratios based on trends and among companies.

Chapter Preview If accounting is the language of business, what is it saying to us?[1] In this chapter we address this question and shows how external interested parties, such as investors and creditors, can use financial statements to evaluate a company. Of course, no one uses financial statements in isolation; they look at

---

*"Conditions for Use of Non-GAAP Financial Measures," RIN3235-A169, Securities and Exchange Commission, effective March 29, 2003.
[1] The phrase "accounting is the language of business" is not attributed to any one person, but we can find its use as early as 1921 in the context of mine accounting [Thomas Orrin McGrath, *Mine Accounting and Cost Principles*, McGraw-Hill, 1921].

additional information about a company and the macroeconomic environment—the industry in which the company operates—and compare the company's statements across time and with members of its peer group, such as other companies in the same industry, or industry averages.

We begin our coverage of financial analysis with a discussion of the challenges of using accounting information to evaluate a company's performance or condition. We then examine financial ratios, beginning with liquidity, and then look at the other dimensions of a company's condition and performance, including financial leverage, profitability, and efficiency in putting assets to use. We then look at how we can use ratios to help us judge a company's performance and financial condition. In addition to discussing various ratios, we also look at the DuPont system, which helps us understand the interrelationships among different ratios. Following our discussion of the ratios and the DuPont system, we look at ways to analyze ratios over time and across companies.

We use International Business Machines (IBM) and one of its competitors, Microsoft, to demonstrate the application of ratio analysis. We apply the ratios to IBM using IBM's fiscal 2010 financial statements.

4.1 A FRAMEWORK FOR FINANCIAL ANALYSIS

Analyzing a company's financial statements depends on the reason behind the analysis. A bank making a short-term loan will examine different factors than would the same bank making a long-term loan. Further, in both cases, the bank will look at different factors than would an equity analyst trying to value a company's common shares.[2] In turn, both will explore different factors than would another company interested in buying one of these companies or if one of these companies is interested in possibly lowering its prices to heighten competition. However, in all cases, a major source of information is the company's financial statements, and financial analysis provides a standard framework of analysis. Once you understand the basics of financial analysis, you can apply these tools to forecast a company's use or need for cash over a forecast horizon. This is clearly important, not just for the company, but also for its creditors, like the bank, and investment dealers who advise the company on its financing issues. In this chapter, we introduce the basics of financial analysis and forecasting.

Financial analysis is the evaluation of a company's financial performance and financial condition. Key to this evaluation is the annual report, which is the communication between the management of the company and the owners. The annual report contains financial statements, from which we draw information about the company's assets, liabilities, equity, income, and cash flows, among other things. A financial ratio is nothing more than the ratio of two data items, usually accounts from a company's financial statements. The calculation of a ratio is not difficult, but how we use these ratios to evaluate a company is challenging.

We can classify ratios into five types by what we can learn about a company:

1. Liquidity
2. Efficiency
3. Productivity
4. Financial leverage
5. Shareholder

We provide examples of the ratios that you may find in each category in Figure 4-1 and apply and interpret these ratios in this chapter.

In addition to these ratios, we also examine return ratios, which are "bottom-line" performance measures that involve comparing the net benefit (such as net profit) to the resources deployed (such as total assets). Return ratios, by construction, relate directly to other ratios. As we see later in this chapter, we can analyze why a company's bottom line changes from one period to the next by using financial ratios.

---

[2] It is possible for the same investment bank's credit and equity analysts to offer different advice to their debt and equity clients, because their perspectives differ.

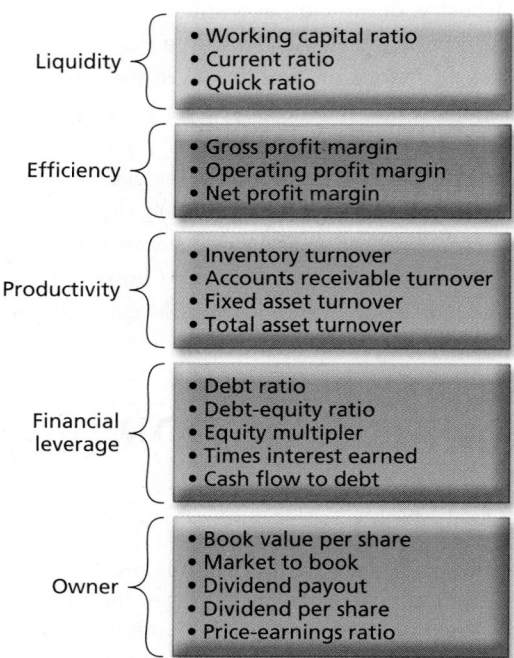

FIGURE 4-1 **Ratios Classified by Type**

We should note that a single ratio does not offer much information. When performing a financial analysis, we need context: other ratios of the same company, the trend of the ratios over time, and comparisons with ratios of other companies in the same line of business. To illustrate this point, consider the current ratio, which is one of the liquidity ratios that we will discuss soon. This ratio is current assets divided by current liabilities. Suppose a company has a current ratio of 2.0. Is this good or bad? We cannot say based simply on this information. A current ratio of 2.0 may be considered good because it means that the company is likely able to pay off its current liabilities using its current assets, with some left over. But a current ratio of 2.0 may also be considered bad if the company's operating cycle is short and its need for liquidity is minimal; a company that maintains a current ratio of 2.0 in this case may have too much invested in low or nonearning assets, which affects profitability.

To judge whether the result of a given ratio is "good" or "bad" requires context. We often use comparisons to provide some context, including:

1. the company's historical ratios, or the trend in its ratios; and
2. the ratios of comparable companies; that is, we can use a similar company or use industry average ratios.

In addition, we need to put any ratio in the context of other dimensions of the company. For example, a company that invests too much in low and non-earning assets may have a current ratio that is higher than its competitors. But when we examine profitability, the company investing too much in current assets will likely have a lower profitability than its competitors because it may not be putting its assets to their best use.

BOTTOM LINE: Interpretation of financial ratios requires context.

Financial Analysis in Perspective

There are actually hundreds of ratios that we could calculate. In addition, there are industry-specific ratios we could add to the mix. For some ratios we calculate the ratio using accounts from one financial statement only, and for other ratios we use accounts from more than one financial statement. Effective use of financial ratios requires understanding the accounting principles that the company uses, the challenges in making comparisons among companies, and the limitations of accounting.

Accounting principles and financial ratios

We construct financial ratios from reported financial statement information. Because we construct ratios using financial statement accounts, these ratios are affected by the principles of accounting applied by the company. Interpreting ratios requires tempering the interpretation with information about the company's accounting policies. For example, if costs of inventory are increasing and the company uses LIFO for its inventory, then its ending inventory is understated, reflecting the oldest costs of inventory. Therefore, interpretation of any ratio using ending inventory must consider the trend in inventory costs and the method of accounting for inventory.

We also must be aware of changes in accounting principles. These changes may be mandatory, when accounting authorities mandate a change in accounting principles, or voluntary, when the company believes that a change in accounting principles is appropriate. No matter the cause, such a change may present a challenge in looking at a company over time. When a company changes accounting principles, it makes a retrospective application; this means that the company restates prior years' accounts as if the new principle had been used all along for any years reported. Therefore, if the company reports the current year's income statement along with the prior two years' statements in its annual report, any change in accounting principle in the current year will be reflected in all three years' statements, but not four years or five years prior. This means that if you compare financial statements from year to year, you may see different data as reported in one year and restated in another.[3]

Another issue that may affect financial statement information is the management of earnings. If managers are compensated based on measures that use financial statement accounts, there is an incentive to manage these accounts. For example, suppose a company pays its top managers a bonus if the return on assets—net profit divided by total assets—is more than 10%. If managers anticipate that the company may not have a 10% return on assets this year, they could manage earnings to either exceed this return hurdle this year or ensure that the company meets this hurdle next year. How could they exceed this hurdle this year? By many means, including extending the depreciable life of assets (therefore reducing depreciation expense) or changing inventory methods (e.g., choosing LIFO in a period of rising inventory costs). How could they increase the chances of exceeding this hurdle next year? By many means, including writing down the value of inventory (taking a loss this year, but having a lower cost of goods sold next year) and writing off goodwill as impaired (taking a loss this year and reducing total assets). When analyzing a company's financial condition and performance, the analyst must keep in mind the potential for the management of financial statement accounts.

BOTTOM LINE: We need to consider accounting principles used by a company, any changes in principles over time, and the potential for the management of financial statements.

Making comparisons among companies

Accounting principles are designed to apply to many different types of firms, and this provides some flexibility in the selection of methods of accounting. Consider some of the possibilities: a company can choose to use LIFO or FIFO accounting for inventory, to use straight-line or double-declining balance for depreciation, or to classify marketable securities as traded securities or available for sale. Therefore, we also must take care in

---

[3] For example, if there is a change in accounting principle for fiscal year 2012 and the company reports 2010 and 2011 income statements as well, the change in principle is applied to 2010 and 2011, as well as to 2012. Therefore, 2011 fiscal year data, as originally reported, may differ from fiscal year 2011 data as restated once the 2012 annual report is issued.

making comparisons among companies because the companies in the comparison may use different accounting principles. For example, suppose a company uses straight-line depreciation and its competitor uses 150% declining balance. If the companies purchase the same type of asset, the first company would report higher net plant and equipment (and, hence, assets) and lower depreciation (and, hence, higher earnings) in the earlier years of the asset's life when compared to its competitor.

As another example, consider comparing two companies that are identical except for the use of different methods of accounting for inventory: one uses FIFO and one uses LIFO. If everything else is equal and there is inflation,

- the company using FIFO will have a cost of goods sold less than that of the company using LIFO, and a gross profit more than that of the company using LIFO, and
- the company using FIFO will have inventory that is higher in value than that of the company using LIFO.

Therefore, the choice of inventory method affects both the balance sheet and the income statement, and therefore affects any ratios calculated using accounts including inventory, cost of goods sold, and gross profit.

In addition, unique factors often drive a particular company's ratios, making it difficult to compare with the ratios of other companies. For example, if a company has made a recent large acquisition of another company, key profitability and turnover ratios often drop. For this reason, it is important to look at a company's ratios over time, but put trends in context of any company-specific events.

Before we calculate financial ratios and compare them among companies, we need to understand the accounting principles that each company uses and the major events affecting a company, and then decide how to make the data comparable. This is not an easy task and is one of the more challenging aspects of financial analysis.

BOTTOM LINE: To perform an effective financial analysis, we need to understand accounting principles used by and major events affecting a company.

Limitations of accounting information

Accounting information is provided based on generally accepted accounting principles. Though accounting authorities seek to develop principles that provide the best information for investors, there are limitations on the usefulness of this information. One of the primary limitations of using accounting information is that accounting provides measurements of the past—what has happened—but we are often using analysis to make decisions that are forward looking. It would be the rare company that stands still from one period to another; most companies change over time, adjusting their products, adjusting the markets in which they provide their products and services, making investments, disposing of nonproducing assets, and so on. Therefore, accounting information, although useful in painting a picture of where the company has been, does not provide information about where the company is going.

Another limitation is that accounting may not capture all information about a company's assets and obligations. A number of off-balance sheet transactions do not affect published financial statements and, hence, financial ratios. For example, companies report operating leases only in footnotes to the financial statements; even though these leases may be essential for the company's operations and may involve multiyear commitments, the obligations under these leases do not show up as part of a company's debt obligation in the balance sheet.

Another limitation is that many accounts are reported at historical cost, which may not be relevant today. Some accounts are recorded at fair value, such as marketable securities; however, other accounts, including property, plant, and equipment, which make up the bulk of many companies' assets, are recorded at the original cost (that is, what the company paid). Unfortunately, this original cost could be a decade or two (or three or more) old, which may not reflect what it is worth to the company. And though accumulated depreciation should reflect the use of the property, plant, and equipment over time, and hence the loss of value, a company may not select a method of depreciation that reflects the reality of how assets lose value over time.[4] Therefore, when we look at the assets in a company's balance sheet, some of these assets are reflected at fair value, whereas others are at historical cost.

So, if there are problems with using accounting information, what is the import of this for financial analysis? It means that when we interpret financial ratios, we need to consider what we are working with.

BOTTOM LINE: We need to understand the data before we apply financial ratio analysis.

1. How does the choice of depreciation affect accounts on the income statement? How does this choice affect accounts on the balance sheet?

2. What types of company events are likely to affect the time-series of accounts that we may observe on the income statement and the balance sheet?

Concept Review Questions

4.2 FINANCIAL RATIOS

A ratio is simply one number divided by another, and a financial ratio is generally constructed by taking the ratio of one account or combination of accounts, to another account or combination of accounts. These accounts may be drawn from the balance sheet, the income statement, or the statement of cash flows. In some cases, we may also use market data, such as the price per share of stock, in a ratio. The goal is to construct ratios that help us understand a company's financial condition or performance.

Liquidity

Financial statement users may have different interests when examining financial statements. Banks that lend to IBM and suppliers shipping to IBM on credit want to know whether the company has the means to pay off its debts. This leads to a focus on the liquidity of the company. **Liquidity** is how easily something can be converted into cash.

liquidity how quickly something can be converted into cash

Liquidity ratios

The focus in analyzing the liquidity of a company is on the overall liquidity of a company's assets and on the assets available to meet current liabilities. We often refer to a company's current assets as the company's **working capital** because these are the assets that are used in the day-to-day operations of the company.[5] A company's **net working capital** is the difference between its current assets and its current liabilities, and considers not only the investment in these operational or current assets, but also the fact that current liabilities free up funds for use in the company.[6]

---

[4] Most companies use straight-line depreciation for financial reporting purposes (though they will most likely use MACRS for tax purposes). However, physical assets do not necessarily lose value in a straight-line manner.

[5] Some define working capital as the difference between current assets and currently liabilities.

[6] This is the same logic that we use in adjusting the traditional cash flow to arrive at the cash flow from operations: Investments in current assets are a use of funds, whereas current liabilities are a source of funds.

working capital ratio
current assets divided by
total assets

In terms of overall liquidity we can use the ratio of current assets to total assets, or the **working capital ratio**:[7]

$$\text{Working capital ratio} = \frac{\text{Current assets}}{\text{Total assets}} \qquad (4\text{-}1)$$

Illustrating with IBM in 2010,

$$\text{Working capital ratio} = \frac{\$48,116 \text{ million}}{\$113,450 \text{ million}} = 0.4242$$

For IBM, this ratio indicates that its assets are liquid, with more than 42% supposedly converting to cash within a year. Overall, IBM's balance sheet is very liquid, indicating relatively small amounts of net fixed assets and large amounts of current assets. So how liquid are these current assets?

current ratio or bankers'
ratio current assets
divided by current
liabilities

Another common liquidity ratio is the **current ratio**, also called the **bankers' ratio,** which we calculate as current assets divided by current liabilities.

$$\text{Current ratio} = \frac{\text{Current assets}}{\text{Current liabilities}} \qquad (4\text{-}2)$$

For IBM in 2010,

$$\text{Current ratio} = \frac{\$48,116 \text{ million}}{\$40,562 \text{ million}} = 1.1862$$

IBM has $1.1862 in current assets for every dollar in current liabilities. This ratio is important for short-term lenders because loans are normally short term and included in current liabilities. So a current ratio of almost 1.2 means that many assets will soon be converted to cash and may be available to help pay off a bank loan. However, if a bank has to seize assets or force a company to liquidate assets, it is a sign that some of its assets are probably not worth much. In particular, the inventory of a bankrupt or failing company is normally not worth its book value, whereas it is unlikely a creditor could ever recover any funds from prepaid expenses, a common component of current assets. For this reason banks also look at the **quick ratio**, or **acid test ratio**, which is cash, plus marketable securities, plus accounts receivable, divided by current liabilities:[8]

quick ratio or acid
test ratio cash, plus
marketable securities
and accounts receivable,
divided by current
liabilities

$$\text{Quick ratio} = \frac{\text{Cash} + \text{Marketable Securities} + \text{Accounts Receivable}}{\text{Current liabilities}} \qquad (4\text{-}3)$$

For IBM in 2010,

$$\text{Quick ratio} = \frac{\$10,661 \text{ million} + 990 \text{ million} + 28,225 \text{ million}}{\$40,562 \text{ million}}$$

$$= \frac{\$39,876 \text{ million}}{\$40,562 \text{ million}} = 0.9831$$

For any company with inventory, the quick ratio is always less than its current ratio. Further, companies that maintain substantial inventories may experience large differences between the quick and current ratios.

We provide the current and quick ratios for IBM and Microsoft over the 2008 to 2010 period in Table 4-1. The liquidity ratios of these two companies differ, both in the absolute

---

[7] There is potential for confusion regarding the term *working capital* because some will refer to the difference between current assets and current liabilities as working capital, whereas others will refer to this difference as net working capital.

[8] Some calculate the quick ratio as current assets minus inventory divided by current liabilities. The problem is that by doing so, we include prepaid expenses and any deferred income taxes classified as short-term as part of the "quick" assets. Although this shortcut is expedient, it is incorrect if the company has prepaid expenses and any short-term deferred income taxes because these are generally not considered available for creditors.

TABLE 4-1 **Liquidity Ratios for IBM and Microsoft, Fiscal Years 2008 Through 2010**

	IBM			Microsoft		
	FY2010	*FY2009*	*FY2008*	*FY2010*	*FY2009*	*FY2008*
Working capital ratio	0.4241	0.4489	0.4474	0.6465	0.6327	0.5940
Current ratio	1.1862	1.3592	1.1548	2.1293	1.8229	1.4469
Quick ratio	0.9831	1.1323	0.9535	1.9047	1.5772	1.2464

value and in the trend over the 2008–10 years. Microsoft experienced an increase in these ratios over this period, whereas IBM demonstrated increased liquidity in 2009, returning to levels similar to 2008 in 2010. Though we may be tempted to say that Microsoft is doing better than IBM in terms of liquidity, we do not have enough information to draw this conclusion. The liquidity ratios are just one piece in the financial analysis puzzle.

The operating cycle

We often look at liquidity ratios along with a company's operating cycle because the operating cycle provides useful information on a company's need for liquidity. The **operating cycle** is the length of time it takes for the company's investment of cash in inventory to be converted into cash in the form of collected accounts. The longer this cycle, the more liquidity a company requires. We can estimate the operating cycle as the sum of the average number of days the company invests in inventory and the average number of days it takes to collect from customers.

operating cycle length of time it takes for the company's investment of cash in inventory to be converted into cash in the form of collected accounts

$$\text{Operating cycle} = \frac{\text{Days of sales}}{\text{in inventory}} + \frac{\text{Days sales}}{\text{outstanding}} \qquad (4\text{-}4)$$

If the amount in inventory is representative of the inventory throughout the year, the ratio of the cost of goods sold to inventory indicates how many times inventory has been created and sold during the year. Dividing this into the number of days in a year provides the **days sales in inventory, or DSI**:

days sales in inventory, DSI, or number of days of inventory average length of time between acquiring and selling inventory

$$\text{Days sales in inventory} = \frac{365}{\dfrac{\text{Cost of goods sold}}{\text{Inventory}}} \qquad (4\text{-}5)$$

The days sales in inventory, which we also refer to as the **number of days of inventory**, is the average number of days the company has the inventory in its possession in the form of raw materials, work-in-process, and finished goods.[9] Another, but mathematically equivalent, formula for the DSI compares the balance in inventory with the average cost of goods sold per day:

$$\text{Days sales in inventory} = \frac{\text{Inventory}}{\left(\dfrac{\text{Cost of goods sold}}{365}\right)} \qquad (4\text{-}6)$$

What if the ending balance of inventory is not typical of inventory levels throughout the year? This is especially important for a seasonal business. We could use monthly or

[9] You may find that some analysts will use revenues or sales in place of cost of goods sold. However, this would distort the number of days because the numerator is in terms of costs to the firm. To be consistent, the denominator must also be stated in terms of the cost to the firm.

quarterly amounts of inventory and then average these.[10] To keep things simple, we will assume that the ending balance of inventory—and other accounts throughout the balance sheet—are representative of the rest of the year.[11] For IBM in 2010:

$$\text{Days sales in inventory} = \frac{365}{\$53,857 \div \$2,450} = 16.6042 \text{ days}$$

or

$$\text{Days sales in inventory} = \frac{\$2,450}{\$53,857 \div 365} = \frac{\$2,450}{\$147.5534} = 16.6042 \text{ days}$$

So in 2010, IBM had almost 17 days of revenues tied up in inventory.

days sales outstanding or average collection period number of days, on average, that accounts receivable accounts are outstanding

The **days sales outstanding (DSO)** or **average collection period** is a measure of the age of the receivables.[12] We calculate this by dividing the credit sales by the accounts receivable because only credit sales generate receivables; cash sales, obviously, generate cash. Because we often do not have revenues amounts broken down by credit and cash, we typically use total revenues or sales in place of credit sales—unless we have information about the use of trade credit.

As most commonly used, we divide the ratio of credit sales to accounts receivable into 365 to estimate the days sales outstanding:[13]

$$\text{Days sales outstanding} = \frac{365}{\dfrac{\text{Credit sales}}{\text{Accounts receivable}}} \qquad (4\text{-}7)$$

which is equivalent to

$$\text{Days sales outstanding} = \frac{\text{Accounts receivable}}{\dfrac{\text{Credit sales}}{365}} \qquad (4\text{-}8)$$

For IBM in 2010,

$$\text{Days sales outstanding} = \frac{365}{\dfrac{\$99,870 \text{ million}}{\$28,225 \text{ million}}} = 103.1554 \text{ days}$$

This means that it takes IBM, on average, 103.1554 days to collect on its receivables. So if IBM's revenues were all on credit, as they probably were because the company does not sell direct to consumers, at the end of 2010 its customers were paying on average 103 days after purchase. If the collection period lengthened, we would check to see whether IBM had changed its credit terms to stimulate revenues or whether its customers were simply delaying payment because of poor economic conditions.

We show the operating cycle in Figure 4-2. As you can see, we are assuming that the company purchases its inventory for cash. If a company purchases its inventory by using trade credit, hence creating accounts payable, the length of time that cash is tied up in operations is less. We refer to the cycle adjusted for the use of trade credit as the

---

[10] One approach is to average the beginning and end of year inventory amounts, but this is flawed: the beginning of the year is the end of the previous fiscal year and, hence, will be at the same point in the seasonal pattern as the end of year inventory.

[11] Is this a problem? If we are consistent in our method, then time-series comparisons and comparisons across companies in the same industry are still appropriate.

[12] This is also referred to as the days sales outstanding or the number of days of sales outstanding.

[13] If you are external to the company and do not have information regarding credit sales and cannot reasonably estimate credit sales, you could use total sales in place of credit sales. However, before you interpret the result, you need to consider the customary practices of the industry and how close credit sales would be to total sales.

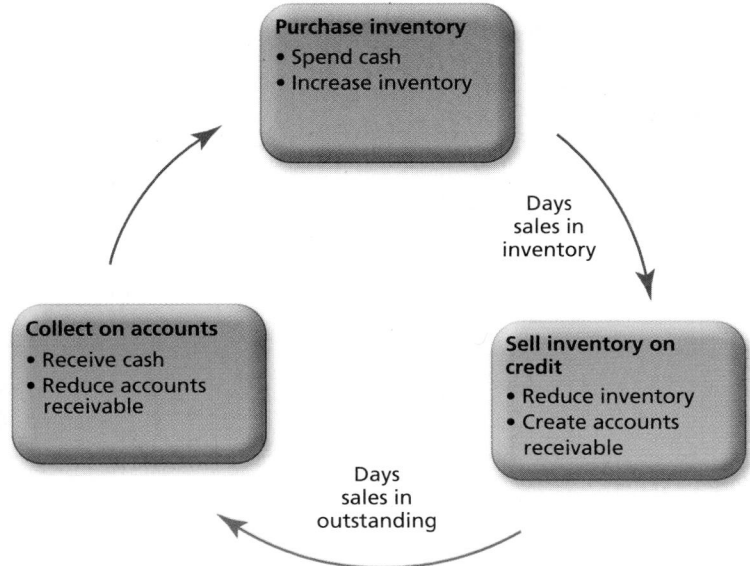

FIGURE 4-2 **The Operating Cycle**

net operating cycle. We can estimate the **net operating cycle**, also known as the **cash conversion cycle**, to provide more information on liquidity, which is the operating cycle, less the days purchases outstanding:

$$\text{Net operating cycle} = \frac{\text{Days of sales}}{\text{in inventory}} + \frac{\text{Days sales}}{\text{outstanding}} - \frac{\text{Days purchases}}{\text{outstanding}} \qquad (4\text{-}9)$$

The **days purchases outstanding (DPO)** is the number of days it takes the company to pay on its trade credit accounts.[14] Because purchases are not paid for immediately, but rather are paid according to the customary credit terms, which vary among industries, the company has more funds available to use in operations. By subtracting days purchases outstanding from the operating cycle, we are considering the benefit from making purchases using trade credit.

We calculate the days of purchases outstanding by dividing the amount of accounts payable from the balance sheet by average day's purchases for the period, and then divide this into the number of days in the year:[15]

$$\text{Days purchases outstanding} = \frac{\text{Accounts payable}}{\dfrac{\text{Purchases}}{365}} \qquad (4\text{-}10)$$

Purchases are not reported in financial statements, so we need to determine this amount using the relationship:

$$\frac{\text{Beginning}}{\text{inventory}} + \text{Purchases} = \frac{\text{Ending}}{\text{inventory}} + \frac{\text{Cost of}}{\text{goods sold}}$$

Solving for purchases:

$$\text{Purchases} = \frac{\text{Ending}}{\text{inventory}} + \frac{\text{Cost of}}{\text{goods sold}} - \frac{\text{Beginning}}{\text{inventory}}$$

net operating cycle or **cash conversion cycle** length of time it takes to convert the investment of cash in inventory back into cash, considering that purchases are acquired using trade credit

days purchases outstanding (DPO) number of days a company takes to pay creditors

---

[14] DPO is also referred to as the *number of days of purchases* and the *days purchases outstanding*.

[15] You may find that some analysts will use cost of goods sold instead of purchases in calculating days purchases outstanding. However, using cost of goods sold instead of purchases makes the bold assumption that the balance in the inventory account does not change from year to year.

TABLE 4-2 Operating Cycle and Net Operating Cycle for IBM for Fiscal Years 2009 and 2010

	in number of days	*FY2010*	*FY2009*
	Days sales in inventory	16.6042	17.5084
Plus	Days sales outstanding	103.1554	102.1256
Equals	Operating cycle	119.7595	119.6340
Less	Days purchases outstanding	52.9316	52.4320
Equals	Net operating cycle	66.8279	67.2020

Graphically, for fiscal year 2010:

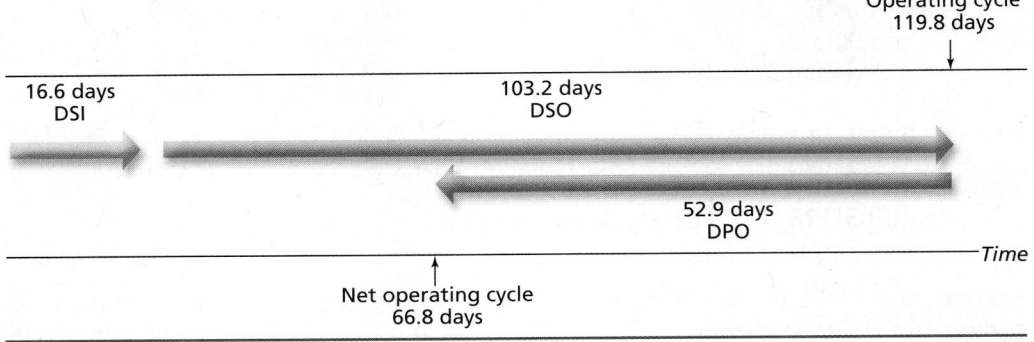

For IBM in FY2010, purchases were, in millions:

$$\text{Purchases} = \$2{,}450 + 53{,}857 - 2{,}494 = \$53{,}814$$

Therefore, IBM's days of purchases outstanding are:

$$\text{Days purchases outstanding} = \frac{\$7{,}804 \text{ million}}{\dfrac{\$53{,}814 \text{ million}}{365}} = 52.9316 \text{ days}$$

In other words, it takes IBM, on average, around 53 days to pay its creditors. We summarize IBM's operating cycle in Table 4-2. As you can see, IBM has a net operating cycle that is positive, which means that although it ties up funds in inventory and receivables from customers, it also uses trade credit, which frees up cash flow.[16]

Efficiency

efficiency ratio or
profitability ratio
measure of how efficiently
a dollar of sales is turned
into profits

Efficiency ratios are measures of how efficiently a company is able to convert a dollar of sales into profits; in other words, how efficiently does it manage its expenses? For this reason, you will often see references to these ratios as **profitability ratios**. The net profit margin is a measure of overall profitability, and we can break it down into its major components. How it is done depends on the type of company and the amount of data presented in its financial statements.

Cost structure and break even

When looking at a company's cost structure, analysts like to think in terms of variable and fixed operating costs, where variable operating costs increase or decrease with the amount of production and sales, and fixed costs do not. Suppose the BullDog Company sells 120 million units at €1 per unit; therefore, BullDog has revenues of €120 million. If variable

---

[16] A negative net operating cycle is not unusual for technology companies, such as Dell Computers.

operating costs are 60% of revenues, this means that the company has a **contribution margin** of 40%, or €0.4 per unit, available to cover to the company's fixed costs and profits. If fixed operating costs are €31 million, Bulldog has an operating profit of €120 million − 72 million − 31 million = €17 million. How many units must BullDog sell to generate an operating profit? In other words, what is BullDog's operating break-even in terms of units produced and sold? We can calculate the **operating break-even** by comparing the fixed costs with the contribution margin:

$$\text{Operating break-even} = \frac{\text{Fixed operating costs}}{\text{Contribution margin}} \quad (4\text{-}11)$$

Therefore, BullDog must sell more than €31 million ÷ €0.4 = 77.5 million units to generate an operating profit.

Suppose that BullDog has interest expense of €5 million. If BullDog sells 120 million units, the company has taxable income of €12 million. With a 35% income tax rate, its net income is €7.8 million. We provide the detail of this example in Table 4-3, which also shows what happens with a 10% increase and decrease in revenues from this base case of 120 million units produced and sold.

If the company sells more and sales increase to €132 million, only the variable costs increase. The gross profit, which is revenues minus variable costs, also increases by 10% to €52.8 million. However, because the fixed production and interest costs stay the same, the taxable income increases from €12 to €16.8 million, and the net profit increases from €7.8 to €10.92 million. Conversely, if revenues decrease by 10% to €108 million, the process works in reverse, and the existence of the fixed costs causes net income profit to drop €4.68 million. You can see the leveraging effect of the fixed costs by looking at a wider range of units sold, from 50 million to 150 million, in Figure 4-3.

This example illustrates that the more fixed costs the company has, relative to its variables costs, the greater its income variability. Note that although sales varied by +/−10%, net income varied by +/−40%. The degree of total leverage of 4 for BullDog shows a significant exposure of profits to variability in sales because every 1% change in sales causes a 4% change in earnings before taxes. This exposure depends on the company's cost structure, which is crucial to the risk of the company.[17]

Clearly, it is important for the company to know its break-even point and how its profits vary with sales. As a result, internally it will have the information to estimate these important values. Externally, however, the company is not required to present this information in its financial statements. All one can do externally is look to see how variable profits are from year to year. Further, the proxies that are available are often poor.

contribution margin portion of each dollar of sales that is available to cover fixed costs, after first satisfying variable costs

operating break-even level of sales at which the company covers all its variable and fixed operating costs

TABLE 4-3 Bulldog Company Profit Margin and Sales Variability

(in millions)	Base case	Increase of 10%	Decrease of 10%
Sales	€120.00	€132.00	€108.00
Variable costs	72.00	79.20	64.80
Contribution margin (40%)	€48.00	€52.80	€43.20
Fixed cost	31.00	31.00	31.00
Operating profit	17.00	21.60	12.20
Interest expense	5.00	5.00	5.00
Income before taxes	€12.00	€16.80	€7.20
Tax	4.20	5.88	2.52
Net income	€7.80	€10.92	€4.68

[17] We discuss this concept in more detail in our discussion of risk and capital structure later in this text.

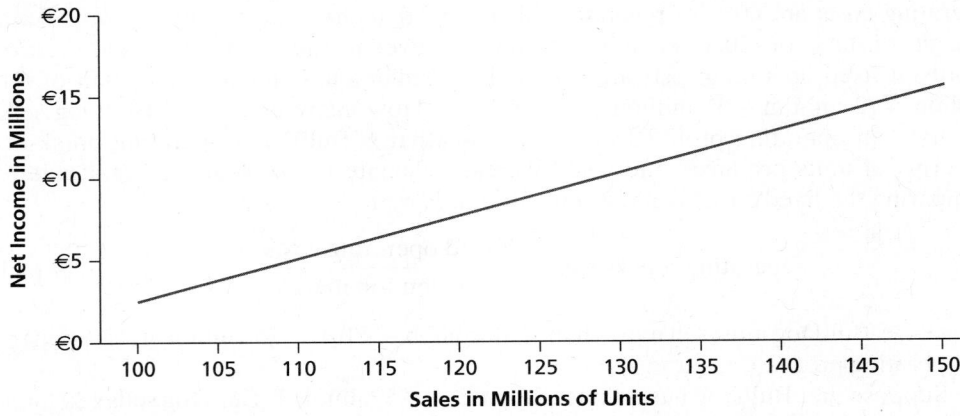

FIGURE 4-3 Net Income for the Bulldog Company for Revenues from 100 to 150 Million Units

From your managerial cost accounting course, you know that cost of goods sold includes variable production costs, as well as the allocation of factory overhead—that is, it includes fixed costs. If the company does only one thing, this factory overhead can include almost all its operating fixed costs, as it does for IBM. Unfortunately, what is presented for IBM does not allow a breakout of variable and fixed costs, so we cannot estimate its break-even point, contribution margin, or the sensitivity of its profits to sales increases or decreases.

EXAMPLE 4.1

Break-Even and Contribution Margins

PROBLEM

Consider a company that has fixed operating costs of $200,000. The company sells its products for $5 per unit, though it costs the company $3 per unit.

1. What is the contribution margin per unit produced and sold?
2. What is the break-even level of sales for this company?
3. If the company sells 75,000 units, will it make a profit?
4. If the company sells 150,000 units, will it make a profit?

Solution

1. The contribution margin is $2 per unit.
2. The break-even level of sales is $200,000 ÷ $2 = 100,000 units
3. No. This is below the break-even level of sales. Operating loss = $375,000 – 225,000 – 200,000 = –$50,000
4. Yes. This is above the break-even level of sales. Operating profit = 750,000 – 450,000 – 200,000 = $100,000

Profit margins

gross profit margin
revenues minus the cost of goods sold, divided by revenues

Consistent with the basic idea of calculating the contribution margin, that is, revenues minus variable costs, we can calculate a variation of it: the **gross profit margin**. This ratio is gross profit (that is, revenues minus the cost of goods sold) divided by revenues:

$$\text{Gross profit margin} = \frac{\text{Revenues} - \text{Cost of Goods Sold}}{\text{Revenues}} \tag{4-12}$$

For IBM in 2010,[18]

$$\text{Gross profit margin} = \frac{\$99,870 \text{ million} - 53,857 \text{ million}}{\$99,870 \text{ million}} = 0.4608 \text{ or } 46.08\%$$

A gross margin of 46.08% indicates that 46.08% of IBM's revenues are available to cover its nonproduction costs. Alternatively, only 53.92% of IBM's revenues actually are used to cover expenses.

The other expenses that companies normally incur apart from cost of goods sold are period costs, which we often loosely refer to as fixed costs because, in the short run, they are unrelated to sales revenues. These costs consist of advertising, research and development, general, selling, and administrative expenses, and amortization expenses. For IBM, these expenses in 2010 are $27,864 million.

The **operating margin**, also known as the **operating profit margin**, is operating profit or income divided by revenues and is a measure of how efficient the company's management is in managing expenses.

operating margin or **operating profit margin** operating income divided by revenues

$$\text{Operating profit margin} = \frac{\text{Operating income}}{\text{Revenues}} \qquad (4\text{-}13)$$

For IBM, this ratio is relatively easy to calculate, but this is not always the case. When analyzing a company's operating performance, analysts use different levels of income in the ratios, depending on their purpose. Consider IBM's income statement:

(in millions)	*2010*
Revenue	$99,870
Cost of revenue	53,857
Gross profit	$46,014
Total operating expenses	26,703
Operating income	$18,150
Other income or expense	1,941
Earnings before interest and taxes	$20,091
Interest expense	368
Earnings before tax	$19,723
Income tax expense	4,890
Net income	$14,833

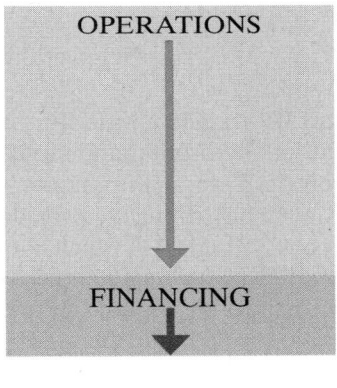

When analyzing operations, the focus is on **operating income** because the difference between operating income (or **operating profit**) and earnings before interest and taxes (EBIT) are the income and expenses that are not specifically related to operations. Some companies do not report these other income or expense items because these items either do not exist or are too small to report, in which case operating income and EBIT are equivalent. In the case of IBM, the difference between operating income and EBIT is small, but if we are focusing strictly on operating performance, we would use operating income in the relevant ratios.

operating income or **operating profit** earnings before interest and before taxes for nonoperating income and expenses

We use these different definitions of income frequently in the text, so be sure you know the differences among gross profit, contribution margin, EBITDA, operating income, EBIT, and net income. We use operating proft to calculate the operating margin, but note that although conceptually this is correct, in many cases companies do not break out their

---

[18] Note that we did not include IBM's investment income as part of sales revenues because this may be income from temporary investments, and we are interested in the profitability of IBM's operations.

TABLE 4-4   Efficiency Ratios for IBM and Microsoft, Fiscal Years 2008 Through 2010

	IBM			Microsoft		
	FY2010	*FY2009*	*FY2008*	*FY2010*	*FY2009*	*FY2008*
Gross profit margin	46.07%	45.73%	44.06%	80.16%	79.20%	80.80%
Operating profit margin	18.17%	17.76%	15.38%	38.68%	36.32%	36.86%
Net profit margin	14.85%	14.02%	11.90%	30.02%	24.93%	29.26%

revenues as diligently as IBM. As a result, we often calculate the operating margin using EBIT. For IBM, the operating margin is 18.17%:

$$\text{Operation profit margin} = \frac{\$18,150 \text{ million}}{\$99,870 \text{ million}} = 0.1817 \text{ or } 18.17\%$$

net profit margin net income divided by revenues

The **net profit margin** provides information on how much of every dollar of sales or revenues are profit available to owners and is the ratio of net income to revenues:[19]

$$\text{Net profit margin} = \frac{\text{Net income}}{\text{Revenues}} \tag{4-14}$$

For IBM the 2010 net profit margin or return on revenues is 14.85%:

$$\text{Net profit magin} = \frac{\$14,833 \text{ million}}{\$99,870 \text{ million}} = 0.1485 \text{ or } 14.85\%$$

So IBM made a little less than 15% on average on the net amount after taxes. We look at the net profit margin to determine how *efficiently* the company converts revenues into profits. Later in the chapter, we expand our analysis to include additional efficiency ratios.

In any event, we provide the efficiency ratios for IBM and Microsoft for three fiscal years in Table 4-4, which allows us to further evaluate IBM's efficiency results. We can see that IBM has maintained steady profitability, steadily increasing its net profit margins, gross profit margins, and operating margins. Microsoft displayed little variability in these ratios, with all the margins being consistently higher than those for IBM.

Productivity

productivity ratios (or **activity ratios** or **asset utilization ratios**) measurements of how productive the company is in generating revenues from its assets

receivables turnover or **accounts receivable turnover** revenues divided by accounts receivables

We use efficiency ratios to measure how efficiently the company turns revenues into profits. The next question is how productive the company is in generating revenues from its assets. The key to looking at different **productivity ratios** is to look at variations of the turnover for each major asset class. For example, we can see how productive the company is in using its investment in receivables, inventory, and plant and equipment because these are the major categories of assets that most companies have. Because these ratios provide information on how effectively the company puts its asset to use, we sometimes refer to these ratios as **activity ratios** or **asset utilization ratios**.

We begin by defining the **receivables turnover** ratio as revenues divided by accounts receivables. The receivables turnover, also known as the **accounts receivable turnover**, indicates how many times, on average, accounts receivable are created and collected during the fiscal period.

---

[19] We use the term *sales* throughout the chapter to represent a company's revenues from the goods and services it sells. When applying these ratios to an actual company, especially a service company or a financial company, you may encounter the term *revenue*.

$$\text{Receivables turnover} = \frac{\text{Credit sales}}{\text{Accounts receivable}} \qquad (4\text{-}15)$$

IBM, like most companies, does not break out revenues into cash and credit sales, at least not in its external financial statements. We therefore must make an assumption regarding the use of trade credit by IBM's customers. For IBM in 2010, assuming that all sales are on credit,

$$\text{Receivables turnover} = \frac{\$99{,}870 \text{ million}}{\$28{,}225 \text{ million}} = 3.5384$$

We can say that IBM turned its accounts receivables over 3.5384 times, on average, during the year. That is, IBM, on average, completes a little over three-and-one-half complete cycles of selling goods on credit and collecting on these accounts. You may begin to notice the relation between this turnover ratio and the days sales outstanding: If you dividend the receivables turnover into 365, you end up with the days sales outstanding.

The second major current asset category is inventory. For IBM, this is $2,450 million in 2010. Conceptually, the **inventory turnover** ratio is calculated as the cost of goods sold divided by inventory because when a widget is sold, its financial cost moves from inventory and is expensed through cost of goods sold. The inventory turnover is how many times, on average, during the fiscal period that inventory is created and then sold:

inventory turnover cost of goods sold divided by inventory

$$\text{Inventory turnover} = \frac{\text{Cost of Goods Sold}}{\text{Inventory}} \qquad (4\text{-}16)$$

For IBM in 2010,

$$\text{Inventory turnover} = \frac{\$53{,}857 \text{ million}}{\$2{,}450 \text{ million}} = 21.9824 \text{ times}$$

Another productivity ratio is the **fixed asset turnover** ratio, which we calculate as the ratio of revenues to net fixed assets, the depreciated value of the fixed assets:[20]

fixed asset turnover revenues divided by net fixed assets

$$\text{Fixed asset turnover} = \frac{\text{Revenues}}{\text{Net fixed assets}} \qquad (4\text{-}17)$$

For IBM in 2010, net fixed assets are $40,259 million – 26,193 million = $14,066 million, so the fixed asset turnover is:

$$\text{Fixed asset turnover} = \frac{\$99{,}870 \text{ million}}{\$14{,}096 \text{ million}} = 7.1001 \text{ times}$$

The **total asset turnover ratio**, often referred to as the **total asset turnover** or simply the **asset turnover**, provides information on how effectively the company puts its assets to work to generate revenues:

total asset turnover ratio (or **total asset turnover** or **asset turnover**) sales or revenues divided by total assets

$$\text{Total asset turnover} = \frac{\text{Revenues}}{\text{Total assets}} \qquad (4\text{-}18)$$

So if every dollar of revenues earned IBM 11.9% in profits, how many dollars of revenues did it generate from each dollar invested in assets, or alternatively what was its turnover ratio?

$$\text{Total asset turnover} = \frac{\text{Revenues}}{\text{Total assets}} = \frac{\$99{,}870 \text{ million}}{\$113{,}450 \text{ million}} = 0.8803$$

For 2010, with total assets of $113,450 million, IBM generated revenues of $99,870 million. In other words, each dollar of assets generated about $0.8803 in revenues. The turnover

---

[20] As companies depreciate their assets, the fixed asset turnover ratio automatically increases, so many analysts also look at the fixed asset turnover ratio by using gross assets, which is the undepreciated cost of the fixed assets (i.e., without any depreciation deducted).

TABLE 4-5 **Productivity Ratios for IBM and Microsoft, Fiscal Years 2008 Through 2010**

	IBM			Microsoft		
	FY2010	*FY2009*	*FY2008*	*FY2010*	*FY2009*	*FY2008*
Receivables turnover	3.5384	3.5740	3.7608	4.8013	5.2213	4.4462
Inventory turnover	21.9824	20.8472	21.4700	16.7500	16.9526	11.7746
Fixed asset turnover	7.0850	6.7607	7.2448	8.1893	7.7554	9.6796
Total asset turnover	0.8803	0.8783	0.9462	0.7256	0.7503	0.8300

ratio is a productivity ratio, as it measures how *productive* the company is in generating revenues from its assets.

We provide some context for IBM's 2010 ratios as calculated earlier by reporting its historical ratios, as well as those for Microsoft, in Table 4-5. There are several findings we should note from Table 4-5.

- IBM collects on its receivables slower than does Microsoft.
- IBM has an inventory turnover that is faster than that of Microsoft.
- IBM's use of its assets is less productive than Microsoft's.

Financial Leverage

financial leverage use of debt, rather than equity, to finance a company

Leverage is synonymous with magnification, and **financial leverage** is the use of debt to finance a company, which results in magnifying the earnings (or losses) to owners. Financial leverage is good when a company is low risk and earns a healthy profit, but when the company loses money, the use of leverage magnifies losses as well. This can get the company into serious trouble.

Financial leverage ratios

We measure financial leverage using a **financial leverage ratio**, which gauges how reliant a company is on debt financing: the greater the financial leverage, the greater the company's reliance on debt financing, and hence, the company assumes more financial risk. This is because debt obligates the company to pay the interest that is contractual, whether the company has earnings or losses. A company financed with nothing but equity can use its discretion on whether to distribute dividends to owners, but a company obligated by debt to pay interest has no choice: The interest and debt repayment are legal obligations, and not paying obligations would have ramifications, such as the creditors being able to force the company into bankruptcy.

For financial leverage, there are three basic ratios: the debt ratio, the debt-equity ratio, and the equity multiplier.[21] The **debt ratio** is the ratio of total debt to total assets:[22]

debt ratio total debt divided by total assets

$$\text{Debt ratio} = \frac{\text{Total debt}}{\text{Total assets}} \qquad (4\text{-}19)$$

interest-bearing debt obligations that require the payment of interest

What are a company's debts? These are the interest-bearing obligations. The **interest-bearing debt** of a company consists of short-term debt such as bank loans and

[21] The term *stock* represents ownership interest at a point in time, not to be confused with equity interests in a corporation.

[22] There are many variations of this ratio that include the use of total liabilities or total long-term debt in the numerator and/or dividing by total capital instead of total assets.

commercial paper, and long-term debt, such as notes and bonds. Of the $90,278 million liabilities of IBM in 2010, only $28,624 are considered debt for purposes of the debt ratio: $4,017 million of the current portion of long-term debt, $2,761 million of notes payable and short-term debt, and $21,846 million long-term debt, for a total of $28,624 million. What makes up the difference between liabilities and debt for IBM? The liabilities that are not part of debt include accounts payables, accrued liabilities, deferred income tax, and pension obligations.

For IBM in 2010, the debt ratio is:

$$\text{Debt ratio} = \frac{\$28,624 \text{ million}}{\$113,450 \text{ million}} = 0.2523$$

The debt ratio reflects how IBM uses other people's money—or does it? IBM's liabilities include money that it owes suppliers and other creditors; the obligations to suppliers make up more than 20% of IBM's liabilities. As long as it stays in business, IBM will continue to generate trade credit as suppliers ship to it and IBM pays them later. But in a broad sense, these liabilities are not debt in the way that bank debt is debt. These liabilities, which we refer to as **operational liabilities**, arise as a result of normal operations, not from someone deciding to invest or lend money to IBM. Therefore, we often calculate ratios that involve liabilities in a manner to focus on the interest-bearing debt.

operational liabilities obligations of a company that arise from normal operations

The sum of interest-bearing debt and shareholders' equity is the company's **invested capital**. Therefore, a variation of the debt-to-assets ratio is the debt-to-invested capital:

invested capital sum of interest-bearing debt and shareholders' equity

$$\text{Debt-to-invested capital} = \frac{\text{Debt}}{\text{Invested capital}} \qquad (4\text{-}20)$$

Another measure of financial leverage is the **debt-equity ratio, D/E**, in which we compare the company's debt with its equity:

debt-equity (D/E) ratio debt to shareholders' equity

$$\text{Debt-equity ratio} = \frac{\text{Debt}}{\text{Shareholders' equity}} \qquad (4\text{-}21)$$

IBM's debt-equity ratio in 2010 is simply debt divided by shareholders' equity:[23]

$$\text{Debt-equity ratio} = \frac{\$28,624 \text{ million}}{\$23,046 \text{ million}} = 1.2420$$

This means that for every dollar of equity contributed by shareholders, IBM borrowed $1.242 in interest-bearing debt.

In addition to the leverage ratios that use debt, some use total liabilities. For example, the ratio of total liabilities to total assets provides a measure of the proportion of a company's assets that are financed with some type of obligation.

A leverage ratio that uses total liabilities indirectly is the equity multiplier. The **equity multiplier** is a financial leverage ratio, which we calculate as the ratio of total asset to equity:[24]

equity multiplier financial leverage ratio that is the ratio of total assets to shareholders' equity

$$\text{Equity multiplier} = \frac{\text{Total assets}}{\text{Shareholders' equity}} \qquad (4\text{-}22)$$

which for IBM in 2010 is:

$$\text{Equity multiplier} = \frac{\$113,450 \text{ million}}{\$23,046 \text{ million}} = 4.9228$$

---

[23] As you examine ratios available by third-party sources, such as Yahoo! Finance, Google Finance, or Reuters, you will see that total debt is sometimes compared with equity in the debt-equity ratio. It is a good idea to check how the third party calculated any ratio that you are relying on in your analysis.

[24] In fact, the leverage ratio is simply one divided by one minus the debt ratio (i.e., $1 \div (1 - 0.2523) = 1.3374$).

The difference between total assets and shareholder' equity is total liabilities. Therefore, the greater a company's total liabilities, relative to its equity, the greater the equity multiplier.

The debt and D/E ratios using only interest-bearing obligations have an advantage over the same ratios that use total liabilities. This is important because it is the promise to pay interest that makes debt risky. IBM does not face risk because its creditors think well enough of it to ship supplies on credit, or because an accountant has decided to generate accruals in terms of future employee benefits. It does face risk through its interest-bearing debt. In this respect, analysts often "net out" (that is, subtract) interest-bearing debt by subtracting cash and marketable securities from total interest-bearing debt. In IBM's case, these two items total $11,651 million.

Coverage ratios

This discussion of the role of interest-bearing debt should remind you that not only is it important to determine the amount or stock of debt, but it is also equally, if not more, important to evaluate how much the debt costs. More generally we look at measures that indicate the *flow* of fixed commitments to income, which provides an estimate of a company's ability to *service* its debt obligations. The most important of these measures is the **times interest earned (TIE)**, or **interest coverage ratio**, which is earnings before interest and taxes (EBIT) divided by interest expense:

times interest earned (TIE) or **interest coverage ratio** earnings before interest and taxes divided by interest expense

$$\text{Times interest earned} = \frac{\text{Earnings before interest and taxes}}{\text{Interest}} \quad (4\text{-}23)$$

We estimate the TIE for IBM in 2010 as:

$$\text{TIE} = \frac{\text{EBIT}}{\text{Interest}} = \frac{\$20{,}091 \text{ million}}{\$368 \text{ million}} = 54.5951 \text{ times}$$

So how do we evaluate the TIE? It means that for every dollar of interest expense, IBM had almost $55 of income available to pay interest and taxes. This emphasizes how little risk IBM's debt imposes on its operations in relation to the profits it generates.[25]

EXAMPLE 4.2

Financial Leverage Ratios

PROBLEM

Using the financial data for the most recent fiscal year of these three companies, calculate the debt ratio and the debt-equity ratio, first using total liabilities and total assets, and then using only interest-bearing liabilities and invested capital:

(in millions)	Company A	Company B	Company C
Accounts payable	$30,000	$50,000	$6,000
Accrued expenses	10,000	20,000	1,000
Short-term debt	5,000	10,000	10,000
Current portion of long-term debt	2,000	5,000	5,000
Long-term debt	30,000	40,000	50,000
Shareholders' equity	80,000	50,000	75,000

---

[25] There are other coverage ratios, which are variations of the TIE that are adjusted to include the impact of other fixed charges, such as preferred share dividends, lease obligations, and sinking fund payments, but we discuss these later when we talk about other contractual commitments attached to different types of securities.

Solution

(in millions)	Company A	Company B	Company C
Total liabilities	$77,000	$125,000	$72,000
Interest-bearing liabilities	$37,000	$55,000	$65,000
Total assets	$157,000	$175,000	$147,000
Invested capital	$117,000	$105,000	$140,000
Using total liabilities			
Debt ratio	0.490	0.714	0.490
Debt-equity ratio	0.963	2.500	0.960
Using interest-bearing debt			
Debt ratio	0.236	0.314	0.442
Debt-equity ratio	0.463	1.100	0.867

A final ratio is the **cash flow to debt ratio**, which is a measure of how long it would take to pay off a company's debt from its cash flow from operations.[26] We calculate this as the ratio of cash flow from operations to debt:

$$\text{Cash flow to debt ratio} = \frac{\text{Cash flow from operations}}{\text{Debt}} \qquad (4\text{-}24)$$

cash flow to debt ratio how long it takes to pay off a company's debt from its cash flow from operations; cash flow from operations divided by debt

For IBM in 2010:

$$\text{Cash flow to debt ratio} = \frac{\$19,549 \text{ million}}{\$28,624 \text{ million}} = 0.6830$$

This ratio indicates that IBM could pay off all its debt in a little less than 2 years if it devoted its operating cash flow to debt repayment. This reflects, once again, IBM's very strong credit position.

So what is the overall assessment of IBM's leverage position in 2010? Its D/E ratio and interest coverage ratios are indicators of the risk that interest-bearing debt imposes on the company. In particular, although the D/E ratio is relatively high, the TIE ratio indicates that IBM's earnings can very easily support the required interest payments. This assessment is borne out once we net out interest expense and look at the ability of IBM to pay off its interest-bearing debt from cash flow from operations.

We provide these ratios in Table 4-6 so that we can look at the trend in IBM's leverage ratios and compare these ratios with those of a comparable company or industry average, in this case, Microsoft. Microsoft had debt, but its interest expense is so small that it is reported as $0 each year.[27]

The trend in IBM's leverage ratios shows that the amount of debt as a percentage of total financing decreased from 2008 to 2010. Comparing IBM with Microsoft, we see the difference in financing decisions: IBM finances a larger portion of its assets with debt, whereas Microsoft does not. Further, Microsoft uses little interest-bearing debt, but rather relies on cash flow from operations.

---

[26] You can find the cash flow from operations on a company's statement of cash flows.

[27] Therefore, it is not possible to calculate coverage ratios for these years.

TABLE 4-6   Leverage Ratios for IBM and Microsoft, Fiscal Years 2008 Through 2010

(in millions)	IBM			Microsoft		
	FY2010	**FY2009**	**FY2008**	**FY2010**	**FY2009**	**FY2008**
Total debt	$28,624	$26,100	$33,926	$5,939	$5,746	$0
Shareholders' equity	$23,046	$22,637	$13,466	$46,175	$39,558	$36,286
Total assets	$113,450	$109,022	$109,525	$86,113	$77,888	$72,793
EBIT	$20,091	$18,548	$17,396	$25,013	$19,821	$23,814
Interest expense	$368	$402	$673	$0	$0	$0
CFO	$19,549	$12,754	$8,203	$24,073	$19,037	$21,612
Ratios						
Debt ratio	0.2523	0.2394	0.3098	0.0690	0.0738	0.0000
Debt-equity ratio	1.2420	1.1530	2.5194	0.1286	0.1453	0.0000
Equity multiplier	4.9228	4.8162	8.1334	1.8649	1.9690	2.0061
Times interest earned	54.5951	46.1194	25.8366	NA	NA	NA
Cash flow to debt	0.6830	0.4887	0.2418	4.0534	3.3131	NA

NA: *Not applicable due to the absence of interest-bearing debt.*

FINANCE in the News | Financial Leverage and Bankruptcy

The use of financial leverage magnifies a company's performance, which is why we see more bankruptcies during periods of recessions than we do during booming economic periods. Consider the ratio of total liabilities to assets of several companies leading up to 2008:

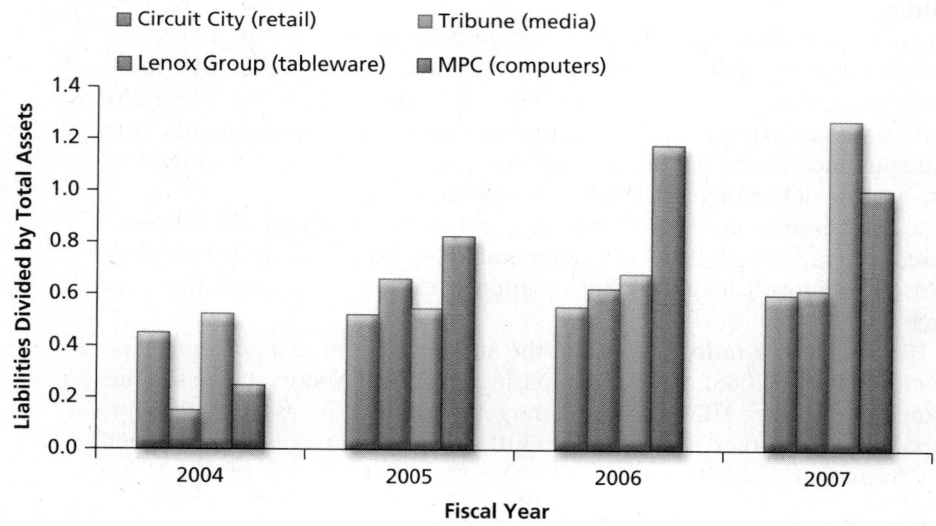

Keep in mind that if liabilities exceed total assets, equity is actually negative. You can see that in the case of Tribune and MPC, there was negative equity prior to the bankruptcy.

Each of these companies filed for bankruptcy in 2008. You can see that in each case the company experienced increasing financial leverage during the four-year period leading up to 2008. In the case of both Tribune and MPC, the debt ratio exceeds 1.0, which means that the company had more debt than assets, and also means that it had negative shareholders' equity.

Circuit City and MPC liquidated following the bankruptcy filings, Lenox was bought during bankruptcy in 2009, and Tribune emerged from bankruptcy in 2011 after selling the Chicago Cubs and Wrigley Field, among other things.

Source of data: Companies' annual 10-K filings with the Securities and Exchange Commission.

Owners' Ratios

When analyzing the company from the perspective of the owners, we use ratios (1) that reflect the dividends paid to owners and (2) that indicate value or relative value.

Dividend ratios

In terms of dividends, one of the most basic ratios an analyst can look at is a company's **dividend yield**, which is the current dividend per share (DPS) divided by the current share price.

$$\text{Dividend yield} = \frac{\text{Dividend per share}}{\text{Price per share}} \qquad (4\text{-}25)$$

dividend yield dividend per share divided by the share price

For IBM, the 2010 DPS was $2.5872, so at the year-end share price of $146.76,

$$\text{Dividend yield} = \frac{\$2.5872}{\$146.76} = 0.0176$$

Because investors are concerned about the company's ability to sustain its dividend payments, we can use the **dividend payout ratio**, or simply the **dividend payout**, to assess this ability. The dividend payout ratio is the DPS divided by the EPS:

$$\text{Dividend payout} = \frac{\text{Dividend per share}}{\text{Earnings per share}} = \frac{\text{DPS}}{\text{EPS}} \qquad (4\text{-}26)$$

dividend payout ratio or **dividend payout** portion of earnings paid out in dividends to owners

We will use the diluted EPS in this equation, although it is also common to use the basic EPS figure. For IBM in 2010, we obtain the following:

$$\text{Dividend payout} = \frac{\text{DPS}}{\text{EPS}} = \frac{\$2.5872}{\$12.0791} = 0.2142$$

This ratio implies that during 2010, IBM paid out 21.42% of its earnings as dividends.

The **plowback ratio**, which indicates the proportion of earnings reinvested in the company, is the complement of the dividend payout ratio:

plowback ratio or **retention ratio** proportion of earnings reinvested in a company

$$\text{Plowback ratio} = \frac{\text{Retained earnings}}{\text{Earnings per share}} = 1 - \frac{\text{DPS}}{\text{EPS}} \qquad (4\text{-}27)$$

We also refer to this ratio as the **retention ratio**. IBM plows back, or retains, $1 - 0.2142 = 0.7858$, or 78.58% of its earnings.

Valuation ratios

Some ratios that are useful in assessing a company's relative value include the earnings per share (EPS), and the **book value per share**, which is the ending shareholders' equity divided by the ending number of shares outstanding.

book value per share shareholders' equity divided by the number of shares outstanding

$$\text{Book value per share} = \frac{\text{Shareholders' equity}}{\text{Number of shares}} \qquad (4\text{-}28)$$

For IBM in 2010,

$$\text{Book value per share} = \frac{\text{Shareholders' equity}}{\text{Number of shares}} = \frac{\$23,046 \text{ million}}{1,227.99 \text{ million}} = \$18.7673$$

If we take a close look at the book value of equity of any company, we see that it likely comprises:

- common stock, or common stock and additional paid-in capital;
- retained earnings;
- accumulated other comprehensive income; and
- Treasury stock.

Taking a close look at IBM, we see for 2010 that the company has book value of equity comprising:

		(in millions)
	Common stock	$45,418
Plus	Retained earnings	92,532
Less	Treasury stock	−96,161
Plus	Accumulated gains and losses not affecting retained earnings	−18,743
Equals	Total stockholder equity	$23,046

For IBM, common stock consists of the par value (20 cents per share), plus the additional paid-in capital. This means that the amount that IBM received from investors when it issued new shares is $45,418 million. These stock issues include its initial public offering. The amount in retained earnings is the accumulation of all the earnings since the company was incorporated in 1911 as the Computing-Tabulating-Recording Co., less any dividends since 1911. This means that the accumulation in retained earnings consists of earnings of different fiscal periods, unadjusted for inflation.

The Treasury stock account is a contra-equity account because it represents an offset or reduction to equity and reflects the cost of shares that IBM bought back from investors. Treasury stock may be set aside for a number of purposes, such as employee incentive programs. These shares may have been bought at any point in time, so the amount paid for these shares is not necessarily what they are worth today.

The account "Accumulated gains and losses not affecting retained earnings" represents the gains and losses that bypass the income statement and go directly to equity and may be positive or negative.[28] The more familiar name for this account is "other accumulated comprehensive income." IBM has, on net, a loss in this account of almost $19 billion.[29]

IBM's book value of equity is $23,046 million. But what is its market value of equity? At the end of fiscal year 2010, IBM had a share price of $146.76 and 1,227.99 million shares outstanding. Therefore, IBM's market value of equity is $180.220 billion.

For a publicly traded company, the market value of equity is the company's **market capitalization**; that is, the total value of the company's shares outstanding. The ratio of the market value to the book value of equity is often simply referred to as the company's **market-to-book value ratio**, or simply the **market-to-book ratio** or **M/B**. The ratio of its market value of equity to its book value of equity is:

$$\text{Market-to-book value ratio} = \frac{\text{Market value of equity}}{\text{Book value of equity}} \tag{4-29}$$

market capitalization total value of the company's shares outstanding, calculated as the product of the market price per share of stock and the number of shares of stock outstanding

market-to-book value ratio or **market-to-book ratio (M/B)** market price per share divided by the book value per share; alternatively, the market capitalization divided by the book value of shareholders' equity

---

[28] For example, from losses when the available-for-sale method is used to account for marketable securities, as we discussed in Chapter 3.

[29] Digging into IBM's footnotes, we see that these accumulated gains and losses are from pension remeasurement and foreign currency translation adjustments.

For IBM in 2008,

$$\text{Market-to-book value ratio} = \frac{\$180,220 \text{ million}}{\$23,046 \text{ million}} = 7.8200$$

In other words, IBM's market value is almost eight times its book value.[30] We can also calculate the market-to-book value ratio as the ratio of the market price per share of stock to the book value per share of stock:

$$\text{Market-to-book value ratio} = \frac{\$146.76}{\$18.7673} = 7.8200$$

One of the most important and widely followed value ratios is the **price-earnings (P/E) ratio**, which is estimated as the share price (P) divided by earnings per share (EPS):

$$P/E = \frac{\text{Price per share}}{\text{Earnings per share}} = \frac{P}{EPS} \qquad (4\text{-}30)$$

> **price earnings (P/E) ratio** share price divided by the earnings per share

Similar to the dividend payout ratio, we use the diluted EPS figure in the denominator, rather than the basic EPS (which is sometimes used). For IBM in 2010, using the market price per share as of the end of 2010,

$$P/E = \frac{\$146.76}{\$12.0791} = 12.1499$$

This means that investors were willing to pay $12.15 for $1 of IBM's 2010 earnings. The higher the ratio, the more investors will pay, and vice versa. Note that P/E ratios increase when share prices increase or when EPS declines. Analysts focus on prices, which are reflected in the numerator of the P/E, and some would argue that a company's shares become too "expensive" when its P/E ratio gets too high. Conversely, others argue that a high P/E ratio is warranted because they expect substantial growth in the company's future earnings or because they feel that the company's shares represent a relatively low-risk investment. In either event, from the company's point of view, higher P/E ratios are a good thing because this suggests that the markets have confidence in the company, all else being equal.

The P/E ratio that we estimated is the *trailing*, or last year's, EPS, and we sometimes refer to this P/E as the **trailing P/E ratio**.[31] When we estimate the P/E ratio based on the current price and by using a forecast or expected EPS, we refer to it as the **forward P/E ratio**:

> **trailing P/E ratio** share price divided by the most recent year's earnings per share

> **forward P/E ratio** share price divided by the expected earnings per share

$$\text{Forward P/E} = \frac{\text{Price per share}}{\text{Expected earnings per share}} \qquad (4\text{-}31)$$

On April 15, 2011, the 2011 EPS estimate for IBM was $13.01, whereas its share price on this same date was $166.21, leaving us with a forward P/E ratio of:[32]

$$\text{Forward P/E} = \frac{\$166.21}{\$13.01} = 12.7756$$

A forward P/E ratio of 12.7756 means that if an investor held the stock for almost 13 years and the EPS stayed the same, that investor would recoup in profits the $12.7756 paid for the stock.[33] The higher the P/E ratio, the longer the shareholder has to wait to

---

[30] In some applications, analysts will use a different timing for the numerator and the denominator because the financial statement data is not known at the end of the year, but rather some time following the end of the year. Therefore, an analyst may use, say, the market price share as of three months following the end of the fiscal year to compare with the end of the fiscal year book value.

[31] Source: Reuters, www.reuters.com.

[32] Source: Reuters, www.reuters.com.

[33] In this sense, the P/E ratio is a simple example of a *payback period*, which we discuss in later chapters in the context of capital budgeting.

recover the cost of his investment in future profits. Generally, low P/E shares are regarded as *value* stocks because the payback period is lower and there is less emphasis on any growth in the forecast EPS. In contrast, high P/E shares are generally regarded as *growth* stocks because investors are relying more heavily on future growth in the EPS.

The P/E ratio and dividend yield are useful value indicators for many companies. However, P/E ratios are meaningless when EPS is negative or is very low, whereas dividend yields are zero for companies that do not pay dividends. In such cases, analysts look for other ratios that provide an indication of a company's relative value, ones that do not rely on earnings.

We summarize the valuation ratios for IBM and Microsoft for fiscal years 2008 through 2010 in Table 4-7. Here are a few facts that we can point out about the relative valuation of IBM and Microsoft:

- Microsoft trades at a market price per share much lower than IBM, but it also has almost seven times as many shares outstanding. In other words, the equity "pie" of Microsoft is cut into more pieces than is IBM's equity, but the resulting market capitalization is larger.
- Though the dividend yields and payouts are similar for the two companies, the dividend per share is higher for IBM because of the fewer shares outstanding.
- The P/E declined over the period for both companies, but more for Microsoft. This is, in part, due to the increasing earnings per share over the period for both companies.

TABLE 4-7 Dividend and Valuation Ratios for IBM and Microsoft, Fiscal Years 2008 Through 2010

(in millions, except for per share and percentages)	IBM			Microsoft		
	FY2010	*FY2009*	*FY2008*	*FY2010*	*FY2009*	*FY2008*
Data						
Number of shares outstanding	1,227.99	1,305.34	1,339.10	9,151	9,380	10,062
Dividends	$3,177	$2,369	$1,551	$4,578	$4,468	$4,015
Net income	$14,833	$13,425	$12,334	$18,760	$14,569	$17,681
Market value per share	$146.76	$130.90	$81.33	$27.91	$30.48	$19.13
Ratios						
Dividends per share	$2.5872	$1.8149	$1.1582	$0.5281	$0.5016	$0.4240
Dividend yield	1.76%	1.24%	0.79%	1.89%	1.65%	2.22%
Dividend payout	21.42%	17.65%	12.57%	24.40%	30.67%	22.71%
Earnings per share	$12.0791	$10.2847	$9.2107	$2.1643	$1.6355	$1.8671
Book value per share	$18.7673	$17.3418	$10.0560	$5.3271	$4.4407	$3.8317
P/E	12.1499	12.7277	8.8300	12.8957	18.6365	10.2461
Market to book ratio	7.8200	8.4628	14.5943	5.2393	6.8637	4.9926
Values						
Market value of equity	$180,220	$191,572	$196,526	$241,924	$271,516	$181,161

1. What is the relationship between a company's inventory and receivable turnover ratios and its operating cycle?

2. When comparing companies, why might an analyst use the companies' operating profit margin instead of the companies' net profit margin?

3. What type of information is provided about a company's financial leverage by the debt ratio, the debt-equity ratio, the TIE ratio, and the cash flow to debt ratio?

4. What useful information do we obtain from the P/E ratio and the M/B ratio?

5. What is the difference between a forward P/E and a trailing P/E?

P/E Ratios and the Economic Environment | LESSONS LEARNED

Consider the P/E ratios of Whirlpool and Wal-Mart over the period 2002 to 2009, which includes the recession that began in December 2007:

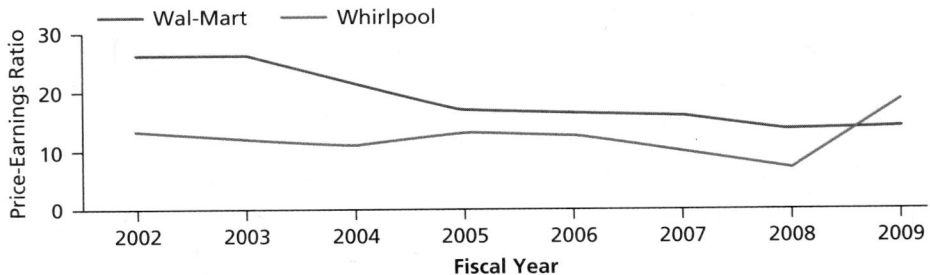

It appears that Whirlpool's P/E ratio improved. Does this mean that investors have revised their expectations of Whirlpool's growth? Does this mean that investors expect Whirlpool to grow more than Wal-Mart? Not necessarily.

Compare the paths of the two companies' P/E ratios with the path of their earnings:

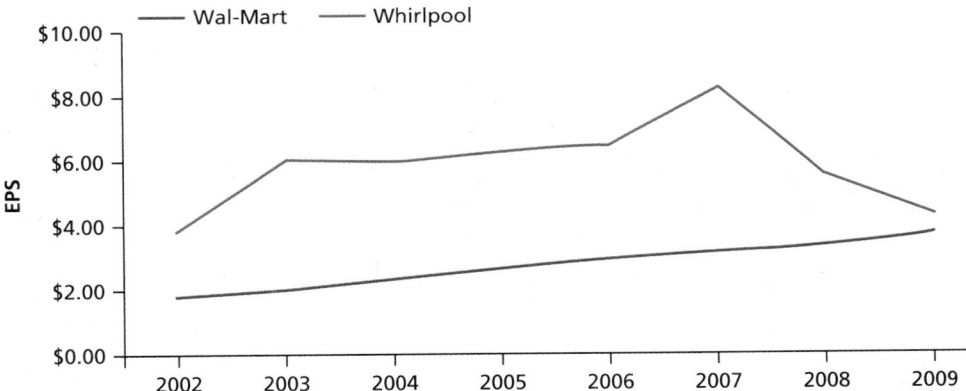

Wal-Mart's earnings appear unaffected by the recession, whereas those of Whirlpool fell during the recession. Wal-Mart typifies a defensive stock, one whose fortunes are relatively unaffected by the economic climate. Whirlpool, on the other hand, is a cyclical stock, whose fortunes move with the general economy.

So why the appearance of improvement for Whirlpool? The P/E's numerator—the price per share—is forward looking, but the denominator—earnings per share—is backward looking. Whirlpool's P/E appears to improve over the recession, but Wal-Mart's P/E does not see such improvement. This is referred to as the Molodovsky effect, which is the overstatement of P/E ratios of cyclical companies, such as Whirlpool in a recession.[34] On the other hand, a defensive stock, such as Wal-Mart, is not as sensitive to the general economy as are other stocks, and its P/E does not tend to be distorted in different economic climates.

---

[34] This observation is attributed to Nicholas Molodovsky, "A Theory of Price Earnings Ratios," *Financial Analysts Journal*, Vol. 51, No. 1 (January/February 1963) pp. 44–50.

4.3   USING FINANCIAL RATIOS

Financial ratios are used for a variety of purposes, but most often as a gauge of a company's financial condition, its ability to meet its obligations, and its performance. We discuss two approaches to using financial ratios: the DuPont system and comparisons of ratios across companies and across time.

Return Ratios and the DuPont System

Return ratios are "bottom-line" ratios that are useful in summarizing a company's performance over a period of time. The two most widely used return ratios are the return on assets and the return on equity.

return on assets (ROA)
net income divided by total assets

The **return on assets (ROA)** is a measure of how well a company's management has put the company's assets to work to produce a profit, and it is the ratio of net income to total assets:

$$\text{Return on assets} = \frac{\text{Net income}}{\text{Total assets}} \tag{4-32}$$

For IBM in 2010,

$$\text{ROA} = \frac{\$14{,}833 \text{ million}}{\$113{,}450 \text{ million}} = 0.1307 \text{ or } 13.07\%$$

return on equity (ROE)
net income divided by shareholders' equity

The **return on equity (ROE)** is the centerpiece of the analysis of a company's financial health. We use ROE to measure the return earned by the owners on their investment in a company. We calculate ROE as the ratio of net income to shareholders' equity:[35]

$$\text{Return on equity} = \frac{\text{Net income}}{\text{Shareholders' equity}} \tag{4-33}$$

The 2010 ROE for IBM Inc. is:

$$\text{Return on equity} = \frac{\$14{,}833 \text{ million}}{\$23{,}046 \text{ million}} = 0.6436 \text{ or } 64.36\%$$

Though at first glance this may seem like a high return on equity, keep in mind that any ratio is affected by both the numerator and the denominator. Therefore, a company may have an ROE that increases over time if its net income increases or its shareholders' equity shrinks.

ROE is not a "pure" financial ratio because it involves dividing an income statement (flow) item by a balance sheet (stock) item.[36] As a result, some people estimate the ROE as net income divided by the "average" shareholders' equity, that is, the average of the starting and ending shareholders' equity. This adjustment acknowledges that net income is earned throughout the year, so it makes sense to divide by an average of shareholders' equity to recognize that not all of those funds were invested throughout the year. For example, the ending shareholders' equity is partly the result of the retained earnings for the year, which in turn is dependent on the net income for the year; however, with three years of data, the use of the average shareholders' equity causes the loss of an observation. As a result, most analysts use the ending shareholders' equity as the denominator simply to get more estimates of the ROE; that way, they can assess a trend over time. However, this

[35] ROE can also be defined as net income available to the common shareholders (i.e., Net income – Preferred dividends) ÷ Common equity (CE). For IBM, there is no difference, because it does not have any preferred equity. For some companies, it can make a difference.

[36] "Pure" ratios involve dividing an income statement item by another income statement item, or dividing a balance sheet item by another balance sheet item.

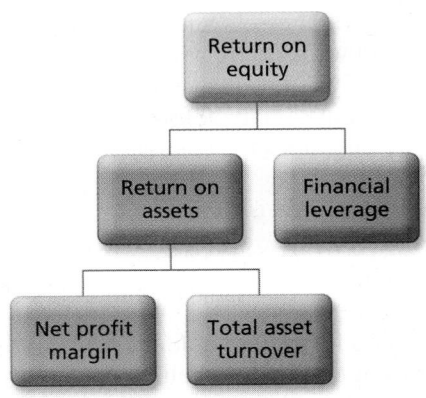

FIGURE 4-4 The DuPont System

tends to understate a company's profitability on average because the ending shareholders' equity will usually exceed the average for the year if the company is profitable.

When we analyze a company, there is a great deal of focus on the return ratios because they tend to capture a great deal of information. We can "decompose" both the return on assets and the return on equity using the DuPont System, which was pioneered by the DuPont Corporation. We provide a variation of the expansion of the return on equity in Figure 4-4.

The **DuPont system** provides a good starting point for any financial analysis and is commonly included in research reports as a way of summarizing a company's key financial ratios. In Table 4-8 we provide the information for IBM for fiscal years (FY) 2009 and 2010. We do not comment on the items in the table now, but you will see how all the reported figures and ratios are related as you proceed through this section, with particular emphasis on the 2010 numbers.

DuPont system method of analyzing return ratios by breaking down these ratios into their components

TABLE 4-8 Return on Equity Analysis of IBM, Fiscal Years 2009 and 2010

From the financial statements	FY2010	FY2009
(in millions)		
Revenue	$99,870	$95,759
Pretax income	$19,723	$18,138
Net income	$14,833	$13,425
Total assets	$113,450	$109,024
Shareholders' equity	$23,046	$22,637
Ratios		
Pretax margin	19.75%	18.94%
× Tax retention rate	75.21%	74.02%
= Net profit margin	14.85%	14.02%
× Turnover ratio	0.8803	0.8783
= Return on assets	13.07%	12.31%
× Leverage	4.9228	4.8162
= Return on equity	64.34%	59.31%

Source: *Data from IBM 10-K filing, 2010*

If we multiply the ROA by total assets and then divide by shareholders' equity, the total asset terms cancel out, and we wind up with the return on equity. More specifically, in the DuPont analysis the financial leverage ratio is the equity multiplier. The equity multiplier is a measure of how many dollars of total assets are supported by each dollar of shareholders' equity, or how many times the company has leveraged the capital provided by the shareholders into total financing.

The 2010 equity multiplier for IBM is 4.9228:

$$\text{Equity multiplier} = \frac{\$113,450 \text{ million}}{\$23,046 \text{ million}} = 4.92276$$

Thus, IBM has *leveraged* every dollar of shareholders' equity into $4.9228 of total financing by using debt and other forms of liabilities to help finance its operations.

The way to interpret this ratio is that every dollar of total assets earned an ROA of 14.85%, but the shareholders didn't provide all this financing. They provided about one-quarter of the money to buy the company's total assets (i.e., $1 \div 4.9228 = 20.31\%$)—that is, the company leveraged up each dollar of shareholders' equity by 4.9228. As a result,

$$\text{Return on equity} = \text{Return on assets} \times \text{Equity multiplier}$$

$$\text{Return on equity} = \frac{\text{Net income}}{\text{Total assets}} \times \frac{\text{Total assets}}{\text{Shareholders' equity}}$$

$$\text{Return on equity} = 0.130745 \times 4.92276$$

$$\text{Return on equity} = 0.6436 \text{ or } 64.36\%$$

What this 64.36% figure means is that part of the reason for IBM's higher ROE is that it is profitable. The rest of the story is that IBM magnified its ROA by using a significant amount of financial leverage. As a result, when we analyze corporate performance, we look at ROE, ROA, and a series of ratios that measure financial leverage.

We can now decompose ROA into two of its major components: the company's net profit margin and its total asset turnover ratio. We know that:

$$\text{Net profit margin} = \frac{\text{Net income}}{\text{Sales}}$$

When we multiply the net profit margin by the asset turnover, the revenues figure on the bottom of net profit margin cancels out the revenues figure on the top of the turnover ratio, leaving net income ÷ total assets, or simply the ROA:

$$\text{ROA} = \frac{\text{Net income}}{\text{Revenues}} \times \frac{\text{Revenues}}{\text{Total assets}} = \frac{\text{Net income}}{\text{Total assets}}$$

As you can see in this equation, the net profit margin and the asset turnover are connected by revenues, which cancel.

Now we have the major ratios of the DuPont formula. Putting them all together produces the following equation:[37]

$$\text{Return on equity} = \frac{\text{Net income}}{\text{Shareholders' equity}}$$

$$\text{Return on equity} = \frac{\text{Net income}}{\text{Revenues}} \times \frac{\text{Revenues}}{\text{Total assets}} \times \frac{\text{Total assets}}{\text{Shareholders' equity}}$$

Return on equity = Net profit margin × Asset turnover ratio × Equity multiplier (4-34)

---

[37] This is the simplest and most commonly used version of the DuPont system. There are other versions, which we do not discuss here, many of which break ROE into five or more components.

TABLE 4-9   The DuPont Breakdown of IBM's Fiscal Year 2010 Return on Equity

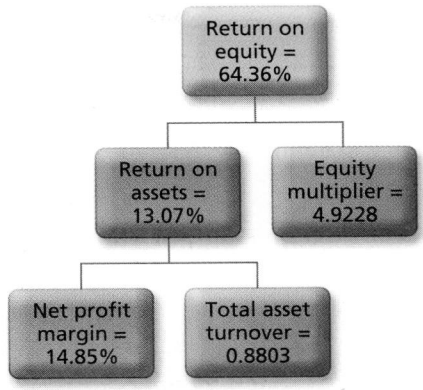

For IBM in 2010,

$$\text{ROE} = \frac{\text{Net income}}{\text{Revenues}} \times \frac{\text{Revenues}}{\text{Total assets}} \times \frac{\text{Total assets}}{\text{Shareholders' equity}}$$

$$= 0.1485 \times 0.8803 \times 4.9228$$

$$= 64.36\%$$

We summarize the breakdown of IBM's 2010 ROE in Table 4-9. Each dollar of equity supported $4.9228 of assets, which in turn generated $0.8803 in revenues, which then yielded a net profit margin of 14.85%. In other words, overall the ROE is determined by leverage, turnover, and profit margin. We summarize IBM's DuPont analysis ratios for fiscal years 2008 through 2010 in Table 4-10. So what does this mean?

What we can observe from Table 4-10 is that:

- IBM is consistently profitable; and
- the net profit margin over this period showed very little variation, but the leverage decreased dramatically from 2008 to 2009 due to a decrease in shareholders' equity during 2008 from share buybacks and pension plan remeasurements.[38]

So how does IBM compare with other information technology companies? Ideally, we would compare IBM to another technology company of similar size, or even an industry average comprising several similar companies. We provide a comparison of IBM with Microsoft later in this chapter.

TABLE 4-10   IBM's DuPont Ratios, Fiscal Years 2008 Through 2010

	FY2010	*FY2009*	*FY2008*
Net profit margin	14.85%	14.02%	11.90%
Total asset turnover ratio	0.8803	0.8783	0.9462
Return on assets	13.07%	12.31%	11.26%
Equity multiplier	4.9228	4.8162	8.1334
Return on equity	64.36%	59.31%	91.59%

[38] Pension plan remeasurements include changes in the assumptions made in terms of the expected return on plan assets and actuarial assumptions.

EXAMPLE 4.3

Applying the DuPont System

PROBLEM

The ABC Company reported the following results:

	Year 1	Year 2
Net income	$500	$600
Total assets	$4,000	$4,500
Shareholders' equity	$3,000	$3,000
Revenues	$10,000	$11,000

Apply the DuPont System to determine why the return on assets and return on equity changed from Year 1 to Year 2.

Solution

	Year 1	Year 2
Return on assets	12.50%	13.33%
Return on equity	16.67%	20.00%

Both the return on assets and the return on equity increased from Year 1 to Year 2. This increase is due to two factors:

1. an increase in efficiency, as represented by the increase in the net profit margin, and
2. an increase in the relative use of debt (vis-à-vis equity):

	Year 1	Year 2
Net profit margin	5.00%	5.45%
Total asset turnover	2.5000	2.4444
Equity multiplier	1.3333	1.5000

Comparisons of Ratios Across Time

Because a given ratio at a given point in time is not meaningful, it is necessary to make comparisons over time and across companies:

- What is the trend in a ratio over time?
- How does the ratio for a company differ from those of its competitors?
- How does the trend in a ratio compare with the trend in the same ratio for a competitor?
- What is the picture of a company's financial health and performance once you look at several different dimensions of the company's condition?

As an example of the time-series analysis of financial ratios, consider Circuit City, a retailer of electronics who filed for bankruptcy in November of 2008. As you can see in Panel A of Figure 4.5, Circuit City's return on equity declined starting after fiscal year 2004, falling to –21.28% in fiscal year 2007. As a first pass in understanding the fall in the ROE, we can look at the DuPont components in Panel B. Circuit City's asset turnover, which represents its productivity, was in a range of 2.5 to 3.3 for the entire 1993–2007 period, and its equity multiplier, representing its financial leverage, was in the range of 1.6 to 2.5 during this same period. What is noticeable, however, is that Circuit City's net profit margin, which captures its efficiency in managing its expenses, fell after 2004. Taking a closer look at how Circuit City operates, the drop in the profit margin follows its elimination of its commission sales force in 2003 and an aggressive expansion into electronics by Wal-Mart stores.

Another consideration is that a company may have had a significant acquisition or a significant divestiture in recent years, which means that looking at trends may not be

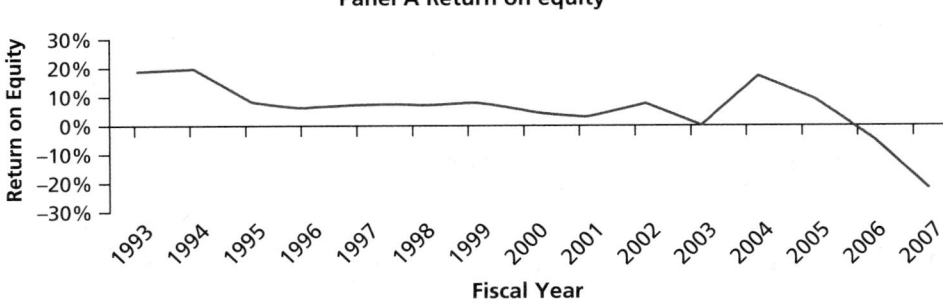

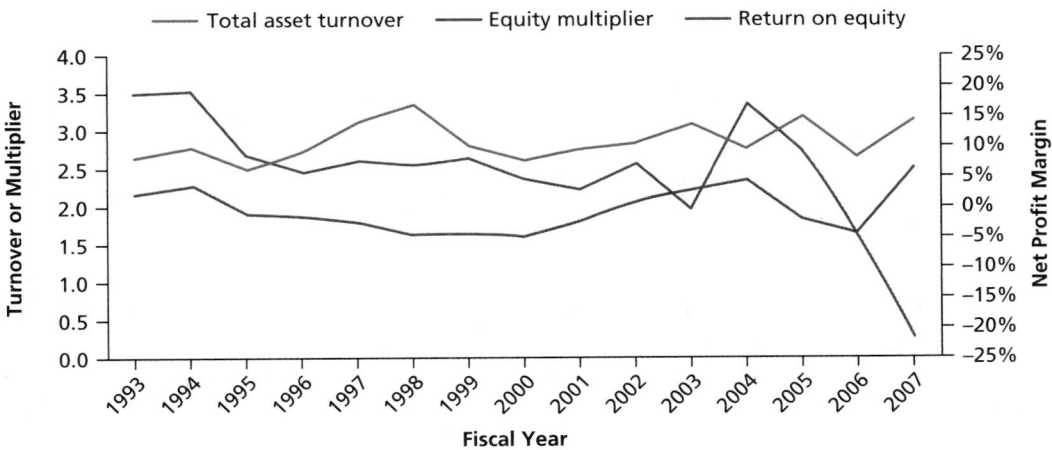

FIGURE 4-5 Circuit City Return on Equity and Return on Equity Components, Fiscal Years 1993 Through 2007

appropriate. For example, if Company A is in an industry with customary credit terms for customers of 40 days, and it acquires another company, Company B, in a different line of business with customary credit terms of 100 days, you will likely observe an abrupt shift in Company A's receivables turnover, average collection period, and operating cycle at the time of the acquisition and in future years. Therefore, you must take care in evaluating trends in ratios.

Comparison of Ratios Across Companies

It is useful to compare the ratios of a company with those of companies in a similar line of business or in the same industry. The issue becomes one of identifying what companies are comparable, and how to make comparisons with the financial ratios of those companies. Often we resort to using industry averages of financial ratios.

Based on the financial ratios and valuations, what do we make of IBM as a potential investment? Comparing IBM to Microsoft:

- IBM has less liquidity than Microsoft;
- IBM has a higher receivables turnover than Microsoft;
- IBM has inventory fewer days than does Microsoft;
- IBM has lower profitability than Microsoft; and
- IBM has more financial leverage than Microsoft, which results in more exaggeration between its return on assets and its return on equity.

Further, IBM plows back almost 80% of its earnings, pays consistent dividends, and has a P/E ratio that is less than the typical stock. As a result, IBM would be considered a value stock. Whether this is an appropriate stock for an investment, however, requires knowing much more about the appropriateness of the stock for the investor's objectives and, hence, the investor's portfolio, issues that we address in later chapters.

Making comparisons, we can contrast one company with another company in the same line of business, as we did with IBM and Microsoft, or we could compare a company with a group of companies in the industry or with the entire industry.

One of the problems that you may encounter is that determining the industry may be a challenge. For example, if you were comparing Walt Disney Company with its industry, do you compare it with amusement parks? Hotels? Entertainment companies? Walt Disney has significant interests in each of these areas. But do other companies have similar interests in similar proportions that would make a good comparable company for Walt Disney Company? Not really.

If you can define the industry and members of the industry, another problem is deciding whether to compare a company with all companies in the industry or a subset. Do you want to compare the company with the leaders in the industry? Do you want to compare the company to those with market shares above a certain threshold? Do you want to compare the company with only domestic competitors, or do you wish to include global competitors? Consider Coca-Cola, a large U.S.-based beverage company. Do we want to compare Coca-Cola with PepsiCo. Inc. and Dr. Pepper Snapple Group? Do we want to include Jones Soda, which has 1/1000 the revenues of Coca-Cola? Do we want to compare Coca-Cola with its global competitors such as Anheuser-Busch Inbev SA, which produces soft drinks as well as beer products? These are all decisions to be addressed in an analysis of Coca-Cola.

Still another problem is determining what type of average to use if you are comparing a company to a group of competitors. Do you use an average that is the equally weighted average of the companies' ratios or a value-weighted average? An equal-weighted average—which is a simple average—considers each comparable company the same importance. A value-weighted average gives more weight to the larger comparables. Calculating an equal-weighted ratio is simple: add up the ratios of the comparables, and divide by the number of comparables. Calculating a value-weighted ratio is also simple: sum the numerators of the ratios of the comparables, sum the denominators of the ratios of the comparables, and then take the ratio of these two sums. When do you use which one? If you are evaluating a company that is seeking to compete with the larger companies in the industry, you likely will want to use the value-weighted average. If, however, you want to compare a company with the typical company in the industry, you most likely will prefer to use the equal-weighted average.

EXAMPLE 4.4	**PROBLEM**	
Equal-Weighted Versus Value-Weighted Averages	Consider the following three companies in an industry, which you would like to use as representing the industry in your analysis:	

	Current assets	Current liabilities	Current ratio
Company Big	$100,000	$50,000	2.00
Company Medium	$50,000	$40,000	1.25
Company Little	$10,000	$10,000	1.00

1. What is the equal-weighted average current ratio?
2. What is the value-weighted average current ratio?

Solution

1. Equal-weighted average current ratio = (2.0 + 1.25 + 1.0) ÷ 3 = 1.4

2. Value-weighted average current ratio = $\dfrac{\$100,000 + 50,000 + 10,000}{\$50,000 + 40,000 + 10,000} = \dfrac{\$160,000}{\$100,000} = 1.6$

If you use industry averages produced by a third-party financial information provider, you need to consider whether the company you are analyzing is in this industry average and consider if this is what you intended. For example, suppose you are analyzing Archer-Daniels Midland (ADM), an agricultural processor in an industry with very few publicly traded companies. If you compare ADM with its competitors and use an industry average provided, say, by Yahoo! Finance, you will be comparing ADM with an average that it plays a large part in (in other words, you are comparing ADM with itself).

Are U.S. GAAP and IFRS Financial Ratios Comparable? | GLOBAL PERSPECTIVE

Though U.S. generally accepted accounting principles (U.S. GAAP) and International Financial Reporting Standards (IFRS) are scheduled to converge into one set of accounting standards, differences currently exist between U.S. generally accepted accounting principles and the International Financial Reporting Standards, which could, potentially, affect the comparability of financial ratios across companies when these companies use different accounting principles. We can get a glimpse of the differences between the two standards by examining a company's reconciliation between financial statements created based on IFRS and financial statements based on U.S. GAAP.

SAP is a German software development company that uses IFRS for its domestic reporting. Though no longer required by the Securities and Exchange Commission, it elects to report using U.S. GAAP for its filings with the U.S. Securities and Exchange Commission.[39] SAP reports for fiscal year 2008:

	IFRS	U.S. GAAP	Difference
Revenue	€11,575	€11,565	€10
Operating expenses	€8874	€8725	€149
Operating profit margin	23.3%	24.6%	

Therefore, the operating profit margin is higher using U.S. GAAP than IFRS for SAP in 2008.

Studies comparing IFRS and U.S. GAAP do not report consistency in terms of whether U.S. GAAP income is higher or lower than IFRS income; the differences are company specific.[40]

Nationally Recognized Statistical Rating Organizations | ETHICS

The subprime crisis and the economic slowdown in 2008 brought to light issues related to nationally recognized statistical rating organizations (NRSROs), more familiarly known as credit rating agencies, and the potential conflicts of interest. These agencies, which include Standard & Poor's, Moody's, and Fitch, provide credit ratings of securities that investors have come to rely on.

NRSROs provide ratings of the creditworthiness of securities such as bonds and mortgage-backed securities. These organizations provide ratings by examining the financial condition of the issuer of the securities. Financial ratios are a significant part of the evaluation of a security issuer's creditworthiness.

Setting the stage for further regulation of NRSROs, the Securities and Exchange Commission (SEC) examined the process of rating and these potential conflicts.[41] Among the many issues cited regarding the credit ratings' role in the crisis were the conflicts of interest that exist between

[39] The U.S. SEC eliminated the requirement of reconciliation between U.S. GAAP and IFRS effective for fiscal years ending after November 15, 2007, Release No. 33-8879 (Dec. 21, 2007), 17 CFR Parts 210, 230, 239 and 249. However, companies may still elect to provide this information.
[40] Betty Chavis and Vivek Mande, "US GAAP/IFRS Convergence: An Analysis of 20 F Reconciliations," working paper, September 2006.
[41] Office of Compliance Inspections and Examinations, Division of Trading and Markets and Office of Economic Analysis, U.S. Securities and Exchange Commission, July 2008.

the issuer and the rating agencies. The model that has been in existence up until now has been the "issuer pays" model:

- The security issuer pays the rating agency to rate the security.
- Up until recently, the rating agency's analysts could participate in the fee-setting negotiations with the issuer.

- The security issuer, especially in the case of the designer/arranger of the security (such as mortgaged-backed securities), has the flexibility of altering the security based on raters' responses so that the security would have the desired rating.

The SEC adopted new rules in 2007 to increase transparency, accountability, and competition among the raters.[42]

Concept Review Questions

1. Why is it not appropriate to interpret a single ratio at a single point in time?

2. Suppose a company observes that its net operating cycle has been declining over time. How would you analyze the net operating cycle to further understand this trend?

3. What factors are the drivers to a company's return on equity?

SUMMARY

- The return on equity is a measure of a company's performance. We can break it down into components—profitability, efficiency, and financial leverage—using the DuPont system to examine changes in a company's return on equity.

- Financial ratios are a useful tool in examining a company's financial leverage, efficiency, productivity, liquidity, and value, either from the perspective of the company's management, or from the perspective of creditors and owners.

- A given financial ratio cannot be examined in isolation, but examining ratios over time for a company or across an industry provides a picture of the company's financial performance and condition.

FORMULAS/EQUATIONS

(4-1)   Working capital ratio $= \dfrac{\text{Current assets}}{\text{Total assets}}$

(4-2)   Current ratio $= \dfrac{\text{Current assets}}{\text{Current liabilities}}$

(4-3)   Quick ratio $= \dfrac{\text{Cash} + \text{Marketable securities} + \text{Accounts receivable}}{\text{Current liabilities}}$

(4-4)   Operating cycle $= \dfrac{\text{Days of sales}}{\text{in inventory}} + \dfrac{\text{Days sales}}{\text{outstanding}}$

(4-5)   Days sales in inventory $= \dfrac{\text{Inventory}}{\text{Average day's sales}}$

(4-6)   Days sales in inventory $= \dfrac{\text{Inventory}}{\left(\dfrac{\text{Cost of goods sold}}{365} \right)}$

---

[42] This was in response to the Credit Rating Agency Reform Act of 2006.

(4-7) $\text{Days sales outstanding} = \dfrac{\text{Accounts receivable}}{\text{Average day's sales}}$

(4-8) $\text{Days sales outstanding} = \dfrac{\text{Accounts receivable}}{\dfrac{\text{Credit sales}}{365}}$

(4-9) $\text{Net operating cycle} = \dfrac{\text{Days of sales}}{\text{in inventory}} + \dfrac{\text{Days sales}}{\text{outstanding}} - \dfrac{\text{Days purchases}}{\text{outstanding}}$

(4-10) $\text{Days of purchases outstanding} = \dfrac{\text{Accounts payable}}{\dfrac{\text{Purchases}}{365}}$

(4-11) $\text{Operating break-even} = \dfrac{\text{Fixed costs}}{\text{Contribution margin}}$

(4-12) $\text{Gross profit margin} = \dfrac{\text{Revenues} - \text{Cost of goods sold}}{\text{Revenues}}$

(4-13) $\text{Operating profit margin} = \dfrac{\text{Net operating income}}{\text{Revenues}}$

(4-14) $\text{Net profit margin} = \dfrac{\text{Net income}}{\text{Revenues}}$

(4-15) $\text{Receivables turnover} = \dfrac{\text{Revenues}}{\text{Accounts receivable}}$

(4-16) $\text{Inventory turnover} = \dfrac{\text{Cost of goods sold}}{\text{Inventory}}$

(4-17) $\text{Fixed asset turnover} = \dfrac{\text{Sales}}{\text{Net fixed assets}}$

(4-18) $\text{Total asset turnover ratio} = \dfrac{\text{Revenues}}{\text{Total assets}}$

(4-19) $\text{Debt ratio} = \dfrac{\text{Total debt}}{\text{Total assets}}$

(4-20) $\text{Debt-to-invested capital} = \dfrac{\text{Debt}}{\text{Invested capital}}$

(4-21) $\text{Debt-equity ratio} = \dfrac{\text{Debt}}{\text{Shareholders' equity}}$

(4-22) $\text{Equity multiplier} = \dfrac{\text{Total assets}}{\text{Shareholders' equity}}$

(4-23) $\text{Times interest earned} = \dfrac{\text{Earnings before interest and taxes}}{\text{Interest}}$

(4-24) $\text{Cash flow to debt} = \dfrac{\text{Cash flow from operations}}{\text{Debt}}$

(4-25) $\text{Dividend yield} = \dfrac{\text{Dividend per share}}{\text{Price per share}}$

(4-26) $\text{Dividend payout} = \dfrac{\text{Dividend per share}}{\text{Earnings per share}} = \dfrac{\text{DPS}}{\text{EPS}}$

(4-27) $\text{Plowback ratio} = \dfrac{\text{Retained earnings}}{\text{Earnings per share}} = 1 - \dfrac{\text{DPS}}{\text{EPS}}$

(4-28) $\text{Book value per share (BVPS)} = \dfrac{\text{Shareholders' equity}}{\text{Number of shares}}$

(4-29) Market-to-book (M/B) $= \dfrac{\text{Price per share}}{\text{Book value per share}}$

(4-30) P/E $= \dfrac{\text{Price per share}}{\text{Earnings per share}} = \dfrac{P}{EPS}$

(4-31) Forward P/E $= \dfrac{\text{Price per share}}{\text{Expected earnings per share}}$

(4-32) Return on assets $= \dfrac{\text{Net income}}{\text{Sales}} \times \dfrac{\text{Sales}}{\text{Total assets}}$

(4-33) Return on equity $= \dfrac{\text{Net income}}{\text{Shareholders' equity}}$

(4-34) Return on equity $=$ Net profit margin $\times$ Total asset turnover ratio $\times$ Equity multiplier

QUESTIONS AND PROBLEMS

Multiple Choice

Use the following information to answer Questions 1 through 6.

Balance Sheet as of December 31, 2012
(in millions)

Cash	$400,000	Accounts payable	$500,000
Marketable securities	500,000	Accrued liabilities	90,000
Inventory	250,000	Wages payable	150,000
Equipment	1,000,000	Long-term debt	2,000,000
Land	2,500,000	Common stock	2,800,000
Patent	980,000	Retained earnings	90,000
Total assets	$5,630,000	Total liabilities and equity	$5,630,000

Income Statement 2012
(in millions)

Sales	$1,090,000
Cost of goods sold	380,000
General, selling, and administration expenses	200,000
Interest	150,000
Earnings before taxes	$360,000
Tax	108,000
Net income	$252,000

1. The debt ratio is *closest* to:
   A. 0.36.   B. 0.49.   C. 0.55.   D. 0.94.

2. The debt-equity ratio and times interest earned ratio are *closest* to:
   A. 0.69; 2.4.   B. 0.69; 3.4.   C. 0.95; 2.4.   D. 0.95; 3.4.

3. The gross profit and the operating margin are *closest* to:
   A. 35%; 23%.   B. 35%; 47%.   C. 65%; 23%.   D. 65%; 47%.

4. The average days sales in inventory is *closest* to:
    A. 240 days.   B. 260 days.   C. 555 days.

5. The working capital ratio is *closest* to:
    A. 7.3%.   B. 18.5%.   C. 20.4%.   D. 24.0%.

6. Invested capital is *closest* to:
    A. $2,890,000.   B. $4,800,000.   C. $4,890,000.   D. $5,630,000.

7. A company with total assets of $100 million, total liabilities of $50 million, and return on assets of 5%, has a return on equity closest to:
    A. 2.5%.   B. 10%.   C. 15%.

8. A company that has an increase in its return on assets, but has no noticeable change in asset turnover, *most likely* has experienced:
    A. a decrease in its net profit margin.   C. a decrease in its financial leverage.
    B. an increase in its net profit margin.   D. an increase in its financial leverage.

9. A company with a net profit margin of 10% and an asset turnover of five times has a return on assets closest to:
    A. 5%.   B. 10%.   C. 15%.   D. 50%.

10. To increase return on equity (ROE),
    A. increase equity, all else being unchanged.
    B. decrease debt outstanding, all else being unchanged.
    C. decrease earnings after tax, all else being unchanged.
    D. decrease the corporate tax rate, all else being unchanged.

Practice Problems and Questions

4.1   A Framework for Financial Analysis

11. Suppose a company extended the useful lives of its equipment this fiscal year.
    A. What types of ratios would be affected? What effect would this have on this year's financial ratios?
    B. What effect would this have on comparisons of this company's ratio over time?

12. The Hungry Caterpillar Company acquired another company this year that is approximately 20% of the size of HCC.
    A. What types of ratios would be affected? What effect would this have on this year's financial ratios?
    B. What effect would this have on comparisons of HCC's ratio over time?

13. Sue Analyst calculated the quick ratio of the Meridian Corporation for 2013 to be 1.5 times. Sue has concluded that this means that the Meridian Corporation has sufficient liquidity because it has 1.5 times the "quick" assets that it needs to meet its short-term obligations. Is Sue's interpretation correct? Explain.

14. Joe Calc has calculated the inventory turnover of the Apple Turnover Company to be thirty times this fiscal year and twenty-five times the previous fiscal year. Joe is interpreting this increase to an improvement in the company's use of its assets, and that thirty times means that the company is doing quite well. Do you agree with Joe? Explain.

15. An analyst has observed that the profitability of the Radford Company improved, with a net profit margin of 10% during the most recent fiscal year, compared to a 9% net profit margin the previous year. The analyst concluded that this improvement in net profit margin means that the company is doing well and being efficient in the management of its expenses. Do you agree with the analyst? Explain.

4.2   Financial Ratios

16. What distinguishes a current ratio from a quick ratio? Why would you prefer to use one versus the other in the financial analysis of a company?

17. What is the relationship between the days sales outstanding and the receivables turnover?

18. What is the relationship between the inventory turnover and the days sales in inventory? Demonstrate this relationship using equations.

19. If a company has a current ratio that is increasing through time, does this mean that the company is doing well? Explain.

20. Is it possible for a company to have a net operating cycle that is negative? Explain.

21. For each of the following, explain what distinguishes the two items listed in each:
    A. Current ratio and quick ratio.
    B. Dividend yield and dividend payout.

22. Which profit margin(s) are affected by a company's financing decisions?

23. What distinguishes total debt from total liabilities?

24. What is invested capital?

25. Chapel Hill Co. reports the following:

Inventories	$650,000
Current assets	$1,200,000
Total liabilities	$3,500,000
Long-term debt	$2,099,000

    What are the current ratio and the quick ratio for the Chapel Hill Co.?

26. Using the calculated ratios provided in this chapter, what is Microsoft's operating cycle for fiscal years 2009 and 2010?

27. The Seattle Settie Company had credit sales of $1 billion for the most recent fiscal year and has a balance of $125 million accounts receivable at the end of the fiscal year. The company would like to reduce the credit terms to match the industry average days' sales outstanding of 35 days. If the company expects credit sales of $1.1 billion next year, what would the balance in accounts receivable be if Seattle Settie achieves the industry average collection period?

28. Complete the following table for Lubbock Lock Company's most recent fiscal year:

Inventory turnover	12 times
Receivables turnover	
Days sales in inventory	
Days sales outstanding	60.833 days
Days purchases outstanding	45.000 days
Operating cycle	
Net operating cycle	

29. Buckeye Tree Company is interested in reducing its investment in inventory to levels that are more comparable to those of its competitors. Its competitors typically have 30 days of inventory on hand, whereas Buckeye currently has 40 days on hand. Buckeye predicts that its average day's sales will remain at $4 million next year.
    A. If Buckeye alters its inventory control to have only 30 days of inventory on hand, what do you expect the change in inventory next year compared to the current year to be?
    B. If Buckeye alters its inventory control to have only 30 days of inventory on hand, how will next period's inventory turnover compare to this period's?

30. If a business has a gross profit margin of 40% and revenues of $100 million, what is its cost of goods sold?

31. Consider the following information from the income statement of the Roanoke River Company and the related profit margins, and complete the table:

Revenues	$1,000
Cost of goods sold	
Gross profit	$400
Selling, general, and administrative expenses	
Operating profit	
Interest	$50
Earnings before taxes	
Taxes	$63
Net income	$188

Gross profit margin	40%
Operating profit margin	30%
Net profit margin	
Tax rate	

32. Suppose a company has a contribution margin of 6%, a unit sales price of $10, and operating fixed costs of $100 million.
   A. What is the break-even level of sales?
   B. What is the company's operating profit margin at the operating break-even level of sales?

33. Suppose a company has a contribution margin of 25%, a unit sales price of $100, and fixed operating costs of $500 million.
   A. What is the operating break-even level of sales?
   B. Graph the operating profit for this company for unit sales ranging from 1 million to 30 million.

34. Consider the following accounting data for Bindee Corporation:

Accounts receivable	$500,000
Accounts payable	$305,000
Inventory	$200,000
Gross profit	$250,000
Revenues	$950,000

   A. Calculate the receivables turnover, inventory turnover, and days sales outstanding.
   B. Interpret the days sales outstanding.

35. Suppose that the Provo Proofing Company (PPC) has an inventory turnover of fifty times for the current fiscal year. If PPC has revenues of $100 million and a gross profit margin of 40% for the year, what is PPC's amount of inventory at the end of the year?

36. If a company has an inventory turnover of four times and a receivables turnover of eight times, what is the company's operating cycle?

37. Consider the following information from a company's balance sheet, in millions:

Accounts payable	$2,000
Wages payable	1,000
Accrued expenses	400
Notes payable	500
Current portion of long-term debt	100
Long-term debt	2,000

A. What is the amount of the company's total liabilities?

B. What is the amount of the company's interest-bearing debt?

38. Luxury retail companies tend to have earnings that vary with the economy. In interpreting the P/E multiple for these companies, would you want to use a trailing P/E or a forward P/E?

39. Suppose a company has a dividend yield of 5%. If the price of a share of the company's stock is $30, what is the dollar amount of dividend per share of stock?

40. An analyst has observed that the Staunton Grocery has a book value per share of $3, compared to its competitor that has a book value per share of $5. The analyst concluded that the Staunton Grocery is not doing as well as its competitors based on this. Do you agree? Explain.

41. Consider the following data for Athens Associates, Inc.:

Shareholders' equity	$945,000
Number of shares outstanding	500,000
Cash dividends	$150,000
Market price of each share	$9.50
Net income	$433,000

Calculate book value per share, dividend yield, dividend payout, and market-to-book ratio.

4.3 Using Financial Ratios

42. Suppose a company's equity multiplier is increasing through time.

A. What does this mean in terms of the company's capital structure?

B. What does this mean in terms of the relationship between the return on assets and the return on equity for the company over time?

43. Consider a company that has a return on assets of 10% and a return on equity of 25%.

A. What is the company's equity multiplier?

B. What is the company's ratio of liabilities to total assets?

44. If a company has a return on equity of 30% and an equity multiplier of 1.5, what is this company's return on assets?

45. Suppose you observe the following for a company:

	Fiscal Year		
Ratio	*20X1*	*20X2*	*20X3*
Return on equity	12%	14%	15%
Return on assets	5%	6%	8%
Net profit margin	3%	2%	2%

What conclusions can you draw from this information regarding the company's financial leverage and productivity?

46. Consider Happy Burger company, which reports the following:

	Fiscal Year		
(in millions)	*20X5*	*20X6*	*20X7*
Total liabilities	$400	$500	$600
Shareholders' equity	$800	$900	$1,000

Has Happy Burger's financial leverage increased or decreased over this 3-year period? Use one or more of the financial leverage ratios to support your conclusion.

47. The Duke Pet Supply Company reported the following financial information for its most recent fiscal year:

Income Statement, for Fiscal Year 2013

(in millions)

Revenues	$1,000
Cost of goods sold	700
Selling, general, and administrative expenses	100
Earnings before interest and taxes	$200
Interest expense	50
Earnings before taxes	$150
Taxes	60
Net income	$90

Balance Sheet, as of December 31, 2013

(in millions)

Cash and cash equivalents	$10
Accounts receivable	40
Inventory	50
Net plant, property, and equipment	800
Intangible assets	50
Total assets	$950
Current liabilities	$75
Long-term debt	300
Shareholders' equity	575
Total liabilities and shareholders' equity	$950

Additional information for the company is also available:

Market value of equity	$700 million
Market value of debt	$400 million
Dividends	$30 million
Number of shares outstanding	10 million

Complete the following table:

Return on assets		Times interest earned	
Return on equity		Inventory turnover	
Current ratio		Receivables turnover	
Quick ratio		Days sales in inventory	
Working capital ratio		Days sales outstanding	
Gross profit margin		Operating cycle	
Operating profit margin		Market-to-book	
Net profit margin		Market value equity per share	
Equity multiplier		Price-earnings ratio	
Debt ratio		Dividend yield	
Debt-equity ratio		Dividend payout	
		Plowback ratio	

48. Tarheel Shoe Company reports income statement and balance sheet information as follows:

Income Statement, for Fiscal Year 2014

(in millions)

Revenues	$10,000
Cost of goods sold	9,000
Selling, general, and administrative expenses	200
Earnings before interest and taxes	$800
Interest expense	$50
Earnings before taxes	$750
Taxes	300
Net income	$450

Balance Sheet, as of December 31, 2014

(in millions)

Cash and cash equivalents	$100
Accounts receivable	300
Inventory	3,000
Net plant, property, and equipment	5,000
Total assets	$8,400
Current liabilities	$500
Long-term debt	600
Shareholders' equity	7,300
Total liabilities and shareholders' equity	$8,400

Additional information for the company is also available for fiscal year 2014:

Market value of equity	$10,000 million
Market value of debt	$600 million
Dividends	$50 million
Number of shares outstanding	50 million

Complete the following table:

Return on assets		Receivables turnover	
Return on equity		Days sales in inventory	
Current ratio		Times interest earned	
Quick ratio		Inventory turnover	
Working capital ratio		Days sales outstanding	
Gross profit margin		Operating cycle	
Operating profit margin		Market-to-book	
Net profit margin		Market value equity per share	
Equity multiplier		Price-earnings ratio	
Debt ratio		Dividend yield	
Debt-equity ratio		Dividend payout	
		Plowback ratio	

49. Disco Disc, Inc., registered a gross profit margin of 75% on revenues of $16 million in 2012. At the end of 2012, Disco Disc, Inc., had total shareholders' equity of $13.8 million. In 2013, the company had net income of $5.2 million and paid out half of this amount in dividends, resulting in shareholders' equity at the end of 2013 of $16.4 million.

A. What would the company's income statement show for the value of cost of goods sold for fiscal year 2012?

B. Other disc-making companies have an average forward P/E ratio of 12.0 at this time. With a share price of $18.20, what are the expected 2012 EPS for Disco Disc if its forward P/E ratio is the same as the industry average?

50. Consider the following information on BASF SE, a German chemical company with sales throughout the world, in billions of Euros:

	2005	2006	2007	2008	2009	2010
Revenues	42.745	52.61	57.951	62.304	50.693	63.873
Net income	3.007	3.215	4.066	2.912	1.41	4.557
Total assets	35.670	45.291	46.802	50.86	51.268	59.393
Stockholders' equity	17.524	18.578	20.098	18.722	18.609	22.657

A. Calculate the return on assets and return on equity for each year.

B. Explain the changes in returns from year to year using the DuPont system.

Cases

Case 4.1 Ratio Analysis of the Backup Zone

The Backup Zone is a business started by two business students. The Backup Zone provides disc backup services for laptops, home computers, notebooks, readers, phones, and other electronic devices.

Balance Sheet for The Backup Zone
End of the Year Indicated

	Year 1	Year 2
Assets		
Current assets (cash)	$1,150	$493
Property and equipment (net)	3,840	3,888
Total assets	$4,990	$4,381
Liabilities and owners' equity		
Interest payable	$200	$160
Tax payable	177	182
Dividends payable	200	210
Long-term debt	3,200	2,400
Total liabilities	$3,777	$2,952
Common shares	1,000	1,000
Retained earnings	213	429
Total owners' equity	$1,213	$1,429
Total liabilities and owners' equity	$4,990	$4,381

Income Statement for The Backup Zone
(For the Full-Year Indicated)

	Year 1	Year 2
Revenues (net of bad debts)	$1,950	$2,200
Selling and administrative expenses	0	220
Loss (stolen equipment)	160	0
EBITDA	$1,790	$1,980
Amortization expense	1,000	1,212
EBIT	790	768
Interest expense	$200	$160
Earnings before tax	590	608
Tax (30%)	177	182
Net income	$413	$426
Earnings per share (100 shares)	$4.13	$4.26
Dividends per share	$2.00	$2.10

A. Find The Backup Zone's return on equity for Years 1 and 2 using the owners' equity figure at the end of each year. Did this ratio improve or get worse between Year 1 and Year 2?

B. Use the definition of the equity multiplier in the DuPont system to determine if The Backup Zone has become more or less leveraged between Year 1 and Year 2.

C. One key part of ROE in the DuPont system is the return on assets. Find the ROA for The Backup Zone and determine if it is increasing or decreasing.

D. The most recent financial statements for a similar company show that its debt ratio was 0.256 and its debt-to-equity ratio was 0.073. At the end of Year 2, was The Backup Zone more or less leveraged than this major competitor? (Note: For comparison with the comparable company, use only the interest-bearing liabilities, i.e., long-term debt, when calculating the financial leverage ratios.)

E. In the DuPont system, there are two components of ROA. Determine whether efficiency or productivity (or both) is responsible for the increase in ROA for The Backup Zone from Year 1 to Year 2.

F. We can calculate cash flow from operations (CFO) as Net income + Noncash expenses + Change in working capital. Calculate the CFO for Year 2, and use this to calculate the cash flow to debt ratio. How many years would it take for the company to pay off its entire debt load if it devoted its cash flow to debt repayment?

G. Find the operating margin for The Backup Zone for both Year 1 and Year 2 (you may assume that the net operating income is equal to the company's EBIT). Was there an increase or a decrease in the operating margin, and is this a good trend or a bad one?

H. Calculate the fixed asset turnover for The Backup Zone for Years 1 and 2 (note that net fixed assets corresponds to "property and equipment (net)" on the company's balance sheet). Has the company become more or less productive in terms of generating revenues from assets?

I. At the end of its most recent fiscal period, a competitor had a working capital ratio of 4.3% and a current ratio of 18.2%. Calculate these ratios for The Backup Zone at the end of Year 1 and Year 2. Is the company more or less liquid than its competitor?

J. A competitor company had net operating income of $4.426 million and revenues of $30.16 million in its most recent accounting period. Find the operating margin for this competitor. Comment on The Backup Zone's level of operating efficiency compared to this real-world business.

Case 4.2 Applying Altman's Model to IBM

Franklin Minton, an analyst for a mutual fund, believes that as a first pass in selecting investments that the company should be considered as not likely to enter bankruptcy, using a model developed by Edward Altman. Altman's model uses financial ratios to classify companies on the likelihood of entering financial distress in the near future. The financial ratios are weighted, and the product of the weights and ratio produces a score, referred to as a Z-score:

$$Z\text{-score} = \left[1.2 \times \left(\frac{\text{Working capital}}{\text{Total assets}}\right)\right] + \left[1.4 \times \left(\frac{\text{Retained earnings}}{\text{Total assets}}\right)\right] + \left[3.3 \times \left(\frac{\text{EBIT}}{\text{Total assets}}\right)\right]$$

$$+ \left[0.6 \times \left(\frac{\text{Market value of equity}}{\text{Book value of liabilities}}\right)\right] + \left[0.999 \times \left(\frac{\text{Sales}}{\text{Total assets}}\right)\right]$$

Altman found that companies with Z-scores above 3.0 are not likely to enter into bankruptcy, and companies with Z-scores below 1.8 are likely to enter bankruptcy. The "gray area," in which it is difficult to predict bankruptcy, lies between 1.8 and 3.0.

1. Classify each of these ratios as productivity, efficiency, liquidity, or financial leverage.

2. Calculate the Z-score for IBM for fiscal years 2008 through 2010, using the financial reports in this chapter and the previous chapter, and classify IBM in terms of likelihood of bankruptcy.

3. Using your calculated Z-scores and the individual components, explain why IBM's Z-score changed from FY2008 to FY2010.

PART 3

THE BASICS OF VALUATION

In finance, the time value of money is an essential building block for valuing stocks, bonds, or any other asset. In this section, we develop the basic discounted cash flow model that is the workhorse of finance. We start with the basic principles and math of the time value of money and then apply the basic discounting framework to valuing bonds and equities. In the process, we develop a model for valuing equities and discuss how equity valuation is related to fundamentals.

CHAPTER 5

THE TIME VALUE OF MONEY

© Masterfile

What does the Credit Card Act of 2009 do for you? The Credit Card Accountability Responsibility and Disclosure Act of 2009, or Credit Card Act of 2009, changed the landscape for credit card companies and consumers with new credit card rules, rules that seek to protect consumers from abuses from credit card companies.[1] These rules also reduce sources of income that these companies sought to offset the risks of default on these debt obligations.

These rules include the following:

1. Credit card marketing to those under twenty-one years of age is restricted, and colleges are required to disclose any contracts with credit card companies that involve selling student and alumni contact information.

2. Credit card companies cannot raise the interest rate on existing balances but only on future purchases, if sufficient notice has been provided. This negates the previous practice of raising the interest rate on existing balances, a practice that spun many credit card debtors into a financial down-spiral.

3. Credit card bills must include a disclosure about how long it would take a person to pay off the balance of the account if only the minimum payments are made. Also disclosed is the amount that would have to be paid each month to have everything paid off within three years.

4. A ban has been placed on universal default, a practice of credit card companies declaring an account in default if the credit card customer has been in default with another obligation. However, universal default can be applied on future purchases if there is sufficient notice.

5. A ban on over-the-limit fees has been placed, except when the credit card holder has agreed to these fees in advance.

6. If a credit card customer has different balances with different interest rates, payments are now allocated in the manner that minimizes cost to the customer, rather than at the credit card company's discretion.

7. Gift cards cannot expire in less than five years, and inactivity fees cannot be imposed within the first twelve months.

These rules, among others, may be effective in encouraging consumers to reduce debt. Consider the disclosure rules on paying off the balance. Suppose you have a balance of $5,000, with the following terms:

• Minimum payment due is 3% of balance
• Interest rate is 15% per year

Unless you have a really clear understanding of the time value of money, you may not have a good idea of how long it will take you to pay off your balance if you make the minimum payment. Under the new rules, your credit card bill will tell you the following:

• It will take fourteen and a half years to pay off the balance if you make only the minimum payment of $150 each month.

• You can pay off the balance in three years if you make a payment of $173.33 each month.

This example may encourage you to pay more than the minimum.

[1] Public-Law 111-24, 123 STAT. 1734, May 22, 2009.

140

Learning Outcomes

After reading this chapter, you should be able to:

LO 5.1 Describe and compare the principles of compound interest and simple interest, and apply these principles to solve present value and future value problems involving a single sum.

LO 5.2 Identify and apply the appropriate method of valuing different patterns of cash flows, including the ordinary annuity, annuity due, deferred annuity, and perpetuity.

LO 5.3 Calculate and compare annual percentage rates and effective annual rates for both discrete and continuous compounding.

LO 5.4 Apply the time value of money mathematics to solve loan and retirement problems.

Chapter Preview We introduced you to the study of finance in Part 1 and examined the importance of company financial statements in Part 2. In Part 3, we discuss the basic valuation process and apply it to financial securities. This valuation process relies heavily on discounting future expected cash flows, one of the tools discussed in this chapter. To understand finance, you need to have a solid foundation in the tools that we present in this chapter, including the math of translating a value from one period to another, time-lines to sort out the various cash flows and values, and identifying the sensitivity of values, both present and future, to interest rates and time.

In this chapter, we introduce you to everyday problems, such as taking out a loan, setting up a series of payments, and valuing them. The ideas in this chapter are important for all types of financial problems: determining payments for a home mortgage, buying versus leasing a new car, appropriately valuing a bond or stock, determining whether a company should expand production or abandon a product line, and deciding how much a company should be willing to pay for another company. Although each situation involves unique circumstances that will be covered in subsequent chapters, the basic framework used to evaluate these problems is the same and relies on material covered in this chapter.

5.1 TIME IS MONEY

In this chapter, we are concerned with the time value of money. The **time value of money** is the concept that money today is more valuable than the same quantity of money in the future. For example, $1 today is worth more than $1 to be received next year or ten years from now. As we saw in Chapters 1 and 2, the financial system is designed to transfer savings from lenders to borrowers so that savers have money to spend in the future. Money, in this sense, represents our ability to buy goods and services; that is, it operates as a medium of exchange and has no value in and of itself. A **medium of exchange** is any instrument that facilitates the exchange of goods or services. Of course, an investor could simply store the money (that is, stash it under the mattress) and spend it in the future; a dollar today is always worth at least a dollar in the future.[2] However, this option ignores the fact that the saver has other uses for that money, which we refer to as an "opportunity cost" or an "alternative use." This results in the time value of money.

A **loan** is a contract in which the borrower uses the funds of the lender, and in exchange the borrower not only repays the amount borrowed but also pays the lender compensation for use of the funds in the form of interest. **Interest** is compensation for the time value of money: In the case of a loan, the borrower is expected to repay an amount loaned plus interest to compensate the lender who did not have the use of the funds during the term of the loan.

The opportunity cost of money is the return that is expected when it is invested in something of similar risk. For this reason, we also refer to the interest rate as the price of money. It helps us analyze the problem of determining the value of money received at different times. Suppose, for example, a person has three choices: receiving $20,000 today,

time value of money idea that money invested today has more value than the same amount invested later

medium of exchange something that provides a way to buy goods and services but has no value in and of itself

loan contract in which the borrower uses the funds of the lender, and, in exchange, repays the amount borrowed plus compensation for the use of the funds

interest compensation for the time value of money

---

[2] This ignores the fact that what we are really concerned about is what that dollar will buy in terms of goods and services, that is, its purchasing power. We discuss this later in the chapter.

$31,000 in five years, or $3,000 per year indefinitely. Making a choice from these different options requires knowing how to value the dollars received at different times; that is, we need to adjust for the time value of money.

To make a decision, we need to know the interest rate. We will use i as a standard notation throughout this textbook for the market interest rate.[3] We will also refer to this market interest rate by several other names later in the textbook, such as the **required rate of return** or **discount rate**. The reason for these different names will become clear later, but in all cases, we are looking at the investor's opportunity cost, that is, what he or she can do with the money being invested. However, first we have to make some basic distinctions in terms of how this interest rate is earned and distinguish between simple interest and compound interest.

required rate of return or discount rate market interest rate or the investor's opportunity cost

Simple Interest

simple interest interest paid or received on only the initial investment

principal amount loaned or the amount of the investment

Simple interest is interest paid or received on only the initial investment (the **principal**). In practice, only a limited number of applications use simple interest, but we introduce it first to contrast it with compound interest, which is the typical type of interest.

Suppose you deposit $100 in an account that pays 5% per year, using simple interest. If you leave your money in this account for three years, what will the balance be in the account? With simple interest, the interest is based on the principal amount, which is $100 in this case. Therefore, the interest is $100 × 0.05 = $5 each year in this example. This means that at the end of three years, there is $100 + $5 + $5 + $5 = $100 + (3 × $100 × 0.05) = $115 in the account.

Because the same amount of interest is earned each year with simple interest, we can use the following equation to find the value of the investment at any point in time:

$$FV_n = PV_0 + (n \times PV_0 \times i) \tag{5-1}$$

where FV_n is the future value at the end of n periods, PV_0 is the principal amount today (period 0), n is the number of periods, and i is the interest rate per period.

Consider another example. Suppose you invest $1,000 today for five years in an account that pays 6% interest. Note that $PV_0 \times i$ = interest, so in applying this equation to this problem means that:

PV = $1,000

$n = 5$

$i = 6\%$

The value in year 5 is $1,000 + (5 × $60) = $1,300. The basic point of simple interest is that to get the future value of an investment, we calculate the annual interest (in our case $60), multiply this by the number of years of the investment, and add it to the starting principal.

Compound Interest

compound interest arrangement in which interest is earned on the principal amount invested *and* on any accrued interest

Compound interest is interest that is earned on the principal amount invested *and* on any accrued interest. Compound interest can result in dramatic growth in the value of an investment over time. This growth is directly related to the number of periods as well as to the level of interest or return earned. Because most financial transactions involve compound interest, you should assume compound interest applies unless explicitly told that the transaction is simple interest.

---

[3] Other common notations for the interest rate are k and r. We use i when we discuss the time value of money because i is the notation used in popular financial calculators.

PROBLEM

Suppose someone invests $10,000 today for a five-year term and receives 3% annual simple interest on the investment. How much would the investor have after five years?

EXAMPLE 5.1
Simple Interest

Solution

Annual interest = $10,000 × 0.03 = $300 per year.

Or

$$FV_5 = \$10,000 + [5 \times \$10,000 \times 0.03] = \$10,000 + 1{,}500 = \$11{,}500$$

Year	Beginning amount	Ending amount
1	$10,000	$10,300
2	10,300	10,600
3	10,600	10,900
4	10,900	11,200
5	11,200	11,500

The interest earned is $300 every year, regardless of the beginning amount, because interest is earned on only the original investment. Interest is *not* earned on any earned interest.

We calculate a future value of a lump sum when interest is compounded by considering interest not only on the principal amount but also on any accumulated interest. Consider an example of how compound interest works. Suppose you deposit $100 in an account that pays 5% interest per year. What is the balance in the account at the end of two years (that is, the future value or FV_2) if interest is compound interest? The answer is $110.25:

$$FV_1 = \$100 + (\$100 \times 0.05) = \$105$$
$$FV_2 = \$105 + (\$105 \times 0.05) = \$110.25$$

Unlike simple interest, the amount of compound interest earned increases every year; the interest rate is applied to the principal plus interest earned, so the value of the investment increases. As a result, the interest received each successive year is greater than that of the previous year because of **compounding**.

Let us look at the first two years of interest by using a little algebra. For the first year, everything is the same as with simple interest; that is, the amount at the end of the first year, which we represent as FV_1, is the starting principal (that is, PV_0) plus the interest, or:

compounding increase in value over time due to interest on both the principal amount and any interest earned up to that point in time

$$FV_1 = PV_0(1 + i)$$
$$FV_1 = \$1{,}000 + (\$1{,}000 \times 0.10)$$
$$FV_1 = \$1{,}000 \times (1 + 0.10)$$
$$FV_1 = \$1{,}100$$

where PV_0 = the present value today (i.e., at time 0). We used a bit of algebra to restate the future value as the principal multiplied by 1 plus the interest rate.

For the second year, the full $1,100 is reinvested; that is, we do not take the $100 of interest out and spend it. As a result, we have the following:

$$FV_2 = \$1{,}100 + (\$1{,}100 \times 0.10) = \$1{,}210 = \$1{,}100 \times (1 + 0.10)$$

using the notation

$$FV_2 = PV_1(1 + i) = PV_0(1 + i)^2$$

In this case, \$1,100 is invested at the beginning of the second year, and it earns 10% percent interest. The interest earned in the second year is \$110: the \$100 interest on the starting principal plus \$10 interest earned on the \$100 of interest reinvested at the end of the first year. We can rearrange all this using algebra to get the formula for the future value at the end of the second year. This is the starting principal, multiplied by 1 plus the interest rate squared. As we increase the number of periods, we get the general formula:

$$FV_n = PV_0(1 + i)^n \qquad\qquad (5\text{-}2)$$

where FV_n is the future value at time n.

We refer to this equation as the basic *compounding equation*, and the last term $(1 + i)^n$ as the **compound factor** or **future value interest factor**. Applying this equation to our example of investing \$1,000 for five years at 10%, we get:

$$FV_5 = \$1,000(1 + 0.10)^5 = \$1,000 \times 1.61051 = \$1,610.51$$

This is \$110.51 more than we would receive for the investment earning simple interest. We show the growth in the \$1,000 over the five years in Figure 5-1. As you can see in this figure, the principal remains constant, the interest on the principal grows at a rate of \$100 per year, and the interest-on-interest grows each year. The **interest-on-interest** is the amount of value attributed to the fact that interest is paid on previously earned interest.[4]

We illustrate what happens with the two types of interest over time in Figure 5-2. Note that for the first few years, the difference between compound and simple interests is minimal, but over time, the difference gets bigger and bigger. You can also see that the value grows in a straight line with simple interest, growing by \$100 each year, whereas the future value with compound interest grows at a rate of 10% per year, which means that the line representing the future values is convex.

You can also solve this example using a financial calculator. Most financial calculators have one set of keys dedicated to the time value of money calculations. Your task is to type in the given values and input them into the calculator's registers by striking the appropriate time value of money key associated with the value. You repeat this process for each of the known values, and then, once you have input all the given values, you strike

---

compound factor or future value interest factor amount that reflects the interest rate and the number of periods, which, when multiplied by a current or present value, results in the equivalent future value

interest-on-interest interest earned on previously accumulated interest

---

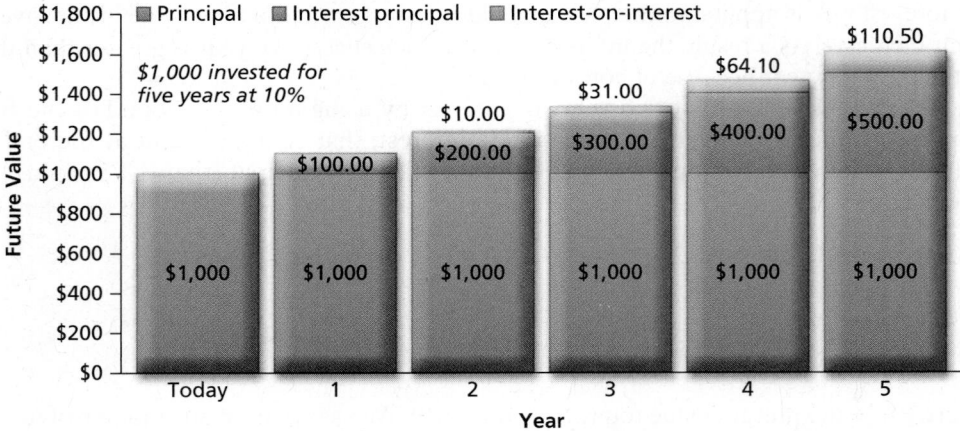

FIGURE 5-1 Growth of Value Over Time with Compound Interest

---

[4] The easy way to determine interest on interest in any problem is to calculate the future value with compound interest and the future value with simple interest and then take the difference. This difference is the interest-on-interest.

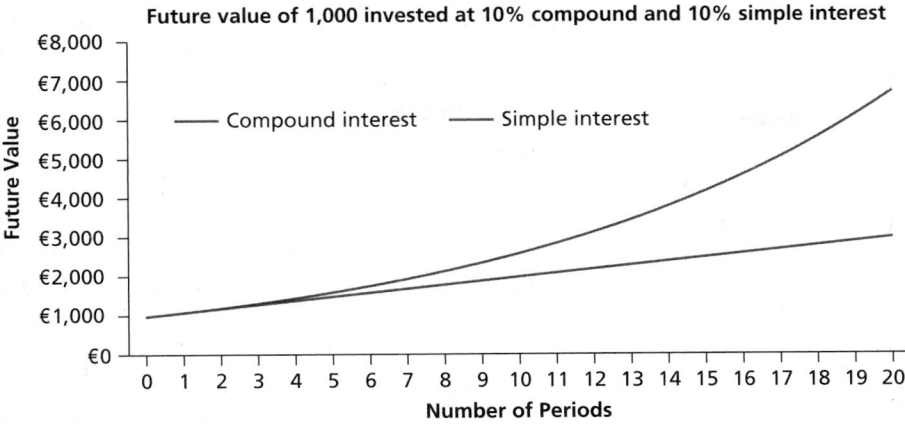

FIGURE 5-2 **Simple Versus Compound Interest**

the key corresponding to the unknown value; the answer then appears in the display window.

If you are using a financial calculator to perform the calculation using basic mathematics, you use the interest rate in a decimal form. However, if you are using the time value of money functions within a financial calculator, you use the interest rate expressed as a whole number; that is, 10% is 10, 5% is 5, and so forth.

Here is something that trips up a lot of people when they first use a financial calculator: The present value must be typed in as a negative number. You enter the PV with a negative sign (on most financial calculators) to reflect the fact that investors must pay money now to get money in the future. Alternatively, we could have left it positive, which would produce a negative sign in front of the FV, which we could simply ignore.[5]

PROBLEM

Suppose you invest $10,000 today for a five-year term and receive 5% annual compound interest.

A. How much would you have after five years?
B. How much interest-on-interest would you earn during the five years?

EXAMPLE 5.2

Compound Interest

Solution

A. Annual interest is earned on the original $10,000 (principal) *plus* on accrued interest. Therefore, the investor would have $12,762.82 at the end of five years:

Year	*Beginning amount*	*Compound interest*	*Ending amount*
1	$10,000.00	$10,000.00 × 0.05 = $500.00	$10,500.00
2	$10,500.00	$10,500.00 × 0.05 = $525.00	$11,025.00
3	$11,025.00	$11,025.00 × 0.05 = $551.25	$11,576.25
4	$11,576.25	$11,576.25 × 0.05 = $578.81	$12,155.06
5	$12,155.06	$12,155.06 × 0.05 = $607.75	$12,762.82

B. The future value with compound interest is $12,762.82. If interest were simple interest only, the future value would be $10,000 + 2,500 = $12,500. Therefore, the interest-on-interest is $12,762.82 – 12,500 = $262.82

---

[5] This is because of the way the manufacturers have programmed the calculator. If do not input the PV as a negative number, inaccuracies may not occur in simple problems, but you may get an error message or incorrect answers in other, more complex problems.

For our example of investing $1,000 for five years at 10%, we input the three known values (PV, *i* and *n*) and solve for the one unknown, which is the future value five years from now. We represent these inputs as the following inputs:

PV = $1,000

$i = 10\%$

$n = 5$

We represent these inputs generically in the remainder of this chapter and throughout the remainder of this text because this sets you up for a variety of calculators and spreadsheets.

Remember, when you enter these values into your calculator or spreadsheet, you enter the present value as a negative number without the comma and currency symbol and you enter the interest rate without the percentage sign and as a whole number (for example, "10") in the financial calculator, and in decimal form (for instance, "0.10") in the spreadsheet. For example, in most financial calculators the inputs for this problem would be the following:[6]

$$1000 \ +/- \ PV \ 10 \ I/YR \ 5 \ n \ FV$$

USING A SPREADSHEET TO SOLVE FOR THE FUTURE VALUE

We can use the FV function in Excel to calculate the future value:

$$= FV(RATE, NPER, PMT, PV, type)$$

where RATE = interest rate (expressed as a decimal)

NPER = number of periods

PMT = the payment amount, which is zero is in this case

PV = present value

type = 0 if it is an ordinary annuity, 1 if it is annuity due.[7]

Note the key difference between the financial calculator function and the spreadsheet function: The interest rate is in decimal form in the spreadsheet, but not with the financial calculator. If we want to determine the future value of $1,000 in five years with 10% interest, we would enter the following in the appropriate cell:

$$= FV(0.10, 5, 0, -1000, 0)$$

This yields 1,610.51.

Another difference between the spreadsheet and the calculator function is that you cannot leave out an element in the spreadsheet function unless it is the optional "type." For example, if the problem does not have a regular payment (that is PMT), and you do not type this in as the third argument in parentheses, the function will interpret the PV you entered as the PMT and the type as the PV, giving you an answer to a completely different problem.

---

[6] Before you begin any calculation using the time value of money in a financial calculator, be sure to clear the calculator's registers (that is, where the data are stored internally); otherwise, old data may be stored. For example, there is no payment (i.e., PMT) in this example. If you had calculated a problem with a payment before this one, you would still have that payment stored in the calculator, and it would be included in this next calculation. To be on the safe side, clear your financial calculator prior to every calculation. Check the owners' manual for the procedure for clearing the registers.

[7] We will explain what the difference is shortly; for now, our examples involve ordinary annuities.

CALCULATOR TOOLS: COMPOUNDING WITH A FINANCIAL CALCULATOR

When calculating a future value, you have the present value, the interest rate, and the number of periods, and you need to determine the future value. In other words, you have three values, and your task is to solve for the one unknown value. Therefore:

PV = 1000
i = 10%
n = 5

and you need to solve for FV.

The actual keystrokes for common financial calculators are the following:

HP10B	**TI BAII**	**HP12C**	**TI83/84**
1000 +/– PV	1000 +/– PV	1000 CHS PV	*Using TVM Solver App:*
10 I/YR	10 I/YR	10 i	N = 5
5 N	5 N	5 n	i = 10
FV	FV	FV	PV = –1000
			PMT = 0
			FV = *Solve*
			P/Y = 1
			C/Y = 1

Warning   Financial calculators are programmed such that any value entered into a registry (i.e., a storage location in the calculator's memory) will remain unless written over or explicitly cleared. For example, if you enter 1000 +/– PV 10 I/YR 5 N in one problem, and then 2000 +/– PV 12 I/YR in the next, the 5 will remain in the number of periods registry. This can be handy in some applications or result in errors if not intended.

You can use either of two approaches to avoid this problem:

1. Type a zero value for any unused variable
2. Clear the calculator before each problem

The best approach depends on both the calculator and what you feel comfortable with. The process of clearing the calculator registries varies by model, so check your manual.

For the calculators that we present in this chapter, you clear by using the following keystrokes:

HP10B	**TI BAII**	**HP12C**	**TI83/84**
■ CLEAR ALL	2nd CLR TVM	f FIN	*Enter 0 in display*

Let us now extend the time horizon in our example of investing $1,000 at 10%. Investing $1,000 for fifty years at an annual interest rate of 10% produces $117,390.85. Note the difference between this amount and the future value of the same $1,000 invested for fifty years, but earning simple interest: ($1,000 + [50 × $100]) = $6,000. You can see the difference that compounding makes over this fifty-year span in Figure 5-3. What is the difference between the two future values after fifty years? You would get $111,390.85, which is the interest-on-interest.

You might be tempted to ask whether a fifty-year term is realistic. It is for many investments. Consider someone who begins investing for retirement in his or her early twenties.

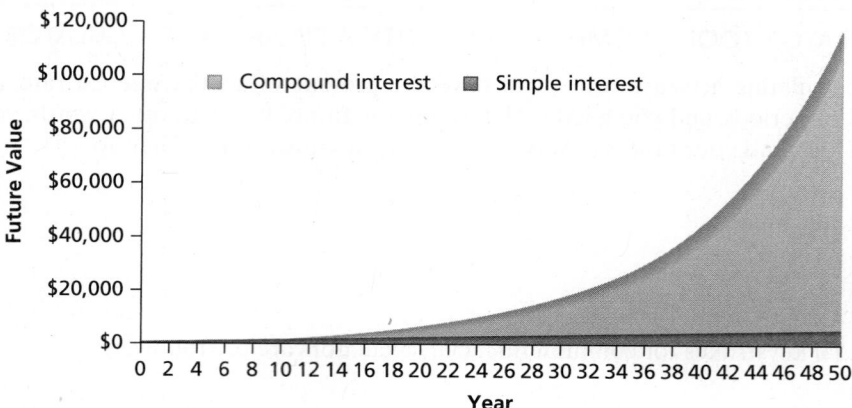

FIGURE 5-3   Simple Versus Compound Interest Over Fifty Years

Those early investments could earn compound returns for forty years or more before the individual retires. Further, assuming the individual does not withdraw all of the retirement savings on his or her retirement day (which would have severe tax consequences) and assuming that this person lives another twenty to twenty-five years after retirement, some investment dollars may remain untouched for more than fifty years.

LESSONS LEARNED

Behold the Miracle of Compounding

Compound interest has been called the eighth wonder of the world. And with good reason. It magically turns a little bit of money, invested wisely, into a whole lot of cash. Even Albert Einstein—a bit of a smarty pants—is said to have called it one of the greatest mathematical concepts of our time.

But you don't need to be a genius to harness the power of compounding. Even the most average of Joes can use it to make money. Trust me. This is *so* much easier than the theory of relativity.

Here's the gist: When you save or invest, your money earns interest or appreciates. The next year, you earn interest on your original money *and* the interest from the first year. In the third year, you earn interest on your original money and the interest from the first *two* years. And so on. It's like a snowball—roll it down a snowy hill and it'll build on itself to get bigger and bigger. Before you know it . . . avalanche!

Harness the power

Here are three steps to help you make the power of compound interest or compound earnings work for you. And when I say "work FOR you," I mean it. Once you set up an account, you don't have to do much else. Just sit back and wait for the money to roll in.

1. **Start young.** When you're in your twenties and thirties, your best friend is TIME. Start rolling your snowball at the top of the hill and you'll have a much bigger mass at the bottom than someone who started halfway down.

    Consider this: Amy, a 22-year-old college graduate, saves $300 per month into an account earning 10% per year for six years. (That's the average annual return of the stock market over time.) Then at age 28, she starts a family and decides to stay home with the children full time. By then, Amy had kicked in $21,600 of her own money. But even if she doesn't contribute another cent *ever*, her money would grow to a million bucks by the time she turned 65.

    Compare that to Jason, who put off saving until he was 31. He's still young enough that becoming a millionaire is within reach, but it will be tougher. Jason would have to contribute the same $300 a month for the next 34 years to earn $1 million by age 65. Although Amy invested less money out-of-pocket — $21,600 over six years vs. Jason's $126,000 over 34 years — her money had more time to grow, or compound. . . . Bottom line: Getting rich is easier and more painless the earlier you start.

2. **Remember that a little goes a long way.** Don't think you have enough money to start investing? You can get into a good mutual fund for as little as $50 a month.

    Let's say a 20-year-old stashes $50 a month into a fund earning 10% annually. He'd have $528,000 by age 65. Not bad for practically starting with pocket change!

    A little bit can make a difference elsewhere in compounding, too. For example, if our 20-year-old earned 9% annually instead of 10%, he would amass only $373,000 in the same period of time. That seemingly small 1% difference in performance resulted in 29% less money over the long haul.

3. **Leave it alone.** The prospect of making a lot of money without doing anything sounds good on paper. But, admittedly, in practice, it can be maddening. Every time you receive your account statement, you watch your balance s-l-o-w-l-y inch up—or even drop. How on earth are you ever going to get rich at this pace?

Investing is a lot like Heinz ketchup: Good things come to those who wait. You must be patient for compounding to work its awesome power. Remember that as your money earns more, it'll earn even *more*. You certainly won't get rich overnight this way. But you will get rich if you start young, invest wisely and leave it alone.

Source: "Behold the Miracle of Compounding," by Erin Burt, *Kiplingers, November 8, 2007, www.kiplinger.com/ columns/starting/archive/2007/st1107.htm.*

In Table 5-1, we provide some evidence regarding the power of compound returns, where we show the future values that would have resulted from investing $1,000 at the beginning of different points in time and what it would be worth today. The dramatic difference in ending values results from differences in the rate of return: If you invested $1,000 at the beginning of 1930 at 1% per year, you would only have $2,217 at the end of 2009. If, instead, you invested $1,000 earning 10% per year, you would have over $2 million at the end of 2009. Now you can see why finance professionals struggle to increase

PROBLEM

Suppose you deposit $10,000 in an account that pays 5% compound interest. At the end of three years, if you have never made any withdrawals:

A. How much will you have in the account at the end of three years?
B. How much interest-on-interest did you earn in your account at the end of three years?

EXAMPLE 5.3

Interest-on-Interest

Solution

A. $FV = \$10,000 (1 + 0.05)^3 = \$11,576.25$
B. $FV_{Simple} = \$10,000 + (\$10,000 \times 0.05 \times 3) = \$11,500$

Interest-on-interest $= \$11,576.25 - 11,500 = \$76.25$

TABLE 5-1 Ending Wealth of $1,000 Invested for Different Investment Periods at Different Rates

Invested at the beginning of:	Results in a value at the end of 2009, if invested at:			
	1% per year	4% per year	7% per year	10% per year
1930	$2,217	$23,050	$224,234	$2,048,400
1940	$2,007	$15,572	$113,989	$789,747
1950	$1,817	$10,520	$57,946	$304,482
1960	$1,645	$7,107	$29,457	$117,391
1970	$1,489	$4,801	$14,974	$45,259
1980	$1,348	$3,243	$7,612	$17,449
1990	$1,220	$2,191	$3,870	$6,727
2000	$1,105	$1,480	$1,967	$2,594

basis point one
one-hundredths
of 1 percent

the returns on their investments even by very small amounts. In fact, it is normal to keep track of returns down to one-hundredth of 1%, which is a **basis point**.[8]

Earning just a few basis points more on one investment causes the future value of the portfolio to compound that much faster. For example, if you invested at the beginning of 1930 and could have earned fifty basis points more than the 7% we show in this table, you would have a value of $325,595 at the end of 2009 instead of $224,234; the fifty basis points produces over $100,000 more wealth over that period.[9]

Until now, we have assumed that the interest rate remains the same each period. There is always the possibility that interest rates earned on investments or paid on obligations may change over time. Though the interest may change, the mathematics do not; we simply cannot use shortcuts, calculator functions, or spreadsheet functions to perform the math. Consider an investment of $20,000 in which you expect to earn 3% the first year, 4% the second year, and 5% the third year. How much is the investment worth in three years? It is worth $22,495.20:

$$FV_3 = \$20,000 \times (1 + 0.03) \times (1 + 0.04) \times (1 + 0.05) = \$22,495.20$$

How much of this investment is interest on the principal, and how much is interest-on-interest? We can use the same approach as we did previously to break down the future value into principal, interest on the principal, and interest-on-interest components:

Year	Beginning value	Interest rate	Interest on the principal	Interest-on-interest	Balance at the end of the year
1	$20,000.00	3%	$600.00	$0.00	$20,600.00
2	$20,600.00	4%	$800.00	$24.00	$21,424.00
3	$21,424.00	5%	$1,000.00	$71.20	$22,495.20

The interest-on-interest is the product of the interest rate for the period and any accumulated interest. Let us consider Year 2 in this example. The interest on the principal amount is $20,000 \times 0.04 = \$800$; the interest-on-interest is $600 \times 0.04 = \$24$. For the third year, the interest-on-interest is $(\$600 + 800 + 24) \times 0.05 = \$71.20$. The interest-on-interest over this three year period is $24 + 71.20 = \$95.20$. Another way of calculating this is to compare the

---

EXAMPLE 5.4

Compounding with Different Rates of Return

PROBLEM

Consider depositing €1,000 in an account that is expected to pay 5% interest for the first three years and 2% for the following three years.[10] What will be the balance in the account six years from now if there are no withdrawals from the account?

Solution

$$FV_6 = €1,000 (1 + 0.05)^3 (1 + 0.02)^3 = €1,000 \times 1.57625 \times 1.061208 = €1,672.73$$

---

[8] Therefore, if an interest rate changes from 5% to 6%, we say that the interest rate has changed by 100 basis points.

[9] Why worry about such a long period? Remember that while you may be currently thinking short term, many financial instruments exist—and are valued—for the long run.

[10] You will notice that the monetary units do not matter. The time value of money mathematics apply whether we are using U.S. or Canadian dollars ($), euro (€), Japanese yen (¥), British pounds (£), or any other currency.

Islamic Law and Interest | GLOBAL PERSPECTIVE

Islamic law promotes a faith-based financial system that forbids interest, or *riba*, on transactions but permits profits from investments, *mudharabah*, that are shared between the parties to the transaction. The prohibition of interest, the sharing of profits, and the prohibition on speculation result in differences between the Islamic financial system and the traditional European and U.S. systems.
  Consider the following:

- A simple savings account, in the U.S. system, results in periodic interest being provided to the depositor in exchange for the bank having the use of the funds.

In the Islamic financial system, the bank cannot pay interest, but the bank may provide a gratuity, a *hibah*, in gratitude for the depositor leaving the funds in the hands of the bank.

- A loan in the U.S. system results in the borrower paying the amount borrowed plus interest. In the Islamic system, the borrower does not pay interest for a loan (a *qard*) but can provide a gratuity to the bank.

Source: Shanmugam, Bala, and Zaha Rina Zahari, *A Primer on Islamic Finance*, CFA Institute, December 2009.

future value with compound interest, the $22,495.20, with the value with simple interest, $20,000 + 600 + 800 + 1,000 = $22,400: $22,495.20 − 22,400 = $95.20.

Discounting

So far, we have been concerned with finding future values, but there is a problem with comparing future values: There are many of them! We could choose an arbitrary common period to make the comparisons, which would solve this problem. The obvious choice is to compare the values at the current time; so, instead of calculating future values, we determine present values. We refer to this process as **discounting**. We will explain it with a simple example.

discounting calculating the present value of a future value, considering the time value of money

Suppose an investor estimates that she needs $1 million to live comfortably when she retires in forty years. How much does she have to invest today, assuming a 10% interest rate on the investment?

First, start with what we already know: the future value formula from Equation 5-2:

$$FV_n = PV_0(1 + i)^n$$

where $(1 + i)^n$ is the compound factor. With a starting present value, we multiply by the compound factor to get the future value. Turning this around, we can divide the future value by the compound factor to arrive at the present value, or, rearranging Equation 5-2 and solving for PV_0,

$$PV_0 = \frac{FV_n}{(1 + i)^n} = FV_n \times \left(\frac{1}{(1 + i)^n}\right) \tag{5-3}$$

This is the basic discounting equation, and the last term, $1 \div (1 + i)^n$, is the **discount factor**.
  So, let us return to our example. With

discount factor value that, when multiplied by the future value, results in the present value of this future value

FV = $1,000,000
$i = 0.10$
$n = 40$

we arrive at the present value of $22,094.93:

$$PV_0 = \$1,000,000 \times \frac{1}{1.10^{40}}$$

$$PV_0 = \$1,000,000 \times \frac{1}{45.259256}$$

$$PV_0 = \$1,000,000 \times 0.02209493$$

$$PV_0 = \$22,094.93$$

Therefore, an investment of \$22,094.93 today, earning a 10% return per year, has a future value of \$1 million in forty years. With a 10% market interest rate, \$22,094.94 today and \$1 million in forty years' time are worth the same:

$$FV = \$22,094.94 \times 1.10^{40} = \$22,094.94 \times 45.25926 = \$1,000,000$$

Now you know why we call this process *discounting*. If people do not want to pay the full price for something, they ask for a discount, that is, they ask for something off the price. In the same way, \$1 million in forty years is not worth \$1 million today, so you discount, or take something off, to get it to its true value. Discounting future values to find their present value is the same process, except that when we know the market interest rate, we can use Equation 5-3 to calculate the value today.

EXAMPLE 5.5

Solving for a Present Value

PROBLEM

Suppose you are considering an investment that promises \$50,000 in three years. If you determine that the appropriate discount rate for this investment, considering its risk, is 15%, what is this investment worth to you today?

Solution

Using the formula:

$$PV_0 = \frac{\$50,000}{(1 + 0.15)^3} = \frac{\$50,000}{1.520875} = \$32,875.81$$

Using a financial calculator:

FV = 50000

$n = 3$

$i = 15$

Solve for PV.

Using a spreadsheet function:

= PV(0.15,3,0,50000)

Note the following important points from the previous examples:

- Discount factors are always less than 1 (as long as $i \geq 0$). This means that future dollars are worth less than the same dollars today, or PV > FV.
- Discount factors are the reciprocals of their corresponding compound factors, and vice versa. In other words, discounting is compounding in reverse.

Compounding and Discounting with Continuous Compounding

Until now, we have used **discrete compounding**; that is, interest is compounded a fixed number of times. There are many applications in finance in which interest is compounded continuously. **Continuously compounded interest** or, simply, **continuous compounding**, means that interest is instantaneous, or compounded an infinite number of times. Though this may seem like an abstract concept, continuously compounded interest is the basis for many financial transactions (such as interest on credit card balances).

Consider a lump sum of $10,000 deposited in an account for six years. If interest is compounded annually, at the end of five years you will have:

$$FV_5 = \$10{,}000\ (1 + 0.05)^6 = \$13{,}400.96$$

If, however, interest is calculated quarterly, the rate per period is 1.25% and there are $4 \times 6 = 24$ periods. The result is:

$$FV_5 = \$10{,}000\ (1 + {}^{0.05}\!/_4)^{24} = \$13{,}473.51$$

Therefore, the inputs for your calculator's calculation are:[11]

PV = $10,000
i = 1.25%
n = 24

If interest is compounded daily:

$$FV_5 = \$10{,}000\ (1 + {}^{0.05}\!/_{365})^{2{,}190} = \$13{,}498.31$$

If interest is compounded continuously, we have to resort to using Euler's e, which is a mathematical constant (approximately 2.71828):[12]

$$FV_5 = \$10{,}000\ e^{0.05 \times 6} = \$10{,}000\ e^{0.3} = \$13{,}498.59$$

where e is the unique Euler constant. You can find this constant on your calculator (usually represented as e) and in a spreadsheet program (usually indicated as EXP). You will notice that as the frequency of compounding increases, the future value increases as well. The limit to this increase is the continuously compounded value.

Discounting works in a similar manner. Suppose you have a goal of having $20,000 in an account at the end of four years. If you make a deposit today in an account earning 6%

discrete compounding compound interest in which interest is paid at specified intervals of time, such as quarterly or annually

continuously compounded interest or **continuous compounding** interest is instantaneous, compounded an infinite number of times

---

[11] You could also adjust the payments per period (often designated as P/YR) and input the 5% rate and the number of periods. We do recommend this approach because many students forget to change the payments per period back to P/YR = 1, which would result in errors in subsequent calculations. The simplest method is to convert i and n and then enter these values in the calculator.

[12] Euler's e is a really cool number because it is used in many ways in mathematics and in finance. Euler's e is (1) the inverse of the natural logarithm, (2) the base of the natural logarithm, (3) a function that is equal to its own derivative, and (4) an irrational number (with so many digits that there are contests for memorizing or programming the decimal digits). There is even a book written about it: *e: The Story of a Number*, by Eli Manor [Princeton University Press (1998)].

interest, how much would you have to deposit as a lump sum today to meet your goal? It will depend on the frequency of compounding:

Frequency of compounding	Present value
Annual	$PV_0 = \dfrac{\$20,000}{(1 + 0.06)^4} = \$15,841.87$
Quarterly	$PV_0 = \dfrac{\$20,000}{(1 + 0.015)^{16}} = \$15,760.62$
Daily	$PV_0 = \dfrac{\$20,000}{(1 + 0.00016438)^{1,460}} = \$15,732.87$
Continuous	$PV_0 = \dfrac{\$20,000}{e^{0.06 \times 4}} = \$15,732.56$

As you can see, the more frequent the compounding, the smaller is the present value.

Determining the Interest Rate

Let us look at the basic valuation equation again:

$$FV_n = PV_0(1 + i)^n$$

We have used this equation to solve for future values (FV) and present values (PV), but note that we can solve for two other values: (1) the interest rate, i, and (2) the period, n. If both the present and future values are known, and we know either the interest rate or the period, we can solve for the last unknown.

For example, suppose you want to find out the interest rate necessary for your investment to double in value in six years:

PV = $1
FV = $2
$n = 6$

And then solve for i:

$$\$2 = \$1(1 + i)^6$$

Rearranging and solving for i produces an interest rate of 12.246%:

$$\frac{\$2}{\$1} = (1 + i)^6 \rightarrow \sqrt[6]{\frac{\$2}{\$1}} = (1 + i) \rightarrow i = \sqrt[6]{\frac{\$2}{\$1}} - 1 = 12.246\%$$

In other words, you can double your money in six years if you can earn 12.246% on your investment.

Let us apply this to a company's dividends per share. International Business Machines (IBM) paid $0.51 in dividends per share during 2000. In 2011, IBM paid $2.90 in dividends. What is the growth rate of IBM's dividends? We know the following:

PV = $0.51 *The starting value of dividends*
FV = $2.90 *The ending value of dividends*
$n = 11$ *The number of periods since 2000*

Solving for i, we have the rate of growth in dividends, which is 17.117%.

Determining the Number of Periods

Now consider another example, this time solving for the number of periods. How long does it take to triple your money if the interest rate is 3% per year? The known values are:

PROBLEM

What would the annual interest rate have to be so that your investment at the end of twenty years:

1) doubled?
2) tripled?
3) quadrupled?

EXAMPLE 5.6

Solving for the Interest Rate

Solution

Formula	Calculator	Spreadsheet	Answer
1) $2 = 1(1+i)^{20}$ $i = \sqrt[20]{\dfrac{\$2}{\$1}} - 1$	$PV = -1; FV = 2;$ $n = 20$	=RATE(20,0,−1,2)	3.526%
2) $3 = 1(1+i)^{20}$ $i = \sqrt[20]{\dfrac{\$3}{\$1}} - 1$	$PV = -1; FV = 3;$ $n = 20$	=RATE(20,0,−1,3)	5.647%
3) $4 = 1(1+i)^{20}$ $i = \sqrt[20]{\dfrac{\$4}{\$1}} - 1$	$PV = -1; FV = 4;$ $n = 20$	=RATE(20,0,−1,4)	7.177%

$PV = \$1$
$FV = \$3$
$i = 3\%$

and the unknown value, the one you solve for is n:

$$\$3 = \$1(1 + 0.03)^n$$

Rearranging and solving for i:[13]

$$\frac{\$3}{\$1} = (1 + 0.03)^n$$

Taking the natural logs of both sides and then solving for n, we find that n is 37.16676:

$$\ln 3 - \ln 1 = n \ln (1.03)$$

$$n = \frac{\ln 3 - \ln 1}{\ln(1.03)} = \frac{1.0986 - 0}{0.029559} = 37.16676$$

$$n = 38$$

Therefore, if you can earn 3% per year on your investment, you will triple your money in 38 years.[14]

When solving for the interest rate or solving for the number of periods, you can use mathematics, as we just did, or use a financial calculator or spreadsheet. It is very important when you use a calculator or spreadsheet that you change the sign on the present value when you enter it. If you do not, the calculator cannot compute a solution.

[13] In this calculation, we take a natural log of a value. While we will not go into all the painful details on what logarithms and base e mean, we can tell you that this allows us to make this equation easier to solve by using the properties of logarithms to bring the exponent n into a linear equation and thus solve for n. How do you take a natural log of something? You probably have a key on your calculator that is labeled "LN" or "ln."
[14] Why not round down to thirty-seven years? Because at thirty-seven years, we have not tripled the money; however, by the time interest is compounded the thirty-eighth time (remember, this is discrete interest), we have tripled the money.

EXAMPLE 5.7

Solving for the Number of Periods

PROBLEM

If you can earn 5% on your investment, how long does it take, rounding up to the next whole compounding period, for your money to:

1. double?
2. triple?
3. quadruple?

Solution

	Formula		Calculator	Spreadsheet	Answer
1) $n =$	$\dfrac{Ln\ 2}{Ln\ 1.05}$	$= \dfrac{0.693147}{0.048790}$	$PV = -1; FV = 2; i = 5$	=NPER(0.05,0,–1,2)	14.2067
2) $n =$	$\dfrac{Ln\ 3}{Ln\ 1.05}$	$= \dfrac{1.098612}{0.048790}$	$PV = -1; FV = 3; i = 5$	=NPER(0.05,0,–1,3)	22.5171
3) $n =$	$\dfrac{Ln\ 4}{Ln\ 1.05}$	$= \dfrac{1.386294}{0.048790}$	$PV = -1; FV = 4; i = 5$	=NPER(0.05,0,–1,4)	28.4134

SUMMARIZING

The equation for the future value, $FV_n = PV_0(1 + i)^n$, has four values, and if we know any three of them we can solve for the last one. We can solve four different types of finance problems using this equation:

1. *Future value problems*: How much will I have in w years at x% if I invest $\$y$?
2. *Present value problems*: What is the value today of receiving $\$z$ in w years if the interest rate is x%?
3. *Determining the interest rate*: What rate of return will I earn if I invest $\$y$ today for w years and get $\$z$?
4. *Determining the number of periods:* How long do I have to wait to get $\$z$ if I invest $\$y$ today at x%?

Concept Review Questions

1. You are given a choice of receiving $1,000 today or $1,000 one year from today. Are you indifferent to the difference between the two choices? Why, or why not?

2. Suppose you are considering lending someone $10,000. If your opportunity cost of funds is 5%, what interest rate should you charge for this loan? Explain your reasoning.

3. An investor wants to calculate the average annual return on an investment. She identified the amount invested and the value of the investment at the end of the investment period. She then calculated the percentage change in the value of the investment from the beginning to the end of the investment period and divided this by the number of years to arrive at the average annual return on the investment. Is this the correct approach? Explain.

5.2 ANNUITIES AND PERPETUITIES

So far, what we have examined are single-sum problems because we were looking at a single investment today and a single payoff in the future or looking at the value today of a future lump sum. In principle, we can solve almost any problem by using the techniques we have discussed because, for example, valuing a series of receipts in the future can be done by valuing each one individually. However, special formulas exist for standard problems in finance, for which the receipts or payments are the same each period.

Ordinary Annuities

Up to this point, we have dealt with PV and FV concepts as they apply to only two cash flows—one today (i.e., the PV) and one in the future (i.e., the FV). In practice, we often need to compare different series of receipts or payments that occur through time. An **annuity** is a series of payments or receipts, which we will simply call **cash flows**, over some period that are for the same amount and paid over the same interval; that is, for example, they are paid annually, monthly, or weekly. Annuities are common in finance: The one you may be familiar with is a personal loan or mortgage payment. This involves identical payments made at regular intervals based on a single interest rate for a loan.

An **ordinary annuity** involves *end-of-period* payments. We have the same values as in our earlier discussion: FV, PV, *n*, and *i*. However, now we have another term, PMT, for the regular annuity payment or receipt. The example below demonstrates how to determine the FV and PV of an ordinary annuity.

Suppose someone plans to invest $1,000 at the end of each year for the next five years and expects to earn 13% per year. How much will the investor have after five years? How much would the investor need to deposit today to obtain the same results?

We can first depict the series of payments in a timeline, which shows when the cash flows occur:

Timelines are very useful in finance, and you may want to develop the habit of displaying the data in a problem in a timeline to avoid any confusion about the timing of cash flows. For example, from the diagram above, we can see that by the end of Year 5, the first deposit of $1,000 will earn a return for four years because there are four years from the end of Year 1 to the end of the problem in Year 5. In contrast, the second payment will earn a return for only three years, the third for only two, the fourth for one year, and the final payment will not earn a return at all.

Future value of an ordinary annuity

Suppose we want to calculate the future value of this series of cash flows, with an interest rate of 13%. Using this information, we could view this as a five-part problem in which we have to find the future value of each of the five payments:

$$FV_5 = \left(\$1{,}000 \times (1.13)^4\right) + \left(\$1{,}000 \times (1.13)^3\right) + \left(\$1{,}000 \times (1.13)^2\right)$$
$$+ \left(\$1{,}000 \times (1.13)^1\right) + \left(\$1{,}000 \times (1.13)^0\right)$$
$$FV_5 = (\$1{,}000 \times 1.63047) + (\$1{,}000 \times 1.44290) + (\$1{,}000 \times 1.27690)$$
$$+ (\$1{,}000 \times 1.130) + (\$1{,}000 \times 1)$$
$$FV_5 = \$1{,}000 \times 6.48027 = \$6{,}480.27$$

annuity regular payments from an investment that are for the same amount and are paid at regular intervals of time

cash flows actual cash generated from an investment

ordinary annuity equal payments from an investment over a fixed number of years, with the payments made at the end of each period

The investor would have $6,480.27 after five years, as we depict in the timeline:

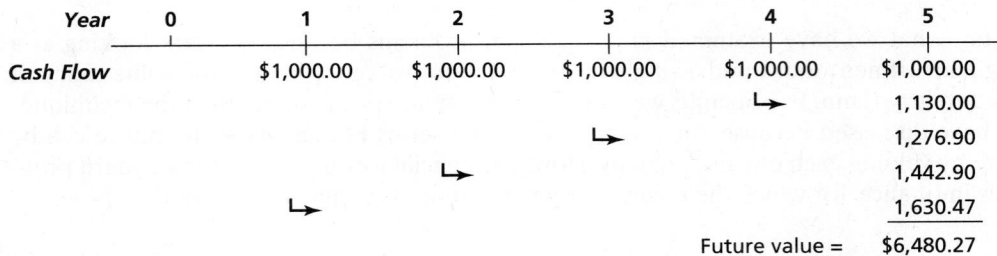

Year	0	1	2	3	4	5
Cash Flow		$1,000.00	$1,000.00	$1,000.00	$1,000.00	$1,000.00
						1,130.00
						1,276.90
						1,442.90
						1,630.47
					Future value =	$6,480.27

When we have to solve a problem that involves valuing a series of even cash flows, we can always do this the long way: determining the future value of each of the cash flows and then summing these future values. This approach is fine in the case of a five-period annuity, but it would be tedious in the case of, say, a twenty-five-year, monthly-payment mortgage with 300 payments.

Fortunately, there is a much quicker way (even without the use of a financial calculator or a spreadsheet). If we look closely at our solution, we can see that we are multiplying $1,000 by the sum of five compound factors based on a 13% return (i.e., the compound factor for i = 13%, with n = 4, 3, 2, 1, and 0, respectively).

The formula for the future value of an ordinary annuity is:

$$FV_n = PMT \sum_{t=1}^{N}(1 + i)^{N-t} = PMT\left[\frac{(1 + i)^N - 1}{i}\right] \tag{5-4}$$

future value annuity factor sum of the individual periods' future value compound factors that, when multiplied by the amount of an annuity, provides the future value of the annuity

where PMT is the end-of-period annuity payment and N is the number of payments. The term in brackets is the **future value annuity factor**. The advantage of Equation 5-4 is that it involves only one factor and it can be easily solved by using a simple calculator. How could you arrive at the future value annuity factor without this formula, but by using a financial calculator? Simply provide a PMT of 1 and then enter i and N; when you solve for FV, this will be the future value annuity factor.

Using this equation, we can solve for the future value as follows:

$$FV_5 = PMT \sum_{t=1}^{5}(1 + 0.13)^{5-t} = \$1,000\left[\frac{(1 + 0.13)^5 - 1}{0.13}\right]$$
$$= \$1,000 \times 6.48027 = \$6,480.27$$

We can derive the future value annuity factor for five years at 13% using a simple calculator.[15] Note that the sum of the compound factors for the N periods is equal to the future value annuity factor for N payments, that is:

$$\text{Future value annuity factor} = \sum_{t=1}^{N}(1 + i)^{N-t} = \left[\frac{(1 + i)^N - 1}{i}\right]$$

In our example,

Year	Cash flow at end of year	Future value interest factor	Future value, end of fifth year
1	$1,000	1.63047	$1,630.47
2	$1,000	1.44290	$1,442.90
3	$1,000	1.27690	$1,276.90
4	$1,000	1.13000	$1,130.00
5	$1,000	1.00000	$1,000.00

Future value annuity factor = 6.48027   FV = $6,480.27

---

[15] Simply substitute 1 for the PMT: i = 13, n = 5, PMT = 1, and solve for FV.

Of course, we could also use a financial calculator or a spreadsheet:[16]

Financial Calculator

PMT = –$1,000

$i = 13$

$n = 5$

PV = 0

Solve for FV.

Spreadsheet

=FV(0.13,5,–1000,0)

Present value of an ordinary annuity

The present value of an ordinary annuity is the discounted value of the series of cash flows, with the first cash flow occurring one period from today. Consider the example of a series of five cash flows of $1,000 to be received at the end of each year if the interest rate is 13%. What is the present value of this series? Taking a closer look, we can solve for the present value by viewing this as a five-part problem for which we have to find the present value of each of the five annual payments:

$$PV_0 = \frac{\$1,000}{1.13^5} + \frac{\$1,000}{1.13^4} + \frac{\$1,000}{1.13^3} + \frac{\$1,000}{1.13^2} + \frac{\$1,000}{1.13^1} = \$3,517.24$$

Or each cash flow is multiplied by the appropriate corresponding discount factor and then summed:

$$PV_0 = (\$1,000 \times 0.54276) + (\$1,000 \times 0.61332) + (\$1,000 \times 0.69305) \\ + (\$1,000 \times 0.78315) + (\$1,000 \times 0.88496) = \$3,517.24$$

Or multiply the periodic cash flow by the **present value annuity factor**, which is the sum of the individual discount factors:

$$PV_0 = \$1,000 \times 3.51724 = \$3,517.24$$

present value annuity factor sum of the discount factors that, when multiplied by the amount of an annuity payment, results in the present value of the annuity

Using a timeline, you can see that we discount the first cash flow one period and the last cash flow five periods:

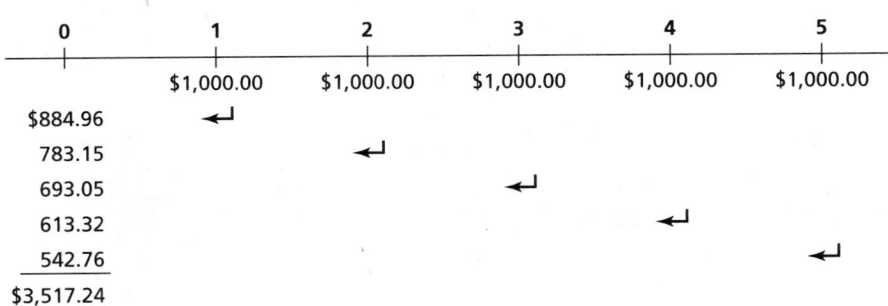

---

[16] You will notice that we use "N" to indicate the number of payments in an annuity, but refer to the "n" in the calculator calculations. This is because the number of payments and number of periods share the same key in the financial calculator.

As before, note that we are using the long way, by multiplying $1,000 by the sum of the relevant five discount factors, which add to 3.51724. Fortunately, the formula for determining the PV of ordinary annuities will do this for us:

$$PV_0 = PMT \sum_{t=1}^{N} \frac{1}{(1+i)^t} = PMT \left[\frac{1 - \frac{1}{(1+i)^N}}{i} \right] \tag{5-5}$$

To further demonstrate the relationship between the discount factors and the present value annuity factor, examine the problem in a table format:

Year	Cash flow at end of year	Discount factor	Present value, today
1	$1,000	0.88496	$884.96
2	$1,000	0.78315	783.15
3	$1,000	0.69305	693.05
4	$1,000	0.61332	613.32
5	$1,000	0.54276	542.76
		Present value annuity factor = 3.51724	PV = $3,517.24

By using this equation to solve this example, we arrive at:

$$PV_0 = \$1,000 \left[\frac{1 - \frac{1}{(1.13)^5}}{0.13} \right] = \$1,000 \times 3.51724 = \$3,517.24$$

Using a calculator or spreadsheet:

Using a financial calculator
PMT = $1,000
$i = 13\%$
$n = 5$
FV = 0

Solve for PV.

Using a spreadsheet
=PV(0.13,5,−1000,0)

Note: You can either change the sign on the PMT to negative or change the sign on the PV once it is calculated.

From this example, we can see that:

lessor person or company that leases out an item

lessee person or company that leases an item, paying a periodic amount in exchange for the use of the item

Annuities Due

Sometimes, annuities are structured such that the cash flows are paid at the beginning of a period rather than at the end. For example, leasing arrangements are usually set up like this, with the **lessee** (the one borrowing) making an immediate payment on taking possession of the equipment, such as a car, to the **lessor** (the one lending). Such an annuity is an **annuity due**. Let us look at an example to see how to evaluate these cash flows.

annuity due annuity for which the payments are made at the beginning of each period

Consider a problem similar to the annuity problem that we just looked at, except that now the payments are made at the beginning rather than at the end of each year. How much will the investor have after five years? How much would the investor have to deposit today to have the same results?

We begin as before by depicting the data in a timeline:

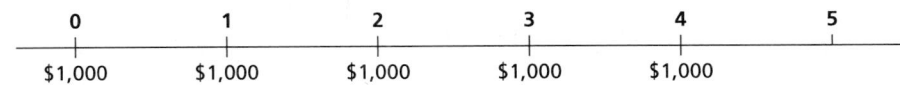

Note that as before, we have five cash flows of $1,000 each. However, each cash flow appears one period *earlier*, and thus each receives an *extra* period of interest at the rate of 13%.

Future value of an annuity due

We can solve for the future value of an annuity due in much the same way as we solved for the future value of an ordinary annuity, but we adjust for the additional compounding that each cash flow receives. Using the "brute force approach," we can find the future value of each of the five payments:

$$
\begin{aligned}
FV_5 &= \$10,00(1.13)^5 + \$1,000(1.13)^4 + \$1,000(1.13)^3 \\
&\quad + \$1,000(1.13)^2 + \$1,000(1.13)^1 \\
&= (\$1,000 \times 1.84244) + (\$1,000 \times 1.63047) + (\$1,000 \times 1.44290) \\
&\quad + (\$1,000 \times 1.27690) + (\$1,000 \times 1.1300) \\
&= \$1,000 \times 7.32271 \\
&= \$7,322.71
\end{aligned}
$$

We illustrate this same compounding in a timeline:

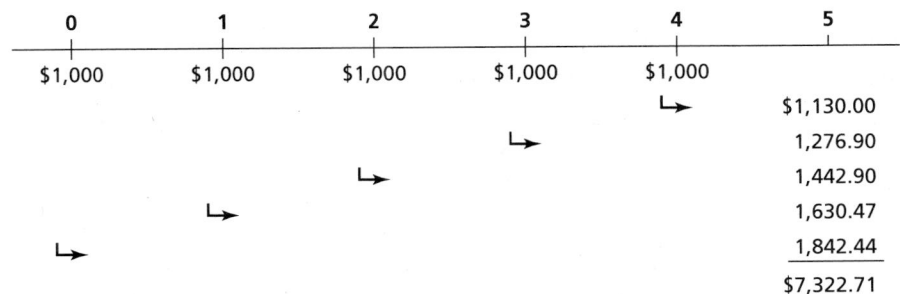

Note that because each flow gets one extra period of compounding at 13%, the net result is that we multiply our answer to the ordinary annuity by 1.13. In other words, the FV (annuity due) = [FV (ordinary annuity)](1 + i):

$$
FV_{5,annuity\ due} = FV_{5,ordinary\ annuity} \times (1 + i) = \$6,480.27 \times 1.13 = \$7,322.71
$$

Therefore, we can alter Equation 5-4 to find the FV of an annuity due as follows:

$$
FV_n = PMT \sum_{t=1}^{N} (1 + i)^t = PMT \left[\frac{(1 + i)^N - 1}{i} \right] (1 + i) \tag{5-6}
$$

However, we can now solve the example as follows:

$$FV_5 = PMT\left[\frac{(1 + 0.13)^5 - 1}{0.13}\right](1 + 0.13) = \$1,000 \times 6.48027 \times 1.13 = \$7,322.71$$

In other words, the value of the annuity due of $7,322.71 is 1.13 times larger than the value of the ordinary annuity that we calculated earlier of $6,480.27. Using a table format and identifying the individual compound factors, we see that the future value of this annuity is the sum of the individual future values, which is also equal to the product of the period cash flow and the sum of the compound factors:

Year	Cash flow at the beginning of the year	Compound factor	Future value
1	$1,000	1.84244	$1,842.44
2	$1,000	1.63047	1,630.47
3	$1,000	1.44290	1,442.90
4	$1,000	1.27690	1,276.90
5	$1,000	1.13000	1,130.00
	Future value annuity due factor =	7.32271	FV =$7,322.71

Using a financial calculator, we first put the calculator in the "Begin", "BEG", "Due" mode, depending on the calculator model, and then:

PMT = $1,000

$i = 13\%$

$n = 5$

Using a spreadsheet function, you indicate the timing of the cash flows using the fifth argument in the function with a "1". The spreadsheet entry is:

$$= FV(0.13, 5, -1000, 0, 1)$$

Present value of an annuity due

As before, to solve for the present value, we could view this as a five-part problem for which we have to find the present value of each of the five payments.

$$PV_0 = \frac{\$1,000}{(1 + 0.13)^4} + \frac{\$1,000}{(1 + 0.13)^3} + \frac{\$1,000}{(1 + 0.13)^2} + \frac{\$1,000}{(1 + 0.13)^1}$$

$$+ \frac{\$1,000}{(1 + 0.13)^0} = \$3,974.48$$

We can also represent in a timeline, noting that the cash flow at the beginning of, say, Year 2 is the same as the cash flow at the end of Year 1:

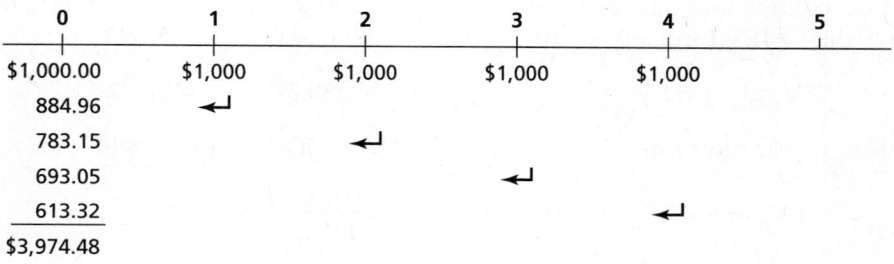

Or we can use a table format:

Year	Cash Flow at the Beginning of the Year	Discount Factor	Present Value
1	$1,000	1.00000	$1,000.00
2	$1,000	0.88496	884.96
3	$1,000	0.78315	783.15
4	$1,000	0.69305	693.05
5	$1,000	0.61332	613.32
		3.97448	$3,974.48

Note that we could also multiply our answer to the ordinary annuity valuation by 1.13, that is, $(1 + i)$:

$$PV_0 = \$1,000 \times 3.51724 \times 1.13 = \$3,974.48$$

Accordingly, we can modify Equation 5-5 to arrive at the formula for determining the PV of an annuity due:

$$PV_0 = PMT \sum_{t=1}^{N} \frac{1}{(1 + i)^{N-t}} = PMT \left[\frac{1 - \dfrac{1}{(1 + i)^N}}{i} \right](1 + i) \tag{5-7}$$

Using this to solve for the present value, we get:

$$PV_0 = \$1,000 \left[\frac{1 - \dfrac{1}{(1.13)^5}}{0.13} \right](1.13) = (\$1,000 \times 3.51724 \times 1.13) = \$3,974.48$$

Deferred Annuities

A **deferred annuity** is simply an annuity that begins two or more periods from the present. These annuities occur when a series of payments or receipts are delayed into the future. The classic example is saving for retirement: When you think about how much you need for your retirement, you usually start with figuring out how much you need to live on each year, and then you back into what you need to have saved by the time you retire. This is a deferred annuity.

deferred annuity annuity that begins two or more periods from the present

Let us start with a very basic example. Suppose you are promised a series of four payments of $1,000 each that begins three years from now, and the appropriate discount rate is 4%. There are three ways to solve this problem:

The long way

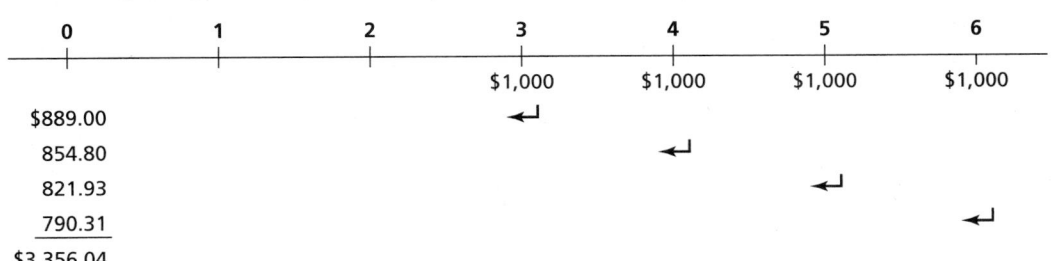

As a discounted ordinary annuity

Using this method, you discount the four $1,000 cash flows as an ordinary annuity. This provides you with a value as of the end of the second period (Remember: The present value of an ordinary annuity is one period before the first cash flow). Discounting this value for two periods provides you with the value today.

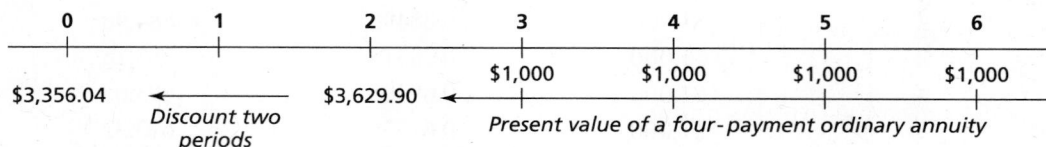

As a discounted annuity due

This method is similar to Method 2, but because of the timing of the valuation, there is one more discount period. Why? Because when you discount the four payments as an annuity due, you get a value coinciding with the first cash flow, which is at the end of the third period.

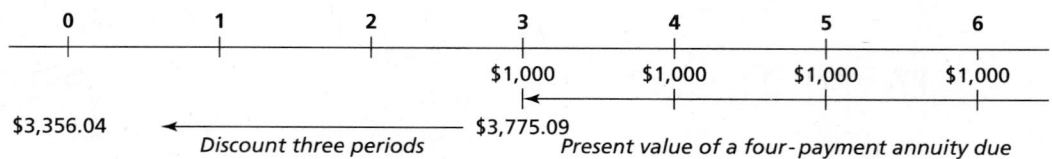

As you can see, you get to the same place using each of the three methods. Which is easier? For very simple problems, it is really a matter of personal choice. For problems involving many more cash flows? Most likely, Method 2 is easier because you can use the built-in calculator or spreadsheet annuity function and, if you are using a financial calculator, you do not have to change any settings on the calculator.

Perpetuities

perpetuity annuity that provides periodic payments forever

A **perpetuity** is a special annuity that goes on forever, so N goes to infinity in the annuity equation. In this case, Equation 5-5 reduces to:[17]

$$PV_0 = \frac{PMT}{i} \tag{5-8}$$

Perpetuities are easy to value because all we do is divide the cash payment or receipt by the interest rate. Consider an investment that promises to pay $2 each year, forever. If the discount rate is 8%, the present value of this investment is $2 ÷ 0.08 = $25.

There is only a small difference in the present value of the cash streams between a perpetuity and an annuity with many payments. For example, the difference between $2 in perpetuity and a fifty-period ordinary annuity of $2 each year is $25 − 24.47 = $0.53. This tells us that the PV of the cash flows of $2 per year from Year 51 to infinity (that is, ∞) is only $0.53. This is a very important result and is the driving force behind many financial innovations because it means that cash flows far into the future are of very little value because of the discounting involved in the time value of money.

---

[17] If N is infinity, then $PV_0 = PMT \sum_{t=1}^{\infty} \frac{1}{(1 + i)^t}$ which reduces to $PMT ÷ i$.

PROBLEM

Consider an annuity of $3,000, with cash flows occurring at the end of each period and an interest rate of 12%.

A. If the cash flows occur for thirty years, what is the present value of this annuity?
B. If the cash flows occur each period, forever, what is the present value of this stream of cash flows?

EXAMPLE 5.8

Annuities and Perpetuities

Solution

A. $$PV_0 = \$3,000 \left[\frac{1 - \frac{1}{(1.12)^{30}}}{0.12} \right] = \$3,000 \times 8.05518 = \$24,165.55$$

B. $$PV_0 = \frac{\$3,000}{0.12} = \$25,000$$

Determining the Number of Periods or the Interest Rate

When we focused on the value of a single sum, whether compounding or discounting, we could solve for the number of periods given a future value, a present value, and an interest rate. We could also solve for the interest rate or return given a future value, a present value, and the number of periods. We can do the same for an annuity or a perpetuity, although using formulas in some cases becomes a bit burdensome. To overcome this, we can rely on financial calculators and spreadsheets to do the heavy lifting in solving these types of problems.

Consider solving for an interest rate, given the present value, the number of payments, and the amount of the payment. This is a common application when the loan terms are disclosed and the borrower wants to know the cost of the loan based on these terms. The general setup for the problem features the present value annuity formula:

$$PV_0 = PMT \sum_{t=1}^{N} \frac{1}{(1 + i)^t}$$

If $10,000 is borrowed, the present value is $10,000. If the payments are $2,000 each, and there are six payments, then:

$$\$10,000 = \$2,000 \sum_{t=1}^{6} \frac{1}{(1 + i)^t}$$

There is no direct solution to the problem; the best we can do is determine that the present value annuity factor is equal to $10,000 ÷ $2,000 = 5. We could use the trial-and-error method to eventually find the interest rate, i, but this becomes quite tedious. Instead, using a calculator:

PV = $20,000

PMT = $2,000

$n = 6$

Solve for i.

You should note that the present value and the payment must have different signs when entered into the calculator, or the program will not be able to determine a solution. Using a spreadsheet function, RATE,

$$= \text{RATE(number of periods, payment, present value, future value)}$$

or

$$= \text{RATE}(6,2000,-10000,0,0)$$

The rate is 5.472%.[18]

We solve for the number of payments in a similar manner. Suppose Company X can borrow $100 million and determines that it can pay this back in semi-annual payments of $4 million each. If the annual rate of interest on this borrowing is 5% but the rate per semi-annual payment is 2.5%, how many payments need to be made by Company X? We again use:

$$PV_0 = PMT \sum_{t=1}^{n} \frac{1}{(1 + i)^t}$$

Substituting the known values for PV_0, PMT, and i:

$$\$100 = \$4 \sum_{t=1}^{N} \frac{1}{(1 + 0.025)^t}$$

Using a financial calculator or a spreadsheet, we can calculate the number of payments as 39.7217:

Financial calculator	*Spreadsheet*
PV = $100	= NPER(0.025,4,−100,0)
i = 2.5%	
PMT = 4	
Solve for n.	

Because these are semi-annual payments, it will take forty payments (with the last payment not quite $4 million) to repay the loan.

EXAMPLE 5.9

Ordinary Annuities and Annuities Due

PROBLEM

Consider two series of cash flows:

Series A: Beginning today, produces a cash flow of $2,000 each month for sixty months.

Series B: Beginning one month from today, produces a cash flow of $2,050 each month for fifty-nine months.

If the discount rate appropriate for both series is 0.5% per month, which series is more valuable today?

Solution

Series B has a larger present value, so it is more valuable today.

---

[18] Be sure to place a zero in the fourth argument because there is future value.

Series A: Present value of a sixty-payment annuity due:

$$PV_0 = \$2,000 \sum_{t=1}^{60} \frac{1}{(1 + 0.005)^{60-t}} = \$2,000$$

$$\left[\frac{1 - \dfrac{1}{(1 + 0.005)^n}}{0.005} \right] (1 + 0.005) = \$103,968.38$$

or a fifty-nine-payment ordinary annuity plus one payment:

$$PV_0 = \left[\$2,000 \sum_{t=1}^{59} \frac{1}{(1 + 0.005)^t} \right] + \$2,000 = \$103,968.38$$

Series B: Present value of an ordinary annuity

$$PV_0 = \left[\$2,050 \sum_{t=1}^{59} \frac{1}{(1 + 0.005)^t} \right] = \$104,517.59$$

SUMMARIZING

Ordinary annuity: The first cash flow occurs one period from today.

Example: Three-payment ordinary annuity

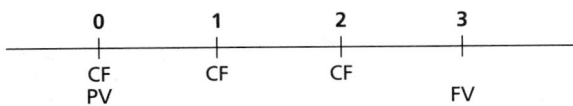

Annuity due: The first cash flow occurs today.

Example: Three-payment annuity due

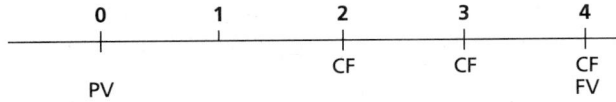

Deferred annuity: The first cash flow occurs beyond one period from today.

Example: Three-payment deferred annuity, with the first payment deferred one period

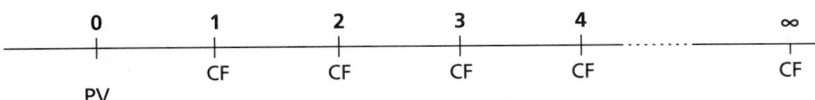

Perpetuity: The first cash flow occurs one period from today, and continues *ad infinitum.*

FINANCE in the News | Structured Settlements

In resolving legal claims, such as injuries from an accident, a prevailing party may accept either a lump-sum payment or a series of payments. When the claimant elects to receive a periodic stream (i.e., an annuity), this is referred to as a *structured settlement*. These payments, in most cases, are tax-free cash flows.

Since the 1970s, specialized companies have been making offers to claimants who may prefer to receive a lump-sum cash payment today in exchange for the annuity. From the point of view of the claimant selling the annuity to these companies, the decision involves comparing the present value of the annuity with the offered lump sum. Because the implicit interest on the annuity payments is not taxed but earnings on any invested lump sum are taxed, receiving the annuity is generally more attractive than receiving the lump sum. However, the claimant's individual situation or age may make the lump sum more attractive.

From the point of view of the structured settlement company, the decision is slightly more complex because the federal government has a punitive tax on the difference between the undiscounted value of the annuity and the amount paid for the annuity at a 40% rate. This tax occurs if the sale of the annuity to the company is not approved by the respective state court.[19] Therefore, from the perspective of the structured settlement company, the decision regarding a transfer that is not approved involves comparing the undiscounted value of the annuity with the lump sum offered for the rights to the structured settlement, after subtracting the 40% excise tax. In other words, if the transfer is not approved by the state court, there is no incentive to transfer. If the state court approves the transfer (considering what is best for the recipient), the decision involves comparing the present value of the annuity with the lump sum offered to the claimant.

Sources: Internal Revenue Service Form 8876 *Excise Tax on Structured Settlement Factoring Transactions*, and Allen, Brad, "How to Evaluate Structured Settlement Buyout Offers," *Fox Business News*, www.foxbusiness.com, June 29, 2010.

Concept Review Questions

1. What is the mathematical relation between an ordinary annuity and an annuity due?

2. When you use a financial calculator or a spreadsheet to calculate the future value of an annuity, at what point in time is the resultant FV for the ordinary annuity? for the annuity due?

3. When solving for the number periods of a lump sum or an ordinary annuity, some perfectionists insist on rounding up the number of periods to the next whole period. What is the basis of the reasoning for this?

5.3 NOMINAL AND EFFECTIVE RATES

So far, we have assumed that payments are made annually and that interest is compounded annually, so we have been able to use quoted rates to solve each problem. In practice, in many situations payments are made (or received) at intervals other than annually (e.g., quarterly, monthly), and compounding often occurs more frequently than annually. We need to be sure that we use the appropriate effective interest rate.

annual percentage rate (APR) or stated rate or nominal rate stated rate of interest, calculated as the product of the interest rate per compounding period and the number of compounding periods

APR Versus EAR: Discrete Compounding

The **annual percentage rate (APR)** is the rate stated for an annual period, assuming no compounding of interest within the year. We often refer to the APR as the **nominal rate** or **stated rate**. Because this rate does not consider compounding, it understates the

[19] Internal Revenue Code Section 5891.

true, effective rate of interest. The **effective annual rate (EAR)** for a period is the rate at which a dollar invested grows over that period. It is usually stated in percentage terms based on an annual period. To determine effective rates, we first recognize that the annual rates of financial institutions will equal the effective annual rate only when compounding is done on an annual basis. We will use some examples to illustrate the process for determining effective rates.

effective annual rate (EAR) rate at which a dollar invested grows over a given period; usually stated in percentage terms based on an annual period

Suppose that an account earns 4% interest per year, compounded quarterly. This means that there is $4\% \div 4 = 1\%$ interest every three months. If you deposit $1 in this account today and leave it in the account for five years, you will have $1.22 at the end of twenty quarters, or five years:

$$FV_5 = \$1(1 + 0.01)^{20} = \$1.22$$

If you have $1 today and $1.22 at the end of five years, you have, effectively, earned 4.06% per year. How did we know this? We took the given values and solved for the annual rate: $PV = \$1; FV = \$1.22; n = 5 \rightarrow$ solve for i.

PROBLEM

Suppose you invest $1,000 today for one year at a quoted annual rate of 16% compounded annually.

1. What is the FV at the end of the year?
2. If interest is compounded quarterly, what is the effective annual rate?

EXAMPLE 5.10

Effective Versus Annual Percentage Rates

Solution

1. $FV_1 = 1,000(1.16)^1 = \$1,160.$

   This means that each $1 grows to $1.16 by the end of the period, so we can say that the "effective" annual interest rate is 16%.

2. When the rate is quoted at 16%, and compounding is done quarterly, the appropriate adjustment (by convention) is to charge $16\% \div 4 = 4\%$ per quarter, so we have

$$FV = \$1,000(1.04)^4 = \$1,170$$
$$EAR = \$1,170 \div \$1,000 - 1 = 17\% \text{ or } (1 + 0.04)^4 - 1 = 17\%$$

We can use the following equation to determine the effective annual rate for any given compounding interval:

$$EAR = \left(1 + \frac{APR}{m}\right)^m - 1 \tag{5-9}$$

where EAR is the effective annual rate, APR is the quoted rate, and m is the number of compounding intervals per year.

If the APR is 4% and interest is compounded quarterly, the EAR is 4.06%:

$$EAR = (1 + {}^{0.04}/_4)^4 - 1 = 4.06\%$$

If we leave $1 in an account that pays interest at the rate of 4%, compounded quarterly, we can determine the future value in five years as:

$$FV_5 = \$1(1 + 0.0406)^5 = \$1.22$$

Or, equivalently,

$$FV_5 = \$1(1 + 0.01)^{20} = \$1.22$$

You can, of course, solve effective interest rate problems using a calculator or a spreadsheet. If interest is compounded more frequently than once per year, you have two, equivalent approaches to solving for a value:

Approach 1 Convert the APR into an equivalent rate per period, and adjust the number of periods, and then solve appropriately.

Approach 2 Solve for the effective annual rate and then use this rate to determine the value.

Solving for the future value, FV = $1,000 × (1 + 0.01)^{20} = $1,000 × 1.22019 = $1,220.19. Consider investing $1,000 for five years in an account that has an APR of 4% and interest is compounded quarterly. What will be in the account at the end of five years?

Approach 1: *Convert the APR into usable inputs*

> PV = $1,000
>> $i = 4\% \div 4 = 1\%$
>> $n = 5 \times 4 = 20$

Solving for the future value, FV = $1,000 $(1 + 0.01)^{20}$ = $1,220.19

Approach 2: *Calculate and then use the effective annual rate*

> PV = $1,000
>> $i = (1 + 0.01)^4 - 1 = 0.040604$ or 4.0604%
>> $n = 5$

Solving for the future value, FV = $1,000$(1 + 0.040604)^5$ = $1,220.19.

As you can see, we end up with the same future value, regardless of the approach.

Let us combine what you know about annuities with what you know about effective annual rates. Suppose that you borrow $10 million and will repay this loan with monthly payments of $0.3 million per month. We calculate the monthly interest rate by solving for i using the trial-and-error method:

$$\$10 = \$0.3 \sum_{t=1}^{60} \frac{1}{(1 + i)^t}$$

Using a calculator:

> PV = $10
> FV = $0
> PMT = $0.3
> $N = 60$

Or, using a spreadsheet,

$$=RATE(60,0.3,-10,0).$$

This produces a monthly rate of 2.175%. However, to enhance comparability with other borrowing arrangements, we should place this rate on an annual basis. The equivalent APR is 2.175% × 12 = 26.1%. The effective annual rate is:

$$EAR = (1 + 0.02175)^{12} - 1 = 29.46\%$$

This is a common type of problem in consumer finance: We know the amount borrowed, what the payments are, and how many payments there will be. While the APR is provided in the fine print, we usually have to calculate the effective rate on our own.

APR Versus EAR: Continuous Compounding

When compounding is conducted on a continuous basis, we use the following equation to determine the effective annual rate for a given quoted rate:

$$EAR = e^{APR} - 1 \qquad\qquad (5\text{-}10)$$

where, once again, e is the unique Euler number (approximately 2.718). For example, if an investment has an APR of 5% and interest is compounded continuously:

$$EAR = e^x - 1 = e^{0.05} - 1 = 5.127\%$$

Using a calculator, we click on the key for Euler's "e" (recall that this is often indicated as e^X), enter the exponent in decimal form, and then subtract one:

$$EAR = e^x - 1$$

Suppose you want to calculate the future value of $10 million invested five years at 6% interest, compounded continuously. The future value is:

$FV_5 = \$10 \text{ million } e^{0.05 \times 6}$

$FV_5 = \$10 \text{ million} \times e^{0.3}$

$FV_5 = \$10 \text{ million} \times 1.349859$

$FV_5 = \$13.49859 \text{ million}$

We calculate the present value with continuous compounding in a similar manner. Suppose you want to find today's value of $1,000 three years from now, with 5% interest, compounded continuously:

$$PV_0 = \frac{FV_3}{e^{i \times n}} = \frac{\$1,000}{1.161834} = \$860.7080$$

You perform this calculation in the calculator using the math function, e^x.

USING A SPREADSHEET FOR CONTINUOUS COMPOUNDING

Suppose you want to calculate the EAR in a spreadsheet for an APR of 5%. Using the spreadsheet function EXP and using "^–1" to invert $e^{i \times n}$, you enter:

$$=EXP(0.05)-1$$

which is 5.127%.

Applying this to a present value problem, calculating the present value of $1,000 to be received at the end of three years with an APR of 5%, continuously compounded:

$$=1000 * (EXP(3*0.05)^\wedge -1)$$

which is $860.7080. The "^" indicates an exponent. Taking something to the power of –1 is the same as taking the inverse.

A few observations about EAR and APR:

- If interest is compounded annually, the EAR is equal to the APR.
- If interest is compounded more frequently than once per year, the effective rate is higher than the quoted rate.
- The more frequent the compounding within a year, the greater is the difference between the EAR and the APR.
- The limit is continuous compounding: The largest difference between the EAR and the APR is when interest is compounded continuously.

EXAMPLE 5.11

Effective Annual Rates for Various Compounding Frequencies

PROBLEM

What are the effective annual rates for the following quoted rates?

A. 12%, compounded annually
B. 12%, compounded semi-annually
C. 12%, quarterly
D. 12%, monthly
E. 12%, daily
F. 12%, continuously

Solution

	Formula	*Calculator*	*Spreadsheet*	*Answer*
A.	$EAR = \left(1 + \dfrac{0.12}{1}\right)^{1} - 1$			12%
B.	$EAR = \left(1 + \dfrac{0.12}{2}\right)^{2} - 1$	NOM=12 P/PYR=2 *Solve for EFF*	=EFFECT(0.12,2)	12.36%
C.	$EAR = \left(1 + \dfrac{0.12}{4}\right)^{4} - 1$	NOM=12 P/PYR=4 *Solve for EFF*	=EFFECT(0.12,4)	12.55%
D.	$EAR = \left(1 + \dfrac{0.12}{12}\right)^{12} - 1$	NOM=12 P/PYR=12 *Solve for EFF*	=EFFECT(0.12,12)	12.68%
E.	$EAR = \left(1 + \dfrac{0.12}{365}\right)^{365} - 1$	NOM=12 P/PYR=365 *Solve for EFF*	=EFFECT(0.12,365)	12.747%
F.	$EAR = e^{0.12} - 1$	EXP or e 0.12 −1	=exp(.12)−1	12.75%

ETHICS | The Cost of Small Consumer Loans

Some borrowers do not have access to conventional loans from banks and instead resort to other loan arrangements, such as payday loans, car title loans, and refund anticipation loans. While these loans are easy to get, there is a very high cost to them. The Consumer Federation of America summarized the cost of unconventional loans:

- A payday loan is a loan for a week or two, until the borrower gets paid. The borrower writes a post-dated check for the amount borrowed plus interest and fees, which is then cashed by the lender at the loan due date. Payday loans may cost more than 500% in financing costs.

- Car title loans require you to hand over your car title if you do not repay the loan. Car title lending costs have an effective interest rate around 300%.

- Refund anticipated loans are generally related to anticipated tax refunds. The borrower borrows the expected amount of the refund, less commission and fees, and the lender receives the anticipated refund. Refund anticipation loans have effective interest of over 500%.

  The Federal Deposit Insurance Company (FDIC) initiated a pilot program in February 2008 to encourage banks to make small loans that are affordable. After one year of this program, involving thirty-one banks, $18.5 million had been loaned through the 16,000 loans.

The new consumer protection agency, created by the Wall Street Reform and Consumer Financial Protection Act of 2010, is charged with overseeing the many forms of consumer lending arrangements, which may provide some degree of uniformity among states regarding payday loans, car title loans, and tax refund anticipation loans.

Sources: Consumer Federation of America, "Research Findings Illustrate the High Risk of High-Cost Short-term Loans for Consumers," February 18, 2009; FDIC Press Release, PR-52-2007: "FDIC Issues Final Guidelines on Affordable Small-Dollar Loans"; and "The FDIC's Small-Dollar Loan Pilot Program: A Case Study after One Year," FDIC Quarterly, 2009, Vol. 3, No. 2.

Concept Review Questions

1. At what frequency of compounding is the effective annual rate equal to the annual percentage rate? Explain your answer.

2. The Truth-in-Lending law in the U.S. requires lenders to disclose the APR for any loan transaction. Does the APR overstate or understate the true cost of a loan? Explain.

5.4 APPLICATIONS

Next, we apply some of the time value of money mathematics to a few examples to demonstrate the basic principles.

Comparing Alternative Savings Plans

Let us consider an example of two investors and the role of compound interest. Each investor follows one of two different investing approaches. Assume each investor earns a 5% annual return.

Investor A: Invests early

Investor A begins investing $2,302.37 per year (at year end) for six years, and then she makes no further contributions. She makes her first payment on her twenty-second birthday and therefore makes her last payment on her twenty-seventh birthday. Note that she invests the same amount each year, so this is an example of an annuity. How much money will she have when she turns sixty-five?

We perceive this as a two-part problem, which we can solve in several ways. One way to solve this is to estimate the future value of the payments as of the last payment and then compound this balance until Investor A turns sixty-five. To do this, we first estimate the future value of the six $2,302.37 payments at the end of six years, or at Investor A's twenty-seventh birthday:

Age	Investor A deposit	Investor A balance in account
22	$2,302.37	$2,302.37
23	$2,302.37	$4,719.86
24	$2,302.37	$7,258.22
25	$2,302.37	$9,923.50
26	$2,302.37	$12,722.04
27	$2,302.37	$15,660.51

Or

$$FV_{27} = PMT\left[\frac{(1 + i)^n - 1}{i}\right] = \$2{,}302.37\left[\frac{(1.05)^6 - 1}{0.05}\right]$$

$$= \$2{,}302.37 \times 6.8019 = \$15{,}660.51$$

Note that the first payment is made on Investor A's twenty-second birthday. Therefore, there have been six payments by the time of her twenty-seventh birthday: five that have earned interest, one that was just made on her twenty-seventh birthday that has not yet earned interest.

We estimate the future value of the accumulated savings after thirty-seven years (i.e., from Investor A's twenty-seventh birthday to her sixty-fifth birthday):

$$FV_{65} = PV_{27}(1 + i)^n = \$15{,}660.51 \times (1.05)^{38} = \$15{,}660.51 \times 6.3855 = \$100{,}000$$

In other words, Investor A will have $100,000 saved by her sixty-fifth birthday.

Investor B: Delayed savings

At age twenty-two, Investor B postpones investing until he reaches age thirty-six, then he invests $1,505.14 per year, starting on his thirty-sixth birthday, for thirty years, with his last payment on his sixty-fifth birthday. How much will he have when he turns sixty-five?

In the case of Investor B, the periodic payment is $1,500, and there are thirty such payments:

$$FV_{65} = PMT\left[\frac{(1 + i)^n - 1}{i}\right] = \$1{,}505.14\left[\frac{(1.12)^{30} - 1}{0.12}\right] = \$1{,}505.41 \times 66.4388$$

$$= \$100{,}000$$

In other words, Investor B arrives at the same balance on his sixty-fifth birthday, but he got there by making thirty payments.

Investor A versus Investor B

In this example, we show how the compounding effect is magnified as the time horizon increases. You can see the difference in the accumulation of funds for the investors in Figure 5-4. By starting earlier, Investor A sets aside less than Investor B does but achieves the same result.

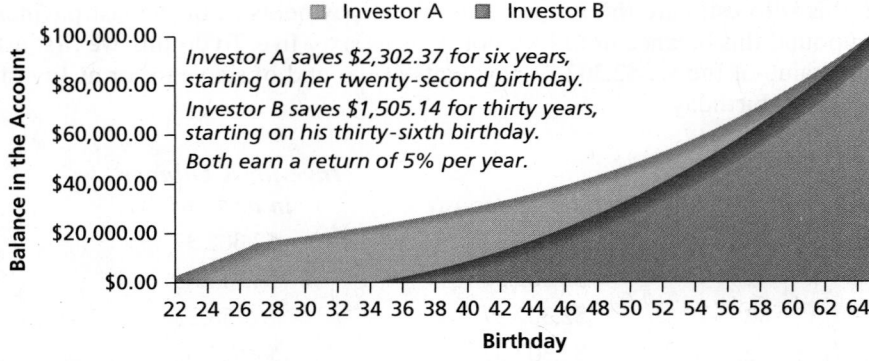

FIGURE 5-4   The Balance in the Investment Accounts for Investor A and Investor B

Loans and Mortgages

One common and important application of annuity concepts is with respect to loan or **mortgage** arrangements. Typically, these arrangements involve "blended" payments for equal amounts that include both an interest component and a principal repayment component. The loan payments are designed to **amortize** the loan, which means paying off a loan over time such that each payment made on the loan consists of principal repayment and interest.[20] In many amortized loans, the principal balance at the end of the loan term is zero. However, in some loans, a lump sum remains at the end of the loan term. We refer to this amount as the *balloon payment*.

Because these loans involve equal payments at regular intervals, based on one fixed interest rate specified when the loan is made, the payments can be viewed as annuities. Therefore, we can determine the amount of the payment, the effective period interest rate, and so on, by using Equation 5-5 and recognizing that the PV equals the amount of the loan.

The process of determining the interest and principal portions of each payment is **amortization**. An **amortization schedule** is a spreadsheet that details how much of each payment is interest and how much is principal, as well as how much of the loan balance remains outstanding after each payment. This is of importance to businesses and individuals, as the interest portion is a deductible expense for tax purposes. We calculate the interest portion by applying the effective period interest rate to the principal outstanding at the beginning of each period. The remaining portion of the payment reduces the amount of principal outstanding.

Consider an example of a three-year $5,000 loan with a 9.07% annual interest rate. To complete an amortization schedule, we first solve for amount of the payment, given:

PV = $5,000

$n = 3$

$i = 9.07\%$

Solving for the PMT using the formula, we find that the periodic payment is $2,000:

$$\text{PMT} = \frac{PV_0}{\left[\dfrac{1 - \dfrac{1}{(1+i)^n}}{i}\right]} = \frac{5,000}{\left[\dfrac{1 - \dfrac{1}{(1.0907)^3}}{0.0907}\right]} = \frac{\$5,000}{2.48685} = \$2,000$$

Using a financial calculator, and remembering to input the present value as a negative value,

FV = $0

PV = $5,000

$n = 3$

$i = 9.07\%$

Solve for PMT.

Using a spreadsheet function, PMT, we enter the interest rate, the number of payments, and the amount of the loan:

=PMT(0.0907,3,5000,0)

We can determine the loan amortization schedule based on the payment, the interest rate, the number of payments, and the amount of the loan. The loan is a simple annual

mortgage loan, usually for real estate, that involves level, periodic payments consisting of interest and principal repayment over a specified payment period

amortize determine the repayment of a loan in which regular payments consist of both interest and principal

amortization process of determining how much of each payment is interest and principal repayment

amortization schedule breakdown of each payment of an amortized loan into interest and principal components

[20] There are, of course, balloon loans, in which a specified lump sum is paid at the end of the loan period. In this case, a portion of the loan is amortized, and a portion of the loan is repaid as a lump sum at the end of the loan period.

payment loan, so the cost of the loan is the annual interest rate multiplied by the outstanding balance. For the first period, this is 9.07% multiplied by $5,000 or $453.50.

Payment	[1] Beginning principal	[2] Payment	[3] Interest $i \times$ [1]	[4] Principal reduction [2] – [3]	[5] Ending principal [1] – [4]
1	$5,000.00	$2,000.00	$453.50	$1,524.24	$3,475.76
2	$3,475.76	$2,000.00	$315.25	$1,662.49	$1,813.27
3	$1,813.27	$2,000.00	$164.46	$1,813.27	$0.00

This is the first charge on the loan payments; the residual, which is $1,524.24 in the first year, goes to reduce the amount of the loan. For the next year, the outstanding balance on the loan is now $3,475.76, and the interest of the loan goes down to $315.25, even though the payment is the same amount, $2,000. You can see this in Figure 5-5. As a result, the amount going toward the repayment of the loan increases to $1,662.49 with the second payment and to $1,813.27 with the third payment.

We can calculate the remaining loan balance, with P representing the number of payments that have been made, using:

$$\text{Remaining principal balance} = \frac{\text{Principal}\left[(1 + i)^N - (1 + i)^P\right]}{(1 + i)^N} \quad (5\text{-}11)$$

So, after the first two payments are made, the remaining loan balance is:

$$\text{Remaining principal balance} = \frac{\$5,000\left[(1 + 0.0907)^3 - (1 + 0.0907)^2\right]}{(1 + 0.0907)^3} = \$1,813.27$$

In practice, loan repayments are often not made on an annual basis, with many calling for quarterly, monthly, or even weekly repayments. For these arrangements, we need to convert the quoted annual rates into effective period rates that correspond to the frequency of payments; in other words, we need to divide the APR by the number of payments in an annual period to determine i, and then n represents the number of payments over the life of the loan.

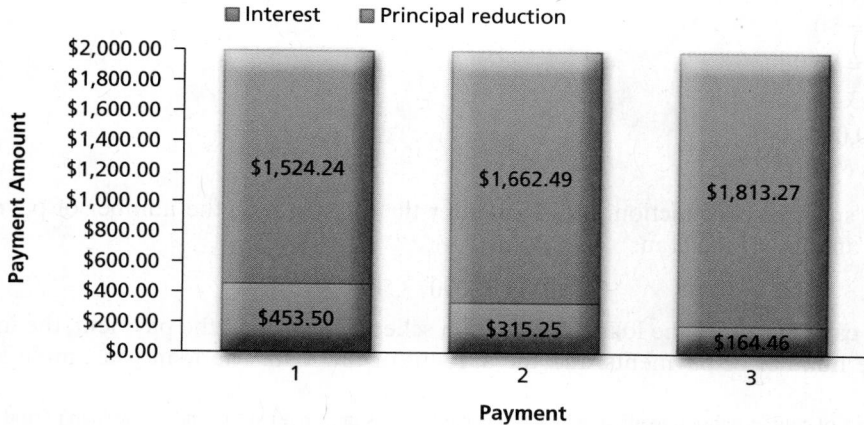

FIGURE 5-5 **Interest and Principal Repayment in an Amortized Three-Year Loan of $5,000 with Interest of 9.07%**

SPREADSHEET APPLICATIONS: AMORTIZING LOANS

Instead of working through the math ourselves, we could use some spreadsheet functions to determine the interest and principal paid with each payment:

$$=IPMT(i, payment\ number, number\ of\ periods, amount\ of\ loan)$$

$$=PPMT(i, payment\ number, number\ of\ periods, amount\ of\ loan)$$

For example, the interest paid with the second payment is:

$$=IPMT(0.097, A3, 3, -5000)$$

and the principal paid with the second payment is:

$$=PPMT(0.097, A3, 3, -5000)$$

The amortization formulas in the spreadsheet are therefore:[21]

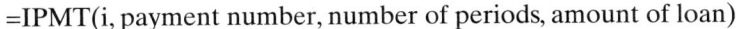

	A	B	C	D	E	F
	Period	*Beginning principal*	*Payment*	*Interest*	*Principal reduction*	*Ending Principal*
1						
2	1	5000	=PMT(0.1,3,–B2,0)	=IPMT(0.1,A2,3,–B2)	=PPMT(0.1,A2,3,–B2,0)	=B2–E2
3	2	=F2	=PMT(0.1,3,–B2,0)	=IPMT(0.1,A3,3,–B2)	=PPMT(0.1,A3,3,–B2,0)	=B3–E3
4	3	=F3	=PMT(0.1,3,–B2,0)	=IPMT(0.1,A4,3,–B2)	=PPMT(0.1,A4,3,–B2,0)	=B4–E4

Mortgages represent an example of a loan that requires that payments be made more frequently than annually. In fact, mortgage payments must be made at least monthly, but some may offer the opportunity to make biweekly or weekly payments.[22] The amortization of a mortgage is similar to the previous example.

Consider a mortgage of $200,000 that is to be repaid over 360 months. If the annual percentage rate on this mortgage is 6%, what are the monthly mortgage payments? The given information is the following:

PV = $200,000
i = 6% ÷ 12 = 0.5%
n = 360

Solving for the payment, using a financial calculator or spreadsheet, provides the answer $1,199.10.

Constructing an amortization schedule, we need to consider that unlike the simple annual payment loan, for which the cost of the loan is the annual interest cost, the cost here is the monthly interest rate of 6% ÷ 12 = 0.5% because we have a monthly amortization schedule. It is this monthly rate applied to the outstanding balance that determines how much of the mortgage's monthly payments represent the cost of the loan. As is clear from the amortization schedule, very little of the early payments go toward reducing the principal—most of the early payments are for interest. This is true for all long-term loans because, by definition, the repayment of the loan is being done over a long period. As time passes, the interest cost of the fixed payments continues to decrease, and the payment of principal correspondingly increases. The reason for this is simply that the interest rate is

[21] The $ next to the cell reference indicates that this is a fixed or absolute reference, so if you were to copy the function (e.g., PMT), it would still refer to the same cell for the principal amount of the loan—and would not change as other relative references change.

[22] As an example of further complications, consider mortgages in Canada. In Canada, mortgages are complicated by the fact that compounding is done on a semi-annual basis, even though payments are made at least monthly.

the cost of borrowing money, and this cost, based on the declining amount of principal that is owed, is subtracted first from the monthly payment—and what is left is used to repay some of the principal amount of the loan. But no matter what, the sum of the interest and principal payments is the amount of the payment.

We amortize this mortgage monthly, using the monthly payment of $1,199.10 and the monthly interest rate of 0.5% for the first five months:

	[1]	[2]	[3]	[4]	[5]
				Principal reduction	Ending principal
	Beginning principal	Payment	Interest $i \times$ [1]	[2] – [3]	[1] – [4]
Period					
1	$200,000.00	$1,199.10	$1,000.00	$199.10	$199,800.90
2	$199,800.90	$1,199.10	$999.00	$200.10	$199,600.80
3	$199,600.80	$1,199.10	$998.00	$201.10	$199,399.71
4	$199,399.71	$1,199.10	$997.00	$202.10	$199,197.61
5	$199,197.61	$1,199.10	$995.99	$203.11	$198,994.50

One question common to a mortgagee—that is, the borrower—would be how much of the loan would be retired after a certain time. We can solve this problem in the same method that we used for the last example, focusing on the ending principal, as compared with the original amount of the loan. In the case of any amortized loan, a high proportion of each of the early payments goes toward interest rather than principal reduction. You can see how the principal remaining on the mortgage falls more rapidly over time in Figure 5-6.[23]

Now let us see what happens if we introduce a balloon payment. A **balloon payment** is a payment that represents repayment of some amount of the principal of loan above and beyond what is paid as part of the amortized loan payments.

balloon payment payment that represents repayment of some amount of the principal of loan above and beyond what is paid as part of the amortized loan payments

Suppose we have a 6% loan of $200,000 for thirty years, with monthly payments, and with a balloon payment of $50,000 at the end of thirty years. What is the monthly payment on this loan? The inputs are similar to our last example, but now we have a future value of $50,000 to consider:

PV = $200,000

FV = $50,000

$i = 6\% \div 12 = 0.5\%$

$n = 360$

The payment in this case is $1,149.326, less than the $1,199.10, with no balloon payment. You can see the difference in the rate of the loan repayment between the loans without

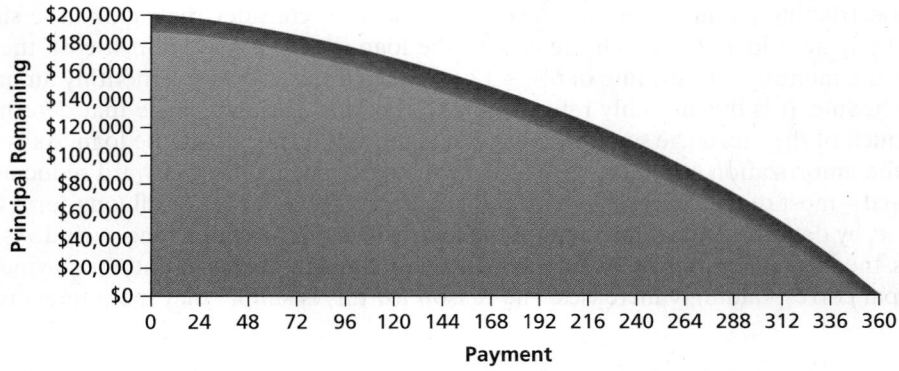

FIGURE 5-6 Principal Remaining on a Mortgage with Loan of $200,000, with Payments of $1,199.10, an Apr of 6%, and 360 Payments

[23] The balance remaining on the loan at any point in time is simply the present value of the remaining payments.

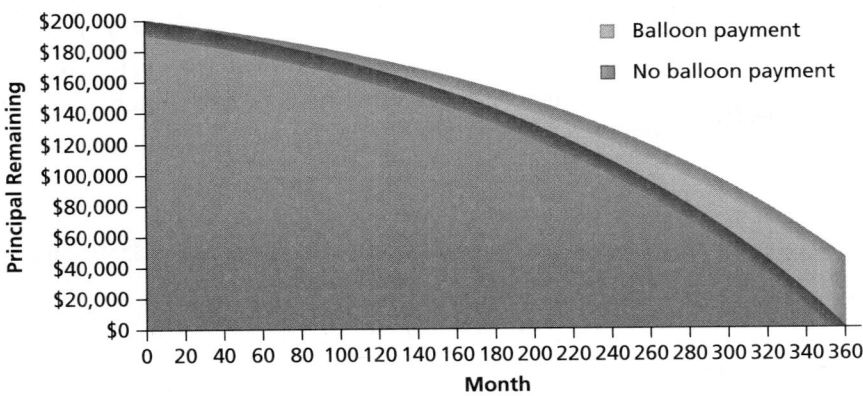

FIGURE 5-7 **Comparison of the Principal Repayment for the Loan of $200,000 at 6% for 360 Months, without and with a Balloon Payment of $50,000 at the End of the Loan Term**

and with the balloon payment in Figure 5-7. For a closer look, you can see the difference in amortization by examining the first six months of payments:

	No balloon payment payment is $1,199.10 per month			Balloon payment payment is $1,149.15 per month		
Month	Interest	Principal repayment	Remaining principal balance	Interest	Principal repayment	Remaining principal balance
1	$1,000	$199	$199,801	$1,000	$149	$199,851
2	$999	$200	$199,601	$999	$150	$199,701
3	$998	$201	$199,400	$999	$151	$199,550
4	$997	$202	$199,198	$998	$152	$199,398
5	$996	$203	$198,994	$997	$152	$199,246
6	$995	$204	$198,790	$996	$153	$199,093

Saving for Retirement

You are advising a client who plans on retiring thirty-five years from today. On retirement, the client wishes to have sufficient savings in his account to guarantee $48,000 each year for twenty years, with his retirement withdrawals beginning one year from his retirement date, for a total of twenty withdrawals. You estimate that at the time of his retirement, your client can sell his business for $200,000. You expect that interest rates will be relatively stable at 8% a year for the next thirty-five years. Thereafter, you expect interest rates to decline to 6%, forever. Suppose your client wishes to make equal, annual deposits at the end of each of the next thirty-five years, how much should he deposit each year to meet his stated objective?

We can visualize the problem using a timeline, using 0 to represent today, D to represent deposits, W to represent withdrawals, and B to represent the proceeds from the sale of the business:

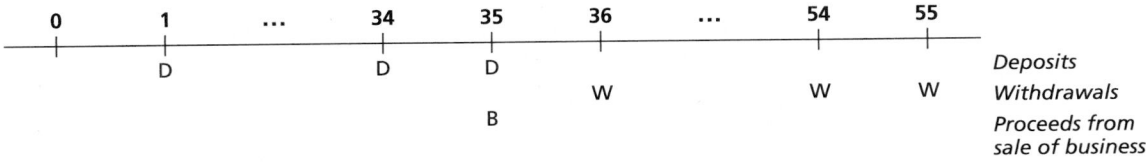

Determine how much the client needs after thirty-five years

At this time, the client wants a twenty-year ordinary annuity of $48,000 because he will be drawing down funds beginning one year from retirement, at a 6% interest rate. In other words, find the PV of a twenty-year annuity, with $i = 6\%$.

$$PV_{35} = \$48,000 \left[\frac{1 - \dfrac{1}{(1.06)^{20}}}{0.06} \right] = \$48,000 \times 11.46992122 = \$550,556.22$$

Using a financial calculator:

$FV = 0$

$PMT = 48,000$

$i = 6$

$n = 20$

Solve for PV.

Using a spreadsheet:

$$=PV(0.06,20,48000,0,0)$$

Your client needs to have $550,556.22 in savings thirty-five years from now so that he can begin to make withdrawals starting thirty-six years from today.[24]

Determine the amount of the periodic savings

In Step 1, it was determined that the client needs $550,556.22 saved thirty-five years from today so that he will have the $48,000 per year that he requires. Subtract the $200,000 you expect the client to get for his business, leaving the amount needed through his investments: $550,556.22 − 200,000 = $350,556.22.

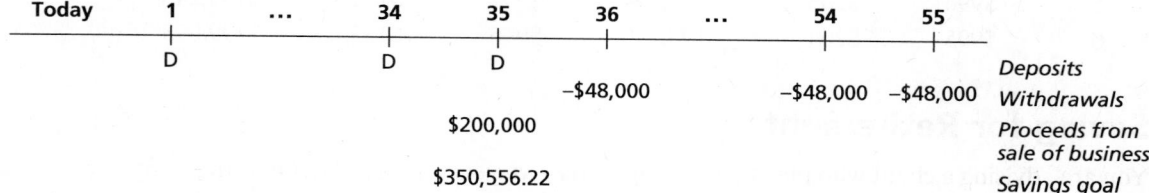

Determine the required year-end payments over the next 35 years

Once you determine the savings goal thirty-five years into the future, now you need to calculate the payment necessary to get there. Using the present value of an annuity formula, substituting the known values and solving for PMT, the payment is $2,034.37:

$$PMT = \frac{\$350,556.22}{\left[\dfrac{(1.08)^{35} - 1}{0.08} \right]} = \frac{\$350,556.22}{172.3168037} = \$2,034.37$$

---

[24] Why do we concern ourselves with thirty-five years from now when the first withdrawal is thirty-six years from now? We calculated the ordinary annuity of $48,000 per year for twenty years. This gave us a present value that is one year before the first cash flow (the assumption built into the math for an ordinary annuity). We could have alternatively calculated the present value of the annuity due as of thirty-six years from today, but then we would have to discount this one period to thirty-five years from now to line it up in time with the $200,000 of proceeds from the sale of the business.

Using a financial calculator:

PV = 0

FV = 350,556.22

$i = 8$

$n = 35$

Solve for PMT.

Using a spreadsheet:

$$=PMT(0.08,35,0,350556.22,0)$$

Therefore, we can represent the cash flows in the timeline:

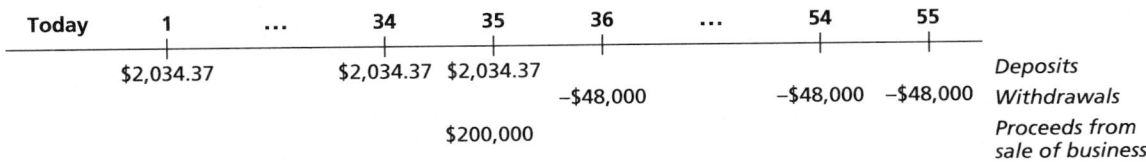

We can see the effects of savings, the business proceeds, and the withdrawals in Figure 5-8. In this figure, we see that the balance in savings:

- grows from both the deposits and the interest on the deposits;
- spikes upward when the business proceeds are received; and
- declines each year after Year 36 by less than the withdrawn amount because of the interest earned on the funds remaining in savings.

Note that this retirement problem appears complicated at first but is quite manageable if you break it down into steps. Timelines are very useful for this purpose because they help us visualize what information we have and what is needed to solve the problem. If you are able to solve these problems, then you have a good understanding of the basic concepts involving the time value of money.

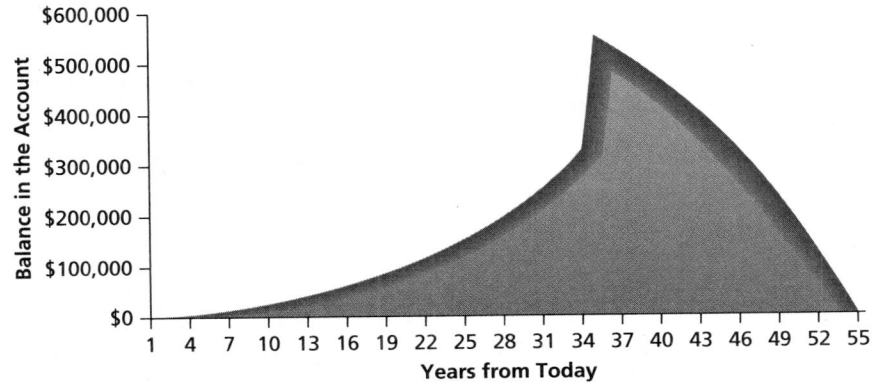

FIGURE 5-8 Growth of the Savings Necessary to Satisfy Retirement Needs

LESSONS LEARNED | I-O Mortgages

Leading up to the Housing Bubble that burst in 2007 and 2008, a popular form of mortgage was the interest-only mortgage, or I-O mortgage. This mortgage required the borrower to pay only the interest for a certain period, typically somewhere in the range of three to ten years, and then the payments were adjusted to pay off the loan, amortized for the remainder of the term of the mortgage.

Consider a $200,000 I-O mortgage that has an annual rate of 5% and requires monthly payments. The payments are I-O for the first ten years, and then the loan is amortized over Years 11 through 30.

The I-O mortgage requires payments of $833 for each month for the first ten years, and $1,319.91 thereafter. A comparable thirty-year, fully amortized mortgage requires a payment of $1,073.64. The payment of interest only means that there is no build-up of equity in the home, as there would be for the fully amortized mortgage: At the end of ten years, there is no equity in the case of an I-O mortgage but $37,316 for the traditional mortgage.

The sudden increase in the mortgage payments once the I-O period is over, combined with the lack of built-up equity, contributed to some of the woes of homeowners as the housing bubble burst.

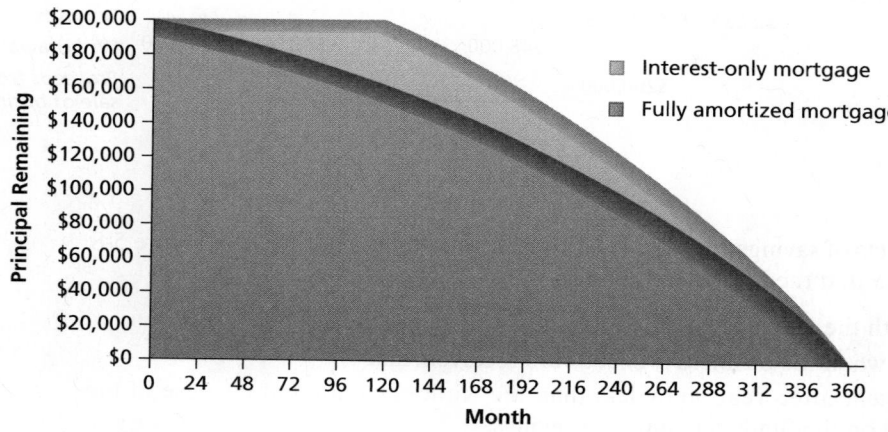

Sources: FDIC, "Interest-Only Mortgage Payments and Option-Payment ARMs," www.fdic.gov/consumers/consumer/interest-only/index.html; Guttentag, Jack, "Interest-only Loans: Not Magic, Usually Not Smart," moneycentral.msn.com/content/banking/homefinancing/p118084.asp; and Bernanke, Ben S. "Monetary Policy and the Housing Bubble," speech to the Annual Meeting of the American Economic Association, January 3, 2010.

Concept Review Questions

1. What are the basic calculation steps for determining how much of a given loan payment is toward interest and how much is toward principal?

2. How do you calculate the amount of principal remaining on a loan at any given point in time during the loan?

3. If a loan is amortized, what is the balance of the loan outstanding after the last payment is made?

SUMMARY

- By applying the process of compounding or discount at an appropriate rate of return, we can calculate economically equivalent values through time. For example, we can calculate the future value five years from now of an amount today. We can also determine the equivalent present value or future value for a series of cash flows.

- Annuities represent a special type of cash flow stream that involve equal payments at the same interval, with the same interest rate being applied throughout the period. We see that these kinds of cash flow streams are commonplace in finance applications (e.g., loan payments) and that there are relatively simple formulas that enable us to determine the present value or future value of such cash flows.

- It is possible to convert a stated rate (that is, the annual percentage rate) into an effective rate, which is important because compounding often takes place at other than annual intervals and the annual percentage rate understates the true, effective rate.

- Time value of money principles may be applied to a number of situations, including the personal finance decisions related to saving for retirement and home mortgage problems.

FORMULAS/EQUATIONS

(5-1) $FV_n = PV_0 + (n \times PV_0 \times i)$

(5-2) $FV_n = PV_0(1 + i)^n$

(5-3) $PV_0 = \dfrac{FV_n}{(1 + i)^n} = FV_n \times \left(\dfrac{1}{(1 + i)^n}\right)$

(5-4) $FV_n = PMT\left[\dfrac{(1 + i)^N - 1}{i}\right]$

(5-5) $PV_0 = PMT\left[\dfrac{1 - \dfrac{1}{(1 + i)^N}}{i}\right]$

(5-6) $FV_n = PMT\left[\dfrac{(1 + i)^N - 1}{i}\right](1 + i)$

(5-7) $PV_0 = PMT\left[\dfrac{1 - \dfrac{1}{(1 + i)^N}}{i}\right](1 + i)$

(5-8) $PV_0 = \dfrac{PMT}{i}$

(5-9) $EAR = \left(1 + \dfrac{APR}{m}\right)^m - 1$

(5-10) $EAR = e^{APR} - 1$

(5-11) Remaining principal balance
$$= \dfrac{Principal\left[(1 + i)^N - (1 + i)^P\right]}{(1 + i)^N}$$

QUESTIONS AND PROBLEMS

Multiple Choice

1. If you invest $1,000 today in an account that pays 5% interest, compounded annually, the balance in the account at the end of ten years, if you make no withdrawals, is *closest* to:

    A. $613.91   B. $1,000.00   C. $1,500.00   D. $1,628.89

2. Which of the following has the largest future value if €1,000 is invested today?

    A. Ten years, with a simple annual interest rate of 8%
    B. Five years, with a simple annual interest rate of 12%
    C. Nine years, with a compound annual interest rate of 7%
    D. Eight years, with a compound annual interest rate of 8%

3. Suppose you deposit $10,000 in an account that pays interest of 4% per year, compounded annually. After five years, the interest paid on interest is *closest* to:

    A. $166.53   B. $200.00   C. $2,000.00   D. $2,166.53

4. Suppose an investor wants to have ¥10 million to retire forty-five years from now. The amount that she would have to invest today with an annual rate of return equal to 15% is closest to:

    A. ¥16,140   B. ¥18,561   C. ¥21,345

5. Maggie deposits £10,000 today and is promised £17,000 in eight years. The implied annual rate of return is *closest* to:

A. 4.36%   B. 6.07%   C. 6.86%   D. 7.88%

6. To triple $1 million, HFund invested today by using an annual rate of return of 9%. The length of time it will take HFund to achieve its goal is *closest* to:

A. 8.04 years   B. 12.75 years   C. 16.09 years

7. Jan plans to invest an equal amount of $2,000 in an equity fund every year end, beginning this year. The expected annual return on the fund is 10%. She plans to invest for twenty years. The amount she expects to have at the end of twenty years is *closest* to:

A. $13,455   B. $102,318   C. $114,550

8. Which of the following credit terms has the highest effective annual rate?

A. 9¾%, compounded daily
B. 9.9%, compounded monthly
C. 9.7%, compounded continuously
D. 9.8%, compounded every other day

9. The present value of a perpetuity with an annual year-end payment of €1,500 and expected annual rate of return equal to 12% is *closest* to:

A. €11,400   B. €12,500   C. €13,500   D. €14,000

10. Consider a mortgage loan of $200,000, to be amortized over thirty years with monthly payments. If the annual percentage rate on this mortgage is 6%, the amount of principal and interest in the second month's mortgage payment is closest to:

A. Principal repayment is $199.10, and interest paid is $1,000.
B. Principal repayment is $200.10, and interest paid is $999.00.
C. Principal repayment is $2,529.78, and interest paid is $12,000.
D. Principal repayment is $2,497.78, and interest paid is $11,848.21.

Practice Problems and Questions

5.1   Time Is Money

11. What is simple interest?

12. Explain how you would calculate the interest-on-interest on an investment.

13. What is the present value of $200,000, discounted five years at 9%?

14. What is the future value of $200,000, compounded five years at 9%?

15. What is the future value of £1,000 invested thirty years at:

A. 8%, compounded annually?
B. 8%, compounded quarterly?
C. 8%, compounded continuously?

16. Consider a company that invests $100,000 in an investment that is expected to earn 4% interest per year, which is reinvested in the investment.

A. What is the value of this investment at the end of four years?
B. Using the time-line below, complete the timeline by indicating the value of the investment at the end of each year in the appropriate box:

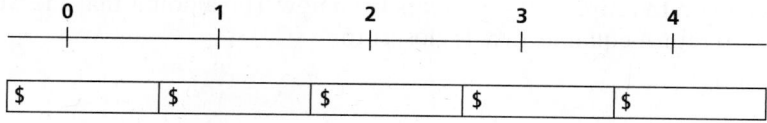

17. Suppose you invest $10,000 today and your investment earns interest at 6% for each of the first two years and 5% for the next two years.

   A. What is your investment worth four years from today?

   B. Diagram the value of this investment using the following timeline, inserting the value of the investment at the end of each year in the appropriate box:

0	1	2	3	4
$	$	$	$	$

   C. What is the amount of interest that you have earned on your investment each year?

   D. What is the amount of interest-on-interest that you earn on your investment over the life of the investment?

18. Complete the following table:

	Present Value	Number of Periods	Interest Rate per Year	Future Value
A.	$100	5	6%	
B.	$1,000	5	6%	
C.	$500	2	2%	
D.	$2,000	10	1.50%	
E.	$3,000	4	4%	

19. Complete the following table:

	Future Value	Number of Periods	Discount Rate per Year	Present Value
A.	$100	5	6%	
B.	$1,000	5	6%	
C.	$500	2	2%	
D.	$2,000	10	1.50%	
E.	$3,000	4	4%	

20. Complete the following table:

	Present Value	Future Value	Number of Periods	Interest Rate per Year
A.	$100	$200	5	
B.	$100	$300		6%
C.	€1,000		5	10%
D.		$30,000	6	7%
E.	$6,000		3	3%

21. An investment adviser promises that you will triple your money in 10 years with Investment A. A comparable investment, Investment B, has a return of 12% per year. Which investment has the highest return?

22. How many years will it take for an investment to double in value if the rate of return is 9%, and compounding occurs:

   A. annually?   B. quarterly?

23. How many years will it take for a balance in a savings account to triple if the interest on the account is 5% a year, compounded continuously?

24. Suppose a company invests $1 million today, and expects this investment to grow in value at the rate of 8% for the first two years, 9% for the next two years, and 7% for the two years after that.

     A. What is this investment expected to be worth in six years?

     B. Calculate and graph the growth in the value of the investment for the six years.

5.2 Annuities and Perpetuities

25. What distinguishes an annuity due from an ordinary annuity?

26. Suppose you have a client who would like a plan for saving for her retirement. She would like to begin saving an amount each year, starting in five years, to provide for her retirement that she plans in thirty years. Her goal is to save $2 million thirty years from today and then live off of her savings for the twenty years after her retirement.

     A. Draw a timeline for this client.

     B. How would you determine how much she needs to save each year to meet her goal? Explain your method.

     C. How would you determine how much she would have to spend each year in retirement? Explain your method.

27. Of the present value of an ordinary annuity and the present value of an annuity due, which has the same number of discount periods as payments?

28. Consider an ordinary annuity consisting of five annual payments of $1,000 each.

     A. As long as the interest rate is greater than or equal to 0%, what is the largest that the present value can be?

     B. As long as the interest rate is greater than or equal to 0%, what is the smallest that the future value can be?

     C. Explain your reasoning for each.

29. Without performing a calculation, select and explain your selection for which of the following will be the larger value for a given number of periods, periodic amount, and interest rate:

- Present value of the ordinary annuity
- Present value of the annuity due
- Future value of the ordinary annuity
- Future value of the annuity due

30. For each of the following, match the loan type with the financial math approach to analyze the problem:

Loan Arrangement	Financial Math Approach
A. Lottery winnings, paid in twenty annual instalments, beginning when the winning ticket is turned in.	1. Present value of an ordinary annuity
B. Mortgage payments, made at the end of each month for thirty years.	2. Present value of an annuity due
C. Three-year subscription to a magazine, paid as a lump sum at the beginning of the three years.	3. Future value of an ordinary annuity
D. Parents set aside $10 at the end of month to save $60,000 for their child's college education.	4. Future value of an annuity due
E. Rent of $450 per month, paid at the beginning of each month.	5. Present value of a lump-sum
	6. Future value of a lump-sum

31. Consider an ordinary annuity of $100 per year, for four years. Assume that the appropriate interest rate for valuing this annuity is 7%.

    A. Complete the following timeline, indicating the following:
       - Cash flows
       - Present value of the annuity
       - Future value of the annuity

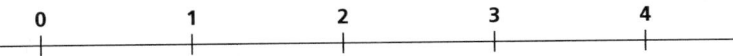

    B. What is the relationship (mathematically) between the present and future values?

32. Complete the following table:

	Payment per Year	Number of Years	Interest Rate per Year	Future Value
A.	$100	5	3%	
B.	$500	6	4%	
C.	$1,000	10	8%	
D.	$450	12	3%	
E.	$10,000	4	4%	

33. Complete the following table:

	Payment per Year	Number of Years	Interest Rate per Year	Present Value
A.	$200	10	3%	
B.	$200	4	4%	
C.	$250	5	10%	
D.	$30,000	3	5%	
E.	$2,100	10	4%	

34. A magazine publisher offers its customers three options on subscriptions:

    Option 1: $50 today for three years.

    Option 2: A two-year rate of $38 paid immediately, followed by a one-year rate of $17 paid at the beginning of the third year.

    Option 3: $17 paid at the beginning of each of the three years.

    A. From the perspective of the company, which option is best if the company's opportunity cost of funds is 8%? Explain.

    B. From the perspective of the subscriber, which option is best in terms of minimizing the cost of subscription if the subscriber's opportunity cost of funds is 5%? Explain.

5.3 Nominal and Effective Rates

35. Under what circumstances, if any, will the annual percentage rate on a loan arrangement be equal to the loan's effective annual rate?

36. If you are a manager at a bank and want to calculate the advertised APR for what the bank is willing to pay, on an effective annual rate basis, how would you go about calculating this APR? Explain your method.

37. Complete the following table:

	Annual Percentage Rate (APR)	Compounding Frequency	Effective Annual Rate (EAR)
Bank V	12%	monthly	
Bank W	5%	semi-annual	
Bank X	8%	continuous	
Bank Y	10%	semi-annual	
Bank Z	5%	quarterly	

38. A credit card company advertises interest rates of 15% on unpaid balances. If interest is compounded daily, what is the effective interest rate that the credit card company charges?

39. Bank A pays 7.25% interest compounded semi-annually, Bank B pays 7.20% compounded quarterly, and Bank C pays 7.15% compounded monthly. Which bank pays the highest effective annual rate on its certificates of deposit?

40. Calculate the effective annual rates for the following:
    A. 24%, compounded daily
    B. 24%, compounded quarterly
    C. 24%, compounded every four months
    D. 24%, compounded semi-annually
    E. 24%, compounded continuously

41. The return on a stock for the most recent quarter was 2%. Suppose this stock is expected to earn 2% each quarter for the rest of the year.
    A. What is the return, stated in terms of an annual percentage rate?
    B. What is the return, stated in terms of an effective annual rate?

42. The Big-Bank would like to pay, effectively, 3% per year, on its preferred checking accounts. What APR must Big-Bank advertise for this account if the interest is compounded monthly? continuously?

5.4 Applications

43. Google, Inc., traded at $100.01 per share on September 3, 2004. On September 3, 2010, Google stock traded at $470.03 per share. What is the average annual return on this stock over this period if Google did not pay dividends? *[Hint: The share price in 2004 is the present value; the share price in 2010 is the future value.]*

44. Roger has his eye on a new car that will cost $20,000. He has $15,000 in his savings account, earning interest at a rate of 0.5% per month.
    A. How long will it be before he can buy the car?
    B. How long will it be before Roger can buy the car if, in addition to savings, he can save $250 per month?

45. Consider a $200,000 10-year loan with an interest rate of 12%, compounded monthly. Payments on the loan are made monthly.
    A. What is the monthly payment required for this loan?
    B. What is the outstanding loan amount after six months.

46. The Athens Company has been awarded a settlement in a lawsuit that that will pay $2.5 million one year from now. However, the company really needs the money today and has decided to take out a loan. If the bank charges an interest rate of 8%, how much can the Athens Company borrow so that the settlement will just pay off the loan?

47. Johann started a small business and was too busy to consider saving for retirement. He sold the business for $600,000, and these proceeds will comprise his retirement savings. If he can invest this total sum and earn 10% per year, how much will his investment be worth in five years? In ten years?

48. Knox Villas has been forced to borrow money to get through the tough economy this year. If the loan is for $2 million at an interest rate of 7%, with payments of interest and principal each year, how much must Knox Villas pay each year if the loan is to be paid off in three years, with end-of-year, equal payments?

49. Jack is 28 years old now and plans to retire in thirty-five years. He works in a local bank and has an annual income of $45,000. His expected annual expenditure is $36,000, and the rest of his income will be invested at the beginning of each of the next thirty-five years (with the first payment on his twenty-ninth birthday) at an expected annual rate of return of 5%. What amount will Jack have saved when he retires if he never gets a raise?

50. Shawna just turned twenty-one years old and currently has no investments. She plans to invest €5,500 at the end of each of the next eight years, starting with her twenty-second birthday. The rate of return on her investment is 4%, continuously compounded.
    A. What will be the balance in her investment account when she makes the last of the eight payments?
    B. Suppose she has an alternative investment, but with similar risk, that can produce a return of 4.2%, compounded annually. Which investment plan should she select?

51. After a summer of travelling (and not working), a student finds himself $1,500 short for this year's tuition fees. His parents have agreed to loan him the money at a simple interest rate of 6%.
    A. How much interest will he owe his parents after one year?
    B. How much will he owe, in total, if he waits to pay for three years?

52. Public corporations have no fixed lifespan; as such, they are often viewed as entities that will pay dividends to their shareholders in perpetuity. Suppose KashKow Inc. pays a dividend of $2 per share every year.
    A. If the discount rate is 12%, what is the present value of all the future dividends?
    B. KashKow Inc. has just declared that its dividend next year will be $3 per share. That rate of payment will continue for an additional four years, after which, the dividends will fall back to their usual $2 per share. What is the present value of all the future dividends?

53. On the advice of a friend, Gilda invests $20,000 in a mutual fund that has earned 10% per year, on average, in recent years. Your own investment research turned up another interesting mutual fund that you recommend to Gilda, which has had an average annual return fifty basis points greater than the one her friend recommended. If she had taken your advice, how much more would her investment be worth after:
    A. one year?
    B. five years?
    C. ten years?

54. To start a new retail guitar business, Keith Richards has three opportunities to borrow the needed $25,000 of funds.
    A. The Local Bank asks him to repay the loan in five equal, end-of-year installments of $6,935.24. What is the bank's effective annual interest rate on the loan transaction?
    B. The Business Development Bank is willing to loan Keith the $25,000 he needs to start his new business. The loan will require monthly payments of $556.11 over five years. What is the effective annual rate on this loan?
    C. The Balloon Bank is willing to offer Keith a loan that has five equal end-of-year installments of $5,000 and a balloon payment of $13,000 along with the last payment. What is the effective annual rate on this loan?
    D. Which is the better deal for Keith, and why?

55. Consider a $50 million loan that is amortized over four years, with end-of-year payments of $19.4 million each.
    A. What is the effective rate of interest on this loan?

B. Complete the amortization table, with table entries in millions of dollars:

Year	Beginning-of-Year Loan Balance	Payment	Interest	Principal Repayment	End-of-Year Loan Balance
1	$50.000				
2					
3					
4					$0.000

56. The fund manager can choose between two investments that have the same cost today. Both investments will ultimately pay $1,300 but at different times, as shown in the table below. If the fund manager does not choose one of these investments, she could leave the funds in a bank account paying 5% per year.

Year	Investment A	Investment B
1	$0	$200
2	$500	$400
3	$800	$700

A. Which investment should she choose?

B. If the cost of each investment is $1,000, should the fund manager invest in one of them, or simply leave the money in the bank account? Would her decision change if the investments instead cost $1,200 each?

C. Suppose the investments cost $1,000. Determine the rate of return on each. If the fund manager can only choose one of them, which should it be?

 57. The following calculation explanation was abstracted from a web site, showing how the total interest on a mortgage is calculated:[25]

"Using your principal and interest (P&I) payment, multiply it by 360 payments, which is thirty years of payments.

Example: $100,000 loan for thirty years at a 5% interest rate will create a $536.82 monthly payment. (This amount does not include taxes or homeowners insurance.) Multiply $536.82 by 360 months. It equals $193,255.20.

Subtract the loan amount from the total you arrive at in Step 1. In the example above, you would subtract $100,000 from $193,255.20, ending with $93,255.20. This represents the amount of interest that is paid over a thirty-year amortized loan, which is commonly how mortgage principal and interest (P&I) is paid."

A. Verify these calculations. Are they correct?

B. Create an amortization table in a spreadsheet for this mortgage, for all 360 months, using the following headings:

Payment	Interest	Principal Repayment	Principal Balance Remaining

C. Do these calculations consider the time value of money? Explain.

 58. Suppose you deposit $100,000 in an account today. And suppose you can earn 4% interest per year on the principal amount and earn 2% interest on any interest earned on interest.

A. Create a worksheet using a spreadsheet program to calculate how much will you have in the account at the end of five years.

[25] Joey Campbell, "How to Calculate Interest Paid Over the Life of a Mortgage," *eHow Money*, www.ehow.com/how_6216640_calculate-paid-over-life-mortgage.html, accessed July 17, 2011.

B. Graph the balance in the account, separating the interest earned on the principal from the interest earned on interest.

Cases

Case 5.1 Saving for Retirement, Considering Different Scenarios

Suppose you are advising a client, Arturo, who is planning for his retirement and wants to have $1 million by the time he retires at age sixty. And suppose you want to lay out alternative savings plans for different return scenarios:

Scenario 1: Steady state
Earns 8% on all funds invested.

Scenario 2: Declining returns
Earns 8% each year for the first five years, 6% for the next five years, and 4% thereafter.

Scenario 3: Increasing returns
Earns 8% each year for the first five years, 10% for the next five years, and 12% thereafter.

Scenario 4: Varying returns
Earns 8% each year for the first five years, 6% for the next five years, and 10% thereafter.

Address the following requirements:

1. Using a spreadsheet program, calculate and graph the balance in savings up to Arturo's sixtieth birthday if he saves $3,000 each year, starting on his twenty-first birthday, under each scenario. His last deposit is on his sixtieth birthday.

2. Suppose your client estimates that once he turns eighty years old, he will need only $48,000 per year for nursing home costs; to simplify, assume payable at the end of the year. Assume that once he retires on his sixtieth birthday, he shifts all of his investments to CDs with a fixed interest rate of 3% per year.

   A. If Arturo plans to live until his ninetieth birthday and leave nothing in his estate, how much is available under each scenario to withdraw from his savings each year starting at his sixty-first birthday until he enters the nursing home? His last withdrawal before the nursing home is on his eightieth birthday.

   B. Calculate and graph the balance in Arturo's savings up through his ninetieth year under each scenario.

Case 5.2 Evaluating an Investment

The Bridgewater Gazebo Company is evaluating a new line of outdoor living outbuildings to add to its successful gazebo line. The expanded manufacturing facilities would cost $1.2 million, but they expect to be able to generate cash flows from this new line that would justify this cost. The current estimates from the project manager, expecting that nearby competitors, such as Yoder Buildings, will enter this line within five years, are the following:

Year	End of Year Cash Flows
1	$100,000
2	$500,000
3	$300,000
4	$300,000
5	$100,000
6 and beyond	$50,000

The discount rate that Bridgewater Gazebo uses to evaluate future cash flows is 8%. *[Hint: The cash flows for Year 6 and beyond are a perpetuity.]*

A. What is the present value of the cash flows on this new line?
B. Should Bridgewater Gazebo enter this line of business? Explain your recommendation.
C. What would be your recommendation if Bridgewater Gazebo used 10% to discount its future cash flows?
D. What would be your recommendation if Bridgewater Gazebo used 12% to discount its future cash flows?

CHAPTER 6

DEBT VALUATION AND INTEREST RATES

At the end of 2010, corporations had over $7.5 trillion of debt outstanding. Because common stock never matures, yet bonds do, many corporations must issue bonds frequently. In 2010, corporations issued four times more debt than equity:

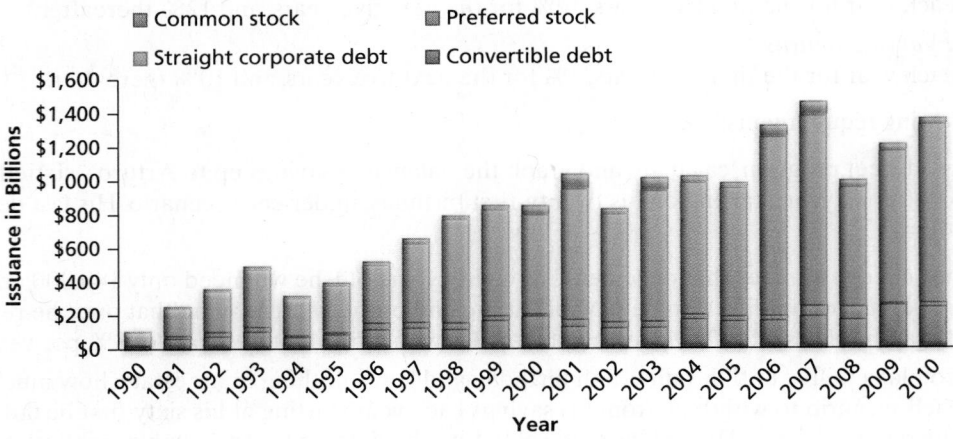

We can see the effect of the credit crunch in 2008 on debt issuance. In 2007, corporations issued over $1.1 trillion of straight corporate debt, whereas in 2008 corporations issued a little over $0.7 trillion in debt. However, the recovery, along with record lower interest rates, encouraged corporate borrowing in both 2009 and 2010.

Source of data: *Securities Industry and Financial Markets Association.*

Learning Outcomes

After reading this chapter, you should be able to:

LO 6.1 Explain the basic features of different types of debt obligations.

LO 6.2 Value debt when given an appropriate discount rate, and explain and demonstrate how bond prices change over time.

LO 6.3 Calculate the yield on a straight bond, a zero-coupon bond, and a callable bond.

LO 6.4 Describe the various government securities, and calculate the value and the yield on Treasury bills.

LO 6.5 List and briefly describe the factors affecting yields on debt securities.

Chapter Preview We introduced the basic time value of money concepts in an earlier chapter, and in this chapter we discuss debt securities, which provide investors with predetermined future cash flows. As such, the analysis of bonds provides an important application of compounding and discounting.

6.1 THE BASICS OF BONDS

A **debt** is a promise by the borrower to repay the amount borrowed, plus interest. Interest on the debt may be periodic, such as paid every six months, or it may all be paid at the debt's maturity along with the principal repayment. We often refer to long-term debt instruments that promise fixed payments to their investors generically as bonds, but to be accurate, we should really use specific terms, depending on the maturity of the debt instrument. A short-term debt obligation with an initial maturity less than 1 year is a **bill** or **paper**; a debt obligation with a maturity between 1 and 7 years is a **note**; and a debt obligation with a term longer than 7 years is a **bond**. Because we value these instruments in the same manner (that is, discounting promised cash flows), we often simply refer to these debt obligations as bonds in our discussion.

The bond market is an important part of the capital market and a major source of financing for companies, as well as for governments and financial institutions. For example, over $1 trillion of bonds were issued in U.S. markets in 2010 by corporations, but only $240 billion in common stock were issued in the same year.[1] Understanding the topics covered in this chapter will deepen your knowledge of how to apply the tools of valuation as well as your familiarity with financial securities.

The key feature of a bond is that the borrower typically agrees to pay the lender a regular series of cash payments, and to repay the full principal amount—that is, the amount borrowed—by the maturity date. We often refer to the borrower as the **issuer** of the bond and the lender or creditor as the **bondholder**. These promises are stipulated in the bond contract and are a fixed contractual commitment. Though many payment structures are possible, the traditional bond provides for identical payments at regular intervals (usually semi-annually or annually), with the full principal to be repaid at the stated maturity date.

We refer to the interest payment as a **coupon** because at one time bonds literally had coupons attached to them, and the investor had to cut the coupon from the bond certificate and send it for payment.[2] Today, almost all bonds are registered, and the payments are made electronically into individual bank accounts, providing a record of who has paid and who has received the interest. Unlike an amortized loan, such as a mortgage, the principal amount of the bond is paid at maturity.[3]

As we have noted, the typical bond is the debt obligation in which the issuer pays interest periodically and then pays the principal amount at maturity along with the last interest payment. We refer to this type of bond as a **straight bond** or a **straight coupon bond**. However, for some bonds the issuer does not commit to paying interest, but rather the bond is sold at discount from its face value. A bond that pays no interest is a **zero-coupon bond** or **zero-coupon note** (or **zero**), which is issued at a discount and repays the face value at the maturity date. The return earned on a zero-coupon bond or note represents the difference between the purchase price and the redemption price. The lower the price paid for the bond, the higher the return. Zero-coupon notes and bonds were initially

debt promise by the borrower to repay the amount borrowed, plus interest

bill or **paper** short-term debt instruments with an initial maturity of less than 1 year

note debt instruments with initial maturities between 1 and 7 years

bond long-term debt instrument in which the borrower promises repayment, usually with interest, with an initial maturity longer than 7 years

issuer party that receives funds in exchange for a security, such as a bond

bondholder party that lends funds by buying a bond issued by another party

coupon interest payment from a note or bond

straight bond or **straight coupon bond** debt obligation that commits the issuer to pay a fixed amount of interest periodically, and then repay the principal amount at maturity

zero-coupon bond or **zero-coupon note** (or **zero**) debt obligation issued at a discount from its face value, pays no coupons, and repays the face value at the maturity date

---

[1] It is true, however, that retained earnings (and, hence, equity) is a major source of funds for corporation. But in terms of investment banking activity in raising capital for corporations, more than four times the amount of bonds are issued compared to equity. This is due, in part, to the fact that equity never matures, yet bonds mature and corporations therefore refinance by issuing additional bonds.

[2] The coupons were attached to the bond and could be mailed in by whoever had the bond. Such bonds were called *bearer bonds* and are still widely used in parts of the world where personal tax rates are high.

[3] In general, when the principal payment is made in one lump sum at maturity, it is called a bullet payment or balloon payment.

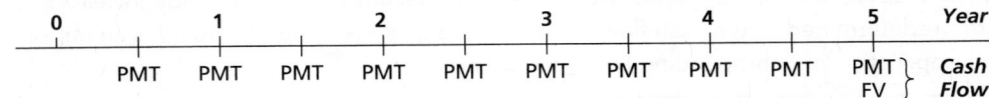

where PMT is the periodic interest payments and FV is the principal repayment

FIGURE 6-1 The Cash Flow Pattern for a Traditional Coupon-Paying Bond

created by financial intermediaries who purchased traditional bonds, "stripped" the cash flows (both the interest and the principal repayment components) from them, and sold the cash flows separately. Today, most zeroes are created this way; however, some are also initially issued as zero-coupon securities.[4]

Bonds are referred to as fixed income securities because the interest payments and the principal repayment are often specified or fixed at the time the bond is issued. In most cases the bond purchaser knows the amount and timing of the future cash payments to be received, barring default by the issuer. However, if the buyer decides to sell the bond before maturity, the price received depends on the level of interest rates at that time.

We depict the typical pattern of cash payments for a semi-annual pay bond using a timeline in Figure 6-1. In the case of a semi-annual pay bond, interest is paid at the end of every six months. We represent the periodic interest or coupon as PMT, and the face value of the bond as FV.

Two things are obvious from Figure 6-1. First, the structure of the payments differs from that of the loan or mortgage because those involve payments consisting of both interest and principal components. In contrast, a typical bond has interest payments throughout its life and a principal repayment at maturity. You can see this in Figure 6-2, where we compare the interest paid on a $1 million loan: If the loan is amortized, you see the pattern in Panel A, and if the loan is a bond, you see the pattern in Panel B. In the case of the amortized loan, principal is paid off over time, whereas in the case of the bond the principal is paid off at the bond's maturity.

Second, we can view a bond as two separate components: an annuity consisting of the identical and regular interest payments, plus a lump-sum principal payment at maturity. In this way, valuing a traditional bond becomes a straightforward application of the time value of money concepts.[5]

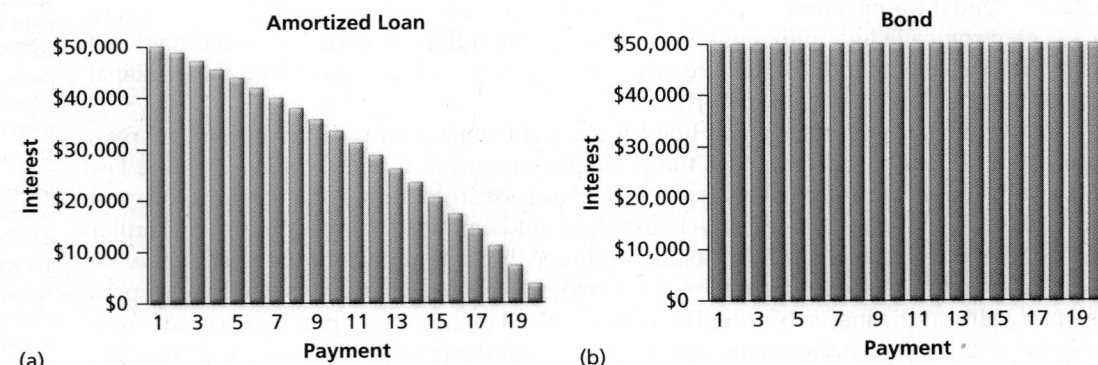

(a)   (b)

FIGURE 6-2 Comparison of Interest on a 20-Year, $1 Million Amortized Loan and a Bond, both with Annual Payments and 5 Percent Interest

---

[4] Zeroes are very popular with financial institutions, which often use them for hedging purposes with respect to their outstanding liabilities. Zeroes are ideally suited for this purpose because, unlike traditional bonds, there are no issues with respect to reinvesting interest payments that are received before maturity.

[5] A coupon bond can be stripped into its coupon and principal components, and these two cash flow streams can be sold separately: The principal portion becomes a zero-coupon bond, whereas the coupon portion becomes an interest-only (IO) security.

Bond Terminology

Before discussing how to value bonds, we introduce some of the terminology and institutional features attached to different types of bonds. Most bonds are sold to a number of investors, and someone must make sure that the payments are made on time. This problem is solved by including all relevant details for a particular bond issue in a **bond indenture**, or **indenture agreement**, that is held and administered by a trust company. This is a legal document that specifies the payment requirements, all other salient matters relating to the issue (such as any assets that might serve as security or **collateral** for the bond), any protective provisions, and other additional features. The trust company then makes sure that these covenant provisions are observed by the issuer.

The **par value** (or **face value** or **maturity value**) represents the amount that is paid at maturity for traditional bonds. The par value of most bonds is $1,000, though bond prices are typically quoted based on a par value of 100. In other words, if the price of a bond is quoted at 99.583, a $1,000 par value bond would be selling for $995.83. The time remaining to the maturity date is the **term to maturity** of the bond. The regular **interest payment** (or **coupon**) is determined by multiplying the **coupon rate** (which is stated on an annual basis) by the par value of the bond. For example, a bond with a coupon rate of 6 percent and a par value of $1,000 would pay coupons of $60 if they are paid annually, or $30 every six months if they are paid semi-annually. Most U.S. corporate bonds pay interest semi-annually; that is, every six months.

Security and Protective Provisions

Though the term is used loosely to encompass many types of debt securities, technically bonds are debt obligations secured by real assets. A bond secured by real property is a **mortgage bond**, and a bond secured by a pledge of other financial assets, such as common shares, bonds, or Treasury bills, is a **collateral trust bond**.

An **equipment trust certificate** is secured by equipment, such as the rolling stock of a railway (that is, vehicles, such as train cars, that move along the railway); the assets pledged as security are owned by investors through a lease agreement with the railway until the loan has been retired. The certificates have serial numbers that dictate their maturity date, with a certain amount maturing every year.

However, not all bonds are secured by real property. For example, a **debenture** is a debt obligation that is not secured by specific asset, but rather is secured by a general claim on the company's unencumbered assets, that is, those assets that have not been pledged as security for other debt obligations. Government bonds are debentures because no specific security is pledged as collateral; however, they are referred to as bonds as a matter of convention.

The indenture agreement is the contract between the issuer of the bond and the bondholders. This agreement not only details the payment schedule and amounts, but also may contain covenants that protect the investor. A **protective covenant** is any clause in the bond indenture that restricts the actions of the issuer. A **negative covenant** prohibits certain actions; for example, a company may be restricted from making a dividend payment larger than a certain amount or prevented from pledging its assets to another lender. A **positive covenant** specifies actions that the company agrees to undertake, for example, to provide quarterly financial statements or maintain certain working capital levels.

Credit Ratings

Credit-rating firms perform detailed analyses of bond issuers and issues to determine the likelihood that the issuer will make the payments of interest and principal repayments on a debt obligation when promised. In the U.S., these firms are known as

---

bond indenture or **indenture agreement** legal document that specifies the payment requirements and all other salient matters relating to a particular bond issue, held and administered by a trust company

collateral assets that can serve as security for the bond in case of default

par value or **face value** or **maturity value** amount paid at maturity for traditional bonds

term to maturity time remaining to the maturity date

interest payment or **coupon** amount paid on a bond at regular intervals

coupon rate percentage of a bond or note's face value that is paid in interest each year

mortgage bond debt instrument that is secured by real assets

collateral trust bond bond secured by a pledge of other financial assets, such as common shares, bonds, or Treasury bills

equipment trust certificate type of debt instrument secured by equipment, such as the rolling stock of a railway

debenture debt instrument secured by a general claim on the issuer's unencumbered assets

protective covenant clause in a bond indenture that restrict the actions of the issuer; covenants can be positive or negative

negative covenant clause in a bond indenture that prohibits certain actions by the issuer

positive covenant clause in a bond indenture that requires specific actions by the issuer

Nationally Recognized Statistical Rating Organizations (NRSROs) credit rating firms that are registered with the U.S. Securities and Exchange Commission

Nationally Recognized Statistical Rating Organizations (NRSROs) and are registered with the Securities and Exchange Commission.[6] The largest NRSROs are Standard & Poor's (S&P), Moody's, and Fitch, but thanks to changes in the regulation of NRSROs, the field has widened and includes DBRS, Ltd.; A. M. Best Company, Inc.; and Kroll Bond Rating Agency, among others. The issuer of a debt obligation contracts with one or more of these NRSROs for a rating based on the creditworthiness of the issuer, tempered by the features of the debt obligation. For example, it is possible for two debt obligations of the same issuer to have different ratings if the issues have different features (e.g., seniority, collateral).

debt rating evaluation by professional debt-rating services after detailed analyses of bond issuers to determine their ability to make the required interest and principal payments

investment-grade debt debt obligation with a credit rating of AAA, AA, A or BBB (or Aaa, Aa, A, Baa)

speculative debt or **high-yield debt** or **junk bond** or **low-grade debt** debt that is not investment grade; debt rated below BBB or Baa

The NRSRO assigns a **debt rating** to a debt obligation to reflect its judgment regarding the issuer's ability to satisfy the promised obligations (that is, interest and principal) when promised. NRSROs use a classification system starting with the highest-rated debt, AAA or Aaa, and then lesser ratings are AA or Aa, A, BBB or Baa, and so on. We provide the debt-rating categories for S&P and Moody's in Figure 6-3.[7]

Investment-grade debt is debt with a rating at or above BBB (Standard & Poor's and Fitch Ratings), Baa (Moody's), or higher; in other words, investment-grade debt comprises the top four major classes. **Speculative debt** has a credit rating below investment grade; if a rated bond is not investment grade, then it is speculative. Other names for speculative debt include **high-yield debt**, **junk bond**, or **low-grade debt**.

These ratings may be modified to indicate the relative ranking within a category, either using numbers or other symbols in addition to the letters (e.g., A1 or A+). This is particularly useful in distinguishing debt in classifications in which there are a large number of debt obligations.

Why have an issue evaluated by a credit-rating firm? Because many investors either want to have or are required to have a third-party assessment of the creditworthiness of the debt. For example, many pension funds are restricted to investing in investment-grade debt. Is all debt rated? No, some issuers will place an issue directly with an investor and need not have the issue rated if the investor does not require it.

S&P	Moody's	Description		
AAA	Aaa	highest credit quality	High quality	Investment grade
AA	Aa	very good quality		
A	A	good quality	Medium grade	
BBB	Baa	medium quality		
BB	Ba	lower medium quality	Non-investment grade	
B	B	poor quality		
CCC	Caa	speculative quality		
CC	Ca	very speculative quality		
D	C	default	In default investment grade	
Suspended		rating suspended		

FIGURE 6-3 Debt-Rating Categories for Standard & Poor's and Moody's

Source: *Standard & Poor's, www.standardandpoors.com; Moody's, www.moodys.com.*

---

[6] As of this writing, there were ten NRSROs.

[7] Rating systems are similar for other rating agencies, such as Fitch. For example, S&P uses AAA for the top-rated bonds, whereas Moody's uses Aaa.

SEC Rules Take Aim at Credit Rating Agencies | ETHICS

As evidenced in the hearings on credit rating agencies in the 2007–2008 financial crisis, there were some problems in the process of credit rating that may have exacerbated the financial crisis:[8]

- An inherent conflict of interest when issuers can "shop" for ratings among the different credit rating agencies.

- A problem when the rating agencies provided advice to those parties creating some structured finance instruments (e.g., mortgage-backed securities) regarding how to ensure that the instruments received the best rating. Hence, the agencies were acting like both the referee and the goalie.

- The mathematical models used by Moody's and S&P for some types of debt had inappropriate assumptions, hence resulting in mislabeling the creditworthiness of some instruments.

- Competition among rating agencies and significant volume of activity created pressures for the rating analysts to "play ball" (that is, give a good rating or be kept from future rating activity).

In response to the problems identified during the subprime crisis in 2007–2008, the Securities and Exchange Commission was charged with the responsibility to improve the credit rating system.[9]

Additional Bond Features

A bond is a contract, and what is in that contract varies from one bond to another. Unlike common shares, each bond contract has to be reviewed separately because they differ from one another. Without recognizing this, the differences can come back to haunt investors years after the bond has been issued.

So far, we have focused our discussion on traditional or regular coupon-paying bonds that provide for full principal repayment at the maturity date. Because bonds can be customized to the needs of the issuer or the investor, we observe many combinations of various features. We describe a few of the features that fall into three groups:

1. Sinking fund and purchase fund provisions
2. Embedded options
3. Floating-rate bonds

Sinking fund and purchase fund provisions

A **sinking fund provision** requires the issuer to set money aside each year so that funds are available at maturity to pay off the debt. Provisions are made in two ways. In the first, the company repurchases a certain amount of debt each year, through a **sinking fund call**, so that the amount of debt decreases. In the second, the company puts funds into a sinking fund trust to buy other bonds, usually government bonds, so that money is available at maturity to pay off the debt. Sinking fund provisions benefit the issuer because the issuer is able to avoid paying the entire face value of the issue at the maturity date.

Bonds with a sinking fund are not always beneficial to investors because in some sinking fund arrangements it may be specified that the bonds will be randomly called based on their serial number and repaid. Therefore, there is a risk that the investor's holding period for the bond will be shortened by the sinking fund call. Further, the bonds are normally called at par value, and the investors may suffer a loss if the bonds are worth more at the time of the repurchase. Finally, as the amount of the issue declines, there may be a loss in liquidity in terms of these bonds trading in the market, resulting in the bonds

sinking fund provision
requirement that the issuer set aside funds each year to be used to pay off the debt at maturity

sinking fund call
repurchase of bonds that have a sinking fund provision permitting the issuer to buy back the bonds

---

[8] *Wall Street and the Financial Crisis: The Role of Credit Rating Agencies*, Permanent Subcommittee on Investigations, U.S. Senate Committee on Homeland Security & Governmental Affairs, April 23, 2010.

[9] At this writing, the SEC has only proposed rules regarding changes, such as increased transparency, training of analysts, and enhancing competition among credit rating agencies.

purchase fund provisions requirements that the repurchase of a certain amount of debt can occur only if it can be repurchased at or below a given price

callable bond debt obligation that gives the issuer the option to repurchase outstanding bonds at predetermined prices at specified times

call price price, generally at a premium over par, at which an issuer can repurchase a bond

putable bond or **retractable bond** debt obligation that allows the bondholder to sell the bonds back to the issuer at predetermined prices at specified times earlier than the maturity date

extendible bond debt obligation that allows the bondholder to extend the bonds' maturity dates

becoming less attractive. These disadvantages are offset, at least in part, by the lowered risk of default as less of the bond issue is outstanding.

A **purchase fund provision** is similar to a sinking fund provision, but requires the borrower to repurchase a certain amount of debt only if it can be bought back from the bondholders at or below a given price. These provisions are generally advantageous to bondholders because they provide some liquidity and downward price support for the market price of the debt instruments.

Embedded options

Issuers of bonds may include any number of embedded options with a debt instrument. These options may provide the issuer more flexibility, the investor more flexibility, or simply make a bond more attractive to investors and, hence, lower the return required by investors.

A **callable bond** gives the issuer the option to "call" or repurchase outstanding bonds at a predetermined **call price** (generally at a premium over par) at specified times. There can be a single call price or a schedule of call prices. These types of bonds create an additional risk for the bondholder because the bond could be called away when interest rates are falling, and hence the bondholder's reinvestment opportunities are lower as well.

Conversely, a **putable bond**, also referred to as a **retractable bond**, allows the bondholder to sell (or "put") the bond back to the issuer at predetermined prices at specified times earlier than the maturity date. In this way, the maturity of the bond is retracted or shortened. In contrast, an **extendible bond** allows the bondholder to extend the maturity date of the bond. In effect, put and retractable features provide bondholders with the flexibility of changing the maturity of the bonds to their advantage.

LESSONS LEARNED | Poison Puts

In the 1980s, there were a number of leveraged buyouts (LBOs) in which a publicly traded company was taken private by an investment group, with this buyout financed significantly by debt. The case of notoriety is that of RJR Nabisco. RJR Nabisco announced that it was going private in a leveraged buyout (LBO) in October 1988. Because the LBO meant that the company was taking on more debt, the existing debt became riskier, and the value of RJR's existing debt fell by almost 20 percent on the announcement of the LBO. In addition, the value of the debt of other large companies fell also on fears that a similar fate awaited these other companies.

In a response to this and a few other cases, investors demanded the ability to sell their bonds back to the company in the event of a merger, a takeover, going private, or a major recapitalization. These putable bonds are sometimes referred to as poison puts because selling bonds back the issuer at face value during one of these events may jeopardize the event—which, to some, is the basic idea of poison puts.

Sources: Burroughs, Bryan, and John Helyar, *Barbarians at the Gate: The Fall of RJR Nabisco,* Harper & Row, Publishers, New York (1991), and Mohan, Nancy, and Carl R. Chen, "A Review of the RJR Nabisco Buyout," *Journal of Applied Corporate Finance,* Summer 1990, Volume 3.2 (2005), pp. 102–108.

convertible bond or **convertible note** debt obligation that can be converted into common shares at a predetermined conversion price at the investor's option

A **convertible bond** or **convertible note** is a debt obligation that can be converted into common shares or other securities of the issuer at a predetermined exchange rate. In this case, the investor has the option to continue to hold the bonds or to exchange the bonds. Companies often issue convertible bonds to make debt issues more attractive to investors, hence lowering the return that investors demand on these securities. These securities are attractive to investors because the investors can benefit from any appreciation of the stock of the company, while at the same time collecting interest. For example, Ford Motor Company issued $2.875 billion of convertible notes in November 2009. Such notes have a fixed coupon rate of 4.25 percent, they mature in 2016, and the issuer has the option to settle any exchange in either stock or an equivalent amount of cash.[10] The exchange

[10] These notes are referred to as 4.25% Senior Notes Convertible, CUSIP 345370CNB.

rate, or conversion rate, is 107.5269 shares per $1,000 note. Therefore, if Ford's common stock price is above $1,000 ÷ 107.5269 = $9.30, investors in these notes can either wait to convert their notes, hoping the price increases even more while they collect interest, or exchange the notes and make a profit.[11]

Convertible bonds are almost always callable, which then gives the issuer the ability to force a conversion at a point in time.[12] If the company calls the bond when it is attractive to the investor to convert it, the investor is faced with a dilemma: have the bond called away at the call price or convert it into shares.

Floating-rate bonds

A **floating-rate bond (floater)** has a coupon that adjusts, with the coupon rate tied to some variable short-term rate, such as the U.S. Treasury bill rate or the LIBOR, although many variations exist.[13] Floaters differ significantly from traditional fixed-coupon bonds because the coupons on floaters increase as interest rates increase and vice versa. Therefore, floaters provide protection against rising interest rates and tend to trade near their par value.

For example, in 2004 Caterpillar Financial Services issued floating-rate demand notes that mature April 15, 2019.[14] The coupon rate is variable, changing periodically to be at least equal to a recent 7-day average yield on money market funds. The result of this floating is that the price of the bond is generally very close to 100.

> **floating-rate bond (floater)** debt obligation that has adjustable coupons that are usually tied to some variable short-term rate

1. In what ways are bonds different from mortgages?

2. Describe the call, conversion, and put features of bonds. Which ones give the issuer more flexibility? Which ones are most attractive to investors?

Concept Review Questions

Issuing Debt in Different Currencies | GLOBAL PERSPECTIVE

Many U.S. companies issue debt denominated in currencies other than the U.S. dollar. For example, Procter & Gamble had $19.647 billion of long-term debt obligations at the end of their 2010 fiscal year. Of this debt:

Currency	Fair Value (in billions)
U.S. dollar	$9.704
Euro	8.061
Japanese Yen	1.129
British Pound Sterling	0.753
Total	$19.647

Procter & Gamble has issued bonds in different currencies at the same time. For example, in 2007 the company issued three types of bonds: 10-year bonds denominated in Euros, 20-year bonds denominated in Euros, and 30-year bonds denominated in U.S. dollars.

Source: Procter & Gamble 2010 10-K filing.

---

[11] Ford's stock price rose above $9.30 in December 2009 and remained above this price until at least the end of 2011. As of the end of 2011, only $883 million of this issue has not been converted by bondholders, and the bonds are trading around 139.

[12] Convertible bonds may be issued with a feature that allows conversion once the bonds have been called, or they may be issued with a feature that prohibits conversion once a call has been announced. Forcing conversion can only occur if bonds or notes allow conversion at call.

[13] London Interbank Offering Rate (LIBOR) is an average of rates that banks would charge to their best customers.

[14] These are medium-term notes issued by the financing subsidiary of Caterpillar [CUSIP 14911QTQ4].

6.2 BOND VALUATION

We are now ready to examine how to value a bond. Once investors know the face value, the term to maturity, and the coupon rate, they know both the amount and the timing of all the future promised payments on a bond. The value of a bond is determined by discounting these future payments by using an appropriate discount rate, often referred to as the **yield to maturity (YTM)** or **market rate of interest**. This market rate of interest is a function of market conditions, that is, other market interest rates, as well as of issue and issuer specific factors.

Valuing Straight Bonds

The value of a straight bond is the present value of the future cash flows on the bond, which consist of interest payments and the par value repaid at maturity. We can use the following equation to value the bond:

$$\text{Value of a bond today} = \text{Present value of coupon payments} + \text{Present value of maturity value}$$

or,

$$PV_0 = \left(\sum_{t=1}^{N} \frac{PMT_t}{(1 + r_b)^t} \right) + \frac{FV_N}{(1 + r_b)^N} \tag{6-1}$$

where PV_0 = bond value;
PMT_t = periodic interest (or coupon) payments;
r_b = bond discount rate (or market rate);
N = number of periods remaining to maturity;
FV_N = face (par) value of the bond.

Valuing a straight coupon bond is an example of applying time value of money concepts. Equation 6-1 should look familiar: It is simply the combination of the formulas for the present value of an annuity and the present value of a lump sum. We discount the interest as an ordinary annuity, and we discount the par value as a lump sum. In terms of notation that we have used previously, the coupon payments are the payments, PMT, that occur at regular intervals of time throughout the life of the bond.

Most U.S. bonds pay coupons semi-annually, although many non-U.S. bonds are annual-pay bonds. The valuation process is not different for semi-annual pay bonds and annual-pay bonds, but we must make the appropriate adjustments when dealing with semi-annual periods rather than annual ones. Specifically, we must divide the annual coupon payments by two to determine the amount of semi-annual coupons and multiply the number of years to maturity by two to obtain the number of semi-annual periods to maturity. Finally, we need a semi-annual discount rate because that coincides with the frequency of payments. For bonds, as a matter of convention, the appropriate adjustment is to divide the yield to maturity, which is the market bond yield, by two to obtain the six-month market yield.[15]

Consider a semi-annual bond with a face value of $1,000, matures in 5 years, has a coupon rate of 6.5 percent, and is priced to yield 5 percent. The inputs are:

PMT_t = ($1,000 × 0.065) ÷ 2 = $32.50
r_b = 0.05 ÷ 2 = 0.025 or 2.5%
N = 5 × 2 = 10 six-month periods
FV = $1,000

---

[15] Notice that this implies the bond yields are not effective rates, but rather are analogous to annual percentage rates.

We use the phrase "priced to yield" because we are saying that if you buy the bond at this price, whatever it turns out to be, you will have a return on your investment equal to the yield to maturity. Of course, there is an assumption underlying the math: When you receive the coupon payment, you will reinvest it in a similar-yielding investment.

We can solve this as the sum of the parts (that is, the present value of the FV, plus the present value of the annuity of PMT_t),

$$PV = \left(\sum_{t=1}^{10} \frac{\$32.50}{(1 + 0.025)^t} \right) + \frac{\$1,000}{(1 + 0.025)^{10}}$$

$$= \frac{PV \text{ of an}}{\text{annuity}} + \frac{PV \text{ of a}}{\text{lump-sum}}$$

$$= \$284.44 + 781.20$$

$$= \$1,065.64$$

or, simply use a financial calculator or spreadsheet to solve this in one calculation:

HP10B		TI BAII		HP12C		TI83/84	Spreadsheet
32.5	PMT	32.5	PMT	32.5	PMT	N = 10	=PV(0.025,10,32.5,1000)
2.5	I/YR	2.5	I/Y	2.5	i	I% = 2.5	
10	N	10	N	10	n	PV = Solve	
1000	FV	1000	FV	1000	FV	PMT = 32.5	
PV		CPT	PV	PV		FV = 1000	
						P/Y = 1	
						C/Y = 1	

What if this same bond was priced to yield 8 percent (that is, its yield to maturity is 8 percent)? In this case, the bond would sell for less than its face value of $1,000. Using the sum of the pieces,

$$PV = \left(\sum_{t=1}^{10} \frac{\$32.50}{(1 + 0.04)^t} \right) + \frac{\$1,000}{(1 + 0.04)^{10}}$$

$$= \$263.60 + 675.56$$

$$= \$939.17$$

or, simply use a financial calculator or spreadsheet to solve this in one calculation:

HP10B		TI BAII		HP12C		TI83/84	Spreadsheet
32.5	PMT	32.5	PMT	32.5	PMT	N = 10	=PV(0.04,10,32.5,1000)
4	I/YR	4	I/Y	4	i	I% = 4	
10	N	10	N	10	n	PV = Solve	
1000	FV	1000	FV	1000	FV	PMT = 32.5	
PV		CPT	PV	PV		FV = 1000	
						P/Y = 1	
						C/Y = 1	

What if this same bond were priced to yield 6.5 percent?

$$PV = \left(\sum_{t=1}^{10} \frac{\$32.50}{(1 + 0.0325)^t} \right) + \frac{\$1,000}{(1 + 0.0325)^{10}}$$

$$= \$273.73 + 726.27$$

$$= \$1,000$$

or, simply use a financial calculator or spreadsheet to solve this in one calculation:

HP10B		*TI BAII*		*HP12C*		*TI83/84*	*Spreadsheet*
32.5	PMT	32.5	PMT	32.5	PMT	N = 10	=PV(0.04,10,32.5,1000)
3.25	I/YR	3.25	I/Y	3.25	i	I% = 3.25	
10	N	10	N	10	n	PV = *Solve*	
1000	FV	1000	FV	1000	FV	PMT = 32.5	
PV		CPT	PV	PV		FV = 1000	
						P/Y = 1	
						C/Y = 1	

What this means is that if an investor bought the bond at its par value of $1,000 and held it to maturity, he or she would earn a return equal to the coupon rate of 6.5 percent if the investor reinvested each coupon to provide a return of 6.5 percent. To see this, let's assume that each cash flow is reinvested at 6.5 percent (3.25 percent each six-month period) until maturity:

Year	Six-month Period	Cash Flow	Number of Periods of Compounding	Future Value of Cash Flow
	1	$32.50	9	$43.34
1	2	32.50	8	41.98
	3	32.50	7	40.65
2	4	32.50	6	39.38
	5	32.50	5	38.14
3	6	32.50	4	36.94
	7	32.50	3	35.77
4	8	32.50	2	34.65
	9	32.50	1	33.56
5	10	1,032.50	0	1,032.50
			Total future value =	$1,376.89

Therefore,

FV = $1,376.89

PV = $1,000

N = 10

When we solve for i, $i = 3.25\%$, and the yield is 2×3.25 percent $= 6.5$ percent. In other words, the person would invest $1,000 and get a 6.5 percent return on that investment per year; that is, $65 in interest each year, any interest on reinvested interest, and then receive $1,000 back at maturity. Thus, when market rates equal the coupon rate, bonds trade at par.[16]

SUMMARIZING	*Element*		*Calculator*
	Coupon payment $\div$ 2	=	PMT
	Number of years to maturity $\times$ 2	=	N
	Yield to maturity $\div$ 2	=	i
	Face value	=	FV

[16] Bonds are often issued at (or very close to) par by setting the coupon rate equal to the market rate at the time of issue.

Bond prices are typically quoted in terms of value per $100 of face value. For example, if a $1,000 face value bond sells at $990, its bond quote is 99. As another example, if a $500 face value bond sells for $495, its bond quote is $495 ÷ $500 = 99. Using bond quotes, we eliminate the need to know a bond's face value.

Consider the bond that matures in 5 years, has a coupon rate of 6.5 percent, and is priced to yield 8 percent. What is the appropriate quote for this bond?

	Using Dollar Amounts, Assuming a $1,000 Face Value	Stating Monetary Amounts as a Percentage of Face Value
Coupon	$32.50	3.25
N	10	10
FV	$1000	100
i	4%	4%

You will notice that the only inputs changing are the coupon and the future value. In equation form, the value of the bond is:

$$PV_0 = \left(\sum_{t=1}^{10} \frac{3.25}{(1 + 0.04)^t} \right) + \frac{100}{(1 + 0.04)^{10}} = 93.9$$

The quote of 93.9, therefore, is stating the price as a percentage of face value. If the face value is $1,000, the value of the bond is $939.

SPREADSHEET TOOLS: VALUING A BOND

There are two ways that you can value a bond using spreadsheet functions. The first, the simplest, is to use the PV function, which calculates the present value of specified periodic cash flows (the PMTs) and the present value of a lump sum (the FV). For example if you want to calculate the value of a bond that has a coupon rate of 8 percent (paid semi-annually), 5 years to maturity, a face value of $1,000, and is priced to yield 10 percent:

$$=PV(r_b,N,PMT,FV)$$

$$=PV(0.05,10,40,1000)$$

This returns a value that is negative, −922.78, so we then multiply the result by −1 to arrive at the present value of $922.78.

Another way to calculate the value of the bond is to use the PRICE function, which provides the value per $100 face value. The PRICE function requires a settlement date (that is, the day you want the price of the bond), maturity date, the coupon rate, the yield, the redemption value (that is, the face value), and the frequency of interest payments within a year:

= PRICE (settlement date, maturity date, coupon rate, yield to maturity, redemption value, frequency)

Because we are not provided the detailed dates of a bond in most of our problems, we can use spreadsheet functions to help us. The function NOW() provides today's date. If we use NOW() * (365 * N), with N as the number of years, we can arrive at the maturity date N years from today. This way we do not have to know the precise maturity date of a bond to value it. However, to be more precise, we would want to adjust for leap years.

In our example, =PRICE(NOW(), NOW()+(365*5),0.08,0.10,100,2)

This provides us 92.281 (the bond quote in terms of per $100 face value), which we then multiply by 10 to get the value of $922.81.

premium amount by which a bond's value is above its face value

discount amount by which a bond's value is below its face value

When a 6.5 percent coupon bond yields 5 percent, the bond is selling at a **premium** from its face value. That is, when investors demand a 5 percent return and the bond provides a coupon greater than that, the bond's price will be bid upward until buying at the market price provides the investor with a market yield of 5 percent. When the 6.5 percent coupon bond is yielding 8 percent, it is selling at a **discount** from its par value. Because the future payments are fixed, the only way to get a return higher than the coupon rate on this bond is to pay less than the par value for it. The preceding examples illustrate the most important property of fixed income investments, such as bonds: *If interest rates increase, the market prices of bonds decline and vice versa.*

EXAMPLE 6.1

Bond Valuation

PROBLEM

Determine the value of a 15-year semi-annual pay bond with a coupon rate of 5 percent, when the appropriate market rate is 6 percent.

Solution

Assuming $1,000 par value:

$$PV = \sum_{t=1}^{30} \frac{\$25}{(1+0.03)^t} + \frac{\$1,000}{(1+0.03)^{10}} = \$901.9978$$

Using a financial calculator

Assuming a $1,000 Face Value		Using Bond Quote Terms	
FV	1000	FV	100
PMT	25	PMT	2.5
i	3	i	3
N	30	N	30
Solve for PV		*Solve for PV*	

Using a spreadsheet

Using the PV function, =PV(0.03,30,25,1000) or =PV(0.03,30,2.5,100)

Consider a bond that has a 5 percent coupon that matures in 15 years. If the yield is less than 5 percent, the bond trades at a premium. If the yield is greater than 5 percent, the bond trades at a discount, as you can see when we look at yields to maturity ranging from 0% to 10% in the table at the top of the next page.

You can also see this inverse relationship between yields and bond values in Figure 6-4, in which we depict the bond price-yield curve for this bond for yields from 0% to 20%. You can see that the relationship between market rates and bond price is not linear; the curve representing this relationship is convex.[17]

The shape of this curve shows two additional factors in the relationship between bond prices and market rates. First, for a given change in interest rates, bond prices increase more when rates decrease than they will decrease when rates increase. Note, for example, that the curve is steeper to the left of any point than it is to the right, so the impact of decreasing interest rates is different from the effect of increasing ones. Second, the curve is steeper for lower interest rates, which means that a given change in interest rates will have a much greater impact on bond prices when rates are lower than if they are higher.

---

[17] A curve is convex if all lines connecting any two points on the curve lie above the line. The convexity is evident if we look at the bond pricing equation, in which the discount rate is raised to powers other than one.

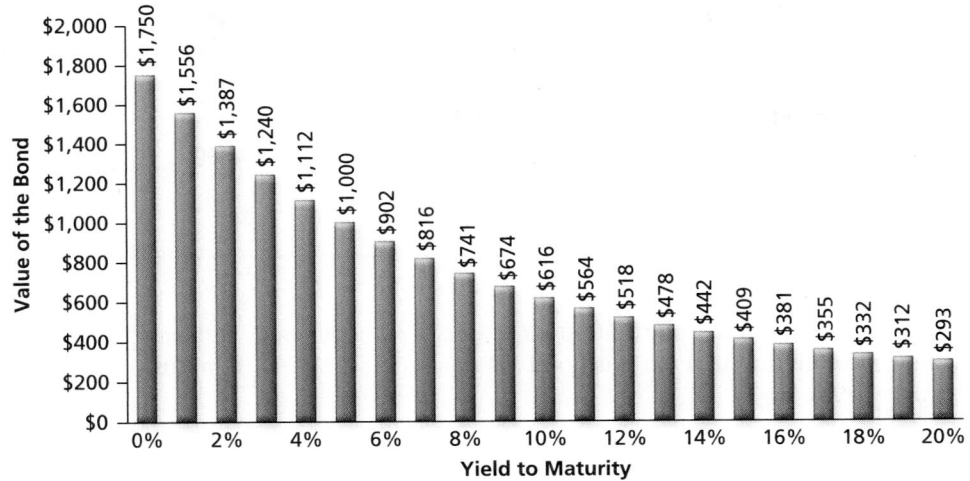

FIGURE 6-4 **Value of a $1,000 Face Value Bond, with a 5% Coupon Maturing in 15 Years, for Different Yields to Maturity**

Yield to Maturity	Discount Rate Per Period	Number of Periods	Coupon Payment	Future Value	Present Value	
i × 2	i	N	PMT	FV	PV	
0%	0.0%	30	$25	$1,000	$1,500.00	
1%	0.5%	30	$25	$1,000	$1,379.75	
2%	1.0%	30	$25	$1,000	$1,270.68	} Premium
3%	1.5%	30	$25	$1,000	$1,171.69	
4%	2.0%	30	$25	$1,000	$1,081.76	
5%	2.5%	30	$25	$1,000	$1,000.00	← At par
6%	3.0%	30	$25	$1,000	$925.61	
7%	3.5%	30	$25	$1,000	$857.88	
8%	4.0%	30	$25	$1,000	$796.15	} Discount
9%	4.5%	30	$25	$1,000	$739.84	
10%	5.0%	30	$25	$1,000	$688.44	

The second-most important property of bonds is that *the longer the time to maturity, the more sensitive the bond price is to changes in market rates.* Intuitively, this makes sense because the longer the term to maturity, the longer the investor has locked in fixed payments based on the bond's coupon rate. When market rates rise above this rate, the bond price will fall more because the coupon rate is unattractive relative to prevailing rates for a longer period. The longer an investor is locked in, the greater the disadvantage and the more the bond price will fall to adjust. Similarly, when rates fall below the coupon rate, the longer an investor is locked in, the greater the attractiveness of the higher coupon.[18]

Consider a bond that has a $1,000 face value and a 7 percent coupon, paid semiannually. And let's compare the bond with two different maturities: 5 years and 20 years. If the yield to maturity of both bonds is 6 percent, the value of the bonds is $1,042.65 and $1,115.57, respectively. But if the yield to maturity changes from 6 percent, which bond's price is more sensitive to this change?

[18] What determines when all the adjusting is done? When the bond price has reached a level such that if the investor buys it at the price and holds it until maturity, the investor will earn the market yield at the time of the purchase of the bond.

Yield to Maturity	5 Years to Maturity	20 Years to Maturity
5 percent	$1,087.52	$1,251.03
6 percent	$1,042.65	$1,115.57
7 percent	$1,000.00	$1,000.00

EXAMPLE 6.2

Estimating Prices for Bonds with Different Terms to Maturity

PROBLEM

Consider the semi-annual pay $1,000 par value 5 percent bond, with market rates at 6 percent. Calculate the value on this bond assuming that the term to maturity is:

1. 5 years.
2. 30 years.

Solution

1. 5 years. $PV = \sum_{t=1}^{10} \frac{\$25}{(1 + 0.03)^t} + \frac{\$1,000}{(1 + 0.03)^{10}} = \$957.349$

Using a financial calculator

Given information:

FV	1000
PMT	25
i	3
N	10

Solve for PV

Using a spreadsheet

Using the PV function,

=PV(0.03,10,25,1000).

2. 30 years. $PV = \sum_{t=1}^{60} \frac{\$25}{(1 + 0.03)^t} + \frac{\$1,000}{(1 + 0.03)^{10}} = \$861.622$

Using a financial calculator

Given information:

FV	1000
PMT	25
i	3
N	60

Solve for PV

Using a spreadsheet

Using the PV function,

=PV(0.03,60,25,1000).

And therefore,

Percentage Change in Price if Yields Change from 6 Percent to:	5 Years to Maturity	20 Years to Maturity
5 percent	4.303%	12.142%
7 percent	−4.091%	−10.360%

As you can see, the 20-year maturity bond's price is more sensitive to changes in the yield than the 5-year bond.

The sensitivity of bond values to interest rates is directly related to interest rate levels and to the term to maturity. It is also related to the level of the coupon rate associated with the bond, though this factor is much less important than either interest rate levels or the term to maturity. In particular, bond values are more sensitive to changes in interest rates for bonds with lower coupon rates than they are for higher-coupon-paying bonds. This is intuitive, if we recall that the compounding or discounting effect is accentuated with time, which suggests that a change in the discount rate has the greatest impact on the most distant cash flows, including the par value to be received at maturity in the case of bonds. For bonds that pay lower coupons, the principal repayment, which occurs at the maturity date, represents a higher proportion of the total payments to be received by the bondholder. As a result, their prices fluctuate more for a given change in interest rates than will otherwise identical higher-coupon-paying bonds.

EXAMPLE 6.3

Estimating Prices for Bonds with Different Coupon Rates

PROBLEM

Consider two bonds that have 15 years remaining to maturity, one with a 5 percent coupon rate, and the other with a 7 percent coupon rate.

1. What is the value of these two bonds if the yield to maturity is:
   a. 5 percent?
   b. 7 percent?

2. Which bond's value is more sensitive to the change in the yield from 5 percent to 7 percent?

Solution

5% COUPON BOND

1a. at 5% the value of the bond is $1,000:

$$PV_0 = \sum_{t=1}^{30} \frac{\$25}{(1 + 0.025)^t} + \frac{\$1,000}{(1 + 0.025)^{10}} = \$1,000$$

Using a financial calculator

Given information:

FV	1000
PMT	25
i	2.5
N	30

Solve for PV

7% COUPON BOND

1a. at 5% the value of the bond is $1,209.30:

$$PV_0 = \sum_{t=1}^{30} \frac{\$35}{(1 + 0.025)^t} + \frac{\$1,000}{(1 + 0.025)^{10}} = \$1,209.30$$

Using a financial calculator

Given information:

FV	1000
PMT	35
i	2.5
N	30

Solve for PV

Using a spreadsheet

Using the PV function, =PV(0.025,30,25,1000).

1b. at 7%, the value of the bond is $816.08

$$PV_0 = \sum_{t=1}^{30} \frac{\$25}{(1 + 0.035)^t} + \frac{\$1,000}{(1 + 0.035)^{10}} = \$816.08$$

Using a financial calculator

Given information:

FV   1000
PMT 25
i   3.5
N   30
Solve for PV

Using a spreadsheet

Using the PV function, =PV(0.035,30,25,1000).

Using a spreadsheet

Using the PV function, =PV(0.025,30,35,1000).

1b. at 7%, the value of the bond is $1,000

$$PV_0 = \sum_{t=1}^{30} \frac{\$35}{(1 + 0.035)^t} + \frac{\$1,000}{(1 + 0.035)^{10}} = \$1,000$$

Using a financial calculator

Given information:

FV   1000
PMT 35
i   3.5
N   30
Solve for PV

Using a spreadsheet

Using the PV function, =PV(0.035,30,35,1000).

2. The bond with the 5 percent coupon has a value more sensitive to the change in yield.

The percentage change in the price of the first bond:

$$\% \text{ change} = \frac{\$1,000 - 816.08}{\$1,000} = -18.39\%$$

The percentage change in the price of the second bond:

$$\% \text{ change} = \frac{\$1,209.30 - 1000.00}{\$1,209.30} = -17.31\%$$

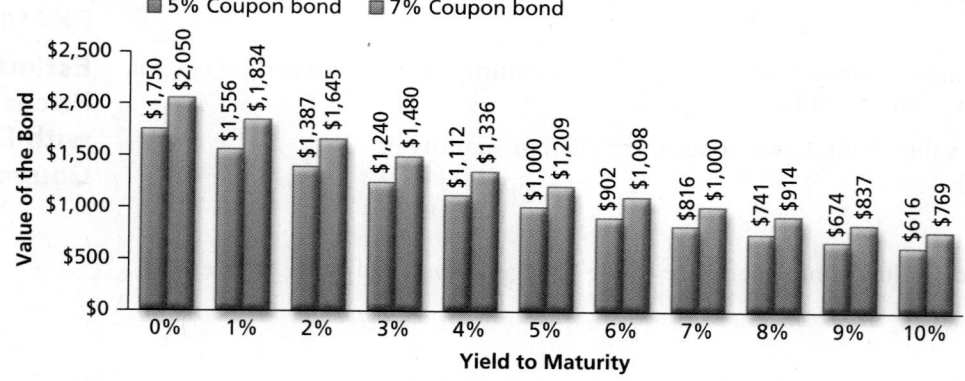

The sensitivity of bond prices to changes in interest rates is **interest rate risk**. All else constant, longer-term bonds with lower coupon rates and with lower market yields have greater interest rate risk than will shorter-term, higher coupon bonds with higher market yields. An important measure of interest rate risk, **duration**, incorporates all these factors into a single measure. Duration is the sensitivity of a bond's value to a change in interest rates; the greater the sensitivity, the greater the duration. The calculation of duration is beyond the scope of this book, but you already have an idea of what contributes to the sensitivity to interest rates, based on the examples and graphs so far:[19]

interest rate risk sensitivity of bond prices to changes in interest rates

duration measure of interest rate risk that incorporates several factors

- The lower the market yields, the higher the duration (compare the slope of the graph of bond values for lower yields versus higher yields; the slope [and, hence, sensitivity] is greater at lower yields).

[19] Duration is a measure of the time-weighted cash flows of a bond: The sooner the cash flows are received, the lower the duration.

- The longer the maturity, the higher the duration (compare the sensitivity to a yield change in the example of 5-year and 20-year maturity bonds).
- The lower the coupon, the higher the duration (compare the example bonds with 5 percent and 7 percent coupons; the bond with the 5 percent coupon has a greater sensitivity for the yield change).

Valuing Zero-Coupon Bonds

Zero-coupon bonds are easy to evaluate by using a variation of Equation 6-1 in which we drop the first term because there are no interest payments to discount. This leaves us with Equation 6-2:

$$PV_0 = \frac{FV_N}{(1 + r_b)^N} \tag{6-2}$$

Remember that, by convention, we value these bonds assuming semi-annual discounting periods and convert our quoted yield to a semi-annual yield; therefore, the number of periods should also be expressed in terms of semi-annual periods. Although that may seem odd because there are no coupons to reinvest every six months, we do this so that the yields on zeroes are comparable to those of coupon bonds.

Consider a zero-coupon bond that has 5 years remaining to maturity. If the bond is priced to yield 6 percent, the value of the bond, using bond quote terms, is:

$$PV_0 = \frac{100}{(1 + 0.03)^{10}} = 74.409$$

Using a calculator, the inputs are:

FV= 100
i = 3%
N = 10

and you solve for the present value. We provide the value of this zero-coupon bond for different yields to maturity in Figure 6-5. As you can see, there is a curvilinear relationship between the value of the bond and the yield to maturity, which we also found with the coupon bonds.

Notice in the equation and in Figure 6-5 that the value of a zero increases as yields fall and decreases as yields increase, just as is the case for a regular coupon-paying bond. In fact, the market prices of zeroes are even more sensitive to interest rate changes because

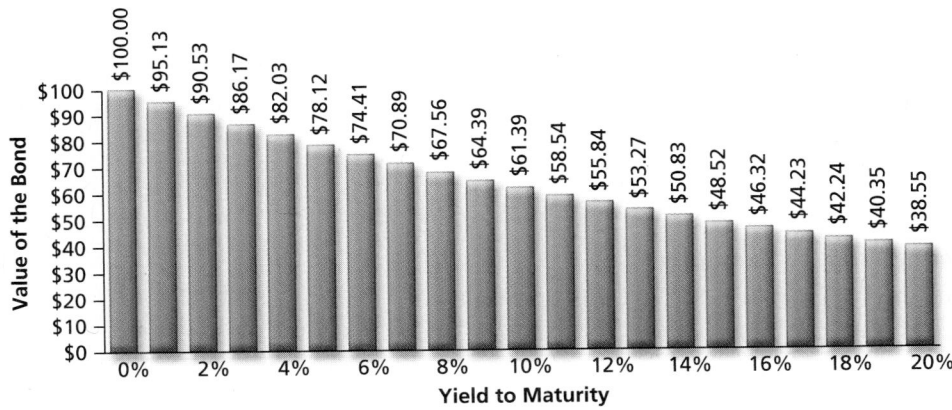

FIGURE 6-5 Value of a Zero-Coupon Bond with 5 Years Remaining to Maturity

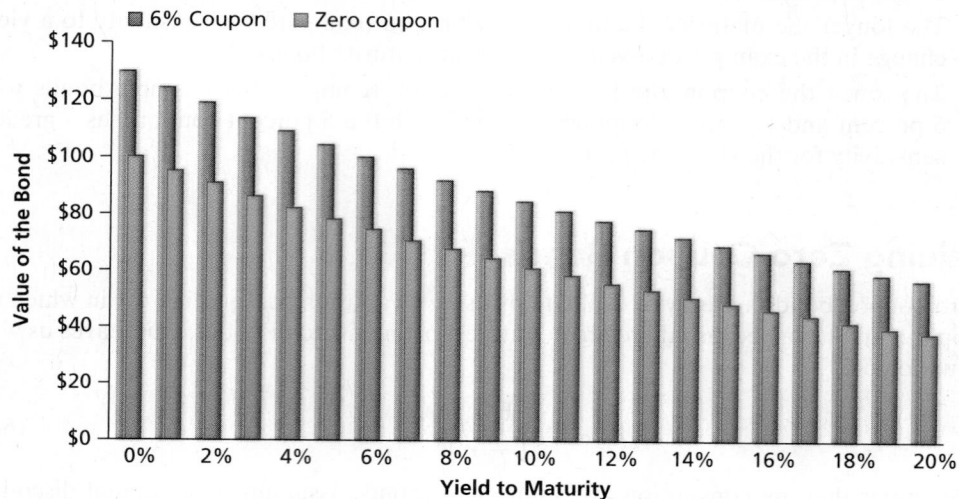

FIGURE 6-6 Value of a Zero-Coupon Bond and a Coupon Bond at Different Yields, Both with 5 Years to Maturity

they make no coupon payments at all. You can see this by comparing the zero-coupon bond that matures in 5 years with a similar bond, but with a coupon rate of 6 percent. If the yield to maturity is 6 percent, the zero-coupon bond has a value of 74, whereas the coupon bond has a value of 100. If the rate goes from 6 percent to 7 percent, the zero-coupon bond's value falls to 71, a drop of 4.73 percent, whereas the coupon bond's value falls to 96, a drop of 4.16 percent. We show this in Figure 6-6, comparing the values of the zero-coupon bond with that of a similar maturity 6% coupon bond.

EXAMPLE 6.4

Valuing a Zero-Coupon Bond

PROBLEM

Determine the value of a 15-year zero-coupon bond with a face value of $1,000 and a market yield of 5 percent.

Solution

$$PV_0 = \frac{\$1,000}{(1 + 0.025)^{30}} = \$476.7427$$

Solution using a financial calculator

Given information:

FV	1000
PMT	0
i	2.5
N	30

Solve for PV

Solution using a spreadsheet

Using the PV function, =PV(0.025,30,0,1000)

A bond quote may differ from the actual prices investors pay for bonds whenever bonds are sold at a date other than the date of a coupon payment. Up until now, we have made an assumption that we are valuing the bond on the coupon date; that is, the owner of the bond has just received a coupon payment, and we have not figured this most recent coupon into the valuation of the bond.

In reality, bonds can trade at any time in the bond's life, so any bond transaction will consider the interest that accrues to bondholders between such payment dates. For example, an investor who held a bond for 45 days since the last coupon has "earned" 45 days of interest, even though he will not receive those 45 days of interest if he sells it now because coupons are paid semi-annually—in fact, the bond purchaser will receive the entire coupon payment on the next scheduled coupon payment date. Based on the convention of a 360-day year (and, therefore, a 180-day coupon period), the seller is due $45 \div (360 \div 2) = 25$ percent of the period's coupon, and the buyer receives the rest; therefore, the price that the buyer must pay is the bond's value as of the most recent coupon, plus the accrued interest (the 25 percent of the coupon in our example). This amount is the **cash price** of the bond. The cash price is often referred to as the **dirty price**, and the price quote of the bond without the accrued interest (that is, as of the most recent coupon) is the **clean price**.

cash price or **dirty price** the actual price paid for a debt obligation that considers the amount of accrued interest on the security

clean price bond quote that does not consider the accrued interest

---

PROBLEM

Consider a $1,000 face value bond with a coupon rate of 5 percent and priced to yield 4 percent. If there were 5 years remaining to maturity as of the most recent coupon payment date, and the bond is sold 30 days into the next coupon period, what is the accrued interest that buyer must pay the seller as part of the bond's price?

Solution

Accrued interest = $(30 \div 180) \times 0.04 \times \$1,000 = \$6.67$

EXAMPLE 6.5

Accrued Interest

---

1. What two time value of money formulas do we need to value a bond?

2. When market interest rates are above the coupon rate on a bond, is it a premium or discount bond?

3. If market interest rates increase, what happens to bond prices? Why?

Concept Review Questions

6.3 BOND YIELDS

Up until now, we have provided the market interest rate, the yield that is needed to value a bond today. However, different types of yields are actually associated with bonds: the yield to maturity, the yield to call, and the current yield.

Yield to Maturity

The discount rate that we use to evaluate bonds is the yield to maturity (YTM). It is the yield that an investor would realize if he or she bought the bond at the current price, held it to maturity, received all the promised payments on their scheduled dates, and reinvested all the cash flows received at this yield. Given the value of a bond and all the details regarding the amount and timing of interest and principal repayments, we can estimate the bond's YTM using Equation 6-1:

$$P_0 = \left(\sum_{t=1}^{N} \frac{PMT_t}{(1 + r_b)^t} \right) + \frac{FV_N}{(1 + r_b)^N}$$

The yield to maturity is r_b if the bond pays annual coupons and is $r_b \times 2$ if the bond pays semi-annual coupons. The challenge is that when we use Equation 6-1 to solve for r_b, we do not find a direct solution. Instead, we must iterate—that is, choose a different value of r_b—until we find a yield that equates the present value with the value of the future flows (interest and principal). Choosing too high a rate will cause the right-hand side of 6-1 to be smaller than the left-hand side; choosing too low a rate will cause the right-hand side of 6-1 to be larger than the left-hand side.

internal rate of return (IRR) return implicit in a set of cash flows, assuming reinvestment of cash flows in a similar-yielding investment

For a bond that pays interest annually, the YTM is r_b; for bonds that pay interest semi-annually, the YTM is $r_b \times 2$. The yield to maturity is an **internal rate of return (IRR)**. An internal rate of return is an investment's effective return, considering the investment's cash flows and any interest earned on reinvesting these cash flows. Implicit in the math of the bond valuation formula (Equation 6-1) is that when the investor receives the cash flows (the PMT), these are reinvested in a security with a similar yield.

The YTM therefore represents the return on the bond, assuming:

1. the bond is held to maturity, and
2. all cash flows—that is, the interest—can be reinvested in similar yielding investments.

Unfortunately, solving for r_b in Equation 6-1 and, hence, the YTM, is difficult because of the various powers involved in the equation, making it impossible to find the algebraic solution. We must therefore resort to using a financial calculator, a spreadsheet program, or time-consuming trial and error.[20,21]

Consider a semi-annual bond that has a face value of $1,000, matures in 5 years, and has a coupon rate of 6.5 percent. If the bond has a current market value of $980, what is the bond's yield to maturity? Assuming that the bond has semi-annual interest, which we assume unless specified otherwise,

PMT = ($1,000 × 0.065) ÷ 2 = $32.50
N = 5 × 2 = 10 six-month periods
FV = $1,000
PV = $980

Solving this would require a trial-and-error approach—solving for the YTM that causes the right-hand side of this equation to be equal to the left-hand side, $980:

$$\$980 = \left(\sum_{t=1}^{10} \frac{\$32.50}{(1 + r_b)^t} \right) + \frac{\$1,000}{(1 + r_b)^{10}}$$

The six-month rate is 3.49 percent, so the yield to maturity is 6.98 percent. Better yet, we can use a financial calculator or spreadsheet to solve this:

HP10B		TI BAII		HP12C		TI83/84	Spreadsheet
32.5	PMT	32.5	PMT	32.5	PMT	N = 10	=RATE(10, 32.5,−980, 1000)*2
10	N	10	N	10	n	I% = Solve × 2	
1000	FV	1000	FV	1000	FV	PV = −980	
980	+/−	980	+/−	980	CHS PV	PMT = 32.5	
	PV		PV	i		FV = 1000	
I/YR		CPT	I/Y	× 2		P/Y = 1	
× 2		× 2				C/Y = 1	

[20] Old-fashioned bond tables, which show yields corresponding to various prices, coupon rates, and maturity dates are also available.
[21] An approximation formula does exist, but it can be off by a significant amount sometimes, especially for longer-term bonds that are trading at prices that are quite different from their par value.

PROBLEM

Estimate the YTM on a 20-year 6 percent bond that pays semi-annual coupons and is selling for $1,030.

EXAMPLE 6.6

Estimating the Yield to Maturity on a Semi-Annual-Pay Bond

Solution

$$\$1{,}030 = \left[\sum_{t=1}^{40}\frac{\$30}{(1 + r_b)}\right] + \frac{\$1{,}000}{(1 + r_b)^{40}}$$

$r_b = 2.8729\%$ Therefore, YTM $= 5.7457\%$

Using a financial calculator

Given:

PV	−1030
FV	1000
N	40
PMT	30

Solve for i, then multiply by 2

Using a spreadsheet program

Using the RATE function,   =RATE(N,PMT,PV,FV): =RATE(40,30,-1030,1000)*2

Using the YIELD function,   =YIELD(NOW( ),NOW()+(20*365),0.06,1030,1000,2,1)

It is relatively straightforward to solve for the yield on a zero if we are given the price of the bond. In particular, we can rearrange Equation 6-1 to determine an exact solution for the semi-annual yields to maturity, as shown in Equation 6-3. This value is then doubled to find the annual YTM.[22]

$$\text{YTM} = \left(\sqrt[N]{\frac{FV_N}{PV_0}} - 1\right) \times 2 \tag{6-3}$$

For example, suppose a zero-coupon bond that matures in six years is issued at 78. What is this bond's yield to maturity? The inputs are:

FV = 100
PV = 78
N = 6 × 2 = 12

Solving for the YTM,

$$\text{YTM} = \left(\sqrt[12]{\frac{100}{78}} - 1\right) \times 2 = \left[\left(\frac{100}{78}\right)^{\frac{1}{12}} - 1\right] \times 2 = 4.1842\%$$

---

[22] Notice that this differs from the coupon-paying bonds, for which there was no finite solution for YTM. Another way of representing this equation, which is closest to how you would solve this using a calculator, is

$$r_b = \left[\left(FV_N / PV_0\right)^{1/N} - 1\right] \times 2.$$

EXAMPLE 6.7

Estimating the Yield to Maturity on a Zero-Coupon Bond

PROBLEM

Determine the YTM on a 10-year zero-coupon bond that is presently quoted at 56.

Solution

$$YTM = \left(\left[\frac{100}{56} \right]^{\frac{1}{20}} - 1 \right) \times 2 = 0.058831 \text{ or } 5.8831\%$$

Using a financial calculator

Given information:

FV	100
PV	56
PMT	0
N	20

Solve for i, then multiply by 2. Don't forget to enter the PV as a negative value in your calculator.

Using a spreadsheet

Using the RATE function, =RATE(20,0,−56,100)*2

LESSONS LEARNED | The Yield to Maturity as an Internal Yield

Consider a semi-annual bond that has 3 years to maturity, a coupon rate of 6 percent, and a price of 90. Therefore:

$N = 6$
$PMT = 3$
$FV = 100$
$PV = 90$

Solving for i, $i = 4.9682\%$. Therefore, the yield to maturity is 9.9363%.

Now let's see what happens in terms of cash flows and reinvestment, as we calculate the future value of each cash flow as of the bond's maturity:

Six-Month Period	Cash Flow	Future Value of Cash Flow, Reinvested at 4.9682%
0	−$90	
1	3	$3.8231 ←$3 × (1 + 0.049682)^5
2	3	3.6421
3	3	3.4697
4	3	3.3055
5	3	3.1490
6	103	103.0000
		$120.3894

Investing $90 in this bond will result in $120.3894 in value at the end of six periods or 3 years. Given this information:

$PV = 90$
$FV = 120.3894$
$N = 6$

We solve for i: $i = 4.9682\%$ and YTM = $4.9682\% \times 2 = 9.9363\%$

Bond Quotes | FINANCE in the News

Investors can find bond prices from FINRA, which provides quoted prices on corporate, government, and municipal bonds.[23] Consider a selection of the bonds issued by IBM and outstanding as of July 2009. Per FINRA, we see the following as of July 3, 2009:

Symbol	Coupon	Maturity	Callable	Moody's	S&P	Fitch	Price	Yield
IBM.KG	5.70	09/14/2017	Yes	A1	A+	A+	106.300	4.760
IBM.LA	7.63	10/15/2018	Yes	A1	A+	A+	119.913	4.922
IBM.GT	8.38	11/01/2019	No	A1	A+	A+	125.206	5.186
IBM.GW	7.00	10/30/2025	Yes	A1	A+	A+	112.536	5.799
IBM.KY	8.00	10/15/2038	Yes	A1	A+	A+	131.130	5.781

The price is that of the last sale, stated in bond quote terms (that is, as a percentage of face value). The yield is the yield to maturity on the bond based on this last trade.

We can interpret the quote for IBM's 5.7 bond maturity 2017, with the symbol of IBM.KG, as the following:

- The bond has a coupon of 5.7 percent, but because the market yield of 4.76 percent is less than the coupon rate, the bond trades at a premium from its face value.
- If you own $100,000 of face value of these bonds, the value of your bonds is 106.3 × $100,000, or $106,300.
- The bond is callable, which means that if certain conditions are met, IBM can buy the bond from the investor.
- The bond is rated A1, A+, and A+ by the three agencies, which means that this is an investment grade bond.

Yield to Call

We mentioned earlier that bonds often have flexible maturity dates because some bonds are callable by the issuer, and for some, the maturity can be retracted or extended by the investor. This means that we can calculate the yield to maturity for these different dates. Suppose, for example, that the bond in the previous example was callable after five years at par.[24] This means that it is quite possible that the bond will not be outstanding for 20 years, because it may be called after 5 years. This yield, which is associated with a bond's first call date, is called its **yield to call (YTC)**. We can estimate it in the same way as we estimated the yield to maturity by using Equation 6-1, except that we replace the time to maturity (N) with the time to first call (M), and we replace the face value (FV) with the call price (CP). This gives us the following equation:

yield to call (YTC) return on a callable bond, assuming that the bond is called away before maturity

$$PV_0 = \left(\sum_{t=1}^{M} \frac{PMT_t}{(1 + r_b)} \right) + \frac{CP_t}{(1 + r_b)^M} \tag{6-4}$$

Bonds are callable at a specified price (the call price), but there is often a schedule of call prices associated with a given callable bond. The call price is usually stated as a percentage of par value. Therefore, a call price of 105 indicates that a $1,000 face value bond is callable at $1,050; a call price of 110 indicates that a $1,000 face value bond is callable at $1,100. Generally, we evaluate the YTC based on the bond's first available call.

Consider a semi-annual pay bond with 10 years remaining to maturity, a 6 percent coupon rate, and a face value of $1,000, that is priced to yield 5 percent. If the bond is callable in 2 years at 110, what is the bond's yield to call? First, we need to solve for the current price (PV) based on the yield to maturity of 5 percent:

PMT_t = ($1,000 × 0.06) ÷ 2 = $30
r_b = 0.05 ÷ 2 = 0.025 or 2.5%
N = 10 × 2 = 20 six-month periods
FV = $1,000

---

[23] FINRA is the Financial Industry Regulatory Authority, www.finra.org.
[24] In practice, many callable bonds may have more than one call date.

Solving for PV, the current value of the bond is $1,077.95.

Solving for the yield to call requires using trial and error to solve for YTC in the following:

$$\$1{,}077.95 = \left(\sum_{t=1}^{4}\frac{\$30.00}{(1 + YTC)^t}\right) + \frac{\$1{,}000}{(1 + YTC)^4}$$

Or,

PMT_t = ($1,000 × 0.06) ÷ 2 = $30.00
N = 2 × 2 = 4 six-month periods
FV = $1,100
PV = $1,077.95

Better yet, we can use a financial calculator or spreadsheet to solve this:

HP10B		TI BAII		HP12C		TI83/84	Spreadsheet
30	PMT	30	PMT	30	PMT	N = 4	=RATE(4,30,−1077.95,1100)*2
4	N	4	N	4	n	I% = *Solve* × 2	
1100	FV	1100	FV	1100	FV	PV = −1077/95	
1077.95	+/− PV	1077.95	+/− PV	1077.95	CHS PV	PMT = 30	
I/YR		CPT	I/Y	i		FV = 1100	
× 2		× 2			× 2	P/Y = 1	
						C/Y = 1	

The yield to call is 6.54 percent.

If the call price is above its current market price, it is unlikely that the bond would be called back by the issuer, so the bond will sell based on its YTM rather than its YTC. It would trade at a price based on its YTC if it was likely that the bond would be called, which would occur if the bond were trading above its call price and, correspondingly, if the YTC < YTM. Generally, a callable bond trades at a value that reflects the lower of YTC and YTM.

EXAMPLE 6.8

Estimating the Yield to Call

PROBLEM

Estimate the YTC on a 20-year 6 percent semi-annual pay bond that is callable in 5 years at a call price of $1,050, if the bond pays semi-annual coupons and is selling for $1,030.

Solution

$$\$1{,}030 = \left[\sum_{t=1}^{10}\frac{\$30}{(1 + r_b)}\right] + \frac{\$1{,}050}{(1 + r_b)^{10}}$$

$r_b = 3.0814\%$ Therefore, YTC = 6.1627%

Using a financial calculator
Given:

PV   −1030
FV   1050
N   10
PMT 30

Solve for i, then multiply by 2

Using a spreadsheet program

Using the RATE function, =RATE(N,PMT,PV,FV): =RATE(10,30,−1030,1050)*2

Current Yield

The **current yield (CY)** is the ratio of the annual coupon interest divided by the current market price. As such, it is not a true measure of the return to a bondholder because it disregards the bond's purchase price relative to all the future cash flows and uses just the next year's interest payment. The current yield is also sometimes referred to as the flat or cash yield. We calculate this rate using Equation 6-5:

$$CY = \frac{\text{Annual interest}}{\text{Current market price}} \tag{6-5}$$

> **current yield (CY):** the ratio of the annual coupon interest divided by the current market price

You will notice when working problems involving bonds that the current yield usually does not equal the coupon rate or the YTM. This will be the case, unless the bond is trading at its face value and all three rates—coupon rate, YTM, and CY—are equal. It is clear that whenever bonds trade at a premium, the CY will be less than the coupon rate but greater than the YTM, and whenever they trade at a discount, the CY will be greater than the coupon rate but less than the YTM, as shown here:

Price-Yield Relationships

Bond Price	Relationship
Par	Coupon rate = CY = YTM
Discount	Coupon rate < CY < YTM
Premium	Coupon rate > CY > YTM

Concept Review Questions

1. When calculating a yield to call, what is different from the calculation of a yield to maturity on the same bond?

2. Is the yield to call always greater than the yield to maturity?

6.4 GOVERNMENT DEBT OBLIGATIONS

We refer to a debt obligation of a national government as a **Treasury security** and refer to these obligations as **sovereign debt**.

> **Treasury security** debt obligation of a national government
>
> **sovereign debt** obligation of a national government that is denominated in a currency other than that of the issuing government

Sovereign Debt

National governments issue debt obligations that, in theory, are considered to be risk free because the government can print money or raise revenues through taxes to meet the cash flow obligations of this sovereign debt. We say "in theory" because there have been situations in which this debt has been viewed as not risk free; Venezuela, Russia, Argentina, the Ukraine, and Belize, among other nations, have defaulted on their debt. In some cases the debt is restructured, allowing the nation to repay the debt under more favorable terms.[25]

---

[25] Of course, there is the case of Ecuador in 2008; the government decided simply not to pay its debts on the basis of moral grounds, though the country could likely have paid its debts.

Sovereign debt ratings are similar to those of corporate debt ratings in terms of a ratings scheme, but as you would expect, the factors are different. Sovereign debt ratings consider:

- fiscal performance.
- debt burden.
- external liquidity and international investment position.
- institutional effectiveness.
- political risks.
- monetary flexibility.
- economic structure.
- growth prospects.

Consider the case of Greece (Hellenic Republic), which is part of the European Union. Its debt credit rating has deteriorated over time, as the economic conditions in the country have worsened:[26]

Date	Debt Rating
March 26, 1997	A–
March 13, 2001	A
June 10, 2003	A+
November 17, 2004	A
January 14, 2009	A–
December 16, 2009	BBB+
April 27, 2010	BB+
March 29, 2011	BB–
May 9, 2011	B
June 13, 2011	CCC
July 27, 2011	CC
February 27, 2012	D
May 2, 2012	CCC

These credit ratings reflect the burgeoning debt, relative to the country's gross domestic product; for example, the ratio of debt to GDP climbed from 94 percent in 1999 to 142.8 percent in 2010. In addition, GDP growth went from positive 1 percent in 2008 to negative 2 and 4.5 percent in 2009 and 2010, respectively. Greece is part of the European Union, and as such cannot print more money and must seek assistance from the European Central Bank. Therefore, it has limited flexibility in dealing with its economic woes.

The credit ratings of countries are not all AAA; rather, they reflect the varying economic conditions. For example, you can see that downgrades that reflect the worsening conditions in the European Union:

Country	Rating as of June 30, 2011	Rating as of January 13, 2012
Germany	AAA	AAA
Iceland	BBB–	BBB–
India	BBB–	BBB–

---

[26] Standard & Poor's *Sovereign Rating and Country T&C Assessment Histories,* July 5, 2011; Standard & Poor's *Sovereign Government Rating Methodology and Assumptions,* June 30, 2011; "Ratings on Greece Raised to 'CCC' From Selective Default following Completion of Debt Exchange; Outlook Stable," Standard & Poor's, May 2, 2012. The rating "D" in this case is selective default, which means that it applies to specific obligations, but not all.

Country	Rating as of June 30, 2011	Rating as of January 13, 2012
Israel	AA–	AA–
Italy	A+	BBB+
Japan	AA–	AA–
Mexico	A	A–
People's Republic of China	AA–	AA–
Russian Federation	BBB+	BBB+
Sweden	AAA	AAA
United Kingdom	AAA	AAA
United States	AAA	AA+

The U.S. was not immune to the effects of the economy and its spending on its ratings. On August 5, 2011, Standard & Poor's lowered the rating on the debt of the United States from AAA, which the U.S. had had since 1917, to AA–. This downgrade followed a rancorous debate over the debt ceiling, the budget, and deficit spending.[27,28]

U.S. Treasury Obligations

Obligations of the U.S. government include short-term securities, which we refer to as Treasury bills (or T-bills), medium-term debt that we refer to as notes, and long-term debt (bonds). Treasury securities also include Treasury Inflation Protected Securities (TIPS), which protect the investor against the effects of inflation. You can see the amount of this debt outstanding in each year 1996 through 2010 in Figure 6-7 and can see how the debt of the U.S. came to a crisis in mid-2011. In addition to the marketable U.S. Treasury securities in Figure 6-7 of $8.85 trillion at the end of 2010, the U.S. government indebtedness

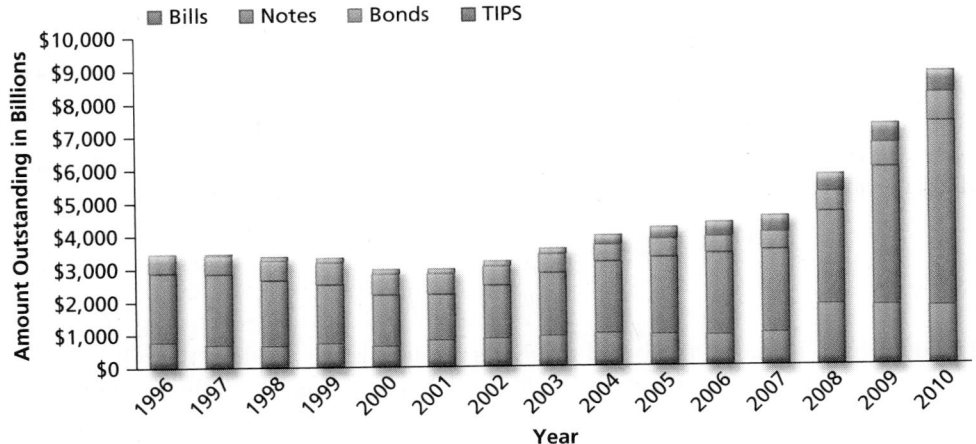

FIGURE 6-7   U.S. Treasury Securities Outstanding
Source of data: *Securities Industry and Financial Markets Association, SIFMA.*

[27] Congress passed the *Budget Control Act of 2011* [Public Law 112-25 S. 365], and the bill was signed into law on August 2, 2011, to increase the debt limit, attempting to avert a credit downgrade or default on the debt. Standard & Poor's downgraded the U.S. debt within one week of this bill being signed into law. This debt crisis brought to the forefront the issue of how much debt the federal government should or could bear.

[28] At the time of this writing, both Moody's and Fitch Ratings rated the U.S. as AAA. However, both agencies had put the U.S. on a "negative watch," which means that conditions are present that may result in a downgrade.

includes U.S. intragovernmental holdings of $4.6 trillion, which, together, came close to hitting the debt limit of $14.29 trillion by mid-2011.[29]

Treasury bills

Treasury bill (T-bill) obligation of the federal government with maturities up to one year that are sold at a discount from face value

A **Treasury bill (T-bill)** is a short-term government debt obligation that matures in 1 year or less. The available maturities are 4 weeks, 13 weeks, 26 weeks, and 52 weeks. Partly because of this short term to maturity, they do not make regular interest payments but rather are sold at a discount from their par (or face) value, which is paid on the maturity date. The discount rate, which is the difference between the face value and the price of the bill, is determined through the U.S. Treasury's auction when the bills are first issued. The interest earned is the difference between the purchase price and the face value.

Treasury securities, including bills, are sold through auctions. Bidding in a government securities auction consists of competitive and noncompetitive bids. The competitive bids comprise 35 percent of an offering, in which the bidder specifies the yield that is acceptable. The noncompetitive bids accept the rate that results from the competitive bids. The rate set by the auction process is the result of a Dutch auction. In a **Dutch auction**, bidders submit the rate and amount that they are willing to buy. The Treasury then determines the rate at which it can sell the amount of securities, accepting all bids at or below the clearing rate. For example, suppose the Treasury wants to sell $50 million of securities and receives the following bids:

Dutch auction bidding process that accepts the bids necessary to sell the intended amount; in the auction of interest-bearing securities, the rate on the securities is set at the rate that is necessary to sell the desired quantity of securities

Bidder	Rate	Quantity in Millions
1	4.5%	$25
2	4.8%	$10
3	5.0%	$15
4	5.5%	$20
5	6.0%	$25

The rate in this case would be set to 5% because at that rate the Treasury would sell the $25 + 10 + 15 = $50 million in securities. Bidders 1, 2, and 3 would receive a rate of 5%, and bidders 4 and 5 would be left out.

Similar to bonds, T-bills can be priced by estimating the present value of the expected future payment (i.e., the par value that is to be repaid at maturity). The value of a T-bill today, P, is the discounted face value, using the annualized rate adjusted to the proportion of the year. In the equation for the valuation of a bill, r_{BEY} is the bond equivalent yield, FV is the face value, and n = the term to maturity expressed as number of days:

$$P = \frac{FV}{1 + \left(r_{BEY} \times \dfrac{n}{365}\right)} \tag{6-6}$$

As evident from its name, the **bond equivalent yield** is the yield on the bill annualized in a manner similar to that of bonds. The logic of this equation is that the present value of the T-bill is the face value, F, divided by 1 plus the rate of interest, where the rate of interest is based on both the bond equivalent yield and the proportion of the year. Therefore, if the bond equivalent yield is 5 percent and the maturity is 90 days, the present value of this bond for each $1 face value is:

$$P = \frac{FV}{1 + \left(0.05 \times \dfrac{90}{365}\right)} = \frac{\$1}{1.01233} = \$0.9878$$

---

[29] The debt ceiling was raised by $500 billion in the *Budget Control Act of 2011*, with further increases conditional on Congressional approval and spending cuts. The debt ceiling was raised again in January of 2012, this time to $16.4 trillion.

PROBLEM

Calculate the value of a 91-day T-bill with a face value of $10,000 that has a quoted yield of 4.20 percent.

EXAMPLE 6.9

Determining the Price of a T-Bill

Solution

$$P = \frac{FV}{1 + \left(0.042 \times \frac{91}{365}\right)} = \frac{\$10,000}{1.010471233} = \$9,896.37$$

Similar to bonds, T-bill prices are usually quoted on the basis of $100 of par value, so the price quote for this T-bill is 98.78.

Rearranging Equation 6-6, we can determine the yield on T-bills using the following equation:

$$r_{BEY} = \frac{FV - P}{P} \times \frac{365}{n} \qquad (6\text{-}7)$$

In the United States, yields on T-bills are also usually quoted based on the **bank discount yield**. The differences arise because of the use of face value instead of price in the denominator of the first term and because 360 days is used instead of 365 days to annualize the rate. The resulting equation is given where r_{BDY} = the bank discount yield:

$$r_{BDY} = \frac{FV - P}{FV} \times \frac{360}{n} \qquad (6\text{-}8)$$

bank discount yield method of stating interest rates that compares the discount with the face value of the security, annualized by 360 divided by the maturity of the security

Suppose a T-bill with 90 days to maturity has a quoted price of 98.78. The bank discount yield for this T-bill is:

$$r_{BDY} = \frac{100 - 98.78}{100} \times \frac{360}{90} = 0.0122 \times 4 = 4.88\%$$

PROBLEM

Estimate the bond equivalent yield, as well as the discount yield, on a 182-day T-bill that is presently quoted at 98.20.

EXAMPLE 6.10

Estimating the Yield on a T-Bill

Solution

$$r_{BEY} = \frac{100 - 98.2}{98.2} \times \frac{365}{182} = 0.01833 \times 2.0055 = 0.03676 \text{ or } 3.676\%$$

$$r_{BDY} = \frac{100 - 98.2}{100} \times \frac{360}{182} = 0.01800 \times 1.97802 = 0.03560 \text{ or } 3.560\%$$

Therefore, the bond equivalent yield is 3.676%, and the discount yield is 3.56%

In addition to the traditional Treasury bills, the U.S. Treasury will also sell a **cash management bill**, which has a variable rate and is not available at every Treasury auction.[30] These bills are issued as needed by the Treasury to meet temporary cash shortfalls of the U.S. government for such uses as paying scheduled Social Security retirement

cash management bills short-term obligations of the U.S. government issued to meet temporary cash needs of the government

---

[30] These bills have been used since 1975.

U.S. Treasury note obligation of the U.S. government that has a maturity of 2, 3, 5, 7, or 10 years and pays interest semi-annually

U.S. Treasury bond obligation of the U.S. government that has a maturity of 30 years and that pays interest semi-annually

I Savings bond debt obligation of the U.S. Treasury that protects the investor against inflation

EE/E Savings bond debt obligation of the U.S. Treasury with a maturity of 20 or 30 years, with a fixed interest rate and interest accrued and paid at maturity

Treasury Inflation Protected Securities (TIPS) bonds issued by the U.S. government that provide investors with protection against inflation

benefits and have maturities that range from a few days to six months.[31] Like the T-bills, these bills are sold at a discount from their face value.

Treasury notes and bonds

A **U.S. Treasury note** has an original maturity of 2, 3, 5, 7, or 10 years, and a **U.S. Treasury bond** has an original maturity of 20 or 30 years. Both notes and bonds pay interest semi-annually. The only distinction between notes and bonds is therefore the maturity. The interest rates on Treasury notes and bonds are determined when these notes and bonds are sold in the Treasury auction. The interest rate is determined at the auction, and this rate becomes the fixed rate until the security matures. The interest earned on U.S. Treasury bonds is taxable for federal income tax purposes, but is not taxed at the state and local level.

In addition to these notes and bonds, the U.S. Treasury also sells bonds as a means for individuals' savings. These savings bonds include the **I Savings bond** and the **EE/E Savings bond**. The I Savings bonds protect against inflation, whereas the EE/E Savings Bonds are 30-year bonds with a fixed interest rate. The interest paid on the savings bonds is not paid to the bondholder as earned; rather, the interest is accrued and paid upon maturity.

The U.S. government also sells **Treasury Inflation-Protected Securities (TIPS)**, which provide investors with protection against inflation by providing a specific real yield. These securities have maturities of 5, 10, or 30 years. Protection from inflation is achieved by pegging the face value to the rate of inflation (as measured by the CPI) and paying interest at the coupon rate applied against the adjusted principal.[32] At maturity, the investor receives the greater of the original principal or the inflation-adjusted principal. The primary difference between the I Savings bond and the TIPS is that the TIPS are marketable (that is, they can be sold among investors), whereas the I Savings bonds are not marketable.[33]

FINANCE in the News | A Point of No Return

In the midst of the financial crisis in 2008, some U.S. Treasury bills had rates that were actually negative at some point during the trading day, Tuesday, December 9, 2008, but ended the trading day at 0.01 percent. In other words, if you bought a Treasury bill when rates were negative, you paid the government for the privilege of owning the bill. Negative rates occurred again in November 2009.

The negative rates in 2008 are blamed on the panic from the Lehman Brothers collapse, but the negative rates in 2009 are explained by the strong demand for bills (especially by banks wanting to spruce up their balance sheets), but insufficient supply, which drove prices up—and yields down.

The U.S. experienced negative Treasury bills once again on the same day as the stock markets fell over 4 percent (August 4, 2011), as investors sold stocks and bought Treasury securities as a "flight to safety." And on December 9, 2008, there was a time during the day when Treasury bill rates were negative, but the day ended with 4-week bills closing at a rate of 0.01 percent and 6-month bills closing at 0.0742 percent.

Sources: U.S. Treasury; Liz Capo McCormick, "Money Market Rates Fall Below Zero as Treasury Bills Retain Haven Demand," *Bloomberg*, August 4, 2011; Daniel Kruger and Cordell Eddings, "Treasury Bills Trade at Negative Rates as Haven Demand Surges," *Bloomberg*, December 9, 2008.

Concept Review Questions

1. How does the formula for determining the price of a T-bill resemble the formula for determining the price of a zero-coupon bond? Why is this so?

2. How does the U.S. bank discount yield differ from U.S. bond equivalent yield?

[31] U.S. Government Accountability Office, *Debt Management: Treasury Has Refined Its Use of Cash Management Bills, but Should Explore Options That May Reduce Cost Further*, GAO-06-269, March 2006.
[32] For example, for 100 of principal, an inflation rate of 2 percent would result in an adjusted principal of $100 \times 1.02 = 102$.
[33] The I Savings bonds can be redeemed after twelve months, with a penalty.

6.5 INTEREST RATES

Interest rates are usually quoted on an annual percentage basis. As we discussed earlier, the interest rate is the price of money, which is determined by the laws of supply and demand, as for any other commodity. In the case of interest rates, it is the supply and demand for loanable funds. All else constant, as the demand for loanable funds decreases, so does the price, and as a result interest rates increase; conversely, interest rates decrease as the supply of loanable funds increases. The interest rate that we have been discussing so far is the **nominal interest rate** because this is the rate charged for lending today's dollars in return for getting dollars back in the future, without taking into account the purchasing power of those future dollars.

nominal interest rate rate charged for lending today's dollars in return for getting dollars back in the future, without taking into account the purchasing power of those future dollars

Base Interest Rates

We refer to the base rate as the **risk-free rate** (r_f), which is the compensation for the time value of money. We will discuss risk at length shortly, but the term risk-free, although conventional, is a bit of a misnomer; what it actually refers to is **default free**: Investors know exactly how many dollars they will get back on their investment. It is common to use the yield on short-term government Treasury bills (T-bills), which are discussed in greater detail later in this chapter, as a proxy for this risk-free rate. Federal government T-bill yields are generally considered risk-free because they possess no risk of default, but the U.S. government debt crisis in 2011 has brought attention to the possibility that there may be some risk of default. Further, government T-bills have very little interest rate risk because their term to maturity is very short.

risk-free rate (r_f) compensation for the time value of money

default free no risk of nonpayment

As a result, we have the following *approximate* relationship:

$$r_f = \text{Real rate} + \text{Expected inflation}$$

This relationship is an approximation of the direct relationship between inflation and interest rates that is often referred to as the "Fisher relationship," after Irving Fisher. Using this relationship, if the risk-free rate of interest is 3 percent and the expected inflation rate is 1.8 percent, the real rate is 3 percent − 1.8 percent = 1.2 percent.

What the Fisher effect means is that investors attempt to protect themselves from the loss in purchasing power caused by inflation by increasing their required nominal yield. As a result, interest rates will be low when expected inflation is low and high when expected inflation is high. More precisely, the Fischer relationship is the following:

$$r_f = [(1 + \text{Real rate})(1 + \text{Expected inflation})] - 1 \qquad (6\text{-}9)$$

Applying a bit of algebra, we see that the risk-free rate is not only the sum of the real rate and the expected inflation rate, but also the cross-product term, real rate × expected inflation:

$$r_f = 1 + \text{Real rate} + \text{Expected inflation} + (\text{Real rate} \times \text{Expected inflation})$$

We often see the approximation simply because the cross-product term (the rightmost term) is generally so small when inflation rates are low.

We show the annual rate of change in the consumer price index (CPI), the yield on a 3-month U.S. Treasury bill, and the yield on a 10-year U.S. Treasury bond in Figure 6-8. The level of nominal interest rates generally tracks the increase in inflation throughout the 1960s, until inflation peaked at more than 12 percent in 1973. Since then, interest rates have generally declined with the rate of inflation. As we just discussed, one measure of the real rate is the difference between the ongoing expected inflation rate and the level of nominal interest rates. This difference was much larger from 1981 until recently than it was in the 1960s because the capital market persistently failed to take into account the inflationary pressures in the economy at that time. Interest rates were at historical lows

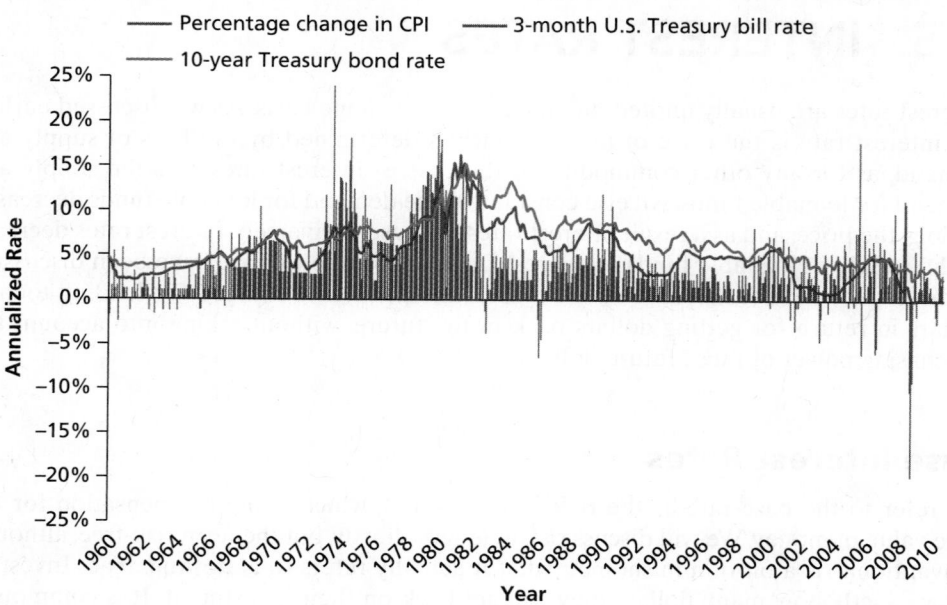

FIGURE 6-8   Interest Rates and Inflation, January 1960–July 2011
Source of data: *Federal Reserve Bank of St. Louis, FRED II.*

EXAMPLE 6.11	PROBLEM
Real Rate of Return	If T-bill rates are presently 4.5 percent and the expected level of inflation is 2.0 percent, estimate the real rate of return.

Solution

Using the Fisher relationship of $r_f = [(1 + \text{Real rate})(1 + \text{Expected inflation})] - 1$, and inserting the known values:

$$0.045 = [(1 + \text{Real rate}) \times (1 + 0.02)] - 1$$

Rearranging to solve for the real rate:

$$\text{Real rate} = (1.045 \div 1.02) - 1 = 2.451\%$$

---

in 2008, with deflation (that is, negative inflation) occurring in some periods, especially in late-2008.

The Term Structure of Interest Rates

So far, we have discussed the major factors affecting the base level of interest rates or r_f, which we proxy as the yield on short-term government T-bills. The yields on other debt instruments will differ from r_f for several reasons. One important factor affecting debt yields is related to its term to maturity. This is obvious if we look at bond quotes, where we can see various yield levels for bonds with different maturity dates, even though the bonds were issued by the same entity.

The relationship between interest rates and the term to maturity on underlying debt instruments is the **term structure of interest rates**. In Figure 6-9 we provide a graphical representation of this relationship, the **yield curve**. The curve is based on debt instruments that are from the same issuer, or else default risk, as well as other risk factors, will affect the difference in yields, in addition to maturity differentials. Therefore, the yield curve is almost always constructed by using sovereign debt issues because they possess the same default risk and levels of liquidity, as well as similar issue characteristics; in Figure 6-9, for example, we have graphed the U.S. term structure using the federal government debt obligations. In addition, the government tends to have a large number of issues outstanding at any given time; therefore, we can construct a yield curve with rate estimates for a wide variety of maturities.

One of the yield curves we depict in Figure 6-9 is for July 1, 2009. This yield curve is slightly upward sloping, with longer maturity securities that have higher yields than the shorter-term securities; that is, although long-term government bonds are virtually free from default risk in the same manner as short-term government T-bills are, long-term bonds typically yield more than medium-term bonds, which generally yield more than T-bills.

Although yield curves are usually upward sloping, they can assume a wide variety of shapes, as we show using March 1, 2007, yields in Figure 6-9. The downward-sloping (or inverted) yield curve for 2007 is less common, with short-term rates exceeding long-term rates. These "inverted" yield curves are unusual, and some market participants believe they indicate that short-term rates will fall. In fact, the inverted yield curve precedes the economic recession of 2008. Another, less common shape, is the relatively flat yield curve, which indicates that long- and short-term rates are very similar.

Several theories that attempt to account for the various shapes and movements of the yield curve incorporate liquidity, investor preferences, and supply and demand. We describe the most popular theories in Appendix 6A (available online).

> **term structure of interest rates** relationship between interest rates and the term to maturity on underlying debt instruments
>
> **yield curve** graphical representation of the term structure of interest rates, based on debt instruments that are from the same issuer

Yield Premiums

In addition to differences in terms to maturity, the yield on bonds will differ from the risk-free rate because of additional risks or features associated with these instruments. The difference between any two interest rates is the **spread**. The spread is often quoted in

> **spread** difference in yields, generally expressed in basis points

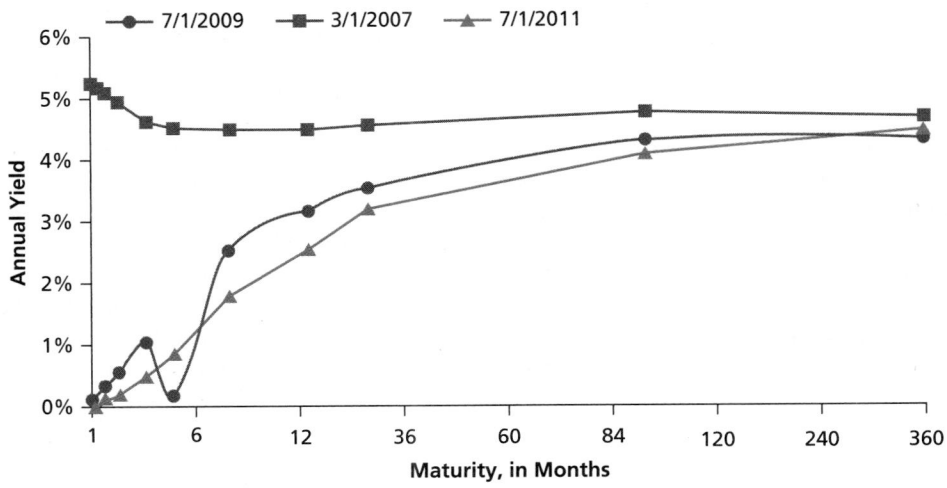

FIGURE 6-9 U.S. Government Yield Curve

Source of data: *U.S. Treasury, www.treasury.gov.*

terms of a **basis point (bp)**, where one basis point is 1/100th of a percent. Therefore, if the yields on two investments are 4 percent and 5 percent, respectively, the spread is 100 basis points, or 100 bps. One of the most commonly referenced spreads is between the yield on a security and the yield on a similar maturity Treasury security. In other words, investors expect extra compensation for assuming additional risks, and therefore they require higher returns. We can express this relationship using the following equation:

$$r_b = r_f + \text{Risk premium} \tag{6-10}$$

We have already discussed the maturity yield differential, and we now turn our attention to the last term in Equation 6-10. The **risk premium** compensates the investor for the assumption of additional risks, which may include some or all of the following: (1) default or credit risk, (2) liquidity, and (3) issue-specific features. We discuss each of these in turn.

The most obvious difference in yield arises because of the different levels of **default risk** associated with the bond issuer. In other words, bondholders require higher yields to compensate them for the possibility that the borrower may default on the promised debt payments. For example, if we consider three bond issues that have similar coupon rates and mature on or about the same date, we can observe that their yields differ when they are from different issuers, which reflects different levels of default risk. Consider a snapshot of yields on the following bonds as of August 2, 2011:[34]

Issuer	CUSIP	Rating	Maturity	Coupon Rate	Yield to Maturity
Procter & Gamble	742718DA4	Aa3	08/15/2014	4.95%	0.741%
Coventry Health Care Inc.	222862AH7	Ba1	08/15/2014	6.30%	3.239%
Springleaf Finance Corp.	02639EMM3	B3	08/15/2014	5.75%	8.250%
Procter & Gamble	742718DF3	Aa3	03/05/2037	5.55%	4.311%
News America	652482BN9	Baa1	03/01/2037	6.15%	5.929%
American Stores Co. LLC	030096AH4	B2	05/01/2037	7.50%	9.733%

You should notice a few things from this snapshot:

- The lower the bond rating, the higher the yield to maturity. Compare the bonds maturing August 15, 2014. Procter & Gamble's bond's yield is less than those of Coventry and Springleaf. This difference in yields reflects the default risk.
- The longer the maturity, the higher the yield. This is because the yield curve on this date is upward sloping. Compare the two similar-rated Procter & Gamble bonds: the shorter-maturity bond has a lower yield.

Most of the differences in yields for bonds of the same term to maturity we observed as we move from government bonds to corporate bonds are due to differences in the default risk associated with the issuers. We refer to this difference as the **default spread**.

A portion of the spread between corporate yields and Treasury yields for similar maturity bonds is also due to the fact that government bonds trade more actively than most investment-grade corporate bonds, which trade more actively than junk bonds. In other words, some bonds are more liquid than others; they are easier to buy and sell, and the required price concessions are lower. Bonds that are less liquid may have to offer investors a higher yield to compensate them for this illiquidity. This additional yield is referred to as the **liquidity premium**.

risk premium difference in yield that compensates the investor for the assumption of additional risks

default risk uncertainty associated with the bond issuer and its ability to pay

default spread difference in yields attributed to the difference in default risk of the securities

liquidity premium additional yield offered on bonds that are less liquid than others

---

[34] The CUSIP is a unique identifier for the bond: the first six characters identify the issuer and the last three characters identify the specific security issue of that issuer. Hence, the identifiers for the Procter & Gamble bonds differ only with the last three characters (DA4 v. DF3).

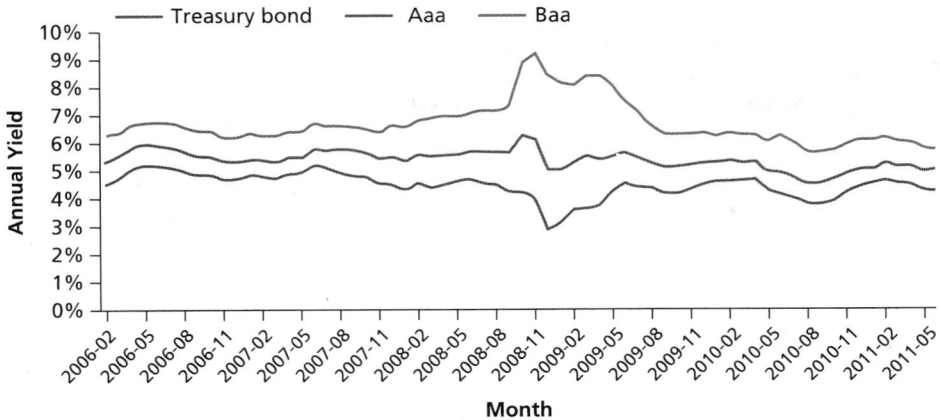

FIGURE 6-10   **Yield for U.S. Treasury Bonds and Aaa and Baa Corporate Bonds, February 2006 through July 2011**
Source of data: *Federal Reserve Bank of St. Louis, FRED II.*

An **issue-specific premium** arises when bonds have features that cause them to be more or less attractive to investors, relative to straight (option-free) bonds. For example, as discussed previously, the call feature is detrimental to bondholders. The reason is that these bonds are likely to be called by the issuer when interest rates are low (so that they can be refinanced at lower rates), which is exactly when the market prices of these bonds are increasing. As a result, investors will not pay as much for a callable bond as they would for an otherwise identical noncallable bond (i.e., they will demand a higher return). Conversely, retractable bonds permit investors to sell the bonds back to the issuer at predetermined prices when interest rates rise (and bond prices fall), which provides protection against rising rates. Similarly, extendible bonds will only be extended by investors if the coupon rates on such bonds are competitive; if rates increased, the investors would choose not to extend and could invest in other bonds that offer higher coupon rates. Therefore, extendible and retractable bonds, as well as convertible bonds, offer investors an additional privilege, and so they will trade at higher prices than otherwise identical straight bonds (i.e., they will provide a lower return).

All three of these factors are embedded in the corporate spread over equivalent maturity U.S. government bonds. In practice, it is very difficult to separate these three components of the corporate spread. In Figure 6-10, we graph the historic rates among Aaa corporate, Baa corporate, and the equivalent maturity U.S. government bonds.

The spread between Aaa and Baa rates was around 150–170 bps in 2006, but this spread widened in late 2008 and 2009 to over 500 bps in some months. Similarly, the spread between the U.S. government bonds and Aaa bonds was less than 100 bps in 2006, but widened to 200 bps in later 2008. In other words, the default spreads widened as the economy entered into the 2008 recession. This is generally the case: Default spreads widen in economic downturns. In fact, the credit spreads began to widen six months prior to the recession. The spreads between the yields of AAA-rated bonds and Treasuries began increasing in June 2008 and peaked in November 2008 at 325 basis points, coinciding with the collapse of Lehman Brothers.[35,36] At that same time, the spread between the yields on BAA rated bonds and Treasuries was 634 basis points. The spreads narrowed again in mid-2009 through mid-2011.

issue-specific premium additional yield, relative to straight, option-free bonds, required by investors when bonds have features that cause them to be more or less attractive to investors

---

[35] A basis point is 1/100th of a percent.
[36] We discussed the 2007–08 financial crisis in Chapter 1. One of the key events was the collapse of Lehman Brothers.

LESSONS LEARNED | Credit Spreads and the Economy

Corporate bond yields change along with the changing economy. Not only do credit spreads, the difference between corporate bond yields and Treasury yields, increase in a recession, but also the spread between yields on corporate bonds that have different credit risk increases, as indicated by the spread between yields on AAA rated bonds and BAA rated bonds. We can see these characteristics when examining the credit spreads leading up to and beyond the recession that began in December 2007:

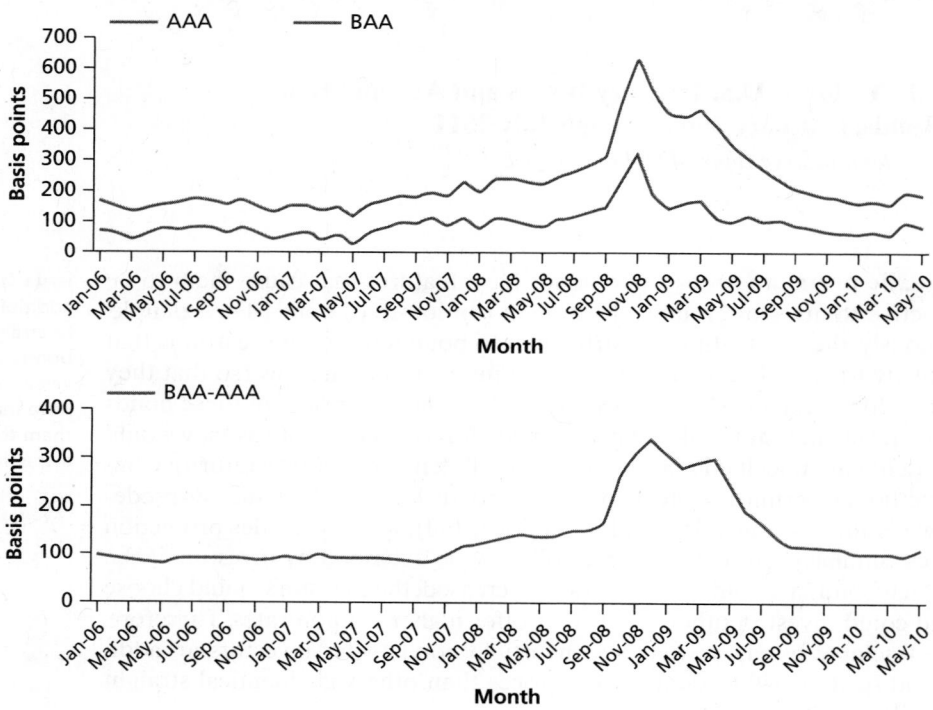

In fact, the credit spreads began to widen six months prior to the recession. The spreads between the yields of AAA rated bonds and Treasuries began increasing in June 2008 and peaked in November 2008 at 325 basis points, coinciding with the collapse of Lehman Brothers.[37,38] At that same time, the spread between the yields on BAA rated bonds and Treasuries was 634 basis points. The spread between yields on AAA and BAA rated bonds began increasing in October 2007 and then peaked in the month following the start of the recession, December 2008, at 338 basis points. The spreads narrowed again during the recovery period in 2010.

Source of data: *Federal Reserve Bank of St. Louis, FRED II.*

Concept Review Questions

1. How does the expected rate of inflation affect nominal interest rates?

2. What is the relationship between the default spread and the economic environment?

SUMMARY

- The traditional coupon-paying bond has a series of cash payments of interest every six months, with the principal repayment at maturity. However, bonds may also have features such as sinking funds, embedded options, and floating rates. In addition, some bonds do not pay interest and, hence, are priced at a discount from their face value.

- We value debt obligations as we do any stream of cash flows. The key for bond valuation is that we understand the timing of the bond's cash flows and the appropriate discount rate.

- One of the most important factors affecting bond prices is the level of interest rates. There is an inverse relation between the yield on a bond and its value.

- Treasury securities include short-term securities, notes, and bonds. The short-term securities, Treasury bills, are priced at a discount because these securities do not bear interest.

FORMULAS/EQUATIONS

(6-1) $PV_0 = \left(\sum_{t=1}^{N} \frac{PMT_t}{(1 + r_b)^t} \right) + \frac{FV_N}{(1 + r_b)^N}$

(6-2) $PV_0 = \frac{FV_N}{(1 + r_b)^N}$

(6-3) $YTM = \left(\sqrt[N]{\frac{FV_N}{PV_0}} - 1 \right) \times 2$

(6-4) $PV_0 = \left(\sum_{t=1}^{M} \frac{PMT_t}{(1 + r_b)^t} \right) + \frac{CP_M}{(1 + r_b)^M}$

(6-5) $CY = \dfrac{\text{Annual interest}}{\text{Current market price}}$

(6-6) $P = \dfrac{FV}{1 + \left(r_{BEY} \times \dfrac{n}{365} \right)}$

(6-7) $r_{BEY} = \dfrac{FV - P}{P} \times \dfrac{365}{n}$

(6-8) $r_{BDY} = \dfrac{FV - P}{FV} \times \dfrac{360}{n}$

(6-9) $r_f = [(1 + \text{Real rate})(1 + \text{Expected inflation})] - 1$

(6-10) $r_b = r_f + \text{Risk premium}$

QUESTIONS AND PROBLEMS

Multiple Choice

1. Which of the following statements concerning bonds is most likely *incorrect*?
   A. Periodic payments on bonds involve payments that include principal and interest.
   B. Bondholders are paid a series of fixed periodic amounts before the maturity date.
   C. The bond indenture is a legal document, specifying payment requirements and so on.
   D. Bonds have a fixed maturity date at which time the issuer repays the full principal amount.

2. Which of the following statements is most likely *incorrect*?
   A. All debentures are secured bonds.
   B. Extendible bonds allow bondholders to extend the maturity date.
   C. Callable bonds give the bond issuer an option to buy back the bond at a predetermined price.
   D. Convertible bonds give the bondholders an option to convert into another security at a predetermined conversion ratio.

3. The bond quote of a 5-year, 7 percent, semi-annual coupon bond when the market rate is 8 percent is *closest* to:
   A. 95.94.   B. 96.01.   C. 100.00.   D. 100.84.

4. The bond quote of a 5 percent, semi-annual pay bond with 5 years to maturity and priced to yield 8 percent is *closest* to:

    A. 80.70.   B. 87.83.   C. 88.02.   D. 100.00.

5. Consider bonds A, B, C, and D, each with a par value of $100 million. Which of the following bond's price is most sensitive to market rate changes?

    A. Bond A: 5-year, 5 percent coupon rate, yield 5.5 percent
    B. Bond B: 3-year, 8 percent coupon rate, yield 5.6 percent
    C. Bond C: 7.5-year, 4.5 percent coupon rate, yield 5.5 percent
    D. Bond D: 10-year, 4.5 percent coupon rate, yield 5.5 percent

6. The yield to maturity on a 6-year, 7 percent, semi-annual coupon bond, which is now priced at 99.3, is *closest* to:

    A. 3.632 percent.   B. 7.089 percent.   C. 7.145 percent.   D. 7.148 percent.

7. Which of the following statements is *correct*?

    A. If a bond is selling at a discount, the coupon rate < current yield < YTM.
    B. The current yield is the ratio of the annual coupon payment divided by the par value.
    C. When the coupon rate is higher than the market rate, the bond is priced at a discount.
    D. When the market rate is higher than the coupon rate, the bond is priced at a premium.

8. Which statement is *incorrect*?

    A. A sovereign debt is a bond issued by a government.
    B. A debt rating of AAA is a worse rating than BB for S&P.
    C. The risk premium in the bond yield reflects default risk, liquidity risk, and issue-specific features.

9. The quoted price of a 182-day T-bill that has a face value of $10,000 and a bond equivalent yield of 5.5 percent is *closest* to:

    A. 94.7867.   B. 97.3307.   C. 99.7276.

10. Which of the following statements is *false*?

    A. TIPS provide protection against the effects of inflation.
    B. Zero-coupon bonds are priced at a discount from face value.
    C. Floating-rate bonds provide the investor protection against decreasing interest rates.
    D. Zero-coupon bonds are often created when cash flows are stripped from traditional bonds.

Practice Problems and Questions

6.1   The Basics of Bonds

11. Describe the cash flows associated with a bond in terms of amount and timing.

12. Distinguish between positive and negative bond covenants.

13. In a callable bond, which party—the issuer or the investor—has an option? Describe the option and what would make it more valuable.

14. Distinguish between a callable bond and a putable bond.

15. Explain the role of a bond indenture in protecting the bond investor.

16. Explain the role of credit ratings in evaluating a bond.

6.2   Bond Valuation

17. Describe the relationship between market rates and bond prices.

18. Calculate the price of the following bond: a face value of $1,000; a coupon rate of 8 percent, and coupons are paid semi-annually; the yield to maturity is 5 percent; the term to maturity is 10 years.

19. Calculate the value of a zero-coupon bond that has 5 years to maturity and is priced to yield 8 percent.

20. Consider a 10-year, $100 face value zero-coupon bond.
    A. If the yield is 14 percent, what is the value of this bond?
    B. If the price quote is 76, what is the yield to maturity on this bond?

21. Consider a bond that pays 6 percent interest in the first 2 years, 5 percent interest in the next 2 years, and 4 percent interest in the next 2 years. If this bond is priced to yield 5 percent, what is the value of the bond? Assume semi-annual compounding and 6 years remaining to maturity.

22. Complete the following table:

	Coupon Rate Paid Semi-annually	Yield to Maturity	Number of Years to Maturity	Face Value	Value
A.	5%	8%	10	$1,000	
B.	7%	8%	20	$1,000	
C.	5%	8%	7	$500	
D.	3%	3%	8	$1,000	
E.	9%	10%	10	$1,000	

23. At maturity, each of the following zero-coupon bonds (pure discount bonds) will be worth $1,000. For each bond, calculate the missing quantity in the following table.

Bond	Price	Maturity (Years)	Yield to Maturity
A	$409	30	
B	$127		7%
C		10	5%

 24. Consider a bond that has 20 years to maturity, a coupon rate of 5 percent, and is currently priced at 7 percent.
    A. Calculate and graph the value of the bond until maturity if the yield to maturity remains the same until the bond matures.
    B. Describe the path of the bond's value until maturity.

 25. Calculate, using both a calculator and a spreadsheet program, the value of a bond with a face value of $1,000, a coupon rate of 6 percent (paid semi-annually), and 3 years to maturity when the yield to maturity is:
    A. 5 percent.   B. 6 percent.   C. 7 percent.

 26. Suppose that 1 year ago a company issued a 5-year semi-annual pay bond with a $1,000 face value and a 12 percent coupon.
    A. If the market yield is 11 percent when these bonds are issued, what was the price of the bonds at issuance?
    B. If the market yield is now 6.5 percent, what is the price of the bond that pays coupons semi-annually?
    C. Using a spreadsheet, calculate and graph the value of this bond for yields ranging from 0 percent to 15 percent in increments of 0.5 percent for both the original maturity and now.

6.3 Bond Yields

27. If a bond is trading at a discount from its face value, what is the relationship between the coupon rate and the yield to maturity?

28. What assumption is made about reinvesting coupons when we calculate the yield to maturity on a bond?

29. Complete the following table, indicating whether the bond will trade at a premium or a discount from its face value:

Bond	Coupon Rate	Yield to Maturity	Discount or Premium?
A	5%	4.5%	
B	6%	9%	
C	4%	8%	
D	9%	8%	
E	12%	15%	

30. Complete the following table:

Value	Coupon Rate Paid Semi-annually	Number of Years to Maturity	Face Value	Call Price	Number of Years until First Call	Yield to Maturity	Yield to Call	Lower of the Yield to Maturity and the Yield to Call
A. $1,000	6%	10	$1,000	101	4			
B. $1,100	9%	10	$1,000	101	4			
C. $990	5%	10	$1,000	101	4			
D. $800	4%	10	$1,000	101	4			
E. $1,025	3%	10	$1,000	101	4			

31. Consider a zero-coupon bond that has 10 years remaining to maturity and has bond quote of 75. What is the yield to maturity on this bond?

32. Complete the following table for these zero-coupon bonds:

Bond	Quote	Years Remaining to Maturity	Yield to Maturity
X	70	5	
Y	80	3	
Z	65	10	

33. Complete the following table for these zero-coupon bonds:

Bond	Quote	Years Remaining to Maturity	Yield to Maturity
M	60	6	
N	55	20	
O	70	5	

34. Complete the following table:

Bond	Value	Coupon Rate Paid Semi-annually	Number of Years to Maturity	Face Value	Yield to Maturity
A	$1,000	5%	10	$1,000	
B	$1,240	5%	15	$1,000	
C	$100	7%	5	$100	

35. You find the following data on two bonds at a time when the market yield is 7 percent:

Bond	Coupon Rate	Quote
A	6%	95.842
B	8%	104.158

These bonds are otherwise identical (5 years to maturity, semi-annual coupon payments). Which bond's price will change by more (and by how much) if the market yield increases by 100 basis points?

36. A 10-year bond has just been issued with its coupon rate set equal to the current market yield of 6 percent. How much would the price of the bond change (in percentage terms) if the market yield suddenly fell by 50 basis points? How much would the price change if the yield rose by 50 basis points?

37. Complete the following table:

	Coupon Rate	Quoted Price	Number of Years Remaining to Maturity	Yield to Maturity	Current Yield
A.	5%	78	5		
B.	8%	110	10		
C.	9.5%	98	20		
D.	2%	105	10		
E.	0%	75	5		

38. Consider a bond that has a 4.875 percent coupon, paid semiannually, 5 years remaining to maturity.

   A. Using a spreadsheet program, calculate and graph the yield to maturity and the current yield for this bond for bond quotes from 80 to 120 in increments of 1. [Horizontal axis: bond quotes | Vertical axis: Yield to maturity and current yield]

   B. Describe the relationship that you observe between the yield to maturity, the current yield, and the bond quotes.

6.4 Government Debt Obligations

39. Distinguish between a Treasury bill and a Treasury bond in terms of maturity and how yields are quoted.

40. Calculate the bank discount yield on a 92-day U.S. T-bill that is currently quoted at 98.0468.

41. Complete the following table for the following Treasury bills:

	Face Value	Number of Days to Maturity	Bond Equivalent Yield	Value of the Bill
A.	$100,000	90	3.00%	
B.	$100,000	60	2.50%	
C.	$1,000,000	30	1.75%	

42. Complete the following table for the following Treasury bills:

	Face Value	Number of Days to Maturity	Bond Equivalent Yield	Value of the Bill
A.	$100,000	25	1.60%	
B.	$100,000	55	2.00%	
C.	$1,000,000	25	1.00%	

43. Complete the following table for the following Treasury bills:

	Face Value	Price	Number of Days to Maturity	Bond Equivalent Yield	Bond Discount Yield
A.	$100,000	$99,000	60		
B.	$100,000	$99,500	30		
C.	$1,000,000	$999,000	90		

44. Complete the following table for the following Treasury bills:

	Face Value	Price	Number of Days to Maturity	Bond Equivalent Yield	Bond Discount Yield
A.	$100,000	$99,500	20		
B.	$100,000	$99,900	10		
C.	$1,000,000	$999,500	20		

45. Using both your calculator and a spreadsheet, complete the following table for the following Treasury bonds, calculating the yield to maturity:

Bond	Coupon Rate	Years to Maturity	Value	Yield to Maturity
A	5%	10	101	
B	6%	20	102	
C	4%	30	99	
D	5%	15	90	
E	6%	20	105	

46. Consider a 91-day Treasury bill
    A. Calculate and graph the value of this security for bond-equivalent yields from 0 percent to 7 percent.
    B. Describe the relationship between the bond-equivalent yields and the value of the bill.

6.5   Interest Rates

47. Describe what is meant by the "Fisher relationship."

48. Bo Ulder explained to you that the risk-free rate is 2%, which is the sum of the real rate of interest and the expected inflation rate. Is Bo correct? Explain.

49. Explain why we may observe different yields on bonds issued by the same company.

50. Consider two bonds issued by Avis Budget Car Rental LLC, both of which have a maturity date of January 15, 2019, and a coupon rate of 8.25 percent. One issue, CAR.AA, has a price of 101.464, and the other issue, CAR.GO, has a price of 104.750. What could explain the different values of these two bonds?

51. Complete the following table, calculating the risk-free rate of interest:

	Real Rate	Expected Inflation	Risk-free Rate
A.	3.00%	0.00%	
B.	2.00%	1.00%	
C.	1.00%	3.00%	
D.	1.50%	2.00%	
E.	2.00%	1.50%	

52. Complete the following table, calculating the risk-free rate of interest:

	Real Rate	Expected Inflation	Risk-free Rate
A.	1.50%	0.50%	
B.	1.00%	1.00%	
C.	1.20%	2.00%	
D.	0.50%	2.00%	
E.	1.00%	2.00%	

53. The two bonds below are identical (face value of $1,000, 8 percent coupon rate paid semi-annually), except that they mature at different times:

Bond	Time to Maturity	Quote
C	3 years	102.664
D	8 years	106.047

If the market yield, currently 7 percent, falls by 100 basis points, which bond's price will change more, and by how much? Why?

54. Consider two bonds, Bond One and Bond Two, with the following characteristics:

Feature	Bond One	Bond Two
Maturity	3 years	8 years
Coupon rate	6%	5%
Coupon frequency	Semi-annual	Semi-annual

A. Calculate the value of each bond if the yield to maturity for each is 5.5 percent using the PRICE spreadsheet function.
B. Using a spreadsheet program, calculate the value of each bond for each yield to maturity from 0 percent to 15 percent.
C. Using a spreadsheet program, graph the values of each bond for yields to maturity ranging from 0 percent to 15 percent on one graph.
D. What conclusions can you draw regarding the sensitivity of the bonds' values to changes in the yield to maturity?

55. Consider three bonds, Bond Three, Bond Four, and Bond Five, with the following characteristics:

Feature	Bond Three	Bond Four	Bond Five
Maturity	10 years	20 years	15 years
Coupon rate	8%	5%	0%
Coupon frequency	Semi-annual	Semi-annual	N/A

A. Calculate the value of each bond if the yield to maturity for each is 7 percent.
B. Using a spreadsheet program, calculate the value of each bond for each yield to maturity from 0 percent to 15 percent.
C. Using a spreadsheet program, graph the values of each bond for yields to maturity ranging from 0 percent to 15 percent on one graph.
D. What conclusions can you draw regarding the sensitivity of the bonds' values to changes in the yield to maturity?

Cases

Case 6.1 Slice & Dice

The Slice & Dice Investment Co. needs some help understanding the intricacies of bond pricing. It has observed the following prices for zero-coupon bonds that have no risk of default:

Number of Years to Maturity	Price per $1 Face Value
1 year	0.97
2 years	0.90
3 years	0.81

A. How much should Slice & Dice be willing to pay for a 3-year bond that pays a 6 percent coupon, assuming annual coupon payments start 1 year from now?

B. What is the yield to maturity of this 3-year coupon bond?

C. Suppose Slice & Dice purchases this coupon bond, and then "un-bundles" it into its four component cash flows: three coupon payments and the par value amount. At what price(s) can the company re-sell each of the first three cash flows (the coupon payments) today?

D. The remaining cash flow (the face value amount) is a "synthetic" 3-year zero-coupon bond. How much must this zero-coupon be sold for if Slice & Dice is to break even on the investment?

CHAPTER 7

EQUITY VALUATION

© Masterfile

What determines the value of stock? Old ideas are still new. We have long recognized that the value of the stock of a corporation is not likely the same as the value of the stock on the company's books. For example, for a company without any debt, it was recognized over one hundred years ago that:[1]

> If a company has special privileges or monopoly of any kind of business, its franchises may have a separate and independent value, and the value of the stock of the company may exceed largely the value of all the tangible property of the corporation. [p. 159]

The valuation of stock based on the future dividends of a company has also long been recognized. For example, Benjamin Graham and David Dodd, back in 1934, remarked:[2]

> the investor may look to future dividends or even to future enhancement of market value, instead of to the current dividend. [p. 320]

The many forces that influence the value of stock were recognized in the early 20th century and beyond. For example, Charles A. Conant wrote in 1905:[3]

> Among the influences which affect prospective earning power, are all the facts and rumors which indicate the economic future,—not only whether crops are to be large or small, but whether consumption is to be greater or less, whether given properties are managed well or ill; whether the rate of growth of population and wealth promises increased earning power in the future, or whether competitive establishments threaten to reduce the margin or profit; whether legislatures are disposed to grant new franchises and continue old ones, or to impose direct burdens to be paid out of dividends and indirect burdens, which gradually cripple the producing power and the initiative of the community. [p. 351]

In other words, it's complicated. But that is what makes the value of stock interesting and rewarding.

Learning Outcomes

After reading this chapter, you should be able to:

LO 7.1 Describe the basic characteristics of equity securities, and identify the primary factors that affect stock values.

LO 7.2 Estimate the value of these securities using the most common dividend discount models.

LO 7.3 Apply multiples to value stock, and relate valuation models to commonly used ratios or multiples.

---

[1] *The Pacific Reporter*, Volume 2, "Ryan v. Board County Commissioners Leavenworth Coal Co., and Others," Filed July 5, 1883, pp. 156–161.
[2] Benjamin Graham and David Dodd, *Security Analysis* (New York: McGraw-Hill, 1934), p. 320
[3] Charles A. Conant, "How the Stock-Market Reflects Values," *The North American Review*, Vol. 180, No. 580 (March 1905) pp. 347–359.

Chapter Preview In this chapter, we apply the time value of money principles and mathematics to value the equity of a company. We began by examining how to evaluate both preferred and common equity based on the present value of their expected future dividend stream. We proceed to show how this approach is related to the fundamental factors that affect stock prices, including future profitability, dividends, interest rates, and risk. We conclude with a discussion of relative valuation approaches and show how they too can be related to company fundamentals.

7.1 EQUITY SECURITIES

equity security
ownership interest in an underlying entity, usually a corporation or a partnership

stock ownership interest in a company

share or **share of stock** security that represents a portion of the stock of a company

shareholder or **stockholder** owner of an equity security of a company

cash dividend payments to owners in the form of cash

common stock residual ownership of a corporation

A corporation will issue an **equity security**, which is a financial instrument that represents ownership in the corporation. We often refer to this financial instrument as the **stock** of the company. A unit of ownership is represented by a **share** or a **share of stock**, and an owner of a share is a **shareholder** or **stockholder**. Because a corporation has a perpetual life, the owners of these securities own a security that has no fixed maturity date. Companies that issue equity securities may choose to pay a **cash dividend**, which is paid from after-tax earnings. Unlike interest payments on debt obligations, dividends are not a tax-deductible expense to the paying corporation.[4]

A corporation, at a minimum, has **common stock**, but it may also choose to issue **preferred stock**. Preferred stock and common stock both represent ownership interest, or equity, but preferred shareholders, as the name implies, have a prior claim to income and assets of the company relative to common shareholders. Common shareholders are the residual claimants of the corporation, which means that they are entitled to income remaining only after all creditors and other, more senior claimants, including preferred shareholders, have been paid. Similarly, in the case of liquidation of the corporation, common shareholders are entitled to the remaining assets only after all other claims have been satisfied. As owners, they can exert control over the corporation through their power to vote, which allows them to elect the board of directors and vote on major issues, such as takeovers, corporate restructuring, and so on.

By far, the most common type of equity security is the common share, which represents a certificate of ownership in a corporation. A purchaser of 100 shares of common stock owns $100/n$ percent of the corporation, where n is the total number of shares of common stock outstanding. A publicly traded corporation may have millions or even billions of common shares outstanding at a point in time. For example, at their June 30, 2012, fiscal year end, Microsoft had 8.383 billion shares of stock outstanding.[5]

Preferred stock provides the owner with a claim to a fixed amount of equity that is established when the shares are first issued. Most preferred stockholders have preference over common stockholders with respect to income and assets (in the event of liquidation), but they rarely have any voting rights. Traditionally, preferred stock has no maturity date, but over the past 30 years preferred stock has been increasingly issued with a fixed maturity date, similar to a bond. The main difference between preferred stock and a bond is that the board of directors declares the dividends and until then, and unlike an interest payment, dividends are not a legal obligation of the company. Usually, no payments can be made to common shareholders until preferred shareholders have been paid the dividends they are due in entirety.

From the perspective of the company issuing the stock, dividends are not considered a cost of doing business, and therefore they are not deductible for tax purposes by the paying company. This is different than the interest paid by the company issuing bonds; interest is a deductible expense for tax purposes.[6] From the perspective of the investor

---

[4] Corporations that receive dividends from other corporations may be able to deduct some or all of these dividends from income and therefore reduce the burden of double taxation, as we described in Chapter 3.

[5] Source: Microsoft Corporation 10-K filing with the SEC, filed July 28, 2011.

[6] The U.S. Internal Revenue Code, a result of federal legislation, has always viewed interest as a necessary and ordinary cost of doing business and, hence, has allowed interest to be deducted; dividends were not viewed as necessary and ordinary costs of doing business and therefore are not deductible for tax purposes.

of bonds and stocks, we also see a difference in the tax treatment: Interest received on bonds is taxed as income of the bond investor, whereas the dividend received by a shareholder may be subject to special treatment. In the case of a corporation owning stock in another corporation, a portion or all of the dividend income may be deducted for tax purposes, hence escaping some or all taxation on this income.[7] For individual owners of stock, the dividend income may be taxed at a lower rate than other income, including interest income.[8] Because of the tax implications:

- from the perspective of the company issuing the securities, debt financing is a lower cost of financing because interest is deductible and dividends are not;
- from the perspective of the corporate investor, stock is preferred to bonds because the dividend income is, at most, partially taxable, whereas interest income is taxed fully; and
- from the perspective of the individual investor, a dollar of income from dividends is preferred to a dollar of income from bonds for tax purposes because dividends are taxed at a lower rate than interest income.

Apart from the tax implications, a dollar of income from debt is less risky than a dollar of income from equity for a given company because creditors have a claim to income and assets prior to shareholders. Therefore, an investor would need to consider the benefits that shares offer from a tax perspective with the additional risk.

The Basics of Valuing Equity

Equity securities may have cash flows in the form of cash dividends, which are paid at the discretion of the board of directors. Therefore, valuing equity is more challenging than, say, valuing bonds. This is because with bonds there is a legal commitment to paying interest and repaying the principal, but with equity there is no such commitment associated with dividends. Therefore, valuing equity requires estimating future dividends.

In the case of preferred stock, the dividends are generally fixed in terms of the payment frequency and the amount, but these still are paid at the discretion of the company's board of directors. Therefore, a company can choose not to pay preferred dividends, with the only consequence (technically) being that the company cannot pay dividends on common shares until the preferred dividends are paid. However, practically speaking, this would send a negative signal to the capital markets, which would likely have a negative effect on the value of the company's financial securities (i.e., bonds, preferred shares, and common shares). Hence, companies are generally reluctant to omit these dividends if at all possible. We refer to preferred stock with a fixed dividend, no maturity, and no embedded option as **straight preferred stock**. We do this to distinguish these from preferred stock with dividends that vary from period to period (as is the case of adjustable rate preferred stock), preferred stock that, essentially, matures, and preferred stock with an embedded option such as preferred stock convertible into common shares or preferred stock that is callable.

straight preferred stock preferred stock with no embedded option, for which the issuer promises to pay a fixed, periodic dividend

We generally value preferred stock using discounted cash flow methods, discounting the expected dividends at a discount rate that reflects the uncertainty associated with the payment of these dividends. In the case of straight preferred stock, the valuation is simply the present value of the perpetual stream of cash dividends.

Because common stock is the last in line in terms of the pecking order of claims on a company and because some companies simply reinvest earnings instead of paying them

[7] We reviewed this provision in more detail in an earlier chapter.

[8] There are various ways that dividend income received by individuals has gotten special treatment in the U.S., including a lower rate for dividends on stocks held a specified period (e.g., six months) and an exclusion of a specified dollar amount of dividends from taxation. The current law, set to expire in 2012, taxes dividend income that qualifies at either 15 percent or 0 percent, depending on the taxpayer's income level. Qualifying dividends under current law are dividends on stocks of U.S. companies held for 61 days around a dividend payment date.

method of multiples
approach to valuing an
entity or the equity of
an entity by applying
the market multiples of
comparable companies

out to shareholders, there are two common approaches to valuing common stock: the discounted cash flow approach, with its many variations, and the **method of multiples**, using the market's evaluation of the value of equity of similar companies to value the a company's equity. The discounted cash flow approach requires an estimate of the **required rate of return**, which is the minimum return that investors expect to earn on the investment in the stock. In the method of multiples, we approach valuation at a different angle: We estimate values based on the market's assessment of comparable companies.

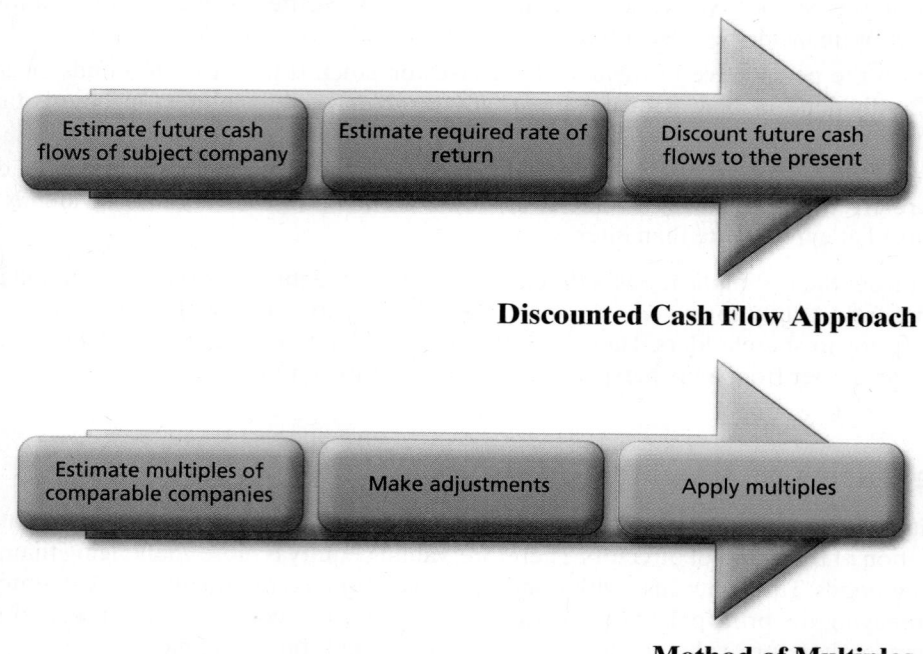

Discounted Cash Flow Approach

Method of Multiples

Why do we need two approaches to value common stock? Because unlike bonds and preferred stock, the future cash flows to owners are uncertain in both the amount and the timing. Also, because the cash flows depend on dividend policies and how the market values these dividends, one approach may be more appropriate for some types of companies, and the other approach may be more appropriate for other types of companies. Do analysts really use these models? Yes, as we show in Table 7-1. Analysts use both approaches, though there are many variations of each approach, as you will see in this chapter.

The Required Rate of Return

Key to the discount models used to value preferred and common stock is the required rate of return. The required rate of return becomes a benchmark for valuation: If a company returns more than required, the value of the stock rises; if a company returns less than required, the value of the stock falls. The difficulty is that we cannot observe this required rate of return directly. We can back into this return by looking at how the market values a company's stock, given a projection of dividends, but we cannot simply look up the required rate of return.

We generally think of the discount rate for equities as the sum of the risk-free rate of return—that is, the compensation for the time value of money—plus a premium for bearing risk:

$$r_e = r_f + \text{Risk premium} \tag{7-1}$$

where r_e is the required return on an equity security and r_f is the risk-free rate of return. The risk-free rate comprises the real rate of return plus expected inflation, and we often use the

TABLE 7-1 Common Share Valuation Approaches

Method Used	*Percentage*
Price-earnings (P/E) approach	88.1
Discounted free cash flow approach	86.8
Enterprise value multiple	76.7
Price-to-book-value approach	59.0
Price-to-cash-flow approach	57.2
Price-to-sales approach	40.3
Dividend-to-price or price-to-dividend approaches	35.5
Dividend discount model	35.1

Source: *Model Selection from "Valuation Methods" Presentation, October 2007, produced by Tom Robinson, Ph.D., CFA, CPA, CFP®, Head, Educational Content, CFA Institute. Copyright 2007, CFA Institute. Reproduced and republished from* Valuation Methods *with permission from CFA Institute. All rights reserved.*

return on Treasury bonds to represent this rate of return.[9] The **risk premium** is based on an estimate of the risk associated with the security; the higher the risk, the higher the risk premium because investors require a higher return as compensation for bearing more risk.[10]

Irrational Exuberance I, II, and III | LESSONS LEARNED

One of the lessons of the recent financial crisis is that we don't always take these lessons to heart. Consider a few of the recent bubbles in our financial history. Alan Greenspan, former chairman of the Federal Reserve Bank of the U.S. noted in a speech in 1996:[11]

> Clearly, sustained low inflation implies less uncertainty about the future, and lower risk premiums imply higher prices of stocks and other earning assets. We can see that in the inverse relationship exhibited by price/earnings ratios and the rate of inflation in the past. But how do we know when irrational exuberance has unduly escalated asset values, which then become subject to unexpected and prolonged contractions as they have in Japan over the past decade?

His comments were followed by declines in the stock markets around the world.

Robert Shiller used the phrase "irrational exuberance" in describing the dot.com frenzy in markets around the world, with stocks with little or no earnings prospects having values that made little sense using almost any one of the valuation models. In his book *Irrational Exuberance*, published in 2000, he discussed speculative bubbles in general, but also the speculative bubble that is often referred to as the "dot.com" or "Internet Bubble."[12] The publication of this book preceded the bursting of the Internet bubble in 2001.

Shiller's second edition of his book, published in 2005, added an analysis of the real estate bubble.[13] He discussed the problems associated with personal bankruptcies leading to financial difficulties for financial institutions. The publication of this book preceded the subprime mortgage-fueled boom that went bust in 2007.

The challenge, as you can see, is that the participants in markets do not always learn and there is a psychological dimension to how market participants value stocks.

---

[9] Because stock is a long-term investment, we generally use the interest rate on a long-term security to proxy the risk-free rate using the rate on a default-free long-term security. You may see applications in which the rate on a Treasury bill is used, but this may understate the appropriate risk-free rate when there is a normal, upward-sloping yield curve.

[10] We discuss the factors affecting the risk premium and methods for estimating a discount rate for equities in later chapters.

[11] Greenspan, Alan. "The Challenge of Central Banking in a Democratic Society," speech to the American Enterprise Institute, December 5, 1996.

[12] Shiller, Robert, *Irrational Exuberance* (Princeton, NJ: Princeton University Press, March 2000).

[13] Shiller, Robert, *Irrational Exuberance* (Princeton, NJ: Princeton University Press, 2005).

1. What distinguishes an equity security from a debt security that is relevant for valuation purposes?

2. What is the relationship between the required rate of return and the risk of the security being valued?

7.2 DISCOUNTED CASH FLOW APPROACHES TO VALUING EQUITY

A commonly used approach for valuing equity securities follows the discounted cash flow approach used to estimate the value of bonds. In particular, we estimate the expected future cash flows associated with the security and then determine the discounted present value of those future cash flows, based on an appropriate discount rate (r_e).

Valuing Preferred Stock

As mentioned previously, traditional preferred stock has no maturity date and pays dividends of a fixed amount at regular intervals indefinitely (that is, to infinity, ∞), as we depict in Figure 7-1, where we represent the periodic dividend payment as D_p.

Because the payments are essentially fixed when the preferred shares are issued, they are often referred to as fixed-income investments. The payment of a fixed dividend amount at regular intervals indefinitely means we can view these investments as *perpetuities*. We can estimate the value of preferred shares using Equation 7-2, the equation that determines the present value of a perpetuity, where P_p is the present value of the preferred stock, D_p is the periodic dividend amounts (or payments), and r_p is the required rate of return on the preferred shares (or discount rate):

$$P_p = \frac{D_p}{r_p} \tag{7-2}$$

The amount of the dividend payments is usually based on a stated par (or face) value and a stated dividend rate, which is similar to the coupon rate on a bond. For example, a preferred share with a par value of $100 and an 8 percent dividend rate would pay an annual dividend of $8 per year. In practice, dividends are paid quarterly; however, for illustration purposes, we assume they are paid annually.[14] This assumption has little influence on the valuation because of the long time involved (i.e., assuming the dividends are paid to infinity).

Consider an example. Suppose a preferred stock has a par value of $50 per share and a dividend rate of 8 percent. If the required rate of return for this preferred stock is 6 percent, what is the value of a share of this stock? The dividend is $50 \times 0.08 = $4 per share, which we discount at the rate of 6 percent:[15]

$$P_p = \frac{\$50 \times 0.08}{0.06} = \frac{\$4}{0.06} = \$66.67$$

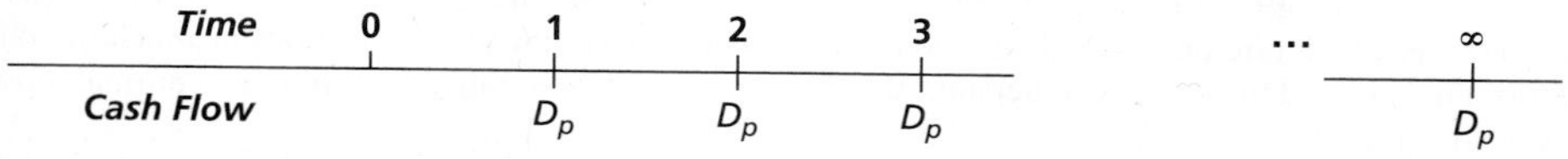

Time	0	1	2	3	...	∞
Cash Flow		D_p	D_p	D_p		D_p

FIGURE 7-1 The Cash Flow Pattern for a Straight Preferred Stock

[14] We will also assume annual dividends when valuing common shares, even though they also usually pay quarterly dividends.
[15] Another way of stating this is saying that we capitalize the $4 at 6 percent.

The stock trades at a premium to its face value. What if the required rate of return is 10 percent, instead of 6 percent?

$$P_p = \frac{\$50 \times 0.08}{0.10} = \frac{\$4}{0.10} = \$40$$

In this case, the stock trades at a discount to its face value. What if the required rate of return is 8 percent instead of 6 percent?

$$P_p = \frac{\$50 \times 0.08}{0.08} = \frac{\$4}{0.08} = \$50$$

In this case, the stock is valued at its par value. Notice that, similar to bonds, preferred shares will trade:

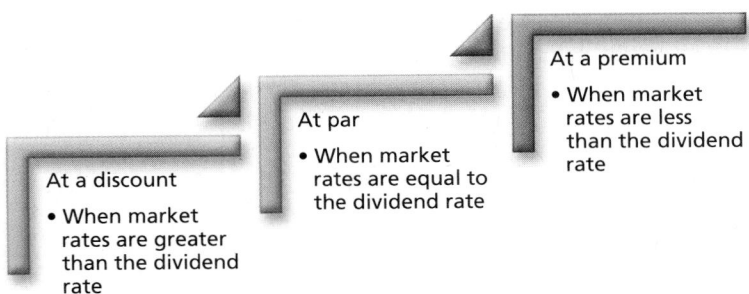

At a premium
• When market rates are less than the dividend rate

At par
• When market rates are equal to the dividend rate

At a discount
• When market rates are greater than the dividend rate

Also note that the market value of preferred shares increases when market rates decline, and vice versa.

PROBLEM

Determine the value of a $50 par value preferred share that pays annual dividends based on a 7 percent dividend rate, when the market yield is:

a. 7 percent.

b. 8 percent.

c. 6 percent.

EXAMPLE 7.1

Determining the Value of Preferred Stock

Solution

First, calculate the expected dividend per year: $D_p = \$50 \times 0.07 = \$3.50$
Then, capitalize this dividend at the appropriate required rate of return:

a. $P_p = \dfrac{D_p}{r_p} = \dfrac{\$3.50}{0.07} = \$50$

b. $P_p = \dfrac{\$3.50}{0.08} = \$43.75$

c. $P_p = \dfrac{\$3.50}{0.06} = \$58.33$

We can rearrange Equation 7-2 to determine the required rate of return on the preferred shares for a given market price, as follows:

$$r_p = \frac{D_p}{P_p} \tag{7-3}$$

If a preferred stock that pays an annual dividend of $2 per share is selling at $25 per share, the required rate of return on this preferred stock is $2 ÷ $25 = 8 percent.

Consider Consolidated Edison Co.'s 4.65% Series C Cumulative Preferred Stock. Each share of this stock has a par value of $100, and the annual dividend, D_p, is $4.65. Because Consolidated Edison pays dividends on this stock every three months (January, April, July, and October), it pays $4.65 ÷ 4 = $1.1625 every three months. On October 26, 2011, this stock had a price of $99.50. We can infer that its required rate of return on this date was r_p = $4.65 ÷ $99.50 = 4.673 percent. Looking back to an earlier date, the stock traded at $90.35 per share on August 9, 2011, which means that the required rate of return was $4.65 ÷ $90.35 = 5.1467 percent.

EXAMPLE 7.2

Estimating the Required Rate of Return on Preferred Stock

PROBLEM

Determine the required rate of return on preferred shares that provide a $6 annual dividend if they are presently selling for $70.

Solution

$$r_p = \frac{D_p}{P_p} = \frac{\$6}{\$70} = 8.57\%$$

Valuing Common Stock

Valuing common shares involves several complications that arise with respect to the appropriate future cash flows that should be discounted. Which cash flows should be discounted? Dividends? Free cash flow? One of the most popular discounted cash flow valuation models, which we discuss next, uses dividends. However, unlike bonds or even preferred shares, there is no requirement that common shares pay dividends at all. In addition, the level of dividend payments is discretionary, which implies we must make *estimates* regarding the *amount* and *timing* of any dividend payments. So, you can see why valuing common stock is treacherous.

The basic dividend discount model

dividend discount model (DDM) model for valuing common shares that assumes common shares are valued according to the present value of their expected future dividends

In the **dividend discount model (DDM)** we assume that common shares are valued according to the present value of their expected future cash flows—specifically, dividends. Based on this premise, we estimate today's value, based on an *n*-year holding period:

$$P_0 = \frac{D_1}{(1 + r_e)^1} + \frac{D_2}{(1 + r_e)^2} + \cdots + \frac{D_n + P_n}{(1 + r_e)^n} \tag{7-4}$$

where
P_0 = the value of a share of common stock today
D_t = the expected dividend at the end of year t
P_n = the expected share value after n years
r_e = the required return on the common shares

We diagram this in a time line on Figure 7-2. As you can see, there are two cash flows in the *n*th period: the expected dividend in that period, plus the expected value of the stock. You will notice that in the case of the value of a preferred share, we used a constant dividend amount (D_p), whereas for common shares we use a dividend that may be different each period (hence, we subscript the dividend in Equation 7-4 and Figure 7-2 to indicate the period). This is because most preferred shares have a stated, constant dividend, whereas common share dividends tend to change over time, at the discretion of the company's board of directors.

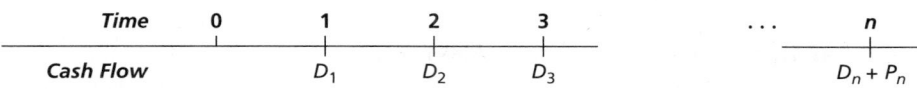

Time	0	1	2	3	...	n
Cash Flow		D_1	D_2	D_3		$D_n + P_n$

FIGURE 7-2 The Cash Flow Pattern for a Share of Common Stock

Consider a stock that is expected to pay $2 at the end of the first year and $3 at the end of the second year. If the stock is expected to have a value of $20 at the end of 2 years, what is the value of the stock today if the required rate of return is 8 percent?

$$P_0 = \frac{\$2}{(1 + 0.08)^1} + \frac{\$3}{(1 + 0.08)^2} + \frac{\$20}{(1 + 0.08)^2}$$

$$= \$1.8519 + \$2.5720 + \$17.1468$$

$$= \$21.5707$$

PROBLEM

An investor buys a common share and estimates she will receive an annual dividend of $0.50 per share in 1 year. She estimates she will be able to sell the share for $10.50. Estimate its value, assuming the investor requires a 10 percent rate of return.

Solution

$$P_0 = \frac{\$0.50 + \$10.50}{(1 + 0.10)^1} = \$10.00$$

EXAMPLE 7.3

Estimating the Value of a Share for a One-Year Holding Period

---

In the dividend discount model, the value at any point (say, time n) is equal to the present value of all the expected future dividends from period $n + 1$ to infinity. So the price next year, for example, is the present value of the expected dividend and share value for year 2. By repeatedly substituting for the future share value, we replace it with the present value of the dividend and share value expected the following year. As a result we remove P_n in Equation 7-4 and eventually get the following:

$$P_0 = \frac{D_1}{(1 + r_e)^1} + \frac{D_2}{(1 + r_e)^2} + \cdots + \frac{D_\infty}{(1 + r_e)^\infty} = \sum_{t=1}^{\infty} \frac{D_t}{(1 + r_e)^t} \qquad (7\text{-}5)$$

In other words, the value today is the present value of all future dividends to be received (i.e., from now to infinity).

Why use dividends? Well, if an investor buys a particular stock, the only cash flows that he or she will receive until the investor sells the stock will be the dividends. Although a company's residual earnings technically belong to the common shareholders, corporations generally do not pay out all their earnings as dividends. Of course, earnings are important too—without them the corporation could not sustain dividend payments for long. In fact, earnings receive more attention from investors than any other single variable. However, corporations typically reinvest a portion of their earnings to enhance future earnings and, ultimately, future dividends.

Equation 7-5 is the workhorse of share valuation because it says that the value of a share is the present value of expected future dividends. However, by repeatedly substituting for the share value, we are implicitly making a very important assumption: Investors are rational. We assume that at each time, investors react rationally and value the share based on what they rationally expect to receive the next year. This assumption specifically rules out "speculative bubbles," or what is colloquially known as the "bigger fool theorem."

Suppose, for example, a broker tells a client to buy XYZ at $30. The investor says, "No, it's only worth $25." The broker replies, "I know, but there is momentum behind it and

I am seeing a lot of interest. I think it will go to $40 by next year." The investor is a fool to pay $30 for something he or she thinks is worth $25, but it is not the fool theorem but the *bigger* fool theorem. If the investor does buy it, he or she *is* a fool, but he or she is also assuming that an even bigger fool will buy it in a year's time for $40.

This type of speculative bubble, in which prices keep increasing and become detached from reality, is specifically ruled out by the assumption of rational investors coolly calculating the present value of the expected cash flows at each time, so that prices never get detached from these fundamentals. Of course, there have been speculative bubbles when it has been very difficult to estimate these fundamental values.[16] However, we cannot build models based on irrationality, so we continue with the development of models based on fundamental cash flows.

Valuation with constant growth

growth rate rate of increase in an amount or value

It is impractical to estimate and discount *all* future dividends one by one, as required by Equation 7-5. Fortunately, we can simplify this equation into a usable formula by making the assumption that dividends grow at a constant rate (g) indefinitely. This **growth rate** represents the annual growth in dividends, ad infinitum.[17]

Once we make the assumption about constant growth, we can estimate all future dividends, assuming we know the most recent dividend paid (D_0):

$$D_1 = D_0(1 + g)$$

$$D_2 = D_1(1 + g) = D_0(1 + g)^2$$

$$D_3 = D_2(1 + g) = D_0(1 + g)^3$$

and so on.

Therefore, under the assumption of constant growth in dividends to infinity, Equation 7-5 reduces to the following expression:

$$P_0 = \frac{D_0(1 + g)^1}{(1 + r_e)^1} + \frac{D_0(1 + g)^2}{(1 + r_e)^2} + \ldots + \frac{D_0(1 + g)^\infty}{(1 + r_e)^\infty} \tag{7-6}$$

growing perpetuity stream of cash flows that grows at a constant rate, forever

constant growth DDM version of the dividend discount model for valuing common shares that assumes that dividends grow at a constant rate indefinitely

In Equation 7-6, we are, essentially, multiplying the dividend today, D_0, by a factor of $(1 + g) \div (1 + r_e)$ every period. This represents a **growing perpetuity**, which we can solve easily because it represents the sum of a geometric series. In fact, Equation 7-6 reduces to the following expression, which is the constant growth version of the dividend discount model, or simply the **constant growth DDM**:

$$P_0 = \frac{D_0(1 + g)}{r_e - g} = \frac{D_1}{r_e - g} \tag{7-7}$$

We should note a few features of Equation 7-7:

1. This relationship holds only when $r_e > g$. Otherwise, the answer is negative, which is uninformative.[18]

2. Only *future* estimated cash flows and estimated growth in these cash flows are relevant in the valuation.

---

[16] In Appendix 7A, we review the famous bubble involving the South Seas Company in 1720, in which Sir Isaac Newton almost bankrupted himself and then proclaimed, "I can calculate the motions of the heavenly bodies, but not the madness of people." The madness of people was the way in which the share price of the South Seas Company became completely detached from its fundamentals. The Internet bubble of the late 1990s, in which shares of Internet stocks rose without regard to fundamentals—and then crashed—indicates that the madness of people may not have changed much in almost 300 years.

[17] This growth rate is the same rate we looked at in our study of the time value of money, but forward looking instead of looking at the past. As a refresher, consider that if a company's dividend was $2 in 2007 and $4 in 2012, the average rate of growth in the dividend in these 5 years is 14.87 percent [$FV = 4$; $PV = 2$; $n = 5$; solve for i].

[18] The negative answer occurs because if $g > r$ in Equation 7-6, each future dividend is worth more than the previous one. The value never converges but increases to infinity.

3. The relationship holds only when growth in dividends is expected to occur *at the same rate indefinitely*.

4. If there is no growth (that is, $g = 0$ percent), this collapses to the value of a perpetuity.

Does the constant growth model actually fit companies? Consider the Hershey Foods Corporation. Hershey pays a dividend to its common stockholders each quarter, as we indicate in Figure 7-3. The dividends have grown at an average annual rate of 6.9939 percent, having grown from $0.092 per share to $1.28 per share over the period 1971 through 2010.[19] In Figure 7-3 we also compare the actual dividend growth with what dividends would have been if the growth had been perfectly constant. As you can see, Hershey's dividend growth is approximated well by assuming constant growth.

PROBLEM

Assume a company is currently paying $1.10 per share in common stock dividends. Investors expect dividends to grow at an annual rate of 4 percent indefinitely, and they require a 10 percent return on the shares. Determine the value of a share of this stock.

Solution

First, calculate the next period's dividend:

$$D_1 = D_0(1 + g) = \$1.10 \times (1 + 0.04) = \$1.144$$

Then, using next period's dividend, the required rate of return, and growth rate, calculate the value today:

$$P_0 = \frac{D_1}{r_e - g} = \frac{\$1.144}{0.10 - 0.04} = \$19.07$$

EXAMPLE 7.4

Using the Constant Growth Dividend Discount Model to Estimate a Share's Value

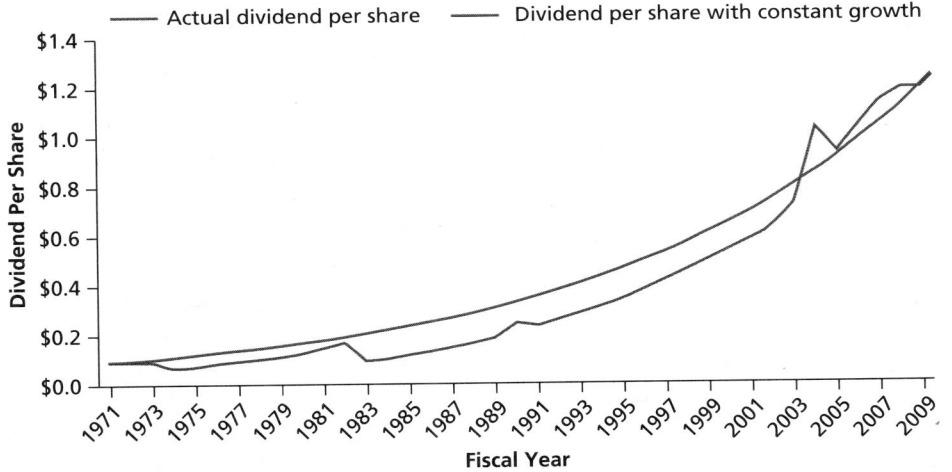

FIGURE 7-3 Hershey Foods Corporation Common Stock Dividends, 1971 Through 2010

Source: *Hershey Foods Corporation 10-K filings and annual reports, various years.*

---

[19] We adjusted the dividends for Hershey's stock splits. Because a stock split increases the number of shares proportionately, we adjusted the historical dividends downward to reflect a split. For example, Hershey split its stock 2 for 1 in 2004, doubling the number of shares outstanding. Hence, we divided the dividend in 2003 by two to put it on the same basis as 2004 dividends. We will cover stock splits in more detail in a later chapter.

Estimating the required rate of return

We can rearrange the constant growth dividend discount model to estimate the rate of return required by investors on a particular share, as follows:

$$r_e = \frac{D_1}{P_0} + g \tag{7-8}$$

The first term ($D_1 \div P_0$) in Equation 7-8 is the expected **dividend yield** on the share. Therefore, we may view the second term, g, as the expected **capital gains yield** (or, simply, **capital yield**) because the total return must equal the dividend yield plus the capital gains yield. It is important to recognize that this equation provides an appropriate approximation for required return *only* if the conditions of the constant growth dividend discount model are met (i.e., in particular the assumption regarding constant growth in dividends to infinity must be satisfied).

Consider a common stock that has an annual dividend of $2 per share. If the value of a share of this stock is $20 and the expected growth rate is 4 percent, the dividend yield is $2 ÷ $20 = 10 percent, and the required rate of return is 10 percent + 4 percent = 14 percent.

Let's take another look at Hershey common stock. The current dividend yield on Hershey common stock is $1.28 ÷ $47.15 = 3.5764 percent. Combining this with the dividend growth rate of 6.9913 percent, we estimate Hershey's required rate of return of 3.5764 percent + 6.9913 percent = 10.5677 percent.

EXAMPLE 7.5

Estimating the Required Rate of Return Using the Dividend Discount Model

PROBLEM

The market value of a company's shares is $12 each, the estimated dividend at the end of this year, D_1, is $0.60, and the estimated long-term growth rate in dividends, g, is 4 percent. Estimate the implied required rate of return on these shares.

Solution

$$r_e = \frac{D_1}{P_0} + g = \frac{\$0.60}{\$12} + 0.04 = 0.05 + 0.04 = 0.09 = 9\%$$

This result suggests that the expected return on these shares comprises an expected dividend yield of 5 percent and an expected capital gains yield of 4 percent.

Estimating the Value of Growth Opportunities

The constant growth dividend discount model can also provide a useful assessment of the market's perception of growth opportunities available to a company, as reflected in its market value. Let's begin by assuming that a company that has no profitable growth opportunities should not reinvest residual profits in the company, but rather should pay out all its earnings as dividends. Under these conditions, we have no growth (that is, $g = 0$), EPS_1 represents the expected earnings per common share in the upcoming year, and earnings per share are equal to dividends, $D_1 = EPS_1$. Under these assumptions, the constant growth dividend discount model reduces to the following expression:

$$P_0 = \frac{EPS_1}{r_e} \tag{7-9}$$

It is unlikely to find a company that has exactly "zero" growth opportunities, but the point is that we can view the share value of any common stock (that satisfies the assumptions of the constant growth dividend discount model) as comprising two components: its no-growth component, and the remainder, which is attributable to the market's perception of the growth opportunities available to that company. We denote this as the **present value of growth opportunities (PVGO)**. Therefore, we get Equation 7-10:

$$P_0 = \frac{EPS_1}{r_e} + PVGO \qquad (7\text{-}10)$$

present value of growth opportunities (PVGO) amount of the value of an asset that is attributable to the expected growth opportunities of the asset's cash flows

If a company's common stock has a market value of $25, the expected earnings per share for next year is $1, and the required rate of return is 10 percent, the stock's present value of growth opportunities is $15:

$$\$25 = \frac{\$1}{0.10} + PVGO$$

Rearranging,

$$PVGO = \$25 - 10 = \$15$$

EXAMPLE 7.6

Estimating the Present Value of Growth Opportunities

PROBLEM

A company's shares are selling for $20 each in the market. The company's EPS is expected to be $1.50 next year, and the required return on the shares is estimated to be 10 percent. Estimate the present value of growth opportunities per share.

Solution

We can solve this for PVGO by rearranging Equation 7-10:

$$PVGO = P_0 - \frac{EPS_1}{r_e} = \$20 - \frac{\$1.50}{0.10} = \$20 - \$15 = \$5.00$$

Returning once again to Hershey Food's common stock, we observe the year-end stock price for 2010 as $47.15 per share, and its earnings per share for 2011 are expected to be $2.83 per share. Therefore, using the 10.5677 percent cost of equity, the present value of growth opportunities is $20.37:

$$PVGO_{Hershey} = \$47.15 - (\$2.83 \div 0.105677) = \$47.15 - 26.78 = \$20.37$$

Extending the Dividend Discount Model

The constant growth dividend discount model predicts that, all else remaining equal, the value of common shares (P_0) will *increase* as a result of:

- an increase in the dividend;
- an increase in the expected growth rate of dividends; or
- a decrease in the required rate of return.

This list illustrates the intuitive appeal of the dividend discount model because it links common share values to three important fundamentals: corporate profitability, the general level of interest rates, and risk. In particular, expected dividends are closely related to profitability, as is the growth rate of these dividends, whereas the required rate of return is affected by the base level of interest rates (r_f) and by risk (as reflected in the risk premium required by investors). In particular, all else being equal, the dividend discount model predicts that common share prices will be higher when profits are high (and expected to grow), when interest rates are lower, and when risk premiums are lower.

We can generally assume that current dividends (D_0) are given, so it is the movements in r_e and g that determine the value of a share (i.e., because $r_e - g$ is the denominator and because $D_0(1 + g)$ is the numerator). Suppose a company currently pays $2 per share each year in dividends, the expected rate of growth in dividends is 5 percent, and the required rate of return is 8 percent. The value of a share of this company's stock is $70:

$$P_0 = \frac{\$2(1 + 0.05)}{0.08 - 0.05} = \frac{\$2.10}{0.03} = \$70$$

But what happens if we vary the inputs? What if . . .
. . . the growth in dividends in 6 percent instead of 5 percent?

$$P_0 = \frac{\$2(1 + 0.06)}{0.08 - 0.06} = \frac{\$2.12}{0.02} = \$106$$

. . . the required rate of return is 9 percent instead of 8 percent?

$$P_0 = \frac{\$2(1 + 0.05)}{0.09 - 0.05} = \frac{\$2.10}{0.04} = \$52.50$$

We show what happens when we vary the growth rate and when we vary the required rate of return in Figure 7-4. As you can see in this figure, there is a positive relation between the growth rate and the value of the stock, and there is a negative relation between the required rate of return and the value of the stock.

EXAMPLE 7.7

Valuing Shares Using the Constant Growth Dividend Discount Model

PROBLEM

Consider a company that is currently paying $1.10 per share in dividends.

a. If investors expect annual growth in dividends to be 3 percent and the estimated required rate of return to be 10 percent, what is the value of these shares?
b. If investors expect annual growth in dividends to be 3 percent and the estimated required rate of return to be 11 percent, what is the value of these shares?

Solution

$$D_1 = \$1.10 \times (1 + 0.03) = \$1.133$$

a. $P_0 = \$1.133 \div (0.10 - 0.03) = \$16.1857$

b. $P_0 = \$1.133 \div (0.11 - 0.03) = \$14.1625$

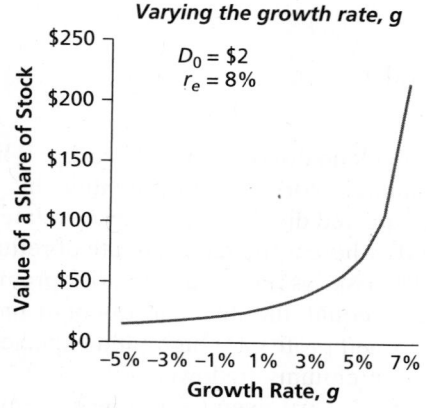

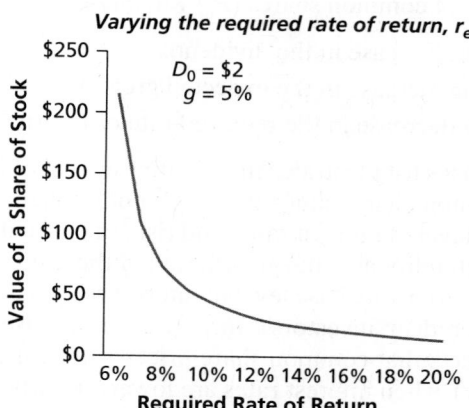

FIGURE 7-4 Comparison of the Value of Stock with Varying Growth Rates and Varying Required Rates of Return

Estimating the inputs into the constant growth dividend discount model generally requires a great deal of analysis and judgment. Assuming we know the most recent year's dividend payment, D_0, we need to estimate the required rate of return, r_e, and the expected growth in dividends, g, because $D_1 = D_0 (1 + g)$. As discussed earlier, the required rate of return for equity will equal the risk-free rate of return plus a risk premium, as depicted in Equation 7-1.[20]

We can use several methods to estimate the expected annual growth rate in dividends. One of the most common approaches is to determine the company's **sustainable growth rate, SGR**, which can be estimated by using the following equation:

$$\text{SGR} = b \times \text{ROE} \tag{7-11}$$

where b is the company's earnings retention ratio and ROE is company's return on common equity (i.e., net income ÷ common equity).[21] The **retention ratio** is the complement of the dividend payout ratio; in other words, $b = 1$ – dividend payout ratio. Another name for the retention ratio is the **plowback ratio**, named as such because these are the earnings that are *plowed back* into company.

From Equation 7-11 we see that growth in earnings (and dividends) is positively related to the proportion of each dollar of earnings reinvested in the company, b, as well as positively related to the company's return on equity. For example, a company that retains all its earnings and earns 10 percent on its equity would see its equity base grow by 10 percent per year. If the same company paid out all its earnings, then it would not grow. Similarly, a company that retained a portion, b, would earn 10 percent on that proportion, resulting in $g = b \times \text{ROE}$.[22]

> **sustainable growth rate (SGR)** earnings retention ratio multiplied by return on equity

> **retention ratio** or **plowback ratio** proportion of earnings reinvested in the company; the complement of the dividend payout ratio

---

PROBLEM

A company has an ROE of 12 percent, and its dividend payout ratio is 30 percent. Use this information to determine the company's sustainable growth rate.

Solution

$$g = b \times \text{ROE} = (1 - 0.30) \times (0.12) = 0.70 \times 0.12 = 0.0840 = 8.40 \text{ percent}$$

EXAMPLE 7.8

Estimating a Company's Sustainable Growth Rate

We can use the DuPont system to decompose ROE into three factors, as we show in Equation 7-12:

$$\text{ROE} = (\text{Net income} \div \text{Revenues}) \times (\text{Revenues} \div \text{Total assets}) \times (\text{Total assets} \div \text{Equity})$$

or, equivalently,

$$\text{ROE} = \text{Net profit margin} \times \text{Turnover ratio} \times \text{Equity multiplier} \tag{7-12}$$

The ROE, and hence g, increases with higher profit margins, higher asset turnover, and higher debt (although higher debt implies higher risk and, therefore, higher r_e).

We should note, however, that companies' return on equity can be quite variable, so what we are looking for is really the long-term trend. Consider International Business Machines (IBM), a U.S. technology service provider. As we show in Figure 7-5, Panel A, IBM's return on equity was relatively constant until 1990, which marks IBM's

---

[20] We defer further discussion of estimating the discount rate for equities to later chapters in this text.

[21] You may notice that we refer to this equity as common equity, but we made no such distinction in prior chapters. Because common equity is the residual ownership of the company, the growth pertains to returns to common shareholders; the return to preferred shareholders is fixed.

[22] A major weakness of this approach is its reliance on accounting figures to determine ROE because it is based on book values and the accrual method of accounting. As a result, it may not represent the "true" return earned on reinvested funds.

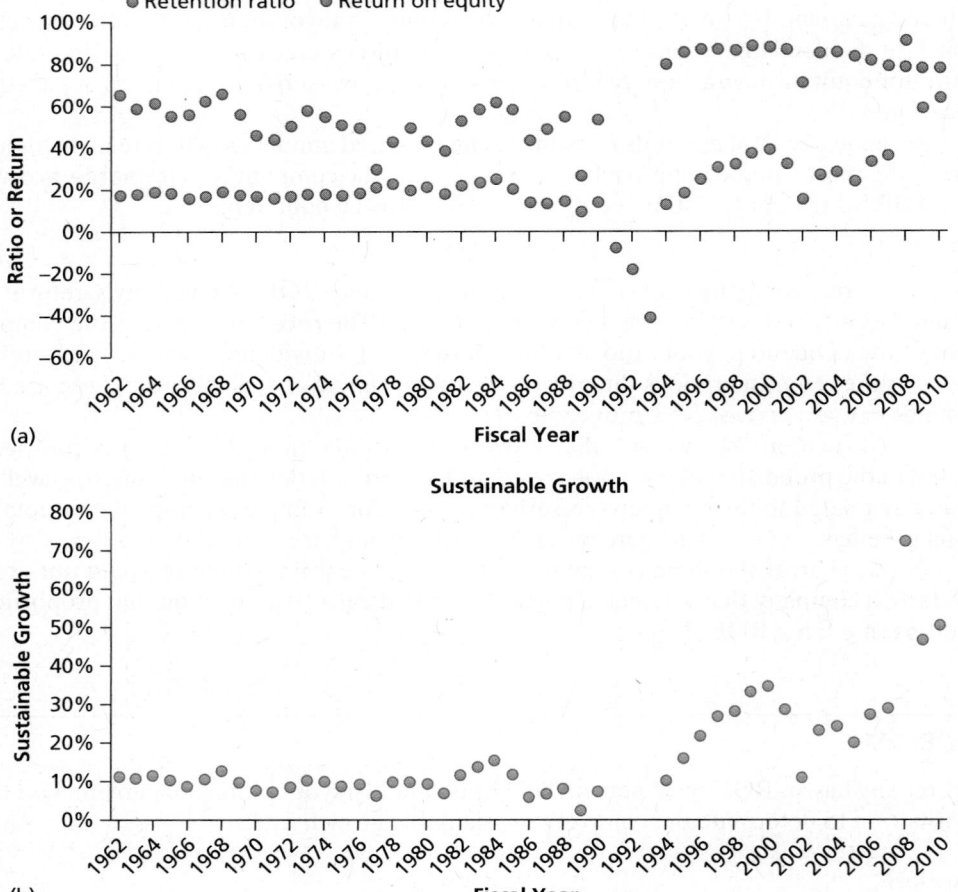

(a)

(b)

FIGURE 7-5 International Business Machines' Retention Ratio and Return on Capital, 1962 Through 2010

Source of data: *International Business Machines Annual Reports, various years, and 10-K filings.*

diversification from computers into technology services and consulting; this also marks when IBM's return on equity increased, in general, but also became more variable.[23]

Considering the variability of the return on equity and the retention ratio, as illustrated using IBM, we need to focus on the long-term trend, rather than a particular year's calculated SGR. For example, we might estimate IBM's retention ratio beyond 2011 to be around 80 percent and its return on equity as 35 percent, which typifies the 1994–2008 period. This implies a sustainable growth of IBM as 28 percent; however, in practice such a high rate of growth is not sustainable in the long run.

Another approach to estimating *g* is to examine historical rates of growth in dividends and earnings levels, including long-term trends in these growth rates for the company, the industry, and the economy as a whole. Predictions regarding future growth rates can be determined based on these past trends by using geometric or arithmetic averages or by using more involved statistical techniques, such as regression analysis. Finally, an important source of information regarding company growth, particularly for the near term, can be found in analyst estimates. Investors are often especially interested in "consensus" estimates because market values are often based to a large extent on these estimates.

---

[23] 1993 marks the beginning of a new phase in IBM's financial history as it defines its new business lines with a new CEO, Louis Gerstner, Jr. at the helm. IBM experienced losses in 1991, 1992, and 1993, but maintained its dividend; hence, its retention ratio and sustainable growth are not defined with losses.

PROBLEM

A company just paid an annual dividend of $1.00 per share and had earnings per share of $4. Its projected values for net profit margin, asset turnover, and the leverage ratio are 4 percent, 1.25 times, and 1.40, respectively. Estimate the company's sustainable growth rate.

Solution

Step 1: Calculate the return on equity

$$\text{ROE} = 0.04 \times 1.25 \times 1.40 = 0.07 = 7.00\%$$

Step 2: Calculate the retention rate

$$\text{Payout ratio} = \text{DPS} \div \text{EPS} = \$1 / \$4 = 0.25, \text{ so } b = 1 - 0.25 = 0.75$$

Step 3: Calculate the sustainable growth rate

$$g = b \times \text{ROE} = 0.75 \times 7.00\% = 5.25\%$$

EXAMPLE 7.9

Estimating a Company's Sustainable Growth Rate Using the DuPont System

It is important to remember in the application of any of these approaches that we are estimating future growth, and the inputs require judgment on the part of the analyst. If researchers believe past growth will be repeated in the future or want to eliminate period-to-period fluctuations in the plowback and return on equity, they may choose to use 3- to 5-year averages for these variables. Conversely, if the company has changed substantially, or analysts have good reason to believe the ratios for the most recent year are the best indicators of future sustainable growth, they will use these figures. In addition, an analysis of macroeconomic, industry, and company-specific factors may lead researchers to develop predicted values for these variables, independent of their historical levels.[24]

A key element in estimating future growth is to consider the company's ability to sustain growth. If the company has a competitive advantage that may be whittled away over time by its competitors, the best long-term growth rate may be the industry's growth rate, or even the long-term growth rate of the general economy. Therefore, the best estimate of growth may not be determined by the numbers, but by the application of judgment that considers not only the company's past, but also the many factors that affect its future.

Valuation With Multistage Growth

As we have noted, the constant growth dividend discount model relationship holds only when we are able to assume constant growth in dividends from now to infinity. In many situations it may be more appropriate to estimate dividends for the most immediate periods up to some point in time, after which it is assumed there will be constant growth in dividends to infinity. Several situations lend themselves to this structure. For example, it is reasonable to assume that competitive pressures and business cycle influences will prevent companies from maintaining extremely high growth in earnings for long periods. In addition, short-term earnings and dividend estimates should be much more reliable than those covering a longer period, which are often estimated by using some very general estimates of future economic, industry, and company conditions. To use the best information available at any point, it may make the most sense to estimate growth as precisely as possible in the short term, before assuming some long-term rate of growth. In practice, the discounted cash flow approach assuming multistage growth is used often by analysts.

---

[24] Some evidence indicates that using macroeconomic factors and company-specific factors, such as the independent auditor's opinion, are useful in predictions.

We can apply Equation 7-13 when steady growth in dividends to infinity does not begin until period t:

$$P_0 = \frac{D_1}{(1 + r_e)^1} + \frac{D_2}{(1 + r_e)^2} + \dots + \frac{D_t + P_t}{(1 + r_e)^t} \qquad (7\text{-}13)$$

where $P_t = \dfrac{D_{t+1}}{r_e - g}$. Notice that this is Equation 7-4, with n replaced by t and with an estimate for the future share price, P_t.

In Figure 7-6 we depict the cash flows associated with this type of a valuation framework, but with one growth rate for a finite number of periods and another growth rate following in perpetuity. This well-known version of the multiple-growth dividend discount model is the **two-stage growth rate model**, which assumes growth at one rate for a certain period, g_1, followed by some steady growth rate to infinity at g_2. This model is applied often to start-up companies, in which growth for the first few years is expected to be high, but then slowing as the company, industry, or product matures. In the example in Figure 7-6, dividends grow at a rate g_1 for 4 years, and then beginning in the 5th year, dividends begin to grow at a rate of g_2. This means that the dividend in year 5, D_5, is affected by the growth rate for the first 4 years, as well as the growth rate in the 5th year:

$$D_5 = D_4(1 + g_2) = D_0(1 + g_1)^4(1 + g_2)$$

> **two-stage growth rate model** valuation model for equity in which there are two stages, each with a different growth rate

Essentially, whenever we use multiple period growth rates, we estimate dividends *up to the beginning* of the period in which it is reasonable to assume constant growth to infinity. In Figure 7-6, constant growth begins after the fourth period. Then we can use the constant growth dividend discount model to estimate of the market value of the share at that time; in the case of Figure 7-6, we estimate the value of a share at the end of the fourth period, which is the present value of the dividends from period 5 on, growing at a constant rate g_2:

$$P_4 = \frac{D_5}{(1 + r_e)^5} + \frac{D_6}{(1 + r_e)^6} + \frac{D_7}{(1 + r_e)^7} + \dots + \frac{D_\infty}{(1 + r_e)^\infty} = \frac{D_4(1 + g_2)}{(r_e - g_2)} = \frac{D_5}{(r_e - g_2)}$$

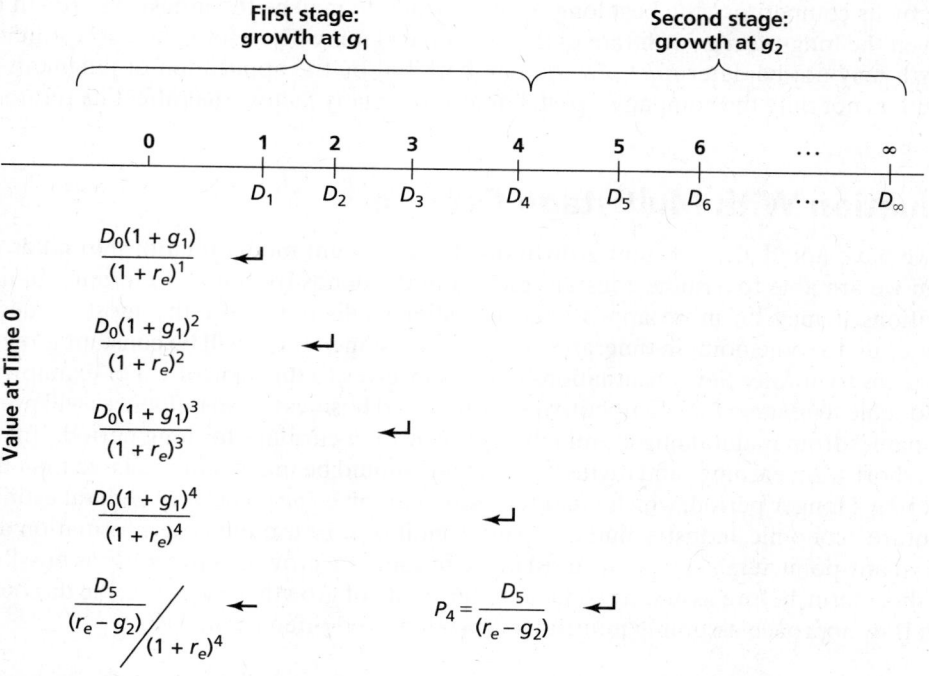

FIGURE 7-6 The Cash Flow Pattern for Multiple Stage Growth in Dividends

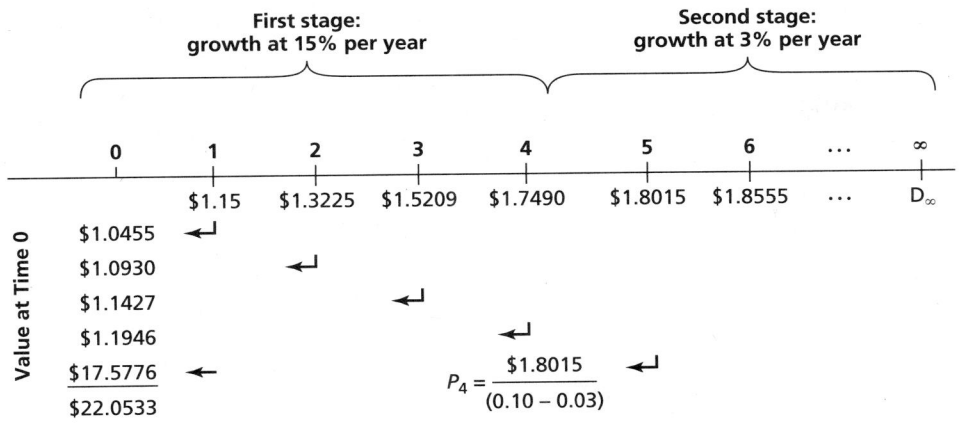

FIGURE 7-7 **The Cash Flow Pattern for Multiple Stage Growth in Dividends**

Finally, we discount all the estimated dividends up to the beginning of the constant growth period, as well as the estimated market value at that time.[25] This provides us with today's estimate of the share's market value.

Let's put some numbers to this problem. Assume that the current dividend is $1 and that dividends are expected to grow at a rate of 15 percent for the first 4 years, 3 percent thereafter. If the required rate of return is 10 percent, what is the value of share of stock today? As you can see in Figure 7-7, the value of the stock today is $22.0533, which is comprised of the present value of the first four dividends and the present value of the value of a share four years from today.

PROBLEM	EXAMPLE 7.10

A company is expected to pay a dividend of $1.00 at the end of this year, a $1.50 dividend at the end of year 2, and a $2.00 dividend at the end of year 3. It is estimated dividends will grow at a constant rate of 4 percent per year thereafter. Determine the market value of this company's common shares if the required rate of return is 11 percent.

EXAMPLE 7.10

Using the Multistage Dividend Discount Model

Solution

First, estimate dividends up to the start of constant growth to infinity. In this example, they are all given, so no calculations are required:

$D_1 = \$1.00$

$D_2 = \$1.50$

$D_3 = \$2.00$

Second, estimate the value at the beginning of the constant growth to infinity period:

$$D_4 = \$2.00 \times (1 + 0.04) = \$2.08$$

$$P_3 = \frac{D_4}{r_e - g} = \frac{\$2.08}{0.11 - 0.04} = \$29.71$$

Third, discount back the relevant cash flows to time 0:

$$P_0 = \frac{1.00}{(1 + 0.11)} + \frac{1.50}{(1 + 0.11)^2} + \frac{2.00 + 29.71}{(1 + 0.11)^3} = 0.90 + 1.22 + 23.19 = \$25.31$$

[25] Recall that P_t represents the present value of all the expected dividends from time $t + 1$ to infinity, so we are essentially discounting *all* the expected future dividends associated with the stock.

Using a financial calculator, enter the cash flows and interest rate, then solve for the NPV:

CF_t	1.0
CF_t	1.5
CF_t	31.71　← 29 + 2.71
i	11

Solve for the NPV

Using a spreadsheet, type the cash flows in the appropriate cells and using the NPV function:

	A	B
1	1	
2	1.5	
3	31.71	
4		= NPV(.11, A1:A3)

Limitations of the Dividend Discount Model

Although the dividend discount model provides a great deal of insight into the factors that affect the valuation of common shares, it is based on several assumptions that are not met by a large number of companies. In particular, it is best suited for companies that (1) pay dividends based on a stable dividend payout history that they want to maintain in the future, and (2) are growing at a steady and sustainable rate. As such, the dividend discount model works reasonably well for large corporations in mature industries with stable profits and an established dividend policy.[26]

Not surprisingly, the dividend discount model does not work well for many resource-based companies, which are cyclical in nature and often display erratic growth in earnings and dividends. In addition, many of these companies (especially the smaller ones) do not distribute dividends to shareholders. Consider Hecla Mining, which mines for metals including silver, gold, lead, and zinc. Looking at Hecla's net income, you can see that its earnings were relatively stable until 1975, as we show in Figure 7-8, but the company paid dividends on and off until 1991; when net income became quite variable, dividends ceased.

The dividend discount model will also not work well for companies in distress, companies that are in the process of restructuring, companies involved in acquisitions, and private companies. Finally, if a company enters into substantial share-repurchase arrangements, we must adjust the model because share repurchases also represent a method of distributing wealth to shareholders.

Due to the limitations of the dividend discount model, and because common share valuation is a challenging process, involving, as it does, predictions for the future, analysts often use several approaches to value common shares. Aside from the relative valuation approaches discussed in the next section, another discounted cash flow approach—using the free cash flow instead of dividends—is used frequently. The free cash flow approach is implemented almost identically to the dividend discount model, except that instead of discounting estimated future dividends, you discount expected future free cash flows. The underlying rationale is that dividends are discretionary, and many firms may choose not to

[26] When we look at dividends for companies, we need to also consider the effects of severe economic environments. For example, many mature, steady-dividend-paying companies cut their dividends during the 2007–08 financial crisis, but have since resumed these dividends, albeit at lower rates. General Electric, with a history of steadily increasing dividends, cut its dividend in mid-2009 from $0.31 each quarter to $0.10 each quarter, but then resumed a pattern of steadily-increasing dividends in the quarters that followed.

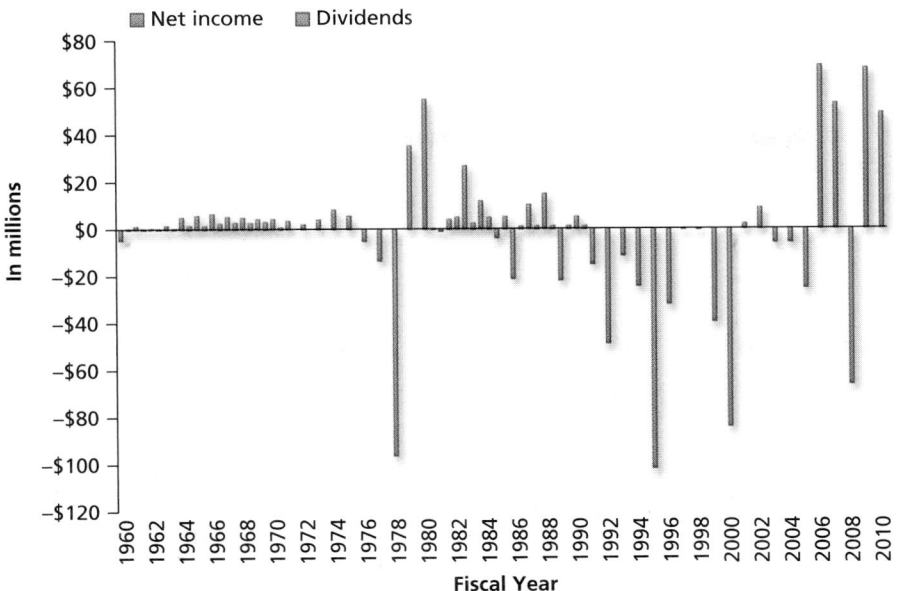

FIGURE 7-8 Hecla Mining Net Income, 1960 Through 2010

Source of data: *Hecla Mining Annual Report and 10-K filings, various years.*

pay out the amount of dividends they could. Therefore, instead of using dividends, you use free cash flow, which is in some sense a measure of what a firm could pay out if it chose to.

We will not discuss this model in detail but will note that there are two variations of this approach:

1. using free cash flows to equity holders and discounting them using the required return to equity holders (as in the dividend discount model); and

2. using free cash flows to the firm, and discounting them using the firm's weighted average cost of capital. This approach is often more appropriate when firms do not pay out a significant portion of their earnings as dividends, or pay out well below their capacity.

BP and Its Dividend | ETHICS

BP PLC is a British limited company in the energy industry, with fiscal year 2009 revenues of $239 billion. From 2005 to 2009, the dividends on BP shares grew at an average rate of 17.4 percent per year, increasing each year despite the fact that the earnings to shareholders declined in 2009. BP had not reduced its dividends since 1992.

In April 2010, BP declared a dividend of $10 billion, with payment in June 2010. BP experienced a disaster with its Deepwater Horizon drilling operation, which exploded on April 20, 2010, resulting in a massive oil spill in the U.S. Gulf of Mexico. BP faced a dilemma regarding paying its dividend while still wrangling with the 2010 oil spill in the Gulf. The spill resulted in not only direct and future costs to BP, but also a problem: The company had committed to shareholders to pay the dividend, but there was pressure by politicians for BP to not pay the dividend. Should BP disappoint the pensions and other investors who depend on the dividend? Should BP consider the political fallout and cut the dividend?

In the first two quarters of 2010, BP took a $32.2 billion charge for current and anticipated spill-related costs. In the quarter ending June 30, 2010, BP had current assets of $77 billion, equity of $85 billion, cash flow from operations of $14 billion, but a loss after the spill charge, of $17 billion. For the fiscal year 2010 BP was expected to generate profits, and the charge for the spill was manageable considering the earnings of the company.

BP resolved this dilemma by canceling its dividend for 2010, but promised to consider paying a dividend in the future. By not paying a dividend, BP contributed to a fund to pay for spill-related costs, as well as pay down its debt. BP resumed its dividend in 2011.

Sources: Barr, Colin, "BP Slashes Dividend," *Fortune*, June 16, 2010; Herron, James, "BP Takes Heat from Two Sides on Dividend," *Wall Street Journal*, June 9, 2010; www.bp.com.

1. In what ways are preferred shares different from bonds, and how do these differences affect the valuation of preferred shares?

2. According to the dividend discount models used to value common stock, what factors are important in this valuation, and what relationship do they have to the value of a share of stock?

7.3 USING MULTIPLES TO VALUE EQUITY

We can use relative valuation to estimate the value of common shares by comparing the market values of similar companies, relative to a common variable, such as earnings, cash flow, book value, or sales. Because relative valuation relies on multiples, we refer to this methodology as the method of multiples. Conceptually, relative valuation appears simple to apply: All we need to do is find a group of comparable companies and then use their financial data and market values to infer the value of the company in question. However, finding comparable companies is difficult: What company is similar to Microsoft, for example? Even after we find a group of comparable companies, we have to estimate the appropriate multiple because values will differ even for comparable companies, so the exercise involves substantial analysis and judgment.

Using the Price-Earnings Ratio

We illustrate the approach by using the most commonly used relative valuation multiple: the **price-earnings (P/E) ratio**. The P/E ratio represents the number of times investors are willing to pay for a company's earnings, as expressed in the share price, or the share price divided by the earnings per share. The P/E approach is implemented by estimating the company's earnings per share (EPS) and multiplying it by a justifiable P/E multiple. The **justified P/E** is the multiple that is considered sustainable over the long term. The typical P/E formulation for valuation purposes uses estimated earnings per share (EPS$_1$) for the next 12 months. The basic valuation equation can then be expressed as shown in Equation 7-14:

> **justified P/E** multiple that is considered sustainable over the long-term

$$P_0 = \text{Estimated } EPS_1 \times \text{Justified P/E} = EPS_1 \times (P_0 / EPS_1) \qquad (7\text{-}14)$$

Notice that the P/E ratio used in Equation 7-14 is based on expected future earnings (Estimated EPS$_1$) and is therefore the *leading P/E ratio*. By comparison, when we analyze financial ratios, the reported P/E ratios are often based on earnings over the previous 12 months (EPS$_0$), resulting in *lagging P/E ratios*. For valuation purposes, we typically focus on the leading P/E ratio because market values are based on expectations about the future.

Using the P/E ratio is easy: If the company's forecast earnings per share are $2 and the P/E ratio for comparable companies is 20, we would arrive at a share value of $40 using the P/E approach. We can see from this example why this approach is also called "using multiples." In this case, the multiple of earnings is 20 times. In this sense the multiple is an example of a payback period. The higher the multiple, the longer the payback period and the more the investor is expecting earnings to increase. Alternatively, it could be that the shares are simply more expensive shares.

> **relative valuation** valuing a company relative to other comparable companies

We can also see why the approach is commonly called **relative valuation**: We are valuing the company relative to other comparable companies. This means that if the comparable companies are all overvalued, using the P/E approach will overvalue the company

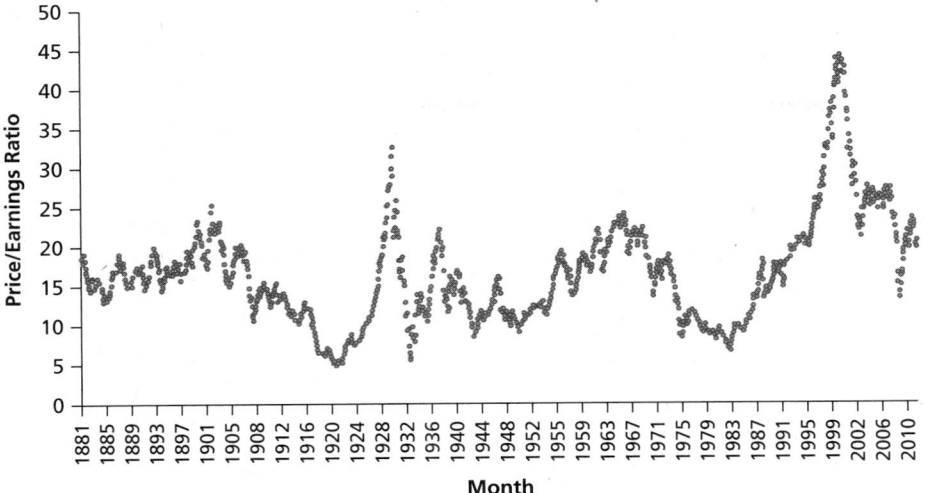

FIGURE 7-9 Price-Earnings Ratio for the S&P 500 Index, January 1881–November 2011

Source of data: *Robert Shiller, www.yale.edu.*

in question. What this means is that if the market is in a "speculative bubble," the P/E approach will not detect it directly. What is then needed is some yardstick or benchmark P/E. We can ballpark this by looking at the P/E ratio for the S&P 500 Composite Index, which we show in Figure 7-9.

The P/E is based on trailing or lagged earnings for the companies in the S&P 500 Index, and it vividly demonstrates the problems with the P/E ratio: Very low earnings cause the value of the P/E to skyrocket. In the early 1990s, the U.S. experienced a bubble in Internet stock, causing the average P/E ratio to increase to 45 times. Then during the slowdown in 2002 and the puncturing of the Internet bubble, price-earnings ratios fell, recovering slightly.

What we see in Figure 7-9 is the **Molodovsky effect**. This effect is named after Nicholas Molodovsky, who observed that P/E ratios are overstated in slow economic periods.[27] The numerator in the trailing P/E ratio is the current price, which reflects investors' expectations about future earnings and cash flows to investors, whereas the denominator reflects the most recent earnings experience. Because of the forward-looking nature of prices, the P/E ratios of cyclical stocks tend to have prices looking forward to better economic times, but earnings that reflect poor economic times. Therefore, high P/E ratios during recessions, for example, are likely overstated. On the other hand, if investors are forecasting declining earnings, a trailing P/E may be understated.

Molodovsky effect trailing P/E ratios of cyclical companies are overstated during low points of the economic cycle

Recognizing these problems, we can see that typically the P/E is in the range of 15 to 20 times. When P/E ratios fall to the lower band of this range, we tend to think the stock market is undervalued; when the P/E creeps above 20, we take it as a warning signal that equities are overvalued. At the end of the 2007–2009 recession, both the stock market and earnings prospects fell, but in late 2009 investors priced stocks expecting that earnings would recover.[28]

The P/E ratio is an attractive (and commonly reported) statistic for investors and analysts for several reasons. First, it relates the price to the earnings owned by the shareholders. Second, it is easy to compute and as a result is commonly available. This makes

[27] Molodovsky, Nicholas, "Some Aspects of Price-Earnings Ratios," *Financial Analysts Journal*, May 1953, Vol. 9, No. 2, pp. 65–78.
[28] The National Bureau of Economic Research indicates that this recession began in December of 2007. The previous recession was from March 2001 through November 2001 [www.nbre.org/cycles/].

comparisons relatively straightforward. Third, it is intuitive, as it indicates the payback period and thus can be related to a number of other company characteristics, such as growth opportunities and risk.

We need two estimates to calculate Equation 7-14. Unfortunately, obtaining reasonable estimates requires a substantial amount of analysis and also an element of judgment. EPS_1 can be determined by using several approaches, which are similar to those described earlier for estimating future dividends. In particular, we can analyze historical earnings data, project trends, and the company's present situation and forecast future earnings.[29] In addition, the use of analyst estimates (and consensus estimates) may provide reasonable forecasts of EPS_1.

Estimating justifiable P/E ratios is even more involved, and there are several approaches we can use. One common approach is to find comparable companies and estimate an appropriate P/E ratio for the company being analyzed, based on a comparison of this company with the others, in terms of risk and growth opportunities. This approach often involves using an industry average P/E ratio, which is then scaled up or down, based on an assessment of whether or not the company is above or below average. Unfortunately, this approach involves a great deal of subjectivity regarding several company-specific characteristics, including risk, potential for growth, and the overall financial health of the company. Further, differences in accounting among companies may require some adjustments for comparability among companies. In addition, this approach may build market errors into the value estimation process. For example, even though a company may be average within its industry, the industry average P/E ratio may be too high if the industry's earnings are currently depressed (understating the denominator), but the market anticipates that earnings will recover for a particular industry at a particular time. Another commonly used approach is to examine historical averages for the company or the company's industry. However, using historical averages may be inappropriate if the company has changed substantially and as market and industry conditions change.

Potential problems are associated with the use of industry or historical averages to estimate the appropriate P/E ratio, so it is beneficial to obtain corroborating estimates based on economic, industry, and company fundamentals, if possible. Fortunately, we can estimate the P/E ratio by relating it to the fundamentals in the dividend discount model.[30] We illustrate this by using the simplest DDM model: the constant growth model:

$$P_0 = \frac{D_1}{r_e - g}$$

Dividing both sides of this equation by expected earnings (EPS_1), we get Equation 7-15:

$$\frac{P_0}{EPS_1} = \frac{D_1 / EPS_1}{r_e - g} \tag{7-15}$$

We are left with the P/E ratio on the left side of Equation 7-15 and the expected dividend payout, required rate of return, and growth rate on the right-hand side. Notice that it is *expected earnings*, not historical earnings, that are relevant. Also note that r_e and g are typically the most important factors in the determination of the P/E ratio because a small change in either can have a large effect on its value. Based on Equation 7-15, the following relationships should hold, all else being equal:

- The higher the expected payout ratio, the higher the P/E.
- The higher the expected growth rate, g, the higher the P/E.
- The higher the required rate of return, r_e, the lower the P/E.

---

[29] You can also refer to our discussion of forecasting financial statements in Chapter 4.

[30] Similar to the DDM, this approach for estimating P/E ratios will work best for companies with relatively stable dividend and growth patterns.

However, "all else being equal" is a brave assumption because many of these variables are interrelated. For example, raising the payout ratio and thus increasing the dividend seems to increase the P/E, but raising the payout may also reduce growth because one estimate of the growth rate is the sustainable growth rate, where $g = (1 - \text{Payout}) \times \text{ROE}$. We might also try to increase the growth rate by taking on risky investment projects that could increase future earnings and dividends, but this could also cause the required rate of return to increase (i.e., recall $r_e = r_f + \text{Risk premium}$). However, what we can say is that P/E ratios tend to be higher when future growth in earnings and dividends is also expected to be high and when interest rates or risk premiums are low (because they both affect r_e).

EXAMPLE 7.11
Using the P/E Ratio Approach

PROBLEM

Assume that a company has just reported an EPS of $2.00 and expects to maintain a 40 percent payout ratio. Estimate the company's P/E ratio and its market value, assuming its ROE is 10 percent and that investors require a 9 percent return on their shares.

Solution

First, estimate $g = (1 - \text{payout}) \times \text{ROE} = (1 - 0.40) \times 10\% = 6.00\%$.

Second, estimate $EPS_1 = (EPS_0)(1 + g) = (2.00 \times 1.06) = \$2.12$.

Third, estimate $\dfrac{P}{E} = \dfrac{D_1/EPS_1}{r_e - g} = \dfrac{0.40}{0.09 - 0.06} = 13.33$

Fourth, estimate $P_0 = EPS_1 \times P_0/EPS_1 = \$2.12 \times 13.33 = \$28.26$.

We assume that the payout ratio remains constant at 40 percent, but we vary the main subjective inputs, r_e and g, to assess the effect on the P/E ratio and on value.

EXAMPLE 7.12
Varying the Inputs of the P/E Ratio Approach

PROBLEM

Suppose a company has EPS of $2.00 and a payout ratio of 40 percent. Value a share of common stock assuming:

a. a growth rate of 5 percent and a required rate of return of 10 percent.
b. a growth rate of 7 percent and a required rate of return of 8 percent.

Solution

a. $EPS_1 = \$2.00 \times 1.05 = \$2.10$

$\dfrac{P}{E} = \dfrac{0.40}{0.10 - 0.05} = 8$

So, $P_0 = \$2.10 \times 8.00 = \$16.80$

b. $EPS_1 = \$2.00 \times 1.07 = \$2.14$

$\dfrac{P}{E} = \dfrac{0.40}{0.08 - 0.07} = 40$

So, $P_0 = \$2.14 \times 40.00 = \$85.60$

Notice the wide range of P/E and value estimates that arise for relatively small changes in our estimates of r_e and g.

Aside from the difficulties in estimating an appropriate P/E ratio and in estimating future EPS, there are several other practical concerns regarding the use of P/E ratios:

- The P/E ratio is uninformative when companies have negative or very small earnings.[31]
- The P/E ratio may be highly variable across an industry.
- The volatile nature of earnings implies a great deal of volatility in P/E multiples. For example, the earnings of cyclical companies fluctuate quite dramatically throughout a typical business cycle.
- Net income, and hence earnings per share, is susceptible to the influence of accounting choices and earnings management.

For these reasons, P/E ratios are often based on smoothed or normalized estimates of earnings for the forecast year. This is also the reason analysts use other, similar relative value approaches along with a P/E analysis.

LESSONS LEARNED | Low Price-Earnings Ratio

Are low-P/E stocks good buying opportunities? Some may refer to low-P/E stocks as "cheap," but cheap does not always mean it's a good deal. Here are a few reasons:

- A low P/E ratio may mean that the company is likely headed for trouble. Look at any company that is in financial distress, and you will see a falling share price and shrinking earnings—it may be that the share price, which is forward-looking—shrinks faster than reported earnings.
- Some argue that a stock with a low P/E may be undervalued. But isn't the value of the stock in the market

the value of the stock? Could the market—the millions of investors who watch the value of stocks—be so wrong as to make such a mistake in valuing a stock? Not likely so.

- A P/E may be low because of inflation. In periods of high inflation, the deductions for depreciation are based on historical costs, and the cost of goods sold may reflect historical, not replacement, costs. In this case, high inflation will result in overstated earnings, hence resulting in a low P/E.

Additional Multiples or Relative Value Ratios

The **market-to-book (M/B) ratio** is the market value per share divided by the book value per share. Equivalently, we can calculate the market-to-book ratio as the ratio of the market capitalization of the common stock divided by the book value of common equity. Recall that the book value per share equals the book value of equity (i.e., assets – liabilities) divided by the number of common shares outstanding. As such, valuing stocks relative to their M/B is an attractive approach for several reasons. Book value provides a relatively stable, intuitive measure of value relative to market values that can be easily compared with those of other companies, provided accounting standards do not vary greatly across the comparison group. It eliminates several of the problems arising from the use of P/E multiples because book values are rarely negative and do not exhibit the volatility associated with earnings levels. However, book values may be sensitive to accounting standards and may be uninformative for companies that do not have a large proportion of fixed assets (such as service companies) or that have negative equity.

The use of the M/B ratio fell out of favor in the 1980s and 1990s because of high rates of inflation that distorted the M/B ratio. This is because using historical cost accounting in an inflationary period results in understated carrying or book values. However, the low

[31] We can sometimes get very large or meaningless numbers for the P/E ratio, even when we aggregate across all companies. For a particular company, the possibility of these problems is much higher.

rate of inflation of the last 10 to 15 years has removed most of these problems, whereas changes in accounting standards have made the book value of equity more useful.[32]

The **price-to-sales (P/S) ratio** has several properties that make it attractive for valuation purposes. Similar to the P/E and M/B approaches, we implement it by multiplying a justifiable P/S ratio by the revenue per share. Unlike earnings and book values, sales (or revenues) are relatively insensitive to accounting decisions and are never negative.[33] Sales are not as volatile as earnings levels, hence P/S ratios are generally less volatile than P/E multiples. In addition, sales figures provide useful information about corporate decisions, such as pricing. However, sales do not provide information about expenses and profit margins, which are important determinants of company performance.

Another commonly used relative valuation ratio is the **price-to-cash-flow (P/CF) ratio**, where cash flow (CF) is often estimated as cash flow from operations.[34] By focusing on cash flow rather than on accounting income, this ratio alleviates some of the accounting concerns regarding measures of earnings.

We can form multiples using earnings before interest and taxes (EBIT) or earnings before interest, taxes, and depreciation and amortization (EBITDA) instead of net income to eliminate a significant proportion of volatility caused in EPS figures by the use of debt, and by depreciation and amortization (which are noncash expenses). Because EBIT and EBITDA are earnings to all suppliers of capital (that is, bondholders and shareholders), we often compare the value of the entity's capital with these earnings. The market value of an entity's capital, less cash and cash equivalents, is the entity's **enterprise value**. The enterprise value is often referred to as the takeover value of the company because this is what another entity would have to pay to purchase the company.[35] Comparing the enterprise value to these measures of earnings, the resultant ratios are **enterprise value to EBIT** and the **enterprise value to EBITDA ratio**. We use the enterprise value in the numerator to reflect the fact that EBIT and EBITDA represent income available to both debt and equity holders.[36]

However, although there are many different valuation ratios or "multiples," they are all related to the fundamental valuation drivers. Suppose an investor requires a 15 percent return on his or her shares, expects the company to pay a $1 dividend, and expects dividends and earnings to grow at 10 percent. In this case, we can use the constant growth model to value the shares at $20.

$$P_0 = \frac{\$1}{0.15 - 0.01} = \$20$$

If 0.5 million shares are outstanding, this company would have a total market value for the equity or equity market capitalization of $10 million.[37]

Suppose the XYZ Company has the forecast income statement and financial data we show Table 7-2. We can link all these valuation multiples using this data.

In valuing this company, one valuation metric is to simply compare dividend yields across other comparable companies. A high dividend yield relative to other companies

price-to-sales (P/S) ratio market price per share divided by sales per share

price-to-cash-flow (P/CF) ratio market price per share divided by per share cash flow

enterprise value market value of an entity's debt and equity, less cash and cash equivalents

enterprise value to EBIT ratio total market value of the company, less cash and cash equivalents, divided by earnings before interest and taxes

enterprise value to EBITDA ratio total market value of the company, less cash and cash equivalents, divided by earnings before interest, taxes, and depreciation and amortization

---

[32] At one point, companies were required to write off goodwill, and this seriously affected both earnings and the book value of equity. Now the goodwill arising from an acquisition is only written off when it is impaired by a drop in value. This is what caused the huge losses to Nortel and JDS Uniphase in 2002.

[33] We use the terms *revenues* and *sales* interchangeably. If we were to be fussy, we would use *sales* when referring to retail firms and *revenues* for all other types of firms.

[34] A number of estimates of cash flow are used in practice. For example, some analysts focus on free cash flow available to shareholders, which is estimated as net income, plus depreciation and deferred taxes, less capital expenditures, the change in net working capital, and net external debt financing.

[35] The reason that cash and cash equivalents are removed is that if the company is taken over the cash and cash equivalents can be used to offset the purchase price of the firm.

[36] Technically, what we would want to use for the market value of capital is the market value of equity, plus the market value of debt capital. Debt capital in this context is the interest-bearing obligations of the company.

[37] The market capitalization is sometimes referred to casually as the "market cap" or simply the "cap."

TABLE 7-2   Forecast Income Statement for XYZ Company

	(in millions)
Earnings before interest taxes, depreciation, and amortization (EBITDA)	$3.3
Less: Depreciation	0.8
Earnings before interest and taxes (EBIT)	$2.5
Less: Interest	0.5
Earnings before taxes (EBT)	$2.0
Less: Income tax (50 percent)	1.0
Net income	$1.0
Dividends	$0.5
Cash and cash equivalents	$1.0
Book value of equity	$5.0
Book value of debt	$6.0
Market value of debt	$5.0
Market value of equity	$10.0

might then indicate an undervalued stock. Another way of looking at the dividend yield is to take its reciprocal and look at the dividend multiple, that is, the market value divided by the dividend. In this case, XYZ's dividend yield is $0.5 ÷ $10.0 = 5 percent, and its stock is selling at 20 times its dividend.

In practice, we don't often talk about the value in terms of a multiple of the dividend because the dividend yield provides the same information, and yields on stocks are often compared directly with yields on income trusts, bonds, and other interest-earning securities. However, the fundamental problem with using dividend multiples is that many companies do not pay dividends.

An alternative to dividends is to examine earnings. In the case of XYZ, with a market value of equity of $10 million and $1 million in net income, the P/E ratio is 10 times. Immediately we can see that although many companies do not pay cash dividends, they should all expect to have some earnings. The problem here is that earnings are cyclical and industry specific, so let's move up the income statement a bit more.

The next item is the earnings before interest and tax (EBIT), which with our example is $2.5 million. The difference between the EBIT and the net income is that the EBIT does not belong to the shareholders because some flows through to the company's creditors and some to the government. This is why we usually calculate the total company value (or enterprise value), that is, the value of the debt plus the value of the equity for all the ratios "above" net income. For our example, this comes to $15 million.[38] The EBIT multiple is $15 million ÷ $2.5 million = 6 times.

However, as we know from our accounting discussion, depreciation is a noncash charge, so we go farther up the income statement and add back depreciation to get EBITDA. This adds back all the accounting items that do not involve cash.[39] Looking at our example once again, with a total enterprise value of $6 + 10 − 1 = $15 million, the EBITDA multiple is 4.5 times. The EBITDA multiple is the most commonly used multiple when companies look at acquiring other companies because it is a good proxy for the cash

---

[38] The debt market value is assumed to be the book value of $5 million.
[39] Depreciation of fixed assets is by far the largest component of these noncash adjustments, but there are also amortizations, such as issue costs attached to debt, as well as other noncash adjustments.

flow that the company generates that can be used by another company. Another useful metric is to look at the contribution generated by the company, which is the EBITDA with all the fixed costs added back. In our example, this is $5 million, giving a multiple of three times. This is useful for companies valuing other companies when they can consolidate operations and remove the fixed costs.

The final valuation multiple uses sales. In our case, the sales multiple is the $10 million in sales divided by $10 million in common equity, with a resulting multiple of 1.0. This multiple is useful if the entire sales of the company could be switched to another company and the existing plant and facilities closed down. Another variant on this is to look at the equity value per unit of sales, in our case, $10 million for 1 million unit sales means that the company's shares are selling for $10 per unit of sales.

If we use these valuation multiples, along with the market-to-book ratio, which in our case is $10 million ÷ $5 million = 2 times, and the company's return on equity (ROE) of 20 percent, we have a comprehensive list of key valuation ratios for the company, all flowing from the fundamental valuation model.

Now let's examine how multiples work with actual companies. Consider IBM and Microsoft. If we look at these two companies for fiscal years 2010 and 2009, as we show in Table 7-3, we see the following:

- IBM is a larger company than Microsoft, as measured by revenues, but slightly larger in size than Microsoft in terms of assets.
- The market assigns a higher multiple to IBM stock for earnings, book value, EBIT, and EBITDA.
- The market assigns a higher multiple to Microsoft for revenues, as indicated with the P/S multiple.

One of the advantages of using multiples is that it doesn't matter what currency you are using: The multiple simply relates the market's valuation to a financial statement item, no matter the currency. Consider Anheuser-Busch Inbev, which is a Belgium beverage firm. Its global competitors include the Japanese beverage companies Kirin Holdings Co. and Asahi Group Holdings, and the French company, Danone. We can compare how the markets value these companies by comparing the multiples of these companies in their home markets:[40]

| | Multiple As of October 2011 | | | |
Company	P/E	P/S	M/B	P/CF
Anheuser-Busch Inbev	18.81	2.41	2.46	9.46
Kirin Holdings Co	42.70	0.44	0.95	5.24
Asahi Group Holdings	14.23	0.54	1.23	6.70
Danone	16.25	1.78	2.74	12.61
Industry	21.50	5.21	1.42	6.61

Source: *Reuters.com.*

Whereas Kirin Holdings receives the highest multiple based on earnings, Anheuser-Busch Inbev has the highest based on sales, and Danone has the highest multiple based on cash flow and book value. In all four cases, however, the price-to-sales multiple is less than the industry average; this industry average may be affected by smaller, relatively young companies that have high sales growth yet do not generate earnings and are perceived as valuable due to their future prospects.

[40] We should note that cross-country comparisons may be affected by accounting standards, which may differ across countries.

TABLE 7-3 IBM and Microsoft Multiples

	IBM		Microsoft	
Fiscal year	*2010*	*2009*	*2010*	*2009*
In millions				
Revenues	$99,871	$95,759	$69,943	$62,484
Total assets	$113,452	$109,022	$108,704	$86,113
Cash and equivalents	$10,661	$12,183	$9,610	$5,505
Book value of debt	$28,624	$26,100	$11,921	$5,939
Book value equity	$23,046	$22,637	$57,083	$46,175
Cash flow from operations	$19,549	$20,773	$26,994	$24,073
EBIT	$18,150	$17,011	$27,161	$24,167
EBITDA	$21,807	$20,784	$29,927	$26,840
Net income	$14,833	$13,425	$23,150	$18,760
Number of shares outstanding	1,287	1,341	8,593	8,927
Per Share				
Price per share	$146.76	$130.90	$26.00	$23.01
Book value per share	$17.91	$16.88	$6.64	$5.17
Sales per share	$77.60	$71.41	$8.14	$7.00
Cash flow from operations per share	$15.19	$15.49	$3.14	$2.70
EBIT per share	$14.10	$12.69	$3.16	$2.71
EBITDA per share	$16.94	$15.50	$3.48	$3.01
Earnings per share	$11.53	$10.01	$2.69	$2.10
Multiple				
P/E	12.734	13.075	9.651	10.949
M/B	8.196	7.754	3.914	4.449
P/S	1.891	1.833	3.194	3.287
P/CF	9.662	8.450	8.277	8.533
EV/EBIT	9.819	9.603	7.872	8.272
EV/EBITDA	8.173	7.860	7.144	7.448

Source of data: *Microsoft Corporation's 2010 10-K filing, IBM Corporation's 2010 10-K filing, and Yahoo! Finance.*

Not all these ratios are equally useful for every company. Cable companies, for example, usually sell on a value per unit of output, in their case, a value per subscriber because the more subscribers a cable company has, the more revenue it can generate. "Old-line" manufacturing companies generally sell on a market-to-book or P/E ratio basis because they tend to have stable earnings. Growth companies tend to sell on EBITDA or sales multiples. However, in all cases, these valuation multiples are simply shortcuts for the fundamental discounted cash flow valuation.

In a Recession, Buy Revenues, Not Earnings

The price-to-sales ratio tells you how many dollars of revenues you are buying for each dollar you pay for a stock.

The price-to-earnings ratio is the most popular metric for getting a quick read on how investors are valuing an individual stock or the overall market. The Standard & Poor's 500 index, for example, sells for 18 times latest 12-month earnings and at 11 and 10 times the consensus forecast for 2008 and 2009, respectively. The P/E ratio, however, has its limitations, especially in sharp economic downturns.

For example, of the Standard & Poor's 500 companies, 60 have posted losses over the latest 12 months. According to consensus estimates tabulated by Thomson IBES, security analysts expect 27 S&P companies to deliver losses in their current fiscal year. Analysts tend to be optimistic, so the actual number of S&P companies reporting fiscal losses will likely be higher—possibly much higher. Keep in mind that, at the onset of a downturn, a low P/E can be a warning of an impending collapse in earnings, not a sign of a cheap stock. Once earnings slip into negative territory, the P/E becomes a nonmeaningful, useless statistic.

The price-to-sales ratio (stock price divided by sales per share, or PSR) does not suffer such limitations. *Forbes* columnist and investment manager Kenneth Fisher has been a long-time proponent of the PSR.

In short, the PSR tells you how many dollars of revenues you are buying for each dollar you pay for a stock. If a stock has a PSR of 0.5 it means you are buying two dollars of revenues for each dollar of stock price.

PSRs can also tell you a great deal about the earning power of company. Supermarkets, for example, only make a few pennies of net profit for each dollar of revenue. The median PSR for large supermarket chains is only 0.2. In contrast, a high-margined business such as software has a median PSR of 3.1

Revenues, too, are not immune from slippage during a business slump but they are usually more resilient than earnings. It does not matter, of course, how good a deal you get investing in corporate revenues if management is unable eventually to turn a corporate revenue stream into profits. The trick is to seek out companies selling for low PSRs relative to their long-term history and/or industry average, where management seems capable of improving margins or restoring a money-losing business to profitability.

Steve Kichen, "In a Recession, Buy Revenues, Not Earnings," *Forbes.com*, November 10, 2008.

---

1. Why can the P/E ratio be viewed as a type of payback period?

2. What fundamental factors drive P/E ratios?

3. What other relative valuation multiples are useful in valuation?

Concept Review Questions

SUMMARY

- A value of a share of stock is the future value of future cash flows to that share. In terms of preferred and common stock, the value of a share is the present value of expected future dividends.

- The valuation of preferred stock is rather straightforward; we typically use the present value of a perpetuity formula to estimate the value of a share of preferred stock.

- Because the dividend rate on common stock is not set, but rather the amount and timing of dividends is left to the discretion of the board of directors, the valuation of a share of common stock is more complicated than the value of preferred stock. A useful model is the dividend discount model, assuming a constant growth in dividends. This model can be modified to consider multiple stages of growth, and other patterns of future dividends.

- A value of a share of stock can also be estimated by looking at how the market values comparable companies. Using the multiples of the market value of comparable companies' stocks to these companies' respective earnings, cash flows, sales, or other measure of performance, we can then apply these multiples, such as the price-earnings ratio, to value a company's stock.

- The constant growth version of the DDM is related to the fundamentals that affect stock values (i.e., future profitability and dividends, interest rates, and risk), which we can then associate with multiples.

FORMULAS/EQUATIONS

(7-1) $r = r_f + \text{Risk premium}$

(7-2) $P_p = \dfrac{D_p}{r_p}$

(7-3) $r_p = \dfrac{D_p}{P_p}$

(7-4) $P_0 = \dfrac{D_1}{(1 + r_e)^1} + \dfrac{D_2}{(1 + r_e)^2} + \cdots + \dfrac{D_n + P_n}{(1 + r_e)^n}$

(7-5) $P_0 = \dfrac{D_1}{(1 + r_e)^1} + \dfrac{D_2}{(1 + r_e)^2} + \cdots + \dfrac{D_\infty}{(1 + r_e)^\infty} = \sum\limits_{t=1}^{\infty} \dfrac{D_t}{(1 + r_e)^t}$

(7-6) $P_0 = \dfrac{D_0(1 + g)^1}{(1 + r_e)^1} + \dfrac{D_0(1 + g)^2}{(1 + r_e)^2} + \cdots + \dfrac{D_0(1 + g)^\infty}{(1 + r_e)^\infty}$

(7-7) $P_0 = \dfrac{D_0(1 + g)}{r_e - g} = \dfrac{D_1}{r_e - g}$

(7-8) $r_e = \dfrac{D_1}{P_0} + g$

(7-9) $P_0 = \dfrac{EPS_1}{r_e}$

(7-10) $P_0 = \dfrac{EPS_1}{r_e} + PVGO$

(7-11) $SGR = b \times ROE$

(7-12) $ROE = \text{Net profit margin} \times \text{Turnover ratio} \times \text{Leverage ratio}$

(7-13) $P_0 = \dfrac{D_1}{(1 + r_e)^1} + \dfrac{D_2}{(1 + r_e)^2} + \cdots + \dfrac{D_t + P_t}{(1 + r_e)^t}$

(7-14) $P_0 = \text{Estimated } EPS_1 \times \text{Justified P/E} = EPS_1 \times (P_0/EPS_1)$

(7-15) $\dfrac{P_0}{EPS_1} = \dfrac{P}{E} = \dfrac{D_1/EPS_1}{r_e - g}$

QUESTIONS AND PROBLEMS

Multiple Choice

1. Which of the following is a correct characterization of the cash flows of a bond and a stock?

	Bond	*Stock*
A.	Discretionary	Discretionary
B.	Discretionary	Legal obligation
C.	Legal obligation	Discretionary
D.	Legal obligation	Legal obligation

2. Which of the following is a correct characterization of the tax deductibility of payments by a company paying interest and dividends?

	Bond	*Stock*
A.	Deductible	Deductible
B.	Deductible	Not deductible
C.	Not deductible	Deductible
D.	Not deductible	Not deductible

3. The government Treasury bond yield is 4 percent, and the risk premium of the Boise Company is 6.5 percent. Boise's common stock's required rate of return is *closest* to:

   A. 0.26 percent.   B. 2.5 percent.   C. 10.5 percent.   D. 17 percent.

4. Bismarck Inc. just paid a dividend of $2.00 per share, which is expected to grow at a constant rate of 4.5 percent, indefinitely. The T-bond rate is 3 percent, and the risk premium of Bismarck's common stock is 6.5 percent. Bismarck Inc.'s value of a share of its common stock is *closest* to:

   A. $1.80.   B. $40.00.   C. $41.80.   D. $42.60.

5. Bloomfield Holdings recently paid an annual dividend this year of $1.50 per share, and its estimated long-term growth rate in dividends is 4 percent. The current market price of each share is $26. The implied rate of return on the share for Bloomfield stock is *closest* to:

   A. 6 percent.   B. 9.77 percent.   C. 10 percent.   D. 10.24 percent.

6. Firestone Co. just paid a dividend of $1.50 per share, and its EPS is $9.00. Its book value per share is $36. Firestone's sustainable growth rate is *closest* to:

   A. 0.69 percent.   B. 4.17 percent.   C. 16.67 percent.   D. 25 percent.

7. The sustainable growth rate is *negatively* related to:

   A. payout ratio.   B. retention ratio.   C. net profit margin.   D. leverage ratio or equity multiplier.

8. Which of the following is *not* a workable assumption in the constant growth dividend discount model?

   A. Dividends do not grow.
   B. Dividends are expected to decline at a constant rate.
   C. The required rate of return is less than the growth rate.

9. Using the method of multiples to value the equity of a private company, you've concluded that the comparable companies had price-earnings ratios around 15. If the private company's earnings are $3 million, the value of the private company's equity is *closest* to:

   A. $0.2 million.   B. $5 million.   C. $15 million.   D. $45 million.

10. A company with a current dividend of $2 per share, an earnings per share of $5, expected dividend growth of 5 percent, and a required rate of return of 8 percent, is expected to have a price-earnings ratio *closest* to:

    A. 5.25 times.   B. 13.33 times.   C. 14.00 times.   D. 70.00 times.

Practice Questions and Problems

7.1 Equity Securities

11. Describe preferred stock in terms of seniority, maturity, and dividends.

12. Compare how dividend income is taxed in the U.S. compared to interest income. Which is likely taxed at a lower rate?

13. What distinguishes preferred stock from common stock?

14. Why is it more likely that you can use the formula for the present value of a perpetuity to value a share of preferred stock than it is for a share of common stock?

15. If a share of preferred stock has a face value of $50 and a dividend rate of 3 percent per year, what is the annual dividend on this stock?

7.2 Dividend Discount Valuation of Equity

16. State the relationship that the required rate of return, the expected growth rate, and expected dividends have with the market value of a share of stock according to the constant growth dividend discount model.

17. Describe how to estimate the present value of growth opportunities (PVGO) and what it represents.

18. The Alabama Power Company had 6.48 million shares of its 5.2% preferred stock outstanding as of the end of 2011. The stated par value of each share is $25.
    A. What is the amount of dividend paid on each share, each quarter?
    B. If the stock is trading at $25.70, what is the required rate of return on this stock?
    C. If the required rate of return is 6 percent, what is the market value of this preferred stock per share?

19. Bayer AG paid the following dividend per share:

Year	Dividend
2004	€0.55
2005	€0.95
2006	€1.00
2007	€1.35
2008	€1.40
2009	€1.40
2010	€1.50

   A. What is the average annual growth rate of dividends from 2004 to 2010?
   B. What is the average annual growth rate of dividends from 2007 to 2010?

20. Fill in the missing information in the following table for preferred shares A through G:

Company	Value Per Share	Par Value	Required Rate of Return	Dividend Rate	Dividend
A		$100	8%	5%	$5.00
B	$33.33	$50	3%		
C	$90.00	$75			$4.50
D	$116.67	$50		14%	$7.00
E	$30.00	$30	7%		$2.10
F		$100	4%		$7.00
G			7%	9%	$9.00

21. Fill in the missing information in the following table pertaining to the value of common stocks using the constant growth dividend discount model:

Company	Value of a Share Today	Required Rate of Return	Dividend Growth	Current Dividend	Dividend Expected One Year from Today
A		15%		$4.50	$5.00
B	$600	3%	1%		
C	$70		5%		$8.00
D	$55			$10.00	$11.00
E		14%	6%	$9.50	
F		15%	0%		$18.00
G	$40	5%	–2%		

22. Determine the present value of growth opportunities for a company with a leading EPS of $1.85, a required rate of return of 8 percent, and a current stock price of $50.

23. The Ames Company's current dividend is $3.60. Dividends are expected to grow by 9 percent for years 1 to 3, by 6 percent for years 4 to 7, and by 2 percent thereafter. The required rate of return on the stock is 12 percent. What is the value of a share of stock today for the Ames Company?

24. The Charlotte Clothing Company's current dividend is $4.00. Dividends are expected to grow by 25 percent for years 1 to 3 and by 10 percent thereafter. The required rate of return on the stock is 15 percent. What is the current value of a share of stock of the Charlotte Clothing Company?

25. The Tallahassee Company's preferred shares have a par value of $50, and a dividend rate of 7 percent and trade at a price of $70. The St. Pete Company's preferred shares have a par value of $60 and a dividend rate of 4 percent and trade at a price of $45. Which company's preferred stock is riskier?

26. The Orono Company is expected to earn $10,000,000 next year. There are 2,000,000 shares outstanding, and the company uses a dividend payout ratio of 40 percent. The required rate of return for companies like the Orono Company is 8 percent. The current share price of Orono Company common stock is $75.
    A. What are the expected earnings per share for the Orono Company?
    B. What are the expected dividends per share for the Orono Company?
    C. What is the present value of growth opportunities for this company?

27. The Boulder Granite Company's most recent earnings were $300,000. From these earnings, it paid dividends on common equity totaling $175,000. There are 50,000 common shares outstanding. The ROE for Boulder is 12 percent. Determine the following:
    A. Earnings per share. Which can you calculate: leading or lagging EPS?
    B. Dividends per share
    C. Earnings retention ratio
    D. Sustainable growth rate

28. The Milliken Corporation has issued $1 million in preferred shares to investors with a 7.25 percent annual dividend rate on a par value of $100. Assuming the company pays dividends indefinitely and the required rate is 10.5 percent, calculate the value of the preferred stock.

29. The Tampa Company currently doesn't pay any dividends, but is expected to start paying dividends 5 years from today. The first dividend is expected to be $1.00 and to grow at 6 percent thereafter. The required rate of return for the company is 10 percent. What is the current value of a share of Tampa Company stock?

30. The Tucson Tomato Company's current dividend is $5. You expect the growth rate to be 0 percent for years 1 to 5, and 2 percent for years 6 to infinity. The required rate of return on this company's equity is 10 percent. Determine the following:

    A. The expected dividend at the end of year 5.

    B. The expected dividend at the end of year 6.

    C. The expected value of the stock at the end of year 5 (immediately after the year 5 dividend).

    D. The price of the stock today.

31. The Belvedere Butler Services, Inc.'s current dividend is $5. You expect the growth rate to be 8 percent for years 1 to 5, and 2 percent from years 6 to infinity. The required rate of return on this company's equity is 10 percent. Determine the following:

    A. The expected dividend at the end of year 5.

    B. The expected dividend at the end of year 6.

    C. The expected value of a share of the stock at the end of year 5 (immediately after the year 5 dividend).

    D. The value of a share of the stock today.

32. Victor Blazquez is interested in investing in the XML Software Company. XML's current dividend is $5.50, and XML shares are selling for $180. The required rate of return for companies like XML is 8 percent. Victor has conducted an extensive analysis of the company and believes that the dividend growth rate should be 5 percent.

    A. Should Victor buy the stock at $180? Why or why not?

    B. Do you expect the value of a share of the stock to stay at $180? Explain your answer.

 33. Consider a company that has common stock with a dividend this year of $1. The dividend is expected to grow at a rate of 10 percent per year for the next 5 years, and then grow at a rate of 3 percent per year thereafter. The required rate of return on this stock is 6 percent.

    A. Using a spreadsheet, calculate and graph the dividends on this stock for the current year and for each of the next 25 years.

    B. Using a spreadsheet, calculate and graph the value of the share of stock for the current year and for each of the next 25 years.

    C. Compare the graphs that you prepared for A and B. What is the relationship between these two graphs?

7.3 Using Multiples to Value Equity

34. What is the relationship between a company's sustainable growth rate and its return on equity?

35. What is the Molodovsky effect? What is the relevance of this effect on the interpretation of P/E ratios?

36. Consider a company with the following characteristics:

    • Book value per share of $4.00

    • Market value per share of $6.00

    • Number of shares of common stock outstanding of 5 million

    A. What is this company's market capitalization?

    B. What is this company's market-to-book ratio?

37. Consider a company that pays out 25 percent of its earnings in dividends, has dividends that are expected to grow at a rate of 5 percent per year, ad infinitum, and has a price-earnings ratio of 10 times. What is the required rate of return on this company's common stock?

38. Calculate the leading P/E ratio, given the following information: retention ratio = 0.6, required rate of return = 10 percent, and expected growth rate = 5 percent.

39. Athens, Inc. just paid a dividend of $4, and its current earnings per share is $5. The current Treasury bond rate is 3 percent, and Athens's risk premium is 12 percent. The net profit margin, asset turnover, and debt-to-equity ratio are 20 percent, 1.5 times, and 0.67, respectively. Calculate the sustainable growth rate for Athens, Inc.

40. The LMX Company is expected to pay a $2 dividend in one year. The required rate of return is 9 percent. The company uses a dividend payout ratio of 25 percent. Calculate the leading P/E ratio in the following cases:

   A. Expected growth rate = 4 percent

   B. Expected growth rate = 8 percent

   C. If a company is expected to have a constant dividend growth rate, do you expect the P/E ratio to change over time? Explain your answer.

 41. A financial analyst has completed a fundamental analysis of the PDP Company. PDP is a young company and expects to invest heavily in facilities and research and development during the next 5 years; it expects to reap the benefits of its research and development during years 6 to 10; however, it expects rivals to enter the market and margins and profitability to stabilize at a lower level after year 10. The details of the analysis are presented here:

Fundamental Analysis of the PDP Company

Period	Net Profit Margin	Turnover	Equity Multiplier	Dividend Payout Ratio
Years 1–5	1%	0.75	3.0	0.05
Years 6–10	15%	2.00	1.5	0.10
Years 11–?	5%	1.40	1.0	0.50

The current dividend for PDP is $3.00 and the required rate of return for this type of company is 15 percent. Determine the current stock value for a share of PDP stock.

Cases

Case 7.1 Big G Company

An analyst is concerned about the effect of errors in his estimates of the future dividend payout ratio for the Big G Company. Assume that the current dividend is $1, return on equity is fixed at 10 percent, and the required rate of return is 15 percent. Using a spreadsheet program, complete the following:

   A. Calculate the value of a share of stock today for dividend payout ratios ranging between 5 percent and 75 percent in 5 percentage point increments.

   B. Graph the relationship between the stock value and the dividend payout ratios.

   C. Describe the relationship between the stock value and the payout ratios. Is the percentage change in the stock price for a 5 percentage point change in dividend payout ratio constant?

Case 7.2 The Denver Company

The Denver Company is expected to pay a $1.50 dividend next year. Dividends are expected to grow at 3 percent forever, and the required rate of return is 7 percent.

   A. Calculate each of the following:

      1) The value of a share of Denver stock today.

      2) The expected dividend yield.

      3) The expected capital gains yield.

   B. In one year, immediately after the dividend is paid,

      1) What is the value of a share of the stock?

      2) What was the one-year holding period return?

      3) Looking forward one year, what are the expected dividend and capital gains yields?

   C. In year 10, immediately after the dividend is paid,

      1) What is the value of a share of the stock?

      2) What was the 1-year holding period return (year 9 to 10)?

      3) Looking forward 1 year, what are the expected dividend and capital gains yields?

D. Using a spreadsheet,

1) Calculate the dividends for years 1 through 30 into the future.

2) Calculate the expected price at the end of years 1 through 30 into the future.

3) Plot these dividends and prices starting today and extending through 30 years from today.

Case 7.3 Nova Lobster Company

The Nova Lobster Company (NLC) is a privately held lobster farming company. It has hired the Naslaan Consulting Company to help evaluate an offer for the company from Star Lobster Company. Currently NLC has a net income of $150,000 on sales of $350,000, and it processes 250,000 lobsters each year. The total assets are $2,500,000, and the book value of equity is $2,000,000. The company is the sole source of income for the owners, the Wong family, and consequently the dividend payout ratio is 65 percent. The risk-free rate is 2 percent, and the appropriate risk premium for this company is 5 percent.

A. There are three other publicly traded lobster farming companies. Summary data on those companies is presented here:

Company	SeaLobster	ToroLobster	AgriLobster
Price per share	$25	$10	$15
Number of shares outstanding	1,000	10,000	500,000
Market value of company per lobster processed	5	7	12
P/E	15	5	35

Given the data on these companies, determine the value of NLC. Discuss the strengths and weaknesses of the comparable companies' approach to valuation.

B. StarLobster believes that it can make several changes to the operations of NLC that will increase value. It believes that it can improve the net profit margins to 50 percent without changing the turnover ratio. It will also increase the equity multiplier (i.e., total assets divided by equity) to 1.50 and reduce the dividend payout ratio to 40 percent. What is the maximum price StarLobster should consider?

A SHORT PRIMER ON BUBBLES[41]

In 1711, the South Seas Company (SSC) was given a monopoly on all English trade to the South Seas, that is, South America.[42] Unfortunately, South America was largely under the control of Spain, and England was at war with Spain. Nevertheless, the hope was that in the ensuing peace, England would be able to dictate a freeing up of trade to the company's benefit. As it turns out, the peace would be to England's benefit, but not very much to the company's. Meanwhile, John Law, a Scottish promoter in France, had set up the Mississippi Company, which was draining investment from England to France. In response, the South Seas Company offered to have investors convert England's national debt into shares of the company. The company would pay a one-time fee to the government for this conversion and receive the fixed annual payments on the national debt. The certainty of receiving the interest payments would allow the company to borrow to fund its South Seas trade.

It was an audacious plan in an age of optimism and jubilation at England's defeat of both Spain and France. In April 1720, the government accepted the offer, and the stock price took off. It was clear that the plan could only be accepted if the stock price went up enough to encourage investors to convert their national debt into SSC equity. Consequently, the company issued shares on an installment basis. As the cash came in, the company lent it back so that investors could buy more shares. The stock took off and in doing so sucked in a whole group of neophyte investors.

It also spawned imitators. One of the most interesting of these declared that it was "a company for carrying on an undertaking of great advantage, but nobody was to know what it is." Prices soared, and small investors got in for fear of missing out. Sir Isaac Newton sold his stock in the SSC in April 1720 for a 100 percent gain. However, SSC's stock price rocketed up from 300 pounds to its peak of more than 1,000 pounds, and he bought back in. In August the bubble burst, and by September prices were back to 300 pounds. The *London Gazette* was full of bankruptcies, and Isaac Newton lost 20,000 pounds; philosophically, he made his famous statement, "I can calculate the motions of the heavenly bodies, but not the madness of people."

We have learned from this, haven't we? Leaving aside the Great Crash of 1929, there is the little matter of the Crash of 2000 and our recent experience with technology and Internet stocks. The most recent crashes stemmed from the high valuation of the equity market as a result of the long bull markets of the late 1990s.

Long bull markets pull in inexperienced investors who have unrealistic expectations. Over long periods, equity market average returns have exceeded 10 percent a year, which is not enough to get investors really excited. However, a couple of 25 percent plus years bring in the people who then come to expect 25 percent plus returns. Moreover, plenty of people are willing to tell them that they can get 25 percent returns and that this time it is different: It is a new world of investing with new metrics.[43]

---

[41] This appendix is based on Laurence Booth, "Investments, 'Alternative' Investments and Bubbles." *Advisor's Guide to New Investment Opportunities*, 2002, pp. 12–19.

[42] See Jim Harrison, "The Damn'd South Sea," *Harvard Magazine*, May–June 1999.

[43] The Ponzi scheme operated for 20 years by Bernard Madoff is an example of how people can be swayed to invest funds for outsized returns. A Ponzi scheme, basically, is paying returns to old investors with the funds of new investors. The Madoff scheme fell apart in December 2008, and Bernard Madoff was sentenced to prison for securities and mail fraud, among other felonies.

In the September 1999 issue of *Atlantic Monthly*, James Glassman and Kevin Hassett discussed the advice in their book that the Dow will go to 30,000. They stated (page 37), "Stocks were undervalued in the 1980s and 1990s and they are undervalued now. Stock prices could double, triple or even quadruple tomorrow and still not be too high." They went on to suggest (page 42), "A profound change has occurred in the attractiveness of stocks since the early 1980s, as investors have become more rational. The old limits of yields and P/Es do not apply anymore, if they ever did." And finally (page 56), "In truth there is no extra risk in stocks."[44]

It is a familiar refrain during times of speculative bubbles that this time it is different. After all, the little investors get in only after a run-up in prices, so it has to be "different this time," otherwise, they have missed the boat. On May 15, 1929, the *Outlook* and *Independent* remarked, "But apparently there has been a fundamental change in the criteria for judging security values. Widespread education of the public in the worth of equity securities has created a new demand." Similarly, before the correction in 1969, *Barron's* stated, "The failure of the general market to decline during the last three years despite its obvious vulnerability, as well as the emergence of new investment characteristics, has caused investors to believe that the U.S. has entered a new investment era to which old guidelines no longer apply."[45]

The fact is that "old guidelines" are perennial; the only thing that changes is that the old investors die off and a new generation has to learn the same old lessons. Does that 1720 English company that promised "carrying on of an undertaking of great advantage, but nobody to know what it is" sound familiar? It should. On January 25, 2000, Michael Lewis, the author of *Liar's Poker*, pointed out that an Internet company, NetJ.com, had filed statements with the U.S. Securities and Exchange Commission with the confession that "the company is not currently engaged in any substantial activity and has no plans to engage in any such activity in the foreseeable future." The company had $127,631 in accumulated losses and so little money on hand that the directors would have had to chip in to pay any filing costs to raise capital. The only snag was NetJ.com had a market capitalization of $22.9 million.

---

[44] They also go through an interesting valuation of Cisco (page 52), in which they state, "Using the standard formula for calculating a stock's present value according to the flow of cash it generates over time, we find that Cisco's PRP should be $399 a share. In other words, Cisco's price last June would need to sextuple. Its P/E would rise to 539 (No that's not a misprint)." As we read this, Cisco's price is $18.56. James Glassman and Kevin Hassett, "Dow 36,000," *Atlantic Monthly*, 284, no. 3 (September 1999).

[45] Quoted in Jim Stack, *The New Paradigm Era or Bubble* (Whitefish, MT: InvesTech Research, 1997).

PART 4

CAPITAL MARKET THEORY AND FINANCIAL MANAGEMENT

In this section of the text, we develop the key topics of risk, return, portfolio theory, asset pricing, and market efficiency. In Chapter 8, we discuss various measures of risk and methods for estimating the required rate of return for assets and portfolios. We provide a discussion of market efficiency and asset pricing in Chapter 9.

CHAPTER 8

RISK, RETURN, AND PORTFOLIO THEORY

Diversification   One of the most important elements to come out of academic research for investment management, financial management, and even personal finance, is the idea of diversification. Diversification is the idea that you can reduce risk by investing in investments whose returns are not in perfect synch with one another. The basic idea has been around for a very long time: Don't put all your eggs in one basket.

To illustrate how this works, consider the investment of $1 at the end of 2000 in either small corporate stocks or long-term government bonds:

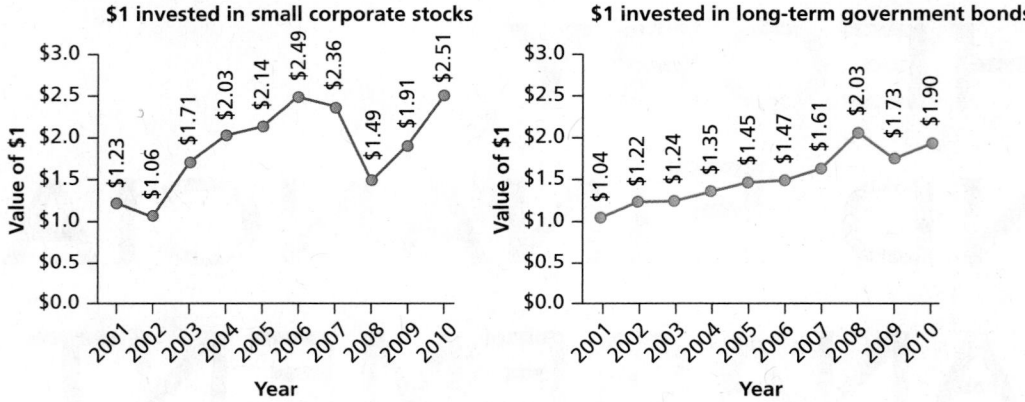

You would have more from the stock investment ($2.51 v. $1.90), but you would also have more variability in your portfolio's value. Now let's see what would you have had if you invested half your portfolio (that is, 50¢) in small corporate stocks and half in U.S. government bonds:

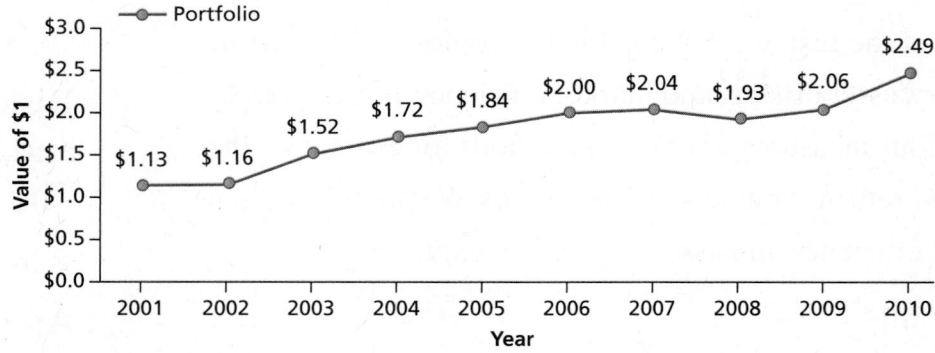

By investing in both stocks and bonds, you reduce the year-to-year fluctuations in your portfolio value because the returns on stocks and government bonds do not always move together. And, instead of $2.51, you wind up with $2.49, which is not much of a sacrifice to achieve less volatility. This is the beauty of diversification: *reduce risk without sacrificing much return.*

Source of data: *Morningstar.com* and *OnlyGold.com.*

Learning Outcomes

After reading this chapter, you should be able to:

LO 8.1 Distinguish between ex post and ex ante returns and calculate ex post and ex ante returns.

LO 8.2 Estimate expected returns and risk for individual assets.

LO 8.3 Describe what happens to risk and return when assets are combined in a portfolio.

LO 8.4 Explain what is meant by an "efficient frontier."

LO 8.5 Justify the importance of diversification for financial managers and investors.

Chapter Preview Financial management requires making decisions now that have uncertain payoffs in the future. This uncertainty is pervasive throughout financial decision making, which means that the financial manager must identify, measure, and manage risk.

In this chapter we describe ways to measure, analyze, and manage risk. Although our goal is to put this in the context of decision making within a business entity, we introduce the concepts, mathematics, and methods using generic assets and securities. We develop the basic terminology and concepts and then establish the relationship between risk and return. We also demonstrate the benefit from diversification, whether what we are diversifying is a portfolio of stocks or a collection of products in a business entity.

8.1 MEASURING RETURNS

What is risk? One definition is that **risk** is the chance or possibility that outcomes may not turn out as expected.[1] Recognizing that we often are not concerned about making too much money, but rather are concerned about losses, a common definition of risk is the possibility of incurring harm or the chance of a loss.

risk chance that future outcomes may not turn out as expected

Up until now, we have measured returns in term of the percentage change in a value over a period, considering not only the change in the value of something, but any associated cash flows as well. And we were often measuring these returns over some past period. When we are making financial decisions, however, we are regularly faced with estimating returns for some future period, rather than simply looking back on what has occurred. Therefore, we must distinguish between returns measured in the past and those estimated for a future period.

Ex Post Versus Ex Ante Returns

Let's first distinguish between an **ex post return** and an **ex ante return**. Ex post means "after the fact," so ex post returns are past or historical returns. Ex ante means "before the fact," so ex ante returns are expected returns. Advertisements for mutual funds and other investments show historical or ex post returns, and then in smaller print have a disclaimer that past returns do not necessarily reflect future, or ex ante, returns. Of course, what investors are interested in are these future or expected returns, but their judgment in terms of what they can reasonably expect is informed by what has happened in the past.

ex post return past or historical, return

ex ante return future or expected return

So how can investors measure these ex post or historical returns? As we saw in previous chapters, the return on an investment consists of two components: the income yield and the capital gain (or loss) yield. The **income yield** is the return earned in the form of a

income yield return earned by investors as a periodic cash flow

---

[1] We could distinguish between uncertainty and risk. In common use, these two are used interchangeably. However, the term *risk* is used when we are able to estimate probabilities associated with possible future outcomes, whereas we use the term *uncertainty* when we cannot.

periodic cash flow received by the investors. These cash flows are interest payments from bonds and dividends from equities. When we refer to this yield for a security, there are two types of yield: the cash flow yield, which is the ratio of the periodic cash flow to the security's price, and the capital yield, which is the ratio of the price change to the share price.[2] We show this in Figure 8-1 for the S&P 500 over time.

$$\text{Income yield} = \frac{CF_1}{P_0} \qquad (8\text{-}1)$$

where CF_1 is the expected cash flows to be received and P_0 is the purchase price today.

We provide the monthly dividend yield on the S&P Index in Figure 8-1 from 1871 through October 2011.[3] As you see in this figure, the dividend yields appear to have a cyclical pattern, but the trend in the last 30 years has been declining dividend yields.

The dividend yield may change for two reasons: (1) changes in the dividends per share, or (2) changes in the stock prices of the dividend-paying companies. The apparent increases in dividend yields in late 2008 and early 2009 are primarily from the decrease in the share prices—that is, the denominator in the dividend yield formula. But the dividend yield does not tell the whole story. The **capital gain** (or **capital loss**) component measures the appreciation (or depreciation) in the price of the asset from some starting price, usually the purchase price or the price at the beginning of the year. Dividing this gain or loss by the price produces the capital gain (or loss) yield or return, as expressed in Equation 8-2.

$$\text{Capital gain or loss return} = \frac{P_1 - P_0}{P_0} \qquad (8\text{-}2)$$

where P_1 is the selling price 1 year from today.

Creating a generic equation for a return that we could apply to stocks, bonds, or any other asset, we add the income yield and the capital gain (or loss) yield together to get the

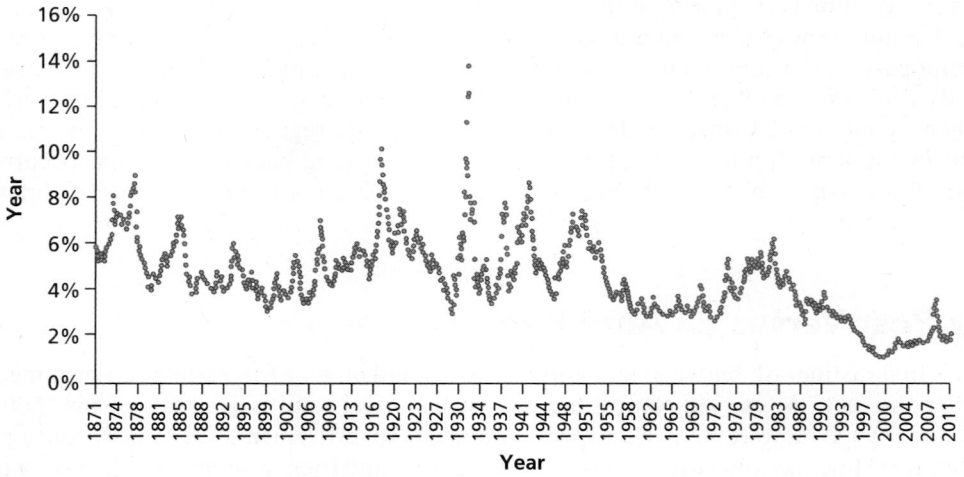

FIGURE 8-1   S&P 500 Monthly Dividend Income Yields, 1871 Through October 2011

Source of data: *Robert Shiller, www.yale.edu.*

---

[2] When we refer to this yield for a bond, there are several types of yields: the current yield, which is the ratio of the annual interest to the current bond price, the yield to maturity, which is the internal rate of return on the bond, and the yield to call, which is the internal rate of return on a callable bond assuming the bond is called at the first opportunity.

[3] The dividend yield depicted here is measured as D_0/P_0, i.e., using dividends paid over the last 12 months, not the expected dividends.

complete picture of the return from investing in bonds versus common shares. The **total return** is the sum of the income yield and the capital gain yield:

total return income yield plus the capital gain (or loss) yield

$$\text{Total return} = \text{Income yield} + \text{capital gain (or loss) yield}$$

$$\text{Total return} = \frac{CF_1}{P_0} + \frac{P_1 - P_0}{P_0} = \frac{CF_1 + P_1 - P_0}{P_0} \qquad (8\text{-}3)$$

Suppose a stock was purchased a year ago for $25 and is currently worth $30. If the stock paid a dividend of $1 at the end of the year, then:

- the total return is ($30 − 25 + 1) ÷ $25 = 24 percent,
- the capital yield is ($30 − 25) ÷ $25 = 20 percent, and
- the income yield is $1 ÷ $25 = 4 percent.

Consider another example, using the stock price and dividends for IBM Corporation. At the end of 2009, IBM had a stock price of $130.90 and at the end of 2010 IBM had a stock price $146.76. During 2010, IBM paid four dividends, totaling $2.50. The return on IBM stock for 2010 is:

$$\text{Total return}_{2010} = \frac{\$2.50}{\$130.90} + \frac{\$146.76 - 130.90}{\$130.90} = 1.91\% + 12.12\% = 14.03\%$$

In other words, in 2010 IBM had a dividend yield of 1.91 percent and a capital yield of 12.12 percent, for a total return of 14.02 percent. During 2011, a share of IBM stock received a dividend of $2.90 and the closing price for 2011 was $183.88. Therefore, IBM's return for 2011 is:

$$\text{Total return}_{2011} = \frac{\$2.90}{\$146.76} + \frac{\$183.88 - 146.76}{\$146.76} = 1.98\% + 25.30\% = 27.28\%$$

We provide the total return, indicating the dividend and capital components, for the S&P 500 from 1970 through 2010 in Figure 8-2. As you can see in this graph, in most years the dividend component is a small part of the return on the S&P 500. However, in some years, such as 1994, the dividend yield is a substantial part of the return, and in other years, such as 2000–2002, and 2008, the dividend yield is a small offset of the large capital loss.

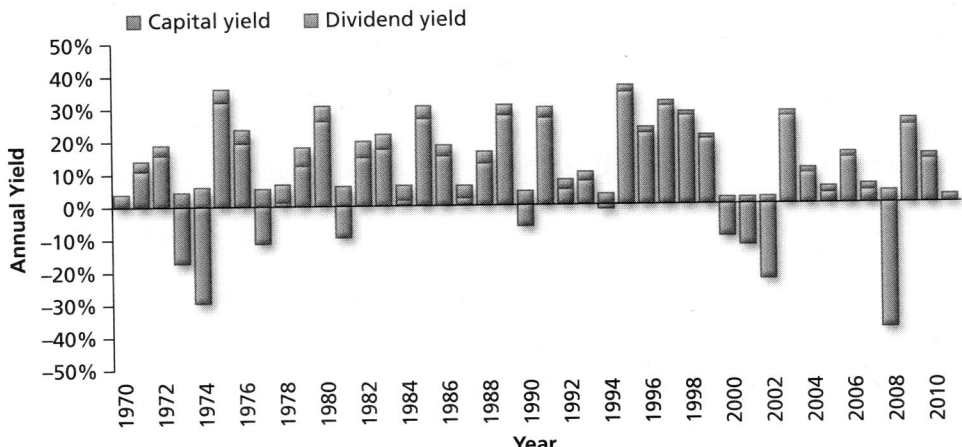

FIGURE 8-2 Dividend and Capital Gain or Loss Components of the Return on the S&P 500 Index, 1970–2011

Source of data: *Standard and Poor's, www.standardandpoors.com,* and *Robert Shiller, www.yale.edu.*

EXAMPLE 8.1

Calculating Returns

PROBLEM

Estimate the income yield, capital gain (or loss) yield, and total return for the following securities over the past year:

1. An investment in a security of $990 that is currently selling for $995 and provides a cash flow to the investor of $60 at the end of each year.
2. A stock that was purchased for $20, provided an annual dividend of $1 and is currently worth $19.50.

Solution

1. $CF_1 = 0.06 \times \$1,000 = \$60$; $P_0 = \$990$; $P_1 = \$995$

   Income yield $= \$60/\$990 = 0.0606 = 6.06\%$

   Capital gain return $= (\$995 - \$990) \div \$990 = 0.0051 = 0.51\%$

   Total return $= 6.06\% + 0.51\% = 6.57\%$

   Or, total return $= (\$60 + 995 - 990) \div \$990 = 0.0657 = \mathbf{6.57\%}$

2. $CF_1 = \$1.00$; $P_0 = \$20$; $P_1 = \$19.50$

   Income yield $= \$1/\$20 = 0.0500 = 5.00\%$

   Capital loss return $= (\$19.50 - 20.00) \div \$20 = -0.0250 = -2.50\%$

   Total return $= 5.00\% - 2.50\% = 2.50\%$

   Or, total return $= (\$1 + 19.50 - 20) \div \$20 = 0.0250 = \mathbf{2.50\%}$

When calculating a holding period return on a stock or a bond, it does not matter whether or not the stock or bond is sold in calculating the rate of return. This may seem obvious to most people, but psychologists have observed that people make different decisions if they own something than if they don't. For example, people will keep something for years because it cost $100 and is "valuable," even after they see the identical thing in a flea market selling for $1 and yet wouldn't buy it for $1. Owning assets includes an attachment effect, and with such an attitude, many people refuse to accept capital losses in the total return calculation until they actually sell the asset and realize them. Until then, people refer to them as a **paper loss**, with the implication that they are not real. This attitude is reinforced by the tax rules: Capital gains and losses are only taxable on realization.

paper loss capital loss that people do not accept as losses until they actually sell and realize them

A second important point is that whether or not we include paper gains and losses, in part, depends on our investment horizon. For example we can look at rates of return over daily, weekly, monthly, annual, or even longer periods. A **day trader** is someone who buys and sells based on intraday price movements. In that case, the total return for a day's trading includes the effect of capital gains and losses daily and sometimes over even shorter periods. In contrast, most people review their investments less frequently, perhaps quarterly or sometimes annually. For them the intraday price variability and total return are not as big a concern. What is of concern is the total return over, say, a quarter or a year. They are much less concerned about rates of return over shorter periods or the paper losses that are involved.[4]

day trader someone who buys and sells based on intraday price movements

[4] This brings to mind the philosophical question, Does a falling tree in a forest make a noise if there is no one there to hear it? Similarly, does a daily total return matter to an investor who only reviews his or her investments once a month?

The contrary view is that investors have to **mark to market** the prices of all financial securities over the relevant investment horizon. This means that investors always carry securities at the current market value regardless of whether they sell them. As a result, the total return includes the effect of paper gains and losses on securities not yet sold. This view is based on the basic opportunity cost argument: What is the alternative use for the funds tied up in the investment? Clearly, an investor cannot sell the security at its historical cost; he or she can sell at the current market value, and this is the value that can be reinvested elsewhere. We focus on the mark to market and consider the total return as including paper gains and paper losses over the relevant investment horizon because this reflects the economic value of past investment decisions.

Measuring Average Returns

How can we measure these ex post or historical returns? Two often-used statistical measures are the arithmetic mean and the geometric mean. The **arithmetic mean** or **arithmetic average** is commonly used to summarize data. We calculate the arithmetic mean return as the sum of all the returns divided by the total number of observations, as we express in Equation 8-4:

$$\text{Arithmetic mean return} = \frac{\sum_{i=1}^{n} r_i}{n} \qquad (8\text{-}4)$$

arithmetic mean or **arithmetic average** sum of all observations divided by the total number of observations

where r_i is the individual returns for period i, and n is the total number of observations.

The **geometric mean**, in contrast, measures the average or compound growth rate over multiple periods. For investments, this is the growth rate in the value invested or equivalently the compound rate of return:

geometric mean average or compound growth rate over multiple time periods

$$\text{Geometric mean return} = \sqrt[n]{(1 + r_1) \times (1 + r_2) \times (1 + r_3) \times \ldots \times (1 + r_n)} - 1 \quad (8\text{-}5)$$

or, equivalently,

$$\text{Geometric mean return} = [(1 + r_1) \times (1 + r_2) \times (1 + r_3) \times \ldots \times (1 + r_n)]^{1/n} - 1$$

Consider a set of returns on two stocks:

Year	Stock 1	Stock 2
1	5%	5%
2	2%	−1%
3	3%	10%
4	2%	−3%
5	4%	5%

The arithmetic mean of both stocks' returns is 3.2%. The geometric mean return for Stock 1 is:

$$\text{Geometric mean return of Stock 1} = [1.05 \times 1.02 \times 1.03 \times 1.02 \times 1.04]^{1/5} - 1 = 3.193\%$$

The geometric mean return for Stock 2 is:

$$\text{Geometric mean return of Stock 2} = [1.05 \times 0.99 \times 1.10 \times 0.97 \times 1.05]^{1/5} - 1 = 3.095\%$$

Notice that the geometric mean is less than the arithmetic average. This will always be the case unless the returns are identical. The more the returns vary, the bigger the difference between the arithmetic and geometric means.

EXAMPLE 8.2

Calculating the Arithmetic Average and the Geometric Mean

PROBLEM

Estimate the arithmetic mean and the geometric mean for the following returns:

Observation	Return
1	4.3%
2	3.2%
3	5.6%
4	10.5%
5	−7.6%

Solution

$$\text{Arithmetic mean} = (0.043 + 0.032 + 0.056 + 0.105 - 0.76) \div 5 = 16 \div 5 = \textbf{3.20\%}$$

$$\text{Geometric mean} = [1.043 \times 1.032 \times 1.056 \times 1.105 \times 0.924]^{1/5} - 1$$

$$= (1.1605455)^{1/5} - 1$$

$$= 1.0302 - 1 = 0.0302 \text{ or } \textbf{3.02\%}$$

We report the arithmetic and geometric average annual rates of return on the S&P 500 over various intervals of time in Table 8-1. These returns assume that the investor buys and holds the security for each year, but using different starting points in time. Note that we provide the standard deviation of the annual returns in the last row of Table 8-1. The standard deviation measures the "typical" variation of the return: The larger the standard deviation, the more variable the return.[5] The squared standard deviation is the variance. Approximately, the difference between the arithmetic and geometric return is half this variance.

As we indicated before, the more variable the annual returns, the bigger the difference between the arithmetic and geometric measures of return. Looking again at Table 8-1, the biggest difference is for the more recent intervals of time. So when should we use the arithmetic mean to describe the average return from an investment? And when should we use the geometric mean to describe the average return from an investment? The answer depends on what we are trying to determine.

TABLE 8-1   Average and Standard Deviations of Monthly Returns, 20 Years Ending June 2010

	5 Years Ending June 2010	10 Years Ending June 2010	20 Years Ending June 2010
Arithmetic average monthly return	2.049%	1.673%	2.623%
Geometric average monthly return	0.964%	1.578%	2.548%
Standard deviation of monthly returns	4.725%	4.364%	3.877%

Source of data: *Robert Shiller, Yale University.*

---

[5] Remember from statistics that the standard deviation for a sample of observations is the square root of the variance. The variance is the sum of the squared deviations of each observation from the mean, divided by the number of observations less one.

The arithmetic mean is appropriate when we are trying to estimate the typical return for a given period, such as a year. So if we wanted to know the best estimate for the rate of return over the next year, we would use the arithmetic mean of the annual rates of return because, by definition, this measures the average annual rate of return. We use the geometric mean when we are interested in determining the "true" average rate of return over multiple periods, for instance, if we wanted to know how our investment (and wealth) will grow over time. We use the geometric mean because it measures the compound rate of growth in our investment value over multiple periods. In this sense, the difference between the arithmetic mean and geometric mean is dependent on the relevant investment horizon.

Consider an investment in a stock that pays no dividend. You purchase the stock initially for $20 per share, and the stock has the following values over the 3-year holding period:

Year	Price of the Stock
Initial	$20
1	$25
2	$26
3	$20

What is the return on this investment? Let's first calculate the return each year:

Year	Price of the Stock	Annual Return
Initial	$20	
1	$25	25.000%
2	$26	4.000%
3	$20	–23.077%

What is the average annual return on this stock? By comparing the initial value with the value at the end of 3 years, we see that there is no return—the stock is worth the same at the end of three years as initially. If we calculate the arithmetic average of the annual returns, we end up with 1.974 percent. If, on the other hand, we calculate the geometric mean return, we have 0 percent, which confirms our basic comparison of initial and at-the-end-of-3-years values:

Year	Price of the Stock	Annual Return		1 + Annual Return
Initial	$20			
1	$25	25.000%		1.25000
2	$26	4.000%		1.04000
3	$20	–23.077%		0.76923
		Sum = 5.923%	Product =	1.00000
		Arithmetic mean = 1.974%	Geometric mean =	0.000%

Why do the arithmetic mean return and the geometric mean return differ? The arithmetic mean simply averages the annual rates of return without taking into account that the amount invested varies across time. For this reason, the geometric mean is a better average return estimate when we are interested in the rate of return performance of an investment over time.

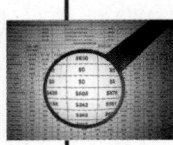

SPREADSHEET APPLICATION: MEANS

Spreadsheets have built-in functions for both the arithmetic mean and the geometric mean:

Arithmetic mean: = AVERAGE(values)

Geometric mean: = GEOMEAN(values)

When working geometric with returns, or any values less than 1.0, you have to take care to add one to the values; the spreadsheet function will not do this automatically.

Consider the case of calculating the mean for the following returns:

	A	B
	Observation	*Return*
1		
2	1	5%
3	2	1%
4	3	0%
5	4	−3%
6	5	5%

We calculate the arithmetic mean using = AVERAGE(B2:B6).

For the geometric mean, we first add one, then calculate the geometric mean, and then subtract one:

	A	B	C
	Observation	*Return*	*Return + 1*
1			
2	1	5%	1.05
3	2	1%	1.01
4	3	0%	1.00
5	4	−3%	0.97
6	5	5%	1.05

And we calculate the geometric mean using = GEOMEAN(C2:C6) − 1. Alternatively, we could use = (PRODUCT(C2:C6)^(1/5)) − 1.

Estimating Expected Returns

Although it is important to be able to estimate the ex post returns realized from past investments, financial managers are generally interested in the returns they expect to realize from an investment made today. In practice, the **expected return** is often estimated based on historical averages, but the problem is that there is no guarantee that

expected return
estimated future return

the past will repeat itself. For example, 1938 to 2009 included World War II (1939–45), a period of significant inflation (1970s and into the 1980s), a recession in the early 1990s that followed the 1987 stock market collapse and the savings and loan crisis, and the 2007–08 financial crisis. For investors interested in expected returns, such events as these can have unexpected effects.

An alternative approach is to use all available information to assess the most likely values under various future scenarios, and then attach probabilities to the likelihood of each occurring. When this approach is used, the expected value is estimated as the weighted average of the expected outcomes under each scenario, where the weights correspond to the probabilities of each scenario actually occurring:

$$\text{Expected value} = \sum_{i=1}^{n} (\text{outcome}_i \times \text{probability}_i) \qquad (8\text{-}6)$$

where outcome$_i$ is the likely outcome (in this case, the return on the investment) in scenario i, and probability$_i$ is the probability of state i occurring.[6]

Suppose you have two possible returns on an investment:

Scenario	Probability of Occurrence	Return on Investment
Outcome 1	60%	15%
Outcome 2	40%	–5%
	100%	

The expected return is the weighted average of the possible returns, where the weights are the probabilities:

Scenario	Probability of Occurrence	Return on Investment	Probability × Return on Investment
Outcome 1	60%	15%	0.09
Outcome 2	40%	–5%	–0.02
		Expected return, $E(r)$ =	0.07

We calculate the expected return by weighting the possible returns by the probabilities. Where do these probabilities come from? For example, economists might make estimates of different economic growth scenarios for the upcoming year, and then security analysts will estimate the prospects for each firm. Consider the distribution of the annual returns for the S&P 500, as we show in Figure 8-3. Though the past is not a precise forecaster of the future, an analyst could use this information on historical frequencies to formulate an estimate of the likelihood of monthly returns in the future.

[6] If we are dealing with returns, we often express this formula as $E(r) = \sum (r_i \times p_i)$, where E(r) is the expected return and r_i is the return in scenario i.

EXAMPLE 8.3

Estimating Expected Values

PROBLEM

Consider the expected cash flows from a project, in millions of dollars:

Scenario	Probability	Possible Outcome (in millions)
High	10%	$100
Medium	60%	$50
Low	30%	$20

What is the expected cash flow for this project?

Solution

Scenario	Probability	Possible Outcome (in millions)	Probability-weighted Outcome
High	10%	$100	$10
Medium	60%	$50	30
Low	30%	$20	6
		Expected cash flow =	$46

Therefore, the expected cash flow from this project is $46 million.

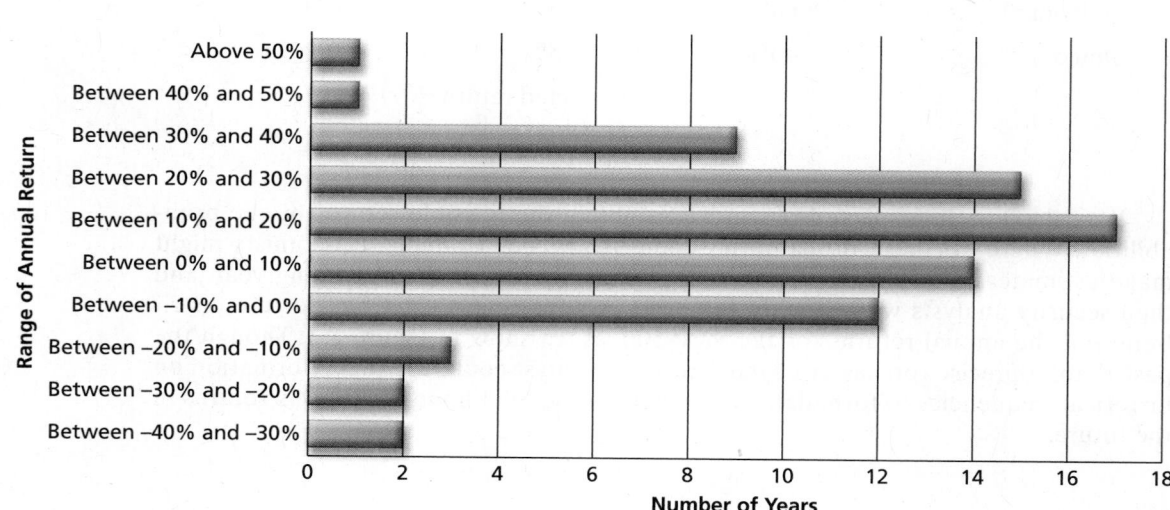

FIGURE 8-3 Distribution of Annual Returns on the S&P 500 Index

Source of data: *Standard and Poor's, www.standardandpoors.com*

There are pros and cons to each method for determining expected rates of return. For short-term forecasts the scenario-based approach makes more sense because where we are today has a huge bearing on what is likely to happen over a short period. However, for longer-run forecasts, the historical approach tends to be better because it reflects what actually happens even if it was not expected. In the next sections, we will use the scenario-based approach.

Concept Review Questions

1. What is the difference between ex ante and ex post returns?

2. Why does the income and capital gains component of the total return differ between common shares and bonds?

3. Why is the geometric mean return a better estimate of long-run investment performance than the arithmetic mean return?

8.2 MEASURING RISK

We have already touched on *risk* several times. Risk is the probability of incurring harm, and for financial managers harm generally means losing money or earning an inadequate rate of return. In the rest of this chapter, we use *risk* to mean the probability that the actual return from an investment is less than the expected return. This means that the more variable the possible return, the greater the risk. We normally see a trade-off between risk and return: Assets offering higher expected rates of return tend to be riskier than those offering a lower rate of return.

The Standard Deviation: Ex Post

Measuring risk requires capturing the variability or dispersion of possible outcomes. One measure of dispersion is the range. The **range** is the difference between the highest value and the lowest value, and therefore it does not capture the variability of returns *between* these two values. However, a more common measure of risk is the **standard deviation**, which uses all the observations and provides a measure of how disperse the observations are from the average. When we are dealing with a sample of observations using information that has occurred (that is, ex post), we can also refer to this standard deviation as the **ex post standard deviation**.

range measure of dispersion calculated as the difference between the maximum and minimum values

standard deviation measure of risk; measure of dispersion

   We often look back on historical returns to gauge the risk to expect in the future. If σ is the standard deviation, $\bar{x}$ is the average return, x_i is the observation in year i, and N is the number of observations, we calculate the standard deviation for a series of historical or ex post returns or cash flows as:

ex post standard deviation measure of risk for a set of observations

$$\text{Ex post standard deviation} = \sqrt{\frac{\sum_{i=1}^{N}(x_i - \bar{x})^2}{N - 1}} \qquad (8\text{-}7)$$

This is the sample standard deviation, where the sample consists of N observations on returns, cash flows, or other measureable outcome. The term inside the square root sign in Equation 8-7 is the variance, which we denote as σ^2. Therefore, the standard deviation is the square root of the variance, and, conversely, the variance is the square of the standard deviation. We focus on the standard deviation because it is easier to interpret: The standard deviation for a return series is expressed in the same units as the returns, that is, as a percentage. In contrast, the variance is expressed in units of squared returns, which makes its interpretation less obvious.

variance standard deviation squared; denoted as σ^2 and expressed in units of squared units

EXAMPLE 8.4

Calculating the Ex Post Standard Deviation

PROBLEM

Consider the cash flows generated from each of the five divisions of Company X for this past fiscal year, in millions of dollars:

Division	Cash Flow (in millions)
1	$500
2	$100
3	$25
4	$400
5	$300

What is the standard deviation of these cash flows?

Solution

Division	Cash Flow (in millions)	Deviation from the Mean	Squared Deviation
1	$500	$235	55,225
2	100	–165	27,225
3	25	–240	57,600
4	400	135	18,225
5	300	35	1,225
Sum	$1,325		Sum = 159,500
Mean	$265		

The standard deviation is the square root of 159,500 / 4 or $199.6873.

SPREADSHEET APPLICATIONS: THE STANDARD DEVIATION

Spreadsheets make it easy to calculate the standard deviation. Consider the following observations:

	A	B
1	*Observation*	*Return*
2	1	5%
3	2	1%
4	3	0%
5	4	–3%
6	5	5%

We calculate the standard deviation using = STDEV(B2:B6), and the variance using = VAR(B2:B6).

The Standard Deviation: Ex Ante

Though an ex post standard deviation is useful in gauging risk, what we really need for decision making, if we can formulate expectations about the asset's future cash flows or returns, is an **ex ante standard deviation**; that is, a standard deviation that is formulated based on *expectations* about the future. We can use Equation 8-8 to estimate the scenario-based standard deviation.

$$\text{Ex ante standard deviation} = \sqrt{\sum_{i=1}^{n} p_i (r_i - E(r))^2} \tag{8-8}$$

ex ante standard deviation weighted standard deviation, with the likelihood of each occurrence used as the weight applied to the squared deviation from the expected value; a forward-looking measure of risk

We refer to this as the ex ante measure because we are explicitly taking into account updated probabilities of future events happening. In this application, r_i is one of the possible outcomes and $E(r)$ is the calculated expected value of the possible outcomes. As you can see in this equation, the standard deviation is the result of weighting the squared deviations from the expected value by the likelihood of the outcome occurring.

Consider our previous example, with an expected return of 7 percent, which we calculated based on the possible outcomes and the likelihood of the possible outcomes:

Scenario	Probability of Occurrence	Return on Investment
Outcome 1	60%	15%
Outcome 2	40%	–5%
	100%	

We calculate the variance and standard deviation of the variance by applying Equation 8-8:

Scenario	Probability of Occurrence p_i	Possible Return on Investment r_i	Probability × Return $p_i \times r_i$	Deviation: Return less Expected Return $(r_i - E(r_i))$	Deviation Squared $(r_i - E(r_i))^2$	Deviation Squared, × Probability $p_i(r_i - E(r_i))^2$
Outcome 1	60%	15%	0.09000	0.08000	0.00640	0.00384
Outcome 2	40%	–5%	–0.02000	–0.12000	0.01440	0.00576
		Expected return, $E(r) = 0.07000$			Variance = 0.00960	

Standard deviation = 0.09798

where the standard deviation is $\sqrt{0.0096} = 0.0978$.

	Ex Post Standard Deviation	Ex Ante Standard Deviation
Perspective	Looking back on what has occurred.	Looking forward to what may happen.
Observations	Observations from the past.	Possible outcomes in the future.
Calculation of the variance	Average of the squared deviations of observations from the mean of the observations.	Weighted average of the squared deviations of possible outcomes from the expected outcome, where the weights are the probabilities.
Formula for the standard deviation (σ)	Ex post $\sigma = \sqrt{\dfrac{\sum\limits_{i=1}^{N}(x_i - \bar{x})^2}{N-1}}$	Ex ante $\sigma = \sqrt{\sum\limits_{i=1}^{n} p_i(r_i - E(r))^2}$

EXAMPLE 8.5

Estimating the Ex Ante Standard Deviation

PROBLEM

Estimate the standard deviation of the possible cash flows of a company based on possible economic climates:

	Probability	Possible Cash Flow (in millions)
Good	25%	$1,250
Fair	55%	$1,000
Poor	20%	$750

Solution

	Probability	Possible Outcome (in millions)	Probability-weighted Outcome (in millions)	Deviation from Expected Cash Flow (in millions)	Squared Deviation	Probability-weighted Squared Deviation
Good	25%	$1,250	$313	$238	56,406	14,102
Fair	55%	$1,000	$550	–$13	156	86
Poor	20%	$750	$150	–$263	68,906	13,781
		Expected cash flow = $1,013			Variance = 27,969

Standard deviation = $\sqrt{27{,}969}$ = $167.239

Concept Review Questions

1. Why is the range sometimes a poor measure of risk?

2. What is the difference between a scenario-based (probability) estimate of risk versus a historical data-based estimate of risk?

3. Why would we sometimes want to use scenario-based risk measures rather than the standard deviation of actual returns over a long period?

8.3 EXPECTED RETURN AND RISK FOR PORTFOLIOS

A **portfolio** is a collection of assets that are combined and considered a single asset. In the case of securities, a portfolio is a collection of stocks, bonds, and other financial assets. In the case of a company, a portfolio is the collection of the products or services the company produces. A portfolio therefore may refer to the holdings of a single investor, as well as to holdings that are managed as a unit by one or more portfolio managers on behalf of their clients, or a corporation or other business entity.

It is a basic proposition in finance that assets should be managed within a portfolio rather than individually because risk-reduction gains are possible by combining assets into a portfolio. We will be using the statistical ideas that we have just discussed to explore portfolio theory and the implications for financial managers. The basic idea is as simple as the old adage "Don't put all your eggs in one basket": Investors should diversify their investments so that they are not unnecessarily exposed to a single negative event. Modern portfolio theory (MPT) takes this basic idea and shows how to form portfolios with the highest possible expected rate of return for any given level of risk. First, we examine how to calculate the expected return and risk of a portfolio.

portfolio collection of assets, such as stocks and bonds, that are combined and considered a single asset

Calculating a Portfolio's Return

The expected return on a portfolio is simply the weighted average of the expected returns on the individual assets in the portfolio. Let $E(r_p)$ represent the expected return on the portfolio, $E(r_i)$ the expected return on asset i, and w_i the portfolio weight of asset i.[7] The expected return on a portfolio is:

$$E(r_p) = \sum_{i=1}^{n} (w_i \times E(r_i)) \tag{8-9}$$

The portfolio weight of a particular asset is the percentage of the portfolio's total value that is invested in that asset. These weights sum to one because 100 percent of the portfolio must be invested in something, even if it is in cash.

Consider investments X and Y, which have three different possible outcomes: Good, OK, and Bad:

Scenario	Probability of Possible Outcome	Possible Return on Investment X	Possible Return on Investment Y
Good	35%	15.0%	4.0%
OK	55%	10.0%	6.0%
Bad	10%	−5.0%	8.0%

---

[7] Confused about $E(r)$ and $E(r_i)$? It's easy to get confused. Unfortunately, in the realm of portfolio theory and statistics we have many expected returns to contend with. Here is the difference: When we are dealing with a probability distribution, the expected value is the measure of central tendency (a type of weighted average) for that probability distribution. When we are dealing with portfolio returns, these are all expected returns for the individual assets (hence, the subscript i).

The expected return on both investments is the same, 10.5 percent:

Scenario	Probability of Possible Outcome	Possible Return on Investment X	Probability-weighted Return on Investment X	Possible Return on Investment Y	Probability-weighted Return on Investment Y
Good	35%	15.0%	5.25%	4.0%	1.40%
OK	55%	10.0%	5.50%	6.0%	3.30%
Bad	10%	–5.0%	–0.50%	8.0%	0.80%
	100.00%		$E(r_X) = 10.25\%$		$E(r_Y) = 5.50\%$

Now consider a portfolio that has these two investments, Investment X and Investment Y, with $150,000 and $250,000 invested, respectively:

Investment	Amount Invested	Expected Return
Investment X	$150,000	10.25%
Investment Y	250,000	5.50%
Total	$400,000	

The weights associated with each investment are:

Investment X: $150,000 ÷ 400,000 = 37.5%
Investment Y: $250,000 ÷ 400,000 = 62.5%

The expected return on the portfolio comprised of investments X and Y is therefore 7.281 percent:

Investment	Weight w_i	Expected Return $E(r_i)$	$w_i \times E(r_i)$
Investment X	37.5%	10.25%	0.03844
Investment Y	62.5%	5.50%	0.03438
	100.0%	$\sum_{i=1}^{2}[w_i \times E(r_i)] = 0.07282$	

We can simplify the expected return formula in the two-asset case to make it more informative. Let us define w as simply the weight placed on asset X, so that $(1 - w)$ is the weight placed on asset Y. The expected return on X is 10.25 percent and the expected return on Y is 5.5 percent. In this case, we can rearrange the expected return for a two-asset portfolio, $E(r_p)$:

$$E(r_p) = E(r_Y) + w[E(r_X) - E(r_Y)] \qquad (8\text{-}10)$$

For example, if we place a weight of 0 in X, then by definition 100 percent is invested in Y, and we expect to earn 5.5 percent, the expected return on Y. Conversely, if we invest 100 percent in X and nothing in Y, then we expect to earn 10.25 percent. Incrementally, as we increase w and put more money (weight) in X, then the return on the portfolio approaches 10.25 percent.

EXAMPLE 8.6

Estimating the Expected Portfolio Return

PROBLEM

Consider a company that has two divisions: Division One, with an expected return of 25 percent, and Division Two, with an expected return of 30 percent. The total value of the company is $500 billion, $300 billion attributed to Division One and $200 billion attributed to Division Two. What is the expected return on this company?

Solution

The company is a portfolio comprised of two divisions. The expected return on this company is the weighted average of the expected returns on the two divisions, or 27%:

Division	Value (in billions)	Weight	Expected Return	Weighted Expected Return
One	$300	60%	25%	15%
Two	200	40%	30%	12%
	$500		Portfolio return = 27%	

We graph this relationship between the weights and the expected return in Figure 8-4. Note that the graph sets the base return at 10.5 percent, where nothing invested in X, and then increases to 10.25 percent as we invest more and more in X.[8]

Regardless of the number of assets held in a portfolio or the portfolio weights, the expected return on the portfolio is *always* a weighted average of the expected return on each individual asset. However, this is *not* the case for the portfolio standard deviation because we must account for correlations, or comovements, among the individual asset returns included in the portfolio, which in turn affect the variability in total portfolio returns. Therefore, the standard deviation for a portfolio will reflect the weighted impact of the individual assets' standard deviations and the relationship among the comovements of the returns on those individual assets.

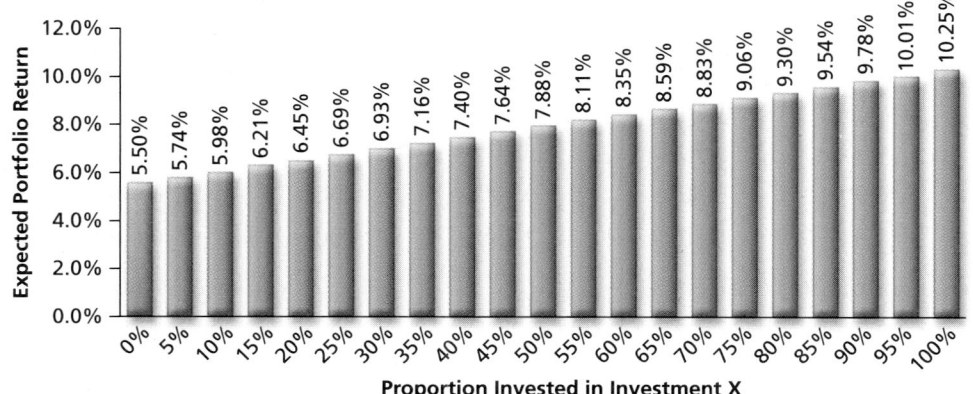

FIGURE 8-4 **Expected Return on a Portfolio Comprising Investments X and Y**

[8] For the purposes of this discussion, we have limited the investment weights to a range from 0 percent to 100 percent. However, if we are allowed to short sell either asset, then the weights can be less than 0 (i.e., negative) and more than 100 percent. Short selling means investors sell shares in a stock that they do not own. This can be done through a broker who "lends" investors shares that they can sell on the condition that the investors agree to "replace" these borrowed shares in the future (i.e., by buying them in the market). Thus, it provides investors with a way to profit from the belief that share prices will decrease. There are several technicalities associated with short selling that we will not discuss here. The main implication of short selling for our present discussion is that investors can maintain a negative position in one of the two stocks, so they can short sell A and use the proceeds to invest in B and vice versa.

We estimate the standard deviation of a two-asset portfolio using Equation 8-11. Notice that the first two terms inside the square root sign account for the weighted individual asset standard deviations (or variances), whereas the third term accounts for the weighted comovement of the returns on the two assets. We denote this as COV_{XY}, which is the **covariance** of the returns on X and Y. A covariance is simply a statistical measure of how two variables move together—how they covary. The covariance is in terms of squared units (e.g., squared returns, squared dollars, etc.). The standard deviation of the portfolio's returns, using the covariance of X and Y, is:

covariance statistical measure of the degree to which two or more series move together, or covary

$$\sigma_p = \sqrt{w_X^2\,\sigma_X^2 + w_Y^2\,\sigma_Y^2 + 2\,w_X\,w_Y\,COV_{XY}} \qquad (8\text{-}11)$$

where σ_P = the portfolio standard deviation.

We calculate the variances of the investments' returns as:[9]

Investment X

Scenario	Probability of Occurrence p_i	Return on Stock r_i	Probability × Return $p_i \times r_i$	Deviation: Return less Expected Return $(r_i - E(r_i))$	Deviation Squared $(r_i - E(r_i))^2$	Deviation Squared, × Probability $p_i(r_i - E(r_i))^2$
Good	35.00%	15.0%	5.25%	4.75%	0.002256	0.0007897
OK	55.00%	10.0%	5.50%	−0.25%	0.000006	0.0000034
Bad	10.00%	−5.0%	−0.50%	−15.25%	0.023256	0.0023256

Expected return, $E(r_X) = 10.250\%$ Variance = 0.0031188

Standard deviation = 0.0558458

Investment Y

Scenario	Probability of Occurrence p_i	Return on Stock r_i	Probability × Return $p_i \times r_i$	Deviation: Return less Expected Return $(r_i - E(r_i))$	Deviation Squared $(r_i - E(r_i))^2$	Deviation Squared, × Probability $p_i(r_i - E(r_i))^2$
Good	35.00%	4.0%	1.40%	−1.50%	0.000225	0.0000788
OK	55.00%	6.0%	3.30%	0.50%	0.000025	0.0000138
Bad	10.00%	8.0%	0.80%	2.50%	0.000625	0.0000625

Expected return, $E(r_Y) = 5.500\%$ Variance = 0.0001550

Standard deviation = 0.0124499

We see that Investment X has a higher expected return than Investment Y, but also a larger standard deviation.

We calculate the covariance of the returns on asset X and asset Y, COV_{XY}, as follows:

$$COV_{XY} = \sum_{i=1}^{n} p_i(r_{X,i} - \bar{r}_X)(r_{Y,i} - \bar{r}_Y) \qquad (8\text{-}12)$$

[9] You may notice that (1) it is important to use many decimal places, and (2) there may be slight differences due to rounding.

where $r_{X,i}$ = the ith return on asset X. The covariance between investments X and Y is -0.0003625:

Possible Outcome	Probability of Possible Outcome	Return on Investment X	Return on Investment Y	Deviation for Investment X $(r_{X,i} - r_X)$	Deviation for Investment Y $(r_{Y,i} - r_Y)$	Product of the Probability and the Deviations $p_i(r_{X,i} - r_X)(r_{Y,i} - r_Y)$
Good	35.00%	15.0%	4.0%	4.75%	−1.50%	−0.0002494
OK	55.00%	10.0%	6.0%	−0.25%	0.50%	−0.0000069
Bad	10.00%	−5.0%	8.0%	−15.25%	2.50%	−0.0003813
	Expected return = 10.250%		5.50%			Covariance = −0.0006375

This covariance indicates that the two returns tend to move in the opposite direction.

If we construct a portfolio comprising 37.5 percent of Investment X and 62.5 percent of Investment Y, the portfolio standard deviation is:

$$\sigma_p = \sqrt{w_X^2 \sigma_X^2 + w_Y^2 \sigma_Y^2 + 2\, w_X\, w_Y\, COV_{XY}}$$

$$= \sqrt{(0.375)^2(0.00311875) + (0.625)^2(0.00015500) + 2(0.375)(0.625)(-0.00063750)}$$

$$= \sqrt{0.00043857 + 0.00006055 - 0.0002988}$$

$$= \sqrt{0.000200293}$$

$$= 0.01415249 \; or \; 1.415249\%$$

Remember that the term σ_X^2 and σ_Y^2 are the variance of the possible returns on Investment X and Y, respectively. Notice that the portfolio standard deviation of 1.415 percent is *less than* the weighted average of the standard deviations of each individual asset, which is 2.8723 percent [that is, $(0.375 \times 0.05584577) + (0.625 \times 0.01244990)$]. This is always the case, except for one special situation, which we discuss momentarily.

What happens to the portfolio's standard deviation if we vary our investment in the riskier asset? We graph this in the case of the portfolio comprising Investments X and Y in Figure 8-5.

Notice that we start out with the standard deviation of the portfolio at 1.245 percent because all funds are in Y, and we finish up at 5.585 percent because all funds are in X, but

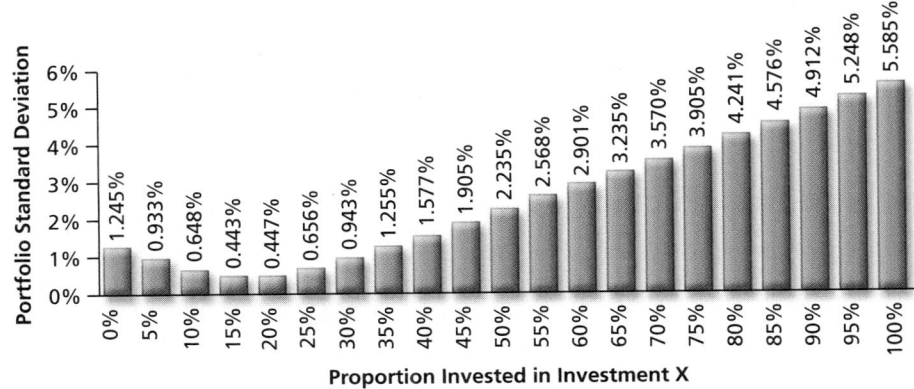

FIGURE 8-5 Portfolio Risk as Weights in Assets Change

EXAMPLE 8.7

Estimating a Covariance

PROBLEM

Consider the portfolio comprising two assets, Asset M and Asset N, with the following possible returns for two different scenarios, Up and Down:

Market Condition	Probability	Return on Asset M	Return on Asset N
Up	40%	10%	40%
Down	60%	–5%	–20%

What is the covariance of the returns on the two assets that comprise this portfolio?

Solution

First, we calculate the expected return for each asset:

Market Condition	Probability-weighted Outcome of Asset M	Probability-weighted Outcome of Asset N
Up	4.00%	16.00%
Down	–3.00%	–12.00%
	Expected return = 1.00%	Expected return = 4.00%

Then we calculate the deviation of the possible return from the respective expected return, and then probability weight the product of these deviations. This process produces a covariance of 0.02160:

Market Condition	Probability	Deviation for Asset M	Deviation for Asset N	Product of the Probability and the Deviations
Up	40%	9.00%	36.00%	0.01296
Down	60%	–6.00%	–24.00%	0.00864
				Covariance = 0.02160

in between it is not a straight line. In fact, the lowest standard deviation in Figure 8.5 is when there is 85 percent invested in Y and 15 percent invested in X. In this case, the standard deviation is 0.0443 percent. This is a clear win for the investor: an expected return of 6.21 percent (see Figure 8-4) and virtually no risk (see Figure 8-5).

Correlation Coefficient

correlation coefficient
statistical measure that identifies how asset returns move in relation to one another; denoted by ρ

Although covariance provides a useful measure of the relationship of the comovements of returns on individual assets, it is difficult to interpret intuitively because, as was the case with the variance, the unit is percent squared. Fortunately, covariance is related to another statistical measure, the **correlation coefficient** (ρ_{AB}), which we can interpret more intuitively: The correlation coefficient ranges from –1 (perfect negative correlation) to +1 (perfect positive correlation). The correlation coefficient is related to covariance and individual standard deviations according to the relationship in Equation 8-13:

$$\rho_{XY} = \frac{COV_{XY}}{\sigma_X \sigma_Y} \qquad (8\text{-}13)$$

We can also solve for covariance by rearranging this equation:

$$COV_{XY} = \rho_{XY}\, \sigma_X \sigma_Y \qquad (8\text{-}14)$$

The correlation between the returns on Investment X and Y is close to 1.0:[10]

$$\rho_{XY} = \frac{COV_{XY}}{\sigma_X \sigma_Y} = \frac{0.0012}{0.02450 \times 0.04899} = 0.999992$$

Finally, we can replace the covariance term in Equation 8-11 to produce Equation 8-15, which is commonly used to estimate portfolio standard deviation when there are two assets:

$$\sigma_p = \sqrt{w_X^2 \sigma_Y^2 + w_Y^2 \sigma_Y^2 + \underbrace{2\, w_X w_Y \rho_{XY} \sigma_X \sigma_Y}_{COV_{XY}}} \qquad (8\text{-}15)$$

Using the values from our Investment X and Investment Y example,

$$\sigma_p = \sqrt{(0.375)^2(0.00311875) + (0.625)^2(0.00015500) + 2(0.375)(0.625)(-0.91690440)(0.05584577)(0.01244990)}$$

$$= \sqrt{0.00043857 + 0.00006055 - 0.00029883}$$

$$= \sqrt{0.000200293}$$

$$= 0.01415249 \text{ or } 1.415249\%$$

Notice that this is the same answer we got when we used the covariance, but we expect this because of the relation between the correlation coefficient and the covariance. We can now separate the standard deviation component from the correlation component. This is useful because we already have the standard deviation of both assets in the first two terms, so the correlation coefficient is the only *new* information.

EXAMPLE 8.8

Estimating the Correlation of Returns

PROBLEM

Consider the portfolio comprised of two assets, Asset Three and Asset Four. What is the correlation between the returns on Asset Three and Asset Four, based on the following information?

Covariance of Three and Four	−0.00045
Standard deviation of the returns on Three	0.04
Standard deviation of the returns on Four	0.03

Solution

$$\text{Correlation} = -0.00045 \div (0.04 \times 0.03) = -0.375$$

---

[10] When we are dealing with only a couple or a few possible outcomes, the correlations tend to be either very high or very low. We see correlations more representative of what we see in practice when we allow for more possible returns—beyond three—for each asset.

The correlation coefficient measures how asset returns move in relation to one another. It is a relative measure that has a maximum value of +1.0, which denotes perfect positive correlation, and a minimum value of −1.0, which denotes perfect negative correlation. Positive correlation coefficients imply that the returns on asset A tend to move in the *same* direction as those on asset B. In other words, when the returns on asset B go up, the returns on asset A also tend to increase, and vice versa. It doesn't mean to say that they always go up together; if they did, they would be perfectly positively correlated. Negative correlation coefficients imply the opposite: The returns on asset A tend to move in the opposite direction to those on asset B. In other words, on average, when the returns on asset B go up, the returns on asset A tend to decrease, and vice versa.

The closer the absolute value of the correlation coefficient is to 1, the stronger the relationship between the returns on the two assets. In fact, when $\rho_{AB} = +1$, that is, perfect positive correlation, and if we know the return on one asset, we can predict the return on the other asset with certainty.[11] The same applies when we have $\rho_{AB} = -1$, that is, perfect negative correlation, which implies the returns have a perfect negative relationship with each other. When $\rho_{AB} = 0$ (i.e., zero correlation), there is no relationship between the returns on the two assets; therefore, knowing the return on one asset provides no useful information for predicting the return of the second asset. We illustrate correlation in Figure 8-6, including perfect positive and negative correlation, positive correlation, negative correlation, and no correlation. You can recognize perfect positive and perfect negative correlation right away because the pairwise observations of returns lie on a perfectly straight line.

Focusing on securities, the extreme correlation coefficient values described earlier do not occur for traditional common stock in practice because so many different factors influence stock returns. Generally, security returns display positive correlations with one another but these correlations are less than one. This is logical because most stocks tend to follow the movements of the overall market. As expected, the correlations tend to be higher among securities whose companies are similar in nature, for example, if they are in the same industry, are about the same size, and so on.

Correlation Coefficients and the Portfolio Standard Deviation

As we discussed earlier, the correlation between the returns on the two assets included in a portfolio affects the portfolio's standard deviation of returns. Holding the weights and the individual standard deviations constant, it is clear that the lower the correlation coefficient, the lower the portfolio's standard deviation.

We illustrate this in Figure 8-7, using a portfolio of two assets, with equal weights. The standard deviation of the monthly returns of the two assets is 5 percent and 2 percent, respectively. As you can see in this figure, the portfolio standard deviation is lowest when there is a negative correlation of −1.0, and highest when there is a positive correlation of 1.0. Also, the portfolio standard deviation is less than the weighted average of the individual assets portfolios, 3.5 percent, for all correlations except for when correlation is equal to 1.0.

We can learn a few things from this figure:

- As long as the correlation is not perfect, that is, correlation of 1.0, the portfolio's standard deviation is less than the weighted average of the two assets' standard deviation. *This result is very important because we have just shown the secret of modern portfolio theory: By combining assets into portfolios, we can reduce risk.*

---

[11] Technically, when $\rho = +1$ or -1 and we plot the returns of one asset on the x-axis and the returns on the other asset on the y-axis, we can draw a straight line through the points, and all of them will lie on the line. Such a line would be upward sloping when $\rho = +1$, and it would be downward sloping when $\rho = -1$.

- The slope of the relationship between the portfolio standard deviation and correlation is not linear.
- With perfect, negative correlation, the variability of the portfolio is reduced to almost zero, which means there is almost no risk. In fact, whenever the correlation coefficient equals −1, there exists one set of portfolio weights for the two assets such that we can eliminate risk completely.

This suggests that to discuss how the standard deviation and expected return of a portfolio varies as we change its composition, we can look at three special cases: when the correlation coefficient between the two assets is 0, +1, or −1.

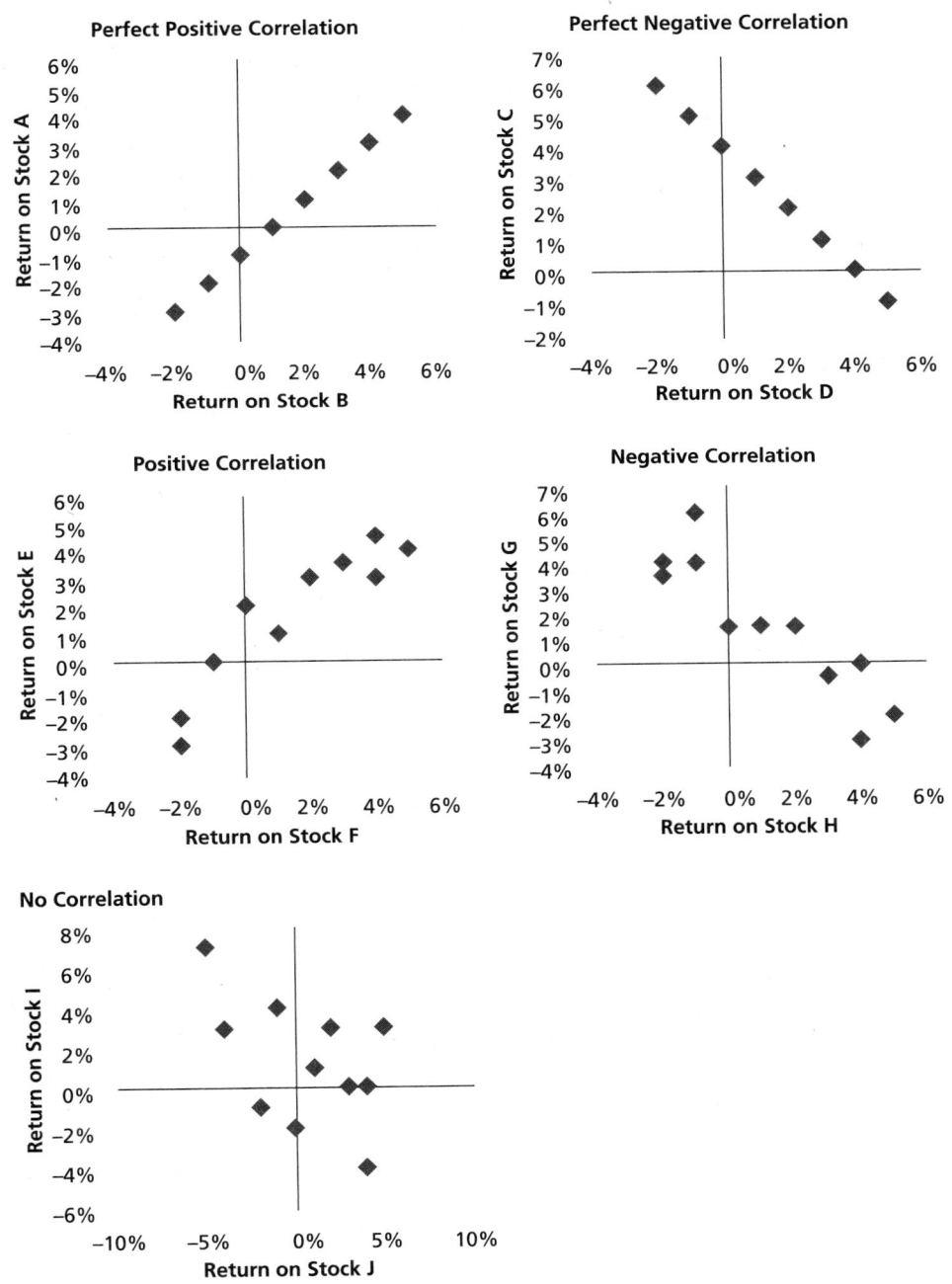

FIGURE 8-6 **Correlation between the Returns on Stocks**

SPREADSHEETS: CORRELATION

We can use spreadsheets to calculate the correlation between or among any series. Consider the annual returns for small stocks, long-term government bonds, and gold in the following spreadsheet:

	A	B	C	D
1	*Year*	*Small Company Stocks*	*Long-term Government Bonds*	*Gold*
2	2001	22.77%	3.70%	1.41%
3	2002	–13.28%	17.84%	23.96%
4	2003	60.70%	1.45%	21.74%
5	2004	18.39%	8.51%	4.40%
6	2005	5.69%	7.81%	17.77%
7	2006	16.17%	1.19%	23.92%
8	2007	–5.22%	9.88%	31.59%
9	2008	–36.72%	25.87%	3.97%
10	2009	28.09%	–14.90%	25.04%
11	2010	31.26%	10.14%	30.60%

We can calculate the correlation between the return on the small company stocks and long-term government bonds using the CORREL function: =CORREL(B2:B11,C2:C11). This results in a correlation of –0.71.

We can also use the spreadsheets' data analysis tools to calculate all of the pairwise correlations among the three investments: Data > Data Analysis > Correlation

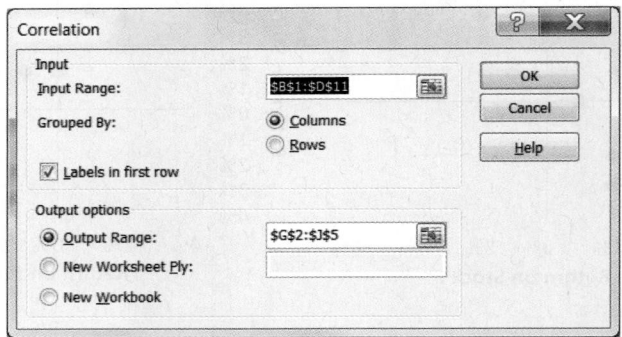

The result is a correlation matrix:

G	H	I	J
	Small Company Stocks	*Long-term Government Bonds*	*Gold*
Small company stocks	1		
Long-term government bonds	–0.71171	1	
Gold	0.218616	–0.27263	1

This tells us that the returns on long-term government bonds are negatively correlated with the returns on both small company stocks and gold, and that the returns on small company stocks and gold are positively correlated.

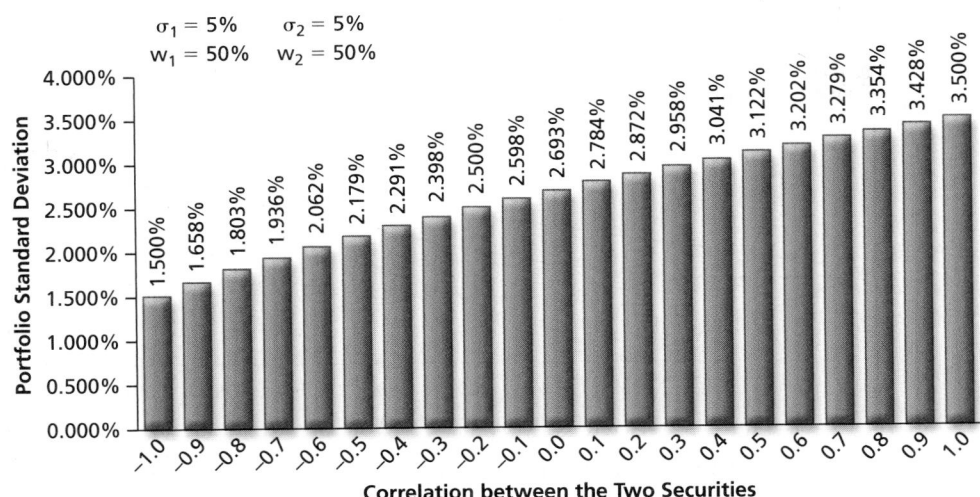

FIGURE 8-7 **Portfolio Standard Deviation of a Portfolio Comprising Two Investments with Different Correlations**

Let's go back to Equation 8-15, for the portfolio standard deviation of two assets, X and Y, which for ease of reference we repeat here.

$$\sigma_p = \sqrt{w_X^2 \sigma_X^2 + w_Y^2 \sigma_Y^2 + 2\, w_X w_Y \rho_{XY} \sigma_X \sigma_Y}$$

The three special cases produce simplified versions of the standard deviation of the portfolio's return.

$$\text{If } \rho = +1 \; \sigma_p = \sqrt{w_X^2 \sigma_X^2 + w_Y^2 \sigma_Y^2 + 2\, w_X w_Y \sigma_X \sigma_Y}$$

$$\text{If } \rho = 0 \; \sigma_p = \sqrt{w_X^2 \sigma_X^2 + w_Y^2 \sigma_Y^2}$$

$$\text{If } \rho = -1 \; \sigma_p = \sqrt{w_X^2 \sigma_X^2 + w_Y^2 \sigma_Y^2 - 2\, w_X w_Y \sigma_X \sigma_Y}$$

The zero correlation coefficient case is obvious as the covariance term disappears. However, in the other two cases, the correlation coefficient also disappears because it is either +1 or −1.[12] This allows us to simplify the equation for the standard deviation of the portfolio return. We showed earlier how the portfolio risk (standard deviation) varied with the composition of the portfolio (i.e., for the weights invested in X and Y). Now we can consider how the variability changes with the portfolio composition for these three special cases—correlations of 1.0, 0.0 and −1.0. We show the results in Figure 8-8.

Note that with perfect positive correlation, the variability changes in a linear (straight line) fashion with the portfolio weights. As we discussed before, in this case the standard deviation of the portfolio is a weighted average of each asset's standard deviation. However, when the correlation is less than perfectly positive, the relationship is "bowed," and it gets more bowed as the correlation decreases until, with a perfect negative correlation, we can remove all risk. In this case, the bow becomes two straight lines that touch the horizontal axis. At this point in the $\rho = -1$ case, we can create a portfolio with a standard deviation of zero and no variability at all. In this example, if we invest 30 percent in Investment X, with the remainder in Investment Y, we have no portfolio risk when the correlation between the returns on X and Y is −1.0. In other words, we have to put *more* in the lower-variability Investment X to compensate for the fact that it does not move as much as Investment Y.

---

[12] We now get a perfect square: For a perfect positive correlation, think $(a + b)^2$, and for a perfect negative correlation, $(a - b)^2$, where a is the standard deviation of asset A times its portfolio weight (i.e., $w_X \sigma_X$) and b is the same for asset B (i.e., $w_Y \sigma_Y$).

Portfolio has two assets, Investments X and Y. Investment X has a standard deviation of 2.920%, and Investment Y has a standard deviation of 1.245%

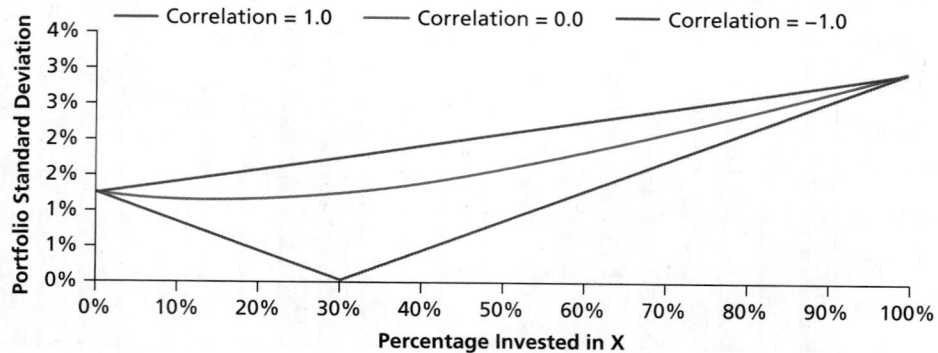

FIGURE 8-8 Portfolio Risk and Composition

hedging offsetting an investment position to reduce risk

The perfect negative correlation case is of great importance in managing risk, because it is the basis of **hedging**, which is to take an offsetting position to minimize risk. The principle of hedging helps us to understand the relationship between correlation and covariance. Note that although the two assets are perfectly negatively correlated, we do not create an equally weighted portfolio, investing the same amount in each asset.

GLOBAL PERSPECTIVE | The Linkage Between the U.S. and the European Union Economies

Financial markets in the United States have been buffeted by the European problems. Over the four-week period leading up to May 6, just prior to news that EU members would be meeting to craft the most recent package, broad U.S. stock price indexes declined and implied volatility on equities rose sharply, reflecting some increased aversion to risk. The flight to quality also showed through to U.S. Treasury yields and the foreign exchange value of the dollar, with the 10-year Treasury yield declining 50 basis points over the four-week period and the dollar climbing more than 6 percent against the euro. Following the announcement of the May 10 package, Treasury yields moved back up slightly and equity prices rebounded, but these moves were subsequently reversed and the dollar rose further against the euro.

These effects on U.S. markets underscore the high degree of integration of the U.S. and European economies and highlight the risks to the United States of renewed financial stresses in Europe. One avenue through which financial turmoil in Europe might affect the U.S. economy is by weakening the asset quality and capital positions of U.S. financial institutions. There are, to be sure, good reasons to believe that these institutions can withstand some fallout from European financial difficulties. In the past year, the Federal Reserve has pressed the largest financial institu-

tions to raise substantial additional capital. Moreover, the direct effect on U.S. banks of losses on exposure to one or more sovereigns in peripheral Europe—which, in the current context of sovereign debt concerns, is generally understood to mean Greece, Portugal, Spain, Ireland, and Italy—would be small. According to the Federal Financial Institutions Examination Council, almost all U.S. exposure to peripheral European sovereigns is held by 10 large U.S. bank holding companies, whose balance sheet exposure of $60 billion represents only 9 percent of their Tier 1 capital. However, if sovereign problems in peripheral Europe were to spill over to cause difficulties more broadly throughout Europe, U.S. banks would face larger losses on their considerable overall credit exposures, as the value of traded assets declined and loan delinquencies mounted. U.S. money market mutual funds and other institutions, which hold a large amount of commercial paper and certificates of deposit issued by European banks, would likely also be affected.

Extracted from Daniel K. Tarullo, Testimony on the International Response to European Debt Problems, Before the Subcommittee on International Monetary Policy and Trade and Subcommittee on Domestic Monetary Policy and Technology, Committee on Financial Services, U.S. House of Representatives, Washington, D.C., May 20, 2010.

The Financial Crisis and Risk Models | LESSONS LEARNED

The essential problem is that our models—both risk models and econometric models—as complex as they have become, are still too simple to capture the full array of governing variables that drive global economic reality. A model, of necessity, is an abstraction from the full detail of the real world. In line with the time-honored observation that diversification lowers risk, computers crunched reams of historical data in quest of negative correlations between prices of tradeable assets; correlations that could help insulate investment portfolios from the broad swings in an economy. When such asset prices, rather than offsetting each other's movements, fell in unison on and following August 9 last year, huge losses across virtually all risk-asset classes ensued.

The most credible explanation of why risk management based on state-of-the-art statistical models can perform so poorly is that the underlying data used to estimate a model's structure are drawn generally from both periods of euphoria and periods of fear, that is, from regimes with importantly different dynamics.

The contraction phase of credit and business cycles, driven by fear, have historically been far shorter and far more abrupt than the expansion phase, which is driven by a slow but cumulative build-up of euphoria. Over the past half-century, the American economy was in contraction only one-seventh of the time. But it is the onset of that one-seventh for which risk management must be most prepared. Negative correlations among asset classes, so evident during an expansion, can collapse as all asset prices fall together, undermining the strategy of improving risk/reward trade-offs through diversification.

Extracted from Alan Greenspan, "We Will Never Have a Perfect Model of Risk," *Financial Times*, March 16, 2008.

Concept Review Questions

1. What is the relationship between the returns on individual assets in a portfolio and the portfolio's expected return and standard deviation of returns?

2. What is the relationship between the covariance and the correlation coefficient?

3. Why can you always remove all risk in a two-asset portfolio if the assets are perfectly negatively correlated?

8.4 THE EFFICIENT FRONTIER

In the previous section, we examined the return and the standard deviation of a two-asset portfolio, where the two assets have different expected returns and standard deviations. We have shown how the expected return of a two-asset portfolio changes as we shift the proportion invested from the lower to the higher return asset. We have also shown how the portfolio standard deviation changes as we shift the weight from the lower risk to the higher risk asset. We also demonstrated the role of the correlation between the two assets' returns in the standard deviation of the portfolio: There is a mix of each asset that minimizes the portfolio's standard deviation.[13]

The Role of Correlation

Let's consider another example, this time involving Asset One and Asset Two:

Asset	Expected Return	Standard Deviation
One	15%	4%
Two	5%	1%

[13] We limited the investment in any one asset to the 0–100% range. Allowing short selling, that is, which would result in a negative weight for an asset, would, for lower return levels, create a greater standard deviation (and the graph would resemble a boomerang).

First, let's assume a correlation of 1.0. If we calculate the return and standard deviation of every two-asset portfolio comprised of One and Two, using the different possible weights, and plot these results with expected return on the vertical axis and standard deviation on the horizontal axis, we arrive at the relationship we depict in Panel A of Figure 8-9, which represents all possible portfolio combinations that can be constructed by varying the weights in our two assets, One and Two. As you can see, this is a straight line: If the returns of the two assets are perfectly correlated, the standard deviation is:

$$\sigma_p = \sqrt{w_{One}^2 \, \sigma_{One}^2 + w_{Two}^2 \, \sigma_{Two}^2 + 2 \, w_{One} \, w_{Two} \, \sigma_{One} \, \sigma_{Two}}$$

Now let's assume that the correlation between the returns of Asset One and Asset Two is 0.5. This means that 0.5 is multiplied in the last of the terms in the square root:

$$\sigma_p = \sqrt{w_{One}^2 \, \sigma_{One}^2 + w_{Two}^2 \, \sigma_{Two}^2 + 2 \, w_{One} \, w_{Two} \, \sigma_{One} \, \sigma_{Two} 0.5}$$

or, multiplying 2 and 0.5 and simplifying,

$$\sigma_p = \sqrt{w_{One}^2 \, \sigma_{One}^2 + w_{Two}^2 \, \sigma_{Two}^2 + w_{One} \, w_{Two} \, \sigma_{One} \, \sigma_{Two}}$$

Therefore the influence of the last term on the variance is one-half what it was when the correlation was 1.0. This means that except for the extremes when one of the weights is zero, the standard deviation will be less than when the correlation was perfectly 1.0. You can see this in Panel B of Figure 8-9.

What happens to the return-standard deviation relationship when the correlation between the returns of Asset A and Asset B is negative? This means that the influence of the last term in the standard deviation formula is negative, reducing the portfolio standard deviation:

$$\sigma_p = \sqrt{w_{One}^2 \, \sigma_{One}^2 + w_{Two}^2 \, \sigma_{Two}^2 - w_{One} \, w_{Two} \, \sigma_{One} \, \sigma_{Two}}$$

You can see the effect on the standard deviation in Panel C of Figure 8-9. What we show in Figure 8-9 is what is referred to as the "frontier," which is the possible set of portfolios that we can create based on the expected returns, standard deviations, and the correlation between the two assets. As long as the correlation coefficient is not close to either extreme value (i.e., −1 or +1), the parabola shape prevails, as we show in Panels B and C of this figure. Further, because risky assets tend to have positive correlation coefficients that are less than one, the frontier in Panel B is most representative of the return and standard deviation relationship for portfolios formed by using most assets.

Modern Portfolio Theory

modern portfolio theory set of theories that explain how rational investors, who are risk averse, can select a set of investments that maximize the expected return for a given level of risk

risk averse to dislike risk, and require compensation to assume additional risk

We can generalize from the two-asset to the *n*-asset case, for which the expected return is the weighted average of the expected returns on the individual assets, regardless of the number of assets in the portfolio. As a result, Equation 8-9 for estimating portfolio expected returns still applies, and the portfolio weights still must sum to 100 percent. However, calculating the standard deviation on a portfolio of more than two assets becomes cumbersome quite quickly as the number of assets increases, and we will leave that for your further studies in Finance. Harry Markowitz, who is considered the father of modern portfolio theory, was awarded the 1990 Nobel Prize in Economics as a result of his work in this field during the 1950s.[14] **Modern portfolio theory (MPT)**, in a nutshell, is the set of theories that explain how rational investors, who are risk averse, can select a set of investments that maximize the expected return for a given level of risk. A **risk-averse** investor is one that likes return but doesn't like risk; therefore, to be enticed to take on more risk requires a higher expected return.

[14] Harry Markowitz, "Portfolio Selection," *Journal of Finance*, Vol. 7, No. 1 (March 1952) pp. 77–91.

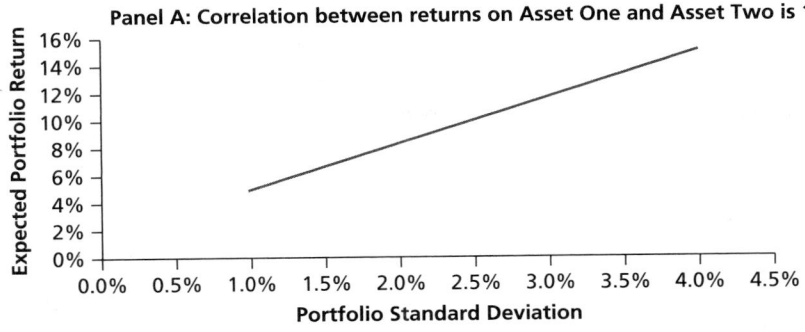

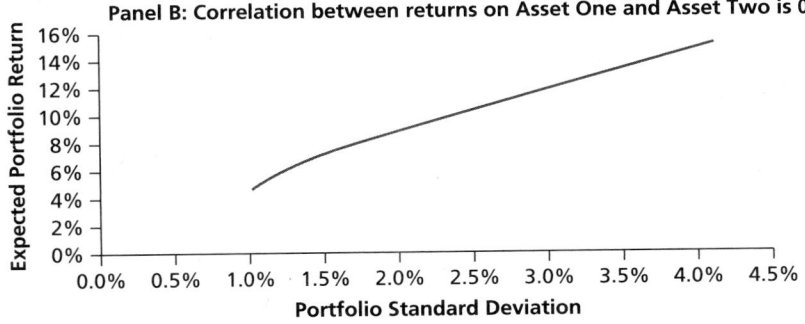

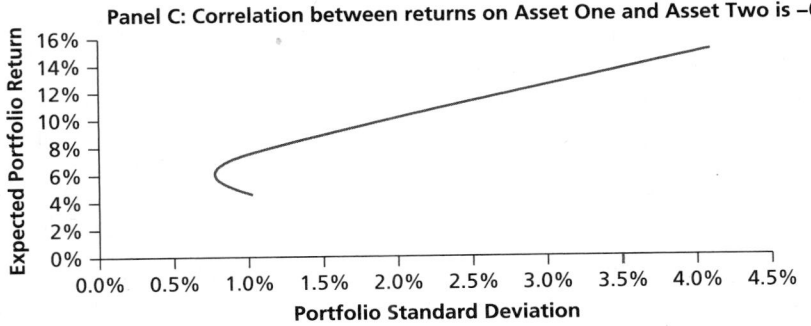

FIGURE 8-9 **Two-Asset Portfolios Formed Using Asset One and Asset Two**

One of Harry Markowitz's main contributions was to show investors how to diversify their portfolios optimally. His arguments are based on several assumptions, the most important of which are:

1. Investors are rational decision makers.
2. Investors are risk averse.
3. Investor preferences are based on a portfolio's expected return and risk (as measured by variance or standard deviation).

Based on these assumptions, Markowitz introduced the notion of an **efficient portfolio**, which dominates other portfolios that could be constructed from a given set of available assets. Efficient portfolios are those that offer the highest expected return for a given level of risk, or offer the lowest risk for a given expected return. Investors can identify efficient portfolios by specifying an expected portfolio return and minimizing the portfolio risk at this level of return, or by specifying a portfolio risk level they are willing to assume and maximizing the expected return given that level of risk.

The first step in the Markowitz analysis is to determine the expected return-risk combinations available to investors from a given set of assets, by allowing the portfolio

efficient portfolio collection of investments that offers the highest expected return for a given level of risk, or offers the lowest risk for a given expected return

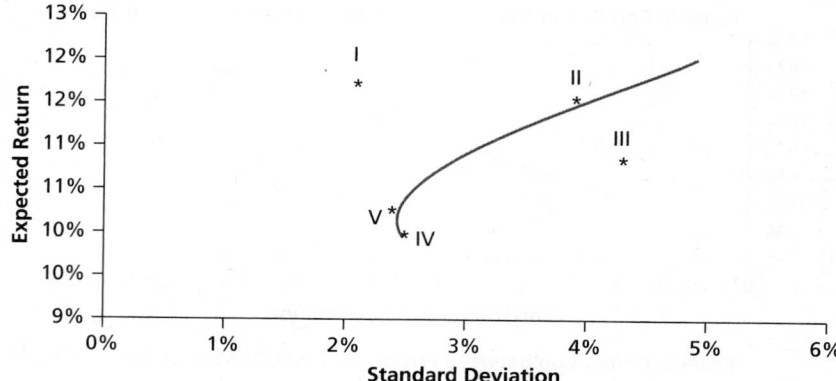

FIGURE 8-10 **The Efficient Frontier**

weights to vary, just as we did in Figure 8-9 when we considered only two assets. The entire curve is referred to as the **minimum variance frontier**, which we illustrate in Figure 8-10. Although our discussion has focused on plotting expected return against standard deviation, remember that the variance is just the standard deviation squared.

Notice that the shape is virtually identical to the frontier we constructed using only two assets in Figure 8-9. However, although the shape is similar, by using all available assets, we will be able to generate a set of more efficient portfolios, in the sense of offering higher expected return for a given risk level, or lower risk for a given expected return level.

The other difference between Figures 8-9 and 8-10 is the five portfolios marked I through V that we include in Figure 8-10. We can create all the portfolios that lie along the efficient frontier, including II, IV, and V, by combining the underlying assets. A portfolio along the efficient frontier is an **attainable portfolio**. Portfolios I and III, conversely, which lie above and below the efficient frontier, respectively, are *not* attainable:

- Portfolio I is not attainable in the sense that there is no way that the underlying assets can be combined in such a way to achieve this combination of expected return and risk. It is simply impossible.

- Portfolio III is unattainable in a different sense: It can be attained only by deliberately wasting money—that is, by simply not investing some portion of wealth and leaving money to earn zero return. It means that the portfolio is not formed by efficient combinations of the underlying assets.

This leaves us with portfolios II and V, which do lie on the minimum variance frontier. Here we can ignore portfolio IV because it is a *dominated* portfolio, even though it lies on the minimum variance frontier. Like portfolio III, which is inefficient (as well as dominated), portfolio IV offers a lower expected rate of return for the same risk as another portfolio on the upper half of the minimum variance frontier. We can see this by drawing a vertical line though IV. The point where it intersects the top part of the minimum variance frontier indicates a portfolio with the same standard deviation of return but a higher expected rate of return. Portfolio V is a special portfolio: it lies on the efficient frontier and also has the minimum amount of portfolio risk available from any possible combination of available assets. It is the **minimum variance portfolio (MVP)**.

The importance of the MVP is that portfolios that lie below it on the bottom segment of the minimum variance frontier are dominated by portfolios on the upper segment. The segment of the minimum variance frontier above the global minimum variance portfolio, therefore, offers the best risk-expected return combinations available to investors from this particular set of assets. This segment includes the set of efficient portfolios that comprise the **efficient frontier**. Rational, risk-averse investors are interested in holding only those portfolios, such as portfolio II, that offer the highest expected return for their given

minimum variance frontier curve in return–standard deviation space, produced when determining the expected return-risk combinations available to investors from a given set of assets by allowing the portfolio weights to vary

attainable portfolio collection of investments that may be constructed by combining the underlying assets and lies along the minimum variance frontier

minimum variance portfolio (MVP) portfolio that lies on the efficient frontier and has the minimum amount of portfolio risk available from any possible combination of available assets

efficient frontier set of portfolios that offers the highest expected return for their given level of risk

level of risk.[15] In this sense, these portfolios are not dominated by other attainable portfolios. In fact, the efficient frontier is the cornerstone of modern portfolio theory.

Finally, the particular portfolio chosen by an investor will depend on his or her risk preferences. A more aggressive (i.e., less risk averse) investor might choose Portfolio II in Figure 8-10, whereas a more conservative (i.e., more risk averse) investor might prefer Portfolio V (i.e., the MVP).

Concept Review Questions

1. How do you form the minimum variance frontier in the two-asset case?

2. What assumptions about investors underlie Markowitz's theories regarding efficient portfolios?

3. What are the implications of portfolio theory for the financial manager?

8.5 DIVERSIFICATION

We previously demonstrated that the expected portfolio return is *always* a weighted average of individual asset returns, and as long as the correlation between the two assets' returns is less than perfect, positive correlation, portfolio risk is always *less than* a weighted average of the risk of the two assets that comprise the portfolio. Therefore, there is a benefit to combining assets into portfolios. In other words, we can eliminate risk by investing our funds across several assets, or by "not putting all our eggs in one basket." This principle is **diversification**. We have already seen how Markowitz showed that efficient diversification leads investors to hold a portfolio along the efficient frontier, which is one of the cornerstones of modern portfolio theory. However, we have also seen that calculating all those correlation coefficients and generating the efficient frontier is not easy.

diversification reduction of risk by investing funds across several assets

Diversification and Risk

Let's first look at what happens if there is simply random or naïve diversification. **Random diversification** or **naïve diversification** refers to the act of randomly diversifying without regard to relevant investment characteristics, such as company size, industry classification, and so on.[16] That is, in the case of stocks, an investor randomly selects a relatively large number of stocks.[17] We can see this in Figure 8-11, in which we graph the average portfolio standard deviation against the number of assets in the portfolio.[18]

random diversification or **naïve diversification** randomly buying assets without regard to relevant investment characteristics

The benefits of random diversification do not continue indefinitely. As more and more assets are added, the marginal risk reduction per asset becomes extremely small, eventually producing an almost negligible effect on total portfolio risk. In the case of stocks, for example, going from 10 to 20 stocks eliminates an additional 7 percent of the monthly portfolio standard deviation, and going from 20 to 30 stocks eliminates only 3 percent of the monthly standard deviation. Thus, although a large number of securities is not required to achieve substantial diversification benefits, the monthly portfolio risk levels out as additional securities are added to the portfolio.

[15] We will talk more about risk aversion in the next chapter.

[16] This is commonly represented in cartoons as someone throwing darts into a dartboard to randomly pick stocks. Nowadays we do it with computers.

[17] When investors relied on stock quotes printed in the newspaper, this was referred to as choosing stocks using darts on the stock pages. With most investors using the Internet for stock quotes, this doesn't work too well.

[18] How do we create Figure 8-11? What this represents is the portfolio standard deviation for each size portfolio. The standard deviation that we graph is the average standard deviation for portfolios created by randomly drawing securities for a portfolio consisting of one stock, and then repeating this for a large number (e.g., 10,000) of random draws. This is repeated for portfolios consisting of two stocks, and so on.

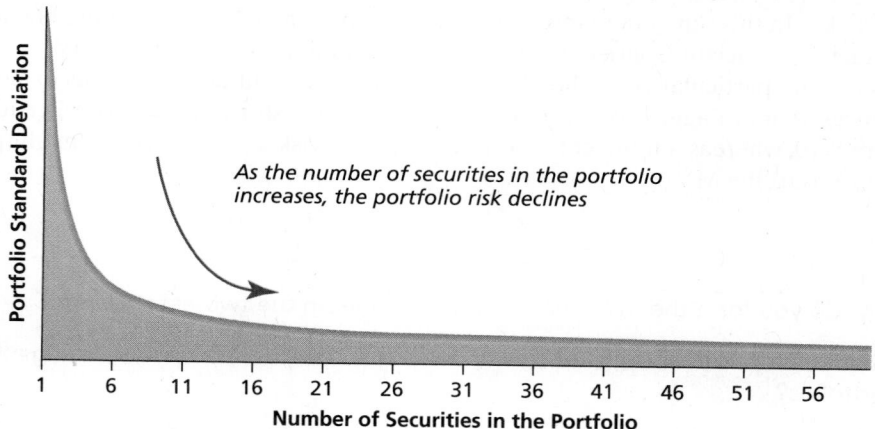

FIGURE 8-11 Portfolio Risk for Different Size Portfolios, Assuming Naïve Diversification

ETHICS | Socially Responsible Investing and the Fiduciary Duty

The portfolio manager of a fund has a fiduciary duty to the beneficiaries of the fund to act "with the care, skill, prudence and diligence under the circumstances prevailing that a prudent man acting in a like capacity and familiar with such matters would use in the conduct of an enterprise of like character with like aims." ERISA Section 404(a)(1)(B).

So how does this fiduciary duty translate if the portfolio manager focuses on socially responsible investments (SRI)? If making decisions that are consistent with SRI do not lead to the risk and return that are possible without constraining the feasible set of investments to be consistent with SRI, is the portfolio manager being prudent?

If the set of feasible investments is limited, there is a possibility that SRI investing will not permit fund managers to take advantage of the reduction in risk through diversification. So far, the evidence with respect to how SRI funds perform relative to other funds is mixed; some studies find that SRI funds underperform other funds, whereas other studies find that there is no difference in performance.[19]

Decomposing Risk

unique risk or nonsystematic risk or diversifiable risk company-specific part of total risk that is eliminated by diversification

market risk or systematic risk or nondiversifiable risk systematic part of total risk that cannot be eliminated by diversification

The part of the total risk that *is* eliminated by diversification is the company-specific **unique risk**, which we sometimes refer to as **nonsystematic risk** or **diversifiable risk**. The part that is *not* eliminated by diversification is the **market risk**, which is also referred to as **systematic risk** or **nondiversifiable risk**. A portion of the risk cannot be eliminated because all the securities in the portfolio are directly influenced by overall movements in the general market or economy. We also refer to market risk as beta risk because we often measure this risk as the coefficient when we regress excess returns on a stock (that is, returns above and beyond the return on a risk-free asset) against the excess returns on the market. We show the total and market risk components in Figure 8-12.

$$\text{Total risk} = \text{Market risk} + \text{Unique risk} \qquad (8\text{-}16)$$

or, equivalently,

$$\text{Total risk} = \text{Systematic risk} + \text{Nonsystematic risk}$$

[19] For an overview of the issues and evidence, see "Socially Responsible Investing: Is Your Fiduciary Duty at Risk?" by William Martin, *Journal of Business Ethics*, Vol. 90 (2009), pp. 549–560.

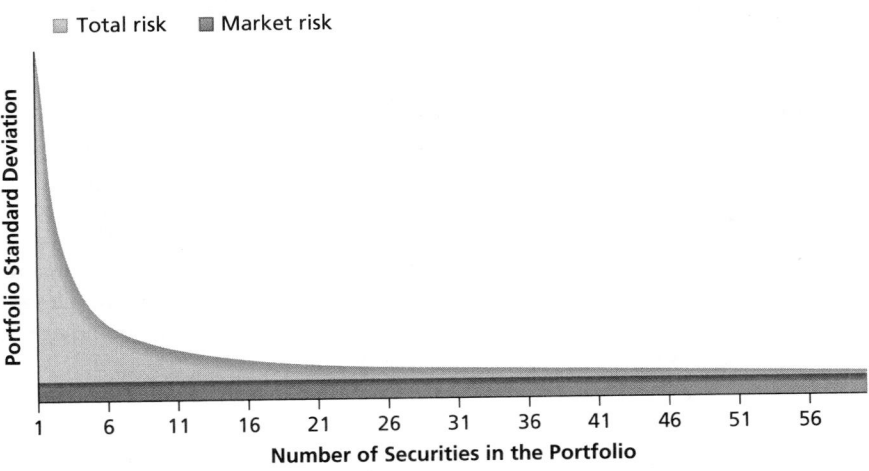

FIGURE 8-12 Total and Market Risk for Different Size Portfolios, Assuming Naïve Diversification

In the case of portfolios of securities, diversification can be achieved more efficiently when we take a more structured approach to forming portfolios by consciously selecting securities that can be expected to have lower correlations among their returns, that is, to choose them from different industries, countries, and so on. In the case of a company, diversification requires selecting products or projects whose cash flows are not highly correlated with one another.

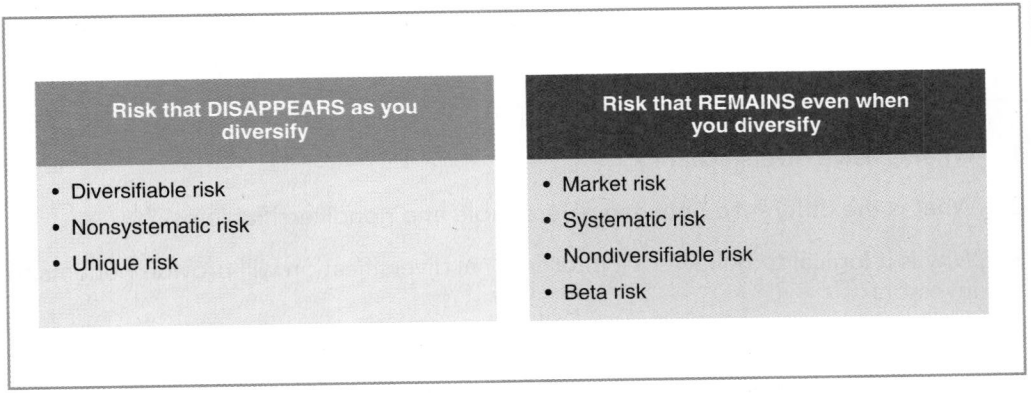

SUMMARIZING: RISKS

Risk that DISAPPEARS as you diversify	Risk that REMAINS even when you diversify
• Diversifiable risk • Nonsystematic risk • Unique risk	• Market risk • Systematic risk • Nondiversifiable risk • Beta risk

Everything That Falls Must Converge | FINANCE in the News

Assets have high correlations during stressful times, meaning diversification isn't the silver bullet it's touted as.

The writer Flannery O'Connor titled one of her stories "Everything That Rises Must Converge." And while it is unknown whether the markets have a sense of irony, it can be said that their recent behavior has inverted O'Connor's title quite neatly. For in the last quarter of 2008 most major asset classes converged, but on the way down.

In less highfalutin' terms, the end of 2008 was when the gospel of diversification was dealt a serious blow. Domestically the Russell 3000 and the Standard & Poor's 500 both collapsed. Globally major indexes like the FTSE 100 and the Nikkei 225 ended the year in the red. Indeed stocks all hung together, but not for the better.

It wasn't just stocks. The benchmark 10-year Treasury fell off a cliff, oil prices took a spill and even gold ended the quarter lower, although the metal's drop was relatively slight by comparison. Real estate, of course, continued to be a bloodbath. The S&P/Case-Shiller U.S. National Home Price Index recorded an 18.2% decline in the fourth quarter of 2008 vs. the fourth quarter of 2007, the largest in the series' 21-year history. Truly there was nowhere to run and nowhere to hide as everything converged.

These convergences are problematic because they show that diversification meant the least when it was needed the most. As investors, we are always told to not put all our eggs in one basket, but as 2008 closed out this strategy didn't perform as hoped. You could almost say that what this strategy yielded instead was simply more eggs in more baskets falling at the same time, and yet somehow still ending up on our faces.

The question then becomes whether diversification is merely a truism with little truth in it or whether investors are right to continue to try and parcel out their way to less volatility.

David Joy, chief market strategist at RiverSource Investments, says that while only time will give a clear answer to this question he believes the fourth quarter's close correlations were an aberration. The reason their asset classes moved in tandem is because hedge funds did all they could to dump any assets that had any liquidity at all. Noting this, he says that diversification should still have some value but that "alternative assets, with very low correlations to broad asset categories, are increasing in importance in the search for diversification."

For the wealthy, such alternative assets could include hedge funds and venture capital projects. For those with fewer riches, gold and other precious metals could be areas worth investigating.

Vahan Janjigian, chief investment strategist at Forbes, is more skeptical about the value of diversification. "When there are market panics and widespread selling, diversification does not do much good," he says. Which is not to say investors shouldn't diversify, he says, but investors should realize that it doesn't bullet-proof your portfolio. Like most pieces of inherited market wisdom, diversification offers no refuge from keeping a constant eye on your portfolio, and it should not offer false peace of mind.

Marc Lowlicht, the head of the wealth management division at Further Lane Asset Management, hopes that diversification works once again, or it will become increasingly hard to manage risk. But if diversification continues to proven ineffectual he forecasts having to use various hedging strategies in order to gain more upside on his client's investments.

Still, Lowlicht remains confident, at least for now, that once the great deleveraging is over that asset classes will start to diverge once again. Should the markets rise and converge, however, all bets are off.

Source: Serchuk, David, "Everything That Falls Must Converge," *Forbes*, May 14, 2009.

Concept Review Questions

1. What is naïve diversification?

2. What is the difference between diversifiable and nondiversifiable risk?

3. Why is it logical to believe that international diversification will provide benefits to investors?

8.6   A COMPREHENSIVE EXAMPLE

We demonstrate the measurement of risk and the concept of diversification with an example using two assets. Suppose you are given the following information for two investments, A and B, where the return on each varies with the state of the economy:

State of the Economy	Probability of Occurrence	Return on Investment A	Return on Investment B
High growth	10%	60%	5%
Moderate growth	20%	20%	25%
No growth	50%	10%	5%
Recession	20%	−25%	0%
	100%		

The Expected Return

We calculate the expected return for each investment using a weighted average of the possible outcomes, where the weights are the probabilities of each outcome:

$$E(r_A) = (0.10 \times 0.60) + (0.20 \times 0.20) + (0.50 \times 0.10) + (0.20 \times -0.25) = 10\%$$

$$E(r_B) = (0.10 \times 0.05) + (0.20 \times 0.25) + (0.50 \times 0.05) + (0.20 \times 0.00) = 8\%$$

Therefore, Investment A has a higher expected return than Investment B. You may find it easier to perform this calculation in table form. In this case the calculation is:

State of the Economy	Probability of Occurrence	Return on Investment A	Probability × Return on Investment A	Return on Investment B	Probability × Return on Investment B
High growth	10%	60%	0.06	5%	0.005
Moderate growth	20%	20%	0.04	25%	0.050
No growth	50%	10%	0.05	5%	0.025
Recession	20%	−25%	−0.05	0%	0.000
			$E(r_A) = 0.10$		$E(r_B) = 0.080$

The Standard Deviation

The expected return on Investment A is 10 percent and the expected return on Investment B is 8 percent. What is the standard deviation of each investment's possible returns? To calculate the standard deviation, we must first calculate the variance of each investment's possible returns, which requires:

1. comparing the possible outcomes with the expected value of the outcomes,
2. squaring this deviation from the expected value, and then
3. weighting the squared deviation by the probability associated with the possible outcome.

The calculation for each investment is:

$$\sigma_A^2 = 0.10(0.60 - 0.10)^2 + 0.20(0.20 - 0.10)^2 + 0.50(0.10 - 0.10)^2 + 0.20(-0.25 - 0.10)^2$$

$$\sigma_A^2 = 0.00515$$

$$\sigma_B^2 = 0.10(0.05 - 0.08)^2 + 0.20(0.25 - 0.08)^2 + 0.50(0.05 - 0.08)^2 + 0.20(0.0 - 0.08)^2$$

$$\sigma_B^2 = 0.00760384$$

In tabular form,

State of the Economy	Probability of Occurrence	Return on Investment A	Deviation from the Expected Return for Investment A	Squared Deviation for Investment A	Weighted Squared Deviation for Investment A
High growth	10%	60%	0.06	0.2500	0.02500
Moderate growth	20%	20%	0.04	0.0100	0.00200
No growth	50%	10%	0.05	0.0000	0.00000
Recession	20%	−25%	−0.05	0.1225	0.02450
					$\sigma_A^2 = 0.05150$

State of the Economy	Probability of Occurrence	Return on Investment B	Deviation from the Expected Return for Investment B	Squared Deviation for Investment B	Weighted Squared Deviation for Investment B
High growth	10%	5%	−0.03	0.0009	0.00009
Moderate growth	20%	25%	0.17	0.0289	0.00578
No growth	50%	5%	−0.03	0.0009	0.00045
Recession	20%	0%	−0.08	0.0064	0.00128

$$\sigma_B^2 = 0.00760$$

The standard deviation of each investment's return is the square root of the respective variance:

$$\sigma_A^2 = \sqrt{0.00515} = 22.69\%$$
$$\sigma_B^2 = \sqrt{0.00760} = 8.72\%$$

Notice that Investment A has the higher standard deviation than Investment B; therefore, it appears to have the more risk, based on the variability of the forecast return around its expected return.

Suppose you create a portfolio that has 30 percent invested in Investment A and 70 percent invested in Investment B. What is the expected return on this portfolio? The expected return on this portfolio, $E(r_p)$, is the weighted average of the returns on the investments, 8.6 percent:

$$[w_A \times E(r_A)] + [w_B \times E(r_B)] = (0.30 \times 10\%) + (0.70 \times 8.0\%) = 8.6\%$$

Covariance

What is the covariance between the returns of Investment A and those of Investment B? We go back to the probability distribution of each investment's returns, calculate the probability-weighted return for each possible economic scenario, and then calculate the variance of these weighted returns. This variance is the covariance between the returns on Investment A and the returns on Investment B:

State of the Economy	p_i	Return on Investment A	Return on Investment B	Calculation	Result
High growth	10%	60%	5%	$0.10 \times (0.60 - 0.10) \times (0.05 - 0.08)$	−0.0015
Moderate growth	20%	20%	25%	$0.20 \times (0.20 - 0.10) \times (0.25 - 0.08)$	0.0034
No growth	50%	10%	5%	$0.50 \times (0.10 - 0.10) \times (0.05 - 0.08)$	0.0000
Recession	20%	−25%	0%	$0.20 \times (-0.25 - 0.10) \times (0.00 - 0.08)$	0.0056

$$COV_{A,B} = 0.0075$$

Correlation

The correlation between the returns on Investments A and B is related to the investments' respective standard deviations. More specifically, the correlation is the ratio of the covariance of returns of the two investments, divided by the product of their respective standard deviations:

$$\rho_{AB} = \frac{COV_{AB}}{\sigma_A \sigma_B} = \frac{0.0075}{(0.22669)(0.0872)} = 0.379$$

The Portfolio's Risk

We use the following information to calculate the portfolio risk:

w_A = 30%   *The proportion invested in Investment A*

w_B = 70%   *The proportion invested in Investment B*

σ_A = 22.69%   *The standard deviation of the returns on Investment A*

σ_A = 8.72%   *The standard deviation of the returns on Investment B*

ρ_{AB} = 0.379   *The correlation between the returns of Investment A and Investment B*

Using Equation 8-11, we calculate a portfolio standard deviation of 10.73 percent:

$$\sigma_p = \sqrt{(0.30)^2(0.2269)^2 + (0.70)^2(0.0872)^2 + 2(0.30)(0.70)(0.0075)}$$

$$\sigma_p = \sqrt{0.0046335 + 0.003725 + 0.003149} = \sqrt{0.01151} = 10.73\%$$

Using Equation 8-15, we arrive at the same portfolio standard deviation:

$$\sigma_p = \sqrt{(0.30)^2(0.2269)^2 + (0.70)^2(0.0872)^2 + 2(0.30)(0.70)(0.379)(0.2269)(0.0872)}$$

$$\sigma_p = \sqrt{0.0046335 + 0.003725 + 0.003149} = \sqrt{0.01151} = 10.73\%$$

Sensitivity Analysis

The calculation of the standard deviation is based on a number of estimates about the future. We can perform sensitivity analysis on the portfolio's risk based on varying different parameters. Consider if we vary the proportions invested in Investment A and Investment B:

Scenario	Proportion Invested in Investment A	Proportion Invested in Investment B	Expected Return on the Portfolio	Standard Deviation of the Returns on the Portfolio
1	100%	0%	10.000%	22.69%
2	30%	70%	8.600%	10.73%
3	70%	30%	9.400%	17.05%
4	0%	100%	8.000%	8.72%

A few observations:

- If the entire portfolio is invested in Investment A (Scenario 1), the risk of the portfolio is the same as that of Investment A: 22.69 percent.
- If the entire portfolio is invested in Investment B (Scenario 4), the standard deviation of the portfolio is the same as that of Investment B.
- The greater the proportion of the portfolio invested in Investment A, the higher the portfolio risk, but also the higher the expected return.

If we vary the estimate of, say, the probabilities of the possible outcomes, we end up with different expected values and standard deviations. Consider a change in the probabilities associated with each state of the economy:

State of the Economy	Probability	Return on Investment A	Return on Investment B
High growth	20%	60%	5%
Moderate growth	20%	20%	25%
No growth	50%	10%	5%
Recession	10%	–25%	0%

If 30 percent is invested in Investment A and 70% in Investment B:

Statistic	Investment A	Investment B	Portfolio
Expected return	19%	9%	11.5%
Standard deviation	23.88%	8.38%	9.87%

Covariance of returns	0.002775	
Correlation of returns	0.138646	

The change in the probabilities associated with the different outcomes changes all of the parameters: expected returns, standard deviations, covariance, and correlation. As you can see from these examples, it is important to consider the sensitivity of the estimates used in the evaluation of a portfolio's expected return and risk.

Concept Review Questions

1. What is the relation between the covariance and the correlation of two assets' returns?

2. What is meant by stating that a portfolio lies on the efficient frontier?

3. What is the role of correlation in a portfolio's risk?

SUMMARY

- In financial decision making and analysis, we use both ex post and ex ante returns on investments: We use ex post returns when we look back at what has happened, and we use ex ante returns when we look forward, into the future.

- One measure of risk is the standard deviation, which is a measure of the dispersion of possible outcomes.

- When we invest in more than one investment, there may be some form of diversification, which is the reduction in risk from combining investments whose returns are not perfectly correlated.

- If we consider all possible investments and their respective expected return and risk, there are sets of investments that are better than others in terms of return and risk. These sets make up the efficient frontier.

- If we consider a company as a portfolio of investments, diversification plays a role in financial decision making. Financial managers need to consider not only what an investment looks like in terms of its return and risk as a stand-alone investment, but more important, how it fits into the company's portfolio of investments.

FORMULAS/EQUATIONS

(8-1) Income yield $= \dfrac{CF_1}{P_0}$

(8-2) Capital gain or loss return $= \dfrac{P_1 - P_0}{P_0}$

(8-3) Total return $= \dfrac{CF_1 + P_1 - P_0}{P_0}$

(8-4)   Arithmetic mean $= \dfrac{\sum_{i=1}^{n} r_i}{n}$

(8-5)   Geometric mean $= \sqrt[n]{(1 + r_1) \times (1 + r_2) \times (1 + r_3) \times \ldots \times (1 + r_n)} - 1$

(8-6)   Expected value $= \sum_{i=1}^{n} (outcome_i \times probabilty_i)$

(8-7)   Ex post standard deviation $= \sqrt{\dfrac{\sum_{i=1}^{N} (x_i - \bar{x})^2}{N - 1}}$

(8-8)   Ex ante standard deviation $= \sqrt{\sum_{i=1}^{n} p_i (r_i - E(r_i))^2}$

(8-9) $E(r_p) = \sum_{i=1}^{n} (w_i \times E(r_i))$

(8-10) $E(r_P) = E(r_Y) + w[E(r_X) - E(r_Y)]$

(8-11) $\sigma_p = \sqrt{w_X^2 \sigma_X^2 + w_Y^2 \sigma_Y^2 + 2w_X w_Y COV_{XY}}$

(8-12) $COV_{XY} = \sum_{i=1}^{n} p_i (r_{X,i} - \bar{r}_X)(r_{Y,i} - \bar{r}_Y)$

(8-13) $\rho_{XY} = \dfrac{COV_{XY}}{\sigma_X \sigma_Y}$

(8-14) $COV_{XY} = \rho_{XY} \sigma_X \sigma_Y$

(8-15) $\sigma_p = \sqrt{w_X^2 \sigma_X^2 + w_Y^2 \sigma_Y^2 + 2w_X w_Y \rho_{XY} \sigma_X \sigma_Y}$

(8-16)   Total risk = Market risk + Unique risk

QUESTIONS AND PROBLEMS

Multiple Choice

1. An investor purchased a company's stock at $25 1 year ago and it is now worth $24. The company paid a quarterly dividend of $1 per share during the year. The capital gain or loss return for this stock is closest to:

   A. –16 percent.   B. –4 percent.   C. 4 percent.   D. 12 percent.

2. An investor purchased a stock at $25 1 year ago and it is now worth $24. It paid a dividend of $4 per share at the end of the year. The total return for this stock is *closest* to:

   A. 0 percent.   B. 4 percent.   C. 16 percent.   D. 12 percent.

3. Which of the following is *incorrect*?

   A. The geometric mean of 50 percent and –50 percent is –13.4 percent.

   B. The arithmetic average is always less than the geometric mean of a series of returns.

   C. The income yield of an asset that has a $3 cash flow during a period with a beginning price of $15 is 20 percent.

   D. The greater the dispersion of a distribution, the greater the spread between the geometric mean and the arithmetic average.

4. The expected return on a stock that has a 30 percent probability of a 30 percent return, a 20 percent probability of a 40 percent return, and a 50 percent probability of a 15 percent return, is *closest* to:

    A. 15 percent.   B. 20 percent.   C. 24.5 percent.   D. 35.5 percent.

5. Consider a stock that has a 30 percent probability of a 30 percent return, a 20 percent probability of a 40 percent return, and a 50 percent probability of a 15 percent return. The standard deviation is *closest* to:

    A. 10.11 percent.   B. 10.25 percent.   C. 11.12 percent.   D. 12.00 percent.

6. Which of the following is *false*?

    A. Standard deviation is easier to interpret than variance as a measure of risk.

    B. Covariance measures the comovement between the returns of individual assets.

    C. The expected return of a portfolio is always the weighted average of the expected return of each asset in the portfolio.

    D. The standard deviation of a portfolio is always the weighted average of the standard deviations of individual assets in the portfolio.

7. The correlation coefficient:

    A. may be greater than +1.

    B. measures how asset returns move in relation to one another.

    C. equals covariance multiplied by the individual standard deviations.

    D. shows a stronger relationship between the returns of two assets when its absolute value is closer to 0.

8. The correlation coefficient between the returns on a portfolio and a potential investment of the portfolio that most likely will provide the greatest diversification benefits for a given portfolio is:

    A. −0.9.   B. 0.0.   C. 0.5.   D. 1.0.

9. Consider a portfolio consisting of two assets, A and B. The expected return on A is 5 percent, whereas the expected return on B is 10 percent. If the market value of A is €100 and the market value of B is €300, the expected return on this portfolio is *closest* to:

    A. 7.5%.   B. 8.75%.   C. 13.17%.

10. Which of the following statements is incorrect?

    A. Investors can reduce a portfolio's risk by diversifying.

    B. The portfolios that lie along the efficient frontier provide the greater expected return for a given level of risk.

    C. Portfolios that lie on the part of the efficient frontier that is below the minimum-variance portfolio are the most attractive portfolios for investors.

    D. Adding a security to a portfolio that has returns that are negatively correlated with the existing portfolio will result in a portfolio risk that is less than the weighted average of the individual securities' standard deviations.

Practice Questions and Problems

8.1 Measuring Returns

11. Distinguish between ex post and ex ante returns on investments. Which, if any, would a financial manager find useful in evaluating an investment?

12. Describe the circumstances in which a financial manager or analyst would use the arithmetic mean to describe a return series.

13. Describe the circumstances in which a financial manager or analyst would use the geometric mean to describe a return series.

14. Suppose a financial manager is evaluating the performance of the following investments made last year, all values in millions:

	Investment One	Investment Two	Investment Three
Initial investment	$10	$20	$15
Cash flow, year 1	$1	$2	$5
Value of investment, end of year 1	$10	$18	$12

What is the income yield, capital yield, and total yield for each investment?

15. An analyst's file on the daily performance of the Houston Company has been partially completed.
    A. Complete the table, filling in the missing data.

The Houston Company Stock Performance

Quarter	Opening Price	Dividend	Closing Price	Income Yield	Capital Yield	Total Return
1	$20	$1.00	$21	5.00%	5.00%	
2	$21		19	4.76%		–4.76%
3	$19	$0.50	21		10.53%	
4		$0.50	22	2.38%		

B. What is the geometric mean return for the year for the Houston Company stock?

16. Calculate the annual arithmetic mean and geometric mean return on the following security, and state which method is more appropriate for the situation: purchase price = $30; 1st-year dividend = $5; price after 1 year = $35; 2nd-year dividend = $8; selling price after 2 years = $28.

8.2 Measuring Risk

17. What is the difference between an ex ante standard deviation and an ex post standard deviation?

18. Why might a financial manager estimate and use the ex post standard deviations of a company's past capital investments when evaluating new capital projects?

19. You observed the following daily returns for two companies: ABC and DEF.

	Daily Returns	
	ABC	DEF
Monday	3%	2%
Tuesday	2%	8%
Wednesday	–8%	14%
Thursday	–10%	12%
Friday	7%	3%

Calculate, for each stock, the:
  A. Geometric mean daily return
  B. Arithmetic mean daily return
  C. Standard deviation of daily returns

20. Calculate the expected return and the standard deviation of the returns for the following investment:

Conditions	Probability	Possible Return
Boom	15%	10%
Stable	60%	5%
Recession	25%	1%

21. Calculate the expected return and the standard deviation of the returns for the following asset:

Conditions	Probability	Possible Outcome
Best	20%	25%
OK	60%	15%
Lousy	20%	−5%

22. The analysts at Food Products Inc. have conducted an extensive analysis of the economy and have concluded that the probability of a recession next year is 25 percent, a boom is 15 percent, and a stable economy is 60 percent. The CFO has estimated that the earnings per share will be $1 if there is a recession, $2 if there is a boom, and $1.25 if the economy is stable.
    A. What is the expected earnings per share for Food Products, based on the analysts' and CFO's expectations of the economy?
    B. What is the standard deviation of the possible earnings per share?

23. You have observed the following returns:

Period	Return
1	10 percent
2	−8 percent
3	5 percent
4	2 percent
5	−20 percent

    A. Calculate the geometric mean return.
    B. Calculate the arithmetic mean return.
    C. Calculate the variance and standard deviation of these returns.

24. On January 1, 2013, the Absent Minded Profs published the following forecasts for the economy:

State of the Economy	Probability	Forecasted Quarterly Return
Poor	20%	−3%
Average	50%	5%
Boom	30%	8%

During 2013, you observed quarterly returns of 2 percent, −5 percent, 3 percent, and 8 percent.
    A. Calculate the ex ante expected quarterly return.
    B. Calculate the ex ante standard deviation of quarterly returns.
    C. Calculate the ex post average quarterly return.
    D. Calculate the ex post standard deviation of quarterly returns.
    E. Explain the difference between the ex ante and ex post returns.

 25. Calculate the ex post standard deviation of returns for the following:

Period	Return
1	50 percent
2	30 percent
3	20 percent
4	35 percent
5	55 percent

8.3 Expected Return and Risk of Portfolios

26. Distinguish between a correlation and a covariance.

27. Why would a financial manager be concerned about the correlation among a company's different products when making investment decisions?

28. Suppose you determine that the correlation between the returns on two products is 0.4. What does that mean?

29. Suppose a company has the following three products: peanut butter, toothpaste, and computers. What is likely to be the correlation (positive, negative, or zero) among the cash flows of these products? Explain.

30. Consider a portfolio consisting of two assets, A and B. The expected return on A is 5 percent, whereas the expected return on B is 10 percent. If the market value of A is £750 million and the market value of B is £250 million, calculate the expected return on this portfolio.

31. The managers of the Dayton Fund are exploring different portfolio allocations between two stocks. Complete the following table.

	Case 1	Case 2	Case 3	Case 4	Case 5
Amount invested in Stock 1	$500		$100	$200	
Amount invested in Stock 2	$500	$1,600	$5,000	$300	$900
Total invested	$1,000	$2,000	$5,100	$500	$1,000
Weight in Stock 1	50%		2%	40%	
Weight in Stock 2		80%			90%
Expected return of Stock 1	8%	3%	10%	5%	1%
Expected return of Stock 2		5%		6%	10%
Expected return on the portfolio	5.5%	4.6%	5.1%		

32. Your portfolio consists of two assets: Ice-T and Mr. B. The expected return for Ice-T is 8 percent, while for Mr. B it is 3 percent. The standard deviation is 4 percent for Ice-T and 14 percent for Mr. B. If 15 percent of the portfolio is invested in Ice-T, calculate the portfolio standard deviation if:

A. the correlation between the stocks is 0.75.
B. the correlation between the stocks is –0.75.

33. An investor owns a portfolio of $30,000 that contains $10,000 in Bluechip Inc. stock, with an expected return of 12 percent; $5,000 in bonds, with an expected return of 8 percent; and the rest in Redchip Inc. stock, with an expected return of 20 percent. Calculate the expected return of his portfolio.

34. The Diverse Funds are exploring the risk of different portfolio allocations between two stocks. Complete the following table.

	Case 1	Case 2
Weight in Stock 1		15%
Weight in Stock 2	25%	
Standard deviation of Stock 1	15%	2%
Standard deviation of Stock 2	3%	10%
Covariance between Stocks 1 and 2		
Correlation between Stocks 1 and 2	–0.20	0.40
Portfolio variance		
Portfolio standard deviation		

35. Analysts have reported the following return data on six stocks:

Day	XYZ	ABC	DEF	GHI	JKL	MNO
Monday	1%	–18%	3%	6%	7%	3%
Tuesday	2%	–15%	8%	3%	5%	–4%
Wednesday	3%	–12%	13%	1%	3%	8%
Thursday	4%	–9%	18%	3%	2%	–2%
Friday	5%	–6%	22%	–5%	0%	0%

   A. Graph the returns of each stock (ABC, DEF, GHI, JKL, and MNO) over time.
   B. Based on the five graphs, which stocks are positively correlated with XYZ?
   C. Based on the five graphs, which stocks are negatively correlated with XYZ?
   D. Based on the five graphs, which stocks are uncorrelated with XYZ?

8.4   The Efficient Frontier

36. What is an efficient frontier?

37. State three of the most important assumptions underlying Markowitz's notion of efficient portfolios.

38. What is the role of the decision maker's risk aversion in selecting a portfolio?

39. Complete the following table, indicating whether each of the following portfolios cannot lie on the efficient frontier?

Portfolio	Expected Return	Standard Deviation of Returns	Cannot Lie on the Efficient Frontier? Yes or No
A	6%	10%	
B	7%	12%	
C	5%	10%	
D	7%	11%	
E	6%	11%	

8.5   Diversification

40. Evaluate the following statement:
    "Diversification can only exist when the assets' returns are negatively correlated."

41. For each of the following identify the risk:

Characteristic	Type of Risk
Risk that can be eliminated by diversifying	
Risk that remains after diversifying	
Unavoidable risk	

42. Some companies embark on acquisitions for the purposes of diversifying their business, arguing that by acquiring a company that operates in a different line of business, they are reducing the risk of the company as a whole.

   A. What would be the benefit, if any, from this form of diversification to the financial management of the company? Explain.
   B. Would this diversification benefit shareholders of the companies performing this type of diversification? Explain.

43. The New Bedford Analysts have recently published a study claiming that the benefits to diversification are constant. In other words, adding one more stock to a three-stock portfolio will have the same impact as adding one more stock to a 500-stock portfolio. Evaluate this claim.

44. Consider a portfolio that has five investments. The financial manager is considering adding a sixth investment to the portfolio. The possible candidates are:

Security	Expected Return	Standard Deviation of Returns	Correlation with the Company's Existing Investments
A	10%	10%	0.9
B	9%	9%	–0.2
C	9%	8%	–0.2
D	8%	8%	0.0

Which investment do you recommend, and why?

45. A financial analyst with the Auburn Cat Supply Company has developed forecasts for a new cat food product, the Natural Tiger. The analyst is preparing a presentation on the return and risk of this new product and wants to be prepared for questions of how this product will fit into the current lineup of products. The analyst has gathered the following forecasts:

State of the Economy	Probability	Return on Auburn Cat Supply Company	Return on Natural Tiger
High growth	10%	20%	6%
Moderate growth	30%	10%	8%
No growth	50%	3%	12%
Recession	10%	–5%	15%

A. Calculate the expected return for both the company and the new product.
B. Calculate the standard deviation of returns for both the company and the new product.
C. Calculate the covariance and correlation between the returns for the company and the new product.
D. Assume that after investing the product, the company is comprised of 80 percent of products before Natural Tiger, and Natural Tiger is the remaining 20 percent. Should the analyst recommend the new product? Explain.
E. Assume that after investing the product, the company is comprised of 90 percent of products before Natural Tiger, and Natural Tiger is the remaining 10 percent. Should the analyst recommend the new product? Explain.
F. Using a spreadsheet, calculate and graph the expected return and standard deviation of the Auburn Cat Supply Company using different weights for Natural Tiger, ranging from investing such that Natural Tiger comprises 50 percent of the Auburn Cat Supply Company after investment, to 0 percent, in increments of 5 percent. What level of investment would you recommend, relative to the Auburn Cat Supply Company, based on your analysis? Why?

46. Consider the returns on the following ex post returns on three investments:

Year	Investment 1	Investment 2	Investment 3
1	2%	10%	–3%
2	2%	7%	9%
3	3%	8%	–2%
4	4%	9%	12%
5	4%	6%	0%
6	3%	9%	15%
7	3%	10%	–1%
8	3%	5%	20%
9	2%	8%	12%
10	3%	8%	18%

A. What is the arithmetic mean annual return for each investment over these 10 years?

B. What is the geometric mean annual return for each investment over these 10 years?

C. What is the standard deviation of returns for each investment?

D. What is the correlation of returns among each pair of investments (that is, Investment 1 and 2, Investment 1 and 3, and Investment 2 and 3)?

E. If Investment 1 represents a company's existing investments and Investments 2 and 3 are possible investments, which investment, 2 or 3, offers the most diversification potential? Why?

Case

Case 8.1 The Boise Boyz Company

The Boise Boyz Company (BBC) currently has a single line of business, buoys. The company is considering the purchase of one of two companies, each in a different line of business: The Treasure Search Company (TSC) and the Old Lady Knitting Company (OLKC). BBC is four times as large as TSC and OLKC, each considered alone. The financial analysts of BBC have worked up some numbers to present to the CFO, Bobby Boyz, regarding returns on BBC and the two other companies for the next year. The analysts project the following:

Economic Environment	Probability	Returns		
		BBC	TSC	OLKC
Economic recovery	20%	15%	20%	11%
Stagnant economy	50%	8%	10%	10%
Recession	30%	1%	–10%	9%

Answer the following questions regarding the evaluation of the acquisition of TSC and OLKC, using a spreadsheet to perform the calculations:

A. What is the expected return and standard deviation of these returns for each company?

B. What is the expected return if BBC acquires TSC? OLKC?

C. What is the standard deviation of the portfolio consisting of BBC and TSC? BBC and OLKC?

D. Based on the expected return and the portfolio standard deviation, which acquisition is preferred: TSC or OLKC? Explain your reasoning.

CHAPTER 9

ASSET PRICING

© mathieukor/iStockphoto

Hither or Whither the Random Walk? Now in its tenth edition, the popularity of Burton Malkiel's book, *A Random Walk Down Wall Street*, has survived investors' fascination for small stocks, the Internet bubble, and the fervor and fury over mortgage-backed securities.[1] First published in 1973, it has stood the test of time and the market's ups and downs.

The basic message of the book is that the markets are efficient and that it is not possible to beat the market on a risk-adjusted basis. Burton Malkiel dispels the notion that you can earn abnormal returns—that is, those in excess of what you expect based on the amount of risk—using technical analysis or fundamental analysis.

Does this mean that you cannot earn profits when trading in stock? No, but don't expect to earn profits in excess of those adequate for the amount of risk on a consistent basis. Does this mean you should not analyze stocks? No, because fundamental analysis is useful in determining whether a stock fits in your portfolio in terms of returns and risk.

Learning Outcomes

After reading this chapter, you should be able to:

LO 9.1 Describe the importance of the efficient frontier in portfolio selection.

LO 9.2 Describe how the capital market line and returns are determined from modern portfolio theory, and explain the relationship between the capital asset pricing model's security market line and the capital market line.

LO 9.3 Discuss implications of the capital asset pricing model for risks that investors face.

LO 9.4 Describe the basics of models of asset pricing that are alternatives to the CAPM.

LO 9.5 Explain what is meant by market efficiency, and differentiate among different levels of efficiency.

LO 9.6 Discuss the implications of behavioral finance in financial decision making.

Chapter Preview Our focus in this chapter is on the asset pricing models, which help us understand the relation between return and risk and how assets are priced considering risk. We begin our discussion with an overview of the efficient frontier, which is the set of assets that offer the best opportunities in terms of risk and return. We then build on the idea of an efficient frontier, introducing the capital asset pricing model, which describes how assets are priced by market participants. We also look at alternative asset pricing models and then shift our focus to market efficiency. We conclude the chapter with a discussion of the behavior of financial decision makers that does not always match up with what our asset pricing models assume and learn how this behavior may affect decisions.

---

[1] Burton G. Malkiel, *A Random Walk Down Wall Street*, 10th ed. (New York: W. W. Norton & Company, 2011).

9.1   THE EFFICIENT FRONTIER

Which would you rather have?

Receive $100 if a coin flip
produces a head
Pay $100 if a coin flip produces a tail   or $50

This is a fair gamble because the expected payoff is $0, that is, the expected payoff is [$100 × 0.50] + [–$100 × 0.50] = $0. If someone turns down a fair gamble, he or she is likely risk averse. A risk-averse person prefers the risk-free situation—that is, not gambling on a risky situation where there is an equal probability of winning or losing the same amount of money. We assume that investors are risk averse when choosing among different investments: Investors are not willing to undertake fair gambles.

The Role of Risk

The corollary to turning down a fair gamble is that the risk-averse person requires a **risk premium** to enter into a risky situation. For example, someone might be willing to undertake a gamble if the head's payoff is $150 instead of $100. In this case, the expected payoff increases to $25, and it is no longer a fair gamble because there is a risk premium of $25. Another person may require that the head's payoff increases to $200 before undertaking the gamble, so the risk premium increases to $50. The second individual is more risk averse and requires a larger expected payoff or risk premium to get into the risky situation. Generally, investor behavior is consistent with risk aversion and the existence of risk premiums to induce individuals to bear risk. We can represent this risk aversion by the required risk premium per unit of risk, with higher risk premiums indicating greater risk aversion.

We can also reverse the situation and put the individual in a risky situation and ask how much he or she is willing to pay to get out of the risky situation. Suppose, for example, someone faces a fair gamble; how much would he or she pay to get out of it? A very risk averse individual would pay a large amount, say $25, to get out of the fair gamble with equally likely payoffs of +/–$100. In this case, instead of calling the increased payoff a risk premium, we refer to the payment to get out of a risky situation as an **insurance premium**.

insurance premium payment to get out of a risky situation

The Efficient Frontier with Risk-Free Borrowing and Lending

The existence of insurance markets indicates how risk aversion creates a demand to remove risk, whereas the existence of capital markets indicates how risk aversion generates risk premiums required to induce people to bear risk. We assume that investors are risk averse, that is, they require a risk premium to bear risk. We also assume that the more risk averse an investor, the higher the risk premium the investor requires. Further, we assume that we can represent risk by the standard deviation of the return on the portfolio.[2]

These assumptions lead to the result that investors choose only portfolios on the efficient frontier. The efficient frontier represents all portfolios of risky assets that have better risk-return situations than other portfolios of risky assets, which we represent in Figure 9-1.

---

[2] This is a simplification, but helps illustrates the point. The standard deviation assumes that the individual is just as concerned about making too little as making too much return on an investment. There are metrics that we could use to address this (e.g., semivariance), but this is beyond the scope of this book.

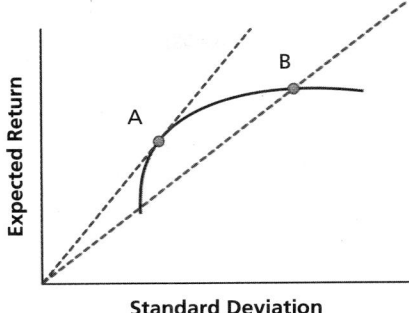

FIGURE 9-1 The Efficient Frontier

We can't say where a particular person's preference falls on the efficient frontier because individuals differ in terms of their risk aversion. But a very risk-averse individual may choose portfolio A, and a less risk-averse individual may choose portfolio B. Why do we know that the investor choosing A is more risk averse than the investor choosing B? The line going through A to the origin is steeper than the line through B and the origin. The slope of the line is the height (the expected return on the portfolio) divided by the length (the standard deviation of the portfolio). Because the line through A is steeper than the line through B, the individual who invests in A requires a higher expected rate of return per unit of risk—that is, he or she is more risk averse.

Many lines go through the origin and touch different points on the efficient frontier: the flatter the line, the less risk averse the investor. Investors choose a portfolio with a lower expected rate of return per unit of risk and gradually move out along the efficient frontier. Apart from knowing that investors differ in terms of their risk aversion, we know only that their preferred portfolio lies somewhere along the efficient frontier.[3]

The origin is the point with a zero expected rate of return and zero risk. Another way of describing a risk-free asset is that it has zero risk, such as a government's Treasury security, where the return on the asset is guaranteed with no possibility of earning more or less. We usually use a Treasury security as the risk-free asset simply because they are obligations of the government, which also has a monopoly on issuing government bank notes; Treasury securities are default free because investors generally believe that they will always be paid off in full.

Risk-Free Investing

Consider any point on the efficient frontier in Figure 9-1. Now, assume an investor places a portion w of his or her wealth in the risky portfolio X and the remainder $(1 - w)$ in the risk-free asset, a U.S. Treasury bond. Remember that the expected return on a portfolio is always a weighted average of the expected returns on the individual assets, so we can estimate the expected return on this portfolio as:

$$E(r_p) = r_f + w[E(r_X) - r_f] \qquad (9\text{-}1)$$

where $E(r_p)$ is the expected return on the portfolio, r_f is the expected return on the risk-free asset, $E(r_X)$ is the expected return on the risky portfolio X, and w is the proportion of the portfolio invested in the risk portfolio.

Suppose the investor begins with a 100 percent investment in the risk-free asset; that is, $w = 0$. As the investor shifts the portfolio, adding more of the risky asset, w increases,

---

[3] The previous discussion may be a bit light for those with extensive economics training. We could represent each individual by his or her indifference curve, symbolizing his or her risk aversion and personal trade-off between risk and return. However, this adds little to our discussion.

so the investor increases the expected return on the portfolio, $E(r_p)$, at the cost of reducing the investment in the risk-free asset. As a result, the expected return on the portfolio increases by the difference: $E(r_X) - r_f$.

If the return on the risk-free asset is 3 percent and the return on the risky portfolio X is 11 percent, a portfolio consisting only of the risk-free asset has an expected return of 3 percent, whereas a portfolio consisting of only the risky portfolio X has an expected return of 11 percent. However, a portfolio consisting of equal parts of the risk-free and risky portfolio X has an expected return of:

$$E(r_p) = (0.50 \times 0.03) + (0.50 \times 0.11) = 0.07 \text{ or } 7\%$$

We can estimate the standard deviation on this portfolio as:[4]

$$\sigma_p = \sqrt{w_X^2 \sigma_X^2 + w_Y^2 \sigma_Y^2 + [2\,w_X w_Y \sigma_X \sigma_Y \rho_{XY}]}$$

where σ_X^2 and σ_Y^2 are the standard deviations of the returns on assets X and Y, respectively, w_X and w_Y are the proportions invested in X and Y, respectively, and ρ_{XY} is the correlation of returns between X and Y.

If we replace portfolio Y with the risk-free security, $(1 - w)$ for w_Y, we arrive at the following:

$$\sigma_p = \sqrt{w^2 \sigma_X^2 + (1 - w)^2 \sigma_{r_f}^2 + [2\,(1 - w)\,w\,\rho_{X,r_f} \sigma_X \sigma_{r_f}]}$$

We know exactly what we are going to get from the risk-free asset, so the standard deviation of its return is zero; that is, $\sigma_{r_f} = 0 = 0$. Because the return does not vary, the correlation between the return on the risk-free asset and that on the risky portfolio X is also zero. Therefore, the standard deviation with $\sigma_{rf} = 0$ and $\rho_{X,rf} = 0$ reduces to:

$$\sigma_p = \sqrt{w^2 \sigma_X^2}$$

Taking the square root of the final term leaves us with Equation 9-2:

$$\sigma_p = w\sigma_X \tag{9-2}$$

In other words, portfolio risk increases in direct proportion to the amount invested in the risky asset, w. Therefore, the higher the proportion of the portfolio allocated to the risky asset, the higher the portfolio risk.

If the standard deviation of the returns on risky portfolio X is 20 percent, a portfolio comprising equal parts of the risk-free asset and the risky portfolio X will have a standard deviation of:

$$\sigma_p = 0.5 \times 0.20 = 0.10 \text{ or } 10\%$$

If, on the other hand, only 25 percent of the portfolio is invested in the risk-free asset and 75 percent is invested in portfolio X, the portfolio's standard deviation is:

$$\sigma_p = 0.75 \times 0.20 = 0.15 \text{ or } 15\%$$

Because both the expected return and the standard deviation of a portfolio comprising any risky portfolio and a risk-free asset can be represented by a line that is based on the weights invested in r_f and in the risky asset, we can express all the expected returns and risks for various portfolio combinations as a straight line. We can show this by rearranging Equation 9-2 in terms of the portfolio weight:

$$w = \frac{\sigma_p}{\sigma_X}$$

and substituting for w in Equation 9-1, we can solve for the return on the portfolio, $E(r_p)$:

$$E(r_p) = r_f + \left(\frac{E(r_X) - r_f}{\sigma_X} \right) \sigma_p \tag{9-3}$$

---

[4] This equation was introduced in Chapter 8.

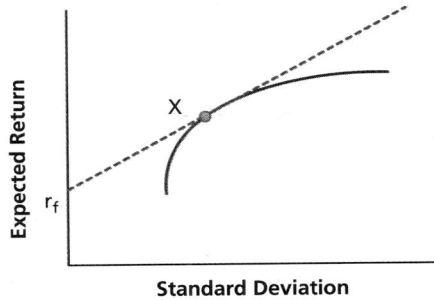

FIGURE 9-2 Portfolio of the Risk-Free Asset and Risky Assets

Equation 9-3 is the equation of a straight line when we graph the expected return against the portfolio standard deviation: The line intersects the vertical axis at the risk-free rate and then has a constant slope. The slope is the rise over the run, or the increased expected return divided by the increased risk. The increased expected return, as discussed, is the incremental return on the risky portfolio minus the lost return by taking money out of the risk-free asset. We represent this portfolio in Figure 9-2.

We interpret this figure the same as before: if $w = 0$, all the investment is in the risk-free asset (e.g., Treasury security), and the portfolio has no risk and earns r_f. As w increases, the expected return on the portfolio increases by $E(r_X) - r_f$ and its risk by σ_P, until $w = 100$ percent and the portfolio expected return is $E(r_X)$ and its risk is σ_X.

Consider portfolio T in Figure 9-3. All portfolios composed of risky portfolio T and the risk-free rate lie along the line from r_f to T and offer a higher expected rate of return for the same risk as do portfolios composed of the risk-free rate and risky portfolio X. Portfolio T is the **tangent portfolio**; graphically, it is the risky portfolio on the efficient frontier whose tangent line cuts the vertical axis at the risk-free rate. Portfolios composed of the risk-free asset and portfolio T offer the highest expected rate of return for any given level of risk and represent the **new efficient frontier** (or **super-efficient frontier**), which we depict in Figure 9-4.

Consider, for example, portfolio X, which was optimal for a very risk-averse investor before we considered investing in the risk-free asset. Now this investor could hold a portfolio of the risk-free asset and the risky portfolio T that offers a higher expected rate of return for the same risk as X. This is the new portfolio X+. What this demonstrates is that a portfolio partially invested in the risk-free asset reduces the portfolio risk but can achieve a higher expected rate of return than any portfolio on the efficient frontier of risky assets.

tangent portfolio risky portfolio on the efficient frontier whose tangent line cuts the vertical axis at the risk-free rate

new efficient frontier or **super-efficient frontier** portfolios composed of the risk-free rate and the tangent portfolio that offer the highest expected rate of return for any given level of risk

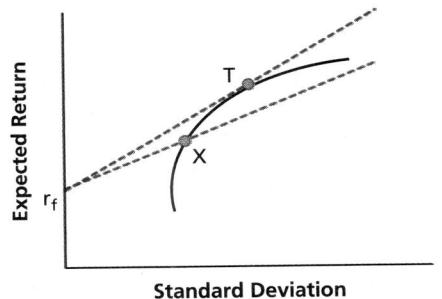

FIGURE 9-3 Efficient Portfolios

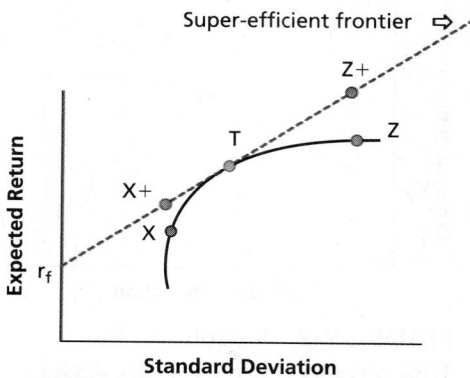

FIGURE 9-4 The New Efficient Frontier

EXAMPLE 9.1

Expected Return and Standard Deviation for a Two-Asset Portfolio That Includes Investment in a Risk-Free Asset

PROBLEM

Assume that a portfolio R has an expected return of 10 percent, with a standard deviation of 25 percent, and that the risk-free rate is 4.5 percent. Estimate the expected return and standard deviation for a portfolio that has 30 percent invested in the risk-free asset and 70 percent in R.

Solution

$w = 0.70; (1 - w) = 0.30$

Therefore,

$E(r_p) = (0.30 \times 4.5\%) + (0.70 \times 10\%) = 1.35\% + 7.0\% = 8.35\%$

and

$\sigma_p = 0.70 \times 25\% = 17.50\%$

Risk-Free Borrowing

Now consider a less risk-averse investor who held portfolio Z in Figure 9-4. That investor could now hold portfolio Z+ and also get a higher expected rate of return for the same level of risk as Z. However, getting to portfolio Z+ involves having more than 100 percent invested in the risky portfolio T ($w > 100$ percent) and thus a negative or **short position** in the risk-free asset.

short position negative position in an investment

We create a short position in the risk-free asset by borrowing. One way to do this is to buy stocks on margin, which means the investor can borrow part of the purchase price from a broker.[5] For example, some stocks have margin requirements as low as 30 percent, indicating an investor could buy $1,000 worth of stocks by investing only $300 and borrowing the remaining $700 from a broker. In this case, the portfolio weights are $w = 1,000 \div 300$ or 333 percent in the risky asset and –233 percent in the risk-free asset. Of course, investors must pay interest on the borrowed money. For simplicity, we assume that they can also borrow at the risk-free rate.[6]

---

[5] In the case of an interest-bearing debt instrument, if you invest in the debt instrument and receive income, you have a *long* position; if you are on the other side of the transaction, the borrower, you have a *short* position.
[6] Although borrowing rates are generally higher than the risk-free rate in practice, this assumption can be relaxed without greatly affecting our key results.

Consider an investor who invests $10,000 in a portfolio of risky assets, portfolio V. Portfolio V has an expected return of 12 percent and a standard deviation of returns of 25 percent. If, in addition, the investor borrows $5,000 at the risk-free rate of 3 percent and invests it in portfolio V, the total invested in portfolio V increases to $15,000. What is the expected return on this investment? The expected return calculation requires us to first calculate the weights:

$$w = \$15,000 \div \$10,000 = 1.5$$
$$(1 - w) = 1 - 1.5 = -0.5$$

In other words, there is a short position, borrowing at the risk-free rate. The expected return on the portfolio is therefore:

$$E(r_p) = (-0.50 \times 0.03) + (1.50 \times 0.12) = -0.015 + 0.18 = 0.165 \text{ or } 16.5\%$$

The standard deviation of the investor's investment, considering both the investment in the risky portfolio V and the borrowing, is the weight invested in the risky portfolio (150 percent, in this example), multiplied by the standard deviation of the returns on the risky asset (the 25 percent):

$$\sigma_P = w\sigma_X = 1.50 \times 0.25 = 0.375 \text{ or } 37.5\%$$

PROBLEM

Assume that an investor invests all her wealth, $1,000, in a portfolio that has an expected return of 10 percent and a standard deviation of 25 percent. She borrows an additional $700 at the risk-free rate of 4.5 percent, which she also invests in the portfolio. Estimate the expected return and standard deviation for this portfolio.

Solution

$$w = 1,700 \div 1,000 = 1.70;$$

$$(1 - w) = 1 - 1.70 = -0.70$$

Therefore,

$$E(r_p) = (-0.70 \times 0.045) + (1.70 \times 0.10) = -0.0315 + 0.17 = 0.1385 \text{ or } 13.85\%$$

$$\sigma(r_p) = 1.70 \times 0.25\% = 0.425 \text{ or } 42.50\%$$

EXAMPLE 9.2

Expected Return and Standard Deviation for a Two-Asset Portfolio That Includes Borrowing at the Risk-Free Rate

The Separation Theorem

We showed earlier that any point along the tangent line from the risk-free rate is attainable by either investing or borrowing at r_p and then investing all remaining proceeds in the risky portfolio T. From Figure 9-4, we see that all the portfolios along this line dominate all the portfolios on the efficient frontier, except for point T. As we showed, X+ is better than X and Z+ is better than Z. Therefore, allowing for the possibility of risk-free investing and borrowing expands the efficient set and provides investors with *more* portfolios from which to choose. This line is the new (or super) efficient frontier. The efficient frontier that we started with is the *efficient frontier of risky portfolios*, which distinguishes it from the efficient frontier of the risk-free asset and the tangent portfolio.

Investors can achieve any point on this new efficient frontier by borrowing or investing desired amounts at the risk-free rate and investing the remainder in one portfolio of risky assets, which is the tangent portfolio T. Therefore, each investor can choose the point on this line that suits his or her personal risk preferences: More risk-averse investors can choose portfolios, like X+, that are heavily invested in the risk-free asset, whereas more aggressive investors can choose portfolios, like Z+, that involve borrowing.

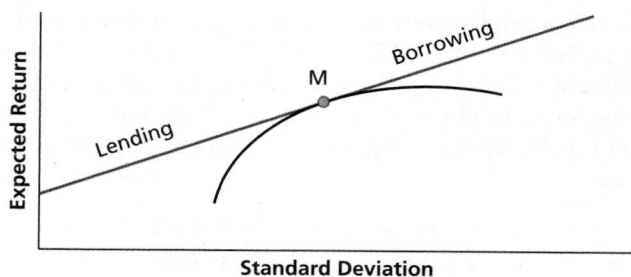

FIGURE 9-5 Separation Theorem

Suppose investors all agree on the expected rates of return and the risk attached to each security. In that case, the efficient frontier of risky assets is the same for all investors. This would occur, for example, if the investors were clients of an investment company that estimated all these values and then discussed the best portfolio for a particular client. It would no longer be necessary to match each investor's risk preferences with a specific risky portfolio. Instead, the investment company would recommend the same tangent portfolio to all its clients. It might then refer to this portfolio as its model portfolio, and some investors would invest in this and the risk-free asset, whereas others would borrow to invest in the model portfolio.

Suppose further that all investment companies agreed on the set of expected returns and the risk attached to the securities. In that case, the tangent or model portfolio would also be the same. This result provides the basis for the **separation theorem**, which is that the investment decision (that is, how to construct the portfolio of risky assets) is separate from the financing decision (that is, how much should be invested or borrowed in the risk-free asset). In other words, the tangent portfolio T is optimal for every investor regardless of his or her degree of risk aversion. Further, if everyone holds the same portfolio, it must be the **market portfolio** of all risky securities, which we represent as M, as we show in Figure 9-5, because every security has to be held by someone. This is an equilibrium condition because supply equals demand for all the risky securities, and we replace T with M, which is not just the tangent portfolio but also the market portfolio. This hypothesis is the basis for the most common model we use in finance to price securities, which we discuss in the next section.

separation theorem theory that the investment decision (how to construct the portfolio of risky assets) is separate from the financing decision (how much should be invested or borrowed in the risk-free asset)

market portfolio portfolio that contains all risky securities in the market

---

Concept Review Questions

1. What is risk aversion, and how do we know investors are risk averse?

2. What is the risk of a portfolio consisting of a risk-free asset and a risky security?

3. Why is the tangent portfolio so important?

4. How do we generate a portfolio with a higher expected rate of return than that of the tangent portfolio?

9.2   THE CAPITAL ASSET PRICING MODEL

capital asset pricing model (CAPM) pricing model that describes the expected return as the sum of the risk-free rate of interest and a premium for bearing market risk

William Sharpe and John Lintner are credited for developing the **capital asset pricing model (CAPM)**, which is a model that describes expected returns in terms of the risk-free rate of interest and a premium for bearing market risk.[7] The initial development of the CAPM is based on a number of assumptions that we have already briefly discussed:

[7] William F. Sharpe ["Capital Asset Prices: A Theory of Market Equilibrium under Conditions of Risk," *Journal of Finance*, Vol. 19 (1964): 425–442] and John Lintner ["The Valuation of Risk Assets and Selection of Risky Investments in Stock Portfolios and Capital Budgets," *Review of Economics and Statistics,* Vol. 47 (1965): 13–37]. William Sharpe won the Nobel prize for developing the best-known equilibrium asset pricing model, which relates expected returns to risk.

1. All investors have identical expectations about expected returns, standard deviations, and correlation coefficients for all securities.

2. All investors have the same one-period time horizon.

3. All investors can borrow or lend money at the risk-free rate of return (r_f).

4. There are no transaction costs.

5. There are no personal income taxes so that investors are indifferent between capital gains and dividends.

6. There are many investors, and no single investor can affect the price of a stock through his or her buying and selling decisions. Therefore, investors are price takers.

7. Capital markets are in equilibrium.

These assumptions may appear unrealistic at first. For example, we need the assumption of identical expectations so that the efficient frontier of risky portfolios is the same for all investors. However, not all investors have the same impact in the market; the most important are the big institutions that invest most of the money. They all have access to the same information, and they all have expert analysts analyzing the data. Similarly, borrowing rates differ from lending rates for small investors, but for large institutional investors, the difference is not material. The same applies to transaction costs. The result is that most of the assumptions can be relaxed without significantly affecting the CAPM or its main implications. However, before discussing the CAPM, we discuss what happens to the overall capital market.

The Market Portfolio and the Capital Market Line

The assumptions for the CAPM listed earlier give rise to the following very important implications, which we discussed previously:

1. The "optimal" risky portfolio is the one that is tangent to the efficient frontier on a line that is drawn from the risk-free rate, as we show in Figure 9-4. This portfolio is the same for all investors.

2. This optimal risky portfolio is the market portfolio that contains all risky securities. The value of this portfolio is the aggregate of the market values of all the individual assets in the portfolio. Therefore, the weights of these assets in the market portfolio are their proportionate weight in its total value.

As we have discussed, the second implication results from our assumption that market equilibrium exists. This implies that supply equals demand—in other words, all assets are assumed to be bought and sold at the equilibrium price established by supply and demand. Because all assets trade, it must mean that they are correctly priced to adequately compensate investors for the associated risks. For example, if an asset is priced too high, and therefore the expected rate of return is too low, demand for it would fall, as would its price. Market clearing implies that the price would eventually fall to an equilibrium level. Because the market consists of all available assets, and all these assets are assumed to be priced correctly to reflect adequate compensation for the associated risk, the market portfolio is the most efficient (or optimal) portfolio, with respect to the weights attached to the individual securities in the market portfolio.

Theoretically, the market portfolio should contain all risky assets worldwide, including stocks, bonds, options, futures, gold, real estate, and so on, in their proper proportions. Such a portfolio, if it could be constructed, is completely diversified. However, in practice, the market portfolio is unobservable, so we use proxies to measure its behavior. It is common to use stock market indexes, such as the S&P 500 Composite Index in the United States. We graph the relationship between expected return and standard deviation implied by the capital asset pricing model in Figure 9-6. This graph is similar to Figure 9-4, but we do not include the efficient frontier portion, and the only portfolio is M, the tangent portfolio, because the market portfolio (M) is the optimal portfolio of risky securities that is combined with the risk-free asset. Recall that this line produces the highest attainable expected return for any given risk level; therefore, it includes only efficient portfolios.

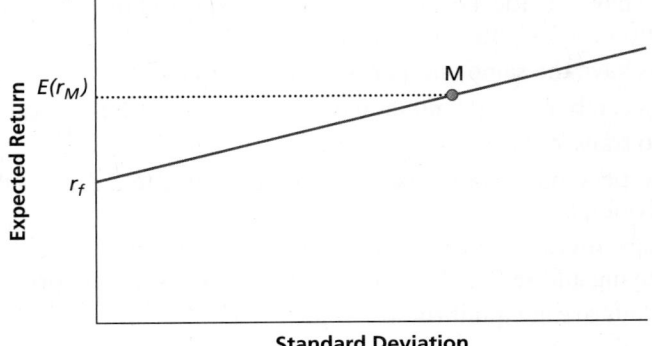

FIGURE 9-6 The Capital Market Line

capital market line (CML) line depicting the highest attainable expected return for any given risk level that includes only efficient portfolios

Further, all rational, risk-averse investors will seek to be on this line. In Figure 9-6, this line is the **capital market line (CML)**.

We can see from Figure 9-6 that the CML has an intercept of r_f, just as with any portfolio consisting of the risk-free asset and a risky portfolio. But the risky portfolio is not arbitrary: Now it is the market portfolio. So we have a special version of Equation 9-3:

$$\text{Slope of the CML} = \frac{E(r_M) - r_f}{\sigma_M} \qquad (9\text{-}4)$$

market price of risk incremental expected return divided by the incremental risk; indicates the additional expected return that the market demands for an increase in risk

As in Equation 9-3, the slope of the capital market line is the incremental expected return divided by the incremental risk. This special trade-off of risk and return is the **market price of risk** for efficient portfolios; in other words, this is the equilibrium price of risk in the capital market. It indicates the additional expected return that the market demands for an increase in a portfolio's risk. Adding the risk-free rate, r_f, gives the CML as

$$E(r_p) = r_f + \left[\frac{E(r_M) - r_f}{\sigma_M} \right] \sigma_p \qquad (9\text{-}5)$$

$E(r_M)$ = the expected return on the market portfolio M;

σ_M = the standard deviation of returns on the market portfolio; and

σ_p = the standard deviation of returns on the efficient portfolio being considered.

The CML is a special version of Equation 9-3 in another important way. The CML indicates an expected rate of return, yet we have made enough assumptions to identify the portfolio as the market portfolio and as an equilibrium condition in the capital market, where supply equals demand. As a result, the CML describes not just an expected rate of return but also the appropriate return for the risk, which is the **required rate of return,** that we denote as $E(r_p)$.

Having defined the CML, we can focus on the difference between expected and required rates of return. Consider the CML that we show in Figure 9-7, and we are looking at three portfolios: D, E, and F.

- Only portfolio E lies on the CML. For this portfolio, the expected rate of return is the same as the required rate of return, so the portfolio is fairly priced.

- The expected return on Portfolio F is higher than that of E. However, this portfolio is below the CML, which indicates that the required rate of return is higher than this expected rate of return. If we look at just the expected rate of return, F would seem to be a good buy, but this is wrong because it is a very risky portfolio. Given its risk, it is a bad buy, and its price would drop, forcing up its expected rate of return until it was fairly priced and the expected and required rates of return were the same.

PROBLEM

Assume the expected risk-free rate is 4.5 percent. The expected return on the market is 10 percent, and it has a standard deviation of 20 percent. Determine the expected return necessary for investors to hold an efficient portfolio with a standard deviation of 25 percent.

EXAMPLE 9.3
Using the CML

Solution

$$E(r_p) = E(r_f) + \left[\frac{E(r_M) - E(r_f)}{\sigma_M} \right] \sigma_p$$

$$= 0.045 + \left[\frac{0.10 - 0.045}{0.20} \right] \times 0.25$$

$$= 0.045 + (0.275 \times 0.25)$$

$$= 0.045 + 0.06875 = 11.375\%$$

Notice that the required return on the portfolio is greater than that expected for the market portfolio because it has a higher standard deviation.

- Portfolio D presents the opposite situation: It has a high expected rate of return and relatively low risk. In this case, the expected rate of return exceeds the required rate of return, and investors would bid up its price and cause its expected rate of return to fall until it lies on the CML.

It is also important to recognize that:

1. The CML must always be *upward sloping* because the risk premium always be positive with risk averse investors, and
2. The CML predicts *required* returns.

As a result, risk-averse investors will not invest unless they expect compensation for bearing risk. The greater the risk, the greater the required rate of return.

However, there is a big difference between ex post and ex ante returns. After the fact (ex post) returns can be, and often have been, less than the Treasury rate. If this were never the case, investing in the equity market would have no risk, and no one would hold Treasury securities. The observation of ex post poor returns on risky securities does not negate the validity of the CML, however; it merely indicates that returns actually realized

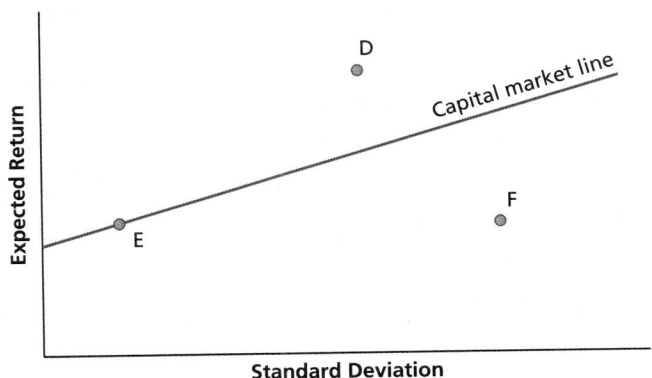

FIGURE 9-7 Expected and Required Rates of Return

differed from those that were expected. Another way of saying this is that investors sometimes get it wrong, and they do not get what they expected. Of course, if investors were never wrong, there would be no risk in the equity market.

The ideas that we have just described are a critical part of the evaluation of investment performance in a financial system. Consider the slope of the CML. In equilibrium, all portfolios should lie along the CML, investors will bid up those offering higher expected returns than the required rate of return, and investors will bid down those offering lower returns than the required rates of return. The CML is based on expected rates of return, so it is ex ante. However, if expectations are realized (that is, on average the actual return is what was expected), we can use the CML to judge the performance of different portfolios ex post, that is, actual portfolio performance.

FINANCE in the News | Efficient Frontier

The true challenge to investment professionals today is to find an investment solution that can assemble non-correlated asset classes that are liquid, transparent and still appropriate for individual investor's risk profiles wherein the Efficient Frontier meets the client's "indifference curve."

A security's real risk is the variability of its returns that cannot be diversified away, called systematic beta risk. Systematic beta risk has increased significantly on many traditional strategic asset allocation models, causing considerable damage to account values and in some cases, panic by clients. Non-correlation is the major influence in this increased systematic beta risk crisis challenging the efficacy of strategic investment portfolios, and investment professionals are desperate to find alternative solutions.

Excerpt from "The Dubious Efficiency of the Efficient Frontier," by Andrew Hanlon, *Forbes*, April 9, 2009.

Risk-Adjusted Performance and the Sharpe Ratio

When the ideas underlying the CML are used in this way, it leads to the **Sharpe ratio,** the ratio of *ex post* excess returns to risk[8]:

$$\text{Sharpe ratio} = \frac{r_p - r_f}{\sigma_p} \qquad (9\text{-}6)$$

Sharpe ratio or **reward-to-variability ratio** or **reward-to-risk ratio** measure of portfolio performance that describes how well an asset's return compensates investors for the risk taken

We also refer to the Sharpe ratio as the **reward-to-variability ratio** or the **reward-to-risk ratio** because this ratio is a comparison of the return, in excess of the risk-free rate, to risk. This measure is commonly used to evaluate the historical (that is, ex post) performance of portfolio managers. When comparing two investments, the investment with the higher Sharpe ratio is preferred because the investment with the higher Sharpe ratio provides the greater reward per unit of risk. The ex ante Sharpe ratio of the market portfolio is the slope of the CML.

Suppose a portfolio has an expected return of 5 percent and a standard deviation of returns of 8 percent. If the risk-free rate of interest is 3 percent, the Sharpe ratio is:

$$\text{Sharpe ratio} = \frac{0.05 - 0.03}{0.08} = 0.25$$

We have derived the Sharpe ratio in terms of "expected" (i.e., ex ante) returns in our discussion. However, in practice, it is a commonly used measure of ex post (i.e., realized) returns, where we replace expected returns with historic realized returns. For example, a

[8] This ratio is named after William Sharpe of Stanford University, who developed it and first applied it to assessing portfolio performance.

EXAMPLE 9.4

Sharpe Ratios

PROBLEM

a. Calculate the Sharpe ratio for each of the following securities, assuming a risk-free rate of 3 percent:

Security	Expected Return	Standard Deviation of Returns
A	4%	3%
B	5%	5%
C	4.5%	7%
D	3.5%	2%

b. Which security has the best reward-to-risk ratio?

Solution

a.

Security	Sharpe Ratio
A	0.33
B	0.40
C	0.21
D	0.33

b. Security B has the highest Sharpe ratio.

---

stock has return of 6 percent and a standard deviation of returns of 7 percent. If the return on the risk-free security is 2 percent, the Sharpe ratio of the stock is 0.571:

$$\text{Sharpe ratio} = \frac{0.06 - 0.02}{0.07} = 0.5714$$

---

1. What is the market price of risk according to the CML?

2. If the expected return on a diversified portfolio lies above the CML, should an investor buy or sell it?

3. When is the expected return equal to the required return?

4. Why is the Sharpe ratio frequently referred to as a "risk-adjusted" measure of performance?

9.3 THE CAPM AND MARKET RISK

The CML provides a method of estimating the required return on equity assets relative to their risk, but it applies only to efficient portfolios and not to individual securities. In addition, the risk premium is based on portfolio risk, as measured by the standard deviation of the return on the portfolio. In financial management, we are usually concerned with the risk associated with individual firms and the required return for investing in them. From the principles of diversification, we know that as the number of securities included

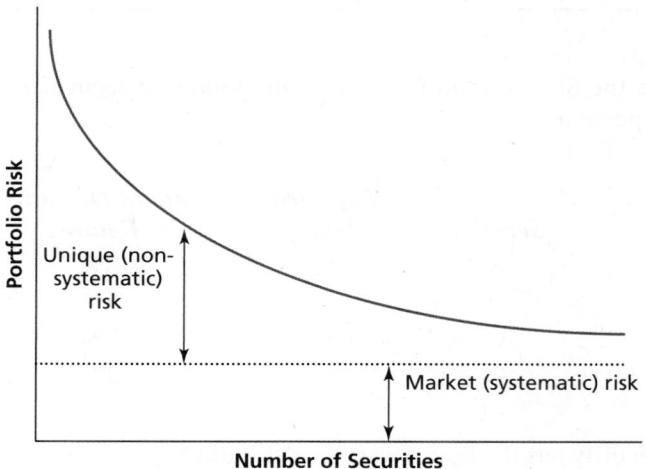

FIGURE 9-8   Portfolio Risk and Diversification

in a portfolio increases, unique (nonsystematic or diversifiable) risk is eliminated, and only market (systematic or nondiversifiable) risk remains. We depict this relationship in Figure 9-8.

We show the average risk of an individual security in Figure 9-8, where the curve gets very close to the vertical axis, that is, a one-stock portfolio. Therefore, by randomly building diversified portfolios, the risk of a portfolio falls until it reaches a baseline, and we cannot reduce risk below this market level. What this means is that part of an asset's risk is diversifiable. Further, if it can be diversified away by holding a portfolio of more than, say, 20 different assets, it is not important to rational investors. This is the key insight of the CAPM.

GLOBAL PERSPECTIVE | Is There Still a Benefit from International Diversification?

The implication of modern portfolio theory and the capital asset pricing model is that investors can benefit from holding a well-diversified portfolio. Investing internationally has been seen as one way to enhance diversification, reducing the level of market risk below the level available domestically. This is because different countries have different economic growth and different timing and extent of expansions and contractions in their business cycle.

But is this still true? With market integration on a global scale, increased international trade and flow of funds, and increased cooperation among central banks in times of economic stress, is there still diversification benefit from investing internationally?

Much of the evidence suggests that there is a little benefit from international diversification in developed markets, but some diversification benefit remaining in emerging markets, where an emerging market is a market in an economy in which there is low to middle per capita income.[9] Therefore, an investor in the U.S. is not likely to achieve much diversification by investing in Germany or Japan. But a U.S. investor may achieve diversification by investing in Morocco or Indonesia.

So, yes, it is possible to reduce risk by investing internationally, but the benefit depends on which country.

---

[9] Peterson Christoffersen, Vihang R. Errunca, Kris Jacos, and Xisong Jin, "Is the Potential for International Diversification Disappearing?" working paper, March 16, 2010, Available at SSRN: ssrn.com/abstract=1573345.

Beta

In the CAPM, rational investors are not compensated for unique or diversifiable risk because it can be eliminated through diversification. This implies that market risk is the appropriate measure of risk to determine the risk premium required by investors for holding a risky security. We now introduce a new term, **beta (β_i)**, which is a commonly used measure of market risk that relates to the extent to which the return on an asset moves with that on the overall market.

We typically estimate beta by first plotting the returns on an individual security on the vertical axis relative to the returns for the market, which we plot along the horizontal axis, and then fitting a line through the observations, as we show in Figure 9-9. The line is the **characteristic line**, and we determine it by using a statistical technique called regression analysis. Regression is a statistical method of determining the best fitting line that depicts the relationship between two variables; in this case, between the return on an asset and the return on the market portfolio. The slope of the line is the asset's beta coefficient. For example, in Figure 9-7, the slope coefficient is 0.85, which indicates that if the return on the market portfolio goes up or down by 1.0 percent, the return on this asset is expected to go up or down by 0.85 percent, respectively; that is, it changes by 0.85 of the return on the market.[10]

Estimating beta coefficients is tricky because we are interested in the extent that an asset's returns move with the market over a future period. We typically estimate beta coefficients by using historical data, which assumes that what has happened in the past is a good predictor for the future. Typically, betas for securities are estimated by using 60 months of monthly returns, but sometimes 52 weekly returns are used. Betas change through time as the risk of the underlying asset or portfolio changes. This is particularly important for individual securities, for which betas can change quite dramatically over relatively short periods. Conversely, betas estimated for large portfolios or for industries are much more stable because of averaging over many assets. Therefore, estimates of portfolio betas show less change from period to period and are much more reliable than are the estimates for individual assets.

beta (β_i) measure of market risk, or performance volatility, that relates the extent to which the return on an asset moves with that on the overall market; the covariance between an investment and the market divided by variance of the market

characteristic line line of best fit through the returns on an individual asset, plotted on the vertical axis, relative to the returns for the market, plotted along the horizontal axis

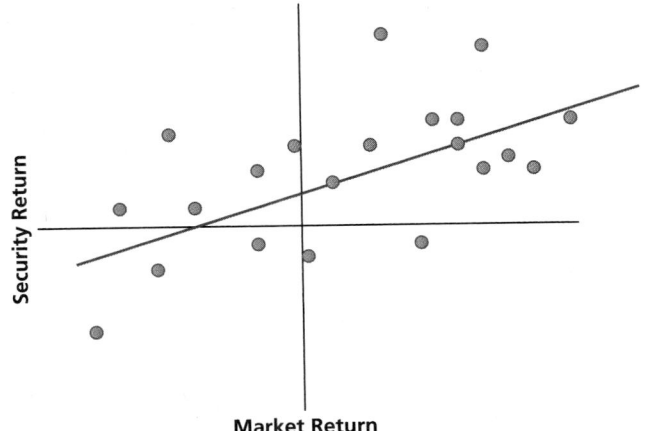

FIGURE 9-9 **The Characteristic Line for Security A**

---

[10] The characteristic line is also often estimated by using excess returns. The excess return is calculated by subtracting the risk-free rate from both the return on the stock and the return on the market. In excess return form, the same analysis applies.

Under some common statistical assumptions, we can estimate betas by using Equation 9-7:[11]

$$\beta_i = \frac{\text{Covariance of returns in security } i}{\text{Variance of the market portfolio's returns}} = \frac{COV_{i,M}}{\sigma_M^2} = \frac{\rho_{i,M}\sigma_i}{\sigma_M} \quad (9\text{-}7)$$

In Equation 9-7, we can see that the beta of an individual asset is the ratio of the covariance of that asset's return with the market, compared to the total variance of the market portfolio's returns.

Beta is a measure of the risk of an individual asset, stock, or portfolio relative to the market portfolio. A beta of 1 implies that if the market return increased (or decreased) by 1 percent, the return on the security (or portfolio) would, on average, increase (decrease) by 1 percent. Therefore, the market portfolio, by definition, has a beta of 1. An asset with a beta of 1.2 has returns that are 1.2 times as volatile as market returns, both up and down. In other words, if the market increased 10 percent, that security's returns would increase by 12 percent, and so on.[12]

Consider an example. Stock One has a beta of 0.8, whereas Stock Two has a beta of 1.2. If the returns on the market increase by 3 percent, we expect:

- Stock One returns to increase by $0.8 \times 0.03 = 0.024$ or 2.4%
- Stock Two returns to increase by $1.2 \times 0.03 = 0.036$ or 3.6%

If the returns on the market decline by 3 percent, we expect:

- Stock One returns to decline by $0.8 \times 0.03 = 0.024$ or 2.4%
- Stock Two returns to decline by $1.2 \times 0.03 = 0.036$ or 3.6%

<table>
<tr><td rowspan="10" style="background:gray">SUMMARIZING: BETAS AND MARKET RISK</td></tr>
</table>

Beta		*Market Risk*
Greater than 1.0	$\beta_i > 1$	More market risk than the average security in the market
Equal to 1.0	$\beta_i = 1$	Market risk the same as the average security in the market
Less than 1.0	$\beta_i < 1$	Less market risk than the average security in the market
0	$\beta_i = 0$	No market risk (e.g., risk-free security)
Less than 0.0	$\beta_i < 0$	Negative correlation with the market return[13]

[11] The characteristic line is also often estimated by using excess returns. The excess return is calculated by subtracting the risk-free rate from both the return on the stock and the return on the market. In excess return form, the same analysis applies.

[12] You may notice that beta is an elasticity measure: It captures the sensitivity of the return on the stock to changes in the return on the market.

[13] According to Equation 9-7, negative betas can only occur if an asset has a negative correlation coefficient with market returns, which is uncommon. This is the only way a negative beta is possible because the standard deviation terms in Equation 9-7 are always positive. Gold stocks have sometimes had negative betas because the price of gold tended to go in the opposite direction of the market; investors would invest in gold when they were nervous about future market movements. However, this relationship is not as strong as it used to be, and negative betas rarely occur, even for gold stocks.

PROBLEM

The returns on stock X have a standard deviation of 25 percent and a correlation coefficient of 0.70 with market returns, which have a standard deviation of 20 percent. Estimate the beta for stock X.

EXAMPLE 9.5

Estimating Beta

Solution

$$\beta_x = \frac{\rho_{x,M}\sigma_x}{\sigma_M} = \frac{0.70 \times 0.25}{0.20} = 0.875$$

Notice that even though stock X has a higher standard deviation than the market, its beta is less than one because of the correlation coefficient of 0.70.

Consider how we would estimate a beta using historical stock returns. We would need a large number of monthly, weekly, or daily returns on the stock, along with the same number of monthly, weekly, or daily returns on a market index. Using this data, we can then use statistical packages or spreadsheets to estimate the regression line; the slope of the line is the estimate of the security's beta.

Let's see how this works using Microsoft Corporate common stock.

1. We collect monthly returns (including dividends), on Microsoft common stock (MSFT) from January 2006 through December 2010.[14]

2. We collect monthly returns on the Standard & Poor's 500 Index (S&P 500) for the same months.[15]

3. We put both time-series in a workbook and regress the returns on Microsoft stock against the returns on the S&P 500.

	A	B	C
		Return on	*Return on*
1	*Month*	*MSFT*	*S&P 500*
2	Jan-06	7.65%	2.55%
3	Feb-06	–4.23%	0.05%
4	Mar-06	1.27%	1.11%
5	Apr-06	–11.25%	1.22%
6	May-06	–5.84%	–3.09%

4. We use the spreadsheet SLOPE function to estimate the beta:

=SLOPE(B2:B61,C2:C61)

which produces a beta estimate of 1.0719. We can see this graphically when we see the scatterplot of the returns on MSFT and those on the S&P 500 (see next page).

The slope of the line, which represents the average relationship between the returns on MSFT and the S&P 500, is 1.0719.

[14] Sources of the data needed to calculate these returns include Yahoo! Finance and Google Finance. Don't forget to include dividends in your calculation of the monthly return.

[15] Sources of the data needed to calculate these returns include Robert Shiller (available at his web site at www.econ.yale.edu/~shiller/data.htm; however, the dividends on the S&P 500 have been smoothed in his spreadsheet), Yahoo! Finance, YCharts.com, and many other financial sites. You may find slight differences in returns due to different assumptions regarding when to include dividends: during the month at which the dividend is ex-dividend (that is, no longer trades with the stock), or the month the dividend is payable.

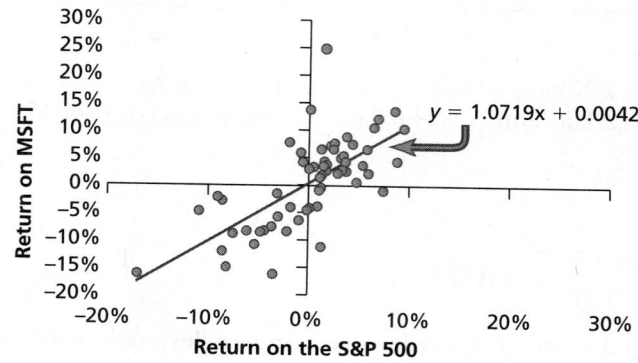

Betas tend to vary a great deal across companies in different industries because they possess different risk profiles. Although betas tend to be more similar for companies operating in the same industry, they can still vary substantially because even companies within the same industry can differ substantially across various dimensions, such as financial risk, size, and so on. Betas also may change over time; for example, high-growth companies tend to have betas much larger than 1.0, but over time, as the company matures and growth slows, the beta approaches 1.0. We provide examples of betas in Table 9-1.

Unlike portfolio standard deviations, portfolio betas are weighted averages of the betas for the individual securities in the portfolio. Therefore, we can estimate the beta for an n-security portfolio by using Equation 9-8:

$$\beta_p = w_A\beta_A + w_B\beta_B + \ldots + w_n\beta_n \tag{9-8}$$

Consider a portfolio with one-quarter of its investment in Lockheed Martin and the remainder invested in Big Lots. Using the data in Table 9-2, the beta for this portfolio is 1.165:

$$\beta_p = (0.25 \times 1.09) + (0.75 \times 1.19) = 1.165$$

TABLE 9-1   Estimated Betas for U.S. Companies

Company	Ticker	Industry	Beta
Boeing Company	BA	Aircraft manufacturing	1.24
Lockheed Martin	LMT	Aircraft manufacturing	1.09
Coca-Cola Company	KO	Beverages	0.60
Pepsico, Inc.	PEP	Beverages	0.54
Celanese Corporation	CE	Chemicals	2.78
Eastman Chemical Corporation	EMN	Chemicals	1.84
Johnson & Johnson	JNJ	Consumer products	0.53
Procter & Gamble Company	PG	Consumer products	0.57
Big Lots	BIG	Discount retail	1.19
Family Dollar Stores	FDO	Discount retail	0.17
International Business Machines	IBM	Information technology	0.79
Microsoft	MSFT	Information technology	1.01
Target Corporation	TFT	Retail	1.16
Wal-Mart Stores	WMT	Retail	0.20
PPG Industries	PPG	Specialty chemicals	1.16
Valspar Corporation	VAL	Specialty chemicals	0.97

Source: *Yahoo! Finance.*

We can see from this result why diversified portfolios end up with only market risk. First, the beta on the market portfolio, by definition, is 1.0. We can see this from Equation 9-7 by substituting M for the standard deviation of the security and noting that an asset is perfectly correlated with itself! So, if the average beta is 1.0, as we randomly add securities to a portfolio, we eventually end up with an average risk portfolio with a beta of 1.0, composed of all market risk. This is also why most large portfolios made up of a large number of securities are essentially the same as the market portfolio and earn the same rate of return.[16]

PROBLEM

An investor has a portfolio that consists of $10,000 invested in stock B, which has a beta of 1.2; $20,000 in stock C, which has a beta of 0.8; and $20,000 in stock D, which has a beta of 1.3. Estimate the beta of this portfolio.

EXAMPLE 9.6

Estimating a Portfolio Beta

Solution

$$w_B = \frac{10,000}{(10,000 + 20,000 + 20,000)} = 0.20; \; w_c = \frac{20,000}{50,000} = 0.40; \; w_D = \frac{20,000}{50,000} = 0.40$$

$$\beta_p = w_B\beta_B + w_C\beta_C + w_D\beta_D$$
$$= (0.20 \times 1.2) + (0.40 \times 0.8) + (0.40 \times 1.3)$$
$$= 0.24 + 0.32 + 0.52$$
$$= 1.08$$

The Security Market Line

An important result of the capital asset pricing model is that investors should be compensated for market risk, as measured by beta. Though we will leave the derivation to investments texts, we can use the capital market line to derive the **security market line (SML):**[17]

$$E(r_i) = r_f + [E(r_M) - r_f]\beta_i \qquad (9\text{-}9)$$

where $E(r_i)$ is the expected return on the asset (or portfolio) i. The term $E(r_M) - r_f$ is the expected **market risk premium** and is also a function of market conditions. When we multiply an asset's beta by the market risk premium, we get an asset's risk premium. Adding the asset's risk premium to the risk-free rate gives us the required rate of return on the asset.

Suppose the risk-free rate is 3 percent and the expected return on the market is 9 percent. If an asset's beta is 1.2, the expected return on this asset is 9.2 percent:

$$E(r_i) = 0.03 + [(0.09 - 0.03) \times 1.2]$$
$$= 0.03 + [0.06 \times 1.2] = 0.02 + 0.072 = 0.092 \text{ or } 9.2\%$$

The market risk premium in this case is 6 percent, and the risk premium for this asset is 7.2 percent.

The SML is the most widely used contribution of the CAPM, and we depict this graphically in Figure 9-10. The SML represents the trade-off between market risk and the required rate of return for any risky asset, whether it is an individual asset or a portfolio.

security market line (SML) relationship between market risk and the required rate of return for any risky security, whether an individual asset or a portfolio

market risk premium risk premium as a function of market conditions; the expected return on the market minus the risk-free rate

---

[16] This is what is commonly referred to as closet indexing because although they charge large fees, most mutual funds have similar performance.

[17] For a formal derivation of the SML from the CML, refer to almost any investment textbook. To avoid confusing the SML and the CML, remember that the CML is a depiction of the relationship between expected return and total risk, whereas the SML is a depiction of the relationship between expected return and market risk.

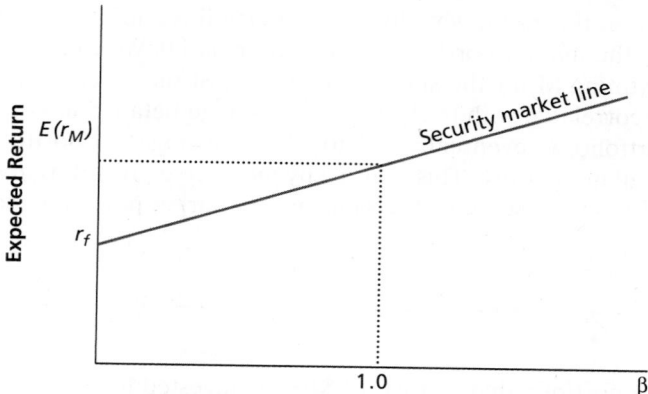

FIGURE 9-10 The Security Market Line

The SML is upward sloping, which indicates that investors require a higher expected return on higher-beta assets. In essence, the SML formalizes the notion we discussed before: The required rate of return on an asset equals the risk-free rate plus a risk premium. The size of the risk premium varies directly with an asset's market risk, as measured by beta, in the SML.

According to the SML, assets or portfolios with betas greater than the market beta of 1.0 will have larger risk premiums than the "average" asset and will therefore have higher required rates of return. Conversely, assets with betas less than that of the market are less risky and will have lower required rates of return.

EXAMPLE 9.7

Using the SML

PROBLEM

Given an expected return on the market of 10 percent and a risk-free rate of 4.5 percent, estimate:

a. the market risk premium.
b. the required return for Security X that has a beta of 0.875.
c. the required return for a portfolio that has a beta of 1.08.

Solution

a. $E(r_M) - r_f = 0.10 - 0.045 = 5.5\%$
b. $E(r_X) = r_f + (E(r_M) - r_f)\beta_X = 0.045 + (0.055 \times 0.875)$
   $\qquad = 0.045 + 0.04813 = 9.313\%$

   Notice that the required return for X is *less* than the expected market return because its beta is *less* than one.

c. $E(r_p) = r_f + (E(r_M) - r_f)\beta_p = 0.045 + (0.055 \times 1.08) = 0.045 + 0.0594 = 10.44\%$

   Notice that the required return for this portfolio is greater than the expected market return because its beta is greater than one.

The SML and Security Valuation

In equilibrium, the expected return on all properly-priced assets will lie *on* the SML, just as the expected return on all portfolios will lie on the CML. As with the CML, when investors expect a return equal to the required return, the asset is correctly priced. However, at any given time, some assets may be temporarily mispriced according to CAPM.

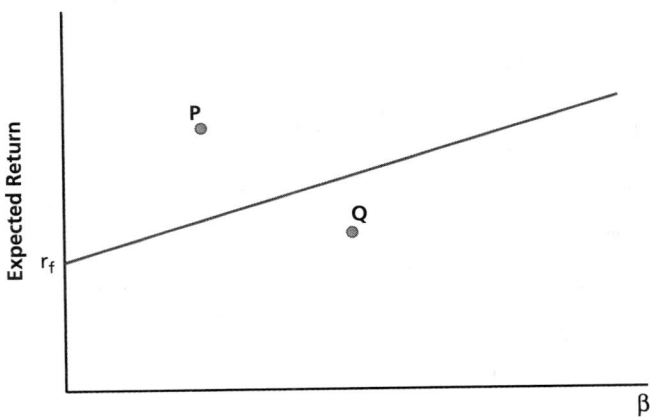

FIGURE 9-11 **The SML and Security Valuation**

Whenever analysis suggests that the expected return on an asset differs from its required rate of return according to CAPM, that asset is considered undervalued or overvalued. Assets or portfolios that have expected returns greater than their required rate of return are undervalued because they provide investors with an expected return that is higher than the return required given their risk. Similar to the CML, undervalued securities will lie *above* the SML, reflecting the fact that the expected return exceeds the required return, which is the return along the SML that corresponds to the beta coefficient. Asset P in Figure 9-11 represents an example of an undervalued security. Similarly, assets or portfolios whose expected returns are less than their required rate of return, such as Q in Figure 9-11, are overvalued and will lie below the SML.

If markets are efficient, we would expect prices to be correct. Therefore, whenever rational investors observe an undervalued asset, such as P, they will rush to purchase it because it offers a higher expected return than its required return. As a result of this increase in demand for asset P, its price will increase until it eventually equals the price level at which its expected return equals the required return according to the SML. In other words, asset P's price will adjust until it lies along the SML. In similar fashion, selling pressure for asset Q (which is overvalued) would increase, causing Q's price to decline until it too lies along the SML.

This discussion of the security market line is very similar to the discussion of the capital market line. The primary difference is the measure of risk: For individual assets, the measure of risk is beta, whereas for diversified portfolios, it is the standard deviation.

Using the SML to Estimate Long-Term Discount Rates

Technically, the CAPM is a one-period model, and some analysts will use Treasury bill rates instead of the government Treasury bond rate as the appropriate risk-free rate.[18] However, financial analysts often use the CAPM to estimate the required return on common shares over many periods, such as when they are trying to estimate the share price using the dividend discount model or free cash flow models. In these applications, which are the most common for financial managers, the rate on a Treasury note or bond would be most appropriate as the rate on a risk-free security. These models require the discounting of expected cash flows that occur over many periods in the future. It is also common to use the CAPM to estimate the cost of a firm's common equity financing component when estimating the firm's overall cost of capital. This cost of capital is then used to discount the expected future cash flows associated with capital expenditure decisions.

[18] The Treasury bill rate is sometimes used for the risk-free rate in the CAPM because this rate provides a better one-period rate of return. However, short-term rates tend to fluctuate widely.

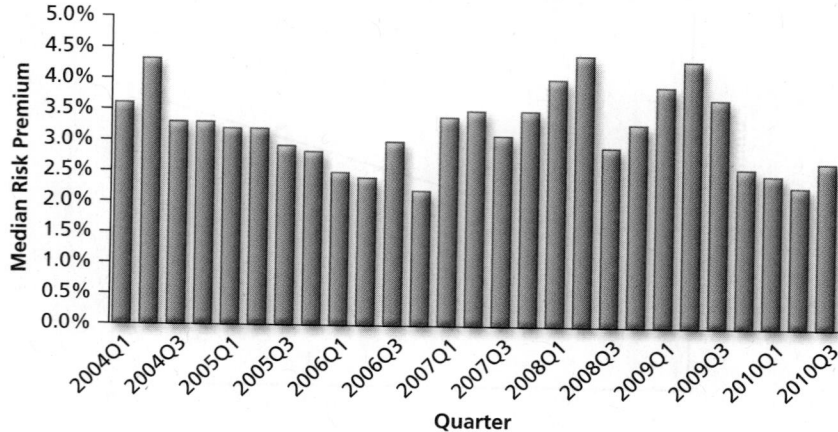

FIGURE 9-12 Estimated Market Risk Premiums
Source of data: *John R. Graham and Campbell R. Harvey, "The Equity Risk Premium in 2010," Working paper, Duke University, ssrn.com/abstract=1654026, Table 1.*

Estimates of the market risk premium are sensitive to the period used in estimating this premium, as well as the method of estimation. For example, if you are using ex post data, you are using an observation that occurred, rather than the whole spectrum of possible returns that investors considered in pricing assets at that time. Ex post measures of market risk premiums in the U.S. range from 6 percent to close to 13 percent, depending on the time period considered.[19] However, several researchers have argued that these ex post estimates overestimate the ex ante market risk premium.[20] Researchers estimating the ex ante market risk premium, which is what is relevant in asset pricing, observe values for the U.S. that are much less than ex post estimates.[21]

We show the expected market risk premiums according to a recent survey of CEOs by John R. Graham and Campbell R. Harvey in Figure 9-12.[22] Notice that (1) risk premiums are variable, and (2) risk premiums have declined since their peak in 2009, and in mid-2010 they were around 2.5 to 3 percent. The risk premiums cited in the Graham and Harvey study are less than those reported by Pablo Fernandez in his survey of professors, analysts, and companies. Fernandez finds that the risk premiums estimated in 2011 were around 5 to 5.5 percent in the U.S. and in the range of 4.5 to 6 percent in most developed nations.[23]

Concept Review Questions

1. Why is beta a measure of market risk for an asset?

2. If an asset's correlation with the market return increases, will its beta increase or decrease?

3. What is a characteristic line, and why is it useful?

4. If the market risk premium increases, will securities become overvalued or undervalued?

---

[19] E. Scott Mayfield, "Estimating the Market Risk Premium," *Journal of Financial Economics*, Vol. 73, No. 3 (September 2004): 465–496, Table 5.

[20] Eugene F. Fama and Kenneth R. French, "The Equity Premium," *Journal of Finance*, Vol. 57, Issue 2 (2002): 637–659.

[21] Fama and French (2002) estimate market risk premiums of 2.55–4.32% for the 1951–2000 period.

[22] John R. Graham and Campbell R. Harvey, "The Equity Risk Premium in 2010," Working paper, Duke University, ssrn.com/abstract=1654026.

[23] Pablo Fernandez, Javier Aguirreamalloa, and Luis Corres, "Market Risk Premium Used in 56 Countries in 2011: A Survey with 6,014 Answers," Working paper, IESE Business School, University of Navarra, May 2011.

9.4   ALTERNATIVE ASSET PRICING MODELS

The CAPM is a "single-factor" model because it suggests that the required return on capital assets—that is, stocks—is determined by only one risk factor: market risk. CAPM is often criticized because it is based on several assumptions, many of which are called into question in the real world. In addition, a substantial amount of empirical evidence finds that the CAPM does not hold well in practice. In particular, although empirical estimates of the ex post SML suggest that it is, indeed, an upward-sloping straight line, the ex ante y-intercept has been found to be higher than $E(r_f)$, and the slope of the SML is less than that predicted by theory—that is, it is "flatter" than it should be. Although this research remains very controversial, a 1992 study of U.S. stock returns by Fama and French concluded that beta, the sole risk factor in the CAPM, possessed no explanatory power for predicting stock returns.[24] In addition, they found that two other factors (discussed in the next subsection) do a much better job of explaining common stock returns.

Richard Roll in 1976 identified an important theoretical problem associated with tests of the CAPM, and this identification is commonly referred to as Roll's critique.[25] Roll argued that the CAPM cannot be tested empirically because we cannot observe the market portfolio, which consists of all risky assets. Therefore, researchers are forced to use market proxies, which may or may not be the optimal mean-variance efficient portfolio. In effect, Roll argued that tests of the CAPM are actually tests of the mean-variance efficiency of the chosen market portfolio. He showed that the basic CAPM results hold whenever the chosen proxy is mean-variance efficient and do not hold if the converse is true. As a result the empirical tests have no power.

Despite the criticisms of the CAPM, it remains a commonly used method of estimating the required rate of return on individual assets used by both academics and practitioners. One of the main reasons for its staying power is its intuitive appeal for assessing the trade-off between risk and expected return and the observation that individuals hold diversified portfolios. Further, the other options have had at least as much difficulty generating statistical support as has the CAPM. However, in response to some of the problems associated with the CAPM, alternative asset pricing models have been developed, and we discuss two of the better-known alternatives in the next section. In contrast to the CAPM, both of these models are multifactor models because they assume that more than one factor affects asset returns.

Fama and French Model

Professors Eugene Fama and Kenneth French examined a large number of companies' security returns and financial statement data and found that two factors affected stock returns in addition to market returns. Based on this discovery, they developed a three-factor pricing model. Like the CAPM, their model includes an overall market factor; however, it also includes the market value of equity and the ratio of the book value of equity to the market value of equity.[26]

The **Fama–French model** became popular because some believe that it does a better job than the CAPM of explaining ex ante stock returns. For example, Ibbotson Associates, Inc., a major provider of financial information, now gives estimates of the required return

Fama–French model pricing model that uses three factors (a market factor, the market value of a firm's common equity, and the ratio of a firm's book equity value to its market value of equity) to relate expected returns to risk

---

[24] See E. Fama and K. French, "The Cross Section of Expected Stock Returns," *Journal of Finance, 47* (1992): 427–65.

[25] See R. Roll, "A Critique of the Asset Pricing Theory's Tests; Part I: On Past and Potential Testability of the Theory," *Journal of Financial Economics, 4* (1976): 129–76.

[26] See Eugene Fama and Kenneth French, "Size and Book-to-Market Factors in Earnings and Returns," *Journal of Finance, 50* (1995): 131–55.

LESSONS LEARNED | Debunking Beta

It's time to delete the CAPM from business school textbooks. The theory has done more harm than good for investors. Ever since the 1980s CAPM has been widely accepted by almost all sophisticated trading and money management firms practicing Modern Portfolio Theory to price stocks. It's baked into most Wall Street computer models. Indeed, most of the big firms and their chief risk officers focus on beta but—at least until recently—have ignored most other types of risks. Little things like leverage and liquidity. I believe that this contributed to the severity of at least three major crashes since the 1980s: the Crash of 1987, Long-Term Capital in 1998 and the subprime debacle we are still working through.

In the years leading up to the 2007–08 crash, leverage and liquidity were not considered risky on subprime bonds. After all, the beta of these bonds was relatively low,

despite the garbage they were holding and the leverage they piled on. When housing prices fell, the markets collapsed.

The low-beta ABX.HE.BBB investment-grade mortgage bond index, for example, sank into a black hole. Most investment banks, banks and many hedge funds were heavily margined in bonds of this type, anywhere from 25-to-1 to 40-to-1. At 30-to-1 leverage it takes a drop of only 3.3% to wipe out invested capital.

But the ABX mortgage index did not decline 3.3%; it dropped 98%. The loss was a stunning—2,940%. Banks lost billions and buyers disappeared. That's why Bear Stearns, Lehman and Washington Mutual no longer exist. Thank you, CAPM.

Extracted from David Dreman, "Debunking Beta," *Forbes*, September 27, 2010.

---

on equity for companies based on this model, in addition to estimates determined by the more widely recognized CAPM. However, the FF model has been criticized because it is not based on sound economic fundamentals, whereas the CAPM is based on economic reasoning and fundamentals. Further, many believe that the FF model is simply an example of data mining, in which the data have been examined so many times that eventually some variables are bound to be discovered that explain returns better than the CAPM does.[27]

Arbitrage Pricing Theory

arbitrage pricing theory (APT) pricing model that uses multiple factors to relate expected returns to risk by assuming that asset returns are linearly related to a set of indexes, which are proxy risk factors that influence asset returns

arbitrage process of taking advantage of different pricing for the same item in different markets

no-arbitrage principle rule that two otherwise identical assets cannot sell at different prices

Another well-known multifactor asset-pricing model is the **arbitrage pricing theory (APT)**. The APT requires very few assumptions, unlike the CAPM. In particular, the APT does not depend on the existence of an underlying market portfolio, and it allows for the possibility that several types of risk may affect asset returns. **Arbitrage** is the process of taking advantage of different pricing for the same item in different markets; if this different pricing exists, you would buy the item in the market with the cheaper price and sell it in the market where it has a higher price, making a profit from simple buying and selling. In fact, APT is based on the **no-arbitrage principle**, which states that two otherwise identical assets cannot sell at different prices.

Development of the formal APT assumes, as we have noted, that asset returns are linearly related to a set of indexes, which are proxy risk factors that influence asset returns. The underlying risk factors in the APT represent broad economic forces, which are unpredictable. We express the APT in Equation 9-10:

$$E(r_i) = a_0 + b_{i1} F_1 + b_{i2} F_2 + \ldots + b_{in} F_n \tag{9-10}$$

---

[27] This reminds us of the quote from economist Ronald Coase: "If you torture the data long enough, it will confess" [from a 1960s talk to the University of Virginia]. The Fama–French model is derived from the examination of the historical relation between a large number of financial statement data and stock returns, with a few of these financial statement items bubbling to the top in terms related to returns. This is always a risky approach to model building because what happened in the past does not always happen in the future.

where $E(r_i)$ = the expected return on asset i

a_0 = the expected return on a asset with zero systematic risk

b_i = the sensitivity of asset i to a given risk factor

F_i = the risk premium for a given risk factor

In Equation 9-10, you can see that an asset's risk is based on its sensitivity to basic economic factors, and the expected return increases proportionate to this risk. The sensitivity measures (b_i) have a similar interpretation to beta in the CAPM because they measure the relative sensitivity of a asset's return to a particular risk premium. In fact, the APT is equivalent to the CAPM if there were only one risk factor—that is, market returns—influencing asset returns.

The main problem with the APT is that the factors are not specified ahead of time. In fact, APT does not even specify the number of risk factors that exist or state which factors are the most important. As a result, these factors, as well as their relative importance, must be identified empirically.

Most empirical evidence suggests that three to five factors influence asset returns and are priced in the market. For example, Roll and Ross identify the following five systematic factors:[28]

1. Changes in expected inflation
2. Unanticipated changes in inflation
3. Unanticipated changes in industrial production
4. Unanticipated changes in the default-risk premium[29]
5. Unanticipated changes in the term structure of interest rates

The key is that these factors represent surprises because what is expected is already built in to the current price of an asset.[30] In other words, surprises drive returns because it is the new information—the surprise—that causes participants to revalue assets and, hence, generate returns.

A challenge in using the APT in financial decision making is that identifying these factors can be criticized as data mining and as such may be hazardous. Factors or their importance may change over time, making it difficult to use these factors in forward-looking decision making.

Summary of Alternatives

So, if these alternative models all have warts, and the CAPM has its warts, which model should you use, if any? The problem is that none of these models will help you earn abnormal returns on your investments. These models were developed to understand better how investors price assets. In addition to helping us understand what is important in the pricing of securities (risk and return), these models also rationalize what moves market prices (surprises).

1. Why do we refer to the CAPM as a single-factor model?

2. Describe some of the criticisms of the CAPM, including Roll's critique.

3. Briefly describe the strengths and weaknesses of the Fama–French model and the APT.

Concept Review Questions

[28] Richard Roll and Stephen Ross, "An Empirical Investigation of the Arbitrage Pricing Theory," *Journal of Finance, 35*, no. 5 (December 1980): 1073–1103.

[29] This variable is commonly defined as the yield on long-term corporate bonds minus the yield on long-term government bonds.

[30] And because they are surprises, there is no way to anticipate these.

9.5   MARKET EFFICIENCY

Financial managers need to know what investors want when they make investments, whether these investments are bonds, stocks, land, or plant and equipment. Financial managers also must know the required rates of return for different investments to make informed decisions. Once financial managers know what investors require, they can then make decisions that enhance shareholder value. Never forget that financial managers have a responsibility, as well as a legal obligation, to act in the owners' best interests. Correctly estimating discount rates is only part of the problem. A second important element is whether or not market prices correctly reflect the actions of managers. This brings up the question of market efficiency.

Defining Market Efficiency

efficient market market in which prices reacts quickly and relatively accurately to new information

An **efficient market** is one in which the prices of all assets accurately reflect all relevant and available information about the assets. This definition implies that asset prices in efficient capital markets are "correct." In other words, the current price of a common share reflects all known information, both past and present, about the corporation, including information about a company's earnings, financial strength, management strengths and weaknesses, and future plans as announced through press releases and the management discussion and analysis (MD&A) in its financial statements. Prices reflect rational expectations about what is expected to happen in the future and therefore mirror today's beliefs about future interest rate changes, future profits, potential mergers, and so on. Events that cause these beliefs about the future to change will have a corresponding impact on today's prices.

efficient market hypothesis (EMH) theory that markets are efficient and therefore, in its strictest sense, implies that prices accurately reflect all available information at any given time

The **efficient market hypothesis (EMH)** formalized the concept of an efficient market into a theory that markets are efficient, and therefore, in its strictest sense, it implies that prices accurately reflect all information at any point in time. Because the strictest form of the EMH represents such a high hurdle, we commonly break the EMH down into three different, and cumulative, levels based on the extent that prices reflect different types of available information: the weak form, semi-strong form, and strong form. For example, because of the cumulative nature of the definition, a market that is strong form efficient is also weak form and semi-strong form efficient.

Weak form of market efficiency

weak-form efficient characteristic of a market in which asset prices fully reflect all market data, which refers to all past price and volume trading information

If a market is **weak-form efficient**, asset prices fully reflect all market data, which refers to all past price and volume trading information. If markets are weak-form efficient, historical trading data is already reflected in current prices and should be of no value in predicting future price changes. In other words, it is not possible to generate an **abnormal profit**, a profit in excess of that expected for the asset's level of risk on a consistent basis.

abnormal profit profit in excess of those expected for the asset's level of risk

random walk hypothesis theory that prices follow a random walk, with price changes over time being independent of one another

If a market is weak-form efficient, current market prices reflect all historical trading data. Therefore, past price changes (and total returns) should be unrelated to future price changes. This idea is related to the **random walk hypothesis**, in which prices follow a random walk, with price changes over time being independent of one another. This hypothesis is logical if information arrives randomly, as it should, and if investors react to it immediately.

technical analysis study of historical trading information to identify patterns in trading data that can be used to invest successfully

Technical analysis involves the analysis of historical trading information to attempt to identify patterns in trading data that can be used to invest successfully. Most of the empirical evidence regarding the profitability of technical analysis in U.S. stock markets and markets in other developed countries suggests that technical trading rules, on average, have not been able to outperform a simple buy-and-hold strategy once we consider risk and trading costs. This is not to say that there are no opportunities in emerging markets; evidence suggests that emerging markets such as China, Bangladesh, and Turkey are not considered weak-form efficient and that technical analysis may provide abnormal returns.[31]

In addition to tests of specific technical trading rules, there is research that examines market anomalies based on the calendar (so-called calendar anomalies), which are patterns, such as the day-of-the-week or month-of-the-year that may produce profitable trading strategies. For example, there was evidence beginning in 1980 that Friday returns are larger than Monday returns, providing a profitable trading opportunity.[32] However, over time this "anomaly" disappeared.[33] Though these patterns are interesting to note, it would be difficult and very risky to attempt to exploit them because the evidence refers to averages that are observed in the past, which means (1) they do not occur all the time, and (2) anyone attempting to exploit these anomalies would incur trading costs that likely offset any potential profit. However, there is evidence that using some strategies, such as trading based on the day of the week, is profitable in some developing markets.[34] The bottom line is that securities markets in developed countries are weak-form efficient, but there remain inefficiencies in developing nations' markets.

Semi-strong form of market efficiency

In a market that is **semi-strong-form efficient**, asset prices reflect all publicly known and available information. For stock markets this includes information about earnings, dividends, corporate investments, management changes, and so on. This also includes market data, which are publicly available. Therefore, this version of the EMH encompasses the weak form. In other words, if a market is semi-strong efficient, then it must also be weak-form efficient.

A market that quickly incorporates all publicly available information into its prices is semi-strong efficient. In such a market, it would be futile to act on publicly available information, such as earnings announcements, merger announcements, and so on, in an attempt to consistently generate abnormal profits.[35]

One way of testing for semi-strong market efficiency is to examine the speed of adjustment of stock prices to announcements of significant new information. In a semi-strong efficient market, prices would adjust quickly and accurately to this new information so that investors could not act on it after its announcement and earn abnormally high risk-adjusted returns. In contrast, if the market overreacts or underreacts, or if time lags exist in stock price adjustments, and investors could exploit these flaws, then the market is not semi-strong efficient.

Most of the tests of semi-strong-form efficiency in securities markets take the form of an **event study**: Researchers examine stock returns to determine the impact of a particular event on stock prices. The vast majority of these studies support the notion that the market adjusts to new public information rapidly and accurately, and that investors could not earn abnormal profits based on inefficient market reactions to significant information

semi-strong-form efficient characteristic of a market in which all publicly known and available information is reflected in security prices

event study statistical examination of stock returns to determine the effect of a particular event on stock prices

[31] See, for example, Suzanne Fifield, David Power, and C. Donald Sinclair ["An Analysis of Trading Strategies in Eleven European Stock Markets," *European Journal of Finance*, Vol. 11, No. 6 (2005), 531–548] and Asma Mobarek, A. Sabur Mollah, and Rafiqul Bhuyan ["Market Efficiency in Emerging Stock Market," *Journal of Emerging Market Finance*, Vol. 7, No. 1 (January 2008): 17–41], and Kong-Jun Chen and Xiao-Ming Li ["Is Technical Analysis Useful for Stock Traders in China? Evidence from the Szse Component A-Share Index," *Pacific Economic Review*, Vol. 11, No. 4 (2006): 477–488].

[32] Kenneth R. French, "Stock Returns and the Weekend Effect," *Journal of Financial Economics*, Volume 8, Issue 1 (March 1980): 55–69.

[33] See, for example, Seyed Mehdian and Mark J. Perry ["The Reversal of the Monday Effect: New Evidence from US Equity Markets," *Journal of Business Finance & Accounting*, Vol. 28, No. 7 (September/October 2001): 1043–1065].

[34] See, for example, Francesco Guidi, Rakesh Gupta, and Suneel Mahesdhwari ["Weak-Form Market Efficiency and Calendar Anomalies for Eastern Europe Equity Markets," *Journal of Emerging Market Finance*, Vol. 10, No. 3 (December 2011): 337–389].

[35] Does this mean that financial analysis is fruitless? No, because analysts use information to formulate valuation estimates and to measure the risk of an asset. The measurement of risk and return is crucial to the formation and maintenance of security portfolios.

announcements.[36] Consider, for example, the market reaction to a surprise in earnings. If earnings are a surprise—better than expected or worse than expected—the earnings announcement provides information to the market. In an efficient market, we expect the share price to react quickly to this information. Early studies claimed that there was a quick reaction, but that some of the reaction lingered for days, supporting the idea that markets were not semi-strong efficient. However, subsequent evidence indicates that much of what was viewed as a delayed reaction could be explained once we control for transactions costs and risk.[37]

The other common test of semi-strong efficiency is to examine strategies that earn abnormal risk-adjusted returns over the long term. Perhaps the strongest evidence of semi-strong market efficiency is the fact that professional fund managers, with all of their training, expertise, technological capability, and access to data, do not outperform the market on a risk-adjusted basis, on average. In fact, most studies indicate the performance of the average active portfolio manager, after expenses, is actually worse than the performance of their passive benchmarks. Some studies suggest they may underperform their benchmarks by as much as 50 to 200 basis points (that is, 0.5% to 2%). Adding further support for capital markets as semi-strong efficient, evidence also suggests that pension fund managers consistently underperform their benchmarks.

Strong form of efficient markets

strong-form efficient characteristic of a market in which stock prices fully reflect all information, which includes both public and private information

If a market is **strong-form efficient**, asset prices fully reflect all information, which includes both public and private information. Public information is any information that is readily available to investors, whereas private information is any information not available, which we generally think of as inside information.[38] This would include, for example, an acquisition that is being planned yet has not yet been disclosed. It is obviously the most stringent form of market efficiency, and it encompasses both the weak and semi-strong versions because market data and all other publicly available information must be reflected in prices, as well as any private information that is possessed by some market participants but not by all. In such a market, no investor could take advantage of the possession of superior information or the superior processing of information to identify mispriced securities because the prices would already properly reflect all information. Obviously, this is a very strong assertion. For example, it asserts that insiders could not profit from private inside information.

If a market is strong-form efficient, this suggests that insiders cannot profit from inside information that is not known to the public because prices would already reflect this information. However, it seems impossible that prices could reflect information that is not yet publicly available. Strong-form market efficiency tests examine whether any group of investors has information (public or private) that allows them to earn abnormal profits consistently. Therefore, it is common to examine the performance of groups that are thought to have access to "private" information, such as insiders. Given their access to privileged information, it is not surprising that several studies have found that they have consistently earned abnormal returns on their stock transactions, which refutes strong-form efficiency. However, some studies have found that they perform only slightly better than average. It should be noted that the trading activity of insiders is restricted to protect the general investing public. Therefore, their potential to exploit this insider knowledge is quite limited. We can conclude that it is not surprising that, on balance, the evidence does not support this version of the EMH.

---

[36] Usually, abnormal returns are defined as those that exceed the expected return on a stock according to a model of stock returns, such as the CAPM.

[37] Dongcheol Kim and Myungsun Kim, "A Multifactor Explanation of Post-Earnings Announcement Drift," *Journal of Financial and Quantitative Analysis*, Vol. 38, No. 2 (June 2003): 383–398.

[38] Several definitions exist for "insiders." We suggest the use of a broad definition that includes any party that has access to private information about an asset as a result of a special relationship with the underlying entity. For example, this would include anyone who sat on the board of directors for a corporation, as well as that company's officers, lawyers, bankers, and so on.

Strong form	• Public and private information
Semi-strong form	• Publicly available information
Weak Form	• Past prices, volume, and other market information

Trading on Private Information | ETHICS

If a market is strong-form efficient, it would not pay for someone to trade on inside information because this information would already be reflected in asset prices. However, we know that individuals have traded on private information, made profits, and been caught.

In 2010, the Securities and Exchange Commission focused on hedge funds and the potential for insider trading. The heart of the issue is the following:

1. If markets are efficient, then hedge funds should not be able to earn abnormal profits.

2. If hedge funds have an advantage regarding information on publicly traded companies, this provides an unfair advantage to this group of investors.

One of the more recent large cases involved a hedge fund advisory firm, Galleon Management LP. Not only was Galleon and the hedge fund's manager charged, but also the individuals supplying the insider information were.[39] For example, Rajat K. Gupta was charged in October 2011 for illegally tipping Raj Rajaratnam, providing information from his serving on boards of Goldman Sachs and Proctor & Gamble.

Not to be outdone by hedge funds, some members of the U.S. Congress have traded on insider information and profited nicely. Though members of Congress are not insiders in the sense of a CEO or a CFO, they are privy to information that is nonpublic, but profitable to trade on. As exposed in Peter Schweizer's 2011 book *Throw Them All Out*, the insider trading laws that forbid trading on material, nonpublic information—at least up until the book exposed the issue—were not enforced with respect to the trading by members of Congress and their families.[40] In response to this exposure, the Stop Trading on Congressional Knowledge Act (or the STOCK Act), was signed in to law in April, 2012.[41]

Market Efficiency Assumptions

For prices to be correct, the market must react quickly and accurately to new information. Several conditions must exist before markets can operate efficiently. One critical piece of this puzzle is that all market participants are treated fairly; that is, the market is a level playing field. This requirement is the reason that such a heavy emphasis is placed on **disclosure**; that is, the revelation of all material facts so that everyone in the market is buying and selling based on the same disclosed material facts about the firm.

A lack of disclosure is one reason that smaller, more loosely regulated markets tend to be less efficient, and that the prices in these markets do not accurately reflect available information. In this case, information is either not disclosed, is disclosed late, or is disclosed in such a way that not all market participants are aware of what is going on. Information disclosure is a very important part of **securities law**, and significant attention is

disclosure revelation of all material facts so that everyone in the market is buying and selling based on the same material facts about the firm

securities law body of law that ensures, through capital market regulations, that all investors have equal access to, and an equal opportunity to react to, new and relevant information and that governs the buying and selling of assets

[39] *SEC v. Galleon Management, LP, Raj Rajaratnam, Rajiv Goel, Anil Kumar, Danielle Chiesi, Mark Kurland, Robert Moffat and New Castle LLC* Civil Action No. 09-CV-8811.
[40] Peters Schweizer, *Throw Them All Out* (New York: Houghton Mifflin Harcourt Publishing Company, 2011).
[41] Public Law 112-05, signed into law April 4, 2012.

devoted to the maintenance and enforcement of these capital market regulations designed to ensure that all investors have equal access to, and an equal opportunity to react to, new and relevant information. For example, insider trading laws prevent insiders from acting on private information before that information is made public.

The technical definition of market efficiency suggests that market prices are *always* correct, which requires instantaneous and perfect price adjustments in response to the arrival of new information in the marketplace. This type of efficiency is not a practical reality; however, efficient markets do react quickly and relatively accurately to new information, and therefore prices are correct on average. We can expand on this logic and note that market efficiency is a matter of degree. In other words, more efficient markets process information faster and more accurately than do inefficient ones; therefore, the prices in these efficient markets are closer to the true values.

The following assumptions underlie the existence of efficient markets:

1. A large number of rational, profit-maximizing investors exist, who actively participate in the market by analyzing, valuing, and trading assets. The markets are assumed to be competitive, which means that no one investor can significantly affect the price of an asset.

2. Information is costless and widely available to market participants at the same time.

3. Information arrives randomly, and therefore announcements are not related to one another.

4. Investors react quickly and fully to the new information, which is reflected in stock prices.

Though these conditions are stringent and are not met in the strictest sense in the real world, they are not unreasonable today. A large number of market participants actively follow the prices of securities trading in the market and devour information that may affect these prices. For example, all the major investment banks have securities analysts whose job is to monitor companies and regularly report on their value through earnings forecasts and buy/sell/hold recommendations. We refer to this type of analyst as a **sell-side analyst** because they work for the investment banks that underwrite and sell assets to the public. Many institutions invest in assets, such as insurance companies, mutual funds, and pension funds. For example, CNA Financial, an insurance holding company, had over \$55 billion of assets at the end of 2010, \$42.6 billion of which are investments in fixed-income securities, equity securities, and short-term investments, among other investments. These institutions also employ assets analysts to evaluate the research and recommendations produced by the sell-side analysts. Because these institutions buy assets, we refer to this type of analyst as a **buy-side analyst**.

With all these analysts following publicly traded companies, we might expect prices to be rational and based on available information and economic fundamentals. In addition, an abundance of free or inexpensive information is available about most actively traded securities, and some would even argue that an overabundance of such information makes it difficult to "separate the wheat from the chaff." This information generally arrives randomly and is not predictable; if it were predictable, the prices would already reflect the information. Therefore, it is reasonable to assume that markets *could* be efficient. However, whether they are efficient or not is another matter because the analysts and market participants are human and may not process this information efficiently.

sell-side analyst person whose job it is to monitor companies and regularly report on their value through earnings forecasts and buy/sell/hold recommendations; employed by the investment banks that underwrite and sell securities to the public

buy-side analyst person whose job it is to evaluate the publicly available information for institutions in the capital market that invest in securities

Anomalies

anomaly mispricing of an asset such that the pricing of the asset is not consistent with efficient markets

Researchers have documented numerous anomalies in security pricing over the past few decades. An **anomaly** is a mispricing of an asset such that the pricing of the asset is not consistent with efficient markets. In other words, the pricing of an asset is not associated with relevant information about the asset that is known to all market participants. The presence of an anomaly would permit an investor to consistently earn abnormal profits from using a strategy to exploit an anomaly. Therefore, if you do some data snooping and discover that there is a relationship, say, between a company's stock price and the first letter of the company's name, such that you could make money by buying the stock of companies whose name starts with M and selling companies' stock whose name begins with P, this may be present for the time period of your study. But there are three questions to ask:

1. Could you make a profit after considering transactions costs for your trades?
2. Could you make a profit after adjusting for the market risk of the stocks?
3. Could you make a profit consistently in any other time period (especially going forward) using this strategy?

The answer is, "Probably not."

What are the types of anomalies that researchers have found? We list a few of these in Table 9-2. Consider a few of these:

- The size effect is that small capitalization stocks outperform large capitalization stocks, which indicates that the market is not weak-form efficient.
- The January effect is that returns in January are higher than the rest of the year. This indicates that the market is not weak-form efficient.
- The earnings surprise anomaly is that when earnings are released by a company and there is an unexpected portion, the market not only reacts immediately, but also continues to react for some days following the earnings announcement. This is evidence against semi-strong market efficiency.
- The value anomaly is that value stocks (that is, low market/book ratios) outperform other securities, which would indicate that the market is not semi-strong-form efficient.

Though these anomalies are documented as statistically significant in some periods, the issue becomes one of whether these anomalies are economically significant, that is, they are not profitable on a risk-adjusted basis after considering transactions costs.

While we will not go into detail on the evidence regarding these, the general conclusions are the following:

- Some anomalies, such as the size, the January, or day-of-the-week effects, do not persist over time. This may be due to either the anomaly being time specific or to the anomaly disappearing because investors have exploited the anomaly and therefore the stocks then become correctly priced.
- Some anomalies, such as momentum, can be explained by rational behavior or a factor that is not accounted for in pricing models. What appears to be an anomaly may, in fact, be a rational response to information that is disseminated slowly.
- Some anomalies, such as the value and small firm effect, may be attributed to the use of the CAPM in the analysis, but these anomalies most likely are not apparent if a more robust model, such as the Fama–French model, were used in developing expected returns and asset pricing.

TABLE 9-2 Examples of Anomalies Documented by Researchers

Cross-Sectional Anomalies	Time-Based Anomalies	Other Anomalies
• Book-to-market ratio	• January	• Earnings surprise
• P/E ratio	• Day-of-the-week	• Initial public offerings
• Value	• Weekend	
• Small firm	• Time-of-day	
• Size	• Momentum	
	• Overreaction	

- Some anomalies, such as earnings surprise and initial public offerings, do not exist once transactions costs and risk are adequately accounted for in the analysis.
- Some anomalies, such as the overreaction anomaly and the initial public offering effect, may be explained by investor behavior that is not captured in pricing models. However, it may not be possible to earn abnormal returns once transactions costs and risk are properly considered.

The late Professor Fischer Black, who summed up anomalies succinctly in his discussion of expected returns, remarked that "so called 'anomalies' don't seem anomalous to me at all. They seem like nuggets from a gold mine, found by one of the thousands of miners all over the world."[42]

LESSONS LEARNED | Wacky Indicators

In addition to the technical analysis and calendar-based anomalies that investors have used to chase abnormal returns, a number of indicators fall into the category of superstitious indicators:

Super Bowl winners	If a former member of the American Football League wins, the stock market will experience a down year.
Butter production in Bangladesh	The return on the S&P Index will be twice that of the change in butter production in Bangladesh.
Triple Crown	If a horse wins the Triple Crown (that is, wins the Kentucky Derby, the Belmont Stakes, and the Preakness Stakes), the stock market will have a bad year.
Hemlines of women's dresses	There is a positive relationship between movement in the market and hemlines: if hemlines get shorter, prices go up, and vice versa.
Sports Illustrated Swimsuit Model	The market does well when the swimsuit model chosen for the cover is of U.S. nationality.

If you plan to start trading based on any of these, please note that they have been, largely, debunked.

Implications

Overall, based on the available empirical evidence with regard to capital markets of the United States and most developed markets, these markets are weak-form and semi-strong-form efficient, but not strong-form efficient.

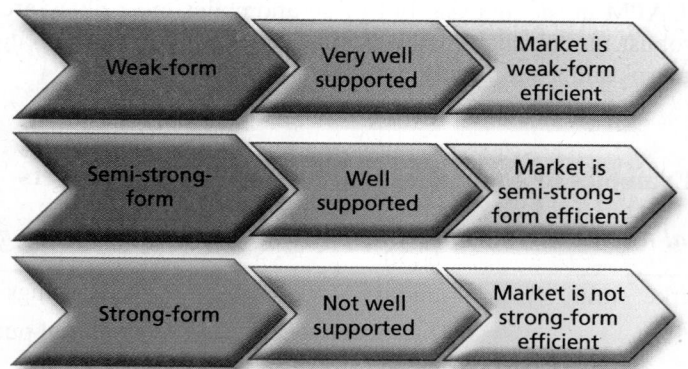

The EMH states that security prices fully and accurately reflect all available information at any given time. The evidence suggests that market efficiency does hold. The implications for investors and for corporate officers include:

1. Technical analysis is not likely to be rewarded in the form of abnormal returns because markets appear to be weak-form efficient.
2. Fundamental analysis, based on the use of various forms of publicly available information, is likely to be unsuccessful at generating abnormal profits. The implication is that to benefit from the use of such data, the analysis must be of superior and consistent quality.

In light of items 1 and 2 just listed, active trading strategies are unlikely to outperform passive portfolio management strategies on a consistent basis. An **active trading strategy** includes trading based on timing the market, trends, or other criteria. A **passive investment strategy** involves buy-and-hold strategies and the purchase of such products as index mutual funds or exchange-traded funds (ETFs) that replicate the performance of a market index. The lack of success for active strategies is partially attributable to the extra costs associated with collecting and processing information, as well as to the additional trading costs associated with active strategies. These extra costs can be justified only if the approach generates sufficient additional returns to compensate for them. Passive strategies minimize these costs.

active trading strategy trading based on timing the market, trends, or other criteria

passive investment strategy buy-and-hold strategies and the purchase of such products as index mutual funds or exchange-traded funds (ETFs) that replicate the performance of a market index

Two of the most important implications of efficient markets for financial managers are as follows:

1. The timing of security issues or repurchases is unimportant in an efficient market because prices will be correct on average. In other words, prices will not become inflated, so there is no optimal time to sell new securities, and securities will not be undervalued, so there is no optimal time to repurchase outstanding securities.
2. If short-run momentum and overreaction continue, we would expect the opposite: that corporations issue equity after a price run-up and repurchase shares after a price decline. Therefore, managers should monitor the price of the company's securities and see whether price changes reflect new information or short-run momentum and/or overreaction.

Market Efficiency Around the World | GLOBAL PERSPECTIVE

The International Monetary Fund has promoted the distribution and transparency of economic and financial data in capital markets to encourage the efficiency of capital markets around the world. The IMF's program includes the Special Data Dissemination Standard (SDDS) in 1996 and the General Data Dissemination Initiative in 1997.

As of 2010, 153 of the IMF's 185 member nations participate. The data available include economic data such as the consumer price index, trade data, demographic data, and national accounts. Market data include exchange rates, interest rates, and stock market indices.

Data on any of these 153 nations can be accessed through www.imf.org.

Concept Review Questions

1. Define market efficiency in terms of information.
2. Discuss the reasonableness of the assumptions underlying market efficiency.
3. What are the main implications of the efficient markets hypothesis for financial managers?
4. If someone discovers that stock returns for stocks with a ticker symbol of one character are higher than stock returns for stocks with a ticker symbol of three characters, what would you want to know before putting your money into this strategy?

9.6 BEHAVIORAL FINANCE AND FINANCIAL MANAGEMENT

behavioral finance study of how human behavior affects economic decision making

Behavioral finance is the study of how human behavior affects economic decision making. While we devise theories that depend on rational, risk-averse investors, there is always the possibility that financial managers do not act this way and, in fact, make decisions that are biased. Why look at behavioral finance? Because decisions are not made by computers; no matter how much decisions depend on formulas and models, there is always a human element somewhere along the way, either through the inputs to the formulas and models or through the interpretation of the results of the formulas and models.

Cognitive Biases

Individuals' behaviors enter into decision making, whether intentional or subconsciously. Asset pricing models, in particular, make certain assumptions about behavior (e.g., risk averse, rational). But what happens if these assumptions are not true? What can be done to ensure that personal biases do not enter into decision making? An important step is to understand psychology and the cognitive biases that may exist.

cognitive bias mistake in decision making that results from one's own preferences and beliefs

A **cognitive bias** is a mistake in decision making that results from one's own preferences and beliefs. These biases result in decisions that are not consistent with pure scientific or statistical reasoning. The many sources of bias include overconfidence, loss aversion, the disposition effect, representativeness, anchoring, framing, and mental accounting. Though this is not a complete list of such biases, by discussing a few of these biases briefly, you can get an idea of how behavior may affect financial decision making and the need for monitoring and mechanisms to minimize the effects of these biases.

Overconfidence

People, including and perhaps even more so financial professionals, are generally overconfident about their abilities. There are many ways that this becomes apparent when we observe behavior. For example, a decision maker who has a good understanding of the role of diversification may nevertheless choose an investment portfolio without adequate diversification because of overconfidence in his or her ability to select investments.

One result of this overconfidence in the stock market is that individuals who are more overconfident tend to trade more often than others, generally to the detriment of the value of their portfolio. Overoptimism is quite common in speculative bubbles in markets.

Overoptimism also affects the outlook of companies' top management. In the Duke/CFO Magazine Optimism Index, CFOs are generally more optimistic about their own company's prospects compared to how they perceive the economy in general.[43] Overconfidence can lead to subconsciously biasing investment project choices toward projects that the financial manager believes are more profitable. How could this be possible? Many subjective inputs contribute to capital investment decisions, as you will see in later chapters, which a manager can use to manage the outcome of the analysis, making a project appear more profitable or less risky. And this does not have to be intentional; this could be subconscious.

People tend to differ in the degree of overconfidence, with men more overconfident than women and entrepreneurs more overconfident than other persons in the business. But this is not necessarily a bad thing because this optimism is what helps individuals take on outsized risk related to new businesses, inventions, and new products.

BOTTOM LINE: Overconfidence may lead to poor or risky decision making.

---

[43] The average of CFO's assessments of prospects should coincide with the average assessment of the economy as a whole, but it does not.

Loss aversion

In asset pricing models, we base the theories on risk aversion. However, loss aversion has different implications for pricing. **Prospect theory** is the area of study of how individuals make choices given information about probabilities. According to prospect theory, individuals tend to be risk averse when there are gains, but tend not to be risk averse—and, in fact, are risk seekers—when considering losses.[44] The different type of risk preference for gains and losses arises from **loss aversion**, which is a willingness to avoid losses that is disproportionate to the willingness to seek similar-sized gains.

The basic idea is the following: Individuals do not weigh probabilities as we would expect based on probabilities. Consider the following choice:[45]

Choice 1	*Choice 2*
50 percent chance to win $1,000	$450 for sure
50 percent chance to win nothing	

Which would you prefer? If you apply the expected value calculations that we covered in an earlier chapter, you would see that Choice 1 has an expected value of $500. However, as this problem is framed, many will choose Choice 2, letting certainty outweigh the expected value.

What are the implications for financial management? Loss aversion implies that decision makers may give more weight to certainty and therefore not think in terms of the statistical expected value. Loss aversion also implies that managers may focus too much on what has already been spent—a sunk cost—in making decisions.

Closely related to loss aversion is the disposition effect. The **disposition effect** is the behavior of individuals in which they avoid realizing any paper losses, but tend to realize paper gains. In other words, people tend to hang onto losers longer than they should. We can see this in any stock market: In a bull market, in which stock prices are climbing, there is increased trading volume; in a bear market, in which stock prices are declining, there is decreased trading volume.

This may explain why markets may not react to news as quickly as we would expect in an efficient market because some investors will hesitate in selling when there is bad news, hence perpetuating a drop in a stock's price, and will sell quickly when the price rises, hence dampening the initial response to good news.

BOTTOM LINE: Financial managers may not be willing to abandon an investment project that is not turning out as expected.

Representativeness and anchoring

Representativeness is the tendency for people to judge something, such as an investment, by the degree to which this something resembles something else in the person's experience. In other words, an individual will overweight most recent events, giving less weight to long-term averages. For example, when the market falls significantly, it is this fall that most investors consider, not the rise before that fall.

It is all too often that employees invest in the employer's own stock. An example may be an employee of a food processor selecting food processor stocks in his or her personal investment portfolio, despite the heavy investment in food processing of his total portfolio in the form of in-human capital investment through the employee's career. The familiarity with the employer or the industry may deter an investor from fully diversifying a portfolio.

prospect theory the area of study of how individuals make choices given information about probabilities and outcomes

loss aversion willingness to avoid losses that is disproportionate to the willingness to seek similar-sized gains

disposition effect behavior of individuals in which they avoid realizing any paper losses, but tend to realize paper gains

representativeness tendency for people to judge something, such as an investment, by the degree to which this something resembles something else in the person's experience

[44] Prospect theory was developed by Daneil Kaheman and Amos Tversky, "Prospect Theory: An Analysis of Decision Under Risk," *Econometrica*, No. 37 (1979): 264–291.

[45] This example is modeled from the A–B choice in Kahneman and Tversky, ibid.

Closely related to representativeness is anchoring. **Anchoring** is the tendency to use inappropriate or irrelevant factors in decision making. Consider forecasting a time series. If individuals are asked to forecast the following:

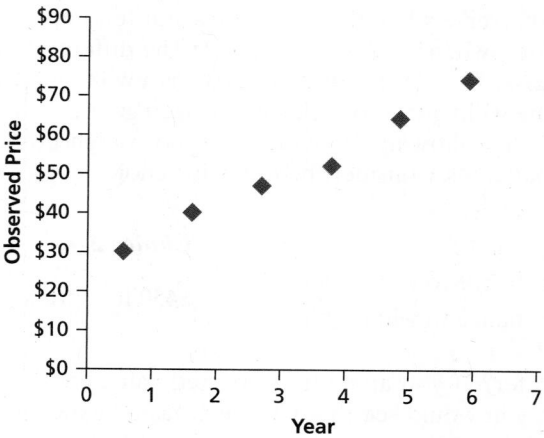

people tend to underestimate the seventh observation due to anchoring, predicting the observed price lower than the statistical trend line:

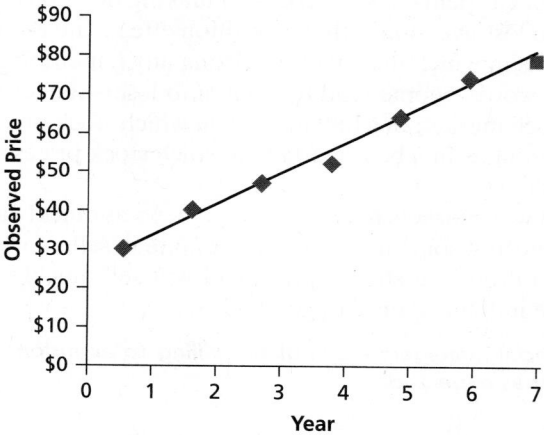

If a decision is anchored, this means that the decision is influenced by how something is presented. Consider two series of numbers:

Series A:	44	48	63	72	88
Series B:	101	81	50	43	40

Without resorting to your calculator, which series has the highest mean? If you chose Series B, you are likely anchoring your answer on the first few observations of each series. Although the average is the same for both series—63—there is a tendency to let the first observations in the series influence the choice. Related to this is the investment in projects for which the manager has the most familiarity, rather than those projects that offer the most diversification.

BOTTOM LINE: Past experiences, especially the most recent past, may unduly affect the forecasts that are made for capital projects or investments made today.

Framing

Framing is the manner in which something is presented, which may influence how someone feels about this something. Consider the classic example of specials. Most of the time you see "happy hour" specials with some type of discount (e.g., two for one) during certain hours, corresponding to the period of time in which there is the slowest bar traffic. Therefore, by arriving during happy hour, the individual believes that they are getting a deal. Now let's turn this around and have the same exact pricing, but a different advertisement, or framing. What if the advertisement were, instead, that you pay full price during happy hour, but pay more than full price when it is not happy hour? The way this is framed, you may come away feeling that you would not like to visit the bar during any time but happy hour because you would have been taken advantage of otherwise. You may no longer feel that happy about happy hour; rather, you may feel quite negative about the bar from this advertisement. Your attitude is shaped by this framing.

framing manner in which something is presented, which may influence how someone feels about this something

BOTTOM LINE: How an investment opportunity or project is presented and evaluated may influence its acceptability.

Mental accounting

Mental accounting is the process of investors separating money into different accounts in their thought process, which affects decision making. For example, a financial manager may view funds generated internally as free or low-cost capital and treat funds raised from a stock issue as costly, even though they are—with the exception of flotation costs—the same cost.[46] Another example of mental accounting is evaluating investments in a company as separate "silos," instead of taking the companywide perspective.

mental accounting process of investors separating money into different accounts in their thought process

BOTTOM LINE: Mental categorization of funds may not be optimal when making decisions to maximize shareholder wealth.

Implications of Behavior in Financial Decision Making

Most asset pricing models assume that investors are rational, and the value of an asset reflects rational decision making. We also assume that investors are risk averse but are willing to take on risk if compensated for this risk in the form of higher expected returns. So what if these assumptions are not true? What are the implications?

Despite the long list of assumptions, and despite the role of human behavior in decision making that may not be rational or risk averse, the CAPM model has generally withstood a barrage of attacks. This is because the basic conclusion of expected returns determined by the time value of money and a premium for bearing market risk still stands. Therefore, using the CAPM in determining the cost of funds, one of the more prominent uses in financial management, is still acceptable.

Another implication of human behavior in decision making is that any system of governance should build in protections against behaviors that may be detrimental to the goal of the firm. Policies and procedures can be developed that guard against overconfidence, disposition effect, mental accounting issues, and framing.

1. How does loss aversion affect decision making?

2. Can a financial manager be ethical and still be overconfident?

3. If not all investors are risk averse, can the CAPM still hold true? Explain.

Concept Review Questions

---

[46] This is similar to the mental accounting mistake that many individuals make when looking at tax refunds. A tax refund is simply what was overpaid to the government over a period, but many individuals treat the refund as "found money."

SUMMARY

- The efficient frontier is the set of portfolios that provides the best return for a given level of risk (or, similarly, the lowest risk for a given level of return). If we combine borrowing or lending at the risk-free rate of interest, the set of investment opportunities improves.

- The capital market line depicts the required return for efficient portfolios based on their standard deviations, whereas the security market line depicts the relation between the required return and market risk, as measured by beta.

- An efficient market is a market in which asset prices reflect available information quickly and accurately. The EMH is commonly broken down into three forms that are based on the extent to which prices reflect different types of available information. The weak-form EMH states that security prices reflect all market data; the semi-strong form states that prices reflect all publicly known and available information; and the strong form states that prices reflect all public and private information

- An implication of the capital asset pricing model for financial decision making is that return on an investment is consistent with the amount of market risk of the investment, not on the investment's total or stand-alone risk. The implications of market efficiency for financial decision making include the (1) inability to time security offerings and (2) the expectation of returns commensurate with market risk.

- Behavioral finance is an area of study that examines how human behaviors can enter into decision making. Cognitive biases can enter into decision making, resulting in decisions that are not in the best interest of owners.

FORMULAS/EQUATIONS

(9-1) $E(r_p) = r_f + w[E(r_X) - r_f]$

(9-2) $\sigma_p = w\sigma_X$

(9-3) $E(r_p) = r_f + \left(\dfrac{E(r_X) - r_f}{\sigma_X}\right)\sigma_p$

(9-4)   Slope of the capital market line $= \dfrac{E(r_M) - r_f}{\sigma_M}$

(9-5) $E(r_p) = r_f + \left[\dfrac{E(r_M) - r_f}{\sigma_M}\right]\sigma_p$

(9-6) $\beta_i = \dfrac{COV_{i,M}}{\sigma_M^2} = \dfrac{\rho_{i,M}\sigma_i}{\sigma_M}$

(9-7)   Sharpe ratio $= \dfrac{r_p - r_f}{\sigma_p}$

(9-8) $\beta_p = w_A\beta_A + w_B\beta_B + \ldots + w_n\beta_n$

(9-9) $E(r_i) = r_f + (E(r_M) - r_f)\beta_i$

(9-10) $E(r_i) = a_0 + b_{i1}F_1 + b_{i2}F_2 + \ldots + b_{in}F_n$

QUESTIONS AND PROBLEMS

Multiple Choice

1. Which of the following statements is *false*?
   A. The standard deviation of a risk-free asset is zero.
   B. The covariance of any combination of a risky security and a risk-free asset is zero.
   C. Portfolios on the efficient frontier dominate all other attainable portfolios for a given risk or return.
   D. The risk measurement associated with the security market line (SML) is the standard deviation of the portfolio.

2. If Portfolio A lies above the security market line, Portfolio A is:
   A. overvalued.
   B. undervalued.
   C. undetermined.
   D. properly valued.

3. The expected return and standard deviation of a portfolio consisting of $2,000 invested in the risk-free asset with an 8 percent rate of return, and $8,000 invested in the risky security with a 20 percent rate of return and a 25 percent standard deviation, is *closest* to:

Expected Return	*Standard Deviation*
A. 5 percent	10.4 percent
B. 10.4 percent	5 percent
C. 17.6 percent	20 percent
D. 20 percent	17.6 percent

4. Which of the following statements is *false*?
   A. The market portfolio is observable.
   B. Systematic risk cannot be diversified away.
   C. The *y*-intercept of both the SML and the CML is the risk-free rate of interest.
   D. The market portfolio includes all risky assets, including stocks, bonds, real estate, derivatives, and so on.

5. Systematic risk:
   A. is also called unique risk.
   B. does not change throughout time.
   C. equals total risk divided by nonsystematic risk.
   D. measures of portfolios are more stable than those of individual assets.

6. Which of the following statements about an efficient market is false?
   A. Prices reflect all relevant and available information.
   B. Prices react to new information quickly and correctly.
   C. Price changes follow predictable patterns through time.
   D. Prices reflect such information as a company's financial strength and earnings.

7. Which of the following is *useful* in attempting to identify mispriced securities if a market is semi-strong efficient, yet not strong-form efficient?
   A. Earnings expectations
   B. Past stock price changes
   C. Relevant insider information
   D. Past and current published trading volumes

8. Which of the following statements is true?
   A. The weak form of the efficient market hypothesis encompasses the semi-strong form.
   B. The strong form of the efficient market hypothesis encompasses the semi-strong form.
   C. The semi-strong form of the efficient market hypothesis encompasses the strong form.
   D. The strong form of the efficient market hypothesis does not encompass the weak form.

9. An event study is most often used to evaluate:
   A. whether a market is weak-form efficient.
   B. whether there is insider trading for a stock.
   C. the effect of information as it reaches market participants.

10. A portfolio manager who believes that markets are semi-strong efficient would most likely use:

    A. active trading strategy.

    B. passive investment strategy.

Practice Questions and Problems

9.1   The Efficient Frontier

11. What does the efficient frontier represent?

12. If a portfolio does not lie on the efficient frontier, what does this mean about this portfolio?

13. Determine if you are risk averse or risk loving. For the following decisions, indicate if they are consistent with risk aversion or risk loving:

    A. Buying a lottery ticket

    B. Buying fire insurance for your house

    C. Backing up your computer

14. The Mason Consulting firm has been hired to conduct an investigation of the advice the Sketchy Brokerage Company has been giving its clients, and the investigation might result in a lawsuit. Mason observes that clients have been placed in the following portfolios:

Investor	Portfolio	Expected Return	Standard Deviation
A	A	2.0%	0.40%
B	B	4.0%	0.60%
C	C	5.0%	0.30%
D	D	7.0%	0.50%
E	E	9.0%	0.45%
F	F	10.0%	0.70%

Evaluate the advice the broker has been giving his clients (assume that investors can only invest in one of the six portfolios).

    A. Which investors are holding inefficient portfolios?

    B. What changes would you make to their investments—how will this improve their portfolio?

    C. Mr. Al Locate, the broker under investigation, argues that these portfolios are appropriate because these investors are risk loving. Are inefficient portfolios appropriate for risk-loving investors?

    D. Of the investors who are holding efficient portfolios, who is:

       i) The most risk averse

       ii) The least risk averse

15. Suppose that an investor invests all his wealth, $10,000, in a portfolio that has an expected return of 10 percent and a standard deviation of 20 percent. He borrows an additional $5,000 at the risk-free rate of 3 percent, which he also invests in this portfolio. What is the estimated expected return and standard deviation for this portfolio?

9.2   The Capital Asset Pricing Model

16. According to the CAPM, what are the primary determinants of an asset's return?

17. Why might a financial manager care about the CAPM and a company's beta?

18. Calculate the missing values for the following four efficient portfolios. The expected return on the market is 8 percent, with a standard deviation of 5 percent, and the risk-free rate is 2 percent.

Investor	Weight in Risk-free Asset	Expected Portfolio Return	Portfolio Standard Deviation
Charles	25%		
Fritz	40%		
Eddy	50%		
Nellie	75%		

19. Jackie borrowed $800 at the risk-free rate of 8 percent. She invested the borrowed money and $1,000 in a portfolio with a 15 percent rate of return and a 30 percent standard deviation. What is the expected return and standard deviation of her portfolio?

20. Stock FM has a standard deviation of 30 percent. It has a correlation coefficient of 0.75 with market returns. The standard deviation of market return is 20 percent, and the expected return is 16 percent. The risk-free rate is 6.5 percent. What is the required rate of return of Stock FM? Compare FM's required return to the expected market return.

21. Three investors are having an argument about investments and have come to you for advice. The set of possible investments are A, B, and C:

Risky Portfolio	Expected Return	Standard Deviation
A	7%	5%
B	13%	7%
C	17%	11%

Assume you cannot mix risky investments. Investor 1 says that they should all invest in portfolio A because it has the lowest risk. Investor 2 says that they should all invest in portfolio C because it has the highest return. Investor 3 is just confused.

A. If there is no risk-free asset, can you recommend the same portfolio for each of the friends? Why or why not?

B. If the expected risk-free rate is 2 percent, can you recommend the same set of risky assets for each of the friends? Why or why not?

C. Does the existence of a risk-free asset make the friends better off? Explain your reasoning.

9.3 The CAPM and Market Risk

22. What does beta in the CAPM represent?

23. What is the beta of the:
   A. risk-free asset?
   B. market portfolio?

24. Which of the following are examples of systematic and unsystematic risks:
   A. Inflation risk
   B. CFO's fraudulent activities
   C. Changes in interest rates
   D. Product tampering
   E. Political risk
   F. CEO's aversion to working on Fridays

25. You are on the board of directors of the BY Company. The stock price of BY has suddenly increased by 20 percent, and the CEO has come to the board asking for a substantial pay increase. The CEO argues that the company's prospects have dramatically improved—after all, why else would the stock price increase? Do you feel that the CEO should receive a large pay increase?

26. The manager of the Mountaineer Company is puzzled. Analysts are saying that the future prospects for his company are poor because the stock price has dropped 5 percent.

   A. Explain to the manager the relationship between stock prices and market expectations.

   B. Would you be as concerned about the company's future prospects if the company had a beta of 1.5 and the market has fallen 4 percent?

27. Which security, A, B, or C, will provide the greatest return per unit of risk when combined with the risk-free asset with a 5 percent rate of return?

Security	Expected Return	Standard Deviation of Returns
A	20%	5%
B	17%	11%
C	28%	20%

28. Determine the beta of a company's stock based on the following information:

Market expected return	8 percent
Standard deviation	3 percent
Risk-free rate	3 percent
Current dividend	$4.50
Dividend growth rate	5 percent
Current stock price	$25

29. Using the relationship between individual security betas and the portfolio beta, complete the following table:

	Security 1 Beta	Security 2 Beta	Weight in Security 1	Portfolio Beta
Case 1	0.40	1.50	0.60	
Case 2		0.45	0.80	0.49
Case 3	1.10	1.90		1.50
Case 4	1.25	0.40	0.75	
Case 5	1.30		0.15	1.895

30. Estimate the beta of a stock with the following characteristics:
   - market risk premium is 20 percent;
   - risk-free rate of interest is 10 percent;
   - the current stock price per share is $10;
   - expected dividend at the end of the year is $2.50; and
   - expected price per share in one year is $12.50.

   Assume the market is in equilibrium.

31. Suppose you have a portfolio now that has $100 in Stock A with a beta of 0.9, $400 in Stock B with a beta of 1.2, and $300 in the risk-free asset. You have another $200 to invest and wish to achieve a beta of your portfolio that is the same as the market beta. What would the beta of the stock added to your portfolio do to achieve this goal?

32. The Redrock Consulting firm is valuing the Vancouver Rain-Making Company (VRMC) and needs to calculate the following:

A. The required rate of return of the VRMC, assuming the market risk premium is 8 percent, the risk-free rate is 2 percent, and its common stock's beta is 1.2.

B. The price of VRMC based on the current dividend of $1.25 and a dividend growth rate of 3 percent.

33. The Wise Advisers are following five different stocks and need to issue a recommendation (buy, hold, or sell) to their customers. The market return is 7 percent with a standard deviation of 4 percent. The risk-free rate is 3 percent. The CAPM is assumed to hold.

Security	Expected Return	Standard Deviation	Beta	Recommendation
ABC	5%	9%	1.50	
DEF	10%	3%	1.10	
GHI	6%	10%	.95	
JKL	9%	4%	.75	
MNO	14%	6%	1.25	

To determine the recommendations, begin by calculating the required returns for each security using the capital asset pricing model. Comparing the expected and required returns will indicate which securities are under, over, or correctly priced.

9.4 Alternative Asset Pricing Models

34. Describe and provide an example of an arbitrage opportunity.

35. What type of factors drive returns in the arbitrage pricing theory?

36. Consider two analysts, Joe and Jane. Joe is convinced that the only relevant factor in explaining stock returns is the market return. Jane believes that surprises drive returns. Classify each analyst according to the asset pricing model that is most consistent with their beliefs.

37. Consider two portfolios, A and B. Portfolio A has a beta of 1.0 and an expected return of 15 percent. Portfolio B has a beta of 0.8 and an expected return of 12 percent. If the risk-free rate of return is 5 percent, how can you take advantage of this arbitrage opportunity according to the arbitrage pricing theory?

9.5 Market Efficiency

38. What distinguishes a weak-form efficient market from a semi-strong-form efficient market?

39. What distinguishes a semi-strong-form efficient market from a strong-form efficient market?

40. Why would a financial manager of a corporation be interested in whether financial markets are efficient?

41. If insiders can make abnormal profits by trading in the company's stock,

A. what does this say about the efficiency of the stock market?

B. would this activity be legal? Explain.

42. If a mutual fund claims that it can "beat the market on a risk-adjusted basis," what does this say about the efficiency of the market if this statement is true?

43. If a trader uses technical analysis and claims that she can "beat the market on a risk-adjusted basis," what does this say about the efficiency of the market if true?

44. The CEO of the Yucca Diet Pill Company has hired IB Consulting to advise her on issuing new stock. Her company will need to issue more stock soon to finance the development of a new product—the Yucca Hair Growth formula. The CEO has noticed that, on average, the stock price of diet pill companies is higher in the

spring than the rest of the year. She would like to issue the Yucca stock in the spring to obtain the highest price possible. Given your understanding of the efficiency of the market, what advice do you have for this CEO regarding the timing of the new stock issue of the Yucca Diet Pill Company?

45. On the morning of March 15, the Ames Company announced that it will pay its first dividend of $5 this year. The ex-dividend date will be July 3.

   A. If the announcement is a complete surprise to the market, what do you expect will happen to the stock price on March 15?

   B. If the announcement has been forecasted by the financial analysts, what do you expect to happen to the stock price on March 15?

   C. What do you expect to happen to the price of Ames stock on July 3?

46. On Monday evening, the East Tennessee Steam Engine Company announced that it would be restating its financial statements for the last 5 years, and the CFO was also arrested for fraud. Interpret the following Tuesday stock reactions:

   A. Stock price drops

   B. Stock price does not change

9.6   Behavioral Finance and Financial Management

47. Is loss aversion the same thing as risk aversion? Explain.

48. If a financial manager is interested in maximizing owners' wealth, how could the manager be overconfident and still be honest?

49. If a person gives too much weight to recent information, rather than long-term averages, what type of behavior does this exhibit? Explain.

50. A financial manager refuses to abandon an unprofitable project and believes that if the company sticks with this project it will be profitable. The manager is most likely exhibiting what type of behavior?

Cases

Case 9.1 Morgantown Company Stock

On Monday, February 18, the stock of the Morgantown Company was trading at $25 per share. The CEO was satisfied with this price, as it reflected the prospects of Morgantown in terms of the future dividend growth and required rate of return. The company's scientists worked all Monday night to complete a project, which will dramatically improve the quality of Morgantown's products and result in a huge increase in sales for the next 10 years.

   A. If markets are efficient and reflect available information, explain why the stock price of Morgantown should or should not reflect the top-secret project's prospects on Monday, February 18, and on Tuesday, February 19.

   B. The CEO of Morgantown has been watching the company's stock price and noticed that the stock price increased during trading on Tuesday, even though the market, in general, was flat. Why might the stock price be increasing on Tuesday, February 19, even though the company has not made any announcements regarding the top-secret project?

   C. The U.S. Securities and Exchange Commission's Regulation FD requires that companies disclose information to all investors at the same time.[47] To avoid any problems with this regulation, the management of Morgantown decides to issue a press release about the top-secret project on Wednesday, February 20. What, if anything, do you expect to happen to the stock price of Morgantown once this press release is issued? Why?

---

[47] 17 Code of Federal Regulation Parts 240, 243, and 249, RIN 3235-AH82, effective October 23, 2000.

Case 9.2 JPMorgan Chase's Sinking Profit

On Saturday, January 14, 2012, JPMorgan Chase (ticker symbol JPM), announced a drop in profit of 23 percent for the fourth quarter of 2011, compared to the same quarter a year earlier. This drop in profit is attributed to a drop in investment banking activity, but it was offset somewhat by a reduction in defaults on mortgages and credit-card debt.

A. What do you believe should have happened to JPMorgan's common stock on Friday, January 13, 2012? Why?

B. What do you believe should have happened to JPMorgan's common stock on Tuesday, January 17, 2012, which is the first trading day following this announcement? Why?

C. Download daily stock prices for JPM for the ten trading days before and after this announcement, and calculate the return for each trading day. Do the same for the S&P 500. Using a beta of 1.35, estimate the expected return on JPM stock for each day based on the security market line.

D. Using the analysis in C, estimate the abnormal return for each trading day:

Abnormal return = Actual return – return expected using the SML

Relate your findings to the earnings announcement.

PART 5

Long-Term Investment Decisions

The long-term, capital decisions of a company are important for the sustainability of a company. Without new capital investments and assessment of existing investments, a company will not grow and create value. In Part 5, we focus on decision making involving the investment in long-term assets. We discuss different evaluation techniques in Chapter 10 and then focus on estimating future cash flows from a project in Chapter 11.

CHAPTER 10

CAPITAL BUDGETING DECISIONS

© Stigur Karlsson/iStockphoto

Many working business professionals consider returning to school to earn an MBA. But is it worth it? It depends. Antony Davies and Thomas Cline considered the cost and potential earning power from individuals who pursued an MBA in the years 1993–2000, and found:

- The return on investment in an MBA was better than Treasury Bills, the return on triple-A rated bonds, and the Dow Jones Industrial Average.

- The payback period, in years to recover tuition and fees, is 8–10 years.

- The NPV—the present value of the benefits from increased salary and benefits, less the present value of the costs of tuition and fees—ranges from $360,000 (in 1993) to around $700,000 in 1998, with the NPV in 2001 of $550,000.

They also observed that there is variation in the benefits from an MBA. In other words, your experience may differ from that of the "average."

Source: *Antony Davies and Thomas Cline, "The ROI on the MBA, BizEd, January/February 2005, pp. 42–45.*

Learning Outcomes

After reading this chapter, you should be able to:

LO 10.1 Describe the process of basic capital budgeting.

LO 10.2 Compare and apply capital budgeting techniques used to evaluate long-term investments, including the net present value and internal rate of return techniques.

LO 10.3 Reconcile the approach to capital budgeting that is consistent with value maximization with the capital budgeting techniques used in practice.

Chapter Preview In this chapter, we discuss long-term investment decisions made by companies; that is, investments in real assets, such as plants and equipment. In previous chapters, we have seen that a company's investment decisions are critical to its value because market values are based on the expected future growth in company earnings, dividends, and distributable cash flows.

We revisit several concepts that we discussed when describing how to value bonds and shares. In particular, we emphasize that the basic techniques are similar: estimate future cash flows from the investment, determine appropriate discount rates, convert those expected future cash flows into their corresponding present values, and compare these present values with the cost of the investment. The essential difference between valuing shares and valuing projects or companies is not in the approach, but rather in the judgment necessary because of the differing quality of the inputs.

10.1 THE CAPITAL BUDGETING PROCESS

A **capital expenditure** is a company's investment in long-lived assets, which may be tangible assets, such as property, plants, and equipment, or intangible assets, such as research and development, copyrights, brand names, and franchise agreements. Tangible assets are hard, physical assets, whereas intangible ones are more abstract; it is easier for a company to borrow against tangible assets than against intangible ones.[1]

capital expenditure investment in long-lived assets, which may be tangible or intangible

What Is Capital Budgeting?

Long-term investment decisions determine a company's future direction and may be viewed as the most important decisions a company makes because its capital expenditures usually involve large amounts of money, and the decisions are frequently irrevocable. For example, Buckeye Partners, L.P., owns 5,400 miles of pipelines for petroleum products in the U.S. Once these pipeline assets are in place, they are largely unique to that application and have very little alternative use. It is therefore important that the decision to make capital investments is made on sound financial and economic grounds. The irrevocable and unique nature of real investments has its parallel in investments in intangible assets, where a decision to bring out a new soft drink, for example, with the attendant product development costs and marketing campaign, is also irrevocable. In this case, it is almost impossible to get back the investment costs of a failed new product launch.

The importance of capital investment decisions lies in their ability to affect the risk of the company. In some cases, the very survival of the company depends on the success of a new product produced from prior investment decisions. Apple Computer (AAPL), for example, was revived in the 2000s when it brought out the iPod, and later iTunes, the iPhone, and the iPad.[2] New products can also provide a much-needed boost to maintain competitiveness or increase market share. For instance, McDonald's (MCD) had a resurgence of sales when it introduced espresso-based coffee, McCafe, in 2009, which allows McDonald's to compete with coffee chains, such as Starbucks.

Capital budgeting refers to the process through which a company makes capital expenditure decisions:

capital budgeting process through which a company makes capital expenditure decisions by identifying investment alternatives, evaluating these alternatives, implementing the chosen investment decisions, and monitoring and evaluating the implemented decisions

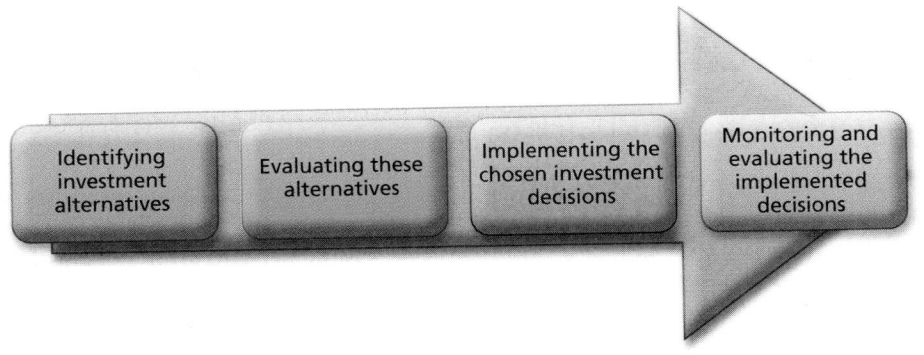

[1] Under U.S. and International Financial Reporting Standards (IFRS), most spending to generate intangible assets, such as research and development (R&D) and advertising, is expensed rather than capitalized. Therefore, these items do not generally appear on the balance sheet as an asset. As a result, most intangible assets that appear on the balance sheet result from a company taking over another at a premium to its book value. The acquiring company allocates this premium among identifiable intangible assets, with any not otherwise allocated premium ending up in the account referred to as goodwill.

[2] See "Apple's Remarkable Comeback Story," Amanda Cantrell, *CNNMoney.com*, March 29, 2006.

We focus most of our discussion on the general framework that should be used to evaluate various investment alternatives because the remaining decisions are company specific. First, we briefly discuss the goals of this process.

Where Does Value Come From?

A company that does not invest effectively will find itself at a competitive disadvantage, which in the extreme will affect its long-term survival. In the short run, poor investment decisions will make a company less attractive than those that have better prepared themselves for the future. This will manifest itself in the market price of its debt and equity securities, which will decline and hence increase its cost of capital.

To fully understand where value comes from, we need to apply basic economic principles. Recall from economics that to earn more than a "normal" profit, a company must have some type of comparative or competitive advantage. A **normal profit** is the return on an investment that compensates the investor for explicit and implicit costs, where implicit costs include the opportunity cost of the investor's capital. **Economic profit**, on the other hand, is the return on an investment *in excess* of the normal profit. This is the essence of creating value: generating economic profits through capital investment.

A **comparative advantage** is the ability of a company to produce a product at a lower cost than its competitors. This includes the innate advantage that a company has over other companies due to access to resources, inputs, or markets. Examples of such access include ownership of oil fields, mines, chemicals, land, or production of inputs.[3]

A **competitive advantage** is any strategy or company action that reduces the competition that the company experiences. These advantages include patents, copyrights, and trademarks, which may keep competitors at bay, or at least slow down imitations of products. Another competitive advantage is economies of scale; if a particular good can produce a lower cost if the scale of production is increased, this will discourage competitors from entering the market because it would be difficult for any entrant to compete against an existing, larger producer. Still another example of a competitive advantage is when a government grants a monopoly to a company, such as a cable company or an electric utility, which then creates a barrier keeping any other potential competitors out of the market.[4,5]

Michael Porter, a professor at Harvard Business School, reframed these basic economic principles by identifying five critical factors that determine the attractiveness of an industry in terms of the ability to generate economic profit:

1. entry barriers,
2. the threat of substitutes,
3. the bargaining power of buyers,
4. the bargaining power of suppliers, and
5. rivalry among existing competitors.[6]

These are often referred to as the **five forces**. Porter argues that, after inception, companies have little immediate control over the attractiveness of their industry. This implies that industry structure is a significant input into every company's investment decisions and

normal profit return on an investment that compensates the investor with the explicit and implicit costs, where implicit costs include the opportunity cost of the investor's capital

comparative advantage innate advantage that a company has over other companies due to access to resources, inputs, or markets

competitive advantage any strategy or feature that reduces the competition that the company experiences

five forces based on the work of Michael Porter, the five critical factors that determine the profitability and, hence, attractiveness of investing an industry: entry barriers, the threat of substitutes, the bargaining power of buyers, the bargaining power of suppliers, and rivalry among existing competitors

---

[3] The idea of comparative advantage is not new. It was first discussed by economist David Ricardo in 1817 [*On the Principles of Political Economy and Taxation*, London: John Murray, 1817].

[4] For a discussion of the cable monopolies, see Clint Bollick, "Cable Television: An Unnatural Monopoly," Cato Policy Analysis, No. 34, Cato Institute, March 13, 1984.

[5] We can distinguish comparative and competitive advantages by noting that comparative advantages are static, whereas competitive advantages are created by the company and, hence, are dynamic. That is, a company could overcome the comparative advantage of a competitor with a competitive advantage. For example, suppose a company owns all oil fields, which would be a comparative advantage; another company could innovate by creating lower-cost synthetic oil that could compete against the company with the oil fields.

[6] Michael E. Porter, "The Five Competitive Forces That Shape Strategy," *Harvard Business Review*, January 2008.

profitability. However, Porter points out that a company *may* exert control over the manner in which it strives to create a competitive advantage within their industry. Obviously, these decisions are also closely related to a company's long-term investment decisions.

Michael Porter argues that companies can create competitive or comparative advantages for themselves by adopting one of the following strategies:

1. *Cost leadership: strive to be a low-cost producer.* This strategy is viable for companies that are able to take advantage of economies of scale, proprietary technology, or privileged or superior access to raw materials. Investment outlays should be made in accordance with a company's potential advantage. For example, if economies of scale or technological advantages are possible, companies should invest in a manner that will enable them to exploit these opportunities.

2. *Differentiation: offer "differentiated" products.* Companies may provide products that are differentiated from others in several ways. The most obvious is to have a product that is itself unique by virtue of its physical or technological characteristics. However, companies may also differentiate their products by providing customers with unique delivery alternatives or by establishing a marketing approach that distinguishes their products from those of their potential competitors.

Either of these strategies can be applied with a broad, industrywide focus, or with a narrow, industry-segment focus, and both have their corollary in capital investment decisions. As we will discuss, cost leadership usually follows from replacement decisions, when companies are constantly striving to use the latest technology to lower the costs of production. Product differentiation usually follows from new product development decisions, such as the launch of a new soft drink or a new model of a car.

Basic economic principles, echoed by Michael Porter, suggest that it is difficult to sustain a competitive advantage once one has been created. This is particularly true in industries where competition is heated or there are low barriers to entry. Therefore, companies must continually plan (and invest) strategically. This brings up the question: What is the relationship between corporate strategy and the capital investment decision?

A Perspective on Capital Budgeting Decision Making

It is a basic premise of finance that when a senior executive justifies a project on nonfinancial grounds, either the analysis is not rigorous enough, with the advantages not fully developed, or it is a pet project and should not be pursued. Every project is amenable to the analytical techniques that we discuss later—the only difference is that the inputs are more qualitative the more strategic the analysis. However, this does bring up a basic distinction—the difference between bottom-up and top-down analysis.

Bottom-up analysis is based on the idea that a company is simply a set or portfolio of capital investment decisions. Equipment replacement is a typical bottom-up analysis, in which an engineer estimates the savings in terms of labor hours, power, material costs, and so on, from replacing one piece of equipment with another. A financial analyst then translates these savings into financial parameters to see whether the replacement savings are worth the cost of the equipment. However, at no point does either the engineer or the financial analyst consider whether the company should continue in this business. An analogy might be the engineer on the *Titanic* deciding to replace some equipment just after the ship struck the iceberg! In isolation, it might be a good decision, but obviously it is irrelevant on a larger scale.

bottom-up analysis investment strategy in which capital investment decisions are considered in isolation, without regard for whether the company should continue in this business or for general industry and economic trends

top-down analysis investment strategy that focuses on strategic decisions, such as which industries or products the company should be involved in, looking at the overall economic picture

In contrast, **top-down analysis** focuses on the strategic decisions about which industries or products the company should be involved in. It is the basic decision of whether Ford should produce passenger cars or trucks, rather than of which passenger cars should be developed. The auto industry has undergone drastic changes that include splitting off divisions and product lines, through closures, sale, or spin-offs. For example, shortly before declaring bankruptcy in June 2009, General Motors discontinued its Pontiac brand.

Top-down: Start with strategy and find profitable investments that fit this strategy

Bottom-up: Start with the most profitable, potential investments

In looking at bottom-up versus top-down analysis, the capital budgeting framework is identical. What is different is the quality of the estimates. In replacement decisions, it may be easier to specify the degree of risk because the analyst can estimate the cost savings with more clearly defined probabilities. It may be possible, for example, to estimate that that there is a 30 percent chance of saving $5 million and a 70 percent chance of saving $100 million per year. In this way, replacement decisions are similar to the evaluation of equity investments for which there is a long price history, and means, variances, and so on can be estimated to say there is a 50 percent chance of a share going up 15 percent in price and a 50 percent chance of it going down 5 percent.

In contrast, top-down or strategic decisions often involve a situation of uncertainty, in which it is almost impossible to place probabilities on the possible outcomes.[7] In these situations, it is important for the analysis to involve different scenarios, so that the company can better assess the risk of a project.[8] This flexibility in top-down decision making is an application of the theory of option pricing to capital investment decisions, **real option valuation (ROV)**. ROV, in a nutshell, is the valuation of a capital investment considering the value of all the options that the investment provides, such as the option to expand, abandon, or delay.[9] ROV is very difficult to implement, but it is important in financial management because many capital investment decisions involve one or more of these options.

real option valuation (ROV) valuation of a capital investment considering the value of all the options that the investment provides, such as the option to expand, abandon, or wait

Discounted Cash Flow and Maximizing Owners' Wealth

The goal of the company should be to maximize owners' wealth, and many techniques are available for making capital investment decisions that are consistent with this overriding objective. These techniques are **discounted cash flow (DCF)** methodologies, and as their name suggests, they are the capital investment analogues to the DCF valuation techniques discussed earlier. DCF valuation involves estimating future cash flows and comparing their discounted values with investment outlays required today. In this way, they are technically identical to the approaches used to evaluate bonds and stock.

discounted cash flow (DCF) determining a value today by estimating future cash flows and comparing their discounted values with the cash outlay today

[7] This distinction between risk and uncertainty is attributed to Frank Knight, *Risk, Uncertainty, and Profit* (Boston: Hart Schaffner & Marx; Houghton Mifflin Co., 1921).

[8] We discuss scenario analysis in Chapter 11.

[9] We discuss real options and real options valuation in Appendix 11B.

The only practical difference is that whereas the cash flows are fixed in valuing bonds and shares in the sense that the analyst cannot change them, in making capital investment decisions the analyst can change the underling cash flows by changing the structure of the project. For example, the company can decide to defer a project for a year or, after the analysis, decide to change the form of a product. If it is a new car development, for example, some parts may become optional extras to hit a target price point, or a substitute sweetener may be used in a new soft drink. As a result, the application of DCF valuation techniques in capital investment decisions is, by nature, more of an iterative process than a one-time decision.

In this chapter, we focus on the application of the approaches themselves and discuss their relative advantages, assuming that we already know the expected cash flows. In this way we can focus on the capital budgeting framework and techniques that we may use to evaluate project cash flows.[10]

Concept Review Questions

1. Contrast top-down versus bottom-up analysis.

2. In what ways are discounted cash flow methods used in capital investment analysis similar to methods for valuing common shares, and in what ways are they different?

10.2 EVALUATING INVESTMENT PROJECTS

A financial manager can use a number of approaches to evaluate an investment. These approaches include measures of an investment's contribution to the company's value, measures of the return on the investment, and measures of the time it takes to recover the original investment.

The Net Present Value Method

The **net present value (NPV)** of an investment is the estimated value added of a project, which we calculate as the sum of the present value of all future after-tax incremental cash flows generated by an initial cash outlay, less the present value of the investment outlays. In other words, the NPV is the present value of the expected cash flows net of the costs needed to generate them. We depict this process graphically in Figure 10-1, where, for simplicity, there is a single outlay at time zero, each cash flow is represented by CF and a subscript indicating the period end, and the final cash flow occurs at the end of period n.[11] Each of these cash flows are incremental cash flow related to a project. Put another way, these cash flows represent how a business entity's cash flows change if they were to take on this project.[12]

net present value (NPV) added value from a capital project; sum of the present value of all future cash flows generated by an initial cash outlay, less the present value of the investment outlays

---

[10] We discuss the estimation of cash flows in detail in Chapter 11.

[11] We've simplified the project's cash flows to assume that all the project's cash outflows occur immediately (today, which we designate as time 0). If the project's cash outflows occur over time, we would discount these to the present.

[12] We discuss the calculation of cash flows in Chapter 11. Though covered in this later chapter, the basic idea is that this cash flow includes any relevant cash flow, including taxes.

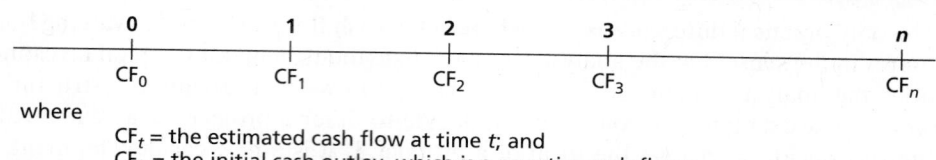

where

CF_t = the estimated cash flow at time t; and
CF_0 = the initial cash outlay, which is a negative cash flow.

FIGURE 10-1 The Cash Flow Pattern for a Traditional Capital Expenditure

We use the project's cost of capital, which is the cost of capital that reflects the riskiness of the project's cash flows: the greater the riskiness of a project's future cash flows, the greater the cost of capital. We represent the NPV of an n-year project as Equation 10-1:

$$NPV = \frac{CF_0}{(1+i)^0} + \frac{CF_1}{(1+i)^1} + \frac{CF_2}{(1+i)^2} + \frac{CF_3}{(1+i)^3} + \ldots + \frac{CF_n}{(1+i)^n} \qquad (10\text{-}1)$$

where CF_t is the estimated incremental cash flow at time t;
        CF_0 is the initial incremental cash outlay; and
        i is the project's cost of capital.

Therefore, the project's cost of capital is the discount rate applied to the project's cash flows. We can rewrite the formula for the NPV as simply:

$$NPV = \sum_{t=0}^{n} \frac{CF_t}{(1+i)^t} \qquad (10\text{-}2)$$

risk-adjusted discount rate discount rate that reflects the overall riskiness of the project

We have discussed previously that the market value of any company in an efficient market is the present value of its expected incremental cash flows, discounted at an appropriate **risk-adjusted discount rate**, which is based on the overall riskiness of the project. In other words, the risk-adjusted discount rate is the project's cost of capital. Therefore, we can say that projects that have a positive net present value add value to the company and should be accepted: A positive NPV implies that the present value of the expected future cash flows exceeds the cash outlay today—that is, it increases the value of the company. Because the company's creditors have a fixed claim on the company's income, regardless of the value of the project, this NPV trickles down to the shareholders and increases the market value of the company's common shares. In this way, accepting positive NPV projects maximizes the company's market value and creates shareholder value. In contrast, accepting negative NPV projects destroys company value and should be rejected because, by definition, the destruction of shareholder value is not in the best interest of the shareholders.

We would expect positive NPVs to arise only in situations in which a company has a competitive advantage. Because of the competitive nature of today's business environment, we would not expect to see an abundance of such opportunities, nor would we expect them to persist for very long. Therefore, projects that produce an NPV of $0 will be the norm where companies operate in competitive markets. These projects should be accepted because they provide the appropriate return required to compensate for the financing costs (and risks) associated with the investment.

Let's consider an example. Suppose the Duke Company has an investment that requires a $12 million cash outlay today. It estimates that the expected incremental cash flows associated with this investment are $5 million at the end of years 1 and 2 and $8 million at the end of year 3. Using a 15 percent discount rate, what is this project's NPV? One way to approach this is that we could lay out all the cash flows in a timeline and then discount each cash flow back to the present, summing the present values. Using 0 to indicate today and then laying out the end-of-year cash flows:

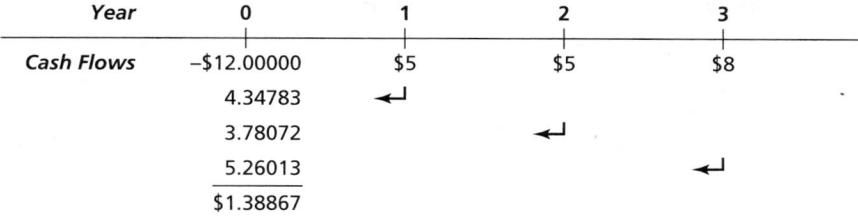

Year	0	1	2	3
Cash Flows	−$12.00000	$5	$5	$8
	4.34783	↵		
	3.78072		↵	
	5.26013			↵
	$1.38867			

Using Equation [10-2]:

$$NPV = CF_0 + \frac{CF_1}{(1+i)^1} + \frac{CF_2}{(1+i)^2} + \frac{CF_3}{(1+i)^3}$$

$$NPV = \left[\frac{-\$12}{(1+0.15)^0} \frac{\$5}{(1+0.15)^1} + \frac{\$5}{(1+0.15)^2} + \frac{\$8}{(1+0.15)^3} \right]$$

$$NPV = -\$12 + 4.34783 + 3.78072 + 5.26013$$

$$NPV = \$1.38867 \text{ million}$$

Therefore, the Duke Company should accept this project because it has a positive NPV and would increase company value by $1.38867 million.

CALCULATOR TOOLS: SOLVE FOR THE NPV

Consider the set of cash flow from the Duke Company example. The calculator program requires that you enter the cash flows in sequence.

TI BA II Plus	HP10B	HP12C	TI-83/84
CF 2nd CLR WORK	CLEAR ALL	f REG	{5,5,8}
−12 Enter ↓	+/− 12 CF	12 CHS CF_0	STO L1
5 Enter ↓ ↓	5 CF	5 CF_j	Apps Finance 7
5 Enter ↓ ↓	5 CF	5 CF_j	NPV(.15, −12, L1)
8 Enter ↓	8 CF	8 CF_j	ENTER
NPV 15 Enter ↓	15 I/YR	15 i	
CPT	NPV	f NPV	

SPREADSHEET APPLICATIONS: SOLVE FOR THE NPV

Consider the set of cash flow from the Duke Company example. The NPV function in a spreadsheet requires you to enter the cash flows in order, starting with the *first* year's cash flow and then subtracting the initial cash outlay, which is $12 million in this example. You can simply type in:

$$= NPV(0.15, 5, 5, 8) - 12$$

or you can include the data in cells and use cell-referencing:

	A
1	.15
2	−12
3	5
4	5
5	8
6	=NPV(A1,A3:A5)+A2

EXAMPLE 10.1

Calculating the NPV

PROBLEM

Consider an investment that requires an outlay of $5 million initially, with expected cash flows of $1 million, $0, and $5 million, respectively, for the following 3 years.

  a. What is the net present value of this investment if the discount rate is 5 percent?
  b. What is the net present value of this investment if the discount rate is 8 percent?

Solution

  a. NPV = −$5 + 0.95238 + 4.31919 = $0.27157 million
  b. NPV = −$5 + 0.92593 + 3.96916 = −$0.10491 million

The Internal Rate of Return

The **internal rate of return (IRR)** is the discount rate that makes the NPV equal to zero for a given set of cash flows.[13] This implies that it is the discount rate that sets the present value of future cash flows equal to the initial cash outlay. Or, in other words, the NPV is equal to zero. In this way, it is a rate of return that is internal to this particular set of cash flows; for this reason, we often refer to it as the economic rate of return of a given project. Consider Equation 10-1 once again:

$$\text{NPV} = \frac{CF_0}{(1+\text{IRR})^0} + \frac{CF_1}{(1+\text{IRR})^1} + \frac{CF_2}{(1+\text{IRR})^2} + \frac{CF_3}{(1+\text{IRR})^3} + \cdots + \frac{CF_n}{(1+\text{IRR})^n}$$

Setting the NPV to zero and simplifying,

$$0 = \frac{\sum_{t=0}^{n} CF_t}{(1+\text{IRR})^t} \tag{10-3}$$

The general rule for IRR evaluation criteria is that a company should accept a project whenever the IRR is greater than the appropriate risk-adjusted discount rate, which is the project's cost of capital. Just like NPV, the IRR represents a discounted cash flow approach; in general, it will lead to the same accept/reject decisions as NPV. The project's cost of capital, when used in conjunction with the IRR, becomes a **hurdle rate**; the IRR must exceed the project's cost of capital or hurdle to be acceptable. In other words, the project's cost of capital is the minimum acceptable return on the project.

hurdle rate minimum acceptable return on an investment project

An issue with the IRR is that you cannot solve directly for the IRR.[14] There is no finite solution for the IRR when solving Equation 10-3; this means that solving for the IRR requires trial and error. Fortunately, financial calculators and spreadsheets make this process very manageable.

We illustrate the calculation process using the example with a $12 million outlay and end-of-year cash flows of $5, $5, and $8. The IRR is the value that solves the following expression:

$$\left[\frac{\$5}{(1+\text{IRR})^1} + \frac{\$5}{(1+\text{IRR})^2} + \frac{\$8}{(1+\text{IRR})^3}\right] = \$12$$

Solving by trial and error is very complicated, even for this simple three-period problem. We know from our earlier calculation that the project's NPV is positive at the discount

[13] The IRR is the same as the yield to maturity (YTM) for a bond that we estimated earlier. In fact, the yield to maturity is the IRR of a bond for a given purchase price.

[14] Looking at Equation 10-3, we can see this if we multiply through by $(1+\text{IRR})^n$; it then becomes clear that in finding the IRR, we are solving for the roots of an nth order polynomial.

rate of 15 percent. Therefore, we know that the NPV will be zero at some discount rate greater than 15 percent. Trying different discount rates, we see that the NPV changes from positive to negative between the discount rate of 21 percent and 22 percent. Therefore, we know that the IRR is between 21 percent and 22 percent:

Discount Rate	NPV
20%	$ 0.27
21%	$ 0.06
22%	$ (0.14)
23%	$ (0.33)

NPV is $0 between 21% and 22%

This is one case for which it is worthwhile to use a financial calculator or spreadsheet—and this is only a three-period project; imagine if it were a 20-year project.

SPREADSHEET APPLICATIONS: THE IRR

We can also calculate the IRR using a calculator or spreadsheet, using the IRR function and the following data:

	A	B
1	CF_0	−30
2	CF_1	5
3	CF_2	5
4	CF_3	5

The IRR function in this case, using cell-referencing, is =IRR(B1:B4).

Notice that the IRR of 21.31 percent exceeded the company's cost of capital of 15 percent, which implies that the project increases shareholder value and should be accepted. This will always be the case when the NPV is positive, as it is in this case. In fact, this should be obvious when we look at Equations 10-1 and 10-2, because the NPV will equal zero when the IRR = i. Therefore, when IRR exceeds the project's cost of capital, the NPV will be positive because the NPV will be higher when we use a *lower* discount rate than it will when we use the *higher* discount rate (i.e., IRR). This is very intuitive: A positive NPV implies that a project earns a return (IRR) that is higher than the cost of funds. Similarly, we can say that a negative NPV implies that IRR is less than the project's cost of capital, and vice versa. We can see this in Figure 10-2, where we graph the NPV of this project on the vertical axis, against the discount rate on the horizontal axis. We refer to this illustration as the project's **net present value profile** (or **NPV profile**). The IRR is the rate at which the curve representing the NPVs crosses the horizontal axis.[15]

net present value profile or **NPV profile** graph of a project's net present value against the discount rate

An issue with the IRR is that the IRR is not meaningful if there is more than one sign change in cash flows. Every time the sign of the polynomial changes (that is, the cash flows change from positive to negative or negative to positive), there is a root, so for complex cash flow streams we often find that there is more than one IRR, or more than one root.[16]

[15] Another name for a graph of this relationship is the *investment profile*.

[16] As previously mentioned, this will not be true if we pick the wrong IRR when there are multiple reversals in the signs of the cash flows. This does not happen often in normal projects, but it does happen sometimes, to the surprise of analysts who forget this fact.

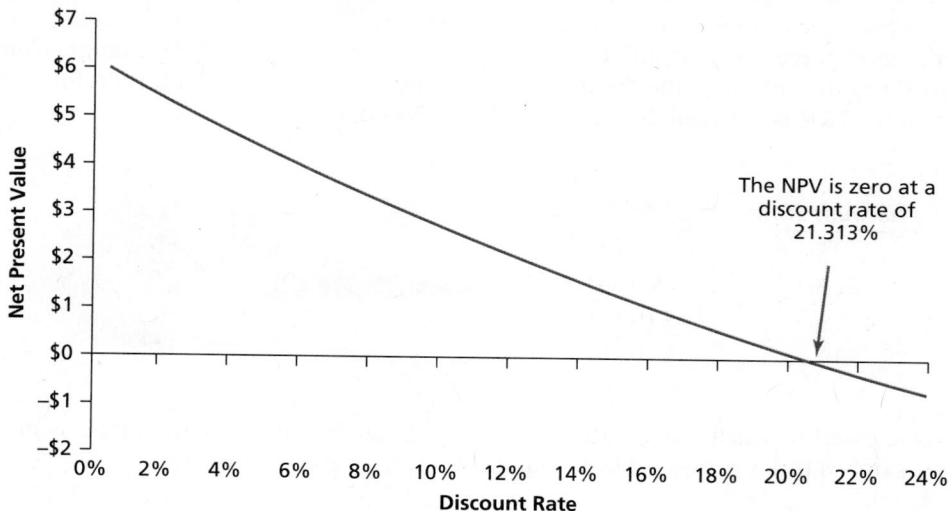

FIGURE 10-2 **The Net Present Value of the Duke Company Project for Different Discount Rates**

EXAMPLE 10.2	PROBLEM
Calculating the IRR	Consider an investment that requires an outlay of $5 million initially, with expected end-of-year cash flows of $1 million, $0, and $5 million, respectively, for the end of the following 3 years. What is the internal rate of return of this investment?

Solution

The NPV is positive when the discount rate is 5 percent, but negative when the discount rate is 8 percent. Therefore, we know that the IRR falls between 5 percent and 8 percent. Through trial and error, we find:

Discount Rate	NPV (in millions)
5%	$0.27157
6%	$0.14149
7%	$0.01607
8%	−$0.10491

Therefore, we can conclude that the IRR is between 7 percent and 8 percent. Using a financial calculator or a spreadsheet program, we find the precise IRR of 7.1308 percent.

A Comparison of NPV and IRR

We can see the relation between the NPV and the IRR using the NPV profile, such as the one we show in Figure 10-3 for two separate projects. NPV profiles depict the NPV of a project for various discount rates.

Consider the cash flows for Project A and Project B:

Period	End of Period Cash Flows	
	Project A	Project B
0	−£1,000	−£1,000
1	£500	£0
2	£500	£0
3	£500	£1,700

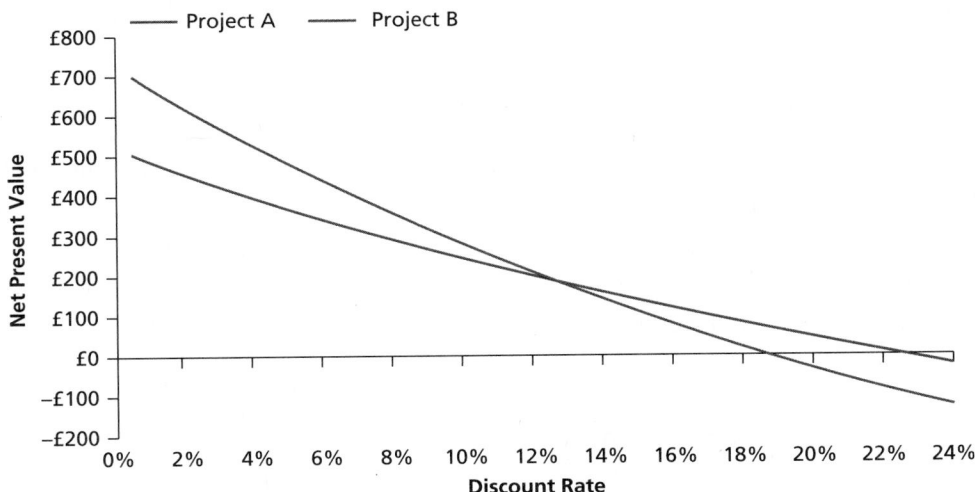

FIGURE 10-3 NPV Profiles for Two Projects, A and B

In Figure 10-3, we graph the NPV against the discount rate for both projects. As you can see, the NPV depends critically on the appropriate discount rate, obvious from Equation 10-2. As the discount rate increases, the NPV decreases and eventually becomes negative for higher discount rates. By definition, we know that the IRR occurs at the discount rate that makes the NPV = £0. This corresponds to the point at which the NPV curve crosses the x-axis in Figure 10-3. For project A, the IRR is 23.375 percent, whereas for project B, the IRR is 19.348 percent. The diagram shows that whenever the discount rate exceeds the IRR, we have a negative NPV, and whenever the discount rate is less than the IRR, we have a positive NPV. Recall that we have previously noted these relationships between NPV and IRR.

Whether or not the projects should be accepted depends on the discount rate. We can make several useful observations from Figure 10-3:

- Project A should be accepted if the **project cost of capital** is less than 23.375 percent because the NPV will be positive for these discount rates and because IRR is greater than the project cost of capital.

- If the project cost of capital is greater than 23.375 percent, Project A should be rejected, because the NPV will be negative, and IRR is less than the project's cost of capital.

- Project B should be accepted if the project's cost of capital is less than 19.348 percent, and it should be rejected if the project's cost of capital is greater than 19.348 percent.

project cost of capital discount rate that reflects the return suppliers of capital require considering the project's risk

So, if we are independently evaluating a project by using either the NPV or IRR evaluation criteria, we should arrive at the same conclusion.

In Figure 10-3 we also see that we can rank projects differently by using NPV versus using IRR. Suppose, for example, these two were **mutually exclusive projects**, meaning that a company has to decide between them and can accept only one. Because the IRR of project B is 19.348 percent, whereas the IRR of project A is 23.375 percent, project A will always appear to be superior according to the IRR approach. However, by using the NPV approach, we arrive at different rankings depending on the project's cost of capital (i), because in this example the NPV profiles cross over and have the same NPV at one special discount rate, which is the **crossover rate**. If i is greater than the crossover rate of 12.788 percent, then project A is preferable to project B because it generates a higher NPV, whereas if i is less than 12.788 percent, then project B is preferred. As a result, the NPV rule can rank projects differently from the IRR rule, so which one is better?

mutually exclusive projects projects for which the acceptance of one precludes the acceptance of one or more of the alternative projects

crossover rate discount rate at which the net present value profiles of two projects cross

To answer this question, we have to understand why the slopes of the two NPV profiles differ: The slope reflects the change in the NPV as the discount rate changes. If a project has cash flows that are far in the future, then changes in the discount rate have a big impact on the NPV of the project. In this case project B has cash flows that are farther away, so at high discount rates these cash flows are valued less, and the NPV falls by more than the NPV of project A. As a result, beyond the crossover point, A is preferred to B, because B's far-off cash flows are worth less, whereas at lower discount rates, the reverse happens, and B is preferred to A.

How do we determine this crossover rate? We can guesstimate from the graph, which would mean that the crossover rate is between 12 and 13 percent, or we can use this simple procedure:

1. Calculate the difference in cash flows between the projects for each period; and
2. Calculate the IRR of these differences.[17]

In the example with Project A and Project B,

Period	*End-of-year Cash Flows* Project A	Project B	Difference
0	–£1,000	–£1,000	£0
1	£500	£0	£500
2	£500	£0	£500
3	£500	£1,700	–£1,200

The IRR of the differences is 12.788 percent. Therefore, the crossover rate is 12.788 percent, and this is the discount rate at which our preference changes: Below 12.788 percent, we prefer Project B; above 12.788 percent we prefer project A; at 12.788 percent, we are indifferent between the two projects because they have the same NPV.

In addition to the timing of cash flows, another source of differences between NPV and IRR is the scale factor. The internal rate of return does not consider the scale or size of the project, whereas the NPV does. Consider the example of two projects, Small and Big, each with a project cost of capital of 5 percent:

Year	*End-of-year Cash Flow* Small	Big
0	–$10,000	–$50,000
1	$0	$0
2	$0	$0
3	$12,500	$62,500

The projects have similar timing of cash flows, but the scale is different: Big's cash flows are five times those of Small. Both projects have a positive NPV ($797.97 and $3,989.85, respectively) at the project cost of capital, and the IRR of both projects is 7.72 percent. If these projects are independent, we would choose both projects. However, if these projects are mutually exclusive, using the IRR would not be best because the IRR considers both projects to return the same 7.72 percent. Using the net present value approach, we would choose Big because it provides the greater added value.[18] The bottom line is that the IRR does not consider the scale or size of the project.

Further, the fact that the NPV decision depends on the discount rate, whereas the IRR decision does not, is very important and relates to the different reinvestment rate assumptions of the two techniques:

---

[17] It will not matter whether you subtract A's cash flows from B's, or vice versa—as long as you are consistent for all periods.

[18] If there is a limit to the capital budget, as we discuss later in this chapter, we would need to look at the total net present value of possible projects that fit into the budget, which may imply choosing Small or Big, depending on the budget and the profitability of the other projects under consideration.

- The NPV assumes that all cash flows are reinvested at one consistent discount rate (i.e., the cost of capital).
- The IRR assumes instead that all cash flows are reinvested at the IRR. In other words, the cash flows are reinvested in similar yielding investments.

If we remember that most projects will have low or zero NPV in a competitive market and that the discount rate reflects the opportunity cost or the all-in required return of the company's investors, it is clear that the NPV assumption is more realistic. To put it another way, if an executive estimates an IRR of, say, 30 percent because he or she finds a wonderful project, the executive is then implicitly assuming that the cash flows generated by this wonderful project can be reinvested in another similarly wonderful project. This means that the executive is assuming that he or she has many wonderful projects, which is not normally a very realistic assumption.

Issue	*NPV*	*IRR*
1. Future cash flows change sign	It still works the same for both accept/reject and ranking decisions.	Multiple IRRs may result—in this case, the IRR cannot be used for either accept/reject or ranking decisions.
2. Ranking projects	Higher NPV implies greater contribution to company wealth—it is an *absolute* measure of wealth.	The higher IRR project may have a lower NPV, and vice versa, depending on the appropriate discount rate and the size of the project.[19]
3. Reinvestment rate assumed for future cash flows received	Assumes all future cash flows are reinvested at the discount rate.	Assumes cash flows from each project are reinvested at that project's IRR.

SUMMARIZING: NPV VERSUS IRR

CALCULATOR TOOLS: SOLVE FOR THE IRR

Consider a project that has a $5 million cash outlay today, but is expected to produce end-of-year cash flows of $4, $1, and $2 in the succeeding years. What is the internal rate of return for this project? Answer: 22.808%

TI BA II Plus	HP10B	HP12C	TI 83/84
CF 2nd CLR WORK	CLEAR ALL	f REG	{4,1,2}
−5 Enter ↓	+/− 5 CF	5 CHS CF_0	STO L1
4 Enter ↓ ↓	4 CF	4 CF_j	Apps Finance IRR
1 Enter ↓ ↓	1 CF	1 CF_j	IRR(−5, L1)
1 Enter ↓ ↓	2 CF	2 CF_j	ENTER
IRR ↓	IRR	f IRR	
CPT			

[19] For example, would analysts prefer an IRR of 100 percent on $1,000 or 20 percent on $1 million?

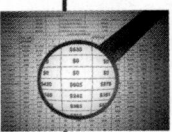

SPREADSHEET APPLICATIONS: SOLVE FOR THE IRR

	A	B
1	0	–5
2	1	4
3	2	1
4	3	2
5	IRR	=IRR(B1:B4)

Answer: 22.808%

The Modified Internal Rate of Return

The assumption built into the internal rate of return mathematics that all cash inflows are reinvested at the internal rate of return may be too aggressive an assumption to make. We can modify this assumption by calculating the return on the project with a more realistic assumption regarding the reinvestment of cash inflows. The result is the **modified internal rate of return (MIRR)** . The accept/reject criteria for the MIRR is similar to that of the IRR: If a project has a MIRR greater than its cost of capital, it is acceptable; if a project has a MIRR less than its cost of capital, it is not acceptable.

Let's start with a Project X that has a project cost of capital of 10 percent and the following cash flows:

Year	End-of-year Cash Flow
0	–$10,000
1	4,200
2	4,200
3	4,200

The IRR of Project X is 12.51 percent, and the NPV is $444.78. To illustrate the role of reinvestment, let's assume that the company has no other projects in which to reinvest any of these cash flows. We calculate the return on Project X in this situation by comparing the investment of $10,000 with what is available at the end of the project. If each cash flow that comes in is deposited in an account that earns no interest, the company will have $12,600 at the end of 3 years. Therefore,

PV = $10,000
FV = $12,600
 N = 3
Solve for $i \rightarrow i = 8.01\%$

Given no other use of the cash, the company has a return, which is the MIRR, of 8.01 percent. Under these circumstances, Project X is not acceptable.

Now let's assume that the company has other investment opportunities available that earn 5 percent. We can represent this in a diagram, indicating the cash flows and how they "grow" when reinvested at 5 percent:

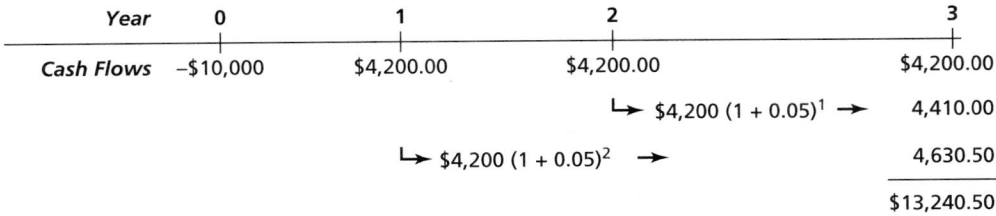

In table form, we have:

Year	End-of-year Cash Flow	Future Value of Reinvested Cash Flows, End of Period 3
0	–$10,000.00	
1	$4,200.00	$4,630.50
2	$4,200.00	4,410.00
3	$4,200.00	4,200.00
Total		$13,240.50

The future value of the reinvested cash flows, FV, is $13,240.50, and therefore the MIRR is 9.81 percent:

$$PV = \$10,000$$
$$FV = \$13,240.50$$
$$N = 3$$
$$\text{Solve for } i \rightarrow i = 9.81\%$$

Again, the project is not acceptable because the return on the project is less than the project's cost of capital.

A common assumption for reinvestment opportunities is to use the company's cost of capital, which is the return on the typical or average project of the company. The reasoning is simple: If the company has cash flows from a project, they are most likely reinvested in a typical project for the company. If the company's cost of capital is, say, 9 percent, the MIRR becomes 11.25 percent.[20] In this case, the project is acceptable because the MIRR of 11.25 percent exceeds the project's cost of capital of 10 percent.

The MIRR is sensitive to the reinvestment assumption, as we show in Figure 10-4, where we graph the MIRR against the reinvestment rate for Project X; the better the reinvestment opportunities, the better the return on the project, as measured by MIRR.[21]

Payback Period and Discounted Payback Period

Companies often use a measure of time to screen or evaluate projects. Conceptually and mathematically easier than the net present value, the internal rate of return, and the modified internal rate of return, the **payback period** is the number of years required to fully

payback period number of years required to fully recover the initial cash outlay associated with a capital expenditure

[20] If you are checking this calculation, the future value of the cash flows, considering reinvestment at 9 percent, is $13,768.02.

[21] Using Microsoft's Excel Solver function, we can solve for the reinvestment rate at which the MIRR is equal to the project's cost of capital. We do this by setting the goal of the MIRR equal to 10 percent and then solve for the reinvestment rate that is applied against the project's cash inflows. For Project X, the project is acceptable as long as the return on reinvested cash flows is equal to or greater than 5.5329 percent.

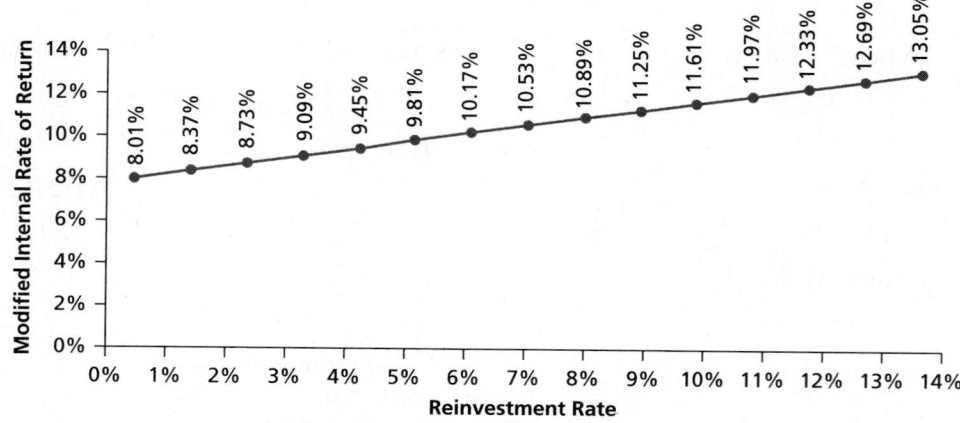

FIGURE 10-4 Modified Internal Rate of Return for Project X

EXAMPLE 10.3

The Modified Internal Rate of Return

PROBLEM

Consider a project with the following cash flows:

Year	End-of-year Cash Flow
0	−$1,000.00
1	$500.00
2	$0.00
3	$800.00

If the project's cost of capital is 11 percent and the reinvestment rate for its cash flows is 9 percent, is this project acceptable based on the modified internal rate of return?

Solution

Year	Future Value of Reinvested Cash Flows, End of Period 3
1	$594.05
2	0.00
3	800.00
	$1,394.05

PV = $1,000
FV = $1,394.05
N = 3
Solve for $i \rightarrow i = 11.71$ percent.

Therefore, the project is acceptable because the MIRR exceeds the project's cost of capital of 11 percent.

---

recover the initial cash outlay associated with the capital expenditure. Shorter payback periods are better, and usually this decision criterion is implemented by choosing a cutoff date and rejecting projects whose payback period is longer than the cutoff period.

SPREADSHEET APPLICATIONS: THE MIRR

You can calculate the modified internal rate of return using the built-in function, MIRR. The function has three arguments:

1. the cells indicating the set of cash flows,
2. the financing rate (that is, the project's cost of capital), and
3. the reinvestment rate.

Consider the example of

	A	B
	Year	End-of-year Cash Flow
1	Year	
2	0	–$1,000.00
3	1	$200.00
4	2	$300.00
5	3	$400.00
6	4	$500.00

Suppose the project's cost of capital is 10 percent, but the reinvestment rate is 5 percent. You calculate the MIRR using:

$$=MIRR(B2:B6,0.1,0.05)$$

to arrive at the MIRR of 10.34 percent.

What is the payback period for our example with an outlay of $12 million and subsequent cash inflows of $5, $5, and $8 million, respectively? We determine this by calculating the cumulative cash flows over time:

Year	End-of-year Cash Flow	Cumulative, Recovered Cash Flows
1	$5	$5
2	$5	$10
3	$8	$18

If the cash flows are received evenly throughout the year, the payback period is 2 + (2/8) = 2.25 years.[22] With a $12 million cash outlay, $10 million is recovered in 2 years, and then the additional $2,000 is recovered one-quarter of the way through the 3rd year, assuming that the cash flows are evenly spaced throughout the year.

The payback period provides a useful intuitive measure of how long it takes to recover an investment, and it is sometimes used as an informal measure of project risk, especially for short-lived projects. This is because in some sense the quicker a company recovers its investment outlay, the less risky the project. However, the payback period has some important drawbacks. In particular, it disregards the time and risk value of money because it treats a dollar of cash flow received in year 3 the same as those received

[22] If the cash flows are period-end cash flows, the payback period is a full 3 years because it is not until the third period, when cash flows are received, that the initial outlay of $12 million is recovered.

EXAMPLE 10.4

Calculating the Payback Period

PROBLEM

Consider an investment that requires an outlay of $5 million initially, with expected end-of-year cash flows of $1 million, $0, and $5 million, respectively, for the following 3 years. What is the payback period on this investment?

Solution

Year	End-of-year Cash Flow (in millions)	Cumulative Cash Flows Recovered (in millions)
1	$1	$1
2	$0	$1
3	$5	$6

If the cash flows are received evenly throughout the year, the payback period is 3 years.[23]

in year 1, and so on. In addition, the payback period does not account for the cash flows received after the cutoff date, which could be substantial for some long-lived projects. Finally, the choice of the cutoff date is somewhat arbitrary and may vary from one company to the next.

discounted payback period number of years required to fully recover the initial cash outlay associated with a capital expenditure, in terms of discounted cash flows

The **discounted payback period** alleviates the first shortcoming of the payback period by accounting for the time value of money. It is defined as the number of years required to fully recover the initial cash outlay in terms of discounted cash flows. Shorter periods are better, and projects with discounted payback periods before the cutoff date will be accepted. Unfortunately, just as was the case for the payback period criterion, the discounted payback period ignores cash flows beyond the cutoff date, and the cutoff date is somewhat arbitrary.

What is the discounted payback period for our example with an outlay of $12 million and subsequent end-of-year cash inflows of $5, $5, and $8 million, respectively, if the discount rate is 15 percent? We determine this by calculating the cumulative discounted cash flows over time:

Year	End-of-year Cash Flow (in millions)	Calculation	Accumulated Discounted Cash Flows (in millions)	
1	$5	$5 \div 1.15 =$	$4.34783	
2	$5	$4.3473 + [$5 \div (1.15)^2] =$	$8.12854	
3	$8	$8.12854 + [$8 \div (1.15)^3] =$	$13.38867	← $12 million recovered

The discounted payback period is 3 years.

The discounted payback period is either the same or longer than for the simple payback period; the future cash flows are worth less because they have been discounted for time and risk. If a company is going to use discounting, it might as well discount all the future cash flows and calculate the NPV. For this reason, the discounted payback period is a sort of compromise between the payback period and the NPV.

---

[23] If the cash flows are period-end cash flows, the payback period is a full 3 years because it is not until the third period, when cash flows are received, that the initial outlay of $5 million is recovered.

PROBLEM

Consider an investment that requires an outlay of $5 million initially, with expected end-of-year cash flows of $1 million, $0, and $5 million, respectively, for the following 3 years. What is the discounted payback period on this investment if the discount rate is 5 percent?

EXAMPLE 10.5

Calculating the Discounted Payback Period

Solution

Year	End-of-year Cash Flow (in millions)	Accumulated Discounted Cash Flow
1	$1	$0.95238
2	$0	$0.95238
3	$5	$5.27157

The discounted payback period is 3 years.

The Profitability Index

The **profitability index (PI)** is another DCF approach used to evaluate capital expenditure decisions. Like the IRR, the PI is a relative measure of project attractiveness. It is defined as the ratio of a project's discounted net incremental after-tax cash inflows divided by the discounted cash outflows, which is usually the initial after-tax cash outlay. We calculate the PI as:

$$PI = \frac{PV(\text{cash inflows})}{PV(\text{cash outflows})} \qquad (10\text{-}4)$$

profitability index (PI) discounted cash flow approach used to evaluate capital expenditure decisions; the ratio of a project's discounted net incremental cash inflows over the discounted cash outflows

It should be obvious from Equation 10-4 that projects with ratios greater than 1 should be accepted because, by definition, they have positive NPVs, whereas projects with ratios less than 1 should be rejected. It is also obvious that larger ratios are favored because their NPVs are higher. The discount rate to be used is the same as the one used for calculating the NPV, and it is usually the project's cost of capital. Therefore, we observe the following relationship between NPV and PI:

$$\text{If} \quad NPV > 0 \quad \text{then} \quad PI > 1$$
$$\text{If} \quad NPV < 0 \quad \text{then} \quad PI < 0$$

What is the profitability index for our example with an outlay of $12 million and subsequent end-of-year cash inflows of $5, $5, and $8 million, respectively, if the discount rate is 15 percent?

Present value of cash inflows = $4.34783 + 3.78072 + 5.26013 = $13.38867 million
Present value of cash outflows = $12 million

and therefore:

PI = $13.38867 million ÷ 12 million = 1.11572 million

We show the relation between the PI and the NPV in Figure 10-5, with the NPV on the left vertical axis and the PI on the right vertical axis. You'll notice that when the NPV is negative, the PI is less than 1.0.

As discussed earlier, the PI produces the same accept/reject decisions as do the NPV and the IRR approaches in the case of independent projects. In addition, the PI does not suffer from two of the weaknesses of the IRR approach because it uses one consistent and reasonable discount rate and because it works even when future cash flows change signs.

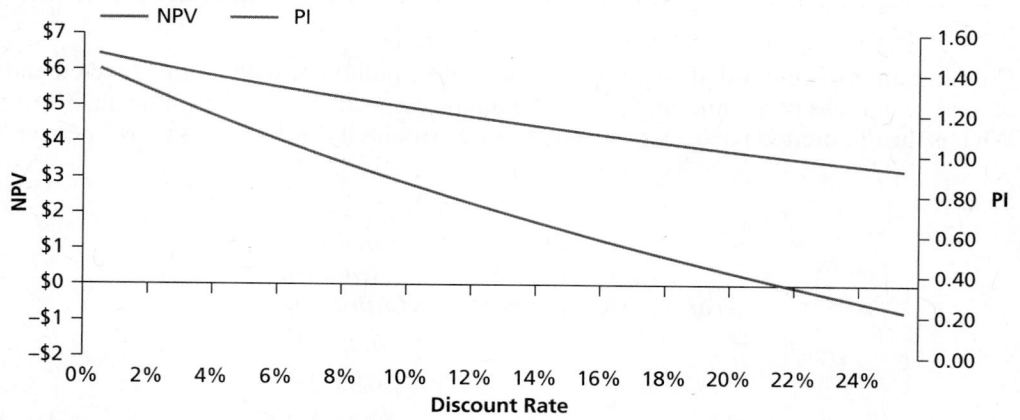

FIGURE 10-5 **NPV and PI for the Duke Company Project**

EXAMPLE 10.6

Calculating the PI

PROBLEM

Consider an investment that requires an outlay of $5 million initially, with expected end-of-year cash flows of $1 million, $0, and $5 million, respectively, for the following 3 years. What is the profitability index on this investment if the discount rate is 5 percent?

Solution

$$\text{PI} = \frac{\text{PV(cash inflows)}}{\text{PV(cash outflows)}} = \frac{\dfrac{\$1}{(1.05)^1} + \dfrac{\$5}{(1.05)^3}}{\$5} = \frac{\$5.27157}{\$5} = 1.0543$$

Therefore, the project should be accepted because the PI > 1.

Like the IRR, the PI is attractive because it can be expressed as a percentage, so a PI of 1.116 could be restated as +11.6 percent.

One weakness that the PI measure shares with IRR is that it is a relative measure and not an absolute measure of wealth, like NPV. Although it is useful as a starting point for ranking projects when some projects must be rejected, final decisions should be based on which projects maximize the total NPV for the company.[24] In this case, the PI is often used when companies are capital constrained, as we discuss later.

A Comprehensive Example

Let's review the different methods of evaluating capital projects by applying these methods to another example. Consider two projects:

Year	End-of-year Cash Flows (in millions)	
	Project M	Project N
2011	–$100	–$100
2012	$0	$55
2013	$0	$55
2014	$0	$55
2015	$240	$55

[24] We will elaborate on this point later in this chapter, when we discuss capital rationing.

Suppose the appropriate cost of capital for each project is 8 percent. What is each project's:

- net present value?
- internal rate of return?
- profitability index?
- payback period?
- discounted payback period?

We can discount each cash flow and then calculate the net present value:

| | **Present Value of Cash Flows (in millions)** | |
	Project M	Project N
1	$0.00	$50.93
2	0.00	$47.15
3	0.00	$43.66
4	$176.41	$40.43
Present value of inflows	$176.41	$182.17
Present value of outflows	−100.00	−100.00
Net present value	$76.41	$82.17

The net present value of both projects is positive; in other words, both projects would enhance the company's value. We could also use a calculator or a spreadsheet to calculate the net present value:

CALCULATOR TOOLS: THE NPV

	Project M			Project N	
TI BA II Plus	**HP10B**	**TI 83/84**	**TI BA II Plus**	**HP10B**	**TI 83/84[25]**
CF 2nd CLR	CLEAR ALL	{0,0,0,240}	CF 2nd CLR	CLEAR ALL	{55,55,55,55}
WORK	+/− 100 CF	STO L1	WORK	+/− 100 CF	STO L2
−100 Enter ↓	0 CF	Apps Finance 7	−100 Enter ↓	55 CF	Apps Finance 7
0 Enter ↓ ↓	0 CF	NPV(8, −100, L1)	55 Enter ↓ ↓	55 CF	NPV(8, −100, L2)
0 Enter ↓ ↓	0 CF	ENTER	55 Enter ↓ ↓	55 CF	ENTER
0 Enter ↓ ↓	240 CF		55 Enter ↓ ↓	55 CF	
240 Enter ↓ ↓	8 I/YR		NPV 8 Enter ↓	8 I/YR	
NPV 8 Enter ↓	NPV		CPT	NPV	
CPT					

The internal rate of return is the rate that equates the present value of the future cash flows with the $100 million investment. Because the net present value of both projects is positive using a discount rate of 8 percent, we know that the internal rate of return of each project is greater than 8 percent. Using a calculator or a spreadsheet, we find the internal rates of return of 24.467 percent and 41.140 percent for Project M and Project N, respectively.

---

[25] We can use any of the storage locations for the array (L1, L2, etc.). By storing each project's cash flows in a different stored array, we can then use this same array (without having to retype it) when we calculate the IRR for each.

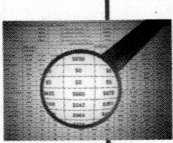

SPREADSHEET APPLICATIONS: THE NPV

	A	B	C
1	*Year*	*Project M*	*Project N*
2	2011	–$100	–$100
3	2012	$0	$55
4	2013	$0	$55
5	2014	$0	$55
6	2015	$240	$55
7			
8	NPV	=NPV(0.08,B3:B6)+B2	=NPV(0.08,C3:C6)+C2

CALCULATOR TOOLS: THE IRR

Project M

TI BA II Plus	HP10B	TI 83/84
CF 2nd CLR	CLEAR ALL	{0,0,0,240}
WORK	+/− 100 CF	STO L1
−100 Enter ↓	0 CF	Apps Finance 8
0 Enter ↓ ↓	0 CF	IRR(−100, L1)
0 Enter ↓ ↓	0 CF	ENTER
0 Enter ↓ ↓	240 CF	
240 Enter ↓ ↓	IRR	
IRR Enter ↓		
CPT		

Project N

TI BA II Plus	HP10B	TI 83/84
CF 2nd CLR	CLEAR ALL	{55,55,55,55}
WORK	+/− 100 CF	STO L2
−100 Enter ↓	55 CF	Apps Finance 8
55 Enter ↓ ↓	55 CF	IRR(−100, L2)
55 Enter ↓ ↓	55 CF	ENTER
55 Enter ↓ ↓	IRR	
IRR Enter ↓		
CPT		

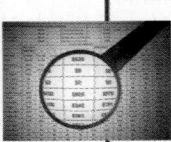

SPREADSHEET APPLICATIONS: THE IRR

	A	B	C
1	*Year*	*Project M*	*Project N*
2	2011	–$100	–$100
3	2012	$0	$55
4	2013	$0	$55
5	2014	$0	$55
6	2015	$240	$55
7			
8	IRR	=IRR(B2:B6)	=IRR(C2:C6)

The profitability index for both is the ratio of the present value of the cash inflows to the $100 million investment. Therefore:

$$\text{Profitability index of Project M} = \frac{\$176.41 \text{ million}}{\$100 \text{ million}} = 1.7641$$

$$\text{Profitability index of Project N} = \frac{\$182.17 \text{ million}}{\$100 \text{ million}} = 1.8217$$

The payback period for Project M is 4 years because there are no cash flows until the 4th year, and that cash flow is sufficient to "pay back" the $100 investment. The payback period for Project N is 2 periods: At the end of the first period, there are $55 million of cash flows, whereas at the end of the second period, the project produces a total of $55 + 55 = $110 cash flows.

We use the discounted cash flows to determine the discounted payback period:

	Discounted Cash Flows (in millions)		*Accumulated Discounted Cash Flows (in millions)*	
Year	*Project M*	*Project N*	*Project M*	*Project N*
2012	$0.00	$50.93	$0.00	$50.93
2013	$0.00	$47.15	$0.00	$98.08
2014	$0.00	$43.66	$0.00	$141.74
2015	$176.41	$40.43	$176.41	$182.17

Project M pays back by the end of 2015, so its discounted payback period is 4 years. Project N, on the other hand, does not accumulate $100 million of cash flows until the 3rd year, so its discounted payback period is 3 years.[26]

We can see the comparison between the two projects by graphing the projects' net present value profiles, as we show in Figure 10-6. The crossover discount rate, the discount rate at which our decision changes between projects, is 5.83 percent. If the discount rate is below 5.83 percent, the best project is Project M; if the discount rate is above 5.83 percent, the best project is Project N.

Summarizing,

Method	*Project M*	*Project N*
Net present value (in millions)	$76.41	$82.17
Internal rate of return	24.461%	41.140%
Profitability index	1.764	1.822
Payback period	4 years	2 years
Discounted payback period	4 years	3 years

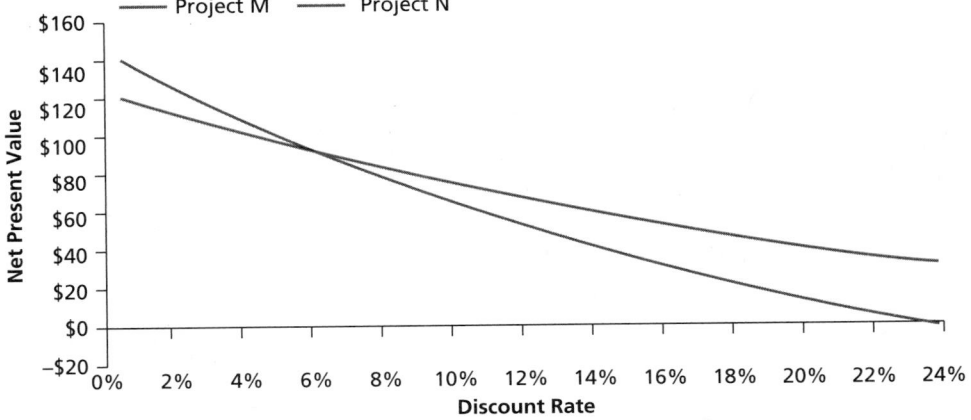

FIGURE 10-6 The NPV Profiles of Project M and Project N

[26] If the cash flows occur evenly throughout each year, we would calculate a fractional payback period. However, because we have assumed end-of-period cash flows for the net present value, internal rate of return, and profitability index, we would have a payback period in whole years.

Based on the net present values and the internal rates of return, both projects are acceptable. If the company must choose between these projects, Project N is preferred because it would add more value to the company when compared to Project M.

What Methods Do Companies Really Use?

John Graham and Campbell Harvey surveyed the chief financial officers (CFOs) of major U.S. companies on how they conducted their capital budgeting.[27] We report their basic results in Figure 10-7. What is clear is that despite the limitations of the IRR method, it is very widely used in practice and just nudges out the NPV as the most important criterion. This is because, in most cases, the IRR gives the "correct" accept/reject decision, and most of the criticisms of the IRR do not often appear in practical applications.

More important, the IRR holds intuitive appeal because it provides a rate of return on particular investment projects that can be compared with the company's financing costs. However, as we pointed out earlier, using this approach can cause problems for the analyst who is unaware of its shortcomings.[28]

GLOBAL PERSPECTIVE | Factoring in Political Risk

Two researchers, Martin Holmen and Bengt Pramborg, surveyed companies regarding the capital budgeting techniques they use when they are making investments in foreign countries.* Investments in foreign countries expose the investor to political risk, which is the risk a company faces that a change in political climate may involve losses (such as expropriation).

They found that in cases in which there is substantial political risk, companies tend to use a method such as the payback period; in cases in which there is little political risk, companies tend to use the net present value method.

* Martin Holmen and Bengt Pramborg, "Capital Budgeting and Political Risk: Empirical Evidence," *Journal of International Financial Management and Accounting*, 20, Issue 2 (Summer 2009): 105–134.

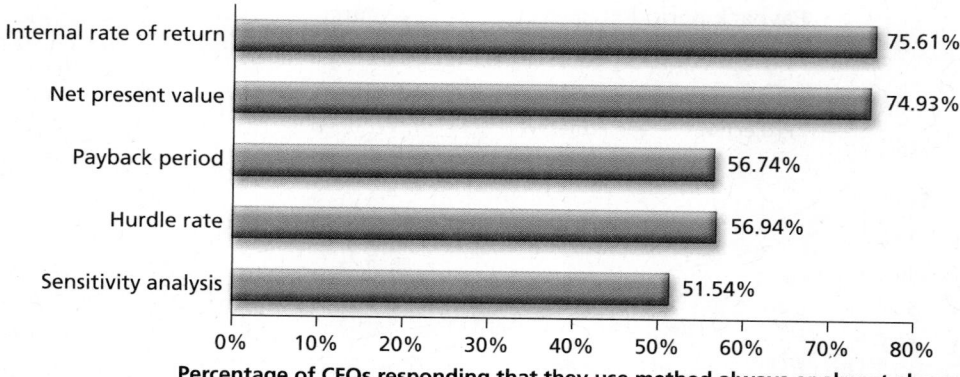

FIGURE 10-7 **Evaluation Criteria Used by Companies**
Source: *Data from Table 2 of John R. Graham and Campbell R. Harvey, "The Theory and Practice of Corporate Finance: Evidence from the Field,"* Journal of Financial Economics, *60 (2001): 187–243.*

[27] John R. Graham and Campbell R. Harvey, "The Theory and Practice of Corporate Finance: Evidence from the Field," *Journal of Financial Economics*, 60 (2001): 187–243.

[28] We have sometimes been approached by former students when they have problems with their analysis. Often, these problems occur because they have forgotten the problems with the use of the IRR.

1. What discount rate do we use to determine the NPV of a project, and why?

2. What are the reinvestment rate assumptions underlying NPV and IRR?

3. What is the crossover rate?

4. Is the PI rule consistent with the NPV rule?

10.3 SPECIAL ISSUES

Independent and Interdependent Projects

Two or more **independent projects** have no relationship with one another. A company's decision to accept one project (e.g., purchase a new computerized accounting system) has no impact on the company's decision to accept another project that is independent of the first one (e.g., replace an aging piece of machinery that is used in the production process). As long as there are no capital spending restrictions, the decision rule is to accept projects that generate a positive NPV (or an IRR > i, or a PI > 1), and reject those that don't.[29] However, many projects are interrelated.

independent projects projects that have no relationship with one another; accepting one project has no impact on the decision to accept another project

The Trouble with IRR | LESSONS LEARNED

Assumptions about reinvestment based on internal rate of return can lead to major capital budget distortions.

Practitioners often interpret internal rate of return as the annual equivalent return on a given investment; this easy analogy is the source of its intuitive appeal. But in fact, IRR is a true indication of a project's annual return on investment only when the project generates no interim cash flows — or when those interim cash flows really can be invested at the actual IRR.

When the calculated IRR is higher than the true reinvestment rate for interim cash flows, the measure will overestimate—sometimes very significantly—the annual equivalent return from the project. The formula assumes that the company has additional projects, with equally attractive prospects, in which to invest the interim cash flows. In this case, the calculation implicitly takes credit for these additional projects. Calculations of net present value (NPV), by contrast, generally assume only that a company can earn its cost of capital on interim cash flows, leaving any future incremental project value with those future projects.

IRR's assumptions about reinvestment can lead to major capital budget distortions. Consider a hypothetical assessment of two different, mutually exclusive projects, A and B, with identical cash flows, risk levels, and durations—as well as identical IRR values of 41 percent. Using IRR as the decision yardstick, an executive would feel confidence

in being indifferent toward choosing between the two projects. However, it would be a mistake to select either project without examining the relevant reinvestment rate for interim cash flows. Suppose that Project B's interim cash flows could be redeployed only at a typical 8 percent cost of capital, while Project A's cash flows could be invested in an attractive follow-on project expected to generate a 41 percent annual return. In that case, Project A is unambiguously preferable.

Even if the interim cash flows really could be reinvested at the IRR, very few practitioners would argue that the value of future investments should be commingled with the value of the project being evaluated. Most practitioners would agree that a company's cost of capital—by definition, the return available elsewhere to its shareholders on a similarly risky investment—is a clearer and more logical rate to assume for reinvestments of interim project cash flows.

When the cost of capital is used, a project's true annual equivalent yield can fall significantly—again, especially so with projects that posted high initial IRRs. Of course, when executives review projects with IRRs that are close to a company's cost of capital, the IRR is less distorted by the reinvestment-rate assumption. But when they evaluate projects that claim IRRs of 10 percent or more above their company's cost of capital, these may well be significantly distorted. Ironically, unadjusted IRRs

---

[29] This issue is discussed in the next section.

are particularly treacherous because the reinvestment-rate distortion is most egregious precisely when managers tend to think their projects are most attractive. And since this amplification is not felt evenly across all projects, managers can't simply correct for it by adjusting every IRR by a standard amount. (The amplification effect grows as a project's fundamental health improves, as measured by NPV, and it varies depending on the unique timing of a project's cash flows.)

How large is the potential impact of a flawed reinvestment-rate assumption? Managers at one large industrial company approved 23 major capital projects over five years on the basis of IRRs that averaged 77 percent. Recently, however, when we conducted an analysis with the reinvestment rate adjusted to the company's cost of capital, the true average return fell to just 16 percent. The order of the most attractive projects also changed considerably. The top-ranked project based on IRR dropped to the tenth-most-attractive project. Most striking, the company's highest-rated projects—showing IRRs of 800, 150, and 130 percent—dropped to just 15, 23, and 22 percent, respectively, once a realistic reinvestment rate was considered. Unfortunately, these investment decisions had already been made. Of course, IRRs this extreme are somewhat unusual. Yet even if a project's IRR drops from 25 percent to 15 percent, the impact is considerable.

John C. Kelleher and Justin J. MacCormack, "Internal Rate of Return: A Cautionary Tale," *The McKinsey Quarterly*, McKinsey & Co., August 2004.

---

contingent projects projects for which the acceptance of one requires the acceptance of another, either beforehand or simultaneously

Capital expenditures can represent **contingent projects**. For example, if a company can implement investment A (e.g., purchase the newest accounting software package) only if it also undertakes investment B (e.g., change the operating system to Microsoft Windows), investment A is contingent on investment B. In other words, one project is feasible only if another project is undertaken either beforehand or simultaneously. For these types of investment projects, the rule is to estimate the total NPV of *all* contingent projects and accept them if this total NPV is positive. In such a situation, it is possible that a project on which others are contingent (e.g., the updating of operating system) can be accepted even if it does not generate a positive NPV on its own. In fact, this is often the case with operating systems. This could occur if the benefits provided by the contingent projects more than offset the losses generated by the initial project.

Mutually exclusive projects, as defined earlier, imply that a company must choose among two or more alternatives. In other words, if a company is considering replacing an old computer system with either system A or system B, it would never buy both, even if the analysis suggested that they both generated positive NPVs.[30] In such a case, the company must decide which project is best. Recall from our previous discussion on IRR versus NPV that whenever a company has to rank projects, NPV is superior.

Capital Rationing

Theoretically, companies should accept all independent projects that generate positive NPVs, which enhance company value. However, in practice, companies often face capital budget constraints, which may force them to turn down attractive projects. Theoretically, these constraints should not exist in efficient markets because companies should always be able to source new financing to take advantage of investment opportunities that generate returns that exceed the cost of raising the required investment funds. However, constraints may arise because of market inefficiencies, which restrict the company's ability to raise funds in the capital markets, or because they are imposed internally (i.e., management sets certain budget limits that cannot be exceeded). When companies face capital budget constraints, it is common to say that **capital rationing** prevails—that is, investment capital must be rationed among available investment projects.

capital rationing allotting investment capital among available investment projects

investment opportunity schedule (IOS) internal rate of return expected on each potential investment opportunity, ranked in descending order

In Figure 10-8 we depict a company's investment decision environment. The company has $25 million of available projects, which are ranked by internal rate of return and plotted in this graph along the **investment opportunity schedule (IOS)**. A company should invest in opportunities along its IOS until the IRR equals its weighted average cost of

---

[30] If A and B are independent projects that generated positive NPVs, a company would accept both projects.

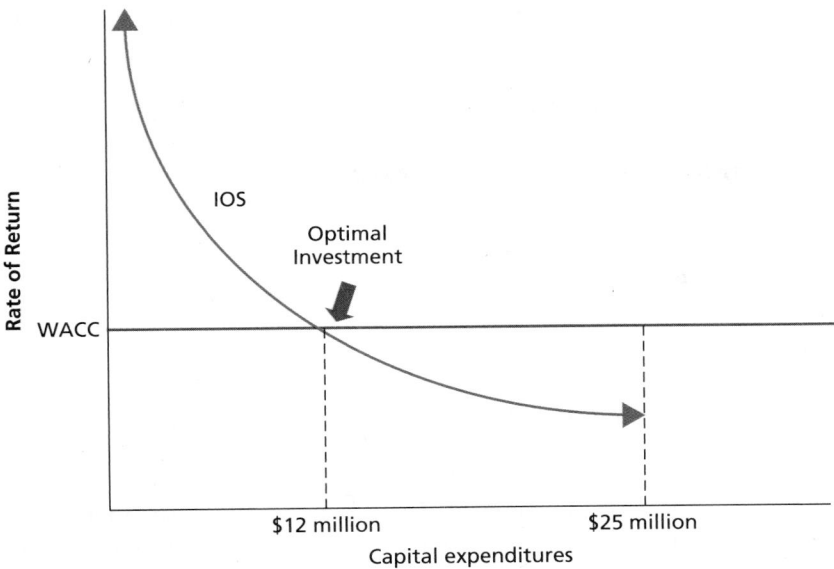

FIGURE 10-8 The Investment Opportunity Schedule and Optimal Investing

capital (WACC)—or equivalently until the last project accepted has an NPV of zero. This would mean that the optimal amount it should invest is $12 million, even though it has $25 million of available projects. However, suppose the company had only $5 million of internal funds; it could not accept all its projects and would be capital rationed, unless it issued new debt or equity.

The important point about capital rationing is that the cost of capital is no longer the appropriate opportunity cost. Now, cash flows generated by a project can be reinvested at a rate higher than assumed by the cost of capital because the company is leaving some positive NPV projects on the table, due to lack of financing. The reinvestment rate assumption underlying the IRR has more validity because the company can reinvest the cash flows from a project at the IRR of the marginal project, rather than at its cost of capital. The problem is that the IOS schedule is rarely a nice smooth downward-sloping function, like the one we show in Figure 10-8.

When companies have to choose among discrete, lumpy projects with limited funds, they have to consider the cost of the investment because this is constrained by the capital budget. In this case, we can first estimate the NPVs and the IRRs, but we can't fully rely on either of them as a criterion because they ignore the cost of the investment and the capital constraint. The PI is often a useful starting point because it gives the highest present value relative to the initial cash outlay, which is constrained. However, the final decision should be based on which combination of projects generates the highest total NPV while satisfying the capital budget constraint. This is because the PI, like the IRR, may lead to incorrect decisions; it is a relative measure.

Consider a company that is evaluating the following independent investments, A through F:

Project	Initial Cash Outlay (CF_0)	NPV	PI
A	€100,000	€13,646	1.136
B	€50,000	–€3,342	0.934
C	€80,000	€10,558	1.132
D	€60,000	€4,320	1.072
E	€75,000	€10,825	1.144
F	€90,000	€7,225	1.080

In the absence of capital rationing, which projects should be selected? If we look at projects ranked by NPV and PI, we see the following rankings:

Rank	Rank Based on NPV	Rank Based on PI
1	A	E
2	E	A
3	C	C
4	F	F
5	D	D
6	B	B

Why do they differ? Because the NPV is in monetary terms, and PI is in relative terms (benefit/cost ratio).

The company should select projects A, C, D, E, and F because they all have positive NPVs and are assumed to be independent. Therefore, the capital spending is €100,000 + 80,000 + 60,000 + 75,000 + 90,000 = €405,000, and the expected value added from this set of projects is €13,646 + 10,558 + 4,320 + 10,825 + 7,225 = €46,574.

Now suppose a capital budget constraint of €250,000 is placed on new investments. Which projects should be selected? The company should take on the combination of positive NPV projects that maximizes total NPV, within the given budget constraints. Possible combinations of projects are the following:

Projects selected	Total NPV	Capital Spending Required	Within the Budget?
A, C, D	€28,524	€240,000	Yes
A, C, E	€35,029	€255,000	No
A, C, F	€42,254	€345,000	No
A, D, E	€28,791	€235,000	Yes
C, E, F	€28,608	€245,000	Yes

If the capital budget constraint is fixed €250,000, the company should select only projects A, D, and E.[31] Why? Because the spending fits in the budget, and this is the set of projects within the budget that has the highest total NPV. What if the budget is €200,000? The company should select projects A and E, requiring an investment of €175,000, with an expected added value of €24,471.

If the company could invest in all projects that have positive NPV, the total investment would be €405,000, and the value added—the sum of the NPVs of these projects—is €46,574. With a budget constrained to €250,000, the total NPV is now only €28,791 under capital rationing, and the "loss" to the company = €46,574 − €28,791 = €17,783. Notice that the loss of €17,783 is the sum of the NPVs of the two forgone positive NPV projects (i.e., C and F). This is detrimental to company value, as it is forced to turn down two "good" positive NPV investments because the company lacks the capital to proceed with them.

Although we have come up with the maximum NPV given the budget constraint, in reality the company would conduct further analysis. For example, the company would forecast its budget for the following year and look at the deferral possibilities. It may be, for example, that E can be deferred, and it is better to go with A and C this year and roll over the excess in the budget to take on E and other projects next year.

---

[31] If there was €5,000 "slack" in the constraint, then the combination of A, C, and E would generate the highest NPV; however, it requires a €255,000 outlay, which exceeds the $250,000 constraint.

Overconfidence and Capital Budgeting | ETHICS

Capital budgeting decisions are, ultimately, made by people, not machines. Though we have tools to quantify the analysis, most of what we are doing is working with estimates: estimates of the initial investment, estimates of future cash flows resulting from the investment, and estimates of the risk associated with the project. Because of the human element, there is a potential for biases in recommending or promoting capital budgets within a company, especially if there is rationed capital. Overconfidence may be reflected in a number of ways, including forecasted cash flows that are too rosy or risk that is understated, and be motivated by compensation formulas, empire building, or simply hubris.

Studies have shown that there is a relationship between a company's CEO overconfidence and investment decisions.[32] Particular to one type of capital budgeting decision, mergers and acquisitions, studies document that the CEO's overconfidence is related to the premium the company pays to acquire other companies: the more overconfident, the higher the premium paid.

Companies can mitigate some of the biases in their capital budgeting processes by requiring specific analyses and data for each capital project, along with supporting assumptions.

The Appropriate Discount Rate

As mentioned earlier, it is usually appropriate to use the project's cost of capital as the discount rate to evaluate a long-term investment project. However, it is often the case that the company's weighted average cost of capital (WACC) is used as the project's cost of capital. The WACC is the after-tax cost of a dollar of additional long-term financing to the company, and we assume that companies will finance long-term investments by using long-term financing. This is appropriate if the project under consideration is an "average" risk investment project for the company—in other words, if it is a typical investment and will not substantially change the asset mix of the company.

However, if a company is considering a project that is atypical, in the sense that it is either more or less risky than the average investment for that company, this fact should be reflected in the discount rate used to evaluate that project. For example, a company could be considering introducing a new product line that entails greater (or lower) risks than its traditional offerings. Under these circumstances, a higher discount rate should be used for projects that possess above-average risk, and a lower discount rate should be used for projects that possess below-average risk. If a company does not adjust the discount rate under these circumstances and merely uses a constant WACC to select investment projects, it will make inappropriate decisions. In particular, this could lead the company to reject positive NPV low-risk projects that appear unattractive if evaluated by using a discount rate that is too high. It could also lead the company to accept negative NPV high-risk projects that appear attractive if evaluated by using a discount rate that is too low.

A good example of this problem was USX Company (USX). For a time, the company comprised two divisions: Marathon Oil Company and U.S. Steel.[33] Suppose, for example, the oil company's WACC was 8 percent and the steel company's was 12 percent, and the overall company was composed of 50 percent of each division, so the company WACC was 10 percent. Applying the company WACC of 10 percent to capital projects would cause some of the steel division's projects with IRRs of 11 percent to be accepted, even if stand-alone steel companies were rejecting similar projects. Likewise, desirable oil projects earning 9 percent would be rejected, even if they were being accepted by

[32] See, for example, David J. Ravenscraft and F. M. Scherer, "Life after Takeover," *Journal of Industrial Economics,* 36, no. 2 (1987): 147–156; Mathew L. A. Hayward and Donald C. Hambrick, "Explaining the Premiums Paid for Large Acquisitions: Evidence of CEO Hubris," *Administrative Science Quarterly,* 42, no. 1 (1997): 103–127.

[33] The two companies ultimately became independent companies, each with its own stock ownership, in 2002. The steel business is now known as United States Steel Company (X) and the oil business Marathon Oil Company (MRO).

EXAMPLE 10.7

Applying the Company's Cost of Capital to All Projects

PROBLEM

Consider a company that has two projects under consideration with the following characteristics:

	End-of-Period Cash Flows	
Year	Project P	Project Q
0	–$10,000	–$10,000
1	$3,000	$4,000
2	$3,000	$3,000
3	$3,000	$2,000
4	$2,000	$3,000

Project P's cost of capital is 3 percent, and Project Q's cost of capital is 9 percent. The cost of capital for the company is 6 percent.

What happens when we use a single cost of capital for both projects and can only invest in one of these projects?

Solution

We may draw an incorrect conclusion regarding whether the projects add value:

	Project P	Project Q
Net present value based on company's cost of capital	–$396.78	$499.09
Decision	Reject	Accept
Net present value based on project's cost of capital	$262.81	–$135.59
Decision	Accept	Reject

equivalent oil companies. If Marathon Oil did this over time, it would gradually become a less valuable oil company, rejecting many opportunities that other oil companies would have accepted.

The common response to the Marathon Oil problem is to estimate risk-adjusted discount rates by adjusting the cost of capital up or down based on the risk level and financing of a specific project under consideration. Marathon Oil would use a discount rate of 8 percent in its oil division and 12 percent in its steel division. Estimating these different discount rates involves estimating betas and the risk associated with the investment and the optimal financing. One method of doing this is the **pure play approach**. This approach involves estimating the weighted average cost of capital of companies in a line of business associated with the project, adjusting for the difference in capital structures between the pure play and the company. Another approach is to estimate beta for the project by regressing the return on assets of the project against that of the market index. Similar techniques can be used to estimate the appropriate project cost of debt and then to estimate the appropriate overall cost of capital.

Several practical difficulties are associated with estimating a project's cost of capital. For example, it may be difficult to find an appropriate company to use as a pure play, and the regression of project return on an index return on assets may lead to an inaccurate beta measure. In addition, intuitive adjustments that are made by managers are subjective in nature and prone to error, but this may be no more prevalent here than in other techniques. However, despite the associated difficulties, estimating risk-adjusted discount rates is preferable to blindly applying one constant discount rate to all projects, regardless of their individual risk characteristics.

pure play approach
estimating betas and the risk associated with an investment and the optimal financing by estimating the weighted average cost of capital of companies in an industry associated with the project

Comparing Evaluation Techniques

The net present value, internal rate of return, modified internal rate of return, and profitability index techniques offer objective criteria when evaluating projects:

| | | Decision Criteria | | |
| | | (i is the project cost of capital) | | |
Evaluation Technique	Metric	Accept	Indifferent	Reject
Net present value	Monetary amount	NPV > 0	NPV = 0	NPV < 0
Internal rate of return	Rate of return	IRR > i	IRR = i	IRR < i
Modified internal rate of return	Rate of return	MIRR > i	MIRR = i	MIRR < i
Profitability index	Index	PI > 1.0	PI = 1.0	PI < 1.0

These methods will generally offer the same accept/reject decisions when evaluating a set of independent projects and when there is no limit on the capital budget. However, when we look at situations in which there are mutually exclusive projects, capital rationing, or different project sizes, we need to take more care in selecting the evaluation technique.

Each technique has its advantages and disadvantages, which we summarize in Table 10-1. As you can see, the net present value technique tends to dominate in terms of consistency with the objective of this decision making, which is to maximize the value of the owners' value.

TABLE 10-1 Comparing Techniques

	Advantages	Disadvantages
Net Present Values	• Considers the time value of money through the discount rate. • Considers all of the project's cash flows. • Has an objective criterion (i.e., accept if NPV is positive).	• Result is in monetary terms, not as the more familiar return. • Sensitive to the project's cost of capital.
Internal Rate of Return	• Considers the time value of money through the hurdle rate. • Considers all the project's cash flows. • Has an objective criterion (i.e., accept if IRR is greater than the project's cost of capital).	• Should not be used when deciding among mutually exclusive projects. • Cannot be used when the signs of cash flows change more than once. • Should not use when the capital budget is limited.
Modified Internal Rate of Return	• Considers the time value of money through the hurdle rate. • Considers all of the project's cash flows. • Indicates the return on the project considering a realistic reinvestment of the project's cash inflows. • Has an objective criterion (i.e., accept if MIRR exceeds the project's cost of capital).	• Should not be used when deciding among mutually exclusive projects. • Should not use when the capital budget is limited.

(Continued)

TABLE 10-1 *(Continued)*

	Advantages	Disadvantages
Payback Period	• Easy to calculate. • A useful initial screening technique. • Measures the liquidity of a project (i.e., how fast cash inflows occur).	• Does not consider the time value of money. • Ignores cash flows beyond the payback period. • Has no objective criterion for what is a good payback period.
Discounted Payback Period	• Indicates whether a project will ever pay back. • Considers the time value of money of the project cash flows.	• Ignores cash flows beyond the payback period. • Has no objective criterion for what is a good discounted payback period.
Profitability Index	• Considers the time value of money through the discount rate. • Considers all the project's cash flows. • Has an objective criterion (i.e., accept if PI is greater than one). • Useful in ranking projects in terms of benefit/cost.	• Should not be used when deciding among mutually exclusive projects.

Concept Review Questions

1. What complications arise when companies are rationed in terms of their available capital budget?

2. Explain how companies should decide which projects to accept and which to reject when capital rationing exists.

3. Distinguish between a project's cost of capital and the company's weighted cost of capital.

SUMMARY

• There are alternative approaches to evaluating capital investment projects. These approaches include the net present value, the internal rate of return, the modified internal rate of return, the profitability index, the payback period, and the discounted payback period.

• The net present value method requires the calculation of the value added from the project, which is the difference between the present value of the cash inflows from a project and the present value of the project's cash outflows, where all cash flows are discounted at the project's cost of capital. A positive net present value indicates that the investment is expected to enhance the value of the company.

• The internal rate of return is the yield on the project, which we derive by solving for the discount rate resulting in a zero net present value. In many cases, a project with an internal rate of return greater than the project's cost of capital is attractive because the project earns more than what the supplier of capital requires considering the project's risk.

- One of the drawbacks of the internal rate of return is that the reinvestment assumption applied to cash flows is the internal rate of return. We can use the modified internal rate of return, with its more realistic reinvestment rate assumption, to overcome this problem. In addition, we should not use the internal rate of return when deciding among mutually exclusive projects or evaluating projects with different initial investments. Another drawback of the internal rate of return is that the internal rate of return should not be used when the sign of the cash flow changes more than once during the life of the project.

- The profitability index is related to the net present value; instead of the difference between the present value of the inflows and outflows, the profitability index is the ratio of these two present values.

- The payback period and the discounted payback period are measures of how long it takes to recover a project's cash outlay in cash inflows and discounted cash inflows, respectively.

- The net present value method is the preferred method because it is consistent with the maximization of shareholder wealth and is not complicated by issues that may cause the internal rate of return to provide misleading results, with respect to mutually exclusive projects, mathematical issues, and an aggressive reinvestment rate.

- If capital is rationed—that is, there is a limit on the capital budget—the focus should be in selecting projects that best enhance shareholder wealth, which means selecting the set of projects that provides the greatest sum of net present values with a sum of initial investments that fit within the budget.

FORMULAS/EQUATIONS

(10-1) $\quad NPV = \dfrac{CF_0}{(1 + i)^0} + \dfrac{CF_1}{(1 + i)^1} + \dfrac{CF_2}{(1 + i)^2} + \dfrac{CF_3}{(1 + i)^3} + \cdots + \dfrac{CF_n}{(1 + i)^n}$

(10-2) $\quad NPV = \dfrac{\sum\limits_{t=0}^{n} CF_t}{(1 + i)^t}$

(10-3) $\quad 0 = \dfrac{\sum\limits_{t=0}^{n} CF_t}{(1 + IRR)^t}$

(10-4) $\quad PI = \dfrac{PV(\text{cash inflows})}{PV(\text{cash outflows})}$

QUESTIONS AND PROBLEMS

Multiple Choice Questions

1. Consider an investment that requires a $10 million initial investment and has a net present value of $6 million. Which of the following statements is *not* correct regarding this investment?

    A. The profitability index is 0.6.
    B. The investment pays back in terms of its discounted cash flows.
    C. The internal rate of return of the project is greater than the project's cost of capital.
    D. Making this investment is expected to increase the value of the company by $6 million.

2.   Which of the following is *not* a critical factor that Porter identified in determining industry attractiveness?
     A. Entry barriers
     B. Rivalry among competitors
     C. Bargaining power of suppliers
     D. Bargaining power of government

3.   The NPV for a project with an after-tax initial investment of $17,000, five equal annual cash flows of $8,000 at the start of each year, beginning with the 3rd year, and a discount rate of 20 percent, is *closest* to:
     A. –$385.49.   B. $1,998.35.   C. $2,937.41.   D. $6,924.90.

4.   Which of the following statements about IRR and NPV is *incorrect*?
     A. NPV and IRR yield the same ranking when evaluating projects.
     B. NPV assumes that cash flows are reinvested at the cost of capital of the company.
     C. IRR may have multiple IRRs when the sign of cash flow changes more than once.
     D. IRR is the discount rate that, when applied to a project's cash flows, results in an NPV equal to zero.

5.   When evaluating two mutually exclusive projects with a crossover rate of 5 percent and $IRR_A < IRR_B$, we prefer project A when the discount rate is:
     A. less than 5 percent.   B. equal to 5 percent.   C. greater than 5 percent.

6.   Consider the following end-of-year cash flows for Projects X and Y:

     Project X: $CF_0 = -\$2,000$ $CF_1 = \$1,000$ $CF_2 = \$1,000$ $CF_3 = \$1,000$
     Project Y: $CF_0 = -\$2,000$ $CF_1 = \$0$ $CF_2 = \$500$ $CF_3 = \$3,000$

     If the discount rate is 15 percent, the decision regarding projects X and Y should be to accept:

	Independent	*Mutually Exclusive*
A.	Both	X
B.	Neither	Y
C.	Both	Y
D.	Neither	X

7.   Consider a project with an after-tax initial investment of $6,000 and expected cash flows of $CF_1 = \$2,500$; $CF_2 = \$4,000$; $CF_3 = \$5,000$, and a discount rate of 20 percent. The IRR is *closest* to:
     A. 15 percent.   B. 25.65 percent.   C. 35.87 percent.

8.   Which of the following would *not* happen if a company uses the company's weighted average cost of capital for all projects, regardless of the individual risks of the projects?
     A. Reject a low-risk project with positive NPV
     B. Reject a high-risk project with positive NPV
     C. Accept a high-risk project with negative NPV
     D. Accept an average-risk project with positive NPV

9.   To estimate risk-adjusted discount rates, a company could use all of the following methods, *except* the:
     A. pure play approach.
     B. cost of capital ± risk premium.
     C. regression of the ROA of the project on the ROA of the whole company.
     D. regression of the return on assets (ROA) of the project on the ROA of market index.

10. We should *reject* a project if:
     A. PI < 1.   B. NPV > 0.   C. IRR > project's cost of capital.   D. MIRR > project's cost of capital.

Practice Questions and Problems

10.1 The Capital Budgeting Process

11. What are capital expenditures?

12. How can an investment project add value to a company?

13. Is the net present value technique consistent with the maximization of owners' equity? Explain.

14. Provide an example of a company that uses cost leadership to give it a comparative or competitive advantage.

15. Provide an example of a company that uses product differentiation to give it a comparative or competitive advantage.

16. Analysts often assume that a company's return on assets will eventually "regress toward the mean," approaching the typical growth in gross domestic product. Is this consistent with Porter's model and basic economic theory? Explain.

10.2 Evaluating Investment Projects

17. For each of the following, describe the basis of accept/reject of a capital project:
    A. Net present value
    B. Internal rate of return
    C. Modified internal rate of return
    D. Profitability index

18. Which of the following techniques is consistent with the maximization of owners' equity? Explain why or why not.
    A. Payback period
    B. Discounted payback period
    C. Net present value
    D. Internal rate of return
    E. Modified internal rate of return

19. List and describe briefly the drawbacks of payback period and discounted payback period.

20. Regarding the net present value profile,
    A. What are the values on the horizontal axis?
    B. What are the values on the vertical axis?
    C. How do you determine the intersection of the profile with the vertical axis?
    D. How do you determine the intersection of the profile with the horizontal axis?
    E. How do you calculate the intersection of any two profiles?

21. If you calculate a project's net present value of $1 million, what is the interpretation of this value?

22. Suppose you are evaluating two mutually exclusive projects, and you calculate the crossover rate as 8 percent. What is the meaning of this rate?

23. If a project has a positive net present value using a discount rate of 5 percent, is the project's internal rate of return greater than or less than 5 percent? Explain.

24. If a project has a positive net present value, is the project's profitability index greater than or less than 1.0? Explain.

25. If a project has a positive net present value, does this project pay back in terms of discounted cash flows? Explain.

26. Consider a project with the following:
    - An after-tax initial investment of $66,777
    - After-tax cash flows at each following six year ends of $20,000 each
    - A year-end cash flow at year 7 of $40,000
    - A discount rate of 10 percent

    A. Draw a time-line of the cash flows for today through period 7.
    B. Is the decision the same using NPV and IRR? Why?

27. Suppose a project has cash inflows following its initial outlay, an NPV of $5,090, and the after-tax initial investment is $10,050.

    A. What is the project's PI?
    B. Should the company accept the project?
    C. Does PI yield the same decision as NPV?

28. Complete the following table by calculating each project's profitability index:

Project	Initial Outlay	Net Present Value	Profitability Index
A	$100,000	$15,000	
B	$10,000	$1,000	
C	$32,000	–$1,000	
D	$40,000	$5,000	

29. Consider a project with the following cash flows:

Year	End-of-year Cash Flow
0	–$100,000
1	$0
2	$90,000
3	$40,000
4	$5,000

    A. Draw a timeline, indicating both the period and the cash flow.
    B. Calculate the project's NPV if the project's cost of capital is 10 percent.
    C. Calculate the project's IRR.
    D. Calculate the MIRR, assuming a reinvestment rate of 10 percent.
    E. Using a spreadsheet, illustrate the project's net present value profile, labeling the axes and indicating the project's internal rate of return on this profile.

30. Consider the following project's cash flows:

Year	End-of-year Cash Flow
0	–$1,000
1	–$2,000
2	$2,000
3	$1,500

A. What is this project's net present value if the discount rate is 6 percent?

B. What is this project's internal rate of return?

C. What is this project's modified internal rate of return if the reinvestment rate is 5 percent?

D. What is this project's modified internal rate of return if the reinvestment rate is 6 percent?

31. SK Inc. has two projects as follows:

	End-of-year Cash Flows				
Project	Year 0	Year 1	Year 2	Year 3	Year 4
E	–€2,500	€800	€1,200	€900	€2,000
F	–€3,000	€750	€1,500	€1,000	€4,000

A. Which project(s) will be selected if it uses the *discounted* payback period method and a discount rate of 12 percent? Explain.

B. What is each project's net present value if the cost of capital for each project is 12 percent?

32. Consider a project with the following cash flows:

Year	End-of-year Cash Flow
0	–$100,000
1	$0
2	$0
3	$0
4	$115,000

A. Draw a time line, indicating both the period and the cash flow.

B. Calculate the project's NPV if the project's cost of capital is 10 percent.

C. Calculate the project's IRR.

D. Using a spreadsheet, illustrate the project's net present value profile, labeling the axes and indicating the project's internal rate of return on this profile.

33. Consider the following end-of-year cash flows for Project C and Project D:

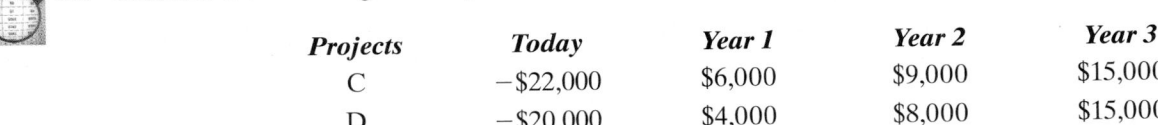

Projects	Today	Year 1	Year 2	Year 3
C	–$22,000	$6,000	$9,000	$15,000
D	–$20,000	$4,000	$8,000	$15,000

A. What is the internal rate of return for each project?

B. Graph the net present value profiles for each project on a single chart, indicating each project's internal rates of return.

C. What is the crossover rate for Projects C and D?

D. If the discount rate for both projects is 10 percent, which project, if any, should be selected?

10.3 Special Issues

34. What is capital rationing?

35. Is capital rationing consistent with the maximization of owners' value? Explain.

36. If two projects are mutually exclusive, which technique(s) should you use?

37. If a project has cash flows that consist of an initial cash outlay, positive cash flows for 5 years, and then a negative cash flow in the final year, what techniques should you use in evaluating this project?

38. Suppose a project has the following cash flows:

Year	End-of-year Cash Flow
20X0	−$100,000
20X1	$0
20X2	$0
20X3	$120,000
20X4	−$2,000

A. If the discount rate is 5 percent, should this project be accepted?
B. If the discount rate is 6 percent, should this project be accepted?
C. What is the internal rate of return for this project?

39. Consider the cash flows for the projects A through D:

Project End-of-year Cash Flows
(in millions)

Year	A	B	C	D
Initial	−$10	−$10	−$10	−$10
1	$2	$0	$0	$5
2	$2	$0	$0	$0
3	$2	$0	$6	$2
4	$2	$0	$0	$0
5	$4	$13	$6	$5

The cost of capital for each project is 5 percent.
A. Calculate the IRR for each project.
B. Calculate the NPV for each project.
C. If the projects are independent, which project or projects should be accepted?
D. If the projects are mutually exclusive, which project or projects should be accepted?

 40. Consider two mutually exclusive projects, named for their planned locations of Corvalis and Portland:

End-of-year Cash Flow

Year	Corvalis	Portland
0	−$9,500	−$9,500
1	$0	$3,000
2	$0	$3,000
3	$0	$3,000
4	$12,000	$2,000

A. If the project discount rate for both projects is 5 percent, what is the appropriate decision?
B. If the project discount rate for both projects is 6 percent, what is the appropriate decision?
C. If the project discount rate for both projects is 7 percent, what is the appropriate decision?
D. Draw the net present value profile for these projects on one graph.

41. Consider the results of the analysis of the following projects:

Project	Initial Outlay	Net Present Value	Internal Rate of Return	Payback Period
A	$10,000,000	$500,000	10%	5 years
B	$5,000,000	−$40,000	9%	4 years
C	$11,000,000	$1,000,000	13%	3 years
D	$2,000,000	$40,000	9%	5 years
E	$3,000,000	−$20,000	12%	4 years
F	$4,000,000	$70,000	7%	3 years
G	$9,000,000	$60,000	3%	5 years

A. If the capital budget is limited to $12 million, which projects, if any, should be selected? Explain.
B. If the capital budget is limited to $20 million, which projects, if any, should be selected? Explain.
C. If the capital budget is limited to $25 million, which projects, if any, should be selected? Explain.

42. Consider the following projects and cash flows:

Dollar Amounts (in millions)	A	B	C	D
Initial cash outlay	−$5	−$15	−$10	−$10
Cash flow, end of period 1	$0	$0	$2	$0
Cash flow, end of period 2	$2	$0	$3	$0
Cash flow, end of period 3	$2	$0	$4	$0
Cash flow, end of period 4	$2	$18	$4	$15
Project discount rate	5%	6%	7%	8%

A. If these projects are independent and there is no capital rationing, which project(s) should you invest in?
B. If these projects are mutually exclusive and there is no capital rationing, which project(s) should you invest in?
C. If these projects are independent and there is a limit on the capital budget of $25 million, which project(s) should you invest in?
D. Draw the net present value profile for each project on a single chart, identifying the internal rate of return of each project.

43. Consider the cash flows for the projects E through H:

Year	E	F	G	H
Initial	−$10	−$10	−$10	−$10
1	$2	$0	$0	$0
2	$2	$0	$0	$0
3	$2	$0	$6	$0
4	$2	$0	$0	$0
5	$4	$13	$6	$13

Project End-of-year Cash Flows (in millions)

The cost of capital for each project is 4 percent.

A. Using a spreadsheet program, calculate the IRR for each project.
B. Using a spreadsheet program, calculate the NPV for each project.
C. If the projects are independent, which project or projects should be accepted?
D. If the projects are mutually exclusive, which project or projects should be accepted?
E. What is the crossover rate for Projects E and F?
F. What is the crossover rate for Projects G and H?
G. Using a spreadsheet program, graph the net present value profiles of Projects E and F on the same chart, indicating the crossover point and internal rates of return.
H. Using a spreadsheet program, graph the net present value profiles of Projects G and H on the same chart, indicating the crossover point and internal rates of return.

Case

Case 10.1 The Austin Saddle Company Expansion

The Austin Saddle Company (ASC) is considering expanding its tannery facilities, increasing its production capacity by 20 percent. The ASC has brought in the marketing, production management, procurement, capital investment, and accounting departments to formulate estimates of the initial cost of the expansion, as well as future cash flow that can be used to evaluate this expansion. The procurement and capital management teams expect that the expansion will require $10 million initially, with the first year's operating cash flows of $2 million. The operating cash flows are expected to grow at a rate of 5 percent each year for 3 years, but then to slow to a 3 percent growth thereafter.

The ASC has a cost of capital of 8 percent, and the expansion project is expected to have risk similar to ASC's typical project.

A. Should ASC expand? Explain your reasoning.
B. If ASC's cost of capital increased to 10 percent, would your recommendation change?
C. At what cost of capital, if any, would your recommendation change? Indicate your decision on a net present value profile of this investment decision.
D. If the growth rate were to be 3 percent, ad infinitum, would your decision change? Explain.

DEALING WITH UNEQUAL LIVES

We have simplified the world in this chapter by assuming that any projects that we are comparing have the same lives. Why is this important? Because if the projects have different useful lives, we would need to make adjustments to make the projects comparable.

Suppose a company is evaluating equipment to use in the new production line. The company can only use one piece of equipment, but the problem is that the two eligible pieces of equipment have different useful lives; Equipment 1 has a useful life of 5 years, and Equipment 2 has a useful life of 4 years:

	End-of-year Cash Flows	
Year	Equipment 1	Equipment 2
0	−$10,000	−$10,000
1	$1,000	$2,000
2	$2,000	$3,500
3	$4,000	$4,500
4	$5,000	$4,000
5	$3,000	

The company expects to have the need for equipment to perform the particular function in the production process for the foreseeable future. To keeps things simple, let's assume that the project cost of capital is 10 percent for each project.

Because these projects are mutually exclusive, we would use the net present value to select the most profitable project, which would be Equipment 1:

	Equipment 1	Equipment 2
NPV	$845.07	$823.71

The issue, however, is that we face the proverbial conundrum of comparing "apples with oranges": These projects are not directly comparable because they provide benefits over different numbers of years.

10A.1 THE COMMON LIFE APPROACH

One way to adjust for this problem is to consider that replacements could be made for each project such that they would have the same useful life. The **common life approach** assumes a finite number of replacements such that each project being compared has the same useful life, the **common life**. The common life for these two projects is 20 years: three replacements of Equipment 1 is equivalent to four replacements of Equipment 2. This is how it works: You invest today in Equipment 1. At the end of 5 years, you invest in Equipment 1 again, with a present value of $845.07. You repeat this at the end of the 10th year and the 15th year. You do likewise for Equipment 2: replace at the end of the 4th, 8th, 12th, and 16th years. This way we have all 20 years covered, as shown in Table 10A-1.

common life approach method of comparing mutually exclusive projects with different useful lives, assuming a finite number of replacements for each project, consistent with the projects' common life

common life revised useful life of projects considering a finite number of replacements such that the projects being compared have the same useful life

TABLE 10A-1 Net Present Values for Reinvestment in Equipment 1 and Equipment 2

Year	Equipment 1	Equipment 2
0	$845.07	$823.71
1		
2		
3		
4		$823.71
5	$845.07	
6		
7		
8		$823.71
9		
10	$845.07	
11		
12		$823.71
13		
14		
15	$845.07	
16		$823.71
17		
18		
19		
20		

The next step is to calculate the net present value of the series of values and then compare these for the two projects:

	Equipment 1	Equipment 2
NPV	$2,946.63	$3,434.76

The value added by Equipment 2 is higher than that provided by Equipment 1. Therefore, we prefer Equipment 1.

10A.2 EQUIVALENT ANNUAL ANNUITY

equivalent annual annuity approach method of comparing mutually exclusive projects that have different useful lives, assuming reinvestment in each in perpetuity

An alternative method of dealing with the unequal lives is to consider reinvestment in each project in perpetuity. Using this approach, which we refer to as the **equivalent annual annuity approach**, we assume that at the end of each project the company will reinvest in the same project, ad infinitum. Although it may appear daunting to consider the mathematics of reinvesting in, say, Equipment 1 every 5 years, forever, there is a simple approach: First calculate the annual annuity amount that is equivalent to the project's net present value, and then assume this annual stream ad infinitum.

For example, the net present value of Equipment 1's cash flows is $845.07. What is this equivalent to in terms of an annuity? Use the NPV as the present value, use the project's life as the number of years, and use the project's cost of capital as the discount rate:

$$PV = \$845.07$$
$$N = 5$$
$$i = 10\%$$
$$\text{Solve for PMT} \rightarrow \text{PMT} = \$222.93$$

We often refer to this annuity amount as the **equivalent annual annuity** because it is the annuity stream that is equivalent to the net present value of the project.

> equivalent annual annuity amount of the annuity that is equivalent to the net present value of a project

With this annual payment, assuming this in perpetuity, we can calculate the present value of the perpetuity:

$$\text{Present value of Equipment 1 in perpetuity} = \frac{\$222.93}{0.10} = \$2,229.28$$

Repeating this for Equipment 2, using $823.71 for the present value and four for the number of years, produces an annuity of $259.86 and a present value of Equipment 2 in perpetuity of $2,598.58.[35] Summarizing,

	Equipment 1	*Equipment 2*
NPV	$846.09	$824.73
EAA	$222.93	$259.86
Present value of perpetuity	$2,229.28	$2,598.58

The two methods—valuing the projects using a common life and using the equivalent annual annuity—can be used in any situation in which the net present value is used.

PRACTICE QUESTIONS AND PROBLEMS

1. Distinguish the use of the common life approach to investment decision making with unequal lives with that of the equivalent annual annuity approach. Be sure to identify the assumptions of each.

2. Suppose you are evaluating three projects, with lives of 5, 6, and 7 years, respectively. What is the common life for these projects?

3. Consider two mutually exclusive projects, Project 1 and Project 2, that have the following cash flows:

	End-of-year Cash Flow	
Year	*Project 1*	*Project 2*
0	−$10,000	−$10,000
1	$1,000	$4,500
2	$2,000	$4,500
3	$4,000	$4,500
4	$5,000	
5	$3,000	
Cost of capital	8%	7%

---

[35] It looks like we could have come to the same conclusion if we had stopped at the amount of the annual annuity. However, if the project cost of capital is different for the two projects, we need to continue on and calculate the present value of the annuity.

A. What is the common life for these projects?
B. What is the net present value of each project?
C. Using the equivalent annual annuity approach, which project is preferred? Explain.

4. Consider three mutually exclusive projects, Projects A, B, and C, that have the following cash flows:

	End-of-year Cash Flow		
Year	Project A	Project B	Project C
0	−$100,000	−$100,000	−$100,000
1	$24,000	$37,000	$0
2	$24,000	$37,000	$0
3	$24,000	$37,000	$0
4	$24,000		$132,500
5	$24,000		
Cost of capital	6%	5%	7%

A. What is the common life for these projects?
B. What is the net present value of each project?
C. Using the equivalent annual annuity approach, which project is preferred? Explain.

CHAPTER 11

CAPITAL BUDGETING: CASH FLOWS AND RISK

Capital spending in the U.S. is cyclical, with less spending during recessionary periods. You can see this over time, using data from the Annual Capital Expenditures Survey (ACES), produced by the U.S. Census Bureau:*

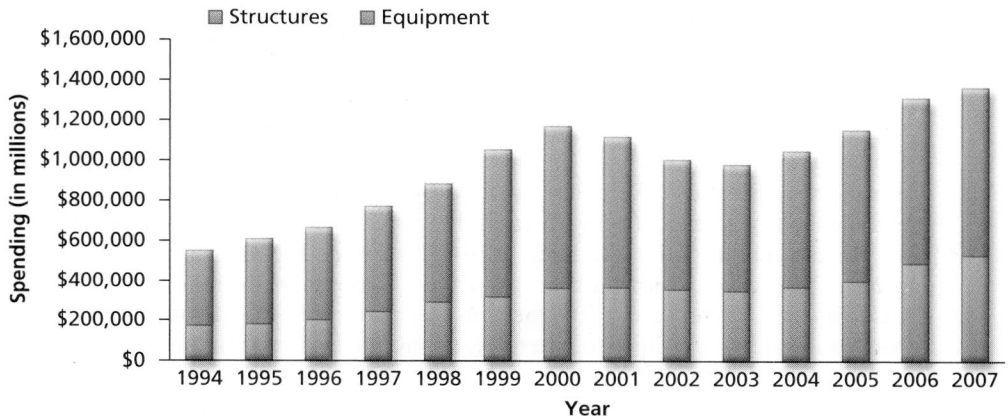

According to the National Bureau of Economic Research, the U.S. economy was in a recession from March 2001 through November 2001.** Capital spending in the U.S. declined in 2001 and continued its decline in 2002 and 2003.

The recession that began December 2007 was expected to have a dampening effect on capital spending in 2008 and beyond. Not only was capital spending affected by lower consumer spending, but companies also found it difficult to raise capital in the financial markets in 2008 and 2009.***

Learning Outcomes

After reading this chapter, you should be able to:

LO 11.1 Identify the relevant cash flows for a capital budgeting analysis.

LO 11.2 Estimate the investment cash flows, operating cash flows, and terminal cash flows of an investment project.

LO 11.3 Conduct a sensitivity analysis to examine the sensitivity of capital investment decisions to the estimates of cash flows.

LO 11.4 Estimate cash flows for a replacement decision.

LO 11.5 Evaluate the effects of inflation on capital budgeting decisions.

---

* Annual Capital Expenditures Survey, U.S. Census Bureau, Historical Data. 2007 is the most recent year available, as of January 2012.

** National Bureau of Economic Research, Business Cycle Expansions and Contractions, www.nber.org/cycles.htm.

*** David Wyss and Beth Ann Bovino, "A Deep and Long Recession," *Business Week*, January 23, 2009.

Chapter Preview In the previous chapter, we discussed capital budgeting techniques used to evaluate capital projects, including the net present value and internal rate of return. We took it for granted in that chapter that we already knew the inputs to the analysis: the net cash flows for each year of the project's useful life. All these methods require an estimate of the present cash outlay, as well as estimates of the future cash flows associated with the investment opportunity. In this chapter, we discuss how to incorporate these inputs into the evaluation process. We need to draw on our previous coverage regarding the company's financial statements, as well as the depreciation for tax purposes.

We begin our discussion by laying out the basic principles of relevant cash flows. We then describe and demonstrate how to estimate the individual cash flows that contribute to a project's net cash flows. Following this, we illustrate how sensitivity analysis can be used to evaluate how the effects of uncertain elements in a capital project can be analyzed. We wrap up the chapter covering specific issues that arise when dealing with replacement decisions and inflation. To provide an additional example of the cash flow determination for a capital project, we provide an integrative problem in Appendix 11A.

11.1 IDENTIFYING RELEVANT CASH FLOWS

One of the most, or perhaps the most, challenging task in capital budgeting is estimating a project's cash flows. We begin by providing some general guidelines for identifying relevant cash flows associated with capital expenditure decisions, along with examples.

In capital budgeting, we need to first determine the appropriate time horizon for the project. We need to know how long a project is likely to continue before it is economically wise to finish or replace it. In this sense, abandonment decisions have to be considered because projects are finished when it is economic to do so and not when the engineer says the assets are no longer functioning.

What Are the Relevant Cash Flows?

The key to determining relevant cash flows is identifying how cash flows of the business change if the business goes ahead with a project:

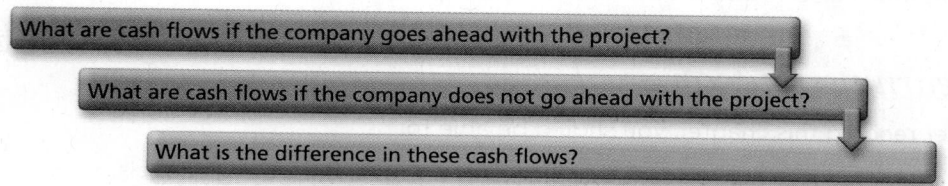

What are cash flows if the company goes ahead with the project?

What are cash flows if the company does not go ahead with the project?

What is the difference in these cash flows?

marginal or **incremental cash flow** the additional cash flow that results from a capital budgeting decision, generated by a new project

In other words, we need to determine each **marginal** or **incremental cash flow** arising from capital budgeting decisions. For example, suppose a company is purchasing equipment that replaces existing equipment. Not only do we consider the cost of the new equipment, but we also consider any cash flows when we dispose of the existing equipment.

What about taxes?

When a company introduces a new product, when it replaces equipment with more efficient equipment, or when it buys physical assets that it will sell at some future point in time, there are likely to be effects of these decisions on the taxable income of the company. Because changes in taxable income result in changes in taxes and, hence cash flows, we need to estimate any and all tax implications for a project's cash flows.

There is also the possibility that tax credits are available for specific capital projects. Periodically throughout the past 50 years, tax credits on investments in capital projects have been available to companies for U.S. federal tax purposes. An investment tax credit is a direct reduction of the company's tax bill at the time the investment is made, which can significantly affect the initial cash outlay for a project.[1]

Using Tax Credits to Compete | GLOBAL PERSPECTIVE

European countries compete for companies to locate within their boundaries. For example, France offers a reimbursement of research and depreciation expenses (through a tax credit) of 40 percent the first year, 35 percent the second year, and 30 percent thereafter up to €100 million, with the possibility of doubling the credit for public-sector research.[2] The goal is to garner jobs and share of investment in Europe by companies in other countries, notably India and China.[3]

Therefore, we when we estimate cash flows, we do this considering any effect on taxes; hence, our goal is to estimate the project's after-tax cash flows. What happens when we apply the net present value or the internal rate of return techniques to analyze these cash flows? We use the project's cost of capital which is on an after-tax basis.[4]

BOTTOM LINE: *Any taxes arising from a project are included in the project's cash flows.*

What about any effect on other products of the company?

Consider a company that is thinking about introducing a new product line that is expected to generate $100,000 per year in additional after-tax cash flows. The introduction of this new product line, however, will likely affect the sales of another product of the same company; more precisely, introducing the new product will cost the company $40,000 in after-tax cash flows as a result of lost sales for an existing product. The $40,000 is the result of cannibalization; **cannibalization** is when a new product competes with, and therefore affects, the sales of another product of the same company. In this example, the incremental cash flows that we use in evaluating the new product line are $60,000 per year (i.e., $100,000 – $40,000).

BOTTOM LINE: *If a proposed capital project would affect the cash flows of other products of the company, the effect on these other products must be considered as part of the determination of the relevant cash flows.*

cannibalization competition of a new product with an existing product of the same company, resulting in diminished sales of the existing product

What if the project affects levels of working capital?

Working capital consists of the short-term assets and liabilities that support the day-to-day operations of a company, including cash, accounts receivable, inventory, or accounts payable. Many capital projects require adjustments in a company's working capital. For example, consider a company that is evaluating a new production process. The process requires the company to hold additional inventory on hand, which would tie up more funds and is reflected in the company's level of working capital. This represents a drain of cash that

[1] In 2011, these credits were limited, for the most part, to alternative fuel production, employment of targeted groups, and research and development. Historically, however, the U.S. has had in place, at different points in time, tax credits for capital spending up to 10 percent of the investment.

[2] Source: *Innovation Comes First*, www.invest-in-france.org.

[3] 2010 Report Job-Creating Foreign Investment in France, investinfrance.org.

[4] We discuss this in more detail later in the chapter.

should be considered in the capital budgeting decision because any funds that are tied up have an associated cost. Of course, another company could be considering a process that requires the company to hold lower amounts of inventory on hand, and this would represent a source of funds for the company, which should also be considered in evaluating the implementation of that process.

The change in working capital affects cash flows: Increases in working capital are decreases in cash flows, and vice versa. A capital project could result in the increase or decrease in any of the working capital accounts. Manufacturing a new product may require having more raw materials on hand (hence, a larger investment in inventory), but replacing existing production line equipment with more efficient machinery may result in having less work-in-process (hence, lowering the investment in inventory). An expansion involving more retail outlets may increase the company's need for cash on hand, as well as inventory on the shelves.

Another reason why we adjust for working capital changes is that we need to adjust for the actual flow of funds. To see how this works, consider a sale to a customer on credit. When the sale is made, there is no effect on cash; cash is not affected until the account is collected:

	Balance Sheet Effect		Income Statement Effect			
Event	Inventory	Accounts Receivable	Sales	Cost of Goods Sold	Net Profit	Cash
Sale of goods on account	↓	↑	↑	↑	↑	No effect
Collect on account		↓				↑

By adjusting for the change in the working capital accounts, we are adjusting for the effect on cash: When the accounts receivable decreases, cash comes into the business from the sale, but not before that time. Considering the different working capital accounts, the adjustment we make in the analysis depends on whether the account is an asset or a liability:

	Effect on Cash Flow of an ...	
Working Capital Account	... Increase in the Account	... Decrease in the Account
Cash	−	+
Accounts receivable	−	+
Inventory	−	+
Accounts payable	+	−

A particularly tricky aspect of dealing with working capital changes is that we always return the company's working capital to the original levels by the end of the project's life. Again, this harks back to the idea that we are looking at how different cash flows are with and without the project. If a project has a useful life of 5 years, this means that after 5 years, the working capital levels should return to the preproject levels.

We often simplify the world when we devise capital budgeting problems that involve working capital changes; we assume that working capital increases abruptly at the beginning of the life of the project and then returns to its preproject levels just as abruptly at the end of the life of the project. A more realistic situation is that working capital changes gradually over the project's life.

BOTTOM LINE: We need to adjust cash flows, particularly the investment cash flow and the terminal cash flow at the end of the estimated project life, to reflect any additional working capital requirements that are associated with the project.

What about sunk costs?

If the company has made an expenditure prior to the decision of whether to invest in a capital project, this expenditure is not relevant to the investment decision; it is a sunk cost. A **sunk cost** is any cost that has been incurred prior to the capital project decision, and these sunk costs are not included in the capital project decision.

sunk costs costs that have already been incurred, cannot be recovered, and should not influence current capital budgeting decisions

You also should ignore sunk costs because the focus of capital budgeting is with *future* cash flows. Suppose a company has spent $50,000 to try to get a project up and running. If something happens to make the project undesirable, the company should not proceed any further; otherwise, it will simply be "throwing good money after bad." In other words, it should accept the $50,000 loss, which makes more sense than losing another $100,000 on the project. Obviously, this is easier said than done.

Other examples of sunk costs include research and development, marketing research, and engineering costs that result in the product idea or develop the estimates for the analysis of the capital project. But what about the use of assets, such as land and buildings, that a company already owns? Suppose, for example, the company bought land 10 years ago for $10 million and has no other use for it. If the company then wants to use this land for a capital project, this $10 million is a sunk cost and therefore does not enter the cash flow analysis for the capital project.

BOTTOM LINE: If the expenditure has already been made, we do not consider this in the cash flow analysis for a capital project.

What about foregone opportunities?

Although sunk costs are irrelevant, we do need to factor **opportunity costs** into cash flow estimates. Opportunity costs represent cash flows that must be forgone as a result of an investment decision. We use the following example to distinguish between sunk costs and opportunity costs. Consider a company that purchased a piece of land several years ago for $150,000. Today, the company is deciding whether or not to use the land as the location for a new storage facility. In this situation, the original outlay of $150,000 is a sunk cost and should be ignored. However, the land cannot be considered "free" because the company always has the option of using it for another purpose or selling it. Assuming the company could sell this land today at a market price of $200,000, this would represent the opportunity cost of using the land for the storage facility; as such, it should be included in the cost of the project.

opportunity costs cash flow that must be forgone as a result of an investment decision

Consider another example. Suppose a company has a building that it purchased 5 years ago for $500 million. And suppose that the company has decided to use a third of this building for the processing of its food product. If the company has no other use for this portion of the building, the cost of the building is a sunk cost and not part of the analysis of the new food product. However, if the company could have rented out that portion of the building for, say, $50 million per year, this $50 million is a foregone cash flow and must be included in the analysis of the new food product.

BOTTOM LINE: Opportunity costs that represent foregone cash flows should be included in the cash flow analysis of a capital project.

What about financing costs?

We do not include associated interest and dividend payments in estimated project cash flows because we account for these in the project's cost of capital; to affect cash flows with these costs would result in double-counting these costs.

When evaluating a project using the net present value, the project's cost of capital is the discount rate applied to the project's cash flows; in the case of evaluating a project using the internal rate of return, the costs of financing the project are captured in the project's cost of capital, which is used as a hurdle rate when compared to the project's internal rate of return.

BOTTOM LINE: Financing costs do not affect the cash flows of a project.

What about benefit or harm to unrelated, third parties?

Also to be ignored are **externalities**. Externalities are the consequences that often result from an investment that may benefit or harm unrelated third parties. An example is a project that generates employment in a depressed region. Although there are intangible benefits for the community and the company, we do not include these in the project's cash flows. Another example is any environmental damage that may occur as a result of a capital project. Any direct costs, such as the cost of mitigation or pollution control devices, would be included in the cash flows of the project because they would be necessary costs related to the investment. In this case, they are not externalities, but rather are costs of the project. Intangible effects, however, would be difficult, if not impossible, to estimate and are not included in the cash flow estimates.

BOTTOM LINE: Costs related to externalities are not considered in a project's cash flows.

What else?

Capital project analysis is challenging primarily because each capital project is unique. Therefore, financial managers must be on the watch for any other cash flow and value effects from a particular capital project.

For example, consider the effect of all project interdependencies on cash flow estimates. If a company is considering projects that are mutually exclusive, the decision to accept one of the projects precludes the acceptance of any other in the set of projects. The other extreme is that projects may be independent; that is, accepting one project would not affect any other project's cash flows. But more realistic situations often include interdependencies.

Consider that companies are, basically, portfolios of projects. A consumer product company, for example, may have many products that are related and may affect each other. If the company has toothpaste products, it also may have floss and mouthwash products. The promotion and sharing of brands and promotions will cause new products to potentially affect existing products, producing cannibalization, as we discussed earlier. But there is also the potential for contingent projects, in which one project's cash flows depend on another project. This includes such contingencies as tie-ins for toys and movies and software and apps for specific operating systems.

Another consideration is that most projects have real options. A **real option** is an opportunity associated with a real asset. Like any other option, a real option is the right, but not the obligation, to undertake an action. Examples of real options include the option to delay a project, the option to abandon a project, or the option to expand a project. For example, the option to delay or wait on a project may provide time for some uncertainties in the economy or regulation to be resolved, providing more certainty in the amount and timing of a project's cash flows. Though difficult to estimate their contribution to a project's value (much of which is beyond the scope of this book), these options are valuable. Our goal in this chapter is to discuss and demonstrate how financial managers estimate cash flows for a project. We reserve the discussion of real options to Appendix 11B.

BOTTOM LINE: Each capital project is unique.

externalities consequences that result from an investment that may benefit or harm unrelated third parties

real option opportunity associated with a real asset, such as the opportunity to delay, abandon, or expand

Concept Review Questions

1. Why do we not deduct interest costs from the cash flows to be discounted?
2. Distinguish between a sunk cost and an opportunity cost. What is an example of each?

11.2 ESTIMATING CASH FLOWS

Sometimes it is convenient to distinguish among three different categories of cash flows and estimate each type of cash flow separately. We discuss each category of cash flow next: the investment cash flow, operating cash flows, and terminal after-tax cash flows.

Considering the cash flows for a project in broad terms, we diagram these in Figure 11-1. We start with the initial investment at the beginning of the project, generate operating cash flows throughout the life of the project, and may have terminal cash flows as we close out the project. The sum of these cash flows for any given year is the net cash flow. Our goal is to estimate the net cash flow for each year in the project's life.[5]

> **SUMMARIZING: WHAT TO DO ABOUT WORKING CAPITAL**
>
> Working capital changes are important to include in the analysis because they help us adjust for the timing of cash receipts, but also capture the opportunity cost of investing in working capital.
>
> Whether you include the cash flow effects from working capital changes in investment cash flows, operating cash flows, and/or terminal cash flows depends on the individual project's scenario. For example, if working capital changes only at the beginning and end of a project, it is easiest to collect these with the investment and terminal cash flows. If, however, working capital changes along with the changes in operations during the life of the project, it is probably easiest to group these with the operating cash flows. The key is not how you classify cash flows from changes in working capital, but rather getting the amount and timing correct.

The Investment Cash Flow

The **investment cash flow** is the total cash outlay that is required to initiate an investment project. Because the investment cash flow often occurs at the beginning of the project, we also refer to this as the **initial cash flow** or **initial cash outlay**. It is the cost of the plant

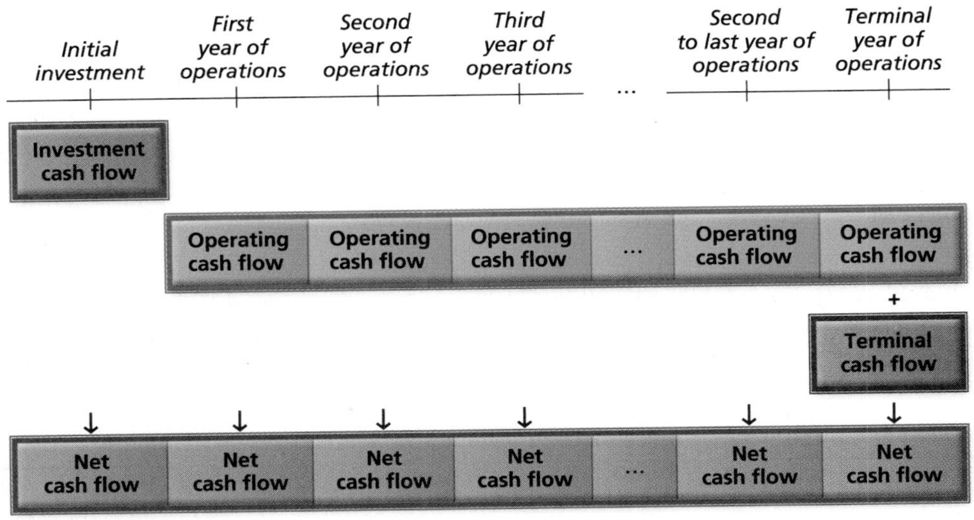

investment cash flow or **initial cash flow** or **initial cash outlay** total cash outlay required to initiate an investment project, including the change in net working capital and associated opportunity costs

FIGURE 11-1 **Typical Project Cash Flows**

[5] We simplify things by assuming that the cash flows only occur at the end of each year. The reason we do this in explaining capital budgeting is to illustrate the approach and techniques. A more realistic analysis would likely involve monthly cash flows and would require more complexity in analyzing the cash flows using the techniques of net present value and internal rate of return, for example.

capital cost cost incurred to make an investment operational, such as machinery installation expenses, land-clearing costs, and so on

or equipment associated with the project, which we call the **capital cost** of an investment, and includes all costs incurred to make an investment operational, such as machinery installation expenses, land-clearing costs, and so on. In most cases, the capital costs are depreciated for tax purposes.

The initial after-tax cash flow includes other cash flows, such as the change in net working capital and any other associated opportunity costs or cash flows. Each capital project has its own specific cash flows at the beginning of the investment decision, but we can generalize these based on a new project and a replacement project:

	New Project	*Replacement project*
	Capital cost	Capital cost
Less	Change in working capital	Change in working capital
Less	Opportunity costs	Opportunity costs
Plus	Tax credits	Tax credits
Plus		Proceeds from sale of replaced equipment
Less		Taxes related to sale of replaced equipment
Equals	Investment cash flow	Investment cash flow

The key to the estimation of the investment cash flow is to make sure that you are consistent in the signs of the flows. Consider an example. The Brennan Co. is evaluating the proposed acquisition of a new milling machine. The machine's base price is $625,000, and it would cost another $25,000 to modify it for special use by the company. The company will need to maintain additional raw materials inventory of $100,000 to use the machine. Brennan Co.'s marginal tax rate is 35 percent. What is the company's associated after-tax cash outlay?

$$\text{Capital cost} = \$625,000 + 25,000 = \$650,000$$

$$\text{Investment cash flow} = -\$650,000 - 100,000 + 0 = -\$750,000$$

Note that the cost of the capital asset is not just the $625,000 purchase price, but also all other cash outlays that are needed to get the equipment operational. In this case, the $25,000 in modifications must be capitalized and then depreciated over the life of the machine because, just like the equipment, these modifications generate benefits over the life of the equipment. Generally, in any analysis, costs have to be divided into capitalized costs and expenses. In most tax systems, anything that generates future benefits is capitalized, and then the value is expensed through depreciation expenses over future periods. In contrast, costs that generate no future benefits can be expensed immediately and so are immediately tax deductible.

EXAMPLE 11.1

Investment Cash Flows

PROBLEM

Consider an investment that requires the purchase of equipment for $1 million and decreases working capital by $0.2 million. The company must spend $0.1 million to install the equipment. What is the investment cash flow for this investment?

Solution

Investment cash flow = –$1 million + $0.2 million – $0.1 million = –$0.9 million.

operating cash flows cash flows that are estimated to occur as a result of the investment decision, comprising the associated expected incremental increase in after-tax operating cash flow

Operating Cash Flows

The **operating cash flow** in a given period t is the incremental operating cash flow, attributed to the operations of the project's investments. In other words, these are the after-tax operating cash flows associated with the project. These cash flows comprise the associated expected incremental increase in after-tax operating income (i.e., the operating cash flows), as well as any incremental tax savings or additional taxes paid in future years that result from the initial investment outlay. The tax savings are associated with the additional depreciation expenses that may be charged for tax purposes as a result of the initial investment.

The amount of depreciation charged for tax purposes is prescribed by U.S. tax law according to the rates prescribed in the **Modified Accelerated Cost Recovery System (MACRS)** for the asset's classified life. There are two important aspects of MACRS. First, the depreciable life of an asset for tax purposes is determined by reference to the tax code; the company does not choose the depreciable life, but rather looks it up. The possible depreciable lives are 3, 5, 7, 10, 15, or 20 years for most property other than real estate. For example, if the company buys a truck, it is classified as 5-year property for tax purposes no matter how long it will be depreciated for financial reporting purposes. Second, MACRS consists of a set of rates applied against the depreciable basis (that is, the capital cost) that are based on declining balance methods 200 percent declining balance for 3-, 5-, 7-, and 10-year assets and 150 percent declining balance for 15- and 20-year assets. Real property is depreciated over 27.5 years or 39 years straight-line depreciation under MACRS, depending on the type, though land is never depreciated.

We summarize the MACRS rates in Table 11-1 for the MACRS lives up to 15 years.[6] Because of the use of a half-year convention, the asset is not fully depreciated—that is, its book value for tax purposes is equal to zero—after 1 year beyond its classified life.[7] For example, if the asset is a 3-year asset, it is fully depreciated after 4 years.

TABLE 11-1 MACRS Rates

Tax rates are effective rate, which are applied against the original cost of the asset

Year	3-year	5-year	7-year	10-year	15-year
1	33.33%	20.00%	14.29%	10.00%	5.00%
2	44.45%	32.00%	24.49%	18.00%	9.50%
3	14.81%	19.20%	17.49%	14.40%	8.55%
4	7.41%	11.52%	12.49%	11.52%	7.70%
5		11.52%	8.93%	9.22%	6.93%
6		5.76%	8.92%	7.37%	6.23%
7			8.93%	6.55%	5.90%
8			4.46%	6.55%	5.90%
9				6.56%	5.91%
10				6.55%	5.90%
11				3.28%	5.91%
12					5.90%
13					5.91%
14					5.90%
15					5.91%
16					2.95%

Rates are those assuming the half-year convention is applied.

[6] The MACRS depreciation is sometimes referred to as the capital cost allowance or cost recovery. See Department of the Treasury, Internal Revenue Service's *Publication 946: How to Depreciate Property* for details on the MACRS system.
[7] For tax purposes, a company may also use a midquarter convention. However, in the interest of keeping the tax depreciation explanation as simple as possible, we are demonstrating MACRS depreciation using the more common half-year convention.

Because depreciation is a noncash expense and we are trying to estimate cash flows, we have two ways to deal with it. The first approach is to deduct the change in depreciation from the change in operating income, then deduct the associated taxes, and finally add the change in depreciation expense back because it is a noncash expense. The second approach is to recognize that depreciation creates tax savings for the company in the amount of the change in depreciation multiplied by the company's marginal tax rate. We refer to this tax savings as the **depreciation tax shield** because the deduction of depreciation to arrive at taxable income shields some income from taxation. We then add this amount to the change in after-tax operating income, which is determined by deducting the taxes associated with the company's before-tax operating income.

We show these two approaches in Table 11-2. This may look complicated on the surface, but Approach 1 is, basically, the income statement for the incremental cash flows, with the noncash charge of depreciation added back to the incremental income to arrive at the cash flow. Approach 2 isolates the depreciation effect by separating the effects of a change in operating income and changes in depreciation. Does it matter which approach you use? Not at all. Which is easier to use? It depends on the problem at hand.

depreciation tax shield tax savings associated with the depreciation deduction for tax purposes, which is the amount of the depreciation expense multiplied by the marginal tax rate

TABLE 11-2 Two Ways to Determine Cash Flows

Approach 1		*Approach 2*	
	Change in revenues		Change in revenues
Less	Change in expenses	*Less*	Change in expenses
Less	Change in depreciation	*Equals*	Change in EBITDA
Equals	Change in taxable income	*Less*	Change in taxes payable
Less	Change in taxes	*Equals*	Change in after-tax operating income
Equals	Change in after-tax income	*Plus*	Change in depreciation tax shield
Plus	Change in depreciation	*Equals*	Operating cash flow
Equals	Operating cash flow		

With respect to the milling machine purchase that Brennan Co. is considering, the company's production department anticipates the machine will generate an additional $525,000 per year in annual operating revenue, whereas the associated annual operating expenses are projected to be $325,000 per year. The economic life of the machine is expected to be 5 years. What is the annual after-tax cash flow for each year?

For each of the 5 years, the change in operating income before depreciation is equal to the change in revenues less the change in operating expenses, or $525,000 – $325,000 = $200,000. The change in operating income before depreciation is the change in EBITDA— earnings before interest, taxes, depreciation, and amortization. Under MACRS, the depreciation for each year is generally different for each year because the tax systems allow the use of an accelerated depreciation system. For example, in the U.S. tax system, the rates for most assets are based on a 200DB system with a half-year convention. The details do not really matter—other than knowing that the rates are different for each year and are applied against the original cost—because the rates prescribed and presented in the tax code are the effective depreciation rates.[8]

---

[8] Consider depreciation that is based on 200DB, with a half-year convention, for a 5-year MACRS asset. 200DB indicates that the annual rate applied to the carrying value (original cost less accumulated depreciation) is what it would be under straight-line, multiplied by 2. The depreciation rate for the second year based on 200DB would be 20% x 2 = 40% of the asset's carrying value. The carrying value is 1 – 0.20, or 80% of the original cost. Therefore, the effective rate is 0.40 x 0.80 = 32%. The 32% is what is reported in the tax cost and is applied against the original cost of the asset.

Looking up the rates for a 5-year asset, and applying these rates to the asset cost of $650,000, we estimate the 5 years of depreciation and the book value of the assets for tax purposes:

Year	Asset Cost	MACRS Rate	Depreciation Expense	Book Value for Tax Purposes
1	$650,000	20.00%	$130,000	$520,000
2	$650,000	32.00%	$208,000	$312,000
3	$650,000	19.20%	$124,800	$187,200
4	$650,000	11.52%	$74,880	$112,320
5	$650,000	11.52%	$74,880	$37,440

We estimate the book value of the asset for tax purposes (that is, the undepreciated cost of the asset) because if the company sells the asset at any time before it is fully depreciated, this book or carrying value is used to compute any gain or loss.

Combining these estimates with the company's tax rate of 35 percent, we can estimate the project's operating cash flow for each year as follows:

Approach 1		Year 1	Year 2	Year 3	Year 4	Year 5
	Change in revenues	$525,000	$525,000	$525,000	$525,000	$525,000
Less	Change in expenses	325,000	325,000	325,000	325,000	325,000
Less	Change in depreciation	130,000	208,000	124,800	74,880	74,880
Equals	Change in taxable income	$70,000	$8,000	$75,200	$125,120	$125,120
Less	Change in taxes	24,500	2,800	26,320	43,792	43,792
Equal:	Change in after-tax income	$45,500	$5,200	$48,880	$81,328	$81,328
Plus	Change in depreciation	130,000	208,000	124,800	74,880	74,880
Equals	Operating cash flow	$175,500	$202,800	$173,680	$156,208	$156,208

Approach 2		Year 1	Year 2	Year 3	Year 4	Year 5
	Change in revenues	$525,000	$525,000	$525,000	$525,000	$525,000
Less	Change in expenses	325,000	325,000	325,000	325,000	325,000
Equals	Change in EBITDA	$200,000	$200,000	$200,000	$200,000	$200,000
Less	Change in taxes payable	70,000	70,000	$70,000	$70,000	$70,000
Equals:	Change in after-tax operating income	$130,000	$130,000	$130,000	$130,000	$130,000
Plus:	Change in depreciation tax shield	45,500	72,800	43,680	26,208	26,208
Equals:	Operating cash flow	$175,500	$202,800	$173,680	$156,208	$156,208

A few observations from this analysis:

1. The use of a declining balance method for depreciation with a half-year convention means that the asset is not fully depreciated at the end of its useful life, which is 5 years in this example. Therefore, in this example, if the company disposes of the asset at the end of 5 years, the asset will have a book value of 5.76% of $650,000 or $37,440, which must be considered when calculating terminal cash flows.

2. Depreciation expense is lower in Year 1 because of the half-year rule, then is the highest in Year 2 and declines thereafter.

3. No matter which of the approaches you use, you get the same operating cash flows.

In this example, we estimated the future cash flows without considering what happens to the machine at the end of its useful economic life. There are often cash flows in the last year that relate to selling or disposing of the asset and returning working capital to its preproject level. In some cases, there may also be expenses related to mitigating the site because of the environmental impact of the project.

EXAMPLE 11.2

Depreciation Tax Shield

PROBLEM

Suppose an asset is classified as a 3-year asset for tax purposes, but has a useful life of 5 years. If the asset has an initial cost of $1 million, what is the depreciation tax shield for each year in the asset's useful life if the tax rate is 40 percent?

Solution

	Year 1	Year 2	Year 3	Year 4	Year 5
MACRS rate	33.33%	44.45%	14.81%	7.41%	0%
Deprecation	$333,300	$444,500	$148,100	$74,100	$0
Tax rate	40%	40%	40%	40%	40%
Deprecation tax shield	$133,320	$177,800	$59,240	$29,640	$0

EXAMPLE 11.3

Operating Cash Flows

PROBLEM

Consider an investment in equipment that does not affect revenues, but reduces expenses. The equipment costs $5 million and is classified as a 3-year asset for tax purposes. The investment does not affect working capital, but it is expected to reduce expenses by $1 million for each of the next 5 years. Once the 5 years are up, the equipment will be worthless and will be scrapped at no cost to the company. If the company's tax rate is 40 percent, what is the operating cash flow for each year of this asset's life?

Solution

Without Effect of Depreciation		Year 1	Year 2	Year 3	Year 4	Year 5
	Change in expenses	$1.00	$1.00	$1.00	$1.00	$1.00
Less	Change in taxes	$0.40	$0.40	$0.40	$0.40	$0.40
Equals	Change in after-tax income	$0.60	$0.60	$0.60	$0.60	$0.60

Effect of Depreciation						
	Change in depreciation	$1.67	$2.22	$0.74	$0.37	$0.00
Multiplied by	Tax rate	40%	40%	40%	40%	40%
Equals	Change in depreciation tax shield	$0.67	$0.89	$0.30	$0.15	$0.00
Summing the change in after-tax income and the change in the depreciation tax shield						
Equals	Operating cash flow	$1.49	$0.90	$0.75	$0.60	$0.60

Terminal Cash Flows

The **terminal cash flow** or **ending cash flow** is the project's cash flow expected in the terminal year of a project, aside from that year's operating cash flow, as determined earlier. It comprises the estimated selling or **salvage value** of the asset.[9]

The salvage value is the estimate of the value of the asset at the end of its useful life; it is, in effect, the estimate of the selling price of the asset at the end of the project. The sale of an asset at the end of the project's life may have tax consequences. First, if the selling price is greater than the original capital cost, a capital gain arises, which is taxable. If a depreciable capital asset is sold below its book value for tax purposes, it generates a capital loss.

Aside from capital gains and losses, additional tax consequences can arise. In particular, depreciation recapture may be generated by the sale of an asset. Under this scenario, the company would have to pay additional taxes on "excess" depreciation charged against the asset or assets if the salvage value is greater than the ending tax book value of the asset. The amount by which the salvage value exceeds the book or carrying value is fully taxable as ordinary income.[10] However, if the salvage value is less than the ending book value, the amount by which the book value exceeds the salvage value is called a terminal loss, which is fully tax deductible.[11] Finally, depreciation recapture may occur if an asset is sold for more than its book value of that asset for tax purposes.

terminal (or ending) cash flow total cash flow expected to be generated in the terminal year of a project, aside from that year's operating cash flow

salvage value estimated sale price of an asset at the end of its useful life

Sell the Asset ...	Capital Gain or Loss	Recapture of Depreciation
for more than the original cost	Salvage value – Original cost = Gain	Original cost – Book value = Recapture
for less than the original cost, but more than the book value	None	Salvage value – Book value = Recapture
for less than the book value	Carrying value – Salvage value = Loss	None

SUMMARIZING: GAIN, LOSS, OR RECAPTURE ON THE SALE OF AN ASSET

Generally, capital gains are rare for depreciable capital assets because these assets typically cannot be sold for more than their original cost after they are put in use. The recapture of depreciation, however, is common because the MACRS rates are likely more accelerated than the actual deterioration of the asset.

[9] In financial accounting, the salvage value is important in the calculation of the depreciation. For tax accounting purposes, salvage value is ignored in the calculation of depreciation. We do not ignore salvage value in the analysis of cash flow for a capital project because this is our best guess of what the company can sell the asset for at the end of the project.

[10] In other words, it is viewed as if the firm charged too much depreciation because the asset is sold for more than its depreciated book value for tax purposes. Therefore, the firm must pay back the amount of taxes it saved by charging too much depreciation.

[11] In this instance, the firm did not charge enough depreciation because the asset was sold below its book value for tax purposes. Therefore, it is permitted to depreciate the asset to its selling price and deduct this charge for tax purposes.

In addition to the salvage value and all the associated tax complications, the working capital associated with the project will be returned to preproject levels, which may represent a cash inflow or outflow. This means that the people to whom you have extended credit will pay off the debts once the project is finished, and all inventory on hand will be sold, so that the net amount after the company has paid its suppliers is available to finance other projects.

We can estimate the ending cash flow with tax implications:

	Estimated selling price of the asset
Less	Taxes on sale
Plus	Change in working capital
Equals	Terminal cash flow

Regarding the project being considered by Brennan Co., the production department estimated that the $100,000 in additional net working capital requirements will be released after the economic life of the machine; therefore, the change in working capital is −$100,000, and the cash flow from this change is +$100,000.[12] Management estimates that at the end of 5 years, the milling machine can be sold for $37,440. What are the terminal cash flow and the present value of this ending cash flow?

Notice in this example that there are no capital gains and no depreciation recapture because the asset is sold for its carrying value of $37,440. Therefore, we can estimate the terminal cash flows as:

$$\text{Terminal cash flow} = \$37,440 + \$100,000 = \$137,440$$

EXAMPLE 11.4

Disposition of an Asset

PROBLEM

Suppose a company has equipment that had an original cost of $10 million, and it sells this equipment 6 years later for $2 million. If the carrying value of this equipment for tax purposes is $1 million, what is the cash flow associated with the sale of this equipment? The company's marginal tax rate is 35 percent.

Solution

Cash flows:
Sale price of $2 million
Tax on recapture of depreciation: $0.35 \times (\$2 - 1) = \$0.35$ million
Cash flow associated with the sale = $\$2 - 0.35 = \$1.65$ million

---

Assembling the Pieces

There are three basic pieces that we have to fit together to evaluate a project:

1. Investment cash flow
2. Operating cash flows
3. Terminal cash flow

The investment cash flow is an outlay that may occur at the beginning of the project or may be spread over several periods, depending on the project. For example, if a company is building a new plant, the outlays may span 2 or 3 years. What is important is to make sure to get the timing of these cash flows correct.

The operating cash flows may be positive or negative, but when we are working with a typical project, these are often positive. When might operating cash flows be

---

[12] This means that the change in working capital provides a cash inflow of +$100,000 as this working capital is reduced.

negative? Examples include when there is a lag between the start-up of the project and revenues, when there are operating expenses that are larger in the beginning of the life of the project that diminish as learning occurs, and when competitors enter the market and the revenues for the product diminish significantly, but operating expenses do not.

The terminal cash flow may be positive or negative. If assets are sold at the end of the project, there is often a positive cash flow after considering taxes on any gain. If remediation of a site is necessary to satisfy environmental laws and regulations, for example, a company may have a significant negative cash flow in the final year.

For each period in a project's life, we sum the cash flows to produce the net cash flow for each period in the life of the project. What are the net cash flows associated with Brennan Co.'s project? Let's assemble the cash flows that we have estimated.

	Initially	Year 1	Year 2	Year 3	Year 4	Year 5
Investment cash flow	−$750,000					
Operating cash flow		$175,500	$202,800	$173,680	$156,208	$156,208
Terminal cash flow						137,440
Net cash flow	−$750,000	$175,500	$202,800	$173,680	$156,208	$293,648

Should Brennan accept or reject this project? This is where the capital budgeting techniques, such as the net present value and internal rate of return, enter the analysis.

Once you have calculated the net cash flow for each year of a project's life, you can apply the capital budgeting techniques to these cash flows to evaluate whether a project is acceptable. Let's apply several of the techniques from Chapter 10 to the Brennan example, assuming a project cost of capital of 9 percent.

Net present value	$17,327.44
Internal rate of return	9.84%
Profitability index	1.02
Payback period	5 years
Discounted payback period	5 years

Therefore, Brennan's capital project is acceptable: It is expected to add value, as indicated by the net present value, and its return exceeds what is required for the project's level of risk (that is, 9 percent).

SUMMARIZING: CONNECTING THE CASH FLOWS WITH THE CAPITAL BUDGETING TECHNIQUES

Because we are working with estimates of what may happen next year, the year after, and on until the expected end of the life of the project, we may want examine the sensitivity of the project's cash flows to the inputs, as we discuss in the next section.

Concept Review Questions

1. Why does the investment cash flow often exceed the purchase price of an asset?

2. How do taxes affect the annual cash flows and terminal cash flows of an investment project?

3. If a project is expected to increase the level of inventories, how does this affect cash flows?

LESSONS LEARNED | Tax Breaks Don't Boost Investment: Study

From 2001 to 2003, 25 companies with big tax breaks cut their capital investments by 22 percent, advocacy group finds.

In an ideal world, tax breaks provide an incentive to companies to plow large sums of money into new plants, equipment, research, people and other things that could spur growth in their businesses and the economy at large.

Alas, it doesn't work out so neatly. Or so a study of 275 profitable Fortune 500 companies by the Citizens for Tax Justice (CTJ) and the Institute on Taxation and Economic Policy (ITEP) suggests. Large tax breaks don't necessarily move corporations to invest more, the report's authors contend.

The study found that 82 companies paid no federal income tax in at least one year during the first three years of the current Bush administration. Indeed, the companies generated so much in the way of excess tax breaks that they received outright federal tax rebates totaling $12.6 billion. In other words, they made more after taxes than before taxes in those no-tax years, the report's authors note.

Further, in 2002 and 2003, the 275 companies sheltered more than half of their profits from tax, according to the report. (The Web site of CTJ, a 501(c)(4) advocacy group, lists "closing corporate tax loopholes" as one of its goals; ITEP refers to itself as "a non-profit, non-partisan research and education organization that works on government taxation and spending policy issues.")

Did companies at least use these enormous tax breaks to invest in their businesses and boost their long-term prospects? Not really, the study suggests. Just seven of the 25 companies with the largest total tax breaks from all sources over the three years increased capital investment from 2001 to 2003, according to the report.

Indeed, the 25 companies in the survey with the biggest total tax breaks cut their capital investments from 2001 to 2003 by 22 percent, on average. In contrast, the remaining 250 companies in the survey reduced their investments by 13 percent.

What's more, just seven of the 25 companies with the largest tax breaks hiked investment over the three-year period—Citigroup, ExxonMobil, Pfizer, Altria, Wachovia, Viacom, and American Express.

The study's authors also point out that tax laws adopted in 2002 and 2003 greatly increased corporate write-offs for accelerated depreciation and made it easier for corporations to use excess tax subsidies to trigger tax rebates, at a three-year cost of $175 billion.

Although backers of such incentives argued that they would spur corporate investment in plant and equipment, "they failed to do so," the study's authors note. For example, the 25 companies that reported the largest tax savings from accelerated depreciation cut their total property and plant and equipment investments by 27 percent from 2001 to 2003, according to the report. The investments of the remaining 250 companies, on the other hand, dipped by only 8 percent.

"We do not mean to imply in our report that corporate tax breaks actively discourage capital investments," said Robert S. McIntyre, director of CTJ and co-author of the report with T.D. Coo Nguyen of ITEP. "But the evidence shows, as it has so often in the past, that business investment decisions are primarily driven by supply and demand, not by government attempts to micro-manage the economy."

The study also found that 28 companies enjoyed negative federal income tax rates over the entire 2001–03 period. Those with large negative tax rates included Pepco Holdings (–59.6 percent), Prudential Financial (–46.2 percent), ITT Industries (–22.3 percent) and Boeing (–18.8 percent).

Half of the $87.1 billion in total tax-breaks over the three years in the companies studied went to just 25 corporations, with each garnering more than $1.5 billion.

Topping the list was General Electric, with $9.5 billion in tax breaks over the three years. It was followed by SBC Communications at $9 billion and Citigroup, IBM, Microsoft, and AT&T, each with about $4.6 billion.

Stephen Taub, "Tax Breaks Don't Boost Investment: Study," CFO.com, September 24, 2004.

11.3 SENSITIVITY TO INPUTS

Much of what goes into the cash flows in the analysis are estimates. Recognizing that estimates are simply that, we may want to perform a *sensitivity analysis*, examining whether the investment is still attractive under varying conditions.

Sensitivity Analysis

Financial analysts use **sensitivity analysis** to examine how an investment's cash flows change as the value of one input is changed. This type of analysis allows companies to determine which of their estimates are the most critical in the final decision, but also provides information for risk management. Obviously, the most critical estimates require the greatest amount of scrutiny on the part of the company.

sensitivity analysis examination of how an investment's value changes as one input at a time is changed

When we use sensitivity analysis, we can examine the cash flows and decision considering one input at a time. Consider the following "what-ifs" of inputs on the Brennan project.

What if:

1. The annual operating income before depreciation is $190,000 instead of $200,000?
   This would affect the operating cash flows and, hence, net cash flows, decreasing them by $10,000 \times (1 - 0.35) = \$6,500$ each year:

	Initially	*Year 1*	*Year 2*	*Year 3*	*Year 4*	*Year 5*
Investment cash flow	−$750,000					
Operating cash flows		$169,000	$196,300	$167,180	$149,708	$149,708
Terminal cash flow						137,440
Net cash flow	−$750,000	$169,000	$196,300	$167,180	$149,708	$287,148

2. What if the asset sold for $100,000 at the end of 5 years, instead of $37,440?
   This would affect the terminal cash flow. Instead of $137,440, the cash flow would be:

$$\text{Terminal cash flows} = \underbrace{\$100,000 - 0.35\,(100,000 - 37,440)}_{\text{recapture of depreciation}} + 100,000$$

$$= \$100,000 \quad - 21,896 \quad + 100,000$$

$$= \$178,104$$

This change would change the Year 5 cash flow by $40,664, from $293,648 to $334,312.

3. What if the tax rate were 25 percent instead of 35 percent?
   This would affect the net operating cash flows each period:

	Initially	*Year 1*	*Year 2*	*Year 3*	*Year 4*	*Year 5*
Investment cash flow	−$750,000					
Operating cash flows		$182,500	$202,000	$181,200	$168,720	$168,720
Terminal cash flow						137,440
Net cash flow	−$750,000	$182,500	$202,000	$181,200	$168,720	$306,160

4. What if there is an additional change in working capital investment?
   In our initial problem, we estimated that inventory would increase by $100,000, which is then restored at the end of the project's life. What if the project requires an additional $40,000 of inventory at the end of the first year of operations, when the project is up and running? In this case, there would be an addition investment cash flow in Year 1, and the working capital recoupment in Year 5 would increase from $100,000 to $140,000, increasing the terminal cash flow to $177,440:

	Initially	Year 1	Year 2	Year 3	Year 4	Year 5
Investment cash flow	−$750,000	−$40,000				
Operating cash flow		175,500	$202,800	$173,680	$156,208	$156,208
Terminal cash flow						177,440
Net cash flow	−$750,000	$135,500	$202,800	$173,680	$156,208	$333,648

SUMMARIZING: SENSITIVITY TO ACCEPTABILITY OF PROJECT TO "WHAT-IFS"

We can use the "what-ifs" to examine the acceptability of a project. Consider Brennan's capital project, using a 9 percent project cost of capital, and the four "what-ifs" that we discuss briefly:

	Base Case	Change in Operating Income	Change in Asset Selling Price	Change in Tax Rate	Change in Working Capital
Net present value	$17,327.44	−$7,955.29	$43,756.25	$45,878.69	$6,627.45
Internal rate of return	9.84%	8.61%	11.05%	11.18%	9.30%
Profitability index	1.02	0.99	1.06	1.06	1.01
Acceptable?	Yes	No	Yes	Yes	Yes

As you can see, "what-ifs" can change the acceptability of the project.

It is also informative to vary the discount rate used in the NPV calculations because this variable is hard to estimate precisely and can change substantially through time as market, industry, and company conditions change. Consider the Brennan example. We can look at the sensitivity of the project's net present value—and hence the project's acceptability—for different discount rates, as we show in Figure 11-2. The project is not acceptable at rates greater than the project's internal rate of return of 9.836 percent.

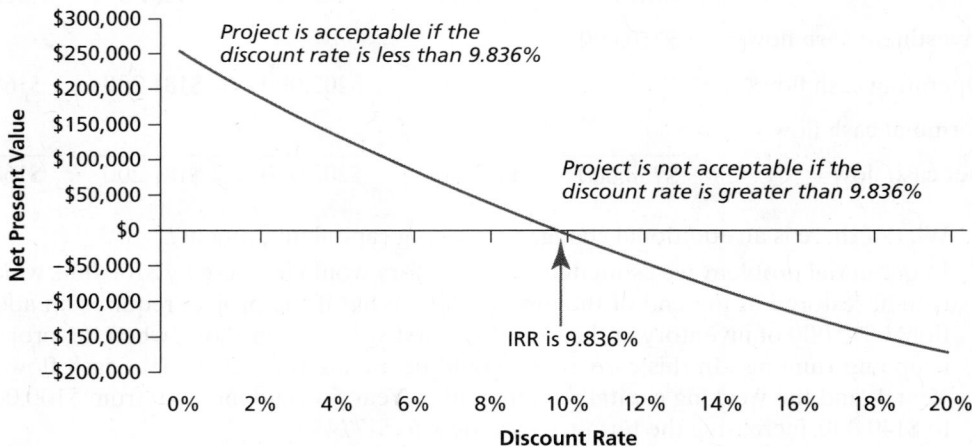

FIGURE 11-2 The Net Present Value of the Project for Different Discount Rates

Scenario Analysis

In practice, companies are dealing with estimates of future cash flows, discount rates, and so on. Because any estimate of the future is subject to error, it is often useful to examine the effect on the attractiveness of a project if one or more inputs turns out different than expected. In other words, companies may want to evaluate the acceptability of projects by using a range of estimates.

Scenario analysis is the examination of how an investment's net cash flows change in response to differing scenarios with respect to the values of one or more estimates, such as sales or costs. It often makes sense to vary more than one input variable at a time because it allows us to account for interactions among the variables and for the fact that many variables can be related to external variables, such as the overall health of the economy or the company's industry. For example, if interest rates decline, it is reasonable to assume that a company's discount rate may decline, and if the product it sells is sensitive to interest rates, it is also reasonable to assume that the operating cash flows associated with a particular capital expenditure could increase under this favorable scenario. Similarly, if the price of oil declines, this may reduce the expected operating cash flows from an investment for an oil producer. The decline in oil prices could also cause the market price of the oil producer's common shares to decline, which could increase its cost of capital.

Scenario analysis is often conducted in the form of a "what-if" analysis, but the scenarios generally involve more than one variable input. These alternatives may reflect, for example, different economic, competitive, or regulatory environments. In practice, it is common to produce a wide variety of what-if scenarios, which can be easily handled through the use of a spreadsheet program, such as Excel.

scenario analysis examination of how an investment's cash flows change in response to varying more than one input variable at a time

---

EXAMPLE 11.5

Scenario Analysis

PROBLEM

A company has a project that requires an initial after-tax cash outlay of $100,000, which is also equal to the capital cost of the assets that are purchased to get the project up and running. The asset will be depreciated as a 5-year asset according to MACRS. The company's effective tax rate is 35 percent. The company makes the following estimates.

	Worst Case	*Base Case*	*Best Case*
Project life	10 years	10 years	10 years
Discount rate	12%	10%	8%
Salvage value	$30,000	$40,000	$60,000
Operating cash flow	$10,000	$15,000	$20,000

Determine the NPV for each scenario.

Solution

Because the asset is a 5-year MACRS asset, its book value at the end of the 10th year is zero. Therefore, the salvage value represents the amount of depreciation recaptured. For example, the cash flow at the end of year 10 for the worst scenario is calculated as $10,000 + $30,000 - (0.35 \times $30,000) = $29,500$. The 10th year's cash flows for the other two scenarios are calculated in a like manner.

	Cash Flows		
Year	*Worst*	*Base*	*Best*
0	-$100,000	-$100,000	-$100,000
1	$10,000	$15,000	$20,000
2	$10,000	$15,000	$20,000

3	$10,000	$15,000	$20,000
4	$10,000	$15,000	$20,000
5	$10,000	$15,000	$20,000
6	$10,000	$15,000	$20,000
7	$10,000	$15,000	$20,000
8	$10,000	$15,000	$20,000
9	$10,000	$15,000	$20,000
10	$29,500	$41,000	$59,000
Discount rate	12%	10%	8%
NPV	−$37,219	$2,193	$52,266

Examining these three scenarios tells the company that although the project seems attractive and has significant upside, it could also turn out to be a losing proposition and is not without risk.

Suppose we are performing sensitivity analysis and assume that a project's incremental revenues are a lot less than originally anticipated, and yet we assume everything else remains the same. Let us also agree that it is unrealistic if the company does not change anything in response to this decline in revenues; a company would not stand by and watch a project deteriorate without doing anything. In practice, companies respond to changing circumstances. That is, they exercise their ability to terminate, adjust, or expand a project—all options—once the project has begun. The option to adjust a real project is a real option. A **real option** is the opportunity, but not the obligation, to undertake an action that changes the capital project. Most capital projects have one or more real options associated with them. We discuss real options in Appendix 11A, though because the mathematics and analytics are beyond the scope of this text, we only scratch the surface of real options in this appendix.

FINANCE in the News | Gas Drillers' Painful Growth Paradox

Growing, growing, gone? America's oil and gas exploration-and-production industry faces a shakeout.

The E&P sector is addicted to high growth. That is expensive: E&P capital expenditure has outstripped cash flow pretty consistently over the past decade, estimates James Murchie, founder of Energy Income Partners LLC. In contrast, Exxon Mobil, consistent winner in terms of return on capital, has reinvested just 41% in that time.

In turn, E&P capex leaves little for dividends and buybacks, meaning investors demand more growth, meaning . . . you get the idea. The model works when commodity prices are rising and capital is plentiful. But the price of natural gas—the fuel that constitutes more than two-thirds of the sector's reserves and production—has slumped on oversupply. That is what happens when every company needs superior growth rates.

Bob Gillon of consultancy IHS Herold points to a structural disadvantage as well. E&P companies' appetite for growth, especially when energy prices are rising, leaves them "having the most amount of money to spend when costs are the highest; the least to spend when costs are the lowest."

A growing realization of the challenge should curtail access to capital. Bank credit lines, predicated on the value of reserves, are being renegotiated.

Consolidation, resisted at the trough of the market, also should pick up. That would help in an industry where the largest company accounts for only 3% of production. That is one reason why U.S. natural gas is so cheap compared with OPEC-influenced oil.

Larger, better-capitalized companies would be better placed to develop America's vast gas reserves without relying on an intravenous drip of capital to fund it. Investors, in turn, could look forward to more sustainable rewards.

Liam Denning, "Gas Drillers' Painful Growth Paradox," *Wall Street Journal*, September 25, 2009.

Simulation Analysis

When examining the role of risk in a project, it is often necessary to apply statistical procedures to analyze the distribution of net cash flows when many inputs are uncertain. This form of the analysis helps us better understand the risk of a project. Let's consider the Brennan project, but look at what happens when just the EBITDA for each year is uncertain.

Suppose that the EBITDA each year has an expected value of $200,000, but is uncertain, normally distributed with a standard deviation of $25,000. To simulate the cash flows and returns on this project, we can use a spreadsheet to draw different values of EBITDA using a random number generator consistent with the distribution. Let's draw 1,000 random EBITDA for each of the 5 years. So what do we get? We get 1,000 sets of net cash flows, from which we can then calculate 1,000 different returns. We show the possible Year 1 net cash flows in Figure 11-3.

As you can see, this appears to be approximately normally distributed; if we were to draw more observations, say, 10,000, the distribution would appear even more bell shaped. With this simulation, we have a distribution of EBITDA and can then calculate a distribution of operating cash flows for each year. With this information, along with the investment and terminal cash flows, we can then estimate the net cash flows for each of the 1,000 draws. From this, we can then calculate the possible returns on this project using the internal rate of return method, as we show in Figure 11-4.

This information can then be used in evaluating the risk of the project and evaluated within the context of a company's risk tolerance. Why didn't we calculate the net present value for each draw? The net present value requires using a cost of capital that reflects the risk of the project. If we are still examining the risk of the project, we cannot determine the project cost of capital. The use of the internal rate of return provides information on the sensitivity of the project's return to the inputs and hence provides information on the project's risk.

---

1. What insights can be gained by using sensitivity analysis, scenario analysis, and simulation analysis?

2. How can a financial manager assess a project's risk using simulation analysis?

Concept Review Questions

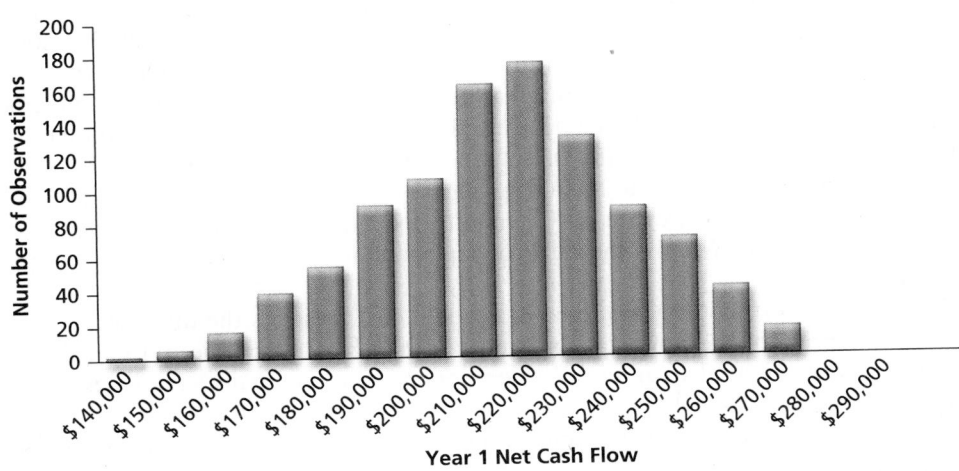

FIGURE 11-3 **Distribution of Year 1 Cash Flows for 1,000 Random Draws of EBITDA**

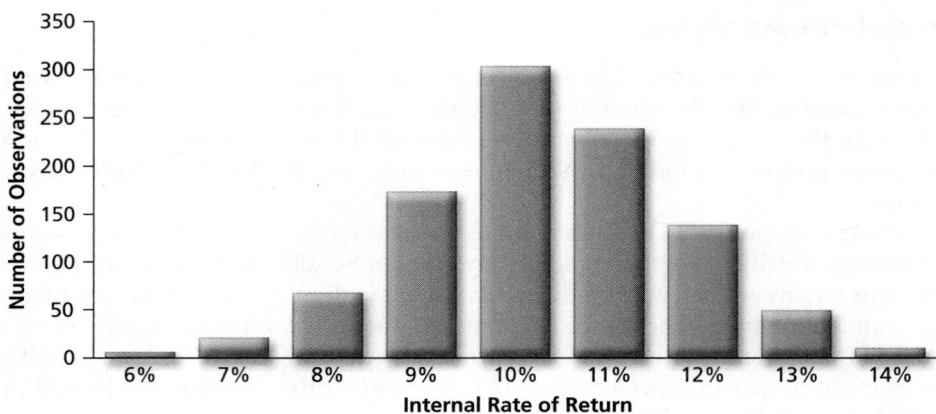

FIGURE 11-4 Distribution of Internal Rate of Returns for 1,000 Random Draws of EBITDA for Each Year

11.4 REPLACEMENT DECISIONS

Earlier in this chapter, we introduced guidelines for estimating cash flows and stated that we should focus on marginal or incremental cash flows that arise as a result of a capital budgeting decision. This refers to the additional cash flows that will be generated for the company. So far, this has been relatively easy to deal with because we have been considering **expansion projects**—that is, projects that would add something extra to the company in terms of additional sales or cost savings. For these types of projects, the new cash flows that arise from the investment decision represent incremental cash flows.

Replacement projects, as their name suggests, involve the replacement of an existing asset (or assets) with a new one. We deal with these types of decisions in the same manner as we deal with expansion problems, except that we must be more aware of focusing on incremental cash flows.

expansion projects
projects that add something extra to the company in terms of sales or cost savings

replacement projects
projects that involve the replacement of an existing asset with a new one

An Example

Suppose the Raleigh Company is considering the purchase of a new machine priced at $350,000 to replace an existing machine. The present market value of the existing machine is $50,000, and it is expected to have a salvage value of $15,000 at the end of 8 years. The existing machine was purchased 3 years ago for $300,000. Management estimates that the company will benefit from the new machine by reducing annual operating expenses by $50,000 over the life of the project, which is expected to be 8 years. This new machine is expected to have a salvage value of $100,000 at the end of 8 years. The company's marginal tax rate is 40 percent. Both machines qualify as 5-year assets for MACRS purposes. What is the NPV of replacement? Should the company replace the existing machine?

We must first estimate the incremental capital cost, which is the difference between the purchase price of the new machine and the salvage price of the old machine. The incremental capital cost also represents a component of the company's incremental initial after-tax cash outlay (ΔCF_0).

The new machine costs $350,000, but we also must consider the sale of the old machine. The old machine was purchased 3 years ago at $300,000. Therefore, the book value of the old machine after 3 years of its life is $86,400:

Year in the Life of the Old Machine	Depreciable Cost of the Old Machine	Depreciation Rate	Depreciation	End-of-period Book Value of the Old Machine
1	$300,000	20.00%	$60,000	$240,000
2	$300,000	32.00%	$96,000	$144,000
3	$300,000	19.20%	$57,600	$86,400
4	$300,000	11.52%	$34,560	$51,840
5	$300,000	11.52%	$34,560	$17,280
6	$300,000	5.76%	$17,280	$0
7	$300,000	0.00%	$0	$0
8	$300,000	0.00%	$0	$0

We therefore need to consider the gain on the sale of the old machine in our analysis. The gain is $13,600, which results in a tax on that gain of $13,600 × 0.40 = $5,440. In this example, there is no mention of opportunity costs arising or of additional working capital being tied up. Putting all this together results in an initial outlay of $255,440:

Purchase of new machine
Initial cost of new machine   −$350,000

Sale of old machine
Proceeds from sale of the old machine $100,000   100,000
Less: Book value of the old machine   86,400
Equals: Gain on the sale of the old machine $13,600
Tax on sale of old machine @ 40%   −5,440
Investment cash flow   −$255,440

Now we need to estimate the operating cash flows for each year. This requires us to estimate the change in the depreciation; that is, how is depreciation different once the new machine replaces the old machine? If depreciation is greater, this provides an increase in the depreciation tax shield; if depreciation is less, this reduces the tax shield.

The old machine is not fully depreciated, so we must compare the depreciation on the new and old machines:

	Year 1	Year 2	Year 3	Year 4	Year 5	Year 6	Year 7	Year 8
Depreciation rate—new	20.00%	32.00%	19.20%	11.52%	11.52%	5.76%	0.00%	0.00%
Depreciation rate—old	11.52%	11.52%	5.76%	0.00%	0.00%	0.00%	0.00%	0.00%

Applying these rates against the original costs of each asset, we can then calculate the change in depreciation:

	Year 1	Year 2	Year 3	Year 4	Year 5	Year 6	Year 7	Year 8
Depreciation—new	$70,000	$112,000	$67,200	$40,320	$40,320	$20,160	$0	$0
Depreciation—old	$34,560	$34,560	$17,280	$0	$0	$0	$0	$0
Change in depreciation	$35,440	$77,440	$49,920	$40,320	$40,320	$20,160	$0	$0

Considering the change in operating income and the change in depreciation, we can then calculate the operating cash flows for Raleigh's replacement project, as we show in Table 11-3.

TABLE 11-3 Operating Cash Flows for the Raleigh Replacement Decision

		Year 1	Year 2	Year 3	Year 4	Year 5	Year 6	Year 7	Year 8
	Change in EBITDA	$50,000	$50,000	$50,000	$50,000	$50,000	$50,000	$50,000	$50,000
Less:	Change in depreciation expense	35,440	77,440	49,920	40,320	40,320	20,160	0	0
Equals	Change in taxable income	$14,560	–$27,440	$80	$9,680	$9,680	$29,840	$50,000	$50,000
Less:	Change in taxes	5,824	–10,976	32	3,872	3,872	11,936	20,000	20,000
Equals	Change in after-tax income	$8,736	–$16,464	$48	$5,808	$5,808	$17,904	$30,000	$30,000
Plus:	Change in depreciation expense	35,440	77,440	49,920	40,320	40,320	20,160	0	0
Equals:	Operating cash flow	$44,176	$60,976	$49,968	$46,128	$46,128	$38,064	$30,000	$30,000

TABLE 11-4 Net Cash Flows Associated for the Raleigh Replacement Decision

		Initially	Year 1	Year 2	Year 3	Year 4	Year 5	Year 6	Year 7	Year 8
	Investment cash flow	–$255,440								
	Terminal cash flow									$21,000
	Change in EBITDA		$50,000	$50,000	$50,000	$50,000	$50,000	$50,000	$50,000	$50,000
Less	Change in depreciation		35,440	77,440	49,920	40,320	40,320	20,160	0	0
Equals	Change in taxable income		$14,560	–$27,440	$80	$9,680	$9,680	$29,840	$50,000	$50,000
Less	Change in taxes		5,824	–10,976	32	3,872	3,872	11,936	20,000	20,000
Equals	Change in after-tax income		$8,736	–16,464	$48	$5,808	$5,808	$17,904	$30,000	$30,000
Plus	Change in depreciation		35,440	77,440	49,920	40,320	40,320	20,160	0	0
Equals	Operating cash flow		$44,176	$60,976	$49,968	$46,128	$46,128	$38,064	$30,000	$30,000
	Net cash flow	–$255,440	$44,176	$60,976	$49,968	$46,128	$46,128	$38,064	$30,000	$51,000

Next, we need to estimate the incremental ending cash flow associated with the replacement decision as follows:

	Sale of new machine	$50,000	
Less:	Tax on sale	20,000	
	Net cash flow from sale of new machine		$30,000
	Foregone sale of old machine	$15,000	
	Foregone tax on sale of old machine	6,000	
Less:	Forgone cash flow from sale of old machine, after tax		9,000
	Ending cash flow, net of foregone opportunity		$21,000

We can then combine these results to determine the NPV of the replacement decision, as we show in Table 11-4. Once we have the net cash flows, we can evaluate these cash flows using the net present value, the internal rate of return, or one of the other evaluation techniques.[13]

Concept Review Questions

1. Discuss any differences in the evaluation of a replacement decision versus an expansion decision.

2. List the cash flows to consider in the investment cash flow associated with a replacement decision.

11.5 INFLATION AND CAPITAL BUDGETING

Because capital expenditures typically involve the estimation of cash flows several years in the future, inflation can play an important role in determining these estimates because it will affect future levels of sales and expenses. In addition, inflation alters the level of interest rates and therefore affects the company's cost of capital that is to be used in discounting these future cash flows.

Nominal Versus Real Cash Flows

Earlier in this chapter, we said that we need to treat inflation consistently. So far, we have been estimating future cash flows on a nominal basis (i.e., estimating the actual cash flow that will result in year 2, etc., without making adjustments for inflation). As a result, we have been discounting these cash flows by using nominal (or actual) discount rates. This approach treats inflation consistently.

An alternative is to estimate future real (that is, inflation-adjusted) cash flows and discount these real cash flows by using real discount rates. However, one difficulty with this approach is that the depreciation tax savings estimates represent the actual amount of depreciation that can be charged in a given year. Therefore, the easiest way to proceed is usually to estimate the nominal cash flows and discount them by using nominal discount rates.

---

[13] We calculate the NPV by discounting the net cash flows. If the project's cost of capital is 10 percent, the net present value of this project's cash flows is –$1,320. Because the net present value is negative, the company should not go ahead with this replacement project.

It is important for companies to consider the effect that inflation will have on both sales and expenses, as well as the discount rate. Although it is often reasonable to assume that sales and expenses will be equally affected by inflation, this will not be the case for all companies or all situations. Much depends on the industry a company is in and on the products it sells. For example, sometimes inflation will have a greater impact on selling prices than it will on expenses, and sometimes the opposite will hold.[14]

Consider a company that has a 3-year project with the following:

- Unit sales are expected to be level at 10,000 units each year for the entire 3 years. The real sales price is expected to be $10 per unit, but the expected sales price inflation is expected to be 4 percent per year.

- Real expenses are expected to be $6 per unit produced and sold, but the expense inflation is expected to be 4 percent per year.

- The initial cost of the asset is $1 million, and there is no salvage value expected.

- Depreciation is calculated using the 3-year MACRS depreciation.

- The company's marginal tax rate is 35 percent.

- The nominal cost of capital for this project is 8 percent.

The net present value of this project is $58,684, as we detail in Table 11-5.

TABLE 11-5 Cash Flows and the Net Present Value with Inflation at 4 Percent Per Year

		Initially	Year 1	Year 2	Year 3
	Unit sales		80,000	80,000	80,000
	Sale price per unit		$21.00	$21.84	$22.71
	Operating expense per unit		$15.00	$15.60	$16.22
	Investment cash flow	−$1,000,000			
	Salvage value				$0
	Tax benefit from loss on disposal				−$74,100
	Terminal cash flow		$0	$0	−$74,100
	Change in revenues		$1,680,000	$1,747,200	$1,817,088
Less	Change in expenses		1,200,000	1,248,000	1,297,920
Less	Change in depreciation		333,300	444,500	148,100
Equals	Change in taxable income		$146,700	$54,700	$371,068
Less	Change in taxes		51,345	19,145	129,874
Equals	Change in income after tax		$95,355	$35,555	$241,194
Plus	Change in depreciation		333,300	444,500	148,100
	Operating cash flow		$428,655	$480,055	$389,294
	Net cash flow	−$1,000,000	$428,655	$480,055	$315,194
	Net present value	$58,584			

[14] For example, from October 2010 to October 2011, the price of wheat increased 9.6 percent, yet the price of flour products rose only 7.4 percent; therefore, a wheat processor was not able to pass along the entire increase in its raw materials to its customers.

TABLE 11-6 Cash Flows and the Net Present Value with Different Inflation Expectations

		Year 0	Year 1	Year 2	Year 3
	Unit sales		80,000	80,000	80,000
	Sale price per unit		$21.00	$22.26	$23.60
	Operating expense per unit		$15.00	$16.20	$17.50
	Investment cash flow	−$1,000,000			
	Salvage value				$0
	Tax benefit from loss on disposal				−$74,100
	Terminal cash flow				−$74,100
	Change in revenues		$1,680,000	$1,780,800	$1,887,648
Less	Change in expenses		1,200,000	1,296,000	1,399,680
Less	Change in depreciation		333,300	444,500	148,100
Equals	Change in taxable income		$146,700	$40,300	$339,868
Less	Change in taxes		51,345	14,105	118,954
Equals	Change in income after tax		$95,355	$26,195	$220,914
Plus	Change in depreciation		333,300	444,500	148,100
	Operating cash flow		$428,655	$470,695	$369,014
	Net cash flow	−$1,000,000	$428,655	$470,695	$294,914
	Net present value	$34,560			

If the inflation expectations change, so that the rate of inflation of revenues differs from that of expenses, we have a different outcome. For example, if the rate of inflation on units sold results in an increase of the sale price by 6 percent per year, and if the rate of inflation on operating expenses per unit is 8 percent each year, we arrive at a net present value of $34,560, as we show in Table 11-6.

Comparing the two analyses, you can see that the depreciation remains the same, but the operating cash flows differ due to the differing inflation rates for revenues and expenses. The difference in rates of inflation can change an acceptable project into an unacceptable project. For example, if the rate of inflation in expenses is 10 percent instead of 5 percent, the net present value of the project is −$5,811, which therefore makes this project unacceptable.

Can there be such disparate inflation rates? Most definitely. Consider the U.S. producer price index (PPI), which is an index of all goods from the perspective of businesses. A nonchocolate confectionary producer in 2010 would have experienced an increase in the price of sugar, a key input, of 21.1 percent, but an increase in the price of its product of only 0.5 percent.[15]

---

1. What is the problem with using a nominal discount rate and nominal cash flows to adjust for inflation?

2. If inflation is expected to increase in the future, how would this affect the profitability of a project? Explain.

Concept Review Questions

[15] U.S. Bureau of Labor Statistics, Producer Price Index, Industry Data.

SUMMARY

- A challenging element of capital budgeting analysis is the estimation of the incremental cash flows of a project. These cash flows include the investment cash flow, operating cash flows, and terminal cash flows. The key is to identify how a company's cash flows change if the company invests in a project.

- Depreciation affects cash flows because the deduction of this noncash expense reduces a company's tax bill; hence, depreciation results in a positive cash flow. We quantify the effect of depreciation with the calculation of the depreciation tax shield.

- Financial managers can use sensitivity analysis and scenario analysis, among other tools, to determine how variations in estimates can affect the attractiveness of project evaluations. Because the inputs to the capital budgeting analysis are estimates, it is important to analyze the sensitivity of capital budgeting decisions to the estimates.

- Inflation may affect the capital budgeting decision. Inflation affects the different elements of a project's cash flows, except for depreciation, which is fixed in amount. Inflation also affects the discount rate. In most analyses, it is easiest to work with nominal cash flows and the nominal discount rate because depreciation is fixed, and its effect in real terms is more challenging to estimate.

QUESTIONS AND PROBLEMS

Multiple Choice Questions

1. When making capital expenditure decisions, companies should not consider which of the following?
   A. Sunk costs
   B. Opportunity costs
   C. After-tax incremental cash flows
   D. Additional working capital requirements

2. If the change in depreciation for a given year of a project is $30,000 and the marginal tax rate is 30 percent, the depreciation tax shield is *closest* to:
   A. $9,000.   B. $27,000.   C. $30,000.

3. If a project is expected to generate annual revenue of $50,000, while incurring an annual cost of $18,000, the effect of the change in revenue and costs on the annual cash flow if the marginal tax rate is 40 percent, is *closest* to:
   A. $12,800.   B. $19,200.   C. $32,000.

4. A company is planning to purchase new, faster printers to replace its existing printers. The capital cost of the new printers = $300,000. The current market price of the old printers = $50,000. The applicable depreciation rate for the first year is 20 percent, the tax rate is 40 percent, and the project's cost of capital is 20 percent. It is estimated that the new printers could last for 5 years. The depreciation tax shield for the first year of operations is *closest* to:
   A. $24,000.   B. $60,000.   C. $120,000.

5. Which of the following items is not included in the calculation of the terminal cash flow?
   A. Salvage value
   B. Operating cash flows
   C. The change in inventory levels
   D. The change in accounts receivable levels

6. The depreciation tax shield is best described as the:

   A. incremental depreciation expense.

   B. depreciation expense on the new asset.

   C. amount of tax savings from deducting depreciation for tax purposes.

7. Which of the following completions is incorrect? An asset that is classified as a 3-year asset for MACRS purposes has:

   A. a zero book value at the end of the 3rd year.

   B. a positive book value at the end of the 3rd year.

   C. been fully depreciated by the end of the 4th year.

8. Suppose a company has an asset that had an original cost of $100,000, that it has depreciated using MACRS as a 3-year asset. If the company sells this asset at the end of the 4th year for $20,000 and has a marginal tax rate of 35 percent, the cash flow from this sale is *closest* to:

   A. $7,000.   B. $13,000.   C. $20,000.   D. $27,000.

9. Consider a project with the following information:

   - Initial cost = $400,050
   - Research and development costs associated with the project = $10,000
   - Associated opportunity costs = $90,000
   - Decrease in inventory = $15,000
   - Installation costs = $5,000

   The investment cash flow is *closest* to:

   A. $480,050.   B. $490,050.   C. $510,050.   D. $520,050.

10. You are given the following information regarding the acquisition of a new machine:

    - The new machine will replace an older machine.
    - The old machine has a book value of $65,000.
    - The purchase cost of the new machine (including shipping and handling) is $120,000.
    - The old machine cost $120,000 and can be sold for $75,000.
    - The company's marginal tax rate is 40 percent.

    The initial investment cash flow is *closest* to:

    A. −$120,000.   B. −$75,000.   C. −$49,000.   D. −$45,000.

Practice Questions and Problems

11.1 Identifying Relevant Cash Flows

11. What is meant by a sunk cost? Provide an example of a sunk cost.

12. Why would you use the marginal tax rate of a company in evaluating a project instead of the company's average tax rate? Explain your answer.

13. Describe how taxes may affect the cash flows from a capital investment project.

14. Two analysts, Arturo and Victor, are in disagreement about how to treat research and development in capital project analysis. Arturo believes that these are sunk costs, and therefore should never be included in an analysis. Victor believes that if the decision involves whether or not to invest in research and development, the research and development expenses should affect the investment decision. Who, if anyone, is correct? Explain.

15. Suppose a company is evaluating a project that would require converting an existing building to house the new project. Which of the following costs or expenses should be considered in the new project's cash flows? For each item, provide an explanation.

    A. The cost of the building

    B. The cost of repairs to the heating system of the building to bring the building up to code

    C. The cost of new lighting necessary for the new project's production process

16. Complete the following, identifying each of the following as a sunk cost, externality, or an opportunity cost:

Item		Sunk Cost	Externality	Opportunity Cost
A.	The cost of research and development to develop a new arthritis drug			
B.	The rent that the company could have received if it did not use the building for a new production line			
C.	The reduction in the revenues for a similar product of the company			
D.	The depreciation expense on a machine if replaced with another machine			
E.	The cost of equipment that is currently idle that could be used for the new product			
F.	The increased efficiency of the company due to synergies in the production of the new product			

11.2   Estimating Cash Flows

17. Consider a company that has a marginal tax rate of 40 percent. For each of the following, estimate the effect on cash flow, indicating inflows as positive values and outflows as negative values:

    A. Increase inventory by $30,000

    B. Decrease accounts payable by $20,000

    C. Sale of an asset that had an original cost of $10,000 and a $0 book value for $2,000

    D. Purchase of equipment for $40,000 and incurring $3,000 to install the equipment

    E. Increase accounts receivable by $5,000

18. Consider an asset that has an initial cost of $500,000 and a useful life of 6 years. The company's marginal tax rate is 30 percent.

    A. What is the depreciation tax shield for each year if the asset is classified as a 3-year asset for MACRS purposes?

    B. What is the depreciation tax shield for each year if the asset is classified as a 5-year asset for MACRS purposes?

19. If the U.S. Congress were to lower tax rates for corporations across the board, would this affect capital investment decisions? If so, in what way, and would this encourage or discourage investment activity?

20. Consider the depreciation of an asset that costs a company $1 million and is classified as a 5-year asset for MACRS purposes. Complete the following table, assuming a marginal tax rate of 40 percent:

Year	Depreciation Expense	Depreciation Tax Shield
1		
2		
3		
4		
5		

21. Consider a company that expects the following working capital accounts associated with a 4-year project:

	Initial	Year 1	Year 2	Year 3	Year 4
Inventory	$10,000	$12,000	$12,000	$14,000	$10,000
Accounts receivable	$12,000	$11,000	$12,000	$13,000	$12,000
Accounts payable	$8,000	$9,000	$9,000	$7,000	$8,000

For each year, indicate the cash flow effects of the changes in the working capital accounts.

22. Consider a project that has the following features:
- Requires an investment cash flow of $50,000 for equipment and installation.
- The assets are classified as 3-year MACRS assets.
- There is no expected salvage value for the assets, but the company will have to pay $3,000 at the end of the 3rd year to dispose of the assets to meet local and federal environmental mitigation requirements. The disposal costs are a tax deductible expense.
- Inventory needs will be reduced by $5,000 for the duration of the project.
- The project will increase revenues by $25,000 each year, but will also increase operating expenses by $12,000.
- The marginal tax rate is 35 percent.

Complete the following table:

		Initial	Year 1	Year 2	Year 3
	Cost of equipment				
Less	Disposal costs and any related taxes from disposal				
Less	Change in working capital				
Equals	Nonoperating cash flows				

	Change in revenues				
Less	Change in operating expenses				
Less	Change in depreciation				
Equals	Change in taxable income				
Less	Change in taxes				
Equals	Change in income after tax				
Plus	Change in depreciation				
Equals	Change in operating cash flow				

	Net cash flow				

23. Oxford Inc. has a project that requires purchases of capital assets costing $40,000 and additional raw material inventory of $2,000. Shipping and installation costs are $1,500. Oxford Inc.'s management estimated that the project would generate annual operating cash flows of $5,600 for each of 6 years. At the end of 6 years, the assets can be sold for $4,000, whereas the additional inventory that was tied up will be released. The assets are classified as 3-year assets for MACRS purposes. The tax rate = 40 percent, and the assets' cost of capital is 15 percent.

A. What are the cash flows for each of the 6 years of the project's useful life?
B. What is the net present value of the project?
C. Should Oxford Inc. accept the project? Explain your reasoning.

24. What is the present value of the operating cash flows if the revenue of a project grows at 5 percent, while expense grows at 4 percent, given that revenues in the first year are $15,000 and expenses in the first year are $7,000? Assume the project's cost of capital is 8 percent and the marginal tax rate is 40 percent. The project has an expected useful life of 8 years.

11.3   Sensitivity to Inputs

25. The U.S. government provided bonus depreciation rules for small businesses in the 2008, 2009, and 2010 stimulus legislation. The bonus depreciation rules allow businesses to deduct an additional 50 percent of an asset's cost in the first year for federal tax purposes, along with the regular depreciation based on MACRS applied to the other 50 percent of the asset's cost.

    A. How would this affect the analysis of the cash flows of a project that has depreciable assets?

    B. Would this make projects more or less profitable in terms of value to the owners?

26. Santa Fe Company is considering a project. The initial cost is $60,000, and the company will use $2,000 less in raw material inventory with this project. The project would generate annual revenue of $70,000 and annual costs of $40,000 for 6 years. At the end of the project, the equipment could be sold for $10,000, and the additional raw materials inventory will be released. The equipment is a 3-year asset for MACRS purposes. The tax rate is 40 percent.

    A. What are the cash flows for each of the 6 years of the project's useful life?

    B. What is the NPV of this project if the project's cost of capital is 15 percent?

    C. What is the NPV of this project if the project's cost of capital is 12 percent?

    D. What is project's internal rate of return?

27. The Evansville Egg Company (EEC) is evaluating a new product line. To create this new product line, the company will spend $500,000 for the new equipment. EEC's financial managers are using a 4-year horizon for this new product line and do not expect to be able to sell the equipment, which qualifies as a 3-year asset in MACRS, at the end of the useful life. EEC's financial managers estimate the product line's cost of capital to be 10 percent. The financial managers of EEC are not confident that they can produce a single estimate of revenues and expenses, but with the help of accounting, manufacturing, and marketing management, they can detail three possible scenarios:

	Worst Case	Most Likely	Best Case
Change in revenues per year	$200,000	$250,000	$350,000
Change in expenses per year	$160,000	$190,000	$210,000
Anticipated tax rate	45 percent	38 percent	35 percent

    A. What is the net present value of the new product line under each scenario?

    B. From this information, what do you conclude regarding the acceptability of the new product line?

    C. How important is the depreciation tax shield to the acceptability of the new product line?

11.4   Replacement Decisions

28. Why does the financial analyst need to consider the depreciation of the replaced equipment in the analysis of cash flows of a replacement project?

29. Suppose new equipment costs $100,000, and it replaces equipment that has no resale value. The change in depreciation is the following:

	Year 1	Year 2	Year 3	Year 4
Old equipment	$8,886	$8,886		
New equipment	$33,330	$44,450	$14,810	$7,410

    If the discount rate on this replacement project is 8 percent and the company's marginal tax rate is 40 percent, what is the contribution of the change in depreciation to the value of the replacement decision?

30. Suppose a company is evaluating the replacement of the equipment in its production line. The old equipment was considered a 3-year MACRS asset and was purchased 3 years ago for $100,000. The company's management estimates that the old equipment can be sold for $10,000. What is the cash flow associated with the old equipment if replaced?

31. The Ames Corp. Inc. is now considering replacing some old equipment. The old equipment was bought 5 years ago for $50,000, and Ames's management believes that the equipment could be sold today for $15,000. The new equipment will cost $100,000 and could be sold at the end of 5 years for $30,000. An additional $4,000 in working capital is required and will be released at the end of 5 years. The new equipment is estimated to reduce operating expenses by $20,000 each year. Assume that the marginal tax rate is 40 percent and the project's cost of capital is 10 percent. Both the new and old equipment are classified as 5-year assets under MACRS.

    A. What are the cash flows for each of the 5 years of the project's life?

    B. What is the replacement project's NPV?

    C. Should Ames make this replacement? Explain your answer.

11.5 Inflation and Capital Budgeting

32. If the revenues, expenses, and discount rate of a project are nominal amounts, how can inflation affect the capital budgeting decision?

33. The Richmond Company has a project that requires the purchase of equipment costing $90,000 and additional raw material inventory of $2,000. Richmond's management estimated that the project would generate revenues of $58,000 and operating expenses of $30,000 each year. At the end of 6 years, the equipment will be worthless, and the company will need to pay $5,000 for its disposal. Any additional inventory that was tied up will be released at the end of the project's life. The equipment is classified as a 3-year asset for MACRS purposes. The tax rate = 40 percent, and the project's cost of capital is 15 percent.

    A. What is the NPV of the project?

    B. If the revenues and operating expenses increase at a rate of 4 percent each year, what is the net present value of this project? Does your answer differ from your answer to A above? If so, why?

    C. If the revenues increase at a rate of 3 percent per year and the operating expenses increase at a rate of 5 percent each year, what is the net present value of this project?

    D. Should Richmond accept the project? Explain.

34. The Morgantown Company (MC) has a project that requires the purchase of production equipment that costs $800,000 initially. MC's management estimated that the project would generate revenues of $440,000 and operating expenses of $250,000 each year. At the end of 5 years, the equipment will be sold for $300,000. The equipment is classified as a 3-year asset for MACRS purposes. The tax rate = 35 percent, and the project's cost of capital is 10 percent.

    A. What is the NPV of the project?

    B. If the revenues and operating expenses increase at a rate of 3 percent each year, what is the net present value of this project? Does your answer differ from your answer to A above? If so, why?

    C. If the revenues increase at a rate of 3 percent per year and the operating expenses increase at a rate of 2 percent each year, what is the net present value of this project?

    D. Should MC accept the project? Explain.

Cases

Case 11.1 The Jam Music Company

The Jam Music Company is considering expanding its production line to satisfy the demand for more CDs. The company has commissioned consultant studies for the expansion, spending $200,000 for these studies. The results of the studies indicate that the firm must spend $900,000 on a new building and $300,000 on production equipment if it wants to have state-of-the-art production. The consultants' report predicts that the company can increase its revenues by $400,000 each year, while incurring an increase of $160,000 in expenses. The consultants expect rivals to step up production within 5 years, reducing benefits from the expansion to Jam after 5 years. Therefore, a 5-year time horizon is assumed for this expansion project. The expansion would require that the company increase its current assets by $100,000 initially, but these asset accounts will be returned to previous levels at the end of the project.

Assume that the building is depreciated as a 10-year MACRS asset and that it can be sold at the end of 5 years for $800,000. Further assume that the equipment is depreciated using MACRS over a 5-year period and that it can be sold at the end of 5 years for $150,000. The marginal tax rate of Jam is 40 percent, and the cost of capital for this project is 10 percent.

Requirements

A. Should Jam invest in this project? Explain.

B. What is the internal rate of return on this project?

C. If the increase in revenues is only $350,000 per year, should Jam invest in this project? Explain your answer.

D. If the revenues start at $600,000 for the first year and decline each year by 25 percent, but expenses do not change, should Jam invest in this project? Explain why or why not.

Case 11.2 Can Tax Credits Make Solar Panels Profitable?

Consider the cost of a solar panel system that is intended to replace 25 percent of a home's electricity use.[16] A system that would fit on the roof of a typical home and would reduce electricity usage by 25 percent costs $37,496.36 before any government tax incentives. Currently, the U.S. government provides a 30 percent tax credit in the year of the solar panel acquisition, and the system is exempt from state and local property taxes.[17] The average monthly electrical bill is $200 per month.

The cost of borrowing for a solar panel system through the FHA's Energy Efficient Mortgage (EEM) program, available for energy efficient home improvements, is an APR of 3.35%.[18] The amount of the mortgage is the cost of the panel system, less any federal incentive. The interest on the EEM is tax deductible, but electricity costs are not deductible for the individual homeowner.

Assume that the homeowner has a marginal tax rate of 38 percent and that the installation is at the end of the current year, but the panels are not used until the first month of the coming year. Further, assume that the solar panels have a useful life of 30 years and that at the end of the life of the panels the homeowner must pay a $500 for removal and disposal of the panels at the local dump.

Requirements

A. What is the payback period for a solar panel system?

B. What is the added value of investing in solar panels on a net present value basis?

C. If energy costs were to increase at a rate of 0.25 percent each month, would this affect the attractiveness of the panels? If so, why?

D. What is the minimum percent tax credit necessary to make the solar system attractive to homeowners on a net present value basis, assuming that energy costs do not escalate?

---

[16] Data for the costs and savings are drawn from CoolPlanetBioFuels.com.

[17] See Internal Revenue Service *Form 5695 Residential Energy Credits* for all the current credits.

[18] Based on 2011 rates.

INTEGRATIVE PROBLEM: DAZZLE

We demonstrate the principles of estimating cash flows using a capital budgeting decision involving a consumer products company that is evaluating a new product. We first introduce the capital budgeting problem and then pick the problem apart to find the relevant information for the cash flow analysis.

11A.1 THE PROJECT

Consider the Smile Toothpaste Company (STC), which has a line of successful dental products that are sold in retail outlets across the country. These products include toothpastes, flosses, and rinses. The financial managers of STC are considering the production of a new toothpaste that their research and development team has determined is an improvement over its existing whitening toothpaste. STC's marketing research has concluded that introducing the new toothpaste, Dazzle, next year would be appropriate, and that projected sales, in millions of units, would be the following:

Year	Estimated Units Produced and Sold
2014	750
2015	1,000
2016	1,500
2017	1,250
2018	250

The marketing managers estimate that each tube of Dazzle should sell for $3, and production management has estimated that the cost of each tube is $1.50. Marketing also estimates that advertising and other promotions will cost $200 million in 2014 and 2015, but then fall to $100 million in 2016 and then $50 million each year following.

The marketing research indicates that sales of Dazzle will reduce sales of its other whitening tooth paste, Brilliant, at a pace of approximately 400 million in the first year, 300 in the second year, and then 200 million units per year thereafter. Brilliant sells for $2.5 per tube and costs $1 per tube for manufacturing. STC will need to stock an additional $500 million of raw materials for the paste and tube production at the end of 2013, maintain this level through 2015, then reduce it to $400 million by the end of 2016, $200 million at the end of 2017, and then $0 at the end of 2018.

The company would be able to use vacant space in another production facility to produce Dazzle. This other production facility was built 10 years ago at a cost of $200 million and is being depreciated as a 20-year MACRS asset. Dazzle's production will take up approximately one-quarter of the floor space of this facility. The production equipment to manufacture the Dazzle toothpaste and tube will cost $20 million and will be depreciated as a 7-year MACRS asset. STC expects to be able to sell this equipment at the end of 5 years for $5 million. The equipment will be acquired December 31, 2013, and production begins in January 2014.

The purchasing managers have alerted the capital project's manager that there is uncertainty regarding the input prices for the abrasives, fluorides, and surfactants used in both Dazzle and Brilliant. Though their initial projections are the most likely costs, it is possible that due to potential fluctuations in the raw materials markets in the near-term that the costs may be 20 percent less than or greater than projected for both Dazzle and Brilliant toothpastes. However, due to competition in the consumer market, it is unlikely that STC can pass along any added costs in the sales price.

STC's marginal tax rate is 35 percent, and this project's cost of capital is 10 percent. Based on all this information, should STC go ahead with Dazzle?

11A.2 ANALYSIS OF THE FACTS

We will analyze the facts, picking out the relevant facts for the calculation of the cash flows.

Dissecting the Problem

Capital project analysis is usually quite detailed, and each problem is unique. Therefore, it is important to address all information about the project, assess whether the information is relevant to the analysis, and determine the implications for cash flows. We demonstrate this by taking apart the Dazzle project information.

Consider the Smile Toothpaste Company (STC), which has a line of successful dental products that are sold in retail outlets across the country. These products include toothpastes, flosses, and rinses. The financial managers of STC are considering the production of a new toothpaste that their research and development team has determined is an improvement over its existing whitening toothpaste.

Relevance: This tells us that though this is a new product, it may cannibalize the company's existing products.

STC's marketing research has concluded that introducing the new toothpaste, Dazzle, next year would be appropriate, and that that projected sales, in millions of units, would be the following:

Year	Estimated Units Produced and Sold
2014	750
2015	1,000
2016	1,500
2017	1,250
2018	250

Relevance: We can now sketch out potential sales for the relevant years of 2014 through 2018.

	2014	2015	2016	2017	2018
Expected sales of Dazzle (in millions of units)	750	1,000	1,500	1,250	250

The marketing managers estimate that each tube of Dazzle should sell for $3, and production management has estimated that the cost of each tube is $1.25. Marketing also estimates that advertising and other promotions will cost $200 million in 2014 and 2015, but then fall to $100 million in 2016 and then $50 million each year following.

Relevance: When we put this together with the projected sales volume, we can now estimate the revenues and expenses for Dazzle.

		2014	2015	2016	2017	2018
Dazzle dollar sales	(in millions)	$2,250	$3,000	$4,500	$3,750	$750
Dazzle dollar costs	(in millions)	$1,125	$1,500	$2,250	$1,875	$375
Marketing and promotion	(in millions)	$200	$200	$100	$50	$50

The marketing research indicates that sales of Dazzle will reduce sales of its other whitening toothpaste, Brilliant, at a pace of approximately 200 million units per year. Brilliant sells for $2.5 per tube and costs $1 per tube for manufacturing.

Relevance: This is the information we need to evaluate the cannibalization, and then the incremental revenues and expenses for Dazzle.

		2014	2015	2016	2017	2018
Brilliant sales price	(per unit)	$2.50	$2.50	$2.50	$2.50	$2.50
Brilliant cost per unit	(per unit)	$1.00	$1.00	$1.00	$1.00	$1.00
Change in Brilliant sales	(in millions of units)	−400	−300	−200	−200	−200
Change in Brilliant's dollar sales	(in millions)	−$1,000	−$750	−$500	−$500	−$500
Change in Brilliant's dollar costs	(in millions)	−$400	−$300	−$200	−$200	−$200
Dazzle dollar sales	(in millions)	$2,250	$3,000	$4,500	$3,750	$750
Dazzle dollar costs	(in millions)	$1,125	$1,500	$2,250	$1,875	$375
Change in revenues	(in millions)	$1,250	$2,250	$4,000	$3,250	$250
Change in operating costs	(in millions)	$725	$1,200	$2,050	$1,675	$175
Marketing and promotion	(in millions)	$200	$200	$100	$50	$50

It is easy to get tangled up in figuring out changes when there is cannibalization. Consider the effects for one year, 2014:

	With Dazzle Only	Without Dazzle	Change
Revenues	$2,250	$1,000	$1,250
Operating costs	1,125	400	725
Revenues less operating costs	$1,125	$600	$525

STC will need to stock an additional $500 million of raw materials for the paste and tube production at the end of 2013, maintain this level through 2015, then reduce it to $400 million by the end of 2016, $200 million at the end of 2017, and then $0 at the end of 2018.

Relevance: We use this information to determine the cash flows from the change in working capital.

(in millions)	2013	2014	2015	2016	2017	2018
Working capital level	$500	$500	$500	$400	$200	$0
Change in working capital	+$500	$0	$0	−$100	−$200	−$200
Cash flow from change in working capital	−$500	$0	$0	$100	$200	$200

The company would be able to use vacant space in another production facility to produce Dazzle. This other production facility was built 10 years ago at a cost of $200 million and is being depreciated as a 20-year MACRS asset. Dazzle's production will take up approximately one-quarter of the floor space of this facility.

Relevance: This is a sunk cost and is therefore not relevant for the Dazzle capital budgeting decision.

The production equipment to manufacture the Dazzle toothpaste and tube will cost $3 billion and will be depreciated as a 7-year MACRS asset. STC expects to be able to sell this equipment at the end of 5 years for $0.5 billion. The equipment will be acquired December 31, 2013, and production begins in January 2014.

This provides what we need for the depreciation expense for each year and provides information on the investment cash flow related to the sale of the equipment at the end of the project's life.

		2014	2015	2016	2017	2018
Depreciation rate for equipment	(percent of cost)	10.00%	18.00%	14.00%	12.00%	9.00%
Depreciation expense	(in millions)	$300	$540	$420	$360	$270

If the company sells the equipment at the end of 5 years, this defines the project's useful life for us. This also tells us that because it is a 7-year MACRS asset, selling it at the end of the 5th year means that the equipment has a positive carrying value at that point in time, which we need to know to calculate any gain or loss at the time of this sale.

(in millions)	2014	2015	2016	2017	2018
Book value of equipment	$2,700	$2,160	$1,740	$1,380	$1,110

This means that the company has an expected loss on the equipment of $500 − 1,110 = $610 million. This loss will result in a tax benefit.

The purchasing managers have alerted the capital project's manager that there is uncertainty regarding the input prices for the abrasives, fluorides, and surfactants used in both Dazzle and Brilliant. Though their initial projections are the most likely costs, it is possible that due to potential fluctuations in the raw materials markets in the near-term that the costs may be 20 percent less than or greater than projected for both Dazzle and Brilliant toothpastes. However, due to competition in the consumer market, it is unlikely that STC can pass along any added costs in the sales price.

Relevance: This will give us something to check in sensitivity analysis.

STC's marginal tax rate is 35 percent, and this project's cost of capital is 10 percent. Based on all this information, should STC go ahead with Dazzle?

Relevance: These are the last pieces that we need to put the puzzle together. This will allow us to calculate the tax on the change in taxable income.

	2014	2015	2016	2017	2018
Change in revenues	$1,250	$2,250	$4,000	$3,250	$250
Change in operating costs	725	1,200	2,050	1,675	175
Marketing and promotion	200	200	100	50	50
Depreciation	300	540	420	360	270
Change in taxable income	$25	$310	$1,430	$1,165	−$245
Tax	9	109	501	408	−86
Change in income after tax	$16	$202	$930	$757	−$159

Knowing the tax rate also allows us to calculate the tax benefit from selling the equipment at a loss:

	Sale price	$500
Less	Carrying value for tax purposes	1,110
Equals	Loss on sale	−$600
Multiply	Tax rate	0.35
Equals	Tax benefit from the loss on sale	$214

Assembling the Pieces

We assemble the pieces in Table 11A-1 for the base case of this analysis. Based on the positive net present value and internal rate of return, Dazzle is a profitable project when we use the base analysis: a positive net present value and a rate of return that exceeds the project cost of capital.

TABLE 11A-1 The Dazzle Analysis

		2013	2014	2015	2016	2017	2018
	Purchase of equipment	−$3,000					
Plus	Sale of equipment						$500
Plus	Tax benefit on loss on sale						214
Equals	Investment cash flows	−$3,000	$0	$0	$0	$0	$714
	Change in working capital	−$500	$0	$0	$100	$200	$200
	Change in revenues		$1,250	$2,250	$4,000	$3,250	$250
Less	Change in operating costs		725	1,200	2,050	1,675	175
Less	Change in marketing and promotion		200	200	100	50	50
Less	Change in depreciation		300	540	420	360	270
Equals	Change in taxable income		$25	$310	$1,430	$1,165	−$245
Less	Change in tax		9	109	501	408	−86
Equals	Change in income after tax		$16	$202	$930	$757	−$159
Plus	Change in depreciation		300	540	420	360	270
Equals	Change in operating cash flow		$316	$742	$1,350	$1,117	$111
Sum	Net cash flow	−$3,500	$316	$742	$1,450	$1,317	$1,024
	Net present value	$25.02					
	Internal rate of return	10.24%					
	Payback period	4 years					

Scenario Analysis

The primary uncertainty mentioned in Dazzle's project description is that costs may be 20 percent more or less than expected, and we can infer that these costs adjustments would occur immediately if they did. Let us consider the 20 percent increase in costs as the worst-case scenario and consider the 20 percent decrease as the best-case scenario.

When we look at the worst-case and best-case scenarios, with costs 20 percent more or less, respectively, for both Dazzle and Brilliant, the decision would be different:

Scenario	Net Cash Flows						Net Present Value	Internal Rate of Return
	2013	2014	2015	2016	2017	2018		
Best case	−$3,500	$411	$898	$1,716	$1,535	$1,047	$602.70	15.64%
Base case	−$3,500	$316	$742	$1,450	$1,317	$1,024	$351.81	14.14%
Worst case	−$3,500	$222	$586	$1,183	$1,100	$1,002	−$552.67	4.59%

We would reject the Dazzle project if the costs were 20 percent more, but in the base-case and the best-case scenarios, the project is profitable. These conclusions present an issue for risk management: Is it worth the risk for an unprofitable project? What is the likelihood that the worst-case scenario will occur?

Simulation Analysis

We can extend this, performing a simulation assuming that the price changes of inputs are normally distributed with a mean of 0 percent and a standard deviation of 10 percent.[19] To make this simulation manageable for this example, we assume that that price change, which we draw from a random number generator, is the same for all years.[20]

We draw 1,000 observations from this distribution, which we use to recalculate each year's cash flow given the price change. For example, we show the 2014 cash flow in Figure 11A-1. How do we interpret this chart? First, the mean price change is 0 percent, so the mean of this distribution will have the same net cash flows as our base case.[21] Second, the distribution of these cash flows is wide ranging, from $190 to $480, but it is concentrated around the mean.

The result of performing this simulation for all years is that we generate 1,000 different internal rates of return, as we show in Figure 11A-2. How do we interpret this? This tells us that the project's returns can vary between 2 percent and 19 percent, depending on the price changes for the inputs, but that the return on the project is likely to be centered around 10–11 percent. The issue facing STC, therefore, is whether this project is consistent with the company's risk tolerance.

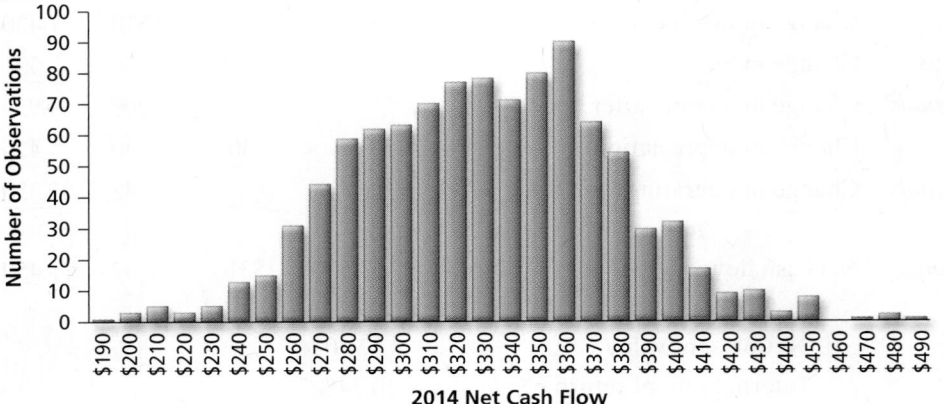

FIGURE 11A-1 Distribution of the Year 2014 Cash Flows Based on 1,000 Different Price Changes

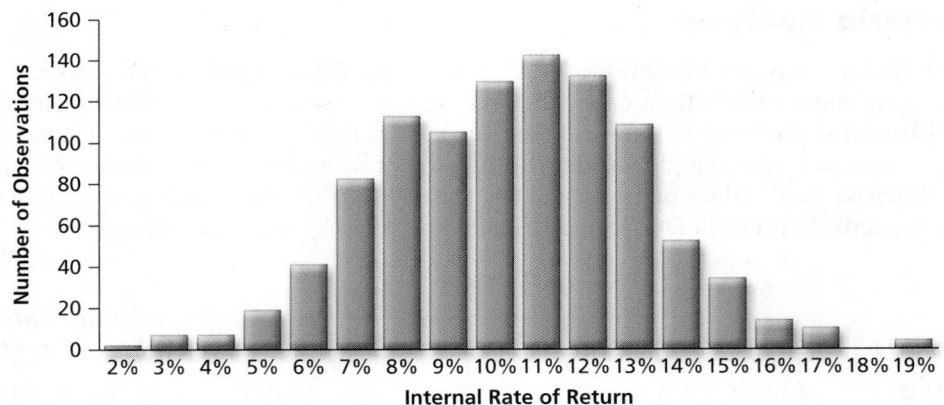

FIGURE 11A-2 Distribution of Internal Rates of Return for the Dazzle Project Based on 1,000 Different Price Changes

---

[19] Therefore, we expect 95 percent of draws from this distribution to be plus or minor two standard deviations (that is, 20 percent) from the base case assumption.

[20] In Microsoft's Excel, we use the Data Analysis tools, specifically the Random Number Generator.

[21] Actually, it is close, but not precisely equal, to the base case. If we had drawn 10,000 observations, the mean would be extremely close to the base case.

PART 6

LONG-TERM FINANCING

The decision a company's managers make regarding how to finance the company's operations and investment activities affects the financial risk the company bears and, ultimately, the cost of its capital. As we saw in Part 5, the cost of capital is a pivotal factor in the capital investment decisions a company makes. Therefore, the financing decision of a company affects its ability to take advantage of future investment opportunities and grow. In Part 6, we look at the different types of financing in Chapters 12 and 13, and then pull all the pieces together in the estimation of the cost of capital in Chapter 14.

CHAPTER 12

DEBT INSTRUMENTS

©Richard Cano/iStockphoto

The Nature of Ratings   Ratings are expressions of opinion about risk, not statements of, or even predictions about, facts. There is not now, nor can there ever be, a science or an orthodoxy for debt ratings. In the most basic sense, all bonds perform in a binary manner. They either pay on time or default. If the future could be known, there would be only two ratings for bonds: ***good*** or ***bad***. Because the future cannot be known, credit analysis resides in the realm of opinion, not fact. The essence of credit rating is the soundness of the judgment that groups bonds into similar classes of risk.

Source: *Letter from Matthew C. Mole, Moody's Investors Service, Inc., to the U.S. Securities and Exchange Commission, in response to the Concept Release Regarding Nationally Recognized Statistic Rating Organizations, www.sec.gov/pdf/mole3.pdf.*

Learning Outcomes

After reading this chapter, you should be able to:

LO 12.1 Describe the basic features of debt financing, and distinguish between short-term funds in the money market and long-term funds in the capital market.

LO 12.2 Distinguish among the different types of short-term financing.

LO 12.3 Explain the different features of corporate bonds, and relate these features to the value of the bond.

LO 12.4 Explain the process of debt ratings, what they mean, and how useful they are in predicting default and recovery rates associated with debt issues.

Chapter Preview Our focus in this chapter is on the contractual obligations between a business entity and its creditors. We discuss both short-term and long-term obligations. We also discuss how independent rating services evaluate and rate these obligations.

12.1   WHAT IS DEBT?

It might seem obvious what debt is. After all, many of us have borrowed money from friends, relatives, or financial institutions. For example, someone might borrow $1,000 at 10 percent interest and agree to pay the loan back in one year's time. In this case, the borrower has to pay back $1,100 at the end of the year; 10 percent interest is the cost of "renting" the $1,000 in principal for the year. In this way, the 10 percent interest rate is the cost of borrowing money.

Debt is a contract between a lender and a borrower that stipulates the terms of repayment of a loan. As a contract, these terms are limited only by the imagination of the contracting parties. However, a critical component is that the interest on debt securities is fully deductible for tax purposes by the borrower and fully taxable for the lender. As a result, one of the major factors determining whether or not a security is debt is its treatment according to the Internal Revenue Code. We will see that many factors determine whether a company issues debt, equity, or some form of hybrid security, but tax consequences are an important factor in this decision.

The simplest sort of debt contract is one that most of us have made by lending a friend a few dollars and telling him or her to pay us back next week. This is obviously a loan, but it is not backed by anything other than the friend's promise to repay in a week's time. If this promise is documented in a written contract that says, "I promise to pay $X to YYY on April 30," it is called a **promissory note**.

All this is straightforward, but it is important to point out that the interest cost and principal repayment in a debt arrangement are each a **fixed contractual commitment**, and failing to honor them has serious ramifications. The fact that the principal and interest payments are fixed contractual commitments is the essential difference between debt and equity. With equity, an investor is an owner, shares in the profits of the business, and has no contractual rights because equity is not a contract in the same way that debt is. Instead, a shareholder owns a share in the business and, as an owner, has the rights allocated in the company's articles of incorporation and bylaws, as well as in the general provisions of corporate and securities laws. However, a shareholder does not have a specific contract that details the cash flows he or she can expect to receive from the investment. An owner is a residual claimant, which means that he or she gets what is left after all the company's contractual commitments are met.

The fact that payments on debt are a fixed, legal commitment puts them in the same category as the company's rental payments on property, its payroll, and its other expenses of doing business. They are legitimate costs of doing business, and the interest paid on debt is tax deductible by the borrowing entity. In contrast, equity costs are not a cost of doing business in the same sense. Instead, they represent returns to the owners of the business after the company has paid all its legitimate expenses. As such, equity securities are treated differently for tax purposes; dividends paid by a corporation are not deductible for tax purposes by the paying corporation.

Suppose, for example, that a company has $10 million in assets and expects to generate 10 percent of this amount, or $1 million, in earnings before interest and tax (EBIT). If the corporate tax rate is 40 percent, the company will pay $400,000 in tax if it makes no interest payments. However, if the company had borrowed $5 million at 7 percent, it would have had a $350,000 interest expense deduction, reducing its taxable income to $650,000 and its tax bill to $260,000. The company's tax bill drops by $140,000 because of its decision to finance part of its operations with debt instead of equity. Therefore:

promissory note written promise to pay back a loan

fixed contractual commitment requirement that the parties involved adhere to specific requirements, such as a specified payment made on a specified date

	Company One $0 Debt	*Company Two* $5 Million Debt
EBIT	$1,000,000	$1,000,000
Interest	0	350,000
Taxable income	$1,000,000	$650,000
Tax (40%)	400,000	260,000
Net income	$600,000	$390,000

Of the $350,000 in interest expense paid by Company Two, only 60 percent, or $210,000, is actually borne by the owners of the company; the other 40 percent, or $140,000, is paid through a reduction in income taxes remitted to the government. We can see this in the fact that net income has dropped by $210,000, despite the increased interest payments of $350,000.

The Cost of Debt

The net cost of the company using debt is the after-tax cost. We start with the yield to maturity on the debt, and then adjust for the tax deductibility of the interest on debt. In our example, the effective cost of debt is the 7 percent interest rate multiplied by one minus the marginal tax rate $(1 - 0.40)$, or 60 percent. This gives the debt cost as 4.2 percent. Using a source of capital that has tax-deductible financing costs is attractive because it reduces the company's income taxes.

after-tax cost of debt net cost of the company using debt, calculated as the before-tax interest cost of the company's debt multiplied by one minus the corporate tax rate

Generally, we can use Equation 12-1 to determine this **after-tax cost of debt** (r_d^*):

$$r_d^* = r_d(1 - T) \tag{12-1}$$

where r_d is the before-tax interest cost of the company's debt, and T is the corporate tax rate. We will generically use r_d as the yield, or required return, on a security and indicate what type of security it is by using subscripts; in this case, we subscript the yield with d, indicating debt. We use the asterisk, *, to indicate when we are referring to the after-tax yield.

Consider an example. Suppose the James Company issued bonds with a coupon rate of 4 percent (paid semi-annually), a face value of $1,000, and 10 years remaining to maturity. A James bond has a value of $1,050 per bond. If James's marginal tax rate is 35 percent, what is its after-tax cost of debt? The yield to maturity on the bond is 1.703 percent $\times$ 2 = 3.406 percent.[1] James Company's after-tax cost of debt is 3.406 percent $\times (1 - 0.35) = 2.214$ percent.

EXAMPLE 12.1

The After-Tax Cost of Debt

PROBLEM

Suppose a company can issue debt with a yield of 8 percent, and the company's marginal tax rate is 35 percent. What is the cost of debt to the company?

Solution

$$r_d^* = 0.08 \times (1 - 0.35) = 0.052 \text{ or } 5.2\%$$

Concept Review Questions

1. Distinguish debt from equity.

2. Explain how to estimate the after-tax cost of debt.

12.2 SHORT-TERM INSTRUMENTS

Companies may want to borrow or lend for the short term or the long term. If they borrow or lend in the short term, they are using the money market, which is the market for short-term financial obligations. For investing purposes, a company may choose to invest in short-term instruments that are issued by the government, or it may choose to invest

---

[1] Based on the financial math introduced in Chapter 5 and applied in Chapter 6, we have FV = 1,000; N = 20; PMT = 20; PV = 1,050, which produces 1.703 percent.

in instruments issued by financial or nonfinancial companies. For borrowing purposes, a company may borrow from a financial institution, such as a commercial bank, or issue short-term securities that can be bought by institutional investors, other companies, or individuals.

Government Treasury Bills

When a government issues a promissory note, we refer to this as a Treasury bill, note, or bond because the promise is issued by the Treasury department of the government. Generally, any debt instrument with a maturity of less than a year is called a *bill* or *paper*, from 1 to 7 years it is called a *note*, and more than 7 years it is a *bond*. We refer to the bills issued by a government as **Treasury bills** or simply as **T-bills.** T-bills are issued for maturities of 4 weeks, 13 weeks, 26 weeks, and 52 weeks.

T-bills, like most money market instruments, are normally sold on a discount basis. In the United States, for example, this means that the U.S. government might auction off $500 million in T-bills, but the bills do not pay a specific interest rate. Instead, they are sold at a discount to their par value, and the interest is earned by the investor when he or she is paid the full par value at the maturity date.

There are two conventions for reporting interest: the bank discount method and the bond equivalent method. Using the **bank discount method**, also referred to as the **discount yield (DY) method**, we compare the price appreciation of the bill (that is, FV – PV) with the face value of the bill (FV), and then annualize by multiplying by 360 divided by the maturity specified in number of days, m:[2]

$$i_{dy} = \frac{FV - PV}{FV} \times \frac{360}{m} \qquad (12\text{-}2)$$

> **bank discount method** or **discount yield (DY) method** convention for specifying the interest on a security that compares the amount of the discount with the face value of the security

We can rearrange Equation 12-2 to solve for the value of the security, based on the discount yield, the price quote, and the maturity:

$$PV = FV\left[1 - \left(i_{dy} \times \frac{m}{360}\right)\right] \qquad (12\text{-}3)$$

Consider a 13-week $1 million T-bill issue priced at 99.0099. The interest is the difference between the market price of $990,099 and the $1,000,000 paid back by the government in 91 days. The discount yield, i_{dy}, is:

$$i_{dy} = \frac{\$1,000,000 - 990,099}{\$1,000,000} \times \frac{360}{91} = 0.009901 \times 3.95604 = 0.039204 \text{ or } 3.9204\%$$

> **bond equivalent method** or **investment yield method** or **coupon equivalent method** convention that specifies the yield on a security by comparing the discount to the value of the security, and then annualizing

We could simplify the calculation by using the quotes, with the face value represented as 100:

$$i_{dy} = \frac{100 - 99.0099}{100} \times \frac{360}{91} = 0.00990099 \times 3.95604 = 0.039204 \text{ or } 3.9204\%$$

Using the **bond equivalent method**, which we also refer to as the **investment yield method** and the **coupon equivalent method**, we annualize the period's return to arrive at the **bond equivalent yield (BEY)**, i_{bey}:

$$\text{Bond equivalent yield} = \frac{\text{Face value} - \text{Price paid}}{\text{Price paid}} \times \frac{365}{\text{Number of days to maturity}}$$

or

$$i_{bey} = \frac{FV - PV}{PV} \times \frac{365}{m} \qquad (12\text{-}4)$$

> **bond equivalent yield (BEY)** yield for a short-term, discount security that is based on comparing the discount with the present value of the security, then annualizing

[2] The 360 days is based on the "banker's year" which is a year comprised of 12 months, each with 30 days. Before the days of financial calculator, this made things much easier for any interest and payment calculations.

The bond equivalent yield for the 13-week T-bill priced at 99.0099 is:

$$i_{bey} = \frac{100 - 99.0099}{99.0099} \times \frac{365}{91} = 0.01 \times 4.01099 = 4.011\%$$

Rearranging Equation 12-3, we can value a T-bill based on the time to maturity, based on a 365-day year, bond equivalent yield:

$$PV = FV\left[1 - \left(i_{bey} \times \frac{m}{365}\right)\right] \tag{12-5}$$

The return in the 91 days is 1 percent, which we convert to an annual rate by multiplying by the number of 91-day periods there are in a year. As you can see when you compare the formulas for the discount yield and the bond equivalent yield, the bond equivalent yield will be larger than the discount yield. Most money market issues are traded on a discount basis, though some commercial paper may be issued in interest-bearing form.

SUMMARIZING: DAY COUNT CONVENTIONS: WHICH TO USE WHEN

You will notice that at times we use 360 days as a year and at other times we use 365. Are we just getting confused? Not really. There are actually different day-count conventions in use, depending on the security and the form of the interest quote (e.g., discount yield). Generally, when we are calculating a discount yield, we use the 360-day year, and when we use the bond equivalent yield we use 365 days.

A number of day conventions are used for debt instruments. Consider the following in which Date1 is the number of days in a period and Date2 is the number of days in the annual period:

Convention

Date1/Date2	Also Known as	What It Means	Examples of Uses
Actual/Actual	ISMA-99 Normal convention	Actual number of days in a month ÷ Actual number of days in a coupon period	Eurobonds
30/360	German convention U.S. convention	Each month has 30 days and each year has 360 days	U.S. corporate bonds U.S. agency issues
Actual/365	English convention	Actual number of days and each year has 365 days (ignores leap years)	U.S. Treasury bonds U.K. Gilt Edged Market
Actual/360	French convention	Actual number of days, but assumes that there are 360 days in a year	U.S. Treasury bills Commercial paper French money markets

PROBLEM

Consider a 182-day T-bill issued at 99.

a. What is the discount yield on this T-bill?

b. What is the bond equivalent yield on this T-bill?

EXAMPLE 12.2

Calculating the Yield on a Treasury Bill

Solution

a. The discount yield is 1%:

$$\text{Discount yield} = \frac{100 - 99}{100} \times \frac{360}{182} = 0.01 \times 1.978 = 0.01978 \text{ or } 1.978\%$$

b. The bond equivalent yield for this discount security is 2.026%:

$$\text{Bond equivalent yield} = \frac{100 - 99}{99} \times \frac{365}{182} = 0.010101 \times 2.0055 = 0.02026 \text{ or } 2.026\%$$

Commercial Paper

Companies can issue **commercial paper (CP)**, which is a name for short-term promissory notes. Unlike T-bills, commercial paper is normally issued with maturities of from 1 day to 270 days, but the typical commercial paper issue is for a maturity of 30 days. Commercial paper is a promissory note with credit risk because the issuer may default on the obligation to pay investors back as promised, though these are typically secured by lines of credit.[3] The dollar amounts involved are frequently very large.

commercial paper (CP) short-term debt instruments, usually unsecured, issued by companies

Yields on commercial paper

Commercial paper is most often issued at a discount from its face value, though issuers may choose to issue the paper as an interest-bearing obligation. In the case of commercial paper issued at a discount, the investor buys the paper at less than its face value and receives this face value at maturity; the difference between the face value and the purchase price, the discount, is the interest that the investor receives on this investment.

We calculate the interest on commercial paper using the bond equivalent yield and a 360-day year. Therefore, if a company issues commercial paper with a face value of $100 million for $99.55 million, and the maturity is 30 days, the bond equivalent yield on this paper is:

$$i_{bey} = \frac{\$100 \text{ million} - \$99.55 \text{ million}}{\$99.55 \text{ million}} \times \frac{360}{30}$$

$$= 0.004520 \times 12$$

$$= 0.05424 \text{ or } 5.424\%$$

Because money market instruments are quoted on an approximate interest rate basis, the 5.424 percent annual rate is equivalent to 0.4520 percent per month. If the issuer does not default on the $100 million commercial paper, the investor receives $100 million after 1 month; if the issuer defaults, the investor gets nothing.

The quoted interest rate is a **promised yield**. The promised yield is the rate investors receive if the issuer does not default and they are paid off on time, as promised. For issues where there is virtually no default or credit risk, these promised yields are also expected rates of return. However, for corporate issues, which have default risk, the expected rate

promised yield quoted interest rate received if the issuer does not default and the investor is paid off on time, as promised

[3] If commercial paper is not secured by lines of credit, the investor has no underlying assets to seize in the event of a default.

of return is always *lower* than the promised yield. The promised yield is the maximum rate the investor can hope to earn by holding the security to maturity.

Because commercial paper has default risk, the yields on commercial paper are higher than those on Treasury bills. The difference between the promised yield on commercial paper and the yield on the equivalent-maturity T-bill is called the **yield spread**. The yield spread is compensation for the possibility that if the commercial paper issuer defaults, the investor gets nothing. The important point to note is that default risk affects promised yields.

yield spread difference between the yield on one debt instrument and the yield on another

---

EXAMPLE 12.3

Calculating the Yield on Commercial Paper

PROBLEM

Consider a 6-month $200 million issuance of commercial paper with a promised yield of 3 percent. The commercial paper is priced at $195 million.

1. What is the discount yield on this paper, assuming a 30-day month?
2. What is the bond equivalent yield on this paper?

Solution

$$i_{dy} = \frac{\$200 - 195}{\$200} \times \frac{360}{180} = 0.025 \times 2 = 0.05 \text{ or } 5\%$$

Assuming a 6-month security matures in 182 days,

$$i_{bey} = \frac{\$200 - 195}{\$195} \times \frac{365}{182} = 0.02564 \times 2.0055 = 0.05142 \text{ or } 5.142\%$$

The actual risk of investing in commercial paper is extremely low because only the more creditworthy companies raise funds in the commercial paper market, and many are secured by lines of credit. Therefore, the yield spread is quite small, as you can see in Figure 12-1, where we plot the yields on 3-month Treasury bills and 3-month commercial paper. The yield spreads are usually larger during periods of economic distress, but even in those periods the spreads are quite small. For example, the largest yield spread in Figure 12-1 occurs in May of 2000; in this month the yield spread was 75 basis points. You can also see the effect of the financial crisis of 2007–2008 on yields and yield spreads. During the early months of the financial crisis, the spreads widened, but once the crisis had ebbed in 2009, the yields remained low, and the spreads narrowed through 2010.

Despite there being low risk in the commercial paper market, assessing default risk requires time as well as analytic skills. This outlay may be worthwhile when investing for a long period, but few investors are inclined to do this analysis for an investment with a 30-day maturity. However, as we noted, default risk does affect yields. Credit rating

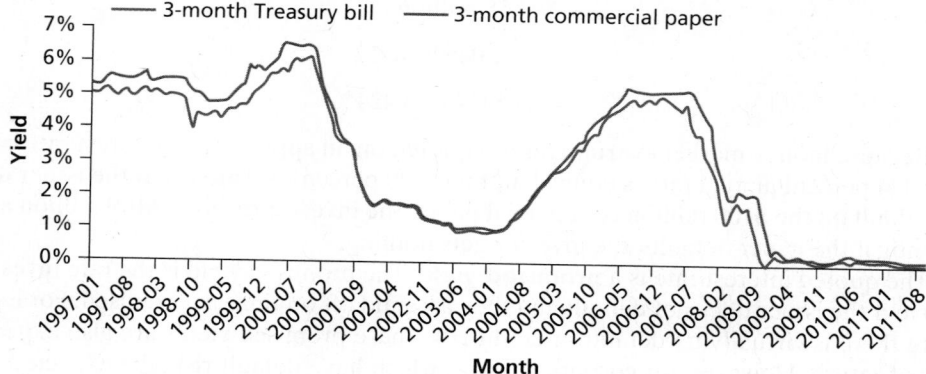

FIGURE 12-1   Yields on 3-month Treasury Bills and 3-month Commercial Paper

Source: *Federal Reserve Bank of St. Louis, Series TB3MS and CPN3M.*

agencies have developed the most basic measure, which provides default or credit ratings to investors, thereby relieving investors of the need to do individual analyses.

The major credit rating firms that rate commercial paper are Standard & Poor's, Moody's Investors Service, and Fitch Ratings. We represent their ratings classifications for commercial paper in Table 12-1.

TABLE 12-1 Credit Ratings on Commercial Paper by Standard & Poor's, Moody's Investors Service, and Fitch Ratings

Description	Standard & Poor's	Moody's Investors Service	Fitch Ratings
Highest short-term credit quality	A-1	Prime-1 or P-1	F1
Good short-term credit quality	A-2	Prime 2 or P-2	F2
Fair short-term credit quality	A-3	Prime 3 or P-3	F3
Speculative short-term credit quality	B	NP	B
High short-term default risk	C		C
Default	D	Default	D

The commercial paper market is only accessible for companies with the very best credit ratings. However, even for these companies, investors are wary of investing in commercial paper unless the companies have **liquidity support**, ensuring that money will be available to pay off the commercial paper if the companies cannot roll it over by selling to new investors. Liquidity support is usually a dedicated backup line of credit from a bank. In this way, the company can draw down on the credit line to pay off the commercial paper if needed when it comes due. The commitment fee to establish a bank line of credit used for liquidity support is about 0.125 percent per year, which adds to the overall cost of a company issuing commercial paper.

Asset-backed commercial paper

Another form of commercial paper is asset-backed commercial paper. **Asset-backed commercial paper (ABCP)** is commercial paper secured with specific assets, such as receivables, and is typically issued by **special purpose vehicles (SPV)**.[4] The SPV is created by the parent company to serve the purpose of buying assets and issuing the commercial paper, with the cash flows of these assets dedicated to repaying the commercial paper. The companies creating the SPV for this purpose are usually banks or other financial institutions, as well as large corporations. Because of the use of the SPV as an entity apart from the creator, the creditworthiness of the ABCP depends, in large part, on the credit quality of the assets backing the ABCP. However, credit enhancements can affect risk, and hence the rating and yield, of the ABCP. Examples of a **credit enhancement** include internal enhancements, such as overcollateralization of the paper (that is, the value of the secured assets is greater than the face value of the commercial paper), or external enhancements, such as insurance. The maturities of ABCP are not longer than 270 days, but are usually between 90 and 140 days.

The market for commercial paper

The issuer of commercial paper can either sell the paper directly to the investor or use a dealer. Issuers that sell directly to investors are usually financial institutions or captive finance companies. Commercial paper sold through a dealer is first sold to the dealer, and

liquidity support ensuring money is available to pay off a debt, often in the form of a dedicated backup line of credit from a bank that ensures companies have money to pay off commercial paper if the companies cannot roll it over by selling to new investors

asset-backed commercial paper (ABCP) short-term debt instrument backed by the cash flows of specific securities, generally held in a special purpose vehicle

special purpose vehicle (SPV) entity created to issue securities and hold assets, often the assets provided by the parent company creating the entity

credit enhancement provision that reduces the default risk of a security, such as overcollateralization or insurance

---

[4] The SPV is referred to as bankruptcy-remote, which means that a default of an obligation of the SPV does not affect the parent company that created the SPV. Other names used for such entities include "conduits," "transformers," and "special purpose entity" or "SPE."

then the dealer uses its resources to sell the commercial paper. Usually, the investment bank charges five basis points (that is, 0.05 percent) as a selling commission, but this is often bid down, depending on market conditions.

The trading or dealing room is a huge room with areas allocated for selling different securities, with each desk flanked by a series of computer screens. The money market desk is an area in which traders sell commercial paper. The traders call major institutional investors and sell them the commercial paper that the bank has arranged to sell on behalf of its clients.

Commercial paper is usually sold on the basis of its credit rating. Though there are few defaults of commercial paper issues, they do occur. The more famous commercial paper defaults are the $82 million Penn Central default in 1970 and the $17 million Mercury Finance default in 1997.

LESSONS LEARNED

The importance of commercial paper in the economy was illustrated during the credit crisis in the fall of 2008. Traditionally, U.S. companies had relied on many different sources of short-term funding, including bank loans and commercial paper. However, during the credit crisis of 2007–2008, banks were unable to lend, so companies turned to issuing more commercial paper. However, immediately following the Lehman Brothers bankruptcy filing on September 15, 2008, a problem arose: There weren't enough investors willing to buy this commercial paper.

Funding Facility to the Rescue

To resolve this problem, on October 7, 2008, the Federal Reserve Bank made an unprecedented move and created a fund (Commercial Paper Funding Facility, CPFF) to purchase highly-rated, unsecured commercial paper.[5] This fund is credited with slowing the decline in borrowing using commercial paper, thus averting a liquidity crisis at companies such as General Electric, by providing a backstop to the commercial paper market.[6] This funding facility appears to have stabilized the market for commercial paper.

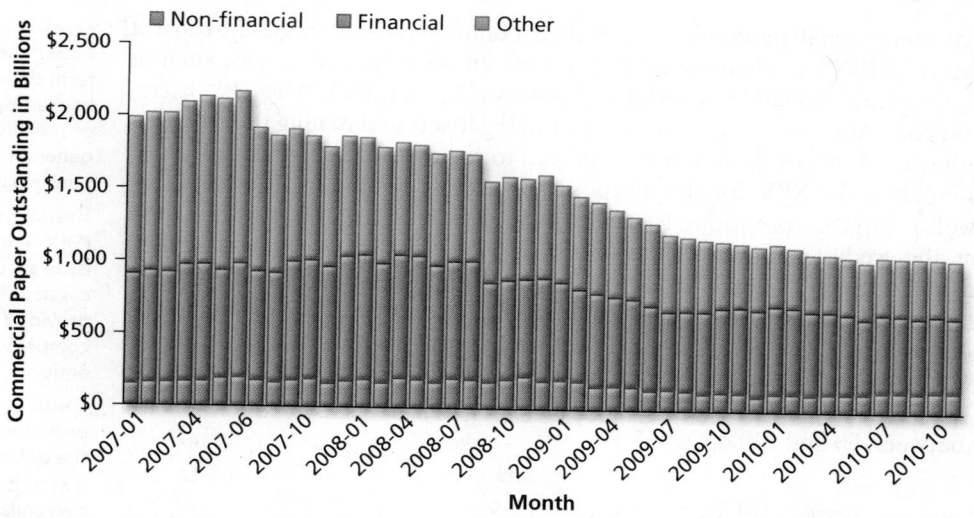

Source of data: Securities Industry and Financial Markets Association.

[5] Press Release, October 7, 2008, Board of Governors of the Federal Reserve System.

[6] Richard D. Anderson, "The Success of the CPFF?" *Economic Synopses*, Federal Reserve Bank of St. Louis, 2009, Number 18.

Bankers' Acceptances

A **bankers' acceptance (BA)** is created as a result of international trade. Typically, an exporter will receive a "bill of exchange" in return for the export of its goods. This bill of exchange is essentially a promissory note issued by the foreign importer, usually guaranteed by its local bank. The exporter will then have this note accepted by its own bank so that it can be sold for cash. Bankers' acceptances are created by international trade.[7]

Bankers' acceptances are usually issued at a discount from their face value, and the maturity may range from 1 to 180 days, though typically the maturity is 90 days. The cost to the company of issuing bankers' acceptances is the yield on the bankers' acceptances plus the bank's **stamping fee** or **acceptance fee**. This fee is usually 0.50 percent to 0.75 percent, depending on the credit risk involved.

Consider an example in which a domestic company, DC, finances a $100,000 transaction with a 180-day bankers' acceptance through USA Bank. USA Bank charges a commission of 0.75 percent, in addition to the 10 percent discount. The foreign company, FC, uses Foreign Bank for its transactions. The following transactions occur:

bankers' acceptance (BA) short-term paper sold by an issuer to a bank, which guarantees or accepts it, obligating the bank to pay off the debt instrument at maturity if the issuer defaults

stamping fee or **acceptance fee** fee paid to the financial institution accepting a bankers' acceptance

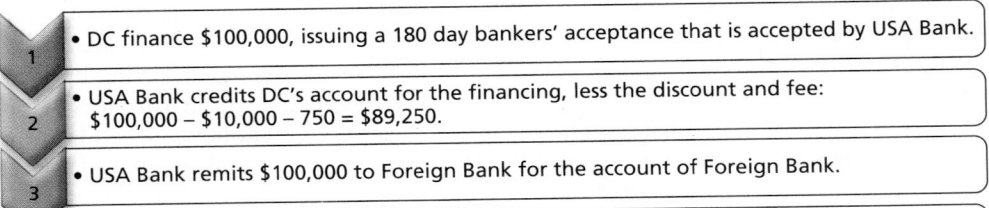

1. • DC finance $100,000, issuing a 180 day bankers' acceptance that is accepted by USA Bank.

2. • USA Bank credits DC's account for the financing, less the discount and fee: $100,000 − $10,000 − 750 = $89,250.

3. • USA Bank remits $100,000 to Foreign Bank for the account of Foreign Bank.

4. • After 180 days (i.e., at maturity), USA Bank charges DC's account for the $100,000.

What is the cost of this financing? We calculate this by comparing the interest, plus fees, paid for the loan with the funds available to DC, adjusting for the length of the credit period:

$$i_{BA} = \frac{\text{Discount} + \text{fee}}{\text{Face value} - \text{discount} - \text{fee}} \times \frac{365}{\text{maturity in days}} \qquad (12\text{-}6)$$

In our example,

$$i_{BA} = \frac{\$10,000 + 750}{\$89,250} \times \frac{365}{180} = \frac{\$10,750}{\$89,250} \times \frac{365}{180} = 0.120448 \times 2.0278 = 0.24244 \text{ or } 24.424\%$$

In short-term financing, commercial banks are very important. For example, when issuing commercial paper, most companies are required to have a backup line of credit to ensure that in the event of a disruption in the money market, funds are available to pay off the commercial paper.[8] Technically, the line of credit is not available if the credit condition of the company deteriorates, and the credit condition is reviewed continually by the bank. Similarly, the banks are critical for the bankers' acceptance market because it is the bank's credit that supports the bankers' acceptance, and not that of the company. However, the commercial paper and bankers' acceptance markets are useful only for companies that have reasonably large and continuous financing needs because commercial paper and bankers' acceptances are sold in large amounts, usually of at least $1 million. For smaller, irregular-sized financing requirements, companies rely more on traditional bank financing. These consist of term loans and lines of credit.

---

[7] Unlike in the United States and most other countries, bankers' acceptances in Canada have nothing to do with trade. They are a method by which lower-rated companies can issue short-term paper into the money market.

[8] Sometimes, external factors, such as an unexpected major default, cause investors to stop buying CP, even though the credit status of an issuer is unchanged.

line of credit basic financing tool provided by banks that establishes a loan with a specified limit to a company based on its creditworthiness

operating or **demand line of credit** lending facility that is made available by the bank for the company's operating purposes and that generally cannot be used to back up a commercial paper program; these demand loans can be cancelled at any time

prime lending rate standard cost of the operating line; the interest rate banks use to calculate their other interest rates

floating interest rate interest rate that changes regularly

term line of credit or **revolving line of credit** line of credit extended by a bank to a company for a specific amount that automatically adjusts as payments are made or received

covenant promise or restriction in a contract

Line of Credit

We have already mentioned a **line of credit** in our discussion of commercial paper because it is a basic financing tool provided by banks. In general, the borrower pays interest on the amount borrowed under the line of credit. In addition to the interest costs, the banks normally charge a commitment fee of around 0.50 percent for setting up the line of credit, which is also charged on the unused balance.

There are different types of lines of credit. The standard line of credit is an **operating line of credit**, also known as a **demand line of credit**. These are lending facilities that are made available by the bank for the company's operating purposes, and they generally cannot be used to back up a commercial paper program. Technically, operating lines of credit are demand loans that can be cancelled at any time. However, in practice, banks are reluctant to do anything that might trigger financial problems for the company because this might leave them legally liable for damages. The structure of lines of credit is a maximum dollar amount that the company can draw down by electronically transferring funds from the operating line to its checking (or current) account.

The standard cost of the operating line is the **prime lending rate**. Prime is an example of a **floating interest rate** because it changes regularly, so the cost of a company's demand loan will float with the bank's prime lending rate. As the prime rate changes, the bank will inform the company of the change in the cost of its loan for the upcoming month. The bank will make loans available to its most creditworthy customers at rates below prime, particularly if they are large enough to access the money market. However, most companies are "prime plus" borrowers, and borrowing rates may be quoted as prime plus 0.5 percent, prime plus 1 percent, and so on.

The second type of bank line adds more stability to the company. This is the **term line of credit** or **revolving line of credit**, which refers to the fact that the amounts owed on the line of credit "revolve" in response to surplus or deficit cash positions experienced by the company as checks are received from customers and the company's checks are cashed by its suppliers. The term is usually at least 364 days and is often out to 5 years, renewable every 6 months. Often a 5-year "revolver" is renewed at the end of each year, making it an "evergreen" 5-year line of credit. Because the revolver is a commitment of credit, the bank has to provide capital against these commitments to ensure the liquidity of the bank. The common 364-day line of credit occurs because more capital is required against a 1-year or 365-day line of credit.

Revolving lines of credit are very flexible financing tools for both the bank and the company. In addition to being used to provide straight borrowings, they are also used to back up commercial paper programs or other commitments, such as forward foreign currency contracts. However, banks have tightened up on the potential uses for these bank lines of credit; the general principle banks use is that lines of credit are for liquidity and not credit-enhancement purposes. This means that the bank will withdraw or adjust the line of credit if a material adverse change occurs, that is, if the credit quality of the company deteriorates. The line of credit is outstanding to provide the company with liquidity that it can draw down only if its credit quality is constant.

Companies have to meet a variety of restrictions to maintain access to the funds in a line of credit. Typically, the maximum value of the line of credit is determined by using a standard formula, such as that it cannot exceed 75 percent of a company's receivables plus 50 percent of its inventory. Normally, the company must provide periodic abbreviated financial statements, sometimes on a monthly basis. The company may then have to meet certain credit restrictions, or **covenants**, such as maintaining the following:

- a minimum current ratio of 1.4 or net working capital of $100 million,
- net worth (shareholders' equity) in excess of $250 million,
- a minimum interest coverage ratio (times interest earned) of 1.75, and
- an asset coverage ratio in excess of 2 and a debt ratio less than 0.75.

The covenants in the revolving loan allow the bank to pull the loan (i.e., demand payment) and prevent the company from drawing it down beyond a certain amount as its credit quality deteriorates. However, the restrictions are only of limited effectiveness because companies usually have more than one bank account, and they know before the bank whether they are going to violate the conditions. In this case, they can simply draw down the line of credit before informing the bank of the violations and transfer the funds to another bank where they have full use of the money. Of course, this will damage their reputation, which could impede their ability to borrow in the future.

In addition to the interest costs, the banks normally charge a commitment fee of around 0.50 percent for setting up the line of credit, which is also charged on the unused balance. As with the operating line, most revolvers are based on prime, with less credit-worthy companies paying higher spreads above prime.

Home Equity Lines of Credit | FINANCE in the News

During the run-up to the housing bubble, many homeowners borrowed against the equity in their homes using a home equity line of credit (HELOC). In many cases, this was borrowing against the home in addition to the home mortgage, and therefore the HELOC became a second mortgage. These home equity lines of credit often had upfront fees and variable interest rates, and some had large balloon payments at the end of the loan, whereas others had low introductory rates that jumped up later.

When home prices started downward, many home-owners with a home equity line of credit found themselves with loans (that is, mortgage plus home equity loan) that far exceeded the value of the home. When the credit market tightened in 2007 and 2008, many banks reduced the outstanding HELOC, which they are permitted to do without prior notice.

Term Loans

The idea behind lines of credit is that the funds are used for working capital purposes: financing receivables, inventory, and ongoing corporate activity. In fact, some more traditional banks still require "cleanup" periods in which the company has a zero balance on its line of credit, to make sure that the bank is not providing permanent financing, which should be financed with longer-term funds. **Term loans** differ from lines of credit because they have a fixed maturity, require repayment to be made on a fixed schedule, and are made to finance longer-term requirements such as equipment purchases.

These loans are structured in a variety of ways. They are usually for at least 3 years and may go out to 10 years or longer. Some involve a **bullet** or **balloon payment**, where only interest is paid until maturity, at which time the entire principal is due and payable. Such loans generally provide permanent financing of the company's operations, rather than financing a particular asset. In contrast, amortizing loans are similar to conventional loans made to individuals, in which a monthly payment consists of both interest and principal payments, similar to a car loan or mortgage, both of which are valued as annuities.

Similar to other forms of bank financing, term loans may be based on the prime lending rate, and thus float with the general level of interest rates. However, term loans are often offered with a fixed interest rate over the term of the loan. In addition, term loans are also offered by insurance companies and specialized business finance companies, often for longer periods than those offered by the chartered banks.

The big advantage of term loans to a borrowing company is that they are easy to arrange. All companies have banking relationships because they need checking accounts to gain access to the payments system, and they also need banks for short-term financing. Consequently, the company's bank already has inside knowledge of its activities, and it

term loan borrowing to finance longer-term requirements, such as equipment purchases, which have a fixed maturity and require repayment to be made on a fixed schedule

bullet payment or **balloon principal** payment (partial or full) paid at maturity of a loan

can readily arrange a term loan if it judges the company to be creditworthy. Further, the term loan can often be structured to fit with a company's operating and revolving lines of credit. For example, sometimes a revolver is structured to switch into a term loan at the end of its 5-year life.

SUMMARIZING:
SHORT-TERM FINANCING

Financial Instrument	Maturity	Types of Interest		Source of Funds	
		Discounted?	Interest Bearing?	Bank Financing	Money Market
Treasury bill	4 weeks–52 weeks	√			√
Commercial paper	1–270 days	√	√		√
Asset-backed commercial paper	90–270 days				√
Bankers' acceptances	1–180 days	√			√
Line of credit			√	√	
Revolving line of credit	364 days–5 years		√	√	
Term loans	3 years–10 years		√	√	

Concept Review Questions

1. Contrast Treasury bills, commercial paper, and bankers' acceptances in terms of who issues them, their basic structure and default risk, and the yields they provide.

2. Briefly describe operating lines of credit, revolving lines of credit, and term loans.

12.3 LONG-TERM INSTRUMENTS

Long-term financing generally refers to any debt issued with a term longer than 1 year and is often called funded debt. The reason for this is that short-term debt is not regarded as permanent capital; therefore, when a company accumulates "too much" short-term debt, it funds this debt by issuing long-term debt. As discussed earlier, banks provide medium-term financing through term loans, which are also provided by insurance companies and other specialized financial companies. These are examples of private financing because there is no offering of the debt to the general public. For bank financing, the company generally does not have to provide any extra information because it already provides information in support of its existing bank relationship.

For term loans from other entities, the company will have to provide an offering memorandum. This document contains much the same type of information as that provided in a prospectus, but in less detail. A **prospectus** is a detailed document that describes the security offering, which is required by the Securities and Exchange Commission for all public offerings; an **offering memorandum**, on the other hand, is less detailed and is used for private placements of securities.

The remaining forms of financing involve public financing, and here it is important to realize that securities laws and regulations, and the required filing of a prospectus, apply to debt as well as equity offerings. Most financing in the capital markets is done by issuers

prospectus detailed document that describes the security offering, which is required by the Securities and Exchange Commission for all public offerings

offering memorandum description of a security's terms, used for private placements of securities

who can raise capital, both debt and equity, through the issue of a short-form prospectus. These filings are made with the Securities and Exchange Commission.

We use terminology that distinguishes debt based on the original term to maturity, whether the debt is backed by specific collateral, and whether the debt can be called back by the issuer or converted into another security by the investor.

Maturity

The **maturity** of a debt obligation is the point in time at which the borrower repays the amount borrowed. This maturity is generally established when the debt obligation is issued. An issuer may specify any length of time to the maturity.

A debt obligation may mature in 5, 10, 50, or 100 years, for example. A source of confusion in debt obligations that are issued by government or corporate entities is that the terms *note* and *bond* are used interchangeably to refer to a debt obligation with a maturity longer than 1 year. In general use, a debt obligation that matures in less than 10 years is often referred to as a **note** or a **medium-term note (MTN)**. An obligation with a maturity between 4 and 10 years is often referred to as an **intermediate-term bond**. We generally refer to debt obligations with terms longer than 10 years as a **bond** or a **long-term bond**. However, the terminology conventions in this area are not hard-and-fast rules. For example, in 1993 Walt Disney Company issued a 7.55 percent coupon medium-term note that matures in July 2093.

A note or bond generally requires the issuer to pay a fixed amount in the future. This fixed amount goes by many names, including **face value**, **maturity value**, and **par value**. If the note or bond specifies the payment of interest, this interest may be a fixed coupon rate, which is specified as a percentage of the par value of the note or bond, or a floating rate, which is specified relative to a reference rate, such as the LIBOR. This fixed amount at maturity and the interest may be in the same currency as the issuer's home country or may be issued in another country's currency.

Security

An issuer may provide collateral for a debt obligation; this collateral is provided to the investor in the case of a default on the obligation. We refer to a debt obligation that is backed by collateral as **secured debt**, where this collateral may be a specific asset, a group of assets, or a specific cash flow. We use the term **debenture** to refer to a debt obligation secured by the general credit of the issuer. Bonds backed by specific collateral include **mortgage bonds**, which are backed by real estate, and **asset-backed notes** or **asset-backed bonds** when backed by a specific asset, a group of assets, or a specific set of cash flows. If a debt security is unsecured, the investors will demand a greater return than for a comparable secured debt of the issuer.

Seniority

There is a pecking order or seniority of debt obligations with respect to claims on the income and assets of the company. We communicate an obligation's seniority by referring to the debt as senior or junior, unsubordinated or subordinated. A **senior debt** is one that has preference over other debt obligations in terms of the issuer's capitalization, whereas a **junior debt** is one that ranks behind other securities in terms of the issuer's capitalization. A **subordinated debt** is unsecured debt that ranks behind—that is, is junior to—other debt of the issuer, and an **unsubordinated debt** is one in which no other unsecured debt ranks ahead of it.

The seniority of a debt obligation affects its risk, and hence its value; the more junior or subordinated a security, the greater the compensation that investors demand for risk.

---

maturity point in time at which the borrower repays the amount borrowed

medium-term note (MTN) debt obligation that matures in less than 10 years

intermediate-term bond debt obligation with a maturity between 4 and 10 years

face value, maturity value, par value promised fixed amount in a note or bond agreement

secured debt debt obligation backed with collateral

asset-backed note or **asset-backed bond** debt obligation that has a specific asset, a group of assets, or a set of future cash flows as collateral

senior debt debt that has preference over other debt obligations in terms of the issuer's capitalization

junior debt debt that ranks behind other securities in terms of the issuer's capitalization

subordinated debt unsecured debt that ranks behind other debt of the issuer

unsubordinated debt unsecured debt that ranks first with the company; no other unsecured debt ranks ahead of it

Indenture Agreements

Debt obligations may have an **indenture agreement**, which is part of the legal agreement between the issuer and the investor. The indenture agreement describes a debt obligation's interest, maturity, any collateral, and other features, such as callability and convertibility.

There is a great deal of flexibility in terms of specifying the covenants in an indenture agreement. As we mentioned earlier in the context of a line of credit, a covenant is a provision that must be satisfied by the issuer. Like other lending agreements, bond indentures have covenants. An **affirmative covenant** is the promises that the issuer makes, such as the timely payment of interest and principal repayment. A **negative covenant**, on the other hand, is a prohibition or restriction. An example of a negative covenant is a clause that may prohibit the issuer from mortgaging, pledging, or otherwise encumbering the assets that are used to secure the debt instrument. Another example of a negative covenant is prohibiting the issuer from paying dividends on common stock if the certain requirements are not met.

Embedded Options

In addition to provisions with respect to maturity, seniority, and collateral, notes and bonds may also have features that give the issuer flexibility in managing their financing costs and that give investors flexibility to convert their investments. These features are options embedded in the debt contract.

Issuers gain flexibility in financing when a debt obligation is callable. A **callable bond** is a bond in which the issuer has the option to buy the bond back from the investor at a specified price, the **call price**. A bond may be callable according to a schedule of call prices, whereby the call price depends on the specific date the security is called from the investor. This **call schedule** is specified in the security's indenture agreement. Generally, if general market interest rates fall, companies are more likely to call a bond; by doing so, they can then issue another bond in its place with a lower interest rate. The terms of a callable bond may be specified so that there is **call protection**, a period of time in which the bond may not be called back from the investor.

The call feature gives the issuer a valuable option to call the bonds back from the investor. Though the valuation of this option is beyond the scope of this text, you can see that this is a call option that becomes more valuable to the issuer the lower the general market rates. The call features does add risk to the investor because as rates are falling, the probability that the security may be called away increases. Therefore, investors will require a greater return on a callable security, compared to that of a similar noncallable security.

Investors gain flexibility when the debt obligation that they invest in is convertible. A **convertible bond** is a debt obligation exchangeable into another security at the option of the investor. A bond may be convertible into a specified number of shares of the issuer's common stock, or any other security of the issuer. The debt's agreement will specify the **conversion ratio**, which is the number of common shares for a given bond.

Suppose a bond with a par value of $1,000 is convertible into 20 shares of common stock of the bond issuer. The **conversion ratio** of this bond is 20. If the stock is selling at $55 per share, the value of the bond if converted, which we refer to as the **conversion value**, is the product of the conversion ratio and the price per common share, or $20 \times \$55 = \$1,100$. This conversion value is the value of the bond if it is converted immediately into common stock. This value establishes a floor for the value of the bond: The value of the bond is the minimum of the conversion value or the value of the bond if it did not have the conversion value, that is, its **straight value**.

The conversion feature gives the buyer of the convertible security a valuable option. If the security into which it is convertible is trading at a price that makes conversion unattractive, the convertible bond will be worth, at minimum, the value of a similar, yet nonconvertible bond. However, the investor of a convertible security has the upside potential of the security into which it is convertible.

Let's consider an example. Suppose the bond of the Fabozzi Company has a 6 percent coupon, paid semi-annually, a face value of $1,000, 5 years remaining to maturity, and it is trading at a yield to maturity of 6.5 percent. Now suppose that this bond is convertible into 15 shares of Fabozzi Company common stock, and that the common stock currently has a market value of $60 per share. What is the value of this bond?

The value of the bond without considering the convertibility is $978.94. This is the bond's straight value. The bond's conversion value is $15 \times \$60 = \$900$. So what value will the bond trade at? It will trade at its straight value because this value is greater than its conversion value. The investor does not have to convert the bond, so he can hold onto the bond and continue to earn interest.

When would the investor want to convert the bond into stock? There is a break-even point of sorts, which we refer to as the **market conversion price**. The market conversion price is the value per share of the stock at which the investor is indifferent between holding the bond and converting it into stock. For the Fabozzi bond, the market conversion price is $978.94 \div 15 = \$65.263$. If the price of the stock is above $65.263, the value of the bond converted into shares is more than the value of the bond; if the price of the stock is below $65.263, the value of the bond as a straight bond is worth more than converting it into stock. Generally, convertible bonds trade at a price above the higher of the market conversion price or the straight bond price, due to the value of the option to convert into shares.

market conversion price value of a share of stock that, considering the conversion ratio of the convertible bond, is equivalent to the value of the bond

---

EXAMPLE 12.4

Convertible Bonds

PROBLEM

Suppose a bond has a conversion feature that specifies the bond can be converted to 10 shares of common stock. The common stock is currently selling for $14 per share. If the bond has a coupon of 5 percent, 5 years remaining to maturity, a face value of $1,000, and is priced to yield 4 percent, what is the:

a. bond's straight value?
b. conversion ratio?
c. conversion value?
d. market conversion price?

Solution

a. Straight value = $[FV = 1000; PMT = 25; N = 10; i = 2\%] = \$1,044.91$
b. Conversion ratio = 10
c. Conversion value = $10 \times \$14 = \$140$
d. Market conversion price = $104.49

Concept Review Questions

1. Describe and distinguish between mortgage bonds, secured debentures, unsecured debentures, and subordinated debt.

2. Discuss the rationale for including debt covenants.

3. Briefly describe the difference between an affirmative covenant and a negative covenant.

12.4 BOND RATINGS

Ratings are essential in the commercial paper market because investments have such a short maturity, making credit analysis expensive. For longer-term debt issues, however, most purchasers, like the major institutions, do their own credit analysis. However, bond ratings are still very important. We provide a summary of the bond ratings from major rating agencies in Table 12-2.

TABLE 12-2 Bond Ratings

Description	Standard & Poor's	Moody's Investors Service	Fitch Ratings	DBRS
Prime, maximum safety	AAA	Aaa	AAA	AAA
High grade, high quality	AA	Aa	AA	AA
Upper medium grade	A	A	A	A
Lower medium grade	BBB	Baa	BBB	BBB
Speculative	BB	Ba	BB	BB
Highly speculative	B	B	B	B
Substantial risk; poor standing	CCC	Caa	CCC	CCC
Extremely speculative		Ca		CC
May be in default		C		C
Default	D		DDD	D
			DD	
			D	

The rating of AAA/Aaa is the highest rating possible. In addition to what you see in Table 12-2, each rating may be modified with a high or low rating to communicate further its creditworthiness within that class. The lowest **investment-grade** bond rating is BBB/Baa, and below this, a bond is commonly referred to as a **junk bond**, although it is more politely referred to as a high-yield bond.

investment grade bond rating that means the issuer is likely to meet payment obligations

junk bond speculative bonds with ratings below investment grade; often called high-yield bonds

Determining Bond Ratings

A bond rating agency determines a bond rating after extensive consultation with the company through a site visit, in which the company can state its view of its business and future prospects, and after examining at least 5 years of historical financial statements. The rating firm usually will already have prior knowledge of the company from its extensive industry surveys. In determining its rating, the rating firm is guided by two basic principles: the stable rating philosophy and the hierarchy principle.

The **stable rating philosophy** is summed up by the idea that the rating is based on structural and not cyclical factors. The fortunes of most companies will fluctuate with the business cycle: When the economy is hot, most companies will make money, and conversely, when it is in recession, most companies will struggle. Holders of 20- or 30-year debt can expect the company to operate though many ups and downs of the business cycle. The rating firm aims to see through these predictable effects and change ratings only when a clear structural change occurs in the company's credit. This sounds easier than it is, because, in practice, it is sometimes difficult to maintain ratings when the economy is

stable rating philosophy ratings based on structural and not on cyclical factors; changes in ratings are made not based on temporary changes in the economy but on clear structural changes in a company's credit

in deep recession, even though the company is responding to that recession in a predictable manner. This is the stage when many rating agencies put companies on **credit watch**, rather than cutting the rating.

The **hierarchy principle** is based on the fact that the rating firm rates debt issues and not companies. Although we think of a rating as applied to a particular company, this is not the case. So the first mortgage bonds of a company might be rated as A (high), unsecured MTNs as A, and junior subordinated bonds as A (low).

In determining its rating, a rating firm typically looks at six basic factors:

1. *Core profitability:* This is an assessment based on standard profit measures, such as the return on equity, return on assets, the "quality" of a company's earnings, its cost structure (e.g., whether it is the low-cost producer or its operating risk), its growth opportunities, and its pricing structure.

2. *Asset quality:* Assets are made up of many different types, so the rating agency looks at the importance of intangibles (for example, how valuable is the goodwill on the company's balance sheet), the market value of the company's assets, and its use of derivatives and risk management to see whether it is managing its operational and market risks effectively.

3. *Strategy and management strength:* Ultimately, a company is comprised of assets and management, so that an assessment of a company's credit risk is vitally concerned with the capabilities of the senior management group. This is particularly important if the company is actively involved in mergers and acquisitions in which a clear strategic approach and skills at integrating acquired companies are valuable.

4. *Balance sheet strength:* If the lenders have to initiate bankruptcy proceedings, it is important to understand where they stand in the overall liabilities of the company, so standard debt ratios, coverage tests, and the amount of financial flexibility available to the company are important. The latter includes an assessment of the company's reliance on short-term debt, its commitment to a capital expenditure program that cannot be easily stopped, and the support potentially available from other parties, such as affiliated companies. Size is important because larger companies are usually less risky and have more market power.

5. *Business strength:* This category includes standard issues, such as market share; growth prospects for the industry; a defensible base of diversified operations; up-to-date management information systems; key intangibles, such as the quality of its workforce; and industry issues, such as the degree of unionization and competition.

6. *Miscellaneous issues:* This is a "catchall" category of issues, such as the quality of the company's accounting statements and whether there have been consistent restatements, the structure of the bond indenture, and the importance of the company and industry to the economy.

Overall, rating debt instruments combines standard financial analysis based on the ratios with a broader company and industry analysis. The result is a mixture of quantitative and qualitative factors.

In Figure 12-2, we graph the yields between AAA/Aaa and BBB/Baa rated bonds, and in Figure 12-3 we show the yield spreads between these two rating classes in basis points. In Figure 12-2 you can see that the yields tend to move together, though not perfectly; the spread between the AAA/Aaa and BBB/Baa yields depends, in part, on the condition of the economy.

The spread experience indicates that during economic slowdowns, there is a *flight to quality*, when investors are reluctant to invest in riskier securities and invest more heavily in low-risk investments. You can see this in Figure 12-3 during the recessionary periods:[9]

credit watch status applied to a company by a rating agency when it is monitoring the company

hierarchy principle theory based on the fact that rating agencies rate debt issues and not companies; rating agencies rate each class of debt lower than the previous class, unless there is very little of the higher-ranked debt outstanding

---

[9] *Business Cycle Expansions and Contractions*, National Bureau of Economic Research.

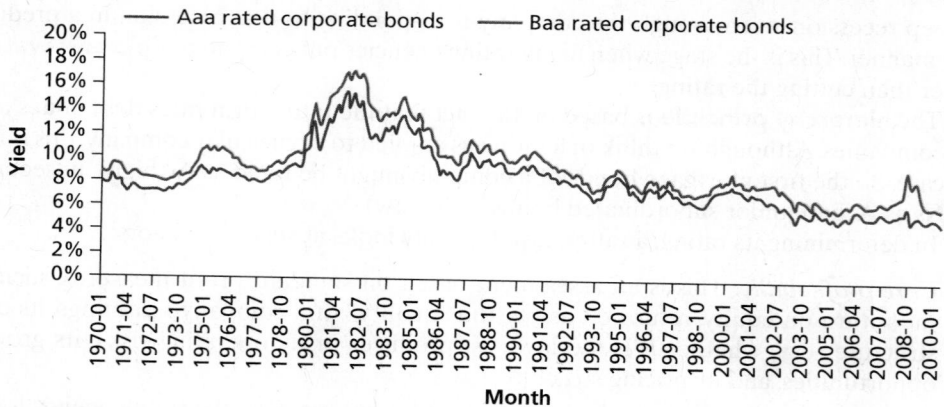

FIGURE 12-2 Yields on Aaa and Baa Rated Corporate Bonds, 1970–2011

Source of data: *Federal Reserve Bank of St. Louis.*

Recession Beginning Month	*Recession Ending Month*
December 1969	November 1970
November 1973	March 1975
January 1980	July 1980
July 1981	November 1982
July 1990	March 1991
March 2001	November 2001
December 2007	June 2009

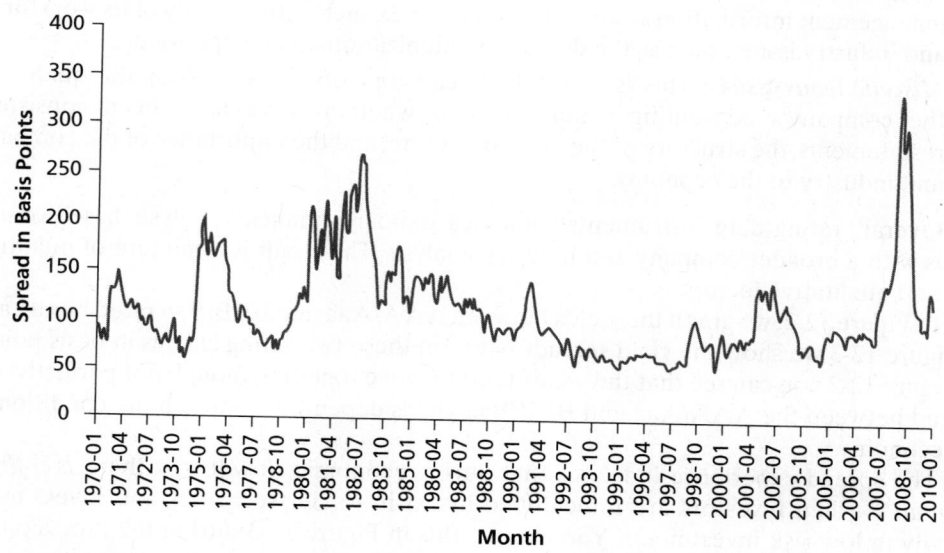

FIGURE 12-3 Yield Spreads Between Aaa and Baa Rated Bonds, 1970–2011

Source of data: *Federal Reserve Bank of St. Louis*

For example, the yield spread between AAA/Aaa and BBB/Baa rated bonds in October 2001 was 88 basis points, and the spread peaked during the 2007–2009 recession in December 2008 at 338 basis points.

During recessionary or slowdown periods, some companies experience financing problems and discover that they cannot access long-term funds on reasonable terms. In fact, these spreads are on **seasoned bond issues** (or actively traded bond issues), and they do not indicate whether or not new funds are available on those terms. For this reason, during these periods, lower-rated companies usually have to finance with shorter-term debt or rely on bank borrowings.

seasoned bond issues actively traded bond issues that have been outstanding for some time

Bond Ratings, Default Rates, and Recovery Rates

Credit ratings are performed by a small number of rating firms, which is the result of the Securities and Exchange Commission requiring that dealers evaluate risk using one of the small number of **Nationally Recognized Statistical Rating Organizations (NRSROs)**. The largest NRSROs are Moody's Investors Service, Standard & Poor's, and Fitch Ratings, and these firms provide 95 percent of the ratings worldwide. The reliance on this small number of NRSROs has been brought into question during recent scandals, as well as during the recent economic problems that were created, in part, by securities that were backed by subprime mortgages, yet received ratings that did not fully reflect their risk.

One problem with bond ratings is the present system of compensating bond rating firms.[10] Currently, the issuer pays the rating firm to rate an issuer, and the issuer can shop around for the best rating among the three NRSROs. This presents a possible conflict of interest: A rating firm that does not provide a sufficiently high rating may not receive future business from the issuer. And because the rating firm relies on the fees it receives from the issuers, this also presents a possible conflict of interest.

Another problem with bond ratings is the speed at which bond raters reflect a company's financial condition. The bond rating firms' actions tend to follow the actual changes in companies' financial conditions.[11] For example, Moody's and Standard & Poor's rated Enron as investment grade up until 4 days before the company's bankruptcy filing.

Still another problem cited regarding NSRSOs is that these firms tended to understate the risk associated with asset-backed securities, specifically subprime-mortgage-backed securities.[12] A number of lawsuits have been filed regarding the rating of these securities.[13]

In response to criticism of the NRSROs, the Securities and Exchange Commission is adopting rules that will encourage competition among NRSROs and increased disclosure of the ratings process. In addition, the SEC is eliminating the requirement that investment risk be assessed using NRSROs, which created an oligopoly in the ratings industry and market participants' reliance on these ratings, to the possible detriment to investors and the markets.[14]

Despite criticisms regarding the ratings assigned to asset-backed securities and the speed of responding to changes in a company's financial condition, the default experience of bonds is consistent with ratings. In Figure 12-4 we provide the default rates on bonds

[10] Testimony of Sean J. Egan, House Committee on Oversight and Government Reform, October 22, 2008.

[11] Testimony of Jonathan R. Macey, House Committee on Financial Services, 109th Congress, 1st session, November 29, 2005.

[12] Jody Shenn, "Moody's Is Least Accurate Subprime-Bond Rating Firm," Bloomberg.com, April 2, 2008.

[13] Martha Graybow, "Credit Rating Agencies Fending Off Lawsuits from Subprime Meltdown," *Reuters*, July 14, 2008, and Robert Cyran, "Hole Poked in Rating Agencies' Lawsuit Shield," *Fortune*, September 4, 2009.

[14] Securities and Exchange Commission, "References to Ratings of Nationally Recognized Statistical Rating Organizations," 17CFR Parts 240, 242, 249 and 270, Federal Register, Vol. 74, No. 195, October 9, 2009.

FINANCE in the News | Competition Among Credit Rating Companies

For much of the 1990s, there were only three Nationally Recognized Statistical Rating Organizations (NRSROs). In an effort to increase the competition among NRSROs, the Securities and Exchange Commission encouraged firms to register as NRSROs and added DBRS and others to the list of NRSROs.

NRSROs are regulated by the Securities and Exchange Act. To become an NRSRO, a firm must register as an NRSRO, which requires completing a Form NRSRO and providing a long list of information that includes financial statements, code of ethics, disclosure of potential conflicts of interest, accessibility of ratings, classes of credit ratings, and credit rating performance statistics.

The NRSROs registered as of the end of 2011, with classes of credit ratings noted, are:[15]

	Classes of Credit Ratings				
	Financial Institutions, Brokers, or Dealers	Insurance Companies	Corporate Issuers	Issuers of Asset-Backed Securities	Issuers of Government Securities, Municipal Securities, or Securities Issued by a Foreign Government
A. M. Best Company		✓	✓	✓	
DBRS Ltd.	✓	✓	✓	✓	✓
Egan-Jones Rating Company	✓	✓	✓	✓	✓
Fitch Ratings	✓	✓	✓	✓	✓
Japan Credit Rating Company	✓	✓	✓		✓
Kroll Bond Rating Agency, Inc.[16]	✓	✓	✓	✓	✓
Moody's Investors Service, Inc.	✓	✓	✓	✓	✓
Morningstar Credit Ratings, LLC				✓	
Standard & Poor's Ratings Services	✓	✓	✓	✓	✓

Despite the expansion of the number of NRSROs, the largest three credit rating services—Fitch, Moody's, and Standard & Poor's—still dominate the credit rating industry:[17]

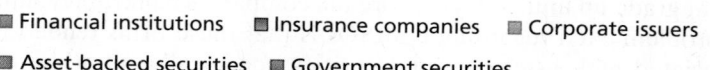

■ Financial institutions   ■ Insurance companies   ■ Corporate issuers
■ Asset-backed securities   ■ Government securities

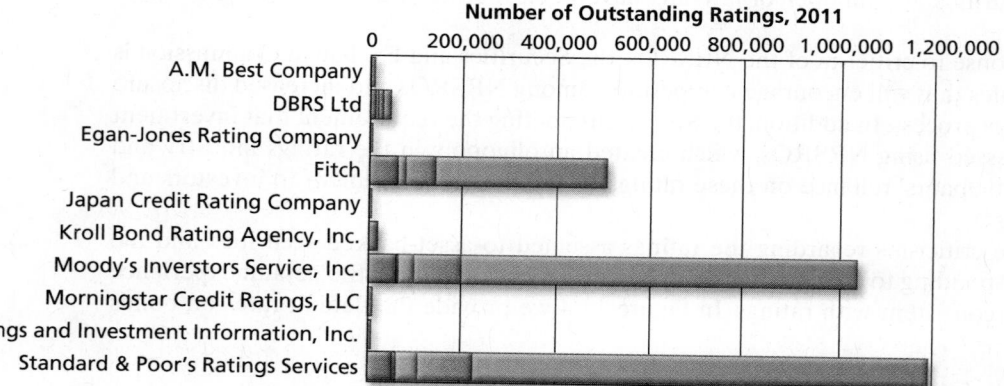

Number of Outstanding Ratings, 2011

Source of data: "2011 Summary Report of Commission Staff's Examinations of Each Nationally Recognized Statistical Rating Organization," Staff of the U.S. Securities and Exchange Commission, September 2011.

[15] Ratings and Investment Information, Inc., was granted registration as an NRSRO in 2007, but withdrew in October 2011 (effective November 2011).

[16] Formally known as LACE Financial Corp.

[17] A. M. Best has a sizeable portion (25.58 percent) of the ratings of insurance companies, though insurance company ratings are less than 1 percent of all outstanding ratings.

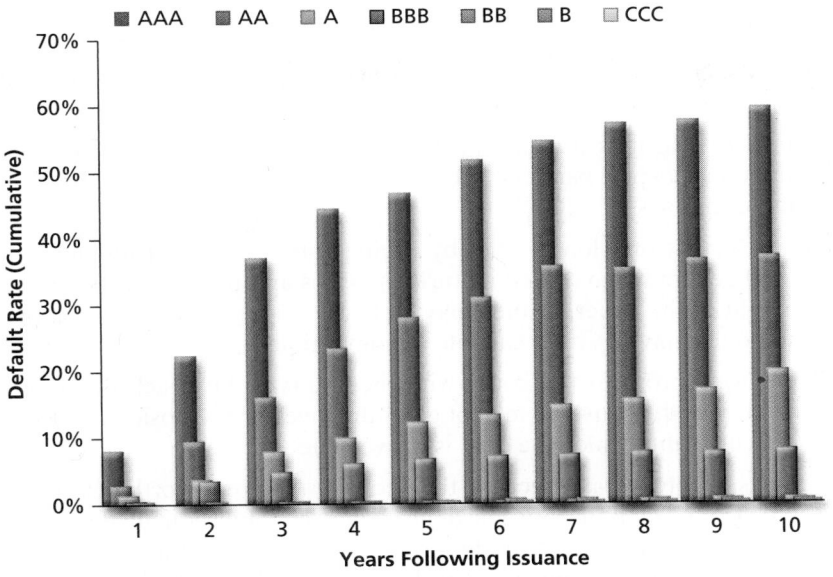

FIGURE 12-4   Default Rates by Rating, 1971 Through 2006

Source: *Edward I. Altman, "About Corporate Default Rates," working paper, New York University, Table 15-2.*

for different rating classes and for different numbers of years following the securities' issuance.[18] As you can see in this graph, the default rates for AAA/Aaa rated bonds is very low when compared to other bond classes, and the default rates of noninvestment-grade bonds (BB/Ba, B, and CCC/Caa) are comparatively high. For example, 2.84 percent of B rated bonds default within 1 year of issuance, but 37.06 percent of these bonds have defaulted by 10 years following issuance.

The data on default and recovery rates indicate what we would expect: High-risk bonds have a higher probability of defaulting as well as a lower recovery rate. Ed Altman, an expert on corporate bankruptcy, high-yield bonds, distressed debt, and credit risk analysis examined the relationship between default rates and recovery rates for bonds over the period from 1982 through 2005.[19] He observed an inverse relationship between the default rates and recovery rates, which is reasonable when you consider what happens when companies are in financial distress. As an industry struggles, many companies in that industry may face default on their securities. When this happens, these struggling companies attempt to liquidate their inventories and other assets at the same time, producing less in return on these assets. This then affects how much creditors are able to get from these distressed companies, which then reduces the recovery rate on these bonds.

Concept Review Questions

1. Differentiate investment-grade debt from junk debt.

2. Briefly describe the main factors rating agencies consider in determining debt ratings.

3. Briefly summarize the evidence regarding how well debt ratings work.

[18] Credit rating firms report periodically on their accuracy of their ratings. For example, Moody's Investors Service reports that the historical average of their accuracy is 84 percent for 1 year ahead accuracy and 72 percent for 5 years ahead accuracy. Moody's also reports that the average rating it assigns to a company prior to the company's bankruptcy is B2, which is a non-investment-grade rating, and the default rates of debt they rate as investment grade is in the range of 0 to 3 percent.

[19] Edward I. Altman, "Credit Risk and the Link between Default and Recovery Rates," in *Global Perspectives on Investment Management*, edited by Rodney N. Sullivan (Charlottesville, VA: CFA Institute, 2006).

SUMMARY

- Debt is a fixed contractual commitment, which may be a short-term or a long-term commitment.

- Money market securities are normally traded on a discount basis and include Treasury bills, commercial paper, bankers' acceptances, and bank financing through lines of credit and term loans.

- Companies finance on a longer term by issuing notes or bonds. These notes may bear interest and generally have fixed maturities. Notes and bonds may be backed by the general credit of the issuer, or they may be backed by specific collateral. In addition, notes and bonds may be either callable or convertible.

- A callable bond provides the issuer with the ability to buy back the debt from the investor, whereas the convertible debt gives the investor the upside potential derived from the security into which the debt is convertible.

- Debt ratings are important because they convey the creditworthiness of the issuer. There is a strong relation between debt ratings and subsequent defaults, whereby securities rated as investment grade have low default rates and securities rated as noninvestment grade have much higher default rates. However, some issues regarding debt rating firms bear further study.

FORMULAS/EQUATIONS

(12-1) $r_d^* = r_d(1 - T)$

(12-2) $i_{dy} = \dfrac{FV - PV}{FV} \times \dfrac{360}{m}$

(12-3) $PV = FV\left[1 - \left(i_{dy} \times \dfrac{m}{360}\right)\right]$

(12-4) $i_{bey} = \dfrac{FV - PV}{PV} \times \dfrac{365}{m}$

(12-5) $PV = FV\left[1 - \left(i_{bey} \times \dfrac{m}{365}\right)\right]$

(12-6) $i_{BA} = \dfrac{\text{Discount} + \text{fee}}{\text{Face value} - \text{discount} - \text{fee}} \times \dfrac{365}{\text{maturity in days}}$

QUESTIONS AND PROBLEMS

Multiple Choice

1. Which of the following statements about debt is *incorrect*?
    A. Interest payments are tax deductible.
    B. Interest payments and principal payments are fixed commitments.
    C. Debt indenture is a legal document, specifying payment requirements, and so on.
    D. Bond issuers are paid a series of fixed periodic amounts before the maturity date.

2. If the marginal tax rate is 40 percent and the before-tax cost of debt is 8 percent, the after-tax cost of debt is *closest* to:
    A. 3.2%.   B. 4.8%.   C. 6.0%.   D. 7.5%.

3. If the promised yield on 30-day commercial paper is 5 percent, the yield on the 91-day T-bill is 3 percent, and the yield on the 30-day T-bill is 2 percent, the promised yield spread is *closest* to:
    A. 2%.   B. 3%.   C. 4%.   D. 5%.

4. Which of the following money market instruments could a company without a very sound credit rating use when seeking financing?
    A. Bill of exchange   B. Commercial paper   C. Bankers' acceptance

5. Which of the following reflects the negative pledge clause?
   A. The issuing company must make its interest payments.
   B. The issuing company must fulfill its supplies to promised customers.
   C. The issuing company has to maintain a current ratio of more than 2.5.
   D. The issuing company must not issue any new debt with existing assets as collateral.

6. Which of the following statements about lines of credit is *false*?
   A. A revolver is usually at least 364 days.
   B. Prime is the cost base of a revolver and is a floating rate.
   C. An operating or demand line of credit is the standard type.
   D. A revolver has more stability than an operating line of credit.

7. Which of the following ratings represents the *higher* credit quality?
   A. A   B. AA   C. BB   D. CCC

8. Consider a convertible bond with a face value of $1,000 and a conversion ratio of 30. If the bond is convertible into common stock of the issuer, and the common stock is trading for $40 per share, the conversion value of this bond is *closest* to:
   A. $33.   B. $40.   C. $1,000.   D. $1,200.

9. A commercial paper issued at $98 million with a maturity of 270 days and a maturity value of $100 million has a bond equivalent yield *closest* to:
   A. 2.0%.   B. 2.7%.   C. 2.8%.   D. 7.8%.

10. The after-tax cost of debt for a company that issues a bond with a yield of 6 percent, if the company's tax rate is 38 percent, is *closest* to:
    A. 2.2%.   B. 2.28%.   C. 3.72%.   D. 6.00%.

Practice Questions and Problems

12.1   What Is Debt?

11. Why do we adjust for taxes in determining the cost of debt?

12. Why do we use the marginal tax rate in calculating the cost of debt instead of the average tax rate for the company?

13. Complete the following table:

Case	Before-tax Cost of Debt	Marginal Tax Rate	After-tax Cost of Debt
A	5%	30%	
B	6%		3.60%
C		20%	7.20%
D	10%	45%	
E	8%		5.60%

14. What would happen to the cost of debt if the marginal tax rate increases?

15. Rasda would like to borrow $150,000 to expand her small business, but needs to understand the impact of the 8 percent interest payments. Last year, her company did not pay any interest and had total earnings before tax of $123,500. The tax rate was 30 percent. Determine the company's net income for the year. Assuming

that earnings before interest and taxes and the rate of taxation will not change, calculate how much the net income figure will change if Rasda proceeds with the loan.

A. Explain to Rasda why her company's net income does not fall by the amount of the interest payments.

B. The cost of the loan Rasda needs for her business is 8 percent per year. Given that the company's net income will fall by less than the amount of interest paid, is Rasda correct in thinking that the after-tax cost of the loan is lower than 8 percent? With a tax rate of 30 percent, what is the after-tax cost of this loan?

12.2 Short-Term Financing

16. Describe briefly what is meant by a "credit enhancement," and provide one example of a credit enhancement.

17. Calculate the price of a 90-day T-bill if the face value is $1 million and the discount yield is 4.8 percent.

18. Calculate the price of a 52-week T-bill if the face value is $1 million and the bond equivalent yield is 3 percent.

19. Suppose you are told that the discount yield of a 13-week T-bill is 3 percent. What is the bond equivalent yield for this T-bill?

20. Determine the selling price of a U.S. T-bill that has a quoted annual interest rate of 2.1 percent and will mature in 180 days. Assume a par value of $1,000.

21. As the newly appointed treasurer for Big Corp., you have to decide how to raise $50 million in short-term financing. You believe you could issue commercial paper with a promised yield of 9 percent. However, your bank will charge a commitment fee of 0.125 percent on the line of credit to back up this paper, as well as 0.125 percent as a selling commission. As an alternative, the bank suggests using bankers' acceptances, which would have a lower yield of 8.75 percent. The bank's stamping fee for these bankers' acceptances is 0.625 percent. Which financing alternative should you choose?

22. Fayettevile Corporation has a revolving line of credit on which it owes $50 million. One of the restrictions imposed with this financing arrangement is that the company must maintain a minimum interest coverage ratio of 1.75. If this is the only borrowing, and the annual interest rate is 9.75 percent, how much does the company have to earn to live up to the covenant?

23. In your job as treasurer of Little Rock Quarry, you have to arrange for a line of credit for the company. The following is taken from the company's most recent balance sheet.

Cash	$1,271,987
Accounts Receivable	18,536,000
Inventory	74,196,000
Total current assets	$94,003,987
Property and Equipment (net)	126,323,000
Goodwill	46,888,000
Total Assets	$267,214,987

The bank will provide credit up to 75 percent of the value of receivables and 50 percent of the inventory value. What is the maximum credit limit that Little Rock can obtain?

24. Denver Corp.'s bank is willing to provide it with a 10-year term loan for $50 million. The annual payments on this loan will be $5 million, and there is a bullet payment of $50 million at maturity. What is the interest rate being charged by the bank?

25. Using a spreadsheet, calculate and graph the discount and bond equivalent yields on a 30-day Treasury bill for prices from 98 to 100, in increments of 0.1 in value. Describe the relationship between the Treasury bill price and its discount and bond equivalent yields.

12.3 Long-Term Financing

26. Compare an affirmative covenant with a negative covenant, giving an example of each.

27. Why would a company issue secured debt instead of a debenture? Explain.

28. Why would a company consider issuing a long-term debt obligation if it can borrow funds by issuing commercial paper?

29. Why would a company issue convertible debt instead of straight debt?

30. Consider a bond that is both callable and convertible, and address the following question: "Can the issuer of a callable, convertible bond force investors to convert the bonds to stock?"

31. Rank the following from lowest to highest cost of financing of a given company:

   A. Senior, secured debt   B. Debenture   C. Commercial paper

32. Complete the following table for each convertible bond:

Bond	Face Value	Coupon Rate	Number of Years to Maturity	Yield to Maturity	Conversion Ratio	Price of Common Stock	Conversion Value	Straight Value	Market Conversion Price	What Price Will the Bond Trade at?
A	$1,000	5%	10	6%	10	$100.00				
B	$1,000	6%	5	5%	25	$40.00				
C	$1,000	4%	3	4%	50	$18.00				
D	$1,000	3%	15	4%	40	$20.00				
E	$500	6%	10	7%	10	$49.00				

12.4 Bond Ratings

33. List and briefly describe the five basic factors used to determine a credit rating.

34. Consider the following ratings of bonds:

   AAA   A   BB
   AA   BBB   B

   A. Which rating classes are considered investment grade?
   B. Which rating classes are considered speculative?

35. Once a bond is issued by a company, why would the company be concerned about its debt rating?

Case

Case 12.1 General Electric's Bond Rating Downgrade

General Electric (GE) is a U.S. conglomerate whose lines of business include technology, financial services, infrastructure, health care, and media. GE held onto its AAA bond rating until March 2009. At that time, Standard & Poor's downgraded GE to AA+. Consider General Electric's financial statements for fiscal years 2006 through 2008 (in thousands):[20]

Balance Sheets	*As of Fiscal Year Ending*		
	12/31/2006	*12/31/2007*	*12/31/2008*
Cash, cash equivalents, and short-term investments	$6,2101	$61,175	$89,633
Receivables, short-term	13,954	22,259	21,411
Inventories	11,401	12,897	13,674
Net property, plant, & equipment	74,966	77,895	78,530
Receivables, long-term	354,180	396,518	381,220
Assets held for sale, long-term	0	0	10,556
Long-term investments	30,337	34,592	31,461
Intangible assets	86,433	97,294	96,736
Prepayments, long-term	15,019	20,190	0
Deferred long-term assets	1,380	1,282	1,230
Discontinued operations long-term asset	0	6,769	1,723
Other assets	47,468	64,466	71,595
Total assets	$697,239	$795,337	$797,769
Accounts payable & accrued expenses	$29,823	$34,383	$36,695
Accounts payable	21,697	21,398	20,819
Accrued expenses	8,126	12,985	15,876
Current debt	172,153	195,101	193,695
Other current liabilities	18,538	16,629	18,220
Long-term debt and leases	260,804	319,015	330,067
Discontinued operations, long-term	475	1,828	1,432
Deferred long-term liabilities	14,171	12,144	4,584
Minority interests	7,578	8,004	8,947
Other liabilities	81,383	92,674	99,464
Total liabilities	$584,925	$679,778	$693,104
Common share capital	669	669	702
Additional paid-in capital	25,486	26,100	40,390
Retained earnings	107,798	117,362	122,123
Accumulated other comprehensive income	3,254	8,324	–21,853
Treasury stock	24,893	36,896	36,697
Total equity	$112,314	$115,559	$104,665
Total liabilities & equity	$697,239	$795,337	$797,769

[20] The data is from General Electric's financial statements, as reported in its 10-K filings each year. The financial statements have been simplified somewhat to reduce the number of accounts that you need to work with.

Income Statements

	Fiscal Year Ending		
	12/31/2006	*12/31/2007*	*12/31/2008*
Total revenue	$163,391	$172,738	$182,515
Direct costs	100,449	104,927	120,712
Gross profit	$62,942	$67,811	$61,803
Total indirect operating costs	37,414	40,297	42,021
Operating income	$25,528	$27,514	$19,782
Total nonoperating income	908	916	641
Earnings before tax	$25,528	$27,514	$19,782
Taxation	3,954	4,130	1,052
Minority interests	908	916	641
Discontinued operations	163	−260	−679
Net income	$20,829	$22,208	$17,410

Statements of Cash Flows

	Fiscal Year Ending		
	12/31/2006	*12/31/2007*	*12/31/2008*
Net income	$20,829	$22,208	$17,410
Adjustments from income to cash	14,784	15,707	18,405
Change in working capital	−3,124	4,413	1,006
Other operating cash flows	−1,843	3,639	11,780
Cash flow from operations	$30,646	$45,967	$48,601
Purchase of property, plant, and equipment	−$16,650	−$17,870	−$16,010
Proceeds from property, plant, and equipment	6,799	8,460	10,975
Change in business activities	857	−5,618	−18,577
Other investing cash flows	−42,408	−57,396	−17,289
Cash flow from investing	−$51,402	−$72,424	−$40,901
Change in short-term debt	$4,582	$2,339	−$34,221
Change in long-term debt	39,016	51,040	53,909
Change in equity	−8,554	−12,319	13,722
Payment of dividends	−10,420	−11,492	−12,408
Other financing cash flows	−1,394	−1,356	3,634
Cash flow from financing	$23,230	$28,212	$24,636
Cash from discontinued operations	———	−284	180
Change in cash	$2,474	$1,755	$32,336

A. Leading up to the downgrade, analyze GE's financial condition and performance and discuss why you believe that GE was downgraded, based solely on these financial statements.

B. What factors, other than historical performance, are important in a bond rating?

C. Consider GE's fiscal year 2009 results:

Balance Sheet	As of 12/31/2009	Income Statement	For Fiscal Year Ending 12/31/2009
Cash, cash equivalents, and short-term investments	$124,201	Total revenue	$156,783
Receivables, short-term	16,458	Direct costs	108,635
Inventories	11,987	Gross profit	$48,148
Net property plant, and equipment	69,212	Total indirect operating costs	37,804
Receivables, long-term	345,465	Operating income	$10,344
Assets held for sale, long-term	34,111	Taxation	−1,090
Long-term investments	35,203	Minority interests	216
Intangible assets	77,503	Discontinued operations	−193
Deferred long-term assets	3,613	Net income	$11,025
Discontinued operations long-term asset	1,520		
Other assets	62,545	**Statement of Cash Flows**	**For Fiscal Year Ending 12/31/2009**
Total assets	$781,818	Net income	$11,025
		Adjustments from income to cash	19,052
Accounts payable & accrued expenses	$33,036	Change in working capital	3,394
Accounts payable	19,703	Other operating cash flows	−8,878
Accrued expenses	13,333	Cash flow from operations	$24,593
Current debt	133,054		
Other current liabilities	52,309	Purchase of property, plant, and equipment	−$8,634
Long-term debt & leases	338,215	Proceeds from property, plant, and equipment	6,479
Discontinued operations, long-term	1,301	Change in business activities	3,982
Deferred long-term liabilities	2,173	Other investing cash flows	41,170
Minority interests	7,845	Cash flow from investing	$42,997
Other liabilities	96,594		
Total liabilities	$664,527	Change in short-term debt	−$29,727
		Change in long-term debt	−2,219
Common share capital	$702	Change in equity	623
Additional paid-in capital	37,729	Payment of dividends	−8,986
Retained earnings	126,363	Other financing cash flows	−3,204
Accumulated other comprehensive income	−15,265	Cash flow from financing	−$43,513
Treasury stock	32,238	Cash from discontinued operations	184
Total equity	$117,291	Change in cash	$24,077
Total liabilities & equity	$781,818		

Was Standard & Poor's downgrade consistent with the performance and condition of GE during the fiscal year following the downgrade? Explain.

CHAPTER 13

EQUITY AND HYBRID INSTRUMENTS

© Daniel Stein/iStockphoto

TARP & Preferred Stock The rescue of banks during the 2008 economic crisis was done, in part, with preferred stock. Though preferred stocks are not often used as a source of capital in the U.S., this was the security of choice in the financial institutions' rescue. The program allowed "Qualified Financial Institutions" (QFI) to sell the U.S. Treasury senior preferred stock that is greater than 1 percent of its risk-weighted assets, but not more than the lesser of $25 billion or 3 percent of its risk-weighted assets.[1]

This preferred stock has the following features:

- A liquidation preference of $1,000 per share.
- *Pari passu* with other preferred shares, which means it is on equal footing with the QFI's other preferred stock.
- A cumulative dividend of 5 percent per year for the first 5 years, 9 percent thereafter (if the QFI is not a subsidiary of a holding company).
- Nonvoting unless dividends are passed over for six dividend periods.
- A term of ten years.

Also, the U.S. Treasury will receive warrants to purchase the common stock of a QFI with a market price of 15 percent of the senior preferred issue amount. Among other restrictions, there are restrictions on the payment of dividends to common shareholders of the QFI, as well as the payment of executive compensation to executives of the QFI.

As they have been able to do so, QFIs repurchased the preferred stock from the U.S. Treasury, including Goldman Sachs ($10 billion), JPMorgan Chase & Co. ($25 billion), and BB&T ($3.1 billion) in June of 2009; Bank of America ($25 billion) and Wells Fargo ($25 billion) in December 2009; and PNC Bank ($7.6 billion) in February 2010, with General Motors ($2.1 billion) in December 2010. In addition, the U.S. Treasury began in 2012 to auction off their preferred stock holdings to investors.

Sources: *"TARP Capital Purchase Program, Senior Preferred Stock and Warrants, Summary of Senior Preferred Terms," United States Treasury, October 14, 2008; Goldman Sachs Repurchases TARP Preferred Stock, Goldman Sachs press release, June 17, 2009; "Ten Major Financial Institutions Repay TARP Money," RTTNews, June 17, 2009; www.financial stability.gov*

[1] Risk-weighted assets equal the weighted average of the QFI's assets, with higher weights assigned to riskier assets; a risk-free asset would have weight of 0 percent, whereas a risky asset may have a weight of 100 percent.

Learning Outcomes

After reading this chapter, you should be able to:

LO 13.1 Identify the accounts that contribute to the shareholders' equity of a company.

LO 13.2 Describe the rights and other features of common stock.

LO 13.3 Distinguish between common stock and preferred stock, especially with respect to rights, income, and embedded options.

LO 13.4 Describe the variety of hybrid financing options available to companies and how they are constructed by combining the basic characteristics of debt and equity to various degrees.

Chapter Preview All companies have equity, which represents the owners' interest in the company. The equity of the owners of corporations is represented by shares of stock. All corporations will have common stock, and some corporations will have preferred stock, which has rights superior to that of common stock. In this chapter, we discuss the features and rights of common and preferred stock. In addition, we discuss hybrid securities, which take on characteristics of both equity and debt.

13.1   SHAREHOLDERS' EQUITY

common share certificate of ownership in a corporation

preferred share certificate of ownership of a fixed claim on the equity of a corporation

An **equity security** is an ownership interest in an underlying business entity. The owners of the equity of a corporation are shareholders. All corporations have common equity, and the owners of this common equity, common shareholders, are the true "owners" of the corporation. A **common share** of stock is a certificate of ownership, representing a proportionate share of the common equity interest in a corporation. A corporation may also have preferred equity, which is senior to common equity with respect to claims on income and assets, and a **preferred share** is a certificate of ownership in the preferred equity of a corporation.

Not all common shares are created equal; we show that the basic rights provided to common shareholders can be distributed among different classes of common shares. In particular, some shares have voting rights, others do not, and some of them have dividends and some do not. Preferred shares come in a wide variety of forms as well because of the different uses of these shares. As a result, some preferred shares are very similar to commercial paper, notes, or long-term financing, with the major difference being that preferred shares pay dividends rather than interest.

Companies can use debt or equity financing, and within equity financing they have some latitude. Ultimately, financial decision makers are interested in how the choices of financing affect the company's cost of capital, as well as the company's flexibility in the future.

shareholders' equity ownership interest of the corporation, as represented on the balance sheet

treasury shares shares of stock bought back by the issuer

accumulated comprehensive income or loss income or loss that bypasses the income statement, going directly to equity

Shareholders' equity is the ownership interest of a corporation. In general, shareholders' equity consists of the capital that owners paid in to buy the initial shares of stock and accumulated earnings, less any dividend paid. You may also notice adjustments to equity on a company's balance sheet for shares bought back by the company and accumulated comprehensive income or loss. The shares bought back by the company are **treasury shares** and are a contra account to equity—that is, the amount paid for these shares is subtracted from equity. The **accumulated comprehensive income or loss** consists of income or losses that bypassed the income statement and went directly to equity. Items that contribute to the accumulated comprehensive income or loss include unrealized gains or losses on marketable securities that are available for sale, foreign currency translation gains or losses, gains or losses on certain hedges using derivatives, and adjustments for underfunded pension plans.[2]

Let's look at an actual company, Archer-Daniels-Midland Company (ADM), to illustrate the reported interests of shareholders. We provide the shareholders' equity detail for

---

[2] Financial Accounting Standards Boards Statement 130, *Reporting Comprehensive Income*, June 1997.

TABLE 13-1 Shareholders' Equity Ratios for Archer-Daniels-Midland Company

	Fiscal Year End	
(in millions)	*June 30, 2008*	*June 30, 2009*
Common stock	$5,039	$5,022
Reinvested earnings	7,494	8,832
Accumulated other comprehensive income (loss)	957	−355
Total shareholders' equity	$13,490	$13,499

ADM for the fiscal years ending June 30, 2008, and June 30, 2009, from ADM's balance sheet in Table 13-1. ADM's shareholders' equity is rather simple:

- The common stock account represents what is paid in by shareholders when shares are first issued.[3]
- The reinvested earnings are the sum of earnings of the company since its incorporation, less any dividends paid since its incorporation. This is the retained earnings of the company.
- The accumulated other comprehensive income (loss) is the sum of the "other comprehensive income" items of the company over fiscal years since 1997, which represent gains, losses, and adjustments that are not reported in the income statement, but that affect shareholders' equity.

In more complex cases, you may also find:

- Preferred stock that is issued and outstanding.
- Preferred stock that is authorized, but not issued. For example, at the end of fiscal year 2009, Yahoo! had 10,000 shares of preferred stock authorized, but none issued. This is generally stock that may be used as a takeover defense.
- Common stock is broken down into two accounts: One account is the par value of the shares issued, whereas the other is the amount paid for shares in excess of par value. The latter is often referred to as "Paid-in capital" or "Additional paid-in capital."

PROBLEM

The following is the information provided in E. I. du Pont Nemours' fiscal year 2009 balance sheet:

EXAMPLE 13.1

Common and Preferred Equity

	Carrying Value (in millions)
Preferred stock, without par value, 23 million shares authorized,	
$4.50 Series − 1,670,000 shares, callable at $120	$167
$3.50 Series − 700,000 shares, callable at $102	70
Common stock, $0.30 par value, 1.8 billion shares authorized, 990,855,000 issued	297
Additional paid-in capital	8,469
Reinvested earnings	10,710
Accumulated other comprehensive loss	−5,771
Common stock held in treasury, at cost 87,041,000 shares	−6,727

[3] This is only stock that is newly issued, as in the case of shares in the company's initial public offering, subsequent stock offerings of the company, and stock used in executive stock compensation that is not purchased in the open market.

Calculate the following:

   a. Du Pont's preferred equity
   b. Du Pont's common equity
   c. Du Pont's total shareholder equity

Solution

   a. $167 + 70 = 237 million
   b. $297 + 8,469 + 10,710 - 5,771 - 6,727 = $6,978$ million
   c. $237 + 6,978 = $7,215$ million

Dividends

ADM has paid dividends for over 77 years and generally raises its dividend every year. ADM's common stock dividend for the fiscal year June 30, 2009, is $0.54. Its dividend yield, based on the four quarters of dividends during its fiscal year ended June 30, 2009, and its price at the beginning of the fiscal year of $33.30, is 1.62 percent:

$$\text{Dividend yield} = \frac{\text{Dividend per share}}{\text{Price per share}} = \frac{\$0.54}{\$33.30} = 0.0162 \text{ or } 1.62\%$$

The tax laws in the U.S. specify that some or all of the dividends received by a corporation from another corporation are not taxed.[4] In general, a corporation that receives dividends from another corporation is allowed to then deduct 70 percent of these dividends in calculating taxable income. If the corporation receiving the dividends owns 20 percent or more of the paying corporation's stock, the deduction increases to 80 percent. If the paying corporation is wholly owned by the receiving corporation, all the dividends are deducted to arrive at taxable income. This is intended to mitigate some of the double taxation of income at the corporate level. In contrast, interest income is taxable between corporations because, as we discussed before, interest expense is tax deductible.

Consider an example. Suppose Corporation B buys the stock of Corporation A. And suppose that Corporation B has a tax rate of 40 percent and taxable income of $5 million before considering dividends. If Corporate A pays $1 million of dividends to Corporation B, what are the consequences to Corporate B? It will depend on the dividends received deduction:

(in millions)		Dividend Received Deduction Rate		
		70%	80%	100%
	Income before dividends	$5.000	$5.000	$5.000
Plus	Dividends received	1.000	1.000	1.000
Less	Dividends received deduction	0.700	0.800	1.000
Equals	Taxable income	$5.300	$5.200	$5.000
Less	Tax	2.120	2.080	2.000
Equals	Income after taxes	$3.180	$3.120	$3.000

What are the consequences to Corporation A? Corporation A cannot deduct dividends that it pays, so its tax situation is not affected by the dividends it pays.

Dividend income is also attractive for individuals because of special treatment in the tax code. For a number of years, dividend income of individuals was taxed the same as the

---

[4] United States Internal Revenue Code Section 243.

taxpayer's other incomes, such as wages. However, in recent years, dividends are taxed at a rate that is lower than the taxpayer's other income if the dividends are considered qualified dividends. A dividend is considered a **qualified dividend** if the taxpayer owned the stock for more than 60 days during the 121-day period that begins 60 days before the ex-dividend date.[5] The ex-dividend date is 2 days before the record date, which is the date the Board of Directors determines to identify which shareholders should receive the forthcoming dividend.[6]

qualified dividend cash dividends from a stock held more than 60 days during the 121-day period beginning before the ex-dividend date

Book Versus Market Value

As of its fiscal year ended June 30, 2009, ADM had 642.039 million shares outstanding. ADM also had shareholders' equity with a book value of $13,499 million. Because ADM has only common shares outstanding, its common equity is also equal to $13,499 million. Each common share had a book value per share of $21.0252, calculated as

$$\text{Book value per share} = \frac{\text{Common equity}}{\text{Number of shares}} = \frac{\$13,499 \text{ million}}{642.039 \text{ million}} = \$21.0252$$

ADM's book value per share indicates the amount of money that its shareholders have invested in the company, which translates into a market-to-book ratio (M/B) of 1.2732:

$$M/B = \frac{\text{Price per share}}{\text{Book value per share}} = \frac{\$26.77}{\$21.0252} = 1.2732$$

If we compare ADM's book value, or carrying value, of shareholders' equity with its market value, we see quite a difference. We calculate the market value of its equity as the number of shares, multiplied by the market value per share at fiscal year end, whereas we take the book values directly from the company's balance sheet:

	Fiscal Year End	
(in millions)	**June 30, 2009**	**June 30, 2008**
Book value of shareholders' equity	$13,499	$13,490
Market value of shareholders' equity	$17,213	$21,735
Market-to-book ratio	1.2751	1.6112

A company's book value of equity changes from year to year because of:

- earnings,
- dividends paid,
- shares issued,
- shares repurchased, or
- other comprehensive income or loss.

Because companies do not issue or repurchase common shares often, the market value of equity changes from year to year primarily because of the market price of the stock. One way to distinguish the book value of equity from the market value of equity is to consider that the book value of equity is backward looking, whereas the market value of equity is forward looking.

---

[5] In other words, dividends will be taxed at a lower rate if the stock is not bought and sold simply to take advantage of a strategy of buying the stock before the ex-dividend date, selling it at or after the ex-dividend date, and then repeating this process in what is referred to as a dividend-capture *strategy*.

[6] We discuss the dividend dates, including the ex and record date, in a later chapter.

13.2   COMMON EQUITY

Common equity is the residual ownership of the company. As such, common shareholders are the last in line if the company is liquidated, waiting in line behind creditors and preferred shareholders. Further, common shareholders may receive dividends only after preferred shareholders receive theirs and in most cases only after interest and any principal due on debt is paid. Though waiting last in line may seem a tough position to be in, if the company generates income or value beyond what is needed to satisfy creditors and preferred shareholders, common shareholders receive this income or value.

Common equity is represented on a company's balance sheet in the accounts of:

- common stock, which is the par value of any issued shares,
- additional paid-in capital, which is the difference between what investors paid for the shares at issuance and their par value,
- retained earnings,
- accumulated comprehensive income or loss, which is any gain or loss that bypassed the income statement and went directly to equity in the balance sheet.

If the company has bought its own shares back from investors, the value of these shares is represented in Treasury stock, which is a contra-equity account (that is, it is a subtraction from equity).

Rights

Generally, owners of common equity interests have the right to:

- vote at any meeting of shareholders of the corporation;
- receive any dividend declared by the corporation; and
- receive the remaining property of the corporation on dissolution.

These three rights then define the basic rights of common shareholders.

In the U.S., corporations are incorporated in a particular state, and businesses operate subject to that state's law.[7] Of the companies listed on the New York Stock Exchange, slightly more than one-half are incorporated in the State of Delaware.[8] This is primarily because corporate law in Delaware has been well tested in the courts and provides barriers to unfriendly takeovers, but other contributing factors include the lower incorporation fees.[9]

The most basic right of common shareholders is the right to vote. Because they own a share of the business, shareholders have the right to make important decisions at the annual shareholders' meeting. These rights include electing the members of the board of directors, appointing the auditors of the company, making changes in the articles of incorporation and bylaws of the company, and voting on major changes in the company's operations. What constitutes a major or fundamental change in the company's operations is difficult to define, but it normally includes a major acquisition of another company through an exchange of shares or the disposition of major assets.

Even these rights, however, can be severely circumscribed. At one time, most equity holders also had a **pre-emptive right**, which was the right to maintain proportional ownership in a company when new shares were issued. If the company were to issue, say, 50 percent more shares in a seasoned offering, each shareholder had the right to buy 50 percent more shares to maintain his or her proportional interest. The pre-emptive right

pre-emptive right right of shareholders to maintain proportional ownership in a company when new shares are issued

---

[7] A corporation that incorporates in one state need not have its headquarters in that state.

[8] The next most popular states of incorporation of NYSE-listed companies are Maryland and Massachusetts.

[9] Still another reason companies cite in favor of incorporating in Delaware is that Delaware, unlike many other states, permits a board of directors comprising a single person.

meant that most new issues of shares were made by means of a **rights offering** to existing shareholders. However, many U.S. companies changed their corporate structure to remove the pre-emptive right, allowing them to sell shares to new investors. For example, Allegheny Energy shareholders voted to remove the pre-emptive right so that the company would have more flexibility in the issuance of new shares through private placement. As a result, very few rights offerings are made, and shareholders cannot prevent their ownership share from being diluted by the sale of new shares to other investors.[10]

rights offering issuance of the opportunity to purchase new shares of stock of a company

The loss of the pre-emptive right has been exacerbated by the fact that most companies have increased the number of authorized shares, so they no longer need shareholder approval to issue more common shares. This means that companies could sell new shares very quickly to major institutional investors, and thus dilute the ownership share of existing investors.

The two remaining rights, to receive a dividend and to receive any remaining property on the dissolution of the corporation, reflect the equity owners' rights as a **residual owner**. For example, the equity holders have no right to a dividend until it is declared by the company's board of directors. Further, there are extensive restrictions on when the company can declare a dividend, the major one being that the company has to have the resources to pay the dividend without impairing its ability to meet its fixed contractual commitments. In this sense, the payment of the dividend reflects the fact that the equity holders are last in line after all other claims on the company's earnings stream have been met. In the same way, if the company is liquidated, all other claimants on the company's assets have to be met before the equity holders receive any payment.

residual owner equity owner who receives any remaining cash flows or property (on the dissolution of the business) after all other commitments have been satisfied

Shareholders have the right to **limited liability**, the restriction that a party cannot be held responsible for obligations beyond a specified amount. The equity holders commit initial equity to the company, but they are legally protected from being forced to put more money into the company. As a result, if the company cannot meet its fixed commitments to pay interest, and so on, the equity holders cannot be forced to inject more money into the company to allow it to meet these commitments. If the creditors then put the company into bankruptcy and there is not enough money to pay off all the claims on the company, again the equity holders cannot be forced to put more money into the company.

limited liability restriction that a party cannot be held responsible for obligations beyond a specified amount

Limited liability ensures that the shareholders can only lose their initial investment, so their downside risk is limited because the most they can lose is their investment, but they have unlimited upside potential. In this sense, common shares have some of the characteristics of call options. We use this insight when discussing financial strategy.

Multiple Classes of Shares

Most corporations have a single class of common stock. However, some corporations will have two classes, with one class publicly traded and another class owned by a small group of investors, such as the founding family. For example, Ford's 71 million Class B shares trade on the New York Stock Exchange, but its other common stock, which does not have a class designation, is held by the Ford family heirs. Ford's founding family owns 5 percent of the company's stock, but controls 40 percent through the founding family class of stock.[11]

Another example of multiple classes of common stock is Berkshire Hathaway. It has two classes: A and B. One share of Class B stock has $1/30$ the rights of a share of Class A stock, but $1/200$ of the voting rights of a Class A share. In addition, a share of Class A stock

---

[10] In fact, a standard takeover defense is to sell shares to a friendly investor, thereby reducing the stake of a potentially hostile acquirer.

[11] Ford's Class B shares are held in a family trust. The problem of what happens after the founder ceases to be involved and gradually the wealth is dispersed over succeeding generations is solved through a trust. Trusts are a standard way of separating ownership from control. For example, inheritances often go to a minor, and the wealth is put into a trust. The minor receives the income from the inheritance but cannot control it until he or she reaches a given age, normally 25. In similar fashion, the shares in the Ford family trust ensure that income flows through to the hundreds of individuals descended from Henry Ford, but all the votes are held by the plan trustees.

is convertible into thirty shares of Class B stock. Class A shares, with the ticker BRKA, trade around thirty times the value of a share of Class B (ticker BRKB). On July 10, 2012, for example, a share of Class A Berkshire Hathaway stock traded at $124,985 per share, whereas a share of Class B stock traded at $83.05 per share.[12]

articles of incorporation rules of the governance of the corporation that are filed with the state of incorporation

How the rights of owners of a corporation are determined lies in the articles of incorporation. The **articles of incorporation** are the rules of the governance of the corporation that are filed with the state of incorporation. If there are multiple classes of stock, the differential rights of voting, rights to income, and claim on assets are detailed in this document. We should note that there is no particular meaning to the designation of the class of stock as "A," "B," or otherwise. This is arbitrary and at the discretion of the issuing company. Class A stock for one company may have more rights than those of Class B for that company, but Class A stock of another company may have fewer rights than those of Class B for this other company. Consider the two classes of common stock of Moog, Inc., a U.S. manufacturer of components for industrial and aircraft applications, which we describe in Table 13-2. In the case of Moog, the Class A shares have voting rights that are less than those of the Class B shares. The Class B shares of Moog trade at a market price close to that of Class A shares, but there is very little trading in Class B shares compared to that of Class A shares.[13] This share structure is relatively simple, and, in fact, companies have few limitations on designing the share structure.

TABLE 13-2 Classes of Moog, Inc., Common Stock

Features	Class A Shares	Class B Shares
Exchange on which stock trades	New York Stock Exchange	New York Stock Exchange
Ticker symbol	MOG.A	MOG.B
Number of shares outstanding	38,718,361	4,015,817
Voting rights	1/10 of a vote per share	1 vote per share
Representation on the board of directors	Elect at least 25 percent of the board of directors, rounded to nearest whole number	Elect 75 percent of the board of directors
Other rights		Convertible at any time into Class A shares on a one-for-one basis

nonvoting shares common shares that have no voting rights

In some cases, a class of shares may actually not have any voting rights; we refer to these shares as **nonvoting shares**. Voting rights mean control and the ability to choose the board of directors and, through them, senior management and the strategic direction of the company. This control value is very important because it means the company can be taken over only by buying the voting shares. In the event of a takeover, voting shares are more valuable than nonvoting shares.

The desire to maintain control by establishing or maintaining classes of shares with different voting rights is common to many family-run businesses, in which the founder needs external capital but wants to maintain control. A classic example was the Four Seasons Hotels Limited (Four Seasons), a chain founded by Isadore Sharpe, whose family controlled 67 percent of the votes through multiple voting shares.[14] In September 1996, Four Seasons proposed to reorganize its two main classes of shares. The subordinated voting shares were to be renamed limited voting shares, and the multiple voting shares owned by the Sharpe family, which already had 12 votes each, were to be renamed variable voting shares. The plan was to increase the voting power of these shares as more limited voting

---

[12] These stock prices are a good example of the scale of stock prices if companies do not split the shares.

[13] The trading volume of Class A shares is 200 times that of Class B shares, even though Class A shares outstanding are less than ten times the number of Class B shares outstanding.

[14] Barbara Shecter, "Four Seasons Plan Assailed," *Financial Post*, September 27, 1996.

shares were issued to keep the Sharpe family at 67 percent of the votes. In essence, without putting up any more money, the Sharpe family would always control the company through these variable voting shares. Many institutional investors refused to invest in limited or nonvoting shares, but on the day the Four Seasons plan was announced, the stock price went up 55 cents and reached a 52-week high.

What the Four Seasons example highlights is the role of the founder of the company. When voting rights are concentrated in the hands of a person who has built the company, investors are often only too happy to see control concentrated in his or her hands because the company *is* the senior management. For this reason, many institutional investors were relatively indifferent to the Four Seasons' plan. The problems arise when the bloodline "thins out," and the second and third generations of the family do not have the managerial skills evident in the original founder, or when the company is sold.

The value of these voting rights very much depends on who has control of the company and whether it is good or bad for shareholder value creation. Empirical studies that have estimated the value of voting rights have produced mixed results, as have studies of the stock market's reaction when companies recapitalize their share structure to create or remove voting differentials. The problem is that differential voting rights may not affect value when the founder runs the company, but they do when that founder ceases to be involved. Regardless, the limited or nonvoting shares usually have a slight premium in terms of the right to a dividend to offset the lost value of control.

Super-Voting Shares and Takeovers | ETHICS

In the 1980s, many companies used dual-class shares as an antitakeover device. A company, wanting to shore up its defenses, would issue a new class of common stock that had superior voting rights, relative to the other class. The company would then sell this class of stock or be in a position to sell it to a "friendly party." This put the acquiring company at a disadvantage because it had access only to the inferior voting publicly traded stock. This, effectively, discouraged the takeover.

The issue of whether takeover defenses, such as this one, are good or bad for the shareholders, or the economy in general, is still debated. Takeover defenses can be used to encourage higher offers and therefore benefit shareholders. However, takeover defenses can also help to entrench management and prevent shareholders from receiving a premium over the current stock price for their shares.

Concept Review Questions

1. What are the basic rights associated with equity securities? How do these differ across different categories or classes of equities?

2. Why do voting rights affect the prices of some common shares and not others?

3. Why is dividend income preferred by both corporations and individual investors?

13.3 PREFERRED EQUITY

Preferred equity is an equity interest in a company that is senior to common equity. On a company's balance sheet, preferred equity is comprised of preferred stock, which is the par value of any issued preferred shares, and additional paid-in capital from preferred shares, which is the difference between what investors paid for the shares at their issuance and the shares' par value.

The most basic type of preferred share is the traditional **straight preferred share**. These are preferred shares that have no maturity date and pay a fixed dividend at regular intervals (usually quarterly). We value these shares as perpetuities. These are the most common type of preferred shares.

straight preferred share preferred share that has no maturity date and pays a fixed dividend at regular intervals, usually quarterly

Maturity

retractable preferred
stock or term preferred
share or redeemable
preferred stock equity
interest that gives the
investor the right to sell
it back to the issuer,
thus creating an early
maturity date

soft-retractable preferred
share equity interest that
gives the issuer the choice
of redeeming the stock
for cash or in its common
shares

mandatory redeemable
preferred stock or
mandatorily redeemable
preferred stock
security that an issuer is
obligated to repurchase
at a specified price at a
specified point in time or
event

trust preferred security
preferred equity security
issued by a trust
created by a company;
the company backs
the obligations of the
preferred security

Straight preferred stock is a perpetual security; it never matures. However, some variations in preferred shares provide a finite life to the stock. For example, **retractable preferred stock**, also known as **term preferred share** or **redeemable preferred stock**, gives the investor the right to sell it back to the issuer, thus creating an early maturity date. Retractable preferred shares permit early retirement, with the typical retraction date being set at 5 years. Therefore, even though the preferred shares may end up being outstanding for longer periods, they are valued as if the maturity is 5 years. A variation on the retractable preferred shares is the **soft-retractable preferred share**. Issuers of these shares have the right to pay cash or in shares of the common stock of the issuer at redemption.

Another form of preferred shares that have a maturity is **mandatory redeemable preferred stock** or **mandatorily redeemable preferred stock**.[15] These shares are redeemed (that is, mature) either at a specified date or as a result of a specified event (e.g., a merger). These shares became attractive for financial institutions to issue in the past decade because these shares are considered equity capital for regulatory purposes.[16]

Another form of preferred stock is a **trust preferred security**, which is popular with financial institutions. In the case of a trust preferred security, the company creates a trust, issues debt to the trust, and then the trust issues preferred stock:

The company issues debt to the trust → The trust buys the company's debt → The trust sells preferred stock to investors

In the case of a financial institution that must meet minimum capital standards, which require a minimum equity based on the riskiness of the institution's assets, the company is actually issuing debt yet can count the preferred stock issued by the trust as equity capital. For example, Wells Fargo Capital VIII, a trust created by Wells Fargo & Company, issued $200 million of 5.625% trust preferred securities in 2003 that are guaranteed by Wells Fargo & Company, one of the largest U.S. financial institutions. These securities are redeemable August 1, 2033, or any time earlier.[17]

Type of Preferred Stock	*Maturity*
Straight	No maturity
Retractable/term/redeemable	Investor has the option to sell it back
Soft retractable	Investor has the option to sell it back, but the issuer has the choice of paying cash or providing common shares
Mandatory/mandatorily redeemable	Issuer must buy back at a specified point in time or when a specified event occurs

[15] Some issues have been referred to as mandatory exchangeable preferred shares.

[16] For example, banks are required to have at least a minimum level of Tier 1 capital (primarily equity) relative to their risk-adjusted assets. Issuing mandatory redeemable preferred stock allows these banks to issue a security with debtlike features (maturity, fixed dividend) that is considered equity.

[17] Per the prospectus, redemption is subject to the approval by the Board of Governors of the Federal Reserve System.

Dividend

The basic type of preferred stock has a dividend that is fixed in amount, which is stated as a fixed dollar amount per period or as a percentage of the par value of the preferred stock. Not all preferred stock has a fixed dividend, however. Some preferred stock has a dividend that has a floating rate. **Floating rate preferred stock** generally has a long maturity date, but the dividend is reset every 3 or 6 months by an auction mechanism so that the dividend yield will be in line with current market interest rates. Alternatively, many of the floating rate preferred shares issued by the major banks have their dividend rate float with 75 percent of some base rate, such as the prime rate or the LIBOR, usually to some maximum rate, but specify a floor or minimum dividend rate. We refer to this form of floating rate stock as **adjustable rate preferred stock (ARPS)**. ARPS have market values very close to their par value because their dividend rate is always very close to the current market rate. For example, Goldman Sachs issued Series A Perpetual Floating Rate Non-cumulative Preferred Stock in April of 2005. The dividend on this preferred stock, paid quarterly, is the 3-month LIBOR rate, plus 75 basis points, with a floor dividend rate of 3.75 percent.[18]

Participating preferred stock is a preferred share that pays a fixed dividend, but its investors will also receive an additional dividend if the dividend on the issuer's common stock exceeds a specified amount. Participating preferred stock is used in some venture capital financing of start-ups and may have a specified "cap" or limit to the participation.

Note that because they do not carry a right to receive a dividend, most preferred shares have a **cumulative provision**, which means that no dividends can be paid on common shares until preferred share dividends, both current and arrears, are paid in full. This ensures that the common shareholders, who have voting rights, don't just suspend payment on the preferred share dividends, while continuing to make dividend payments on the common shares. For some preferred shares, as the arrears accumulate, they give rise to limited voting rights, so that the preferred shareholders can exercise some voting rights over the company. However, like bonds, these rights depend on the structure of the preferred shares.[19]

A common result for companies experiencing financial trouble is to suspend dividend payments on all classes of shares, including preferred shares, to conserve cash. If the company then recovers, it faces the problem of significant cash payments to clear the preferred dividend arrears. In practice, what happens in these situations is that the arrears are often paid through the issue of common shares or some combination of cash and shares. This allows the company to clean up its balance sheet and start fresh.

floating rate preferred stock equity security that has a long maturity date and every 3 or 6 months has its dividend reset by an auction mechanism so that the dividend yield is in line with market interest rates

adjustable rate preferred stock (ARPS) equity security issue for which the dividend yield is pegged to a specific interest rate

participating preferred stock equity issue in which a fixed dividend is supplemented with an additional dividend if the issuer's common stock dividend exceeds a specified threshold

cumulative provision stipulation that no dividends can be paid on common shares until preferred share dividends, both current and arrears, are paid in full

Dividend Type	Description
Fixed	Fixed for the entire life of the preferred stock
Floating	Based on a specified benchmark
Adjustable rate	Based on periodic auctions
Participating	A fixed rate plus a share of income
Cumulative	Any missed dividends must be paid before current dividends to preferred or common shareholders

SUMMARIZING: PREFERRED DIVIDENDS: TYPES

[18] This type of dividend is stated as "maximum of 3.75% or 3mL + 75bp," where "3mL" indicates the three-month LIBOR rate.

[19] Note that many of the short-term preferred shares, particularly those issued by banks, do not have this cumulative feature, because the risk of nonpayment is very low.

Other Features

Preferred stock may also have other features, such as an embedded option. Convertible preferred stock has an embedded option that permits the investor to convert the preferred stock for a specified number of common shares.

convertible preferred stock preferred stock that can be exchanged for a specified number of units of another security

A **convertible preferred stock** is preferred stock exchangeable into another security—usually common stock of the issuer—at the option of the investor. A preferred share may be convertible into a specified number of shares of the issuer's common stock, or any other security of the issuer. At the time of issuance, the preferred stock has a specified **conversion ratio**, which is the number of common shares for a given preferred share. Most convertible preferred stock is callable, which permits the issuer to force conversion in some cases. The way callable preferred can force a conversion is when the call price is unattractive relative to the value of the common stock the investor would receive if converted.

Suppose a share of convertible preferred stock is currently trading for $150 a share, and this stock can be converted into common stock at a rate of one preferred share for five common shares. The value of the preferred stock that is convertible likely differs from that of straight preferred stock because not only does the investor receive the dividend on the preferred stock, but there is also a chance that the conversion would be profitable in the future. Therefore, there will be a **conversion premium** built into the market value of the preferred stock, and the market value of the preferred stock will move in tandem with that of the common stock when the common stock trades at a value that is above the break-even point. The break-even share price in this example is $150 ÷ 5 = $30 per share.

conversion premium difference between the value of a convertible security and the market value of the security into which it is convertible

If a share of common stock is currently trading at $25 per share and there are low expectations regarding the future value of the common stock, the investor would not likely want to exercise her option to convert the preferred stock and would instead hold onto the preferred shares, receiving the dividend. The preferred stock in this case would trade close to its value as straight preferred, which would be the present value of the perpetual dividend stream. If, on the other hand, the common stock were trading, instead, at $35 per share, the preferred stock's market value would, at a minimum, reflect the value of the common stocks when converted, or $35 × 5 = $175.

Consider an example. Ford Motor Company has $50 par value callable convertible preferred stock outstanding, with a dividend of $3.25 per share that is convertible into 2.8249 shares of Ford common stock. In December 2010, Ford common stock was trading around $16.67 a share. At the same time, the Ford preferred stock was trading at approximately $51 per share, which is 3.2 times the value of the common stock. If converted, the investor would receive 2.8249 shares of common stock worth $16.67 × 2.8249 = $47.0911. So why does the preferred stock sell for more than $47.0911? Two reasons:

1. preferred shareholders can hold onto their shares, and these shares will appreciate as Ford's common stock appreciates, hence preferred shareholders have a valuable option, and
2. preferred shareholders receive the $3.25 dividend until they convert.

The difference between the market value of the preferred stock, $51, and the value if converted, $47.0911, is the conversion premium: $51 − $47.0911 = $3.9089.

mandatory convertible preferred stock preferred equity security that must be converted to common shares at or before a specified date

Preferred stock may be **mandatory convertible preferred stock**, which requires conversion at or before a specified date. For example, Mylan Inc. issued 2.139 million shares of 6.5 percent mandatory convertible preferred stock in November of 2007. This stock had a $0.50 par value, with dividends paid quarterly. Each $1,000 of par value of the stock automatically converted on November 15, 2010, into common shares at a rate somewhere between 58.548 and 71.4286 common shares, depending on the price of the common stock at the time. Owners of this preferred stock had the option to convert this stock prior to November 15, 2010.

Most preferred stock is nonvoting, so the investors do not have representation in the issuer's board of directors. Yet, preferred shares may have a contingent voting right, which is a voting right that kicks in when the issuer does not pay the specified dividend.

The Preference for Preferred Shares | GLOBAL PERSPECTIVE

In many European companies and in Canada, the preferred stock may actually have a similar or greater value than the company's common or ordinary shares. This is due to investor preferences for a fixed income stream.

Features also differ slightly from preferred stock in the U.S. For example, preferred stock dividends from European companies are often reinvested automatically in preferred shares, similar to the DRIP plans in the U.S. used for common shares. Another difference is with respect to conversion: In the U.S., the conversion of preferred shares is up to the individual investor, whereas in Germany there must be a majority vote among the convertible preferred stock investors to convert.

Looking at Henkel, a German company, the preferred shares have a market capitalization of €7.7 billion, and the ordinary (a.k.a. common) shares are €9.3 billion:

Shares	Number of shares	Market value (12/1/2011)	Market capitalization
Preferred shares	178,162,875	€43.27	€7,709,107,601
Ordinary shares	259,795,875	€35.78	€9,295,496,408

EXAMPLE 13.2
Convertible Preferred Stock

PROBLEM

A company has issued $100 par callable convertible preferred shares in which each share can be converted into 8 shares of common stock of the issuer. The price of the company's common stock is $12 per share, and the preferred stock can be called at $105 per share.

a. What is the conversion ratio of this preferred stock?

b. If the issuer is intending to call the preferred stock, should the investor accept the call price or should the investor convert the preferred shares into common shares?

Solution

a. Conversion ratio = 8

b. Value if converted, $8 \times \$12 = \$96$; value if wait to be called, $105; therefore, waiting to be called is the wise decision.

The growth in the issuance of preferred stock, with all its variants, has provided a growth in acronyms:

ARPS	Adjustable Rate Preferred Stock or Auction Rate Preferred Stock
PEPS	Premium Equity Participating Security Units
PIERS	Preferred Income Equity Redeemable Shares
PIES	Premium Income Equity Securities
QUIPS	Quarterly Income Preferred Securities
TOPrS	Trust Originated Preferred Securities
TruPS	Trust Preferred Securities

SUMMARIZING: THE ALPHABET SOUP OF PREFERRED STOCK

Issues

Accounting

Preferred stock, like common stock, is a component of shareholders' equity. The preferred stock value in an issuer's balance sheet is similar to that of the issuer's common stock: par value of the preferred stock, plus any additional paid-in capital if investors pay more than the par value of the stock. Unlike the case of common stock, the par value of preferred stock is meaningful because it is most often the basis of dividend calculations.

Some preferred stock is considered a liability for accounting purposes, whereas other preferred stock is considered equity. Preferred stock that is redeemable at the option of the issuer is generally considered equity, whereas preferred stock with a mandatory redemption is generally considered a liability.[20]

Yields and pricing

With respect to yields on preferred shares, the time and risk value of money are important, but so is how dividends are taxed. Dividends received by corporations may not be taxed or may be taxed at a low effective rate as a result of the dividend received deduction. The intent of the dividend received deduction is to mitigate the layers of taxation on corporate income, but it does affect how investors view the yields on preferred stock versus other investments. Further, the capital market is creative in designing securities to match investor demand: Preferred shares have been designed to match similar fixed-income debt securities but with the tax advantage of dividends. Comparisons between preferred shares and debt are never perfect because preferred shares are unambiguously riskier.

The basic risk attached to investing in preferred shares is that they have *equity risk* in addition to the investment risks attached to fixed-income securities. As mentioned earlier, owners of equity securities do not have a contractual right to anything except to the residuals after all others have been paid. If in any quarter, the board of directors decides *not* to pay a dividend, the holders of the preferred shares cannot seek legal action to force payment. This rule gives the company some flexibility if it runs into serious financial trouble because it can conserve cash by suspending the dividend payments. But this flexibility adds risk from the perspective of the preferred stock investor.

Just like bonds and commercial paper, preferred shares are rated by the rating agencies, such as Moody's Investors Service, Standard & Poor's, and Fitch Ratings. The rating classifications are similar to the long-term credit ratings that these services assign to bonds. The relation between risk and expected yields is similar to that of bonds: the greater the risk, the greater the rate of return required by investors.

We have discussed preferred shares in the context of shareholders' equity because legally they are equity securities. However, as the preceding discussion demonstrates, they share many characteristics with debt and are commonly regarded as a **hybrid security**: part debt and part equity. In fact, a continuum of financial securities runs the full range from common shares to what people typically think of as debt. We discuss some of the hybrids in the following sections because they can be very important for corporate financing.

hybrid security security that is part debt and part equity

Concept Review Questions

1. Briefly describe the following types of preferred shares: straight, retractable, and floating rate.

2. Briefly describe the following features that may be associated with preferred shares: cumulative, callable, and adjustable rate.

3. Why are preferred shares sometimes referred to as hybrid securities?

[20] Financial Accounting Standards Board, Statement of Financial Accounting Standards No. 150, "Accounting for Certain Financial Instruments with Characteristics of Both Liabilities and Equity," 2003.

13.4 HYBRID SECURITIES

We now consider the last major class of securities issued by companies, which includes warrants, income bonds, and convertible securities, including convertible bonds and preferred shares.

Warrants

A **warrant** is a security that provides the investor with the option to convert or exchange the warrant into another security, such as a common stock. Warrants are the corporate finance equivalent of call options, with two major differences.[21] First, call options are transactions between two external investors so that what one gains the other loses, but there is no impact on the company. Warrants are issued by companies to raise capital, and when they are exercised, more shares are created. Second, call options are usually issued with very short maturities because they are standardized. Warrants almost always have longer maturities, which makes them more valuable.

As long-term options, warrants are extremely valuable, and they trade at significant premiums over their intrinsic value—that is, they possess a significant time value. The fact that warrants are valuable means that they are frequently used as sweeteners to make issues more attractive and thereby access financing that would not otherwise be available. For example, junior mines (that is, exploration-stage mining companies) often have significant capital expenditures and limited cash flow to meet interest payments on any financing. If they approach a venture capitalist for debt financing, they may be asked to pay a very high interest rate, given the risks involved. This in turn compounds the problem of a lack of cash flow to make the interest payments. In these circumstances, the combination of a low-cost loan and warrants may allow the companies to raise debt. The low interest rate helps alleviate a company's cash flow problems, whereas the warrants make new equity financing available if the company is successful. Investors may be willing to buy these warrants, which may provide a significant payoff if the company does well and its share price increases. In the case of venture financing, used for start-up and growth firms, warrants are often attached to up to 20 percent of the loan.[22]

warrant securities that provide the investor with the option to convert or exchange the warrant into another security, such as a common stock

A call option is the right to buy a specified asset (the underlying) at a specified price (the exercise price) within a specified period of time (the time to expiration).

- The lower the exercise price, the more valuable the option because the cost of buying the underlying is less, and there is a better chance for the value of the underlying asset to be greater than the exercise price.
- The longer the time to expiration, the more valuable the call option because there is more time for the value of the underlying asset to exceed the exercise price.
- The more volatile the value of the specified asset, the more valuable the option because there is a better chance of the underlying asset's price exceeding the exercise price and hence making the option more valuable.
- The greater the market's rate of interest, the greater the value of the option to delay acquiring/investing the underlying stock.

SUMMARIZING: A MINIPRIMER ON OPTIONS

---

[21] A call option is an opportunity, but not a requirement, to buy some specified underlying asset, such as a stock.

[22] In addition, venture financing is often secured by physical assets of the company and accompanied by the right to invest additional funds.

Further, the very risk that makes debt financing expensive also makes the warrants valuable. Call options are more valuable when the underlying asset price is more volatile. This is also true for warrants, which are simply corporate-issued call options. As a general rule, we often see warrants and convertible securities being issued by companies that face significant uncertainty and possess correspondingly low bond ratings. They have difficulty raising debt capital without resorting to the use of some form of sweetener. For these companies, using warrants or adding convertible features reduces the cash outlay for interest payments, thus lowering the risk of financial distress.[23]

Though warrants are often granted along with another security, an issuer can issue warrants that are not attached to another security. We refer to these warrants as **naked warrants**. If the warrants are issued along with another security, they may be **detachable**; if so, the investor may sell the warrants to other investors. Though most detachable warrants are traded over-the-counter, issuers can list warrants on a stock exchange, where they trade much like common stocks. If they are not detachable, issuing bonds plus warrants is similar to issuing convertible bonds.

naked warrant warrant that is issued without being attached to another security issue of the issuer

detachable warrant warrant that can be sold to investors apart from the security with which it was originally issued

FINANCE in the News | Uncle Sam as a Shareholder

Wall Street company Morgan Stanley agreed to pay $950 million to buy back warrants issued to the government as part of the Treasury Department's capital infusion to banks last year.

The payment means the government made $1.27 billion, including dividends, on its $10 billion investment in the company. The government received both preferred stock and warrants on common stock for its investments in banks during the financial crisis. Morgan Stanley was among 10 companies allowed in June to pay back a combined $68 billion.

The company generated a 20% annualized return for the government, said Chairman and Chief Executive John Mack.

"We believe it is vital for our industry to recognize the lessons" of last year's crisis and "make the changes necessary to ensure a similar crisis never occurs again," Mr. Mack added in a statement.

Morgan Stanley's return for the government was slightly less than returns at Goldman Sachs Group Inc.

and American Express Co. but higher than the returns at some smaller banks. Goldman Sachs, which also received $10 billion, paid $1.1 billion last month to repurchase its warrants.

The warrants, which gave the government an option to buy shares in the companies, became more valuable as bank stocks rallied this year.

Morgan Stanley has been negotiating with the Treasury for weeks to repurchase the warrants.

Seven of the 10 financial-services heavyweights that paid back their federal investments also have repurchased the government's warrants.

Wednesday, Bank of New York Mellon Corp. paid $136 million to repurchase warrants. J.P. Morgan Chase & Co., Northern Trust Corp. and Capital One Financial Corp. haven't yet announced warrant-repurchase deals.

Kevin Kingsbury and Aaron Lucchetti, "Morgan Stanley Will Buy Back $950 Million of Warrants," *Wall Street Journal*, August 7, 2009.

Creative Hybrids: Some Examples

income bond debt obligation issued after a reorganization with the interest tied to some cash flow level for the company and with quite long maturity dates

contingent interest interest on a debt security that is paid based on cash flows or earnings

Another security that looks like debt but is closer to equity is an **income bond**. These bonds are generally issued after a reorganization, so that any interest is tied to some cash flow or earnings level for the company, or to the value of the security itself. In other words, interest is **contingent interest**. For example, LabCorp, a U.S. company, issued Zero Coupon Subordinated Notes Due 2021 that have contingent interest. In the case of these bonds, interest is paid every 6 months and is 0.125 percent of the average market

[23] A basic problem of debt financing is that increasing the interest rate for riskier borrowers makes the borrowers even riskier. Using warrants, which lower the interest cost to the debt, results in lower interest payments—and, hence, higher income, relative to using straight debt.

price of the note over a specified trading period. Recently, **cash flow bonds** have been sold with the same objective. In both cases, the maturity dates are generally quite long, usually at least 30 years, and the fact that the "interest" payments are conditional on the company meeting certain thresholds reduces the contractual commitment to pay interest. As a result, income bonds get significant equity weight. This greatly reduces their attractiveness as far as the company is concerned, which is why they have mainly been a "desperation play" after a major reorganization (when the company has lots of tax loss to carry forward and little use for tax shields).

Another way of achieving the same type of objective for some companies is the **commodity bond**. Suppose a gold producer has fixed mine costs to produce gold but then faces uncertain revenues because they are tied to the price of gold. One way to manage this gold price risk is by using derivatives that are tied to the price of gold or through long-term fixed-price contracting. However, an alternative is to tie the bond payments to the price of gold. This can be done in two ways: Either the interest payment is tied to the price of gold, or the principal is. If the principal is tied to the price of gold, then as the gold price increases, so too does the principal, and because interest is expressed as a percentage of the principal, the investor receives more interest. If the bond payments are structured carefully, the interest is tax deductible, but the bonds are less risky to the company because the interest payments are tied to its major risk, which is the price of gold.

Commodity bonds, in which the principal is tied to some external index, are an example of indexed bonds. The most common of these are the real return bonds issued by the U.S. government, referred to as Treasury Inflation Protected Securities (TIPS). In this case, the principal is tied to the consumer price index (CPI), and as the CPI increases, the principal increases and the interest is expressed as a percentage of this increasing principal. In this way, the investor's income increases with inflation, thereby preserving a real rate of return. Real return bonds are not issued by corporations, but they do have an attractive property, which is that the immediate interest payments are much lower than with regular fixed-income bonds.

To return to the problem of tying interest payments to cash flow, another way is to make the interest payments conditional on prior dividend payments. An **adjustable rate convertible subordinated security (ARCS)** does just this. An ARCS has fixed principal and maturity, and the interest normally comprises two parts: a fixed interest rate, and some function of the dividend paid in the prior 6 months. These securities are almost all convertible into common shares, so the dividend is expressed as a percentage of the conversion price. If the conversion price is $50 and the dividend per share is $1, this would be expressed as 2 percent. The ARCS would then pay 5 percent plus twice this 2 percent dividend rate, or 9 percent in total. The ARCS are then subordinated to the company's senior debt.

ARCS combine debt and equity features. Because the interest is represented as a percentage, is tied to the principal value, and legally accrues, it is tax deductible. However, as a deeply subordinated debt issue in which the interest could drop to 5 percent if the dividend is not declared in the prior 6-month period, it has some equity-like features.

1. What distinguishes a hybrid security from a common stock or a bond?

2. Why is preferred stock often referred to as a hybrid security?

Concept Review Questions

SUMMARY

- The shareholders' equity of a company is the book or carrying value of the ownership interest. Shareholders' equity comprises common equity and preferred equity, and we can break down common equity into common stock and retained earnings. There are also adjustments to common equity for treasury shares and accumulated comprehensive income or loss.

- Common equity is the residual ownership of the company. The common equity of a company may have multiple classes of common stock that differ with respect to voting rights and rights to income or assets.

- Preferred stock, although not used as frequently in the U.S. as in other countries, is a source of equity capital for a company. This stock has preference over common stock with respect to claims on income and assets, but its features can be tailored to meeting investors' needs. These features include the dividend, its convertibility into another security, and redemption. For accounting purposes, if the preferred stock looks more like debt than equity, and it is classified as debt on the issuer's financial statements.

- Corporations have choices to make with respect to the type of security they issue—debt or equity—and the features. Many corporations issue securities that are hybrids, which have features of both debt and equity.

QUESTIONS AND PROBLEMS

Multiple Choice

1. A company may issue more than one class of common stock.
   A. True
   B. False

2. Voting rights that are contingent on dividends are most often associated with:
   A. common stock.
   B. preferred stock.
   C. convertible debt.
   D. mandatorily convertible preferred stock.

3. Which of the following is not considered equity for financial reporting purposes?
   A. Preferred shares
   B. Common shares
   C. Callable convertible preferred stock
   D. Mandatory convertible preferred stock

4. Which of the following statements about preferred shares is *false*?
   A. Straight preferred shares have maturity dates.
   B. The most common preferred shares are straight preferred shares.
   C. Floating rate preferred shares dividends are reset periodically.
   D. Retractable preferred shares allow the shareholders to bring forward the maturity date.

5. Which of the following securities is considered a perpetual security?
   A. Common stock
   B. Convertible notes
   C. Convertible bonds
   D. Mandatorily redeemable preferred stock

6. Which of the following statements is *false*?
   A. A convertible security has a specified conversion ratio.
   B. The exercise price is paid in cash when warrants are exercised.
   C. Debt is exchanged for common shares when an investor exercises a warrant.

7. A company with retained earnings of $1,000 million, common stock of $50 million, and paid-in capital of $100 million has a book value of equity *closest* to:

 A. $50 million.

 B. $100 million.

 C. $150 million.

 D. $1,150 million.

8. A company with shareholders' equity of $500 million, no preferred stock, 100 million shares of stock outstanding, and a market price per share of $12, has a book value per share *closest* to:

 A. $5.

 B. $7.

 C. $12.

9. A company that pays $1 million in common stock dividends and a market price per share of $30 for its 1 million shares outstanding, has a dividend yield *closest* to:

 A. 3.3 percent.

 B. 33 percent.

 C. 100 percent.

10. What is the correct ranking of cost to capital for the issuer of the following types of securities, from the highest to the lowest?

 A. Medium-term note debentures, bank loans, mortgage debt

 B. Common shares, medium-term note debentures, mortgage debt

 C. Common shares, convertible preferred shares, straight preferred shares

 D. Convertible preferred shares, convertible bonds, long-term unsecured debt

Practice Problems and Questions

13.1 Shareholders' Equity

11. What is the accumulated comprehensive income or loss that appears in most companies' financial statements?

12. What is treasury stock?

13. What does the account of retained earnings on the balance sheet represent?

14. Consider the following information from Wal-Mart Stores' balance sheet for the fiscal year 2009 (year ending January 31, 2010):

	(in millions)
Preferred stock ($0.10 par value); 100 million shares authorized; none issued	$0
Common stock ($0.10 par value); 11,000 million shares authorized; 3,786 million issued and outstanding	$378
Capital in excess of par value	$3,803
Retained earnings	$66,638
Accumulated other comprehensive loss	$70

 A. What is the total amount of shareholders' equity?

 B. What is the total amount of common equity?

 C. What is the total amount of preferred equity?

 D. What is the book value per share for Wal-Mart's common stock?

15. Consider the following information from the Johnson & Johnson balance sheet for the fiscal year 2009 (year ending January 03, 2010):

	(in millions)
Preferred stock; 2 million shares authorized; none issued	$0
Common stock ($1.00 par value); 4,320,000,000 shares authorized; 3,119,843,000 issued and outstanding	$3,120
Retained earnings	$70,306
Accumulated other comprehensive loss	$3,058
Common stock held in treasury	$19,780

A. What is the total amount of shareholders' equity?
B. What is the total amount of common equity?
C. What is the total amount of preferred equity?
D. What is the book value per share for Johnson & Johnson's common stock?

16. The following is the information provided in E. I. du Pont de Nemours' fiscal year 2010 balance sheet:

	Carrying Value *(in millions)*
Preferred stock, without par value, 23 million shares authorized,	
$4.50 Series − 1,67,000 shares, callable at $120	$167
$3.50 Series − 700,000 shares, callable at $102	$70
Common stock, $0.30 par value, 1.8 billion shares authorized, 990,855,000 issued	$301
Additional paid-in capital	$9,227
Reinvested earnings	$12,030
Accumulated other comprehensive loss	−$5,790
Common stock held in treasury, at cost 87,041,000 shares	−$6,727

Calculate the following:
A. DuPont's preferred equity
B. DuPont's common equity
C. DuPont's total shareholder equity
D. Compare the values for 2010 with DuPont's 2009 values, as shown in Example 13-1. What transactions have occurred to change these equity accounts?

13.2 Common Stock

17. State the three basic rights of common shareholders.

18. On December 2, 2011, Moog Class A stock had a value of $41.25 per share, and Moog Class B stock had a value of $41.10 per share. Using the information in Table 13-2, why would these values be different? Explain.

19. Viacom, Inc., has one class of stock (ticker: VIA) that had a price per share of $51.14 on December 2, 2011, and another class of stock (ticker: VIAB) that had a price of $42.63 per share. There are more shares of VIAB than VIA. The only difference between these two classes is that one is voting and the other is nonvoting. Based solely on the price differential, which class has voting rights? Explain.

20. The hot Internet stock you bought last year doesn't look so hot anymore; in fact, the company has just declared bankruptcy. The creditors, such as equipment suppliers and employees, are owed $1.5 million. How much will the equity holders receive if, when liquidated, the company's assets are worth:
A. $1.7 million.
B. $1.2 million.
C. Suppose the equity holders did not have "limited liability." How much would they receive for each asset value above?

21. With the savings from your summer job you were able to buy 500 shares of a hot new Internet company last year. A few months after your purchase, the company was low on cash and needed to raise more equity capital. The company's charter provided a "pre-emptive" right to shareholders, so you were offered the chance to buy one additional share for each five owned.

    A. What percentage of the company's equity will you own after your initial purchase if there are 500,000 shares outstanding?

    B. How much of the company's equity will you own if you buy the extra shares being offered?

    C. If you decline to buy the additional shares (but they are sold to other investors), how much of the company's equity will you own?

22. When Storrs Fridges needed to raise capital to expand, the founding brothers, David and Douglas Storrs, were concerned about losing control of the company if they sold too many shares. The solution devised by their investment banker was to create two different classes of shares. The brothers would each retain 250,000 Class A shares, which are entitled to two votes apiece. A total of 750,000 common shares, with one vote, would be sold to the IPO investors. What percentage of the company's equity will the brothers own? How much control (percentage of the votes) will the Storrs maintain?

13.3 Preferred Stock

23. Why would the cost of common equity be greater than that of preferred equity for the same company?

24. Consider the preferred stock of Ally Financial: Fixed Rate Cumulative Mandatorily convertible preferred stock, Series F-2. Describe the features of this preferred stock based on this identification.

25. Explain how a company can force conversion in a callable convertible preferred stock issue.

26. Trenton Financial Group has issued convertible preferred shares with a $50 par value. The conversion price for these shares is $12.50 (per common share). Trenton Financial Group's preferred shares also have a call feature that permits the company to repurchase the shares at par value (or, in effect, force the conversion into common shares). Usually, the common stock will be trading at least 20 percent above the conversion price before the call feature is invoked. At what price of its common stock will Trenton Financial Group consider calling the preferred shares?

27. The Lubbock Company has decided to invest some of its excess cash in straight preferred shares issued by other companies. It will earn a yield of 6.5 percent on a $10 million investment. How much net income will Lubbock earn if its corporate tax rate is 30 percent?

28. Frostburg Financial Group has 50,000,000 common shares outstanding, on which it pays a quarterly dividend of $0.20 per share. The company's capital structure also includes 2,000,000 cumulative preferred shares with a $25 par value that yield 8 percent per year (or 2 percent per quarter). After making some bad loans in the subprime mortgage market, Frostburg suffered a big loss and suspended its dividend payments on all forms of equity. Six months later, the company is once again in the black having earned $6,000,000 (after tax), which it intends to pay as dividends.

    A. How much will the common shareholders receive?

    B. The common stock of Frostburg Financial is currently trading at $10.00, while its preferred shares trade at par. Calculate the convertible premium on the preferred shares. What does this premium mean?

13.4 Hybrid Securities

29. What are the differences between a call option and a warrant?

30. Why is preferred stock often referred to as a hybrid security?

31. How would you value a bond whose interest is contingent interest? Explain.

32. Orion's Belt Mining Co. has 12,000,000 common shares outstanding, which are currently trading for $4.75 apiece. In addition, the company has issued 3,000,000 share purchase warrants with a strike price of $4.00 that are just about to expire.

    A. Determine the market value of equity of the company before the warrants are exercised.
    B. What is the total cost to the warrant holders to purchase the new shares?
    C. Calculate the value of the shares that the holders of the warrants will own after they are exercised.
    D. How much would you be willing to pay for each warrant?

Case

Case 13.1 Angel Financing and St. Paul

The St. Paul Company is a start-up venture that designed and operates a web site with job listings for individuals who want to work as a freelancer, whether this be writing, web design, or copyediting. The company helps match freelancers with specific jobs and earns a commission on all placements. The owners of this company, Joss Carpenter and Charisma August, are arranging financing from an angel investor, Whedon Boreanaz. Currently, the company is organized as a partnership, but management is considering incorporating when they are able to secure the financing, with equity owned by Joss, Charisma, and Whedon. Though Joss and Charisma want to be common stock owners when the company incorporates, it has not been decided what type of equity the angel investor should own.

    A. From the perspective of the angel investor, should St. Paul issue common stock or preferred stock in exchange for the financing? Explain your reasoning.
    B. From the perspective of Joss and Charisma, should St. Paul issue common stock or preferred stock in exchange for the financing? Explain.
    C. If the angel investor will only accept common stock, should there be more than one class of stock, each with different rights? Why?
    D. If the angel investor will only accept preferred stock, what features would make this stock more attractive? Explain your answer.

CHAPTER 14

COST OF CAPITAL

How low can it go?   The efforts of the Federal Reserve both before, during, and after the financial crisis of 2007–2008 to keep interest rates low has resulted in historically low costs of capital for companies in the U.S. in 2010 and 2011. The interest rates that corporations are seeing when they issue debt reminds everyone of the 1960s. For example, the yield on AAA-rated bonds was 9.05 percent in 1990, but 4.87 percent in 2010. The result of these low interest rates is that companies are issuing bonds. The cost of equity is also lower, and companies are issuing common and preferred stock. However, the memories of the 2007–2008 financial crisis are fresh, so the investors are being selective; it's *careful money.*

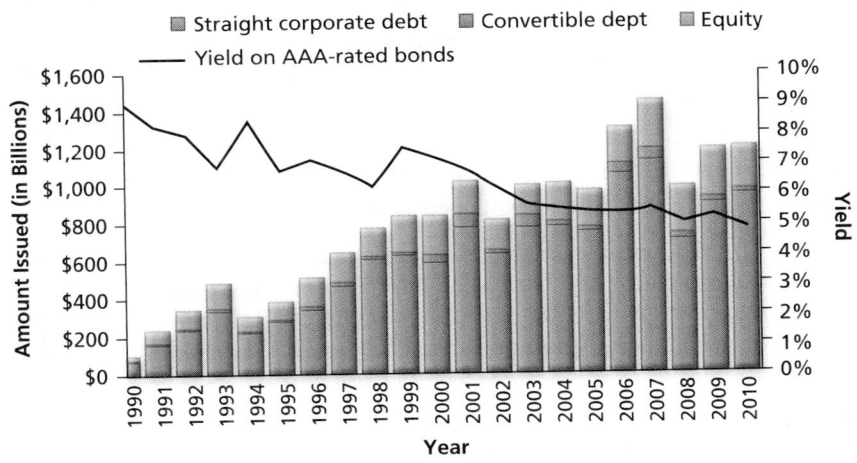

Source of data: *SIFMA.org*

Learning Outcomes

After reading this chapter, you should be able to:

LO 14.1	Explain how the return on equity and the required return by common equity investors are related to a company's growth opportunities.
LO 14.2	List, describe, and apply the steps in estimating a company's weighted average cost of capital, including how to estimate the market values of the various components of capital and how to estimate the various costs of these components.
LO 14.3	Explain how operating and financial leverage affect companies.
LO 14.4	Detail the advantages and limitations of using growth models and/or risk models to estimate the cost of common equity.

14.1 THE MARGINAL COST OF CAPITAL SCHEDULE

cost of capital the return the investor requires

The cost of capital is one of the most basic pieces of information a company needs in investment decision making because this cost is often used as the basis for determining an investment project's hurdle rate or discount rate in making decisions. In investment decision making, the **cost of capital** is the return the investor requires; hence, we refer to the cost of capital as the required rate of return from the perspective of the suppliers of funds (that is, the creditor or owner). Further, the cost of capital is often used in valuing a company, a subsidiary, or any asset, whereby future cash flows are discounted at the cost of capital to estimate a value.

In this chapter we focus on the meaning of the cost of capital, how to calculate it, and the challenges a financial decision maker faces in estimating the cost of capital. You will notice that during this process, we use many of the valuation approaches that you learned in earlier chapters, but we now look at these models from a different perspective: determining the required rate of return, instead of the value.

When a company is making an investment decision, it is determining whether the benefits of the investment (that is, future cash flows) exceed the cost of the investment in terms of not only the outlay, but also the cost of employing capital. When a financial manager evaluates an investment project, the focus is on the incremental cash flows; in other words, the marginal benefit of the project. Consistently, the cost of capital is a marginal cost, the cost of raising an additional dollar of financing. We calculate this marginal cost of capital as the **weighted average cost of capital**, or **WACC**, where:

weighted average cost of capital (WACC) the marginal cost of raising an additional dollar of capital

- the weights are the proportions of capital the company uses when it raises new capital; and
- the costs are the marginal cost for each source of capital.

It may be the case that the component costs change for different levels of financing. Therefore, the WACC would be different for different levels of financing. We often depict this graphically with the **marginal cost of capital schedule**, with the WACC for different levels of financing graphed against the level of financing, as we illustrate in Figure 14-1.

The WACC: The Basics

The basic equation for the WACC is:

$$\text{WACC} = \left(\begin{array}{c} \text{Proportion of} \\ \text{debt financing} \end{array} \times \begin{array}{c} \text{After-tax} \\ \text{cost of debt} \end{array} \right) + \left(\begin{array}{c} \text{Proportion of} \\ \text{preferred stock} \\ \text{financing} \end{array} \times \begin{array}{c} \text{Cost of} \\ \text{preferred equity} \end{array} \right)$$

$$+ \left(\begin{array}{c} \text{Proportion of} \\ \text{common stock} \\ \text{financing} \end{array} \times \begin{array}{c} \text{Cost of} \\ \text{common equity} \end{array} \right)$$

In other words, the costs of the different sources of capital are weighted by the proportion that the source represents in the cost of capital. We can represent this in notation form as:

$$\text{WACC} = \frac{D}{V} r_d^* + \frac{P}{V} r_p + \frac{E}{V} r_e$$

V represents the total value of the company' capital, D represents the value of debt, P represents the value of preferred stock, E represents the value of common equity, and r_d^*, r_p, and r_e represent the marginal costs of capital for debt, preferred equity, and common

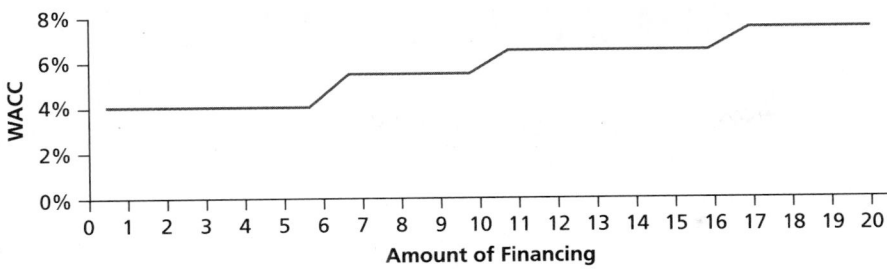

FIGURE 14-1 The Marginal Cost of Capital Schedule

equity, respectively. We can simplify this using the notation for the weights of the different sources of capital, the w_i, as:

$$WACC = w_d r_d^* + w_p r_p + w_e r_e \qquad (14\text{-}1)$$

The reason we designate the cost of debt different than the costs of preferred and common equity (that is, with an " * ") is that the relevant cost of debt is the after-tax cost because of the tax deductibility of interest. Therefore, for every dollar of interest paid, the company only bears a portion of that dollar. In the case of equity, dividends paid to shareholders are not a deductible expense for the paying corporation.

The WACC is the average of the required rates of return on all long-term sources of financing. But because each of the costs is a marginal cost, the WACC is also a marginal cost.

We illustrate the steps in estimating the cost of capital in Figure 14-2 and detail the estimation approach in the sections that follow. In the next section we look at how we determine the weights, and then we look at how we estimate the costs of the different sources of capital. Following the estimation of costs, we show how to put all the pieces together to arrive at a weighted average cost of capital.

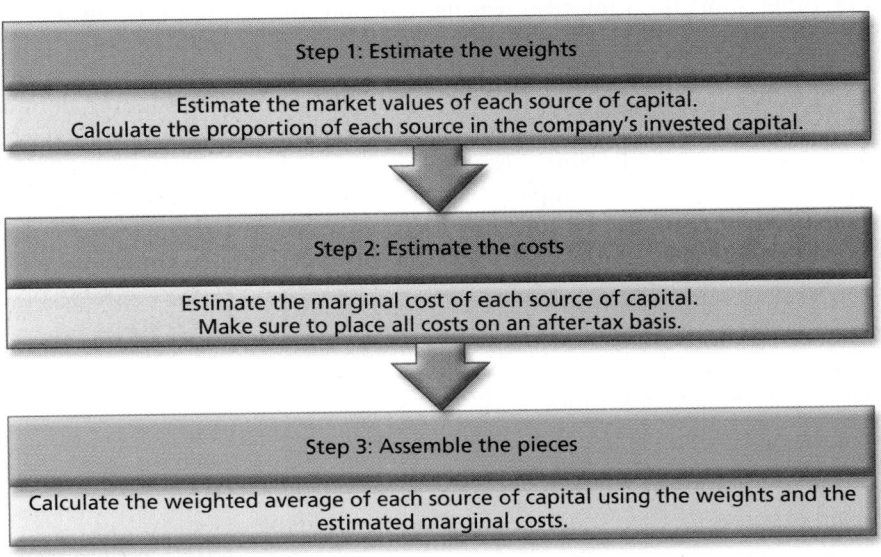

FIGURE 14-2 Steps in Calculating the Weighted Average Cost of Capital

1. Why is the weighted average cost of capital so important?

2. Why do we say that the weighted average cost of capital is a marginal cost of capital?

Concept Review Questions

14.2   ESTIMATING THE WEIGHTS

When calculating the cost of capital, we weight the component costs of capital by the proportion of capital that each source of capital represents when the company raises additional capital. We must first establish what we mean by capital, and then we will deal with the appropriate proportions.

What Is Capital?

Let's begin with a simple balance sheet, as we show in Table 14-1. On the asset side, we have current or short-term assets consisting of cash and marketable securities, accounts receivable, and inventory, plus there are usually some accounting items, such as prepaid expenses. When the current assets are added to the net fixed assets (i.e., gross fixed assets less accumulated depreciation) and any intangibles, we have total assets. On the other side of the balance sheet in Table 14-1, we see how the company finances its total assets.

capital sum of the interest-bearing debt and the equity of a company

The simple definition of **capital** is that it is the sum of the interest-bearing debt and the equity of a company. Debt capital consists of the interest-bearing obligations of the company, whereas equity capital is the sum of the capital of preferred and common shareholders.

Which liabilities do we include in debt capital? Only those that represent long-term sources of financing. We generally consider all interest-bearing debt obligations as debt capital. For example, many accruals are strictly accounting items required to prepare the statements according to generally accepted accounting principles (GAAP). As such, they do not represent a decision on the part of an investor or creditor to finance the company and therefore do not represent debt capital. For example, as long as a company's credit is good, accounts payable arise as a result of a telephone or computerized order, where the invoice arrives with the order. In most cases the supplier is not explicitly thinking of the value of its shipment as an investment in the company.[1] It is simply the way business is done between companies. The only debt capital items in current liabilities are typically bank debt, other short-term interest-bearing debt, and the current portion of any long-term debt that is due within a year. In other words, the debt capital in current liabilities consists of the interest-bearing obligations.

It is important to note that not all long-term liabilities are considered debt capital. Companies report the value of benefits owing to workers that is not fully funded with pension plan assets as a pension liability. Also, there are often deferred income taxes; deferred income taxes are taxes that the company expects to pay in the future. An argument can be made in the financial analysis of a company to include these as a liability (if it is expected that the taxes will be paid) or as equity (if it is expected that the company will always

TABLE 14-1 The Balance Sheet

Cash and marketable securities	
Accounts receivable	Accruals
Inventory	Accounts payable
Prepaid expenses	Short-term debt
Current assets	Current liabilities
Net fixed assets	Long-term debt
Intangible assets	Shareholders' equity
Total assets	Total liabilities and shareholders' equity

[1] Note that this is not always the case. For companies in serious financial trouble, a shipment may be seen as an investment with an explicit interest charge.

have this level of deferred taxes). However, deferred taxes are not considered debt capital because no funds are provided. In almost all cases, these "nondebt" accounting items are ignored in estimating company debt capital.

Another item excluded from debt capital is minority interest because this reflects the amount of shareholders' equity of a subsidiary that is not owned by the shareholders of the parent company.[2] Minority interest is best classified as equity because it is an allocation of ownership, but it does not represent contributed capital. Therefore, we do not consider minority interest as debt or equity capital.

A company's **financial structure** is the entire set of liabilities and equity accounts, whereas the **capital structure** of the company is how this invested capital is financed by debt and equity capital.[3] Therefore, the distinction we are making between a company's financial and capital structure is that the financial structure includes all liability and equity, whereas the capital structure includes only invested capital. **Invested capital** is the sum of the debt capital and equity capital.

We now take as an example the simplified balance sheet in Table 14-2.

- The financial structure is $2,000, consisting of $1,000 of liabilities and $1,000 of equity.
- The capital structure consists of invested capital and is $1,700: $1,000 in shareholders' equity, and $700 of interest-bearing debt (i.e., $50 + $650).

This capital structure results in a debt-to-equity ratio of $700 \div \$1,000 = 0.70$ and a debt-to-invested-capital ratio of $700 \div \$1,700 = 0.41$. This hypothetical capital structure is typical.

The numbers in Table 14-2 come from the company's financial statements and represent historical book values. We can convert them to market values if we have market information.[4] Suppose that the company's equity is selling for 2.5 times its book value, so that its **market-to-book (M/B) ratio** is 2.5. For this example, assuming that the book value of debt is the same as its market value, the total market value of the equity would then be $1,000 \times 2.5 = \$2,500$, and the total market value of the company would be $700 + \$2,500 = \$3,200$. Therefore, the company's market valued debt-to-equity ratio is $700 \div \$2,500 = 0.28$, and the debt to invested capital is $700 \div \$3,200 = 0.22$.

If the company's operating profit after taxes is $500, its **return on invested capital (ROIC)**, defined as operating profit after taxes divided by the book value of invested capital, is 29.31 percent. The company's **return on equity (ROE)**, defined as net income divided by the book value of equity, is $300 \div \$1,000 = 30$ percent.

financial structure liabilities and equity of a company

capital structure how a company finances its invested capital, consisting of debt capital and equity capital

return on invested capital (ROIC) earnings before interest and taxes divided by the book value of invested capital

TABLE 14-2 A Sample Balance Sheet

Cash and marketable securities	$50	Accruals	$100
Accounts receivable	200	Accounts payable	200
Inventory	250	Short-term debt	50
Prepaid expenses	0	Current liabilities	$350
Current assets	$500	Long-term debt	650
Net fixed assets	1,400	Shareholders' equity	1,000
Intangibles	100	Total liabilities and	
Total assets	$2,000	shareholders' equity	$2,000

[2] Minority interest arises when a company reports consolidated financial statements. GAAP requires consolidated statements even when a subsidiary is not 100 percent owned (usually more than 50 percent). As a result, all the subsidiary's debt and assets are included on the consolidated statements, and the part of the subsidiary's equity that is not owned is shown as minority interest.

[3] How the company arrives at these decisions is the focus of another chapter.

[4] Recall that long-term debt will usually be issued at coupon rates that are approximately equal to prevailing market rates so that they are sold at close to their face value. If the interest rates do not change very much, then the market value of such debt will remain close to the book value.

EXAMPLE 14.1
Estimating Debt Capital

PROBLEM

Using the following data from the balance sheet of Microsoft for fiscal year ending June 30, 2010, calculate the total liabilities and the debt for Microsoft:

	(in millions)
Accounts payable	$4,025
Short-term debt	$1,000
Accrued compensation	$3,283
Income taxes	$1,074
Short-term unearned revenue	$13,652
Securities lending payable	$182
Other	$2,931
Long-term debt	$4,939
Long-term unearned revenue	$1,178
Deferred income taxes	$229
Other long-term liabilities	$7,445

Solution

Total liabilities = $4,025 + 1,000 + 3,283 + 1,074 + 13,652 + 182 + 2,931 +

4,939 + 1,178 + 229 + 7,445 = $39,938 million

Note: Assuming the deferred taxes will persist through time and are therefore are most similar to equity, total liabilities = $39,709.

Debt = $1,000 + 4,939 = $5,939 million

Which Weights?

We estimate the proportions of the different sources of capital in the company's capital structure by estimating the proportions that the company uses when it raises new capital. Theoretically, we would like to use the proportions that represent the company's target capital structure, that is, the capital structure that the company aims for over time. However, we cannot observe this target capital structure. As a next-best alternative to the target capital structure, absent other information that may indicate otherwise, we use a company's present capital structure as the best estimate of the target capital structure.

But do we use the book values of the different capital or the market values? We generally use the market values of the capital that the company uses because we assume that the financial decision making of a company is based on market values of capital, rather than on the book values.

Estimating Market Values

Estimating the market value of a company's common equity is quite straightforward whenever a company has shares that are traded publicly. We simply use the market capitalization, which is the product of the company's market price per common share and the number of shares outstanding.[5] If the equity is not publicly traded, we need to use an approach such as the method of multiples to estimate the value based on market multiples of comparable, but publicly traded companies.

---

[5] Notice that in the preceding example we accomplished the same result by multiplying the company's book value of common equity figure by its M/B ratio.

Estimating the market value of a company's preferred shares is also quite straight-forward if they are publicly traded. In the event that the company's preferred shares are not actively traded, we can estimate the market value of the preferred shares by using the present value of a perpetuity equation, where P_p is the price per share, D_p is the dividend per share, and r_p is the required rate of return on preferred shares:

$$P_p = D_p \div r_p \tag{14-2}$$

This valuation assumes, of course, that we have an estimate of the required rate of return.

Estimating the market value of a company's debt can be somewhat more complicated. As mentioned earlier, if interest rates have not changed too much since the debt was first issued by the company, then the book value of the company's long-term debt is close to its market value, so we can use the book value. When a company has bonds outstanding, we can be more precise and use the following bond valuation equation to estimate the market value of those bonds:

$$PV = \left(\sum_{t=1}^{N} \frac{C}{(1 + r_d)^t} \right) + \frac{FV}{(1 + r_d)^N} \tag{14-3}$$

where

PV is the bond value;

C is the interest (or coupon) payment;

r_d is the discount rate (or market rate);

N is the term-to-maturity; and

FV is the face (par) value of the bond.

If the bond pays interest semi-annually, which is the case for most U.S. bonds, the coupon is the coupon paid every 6 months, the discount rate is the 6-month rate, and the term to maturity is in terms of the number of 6-month periods.

If the company has more than one series of bonds or other types of long-term debt issues outstanding, we can repeat this process and add up all the calculated market values to determine the total market value of the company's debt outstanding.

Suppose the financial manager of Company BCD gathers the following information:

	Book value (in millions)
Debt: 8% coupon rate, semi-annual coupons 10 years to maturity	$1.0
Preferred shares: 10% dividend rate	1.0
Common stock: 100,000 shares (originally issued at $15 per share)	1.5
Retained earnings	0.5
Total capital	$4.0

Assume the marginal tax rate is 40 percent. Present market conditions are such that:

- The present market rate on similar risk 10-year bonds is 6 percent.
- Similar risk preferred shares are providing yields of 8 percent.
- The common share price is currently $25.

We first need to estimate the market value proportions of these components assuming the company wants to raise new funds to maintain its present capital structure based on these market value proportions. For long-term debt, the value of debt is:

$$PV = \left(\sum_{t=1}^{20} \frac{4}{(1 + 0.03)} \right) + \frac{100}{(1 + 0.03)^{20}} = 114.8775$$

Or we could use a calculator or spreadsheet program with:

FV = 100
PMT = 4
i = 3%
N = 20

The value of debt is 114.8775 percent of its $1,000,000 face value, or $1,148,775.

The value of the preferred shares is the dividend of 10 percent × $1,000,000 = $100,000, divided by the market rate of 8 percent:

$$P_p = \frac{D_p}{r_p} = \frac{\$100,000}{0.08} = \$1,250,000$$

The value of common equity is the market value per share multiplied by the number of shares, or $25 × 100,000 = $2,500,000.

Putting these pieces together, we have the market value of the capital of Company BCD as:

Capital Source	Notation	Market Value	Proportion
Debt	D	$1,148,775	23.45%
Preferred equity	P	1,250,000	25.52%
Common equity	E	2,500,000	51.03%
Market value of invested capital	V	$4,898,775	100.00%

EXAMPLE 14.2

Calculating the Market Value of Debt

PROBLEM

Consider a company that has $100 million face value of debt outstanding. The debt consists of 20-year bonds with a coupon rate of 5 percent. These bonds have a yield to maturity of 6 percent, paid semi-annually. What is the market value of the company's debt?

Solution

The value of the debt [FV = 100; N = 40; PMT = 25; i = 3%] is 88.4426. Therefore, the market value of the company's debt is 0.884426 × $100 million = $88.4426 million.

Concept Review Questions

1. What is meant by the capital structure of a company?

2. How can we estimate the market value of common equity, preferred equity, and long-term debt?

14.3   ESTIMATING THE COSTS OF CAPITAL

marginal cost of capital
cost of raising one more
dollar of capital

Our objective is to estimate what it would cost the company to raise additional capital—specifically one more dollar of capital. This is the marginal cost of capital. The **marginal cost of capital** is the cost of raising one more dollar of capital. To this end, we need to estimate the marginal costs of each of the sources of capital the company uses.

The Cost of Debt

The cost of debt is the yield or interest on debt if the company borrows one more dollar. If the company has publicly traded debt, you can look at sources such as FINRA for yields.[6] And although that may seem simple, it is more complicated than that because most large companies have many issues of debt outstanding.

Consider the case of Archer-Daniels-Midland, ADM. In October 2009 it had fifteen publicly traded debt issues with remaining maturities ranging from 1 year to 88 years. Though most of these debt issues are debentures with fixed coupon rates, the coupon rates varied depending on when the debt was issued, and some of the issues are callable. Therefore it is not a simple matter to simply revalue the debt at current or expected yields. The current yields vary, depending on the maturity and features, but they generally range between 5.44 percent to 5.74 percent for noncallable debentures with maturities greater than 5 years. Let's use the midpoint of 5.59 percent.

We can estimate ADM's tax rate by looking at its tax footnote in its financial statements. In Note 12 of its June 30, 2009, fiscal year-end report, ADM reports that its effective tax rate is 32.6 percent. It is reasonable that, going forward, future income will be taxed at 32.6 percent.[7]

Putting the before-tax cost of debt of 5.59 percent on an after-tax basis produces a cost of debt of:

$$r_d^* = r_d(1 - T) = 0.0559 \times (1 - 0.326) = 0.03768 \text{ or } 3.768\%$$

PROBLEM

Suppose company ABC can issue new 10-year bonds, with 6 percent, paid semi-annually. Assume a tax rate of 40 percent.

a. What is the company's before- and after-tax cost of debt if these bonds are issued at par value?
b. What is the company's before- and after-tax cost of debt if these bonds are issued at 98?

Solution

a. If the bonds are issued at par, the present value is the same as the par value. Therefore, the yield to maturity is equal to the coupon rate of 6 percent. The after tax cost is $0.06 \times (1 - 0.4) = 0.06 \times 0.6 = 3.6$ percent.
b. If the bonds are issued at 98, the yield to maturity is 6.2723% [FV = 100; PMT = 3; N = 20; PV = 98 → 3.1361% per six months]. The after-tax cost of this debt is 6.2723 percent × (1 − 0.4) = 3.7634% percent.

EXAMPLE 14.3

Determining the Cost of Debt

The Cost of Preferred Equity

We estimate the cost of preferred shares, r_p, at the ratio of the dividend to the current value of a share:

$$r_p = D_p \div P_p \tag{14-4}$$

For example, Company BCD has a 6.2% perpetual, noncumulative preferred stock that has a market value of $21.26 per share and a par value of $25. This implies an annual dividend of 25 × 0.062 = $1.55. Therefore, the cost of this preferred stock to Company BCD is:

$$r_p = \$1.55 \div \$21.26 = 7.29\%$$

[6] The Financial Industry Regulatory Authority (FINRA) is a self-regulator for all securities firms in the U.S. You can find FINRA on the web at www.FINRA.org.

[7] ADM's tax rate is around 31 to 32 percent for most recent fiscal year ends.

EXAMPLE 14.4

Determining the Cost of Preferred Equity

PROBLEM

Suppose a company can issue new preferred shares with a par value of $100 at $98. This preferred stock issue has annual dividends at an 8 percent rate. Estimate the company's cost of preferred equity.

Solution

Based on their $100 par value, we get the following values:

$$D_p = \$8$$

$$P_p = \$98$$

So we have $r_p = D_p \div P_p = \$8 \div \$98 = 8.16\%$

The Cost of Common Equity

When we talk of adjusting for growth, we are referring to forecasting a company's future earnings and dividends. One way of assessing the importance of a company's growth prospects is to look at the stock market's time horizon and estimate the value of the company's current dividend when viewed as a perpetuity, and then compare this value with the stock price. If the values are significantly different, then it means that the stock market is valuing something other than the company's current earnings and dividends.

The value of a common share is the present value of its future dividends. We impose some assumptions to make the valuation workable; otherwise we would be forced into discounting dividends to infinity because common shares have no maturity date.

Growth models and the cost of common equity

The **dividend discount model (DDM)** represents the value of a share of stock today as the present value of all future dividends, discounted at the stock's required rate of return. A special case of the DDM is the constant growth version of the dividend discount model (DDM), which represents the value of a share of stock as the present value of a *growing* perpetuity. The dividend discount model with constant growth is commonly referred to as the **Gordon model** after economist Professor Myron Gordon.

Gordon model model of the value of a share of stock that assumes that dividends are a growing perpetuity

The basic valuation equation with constant growth is:

$$P_0 = \frac{D_1}{r_e - g} \tag{14-5}$$

where the price of a share, P_0 equals the expected next period's dividend, D_1, divided by the return required by common share investors, r_e, minus the forecast long-run growth rate, g, in dividends and earnings, or:

$$\text{Price of a share of stock today} = \frac{\text{Next period's dividend}}{\text{Required rate of return} - \text{Growth rate of dividends}}$$

We can rearrange this equation to estimate the common equity investors' discount rate or required rate of return. This process is the discounted cash flow method for estimating the investors' required rate of return. The equation for doing so is:

$$r_e = \frac{D_1}{P_0} + g \tag{14-6}$$

In this equation, the required rate of return is composed of the expected dividend yield, $D_1 \div P_0$, plus the expected long-run growth rate, g. The long-run growth rate is then the estimate of the increase in the share price and the investors' capital gain. As discussed previously, this is the appropriate cost of equity capital for the company when the company can raise the required funds internally (i.e., using reinvested profits).

Consider a company that has a current dividend of $1 per share and a current share price of $20. If the dividends are expected to grow at a rate of 5 percent per year, what is the required rate of return for this stock? We are given:

$D_0 = \$1$

$P_0 = \$20$

$g = 5\%$

The current dividend is $1, so next period's dividend, D_1, is $1 \times (1 + 0.05) = \$1.05$. We use Equation 14-6 to solve for the required rate of return, r_e:

$$r_e = \frac{\$1.05}{\$20} + 0.05 = 0.0525 + 0.05 = 0.1025 \text{ or } 10.25\%$$

PROBLEM

Assume a company paid a dividend per share this year of $1.00, which is expected to grow at 5 percent per year indefinitely. If its share price is $25, what is the cost of common equity?

EXAMPLE 14.5

Determining the Cost of Common Equity

Solution

First, we need to find D_1:

$$D_1 = D_0(1 + g) = \$1.00(1.05) = \$1.05$$

Now we estimate r_e:

$$r_e = \frac{D_1}{P_0} + g = \frac{\$1.05}{\$25} + 0.05 = 0.042 + 0.05 = 0.0920 \text{ or } 9.20\%$$

Sustainable growth, retention, and the return on equity

One of the issues we face in estimating the value of a share of stock is how to estimate the growth rate. Although the actual growth rate of the value of a share of stock may change from year to year, what we are most concerned with in valuing a stock today is the long-term growth of the stock's value. We can estimate this long-term growth using the sustainable growth rate. **Sustainable growth rate** is the growth we expect a company to be able to sustain in the future. We estimate sustainable growth as the product of the company's retention rate, b, multiplied by forecasted return on equity (ROE):

$$g = b \times \text{ROE} \qquad (14\text{-}7)$$

Even if the company retains all its profits and reinvests them within the company, it is not plausible that it can earn a 20 percent ROE on this investment forever. Such an assumption would imply that no other company can enter the industry and compete with the company to also earn these high ROEs. If other companies can enter the market, which will normally be the case, then these high ROEs will be reduced to normal levels due to competitive pressures.

What has to be remembered is that Professor Gordon developed his model for use in public utility regulation where the allowed ROEs should be reasonable, and we do not get the problem of rapid growth rates. Further, it is a product of regulation that all common equity earns virtually the same regulated ROE. In this case, the average and marginal ROE is exactly the same, and every dollar the company retains earns the same ROE. In contrast, many extremely profitable companies cannot reinvest at the same ROE because they cannot find opportunities as good as their existing ones. In determining the growth rate, the ROE is the future growth rate on incremental investment, and this may be greater or smaller than what the company is currently earning.

However, let's return to the constant growth dividend discount model with the assumption of a constant ROE for the time being. Substituting the sustainable growth rate as expressed in Equation 14-7 into the constant growth dividend discount model in place of g, we get:

$$P_0 = \frac{D_1}{r_e - (b \times \text{ROE})}$$

Further, we can then recognize that the expected dividend per share, D_1, is the expected earnings per share in the next period, EPS_1, multiplied by the dividend payout rate (i.e., one minus the retention rate). This is reasonable because a dollar can either be paid out or retained and reinvested within the company. Making this substitution for D_1 we get:

$$P_0 = \frac{\text{EPS}_1(1 - b)}{r_e - (b \times \text{ROE})}$$

We can see in this equation that the price per share is determined by the company's forecast earnings per share, its dividend payout $(1 - b)$, its ROE, and the required return by common equity shareholders, r_e.

SUMMARIZING: SHARE PRICE AND ITS DETERMINANTS	Based on the relationship in: $$P_0 = \frac{\text{EPS}_1(1 - b)}{r_e - (b \times \text{ROE})}$$ we see that:		

Variable		Relationship with Share Price	
Earnings per share	EPS_1	Positive	An increase in earnings per share increases share price
Retention rate of earnings	b	Depends on ROE	If ROE is positive, the greater the portion of earnings retained, the greater the share price
Return on equity	ROE	Positive	The greater the return on equity, the greater the share price
Required rate of return	r_e	Negative	The higher the required rate of return, the lower the share price

One important use of this equation is to see how growth and the company's ROE affects its share price. Suppose, for example, that the company's retention rate is 50 percent, its cost of equity capital is 12 percent, and its forecasted earnings per share are $2. If the company's ROE is 12 percent, then the forecast growth rate is 6 percent (i.e., 0.12×0.5) and the forecast dividend per share is $1 using the 50 percent payout ratio. In this case, the shares are worth $16.67.

Now suppose instead of a 12 percent ROE, the company is expected to earn 10 percent or 14 percent. At a 10 percent ROE, the company's forecast growth rate drops to 5 percent, and its share price is only $14.29:

$$P_0 = \frac{EPS_1(1-b)}{r_e - (b \times ROE)} = \frac{\$2 \times 0.50}{0.12 - (0.5 \times 0.10)} = \frac{\$1}{0.07} = \$14.29$$

whereas at a 14 percent ROE, the company's growth rate is 7 percent, and its shares are worth $20:

$$P_0 = \frac{EPS_1(1-b)}{r_e - (b \times ROE)} = \frac{\$2 \times 0.50}{0.12 - (0.5 \times 0.14)} = \frac{\$1}{0.05} = \$20$$

What this example illustrates is that the higher the growth rate, the higher the share price, as we show in Figure 14-3. This is because with a higher expected growth rate, investors will forecast larger future dividends and earnings.

Starting with the dividend discount equation for the price of a share of stock,

$$r_e = \frac{D_1}{P_0} + g$$

and rearranging, substituting $EPS_1(1-b)$ for dividends and $b \times ROE$ for the growth rate:

$$r_e = \frac{EPS_1(1-b)}{P_0} + (b \times ROE)$$

In this equation, the first term is the forecast dividend yield and the second is the sustainable growth rate.

However, note what happens when we use this equation to estimate the cost of equity capital for our three growth scenarios, as we depict in Table 14-3. Because the shares were valued using a constant 12 percent discount rate, when we "reverse engineer" from the share price, we get the same 12 percent back as the estimate of the cost of equity capital. In this case, the higher forecast growth rate leads to a higher market price and a lower dividend yield. Generally, companies with high dividend yields have

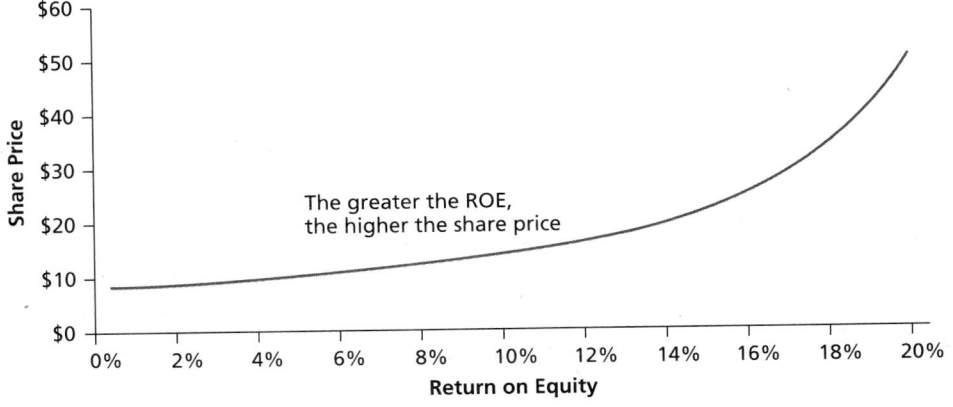

FIGURE 14-3 **Return on Equity and Share Price**

TABLE 14-3 Growth and r_e

ROE	P_0	Expected Dividend Yield	Sustainable Growth Rate	r_e
10%	$14.29	7%	5%	12%
12%	$16.67	6%	6%	12%
14%	$20.00	5%	7%	12%

lower forecast growth rates and vice versa. However, there is no reason for the cost of equity capital to be the same because the composition of the return between dividends and growth changes.[8]

Note that the company's retention rate, and thus its dividend payout ratio, is reflected in the constant growth DDM as "b." In Figure 14-4 we present the share price if this retention rate changes under the three scenarios where the company's ROE is 10, 12, and 14 percent for a wide range of retention rates.

Let's look at the case when the return on equity is 10 percent in Figure 14-4. We already saw that at a 50 percent retention rate, its share price was $14.29, but now we see that its share price *decreases* as the company retains more money and reinvests within the company. In contrast, when the return on equity is 14 percent, the share price increases as the company retains more, whereas for the 12 percent return on equity, the share price is independent of the retention rate.

The reason for these results is that when the company's return on equity is 10 percent, it is less than the investors' required rate of return of 12 percent. As a result, as the company invests more by increasing its retention rate, the shareholders are unhappy. Why would they invest in a company where they require a 12 percent rate of return and be happy with the company returning at 10 percent? In this case, the share valuation model is telling the company's management to reduce investment and return the funds saved as a larger dividend. The shareholders can then take these funds and invest them elsewhere to earn their 12 percent required rate of return. Conversely, where the company is expected to earn 14 percent, the shareholders are saying the opposite: "Don't give us a dividend because we can only earn 12 percent elsewhere, please reinvest more and earn 14 percent." As a result, the share price increases as the company invests more. Finally, for the 12 percent return on equity case, the shareholders are saying: "We don't care what you do

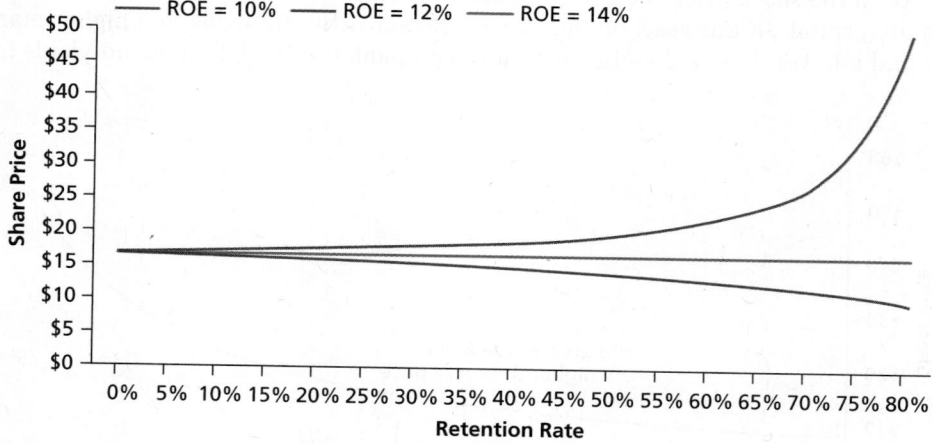

FIGURE 14-4 Share Prices for Different Retention Rates and for Returns on Equity of 10%, 12%, and 14%

---

[8] This is a question of the company's dividend policy, which will be discussed in a later chapter.

because you are not doing anything for us whether you invest or give us a dividend." As a result, there is no impact on the share price.

This example is very important in finance. For a long time it was felt this result was due to the company's dividend policy because the company's retention rate and dividend payout are changing. However, this is not true. What is really changing is the amount of investment the company is making, and the stock market is valuing whether the company is creating or destroying value. When the return on equity is greater than the cost of equity, the company is creating value when it reinvests, and when the return on equity is less than the cost of equity, it is destroying value. This result is independent of how much the company decides to pay out as a dividend because it can always raise money to pay a dividend. This indicates another aspect to the cost of capital: not only is it important to value the company's shares, but it is also a **hurdle rate** for making investment decisions. This is the meaning of the phrase *required return*: Unless an investment jumps this hurdle, it destroys value and should not be undertaken. We discuss this more at the end of the chapter.

The example with the different ROEs and different retention rates also emphasizes another key point: There is a big difference between a *growing* company and a *growth* company. When the return on equity is equal to the cost of equity, the share price was independent of how much the company reinvested. If the company paid out all its earnings and did not grow at all ($b = 0$), the share price is $16.67, whereas if it reinvests all its earnings ($b = 1$) and grows at 12 percent per year, the share price is still $16.67. This is an example of a growing company where if it simply reinvests at its cost of capital, it is "not doing anything" for the shareholders, and they don't care whether it is growing or not. Note also that the earnings yield for this growing company at a 50 percent retention rate is 12 percent, which equals its forecast earnings per share divided by its stock price (i.e., $2 ÷ $16.67). So for growing companies, the earnings yield is a good estimate of their cost of equity capital.

On the other hand, when the return on equity is greater than the cost of equity, the company is doing something that the shareholders cannot do, which is reinvest at 14 percent. We refer to these companies as growth companies and say they have growth opportunities. In this case, note that the earnings yield is $2 ÷ $20 or 10 percent, which underestimates the required return by common shareholders. Finally, some companies destroy shareholder value by investing where $ROE < r_e$. For these companies, the earnings yield is $2 ÷ $14.29 = 14 percent, which overestimates their cost of internal equity. What can a shareholder do if the company does not return what is required? They simply sell their shares (the proverbial "vote with their feet").

Multi-stage growth models

Another version of the dividend discount model to consider is the **multi-stage growth dividend discount model.** In practice there is no limit to the extent of the growth stages, but let's consider a simple case in which the company has some investment today, which we assume equals the company's book value per share (BVPS), which is earning a return (ROE_1) in perpetuity.[9] The company is expected to invest a similar amount next year (Inv), which will earn a return (ROE_2) in perpetuity. This particular version of the multi-stage model can be expressed as:

multi-stage growth dividend discount model version of the dividend discount model that accounts for different levels of growth in earnings and dividends

$$P_0 = \frac{\text{Present value of cash flows of existing assets}}{} + \frac{\text{Present value of growth opportunities}}{}$$

or, using notation,

$$P_0 = \frac{ROE_1 \times BVPS}{r_e} + \frac{\frac{Inv_1}{(1 + r_e)}ROE_2 - r_e}{r_e} \qquad (14\text{-}8)$$

[9] Notice that this will equal EPS_1, which means the value of existing opportunities $= EPS_1 ÷ r$.

The first term in this equation is the present value of the current earnings, as we discussed previously, where the company is expected to earn an ROE_1. The second term represents further investment (Inv_1), which we assume is invested at ROE_2, and is discounted back one period because it is one period further off in the future, but adds a perpetual amount represented by the difference between the company's ROE on this investment of ROE_2 minus r_e. If $ROE_2 = r_e$, then this future investment adds nothing to the value of the company because it does not create value, and the second term is equal zero. However, if $ROE_2 > r_e$, this future investment adds value, with the amount of value depending on the amount of investment (Inv_1) that can be invested at this rate, and by how much ROE_2 exceeds r_e. Equation 14-8 is a basic approach to valuation that breaks out the value of shares into the **present value of existing opportunities (PVEO)**, the first term, and the **present value of growth opportunities (PVGO)**, the second term.

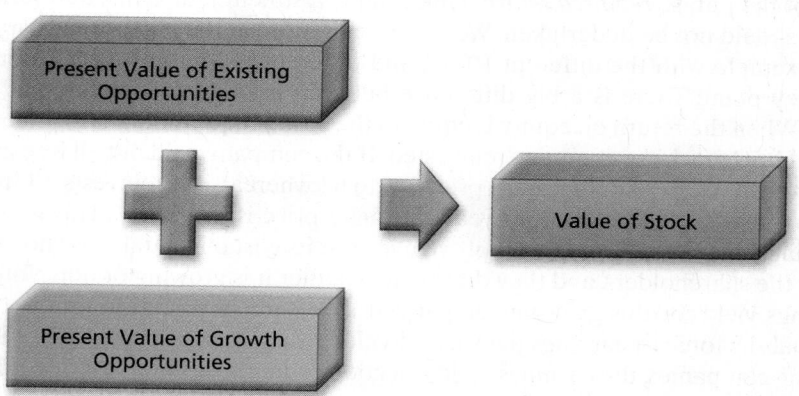

Although these equations make everything seem precise and quite scientific, the financial decision maker must understand the company and the assumptions behind all the parameters in the model before mechanically applying the valuation formulas.

Risk-based models and the cost of common equity

The previous section showed that the dividend discount model could be rearranged to estimate the investors' required return on a company's common shares. However, we also discussed how the model performs poorly when applied to growth stocks, which pay low dividends and/or display high growth rates. In these situations, it makes sense to rely more heavily on **risk-based models**. The most important risk-based model is the **capital asset pricing model (CAPM)**, which states that the expected return on a stock is the sum of the expected risk-free rate of interest and a premium for bearing market risk, specifically the stock's beta multiplied by the difference between the expected return on the market and the risk-free rate of interest.

We can represent the central equation of the CAPM, the security market line (SML), as follows:

$$E(r_i) = r_f + [E(r_M) - r_f]\beta_i \qquad (14.9)$$

In this equation, the required return by common shareholders (r_e) is composed of three terms:

1. The **expected risk-free rate of return,** r_f, which represents compensation for the time value of money.

2. The expected **market risk premium** $[E(r_M) - r_f]$, which is compensation for assuming the risk of the market portfolio; r_M is the expected return on the market.

3. The **beta coefficient** (or simply **beta**), β_i, for the company's common shares, which measures the company's systematic or market risk, and which represents the contribution that this security makes to the risk of a well-diversified portfolio.

The CAPM is derived as a single-period model, but just what is meant by a single period is an unresolved issue because investment horizons differ across investors. In testing the CAPM, it is common use a 30-day time horizon, and yet in making corporate finance decisions, such a short time horizon is rarely useful. In fact, when we talked about the characteristics of common equity, one of the most important is the absence of a maturity date. Although an individual investor may invest for 30 days, at that time, he or she will sell the shares to another investor, so the security is still outstanding. In addition, as we will see when we discuss corporate investment decisions, the cost of capital or WACC is used to evaluate long-term investment decisions made by the company. For this reason, the risk-free rate used in corporate applications of the CAPM is usually the yield on the longest maturity Treasury bond, which is currently the 30-year bond.

We generally use long-run averages supplemented by knowledge of the prevailing economic scenario to estimate the market risk premium. The basic idea is that over long periods, what people expect to happen should eventually be realized, otherwise they are biased in forming their expectations. In contrast, over short periods, it is unlikely that expectations are realized. It's like tossing a die: You may get three consecutive ones, but if you throw it enough times, eventually one-sixth of the time you will get ones, one-sixth of the time you will get twos, and so on. Similarly, we can consider the performance of the S&P 500 Index over the 1988 to 2010 period, as we report in Figure 14-5.

Clearly it is difficult to argue that in any one particular year, the performance of the S&P 500 Index was what had been expected. For example, nobody would have held shares in either 2001 or 2002 if they expected the stock market to go down! So what do we use for the expected market risk premium? A reasonable estimate, derived from academic research, is to use an estimate in the range of 3.5 to 4 percent.[10]

The final piece of information needed to use the SML to estimate required returns is the beta coefficient, which adjusts the risk of the market to the risk of an individual security, so it is an absolute number like 0.50 for a low-risk security and 1.5 for a high-risk security. The beta coefficient measures the degree to which securities move in relation to market movements: The more they move together, the less diversification gains there are and the riskier the security. Betas are normally estimated using the prior 5 years' monthly return data, but it is important to realize that if nothing happened during this period, then that is be reflected in the estimate. Conversely, if something special happened during this period, the beta will

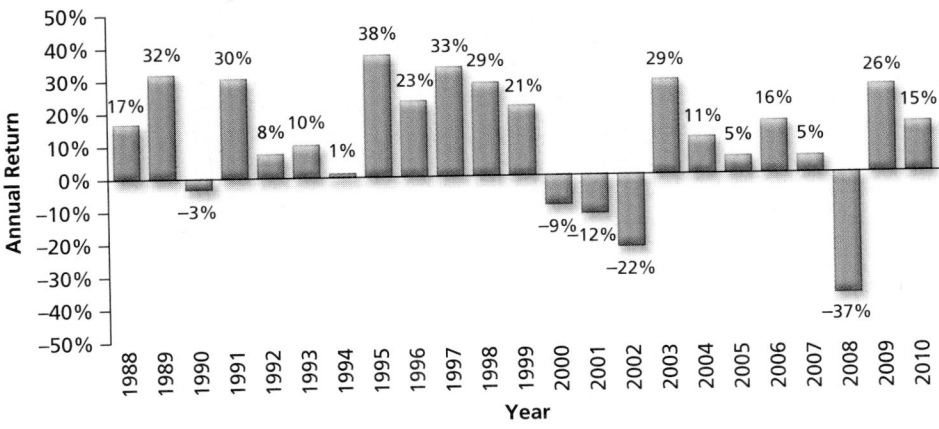

FIGURE 14-5 **Annual Returns on the S&P 500 Index**
Source of data: *Standard & Poor's.*

[10] In surveys of CFOs, John R. Graham and Campbell R. Harvey found that the average, 10-year risk premium is 3.46 percent; though during a recession it tends toward 3.97 percent and is lower, around 3.37 percent, in nonrecessionary periods ["The Equity Risk Premium amid a Global Financial Crisis," working paper, May 14, 2009]. These premiums are similar to what Graham and Harvey had found in their earlier surveys and studies. Eugene F. Fama and Kenneth R. French, in their study of the equity risk premium from 1951 to 2000, find a premium in the range of 2.55 percent to 4.32 percent ["The Equity Premium," *Journal of Finance,* 57, no. 2(2002): 637–659].

reflect it.[11] For this reason, we tend to go back over long periods and again analyze what happened during the estimation period. Consider the common stock of IBM. If we calculate the beta of IBM's stock using the 60 months of returns for the period 2006 through 2010, which includes the financial crisis of 2007–08, we estimate a beta of 0.70. If we calculate the beta over the broader period of 2001 through 2010, which includes a more "normal" market for most of the estimation period, we estimate a beta of 1.04.

As discussed in a previous chapter, if we sum up all the beta coefficients of individual companies, their value-weighted average has to equal 1.0, which is the beta of the market as a whole. For an individual company these may be quite different than 1.0. Consider the examples that we provide in Table 14-4.

The betas that we show in Table 14-4 are wide ranging, from a low of 0.36 for Wal-Mart Stores to a high of 2.42 for U.S. Steel. These betas are calculated using data that span the recent recession, so we need to consider them with the caveat that these may not be representative betas for other economic environments. However, you can see that these betas do tend to differentiate the firms in terms of risk—both operating and financial risk.

EXAMPLE 14.6	**PROBLEM**
Determining the Cost of Common Equity Using CAPM	Assume the beta for a company's stock is 1.15, that the risk-free rate is 4.5 percent, and the market risk premium is 4.5 percent. Estimate the company's cost of equity for internal funds using CAPM.
	Solution
	$r_e = 4.5 + (4.5 \times 1.15) = 9.68\%$

Flotation costs and the marginal cost of capital

In the example in the previous section, we were given the cost of equity, as well as the before-tax cost of debt, which we can adjust to determine the after-tax cost of debt. One complication that arises with respect to all sources of capital, except for internally generated funds, is that the company incurs **issuing costs** or **flotation costs** when new securities are issued. These include any fees paid to the investment dealer and/or any discounts provided to investors to entice them to purchase the securities. As a result, the cost of issuing new securities will be *higher* than the return required by investors because the net proceeds to the company from any security issue will be lower than that security's market price.

issuing costs or **flotation costs** costs incurred by a company when it issues new securities

TABLE 14-4 Betas for a Sample of Companies, December 2011

Company	*Ticker*	*Industry*	*Beta*
Goldman Sachs	GS	Diversified investments	1.39
Intel Corporation	INTC	Semiconductor	1.08
Johnson & Johnson	JNJ	Consumer products	0.54
Microsoft Corporation	MSFT	Software	0.98
Ryder Systems, Inc.	R	Rental and Leasing Services	1.62
United States Steel	X	Metal fabrication	2.42
Wal-Mart Stores, Inc.	WMT	Discount retail stores	0.36

Source of data: *Yahoo! Finance.*

---

[11] Edward Yardeni, "US Stock Valuation Models," Deutsche Bank, October 4, 2000.

Being aware of this fact is particularly important when we consider the cost of common equity to the company. In particular, remember that there are two sources of common equity financing: reinvested earnings, which show up on the company's balance sheet in retained earnings, and new common share issues. When the common equity portion of financing comes entirely from reinvested earnings, the company's cost of equity is equal the return required by its shareholders. However, when the company issues new common shares, it must pay flotation costs for issuing these shares, so the cost to the company is higher than the cost of using internally generated funds.

Adjusting for flotation costs: Two schools of thought

There are two different schools of thought regarding flotation costs. The first school of thought replaces the share price or present value with the proceeds after paying the flotation costs. Therefore, in using the dividend discount model, instead of:

$$r_e = \frac{D_1}{P_0} + g$$

we would use the P_0 less the flotation costs in the denominator of the first term. If we represent the price per share less flotation costs as $P_{0,f}$, we would then have a cost of equity that is slightly higher:

$$r_e = \frac{D_1}{P_{0,f}} + g \tag{14-10}$$

In the case of debt, if the proceeds of the debt issue are not the face value, but rather are P_f, the cost of debt before taxes is the value of r_d that solves the following:

$$P_f = \left(\sum_{t=1}^{N} \frac{C}{(1 + r_d)^t} \right) + \frac{FV}{(1 + r_d)^N} \tag{14-11}$$

What About Companies That Do Business Globally?

GLOBAL PERSPECTIVE

When we calculate the cost of capital in this chapter, we are focusing on the cost of capital for investments made in the same country as the investment, whether that country is the U.S., Canada, France, China, or any other country. This cost of capital represents the marginal cost of capital for a company's average project.

However, when making investments outside a company's home country, it is preferable to use a cost of capital that reflects the country in which the investment is made and the cost of capital appropriate for that country. This international cost of capital is often the starting point for estimating an international project's cost of capital.

How do we estimate an international cost of capital? There are several approaches available, including an international version of the CAPM; however, there is no consensus on the best model. In fact, the most appropriate model may depend on whether the economy is developed or emerging.

What is different in the international cost of capital estimation? One of the primary differences is that the

international cost of capital generally includes a country risk premium, which captures financial, political, and economic risks specific to a country. For example, Duff and Phelps note that Greece has a ratio of government debt to GDP of 115 percent in 2010, which increases both the political and economic risks of investing in that country.

Another factor to consider is that investing in other countries may offer some diversification, hence lowering a company's cost of capital. For example, Duff and Phelps estimate the correlation between return in the U.S. with those of emerging markets and find a correlation of 0.78; therefore, there is some diversification benefit from investing in these countries, and this lowers the cost of equity, and, hence, the weighted average cost of capital.

Sources: Duff & Phelps, *Cost of Capital Estimation in Emerging Markets*, September 30, 2010; Campbell Harvey, "12 Ways to Calculate the International Cost of Capital," working paper, National Bureau of Economic Research, Cambridge Massachusetts, October 11, 2005.

The effect of using the net proceeds instead of the current price or value is to have a higher cost of capital for the respective source.

The other school of thought is to leave the costs as we have calculated them, but then treat the cash flows for the flotation costs as an initial period cash outflow. The argument for this approach is that if we adjust the cost of capital, as in the first approach, we are representing what is a lump sum cash flow as something that affects the costs throughout the life of the project. This is not accurate and does not reflect the realities of the cash flows.

Concept Review Questions

1. Explain the relationship among ROE, retention rates, and company growth.

2. Explain how we can use the CAPM to estimate the cost of common equity.

14.4   ASSEMBLING THE PIECES

Once we have the weights and the costs of the different sources of capital, we calculate the weighted average cost of capital using Equation 14-1 that we introduced earlier:

$$r_a = w_d r_d^* + w_p r_p + w_e r_e$$

Gathering the Information

A financial analyst with the Dozer Company would like to estimate Dozer's cost of capital. He has gathered the following capital structure information using Dozer's most recent balance sheet:

	(in millions)
Current portion of long-term debt	$100
8% bonds	900
Total interest-bearing debt	$1,000
Preferred stock, 1 million $100 par value 7% perpetual preferred shares outstanding	$100
Common stock, 50 million shares outstanding	5
Additional paid-in capital	20
Retained earnings	1,400
Total shareholders' equity	$1,525
Total liabilities and equity	$2,625

Other information that the analyst has gathered:

- Dozer's tax rate is 35 percent.
- The bonds are due in 10 years, pay interest semi-annually, and have a current yield to maturity of 6 percent.
- The preferred stock has a current market value of $110 per share.
- The common stock has a current market value of $80 per share.
- The beta on Dozer's stock is 1.2.
- The expected market risk premium is 4 percent.

- The expected risk-free rate of interest is 2 percent.
- The current dividend on Dozer's common stock is $4 per share, and this dividend is expected to grow at a rate of 3 percent per year.

Calculations

Step 1: Calculate the proportions of capital

The first step in estimating Dozer's cost of capital is to calculate the capital structure proportions. Using book value weights, the capital structure is 39.6 percent debt and 60.4 percent equity: 4 percent preferred and 56.4 percent common. However, we have data available to calculate the market values components, which is the favored approach. We calculate the market value of the components as:

Capital Source	Calculation	(in millions)	Proportion of Total Capital
Debt	FV = 100; N = 20; i = 3%; PMT = 4; $\rightarrow$ PV = 114.877		
	114.877 × $1,000 face = $1,148.77	$1,149	21.85%
Preferred stock	$110 × 1 = $110	110	2.09%
Common stock	$80 × 50 = $4,000	4,000	76.06%
Total capital		$5,259	100.00%

Step 2: Estimate the costs of capital

The cost of debt is rather simple because we are given the current yield to maturity on Dozer's debt, 6 percent. The before-tax cost of debt is 6 percent, so therefore the after-tax cost of debt is $0.06(1 - 0.35) = 0.039$ or 3.9%.

We can infer the cost of preferred stock from the current market value and the dividend stream. We know that the current market value is $110 per share. With a dividend of 7 percent, the dividend per share is $7. Comparing the dividend to the price, we see that the required rate of return on the preferred stock is $7 \div $110 = 0.0636$ or 6.36%.

The cost of equity is a bit more challenging because we have two different ways of estimating the cost. Applying the dividend valuation model, we use the following information:

$D_0 = \$4$

$g = 3\%$

$P_0 = \$80$

Given the current dividend of $4 and the growth rate, we know that the expected dividend for next period, D_1, is $4.12. Putting this together, we see that the cost of equity is 8.15 percent:

$$r_e = (\$4.12 \div \$80) + 0.03 = 0.0515 + 0.03 = 0.0815 \text{ or } 8.15\%$$

If we instead use the CAPM, we have:

$r_f = 2\%$

$E(r_M) - r_f = 4\%$

$\beta = 1.2$

Applying the formula for the security market line,

$$r_e = 0.02 + (1.2 \times 0.04) = 0.02 + 0.048 = 0.068 \text{ or } 6.8\%$$

We arrive at different costs of equity using the DDM and the CAPM. This is to be expected because these models are based on different assumptions and use different elements in the calculation; the DDM focuses on dividend and dividend growth, whereas the

CAPM focuses on risk premiums, the risk-free rate, and beta. Which is correct? We cannot say; all we can say is that these are two plausible estimates. If a company pays dividends and these dividends grow at a constant rate, the DDM may be most appropriate. If a company does not pay dividends, but its stock returns are best explained by the return on the market, the CAPM may be most appropriate.

Step 3: Assemble the pieces

Summarizing, we have the following "pieces" to the cost of capital puzzle:

Piece of the Puzzle		*Estimate*
w_d	proportion of debt	21.85%
w_p	proportion of preferred equity	2.09%
w_e	proportion of common equity	76.06%
$r_d{}^*$	after-tax cost of debt	3.90%
r_p	cost of preferred equity	6.36%
r_e	cost of common equity: DDM	8.15%
r_e	cost of common equity: CAPM	6.80%

Assembling the pieces, if we estimate a cost of capital using the dividend discount model for the cost of equity, assuming constant growth, we arrive at an estimate of 7.184 percent:

$$\text{WACC} = (0.2185 \times 0.039) + (0.0209 \times 0.0636) + (0.7606 \times 0.0815)$$
$$= 0.07184 \text{ or } 7.184\%$$

If, on the other hand, we use the CAPM for the cost of equity estimate, we estimate a cost of capital of 6.1572%:

$$\text{WACC} = (0.2185 \times 0.039) + (0.0209 \times 0.0636) + (0.7606 \times 0.068)$$
$$= 0.061572 \text{ or } 6.1572\%$$

We can state that the cost of capital for Dozer is likely close to the range from 6.1572% to 7.184%.

LESSONS LEARNED | A Losing Formula

Volatile financial markets can wreak havoc with your cost-of-capital calculations—and possibly skew your investment decisions and financial results.

You could always say this about your company's cost-of-capital calculation: however complex it might be, you generally had to do it only once. If only life were still so simple.

Thanks to volatile financial markets and a harsh economy, calculating a weighted average cost of capital that makes sense has become significantly more complex, and carries a far greater margin of error. At least one CFO has resorted to calculating two metrics, one for assessing short-term investment opportunities and another for vetting long-term projects.

Extraordinary times, it seems, demand extraordinary measurements—and hold the potential for extraordinary risks. Underestimate your capital cost and you might take on investments that are not, in fact, economically justifiable. Overestimate and you could wind up not taking on worthy projects.

You could tarnish today's financials, too. Setting your cost of capital too high will artificially boost the cost of your equity-compensation programs this year, and could inflate any impairment charges you must take on goodwill. A botched calculation also could affect the amount of incentive compensation awarded to any employees measured against your company's performance relative to its cost of capital.

The math behind all these calculations hasn't changed, of course, but the integrity of the inputs has. Treasury bond yields—a key component in reckoning the cost of equity, which is one part of a company's weighted average cost of capital—have fallen to historic and, some argue, unsustainable lows. That, warns Roger Grabowski, managing director at financial advisory and investment banking firm Duff & Phelps, could mask the business risks some companies face in this severely depressed economy. "At the very time you would expect that your risk, and therefore your cost of capital, should be higher," he says, "the beginning point of your cost-of-capital estimate is actually very low."

At the same time, Grabowski notes, stock prices have fallen dramatically, but not uniformly, with shares of financial firms and highly leveraged companies falling the hardest. Because stock volatility relative to the broader market is another component of the cost-of-capital calculation, any company whose stock was less volatile than the broader market might also come up with a misleadingly low calculation. Their risk may have declined relative to, say, bank stocks, Grabowski reasons, but not necessarily to the economy.

Of course, for companies that have seen their stocks brutalized and their access to affordable long-term debt choked off, this issue cuts in the other direction. They must worry whether their cost of capital is being artificially inflated. And layered over all of this is the question of whether any of these extreme cost-of-capital inputs are short-term aberrations that should be discounted.

Extracted from Randy Myers, " A Losing Formula," *CFO Magazine*, May 1, 2009.

A Case Study

We provide an example of the estimation of the cost of capital for an actual company so that you can see how all these equations work with actual values. In this example, we estimate the cost of capital of Archer-Daniels-Midland, as of the end of fiscal year 2009. We provide Archer-Daniels-Midland's capital structure, based on carrying values provided in its annual reports in Table 14-5.

U.S. generally accepted accounting principles require a company to report the market value of its liabilities, if it can be reasonably estimated, in footnotes to the financial statements. ADM provides in its debt footnote the amount by which the fair values of its liabilities exceed the carrying value. Using this information, we can calculate the market value of debt.

TABLE 14-5 Archer-Daniels-Midland Capital Structure, for Fiscal Years Ending June 30, 2006, Through June 30, 2009

(in millions)	Fiscal Year End, June 30			
	2009	2008	2007	2006
Interest-bearing short-term debt	$356	$3,123	$468	$549
Current portion of long-term debt	48	232	65	80
Long-term debt	7,800	7,690	4,752	4,050
Total debt capital	$8,204	$11,045	$5,285	$4,680
Shareholders' equity	$13,499	$13,490	$11,253	$9,807
Total capital	$21,703	$24,535	$16,538	$14,486
Debt-to-equity ratio	0.608	0.819	0.470	0.477
Debt to total assets ratio	0.378	0.450	0.320	0.323
Proportion of debt capital	37.8%	45.0%	32.0%	32.3%
Proportion of common equity capital	62.2%	55.0%	68.0%	67.7%

TABLE 14-6   Market Value Capital Structure of ADM, for Fiscal Years Ending June 30, 2006, Though June 30, 2009

(in millions)	Fiscal Year End, June 30			
	2009	2008	2007	2006
Market value of debt[12]	$8,103	$7,789	$4,862	$4,937
Market price per share	$26.77	$33.75	$33.09	$41.28
Number of shares of stock outstanding	643	644	651	654
Market value of equity	$13,499	$13,490	$11,253	$9,807
Total capital	$21,703	$24,535	$16,538	$14,486
Debt-to-equity ratio	0.608	0.819	0.470	0.477
Debt to total assets ratio	0.378	0.450	0.320	0.323
Proportion of debt capital	32.0%	26.4%	18.4%	15.5%
Proportion of common equity capital	68.0%	73.6%	81.6%	84.5%

With respect to the market value of equity, ADM reports the number of shares of common stock it has outstanding in the annual report each year and provides historical share price information on its Investors' Relations portion of its web site. Using these two pieces of information for each year, we can estimate the market value of equity. Based on the market value information in its annual reports, we estimate Archer-Daniels-Midland's market value capital structure, as we show in Table 14-6.

Using the information on the proportions of capital, we need to make an assumption regarding ADM's target capital structure. ADM's use of debt financing has increased slightly over the 4-year period. Though we cannot observe ADM's target capital structure, nor its intentions, we can assume that the most recent capital structure, in market value terms, is the most representative for this company.

With respect to the costs of the individual components, we calculated the after-tax cost of debt in an earlier section as 3.768 percent. This leaves us to calculate the cost of equity. Using the current dividend of $0.56 per share, and expecting this dividend to increase by the historical rate of 7 percent, we therefore expect next period's dividend to be $0.6328 per share. The current market price of ADM stock is $30.66 per share, and the expected long-term growth rate in dividends is 7 percent.[13] Putting this information in the dividend discount model, we have:[14]

$$r_e = (\$0.6328 \div \$30.66) + 0.07 = 0.02064 + 0.07 = 0.09064 \text{ or } 9.064\%$$

Estimating the WACC for ADM, we have:

$$\text{WACC} = (0.32 \times 0.03768) + (0.68 \times 0.09064) = 0.073693 \text{ or } 7.3693\%$$

Although we have used numbers to the fifth decimal place, you should remember that despite looking accurate, these are estimates: Each value in the WACC equation is an estimate, so the final result—in this case a cost of capital of 7.3693 percent—although seemingly precise, is just an estimate.

---

[12] Provided by the company in Note 6 of the respective annual reports.

[13] Per *Value Line Investment Survey*, July 31, 2009.

[14] If we estimate the cost of equity using the CAPM model, using a risk-free rate of 1.5 percent, a market risk premium of 4 percent, and a beta of 0.33, the cost of equity is: $r_e = 0.015 + (0.96 \times 0.04) = 0.0534$ or 5.34%.

SUMMARY

- The WACC is a market value weighted average of the marginal costs of the different sources of capital. If the company earns its WACC, then its present market values are supported; if it is expected to earn less than its WACC, then its market value will fall, and if it is expected to earn more than its WACC, then its market value will increase.

- The weights in the WACC are the proportions that each source of capital represents when the company raises new capital. If we assume that the company is at its target capital structure, then we use the current capital structure as the target capital structure. When calculating the proportions, it is important to use the market value of the different sources of capital, not the book or carrying values.

- A proxy for the before-tax cost of debt is the yield on the company's current debt. We can proxy the cost of preferred equity in a similar manner, looking at how the market currently prices the company's preferred stock.

- The most challenging estimate in the WACC is that for the cost of common equity capital. In estimating this, the financial decision maker can use the dividend discount model (or variants) of this model, or the capital asset pricing model.

- We use the proportions and the costs of each source of capital to estimate the weighted cost of capital. This weighted cost of capital is a marginal cost because each of the component costs is a marginal cost.

FORMULAS/EQUATIONS

(14-1) $\quad r_a = w_d r_d^* + w_p r_p + w_e r_e$

(14-2) $\quad P_p = D_p \div r_p$

(14-3) $\quad PV = \left(\sum_{t=1}^{N} \frac{C}{(1 + r_d)^t} \right) + \frac{FV}{(1 + r_d)^N}$

(14-4) $\quad r_p = D_p \div P_p$

(14-5) $\quad P_0 = \dfrac{D_1}{r_e - g}$

(14-6) $\quad r_e = \dfrac{D_1}{P_0} + g$

(14-7) $\quad g = b \times ROE$

(14-8) $\quad P_0 = \dfrac{ROE_1 \times BVPS}{r_e} + \dfrac{\dfrac{Inv_1}{(1 + r_e)}ROE_2 - r_e}{r_e}$

(14-9) $\quad r_i = r_f + (r_M - r_f)\beta_i$

(14-10) $\quad r_e = \dfrac{D_1}{P_{0,f}} + g$

(14-11) $\quad P_f = \left(\sum_{t=1}^{N} \frac{C}{(1 + r_d)^t} \right) + \frac{FV}{(1 + r_d)^N}$

QUESTIONS AND PROBLEMS

Multiple Choice

1. If an all-equity company is expected to earn and pay out a $5.50 dividend forever (in perpetuity), the value of the company's stock given a cost of equity of 15 percent is *closest* to:

   A. $36.   B. $37.   C. $38.   D. $40.

2. The earnings yield given a $40,000 net income, a $10 market price per share, and 10,000 shares outstanding is *closest* to:

   A. 0.3.   B. 0.4.   C. 0.5.   D. 4,000.

3. What does the company have to earn, based on the following?
   - Market value of debt = $40,000
   - Market value of equity = $69,000

- $r_e = 12.5\%$
- $r_d = 7\%$
- Tax rate $= 35\%$

A. $2,800   B. $8,625   C. $10,099   D. $11,425

4. Which of the following statements is *true*?

    A. When ROE $< r_e$, management is adding value to the company.

    B. When ROE $> r_e$, management is decreasing the company's value.

    C. When ROE $> r_e$, the market price goes above the book value of the investment.

    D. When ROE $= r_e$, the market price goes above the book value of the investment.

5. Which of the following is *not* an input in the calculation of the WACC?

    A. Cost of equity

    B. Corporate tax rate

    C. Book values of equity and debt

    D. Market values of equity and debt

6. To increase the stock price of a company that is assumed to grow at a constant rate g:

    A. increase the cost of equity.

    B. increase the retention ratio.

    C. decrease the dividend payout ratio.

7. Star Inc. just paid a $9.50 dividend, which is expected to grow at a constant rate. Recent EPS is $10.50 and net income is $550,000. Total book equity is $1,100,000, and the cost of equity is 12 percent. The market price per share is *closest* to:

    A. $129.90.

    B. $130.90.

    C. $135.70.

    D. $142.50.

8. Which of the following companies is a growth company?

    A. ROE $> r_e$

    B. ROE $< r_e$

    C. ROE $= r_e$

    D. Net income $= r_e$

9. A company with accounts payable of $1 million, current portion of long-term debt of $2 million, bonds of $3 million, and deferred taxes of $0.5 million has debt capital *closest* to:

    A. $5.0 million.

    B. $5.5 million.

    C. $6.0 million.

    D. $6.5 million.

10. A company's financial analyst has gathered the following information in estimating the company's cost of capital:

- If the company issues debt, the analyst expects the yield on this debt to be 7 percent.
- The company's current dividend on its common stock is $1.5 per share, and the company intends on continuing its policy of increasing this dividend 4 percent each year.
- The current price of its common stock is $20 per share.
- The company has no preferred stock and does not intend on issuing any.
- The company's current capital structure is 35 percent debt and 65 percent equity, but its target capital structure is 40 percent debt, 60 percent equity.
- The company's marginal tax rate is 40 percent.

The company's weighted average cost of capital is closest to:

A. 8 percent.
B. 8.2 percent.
C. 8.7 percent.
D. 8.8 percent.
E. 9.2 percent.

Practice Questions and Problems

14.1 The Marginal Cost of Capital

11. Why is the weighted average cost of capital considered a *marginal* cost of capital?

12. What is the marginal cost of capital schedule?

13. A company is going to finance a new project 100 percent with debt, through a new bond issue. Because the company is using only debt to finance the project, the NPV of the project should be calculated using the cost of debt as the discount rate. Is this statement true? Explain your reasoning.

14. Tony Young has decided to estimate a company's cost of debt as the interest rate on the company's existing debt. He intends to use this interest rate as the before-tax cost of debt. Under what circumstances, if any, would this approach be appropriate?

14.2 Estimating the Weights

15. What is the difference, if any, between debt and liabilities?

16. Why would a company prefer to use market value weights in calculating its cost of capital instead of book value weights?

17. Consider a company that has $1 million face value bonds that are trading at 0.98. What is the market value of the company's debt?

18. If a company has a book value of equity of $20 million and a market-to-book ratio of 1.15, what is the market value of its equity?

19. For each of the following, classify the account as debt capital, equity, or other:

	Debt Capital	Equity Capital	Neither
Accounts payable			
Bank loan			
Bonds payable			
Common stock			
Current portion of long-term debt			
Deferred income taxes			
Notes payable			
Pension liability			
Preferred stock			
Retained earnings			
Taxes payable			
Wages payable			

20. Consider the following:

Book value of debt	$12 million
Book value of equity	$15 million
Market value of debt	$13 million
Market value of equity	$25 million

    What are the weights that this company should use in estimating its cost of capital? Explain your choice.

21. Consider the following information from the balance sheet of Procter & Gamble for the fiscal year 2009 [*Source: Procter & Gamble 10-K for fiscal year 2009*]:

Accounts payable	$7,251
Accrued and other liabilities	8,559
Debt due within one year	8,472
Long-term debt	21,360
Deferred income taxes	10,902
Other noncurrent liabilities (including pensions)	10,189
Total liabilities	$66,733

    What is Proctor & Gamble's debt capital for 2009?

22. Consider the 2010 financial data for ADM (for fiscal year end June 30, 2010):

(in millions)	*2010*
Interest-bearing short-term debt	$1,875
Current portion of long-term debt	$178
Long-term debt	$8,266
Shareholders' equity	$18,808

    A. Complete the following table:

Total debt capital	
Total capital	
Debt-to-equity ratio	
Debt to total assets ratio	
Proportion of debt capital	
Proportion of common equity capital	

    B. Compare the 2010 capital structure with ADM's 2009 and 2008 capital structure (Table 14-5). In what way, if any, did ADM's capital structure change?

14.3 Estimating the Costs of Capital

23. Why do we adjust the cost of debt for taxes, yet we do not adjust the cost of preferred equity or the cost of common equity for taxes?

24. Will the estimate of the cost of equity using the dividend discount model be the same as that determined using the capital asset pricing model? Explain.

25. What is the relationship between the retention rate and the cost of common equity?

26. If a company's yield on its debt increases, what do you expect to happen to the company's cost of debt and weighted average cost of capital? Explain.

27. The Dayton Poultry Equipment Company has been generating a return on equity around 15 percent. If this company increases the portion of earnings that it retains, what do you expect to happen to its stock price? Explain.

28. Consider a company whose stock currently trades for $190 per share. If the current dividend is $2.90 per share and is expected to grow at a rate of 3.44 percent per year, what is the cost of equity for this company based on the constant growth dividend discount model?

29. I. M. Grow Inc. just announced its earnings per share of $3. Its retention ratio is 70 percent. The earnings are expected to grow at 10 percent for 1 year and then grow at 4 percent indefinitely. Given that the cost of equity is 15 percent, what is the market price per share of stock?

30. Calculate the cost of issuing new equity for a company assuming: issue costs are 5 percent of the share price after taxes, market price per share is $20, current dividend per share is $3.50, and the growth rate of dividends is 5 percent.

31. A company has common shares outstanding with a market capitalization rate of 12 percent. The current market price is $13.80, and dividend payments for this year are expected to be $0.28. What is the implied growth rate?

32. Calculate present value of growth opportunities and present value of existing opportunities given the following information:

Return on equity of existing opportunities = 20%
Return on equity of future opportunities = 25%
Further investment = $50
Book value per share = $10
Cost of equity = 15%

33. Consider the following information for a company: current dividend is $2.50, the payout ratio is 70 percent (assuming it is not changing), the return on equity is 15 percent, and the current market price of the stock is $11.50 per share.
   A. What is the cost of equity using a constant growth dividend discount model?
   B. Based on this information, is the current management adding to or reducing the shareholders' value?

34. A company's earnings and dividends are expected to grow at a constant rate indefinitely, and it is expected to pay a dividend of $9.20 per share next year. Expected earnings per share and book value per share next year are $10.50 and $30, respectively. The cost of equity is 12 percent and there are 10,000 shares outstanding. Calculate the company's value assuming that the retention ratio stays the same and the market value of debt is $500,000.

14.4　Assembling the Pieces

35. Consider a company with market values of equity and debt that are $500,000 and $600,000, respectively. The before-tax cost of debt is 6 percent, the risk-free rate of interest is 4 percent, the stock's beta is 1.5, the market risk premium is 10 percent, and the marginal tax rate is 40 percent. What is this company's cost of capital?

36. Consider a company with the following financial statement information:

Balance Sheet

Cash	$140,000	Accounts payable	$200,000
Marketable securities	200,000	Wages payable	100,000
Accounts receivable	40,000	Short-term debt	250,000
Inventory	1,000,000	Long-term debt	690,000
Fixed assets	900,000	Total liabilities	$1,240,000
		Common stock	950,000
		Retained earnings	90,000
Total assets	$2,280,000	Total equity & liabilities	$2,280,000

Income Statement

Sales	$1,200,000
Cost of goods sold	$400,000
Amortization	$90,000
Interest	$56,400
Earnings before taxes	$653,600
Taxes	$261,440
Net income	$392,160
Shares outstanding	300,000

A. What is the cost of equity given a risk-free rate of 5 percent, a beta of 1.2, and an expected market return of 10 percent?

B. What is the market price and market-to-book ratio, assuming the company's stock is a perpetuity and the retention ratio is zero?

C. What is the invested capital and before-tax return on investment for this company?

37. A company has the following capital structure based on market values: equity is 65 percent and debt is 35 percent. The current yield on government T-bonds is 10 percent, the expected return on the market portfolio is 15 percent, and the company's beta is approximated at 0.85. The company's common shares are trading at $25, and the current dividend level of $3 per share is expected to grow at an annual rate of 3.5 percent. The company can issue debt at a 2 percent premium over the current risk-free rate. The company's tax rate is 40 percent, and the company is considering a project to be funded out of internally generated funds that will not alter the company's overall risk. This project requires an initial investment of $11.5 million and promises to generate net annual after-tax cash flows of $1.4 million perpetually. Should this project be undertaken? Explain.

38. A company has the following balance sheet items:

Common stock: 300,000 shares at $8 each	$2,400,000
Retained earnings	$900,000
Debt: 15% coupon, 15 years to maturity	$1,800,000
Preferred shares: 12% dividend	$1,200,000

The before-tax interest cost on new 15-year debt would be 10 percent, and each $1,000 bond would net the company $975 after issuing costs. Common shares could be sold to net the company $8 per share, a 12 percent discount from the current market price. Current shareholders expect a 15 percent return on their investment. Preferred shares could be sold at par to provide a yield of 9 percent, with after-tax issuing and underwriting expenses amounting to 5 percent of par value. The company's tax rate is 45 percent, and internally generated funds are insufficient to finance anticipated new capital projects. Compute the company's marginal cost of capital using the method in which flotation costs are imbedded in the individual costs of capital.

39. A company can issue new 20-year bonds at par that pay 10 percent annual coupons. The net proceeds to the company (after taxes) will be 95 percent of par value. Management estimates that new preferred shares providing a $2 annual dividend could be issued to investors at $25 per share. The company has a beta of 1.20, and present market conditions are such that the risk-free rate is 6 percent, whereas the expected return on the market index is 12 percent. The company's common shares presently trade for $30. The company's tax rate is 40 percent.

A. Determine the company's cost of long-term debt, preferred shares, and common equity financing under the conditions given, using the method in which flotation costs are imbedded in the individual costs of capital.

B. Based on your answer to A, what is the company's weighted average cost of capital assuming that it has a "target" capital structure consisting of 30 percent debt, 10 percent preferred equity, and 60 percent common equity?

C. Suppose everything remains as given, except that the company decides it needs $5 million in total financing. Calculate the company's marginal cost of capital.

D. What is the company's cost of capital, assuming its target capital structure as noted in B, if you use the method in which the costs of flotation do not affect the individual costs of capital?

40. The Laredo Lounge, Inc., plans to issue 20-year bonds with a 12.80 percent coupon rate, with coupons paid semi-annually and a par value of $1,000. The company's tax rate is 50 percent.

A. What is the company's effective annual after-tax cost of debt?

B. Laredo Lounge plans to issue $50 par preferred shares with annual dividends of $6 (i.e., a 12 percent dividend yield). Find the company's cost of preferred stock.

C. Laredo Lounge wishes to make a new issue of common shares. The current market price is $25, next period's dividend is $1.75 (expected dividend at the end of this year), the risk-free rate is 11 percent, the expected return on the market is 18 percent, and the beta is 0.95. The growth rate is 9 percent per year, indefinitely. Calculate the company's cost of issuing new common shares using the:

(a) dividend valuation approach.

(b) CAPM.

D. Find the WACC if the company wishes to raise funds in the following proportions: 30 percent debt, 20 percent preferred stock, and 50 percent common equity. Assume the cost of equity is best estimated using the CAPM.

 41. Consider the example of Archer-Daniels-Midland (ADM) that we used in Section 14.3, but also consider the information for fiscal years 2010 and 2011 from ADM's financial statements:

	2011	2010
Interest-bearing short-term debt	$1,875	$374
Current portion of long-term debt	$178	$344
Long-term debt	$8,266	$6,830
Shareholders' equity	$18,808	$14,609

A. What is the total capital for ADM for 2010 and 2011 in book value terms?

(1) Calculate the debt-to-equity ratio and the debt to total assets ratio for both years.

(2) What are the proportions of debt and equity capital in book value terms?

B. Using additional sources, complete the following:

	2011	2010
Market value of debt		
Market price per share		
Number of shares of stock outstanding		
Market value of equity		
Total capital		
Debt-to-equity ratio		
Debt to total assets ratio		
Proportion of debt capital		
Proportion of common equity capital		

C. Describe how the capital structure has changed in 2010 and 2011, compared to the years 2007 through 2009.

D. What weights would you use in determining ADM's weighted average cost of capital? Why?

Cases

Case 14.1 The Lazquez Company

Suppose you are the assistant to the CFO of the Lazquez Company and are responsible for evaluating how its cost of capital is calculated. The Lazquez Company has the following financial structure:

Accounts payable	$1.0
Wages payable	$0.5
Bank loans	$2.0
Long-term bonds	$10.0
Pension liability	$3.5
Minority interest	$2.0
Common stock (1.5 million shares outstanding)	$1.5
Retained earnings	$10.0
Accumulated comprehensive income or loss	$1.5
Treasury stock	$1

Additional information:
- The market price per share of stock is $20.
- The outstanding bonds have a coupon rate of 6 percent and mature in 10 years.
- The outstanding bonds are currently priced at 110.
- The beta of its common stock is 1.2.
- The expected risk-free rate of interest is 3 percent.
- The expected market risk premium is 4.5 percent.
- The marginal tax rate is 35 percent.

The Lazquez Company currently uses 10 percent as its cost of capital and has been doing so for the past 10 years.
- A. Using Excel, prepare an analysis of the cost of capital for the Lazquez Company, detailing your calculations of the weights and the costs of the different sources of capital. Be sure to note your assumptions and address the sensitivity of your recommendation to the various inputs.
- B. Based on your estimate, what are the implications of the Lazquez Company continuing to use a 10 percent cost of capital?
- C. If Congress lowers the tax rates for corporations, what is the effect on the Lazquez Company's cost of capital? Demonstrate this using your spreadsheet analysis.

Case 14.2 The Cost of Capital of Merck & Co.

You have been assigned to estimate the cost of capital of Merck & Co. based solely on publicly available information. Merck is a pharmaceutical company that develops, manufactures, and markets medicines, therapies, and consumer and animal products. For the fiscal year end December 31, 2009, Merck had the following balance sheet information:

	(in millions)
Loans payable and current portion of long-term debt	$1,379.20
Trade accounts payable	2,236.90
Income tax payable	9,453.80
Dividends payable	1,189.00
6% mandatory convertible preferred stock, $1 par	206.6
Total current liabilities	$15,750.70
Long-term debt	16,074.90
Deferred income taxes and noncurrent liabilities	18,771.50

	(in millions)
Common stock, $0.50 par value	1,781.30
Other paid-in capital	39,682.60
Retained earnings	41,404.90
Accumulated other comprehensive loss	–2,766.50
Stockholders' equity before deduction for treasury	$80,102.30
Treasury stock	21,044.30
Total stockholders' equity	$59,058.00

Source: *Merck & Co. 10-K for fiscal year 2009.*

Other information:

- The market value per share of Merck common stock is $36.20 at the end of 2010.
- The beta of the common stock of Merck is 0.66.
- Merck debt is rated AA by Standard and Poor's and Aa3 by Moody's.
- The yield on Merck's long-term debt at the end of 2010 ranges from 4.099 to 5.243 percent. Merck's long-term debt trades for values ranging from 98.165 to 118.660.
- At the end of 2010, the rate on a 10-year Treasury bond is 3.48 percent.
- The expected market risk premium is in the range of 2.5 to 4 percent.
- The anticipated dividend for 2011 is $1.52 per share.
- The retention rate for Merck is typically 50 percent.
- The annual return on equity for 2010 and 2011 is anticipated to be 20 percent.

A. Using fiscal year 2009 balance sheet information for your best guide to the company's target capital structure for future years, estimate Merck's weighted average cost of capital as of the end of 2010. Be sure to list your assumptions and support your choices.

B. Look up Merck's 2010 and 2011 financial statement from the company's web site, and look up the 10-year Treasury bond rate for 2010 and 2011, as well as the beta and the market value of Merck stock at the end of 2010 and 2011.

    1. If you used the 2009 weights to estimate those for 2010 and 2011, how accurate was this? How has Merck's capital structure changed since 2009?

    2. Based on Merck's information for 2010 and 2011 that you looked up, how accurate were the assumptions that went into the estimate of the cost of capital for 2010?

PART 7

FINANCIAL POLICIES

Having discussed the range of financial securities available to the company, this section considers the critical aspects of financial policy: how a company can combine its outstanding securities to find an optimal financing policy and how it decides its dividend policy. These are two of the most contentious areas of corporate finance, with much of the groundwork laid by Franco Modigliani and Merton Miller, Nobel Prize winners in finance.

CHAPTER 15

CAPITAL STRUCTURE DECISIONS

© Superstock/Age Fotostock America, Inc.

The financial crisis of 2007 and 2008 illustrates the importance of equity capital as a cushion for a company's creditors. The financial crisis of 2007 and 2008 has brought more attention to arcane measures of a financial institution's capital adequacy. Bank capital requirements were established in 1989 by the Bank of International Settlements, in what is referred to as the Basel Accord. These requirements identify capital requirements that are based on what it refers to as Tier 1 and Tier 2 capital, which are, basically:

Tier 1 {
Common stock
Retained earnings
Noncumulative preferred stock
}

Tier 2 {
Hybrid instruments
Subordinated term debt[1]
Reserves
}

Tier 1 capital is considered the bank's primary capital. Regulators use ratios that compare Tier 1 capital with the bank's risk-weighted assets, where risk-weighted assets are the assets of the bank with weights assigned by regulators that range from 0 percent to 100 percent, with 0 percent indicative of the most liquid, safe assets such as cash and government securities. This ratio is, essentially, the complement of a debt-to-assets ratio, but focuses on the risky assets.

Tier 2 capital, which is the supplementary capital up to the same level as Tier 1 capital, is not considered as reliable as Tier 1 capital. The total capital of a bank is the sum of Tier 1 and Tier 2 capital.

Regulators assess a bank's capital adequacy with regard to its ratio of Tier 1 capital to its risk-weighted assets. A bank's Tier 1 capital must be at least 4 percent of its risk-weighted assets, and its total capital must be at least 8 percent of its risk-weighted assets.

During the recent financial crisis, banks were subjected to stress tests, which evaluated whether they would need additional capital to meet capital adequacy measures if the recession persisted. As a result of these stress tests, the regulators required ten large banks to raise capital of $74.6 billion.[2] This led to at least four stock offerings, which would increase Tier 1 capital. However, some banks had an option to sell assets to meet the requirements (that is, reduce the denominator in the capital adequacy ratios).

---

[1] Subordinated term debt is debt that is junior (that is, less priority) than other obligations (such as deposits of customers) that has a maturity of at least 5 years.

[2] "Stress Tests: Ten Banks Need to Raise $74.6 billion in Capital," CNBC.com, Reuters and AP, May 7, 2009.

Learning Outcomes

After reading this chapter, you should be able to:

LO 15.1 Describe how business risk and financial risk affect a company's operating earnings and net income.

LO 15.2 Demonstrate the Modigliani and Miller (M&M) irrelevance argument, list the key assumptions on which it is based, describe the general conclusions of the Modigliani and Miller capital structure theory with regard to the relationship between the value of a company and the capital structure, and compare this to the pecking order theory.

LO 15.3 Explain how other factors such as company size, profitability and growth, asset tangibility, and market conditions can affect a company's capital structure.

Chapter Preview In this chapter we discuss how a company's management determines the company's capital structure. A company may attempt to minimize its cost of capital through its financing choices. Just as a company can increase its value by lowering its production costs, it can increase its value by lowering its capital costs as measured by its weighted average cost of capital. We explore how companies attempt to do so, which is much more difficult than lowering production costs. This involves sophisticated concepts that have been hotly debated for almost 50 years and are still to some extent unsettled.

In discussing these issues, we examine how companies' decisions affect their owners. We also examine how to assess the limits placed on a company's ability to issue debt as creditors and bond-rating agencies assess the risk attached to corporate debt issues. We look at the Modigliani and Miller (M&M) proposition that, under some simplifying assumptions, demonstrates how a company's value is unaffected by the capital structure decision. In addition to the basic M&M proposition, we also show how issuing debt may create value when we relax the two critical assumptions of M&M: that there are no taxes and that there are no bankruptcy or financial distress costs.

After working through the M&M propositions and their implications for capital structure decisions, we look at how companies actually make capital structure decisions.

15.1 OPERATING AND FINANCIAL LEVERAGE

We can break the uncertainty of a company's earnings into three primary sources:

1. **Sales risk**, which is the uncertainty associated with the price and volume that the company produces and sells.
2. **Operating risk**, which is the uncertainty arising from the use of fixed operating costs relative to total operating costs.
3. **Financial risk**, which is the uncertainty arising from the use of fixed-cost sources of financing (that is, debt) relative to equity.

In terms of how these risks affect the company, sales risk affects the company's revenues, whereas, for a given level of sales, operating risk affects the operating earnings of the company. We refer to the combined influence of sales risk and operating risk

sales risk uncertainty regarding the price and quantity of goods and services sold

operating risk uncertainty regarding operating earnings based on the mix of fixed and variable operating costs

financial risk uncertainty regarding the earnings to owners, influenced by the degree to which assets are financed by debt (relative to equity)

business risk uncertainty regarding the operating earnings, which is influenced by both the sales risk and the operating risk of a company

as **business risk** because these are risks that are determined, in large part, on the line of business the company operates. For a given level of operating earnings, financial risk affects the earnings to owners. In the following sections, we look at how these risks affect the earnings and returns of a company.

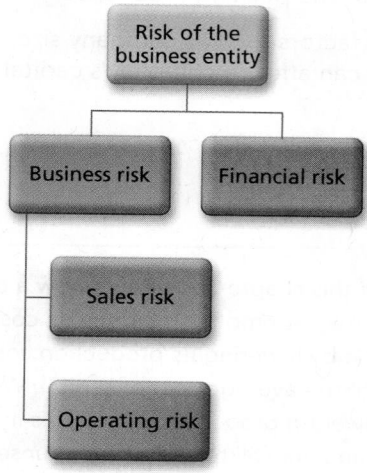

Business Risk

Consider the Gearing Corporation, which produces gaskets. The production of gaskets, no matter the number of units produced and sold, costs $200 per year; therefore, the fixed operating costs are $200 per year. The variable cost of producing a gasket is $0.40, and Gearing sells each gasket for $1.

For now, let us hold the number of units produced and sold to 1,000 units. What does Gearing's income statement look like if it produces and sells 1,000 units?

Revenues	$1,000
Operating expenses	400
Fixed operating expenses	200
Operating income	$400

We now consider what might happen if things changed. Suppose, for example, the company issued a report that sales potential had increased, and it now expected to sell 20 percent more gaskets, so that sales revenues are expected to be $1,200:

Units produced and sold	1,000	1,200
Revenues	$1,000	$1,200
Operating expenses	400	480
Fixed operating expenses	200	200
Operating income	$400	$520

operating leverage volatility in operating income from changes in units produced and sold as a result of the relation between fixed and variable operating costs

In this example, the company's variable costs increase by the same 20 percent that sales increase, to 1,200 units × $0.40 = $480, but operating earnings increase by 30 percent to $520. This is due to **operating leverage**; some of the company's operating costs are fixed and do not increase with sales. The greater the use of fixed costs in the operating cost structure, relative to variable operating costs, the greater the operating leverage.

Now let's consider what happens if sales drop by 20 percent to 800 units:

Units produced and sold	1,000	800
Revenues	$1,000	$800
Operating expenses	400	320
Fixed operating expenses	200	200
Operating income	$400	$280

Operating expenses declined by 20 percent (from $600 to $520), but operating income declined by 30 percent (from $400 to $280).

Degree of operating leverage

We can capture the sensitivity of operating earnings to the fixed operating costs with the **degree of operating leverage (DOL)**, which is that ratio of the percentage change in operating earnings to the percentage change in unit sales:[3]

degree of operating leverage (DOL) measure of the sensitivity of the operating earnings to changes in the number of units produced and sold

$$\text{Degree of operating leverage} = \frac{\text{Change in operating earnings} / \text{Operating earnings}}{\text{Change in unit sales} / \text{Unit sales}}$$

If we substitute Q for unit sales and represent the price per unit as P, the operating cost per unit as V, and the fixed operating cost as F, we can rearrange this to produce the DOL:

$$\text{Degree of operating leverage} = \frac{Q(P - V)}{Q(P - V) - F} \qquad (15\text{-}1)$$

In the case of Gearing,

P = $1

V = $0.4

F = $200

The difference between the sales price and the variable operating cost, P − V, is the **contribution margin**, which, when multiplied by the unit sales, is what is available to cover the fixed operating costs. The DOL therefore depends on the units sold, Q. We qualify our statements about the degree of operating leverage at specific level of units produced and sold. At 1,000 units produced and sold, the DOL is:

DOL = ($1,000 − 400) ÷ ($1,000 − 400 − 200) = $600 ÷ $400 = 1.5

At 1,200 units produced and sold, the DOL is:

DOL = ($1,200 − 480) ÷ ($1,200 − 480 − 200) = $720 ÷ $520 = 1.38

At 800 units produced and sold, the DOL is:

DOL = ($800 − 320) ÷ ($800 − 320 − 200) = $480 ÷ $280 = 1.71

Notice that the difference between the numerator and the denominator is always $200, the fixed operating costs. The fixed operating costs act as the fulcrum in operating leverage.

How do we interpret the DOL? A DOL of 1.5 means that if the quantity produced and sold changes by 1 percent, the operating earnings of the company change by 1.5 percent. In other words, the DOL is a measure of elasticity of operating earnings with respect to the quantity produced and sold. The higher the DOL, the greater the operating leverage and, hence, operating risk.

---

[3] You may recall from economics that this looks like an elasticity measure or, from calculus, the partial derivative of operating income with respect to the quantity produced and sold.

Operating break-even

We can see the effects of operating leverage by looking over a wider range of units produced and sold, as we show in Panel A of Figure 15-1. The effect of operating leverage is to increase the operating profit margin, with small increases for ever-increasing units produced and sold. We can also see the degree of operating leverage over the same range of units in Panel B of this figure. Here you can see that the DOL is negative for some unit sales, peaks, and then declines thereafter.

We can tie together the operating profit margin and the degree of operating leverage by calculating the **break-even point**; that is, the units produced and sold at which the operating profit is zero. We can guesstimate this point using the graph, but we can calculate the precise break-even point by setting the operating profit to zero and then solving for the units, Q:[4]

$$Q(P - V) - F = \$0$$

$$Q(\$1 - 0.4) - 200 = \$0$$

$$Q\$0.6 = \$200$$

$$Q = \$200 \div \$0.6 = 333.33 \text{ units}$$

Sales price per unit = $1
Variable operating cost per unit = $0.4
Fixed operating costs = $200

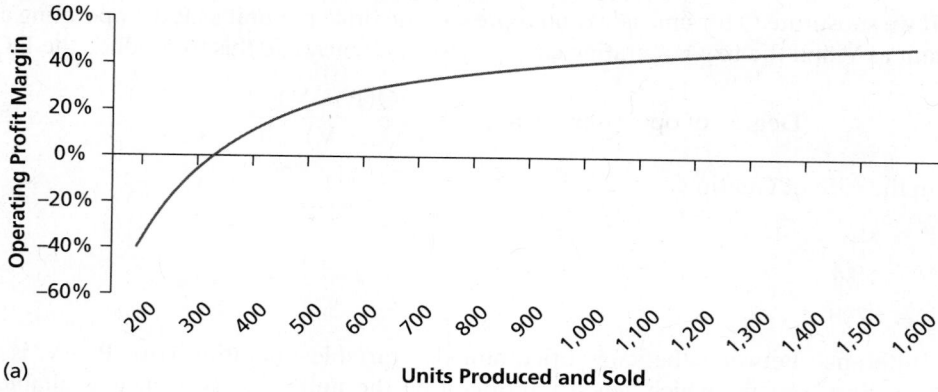

(a)   **Units Produced and Sold**

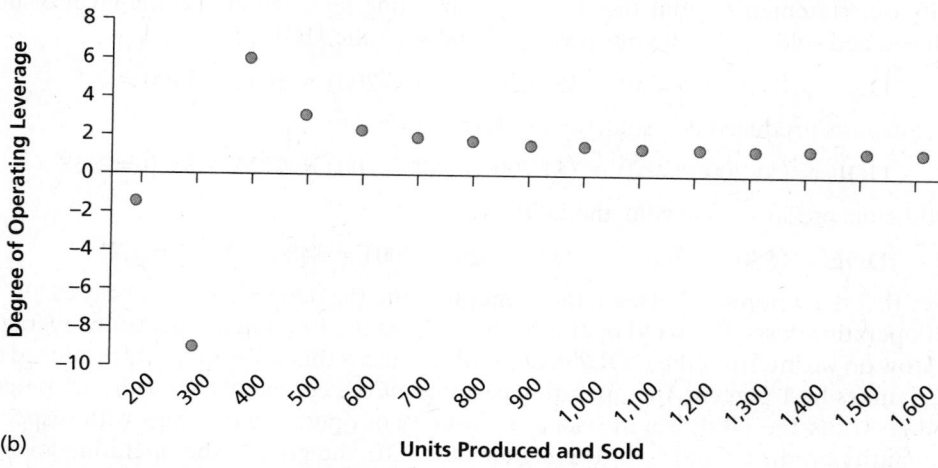

(b)   **Units Produced and Sold**

FIGURE 15-1 Operating Profit and Operating Leverage

[4] The DOL at 333 units is −999, the DOL at 334 units is 501, and the DOL at the break-even units is not defined (dividing by zero). A negative DOL corresponds to operating losses, so our focus is generally on the DOL beyond the break-even point.

We illustrate the operating profit for different levels of units produced and sold in Figure 15-1. The operating profit increases, but not linearly: for the lower level of sales, the company incurs losses; once the company achieves a level of output that covers fixed costs, the profit consists of the contribution margin multiplied by the number of units. We also graph the degree of operating leverage in this figure. As you can see, it is meaningless below a certain point, but then the relationship between DOL and output becomes curvilinear, with steep drops in the DOL for lower levels of output, and then smaller decreases in DOL for higher levels of output.

Sales risk

Now let's introduce sales risk. By consulting with the marketing management of the company, the financial managers at Gearing have determined the price at which they can sell the gaskets based on the volume of sales:

Unit Sales	Price per Gasket
200–799	$1.10
800–1299	$1.00
1300 and above	$0.90

When we introduce the demand function for the product, we introduce more variability in the operating profit margin, as you can see in Figure 15-2. Hence, operating earnings are affected by both sales risk and operating risk.

EXAMPLE 15.1

Operating Leverage

PROBLEM

A company expects to sell 18,000 units of its product at a price of $5 per unit. The variable cost to produce a unit is $3, and the company has fixed operating costs of $30,000. Calculate the following:

A. Contribution margin
B. Operating earnings
C. Degree of operating leverage at 18,000 units
D. Percentage change in operating earnings if the company's sales are 5 percent higher
E. Break-even units produced and sold

Solution

A. Contribution margin = $5 − 3 = $2
B. $[18,000 \times (\$5 - 3) - 30,000] = \$6,000$
C. $[18,000 \times (\$5 - 3)] \div [18,000 \times (\$5 - 3) - 30,000] = 6$
D. $6 \times 5\% = 30\%$ [Check: $18,900 \times (\$5 - 3) - 30,000 = 7,800$, which is 30 percent higher than 6,000]
E. $Q(\$5 - 3) - 30,000 = 0; Q = 30,000 \div 2 = 15,000$ units

---

Financial Leverage

Financial leverage is the use of debt to finance a company's assets. Financial leverage results in earnings to owners that vary more than a similar company that finances its assets with equity. Consider three choices of capital structure for the Gearing Company: Structure One, Structure Two, and Structure Three. With Structure One, Gearing finances its assets solely with equity, whereas with Structures Two and Three, Gearing finances its assets with both debt and equity, as we show in Table 15-1.

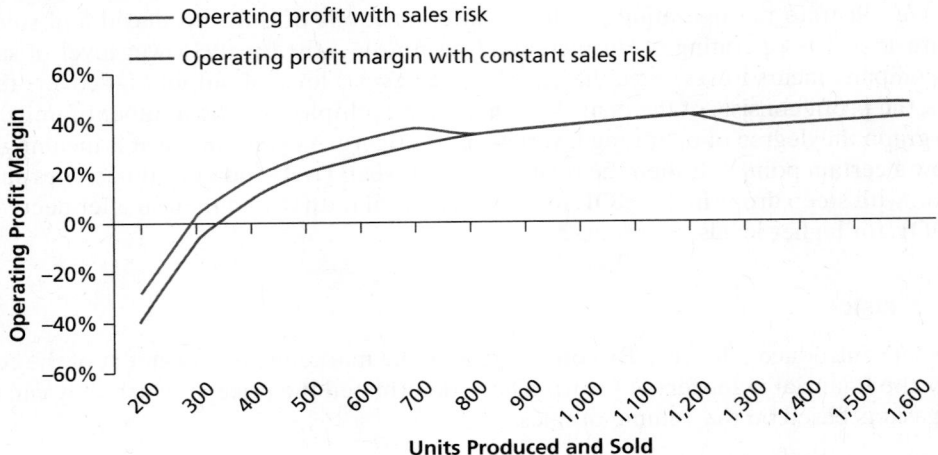

FIGURE 15-2 Operating Profit Margin Using the Demand Function for Sales Price

Invested capital is a sum total of capital in a company's capital structure, consisting of debt and equity. The invested capital for all three structures is the same: $2,000. Now let's consider the income statement of each company, which we show in Table 15-2. For now, we are holding units produced and sold to 1,000, sold at a sales price of $1 per unit.

Returns and financial leverage

We have ratios that we can use to measure the profitability of the companies, including the return on equity and the return on invested capital. As you have seen in previous chapters, we calculate the return on equity (ROE) by comparing net profit with equity:

$$\text{ROE} = \frac{\text{Net income}}{\text{Equity}} \tag{15-2}$$

Therefore, the ROE is affected by interest on debt. The return on invested capital (ROI), on the other hand, is the ratio of operating income to invested capital:

$$\text{ROI} = \frac{\text{Operating income after tax}}{\text{Invested capital}} \tag{15-3}$$

Because we are comparing operating income after tax with invested capital, interest does not enter the picture.

TABLE 15-1 Alternative Financing Strategies for the Gearing Company

	Structure One	Structure Two	Structure Three
Assets	$2,000	$2,000	$2,000
Debt	$0	$500	$1,000
Equity	$2,000	$1,500	$1,000
Number of shares	2,000	1,500	1,000
Debt-to-invested capital	0.00	0.25	0.50
Debt-to-equity	0.00	0.33	1.00

TABLE 15-2   Effect of Alternative Financing Strategies on the Income Statement

	Structure One	Structure Two	Structure Three
Revenues	$1,000	$1,000	$1,000
Operating expenses	400	400	400
Fixed operating expenses	200	200	200
Operating income	$400	$400	$400
Interest	0	25	50
Taxable income	$400	$375	$350
Taxes	140	131	123
Net income	$260	$244	$228

We provide the three returns for each company in Table 15-3, holding operating earnings constant at $400.[5] As you can see, the return on invested capital is the same, no matter the financing. This is because the operating income after tax, which is $400 – 140 = $260, and the invested capital, the $2,000, are same no matter the financing. The return on equity, however, increases with more debt because the operating earnings after tax remain the same, but the amount of equity declines from $2,000 (Structure One) to $1,000 (Structure Three). In the case of Structures Two and Three, Gearing pays the creditors a fixed amount, but anything the company makes beyond that flows to shareholders. Hence, the benefit from financial leverage.

There is, however, a downside to financial leverage. What happens at different levels of operating earnings? Consider each of the three structures, but let's allow operating earnings to change. We show the return on equity for the three structures for operating earnings from a loss of $80 to a profit of $760, which corresponds to unit sales from 200 to 1,600, in Figure 15-3. What you can see in this figure is that the structures that have debt (Two and Three) provide more leverage to a given operating earnings as compared to the structure without financial leverage (One), and that the more debt involved, the greater this leverage.

Degree of financial leverage

We can quantify the financial leverage using the **degree of financial leverage (DFL)**:

$$\text{Degree of financial leverage} = \frac{\text{Operating earnings}}{\text{Operating earnings} - \text{Interest}}$$

Like the degree of operating leverage, there is a "fulcrum"—but this time it is the fixed financing cost associated with chosen capital structure. If we represent the interest

degree of financial leverage (DFL) sensitivity of net income to changes in operating earnings, influenced by the use debt, relative to equity, as a source of capital

TABLE 15-3   Returns: ROI and ROE for the Gearing Capital Structure Choices

	Structure One	Structure Two	Structure Three
Return on invested capital	20%	20%	20%
Return on equity	13%	16%	23%

[5] There will be cases for actual companies in which EBIT is not equal to operating income. Some companies will have nonoperating expenses or income that is not interest, and this will cause a difference between operating income and EBIT.

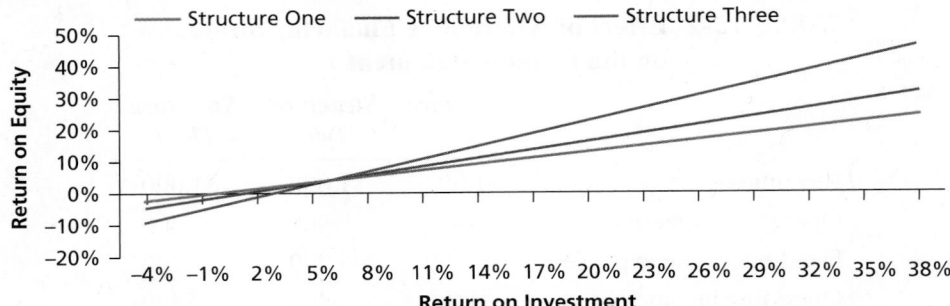

FIGURE 15-3 Return on Equity and Return on Invested Capital for Different Capital Structures

cost as C and use the notation we introduced earlier, the degree of financial leverage (DFL) is:[6]

$$\text{Degree of financial leverage} = \frac{Q(P - V) - F}{Q(P - V) - F - C}$$

Applying this formula, suppose the Gearing Company expects to produce 1,200 units. At this level of production, the degree of financial leverage is:

$$\text{Degree of financial leverage} = \frac{1{,}200(\$1 - 0.4) - 200}{1{,}200(\$1 - 0.4) - 200 - 25} = \frac{\$520}{\$495} = 1.0505$$

What does this mean? It means that a 1 percent change in operating earnings will result in a 1.0505 percent change in net income.

In our example, financial leverage is favorable for the shareholders of a company because it adds to the common shareholders' ROE over most levels of operating earnings. However, remember that the cost of the debt is a fixed contractual commitment of 5 percent before tax.

Financial break-even

Looking back at Figure 15-3, you can see that the ROE–ROI lines intersect. This intersection is a **financial break-even point**. That is, it is the ROI at which the ROE is zero. Using our notation,

financial break-even point return on investment or quantity produced or sold at which a company's ROE is zero

$$\text{ROI} = \frac{[Q(P - V) - F](1 - T)}{D + E} \quad \text{and ROE} = \frac{[Q(P - V) - F - C](1 - T)}{E}$$

If we set ROE equal to zero, insert the values of P, V, F, and C, and then solve for Q, we arrive at a break-even quantity of 375. Using this in the formula for ROI, along with the other parameters, produces an ROI of 1.25 percent. In other words, the ROE is zero for Structure Two when the return on investment is 1.25 percent. Stated another way, the ROE is zero for Structure Two when the company produces and sells 375 units.

The second break-even point is where the two financing strategies produce the same ROE. This point is often called the **indifference point** because it is the ROI at which the ROE is the same, regardless of how the company is financed. We can calculate this point by setting the two ROEs to be the same:

indifference point the quantity produced and sold or return on investment at which two financing strategies provide the same return on equity

$$\text{ROE}_{\text{One}} = \text{ROE}_{\text{Two}}$$

$$\frac{[Q(\$1 - 0.4) - 200 - 0](1 - 0.35)}{\$2{,}000} = \frac{[Q(\$1 - 0.4) - 200 - 25](1 - 0.35)}{\$1{,}500}$$

$$\frac{[0.6Q - 200]0.65}{\$2{,}000} = \frac{[0.6Q - 225]0.65}{\$1{,}500}$$

$$Q = 500$$

[6] You'll notice that we did not include taxes. Because taxes affect both the numerator and the denominator in the same way (that is, multiplying by 1 minus the tax rate), the effect of taxes cancels out.

Inserting the known values, including Q = 500, into the formula for the return on invested capital, we see that the return on invested capital is 5 percent. If we repeat this for $ROE_{One} = ROE_{Three}$ and for ROE_{Two} and ROE_{Three}, we find the same ROI of 5 percent.

The effects of financial leverage

You may have noticed that the cost of debt in our example is 5 percent. We use this example to illustrate that a company using financial leverage to increase the ROE need only earn more than the after-tax cost of debt. From capital budgeting, we know that a company should make investments where it expects to earn more than the project's cost of capital. The project's cost of capital is related to the company's weighted cost of capital (WACC), and the WACC is the weighted average of this after-tax debt cost and the cost of equity. Given that equity is almost always the most expensive form of capital, it follows that the WACC is *always* higher than the after-tax cost of debt.

Remember that the behavior of the ROI reflects the business risk of the company. The expected ROI can be represented by a point estimate, such as 10 percent in our example. However, we have to take into account the business risk of the company, which is the *variability* in the ROI.

We can see from this that the more a company relies on debt financing, relative to equity financing, the greater the variation of returns to equity. The variability of the ROE always increases as the company finances with more debt because there are fixed financial charges that the company has to pay, which are independent of the company's ROI. We can see the downside of this variability when we look at possible ROIs that are negative. The range of ROE values always increases with debt financing, but depending on the numbers, this does not necessarily mean that risk increases. Sometimes the company is better off at all ROI levels with debt financing, regardless of the greater variability in the ROE.

Because the range of ROE values increases with debt financing, the company has to find the cash to cover the fixed interest payments. In the worst case scenario where the company has an ROI of –4 percent, it still has to cover the 5 percent before-tax interest payments. If the company's underlying health remains sound, it can borrow from the bank or use up some of its cash reserves to make these payments. However, sometimes a series of poor operating results can cause serious financial problems for a highly indebted company. This situation can compound as the company's owners might then change their operating procedures once there is a significant risk of financial distress or bankruptcy.

The effects of financial leverage are not confined to companies. In fact they apply to any economic entity, whether a company, an individual, or a government. Financial leverage tends to increase returns at the expense of increased variability and increased risk of financial distress. Consequently the amount of debt a company or individual can carry very much depends on the underlying business risk of the asset being financed.

EPS indifference

Similar to the ROE indifference point, we depict the **EPS indifference point**. We can represent the EPS plotted against the return on investment or the quantity produced and sold; we show the various EPSs plotted against the return on investment in Figure 15-4. As we did with the ROE and ROI indifference points, we can solve for the return on investment at which the earnings per share is the same for the three structures. We first solve for the quantity, Q:

> **EPS indifference point**
> the EBIT level at which two financing alternatives generate the same EPS

$$EPS_{One} = EPS_{Two}$$

$$\frac{[Q(\$1 - 0.4) - 200 - 0](1 - 0.35)}{2,000} = \frac{[Q(\$1 - 0.4) - 200 - 25](1 - 0.35)}{1,500}$$

$$\frac{[0.6Q - 200]0.65}{2,000} = \frac{[0.6Q - 225]0.65}{1,500}$$

$$Q = 500$$

and then calculate the ROI at this quantity, which is 5 percent.

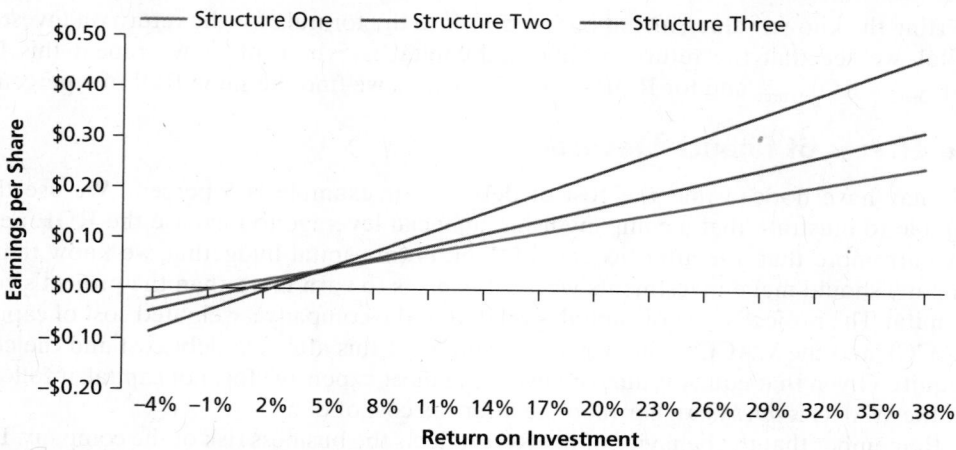

FIGURE 15-4 EPS Indifference Analysis

This analysis provides the company's management with some useful direction in choosing between financing alternatives because companies will generally want to maximize their bottom line as measured by EPS, and they will usually have an estimate of their expected EBIT.

EXAMPLE 15.2
EPS Indifference Analysis

PROBLEM

Consider a company with pretax cost of debt that is 6 percent under the present structure of a D/E ratio of 0.70, and there are 1,000 common shares outstanding. Further, assume that under an all-equity financing plan, the company has 1,280 shares outstanding. What is the EPS indifference EBIT level for a company with $1 million of invested capital?

Solution

First, determine the amount of debt. If D/E is 0.7, and D + E = $10 million, then 0.7E + E = $10 million, and then:

$$D = \$4.12 \text{ million}$$

$$E = \$5.88 \text{ million}$$

Therefore, the interest expense is 6 percent × $4.12 = $0.2472

Next, determine the EPS for each financing structure:

$$\text{EPS}_{70\%\text{D/E}} = \frac{(\text{EBIT} - 0.2472)(1 - 0.4)}{n}$$

$$= \frac{\text{EBIT}(1 - .40) - \$0.14832}{1}$$

$$= \frac{\text{EBIT} - 0.4\text{EBIT} - \$0.14832}{1}$$

$$\text{EPS}_{0\%\text{D/E}} = \frac{(\text{EBIT} - \$0)(1 - .40)}{1.280} = \frac{0.60 \text{ EBIT}}{1.280}$$

Setting the two EPS equations together and solving for EBIT:

$$\frac{(0.6 \times \text{EBIT})}{1.280} = \frac{\text{EBIT} - (0.4 \times \text{EBIT}) - \$0.14832}{1.000}$$

Using a bit of algebra and solving for EBIT,

$$EBIT = \$1.130057 \text{ million}$$

To check your work, substitute the EBIT into each financing arrangement's EPS formula. The EPS for both financing arrangements at this level of EBIT is $0.5297.

Conducting EPS-EBIT indifference analysis is a useful beginning point for companies when trying to evaluate potential financing plans. We discuss some of the additional issues, which are considerable, in the following sections.

Combining Operating and Financial Risk

Up to this point, we have considered operating risk and financial risk separately. However, companies must deal with both of these risks in making decisions. We can see how the two are combined by examining the **degree of total leverage (DTL)**. DTL captures the leveraging effects of both the operating risk and the financial risk, using the sum total of the fixed operating costs and the fixed financing costs as the fulcrum.

Mathematically, the degree of total leverage is the product of DOL and DFL:

degree of total leverage (DTL) sensitivity of net income to changes in unit sales, affected by the company's operating and financial leverage

$$\text{Degree of total leverage} = DOL \times DFL = \frac{Q(P-V)}{Q(P-V)-F} \times \frac{Q(P-V)-F}{Q(P-V)-F-C}$$

$$\text{Degree of total leverage} = \frac{Q(P-V)}{Q(P-V)-F-C} \qquad (15\text{-}5)$$

What this means is that the effects of operating leverage are magnified by a company's financial leverage. Suppose a company has a DOL of 2.0 and a DFL of 1.5. The degree of total leverage for this company is $2.0 \times 1.5 = 3.0$. This means that a 1 percent change in the quantity of units produced and sold will result in a 3 percent change in net income or earnings per share.

What this also means is that risk management within the company requires looking at the company's total risk exposure because of the potential for one type of risk to magnify another risk. This is the essence of enterprise risk management, which looks at the risk of the company as a whole.

Nassim N. Taleb, Daniel G. Goldstein, and Mark W. Spitznagel point out mistakes that are made in risk management.[7] The six mistakes that they highlight are (rephrased slightly):

1. Managing risk by predicting extreme events
2. Using the past to manage risk
3. Not considering advice intended to instruct what not to do
4. Measuring risk by standard deviation
5. Not factoring in human behavior
6. Seeking optimization, without considering vulnerability

SUMMARIZING: RISK MANAGEMENT MISTAKES

[7] Nassim N. Taleb, Daniel G. Goldstein, and Mark W. Spitznagel, "The Six Mistakes Executives Make in Risk Management," *Harvard Business Review,* October 2009.

1. Define business risk and financial risk.

2. How does financial leverage affect the relationship between ROI and ROE?

3. Explain how we determine the ROE and EPS indifference points for a company under various financing alternatives, and why this analysis provides the company with useful information.

15.2   THE MODIGLIANI AND MILLER THEOREMS

Capital structure theory is dominated by the work of economists Franco Modigliani and Merton Miller, who developed capital structure theorems based on a series of assumptions about how financial markets work. It is in fact a very powerful theorem for which (in part) the authors, Franco Modigliani and Merton Miller (also known as M&M), won the Nobel Prize in economics in 1985.[8]

The M&M Theories

Although the theory that they developed does not prescribe a particular capital structure for a company, it does provide a way of looking at the factors that should be considered in selecting a capital structure. The M&M theory comprises three different scenarios:

1. A world without taxes or costs of financial distress
2. A world with taxes, but no costs of financial distress
3. A world with taxes and costs of financial distress

Before we delve into the theory, we need to clarify what we mean by financial distress and costs of financial distress. Suppose, for example, a company has $10 million in cash, its business is failing and is worth only $20 million, but it has a $50 million loan coming due in a year. Clearly if the company doesn't do anything, in a year's time its creditors will insist on payment, and the $20 million business and the $10 million in cash will belong to the creditors. Ignoring any fees and other associated costs, the creditors will get $0.60 on the dollar for their debt, and the shareholders will lose everything. This is a situation of **financial distress**; a company in distress is on the brink of bankruptcy. If the company decides on projects with quick paybacks, rather than projects with positive net present values, there is a cost in terms of foregone opportunities.

financial distress state of business failing where bankruptcy seems imminent if dramatic action is not taken

What are costs of financial distress? They vary by company, and they may be direct or indirect costs. Direct costs include losses related to liquidation from reduced asset prices in distress sales, the loss of the use of tax loss carryovers, and the costs of liquidation in a formal bankruptcy in terms of legal and accounting fees. Although the direct costs of distress can be substantial, even greater losses in value can occur prior to the company deteriorating into a bankruptcy situation. Financial distress is a situation where the company has yet to commit the act of bankruptcy, yet it knows that unless something dramatic happens it will likely go bankrupt. In this situation, where a company may make decisions to meet immediate, short-term cash needs that are not decisions that it would have otherwise made, there are opportunity costs.

---

[8] Franco Modigliani and Merton Miller, "The Cost of Capital, Corporation Finance and the Theory of Investment," *American Economic Review*, 48 (1958): 261–297.

In the theory, an assumption is made regarding the **costs of financial distress**. Costs of financial distress are the legal and administrative costs, as well as losses (including opportunity costs) of a company prior to formal bankruptcy. If there are no costs of financial distress when the company cannot pay its debt obligation, it simply liquidates and pays out these funds to the claimants, both creditors and owners, and does not incur any cost in doing so. This is not realistic, but it is used in the first two parts of the theory to isolate the effects of the deductibility of interest on debt.

costs of financial distress direct costs, opportunity costs, and losses to a company prior to declaring bankruptcy

We discuss the M&M theory briefly in the subsections that follow, but we will not go through the proofs and theorems related to this theory; we will leave that to your further studies in finance. Rather, we focus on the bottom line of each part of the theory and the implications for the financial decision maker.

Part 1: No taxes, no costs of financial distress

In the first part of the M&M capital structure theory, we assume that there are no transactions costs or asymmetric information, no taxes, and no costs of financial distress; in other words, the company operates in a perfect capital market.

Consider the logic. A company's value is the present value of its future cash flows. If there is nothing special about debt financing relative to equity financing—such as interest deductibility or the potential for financial distress—management should be indifferent regarding how to finance the company. The company's value is like a pizza—does how you slice it up into debt or equity affect the size of the pizza? No. Therefore, in a world without taxes and where there is no cost of being in financial distress, the capital structure that a company chooses should not matter, as we show in Figure 15-5.

BOTTOM LINE: The value of the company is not affected by its capital structure.

Part 2: Taxes, but no costs to financial distress

In the second part, M&M starts with the assumptions of the first part, but then introduces taxes, with companies permitted to deduct interest in determining their taxable income. When they do this, capital structure matters: The more debt in the capital structure, the greater the value of the company. The reason for this is that, without costs of financial distress, a company benefits from the tax deductibility of interest, which lowers its tax bill and hence increases its value.

If a company can deduct interest on debt, but financial distress is costless, the value of the company is enhanced by the interest tax-shield. If V_U is the value of the company without debt, D is the amount of debt, r_d is the cost of debt, and T is the tax rate, then:

$$V_L = V_U + \text{Benefit from debt}$$

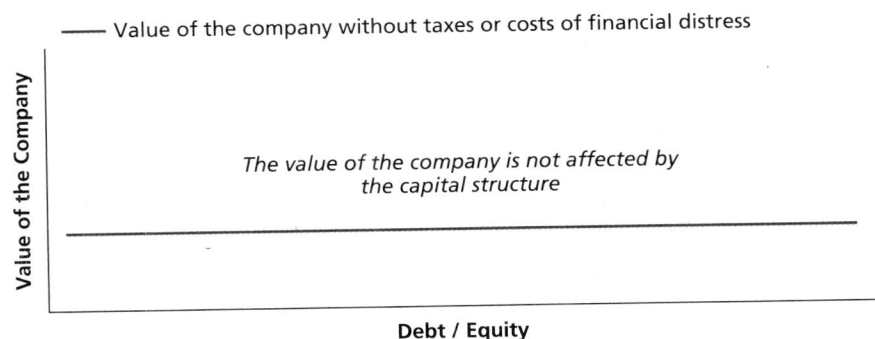

FIGURE 15-5 **Capital Structure in a World Without Taxes or Costs of Financial Distress**

If the company maintains the same capital structure into the future, we can value the benefit from debt as a perpetuity. If the discount rate is the cost of debt, then we can find today's value of the interest tax-shield each year as:

$$\text{Present value of the interest tax-shield} = \frac{r_d \times D \times T}{r_d} = DT$$

Therefore,

$$V_L = V_U + DT \tag{15-6}$$

We illustrate this relationship in Figure 15-6, where we compare the relationship between the value of the company and the debt-equity ratio for both Parts 1 and 2 of the theory.

BOTTOM LINE: If interest on debt is tax deductible but there are no costs to financial distress, the more debt, the greater the value of the company.

Another way of thinking about this is to remember that the value of the company is the value of the equity plus the value of the debt. If the company has no debt outstanding, the value is split between the government in tax revenues and the equity market value because the taxes are proportional to the company's taxable income. If the corporate income tax rate is 40 percent, then the government is getting 40 percent of the overall value and the shareholders, 60 percent. However, if the company issues debt, then the government's share of the pie falls as its tax revenue decreases. Consequently the value of the debt plus the equity goes up.

Consider a company that has $200 of operating income, a tax rate of 40 percent, and the cost of debt of 5 percent. We illustrate the effect of taxes and tax-deductible interest in Figure 15-7, where we plot the income streams of owners, creditors, and the government for different levels of debt financing. As you can see in this figure, the more debt financing, the lower the income to the government because of the interest deductibility.

The tax subsidy to using debt explains why so many corporate financing vehicles are designed with the intention of making the associated payments tax deductible as interest. If the value of the company goes up with the use of debt as it generates a bigger tax shield value and reduces the government share of the value of private enterprise, then the cost of capital must go down.

The bottom line of this part of M&M's theory is that the more debt, the greater the value of the company.[9] Is this realistic? No, because we know that a company that takes on too much debt risks financial distress and, perhaps, bankruptcy. This leads us to the third part of M&M's theory.

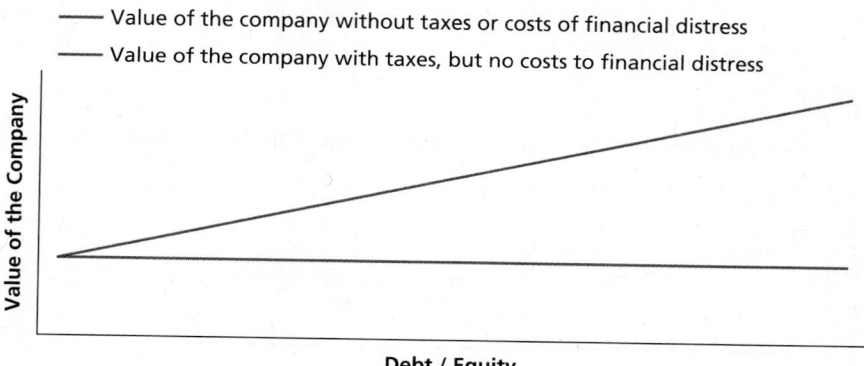

— Value of the company without taxes or costs of financial distress
— Value of the company with taxes, but no costs to financial distress

Value of the Company

Debt / Equity

FIGURE 15-6 M&M with Corporate Taxes

[9] Technically, this would be 99.99 percent debt. If it were 100 percent debt, this debt would, essentially, become the equity of the company.

Distribution of $200 of operating income among the government, owners, and creditors, for different levels of debt financing, with a 5 percent cost of debt and a 40 percent tax rate

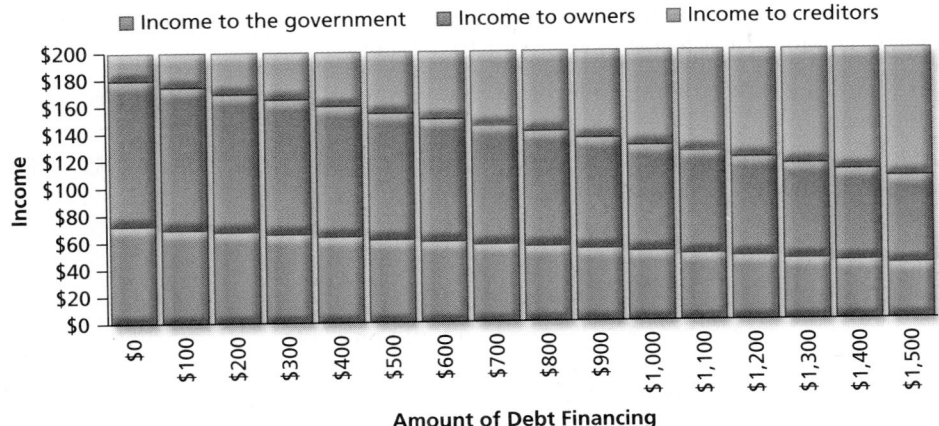

FIGURE 15-7 **Distribution of Income**

Buying Trouble | ETHICS

The Great Atlantic and Pacific Tea Company, most commonly known as A&P, is a retail grocery chain. In 2007, A&P bought another retail grocer, Pathmark. Unfortunately, the debt burden of acquiring Pathmark was too much to bear:

(in millions)	*Before pathmark* Fiscal year ending 2/25/2006	*After pathmark* Fiscal year ending 2/23/2008
Total assets	$2,498.865	$3,647.918
Total liabilities	$1,827.138	$3,229.775
Shareholders' equity	$671.727	$418.143

In other words, A&P increased its assets by almost $1.2 billion, but also increased its debt obligations by more the $1.4 billion. The result? A reduction in the shareholders' equity. A&P's equity was negative in fiscal years ending 2/27/2010 ad 2/16/2011, which can be attributed to the burden of the debt from the acquisition, combined with a decline in the economy.

A&P filed for bankruptcy in 2010.[10] In bankruptcy A&P was able to reduce its debt to $490 million, along with negotiating a new labor agreement. The questions that this bankruptcy raises include:

- Was the Pathmark acquisition appropriate for A&P?
- Were the decisions by management to acquire Pathmark in the best interest of A&P's shareholders?

Part 3: Taxes and costs to financial distress

In the third part, M&M relaxes the assumption of no costs of financial distress. What this means is that if the company assumes too much financial risk, there is a risk that the company will incur costs and possibly bankruptcy. Ultimately, the benefit from the tax

[10] U.S. Bankruptcy Court, Southern District of New York, case 10-24549. A&P exited bankruptcy in early 2012 with an infusion of equity from an investor group.

EXAMPLE 15.3

M&M Introducing Taxes

PROBLEM

Consider companies U and L, each with an expected EBIT of $2 million, which is expected to remain constant indefinitely. Assume that both U and L face a corporate tax rate of 30 percent. Company U has a cost of equity of 10 percent.

A. Estimate the value of the unlevered company (U) assuming its cost of capital is 10 percent.

B. Estimate the value of the identical risk levered company (L), which has $5 million in debt outstanding.

Solution

1. $V_U = \dfrac{\text{EBIT}(1 - T)}{r_U} = \dfrac{\$2(1 - 0.30)}{.10} = \$14 \text{ million}$

Notice the decline of $6 million in U's market value. This is the present value of the future tax payments made to the government.

2. $V_L = V_U + DT = \$14 + (0.30 \times \$5) = \$15.5 \text{ million.}$

   $E_L = V_L - D = \$15.5 - \$5 = \$10.5 \text{ million.}$

Notice that L is worth $1.5 million more than U owing to the tax shield value of debt (DT).

---

deductibility of interest is outweighed by the costs of financial distress. The bottom line: Taking on more debt, relative to equity, will increase the value of the company to a point, after which the costs of financial distress will offset the benefit from interest deductibility.

The important thing about financial distress and bankruptcy costs is that there is a flow of value away from both the debt holders and the equity holders. In the simple M&M world, anyone can buy both the company's debt and equity, and what the equity holder loses, the debt holder gains: This is an example of a *zero-sum game*. All that is happening is that value is being rearranged, but none is being destroyed. The key feature of bankruptcy and financial distress is that value is destroyed. In this way, while the use of debt creates value by reducing the government's share of taxes, it also destroys value by causing increased risk of financial distress and bankruptcy.

bankruptcy legal status of a company that permits the company to deal with debt problems

Bankruptcy is a legal status of a company that permits the company to deal with debt problems. Bankruptcy may occur in one of two ways:

1. The company commits an act of default, such as the nonpayment of interest, and creditors enforce their legal rights as a result; or
2. The company voluntarily declares bankruptcy.

We provide the largest U.S. filings for bankruptcy up through 2010 in Table 15-4. As you can see, most of the filings follow a downturn in the economy. This is consistent with Warren Buffett's observation: "It's only when the tide goes out, you learn who's swimming naked." The Lehman Brothers Holdings bankruptcy filing was the largest at the time of the filing. At the time of its filing, Lehman Brothers had assets of $638 billion and liabilities of $613 billion.[11]

absolute priority rule rule that any assets of the company in liquidation are distributed to creditors, in order of seniority, and, if anything remains, to shareholders

There are two forms of bankruptcy in the U.S.: Chapter 7 and Chapter 11. In Chapter 7, the company's assets are sold and creditors receive funds consistent with the absolute priority rule. The **absolute priority rule** is the rule that in bankruptcy, any assets of the company in liquidation are distributed to creditors, in order of seniority, and, if anything remains, to

---

[11] "Lehman Files for Chapter 11 Bankruptcy," *TheStreet.com*, September 15, 2008.

TABLE 15-4 Largest U.S. Bankruptcy Filings Through 2010

Company	Industry	Year	Total Assets (in billions)
Lehman Brothers Holdings	Investment banking	2008	$638
Washington Mutual Inc.	Financial services	2008	$328
Worldcom	Telecommunications	2002	$104
General Motors	Automobile manufacturing	2009	$91
CIT	Financial services	2009	$71
Enron	Energy	2001	$66
Conseco	Financial services	2002	$61
Chrysler	Automobile manufacturing	2009	$39
Thornburg Mortgage	Financial services	2009	$37
Pacific Gas and Electric	Natural gas and electricity	2001	$36
Texaco	Oil and gas	1987	$35
Financial Corporation of America	Savings and loan	1988	$34
Refco	Financial services	2005	$33
IndyMac Bancorp	Financial services	2008	$33
Global Crossing	Telecommunications	2002	$30

Source: *www.bankruptcydata.com.*

shareholders.[12] In Chapter 11, a plan is designed to rehabilitate the company, reorganizing its claims in an attempt to emerge from Chapter 11 as a viable, going concern. In both cases, the court appoints a trustee to manage the company's affairs, but the purposes are different: In Chapter 7, the trustee manages the dissolution of the company, whereas in Chapter 11 the trustee manages the company's affairs with the creditors' interests in mind.

In Chapter 11 bankruptcy, the court appoints a trustee who then reports back to the court. The monitor has considerable flexibility in preventing creditors from exercising their claims against the company, in restructuring contracts, and in allowing the management of the company to develop a plan to reorganize in the hope of continuing operations. During this period, the company is allowed to raise new financing, called **debtor in possession (DIP) financing**, with a higher priority over existing unsecured claims. It is this financing that provides the company with some breathing space to reorganize and present a plan to all creditors, which the court can impose, providing enough of them agree.

There is very limited scope for preventing creditors from seizing assets, the company cannot raise DIP financing, and there is no provision for imposing a settlement on all creditors, even if a significant majority agree. If a restructuring plan is rejected, then creditors can seize their assets, and the company is liquidated, with anything left after payment to the secured creditors being proportionally allocated to the unsecured creditors.

Either way, reorganization is expensive, with significant legal, accounting, and court fees. All these fees represent an outflow of value that goes to neither the debt holders nor the equity holders. If the company is actually wound up and liquidated, there are even more costs, as the major asset of a failing company is usually a history of tax losses. These losses can be carried forward and used against future profits and are thus valuable to the company. However, if the company is liquidated, these losses disappear. In addition, the process of liquidating a company usually results in sales of assets to third parties at "bargain" prices that are less than their value in place, so again there is a value loss to the company. This is why companies try hard to reorganize prior to a formal bankruptcy and liquidation.

debtor-in-possession (DIP) financing financing specifically for companies in financial distress that provides creditors more seniority than most existing claims of the distressed company

---

[12] The term *absolute* refers to the fact that creditors have an absolute claim over shareholders.

agency costs costs associated with agency problems that arise from the inherent conflicts of interest between managers, owners, and creditors

During periods of financial distress, there is an increase in the agency costs because of the increase in the divergence of interests between equity holders and debt holders. **Agency costs** are any expenses or loss of value due to the inherent conflicts in any agency relationship. Suppose the company has $6 million of assets and $10 million of debt. If the company is liquidated, the debt holders have a chance of getting $0.60 on the dollar back, whereas the equity holders' stake in the company is zero. Therefore, the equity holders (who get to vote) may undertake measures to try to get something for themselves, at the expense of the debt holders. For example, one obvious thing for the shareholders to do is to pay out the $6 million in cash as a dividend. At least this gives them some cash now and in a year's time it simply means that the creditors will be left with nothing. However, as well as being unethical, this is illegal.

ETHICS | Dividend Recaps Versus Fraudulent Conveyance

When a company becomes unable to pay its debts, it is not permitted to pay dividends to its owners. To do so would risk litigation related to fraudulent conveyance (i.e., putting funds out of the reach of the creditors).

What gets tricky is when a private equity firm acquires a company and simultaneously the acquired company borrows heavily (that is, the private equity firm acquires an equity interest in a leverage buyout or LBO), and then pays a rather large dividend to the private equity firm. The "LBO-followed-by-a-large-dividend" process is common in many recent private equity deals, and we refer to this as *dividend recapitalization*. In effect, some of the borrowed funds could wind up as dividends.

If the company becomes insolvent under the weight of all the new debt, is the payment of dividends to the private equity firm considered a fraudulent conveyance? The answer to this question is yet to be resolved in the courts, but hinges, in part, on whether the company's demise was reasonably foreseeable at the time the dividends are paid.[13]

The responsibility of the board of directors is to act in the best interests of the company. For a solvent company this statement means pursuing the best interests of the shareholders. However, for an insolvent company, the responsibility of the board of directors shifts to all the stakeholders in the company, including the creditors. A sudden cash dividend of $6 million shortly before becoming bankrupt would immediately make the board members at the time they were declared personally liable and would cause the court to order the payments reversed.[14]

It's important to note that just because something is illegal doesn't mean there are no other ways of achieving the same result. Funny things happen in failing companies: Assets are sometimes sold to related companies owned by the shareholders at "knock-down" prices, or the company pays for joint venture activities for which there seems on the surface to be little benefit. In all cases, they are simply more sophisticated ways of trying to strip cash out of the company before it goes bankrupt because when it does, these assets belong to the creditors and not the shareholders. Part of the expense of reorganizing or liquidating a company is simply working out what has happened in the previous few years and whether any assets have been fraudulently stripped out of the company.

A more subtle problem than outright fraud is to recognize that the shareholders essentially have a 1-year call option on the underlying company, where the exercise price is the value of the debt.[15] Therefore, shareholders have a call option: Shareholders could dissolve the company, pay off creditors out of assets (if available), and keep whatever remains (if any at all). In 1 year's time, either the value of the company exceeds $10 million or it doesn't. If it does, then the company can refinance and pay off its creditors, and the

---

[13] *Boyer v. Crown Stock Distribution, Inc., et al.*, 587 F.3d 787 (7th Cir. Nov. 21, 2009).

[14] Note that this is also why directors usually resign as the company gets into serious financial trouble.

[15] A call option is the right to buy an asset at a specified price within or at a specified period.

Management Behaving Badly | ETHICS

At the end of 2000, the share price of Enron common stock was $83.13, with a total market value of over $60 billion, and Enron had just experienced two years of significant growth. One year later, a share of Enron stock was worth less than $1.

Though the Enron bankruptcy was November 28, 2001, it has made a lasting impression in terms of the depth of the agency problems and the effects on our current laws. Many issues led to its downfall, but the decisions of its management leading up to bankruptcy illustrate some of the problems that occur when a corporation does not have a good governance system in place to monitor management.

Examples of how Enron's management's self-interest trumped that of creditors and shareholders include:

- During the two years leading up to bankruptcy, Enron paid their top executives well. Each executive considered to be in the 200 best-performing employees of Enron were paid over $1 million each in 2000 and 2001, with one employee paid over $56 million in 2001.
- Management was given near-term exercisable options, which encouraged manipulation of short-term results. In October of 2001, Enron disclosed that it was restating

financial statements for the years 1997 through 2000 for accounting principles violations. Enron had overstated the earnings for those years by over 20 percent and had understated its debt.

- In early 2001, senior management sold stock that they owned prior to the disclosure of Enron's problems; they were selling in an otherwise up market.
- Enron's management had exaggerated the company's water and broadband businesses. Enron wrote down the value of its water and broadband business by over $1 billion in October of 2001.
- In the weeks and days leading up to the company's collapse, Enron paid bonuses to 560 employees that were indicated as key employees, with these bonuses adding up to more than $100 million.

Sources: Joint Committee on Taxation, Senate Committee on Finance "Overview of Executive Compensation Arrangements," Report of Investigation of Enron Corporation and Related Entities Regarding Federal Tax and Compensation Issues and Policy Recommendations, Volume I: Report, February 2003; Paul M. Healy and Krishna G. Palepu, "The Fall of Enron," *Journal of Economic Perspectives*, 17, no. 2 (Spring 2003): 3–26.

---

shareholders will have some residual value. On the other hand, if the value of the company is less than $10 million, the shareholders are protected by limited liability and can simply walk away and hand over the company to the creditors.[16] It is the existence of limited liability and the fact that shareholders are only exposed up to the value of their investment that creates this call option.

If there is no limited liability, the shareholders would have to pay off the $10 million in debt regardless, so they would lose if the underlying company value is less than the face value of the debt.[17] However, with limited liability they can't be forced to make up the losses if the value of the company is less than the face value of the debt that is due. As a result the value of the equity behaves like a call option with the minimum value represented by the horizontal intrinsic value line depicted in Figure 15-8. The importance of understanding the change in the characteristics of the shares in a company in financial distress is that options react differently than ordinary common shares. For example, two major factors increasing the value of a call option are time and risk—both of which increase the option value. So with $6 million in cash (and $10 million in debt), the shareholders have the possibility of increasing the risk of the company and extending the time until they go bankrupt.

Whether or not they can extend the time period will depend on the type of debt that they have outstanding. If the entire $10 million debt is due next year, it would be difficult to extend the period. But if instead, it were long-term debt with only the interest payments due next year, then the company could continue to make the interest payments until all $6 million in assets is used up. During this period, the company could devote all its time

---

[16] This does, of course, raise the ethical issue of such a strategic default.

[17] But, of course, if there was more than $10 million in assets, shareholders would have access to anything above the $10 million.

and energy to survival. This means that normal maintenance may be skipped, machines not replaced, advertising and R&D stopped, and generally the operations allowed to run down. The hope on the part of the shareholders is that something happens to give value to the company, while the worst that can happen is that bankruptcy is delayed. For the creditors, this is a nightmare scenario where they are seeing the value of the operations, as well as the $6 million in cash, go down period by period until by the time they can finally force bankruptcy, they don't get $10 million—they get much less.

The second major problem is that there is an incentive for the shareholders to gamble because they are gambling with the debt holders' wealth. Shareholders might make poor risky investments that they would not otherwise make simply because if the investments pay off, they might get the company out of bankruptcy, and if they don't pay off, it doesn't matter because the shareholders are essentially bankrupt anyway! This incentive often shows up in poorly researched new product introductions where not all the proper R&D has been performed and the product hasn't been properly tested. Unfortunately the opposite also occurs: If the company is going bankrupt, the equity holders have no incentive to put in new money for minor projects, even if they are very profitable, because all this does is create more value for the creditors, not the shareholders.

The problem that all these examples illustrate is that the incentives faced by shareholders and the company change once there is significant bankruptcy risk. Instead of making positive net present value decisions, where the equity holders bear the risk, they face a situation where it is the creditors who bear the risk. This is because the company really belongs to the creditors if debts exceed assets, and yet they cannot alter what the company is doing until the company commits the act of bankruptcy by nonpayment of interest or principal.

During this period of financial distress, the underlying operations of the company are often being poorly managed due to the change in incentive structure. What this means in terms of the M&M argument is that if the company raises too much debt, the underlying EBIT of the levered company will change as poor projects are accepted, good ones are ignored, operations are neglected, or cash is stripped out of the company. Again similar to direct bankruptcy costs, there is a value loss that is not being fully captured by either the debt holders or the equity holders.

Creditors are well aware of these types of actions by distressed companies, which is why they take offsetting measures. One standard way is not to lend long term to risky companies. Instead, debt is short term or includes sinking fund payments that create a continuous cash payment to the creditors, thereby reducing the maturity of the call option. The result is that significant costs are attached to raising too much debt because too much debt increases the risks of financial distress and bankruptcy, and the associated value outflows to third parties. Researchers estimate that the costs of financial distress, both indirect and direct, are 10 to 20 percent of the pre-distress value of the company.[18] This leads to a theory that is referred to as the **static trade-off theory** model, where the company uses debt to maximize its tax advantages up to the point where these benefits are outweighed by the associated estimated costs of financial distress and bankruptcy.

static trade-off theory theory where a company uses debt to maximize its tax advantages up to the point where these benefits are outweighed by the associated estimated costs of financial distress and bankruptcy

We illustrate the model in Figure 15-8. The horizontal line represents the conclusion from the first part of the theory: Without taxes and costs of financial distress, the capital structure of the company does not affect its value. The straight-line at an angle in this figure is the conclusion from the second part of the theory: With taxes, but without costs of financial distress, the more debt the company has, relative to equity, the greater the value of the company. The curved line is the conclusion of the third part: With taxes and costs of financial distress, a company's value increases with increasing levels of debt (relative to equity), to a point at which the costs of financial distress outweigh the benefits from interest deductibility.

BOTTOM LINE: If interest is tax deductible and there are costs of financial distress, there is some optimal capital structure for a company.

[18] Gregor Andrade and Steven Kaplan, "How Costly Is Financial (Not Economic) Distress? Evidence from Highly Leveraged Transactions That Become Distressed," *Journal of Finance*, 53 (1998): 1443–1493.

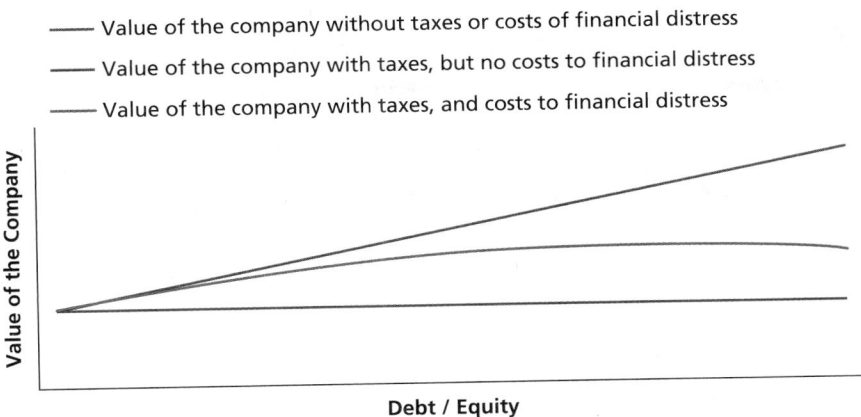

FIGURE 15-8 **Company Value and Financial Distress Costs**

Asbestos and Bankruptcy | ETHICS

During the 1980s and 1990s, many companies that manufactured or used asbestos filed for bankruptcy. One such company was the Johns-Manville Corporation, which filed for bankruptcy in 1982. At the time of the filing, this company was the subject of over 16,000 lawsuits pertaining to asbestos injuries and illnesses, even though it was a large, profitable company.[19] To manage the lawsuits, the Manville Trust was established in 1986 by the bankruptcy plan for Johns-Manville. According to this plan the trust paid claims that resulted from litigation.[20]

(in millions)	Fiscal year	
	1982	*1981*
Total liabilities	$1,170.07	$1,094.53
Shareholders' equity	$1,066.04	$1,203.28
Total assets	$2,236.01	$2,297.81
Debt-equity	1.098	0.910
Debt-total assets	52.33%	47.63%
Operating profit margin	7.32%	7.49%
Net profit margin	–6.92%	1.62%

Today, the Johns-Manville company is a subsidiary of Berkshire Hathaway.[21]

Other Factors That May Affect the Capital Structure Decision

How well does the static trade-off model explain capital structures? It certainly captures the main effects. However, it largely ignores two important issues:[22]

1. **Information asymmetry problems:** the effect of informational differences among shareholders, creditors, and management
2. **Agency problems:** the fact that managers make these decisions on behalf of the shareholders, but they have their own interests at stake as well

---

[19] Its loss in 1982 was preceded by at least 15 years of profitability.

[20] The prediction for the number of claims, at the time of the bankruptcy, was between 83,000 and 100,000 claims.

[21] Berkshire Hathaway bought Johns-Manville in 2001.

[22] Aside from the discussion regarding how agency costs may increase as financial distress costs increase.

FINANCE in the News | General Motors In and Out of Bankruptcy

General Motors (GM), one the largest of the automobile manufacturers, filed for bankruptcy June 1, 2009, as part of a prepackaged plan of bankruptcy. With this prepackaged financing, General Motors created a new entity, which then acquired the profitable assets of the prebankruptcy General Motors. General Motors received debtor-in-possession financing while in bankruptcy from the U.S. Treasury and Export Development Canada.

GM's bankruptcy and bailout timeline:

December	2008	GMAC receives $8.8 billion in bailout funds
		GM receives $0.9 billion in bailout funds (debt obligation)
April	2009	GM receives $2 billion in bailout funds (debt obligation)
May	2009	GMAC receives $7.5 billion in bailout funds (preferred stock)
		GM receives $4.4 billion in bailout funds (debt obligation)
June	2009	GM files for Chapter 11 bankruptcy
		GM receives $30 billion in bailout funds (debt obligation)
July	2009	Emerges from bankruptcy as NGMCO, Inc.; changed name to General Motors Company
		Majority owned by the U.S. government
		GM bailout notes exchanged for preferred and common stock
January	2010	U.S. government provides $3.8 billion to GMAC (preferred stock)
April	2010	GM repays U.S. government loan $4.7 billion
May	2010	GMAC becomes Ally Financial, majority owned by the U.S. government
August	2010	GM files for an initial public offering
November	2010	U.S. government converts $13.5 billion of notes into common stock
December	2010	GM repays $2.1 billion note and partial repayments on other notes

GM is leaner postbankruptcy and has a healthier capital structure:

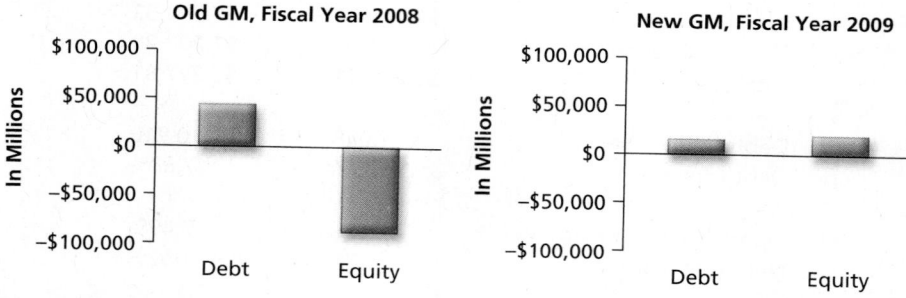

Sources: General Motors 10-K filings and financialstability.gov.

First let's consider the impact of information differences. Suppose a company has a market value of $20 million and after careful consideration decides to undertake a new project that costs $5 million and has a $5 million net present value. The company has 1 million shares outstanding, so the share price prior to undertaking the new project is $20. What should it do, and how should it finance this project? Theoretically the CEO should call a news conference and announce this great new investment, the media and security analysts in attendance should clap their hands, the market value of the company should go up by $5 million to $25 million, and the stock price should rise to $25. The company should then issue 200,000 shares at $25 each to finance the project and spend the $5 million so the total value increases to $30 million and the stock price is $30 million ÷ 1.2 million = $25.

However, the "real" world does not react like this. Investors will yawn, bombard the CEO with questions, and generally be extremely critical because they have heard this story before and cannot distinguish between good companies telling the truth and poor companies spinning a story to boost the stock price. So, more likely what will happen is that the stock price will stay at $20, forcing the company to issue 250,000 shares at $20 to finance the project. Then when the truth is revealed and the project does add value, the company value will later increase to $30 million. So the company value still gets to $30 million, but this time there are 1.25 million shares outstanding and the stock price only reaches $24.

In fact, the situation may be even worse than this because stock prices often drop when a company announces a new share issue. This is because investors suspect that management thinks the stock price is overvalued and that the company is trying to issue common shares while they are trading at inflated prices. Suppose, for example, the stock price drops to $18 on the announcement of the share issue. Then the company will have to issue 277,777 shares to raise the $5 million, and even if the market value gets back up to $30 million, the stock price will only rise to $23.50. In both of these cases, the ownership of this positive NPV project is being shared between the existing shareholders and the new shareholders who are buying in at a below "true" market price.

How can the company handle this problem of information asymmetry? The answer is to raise $5 million in debt. In this case, when the value of the company does rise to $30 million after the profits flow in from the new investment, the equity is worth $25 million and the debt $5 million, but there are still only 1 million shares outstanding, so the stock price rises to $25.

What this suggests is that companies only issue equity as a last resort; instead they finance using internal cash flow, then debt, and, finally, common equity, in what noted financial economist Professor Stewart Myers refers to as a **pecking order**.[23] The pecking order theory is that companies prefer to raise funds starting with internal cash flow, then debt, and finally issuing common stock. Myers's argument that companies follow a pecking order is based on divulging information. If the companies use internal cash flow, then they do not need to have anyone—investment bankers or investors—look closely at what they do. For example, even the shareholders can't force the company to pay a dividend. Similarly, the company can talk to a bank and divulge privileged information to secure a loan. However, when it issues new common shares, as we have seen, the company has to file a prospectus and reveal all material facts that affect the share price. In the process, the company has to be careful not to reveal facts to a competitor that may give it a jump start and allow it to compete away the NPV benefits of the project.

pecking order order in which companies prefer to raise financing, starting with internal cash flow and then debt, and finally issuing common equity

The pecking order was also discussed in a different context by the late financial economist, Gordon Donaldson.[24] Donaldson justified the pecking order through what we would now call agency arguments. He showed that managers' commitment to the company was through their human capital, versus the short-term financial commitment of shareholders. As a result, managers were more concerned about the long-term survival of the company and less inclined to take risks. For these agency reasons, he also argued that managers had a preference for internal cash flow (retained earnings), then debt, and finally issuing new common equity. In an agency model, this financing hierarchy imposes the least risk on the company and requires the least justification by managers.

Regardless of whether it is for agency reasons or information problems, or some combination of the two, we do see companies using the pecking order: Profitable companies tend to have the least debt simply because they don't need it and have more than enough internal funds. Leveraged recapitalizations involve issuing debt and using the funds to buy back shares. These tactics tend to address the issues over time, but only with a significant lag. The real puzzle is that some companies simply don't use much debt and could. Microsoft, for example, is relatively low risk, is highly profitable, and has no significant debt. It could undoubtedly lower its tax bill by using debt financing and buying back shares, and yet it hasn't done so.

---

[23] S. Myers, "The Capital Structure Puzzle," *Journal of Finance* (July 1984): 18; G. Donaldson, "Financial Goals: Manager versus Stockholders," *Harvard Business Review* (May/June 1963): 116–129. Stewart Myers is the Robert C. Merton Professor of Financial Economics at the MIT Sloan School of Management.

[24] G. Donaldson, "Financial Goals: Manager versus Stockholders," *Harvard Business Review* (May/June 1963): 116–129.

LESSONS LEARNED | Record Bankruptcies Despite De-Leveraging

The experience of the 2007–2008 financial crisis changed the game, from a focus on earnings to a focus on strong balance sheets. This is what Jacob Madaline had to say in 2009 about bankruptcies that occurred despite de-leveraging.

It's a race against time as firms struggle to stave off going under, even as they shed debt at a furious pace.

More companies are going to default on their debt even though they are in the process of de-leveraging, says U.S. default expert Edward Altman, a professor of finance at the New York University Stern School of Business. He adds that the bankruptcy rate is going up at a record level and could reach an all-time high by the end of the year. In total he predicts U.S. corporate high-yield default rates will rise between 13% to 15% this year—the previous high was 12.8% in 2002.

De-leveraging will continue as long as the stock market goes up, as leverage is sometimes measured by the amount of debt divided by market value not book value, according to Altman.

Distress exchange—issuing new debt or new equity for the old debt—should become very popular as firms try to avoid bankruptcy and will result in a fast de-leveraging. Already nine companies in the U.S. have used this technique in the first quarter of 2009, according to Altman, vs. 14 in all of 2008. His research shows that 50% of these companies end up in bankruptcy anyway. "This is not enough as the problem is more severe than just reducing debt. This is what Chrysler and General Motors are trying to do, and they will end up bankrupt," he says. In a distress exchange, more than 90% of debt holders have to agree to reduce the debt and this is hard to achieve as investors will get on average $0.50 on the dollar.

On the other hand, tax laws have also made it much easier to reduce debt as the government permits the debt buyers to defer paying taxes for five years on a debt deduction. "A lot of debt is being bought at a discount now," Altman says. "Investors should treat distress exchange as positive if the alternative was to go bankrupt."

Investors should not only look at the leverage levels but also at the nature of the debt—how much is secured and unsecured and how big is the subordinated debt—to better understand what players might influence the future of the company. As companies turn to high-yield debt to finance their operations, the share of senior debt shrinks and junior debt holders have a larger piece of the capital debt structure and a lot of economic clout.

"Even if junior debt holders can't control the assets, they can still put a company into insolvency. They are the 600-pound gorilla in the room and can't be ignored, especially if they bought protection in a form of CDS and might be inclined to push a company into bankruptcy to recover 100 cents on a dollar," says Joel Telpner, partner in banking and finance at the law firm of Mayer Brown in New York.

"Companies are in the survival mood. They are trying to save money to make sure the company gets through the recession," says Campbell Harvey, a professor at the Fuqua School of Business at Duke University. In this tight debt market, supply will eventually win and optimal borrowing will decline as there is less debt supplied by banks and credit is more costly. "This is exactly what happened in the Great Depression. Banks stopped lending, and corporate debt ratios declined," adds Professor John R. Graham, also a professor at Fuqua.

Companies and investors are more interested now in the balance sheet rather than quarterly earnings. Before the recession, Wall Street and investors put primacy on earnings, and this created an incentive for CEOs to borrow more money on a short-term floating rate basis that made their quarterly earnings per share look better, Shubin Stein said.

Now companies are strengthening their balance sheet by paying down their debt, increasing liquidity and lowering their absolute debt levels. Chesapeake Energy, for example, is looking to reduce debt through asset sales and other financing transactions. All together, the oil and gas company sees these transactions raising $1.5 to $2 in 2009 and $1 to $1.5 in 2010, according to reports from Credit Suisse.

Extracted from: Madalina Iacob, "Record Bankruptcies Despite De-Leveraging," *Forbes.com*, May 27, 2009.

Concept Review Questions

1. Explain the impact of taxes and costs of financial distress on M&M's conclusions regarding capital structure.

2. Explain the trade-off in the static trade-off theory.

3. Provide examples of direct and indirect costs of financial distress.

15.3 CAPITAL STRUCTURE IN PRACTICE

We know from theory that the tax deductibility of interest makes debt more attractive than equity, but only to a point because the more debt, vis-à-vis equity, that a company has, the greater the likelihood of incurring costs of financial distress.

Evaluating a Company's Capital Structure

Let's first consider some standard financial ratios that are often used. We can think of these ratios as *stock* or *flow* ratios. Stock ratios are measures such as the debt-to-equity (D/E) and debt ratios. These ratios measure the amount of outstanding debt relative to total assets, total capital, or the amount of equity. Flow ratios include times-interest-earned and cash flow debt ratio. Both stock and flow financial leverage ratios are used by the bond-rating agencies and others as a quick check on the company's financing, and they are also often used to limit the amount of debt a company can raise through its trust indenture. However, we must consider just how useful these ratios really are.

In a previous chapter, we discussed some of the features of different types of debt. For example, we noted that bankers' acceptances have a maturity of 30 days, whereas long-term bond issues are typically for 20 or 30 years. Clearly it matters a great deal to the company if the debt has a 30-day versus a 30-year maturity. For one thing, if the company has to "roll over" its debt every 30 days, it has to be very confident that it has the cash to pay off the debt if the lenders refuse to renew it. Similarly, if the debt has sinking fund payments, where the company is contractually obliged to pay off a certain amount of debt each year, this increases the company's commitments to the debt holders and requires that it have the cash ready to fulfill this commitment. In both cases it is not the *amount* of debt outstanding that matters so much as the *maturity* of the debt. That is why this information is required to be provided in the notes to the company's financial statements. Further, it suggests that the stock ratios are not completely adequate, as they ignore some of the cash flow commitments attached to debt.

It is often explicitly written into the bond indenture where the company cannot issue any more debt unless it has an interest coverage ratio of 2.0 or more, where interest coverage is EBIT divided by interest expense.[25] However, again this does not include all the company's commitments. The most basic limitation is that interest payments are made from cash and not from accounting earnings. Further, similar to the problems with the stock ratios, the interest coverage ratio does not include the impact of any sinking fund payments or other commitments, such as dividends to the preferred shareholders.

Financial ratios

A number of financial ratios help us evaluate just how much of a debt obligation the company has incurred. There are basically two types of financial leverage ratios: ratios that measure the debt burden, and coverage ratios, which measure the company's ability to satisfy its debt obligations. We looked at a number of these ratios in an earlier chapter, which we summarize in Table 15-5.

The challenges in using financial ratios in evaluating a company's debt include the reliance on accounting numbers. Different companies may use different accounting principles, which can possibly distort the accounts, especially in comparisons across companies. Further, the use of historical information presents a challenge. Ratios are formed on the basis of reported financial results, whether annual or quarterly. Nevertheless, these ratios are based on performance in the past, whereas concern over how much debt a company can bear is really an issue about the future.

---

[25] A bond indenture may specify limitations on what a company can do or may specify what a company cannot do.

TABLE 15-5 Financial Leverage Ratios

Ratio	Calculation	Interpretation
Debt ratio	$\dfrac{\text{Debt}}{\text{Total assets}}$	The proportion of total assets financed with debt
Debt-equity ratio	$\dfrac{\text{Debt}}{\text{Equity}}$	How much debt is used to finance the company for every dollar of equity
Equity multiplier	$\dfrac{\text{Total assets}}{\text{Equity}}$	The total assets of the company for every dollar of equity
Times interest earned	$\dfrac{\text{Earnings before interest and taxes}}{\text{Interest}}$	How many times the company can satisfy its interest obligation from operating earnings
Cash flow-to-debt ratio	$\dfrac{\text{Cash flow from operations}}{\text{Debt}}$	The inverse of this ratio is the number of years it would take to pay off the debt using cash flow from operations

The ideal measure is for the company to generate its own forecast of expected cash flows over a short- to medium-term horizon and then work out internally what level of fixed commitments the company can handle without seriously exposing it to harm. The key question is whether the lenders will lend to the company based on its internal scenario-based assessment of how much debt it can carry. This requires that sensitive information be divulged to lenders and that the lenders believe the data. Consequently there is still heavy reliance on standard ratios.

ETHICS | Liar Liar Loans

The subprime crisis of 2007–08 brought attention to the quality of the information on loan applications. During the fast and furious build-up of the housing bubble, many mortgage brokers approved home mortgage loans without proof of income or assets. These loans became known as liar loans or *stated income loans* (i.e., stated but never checked).

The income of home mortgage borrowers with wages or salaries can be easily verified. However, the hunger for commissions on originating mortgages may have encouraged lenders to overlook the verification of income or assets. In one sample of mortgage applications that were approved, 37% of the loans did not involve income verification, and this percentage was much higher in California and Florida.[26] Why would this occur? Because originating loans is profitable, and the lenders sell these loans to investors to shift the risk of the bad loans.

During and following the financial crisis, lenders became more cautious in lending to both individuals and businesses, instituting and maintaining tightened credit standards well into 2012.

Debt ratings

Credit rating services use financial ratios, among other information, to evaluate the creditworthiness of companies and the default risk of debt obligations. Moody's, one of the major rating services, periodically provides data on the most commonly used credit ratios and how they are correlated with their credit ratings. We summarize the most recent report, from 2006, in Table 15-6.[27]

[26] Statement by Steven Krystofiak, President of the Mortgage Brokers Association for Responsiible Lending to the Federal Reserve, August 1, 2006.

[27] Though this may not seem current, the common ratios used in credit evaluations are not revised often.

TABLE 15-6 **Financial Ratios by Moody's Debt Ratings**

Criterion	Investment Grade	Speculative
Interest coverage	6.5 times	2.1 times
Asset coverage[28]	2.4 times	1.4 times
Financial leverage	43.6%	66.8%
Cash flow-to-debt	28.4%	12.7%
Return on assets	6.3%	1.9%
Net profit margin	7.8%	2.1%
Liquidity[29]	4.6%	3.9%

Source: *Data from Moody's Investors Services, "The Distribution of Common Financial Ratios by Rating and Industry for North American Non-Financial Corporations," August 2006.*

Moody's defines these ratios in its own way, but they broadly conform to our previous discussion. Investment-grade companies—companies with at least a BBB bond rating—have higher coverage, less debt (leverage), larger cash flow to debt, less liquidity (cash plus marketable securities as a percentage of total assets), higher profit margins, and higher ROAs than companies with noninvestment-grade bond ratings. Investment-grade companies also tend to have more stable sales and are much larger than speculative companies. All these ratios make sense. Companies with better credit ratings tend to be larger, are more profitable, generate more cash, and have more stable sales, meaning lower business risk.

What we know about capital structure is that companies pay a lot of attention to the impact of issuing debt on their future profit levels and risk, so assessing their underlying business risk is very important. As companies issue more debt, most of their key ratios used by Moody's deteriorate. As a result, their credit rating weakens, and they pay higher interest charges and have to submit to more trust indenture provisions to lessen the risk involved. Knowing how issuing debt affects a company's credit rating is consequently very important. However, the key question is: Does it affect the company's market value? That is, the previous discussion simply indicates whether the company can issue debt or not, and on what terms. It does not answer the question of whether it *should* issue debt.

Altman's Z-score

Another measure of the financial health of a company is the **Altman Z-score**. This is due to the work of Professor Ed Altman and is a weighted average of several key ratios that he found were useful for predicting a company's probability of bankruptcy.[30] His prediction equation is as follows:

Altman Z-score predictive measure of the likelihood of a company filing for bankruptcy, based on the company's financial ratios

$$Z = 1.2X_1 + 1.4X_2 + 3.3X_3 + 0.6X_4 + 0.999X_5 \qquad (15\text{-}7)$$

where:

X_1 is working capital divided by total assets
X_2 is retained earnings divided by total assets
X_3 is EBIT divided by total assets
X_4 is market values of total equity divided by nonequity book liabilities
X_5 is sales divided by total assets

Note that most of the variables are scaled by total assets to standardize them, so we will refer to them by the numerator. However, they all have simple intuitive meanings.

[28] Asset coverage is defined as tangible assets divided by debt.

[29] Liquidity is defined as cash and cash equivalents divided by total assets.

[30] Ed Altman, "Financial Ratios, Discriminant Analysis and the Prediction of Corporate Bankruptcy," *Journal of Finance*, 23 (1968): 589–609.

High working capital generally means more receivables and inventory, which are usually more liquid than fixed assets. The existence of retained earnings generally means that the company has earned money in the past, and therefore it proxies for age and past profitability, among other things. EBIT is a measure of operating profitability. The market value of equity divided by the book value of liabilities is another way of saying a market-value debt ratio. Finally, sales divided by assets is the turnover ratio, so it measures how productively the company is using its assets.

The Altman Z-score was the first of many such measures that attempt to summarize a large number of financial ratios into a simple score. In the case of the Z-score, the larger the better. Altman estimated it using a sample of 66 U.S. manufacturing companies equally divided between companies that did and did not go bankrupt, and his bankrupt companies had an average Z-score of about 1.5. What is interesting is that even though Altman estimated this function more than 40 years ago and with a rather small sample, Moody's (and many other debt analysis reports) still report Altman's Z-score, and it is still working in the sense that the investment-grade companies have higher Z-scores than the noninvestment-grade companies.

Consider Sharper Image, a retailer that filed for bankruptcy in February of 2008. Calculating Sharper Image's Z-score for the years leading up to bankruptcy, we see that the Z-score gave indications that the company was not financially healthy, as you can see in Figure 15-9. We've included the score levels that Altman determined indicated a warning (2.99) and a likely bankruptcy (1.81). In the fiscal year prior to its bankruptcy filing, Sharper Image's Z-score fell below the warning track, into the "likely bankruptcy" range.

Surveys and Observations

John Graham and Campbell Harvey surveyed U.S. companies regarding factors that affect management's decision to issue debt.[31] The most often-cited factor is financial flexibility, followed closely by credit ratings. Other oft-cited factors in their survey include earnings and cash flow volatility, sufficiency of internally generated funds, the level of interest rates, and tax savings from interest deductibility. In a study of capital structure decisions in Europe, Professors Dirk Brounen, Abe de Jong, and Kees Koedijk found that factors that

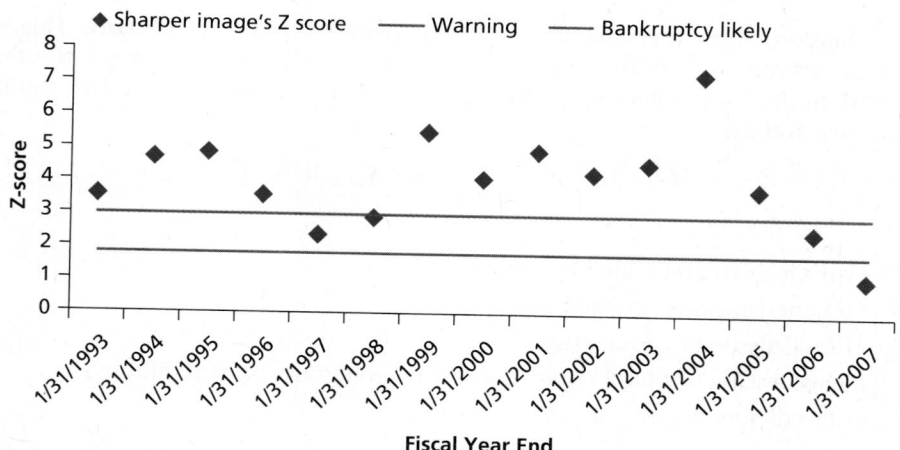

Figure 15-9 Altman Z-Score and Sharper Image
Source of data: *Sharper Image 10-K filings, various years.*

[31] John Graham and Harvey Campbell, "How Do CFOs Make Capital Budgeting and Capital Structure Decisions?" *Journal of Applied Corporate Finance,* 15, no. 1 (Spring 2002): 8–23.

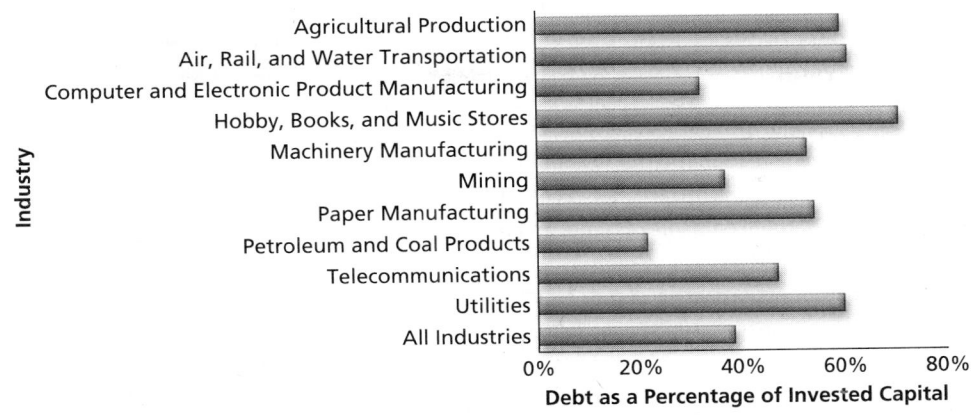

Figure 15-10 Debt as a Percentage of Invested Capital, for Selected Industries

Source: *Statistics of Income, Internal Revenue Service, U.S. Department of the Treasury.*

influence capital structure decisions are similar across the different countries in Europe, despite the institutional and tax differences among these countries.[32]

Consider the capital structure of corporations, by industry, in the U.S. for 2006, which we show in Figure 15-10.[33] As you can see in this figure, the capital structures are quite different among the industries. Basic factors like the nature of a company's assets, its profitability, and growth rate are similar among companies within an industry because they face similar business risk and have similar products, but these factors differ among industries. This is why industry averages are useful proxies for benchmarking capital structure, but they are not the end of the story.

Using surveys, John Graham and Campbell Harvey examine the factors that affect a company's financial decisions. In their analysis of capital structure decision, they found that:[34]

- The majority of companies have a target capital structure, but this is most likely a flexible target, instead of a rigid target.
- Financial managers are concerned with how issuing additional common stock may affect earnings per share.
- Financial managers consider financial flexibility, credit ratings, earnings volatility, internal funds, and interest rates when evaluating issuing additional debt.

In another survey, Professors Henri Servaes and Peter Tufano also found that the majority of companies have target capital structures, but the proportion of companies with a target varies among countries.[35] However, they found that the target capital structure is defined differently among firms, with the most common definitions of the target capital structure, in order of frequency, being the interest coverage, debt to EBITDA, debt to the book value of equity, and the absolute level of debt. In addition, Servaes and Tufano asked the financial managers to identify the factors that are the most important determinants of debt. The leading factors are credit ratings and the ability to continue making investments, as we show in Figure 15-11.

---

[32] Dirk Brounen, Abe De Jong, and Kees C. G. Koedijk, "Capital Structure Policies in Europe: Survey Evidence," ERIM Report Series Reference No. ERS-2005-005-F&A, January 2005.

[33] The most recent data available in 2010 was the data from 2006 tax returns.

[34] John Graham and Campbell Harvey, "How Do CFOs Make Capital Budgeting and Capital Structure Decisions?" *Journal of Applied Corporate Finance,* 15, no. 1 (Spring 2002): 8–23.

[35] Henri Servaes and Peter Tufano, *Corporate Capital Structure. The Theory and Practice of Corporate Capital Structure* (London: Deutsche Bank, January 2006).

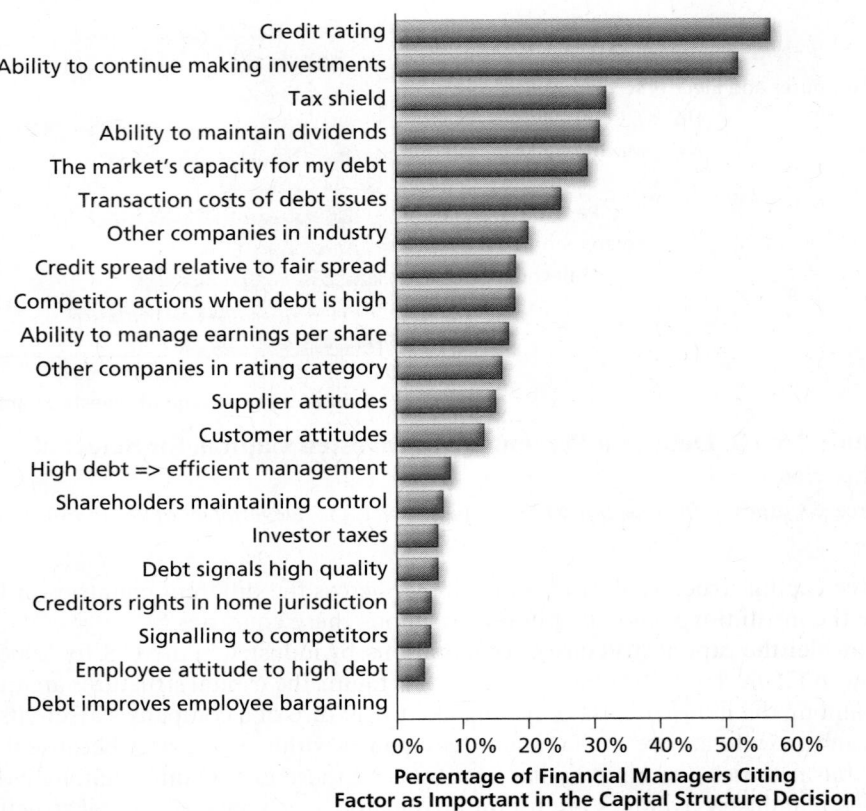

Figure 15-11 **Factors in the Determination of the Level of Debt**

Source: *Based on Figure 21 in Servaes and Tufano (2006).*

Capital Structure Guidance

So what is a company to do? A company selects its capital structure based on a number of factors. Capital structure theory provides a framework for identifying what is important to consider in determining a capital structure, but it is not prescriptive. And surveys and observations provide general information about differences across industries and factors that CFOs feel are most important. But when it comes to identifying the capital structure that a particular company should have, there are no prescriptions. An approach for dealing with this issue is to examine a number of questions, the answers to which will point the way to the target capital structure.

Is the company profitable?

If the company has no profits, then it can't use the tax shields from debt and it might as well finance with equity, or more to the point it has no ability to make interest payments.

What type of assets does the company have?

Lenders make credit evaluations and won't lend if they fear financial distress. In particular, if companies have hard tangible assets, such as property, plant, and equipment, that can be sold elsewhere, then lenders may lend to them even if they are worried about the survival prospects of the company. This is because they can always seize their assets, sell them, and recover most of their principal.

If the company's assets are tangible assets that can be used elsewhere, they can be used as collateral for a secured loan. If the company's assets are not good collateral, then the lender has to look to the company's cash flow rather than its assets for security. If, on the other hand, the assets are not good collateral, the lender will be concerned about its business risk and the variability of its operations.

How risky is the company's underlying business?

It is a basic law of finance based on our discussion of financial leverage that you do not layer significant financial risk on top of significant business risk. Generally, financial markets are size constrained. What this means is that preparing a prospectus and so on is time consuming and costly, so only larger companies access the public markets. Further, larger companies tend to have more diversified operations and more market power. This is not an absolute, but it tends to be the case that larger companies are less risky than smaller companies, so we ask the next question.

Is the company profitable? Is it growing?

Finally there is the basic question of whether the company needs the money, and then it becomes very much a function of its profitability and its growth rate. Growing companies need cash, whereas profitable companies generally spin off cash.

Why might companies deviate from their target capital structure?

The preceding questions go a long way toward determining how much debt a company can carry and what its optimal debt ratio will be. Companies will also deviate from the target capital structure in any given year because raising new capital tends to be "lumpy"; that is, companies are not likely to issue a little bit of equity and a little bit of debt each year, but rather may have a stock issue in one year and a debt issue in the next year.

Of course companies deviate from their target capital structure when they are offered a good deal. Like everyone else, we may do something we didn't intend to if someone offers us a good deal. In terms of financing, this means that if the company observes attractive interest rates for debt financing, it might lean more heavily on debt financing. Similarly, if a company's share price is very high and increasing, it may decide to take advantage of this window of opportunity to issue common shares. This is why we observe more equity financing in a strong equity market than a weak one.[36]

Concept Review Questions

1. What are the main determinants of capital structure?

2. Explain how ratios may be used to assess a company's ability to assume more debt.

3. What is Altman's Z-score, and what does it measure?

SUMMARY

- The basic Modigliani and Miller (M&M) arguments assess whether the capital structure decision creates value. The conclusion was that under some simplifying assumptions, issuing debt does not create value. This is because the company is not doing anything that others can't do just as well; that is, borrow money. In essence, the M&M argument is that companies should stick to doing things where they have a comparative advantage, and it is difficult to see how borrowing money is such because we can all do it.

---

[36] In fact, companies often issue equity when they think it is overvalued. This opportunistic financing causes significant departures from their long-run "target" debt ratios.

- Once we introduce the fact that interest on debt is tax deductible, whereas dividends to the common shareholders are not, it means that there is a tax shield value to raising debt. Hence, there is a transfer of wealth to the private sector from the government as the company finances with debt. This tax incentive to using debt is offset by the resulting financial distress and bankruptcy costs, as discussed in the static trade-off model.

- As its name implies, the static trade-off model does not take into account dynamic effects. The pecking order theory, on the other hand, does account for these dynamic effects as companies tend to first use internal cash flow, then debt, and will only raise new common equity as a last resort. The result is that companies depart from the static trade-off optimal debt ratio over time, and then refinance to bring their debt ratio back in line with their target ratio. Therefore, actual capital structures are constantly changing as companies take advantage of market conditions.

- Capital structure decisions in practice focus on a company's target capital structure and the company's ability to satisfy debt obligations. Financial managers not only worry about how new debt affects a company's credit rating, but they also worry about how capital structure decisions affect dividends and the reported earnings per share.

FORMULAS/EQUATIONS

(15-1) Degree of operating leverage $= \dfrac{Q(P - V)}{Q(P - V) - F}$

(15-2) $ROE = \dfrac{\text{Net income}}{\text{Equity}}$

(15-3) $ROI = \dfrac{\text{Operating income after tax}}{\text{Invested capital}}$

(15-4) Degree of financial leverage $= \dfrac{Q(P - V) - F}{Q(P - V) - F - C}$

(15-5) Degree of total leverage $= \dfrac{Q(P - V)}{Q(P - V) - F - C}$

(15-6) $V_L = V_U + DT$

(15-7) $Z = 1.2X_1 + 1.4X_2 + 3.3X_3 + 0.6X_4 + 0.999X_5$

QUESTIONS AND PROBLEMS

Multiple Choice

1. A company that has a contribution margin of $4 per unit and fixed operating costs of $20,000 breaks even, in terms of operating earnings, at:

    A. 5,000 units.   B. 20,000 units.   C. 80,000 units.

2. Suppose a company sells its product for $3 per unit. The variable cost per unit is $2, and the fixed operating costs are $1,000. The degree of operating leverage at 10,000 units produced and sold is *closest* to:

    A. 1.00.   B. 1.11.   C. 9.00.   D. 10.00.

3. A company with a degree of operating leverage of 1.5 and a degree of financial leverage of 2.0 has a degree of total leverage *closest* to:

    A. 0.5.   B. 1.5.   C. 3.0.   D. 3.5.

4. A degree of operating leverage of 3 means that a:
    A. 1 percent change in operating earnings will result in a 3 percent change in EPS.
    B. 1 percent change in operating earnings will result in a 3 percent change in net income.
    C. 1 percent change in units sold and produced will result in a 3 percent change in net income.
    D. 1 percent change in units sold and produced will result in a 3 percent change in operating earnings.

5. Which of the following statements of rules of financial leverage is *false*?
    A. The use of debt normally decreases the expected ROE.
    B. Debt financing increases the risk to common shareholders.
    C. Debt financing increases the chances of financial distress.
    D. The higher the debt-equity ratio, the steeper the financial leverage line.

6. Which of the following is *not* an assumption of M&M's irrelevance theorem?
    A. There is no tax.
    B. Transactions costs are minimal.
    C. There is no risk of costly bankruptcy.
    D. Two companies exist with different levels of debt.

7. If there are no taxes and no costs of financial distress, the Modigliani and Miller capital structure theory concludes that:
    A. there is an optimal capital structure.
    B. there is no optimal capital structure.
    C. the optimal capital structure is 99.99 percent debt.

8. Which of the companies listed here is the *least* likely to raise debt in the capital market?
    A. A large and profitable company
    B. A less profitable company that has a nonrisky business
    C. A profitable company that has a risky underlying business
    D. A small company that has seen its share price decrease in the past

9. If a company has a debt-equity ratio of 2.0, this is *best* described as:
    A. highly levered.
    B. financially distressed.
    C. the amount of debt per dollar of equity.

10. A company that has an interest coverage ratio of 2 is *best* described as:
    A. having two times as much debt as equity.
    B. cash flow that is twice that of the interest expense.
    C. operating income that is twice that of the interest expense.
    D. one-half of the earnings it needs to meet its financial obligations.

Practice Questions and Problems

15.1 Operating and Financial Leverage

11. What distinguishes the return on invested capital from the return on equity?

12. If a company has a degree of operating leverage of 3.0, what does this mean?

13. Why do we always state that the degree of operating leverage is specific to a level of units produced and sold?

14. How do the degree of operating leverage and the degree of financial leverage interact for a given company?

15. What is the meaning of the operating break-even?

16. Distinguish between sales risk and operating risk. Can a company have a high degree of sales risk, yet a low degree of operating risk? Explain your reasoning.

17. Consider the Gum Company. Gum sells packs of gum for $0.50 each. It costs $0.20 per pack to manufacture and distribute the gum. Gum has fixed operating costs of $5,000 and fixed financing costs of $3,000.

   A. What is Gum's degree of operating leverage at 50,000 packs produced and sold?
   B. What is Gum's degree of financial leverage at 50,000 packs produced and sold?
   C. What is Gum's degree of total leverage at 50,000 packs produced and sold?

18. Analysis of the Fulcrum Corporation indicates that a 10 percent change in operating profit produces a 50 percent change in net income. What is Fulcrum's degree of financial leverage?

19. For each of the following companies,

Company	Quantity	Price per Unit	Variable Cost per Unit	Fixed Operating Cost	Interest
A	3000	$10	$5	$1,000	$100
B	40000	$5	$1	$10,000	$1,000
C	100000	$2	$1	$10,000	$500
D	300	$100	$60	$4,000	$300
E	2000	$30	$25	$4,000	$1,000
F	55000	$20	$15	$20,000	$2,000
G	20000	$25	$20	$8,000	$500

Complete the following table:

Company	Operating Earnings	Contribution Margin	Break-even	Degree of Operating Leverage	Degree of Financial Leverage	Degree of Total Leverage
A						
B						
C						
D						
E						
F						
G						

20. Calculate ROE and ROI given the following:

Sales	$168,000
COGS	$40,000
Amortization	$25,000
SG&A	$16,000
Taxes	$25,200
Before-tax cost of debt	12%
Shareholders' equity	$500,000
Book value of debt (B)	$200,000

21. Calculate the return on equity of a company if:

Return on invested capital = 15%

r_d = 10%

Debt = $150,000

Shareholders' equity = $600,000

Tax rate = 40%

What is the intercept and slope of the financial leverage (ROE–ROI) line? Explain the meaning of the slope.

22. Consider three proposed capital structures, labeled 1, 2, and 3:

	Structure 1	Structure 2	Structure 3
Assets	$10,000	$10,000	$10,000
Debt	$0	$5,000	$8,000
Equity	$10,000	$5,000	$2,000
Cost of debt before taxes		10%	12%
Number of shares	2,000	1,000	400

The company is expected to produce and sell 100,000 items, where each item has a sales price of $1 and a contribution margin of 40 percent. Fixed operating costs are $20,000, and the company's tax rate is 30 percent.

A Calculate the degree of operating leverage for the company at 100,000 items produced and sold.

B. Calculate the following for each proposed capital structure:

(i)   debt-to-invested capital

(ii) debt-to-equity

(iii) return on invested capital

(iv) return on equity

(v)   degree of financial leverage

(vi) degree of total leverage

C. Using a spreadsheet program, graph the earnings per share for each structure on the same graph for units produced and sold ranging from 50,000 to 150,000, in increments of 1,000 units. Discuss the graph in terms of leverage and implications for the company's risk.

D. We have assumed that the value of a share of stock is not affected by the capital structure. What do you expect to be the relation between the value of a share of stock for these different capital structures? Explain your reasoning.

15.2   The Modigliani and Miller Theorems

23. For the M&M irrelevance theorem to hold, what key assumptions must be met?

24. Describe the relationship between the debt ratio and company value when we consider the existence of bankruptcy costs. How do you view the agency costs when bankruptcy occurs?

25. In the M&M no-tax world, consider a company with the following:

Cost of unlevered equity (r_U) = 12%

Cost of debt (r_d) = 9.5%

Debt = $400,000

Net income = $520,000

A. What is the value of the levered company (V_L)?

B. What is the value of levered company (V_L) if the tax rate is 40 percent?

C. What is the cost of levered equity if the tax rate is 40 percent?

26. According to the M&M irrelevance theorem, calculate the market value of the unlevered company and of an identical risk levered company. The expected earnings before interest and taxes of the unlevered company is $1,500,000, which will remain constant indefinitely, and the company's cost of capital is 15 percent. If the levered company has $8.5 million debt outstanding, what's its market value of the equity?

27. Your cousin has just started his MBA and is confused. He understands that without taxes, capital structure is irrelevant. He also understands that with taxes, companies should use 99.99 percent debt. However, his professor is saying that even with taxes there are times that the investor prefers an unlevered company. How is this possible?

15.3 Capital Structure in Practice

28. What is the pecking order according to Myers's argument?

29. Explain the elements of Altman's Z-score, and relate each to a particular dimension of a company's financial condition or performance.

30. List and describe briefly the main factors you need to consider if the CFO of your company asks you to evaluate your company's capital structure.

31. Consider the following information on Laredo Inc., assuming that the book value of equity is the same as its market value of equity:

Current assets	$250,000
Current liabilities	$50,000
Total assets	$600,000
Retained earnings	$190,000
Earnings before interest and taxes	$96,000
Market value of equity	$400,000
Sales	$390,000

A. Calculate Altman's Z-score for Laredo Inc. and then compare this information with Moody's rating chart.
B. Is Laredo Inc. more likely an investment-grade or noninvestment-grade company?

32. Consider the following information on Boston Inc., assuming that long-term liabilities are $400,000 in both years:

	2012	*2011*
Current assets	$500,000	$450,000
Current liabilities	$300,000	$250,000
Total assets	$1,000,000	$950,000
Retained earnings	$300,000	$250,000
Earnings before interest and taxes	$100,000	$80,000
Market value of equity	$2,000,000	$2,100,000
Sales	$3,000,000	$2,800,000

A. Calculate Altman's Z-score for Boston Inc. for both years.
B. Has the Altman Z-score changed from 2011 to 2012? If so, why?

33. An analyst with the Globe Theatre Company has gathered the following information on the company:
- Earnings before interest and taxes is $500,000 per year.
- Cost of capital is 10 percent.
- Before-tax cost of debt is 5 percent.
- The debt is risk free.
- All cash flows are perpetual.

- The current debt-to-equity ratio is two-thirds.
- The corporate tax rate is 40 percent.

The new CEO of the Globe believes that the debt-equity ratio is too high and would like to reduce it to one-third. His intent is to issue stock to repay the debt.

A. What is the effect on the EPS of the Globe Theatre of this change in the debt-equity ratio?

B. What is the effect on the cost of equity for the Globe Theatre if the debt-equity ratio is changed?

Case

Case 15.1 Analyzing Delta Air Lines

Delta Air Lines (DAL) is a U.S.-based company that provides air transportation for both passengers and cargo throughout the world. DAL filed for bankruptcy in 2005, but restructured and emerged from bankruptcy in April of 2007.

Consider the financial statements and accompanying data for Delta Air Lines for the 2007–2009 fiscal years:

Income Statements

(in millions of U.S. dollars)	For Fiscal Year Ending		
	12/31/2007	12/31/2008	12/31/2009
Revenue	17,410	20,269	24,595
Other Revenue, Total	1,744	2,428	3,468
Total Revenue	19,154	22,697	28,063
Cost of Revenue, Total	15,855	20,236	24,886
Gross Profit	1,555	33	–291
Depreciation/Amortization	1,164	1,266	1,536
Unusual Expense (Income)	–1,215	8,427	490
Other Operating Expenses, Total	1,039	1,082	1,558
Total Operating Expense	16,843	31,011	28,470
Operating Income	2,311	–8,314	–407
Other, Net	32	–114	77
Income Before Tax	1,819	–9,041	–1,581
Tax	207	–119	–344
Net Income	1,612	–8,922	–1,237

Balance Sheets

(in millions of U.S. dollars)	As of Fiscal Year Ending		
	12/31/2007	12/31/2008	12/31/2009
Cash & Equivalents	2,648.00	4,255.00	4,607.00
Short Term Investments	138	212	71
Cash and Short-Term Investments	2,786	4,467	4,678
Accounts Receivable—Trade, Net	1,066	1,513	1,353
Total Receivables, Net	1,066	2,652	1,360
Total Inventory	262	388	327
Prepaid Expenses	464	637	846
Other Current Assets, Total	662	830	530
Total Current Assets	5,240	8,974	7,741
Property/Plant/Equipment, Total—Gross	12,309	22,185	23,357

(in millions of U.S. dollars)	As of Fiscal Year Ending		
	12/31/2007	12/31/2008	12/31/2009
Accumulated Depreciation, Total	−608	−1,558	−2,924
Goodwill	12,104	9,731	9,787
Intangibles	2,806	4,944	4,829
Other Long-Term Assets, Total	572	808	749
Total Assets	32,423	45,084	43,539
Accounts Payable	839	1,604	1,249
Accrued Expenses	1,097	1,507	1,663
Notes Payable and Short-Term Debt	295	1,247	139
Current Portion of Long-Term Debt	1,014	1,160	1,533
Other Current liabilities, Total	3,360	5,574	5,213
Total Current Liabilities	6,605	11,092	9,797
Long-Term Debt	7,986	15,411	15,665
Total Long-Term Debt	7,986	15,411	15,665
Total Debt	9,295	17,818	17,337
Deferred Income Tax	855	1,981	1,667
Other Liabilities, Total	6,864	15,726	16,165
Total Liabilities	22,310	44,210	43,294
Common Stock, Total	0	0	0
Additional Paid-In Capital	9,512	13,714	13,827
Retained Earnings (Accumulated Deficit)	314	−8,608	−9,845
Treasury Stock—Common	−148	−152	−174
Other Equity, Total	435	−4,080	−3,563
Total Equity	10,113	874	245
Total Liabilities & Shareholders' Equity	32,423	45,084	43,539

Statements of Cash Flow

(in millions of U.S. dollars)	For Fiscal Year Ending		
	12/31/2007	12/31/2008	12/31/2009
Net Income	1,612	−8,922	−1,237
Depreciation	1,164	1,266	1,536
Deferred Taxes	207	−119	−329
Non-Cash Items	−1,786	8,230	799
Changes in Working Capital	162	−2,162	610
Cash from Operating Activities	1,359	−1,707	1,379
Capital Expenditures	−1,036	−1,522	−1,202
Other Investing Cash Flow Items, Total	411	3,120	194
Cash from Investing Activities	−625	1,598	−1,008
Financing Cash Flow Items	−69	988	−94
Issuance (Retirement) of Stock, Net	0	192	0
Issuance (Retirement) of Debt, Net	−51	536	75
Cash from Financing Activities	−120	1,716	−19
Net Change in Cash	614	1,607	352

Supplemental Data

	For Fiscal Year Ending		
	12/31/2007	*12/31/2008*	*12/31/2009*
Revenue passenger miles, in millions	122,065	134,879	118,943
Passenger load factor	80.3%	81.4%	82.0%
Passenger revenue per available seat mile	$0.111	$0.118	$0.103
Operating cost per seat mile	$0.139	$0.187	$0.123
Average price per fuel gallon	$2.23	$3.16	$2.15
Fuel gallons consumed, in millions	2,534	2,740	3,823

	As of		
	12/31/2007	*12/31/2008*	*12/31/2009*
Common shares outstanding, in millions	292.23	695.14	783.95
Market price per share, end of year	$14.60	$10.57	$11.83

1. What factors contribute to an airline's business risk? Would you consider this risk to be high, moderate, or low? Explain the basis of your assessment.

2. Describe Delta's capital structure, being sure to include an analysis of a few of the capital structure ratios discussed in this chapter.

3. Calculate Altman's Z-score for fiscal years 2008 and 2009, and interpret these Z-scores.

4. Provide an overall assessment of Delta Air Lines' financial condition for the 2 years following its bankruptcy.

CHAPTER 16

DIVIDEND POLICY

© Gary Cameron/Reuters/NewsCom

Jeffrey Immelt Faces More 'Hours of Doom' with GE Dividend Cut *General Electric, which took pride in its long history of paying dividends, was forced to cut its dividend following the 2008–09 recession. While this occurred several years ago, it marks a significant moment in dividend paying history for one of the largest U.S. companies.*

The cracks in Jeffrey Immelt's public optimism came on Feb. 5 [2009], when he joked about his "hour of doom" every morning reading newspaper articles on failed banks, job losses and sinking economies.

The General Electric Co. chief executive maintained then as he had for months that GE could withstand the recession, even as he said he was "prepared" to run the company if it lost its AAA credit rating. Yesterday the GE board ordered the first cut in the dividend since 1938. The lower rating may be next, as Moody's Investors Service said it would keep GE debt on review.

Reducing the annual dividend to 40 cents a share from $1.24 will give Immelt $9 billion in cash that he may use to further shore up a finance unit facing credit losses. The decision to cut was a welcome bow to reality, said Malcolm Polley, chief investment officer of Stewart Capital Advisors in Indiana, Pennsylvania, which holds GE shares among $1 billion in assets.

"Immelt was losing credibility maintaining this steadfast belief they had to keep both their AAA rating and the dividend," Polley said. "It's about time."

Immelt, 53, who succeeded Jack Welch on Sept. 7, 2001, has dealt with the Sept. 11 terrorist attacks and two recessions in his nearly eight-year tenure as CEO. He joined GE in 1982.

As the biggest provider of power-plant turbines, aircraft leasing, jet engines and locomotives, the Fairfield, Connecticut-based company is a bellwether for U.S. trade and industry. More than 40 percent of holders of its 10.5 billion outstanding shares are individual investors.

"Precautionary Action"

GE shares, down 75 percent in the past year, are at their lowest since 1995. The stock fell 59 cents to $8.51 yesterday in New York Stock Exchange composite trading. Immelt, who tripled GE's cash on hand to $48 billion last year through steps such as canceling a stock buyback and raising equity, said as recently as Jan. 23 that GE wouldn't have to cut the dividend. "I hate the fact that there's so much speculation around the dividend and AAA," he said in an interview on the company-owned CNBC television network. "I wish my words could end the speculation. The facts of what we've done here,

I think, should let investors know that we've got the cash, and we've got the operating model that's going to secure the dividend in this environment."

Yesterday, Immelt said in a statement that the move "is the right precautionary action at this time to further strengthen our company for the long-term."

Continued declines in the stock market, the slump in housing prices and rising unemployment likely convinced Immelt that he needed to free up capital to set aside for loss provisions, said Nicholas Heymann, an analyst with Sterne Agee & Leach Inc. who has a "sell" rating on the shares.

42 Percent Decline

"This is certainly a good step, but the problems are probably also of a larger magnitude than might have been perceived even two weeks ago," Heymann said. U.S. unemployment in January reached the highest level since 1992, rising to 7.6 percent. Gross domestic product shrank at a 6.2 percent annual pace from October through December, the most since 1982, the Commerce Department said yesterday.

More than 50 percent of GE's profit in recent years has come from its GE Capital unit, which includes private-label credit cards, real estate, bankruptcy financing and mid-sized company lending, making it a competitor to most banks. The finance unit's profit fell 30 percent to $8.6 billion last year as real estate profit dropped by half and the GE Money consumer division declined by 14 percent. GE forecasts a 42 percent decline this year, to $5 billion. Several analyst estimates are even lower. Heymann forecasts profit of $2.8 billion in 2009.

Extracted from: Peter Robison and Rachel Layne, "Jeffrey Immelt Faces More 'Hours of Doom' with GE Dividend Cut," Bloomberg.com, February 28, 2009.

Learning Outcomes

After reading this chapter, you should be able to:

LO 16.1 Describe the different forms of distributions to shareholders, including cash dividends, stock splits, and stock dividends, and describe the mechanics of dividend payments.

LO 16.2 List and discuss briefly the different explanations for observed distributions.

LO 16.3 Describe current dividend practices.

Chapter Preview The focus of this chapter is on dividends. In this chapter we examine how and why companies pay cash dividends and provide other forms of distributing shares or cash to shareholders. We often refer to the distribution of earnings to owners as the dividend policy, but the decision is actually broader than this, encompassing cash dividends, stock repurchases, and stock dividends.

It might seem obvious that cash dividends matter to the value of a company because we have previously discussed how to value common shares by discounting the expected future dividends. Yet it turns out that this is not the whole story. In this chapter, we discuss possible explanations for why companies pay dividends and then describe what companies actually do.

16.1 DISTRIBUTIONS TO SHAREHOLDERS

A corporation has no legal obligation to make any type of distribution to common shareholders, whether this is a distribution of cash or a distribution of shares. A company's board of directors declares a dividend, and only then does a dividend become a contractual commitment of the company. Shareholders cannot force the members of the board to declare a dividend, and there may be legal restrictions on whether or not the company can declare a dividend. For example, if the company also has preferred shares outstanding, the company must pay the dividend on the preferred shares prior to paying any dividend to common shareholders.

Cash Dividends

We can look at dividends from both a macro- and a micro-level perspective. At the macro level, we can look at dividends paid out of earnings. We show the **dividend payout ratio**, which is dividends as a percentage of earnings, in Figure 16-1 for the stocks that comprise the S&P 500 Index.

We draw a few conclusions from this graph.

- The payout rate is normally around 40 to 60 percent, but increased to over 100 percent during economic downturns, when profits dropped dramatically but dividends remained relatively stable.
- The payout rate has been trending downward over time.
- The median payout for the most recent 10 years is 35.5 percent.

This naturally raises an important question: Why aren't dividends a constant proportion of profits?

We can look at dividends from another perspective. Consider the dividend yield of stocks in the S&P 500 Index, as we show in Figure 16-2. The **dividend yield** is the ratio of the dividend to the price of the stock; with the price of the stock in the denominator,

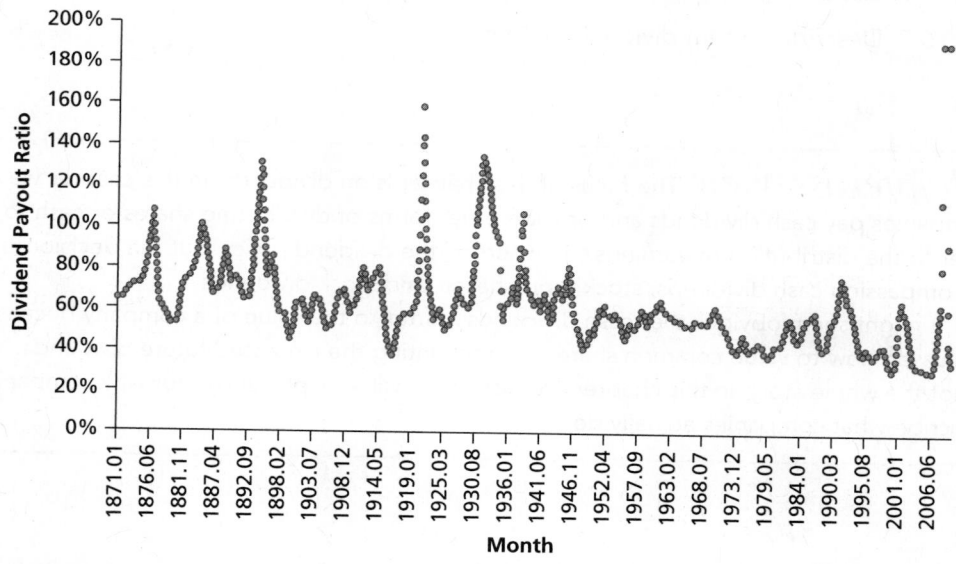

FIGURE 16-1 Aggregate Dividends and Profits, 1871 Through 2010
Source: *Data from Robert Shiller's Stock Market Data Used in "Irrational Exuberance" Princeton University Press, 2000, 2005, updated.*

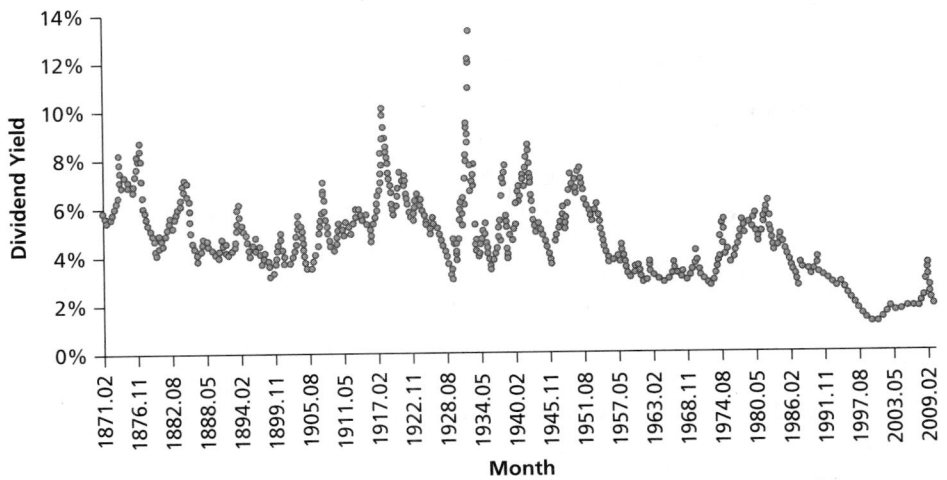

FIGURE 16-2 Dividend Yields of Stocks in the S&P 500 Index, 1871 Through 2010

the dividend yield is affected by the ups and downs of the stock market. The median dividend yield in recent years is around 1.76 percent. The dividend yield has trended downward over the years, with spikes as the U.S. entered economic downturns. These spikes indicate that companies do not adjust dividends instantly when there is an economic downturn.

From the Oracle's Mouth: Its First Div | FINANCE in the News

A few years back, Oracle, a technology company, decided to pay its first dividend. Let's take a look at the reasoning behind this decision.

Software giant's decision to pay a nickel quarterly, described by CFO Jeff Epstein, runs counter to the spate of cuts elsewhere in industry—most dramatically at Alcoa.

Against the grain of company after company slashing dividends, Oracle announced its first payout ever.

The software giant will pay a 5-cent quarterly, for an annual rate of 20 cents, declaring that the dividend policy now will add a new dimension to the way it rewards investors—limited in the past to stock repurchases, acquisitions, and technological improvements. The nickel-a-share will be paid May 8 to stock of record April 8.

Oracle executive vice president and CFO Jeff Epstein noted that non-GAAP operating income was $2.6 billion in the third fiscal quarter, up 15 percent over the same period last year, resulting in operating margins of 46 percent. He also noted the company generated $8 billion in free cash flow in the past 12 months, up 14 percent over the same period last year.

"We are committed to delivering value to our stockholders through technology innovation, strate-gic acquisitions, stock repurchases, and now through a dividend," said Oracle president Safra Catz, who noted the free cash flow position as well, and said that "we are running our business at record operating margins."

The announcement could, of course, signal that the company plans fewer acquisitions as a use for its cash. Technology companies in a growth mode typically preserve cash to reinvest in the business or to buy smaller competitors. But whatever the strategy behind it, the stock jumped nearly 7 percent in after-hours trading Wednesday.

The announcement runs counter to a rash of dividend slashes or eliminations by companies that have long traditions of paying dividends, and regularly raising them. One dramatic slasher this week was Alcoa, which on Monday cut its dividend by 82 percent, to 3 cents a share from 17 cents quarterly, the first time it reduced the payout in more than a quarter century. "Today's actions better prepare Alcoa to manage through a prolonged downturn," Klaus Kleinfeld, Alcoa's president and chief executive, said in his statement.

Source: Stephen Taub, "From Oracle's Mouth: Its First Div," CFO.com, March 28, 2009.

The mechanics of cash dividends

declaration date date on which the board of directors decides that the company will pay a dividend

The actual mechanics of paying a dividend are rather straightforward. The board of directors declares the dividend on a specific date. In the declaration, which occurs on the **declaration date**, the board specifies three items, the:

1. amount of the dividend, generally stated as an amount per share of stock;
2. **record date** or **date of record**, which is the date used to determine the shareholders who will receive the dividend; and
3. **payment date** or **payable date**, which is the day the dividend is actually paid by the company.

record date or **date of record** date that determines the holder of record; the date that determines who receives the forthcoming dividend, as declared by the board of directors

Because shares of stock are traded in markets on a continual basis it can take a day or so to determine who actually owns the shares at a point in time; in this case, who the **holder of record** is on a particular day. This is resolved by the markets, which specify the **ex-dividend date** as two trading days prior to the record date. How this works is as follows:

payment date or **payable date** actual date the dividend is paid to shareholders

- If you buy the stock <u>on</u> the ex-dividend date or later, you do *not* get the forthcoming, declared dividend.
- If you buy the stock <u>before</u> the ex-dividend date and own it at least until the day before the ex-dividend date, you *will* receive the forthcoming dividend.

holder of record person who officially owns a share or shares on a given date

ex-dividend date date on which shares trade without the right to receive a dividend

This explains why we typically see a drop in the share price of a dividend-paying stock from the day before to the ex-dividend date: If you buy the stock on the day before the ex-dividend date, you receive the dividend; if you buy the stock on the ex-dividend date, you do not receive the dividend.

Consider the timeline for the dividend of IBM Corporation paid December 10, 2010, that we show in Figure 16-3. The board of directors declared the dividend in October 2010, setting the record date, the payable date, and the amount. The New York Stock Exchange then determined the ex-dividend date for this dividend. You can see that the price of IBM's stock declined from the day before the ex-date to the close on the ex-date by $0.46. We generally see such a decline; if nothing else is going on with the company and if the market is not moving upward or downward on the ex-date, we generally expect the price to drop by the amount of the dividend, in this case $0.65. But because we cannot hold everything else constant, the drop is approximately (but not exactly) the amount of the dividend in most cases.

special dividend cash dividend paid in addition to the regular dividend

Companies that pay cash dividends tend to do so on a regular basis, whether this is quarterly, monthly, or annually. Companies may also pay a **special dividend**, which, as you might have guessed, are paid infrequently. For example, the board of directors of the

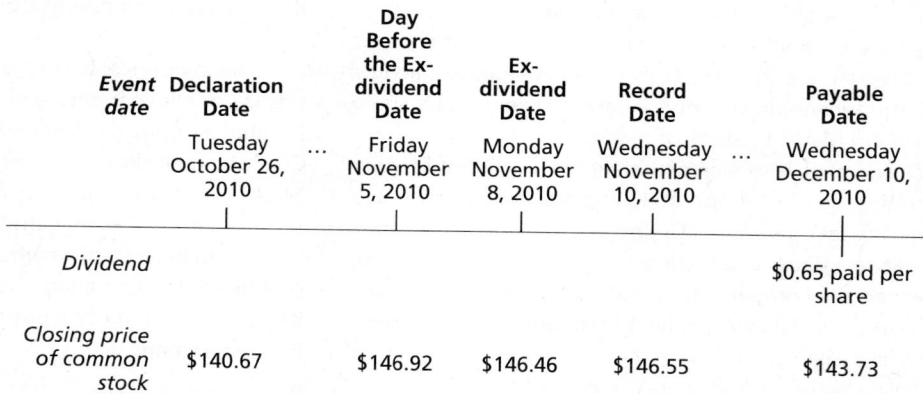

Event date	Declaration Date		Day Before the Ex-dividend Date	Ex-dividend Date	Record Date		Payable Date
	Tuesday October 26, 2010	...	Friday November 5, 2010	Monday November 8, 2010	Wednesday November 10, 2010	...	Wednesday December 10, 2010
Dividend							$0.65 paid per share
Closing price of common stock	$140.67		$146.92	$146.46	$146.55		$143.73

FIGURE 16-3 **Timeline of IBM's Cash Dividend Paid November 8, 2010**

retailer The Buckle, a U.S. retailer, declared a special dividend of $1.80 per share to holders of record on October 15, 2009. This special dividend was in addition to the regular cash dividend of $0.20 per share.[1] Why pay a special dividend? A special dividend is useful when a company has more cash than it needs and wants to distribute this to shareholders, but without the expectation that the regular dividend has increased.

Dividend reinvestment plans

If the investor does not want to receive a dividend, many corporations offer the option of using the cash dividend proceeds to buy new shares by way of a **dividend reinvestment plan (DRIP** or **DRP)**. Why wouldn't an investor want a cash dividend? Because they may want to let their investment in that company grow over time.[2] The company issues shares through the DRIP plan without any brokerage fees or transactions costs. Generally, investors buy as many shares as the cash dividend allows, with the residual deposited as cash. At one time, companies allowed investors to buy the shares through a DRIP at a discount to the closing market price as an incentive for investors to reinvest, but most companies have phased out the discount because the plans became so popular.

> **dividend reinvestment plan (DRIP** or **DRP)** plan allowing cash dividends to be reinvested to buy new shares

DRIPs are popular with both investors and companies. For the company, it means that it can issue shares on a regular basis continuously at no cost, whereas investors perceive that it is paying a regular dividend.[3] For long-term investors who do not rely on income from their portfolios, the automatic reinvestment averages their investment because they are buying shares at a range of prices. It also removes the problem of accumulating funds to reinvest. However, even though less cash is received by the investor, the full cash dividend is still taxable, which represents a disadvantage for taxable investors.

Stock Dividends

A company can also distribute more shares of stock to shareholders through stock dividends. This can be in addition to or in lieu of cash dividends. A **stock dividend** is generally defined as any share distribution, but typically we use the term "stock dividend" when the number of shares issued is less than 25 percent of the outstanding shares.[4] If a company declares a 10 percent stock dividend, each investor will get 10 percent more shares. In terms of accounting, a company paying a stock dividend transfers the value of the shares from retained earnings into the capital stock account. As a result, a company cannot issue a stock dividend if there are no available retained earnings.[5]

> **stock dividend** dividend paid in additional shares rather than cash

A stock dividend will likely have the effect of reducing the share price proportionately. If a company had 10 million shares outstanding and a share price of $20, and then pays a 15 percent stock dividend, the expected share price after the dividend is the total market value of the company, divided by the new number of shares: ($20 × 10,000,000) ÷ (10,000,000 × 1.15) = $17.9 per share.

---

[1] Press release, September 22, 2009, The Buckle, Inc.

[2] This is a form of dollar-cost averaging. Dollar-cost averaging is an investment strategy in which the investor invests the same monetary amount each period in a stock, where sometimes the price is up and sometimes the price is down.

[3] A DRIP also fosters a more ongoing relationship with investors, who often end up holding what we call "odd lots" of shares, so that their total share holdings are in odd numbers such as 123 shares, instead of a round lot of some multiple of 100. This has become less important in recent years as trading has become more efficient and is no longer done in round lots of 100 shares each.

[4] It is quite possible for a company to declare a stock dividend greater than 25 percent. For example, companies could issue a 125 percent stock dividend of a 50 percent stock dividend.

[5] A cash dividend with a DRIP is similar to a stock dividend. In this case, rather than giving the investor cash and then taking it back for shares, the company simply gives more shares.

EXAMPLE 16.1

Stock Dividends

PROBLEM

Suppose a company pays a 5 percent stock dividend. If there were 1 million shares outstanding before this dividend, and the stock price before the dividend was $30,

A. How many shares are outstanding after the dividend?

B. What is the expected price of the stock following the dividend?

Solution

A. $1,000,000 \times 1.05 = 1,050,000$ shares

B. $\$30,000,000 \div 1,050,000 = \$28.57$ per share

Stock Splits

stock split proportionate distribution of shares outstanding, typically involving an increase in shares outstanding of more than 25 percent

Another transaction that is similar, but not identical, to a stock dividend is a **stock split**. Typically, when a company has a goal of issuing more than 25 percent additional shares, it uses a stock split; however, there is no rule or restriction with regard to this.[6] We refer to a stock split in terms of shares after compared to shares before. For example, a 2-for-1 stock split means that if an investor owned 100 shares before the split, he or she owns 200 shares after. As another example, a "3 for 2" stock split results in a 50 percent increase in the shares outstanding; this would be equivalent, in terms of shares before and after, to a 50 percent stock dividend. What is the difference between the stock dividend and stock split? There are some accounting advantages to a stock split because a company does not adjust retained earnings to account for a stock split, but does so for a stock dividend. In the case of a stock split, it is simply an adjustment in the number of shares outstanding.

Both stock dividends and stock splits simply divide the value of the common shares among more shares and, all else constant, reduce the price per share. Why companies do this is something of a mystery because there is no underlying change in the company. One possible explanation is that by increasing the number of shares, the price per share falls, and this may be useful if there is an optimal trading range for the share price. For example, 100 shares at a price of $90 each means a $9,000 trade, but if the share price is $30, then it means a $3,000 trade, which may be more feasible for small investors.[7] Over a long period, a stock price can easily get out of the reach of the typical individual investor. As an example, let's look at the Microsoft Corporation. Microsoft began as a publicly traded company in March of 1986. Since it first started trading, Microsoft has had nine stock splits; seven at 2 for 1, and two at 3 for 2. If Microsoft had *not* split its stock since it first started trading, instead of the price of $27.91 at the end of 2010, Microsoft would be trading at $8,038 per share.

It is difficult to know whether these effects have any economic significance, but continued listing requirements of exchanges require that shares trade at or above a specific dollar value. Though falling below the minimum value does not result in an immediate delisting, a stock with a low price for an extended period will be delisted. For example, a stock listed on the Nasdaq that trades for 30 days below the minimum price of $1 will be notified that it has 180 days to get its stock price above the minimum. During some periods of market disruption, such as the case with the bursting of the Internet bubble,

---

[6] Therefore, if a company would like to increase shares by 25 percent, it could issue a 25 percent stock dividend or have a 1.25:1 stock split.

[7] This argument had some validity a number of years ago when there were significant costs attached to trading shares and round lots of 100 shares cost less than odd lots (that is, less than 100 shares).

the exchanges will waive this continued listing requirement for a period. However, a risk of delisting exists if the stock's price does not get above the minimum level. For example, in October of 2009, the New York Stock Exchange and the NASDAQ warned hundreds of companies of possible delisting if their stock price did not rise above $1 within 30 days. Both markets had waived the minimum price rule during the 2007–2008 financial crisis, but then reinstituted the rule.[8]

Related to the stock split is the **reverse stock split**.[9] Like the stock split that we have already discussed, a company might try to lift its stock price by undergoing a reverse stock split, in which the company issues fewer shares for the existing outstanding shares. For example, a 1 for 2 reverse stock split means that for every two shares an investor owns, the investor receives one in exchange. An investor who owned 100 shares before the reverse stock split owns 50 shares after the split. Why reverse stock split? The typical stock split reduces the share price, so the logic is that the reverse stock split will increase the share price. For example, when companies are warned of a possible delisting due to a low share price, many respond by executing a reverse stock split.[10]

reverse stock split
reduction in shares outstanding by exchanging fewer shares for existing outstanding shares

As we mentioned earlier, with stock splits and stock dividends, the company's value is divided by a greater number of shares, which means the share price should fall; in other words, the shareholders' pie is divided into smaller pieces. If there is an optimal trading range, it might be that the share price does not decrease proportionally with the greater number of shares. This is easy to test. In a pioneering study, Professors Eugene Fama, Lawrence Fisher, Michael Jensen, and Richard Roll examined 940 stock splits in the United States from 1927 to 1959 and found no significant wealth change in the month of the split.[11] However, there were two important results. First, they found that companies that split their stock did so after exceptionally good stock market performance. Consistent with the optimal trading range idea, they split their stock to bring the stock price back to a "normal" range. Second, they found that two-thirds of the companies in their sample increased their aggregate dividend payments, and for those companies the shares performed better in the next year. In contrast, for the one-third of the sample of companies that kept their aggregate dividend constant, the share price underperformed the market.

Although the Fama, Fisher, Jensen and Roll study is quite dated, many researchers have updated these results, and the basic message is the same: In general, North American companies like to keep share prices in a "normal" trading range and use stock dividends and stock splits to keep within that range. Of course, there are exceptions, such as Berkshire Hathaway Class A shares; the company has never split these shares, which have had a value over $120,000 per share.

One observation is that if the price run-up that causes the split results in higher dividends, then the stock price continues to outperform the market; but if there is no change, then the share price slips back. This leads to the conclusion that it is not the stock split or dividend itself that is causing the price behavior, but rather investors' expectations about the company's future performance, and investors take the stock split as a signal that management agrees with this assessment.

---

[8] Waiving of the minimum price rule was necessary because so many stocks fell below the minimum during the market downturn.

[9] Because the prevalence of the reverse stock split has increased in the last decade, many will qualify a stock split as either a forward split (e.g., 2 for 1) or a reverse split (e.g., 1 for 2)

[10] Though the price of a stock in a forward split generally falls proportionately with the split factor (e.g., drops to half its pre-split value before the split), researchers do not find that a reverse stock split increases the stock's value proportionately. The most likely reason for this is that a reverse stock split is executed when the company's stock price has dropped due to financial distress and a reverse stock split does not alter investors' negative view of the company's prospects.

[11] E. Fama, L. Fisher, M. Jensen, and R. Roll, "The Adjustment of Stock Prices to New Information," *International Economic Review*, 10, no. 1 (Feb. 1969): 1–21.

Effect on . . .	Cash Dividend	Stock Dividend	Stock Split
Cash flow	Cash outflow for the total amount of dividends	No cash flow	No cash flow
Retained earnings	Reduce by the amount of the dividends	Reduce by the value of the shares distributed	No effect
Taxable income of investor	Dividend income	No taxable income	No taxable income

FINANCE in the News | Cure for Low Stock Quotes: A Reverse Split

The financial crisis of 2007–08 and the accompanying downturn in the stock market placed the stock of a number of companies in the "too low" range on their respective exchanges. This encouraged a number of companies to reverse split to try to raise their share prices.

Spate of companies giving it a try, often to keep their listing; lately, Progressive Gaming, Emrise, Revlon, and ExpressJet.

Reverse stock splits seem to be going forward for more and more companies—a sign that more share prices are dwindling into below-a-buck territory.

On Tuesday, Progressive Gaming International announced plans for a 1-for-8 reverse split of shares after the close of trading on Sept. 15, the same date Revlon Inc. has picked for the cosmetic company's 1-for-10 move. And Emrise Corp. aims to seek shareholder approval on Nov. 6, although it hasn't yet determined what ratio to apply for its reissuance.

Progressive, which provides products and services used in the gaming industry, said its action is designed to maintain compliance with regulatory agencies, its recent financing transactions and NASDAQ listing requirements. After the split, Progressive will have about 10.8 million shares issued and outstanding, including 2.1 million shares issuable under a convertible note debenture with International Game Technology, and about 800,000 shares issuable under option and warrant agreements. Progressive's stock currently trades at $0.72, near the bottom of its 52-week range of $0.63 to $5.68.

Emrise, which makes electronic devices and communications equipment for aerospace, defense, industrial, and communications applications, said its plan also is designed to maintain its New York Stock Exchange ARCA listing,

establish a share count more appropriate for the company's size, and help shed the negative image of a company whose stock trades below $1. Its shares currently trade around $0.50, down from a 52-week high of $1.04.

Revlon, which previously announced its reverse split for Class A and Class B common, also has some bigger restructuring plans. The company, which is controlled by billionaire Ronald Perelman, said it plans to reduce its debt by $170 million by repaying the $170 million MacAndrews & Forbes Senior Subordinated Term Loan, which matures next Aug. 1. The debt reduction would be achieved in two steps. In the first step, Revlon will use $63 million of the net proceeds from the previously announced July 2008 sale of its Bozzano business in Brazil to repay $63 million of the $170 million M&F Term Loan. The remaining $30 million of net cash proceeds from the sale of the Bozzano business will be used by the company for general corporate purposes.

In the second step Revlon intends to launch, as early as in the fourth quarter of 2008, a $107 million equity rights offering that would allow stockholders to purchase additional shares of Revlon Class A common stock. Revlon intends to use the net proceeds to fully repay the remaining balance of the MacAndrews & Forbes loan.

Revlon has been trading under $1 for most of the year, but in recent weeks has spurted to the $1.40 range.

Meanwhile, last week we reported that ExpressJet Holdings Inc. will ask its shareholders to approve a 1-for-10 reverse stock split at a special meeting scheduled for Oct. 1. Its goal is to remain on the Big Board.

Source: Stephen Taub, "Cure for Low Stock Quotes: A Reverse Split," CFO.com, September 3, 2008.

Share Repurchases

The final aspect of dividend policy we consider is that of share repurchases. A repurchase is an outright purchase of the company's own shares, either through open market purchases through a broker or through a tender offer in which shareholders can elect to sell their shares. To see the effect of a repurchase on share price, consider that the value of a share of stock is the present value of future cash flows. Instead of working just with per share valuation, we need to consider total dividends and total market value of a company. If the company is expected to pay a dividend next period of D_1, has a market value of the shares at the end of next period P_1, and has S_0 shares outstanding, the present value of a share of stock is:[12]

$$P_0 = \frac{\text{Present value of cash flows to shareholders}}{\text{Number of shares}}$$

or, using notation,

$$P_0 = \frac{\frac{D_1 + P_1}{(1 + r_e)}}{S_0} \qquad (16\text{-}1)$$

Let's consider an example of a company with a $50 million value in the next period with 1 million shares outstanding. Further, assume that it has an expected free cash flow of $5 million in the next period.[13] So its value with a $5 a share cash dividend is now $50:

$$P_0 = \frac{\frac{\$5 \text{ million} + \$50 \text{ million}}{(1 + 0.10)}}{1,000,000} = \$50 \text{ per share}$$

However, if instead the company used the $5 million to buy back 100,000 shares at $50 each at the end of the year, then next period the market value of the shares is:

$$P_1 = \frac{\$50 \text{ million}}{900,000} = \$55.55$$

Therefore, the $50 million is spread among fewer shares and so the value of a share increases.

What this example illustrates is that the company can use the $5 million in cash either to pay a cash dividend or repurchase shares, and that share repurchase is simply another form of payout policy. It is an alternative to a cash dividend where the objective is to increase the price per share rather than paying a dividend and forcing the shareholders to immediately pay tax on the dividend. In our example, the $5 million went to shareholders willing to sell their shares, and the value of the equity is then divided among fewer shares.

The advantage of a repurchase for the shareholder is that they can either hold their shares and receive a larger capital gain in the future or sell out now. What sometimes happens is that companies adopt a policy of large, infrequent share repurchase programs. By repurchasing instead of paying a dividend, investors understand that this is a limited commitment; repurchasing stock is unlike increasing a cash dividend, which is seen as a long-term commitment. For example, consider Ahold, an international food retailer based in the Netherlands. Ahold began a share buyback program in March 2011, intending to buy back €1 million of shares over a 12-month period through open market repurchases. Specifying how much they intend to spend and the time frame, the company is limiting its commitment and, hence, expectations by market participants.

---

[12] The market value of stock, or market capitalization, in period 0 is $P_0 \times S_0$, whereas the market value at the end of period 1 is $P_1 \times S_1$.

[13] You will recall from previous chapters that free cash flow is the cash flow generated by the company in excess of the capital expenditures necessary for all positive net present value investments.

A share repurchase program can act like a cash dividend by providing a payout of funds to the shareholders.[14] However, unlike a dividend, share repurchases may be motivated by several other factors, so it is easy to think that it is part of a payout policy when in fact it is not. Several other reasons may motivate share repurchases, including:

Motive for Repurchasing	Explanation
Remove cash without generating expectations for future distributions	Similar to special dividends, a large share repurchase can return cash to the shareholders without generating expectations about receiving similar distributions in the future.
Information or signaling effects	Companies' management may intend a repurchase of shares to signal to the market that it thinks the stock is undervalued.
Offsetting the exercise of executive stock options	Executive stock options are call options granted to senior executives. When exercised, they result in more shares outstanding. Repurchasing shares to meet these exercise requirements leaves the number of shares outstanding constant.
Leveraged recapitalizations	Debt is often raised and the proceeds used to repurchase shares to move the company back to its optimal capital structure.
Repurchase dissidents' shares	A substantial share repurchase program gives the dissidents an opportunity to sell their shares without depressing the market price, thereby removing an "overhang" of shares
Take the company private	A share repurchase to buy all the outstanding company's shares takes the company out of the public markets.

Companies can repurchase their shares by using brokers to purchase the shares in the open market. An **open market repurchase** generally extends over a period of time because a large, sudden purchase may increase the price of the shares.

Another method of repurchasing shares is through a **tender offer**, which is an offer made directly to shareholders to purchase the shares. The tender offer generally states the number of shares the company wants to purchase and describes the process used if more shares are tendered (that is, offered for sale to the company) than the company intends to purchase. The company can specify in the tender offer the price the company is willing to pay per share. If this is the case, the price must be higher than the current market value or there would be no incentive for shareholders to sell their shares.

As an alternative to the fixed-price tender offer, a company can specify a Dutch auction process, in which they specify a range of prices there are willing to pay. In a **Dutch auction tender offer**, shareholders submit bids for the price they are willing to sell their shares; the company will pay the minimum price necessary to acquire the stated number of shares. Suppose a company wants to repurchase 1 million shares, in the range $20 to $30, the current stock price is $18, and shareholders submit the following bids:

open market repurchase method of repurchasing shares in the market through brokers

tender offer offer made directly to shareholders to purchase the shares

Dutch auction tender offer method of repurchasing shares that requests shareholders to submit bids for the price they are willing to sell their shares, and then the company will pay the minimum price necessary to acquire the stated number of shares

Shareholder	Number of Shares Offered	Price
A	200,000	$20
B	300,000	$21
C	200,000	$21
D	100,000	$22
E	300,000	$23
F	200,000	$25

[14] However, in the U.S., repurchasing on a regular basis may be construed as a dividend by the Internal Revenue Service, resulting in a distribution taxable as dividends to shareholders.

The company must pay $23 per share to acquire the shares. Therefore, shareholders A, B, C, D, receive $23 for the shares that they offered. Shareholder E receives $23 for 200,000 of the shares, but the other 100,000 shares are not repurchased by the company. Shareholder F does not participate in the repurchase because he or she asked too much for the shares offered.

Why use a Dutch auction instead of simply stating the purchase price? Because by using the Dutch auction, the company learns the price necessary to get the 1 million shares; if the company had specified $22 they would not likely have gotten the full 1 million shares, and if the company had specified above $23, it would have overpaid.

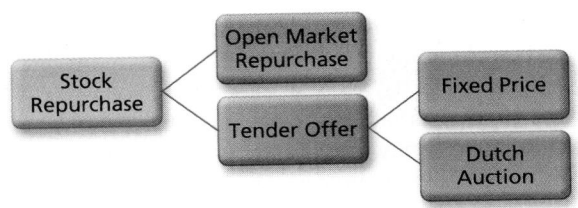

Concept Review Questions

1. Define four important dates that arise with respect to dividend payments.

2. Explain the similarities and differences among stock dividends, stock splits, and repurchases.

16.2   WHY DO COMPANIES PAY CASH DIVIDENDS?

We know that some companies choose to pay dividends, whereas others choose to not pay dividends, and this is true whether we are talking about U.S. companies or companies around the globe. So this leads us to the question, "Why do companies pay cash dividends?" Several explanations of why companies pay dividends include the following:

- Residual cash flow
- Agency costs
- "Bird in the hand"
- Signaling
- Taxes

Residual Theory

One interpretation of the dividend is that the dividend is simply the residual that remains after the company has taken care of all its investment requirements. Therefore, a company only pays a dividend when there is cash flow remaining after funding all positive net present value investment projects. This is the **residual theory of dividends**.[15] In this

residual theory of dividends theory that the dividends paid out should be the residual cash flow that remains after the company has taken care of all of its investment requirements

---

[15] This theory is based, in large part, on Miller and Modigliani: M. Miller and F. Modigliani, "Dividend Policy, Growth, and the Valuation of Shares," *Journal of Business*, 34 (1961): 411–433.

theory, dividends do not affect the value of the company; what *does* affect the value are the investment projects the company undertakes.

If we believe that a company is value maximizing and therefore always accepts the optimal amount of investment, the investing decision is independent of the company's dividend policy. This assumes that companies can always raise the necessary capital to undertake all profitable investments (that is, positive net present value [NPV] projects), so they are not financially constrained.[16] If companies are financially constrained, this irrelevance of dividend policy falls apart. This is because the company must issue new equity to fund dividends.

Let's take an extreme situation where transactions costs are very high and the company cannot raise new capital. In this case, the payment of the cash dividend reduces the amount of money available to invest and causes the company to forgo positive NPV projects. The value of the company falls because the company is not creating value by accepting positive NPV projects.

Faced with significant costs attached to raising new money, cash-poor growth companies have little incentive to pay a dividend because all they are doing is compounding their financing problems. Similarly, companies that face volatile earnings, so that their cash fluctuates significantly from year to year, will attempt to "store" cash from one period to another. As a result, companies maintain their dividend payments conservatively and at a level that minimizes the need to constantly access the capital markets.

The residual theory is consistent with the pecking order explanation of capital structure, which is that managers prefer internal financing to external financing, and the preference of debt to raising new equity through a stock issue. Therefore, the payment of dividends is a distribution of internal equity, which is generally viewed as the preferred source of financing for many companies, to shareholders.[17]

The bottom line of the residual theory is that companies will pay dividends if they do not need additional capital and they have cash flows remaining after all profitable investment projects. If dividends are paid based on residual cash flows, we should see profitable, mature companies paying dividends, but also observe that high-growth companies do not.

Agency Costs

Many researchers have observed that the announcement of a dividend increase is generally associated with the increase in the share price. One possible explanation of this, based on agency theory, is that investors prefer a company to distribute funds rather than possibly invest these in negative net present value projects.

Many investors are very wary of senior management because management tends to view the company as *their* company and not as belonging to the shareowners. The fear is that senior management may waste corporate resources by overinvesting in poor (that is, negative NPV) projects because it is not "their" money but the shareowners'. This view is supported by the very fact that senior management follows a pecking order when raising capital. It means, for example, that shareholders would prefer that cash be disgorged as a dividend and then have management explain why it needs the money back by filing a prospectus and issuing new common shares. From an agency perspective, paying a large dividend and forcing the company to justify future expenditures creates value by controlling management. However, although an agency perspective justifies the stock market's reaction to dividends, it cannot explain the dividend smoothing phenomena.

---

[16] Positive net present value projects are those capital investments that are expected to add value to the business entity.

[17] Based on the pecking order theory, discussed in the previous chapter, internally generated funds are the preferred source of financing.

When Buying Another Company Is Not a Good Idea | ETHICS

Imation is a developer and marketer of media for many different types of electronic devices. In 2011, it made a number of acquisitions that really makes one wonder what the company's management was thinking when they made some of these decisions. How do we know that they made some bad acquisitions? The accounting tells quite a bit.

When a company acquires another company, the purchase price, adjusted for the debts of the acquired company, are allocated among the acquired company's assets based on the fair market value of the acquired company's assets at the time of the acquisition. Anything left over (that is, the purchase price less the fair market of the acquired firm's assets) is recorded as Goodwill, which is listed in a balance sheet below a company's other intangible assets. In other words, Goodwill is how much a company overpaid for an acquisition. Under current accounting rules, a company must revalue this Goodwill each year and write down this Goodwill if it becomes "impaired"; that is, if the value declines.

Imation acquired BeCompliant Corporation in February of 2011, citing potential synergies, with $1.6 million recorded as Goodwill. Within weeks of recording this Goodwill, Imation decided that the entire Goodwill from this acquisition is impaired. In other words, not only do they not know why they overpaid, but by writing off the entire Goodwill from this acquisition, they are claiming that the acquisition price was $1.6 million too much.

In fact, as of March 31, 2011, Imation had Goodwill of $153.9 million and accumulated impairment losses of $153.9 million. In other words, it had written off as impaired all its Goodwill, including that from the BeCompliant acquisition.

Imation is not the only company that creates and then writes off Goodwill as impaired. This case, like others, raises the issue of whether the company resources are being used in shareholders' best interest or are they being wasted?

Source: Imation Form 10-Q filed with the Securities and Exchange Commission May 5, 2011, for the three months ended March 31, 2011.

The "Bird in the Hand" Argument

It is possible that some investors perceive companies that pay dividends to be less risky than companies that do not. It then seems to follow that investors perceive companies that do not pay a cash dividend as riskier; if so, this would result in a higher cost of equity capital and, hence, a lower stock price.

This idea of the **bird in the hand argument** is that a "bird in the hand" (that is, a cash dividend) is worth more than "two in the bush" (twice as much in capital gains).[18] This theory captures the intuition that dividends are more stable than capital gains and, as a result, more highly valued. It is commonly accepted that utilities are less risky than high-tech companies. Further, if you look back at the dividend yields of such companies, you will see that low-risk utilities do indeed have high-dividend yields, and high-risk tech companies rarely pay a dividend. So intuitively, the dividends-are-better argument seems to make sense. In addition, in practice, the share prices of high-dividend-paying stocks have tended to perform as well or better than stocks with low-dividend payouts. In other words, investors need not sacrifice growth for income.

> **bird in the hand argument** notion that a cash dividend is worth more than an equivalent capital gain

It is likely that the dividend yield indicates the risk of the company, and that companies that pay large amounts of dividends are less risky than nondividend-paying companies. Yet, a company that changes its dividend cannot alter the underlying risk of the company; this comes from its underlying operations. In this sense, the dividend should reflect the company's operations through the residual value of dividends, and the company cannot change these underlying operational characteristics by merely changing the dividend.

Signaling

In practice, capital markets are rife with information asymmetries, where some parties know more than others. Despite the main focus of securities regulation, that aims to make all material facts public information, agents in the capital market often have widely different views about a company's future prospects and value.

[18] M. Gordon, "Optimal Investment and Financing Policy," *Journal of Finance*, May 1963.

For example, management usually knows more than external investors, so the company has to have some way of signaling to investors that their press releases can be believed because investors tend to view such information with a great deal of skepticism. One way of doing this is to increase the dividend only when the company believes that it will not have to cut it in the future. The fact that paying a cash dividend reduces the funds available to the company means that management will only do so when they think that their internal funds are increasing and are enough to support the dividend payment.[19] Otherwise, it will impose more transactions costs on the company in having to raise more funds in the future. This signaling model explains why share prices tend to increase on unexpected dividend initiations or increases. In both cases the dividend increase indicates good news because it suggests that management believes it can support the dividend from future earnings.

This signaling model indicates that dividend changes have information content, which provides an important role for dividend policy. The signaling model, when combined with the residual theory of dividends, provides the major theories that explain actual dividend policy. Whereas we can explain the type of companies that should pay a dividend and the general level of the payout using the residual theory of dividends, we can use the signaling model to explain how these dividends should be paid as a slowly adapting dividend per share.[20]

Taxes

Describing how taxes affect financial policy is very difficult because different classes of investors have different tax brackets, so with taxes the general rule is that "one size does not fit all."[21] Corporations pay little or no tax on dividend income if it is from another corporation. This is because of the dividends received deduction, which provides a deduction for 70, 80, or 100 percent of dividends received.[22] As a result, there is a preference by corporate owners of equity for dividend income. For individuals, on the other hand, the preference for dividend versus capital gains income depends on whether the dividends are considered qualifying dividends and whether the price appreciation is short or long term.[23]

The current tax system, with individual investors, corporations, and institutional investors facing different tax rates on dividends, gives rise to **tax clienteles**. High-dividend yield stocks are often referred to as "widows and orphans stocks" because they are often held by lower tax rate investors (often retirees), who rely on the dividends for income. In contrast, low-dividend yield stocks tend to be held by younger investors who have longer-term horizons and are intent on holding for a long time to defer taxes. So, although the payment of a dividend may not have an impact on the general level of share prices, it will be an important influence on the type of investors that a company attracts. The general advice that flows from this is not to drastically change dividend policy because it upsets the existing ownership base.

tax clienteles different preferences for receiving dividend income as a result of investors having different tax situations

Concept Review Questions

1. Explain what is meant by a residual dividend policy.
2. Briefly describe the notion of a tax clientele and how this may affect dividend policies.
3. Explain the "bird in the hand" theory of dividends.

[19] It also means that it is expensive for poor-quality firms to mimic this cash dividend payment.
[20] As modeled by Lintner.
[21] And we should note that this discussion of taxes is not meant as tax advice. Not only do taxes differ by type of entity and jurisdiction, but also tax laws in all countries change frequently enough to make understanding taxes difficult. We are only scratching the surface of taxes and do not intend our discussion to be tax advice.
[22] The percentage of the deduction depends on the ownership interest and extent of control.
[23] Therefore it is obvious that M&M's homemade dividend argument is negated by the existence of differential tax rates, as well as by the existence of transactions costs.

16.3 DIVIDEND POLICY IN PRACTICE

Evaluating Dividend Policies

The dividends of most companies follow some form of pattern, though these patterns may be in terms of a steady payout ratio, a constant dividend per share, or a constantly growing dividend per share. There is no requirement that a company follow a consistent pattern in its dividend, but many shareholders acquire stock with the expectation of dividends following a pattern.

Merck, KGaA

"The objective of our dividend policy is to distribute, on a long-term average, a total dividend equivalent to 30–40% of the Group profit after tax."

Dividend, Merck, Merck Group, www.merckgroup.com

Royal Dutch Shell PLC

"When setting the dividend, the Board of Directors looks at a range of factors, including the macro environment, the current balance sheet and future investment plans. In addition, we may choose to return cash to shareholders through share buybacks, subject to the capital requirements of Shell. It is our intention that dividends will be declared and paid quarterly."

Dividend policy, Shell.com

Barclays Bank PLC

"Barclays declares and pays dividends on a quarterly basis. There are three equal payments in June, September and December each year and a final variable payment in March. We intend our dividend policy to be progressive."

Dividend, group.barclays.com

WWE

"The Company's revised quarterly dividend was set based on targeted ranges for payout ratios and liquidity levels," stated George Barrios, Chief Financial Officer. "Aligning payouts with our current level of earnings and cash flow will significantly enhance our financial flexibility, support our current growth initiatives, and enable us to take advantage of important strategic opportunities in a quickly changing media landscape, including executing on our 'New WWE' initiative."

Press release, WWE, April 28, 2011

We can classify many companies' dividends as falling into one of these patterns:

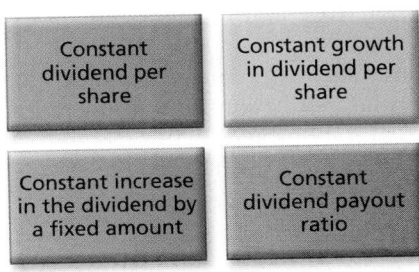

TABLE 16-1 Dividend Ratios

Dividend per share	$\dfrac{\text{Dividend per share}}{\text{Number of shares outstanding}}$	Dollar amount of dividend per share of stock
Dividend yield	$\dfrac{\text{Dividend per share}}{\text{Price per share}}$	Return on stock in the form of a cash dividend
Dividend payout	$\dfrac{\text{Dividend per share}}{\text{Earnings per share}}$	Proportion of earnings paid out in the form of cash dividends
Dividend coverage	$\dfrac{\text{Earnings per share}}{\text{Dividends per share}}$	Number of times a dividend could be paid based on earnings

dividend per share amount of a cash dividend paid by a company

retention ratio proportion of earnings retained in a given fiscal period

dividend coverage ratio ratio of earnings to dividends for a fiscal period

Some companies actually discuss their dividend policy, but in most cases investors are left to infer the policy by looking at what the company has paid in the past. We can evaluate dividend information by using measures of dividend payment, including the ratios that we introduced in an earlier chapter on financial analysis. We summarize these ratios in Table 16-1.

The **dividend per share** is the amount of cash paid per share of stock and is based on the declaration of the company's board of directors. The dividend yield, which is the ratio of the dividend per share to the price per share, depends on both the dividend per share and the share price. We should take care when interpreting a dividend yield. For example, a higher dividend yield may mean that the company is profitable and is confident that it can maintain an increasing dividend; however, a higher dividend yield could also mean that the company's share price is depressed. Similarly, interpreting a lower dividend yield can be difficult because it could mean a low level of dividends, but it could also mean that the price of the stock has risen.

The **dividend payout ratio** is the proportion of earnings that are paid out in a given fiscal period. This is the complement of the **retention ratio**: The greater the dividend payout, the lower the retention ratio. The inverse of the dividend payout is the **dividend coverage ratio**. Like all coverage ratios, this is the number of times the company could pay something, and in this case the "something" is dividends. If the dividend payout is greater than 1 (or the dividend coverage less than 1), this means that the company is paying this period's dividends, at least in part, from retained earnings.

Consider General Electric (GE). We provide the dividend ratios for GE in Figure 16-4 for the fiscal years 1990 through 2010. Looking at the dividend per share, dividends appeared to grow at a constant rate, as evidenced by the curvature of the plot of dividends per share up through 2008. From 1990 through 2008, GE's dividend per share grew at a rate of 12.048 percent. Notice, though, that this pattern is broken in 2009 and 2010. Looking at the dividend payout, as we show in the second graph of this figure, the dividend payout is within the bounds of 33.9 percent to 44.4 percent. Even in 2009 and 2010, when the dividend per share fell, the payout was still within these bounds. The dividend yield, which we show in the third graph in this figure, does not exhibit any particular pattern.

If a company has low variability in its earnings, and earnings grow at a constant rate, it may appear that the company has both a constant payout and a constant-growing dividend period share. This is the case with Johnson & Johnson (JNJ), which we show in Figure 16-5. JNJ's dividend per share increases at a constant rate of 13.633 percent each year, and its payout is within the bounds of 34 to 44 percent.

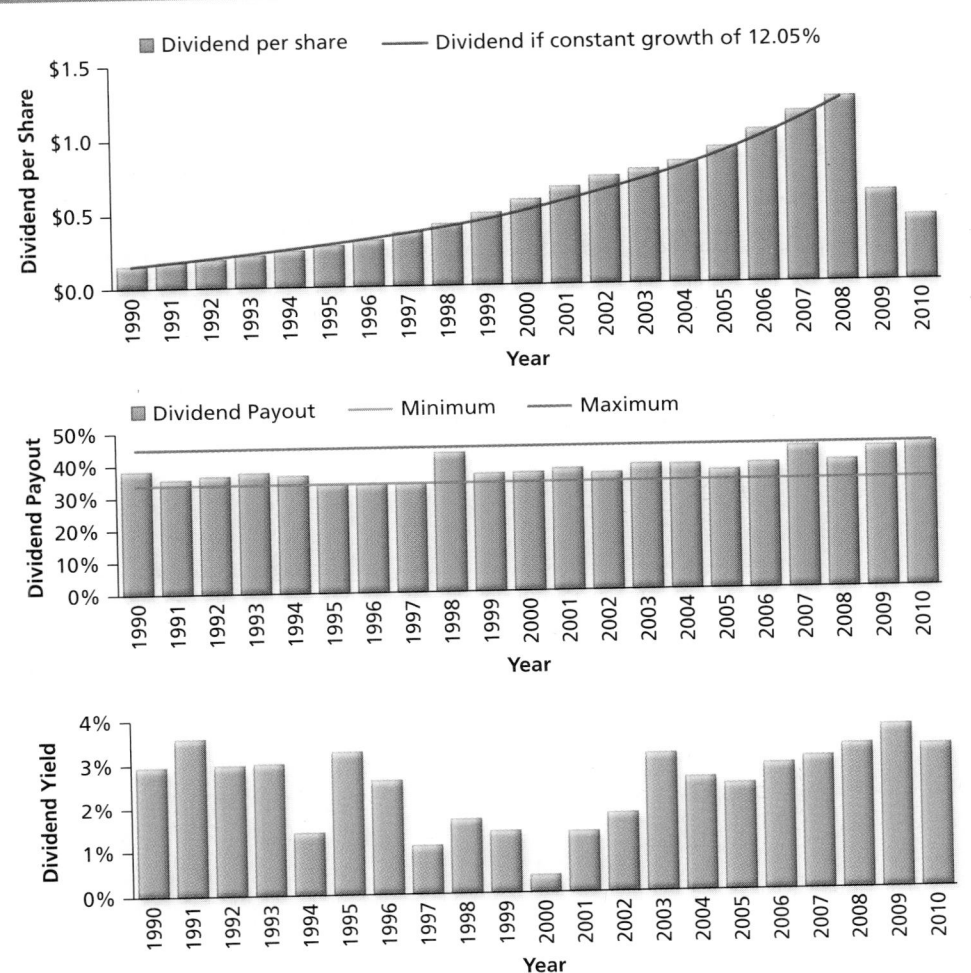

FIGURE 16-4 **General Electric's Dividend**

Source of data: *General Electric's Investor Relations.*

What Do We Know About Dividends?

Observation 1: Dividends follow earnings

We observe that many companies do not vary their dividend each period based on their performance, but rather smooth the dividends over time so that they grow from year to year at a constant rate. Consider Hershey Foods, a producer of confectionary products, based in the U.S. The earnings per share of Hershey vary from year to year, as we show in Figure 16-6, but the dividends grow a steady pace, generally around 8.56 percent per year.

The standard way of explaining observed dividend behavior is to suggest that companies smooth their dividends over time as they move toward a new target level of dividends. The original work was by John Lintner, who suggested using the partial adjustment model that we specify in Equation 16-2:[24]

$$\Delta D_t = \alpha(D_t^* - D_{t-1}) \tag{16-2}$$

[24] J. Lintner, "Distribution of Incomes of Corporations among Dividends, Retained Earnings and Taxes," *American Economic Review,* 46 (1956): 97–113.

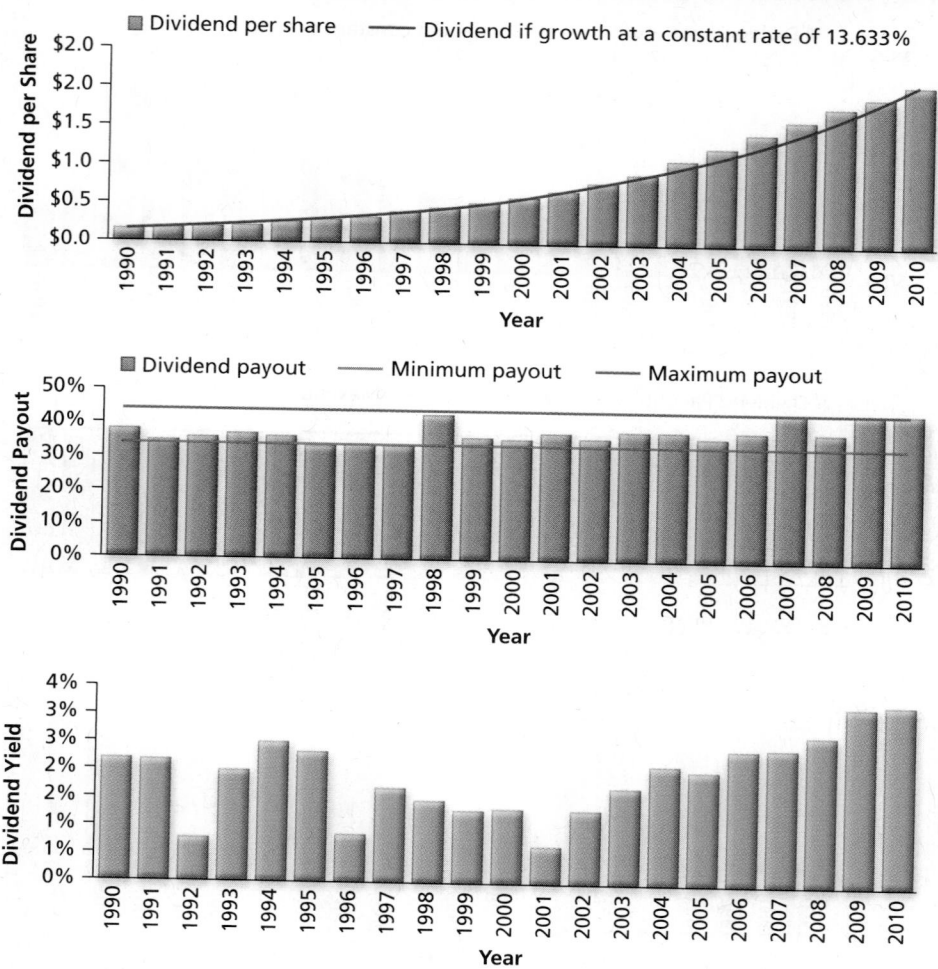

FIGURE 16-5 Johnson & Johnson's Dividend

Source of data: *Johnson & Johnson's Investor Relations.*

This equation simply says that the change in the dividend over any period (that is, ΔD_t) is equal to an adjustment factor (α) multiplied by the difference between the target dividend for the period (D_t^*) and the dividend for the prior period (D_{t-1}). If the company adjusts immediately to the target dividend, then the adjustment coefficient (α) is equal to 1.0, and the cash dividend is always optimal. If it doesn't adjust at all, then the dividend is constant, and α is equal to zero.

In this model, the target dividend (D_t^*) is a function of the company's optimal payout rate of the company's underlying earnings (E_t), which leads to the following model in Equation 16-3:

$$D_t = a + (1 - b)D_{t-1} + cE_1 \tag{16-3}$$

Therefore, current dividends are a function of the previous period's dividends, as well as current earnings.[25]

---

[25] Lintner estimated the coefficient on lagged dividends to be 0.70 indicating an adjustment speed (b) coefficient of 0.30. He also estimated the coefficient on current earnings (c) of 0.15. When the adjustment to the target dividend is complete, Linter's estimates imply an optimal payout ratio of 50 percent (that is, $b \div c$), which is slightly higher than the average payout of 40 percent for U.S companies.

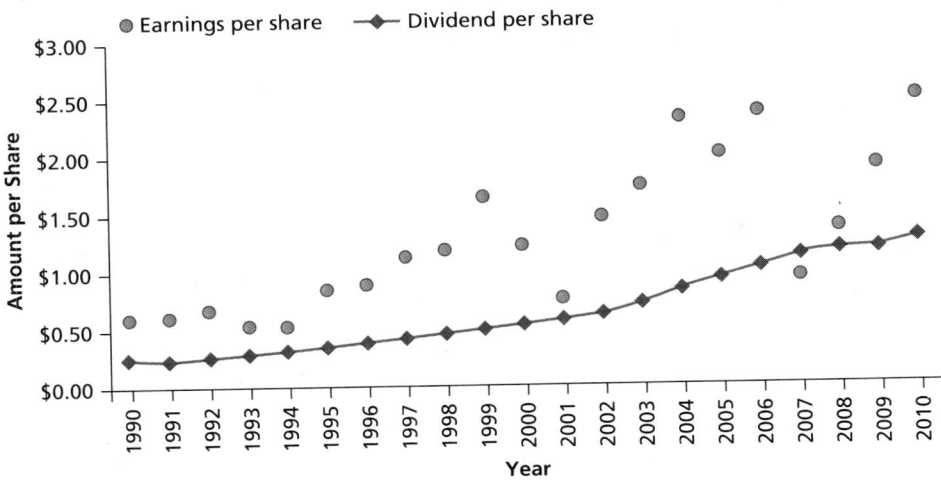

FIGURE 16-6 Hershey Foods Dividends and Earnings

Source of data: *Hershey Foods 10-K, various years.*

<h2>Transparency in Dividends | LESSONS LEARNED</h2>

Most companies that pay dividends follow a policy that resembles a constant dividend, a constantly growing dividend, or a constant dividend payout. Because the policy is rarely stated, we generally infer the policy by looking at the pattern of dividends over time for a company.

Progressive Corporation, an insurance company, follows a transparent approach to dividends, paying dividends that are based on the company's operating performance for the year. This policy was instituted in February of 2006, effective for 2007.[26] Its formula for dividends per share, DPS, is:[27]

$$DPS = \frac{\text{After-tax underwriting income} + \text{Target percentage} + \text{Gain share factor}}{\text{Common shares outstanding at year end}}$$

where the target percentage is specified by the board of directors each year, and the gain-share factor depends on the company's performance relative to profit and growth objectives. The company provides the detailed calculations pertaining to the income and gain-share calculations on its website.

This policy is a departure from traditional policies, but may foreshadow dividend policies to come.

Observation 2: Dividends are sticky

We observe that companies are reluctant to cut dividends when earnings decline, perhaps because of the anticipated market reaction to a dividend cut. Consider Motorola's suspension of its dividend on February 3, 2009. Like many companies that cut their dividend, Motorola's announcement of the dividend cut accompanied its announcement of losses and other negative company news. There was apparently some anticipation of this negative news just before the announcement and then a further drop in share price once the announcement was made, as we show in Figure 16-7.

[26] Charles Carlson, "A Progressive Dividend Policy," *Forbes,* May 19, 2006.

[27] Progressive Corporation Investor Relations, "The Progressive Corporation Annual Variable Dividend Policy," investors.progressive.com/dividend.aspx, accessed December 7, 2011.

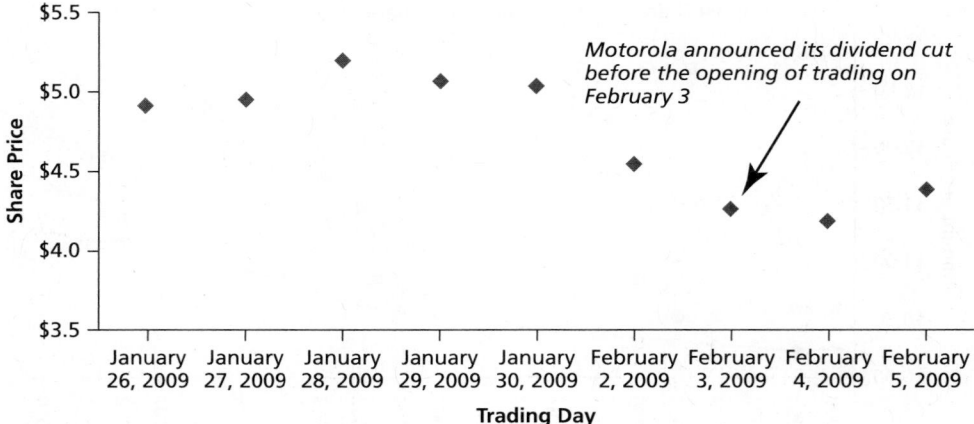

FIGURE 16-7 **Price Reaction to Motorola's Dividend Suspension February 3, 2009**

Source of stock price data: *Yahoo! Finance.*

It would seem reasonable that if a company is cutting its dividend to pursue growth opportunities, investors would reward, rather than punish, the company through its share price. However, even in the case of "growth cuts," the stock market reaction is still negative to news of a dividend cut.[28]

The stigma regarding dividend cuts has been engrained in the memory of many, yet there seems to be a change recently (that is, post the 2007–2008 financial crisis) in how investors perceive dividend cuts. This is likely because many of these cuts were seen by investors as necessitated by the challenging economic and business climate that accompanied the crisis, but also, some of the cuts were required because companies accepted bailout money during the crisis. For example, Discover Financial accepted funds through the Troubled Asset Relief Program in March of 2009 and the following week cut its dividend from 6 cents per share to 2 cents per share. The market response was initially a drop its stock price, but then the stock recovered to its precut levels.

The Evidence

A few of the things that we learn from surveys of financial executives and other observations about dividend policy include:

1. Earnings influence dividend policy.[29]
2. There is a different view of dividend policy between companies in financial and nonfinancial firms. Managers at financial firms are more likely to have explicit payout ratio policies than nonfinancial firms and consider stability of dividends to be more important than their counterparts at nonfinancial firms. Further, financial firms are more likely to be concerned about how their dividend policy compares with that of competitors.[30]
3. There is an aversion to cutting dividends in some countries, although legal and ownership differences may make it more palatable for companies to cut dividends.

[28] See, for example, C. Ghosh and Randall Woolridge, "Stock-Market Reaction to Growth-Induced Dividend Cuts: Are Investors Myopic?" *Managerial and Decision Economics,* 10, no. 1 (March 1989): 25–35.

[29] Alon Brav, John R. Graham, Campbell R. Harvey, and Roni Michaely, "Payout Policy in the 21st Century," *Journal of Financial Economics,* 77, no. 3 (2005): 483–527, and Theodore Veit, "Factors Influencing Dividend Policy Decisions of Nasdaq Firms," *Financial Review,* August 1, 2001.

[30] H. Kent Baker, Samir Sadi, and Shantanu Dutta, "How Managers of Financial versus Non-Financial Firms View Dividends: The Canadian Evidence," working paper, 2008, and Veit (2001).

For example, German companies do not appear to be concerned about the effect of dividend cuts, which may be due to the significant ownership and influence of large banking institutions in German companies.[31]

4. Dividend payouts are influenced by the holdings of top executives of the company, and those companies with executives owning more stock are more likely to increase dividends.[32]

5. Both U.S. and non-U.S. companies' executives view repurchases as attractive not only because of the flexibility repurchases provide, but also the effect on earnings per share.[33] However, repurchases are more common in the U.S. than in other countries.[34]

What we learn about the explanations for dividend policy support the idea that dividends are residual, that dividends are related to earnings, and that repurchases are an alternative to cash dividends.

Concept Review Questions

1. Why are companies hesitant about reducing dividends when earnings fall?

2. What does the evidence imply about how companies manage their dividend payments?

SUMMARY

- Corporations may distribute funds to owners by paying dividends or buying back shares in a share repurchase. Corporations may also provide shareholders with additional shares either through a stock dividend or a stock split, but both of these transactions are merely slicing the equity "pie" into more pieces.

- Investors tend to react favorably to dividend initiations and increases and react unfavorably to dividend cuts or omissions. We gauge investors' reaction to these dividend decisions by looking at the stock price movements associated with dividend policy changes.

- There are various theories and explanations for why companies pay dividends, including the residual theory (companies pay dividends when they have no profitable investment opportunities), agency theory (by paying dividends, companies have to go to the capital market more often, and are therefore monitored more often), the "bird in the hand" explanation (investors prefer the certain cash flow of dividends to the uncertain price appreciation), signaling (by committing to paying more dividends, the company's management is signaling that the company will be able to sustain this dividend into the future), and the dividend tax clientele explanation (some investors prefer dividends because of their tax situation, whereas others do not).

- We observe that companies that do pay dividends do so on a regular basis, either with dividends increasing at a relatively constant rate or a dividend payout rate that is consistent over time. However, in tough economic periods, some companies do cut their dividend and wait to restore their dividend until the economy—and company—has recovered.

---

[31] Francois Degeorge and Ernst Maug, "Corporate Finance in Europe: A Survey," Swiss Finance Institute Research Paper No. 06-17. 2006.

[32] Jeffrey R. Brown, Nellie Liang, and Scott Weisbenner, "Executive Financial Incentives and Payout Policy: Firm Responses to the 2003 Dividend Tax Cut," *Journal of Finance,* 62, no. 4 (August 2007): 1935–1965.

[33] D. Bens, V. Nagar, D. J. Skinner, and M. H. F. Wong, 2004. "Employee Stock Options, EPS Dilution, and Stock Repurchases," *Journal of Accounting and Economics,* 36, no. 1–3 (December 2003): 51–90; and Franck Bancel, Usha R. Mittoo, and Nalinaksha Bhattacharyya, "Cross-country Determinants of Payout Policy: A Survey of European Firms," Working paper, 2005.

[34] Degeorge and Maug.

FORMULAS/EQUATIONS

$$(16\text{-}1) \quad P_0 = \frac{\dfrac{D_1 + P_1}{(1 + r_e)}}{S_0}$$

$$(16\text{-}2) \quad \Delta D_t = \alpha(D_t^* - D_{t-1})$$

$$(16\text{-}3) \quad D_t = a + (1 - b)D_{t-1} + cE_1$$

QUESTIONS AND PROBLEMS

Multiple Choice

1. When is the ex-dividend date if the holder of record date is Thursday, April 14, 2011?
   A. April 12   B. April 13   C. April 15   D. April 16

2. Which of following most likely has a *negative* impact on the share price?
   A. Unexpected dividend increase
   B. Unexpected dividend initiation
   C. Unexpected dividend decrease

3. Which of the following statements regarding motivation for a stock repurchase is most likely *incorrect*?
   A. Companies could be privatized using stock repurchases.
   B. Stock repurchases are sometimes used to buy out dissident shareholders.
   C. Investors consider a company's stock overvalued when a stock repurchase occurs.
   D. Companies can use stock repurchases to move capital structure back to some optimum level.

4. Which of the following is the *correct* ordering in time of the dates associated with a dividend?
   A. Ex-dividend date; declaration date; payable date; date of record
   B. Declaration date, ex-dividend date, date of record, payment date
   C. Declaration date, date of record, ex-dividend date, payment date
   D. Ex-dividend date, declaration date, date of record, payment date

5. If a stock has a current share price of $20, and next year's dividend is expected to be $2, the share price expected one year from today if the cost of equity is 10 percent is *closest* to:
   A. $18.   B. $20.   C. $22.   D. $24.

6. Which of the following will *not* result in an increase in the number of shares outstanding?
   A. A stock split
   B. A stock dividend
   C. A reverse stock split

7. In the partial adjustment model for dividends, a company that immediately adjusts its dividend to the target dividend has an adjustment factor equal to:
   A. –1.   B. 0.   C. 1.

8. A company that has net income of $3 million and pays dividends of $0.6 million has a dividend payout ratio *closest* to:
   A. 1.8 percent.   B. 2 percent.   C. 20 percent.   D. 500 percent.

9. If a stock has a current value of $20 per share and the company pays a dividend of $2 per share, the stock's dividend yield is *closest* to:
   A. 10 percent.   B. 20 percent.   C. 10 times.   D. 20 times.

10. Which theory best describes an investor who prefers receiving a cash dividend rather than relying on the growth of share prices to provide a return on the investment?
    A. Residual theory
    B. Signaling theory
    C. Tax clientele theory
    D. Bird in the hand theory

Practice Questions and Problems

16.1 Distributions to Shareholders

11. Who decides how much and when cash dividends are paid?

12. What is the significance of the date of record?

13. If an investor buys stock on the ex-dividend date, does this investor receive that forthcoming dividend? Explain your answer.

14. Briefly describe the difference between a stock dividend and a cash dividend plus a DRIP.

15. What is the difference to the investor between a cash dividend and a share repurchase?

16. Why might a corporation pay a stock dividend?

17. Why might a corporation pay a stock split?

18. Distinguish between a stock split and a reverse stock split.

19. For each of the following, find the equivalent stock split or stock dividend:
    A. 100 percent stock dividend
    B. 2:1 stock split
    C. 125 percent stock dividend
    D. 1.5:1 stock split

20. Complete the table for each of the following companies:

Company	Number of Shares Outstanding before Split of Dividend	Stock Split or Stock Dividend	Number of Shares Outstanding after Split or Dividend
A	1 million	125% stock dividend	
B	5 million	2:1 stock split	
C	12 million	3:1 stock split	
D	200,000	1.25:1 stock split	
E	10 million	1:3 reverse stock split	

21. Suppose a company's stock is currently trading for $120 per share. The company's board of directors believes that the stock is more attractive if it trades in the range of $25–$45 per share. The board is considering a stock split, a stock dividend, or a stock repurchase. What strategy would you recommend to the board to get the stock price in a more the attractive range?

16.2 Explanations for Paying Cash Dividends

22. Briefly state the underlying idea of the "bird in the hand" argument.

23. Briefly state the tax clientele argument.

24. Describe possible reactions from the market of the following dividend policy changes:

    A. Dividend initiation

    B. Dividend increase

    C. Dividend cut

    D. Dividend suspension

25. List the main reasons why companies repurchase shares.

26. List and describe briefly the methods companies may use to repurchase shares of their own stock.

27. How many new shares does a company have to issue if it is expected to pay out a dividend of $2.50 per share? Currently the company has an operating cash flow of $350 million, and a promising project is available that costs $200 million. There are 100 million shares outstanding with a current price of $40 per share.

28. Coral Gables Inc. (CGI) follows a strict residual dividend policy. The company will have profits of $500,000 this year. After screening all available investment projects, CGI has decided to take three out of the ten projects, and those three will cost $410,000.

    A. What dividends will CGI pay to its shareholders this year?

    B. Its current equity market value is $5,000,500 and the current market price of its shares is $45.60. What is the shortcoming of this policy?

29. What is the change in share price if a company spends its extra $600,000 to buy back stocks at $31 per share instead of paying $600,000 in cash dividends? The next-period market value of equity is $2,500,000, and 100,000 shares are currently outstanding, with a cost of equity of 15 percent.

30. Edmund Fitzgerald, a shipping tycoon, expected his company to earn $1,000,000 per year forever, with no growth. Given a cost of capital of 10 percent, the value of the company is $10,000,000. Edmund identified a new project, which costs $1,000,000 but would earn 11 percent per year forever. To invest in this project, Edmund cancelled this year's dividend. Because he is investing in a positive NPV project, he expected his stock to rise. However, it fell dramatically. Edmund asked his investment banker to explain what happened. Does this mean that investors do not like positive NPV projects?

16.3 Dividend Policy in Practice

31. Explain why companies do not simply pay out dividends as a portion of their profits. What do most companies do in terms of dividend policy?

32. The current stock price of Abacus Industries is $50. For the last 20 years, the company has paid an annual dividend of $5. On June 26, the company announced a dividend of $6 payable on September 10 to shareholders of record at the close of business on September 1.

    A. What do you expect to happen to the price of Abacus stock on June 26?

    B. If the shareholders of Abacus pay no taxes on dividends, what do you expect to happen to the price of Abacus on the ex-dividend date?

    C. If the shareholders of Abacus pay taxes on dividends, do you expect the stock price reaction on the ex-dividend date to be greater, the same, or less than in (B)?

33. The Mortal Coil Company (MCC) currently has cash flow from operations of $10 million, has capital expenditures of $8 million, and pays a dividend of $2 million (all are perpetuities). The company has no growth prospects, and debt- and shareholders expect an annual return of 5 percent. The total number of shares outstanding is 1,000. For the following investors, describe how they can achieve their desired cash flow patterns and the value of their strategy (future value) at the end of the second year. Each investor owns 10 percent of the company, and there are no taxes or transaction costs.

    A. Marie lives in a very high cost city and would like to receive a dividend of $400,000 at the end of Year 1. She needs this money to finance her lifestyle.

B. Charlie has found another investment opportunity that will pay him 15 percent and would also like to receive $400,000 at the end of Year 1.

C. Frank is very frugal and would rather not receive dividends at the end of Year 1.

34. Consider the data for Abbott Labs:

Date	Dividends	Date	Dividends	Date	Dividends
4/11/1983	$0.01562	1/11/1993	$0.07500	7/11/2002	$0.23500
7/11/1983	$0.01562	4/8/1993	$0.08500	10/10/2002	$0.23500
10/7/1983	$0.01562	7/9/1993	$0.08500	1/13/2003	$0.23500
1/9/1984	$0.01562	10/8/1993	$0.08500	4/11/2003	$0.24500
4/9/1984	$0.01875	1/10/1994	$0.08500	7/11/2003	$0.24500
7/9/1984	$0.01875	4/11/1994	$0.09500	10/10/2003	$0.24500
10/9/1984	$0.01875	7/11/1994	$0.09500	1/13/2004	$0.24500
1/9/1985	$0.01875	10/7/1994	$0.09500	4/13/2004	$0.26000
4/9/1985	$0.02187	1/9/1995	$0.09500	5/3/2004	$2.84600
7/9/1985	$0.02187	4/7/1995	$0.10500	7/13/2004	$0.26000
10/8/1985	$0.02187	7/12/1995	$0.10500	10/13/2004	$0.26000
1/9/1986	$0.02187	10/11/1995	$0.10500	1/12/2005	$0.26000
4/9/1986	$0.02625	1/10/1996	$0.10500	4/13/2005	$0.27500
7/9/1986	$0.02625	4/11/1996	$0.12000	7/13/2005	$0.27500
10/8/1986	$0.02625	7/11/1996	$0.12000	10/12/2005	$0.27500
1/9/1987	$0.02625	10/10/1996	$0.12000	1/11/2006	$0.27500
4/9/1987	$0.03125	1/13/1997	$0.12000	4/11/2006	$0.29500
7/9/1987	$0.03125	2/21/1997	$0.13500	7/12/2006	$0.29500
1/11/1988	$0.03125	4/11/1997	$0.13500	10/11/2006	$0.29500
4/11/1988	$0.03750	7/11/1997	$0.13500	1/10/2007	$0.29500
7/11/1988	$0.03750	10/10/1997	$0.13500	4/11/2007	$0.32500
10/7/1988	$0.03750	1/13/1998	$0.13500	7/11/2007	$0.32500
1/9/1989	$0.03750	4/13/1998	$0.15000	10/11/2007	$0.32500
4/10/1989	$0.04375	7/13/1998	$0.15000	1/11/2008	$0.32500
7/10/1989	$0.04375	10/13/1998	$0.15000	4/11/2008	$0.36000
10/6/1989	$0.04375	1/13/1999	$0.15000	7/11/2008	$0.36000
1/8/1990	$0.04375	4/13/1999	$0.17000	10/10/2008	$0.36000
4/6/1990	$0.05250	7/13/1999	$0.17000	1/13/2009	$0.36000
7/9/1990	$0.05250	10/13/1999	$0.17000	4/13/2009	$0.40000
10/9/1990	$0.05250	1/12/2000	$0.17000	7/13/2009	$0.40000
1/9/1991	$0.05250	4/12/2000	$0.19000	10/13/2009	$0.40000
4/9/1991	$0.06250	7/12/2000	$0.19000	1/13/2010	$0.40000
7/9/1991	$0.06250	10/11/2000	$0.19000	4/13/2010	$0.44000
10/8/1991	$0.06250	1/10/2001	$0.19000	7/13/2010	$0.44000
1/9/1992	$0.06250	4/10/2001	$0.21000	10/13/2010	$0.44000
4/9/1992	$0.07500	7/11/2001	$0.21000	1/12/2011	$0.44000
7/9/1992	$0.07500	10/11/2001	$0.21000	4/13/2011	$0.48000
10/8/1992	$0.07500	1/11/2002	$0.21000	7/13/2011	$0.48000
		4/11/2002	$0.23500	10/12/2011	$0.48000

A. Plot these dividends over time in terms of dividend per share and dividend payout.

B. How would you characterize the dividend policy of Abbott Labs in terms of quarterly and annual dividends?

Cases

Case 16.1 Safe-n-Secure

The Safe-n-Secure Company (SNS) is a dividend-paying company; its current dividend yield is 8 percent. Current stock price is $100. The company has paid the same dividend for the last 15 years, and it is not expected to change. Alice believes that the company is an excellent investment opportunity for her clients and has been contacting them. Here are some of the responses she has received:

> Client A: "I need income, I don't trust capital gains—they aren't real, just paper. I'm not interested in this stock; I'd rather just have a bond and get a nice fixed income."

> Client B: "Who cares about dividends? I pay more taxes on the dividends so I want capital gains where I can control the timing of the tax bill. The dividend is too high, and I will pay too much tax so I'm not interested in the stock."

1. Which investor's statement is consistent with the "bird in the hand" argument about dividends?

2. What tax issues is Client B concerned about? What dividend policy would Client B prefer?

Case 16.2 Cautious George Company

The Cautious George Company (CGC) is considering its dividend policy. Currently CGC pays no dividends, has cash flows from operations of $10 million per year (perpetual), and needs $8 million for capital expenditures. The company has no debt, and there is no tax. The company has 2 million shares outstanding, which are currently trading at $50 per share. George, the majority owner of CGC (owns 60 percent), would like to take $20 million of cash out of the company to fund his various charities. You have been hired by CGC to consider different alternatives.

1. George could sell stock to raise the $20 million he requires.
   A. What are the advantages and disadvantages of this strategy?
   B. What do you expect to be the effect on the value of CGC and George's control?

2. CGC could pay a dividend so that George will receive $20 million.
   A. Describe how the company can issue stock to create the dividend.
   B. What is the effect on the value of CGC?
   C. What is the effect on George's level of control of the company?

PART 8

FINANCIAL MANAGEMENT: CAPSTONE

A capstone is the last or finishing stone in a structure, such as an archway. Part 8 is our capstone for the book, because this part gives you an opportunity to apply what you've learned throughout the book. There are several types of decisions that financial managers make that involve both investing and financing, and we cover several of these in Part 8. These decisions include risk management, working capital management, leasing, and mergers and acquisitions. These decisions require the use of the financial math tools, as well as an understanding of accounting relationships, taxes, financial instruments, and investment decision-making.

CHAPTER 17

FINANCIAL PLANNING, FORECASTING, AND RISK MANAGEMENT

A business begins with a plan. If you are just getting started with a business, you will need to construct a business plan, which you use to convince banks and others that they should entrust you with their money and that you will be able to produce the return that they expect.

According to the U.S. Small Business Administration, the key elements to a good business plan are:

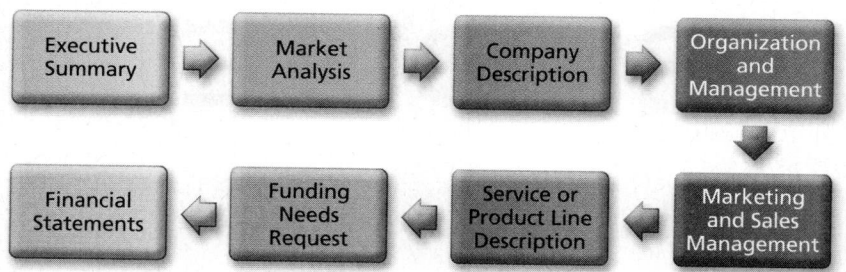

Keep in mind, however, that much of this involves forecasting: What will the market for the product be next year, the year after, and beyond? How will things be managed in the future? Will the service or product be the same next year as this year? What about 4 or 5 years from today? What funds are needed now, and what funds will be needed in the future—and when? What will the financial statements look like based on all this if we look 3, 4, or 5 years into the future?

Common mistakes in business plans include the following:

1. **No plan for progress.** How is the company going to grow? Expand into new markets? Expand the product line? Expand floor space or retail outlets?

2. **Lack of market and industry research.** What is the company's competitive or comparative advantage? How long will it take competitors to imitate your great ideas or products? Are there any changes in regulations coming your way?

3. **Unrealistic assumptions.** You need to make some assumptions, but are these the right ones? Have you considered what happens if the economy changes? Have you considered what happens if styles, demographics, or consumer preferences change?

4. **Incomplete financial statements.** Most business plans require current and forecasted financial statements that are accurate, detailed, and realistic.

5. **Poor design or presentation of the plan.** Bad grammar, redundancy, or a plan that is simply too long can hurt chances of financing.

Sources: *U.S. Small Business Administration,* Essential Elements of a Good Business Plan, *www.sba.gov; Jason Del Rey, "Top Business Plan Mistakes," Inc.com, March 26, 2010; Tim Berry, "Seven Cringe-Worthy Business Plan Mistakes," smallbusiness.foxbusiness.com, June 17, 2011.*

Learning Outcomes

After reading this chapter, you should be able to:

LO 17.1 Examine how budgets and planning operate within a business entity.

LO 17.2 Apply the percentage of sales method of forecasting financial accounts for a business entity.

LO 17.3 Explain how risk is managed within a business entity.

Chapter Preview Finance is forward looking: making decisions today based on forecasts about the future. These forecasts are essential to planning capital investment decisions and financing needs. Financial planning is a challenging part of any financial manager's job. Planning involves not only estimating revenues out into the future, but also projecting costs, anticipating the actions of competitors, forecasting the availability of funds (both short and long term), and analyzing the economy and its effect on the company.

17.1 · THE ROLE OF FINANCIAL PLANNING IN A BUSINESS ENTITY

Financial planning is a dynamic system that includes forecasting revenues, forecasting expenses, planning capital expenditures, managing funding needs, and managing risk. Planning not only incorporates predictions, but also requires examining possible outcomes ranging from a worst-case to a best-case scenario. Financial planning is an ongoing process, with projections adjusted with additional information.

Financial planning begins with the company's strategy, as developed by the company's board of directors or senior management. A company's **strategy** is the direction that the entity intends on moving in the long term. This strategy is the primary focus of the planning process and is used as a benchmark for evaluating performance. Once the company's strategy is clarified, the financial managers solicit the expectations of the sales staff with respect to the quantity and sales price of the company's goods or services. These expectations may be as detailed as being specific as to customers, geographical regions, or products; may be conditional on the economic environment; and may be accompanied by an assessment of the available risks and opportunities. These expectations are then translated into an operating plan, which may be in the form of pro forma statements or a budget.

Probably the most important goal of financial planning is to predict cash flows as accurately as possible. Financial managers can use the budget, generally accompanied by pro forma financial statements, to estimate short-term and long-term financing needs. The estimates that indicate a need for funds help the financial manager prepare for lines of credit, revolving credit agreements, or long-term sources of funds, such as bonds. The estimates that indicate a surplus of funds help the financial manager decide what to do with these funds: Invest them for the short term? Pay down debt? Repurchase stock? Pay a dividend?

Though looking at past trends may be useful, the recent financial crisis has led many CFOs and financial managers to think differently about budgeting and planning because a reliance on historical trends did not work well in understanding and forecasting during this 2007–2008 crisis. An important step in planning is to compare what actually occurs with what is forecasted or budgeted. This comparison, focusing on the deviations, allows introspection into the assumptions of the forecasts, the quality of the estimates, and the relation between the results and the company's strategy.

financial planning dynamic system that includes forecasting revenues, forecasting expenses, planning capital expenditures, managing funding needs, and managing risk

strategy the direction that the entity intends on moving in the long term

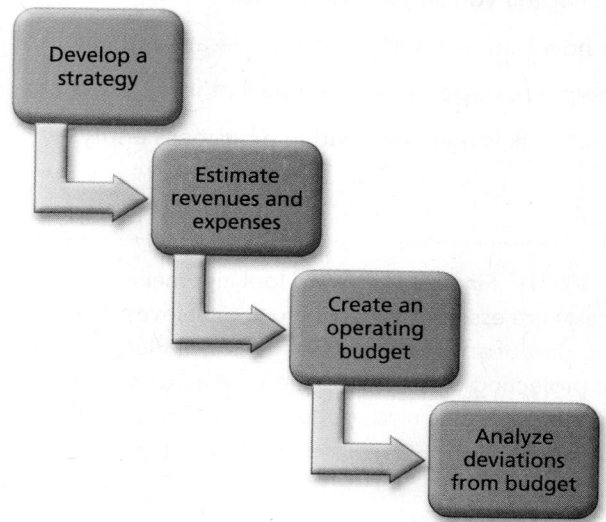

17.2   METHODS OF FORECASTING

Forecasting a business entity's cash flows generally starts with where the company is today, and then predicts how things may change. Financial decision making is, almost always, with uncertainty. Although we may see clearly where a company has been in terms of evaluating and comparing financial ratios and common size statements, making predictions into the future is always with risk.

Consider the case of forecasting the revenues of Wal-Mart Stores. If we look at this company's revenues from 1970 through 2006, which we show in Figure 17-1, we see a steady growth in revenues, but the growth rate has slowed; the growth rate from 1970 to 1971 was 76 percent, for example, whereas the growth rate from 2005 to 2006 was 10 percent. So what should we predict for 2007? 2008? 2009?

If we use a straight line to predict sales, as we show in Figure 17-2, we would predict revenues that are less than the actual revenue:

Year	Actual	Predicted	Difference
2007	$373,821	$236,847	$136,974
2008	$401,087	$245,237	$155,850
2009	$405,046	$253,627	$151,419

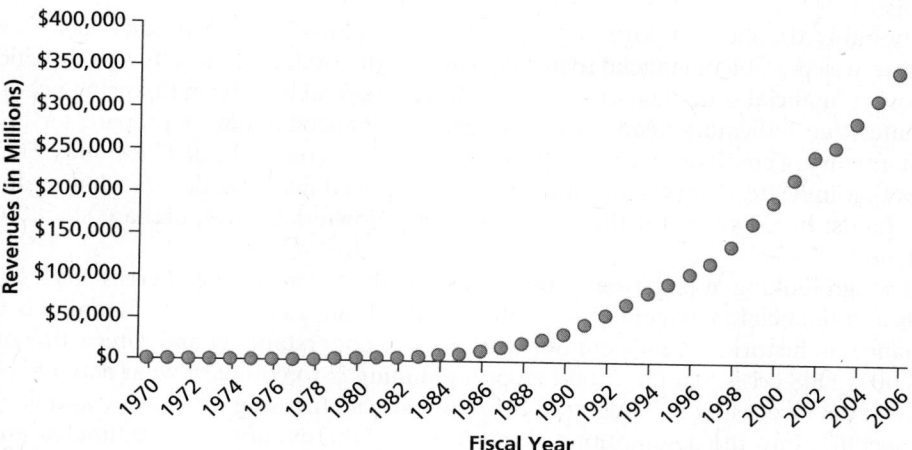

FIGURE 17-1 Wal-Mart Stores Revenues, Fiscal Year 1970 Through 2006

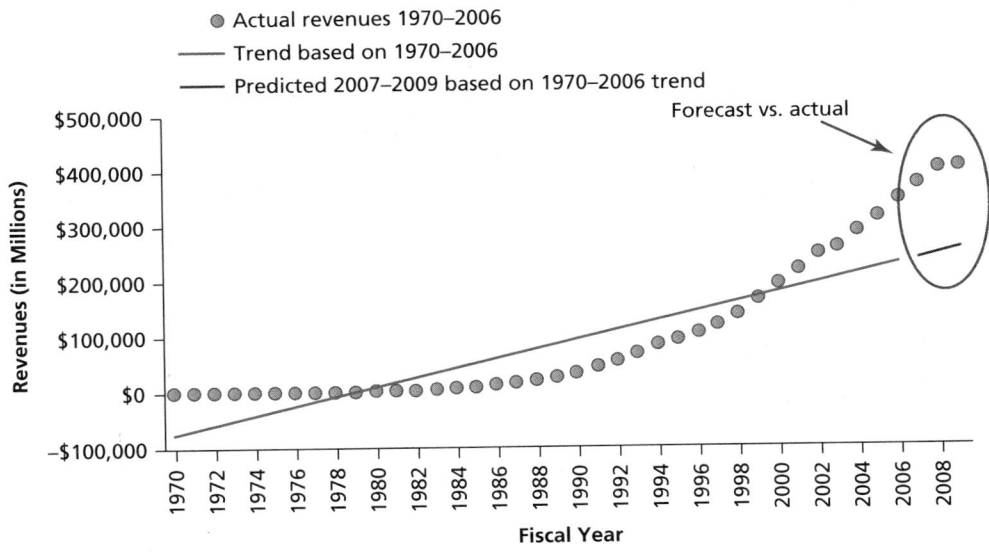

FIGURE 17-2 Wal-Mart Stores Revenues, Fiscal Year 1970 Through 2009

As you can see in Figure 17-2, the actual revenues in the 2007, 2008, and 2009 fiscal years deviated from these, following a path above the trend line.

Using a straight line to predict revenues for a company assumes that the growth of the company's revenues has slowed. Although it is true that Wal-Mart's sales growth has declined over time, the straight-line increase in sales does not depict Wal-Mart's growth. The actual growth in the period of 2004–2006 is 10 percent per year, but the growth slowed to 8 percent in 2007, 7 percent in 2008, and only 1 percent in 2009, as we show in Figure 17-3. What these predictions haven't captured is (1) the force of the economy on revenues, and (2) the natural slowing of growth as a company and its market matures.

FORECASTING WITH SPREADSHEETS

Spreadsheets make it easy to estimate a trend line and to make forecasts. Consider the revenues of Costco for the 10 years 1999 through 2008:

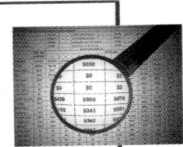

	A	B
1	*Year*	*Revenues*
2	2000	$31,620.72
3	2001	$34,137.02
4	2002	$37,993.09
5	2003	$41,692.70
6	2004	$47,145.71
7	2005	$51,862.07
8	2006	$58,963.18
9	2007	$63,087.60
10	2008	$70,977.48
11	2009	$69,889.00

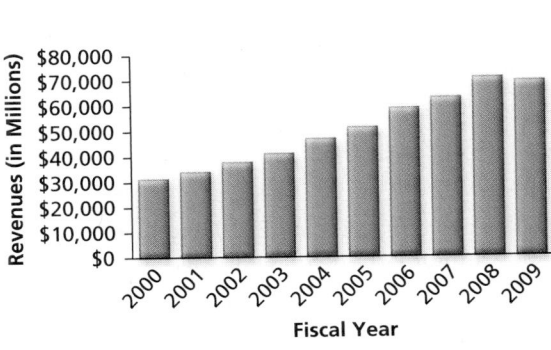

Using Microsoft Excel's Data Analysis group of functions, available in the Data ribbon, we can estimate the line by regressing the revenues on the year:

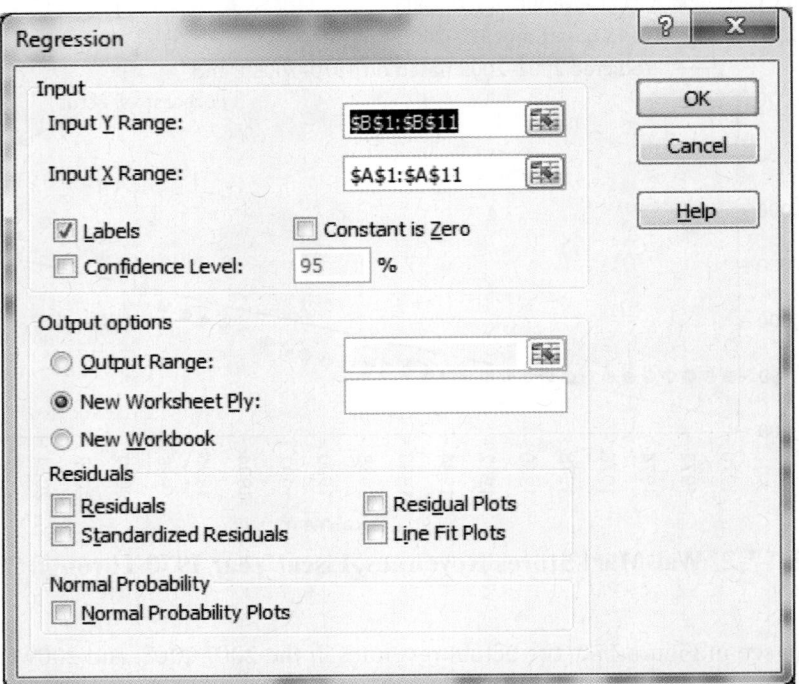

The results, with a few items removed for simplicity:

Regression Statistics

Multiple R	0.9915
R Square	0.9831
Adjusted R Square	0.9810
Standard Error	2001.0680
Observations	10

ANOVA

	df	SS	MS	F	Significance F
Regression	1	1864010526	1864010526	465.5053	0.000000
Residual	8	32034184.6	4004273.08		
Total	9	1896044711			

	Coefficients	Standard Error	t Stat	P-value
Intercept	24539.59	441612.518	−21.461	0.000
Year	4753.322	220.310	21.576	0.000

The intercept is $24,539.59 million with a slope of 4,753.322 million; that is, the average change in revenues each year is $4,753.322 million.

We calculate the predicted 2010 and 2011 revenues by plugging in the time (11 or 12 for the eleventh or twelfth year) for the Year:

2010 Revenues = $24,539.59 million + (4,753.322 million × 11) = $59,961.55 million
2011 Revenues = $24,539.59 million + (4,753.322 million × 12) = $81,579.45 million

The actual revenues for 2010 and 2011, respectively, are $59,961.55 and $81,579.45 million. This means that we overestimated 2010 revenues by $625.13 million and underestimated 2011 revenues by $5,414.55.

There are other methods of forecasting, but at least you get the basic idea: We can use a simple forecasting model to predict a financial account.

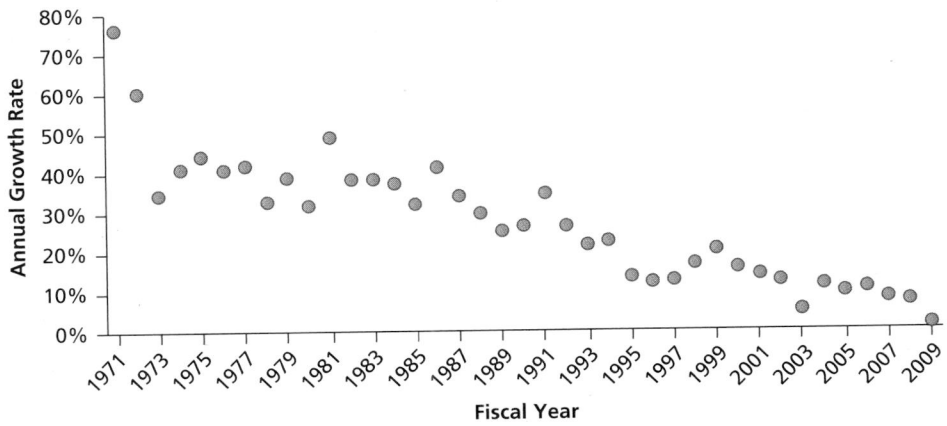

FIGURE 17-3 **Wal-Mart's Annual Growth Rate, Fiscal Years 1971 Through 2009**

When we look at Wal-Mart's year-to-year growth rates, as we show in Figure 17-3, we see that the growth rate has fallen over time. This is consistent with a company passing through the life cycle of an industry: In the 1970s, Wal-Mart was innovative in the discount retail business and in its distribution system. Slowly, however, other companies entered this market and were able to take market share from Wal-Mart. This is the natural progression that we see in most industries over time: Profitability and growth in the early stages invites competition and imitation, which reduces growth and profitability in the industry. The revenues in the latter fiscal years may also be influenced by the slowdown in the economy, resulting from the 2007–2008 financial crisis. Once the recession ended, the question remained of what type of growth the company will experience in 2010, 2011, and beyond.

Looking forward, what is Wal-Mart's sustainable growth? **Sustainable growth** is the feasible growth rate of the company considering what the company earns and how much it plows back into the company. Based on this idea, an estimate of sustainable growth is:

> **sustainable growth** expected growth rate of a business entity considering the entity's return on equity and its earnings retention

$$\text{Sustainable growth rate} = \text{Return on equity} \times \text{Proportion of earnings retained} \quad (17\text{-}1)$$

For Wal-Mart, in the 2009 fiscal year, the return on equity was 20.26 percent, and the proportion of earnings paid out in the form of dividends was 29.4 percent. Therefore the estimate of the sustainable growth going forward from 2009 is $0.2026 \times 0.706 = 14.3$ percent, which would be similar to the pre-recession growth rate.[1] If we apply that growth to the earnings of Wal-Mart for 2010, we would expect earnings of $14,449 million $\times$ 1.143 = $16,515 million, which is close to the $16,389 million actual earnings for fiscal year 2010.

The lesson learned in this exercise is that extrapolating trends from the past into the future must be done with caution. Economic and market forces can easily cause a break in any trend, and any extrapolation must be done considering the company and the industry in which it operates.

The Percentage of Sales Method

The most important input in financial forecasting is an accurate sales forecast because sales growth drives a company's financing requirements. As a result, financial forecasting requires input from most of the divisional managers of the company, but particularly the marketing managers. This will become evident when we consider the most basic forecasting technique: the **percentage of sales method.** We illustrate the process of the percentage of sales method in Figure 17-4.

> **percentage of sales method** approach to forecasting balance sheet and income statement accounts that uses a fixed percentage of sales from the previous period to determine amounts in a future period

---

[1] Performing the same calculation using fiscal year 2008 data, we estimate sustainable growth at 15.6 percent.

ETHICS | Forecasting and Bubbles

One of the challenges of forecasting is that most forecasting incorporates some elements of intuition, experience, and a bit of luck. Even in cases in which sophisticated computer modeling is used to develop a forecast, there is always someone who must create the model and provide the inputs to the model. In other words, forecasting involves the human element. This opens the door for personal biases. For example, if someone is making a case for the investment in a particular capital project, the sales forecast may be "stretched" to make this project look attractive, even if it would not be under most realistic scenarios.

Aside from intentional "stretches," we know that bubbles exist in financial markets. If we simply look at past trends and apply judgment with respect to whether a trend will continue, could bubbles in prices really exist? Most market participants understand that a continued run-up of prices cannot continue forever. So how can bubbles, such as the Internet bubble in the 1990s or the housing bubble leading up to 2007, really continue if decision makers should know that these run-ups cannot continue indefinitely? In both the Internet bubble and the housing bubble, there were many signs that the run-ups could not continue. Bubble theory tells us that a recent past of increasing values can actually confuse or confound the decision maker, leading to forecasting that assumes the past run-up can continue.[2]

The Basics

The percent of sales method is based on the idea that many types of assets and liabilities move along with sales. We can see this when we look at the relation between a company's sales revenue and its assets and liabilities.

A company's CFO and treasurer are concerned with the financial policy variables, which include common equity (whether the company has to issue equity or not), long-term funds (equity plus long-term debt), the capital budget, and the company's total external financing requirement.

external financing requirements (EFR) funds that a company must raise using borrowing or selling equity interests

To illustrate how a plan is constructed, we will assume that the treasurer is interested in total **external financing requirements (EFR)**. Let's look at a simple balance sheet for a hypothetical company, the Dozer Construction Company, and see what this means.

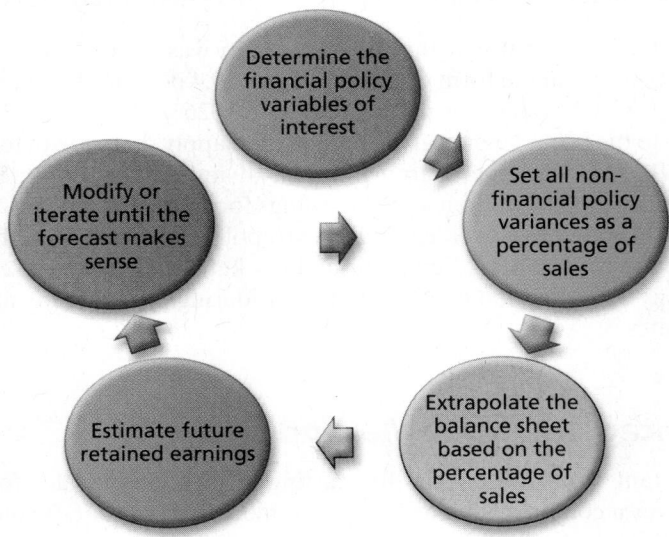

FIGURE 17-4 Financial Forecasting Using the Percentage of Sales Method

[2] Robert J. Shiller, "Bubbles, Human Judgment, and Expert Opinion," *Financial Analyst Journal,* 58, no. 3 (May/June 2002): 18–26.

TABLE 17-1 Balance Sheet for Dozer Construction Company

(in millions)

Cash	$5	Accruals	$5
Securities	10	Payables	5
Receivables	10	Bank debt	20
Inventory	25	Current liabilities	$30
Current assets	50	Long-term debt	40
Net fixed assets	100	Common equity	80
Total assets	$150	Total liabilities and equity	$150

As we see in Table 17-1, this company has total assets of $150 million that have been financed with $80 million of common equity, $40 million of long-term debt, and $20 million of short-term debt. Taken together, these are referred to as invested capital because both the common shareholders and the creditors—the bank and long-term debt investors—have made a decision to invest in the company. In contrast, we often refer to the accruals and payables as **spontaneous liabilities** because as long as the company is in business (i.e., a going concern), it will naturally generate payables and accruals: Suppliers will ship goods on credit, and workers will work and collect their wages at the end of the month. In this sense, when we generate a 5-year financial forecast, we often assume that these accounts vary with sales, and only the financial policy variables will initially be kept constant.[3]

The next step is to convert the nonpolicy variables to a percentage of sales. For the sake of our example, we will assume that sales are $120 million and that the percentages that result from this sales level are reasonable for the future. In practice, we would look at the ratios over the previous 5 years or so, factor in current business conditions for the company (e.g., new orders), and assess what values would be reasonable going forward.

The third step is to extrapolate the balance sheet based on the sales forecast by using these percentages of sales. For our purposes, we will assume that sales are forecast to increase by 10 percent a year. The result is the naive initial forecast that we show in Table 17-2.

The top line is the sales forecast, with sales going from the current level of $120 to $132 million one year out, and then $145 million, and finally $160 million. Then we express all the asset accounts and the spontaneous liabilities as a percentage of sales because these are the nonpolicy variables and are extrapolated based on the sales forecast. Take cash, for example: It is $5 million or 4.2 percent of the $120 million sales level, so based on a 10 percent sales growth forecast, cash increases by 10 percent to $5.50, $6.10, and $6.70 million. The values of the other assets are also increased by 10 percent per year, resulting in a forecast value of $199.60 million for total assets.

On the liability side, as discussed, we assume that spontaneous liabilities increase at the rate of sales, so we get a forecasted value of $13.40 million. Subtracting this figure from the total assets forecast of $199.60 million, we end up with the required invested capital figure of $186.20 million. However, recall that we assumed no change in the amount of invested capital, leaving only $140 million in invested capital, which suggests a shortfall of $46.20 million. This shortfall is the balance sheet *plug*, which we have label as the EFR.[4] Notice that this is a cumulative, not an annual, requirement—that is, the company needs to raise $46.20 million in total financing over the next 3 years.

spontaneous liabilities
accruals and payables that arise during the normal course of business

---

[3] This is not to say that these amounts are ignored: Some financially constrained companies will decide to delay paying bills to meet their financial targets. This means that payables will increase more than proportionally with sales.

[4] Remember, the balance sheet has to balance.

TABLE 17-2 Initial Forecast for Dozer Construction Company

(Dollar amounts in millions)	Year 0	%	Year 1	Year 2	Year 3
Sales	$120		$132	$145	$160
Cash	$5	4.2	$5.5	$6.1	$6.7
Marketable securities	10	8.3	11.0	12.1	13.3
Accounts receivable	10	8.3	11.0	12.1	13.3
Inventory	25	20.8	27.5	30.3	33.3
Net fixed assets	100	83.3	110.0	121.0	133.0
Total assets	$150	125.0	$165.0	$181.6	$199.6
Accruals	5	4.2	5.5	6.1	6.7
Accounts payable	5	4.2	5.5	6.1	6.7
Short-term debt	20	16.7	20.0	20.0	20.0
Long-term debt	40	33.3	40.0	40.0	40.0
Equity	80	66.7	80.0	80.0	80.0
Total liabilities and equity	$150	125.0	$151.0	$152.2	$153.4
Cumulative (EFR)			$14.0	$29.4	$46.2

Adding Complexity to the Simple Forecast

The forecast that we made assuming that any shortfall will result in external financing, without regard to the company's capital structure policy and availability of credit, is extremely naive or simple. For one thing, it ignores any new equity that the company will generate simply by retaining some of its future earnings. For another, it assumes that the existing debt will still be there in 3 years' time. In practice, some of it may need to be refinanced, or the bank may refuse to renew the short-term loans. However, we'll assume that all the debt can be renewed and focus on the retained earnings. To do this, we need to look at the company's income statement in Table 17-3.

The company has a cost structure of 60 percent variable costs and fixed costs of $31 million. So at the current sales level of $120 million, it has EBIT of $17 million, from which it subtracts $5 million in interest on the $60 million of debt and pays 50 percent income taxes or $6 million. As a result, it has net income of $6 million and a net profit margin of 5 percent. However, it pays out 50 percent of its earnings as dividends, so only $3 million

TABLE 17-3 Income Statement for Dozer Construction Company

(in millions)	
Sales	$120
Gross operating profit	48
Fixed costs	31
EBIT	$17
Interest	5
Taxes (50%)	6
Net income	$6
Dividends	$3

TABLE 17-4 First Revision of Forecast for Dozer Construction Company

(Dollar amounts in millions)	Year 0		Year 1	Year 2	Year 3
Sales	$120	%	$132	$145	$160
Cash	$5	4.2	$5.5	$6.1	$6.7
Marketable securities	10	8.3	11.0	12.1	13.3
Accounts receivable	10	8.3	11.0	12.1	13.3
Inventory	25	20.8	27.5	30.3	33.3
Net fixed assets	100	83.3	110.0	121.0	133.0
Total assets	$150	125.0	$165.0	$181.6	$199.6
Accruals	$5	4.2	$5.5	$6.1	$6.7
Accounts payable	5	4.2	5.5	6.1	6.7
Short-term debt	20	16.7	20.0	20.0	20.0
Long-term debt	40	33.3	40.0	40.0	40.0
Equity	80	66.7	83.3	86.9	90.9
Total liabilities and equity	$150	125.0	$154.3	$159.1	$164.3
Cumulative (EFR)			$10.7	$22.5	$35.3

is retained within the company. What is important is that the company's retained earnings as a percentage of sales are its net profit margin multiplied by the proportion of earnings retained, which equals 2.5 percent (i.e., 5% × 0.50) in this example.

If we use this information to revise our earlier simple forecast, we add 2.5 percent of sales each year to retained earnings, which leaves us with our first revision to our naive forecast, which we depict in Table 17-4.

The only difference between this revision and the initial one is that we have taken into account the future retained earnings of 2.5 percent per dollar of sales, which has reduced the EFR by $10.90 million. However, this forecast is still relatively naive and does not make use of skills in financial analysis. We can improve on this naive forecast. To do this, we will go through all the nonfinancial policy assumptions to see whether we can improve on them.

First, we have to recognize that the percentage of sales technique automatically imposes a very strict relationship between assets and sales. For example, when we assume that cash is 4.2 percent of sales, we assume that it will remain so, whether sales are $10 million or $1 billion. Graphically, we are forcing the relationship between cash and sales to be a straight line going through the origin. A more reasonable assumption would be that there are economies of scale to managing cash and that the *marginal* impact of sales growth is less than the average percentage of sales of 4.2 percent. For example, the true relationship at a sales level of $120 million might be $3 million plus 2.5 percent of sales so that the marginal impact of sales growth is only 2.5 percent of sales. In Figure 17-5 we depict the differences in the cash forecasts that arise by changing this assumption.

We can see how cash varies with sales by analyzing the statistical relation between previous sales levels and cash balances. Consider International Business Machines (IBM) and Wal-Mart Stores. If we graph IBM's revenues along with the balance of cash and cash equivalents, as we show in Figure 17-5, Panel A, you can see that the trends of both the cash balance and revenues are similar, though the cash balance is more variable than sales. You see a similar pattern with Wal-Mart, which we show in Panel B of Figure 17-5. If you extend this analysis to other companies, you will see a similar pattern: Cash balances and other operating accounts (such as inventory) tend to move along with revenues.

For now, we will skip marketable securities and consider accounts receivable, addressing the issue of whether assuming a strict percentage of sales is reasonable. In this case, it

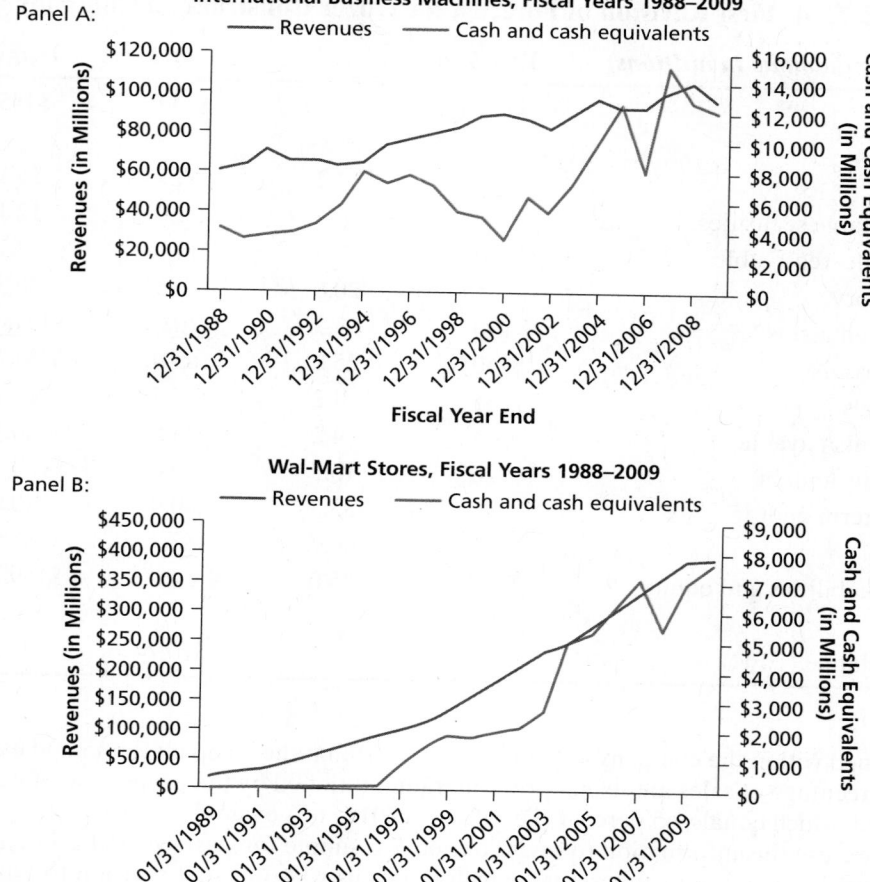

FIGURE 17-5 Revenues and Cash Balances
Source of data: *Companies' 10-K filings at www.sec.gov.*

may be. Previously, when considering the investment in accounts receivable, we showed that the number of days of sales in outstanding receivables (DSO), or the average collection period, gave essentially the same information as the receivables turnover ratio. As long as the company maintains the same credit policy along with the same mix between credit and cash sales, and the economy doesn't crash, then assuming a constant percentage of sales is reasonable. However, if the company anticipates changing its credit policy and granting more lenient credit terms, then the percentage of sales tied up in receivables will increase, as it will if the proportion of credit to cash sales increases. Both of these events might happen in an economic downturn, where the company might use more lenient credit as a way of maintaining its level of sales. Understanding the macroeconomic environment that generates the sales forecast will help the financial manager refine the percentage of sales tied up in receivables. For our purposes, we assume that no slowdown is expected during the forecast period and that estimating receivables at 8.3 percent of sales is reasonable.

We treat inventory in a similar manner to receivables. As long as the inventory turnover ratio is expected to be constant, inventory will increase in line with sales. However, the same qualifications apply in terms of the macroeconomic environment. If a downturn is anticipated, the company might plan to increase the level of inventory to bolster sales by offering immediate delivery. In contrast, the company might believe that it can reduce inventory, either because some of it is obsolete or because it plans to adopt new inventory management systems, such as "just-in-time" inventory planning. However, consistent with our treatment of receivables, we assume that using a constant percentage of sales is reasonable.

Are the assumptions regarding the relation between revenues and the working capital accounts of inventory and receivables reasonable? Let's once again consider IBM and Wal-Mart. IBM sells its services and products primarily to businesses. Therefore, we expect that the ability to extend credit to customers will be important in generating revenues. Therefore, we expect to see that IBM's revenues vary with accounts receivable. Of IBM's revenues, more than one-half is from services, which do not require inventory. It follows that there may not be a strong relationship between revenues and inventory. You can see this in Panel A of Figure 17-6: Receivables follow closely along with revenues, but inventory does not.

Now consider Wal-Mart Stores. Wal-Mart sells primarily to retail customers. Therefore, we do not expect to see a strong relation between revenues and receivables; Wal-Mart extends very little credit.[5] However, Wal-Mart has retail stores that must stock inventory. We expect inventory to move closely with sales. You can see the relationship between Wal-Mart's revenues and its inventory and accounts receivable in Panel B of Figure 17-6. Inventory follows the trend of revenues, but receivables do not.

What the IBM and Wal-Mart Stores examples show us is that whether working capital accounts vary with revenues, or if a particular working account varies with revenues, depends on the type of business. A company that relies on services for most of its revenues

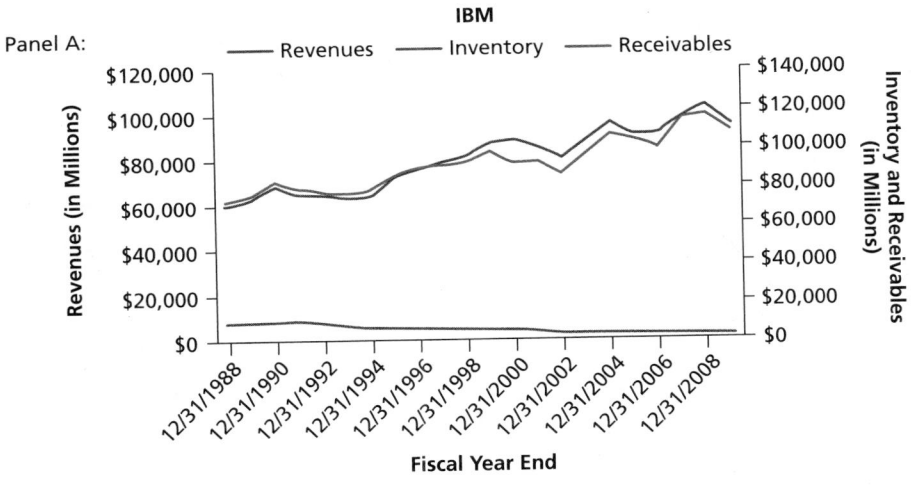

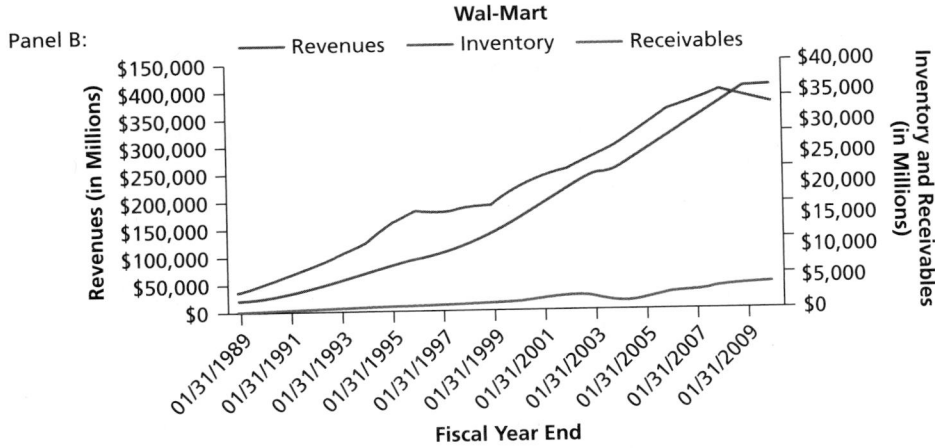

FIGURE 17-6   Revenues, Inventory, and Accounts Receivable for IBM and Wal-Mart, Fiscal Years 1988–2009

Source of data: *Companies' 10-K filings at www.sec.gov.*

[5] In fiscal year ending 1/31/2010, Wal-Mart had receivables of $4 billion, inventory of over $33 billion, and net sales of $408 billion.

will not have significant inventory, and this inventory may bear no relation to revenues. A company that has retail outlets will have a significant investment in inventory, and the level of inventory varies with revenues.

The last asset item is net fixed assets. Here, whether or not the assumption of a constant percentage of sales is reasonable largely depends on whether the company is a retailer, a manufacturer, or a service firm. Further, plant and equipment demands differ as to whether a manufacturer has a single plant or multiple plants, a retailer has one store or many, and so on.

Consider a manufacturer. In a single-plant company, the assumption of a constant percentage of sales tied up in net fixed plant and equipment is usually unreasonable; investment in plant and equipment usually lasts many years, and the company does not replace a part of it each year. Instead, investment in plant and equipment is "lumpy." The company will build its plant and equipment, and then each year the plant and equipment will reduce in value as the company takes depreciation. After a certain number of years, major refurbishment and replacement is needed, and the cycle begins again. For multiplant companies, this effect gets smoothed out because the process is occurring over a large number of plants.

In Figure 17-7 we provide the graphs of revenues and property, plant, and equipment for IBM and Wal-Mart. In the case of IBM, shown in Panel A of this figure, you can see the

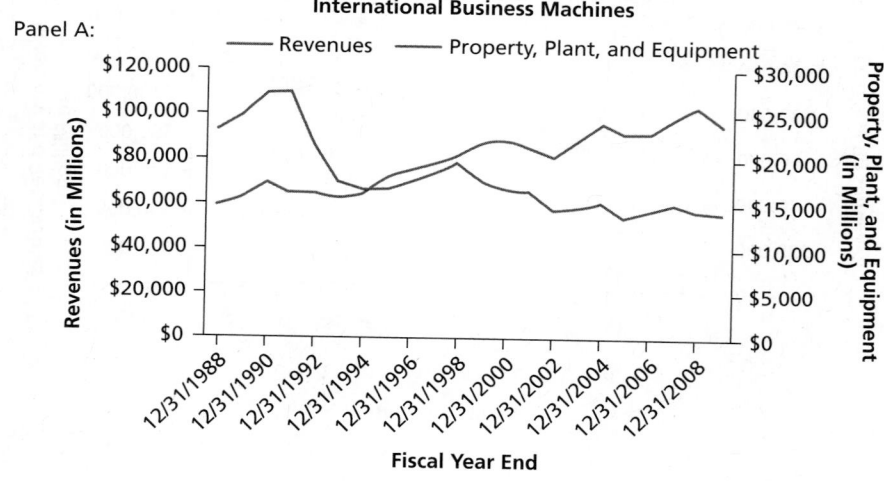

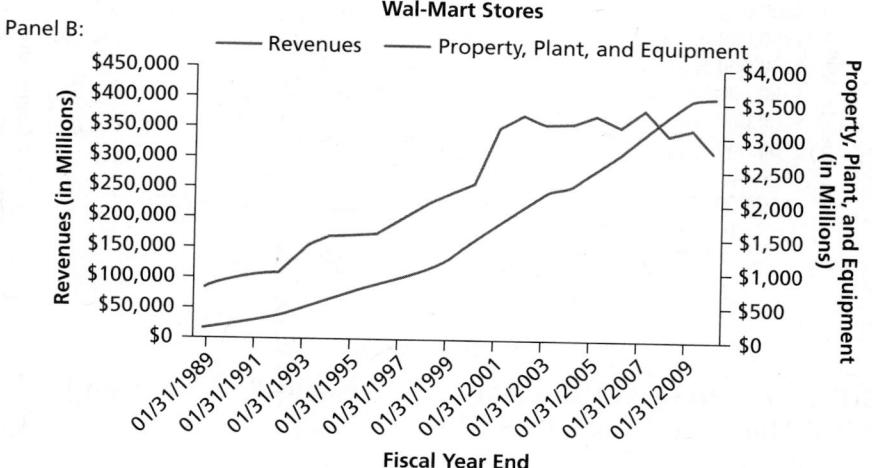

FIGURE 17-7 Revenues and Property, Plant, and Equipment for IBM and Wal-Mart Stores, Fiscal Years 1988–2009

Source of data: *Companies' 10-K filings at www.sec.gov.*

effects of the shift in IBM's revenues from a hardware/software focus to a service focus. There does not appear to be any relationship between revenues and property, plant, and equipment. Contrast this to Wal-Mart, which we show in Panel B of Figure 17-7. Here you can see that there is a positive relation between Wal-Mart's revenues and property, plant, and equipment, but Wal-Mart's revenues are smoother than its property, plant, and equipment, the latter of which is the classic "lumpiness" that we see with companies' capital expenditures.

Returning to our Dozer example, we need to address the issue of why companies hold marketable securities. Generally, companies do not create value by investing in marketable securities; they hold marketable securities as a temporary resting place for cash until it can be used. Suppose the treasurer talks to the controller and realizes that $10 million in marketable securities is needed to fund a plant expansion next year, after which there will be no further capital expenditures over the forecast horizon. In this case, it makes no sense to extrapolate marketable securities into the future. Further, after the plant and equipment are expanded, it will decline in the future as the plant and equipment are depreciated. So we'll assume that the company depreciates the plant and equipment by $10 million per year, but in the first year, it spends the $10 million in marketable securities to maintain the plant and equipment at $100 million.

The final items to consider are the spontaneous liabilities. These act very much like accounts receivable because the major item is accounts payable. As long as the company does not anticipate changing its payment policy, its payables will increase in line with sales, so assuming that payables will remain a constant percentage of sales is reasonable. Making the adjustments discussed earlier, we get the second revision to the forecast, which we show in Table 17-5.

This revision has different implications for the treasurer. Whereas before the company had an external financing requirement, now it would be able to repay some financing obligations because the external funds required is negative. The reasons for this are that the company no longer needs the increase in cash or the marketable securities, and more important, the company does not need to spend money on plant and equipment during the forecast period.

The final step is to consider changes in the net profit margin. Previously, we assumed that the net profit margin remained the same even when sales changed. However, if the

TABLE 17-5 Second Revision of Forecast for the Dozer Construction Company

(Dollar amounts in millions)	Year 0		Year 1	Year 2	Year 3
Sales	$120	%	$132	$145	$160
Cash	$5	4.2	$5.0	$5.0	$5.0
Marketable securities	10	8.3	0.0	0.0	0.0
Accounts receivable	10	8.3	11.0	12.1	13.3
Inventory	25	20.8	27.5	30.3	33.3
Net fixed assets	100	83.3	100.0	90.0	80.0
Total assets	$150	125.0	$143.5	$137.4	$131.6
Accruals	$5	4.2	$5.5	$6.1	$6.7
Accounts payable	5	4.2	5.5	6.1	6.7
Short-term debt	20	16.7	20.0	20.0	20.0
Long-term debt	40	33.3	40.0	40.0	40.0
Equity	80	66.7	83.3	86.9	90.9
Total liabilities and equity	$150	125.0	$154.3	$159.1	$164.3
Cumulative (EFR)			–$11.2	–$21.7	–$32.7

TABLE 17-6 Profit Margin and Sales for the Dozer Construction Company

(Dollar amounts in millions)	Year 0	Year 1	Year 2	Year 3
Sales	$120	$132	$145	$160
Gross margin (40%)	$48	$53	$58	$64
Fixed costs	31	31	31	31
Interest	5	5	5	5
Tax	6	8.5	11.0	14.0
Net income	$6	$8.5	$11.0	$14.0
Net profit margin	5.0%	6.4%	7.6%	8.7%

10 percent sales growth forecast is due to a recovery from a recession, the company may be able to achieve this growth without adding to its fixed costs. In this case, the net profit margin may also increase, if the company's fixed costs are indeed fixed. We report the income statements that arise if we maintain gross profits at 40 percent of sales but maintain fixed costs at $31 in Table 17-6.

Notice that the profit margin increases dramatically from 5.0 percent to 8.7 percent over the 4-year period. This is the typical "recovery from recession" pattern, in which the company lowers fixed costs during a recession, through restructuring and cost cutting, so that the immediate impact of a recovery causes greatly improved profit margins.

Let's consider the company's dividend policy. Companies do not follow a constant dividend payout policy; they tend to cautiously increase dividends in line with sustainable earnings. We'll assume that the treasurer expects the dividend to stay at $3 million for the next 3 years. This means that retained earnings will increase much more quickly than net income. If this higher level of retained earnings is added to our forecast, we get the final forecast, as we show in Table 17-7.[6]

The upshot of this final revision is that the surplus is even greater, and the treasurer has to develop a plan for managing these funds, rather than arranging for the company to raise money. This is quite a different scenario indeed!

Issues

In considering how we changed the simple percentage of sales forecast, we have exaggerated certain effects. For example, fixed costs are only fixed in the sense that they do not vary with sales. However, they still tend to rise over time through wage increases and the general tendency to hire more staff as the company's profits increase. Likewise, it would be difficult for the company to maintain the dividend at $3 million as profits and cash start to pile up.

Alternative assumptions about the macroeconomic environment could soon cause the surplus to become a deficit. For example, if a slowdown is forecast, a stable or declining sales forecast could cause the profit margin to contract, while requiring more receivables and inventory as a percentage of sales. However, this is not the point of the exercise because many different scenarios can be envisioned. What we are demonstrating is how the simple percentage of sales forecasting method, when allied with basic skills in financial analysis, can produce an effective forecast. Note, though, that if it is employed "blindly," it may provide misleading results. Moreover, even though the percentage of sale forecasting method can be improved for short-term forecasts, it is very accurate for multiplant companies over longer periods, which brings us to simple formula forecasting techniques.

[6] Note that some "sophisticated" financial planning models build in a further refinement so that as debt changes, so too does the company's interest charges and net profit margin. This can be done quite easily in Excel by simultaneously solving for all values. However, we find that this extension generally adds little to the usefulness of financial planning, particularly now that interest rates are so low.

TABLE 17-7 Final Revision of Forecast for Dozer Construction Company

(Dollar amounts in millions)	Year 0		Year 1	Year 2	Year 3
Sales	$120	%	$132	$145	$160
Cash	$5	4.2	$5.0	$5.0	$5.0
Marketable securities	10	8.3	0.0	0.0	0.0
Accounts receivable	10	8.3	11.0	12.1	13.3
Inventory	25	20.8	27.5	30.3	33.3
Net fixed assets	100	83.3	100.0	90.0	80.0
Total assets	$150	125.0	$143.5	$137.4	$131.6
Accruals	$5	4.2	$5.5	$6.1	$6.7
Accounts payable	5	4.2	5.5	6.1	6.7
Short-term debt	20	16.7	20.0	20.0	20.0
Long-term debt	40	33.3	40.0	40.0	40.0
Equity	80	66.7	85.5	93.5	104.5
Total liabilities and equity	$150	125.0	$156.5	$165.7	$177.9
Cumulative (EFR)			–$13.0	–$28.3	–$46.3

Concept Review Questions

1. Why is the sales forecast the most critical component of financial forecasting?

2. Describe the basic percentage of sales approach to financial forecasting. What is the main underlying premise to this forecasting approach?

3. What are some of the major limitations of the percentage of sales approach, and how might they be overcome?

This Is What You've Trained for All Your Life | LESSONS LEARNED

It is useful to take a look at how companies wrestled with planning in tough economic times. Looking back to see how companies managed during the 2007–2008 financial crisis, we can see how financial managers adapted.

The recession may not be all kicks, but it's not short of challenges for a CFO. Here's a view of the ups, downs, and demands through the eyes of the finance chief at software company Informatica.

It's a rare CFO who has had much fun during the recession. Earl Fry, who heads up finance for Informatica, a vendor of enterprise data-integration software, certainly isn't one. And that's despite the possibility that the economic ills ultimately will prove to be quite fortuitous for the company.

If there's one thing the recession has done, it's forced companies to rethink processes in a quest to wring out efficiencies. That provides hope for many software firms. Behooving Informatica, companies long afflicted by inertia in their approach to accessing their myriad data silos may at last take a new tack, Fry says. There is pent-up demand—especially, he believes, in the financial-services sector, which comprises about 20% of the company's business.

But there has been no shortage of angst along the way. In the depths of the downturn, the company's previously strong growth pace moderated considerably as large orders fell off. A planned expansion in Europe stalled. A convertible bond offering made in 2006, with the first put option scheduled to come due the year after next, was transformed from a brilliant strategy to a potential bust as Informatica's stock price tumbled.

Fry, Informatica's CFO since 1999, actually noticed the winds of change back in early 2007 and took steps then to slow down the company's spending. He credits his membership on the board of Central Pacific Bank in his native Hawaii with helping to provide him with a bird's-eye view of the unfolding financial crisis.

After the economy melted down last fall, it was gut-check time. Fry recalls going home one evening in late 2008, sharing a bottle of wine with his wife, and feeling somewhat depressed over the many decisions that needed to be made based on "very imperfect" information about business prospects. Finally he said to himself, "Buck up, Fry—this is what you've trained for all your life."

Following is an edited version of Fry's interview with CFO.com, in which he touches on lessons learned from the recession, prospects for recovery, his company's changing liquidity picture, the upcoming rewrite of revenue-recognition rules, and more.

Were the lessons learned from this recession different from those learned from the dot-com bust nine years ago?
Fundamentally those were very different downturns. For the dot-com bust I don't even use the word downturn, because it wasn't broad-based. There was a technology bubble, it burst, and there was a retooling and retrenchment primarily in the technology and software business.

This recession was caused by a massive real estate and financial-driven bubble that built up over the last seven or eight years, or you could even say a couple of decades. The magnitude of this recession is significantly greater.

But one lesson that applies to any downturn is that you have to plan for it. Things are never as good as they seem in an upturn, and if you think about it that way, then you'll be prepared for a downturn and will be able to continue investing in your products and people. Informatica was formed in 1993 around the building of data warehouses. From 2001 through 2004 we stopped growing, but during that time we broadened the technology so it could perform in real time and access more data types. If we had stayed as just a tool for automating data warehouses, even when a recovery happened growth prospects would not have been great.

What are the keys to managing finance during an economic slump?
Always pay attention to your balance sheet. Cash flows are important. Don't get too caught up in the income statement and looking at EPS growth—that's important, but doing that at the expense of cash flows or losing flexibility on your balance sheet is risky.

Also, make sure you're working only on the most important things. In the IT organization, the big projects that will take many years to show some kind of return—you can't do those now. Invest only in things that drive near-term efficiencies.

And, as I mentioned, look for the early warning signs. When things are good, you've got the hiring spigot wide open. When you decide to shut that off, it takes a while to ripple through the organization. So the sooner you can start moderating that, the better off you are.

When we saw things starting to change in early 2007, we had to modify the plan we had just put in place at the start of the year. We made more on-the-fly changes to our operating plan than I've ever done in my 25-year career in Silicon Valley. We had been planning to grow our operations in Europe a lot more. What was happening in the U.S. was broad-based, so we knew there would be a ripple effect. So we said: let's moderate our growth expectations and not put our resources there.

On the other hand, our Latin America business was starting to grow nicely, exceeding its numbers, and we didn't see the same kind of warning signs, so we actually put disproportionately more resources there.

What were the early warning signs you saw in the United States? Were they metric-based macroeconomic issues, or more micro ones, like customers taking a little longer to make decisions or looking for more software options for the same amount of money?
It was a combination of those things. If you rely on any one metric to the exclusion of others, you're going to get burned. If you listen only to what your customers and sales force say to you, you will get burned 100% of the time. They may be right in how they understand the world to be at that particular point in time, but that may not help you in forecasting sales six or nine months out.

The data points we were getting from our field sales team were all flashing green except for one vertical in one region: U.S. domestic financial services. Even there we had a good first quarter in 2007. But the shape of our forecasted pipeline was anomalous, with meaningfully fewer large transactions. What did that mean? By itself, maybe nothing. But being on the bank board and understanding more about the bubble that was cresting in the financial and credit markets, I took that data point as telling me to be careful.

As a CFO, you've got to take every data point you can and form your own picture of the world. I do have a network of other CFOs, but you have to take what they say with a grain of salt. The picture is going to be different in different industries and different parts of the cycle.

Did you have to keep an eye on the balance sheets of your customers because of the credit crunch, or change your credit terms?
We were mindful of it, but only for a very small number of accounts did we change credit terms. By and large we deal with large global companies. Some of them may slow payment down a bit, but I think we had three write-offs in the last five years, all very small."

Extracted from: David McCann, "This Is What You've Trained for All Your Life," CFO.com, September 10, 2009.

17.3 RISK MANAGEMENT

Risk management within a business entity is necessary because of unpredictable events that may have adverse effects on the business. All companies face risk, but the management of these risks affects the company's cost of capital and its value. Part of the challenge in managing risk is that there is an inherent conflict in managing risk: The greater the risk, the greater the expected return. Note that we say "expected" return; the realized return may or may not be greater.

Evaluating Risk in Forecasting

One of the hallmarks of financial decision making is that decisions are made in an environment with uncertainty. No matter the precision of our analysis, the future is not known, and therefore we need to consider the degree of uncertainty associated with our forecasts.

Consider the Dozer analysis from earlier in this chapter. We assumed that sales would grow at a rate of 10 percent per year. What if we had determined from our research that the most likely growth is 10 percent, but that there is a chance that the growth rate may deviate from 10 percent? Let's assume that we have confidence in a 10 percent growth rate, but that we recognize that factors outside our control may affect sales. If we can quantify this, we can run trials on the effect of deviating from a 10 percent growth rate.

Suppose that we expect a 10 percent growth rate, but we realize that there is uncertainty regarding this. Specifically, we believe that the growth rates follow a normal distribution around 10 percent and that the standard deviation is 10 percent. When we used a spreadsheet program to simulate this, we generated 100 random numbers that fit this distribution, where each random number is a possible growth rate. When we do this, we get a distribution of possible growth rates that we illustrate using a histogram in Figure 17-8.

When we apply these growth rates to the relationships in the income statement, we end up with the distribution of net profit margins for Year 1 that we show in Figure 17-9. As you can see, specifying a normal distribution does not guarantee that the resulting distribution of growth rates will be normal. In addition, because of the presence of fixed operating costs, the distribution of the resulting net profit margins is not normal, but rather is skewed positively.

We looked at a single variable in the analysis. A comprehensive analysis of the effect of uncertainty on the forecast requires specifying the inputs that have uncertainty and then examining the possible outcomes once all these uncertain inputs are allowed to vary.

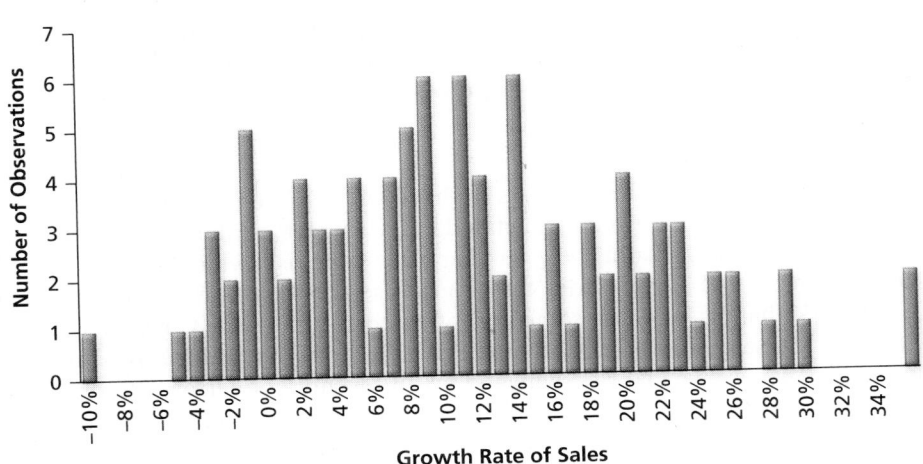

FIGURE 17-8 Distribution of 100 Possible Growth Rates for Dozer, with a Mean of 10 Percent and a Standard Deviation of 10 Percent

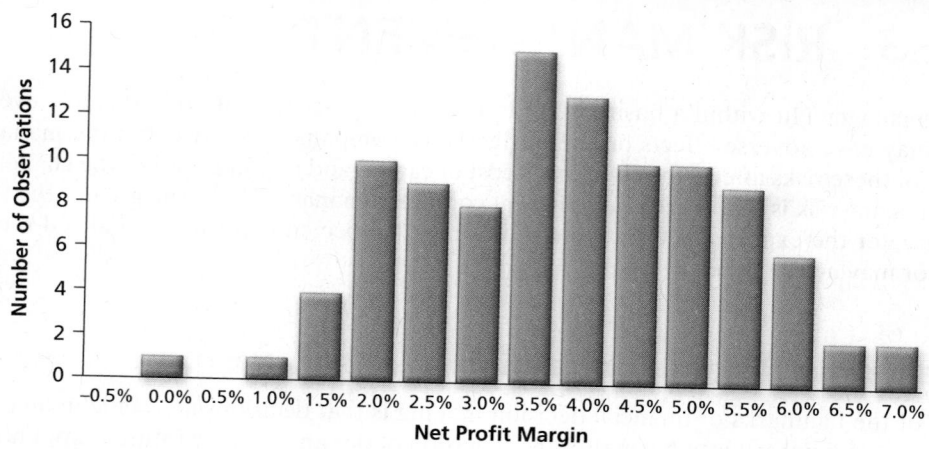

FIGURE 17-9 Distribution of 100 Possible Net Profit Margins for Dozer Resulting from the Randomly Generated Sales Growth

Add-ins are available for spreadsheet programs, including @Risk and Crystal Ball, that make this simulation task more manageable.[7]

Enterprise Risk Management

Whereas budgeting and forecasting appear to be mechanical, it is important to understand that it is not possible to forecast with certainty. There will always be uncertainty and blind spots in planning because consumer behavior is not constant, the economy is continually changing, the competitors' actions are not always predictable, and government regulations can change quickly.

Risk management in an ongoing process that involves:

- the identification of risk,
- the measurement of risk, and
- actions that seek to mitigate these risks.

When we look at the business enterprise as a whole, we refer to risk management as **enterprise risk management (ERM)**.[8] Although enterprise risk management has been around for many years, the most recent financial crisis has emphasized the need to identify and manage risks. A key element of risk management is the business enterprise's **risk appetite**. An enterprise's risk appetite is generally established by the company's board of directors and top management and is a metric that is used in evaluating decisions. Enterprise risk management is an ongoing process, as we depict in Figure 17-10.

enterprise risk management (ERM) process of identifying and managing risks throughout a business enterprise

risk appetite specification of how much risk a company will tolerate

Identify risks

What types of risk do companies face? As we have discussed in previous chapters, every company faces business risk, which is dictated, in large part, by the lines of business in which the company operates. Business risk captures sales risk, which is the uncertainty regarding how many and at what price the goods or services are sold, and operating risk, which is the risk that arises when some operating costs are fixed over a wide range of production or unit sales. In addition, companies may choose to finance their operations with debt, introducing financial risk, which is the uncertainty of earnings to owners that is introduced when a company takes on a legal obligation to pay interest and repay debt.

---

[7] @ Risk is a product of Palisade Corporation, and Crystal Ball is a product of Oracle.

[8] For a more thorough discussion of enterprise risk management, see the report by the Committee of Sponsoring Organizations of the Treadway Commission (COSO), September 2004.

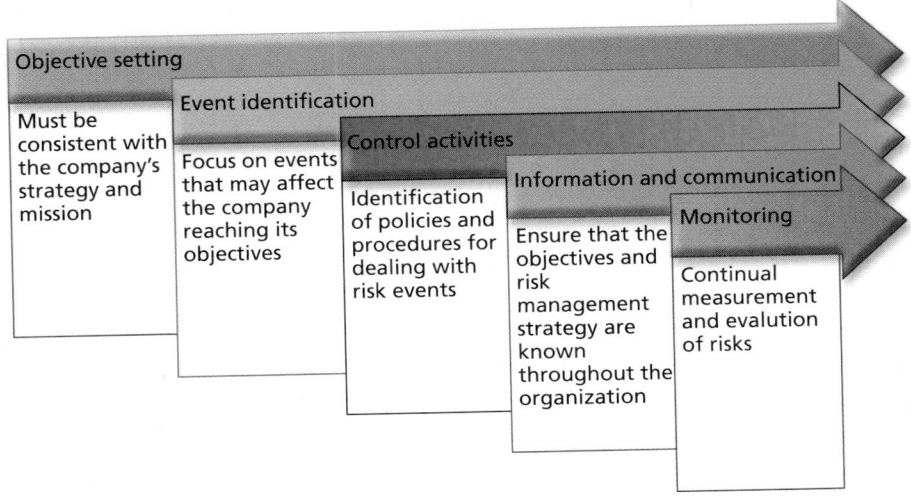

Figure 17-10 Enterprise Risk Management

In addition to business risk, sales risk, and financial risk, companies face many other risks. There are too many to list here, we provide examples in Table 17-8.

An ERM system is useful in managing a company's risks, though some large corporations in the U.S. and Europe do not have such a system in place.[9] One of the impediments to adopting ERM is that an ERM system must be customized for the particular company, which may deter some companies from establishing such a system.

Although a majority of companies surveyed have incorporated enterprise risk management in their decision making, the implementation of such systems tends to vary significantly. In terms of types of risk, most ERM systems consider credit or market risk, compliance risk, and strategic risk; only 58 percent of companies had incorporated human capital or labor risk.[10]

No matter whether a company has an ERM system or not, the Securities and Exchange Commission requires disclosure of a company's risk exposures. At present, companies disclose the list of risks, with some explanation, in the Management Discussion and Analysis (MDA) of the 10-K and 10-Q filings.[11] The types of risks discussed in the MDA include:

- Market for products and services
- Reliance on specific suppliers or customers
- Effect of regulatory changes
- Legal exposures
- Effectiveness of internal controls
- Reliance on key personnel
- Conflicts of interest
- History of operating losses
- Issues related to inadequate disclosure

Following the financial crisis of 2007–2008, the SEC adopted rules, as part of the corporate governance regulation, that require, among other things, additional disclosures of the relationship between corporate governance and risk management, any legal actions that

[9] Alix Stuart, "They'll Take Their Chances," *CFO.com*, September 27, 2010.

[10] Stephen Taub, "Risk Management: More Talk than Action," *CFO.com*, June 23, 2006.

[11] The SEC has been challenging some of the discussion of risks recently if they are not sufficiently detailed or if they are not tailored to the particular company.

TABLE 17-8 Examples of Company Risks

Risk Type	Uncertainty Associated with . . .
Commodity price risk	changes in the price of inputs.
Compliance risk	violating or not conforming to federal, state, and local government rules and regulations regarding disclosures such as those related to security filings or the environment.
Credit risk	payments that are not be made when or in the amounts promised. This pertains to credit extended to customers, as well as default risk in investments.
Environmental risk	pollution or other forms of damage to the environment.
Foreign exchange risk	changes in the relative exchange rate of currencies.
Labor risk	shortages of qualified employees, labor union demands or strikes, and the loss of key personnel to competitors.
Liquidity risk	inability to raise sufficient cash or the inability to sell goods.
Political risk	such issues as the expropriation of assets by a foreign government or a change in import or export rules or taxes, or instability in a country in which the company operates.
Property risk	loss of value or use of productive assets, such as from a natural disaster.
Purchasing power risk	inflation.
Reputation risk	events or actions that damage the trust of customers, employees, suppliers, or investors.
Risk risk	unknown and unaccounted for risks.
Strategic risk	embarking on a strategy that is not the optimal strategy or that may not be possible to achieve given economic or environmental conditions.

involve members of the company's board of directors or company officers, and the board of directors' role in risk oversight.[12]

Measure risks

To manage the risks of a company, we first have to measure risks. In our example using the fictitious Dozer Company, we described how it is possible to capture the uncertainty in sales using simulation. We can use this approach to develop scenarios that incorporate the uncertain elements, specifying the probabilities and possible outcomes, that expose the possible outcomes to decisions under uncertainty.

value at risk (VaR) tool for evaluating the risk of a loss over a specified period

Another risk measure is **value at risk (VaR)**. VaR for a particular investment or financing decision addresses the question: What is the most that I can lose? In assessing risk associated with a future event, we often start with a statistical measure, such as the standard deviation, to capture the dispersion of possible outcomes from the expected outcome. It is important to recognize that measures such as the standard deviation and the coefficient of variation include both good and bad outcomes. An entity may not be worried about generating too much return, but should really be more concerned about the potential for losses. That is where VaR comes in.

VaR is used most often in evaluating risks in portfolios of investments and requires estimating the probabilities associated with downside losses, considering the correlations

[12] Securities and Exchange Commission, 17 CFR Parts 229, 239, 240, 249 and 274, "Proxy Disclosure Enhancements," Release no. 33-9089, December 16, 2009.

that exist among the investments in the portfolio, as well as the investment horizon. VaR, therefore, does not evaluate a particular investment in isolation, but rather considers the entire portfolio of investments. If you think of a business entity as a portfolio of investments, you can begin to see the role of VaR in decision making within a business entity. However, VaR is only as good as its inputs, so reliance on VaR must consider the susceptibility of the model to bad inputs.

Closely related to VaR is **stress testing**, which simulates outcomes based on scenarios with economic downturns or particular stresses, generally with extreme risk exposures. The focus of stress testing is on the negative outcomes and the ability of an entity to survive these outcomes. In other words, stress testing addresses, in the extreme, whether the entity is capable of continuing as a going concern under the worst-case scenario.

stress testing evaluation of outcomes based on economic downturns or particular stresses, generally with extreme risk exposures

Stress Testing | FINANCE in the News

A key tool used by companies and regulators in evaluating the risks of a company is to perform stress testing. Stress testing includes two forms: (1) a simulation of the financial condition and performance of a company if the economy were in a recession, and (2) a simulation of financial condition and performance of a company in response to specific stressors, such as a lack of short-term credit or a significant increase in costs of capital.

Stress testing was key to evaluating banks following the 2007–2008 financial crisis. The Federal Reserve evaluated the nineteen largest banks in the U.S. in mid-2009 and concluded that ten of these banks needed new capital in the event that the recession worsened.[13] The results of these tests affected the U.S. government's

response to provide immediate financing in the form of a capital infusion. Stress testing is not limited to the U.S. Stress testing of financial institutions is performed in the European Union, Hong Kong, and elsewhere. Not only is stress testing used to determine whether banks have sufficient capital to withstand losses, but it is also used to assure the markets of the stability of the banking system.

As an example, consider the stress testing currently performed by the Hong Kong Monetary Authority. Using stress testing, the Authority evaluates stress scenarios including credit risk, economic downturns, a decline in the real estate market, failures of counterparties, changes in yield curve, widening of credit spreads, and dollar interest rate risk.[14]

[13] Board of Governors of the Federal Reserve System, Supervisory Capital Assessment Program, April 24, 2009.
[14] Hong Kong Supervisory Policy Manual, IC-5 Stress-testing.

Stress testing is not only useful to satisfy regulatory requirements, but it is also useful in planning and feedback into the company's strategy. In addition, managers can use stress testing to develop a plan in the event of a crisis, such as a weather-related event (e.g., tsunami, hurricane) or a financial crisis, or to support a request for funding.

Stress testing depends on good-quality inputs and estimates, the ability to develop plausible and useful scenarios, and modeling tools to analyze risk.

Take actions to mitigate risks

If a company evaluates its risk exposure and concludes that the risk exposure is greater than the risk the company should tolerate, it generally has several different ways to reduce its risk, depending on the type of risk. Basically, an entity can assume risk, avoid risk, mitigate risk, or transfer risk.

The easiest way to reduce risk is to avoid it in the first place, making sure to consider risks in making decisions. This means that long-term financing and investment decisions, as well as short-term financing and investment, must incorporate risk in decision making, along with a comparison of the risk of a decision to the company's risk tolerance.

hedge transaction designed to reduce the chance of a loss

short hedge commitment to sell a commodity by selling a futures contract

long hedge commitment to buy a commodity by buying a futures contract

One form of risk mitigation is available through financial transactions, such as hedging a commodity that is a key input into the company's production. A **hedge** is a transaction designed to reduce the chance of a loss. For example, a food processor may use commodity futures to lock in its cost of grains, and a farmer may use commodity futures to lock in the sale price of grains. The farmer that sells the futures contract for the grain is creating a **short hedge** (that is, a commitment to sell), whereas the food processor who purchases a futures contract is creating a **long hedge** (that is, a commitment to buy).

Long hedge → Food processor buys a future contract to lock in future purchase price of commodity

Farmer sells a futures contract to lock in the future sales price of a commodity → Short hedge

credit default swap contract in which one party pays another party to assume a specified risk

insurance contract between two parties in which one party assumes the risk of the other party and receives compensation in the form of an insurance premium

Other financial instruments that can be used to reduce risk, if used properly, include options, forwards, swaps, and securitization. For example, an investor can buy a credit default swap for a particular investment. A **credit default swap** is simply a contract in which one party pays another party to assume a specified risk. In the case of credit default swap, if the credit quality of the issuer of an investment, such as a bond, deteriorates, the seller of the credit default swap will put up collateral and then, in the extreme case in which the issuer defaults, assume the payments in place of the issuer if the issuer fails to do so.

A common form of risk transfer is **insurance**, where the company pays another party to take on a specific risk.[15] Insurance is available for a wide range of risks, including casualty (such as theft or workers' compensation), damage or loss of property, liability, and credit risk. The payment is the **insurance premium**, which is determined based on the likelihood of the risk to occur and the amount of any loss from the event. This is probably the simplest form of risk transfer because an insurance policy shifts the risk to another party, and there is a fixed cost of doing so.

[15] So what is the difference between a credit default swap and insurance? Both can be used to support the claims of bondholders; for example, municipal bond insurance pays creditors if the municipality is not able to do so. The subtle difference between the credit default swap and insurance is that if the credit quality of the insurance debt deteriorates, the seller of the credit default swap may have to provide collateral to the buyer of the swap if the debt is downgraded, but the provider of insurance need not do anything unless the borrower defaults on the debt.

1. What is meant by an enterprise risk management system?

2. What techniques can a financial manager use to reduce a company's risk exposure?

SUMMARY

- Financial planning is an essential function within any business entity. Financial planning requires not only forecasting sales, but also forecasting the company's need for funds in the future.

- Any forecast of a company's revenues should consider not only the trend of sales over the recent periods, but also what is expected for the economy, the industry in which the company operates, and market forces.

- An important aspect of financial planning is risk management. Risk management requires identifying risks, measuring these risks, and taking actions to ensure that the risk the company bears is consistent with the company's risk appetite.

FORMULAS/EQUATIONS

(17-1) Sustainable growth rate $=$ Return on equity $\times$ Proportion of earnings retained

QUESTIONS AND PROBLEMS

Multiple Choice

1. Which of the following accounts are *most* likely to vary along with sales?
   A. Goodwill
   B. Marketable securities
   C. Cash and cash equivalents
   D. Property, plant, and equipment

2. Spontaneous liabilities are *best* described as:
   A. long-term sources of financing.
   B. accounts payable and other short-term operating liabilities.
   C. liabilities that appear to have characteristics more in line with equity.

3. Which of the following accounts is *most* likely to vary with sales for a retail business?
   A. Goodwill
   B. Inventory
   C. Long-term debt
   D. Accounts receivable

4. Predicting revenues into the future should be done with caution because:
   A. companies do not make long-term investments each year.
   B. companies' revenues never follow a trend or pattern over time.
   C. revenues are affected by dividend decisions that the company makes.
   D. revenues are affected by the economic environment, as well as industry and market forces.

5. Sustainable growth is *best* described as related to a company's:
    A. retained earnings.
    B. long-term investments.
    C. return on equity and dividend payout.
    D. financial leverage and return on assets.

6. A company with a return on equity of 20 percent and a dividend payout of 30 percent will have a sustainable growth *closest* to:
    A. 6 percent.
    B. 14 percent.
    C. 20 percent.

7. Enterprise risk management is *best* described as a:
    A. method of shifting risk through insurance and other means.
    B. set of policies and procedures that can be applied to any business entity.
    C. process of identifying, measuring, and managing the risks of a business entity.

8. Stress testing is used to:
    A. predict a company's losses.
    B. predict a company's revenues.
    C. evaluate a company's financial condition if economic conditions deteriorate.
    D. evaluate a company's financial condition if economic conditions were to improve or deteriorate.

9. Enterprise risk management is best described as focusing on:
    A. options.
    B. hedging.
    C. divisional risk management.
    D. risk management for the company as a whole.

10. From the perspective of a farmer who wants to lock in the future price of a crop, the most useful tool is:
    A. selling a futures contract.
    B. buying a futures contract.
    C. selling a credit default swap.
    D. buying a credit default swap.

Practice Problems and Questions

17.1   The Role of Financial Planning

11. What is a company's strategy?

12. What is the relationship between financial planning and a company's strategy?

13. What is the role of budgets in financial planning?

14. Consider Ford Motor Company's statement that appeared in its *2010 Annual Report*:

    The company's four-point plan consists of: balancing our cost structure with our revenue and market share; accelerating development of new vehicles that customers want and value; financing our plan and rebuilding our balance sheet; and working together to leverage our resources around the world.

    What are the implications of this strategy for financial management of Ford?

17.2 Methods of Forecasting

15. Consider the following revenues of a company:

Fiscal Year	Revenues (in millions)
2010	$1,000
2011	$1,050
2012	$1,103
2013	$1,158
2014	$1,216

A. What is the average annual growth rate of the company's revenues?

B. Based solely on the information on the company's revenues for fiscal years 2010 through 2014, what would you predict for the company's revenues in 2015?

16. The Towson Company has a simple balance sheet for the fiscal year ending 12/31/2012, in thousands:

Cash	$100	Accounts payable	$600
Receivables	500	Short-term loan	100
Inventory	800	Current liabilities	$700
Current assets	$1,400	Long-term debt	5,000
Net fixed assets	10,000	Common equity	5,700
Total assets	$11,400	Total liabilities and equity	$11,400

Sales were $15 million in 2012. Consider the following assumptions:

- Sales are expected to grow at an annual rate of 10 percent for both 2013 and 2014.
- Property, plant, and equipment are expected to remain the same as in 2012.
- Long-term debt is expected to remain the same as in 2012.
- Any new financing must be carried out by selling additional equity interests.

Construct Towson's balance sheets for 2013 and 2014, completing the following:

	12/31/2012	As of 12/31/2013	As of 12/31/2014
Cash	$100		
Receivables	500		
Inventory	800		
Current assets	$1,400		
Net fixed assets	10,000		
Total assets	$11,400		
Accounts payable	600		
Short-term loan	100		
Current liabilities	$700		
Long-term debt	5,000		
Common equity	5,700		
Total liabilities and equity	$11,400		

Be sure to list any additional assumptions you made in your analysis.

17. The Boise Company has the following information from its financial statements:

Interest-bearing debt	$900,000
Shareholders' equity	$2,500,000
Sales	$1,050,000
Net income	$670,000
Dividends	$200,000
Sales growth	5 percent

Calculate Boise's sustainable growth rate.

 18. Consider the balance sheet of Yahoo! for fiscal years 2007, 2008, and 2009:

	As of		
	12/31/2009	**12/31/2008**	**12/31/2007**
Cash and cash equivalents	$1,275,430	$2,292,296	$1,513,930
Short-term investments	2,015,655	1,159,691	487,544
Net receivables	1,003,362	1,203,581	1,055,532
Other current assets	300,325	89,930	180,716
Total current assets	$4,594,772	$4,745,498	$3,237,722
Long-term investments	4,723,207	3,372,488	2,542,915
Property, plant, and equipment	1,426,862	1,536,181	1,331,632
Goodwill	3,640,373	3,440,889	4,002,030
Intangible assets	355,883	485,860	611,497
Other assets	194,933	72,111	503,945
Deferred long-term asset charges	0	36,821	0
Total assets	$14,936,030	$13,689,848	$12,229,741
Accounts payable	$1,306,584	$1,073,469	$1,182,350
Short/current long-term debt	0	0	749,628
Other current liabilities	411,144	631,546	368,470
Total current liabilities	$1,717,728	$1,705,015	$2,300,448
Long-term debt	83,021	77,062	0
Other liabilities	0	352,275	28,086
Deferred long-term liability charges	616,645	286,535	356,122
Minority interest	25,316	18,019	12,254
Total liabilities	$2,442,710	$2,438,906	$2,696,910
Common stock	$1,410	$1,595	$1,527
Retained earnings	1,599,638	4,848,162	4,423,864
Treasury stock	–117,331	–5,267,484	–5,160,772
Capital surplus	10,640,367	11,548,393	9,937,010
Other stockholder equity	369,236	120,276	331,202
Total stockholder equity	$12,493,320	$11,250,942	$9,532,831
Total liabilities and equity	$14,936,030	$13,689,848	$12,229,741

Source: *Yahoo! Finance*

Yahoo!'s revenues for the 3 years are as follows:

Fiscal Year	Revenues
2007	$6,969,274
2008	$7,208,502
2009	$6,460,315

A. Which balance sheet accounts tend to vary along with sales?

B. What would you predict for Yahoo!'s fiscal 2010 and 2011 revenues?

C. What were the actual Yahoo! fiscal 2010 revenues? 2011 revenues? (Available at finance.yahoo.com or finance.google.com, and use the ticker symbol YHOO.)

 19. Consider the following revenues for McDonald's, in billions of U.S. dollars (USD):

Year	Revenues (in billions USD)
1998	$8.90
1999	$9.51
2000	$10.47
2001	$11.04
2002	$11.50
2003	$12.80
2004	$14.22
2005	$15.35
2006	$16.08
2007	$16.61
2008	$16.56
2009	$15.46
2010	$16.23

Source: *McDonald's 10-K filings, various years.*

A. Graph revenues from 1998 through 2008.

B. Estimate the trend line of revenues, using revenues from 1998 through 2008.

C. Forecast revenues for 2009 and 2010 and calculate the forecast error for each year. Why might there be forecast errors for these years?

 20. Consider the following revenues for Chocoladefabriken Lindt & Sprungli AG, in billions of Swiss Francs (CHF):

Fiscal Year	Revenues (in billions CHF)
1994	0.765
1995	0.821
1996	0.891
1997	0.864
1998	0.973
1999	1.022
2000	1.344
2001	1.440
2002	1.537

Fiscal Year	Revenues (in billions CHF)
2003	1.591
2004	1.681
2005	1.801
2006	1.995
2007	2.247
2008	2.586
2009	2.946
2010	2.937
2011	2.525
2012	2.579

Source: *Chocoladefabriken Lindt & Sprungli AG annual reports, various years.*

A. Graph revenues from 1994 through 2008.

B. Estimate the trend line of revenues, using revenues from 1998 through 2008.

C. Forecast revenues for 2009 and 2010, and calculate the forecast error for each year. Why might there be forecast errors for these years?

17.3 Risk Management

21. Identify methods companies can use to measure risk.

22. By what means can a company shift risk to another party?

23. How can the risk of a company affect the value of the company?

24. What is VaR, and how does it help a financial manager manage risk?

25. What is the difference between VaR and stress testing?

26. What is a credit default swap?

27. If a company that uses precious metals as inputs to produce its products wants to reduce the uncertainty of the future price of the precious metals, what type of transaction could be used?

Case

Case 17.1 Peterson Wake-Up Calls

Peterson Wake-Up Calls, Inc., was created by a father and son team, Ken and Paul, as a service to college students who need a wake-up call or other reminders. Use these statements to answer the questions about Peterson Wake-Up Calls.

Peterson Wake-Up Calls
Balance Sheet as of End of the Year Indicated

	Year 1	Year 2
Assets		
Current assets (cash)	$1,150	$493
Property and equipment (net)	3,840	3,888
Total assets	$4,990	$4,381

	Year 1	Year 2
Liabilities and Owners' Equity		
Interest payable	$200	$160
Tax payable	177	182
Dividends payable	200	210
Long-term debt	3,200	2,400
Total liabilities	$3,777	$2,952
Common shares	1,000	1,000
Retained earnings	213	429
Total owners' equity	$1,213	$1,429
Total liabilities and owners' equity	$4,990	$4,381

Peterson Wake-Up Calls
Income Statement for the Full Year Indicated

	Year 1	Year 2
Revenues (net of bad debts)	$1,950	$2,200
Selling and administrative expenses	0	220
Loss (stolen equipment)	160	0
Earnings before interest depreciation and amortization	$1,790	$1,980
Amortization expense	1,000	1,212
Earnings before interest and taxes (EBIT)	790	768
Interest expense	$200	$160
Earnings before tax	590	608
Tax (30%)	177	182
Net income	$413	$426
Earnings per share (100 shares)	$4.13	$4.26
Dividends per share	$2.00	$2.10

A. The Petersons are planning their third year of operations. As a first step in the process, create a "Percentage of Sales" balance sheet for Peterson Wake-Up Calls as of the end of Year 2.

B. Suppose the Petersons believe they can increase revenues to $2,600 in Year 3. Use this figure and the percentage of sales balance sheet to forecast the company's balance sheet at the end of Year 3. Remember that the financing components (long-term debt and total owners' equity) should be left unchanged from the Year 2 figures.

   i. The forecast balance sheet does not balance! Determine the amount of external financing required by Peterson Wake-Up Calls based on the initial forecast.

   ii. To achieve the target level of revenues in Year 3 ($2,600), Peterson Wake-Up Calls will have to buy some more equipment. This will increase the amortization expense to $1,422. Selling costs will be the same percentage of sales as in Year 2, and the interest expense for the year will be $120. Use this information to determine the amount of net income the company should expect to earn in Year 3.

   iii. Use the average dividend payout ratio from Years 1 and 2, and the forecast net income figure, to estimate the total amount of dividends that will be paid by the company in Year 3.

   iv. Suppose that Peterson Wake-Up Calls will actually pay $270 in dividends in Year 3. Determine the value of the retained earnings account at the end of Year 3 based on the forecast net income in iii.

v.   The forecast for retained earnings changes the Year 3 forecast for total liabilities and owners' equity to $4,770. With total assets forecast to be $5,177 determine how much external financing will be required in Year 3.

vi. Use the following information to create a revised forecast of the Year 3 balance sheet for Peterson Wake-Up Calls:

  • Cash will increase by the forecast EBITDA amount.

  • Cash will be reduced by $1,050 to purchase new equipment, $552 for Year 2 payables, and $800 for debt repayment.

  • The property and equipment (net) account will increase by $1,050 (wake-up calls) but must be reduced by the $1,422 amortization expense.

  • Interest and tax payable will reflect the respective expenses on the forecast income statement.

  • Dividends payable will be $270.

  • Long-term debt will be reduced by $800, and the retained earnings figure is $718.

With this revised forecast, is any additional external financing required?

CHAPTER 18

DERIVATIVES

© Masterfile

Derivatives: Over the Counter, Out of Sight *Derivatives are extraordinarily useful—as well as complex, dangerous if misused and implicitly subsidized. No wonder regulators are taking a close look.*

1958 American onion farmers, blaming speculators for the volatility of their crops' prices, lobbied a congressman from Michigan named Gerald Ford to ban trading in onion futures. Supported by the president-to-be, they got their way. Onion futures have been prohibited ever since.

Futures are agreements to trade something at a set price at a given date. They are perhaps the simplest example of a derivative, a contract whose value is "derived" from the price of a commodity or another asset. Derivatives continue to be vilified, usually when someone loses a lot of money. Orange County and Procter & Gamble lost fortunes on them in the 1990s. They were at the core of Enron's failure. And in September 2008 they brought American International Group (AIG), a mighty insurer, to its knees. Its fetish for credit default swaps (CDSs), a type of derivative that insures lenders against borrowers' going bust, led it to guarantee at least $400 billion-worth of other companies' loans—including those of Lehman Brothers. The American government forked out $180 billion to save AIG from collapse.

Every catastrophe brings calls for restrictions on derivatives. This year Joseph Stiglitz, a Nobel economics laureate, has said that their use by the world's largest banks should be outlawed. But derivatives have defenders too. Used carefully, they are an excellent—some would say indispensable—tool of risk management. Myron Scholes, another Nobel prize-winner, says a ban would be a "Luddite response that takes financial markets back decades."

Because of the mayhem of the past year or so, lawmakers in America and Europe are on the point of giving derivatives markets their biggest shake-up since the 1970s. For the world's biggest banks, billions of dollars are at stake. For taxpayers, the stakes are just as high.

Derivatives come in many shapes. Besides futures, there are options (the right, but not the obligation, to buy or sell at a given price), forwards (cousins of futures, not traded on exchanges) and swaps (exchanging one lot of obligations for another, such as variable for fixed interest payments). They can be based on pretty much anything, as long as two parties are willing to trade risks and can agree on a price: commodities, currencies, shares, or bonds. Derivatives create leverage too. Contracts are sealed with initial payments that are a small fraction of the potential gain or loss.

In the main, businesses use derivatives to shift risks to other firms, chiefly banks, that are willing to bear them. An airline worried about fuel prices can limit or fix its bills. A bank concerned about its credit exposure to the airline can pass some of its default risk to other banks without selling the underlying loans. About 95% of the world's 500 biggest companies use derivatives. A lack of them can be costly. "The absence of derivatives in iron-ore markets makes negotiations between Australian

643

suppliers and Chinese buyers very confrontational," says Philip Killicoat of Credit Suisse. Earlier this year Rio Tinto's chief negotiator, Stern Hu, was arrested in China during hard bargaining over prices. And the futures ban has not stopped the price of onions from going up and down.

Derivatives have a long history, stretching back thousands of years. In the 17th century the Japanese traded simple rice futures in Osaka and the Dutch bought and sold derivatives in Amsterdam. But trading in financial derivatives really took off only in the 1970s. The fluctuations in currencies and interest rates after the collapse of the Bretton Woods system gave a push to demand. The option-pricing formula developed by Fischer Black and Mr. Scholes, plus advances in computing power, made valuing derivatives much easier. Regulators encouraged them, too. Thrift Bulletin 13, issued by the Federal Home Loan Bank System in 1989, obliged American thrifts to hedge their interest-rate risk.

Derivatives are bought and sold in two ways. Contracts with standardized terms are traded on exchanges. Tailored varieties are bought "over the counter" (OTC) from big "dealer" banks. These banks support the OTC market by hedging their clients' risks with each other or on an exchange.

Excerpt from "Derivative: Over the Counter, Out of Sight," *The Economist*, November 13, 2009.

Learning Outcomes

After reading this chapter, you should be able to:

LO 18.1 Describe the basic elements of an option, explain how these elements affect the pricing of a call or a put option, and calculate the payoffs associated with long and short positions in call and put options.

LO 18.2 Explain the nature of forward and futures contracts, how investors can use these to reduce risk, and how forwards and futures differ from options.

LO 18.3 Describe the basics of swaps, and explain why an investor would be willing to enter into one.

Chapter Preview A derivative is a contract whose value depends on something else. This something else may be an asset, such as a stock, or something quite intangible, such as the weather. In this chapter, we introduce you to several types of derivatives—options, forwards, futures, and swaps—and discuss how these can be used in financial management and, more specifically, risk management.

derivative contract whose value depends on or is derived from a specified asset or variable

underlying or **underlying asset** variable or asset on which derivative is based

option right, but not the obligation, to buy or sell a specific asset at a specific price, within a specified period or on a specific date

forward contract or **forward** agreement in which parties contract today for an exchange to take place sometime in the future

A **derivative** is any contract whose value depends on or is derived from some specified asset or variable. This asset or variable is the **underlying**. If the underlying is an asset, we use the term **underlying asset** in this context. Examples of derivatives are:

- an **option**, which is the right to buy or sell a specific asset at a specific price, within a specified period or on a specific date;
- a **forward contract** or, simply, a **forward**, which permits parties to contract today for an exchange to take place sometime in the future;
- a **futures contract** or, simply, **futures**, which is a standardized forward contract; and
- a **swap**, which is a contract to exchange one set of cash flows for another.

Though many tend to think that derivatives are a rather new type of contract, the fact is that derivatives have been around a long time. Evidence shows that derivatives were created in the nineteenth century BC, written on clay tablets. An early contract was for the delivery of wood at some future point in time.[1] Derivatives have long been used in trade and in speculation.

[1] Marc Van de Mieroop, "The Innovation of Interest. Sumerian Loans," in *The Origins of Value: The Financial Innovations That Created Modern Capital Markets*, ed. William M. Goetzmann and K. Geert Rouwenhorst (Oxford: Oxford University Press, 2005).

644

We can trace the use of derivative contracts through history. For example, derivative securities, in the form of forward contracts that allow contracting for an exchange at some point in the future, date back to the 1600s and the Dutch Tulip Bulb mania. The first traded futures contracts, which are forward contracts that are standardized, also date back to the 1600s in Japan.[2]

In the U.S., the first formalized derivatives market was the Chicago Board of Trade, which was created in 1848. This market arose out the need for farmers and users of food commodities to manage the risks associated with producing and securing these products. The Chicago Mercantile Exchange began trading currency futures contracts in 1972 and followed in 1975 with the trading in interest rate futures, which allows investors and traders to hedge and speculate on interest rates.

Just how important are derivatives to financial decision making? The amount of trading in derivatives has grown significantly over the past three decades, and many of the events leading up to the 2007–2008 economic recession in the U.S. were intertwined with several different types of derivatives.[3]

futures contract or **futures** standardized forward contract

swap contract to exchange one set of cash flows for another

18.1   OPTIONS

In general, an option is a contract that gives the buyer the right, but not the obligation, to buy or sell a specified asset at a specified price within or at a specified point in time. We refer to the right to buy as a **call option**, whereas the right to sell is a **put option**, and we refer to the party who buys the right as the **option buyer** and the party who sells the right as the **option writer**.

call option right but not the obligation to buy an underlying asset at a fixed price within or at a specified time

put option right, but not the obligation, to sell an underlying asset at a fixed price within or at a specified time

Call Options

We begin by considering the characteristics of the basic call option, which is the right, but not the obligation, to buy an underlying asset at a fixed price for a specified time. If the investor in the call option buys the underlying, we refer to this action as the **exercise** of the option. The price at which an investor can buy the underlying asset is the **exercise price** or **strike price**, and the last date at which the option can be converted or exercised is the **expiration date**. We often refer to the amount of time remaining before expiration as the **time to expiration** or the **time to expiry**.

When we refer to a position in a derivative, we often use the term "long" to indicate the investment in the derivative and use the term "short" to indicate the other side of the investment position. Therefore, the position of investing in a call option is a **long call position**.

We begin our discussion assuming that a call option is available on an asset with an exercise price of $50. For the time being, we will not specify the expiration date of the option. If an investor buys the option and then exercises the option when the asset's price is $54, the payoff (without considering how much the investor paid for the option) is $54 − 50 = $4: the investor paid $50 for an asset that is worth $54.

option buyer party who buys an option

option writer party who sells an option

exercise price or **strike price** the price at which an investor can buy the underlying asset

exercise use of the rights of options by buying (in the case of a call option) or selling (in the case of a put option)

expiration date the last date on which options can be converted or exercised

time to expiration or **time to expiry** time remaining for an option before it expires

long call position investment in the right to buy an asset

[2] Ernst Juerg Weber, "A Short History of Derivative Security Markets," Working paper, University of Western Australia.

[3] The Bank of International Settlements reports for the first half of 2011 that the notional amount of over-the-counter derivatives is around $708 trillion, whereas the market value of derivatives is around $20 trillion [Stefan Avdjiev, Andreas Schrimpf, and Chistian Upper, "Highlights of BIS International Statistics," *BIS Quarterly Review*, December 2011, www.bis.org].

payoff proceeds that would be generated from the option if today was the expiration date

We depict the **payoff** for the buyer (that is, holder or owner) of this call for various underlying asset prices in Figure 18-1. The payoff refers to the proceeds that would be generated from the call option if today was the expiration date and the option holder had to decide whether to exercise the option or not. It does not reflect the investor's profits because it does not account for the purchase price of the option, which we discuss later.

Consider a call option with the strike price of $50. If at expiration the underlying asset's price is above $50, say $55, the rational investor exercises the call. This means that he or she pays $50 and "calls" the asset away from the counterparty, that is, the person who has sold the call, the call option writer. The investor could then obtain a payoff of $5 by selling the asset for $55 in the open market. In this case, we say the call is **in the money**. Conversely, if the underlying asset's price is below $50, the call is worthless and would not be exercised. No one would pay the strike price to call the asset away from its owner for $50 when it can be bought for less in the open market. This is the crucial fact about options: They give the owner the right, but not the obligation, to do something. The investor doesn't incur losses in a long call position when the price of the underlying asset is below the strike price, which we refer to as being **out of the money**.[4] As a result, the investor gets the payoff from the option contract above the strike price and gets zero below the strike price. For this reason, options are examples of securities with nonlinear payoffs, as we show in Figure 18-1. Just to make sure that we have all the bases covered, if the value of the underlying asset is equal to the strike price of an option, we refer to this as **at the money**. The **moneyness** of an option is the status of whether the option is in, at, or out of the money.

in the money option would generate a positive payoff if generated today

out of the money option would generate a negative payoff if exercised today

at the money situation in which the value of the underlying asset of an option is equal to the option's strike price

moneyness status of whether the option is in, at, or out of the money

EXAMPLE 18.1

Payoffs for an Investor Who Buys a Call Option

PROBLEM

Complete the following table of the payoffs for various underlying asset prices for a call option buyer who buys a call option with a strike price of $50.

Asset Price ($)

30	40	50	55	60	70
Call Buyer Payoff					

Solution

Asset Price ($)

	30	40	50	55	60	70
Call Buyer Payoff	0	0	0	55 − 50 = 5	60 − 50 = 10	70 − 50 = 20

Out of the Money (30, 40)   At the Money (50)   In the Money (55, 60, 70)

Notice that the payoff is zero for all prices at or below the strike price of $50. Beyond $50, the payoff increases by $1 for every $1 increase in the underlying asset price.

The preceding discussion leaves out one important detail—namely, who the investor is buying the option from. When an investor buys a call option, he or she buys it from some other market participant unrelated to the underlying asset. The person on the other side

---

[4] An option is said to be "at the money" whenever the market price of the underlying equals the strike price.

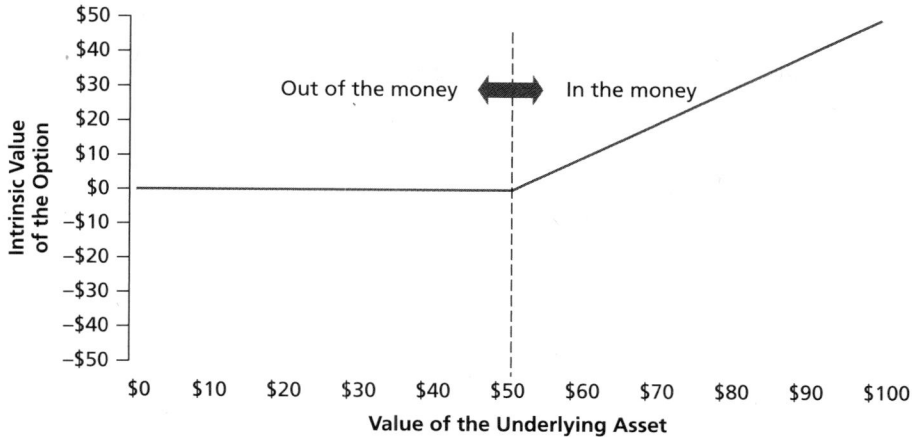

FIGURE 18-1 **Intrinsic Value of a Call Option with an Exercise Price of $50**

of the call option, who *sells* a call option, is the option writer because he or she has written the call option that is purchased by someone else. It is common to say that option writers have assumed a **short position** in the option because a short position involves the sale of something.

If someone sells a call option, the payoff is the mirror image of that received by the person who buys it. For example, we have already looked at the payoff to the $50 call holder and noted that as the asset price increases, say, to $55, the payoff on the call is $5. This $5 payoff occurs as the asset is called away from the option writer for $50 and sold for $55. The payoff to the call option writer is the opposite, as he or she has to go into the market and buy this asset for $55 and then surrender it for only $50, losing $5. Conversely, when a call expires out of the money and is not exercised, the option writer doesn't lose anything.

Price of Underlying Asset	Payoff to Call Option Buyer	Moneyness of Call Option	Payoff to Call Option Writer
$45	$0	Out of the money	$0
$46	$0	Out of the money	$0
$47	$0	Out of the money	$0
$48	$0	Out of the money	$0
$49	$0	Out of the money	$0
$50	$0	At the money	$0
$51	$1	In the money	–$1
$52	$2	In the money	–$2
$53	$3	In the money	–$3
$54	$4	In the money	–$4
$55	$5	In the money	–$5

We depict the payoff for the call option writer of this $50 call in Figure 18-2. Notice that the payoff from writing the call is the mirror image of that from buying the call. So why would anyone want to write such a call option? Because the party buying the option doesn't get the option for free; the call option buyer pays a premium to buy this option, which is where the call option writer makes money.

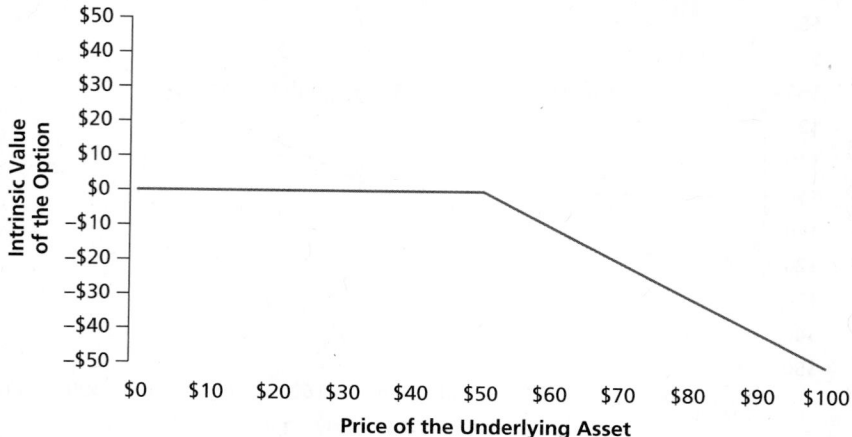

FIGURE 18-2 Payoff to the Call Writer for a Call Option with an Exercise Price of $50

Call option values

So what is the value of the call option? At expiration, the value of the option is the asset price minus the strike price when the call is in the money, and zero when it is out of the money. This is the bold line in Figures 18-1 and 18-2 and is called the **intrinsic value**. We can estimate the intrinsic value of a call option, as shown in Equation 18-1.

> **intrinsic value** value of an option at expiration; it is positive when the option is in the money and zero when it is out of the money

> Intrinsic value of a call option
> = Maximum {Value of the underlying – Exercise price, 0}   (18-1)

In Equation 18-1 you can see that the intrinsic value of a call is the difference between the value of the underlying asset and the exercise price when the call is in the money and equals 0 otherwise.

The intrinsic value is the value of the option on the expiration date. However, before expiration, the value of the call will exceed its intrinsic value because of the option's **time value**.[5] The time value reflects the possibility that the option will be in the money before its expiration. The market value of the option, which we refer to as the **option premium**, is the sum of its intrinsic value and its time value. This relationship is given in Equation 18-2:

> **time value** difference between the option premium and the intrinsic value

> **option premium** value of the option

> Option premium = Intrinsic value + Time value   (18-2)

In other words, up until the option's expiration, the call option is always worth more than its intrinsic value because there is a possibility that the option's underlying will increase in value over time. The longer the time remaining to expiration, the greater the option's time value. We can rearrange this equation to solve for the time value:

> Time value = Option premium – Intrinsic value   (18-3)

Consider two call options on XYZ stock, both with exercise prices of 100: One option expires in January 2013, and the other expires in January 2015. On October 9, 2012, when the stock was trading at $125 per share, the values of these two options were $25.20 and $32.05, respectively. Therefore,

	Option Expiration	
	January 2013	*January 2015*
Intrinsic value	$25.00	$25.00
Time value	0.20	7.50
Value of the call option	$25.20	$32.50

[5] An option's time value is also referred to as its *extrinsic value* or *theta*.

The time value for the call option that expires in January 2015 is greater than the time value for the call option that expires in January 2013.

We can look back at the actual stock prices of XYZ and see whether the options were likely exercised or not. Options expire the Saturday following the third Friday of the month. For XYZ's January 2013 call option, it expired January 16, 2013. The price of a share of XYZ stock at the close of trading just before the option expiration was $132 per share. Therefore, if you had bought the January 2013 call option for $25.20, your profit from this is:

		Per Share
	Value of XYZ stock upon exercise of the call option	$132.00
Less	Exercise the option and buy XYZ stock	100.00
Less	Cost of the option	25.20
Equals	Profit	$6.80

How would your decision change for different values of XYZ stock? As long as you can make a profit from exercising and selling the stock, you can cut your loss:

Value of XYZ Stock	Exercise Price of XYZ Stock	Cost of the Option	Decision	Profit or Loss
$92	$100	$25.20	Do not exercise	−$25.20
97	100	25.20	Do not exercise	−25.20
102	100	25.20	Exercise	−23.20
107	100	25.20	Exercise	−18.20
112	100	25.20	Exercise	−13.20
117	100	25.20	Exercise	−8.20
122	100	25.20	Exercise	−3.20
127	100	25.20	Exercise	1.80
132	100	25.20	Exercise	6.80
137	100	25.20	Exercise	11.80
142	100	25.20	Exercise	16.80
147	100	25.20	Exercise	21.80
152	100	25.20	Exercise	26.80

Therefore, as long as you can recoup some of the $25.20 option premium with a profit on the exercise, you would exercise the call option.

PROBLEM

Assume a call option with a $50 exercise price is selling for $3 in the market. Determine the intrinsic value and time value of this call option, assuming the price of the underlying asset is:

A. $48.

B. $50.

C. $52.

EXAMPLE 18.2

Estimating Call Option Intrinsic and Time Values

Solution

A. $Max(48 - 50, 0) = 0$; Time value $= \$3 - 0 = \$3$

B. $Max(50 - 50, 0) = 0$; Time value $= \$3 - 0 = \$3$

C. $Max(52 - 50, 2) = 2$; Time value $= \$3 - 2 = \$1$

It has long been known that the option value depends on the price of the underlying asset. However, it was not until Fischer Black and Myron Scholes, two finance professors from the University of Chicago, came up with the Black–Scholes option pricing model that the relationship was clearly understood.[6]

The option's value is influenced by the relationship between the price of the underlying asset and the strike price. Because the exercise price is fixed for each call option, this essentially means the price of the underlying asset drives the option's value. As the asset's price falls far below the exercise price, not only is the intrinsic value of the option zero, but so is the time value. This occurs because there is less chance of the price of the underlying asset recovering to exceed the strike price. At the other extreme, when the price of the underlying asset is far above the strike price, the time value gets smaller. So deep in the money and deep out of the money call options are easier to value because their values get closer to their intrinsic values as their time values get smaller.

For example, suppose over the next period it is equally likely that the price of the underlying asset will increase or decrease by $5. If the asset price is currently $10, the call option on this asset is deep out of the money. With a decrease in the asset price to $5, the call option is still deep out of the money. Even with an increase in the asset price to $15, it is still deep out of the money. With deep out of the money calls, the investor needs a sequence of very positive returns on the underlying asset to generate any value. This makes the time value very small.

Now take the opposite situation, in which the asset price is $100, so the intrinsic value of the call option is $50, and it is deep in the money. When the price changes by $5, the intrinsic value of the call option also changes by close to $5. If the time value is zero, the change in the value of the call option is exactly the same as the underlying asset. In the extreme case of a call option on an asset with a strike price of $0, then the call option is deep in the money and exactly the same as the underlying asset.[7]

The importance of the underlying asset's price on the call's value means that a curve connects the intrinsic value of the option when it is deep in and deep out of the money. We illustrate this relationship in Figure 18-3. As you can see in this figure, the value of the call option is related in a nonlinear way to the underlying asset price.

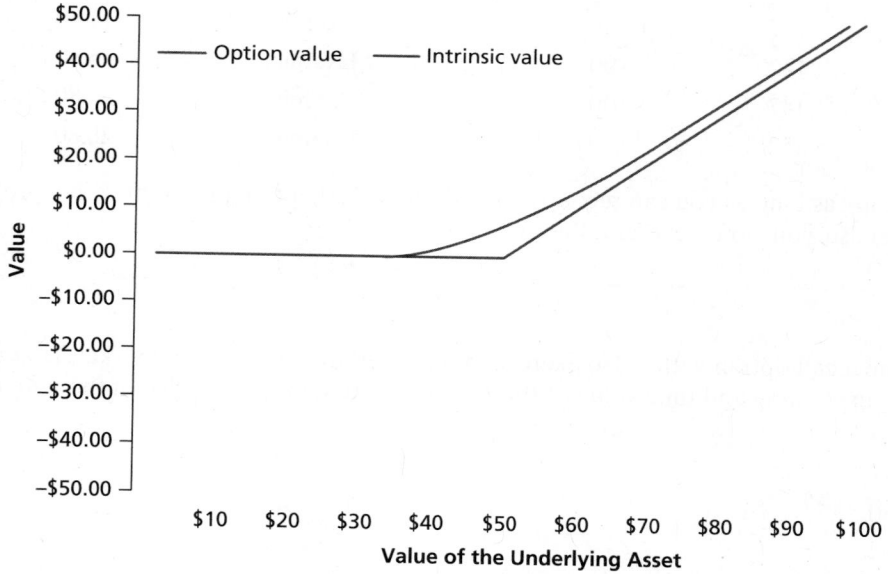

FIGURE 18-3 The Value of a Call Option with an Exercise Price of $50, and the Corresponding Intrinsic Value

[6] Robert Merton was also a pioneer in option pricing. Both he and Myron Scholes won Nobel prizes for their work. Unfortunately Fischer Black died before he could be similarly honored.

[7] This assumes that the value of the asset, like a common share, cannot become negative.

The fact that deep in and out of the money call options are relatively easy to value means that the most difficult options to value are those with a strike price *close* to the price of the underlying. For options that are at the money (i.e., where value of the underlying = exercise price), the time value is at its largest, and by definition, the intrinsic value is zero. Unfortunately, most options start out with the strike price set close to the price of the underlying asset, so they have lots of time value and little intrinsic value. This factor is what makes option valuation complicated.

Factors that affect the value of an option

The price of the underlying asset

First, consider what happens when the price of the underlying asset falls below the exercise price. We know that we are not going to exercise the call and will let it expire worthless, so whether the asset price is $5 or $10 below the strike price doesn't matter. Conversely, it does matter how much the asset price exceeds the exercise price. The call on the low-risk asset will now have an intrinsic value of $5, whereas that on the riskier asset will have an intrinsic value of $10. It is a very important result in option pricing that call options on riskier assets are worth more than those on low-risk assets. The reason for this is that the call protects you from "downside" risk, so how far down you go doesn't matter. All that matters is the upside, or how far above the strike price the asset price can get. Anything that expands the range of outcomes or risk of the underlying asset makes a call option on the asset more valuable.

The time to expiration

Now consider *time*. Risk itself is important, but option values also depend critically on how much time is left until expiration. No matter how risky an underlying asset, if a deep out of the money call option is very close to expiration, say, a day away, it will not be worth much. A deep out of the money call option on a risky asset with a very long time to expiration may be very valuable. Take our previous example of a plus or minus $5 change in the price of the underlying asset. If this is the possible weekly change, then a 1-week call option at $50 is worthless because it is not possible for the price of the underlying asset to exceed $50. However, if the same call has 9 weeks left, it is possible that the price of the underlying asset can increase by $5 each week and go from $10 to $55, thereby giving the call option value.

Over long periods, all sorts of things can happen to give value to the underlying asset and hence the value of a call option on that asset. Call options on risky assets with a long time to expiration are very valuable.

The volatility of the price of the underlying

If a call option is written on an asset whose value does not change much, then there is not a high likelihood that the value of the asset will increase and the option will become valuable. If, on the other hand, a call option is written on an asset whose price changes quite a bit, there is a better chance that the value of this asset will increase and the option become valuable.

Along with the volatility of the underlying's value, we know that value changes compound through time, causing the range of outcomes to increase. This compounding or magnification is greater for high-risk than for low-risk assets, which makes long-dated call options (that is, those with more time to expiry) on risky assets more valuable than similar options on short-dated low-risk assets.

For any given call option, all else constant, its value will *decrease* through time. For example, an at-the-money call option starts out with maximum time value and no intrinsic value. If nothing else changes, and it is still at the money at expiration, then it is worthless. Generally, the time value decreases at an increasing rate as the call gets closer to expiration.

The cash flows on the underlying

Generally, options are not protected from any cash flows generated by the underlying asset, so options on high-dividend-paying stocks or assets with large cash distributions are worth less than those on non-cash flow generating assets.

Why? Consider the case of an option on a stock. Because when the company pays the dividend, the price of the stock declines by approximately the amount of the dividend. If you owned the underlying, you would get the dividend, so this price drop would not matter so much. But if you have the call option on the stock that pays a dividend, you do not receive the dividend, yet the price of the underlying declines by the amount of the dividend. Paying attention to the dividend payments of the underlying asset is important.

The risk-free rate of interest

The final factor that affects option prices is the *risk-free interest rate*. Normally, when interest rates go up, the value of assets goes down. For example, bond prices always decrease when interest rates rise, but equity prices also tend to go down because the equity discount rate increases. However, option prices behave differently because the main effect of increasing interest rates is to decrease the present value of the strike price. An increase in the interest rate has a similar effect on a call option's value as decreasing the strike price. As a result, call options tend to increase with increases in interest rates.

<table>
<tr><td rowspan="2"></td><td colspan="2">*Effect on the Value of a Call Option for . . .*</td></tr>
<tr><td>*an Increase in Factor*</td><td>*a Decrease in Factor*</td></tr>
<tr><td>*Factor*</td><td></td><td></td></tr>
<tr><td>Price of the underlying asset</td><td>+</td><td>−</td></tr>
<tr><td>Strike price</td><td>−</td><td>+</td></tr>
<tr><td>Risk of the underlying asset</td><td>+</td><td>−</td></tr>
<tr><td>Time to expiration</td><td>+</td><td>−</td></tr>
<tr><td>Dividend payments</td><td>−</td><td>+</td></tr>
<tr><td>Interest rates</td><td>+</td><td>−</td></tr>
</table>

SUMMARIZING: FACTORS THAT AFFECT THE VALUE OF A CALL OPTION

That's a lot of factors to consider in a pricing model, and it is important to remember that we considered each of these factors in isolation; that is, the effect of a change in only one factor at a time. In reality, of course, many of these factors are changing all the time and affect one another. For example, an increase in interest rates or a change in risk may have a negative effect on option prices if the indirect effect on the asset price is greater than the direct effects discussed earlier. But, before we consider how to incorporate them into a pricing model, we can place boundaries on the value of the call option by considering the characteristics of put options.

Put Options

As we have noted, a put option gives the owner of the option the right, but not the obligation, to *sell* an underlying asset at a fixed price for a specified time. Consider the value of a put on an underlying asset with a strike price. We depict the payoff for the holder of a put with an exercise price of $50 for values of the underlying assets ranging from $0 to $100 in Figure 18-4.

In considering the behavior of the call option, recall that we first examined a long position in the asset. Because the put is the opposite of a call, we start with the opposite of a long position in the underlying asset, which is a *short position* because holding a put option is having the right to sell the asset. When the underlying asset's value is $55, the investor loses $5. This occurs because he or she has to go into the market and pay $55 to buy the asset to deliver against the forward contract, for which the investor gets only $50. Conversely, if the asset price falls to $45, the investor generates a $5 profit. He or she buys the asset for $45 and then delivers it to meet the forward commitment and receives the $50 exercise price:

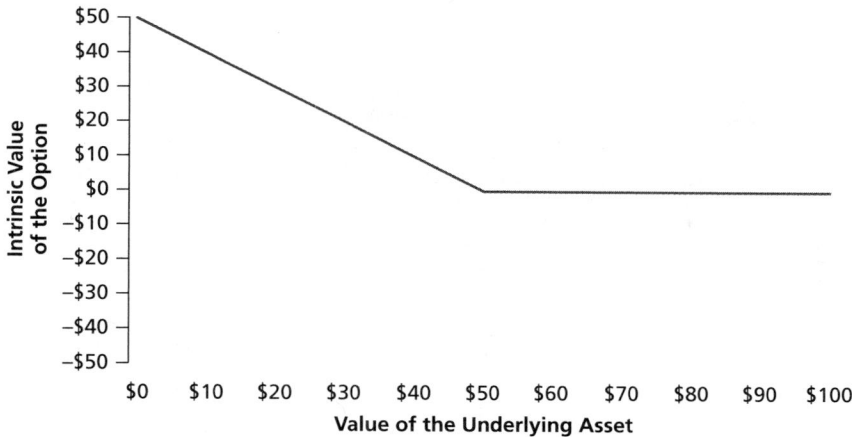

FIGURE 18-4 **Payoff of a Put Option with an Exercise Price of $50**

Price of Underlying Asset	Payoff to Put Option Buyer	Moneyness of Call Option	Payoff to Put Option Writer
$45	$5	In the money	–$5
$46	$4	In the money	–$4
$47	$3	In the money	–$3
$48	$3	In the money	–$2
$49	$1	In the money	–$1
$50	$0	At the money	$0
$51	$0	Out of the money	$0
$52	$0	Out of the money	$0
$53	$0	Out of the money	$0
$54	$0	Out of the money	$0
$55	$0	Out of the money	$0

Graphically, the short position is a 45-degree-angle line going through the value of the underlying $50, as we depict in Figure 18-4. Notice that this is the mirror image of the long position.

Now consider the payoff on the put option. If the asset price increases, then the investor does not exercise the put option because there is no reason to sell the asset for $50 when the investor can sell it in the open market for, say, $55. Conversely, if the asset price drops to $45, the investor exercises the put. It is better to use the put contract and sell it to the counterparty for $50 than to sell it in the open market for $45. The result is the opposite of the call option; put options pay off when the asset price drops below the strike price, and they are worthless when it is above. The put allows an investor to take advantage of the downside risk attached to an asset, just as the call allows an investor to take advantage of the upside.

Now we consider the payoff for the put writer, who has assumed a short position in the put. We know that when the asset's value increases above the strike price, the put expires worthless, so the payoff to both the put owner and writer is zero. When the asset price drops below the strike price, say, to $45, the owner of the put buys the asset for $45 in the open market and sells it to the put writer for $50, making a $5 profit. The put writer's payoff is the opposite of the put holder's because he or she has to pay $50 for an asset that can be sold for only $45, thereby incurring a $5 loss. We depict the payoff for the put writer in Figure 18-5. Notice that it is the mirror image of the put holder's payoff, or is the put holder's payoff folded downward.

EXAMPLE 18.3

Payoffs to Holder of Put Options

PROBLEM

Complete the following table depicting the payoffs for various underlying asset prices for a put option buyer who buys a put option with a strike price of $50.

Asset Price	$30	$40	$50	$55	$60	$70
Put Buyer Payoff						

Solution

Asset Price	$30	$40	$50	$55	$60	$70
Put Buyer Payoff	$20	$10	$0	$0	$0	$0

Notice that the payoff is zero for all prices at or above the strike price of $50. Below $50, the payoff increases by $1 for every $1 decrease in the underlying asset price.

Put option values

We can estimate the intrinsic value of a put option as:

$$\text{Intrinsic value of a put option} = \text{Maximum \{exercise price} - \text{value of the underlying, 0\}} \quad (18\text{-}4)$$

In Equation 18-4, the intrinsic value of a put equals the difference between the exercise price and the value of the underlying when the put is in the money and equals 0 otherwise. Equations 18-2 and 18-3 regarding the time value and option premium of an option apply to puts in the same way as they did for calls.

Consider two put options on IBM stock, each with a strike price of $150. One of the put options has an expiration of January 2010 and a value of $28.70, whereas the other has an expiration of January 2012 and a value of $35.80. Suppose IBM's stock price is $125 in October 2009. The intrinsic value of both put options is $150 – 125 = $25. Therefore, in October 2009,

	Option Expiration	
	January 2010	January 2012
Intrinsic value	$25.00	$25.00
Time value	3.70	10.80
Value of the call option	$28.70	$35.80

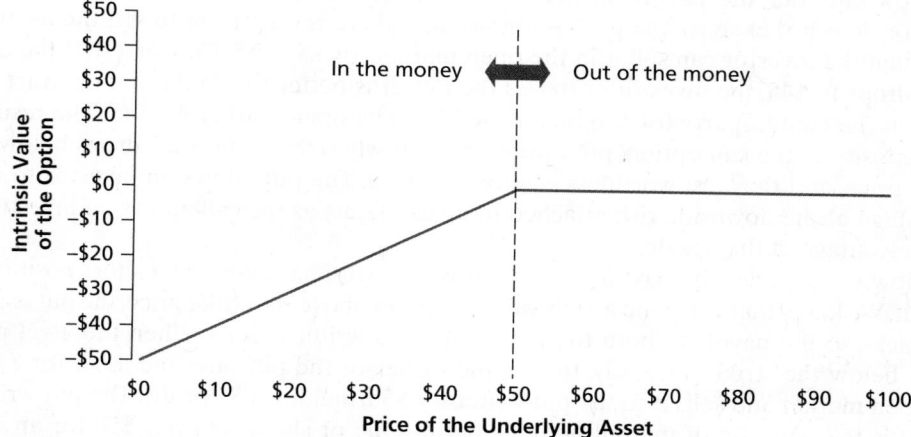

FIGURE 18-5 **Payoff for a Writer of a Put Option with a $50 Exercise Price**

PROBLEM

Assume a put option with a strike price of $50 is selling for $2.25 in the market. Determine the intrinsic value and time value of this put option, assuming the price of the underlying asset is:

A. $48.
B. $50.
C. $52.

Solution

A. Intrinsic value = Max$(50 - 48, 0) = 2$; TV $= 2.25 - 2 = \$0.25$
B. Intrinsic value = Max$(50 - 50, 0) = 0$; TV $= 2.25 - 0 = \$2.25$
C. Intrinsic value = Max$(50 - 52, 0) = 0$; TV $= 2.25 - 0 = \$2.25$

EXAMPLE 18.4
Estimating Put Option Intrinsic and Time Values

The factors that drive put option prices are the same factors that affect call option prices. Though the effects are usually in the opposite direction, there are exceptions. When the asset's value is significantly above the strike price, the put is deep out of the money, so the price approaches its intrinsic value of zero. Conversely, when the asset price drops and is well below the strike price, the put is deep in the money, and again the put's price approaches its intrinsic value. This is opposite the call option, but like the call, the put's maximum time value occurs at the strike price, when its intrinsic value is zero. Opposite to the call, an increase in the asset price decreases the put option value, whereas a higher strike price increases its value. However, an increase in either the expiration date or the risk (uncertainty) in the underlying asset increases the put price in the same manner as it would a call price. A decrease in interest rates or an increase in cash dividend payments increases the put price. All the effects discussed earlier are predictable, given the intuition behind their impact on call prices.

Factor	Effect on the Value of a Put Option for . . .	
	an Increase in Factor	a Decrease in Factor
Price of the underlying asset	−	+
Strike price	+	−
Risk of the underlying asset	+	−
Time to expiration	+	−
Dividend payments	+	−
Interest rates	−	+

SUMMARIZING: FACTORS THAT AFFECT THE VALUE OF A PUT OPTION

Recap: Calls and Puts

Puts and calls have a major difference when it comes to whether or not an investor can exercise the option before the expiration date. Note that a **European option** can be exercised only at maturity, whereas an **American option** can be exercised at any time up to and including the expiration date. This distinction is no longer geographic, as the names imply, because European options are traded in North America and vice versa. For call options on non-dividend-paying assets, the distinction is not important; as long as the

European option option that can be exercised only at maturity

American option option that can be exercised at any time up to and including the expiration date

option can be sold, it should never be exercised before maturity because there is always some time value.[8] However, the distinction may be important for put options.[9] Call and put options are more valuable the more time remaining to expiration and the more volatility in the value of the underlying asset.

<table>
<thead>
<tr><th rowspan="2" style="writing-mode:vertical-rl">SUMMARIZING: FACTORS AFFECTING OPTION PRICES</th><th></th><th>Call Option Value</th><th>Put Option Value</th></tr>
</thead>
<tbody>
<tr><td>Higher asset price</td><td>↑</td><td>↓</td></tr>
<tr><td>Higher exercise price</td><td>↓</td><td>↑</td></tr>
<tr><td>Longer time to expiration</td><td>↑</td><td>↑</td></tr>
<tr><td>Greater volatility</td><td>↑</td><td>↑</td></tr>
<tr><td>Higher interest rates</td><td>↑</td><td>↓</td></tr>
<tr><td>Higher dividends</td><td>↓</td><td>↑</td></tr>
</tbody>
</table>

What if you assembled a position that consists of one call option and one put option, both with the same exercise price? Consider a position with one call and one put option, both with an exercise price of $30. What is the intrinsic value of each option at different values of the underlying around the exercise price? What is the net payoff of this position? The intrinsic value is the difference between the underlying asset's value and the exercise price for the call option and the difference between the exercise price and the value of the underlying asset for the put option. The payoff for this position is the sum of these intrinsic values:

(a) Underlying Value	(b) Exercise Price	(c) = (a) − (b) Intrinsic Value of the Call Option	(d) = (b) − (a) Intrinsic Value of the Put Option	(e) = (c) + (d) Payoff
$25	$30	$0	$5	$5
$26	$30	$0	$4	$4
$27	$30	$0	$3	$3
$28	$30	$0	$2	$2
$29	$30	$0	$1	$1
$30	$30	$0	$0	$0
$31	$30	$1	$0	$1
$32	$30	$2	$0	$2
$33	$30	$3	$0	$3
$34	$30	$4	$0	$4
$35	$30	$5	$0	$5

[8] For interest- or dividend-paying assets, premature exercise may occur in the case of a very large payment that significantly reduces the value of the underlying asset.

[9] Consider what happens if the underlying asset price goes to zero, perhaps because it is a common share and the firm goes bankrupt. Because the underlying asset can never go below zero, the put reaches its maximum value. In this case, all American options would be exercised because the put holder gets the maximum payoff immediately, and that cash can then be reinvested elsewhere.

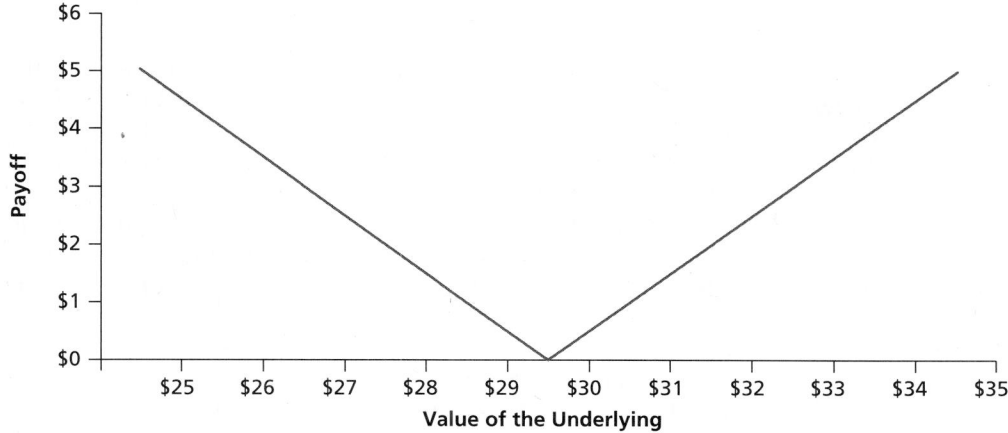

FIGURE 18-6 Payoff Diagram for a Straddle Strategy

In other words, before considering what the investor paid for the options, this position profits when the underlying asset's value is different than the exercise price. In other words, the investor profits when the price moves either direction away from the exercise price, as we show in Figure 18-6.[10] You can see in this figure why this position is referred to as a straddle.

What's the Difference Between Insurance and an Option Strategy?

Investors can use options and other derivatives to protect an investment position from an adverse movement in the price of the underlying; in other words, as part of their risk management.

Let's look at weather derivatives. A weather derivative is an investment vehicle that pays out if a specified weather event occurs (e.g., hurricane, tornado, drought). This type of derivative could be useful in offsetting a risk that is related to weather (e.g., in farming), and can be in the form of an option or a swap. For example, there are cooling degree day options (CDD) and heating degree day options (HDD). In the case of a cooling degree day option, you first average the high and low temperatures each day of the specific location and period. You then compare the average temperature with 65 degrees. If you sum all of these differences for a period of time, you get the value of the contract in degrees; we then convert this to a dollar amount, in the case of this type of option, by multiplying by $20. Sounds complicated, but this is basically valuing deviations in temperatures, with profits going to the party who has the better weather forecast. And you can buy and sell weather derivatives on organized exchanges, such as the Chicago Mercantile Exchange and the NYSE London International Financial Futures Exchange (LIFFE), for weather most anywhere in the world.

Who would invest in weather derivatives? Many manufacturers, producers, and retailers. If you are a supplier of home heating oil, you may want to be protected in case it is an unseasonably warm winter. If you operate outdoor water parks, you may want to hedge the risk of cold weather.

What makes a weather derivative different from, say, traditional options? First, you can't buy the underlying—weather. Second, you can use weather derivatives to hedge against changes in a quantity that someone produces or ships, but these contracts are not as useful when it comes to offsetting the risk related to the price or cost of goods.

Are weather derivatives a form of insurance? Not really. Although weather derivatives can be used to protect the investor or company in the case of a specific weather event, it is not insurance for a couple of reasons. First, if an event occurs in the case of insurance, the insured must file a claim; no such filing is necessary in a weather derivative. Second, the weather derivative can be used in the case of a good outcome (e.g., a weather derivative that pays off if the weather is good) or a bad outcome, whereas insurance is protection against bad outcomes. An example of protecting against a good outcome is the Florida orange grower that wants to be protected in the event that Brazil has good weather—which is bad for the market for Florida oranges.

[10] This position is referred to as a straddle.

Options Markets

Options on stocks and other securities are either traded over the counter, mainly with the major banks, or on organized exchanges. In the U.S., options are traded predominantly on the Chicago Board Options Exchange (CBOE).[11] Option prices are quoted by the strike price and the expiry. For example, consider the quotes for options on IBM stock as of December 16, 2011, that we provide in Table 18-1.

Let's interpret the information in Table 18-1. *Last* is the last price of the option and reflects the price for the most recent transaction. *Bid* is bid price, the price you would get if you sold the option, whereas *Ask* is the ask price, what you would pay for the option. *Volume* represents the number of contracts traded during the trading day, and *Open Interest* is the number of outstanding, open contracts as of this point in time.

For option prices, most of the data are objective and verifiable, such as the strike price, the current price of the underlying asset, the risk-free rate, and the expiration date. The only "soft" number involved in valuing an option is the volatility of the underlying asset's price. However, once we observe the price of the option in a market, we can work backwards, applying a bit of algebra, and calculate the volatility that matches this price. This number is the **implied volatility** of the option.

implied volatility
estimate of the price volatility of the underlying asset based on observed option prices

Several financial services and markets provide the estimate of the implied volatility. For example, the CBOE, through their IVolatility.com service, provides implied volatility indexes and a calculator for the implied volatility for individual options.

TABLE 18-1   Call Option Quotes on IBM Stock as of December 16, 2011

Price of IBM Stock
12/16/2011 = $183.57 per share

Expiration	Strike	Symbol	Last	Bid	Ask	Volume	Open Interest
Jan 12	140	IBMHP.X	42.20	42.05	44.30	5	4,589
Jan 12	180	IBMHT.X	7.70	7.70	7.80	920	10,207
Jan 13	140	IBMJP.X	49.02	48.75	49.25	12	601
Jan 13	180	IBMJT.X	20.60	20.80	21.05	22	1,866
Jan 14	140	IBMAP.X	56.15	52.15	53.10	2	415
Jan 14	180	IBMAT.X	26.20	26.50	27.40	1	173

Source: *Yahoo! Finance, finance.yahoo.com.*

Concept Review Questions

1. Briefly describe the main factors that affect a call option's value, and how they affect the value.

2. Explain how to estimate the intrinsic value and time value for a put option and for a call option.

3. Explain where options are traded.

4. What information do implied volatilities provide?

[11] Trading of options in Europe is performed in a number of exchanges, but the largest is the Eurex, which is operated by the Swiss Exchange and the Deutsche Börse AG.

SEC Charges Monster Worldwide Inc. for Options Backdating Scheme | ETHICS

The SEC brought charges against a number of companies, many of them Internet companies, for backdating executive stock options—that is, changing the date of the option grant back in time. The case against Monster Worldwide is an example of such a backdating scheme and how it affected financial disclosures.

The Securities and Exchange Commission (the "SEC") today charged Monster Worldwide, Inc., for its multi-year scheme to secretly backdate stock options granted to thousands of Monster officers, directors and employees. Monster agreed to pay a $2.5 million penalty to settle the SEC's charges that the company defrauded investors by granting backdated, undisclosed "in-the-money" stock options while failing to record required non-cash charges for option-related compensation expenses.

The SEC's complaint, filed in the District Court for Southern District of New York, alleges that in connection with this scheme, Monster filed false and materially misleading statements concerning the true grant date and exercise price of stock options in its annual, quarterly and current reports, proxy statements and registration statements. Many of these documents also falsely represented

that stock options were being granted at fair market value. Further, Monster failed to record and disclose the compensation expense associated with the "in-the-money" portion of stock option grants. As a result, Monster materially overstated its quarterly and annual earnings in its financial statements and was required to restate its historical financial results for 1997–2005 in a cumulative pre-tax amount of approximately $339.5 million to record additional non-cash charges for option-related compensation expenses.

Without admitting or denying liability, Monster agreed to be permanently enjoined from violations of Section 17(a) of the Securities Act, Sections 10(b), 13(a), 13(b)(2)(A), 13(b)(2)(B), and 14(a) of the Exchange Act, and Rules 10b-5, 12b-20, 13a-1, 13a-11, 13a-13, and 14a-9 thereunder. Monster also agreed to pay a $2.5 million penalty. The Commission took into account the cooperation that Monster provided Commission staff during the course of the investigation.

Sources: United States District Court for the Southern District of New York, Civil Action No. 09 CV 4641 (S.D.N.Y. May 18, 2009), U.S. Securities and Exchange Commission, Litigation Release No. 21042 / May 18, 2009, Accounting and Auditing Release No. 2970 / May 18, 2009.

18.2 FORWARD AND FUTURES CONTRACTS

Forward and futures contracts are commitments by two parties for a transaction at a specific point of time in the future. The contracts may be designed for many different types of underlying assets, and the assets include commodities, energy, equity indexes, interest rates, metals, real estate, and weather. The subtle distinction between the forwards and futures is that a futures contract is a standardized form of a forward contract.

The Basics

As we have mentioned previously, a forward contract is a contract made today for a future delivery of a specified asset. In contrast, a **spot contract** is established today for immediate purchase and delivery of an asset. The definition of immediate delivery depends on the nature of the underlying contract. For foreign exchange contracts, it is generally defined as the next day for exchanging one currency for another for actively traded currencies, and two days for many other less actively traded currencies. In contrast, delivery in a forward contract can be specified for almost any future date.

If you are on one side of a transaction, we refer to the other party as the **counterparty**. One of the risks in using forward contracts is that there is a possibility that one party will default on the obligation; that is, the party obligated to take delivery may not pay what is contracted, or the party obligated to provide the underlying may not deliver it. This creates a risk, which we refer to as **credit risk** or **counterparty risk**. Buying or selling a forward contract requires that a customer have a banking relationship. It is not possible

spot contract agreement for the immediate purchase of an asset

counterparty party on the other side of a forward contract

credit risk or **counterparty risk** uncertainty that a borrower will not repay what is owed or does not have the required payment

for ordinary individuals to access the forward foreign exchange market because forward contracts are not traded in any open market. In this way, forwards are *over-the-counter (OTC)* markets. Because a forward contract involves credit risk, investors may need a line of credit with a bank before it will sell the contract. Once this hurdle has been overcome, forwards are flexible in both the term and the amount of money involved. However, what makes them flexible for corporations also makes them difficult to trade.

Over the past 30 years, a traded instrument has rapidly developed that largely does the same thing: the futures contract. For something to be tradable, it has to be standardized so that people buying or selling it over the telephone or Internet know exactly what they are getting. The dramatic growth in the development of futures markets occurred because these problems have been solved. So let's consider how.

We use currency futures to illustrate how futures work. In Table 18-2, we show foreign exchange rates provided by the Chicago Mercantile Exchange for foreign currency futures. A **foreign currency future** or **currency future** is a contract to exchange two specified currencies at a specified rate at a specified point of time in the future. The **spot price**, which we also show in Table 18-2, is the current or cash price, which for currency exchange is the rate at which one currency is exchanged for the other currency today.

We provide the exchange rate for two currency pairs: the Eurodollar (EUR) for the U.S. dollar (USD), and the Canadian dollar (CAD) for the U.S. dollar in Table 18-2. What do these quotes mean? The reference to EUR/USD means that the EUR is the base currency and the U.S. dollar is the pricing currency:[12]

$$\text{Exchange rate} = {}^{\text{Base currency}}\!/_{\text{Pricing currency}}$$

The exchange rate tells us how much we would get of one currency—the base—in exchange for another—the pricing currency. The quote, therefore, indicates how much of the denominator you get for using one monetary unit of the numerator or base currency. Therefore, EUR/USD 1.3973 means that you can buy 1.3973 U.S. dollars (that is, USD1.3973) for every €1. This also means, if we look at the flipside, that USD/EUR is $1 \div 1.3973 = 0.7159$, or for every USD1 you get €0.7159.

Looking at the quotes on currency futures provides information on investors' forecast for future exchange rates. Because forward rates are the price today for future delivery, they reflect the fact that foreign currency is not worth the same if received at different points in time. If future quotes are higher than spot or near-term quotes, this means that the base currency is appreciating, vis-à-vis the primary currency; if future quotes are lower than the spot or near-term quotes, this means that the base currency is depreciating vis-à-vis the primary currency. For example, according to Table 18-2, if one million U.S. dollars (USD1 million)

foreign currency future or **currency future** contract to exchange two specified currencies at a specified rate at a specified point of time in the future

spot price price that is established today for immediate delivery

TABLE 18-2 Currency Spot and Futures Contract Quotes from the CME Group

	Quoted Rate	
Contract	*EUR/USD*	*CAD/USD*
Spot, July 2009	1.3973	0.8637
Sep 2009	1.3961	0.8631
Dec 2009	1.3957	0.8634
Mar 2010	1.3970	0.8634
Jun 2010	1.3849	0.8638
Sep 2010	1.3852	0.8638
Dec 2010	1.3855	0.8559

Source: *CME Group, www.cmegroup.com, July 9, 2009.*

[12] The pricing currency is also referred to as the quote currency and the counter currency.

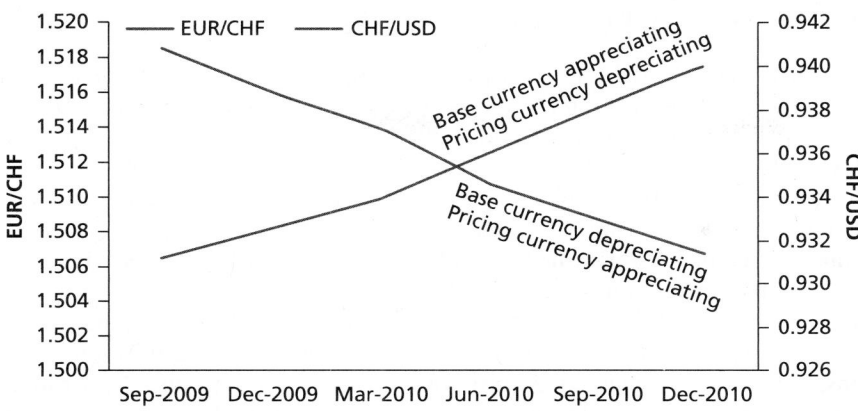

FIGURE 18-7 Futures Contracts as Expectations for Two Currency Pairs
Source: *CME Group, www.cmegroup.com, July 20, 2009.*

is exchanged on the date of these quotes (that is, spot), the investor would get €0.7159 million. However, if the investor wanted to fix a price today for USD1 million to be delivered in December 2010, he or she would only get $1 \div 1.3855 = €0.7218$ million, indicating that investors believe that U.S. dollars will be worth less in the future than they are now. The structure of the futures quotes in Table 18-2 indicates that investors see the Eurodollar depreciating relative to the U.S. dollar.

Interpreting the futures contract quotes we illustrate in Figure 18-7, we see that the U.S. dollar is expected to appreciate relative to the Swiss Franc (CHF): The Sep 2009 CHF/USD contract is 0.9312, which means you get USD0.9312 for every one CHF, whereas the Dec 2010 contract quote is 0.94, which means you get USD0.94 for every one CHF. In Figure 18-7, we also see that the Swiss Franc is expected to appreciate relative to the Eurodollar: The Sep 2010 contract quote is EUR/CHF 1.5185, which means you get CHF 1.5185 for every €1, whereas the Dec 2010 contract quote is 1.5067, which means you get fewer CHF (that is, 1.5067), for every €1.

Futures Contracts

As we mentioned previously, the key difference between a forward contract and a futures contract is standardization of the contract terms. Producing a standardized contract requires that both the underlying asset and the term of the contract be standardized. The term of the contract is set by the individual exchange, but most futures exchanges follow the lead of the CME Group and set delivery months as March, June, September, and December. In practice, physical delivery rarely takes place because most positions are closed out with an offsetting transaction before the final day of trading, which is generally a couple of days before delivery. In this way, futures contracts are designed to share the price risk and not actually transfer the underlying asset. Most futures contracts have a rolling 18-month term, so at any point investors can normally buy and sell futures on the same commodity with six different maturity dates.

To standardize the underlying asset, the exchange specifies precisely what is being traded, so that even though delivery rarely takes place, people know exactly what they are buying or selling. For the rare occasions when delivery does take place, the exchange will specify both the location and how delivery will occur. This is why, for example, the London Metals Exchange keeps a list of recognized warehouses. Further, the exchange performs the function of the counterparty to each transaction, reducing the credit risk associated with these contracts. Finally, the exchange determines how much of the asset is traded in each contract. The actual amount varies with the needs of the individuals who are trading.

The Mechanics of Futures Contracts

clearinghouse company that has the responsibility for reducing the credit risk and making sure that delivery takes place for futures contracts and option contracts

margin good faith deposit with the clearinghouse by both the buyer and the seller to ensure they complete the transaction

initial margin relatively small deposit made with the clearinghouse, usually between 2 and 10 percent of the value of the contract

maintenance margin minimum amount that must be maintained in a margin account

marked to market position valuation that considers all unrealized profits and losses

margin call requirement to add money and increase an equity position to a minimum level

daily resettlement marking to market and adjusting investors' equity positions

settlement price price used to settle futures contracts; usually the daily closing price

notional amount or **notional value** base amount used to determine a position in a futures or options contract

offsetting cancelling a futures position by making an equivalent but opposite transaction

First, let's consider credit risk, which arises with the forward contract because the bank worries a borrower will renege on the forward contract if he or she suffers a loss. To solve this problem, all futures contracts are made with a futures exchange, not with an individual. Investor A might buy a futures contract, and investor B might sell one, but instead of one contract between A and B, the two contracts involve each individual and the exchange. The exchange then assigns responsibility for reducing the credit risk and making sure that delivery takes place to a **clearinghouse**. In the U.S., the CME Group provides the clearing function for its futures contracts.[13]

A **margin** is essentially a good faith deposit made by both the buyer and the seller to ensure they complete the transaction. To make sure that people fulfill their contractual obligations, the futures exchanges enforce two types of margins: an **initial margin** and a **maintenance margin**. In effect, it is a performance bond. The margin is set by each clearinghouse based on the risk involved in the underlying asset: the more risky the asset, the higher the margin. The initial margin is relatively small and varies between 2 percent and 10 percent of the value of the contract, but it is required of both the buyer and the seller. Usually, the brokerage house managing the transaction for the customer imposes a higher margin, particularly for new or smaller clients, but they are not permitted to impose smaller margins.[14]

All futures contracts are then **marked to market** each day, as the value of the contract changes. This means that all profits and losses on a futures contract are credited to investors' accounts every day to calculate the equity position in the underlying contracts. If the equity position increases, the investors can withdraw profits; losses reduce investors' equity positions. Whenever an investor's equity position drops below the maintenance margin requirement (normally 75 percent of the initial margin), he or she will receive a **margin call** and will be forced to contribute more money to increase the equity position. If he or she fails to make this margin call, the position will automatically be closed out. This process of marking to market is called **daily resettlement**, based on the contract's **settlement price**, which is normally, but not always, the daily closing price.

For example, suppose a futures contract is for 1,000 units of some underlying asset and the starting price is $50; the contract value is $50,000, which we refer to as the **notional amount** (or **notional value**) of the contract, even though the investor does not have to come up with $50,000 to enter into it. The buyer and seller of this contract both need to deposit the initial margin requirement, which we assume is $2,000 (i.e., 4 percent of $50,000). Let's also assume that the maintenance margin is 75 percent of the initial margin, which is $0.75 \times \$2,000 = \$1,500$ in this case.

The buyer's commitment is to buy 1,000 units at $50, and the seller's commitment is to sell 1,000 units at $50. If the price closes up $0.25 on the first day, at $50.25, the futures contract is now worth $250 to the buyer. This is because the buyer has contracted to buy the asset for $50,000, and it is now worth $50,250, so the equity increases from $2,000 to $2,250. Conversely the seller's equity has declined from $2,000 to $1,750. Like all futures contracts, the gains and losses offset each other. In this case, the buyer has gained $250 at the expense of the seller, and the clearinghouse will transfer this $250 from the seller's account to the buyer's. The next day, the process starts all over again. If the buyer feels that now that the price has gone up, he or she wants to cancel the contract, the buyer makes an **offsetting** sale, and the purchase is canceled.

[13] With its acquisition of the Chicago Board of Trade in 2007 and the NYMEX Holdings in 2008, the CME Group represents the world's largest futures exchange. In addition to CME Group, other examples include the Canadian Derivatives Clearing Corporation (CDCC), which handles these responsibilities for futures contracts as well as option contracts in Canada, and the LCH.Clearnet, which handles the clearinghouse functions of the International Petroleum Exchange and the London Metal Exchange.

[14] Customers are allowed to post margin by depositing securities, such as T-bills.

The buyer can then withdraw the $2,250.[15] In this case the buyer has a $250 profit on the margin deposit of $2,000.

Suppose instead that both parties leave their contract outstanding, and the next day the price increases again, only this time it jumps to $51. Now the buyer's equity position has increased by $1,000 from its starting position, and the seller's equity position has correspondingly decreased by $1,000. The clearing corporation will have transferred this amount from the margin accounts, and now the seller's equity of $1,000 is below the maintenance margin. This drop in margin would result in the seller getting a call from the broker, telling him or her to post more money or the position will be closed. It is this daily resettling, combined with the enforcement of margin requirements, that ensures both the buyer and the seller meet their commitments. This is the reason the margin is viewed as a performance bond: Both the buyer and the seller have to post margin to make sure that they deliver on their promises. The result is the elimination of credit risk, and individuals can trade futures contracts without worrying about the identity of their counterparty, that is, with whom they are trading. We summarize this example in Table 18-3.

Investors may trade futures on a variety of commodities, ranging from traditional agricultural products to newer energy and base metal contracts. Essentially, we see that futures contracts exist on almost any asset that will generate sufficient interest from companies

TABLE 18-3 Equity in Futures Contracts of 1,000 Units, with an Original Contract Price of $50 Per Contract, an Initial Margin of 4 Percent, and a Maintenance Margin of 75 Percent

	Buyer	*Seller*
Price of contract = $50		
Initial margin	$2,000	$2,000
Equity	$2,000	$2,000
Price of contract = $50.25		
Original contract value	$50,000	$50,000
Contract value	50,250	50,250
Change in contract value	$250	–$250
Margin	2,000	2,000
Equity	$2,250	$1,750
Price of contract = $51		
Original contract value	$50,000	$50,000
Contract value	51,000	51,000
Change in contract value	$1,000	–$1,000
Margin	2,000	2,000
Equity	$3,000	$1,000
Required additional margin	0	500
Equity after margin	$3,000	$1,500

[15] Similarly, the investor with the short position in the futures contract could enter into an offsetting purchase to close the position. Entering into offsetting transactions is the most common way of closing futures positions, and actual delivery of the underlying asset occurs very rarely, in less than 5 percent of all futures transactions.

wanting to hedge risk against changes in their prices or that will generate sufficient speculative trading activity. A **hedge** is a position formulated to reduce or eliminate an exposure to risk, generally by taking a position opposite a position that the investor has already assumed.

Suppose a farmer is concerned about falling prices for corn and would like to make sure that he will be able to sell his corn crop at a reasonable price. And suppose he calculates his cost of producing corn to be $2.50 a bushel. While his corn is still growing, he can sell a futures contract to deliver his corn at a specified future date, say June, for $2.75 a bushel. On the other side of the transaction could be a food processor that would like to buy corn in June at $2.75 a bushel. The food processor would buy corn futures at $2.75 a bushel. In this example, each party reduces their risk by locking in the future price of the corn at $2.75. If the price of corn falls to $2.25 a bushel by June, the farmer has come out ahead because he can sell his corn for a $0.25 profit per bushel; the food processor ends up paying too much in this case. If the price of the corn increases to $3.00 per bushel by June, the farmer still has a profit, but has foregone a potential profit of $0.25 per bushel; the food processor has a cost of $2.75 per bushel in this case, instead of $3.00 per bushel, and therefore has come out ahead. What both parties have done is hedge, which results in a reduction in their exposure to risk.[16]

Also note the intense competition among future exchanges. Competition appears through the introduction of new contracts, such as weather derivatives, futures contracts on real estate, and the consumer price index; some of these survive while others die off through lack of interest. Some of the contracts traded are separated by time zones, so the London Metal Exchange contracts do not really compete with the metal contracts traded in New York because there is a 5-hour time difference. However, the expansion in the trading of financial futures has produced direct competition in some time zones around the world.

open interest number of contracts outstanding; the true amount of futures market activity

Similar to options, the **open interest** represents the number of contracts that are outstanding, so when someone buys and another person sells a futures contact, although two transactions are recorded with the exchange, the open interest is just one contract. The open interest, therefore, represents the true amount of futures market activity. For futures on commodities or some other underlying assets, the open interest tends to exhibit seasonality, so this needs to be considered in interpreting trends in open interest.[17]

Summary of Forward and Futures Contracts

We conclude this section by noting the major differences between forward and futures contracts, which we list in Table 18-4. The bottom line is that forward contracts offer more flexibility because they are customized; however, they possess additional risks because

TABLE 18-4 **Summary: Forwards Versus Futures**

Characteristic	*Forwards*	*Futures*
Contracts	Customized	Standardized
Trading	Dealer or OTC Markets	Exchanges
Default (credit) risk	Important	Unimportant—guaranteed by clearinghouse
Initial deposit	Not required	Initial margin and maintenance margin required
Settlement	On maturity date	Marked to market daily

[16] If instead of a party needing the corn, the buyer of the futures contract is a speculator, they could buy the corn at $2.75 and then turn around and sell it in the cash market for $3.00 per bushel.

[17] You can find detailed information on the open long and short positions in the *Commitments of Traders* report provided each week by the Commodity Futures Trading Commission. www.cftc.gov.

the contracts are not actively traded and because they possess credit risk. In other words, although forwards and futures serve the same basic purposes, one might be preferred over the other in some situations.

Boxed In | FINANCE in the News

Making changes in the regulation of financial instruments and markets following the financial crisis of 2007–2008 is not that simple, with possible unintended consequences. At the end of 2011, some of this regulation is still being developed.

The government's push to standardize over-the-counter derivatives could severely disrupt corporate hedging programs.

Eager to prevent a repeat of last year's financial-market meltdown, in which the federal government was forced to bail out a number of big firms or risk a dominoes-like implosion of the credit-default-swaps market, the Treasury Department has drafted legislation that would impose tight new regulatory controls on the entire over-the-counter derivatives market. That market encompasses not just credit default swaps but all sorts of other derivatives contracts companies use to hedge commodity, interest-rate, and currency risks.

Corporations have largely applauded the Administration's efforts to bring more oversight and transparency to this market. But they have railed against Treasury's recommendation to "standardize" as many OTC transactions as possible and have them cleared on an exchange or through a central counterparty (CCP). Although that would both increase transparency and mitigate counterparty risk, it would also force companies to post collateral—cash or Treasuries—against their hedges based on a daily or twice-daily marking to market of their positions, thus tying up precious cash.

It's not just an issue for large companies. While OTC derivatives can be complex, many kinds of companies take advantage of them, even if only sporadically. According to the International Swaps and Derivatives Association, not only do more than 90% of the *Fortune* 500 use customized derivatives but so do half of midsize companies and thousands of small companies. "I would be shocked if I was talking to a treasurer for even a small $50 million company

that didn't know about their availability," says Tim Murphy, foreign-currency risk manager for $25.3 billion manufacturer 3M. Before joining the company 8 years ago, Murphy spent nearly 12 years on the sell side of the derivatives market, at a bank.

Nash-Finch, a $4.7 billion wholesale grocery distributor, uses swaps to convert some of its floating-rate debt to a fixed rate, or to hedge its price exposure on the 3 million to 6 million gallons of diesel fuel its truck fleet burns through each year. It doesn't use derivatives for trading or other speculative purposes. Despite this small footprint—at the start of this year the company had two interest-rate swaps outstanding with a notional value of $52.5 million, and no diesel-fuel swaps—Nash-Finch may soon be among the many companies whose modest hedging programs are less risky but more complicated and expensive.

That's because the push for centralized clearing would, among other things, jeopardize companies' ability to apply favorable hedge-accounting rules to their derivatives transactions. That accounting treatment is available under FAS 133 only when a derivative is "highly effective" in hedging the underlying risk, meaning that its value moves in a nearly perfect inverse relationship to the value of the underlying exposure.

Finance chiefs fear that standardized contracts might not offer that precision, and without hedge accounting, any fluctuations in the value of a company's derivatives positions would flow through to its income statement rather than its balance sheet, introducing an unwanted new source of volatility to the bottom line.

"If companies can't arrange the perfect hedge, they may be caught in a precarious position," says one treasurer. "It can cause pretty severe income-statement volatility, and that goes contrary to the purpose of hedging."

Source: Randy Myers, *CFO Magazine*, "Boxed In," October 1, 2009.

1. Define initial margin, maintenance margin, margin call, open interest, and notional amount.

2. Explain what is meant by "marked to market."

3. Compare and contrast forwards and futures.

Concept Review Questions

18.3 SWAPS

A **swap contract**, or simply a **swap**, is a contract in which parties agree to exchange a future set of cash flows. A swap contract is a derivative security because the cash flows arising from a swap depend on a specified currency exchange rate, interest rate, or value of another asset. For example, one company may have an advantage in borrowing at a fixed rate of interest, whereas the other party may have an advantage in borrowing at a floating rate. These parties may enter into a swap contract, agreeing to swap—or exchange—the fixed and floating cash flows. These cash flows represent the fixed or floating rate based on a notional amount. In other words, the notional amount is the face value of the contract. They don't really swap these cash flows outright; rather, they calculate the cash flow based on the fixed rate, based on the floating rate, and then net the two out: One party pays the other based on the position they took in the swap.

A swap is an agreement between two parties, the counterparties, to exchange cash flows in the future. Note at the outset that this is a direct agreement between two parties: There is no formal exchange to guarantee performance, so the situation involves a dealer or over-the-counter market, and there is credit risk. As a result, like forward contracts, swaps have evolved into a bank instrument, with the banks or swap dealers serving as intermediaries between the two counterparties to the swap.

Interest Rate Swaps

interest rate swap exchange of interest payments on a principal amount in which borrowers switch loan rates

London Interbank Offering Rate (LIBOR) average of the lending rates of selected European banks to their best customers

plain vanilla swap "fixed for floating" interest rate swap; the simplest and most commonly used type of swap

As with most things, the initial contracts are the simplest and the easiest to understand, so let's start with a simple **interest rate swap**. The interest rate swap is an exchange of floating for fixed interest cash flows, where the floating is often tied to the **London Interbank Offering Rate** or **LIBOR**. The LIBOR is a common benchmark rate in transactions and is an average of the lending rates of selected European banks to their best customers. A "fixed for floating" interest rate swap denominated in one currency is commonly referred to as a **plain vanilla swap**, reflecting the fact that it is the simplest and most commonly used type of swap.[18]

We illustrate the initiation of an interest rate swap by considering two hypothetical companies, Company Fixed and Company Float:

- Company Fixed agrees to pay a fixed rate of 3 percent to Company Float. Company Fixed is the fixed-rate payer, also known as the receive-floating party.

- Company Float agrees to pay at a floating rate of the three-month LIBOR to Company Float. Company Float is the floating-rate payer, also referred to as the receive-fixed party.

The notional amount that these companies agree to is $100 million, with the net cash flow to be paid on a semi-annual basis.

Suppose that LIBOR at the time of the agreement is 3 percent. If interest rates do not change throughout the life of this agreement, then neither company gains or loses with this swap. However, if rates change, there are gains and losses. For example, consider the possible interest at the end of the first 6 months:

Possible LIBOR	Fixed Payment	Floating Payment	Swap Net Cash Flows
2 percent	$1.5 million	$1.0 million	$0.5 million
3 percent	$1.5 million	$1.5 million	$0
4 percent	$1.5 million	$2.0 million	–$0.5 million

The swap net cash flows in this table are from the perspective of the receive-fixed party; the cash flows for the receive-floating party are the negatives of each of these. The

---

[18] In practice, swap dealers will also "pocket" some of the spread as payment for their services.

required payments for interest rate swaps are the **net payments**. This means that instead of exchanging the total interest amounts, interest rate swaps involve exchanging payments representing the *difference* between the fixed and floating rates.

If you parse a multiple-period swap agreement into its individual period cash flows, the swap agreement is really a series of forward-rate agreements. A **forward-rate agreement (FRA)** is a forward contract for an exchange based on fixed and floating interest rates, with the differential paid at the end of the contract. Therefore, an interest rate swap is a series of FRAs, with the differential for each contract resulting in a net payment at the end of each FRA.

Valuing a swap, therefore, requires estimating the future LIBOR rates and how these affect the cash flows to the parties; the fixed rate is known, but the LIBOR rates are unknown.[19]

In addition to simply exchanging a series of interest cash flows based on preferences of the borrowers, swaps are useful when there is comparative advantage in borrowing. A **comparative advantage** with respect to borrowing is when one party can borrow cheaper in one market (say, the floating) than they could in another market (say, the fixed-rate market). For example, high-quality borrowers often have the advantage in borrowing in the fixed-rate market, whereas lower-quality borrowers often have the advantage in borrowing in the floating-rate market. While the high-quality borrower faces lower interest rates in both the fixed- and floating-rate markets, as compared to the lower-quality borrower, the credit spreads may be different in the fixed- and floating-rate markets.

For example, the high-quality borrower may face a 5 percent fixed rate and a LIBOR + 50 basis points in the floating market, but the lower-quality borrower may face a 7 percent fixed rate and a LIBOR + 200 basis points in the floating-rate market.[20] In this case, there is a 200 basis point spread in the fixed market, but only a 150 basis point spread in the floating-rate market. These borrowers can exploit this advantage by having the high-quality company borrow at the fixed rate, having the lower-quality company borrow at the floating rate, and then agree to swap fixed for floating cash flows. In this case there is a 50 basis point difference in the credit spreads, which can be shared by the two parties. How much they gain depends on negotiation between the two. However, in principle there is the spread in the spreads, which totals 50 basis points, and which can be shared in a variety of ways between the two parties.

net payment payment representing the difference between the fixed and floating rates, multiplied by the notional amount of the contract

forward-rate agreement (FRA) a contract for an exchange based on the interest calculated on a notional amount based on the difference between specified fixed and floating interest rates

What's the LIBOR Fuss All About?   GLOBAL PERSPECTIVE

The LIBOR is the "trimmed" average (that is, the outliers are excluded) of the rates banks charge other banks in Britain, and is available for several different maturities.[21] The LIBOR has been around since 1984, when the British Bankers' Association created the BBA interest-settlement rates, and has become the base rate in many variable rate contracts. These contracts include credit card debt, bonds, mortgages, and swaps.

Understating the LIBOR, which is the charge, would result in lower costs of capital for individual and company borrowers with contracts tied to LIBOR, but the flipside is that the lenders are making less money. So why would a large, international bank keep LIBOR artificially low? Because it may have resulted in more profits in investment banking and trading.

It became apparent as far back as 2007 that the LIBOR may understate the true rates, and investigations began into possible "fixing" of the rate. Any manipulation of the LIBOR has significant consequences, spanning the globe. In June of 2012, the U.S. Commodity Futures Trading Commission and the Financial Services Authority (Britain's equivalent to the U.S.'s SEC) fined Barclays Bank $200 million, but the scandal has grown, with investigations centered on Barclays Bank and the Bank of England, but likely to spread their scope to the other international banks. It will take years for the lawsuits to be settled.

Sources: Laurence Knight, "How Big Could the LIBOR Scandal Get?" BBC News, July 15, 2012, www.bbc.co.uk; Federal Reserve Bank of New York, "Statement on Barclays and LIBOR," July 10, 2012, www.newyorkfed.org.

---

[19] If you parse a multiple-period swap agreement into its individual period cash flows, you can see that a swap agreement is really a series of forward-rate agreements.

[20] A basis point is 1/100 of 1%.

[21] The BBA collects rates from sixteen institutions. It disregards the four highest and the four lowest, and averages the remaining eight rates.

The comparative advantage argument is a basic one in finance: Anyone offered a good deal in floating-rate funds, but who doesn't need them, should borrow them anyway and use a swap to exchange it for what is needed and lock in the financing advantage. In addition, although the swap market may have developed in response to such comparative advantages, today's swap markets have evolved beyond that. Today, many firms enter into swap arrangements to convert an existing fixed-rate liability into a floating-rate liability, and vice versa.

Other Types of Swaps

In addition to interest rate swaps, other swaps are available for exchanges of a broad range of cash flows. For example:

currency swap exchange of one currency for another to mitigate risk associated with specific assets or liabilities

commodity swap exchange of a fixed price for the floating price of a commodity

equity swap exchange of a fixed cash flow stream for one based on the return on a stock portfolio

- A **currency swap**, in which a party transforms a liability in one currency for a liability in another currency, or a party transforms an asset in one currency for an asset in another currency.
- A **commodity swap**, in which a party locks in the price of a commodity in exchange for paying a fixed price.
- An **equity swap**, in which a party exchanges a fixed cash flow stream for one based on the return on a stock portfolio.
- A **credit default swap (CDS)**, in which a party pays a fixed amount in exchange for a payoff in the event that the specified, underlying credit instrument (e.g., a bond) defaults.

These swaps allow companies to better manage risks by shifting the risk to other parties who are willing to bear this risk for a price. However, swaps are not without criticism. The lack of a regulated market for credit default swaps has encouraged a call for increased regulation and scrutiny of swap markets, which up until 2009 were largely unregulated.

FINANCE in the News | Credit Swaps Probed for Antitrust Over Trading, Clearing, Data

Both the European Union and the U.S. are investigating sixteen banks that traded credit default swaps as well as Markit, a market information provider, for anticompetitive behavior.[22] The U.S. investigation began in 2009, and the European investigation began in 2011. In addition, the European Commission is also investigating a number of these banks as well as IntercontinentalExchange's ICE Clear Europe, a credit default swaps clearinghouse.

How large a market are we talking about? $21.5 trillion dollars. Why worry? Because a large part of this market (that is, over $3 trillion), involves credit default swaps in sovereign (that is, government) debt.

Sources: "EU Opens Investigations into Credit Default Swaps," *Reuters*, April 29, 2011; "Europe Investigating Banks Over Derivatives," *New York Times*, April 29, 2011; Matthew Dalton, "EU Opens Probes of Swaps Market," *Wall Street Journal*, May 1, 2011.

Concept Review Questions

1. Why would a company want to enter into an interest rate swap?
2. How can swaps be used by a business entity to manage risk?

---

[22] One of the issues is that these sixteen banks are shareholders of Markit.

SUMMARY

- Derivatives have become a significant part of the risk management of companies. Derivatives come in a variety of forms—forward agreements, futures contracts, options, and swaps, to name a few—that investors can use to hedge or otherwise manage risk exposures to commodity prices, securities investments, interest rates, and currencies.

- Investors determine the value of a derivative on the basis of expected future cash flows, though these become a bit more complicated than what we saw earlier with the basics of the time value of money.

- Forwards, futures, and swaps can alter a company's future cash flows, mitigating some of the everyday risks that a company faces.

FORMULAS/EQUATIONS

(18-1) Intrinsic value of a call = Maximum {value of the underlying − exercise price, 0}

(18-2) Option premium = Intrinsic value + Time value

(18-3) Time value = Option premium − Intrinsic value

(18-4) Intrinsic value of a put option = Maximum {exercise price − value of the underlying, 0}

QUESTIONS AND PROBLEMS

Multiple Choice

1. Which of the following statements about a call option is *false*?
    A. On the expiration date, a call option has no time value.
    B. A call option is the right, not the obligation, to buy the underlying asset.
    C. A call option is in the money if the asset price is less than the strike price.
    D. A call option is at the money if the asset price is the same as the strike price.

2. Before the expiration of a call option, if its intrinsic value is $12.50 and the market value of the option is $20, the time value of the option is *closest* to:
    A. $7.50.   B. $12.50.   C. $32.50.

3. Which of the following *increases* the value of a call option?
    A. The price of the underlying asset decreases.
    B. The underlying stock increases its dividend payment.
    C. The volatility of the price of the underlying asset decreases.
    D. The remaining time to expiration of the call option increases.

4. Which of the following *decreases* the value of a put option?
    A. The strike price decreases.
    B. The interest rate decreases.
    C. The underlying asset becomes riskier.
    D. The price of the underlying asset decreases.

5. Consider the following characteristics of an option: Underlying asset price is $45, the exercise price is $40. The intrinsic value of the option:

	if the option is a call option	if the option is a put option
A.	$0	$5
B.	$5	$0
C.	$5	$5
D.	$0	$0

6. Which of the following positions is the *most* risky?
   A. Long a call
   B. Long a put
   C. Short a call
   D. Short a put

7. Which of the following options are in the money?
   A. Price of the underlying asset = $40; Exercise price of the call option = $45
   B. Price of the underlying asset = $40; Exercise price of the put option = $38
   C. Price of the underlying asset = $40; Exercise price of the call option = $38

8. In practice, most futures contracts are closed out by:
   A. cash settlement.
   B. leaving the contracts to expire.
   C. actual deliveries of the underlying assets.
   D. an offsetting transaction before the final day of trading.

9. The primary difference between a forward contract and a futures contract is that:
   A. a futures contract is standardized, but a forward contract is not.
   B. a forward contract is standardized, but a futures contract is not.
   C. futures contracts are for longer maturities than forward contracts.
   D. forward contracts are for longer maturities than futures contracts.

10. A plain vanilla interest rate swap involves:
    A. exchanging USD for EUR.
    B. futures contracts for different currencies.
    C. options on both a forward contract and a futures contract.
    D. an agreement to exchange the net amount of a fixed rate and a floating rate applied to a notional amount.

Practice Questions and Problems

18.1　Options

11. List and briefly describe the factors that affect the value of a call option and a put option.

12. Suppose the call options on ABC and DEF are trading at different prices. Both options have the same strike price and the same time to expiration. Provide two possible explanations for why we observe different prices for these options.

13. You have observed that a very smart and successful investor has bought a call and a put on ABC stock. The options have the same strike prices and expire on the same day. What does the smart investor think is going to happen to the ABC stock? Hint: When will she make money on this investment?

14. When comparing an American option and a European option, both of which have the same underlying stock, the same strike price, and the same expiration, which one is more valuable? Why?

15. Fill in the missing information in the following table:

Long or Short	Call or Put	Strike Price	Value of Option Today	At Expiration		
				Value of Underlying Asset	Payoff (Intrinsic Value)	Profit (Loss)
Long	Call	100	2.50	110		
Short	Call	100	2.50	110		
Long	Put	100	2.50	95		
Short	Put	100	2.50	95		
Long	Call	120	2.50	105		
Short	Call	120	2.50	105		
Long	Put	120	2.50	130		
Short	Put	120	2.50	130		

16. Graph the payoffs (intrinsic values) and profits at expiration for the following option investments (one graph for each option):

A. Long call, strike = $55, cost today = $10
B. Short call, strike = $55, cost today = $10
C. Long put, strike = $55, cost today = $10
D. Short put, strike = $55, cost today = $10

17. Suppose you buy two options on the same underlying stock:

Option A: Call option with an exercise price of $20, three months until expiration, and an option premium of $3.

Option B: Put option with an exercise price of $15, three months until expiration, and an option premium of $3

A. Complete the following table:

Price per Share of the Underlying Stock	Profit	Price per Share of the Underlying Stock	Profit
$8		$17	
$9		$18	
$10		$19	
$11		$20	
$12		$21	
$13		$22	
$14		$23	
$15		$24	
$16		$25	

B. Using a spreadsheet program, graph the profit on this set of options, with the vertical axis indicating the profit and the horizontal axis the price of the underlying stock.

C. Why would someone enter into both of these options at the same time?

18.2 Forwards and Futures

18. Briefly describe what is meant by open interest with respect to futures contracts.

19. What is meant by counterparty risk?

20. What is meant by offsetting?

21. Suppose Party A buys a futures contract for delivery of a commodity at $4 per unit, when the spot price of this commodity is $3.5 per unit. What is Party A expecting to happen to the price of this commodity in the future?

22. If an agricultural producer would like to lock in the price of its products when it takes them to the market, what type of forward or futures contract would it most likely engage in?

23. In the movie *Trading Places*, the Dukes brothers buy orange juice futures, driving up the price, and the other characters, Valentine and Winthorpe, sell orange juice futures. When the news comes out that the orange juice crop is not damaged by a freeze, as the Dukes brothers believed, the price of orange juice futures falls. Which of these parties gains when the orange juice futures price falls?

18.3   Swaps

24. Describe what is meant by a plain vanilla swap.

25. Why would any party want to participate in a currency swap?

26. Diagram the cash flows of an interest rate swap in which one party is a fixed-rate payer and the other party is a floating-rate payer.

   A. Assume first that the fixed rate is 6 percent, the floating rate is LIBOR plus 200 basis points, LIBOR is 3 percent, and the notional amount is $1 million.

   B. Assume that the fixed rate is 5 percent, the floating rate is LIBOR plus 200 basis points, LIBOR is 4 percent, and the notional amount is $1 million.

Case

Case 18.1 The Vanilla Bean Company

The Vanilla Bean Company is able to borrow at a fixed interest rate of 7 percent, but if they borrow at a floating rate, the rate would be the three-month LIBOR, plus 275 basis points. The Vanilla Bean Company prefers to borrow at the floating rate. The Select Ice Cream Company, on the other hand, is able to borrow at a fixed rate of 6 percent, but if it borrows at a floating rate, it would be the three-month LIBOR, plus 225 basis points. The Select Ice Cream Company prefers to borrow at the fixed rate.

   A. Does either party have a comparative advantage in the fixed interest rate market? Does either party have a comparative advantage in the floating interest rate market? Explain.

   B. Would it be advantageous for these two companies to enter into an interest rate swap? If so, what terms would likely be most agreeable to both parties?

   C. If the LIBOR were to increase during the term of an interest rate swap between these two parties, which party would benefit the most?

   D. Diagram an interest rate swap in which the Vanilla Bean Company borrows at a fixed rate and the Select Ice Cream Company borrows at a floating rate.

   E. Assuming a notional amount of $100 million, estimate the net payments, indicating the direction of the cash flow, for each of the following 3-month periods and LIBOR rates:

Period	LIBOR
3 months	2.8%
6 months	3.0%
9 months	3.2%
12 months	3.0%
15 months	3.2%
18 months	3.4%
21 months	3.4%
24 months	3.2%

CHAPTER 19

WORKING CAPITAL MANAGEMENT

Burn, Cash, Burn   Companies in financial distress worry about their cash burn rate. *Cash burn* refers to a company's cash on hand and the rate that cash is used in operations due to negative operating cash flows. The *burn rate* is how long a company can operate before it has to raise funds, either by issuing stock or borrowing. For example, Ford burned through $4.7 billion of cash in the first six months of 2009, but was able to slow that burn with a significant positive cash flow in the fourth quarter 2009, burning just $300 million for the entire year of 2009. The fate of Ford depended on its ability to slow the cash burn, which it did.

Many companies suffer from cash burn leading up to bankruptcy, including United Airlines in 2002 and Consolidated Freightways in 2002. Consider Borders Group, a retail bookstore chain that filed for bankruptcy in 2011. Borders' burned through cash as it approached bankruptcy:

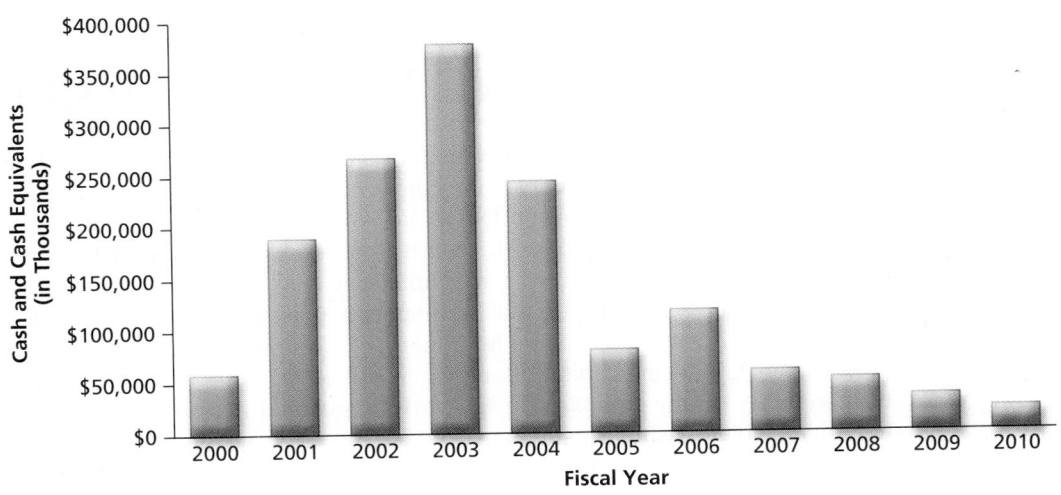

Sources: Bailey, David, "Ford Seen Narrowing Loss, Focus on Cash Burn," *Reuters*, October 30, 2009; B. E. McClure, "Don't Get Burned by the Burn Rate," *Investopedia*, accessed November 1, 2009; William B. Rouse, *Enterprise Transformation: Understanding and Enabling Fundamental Change* (Hoboken, NJ: John Wiley & Sons, 2006); Borders Group 10-K filings, various years.

Learning Outcomes

After reading this chapter, you should be able to:

LO 19.1 Explain why the management of net working capital is critical for the survival of a company, and identify key financial ratios that are used in evaluating working capital management.

LO 19.2 Describe the motives for holding cash and cash equivalents, and explain techniques that financial managers can use to manage cash.

LO 19.3 Explain how credit policies are managed, considering the costs and benefits of extending credit to customers.

LO 19.4 Describe methods of managing inventory and identify the primary costs and benefits associated with inventory levels.

LO 19.5 Calculate the cost of using the different sources of short-term financing, including trade credit, bank loans, bankers' acceptances, and commercial paper.

Chapter Preview In this chapter, we discuss the various dimensions of the management of working capital, where working capital includes cash, accounts receivable, inventory, and the offsetting account of accounts payable. Because working capital is essential for the day-to-day operations of a company, financial managers need to insure that there is sufficient cash on hand and inventory to meet customer needs, while at the same time not having too much investment in cash or inventory on hand. Financial managers must also weigh the benefits of extending credit, thus creating accounts receivables, against the cost of bad accounts and the cost of not receiving payments in cash. As well, financial managers must be aware of the cost of borrowing short-term, whether that be through trade credit, bank loans, or other means.

19.1 ANALYZING WORKING CAPITAL

working capital management manner in which a company manages both its current assets (cash and marketable securities, accounts receivable, and inventories) and its current liabilities (accounts payable, notes payables, and short-term borrowing arrangements)

Working capital is the sum of the company's current assets, whereas **net working capital (NWC)** is the difference between a company's current assets and its current liabilities. **Working capital management** refers to the way in which a company manages both its current assets (i.e., cash and marketable securities, accounts receivable, and inventories) and its current liabilities (i.e., accounts payable, notes payables, and short-term borrowing arrangements). We discuss various methods companies can use to make these decisions. Our focus is on a company's working capital accounts: its current assets and current liabilities.

Managing working capital effectively is critical to both the short-term and the long-term viability of any company. In fact, working capital mismanagement can often cause liquidity problems, which, in the extreme case, can force a company into bankruptcy. Every company has to manage its working capital on a day-to-day basis, whereas the decisions regarding capital structure, dividend policy, and capital budgeting are often episodic decisions that are made quite infrequently by many companies. Consequently, this chapter covers "bread-and-butter" topics that everyone working in a finance capacity in a nonfinancial company has to know.

What constitutes good working capital management? The answer is complicated. However, we can characterize good working capital management as:

1. The maintenance of optimal cash balances.
2. The investment of any excess liquid funds in marketable securities that provide the best return possible, considering any liquidity or default-risk constraints.
3. The proper management of accounts receivables.
4. The development and maintenance of an efficient inventory management system.
5. The selection of the appropriate level of short-term financing in the least expensive and most flexible manner possible.

The purpose of this chapter is to examine the different facets of working capital management within a business enterprise.

Profits are not cash and a company can only pay its bills with cash. A business with profits, but no cash, cannot survive. Therefore, it is important for financial managers to be aware of the cash flow consequences of decisions.

Cash Flow Analysis

Consider the SeeVu Company, which produces touchscreen display screens for e-readers for $75 each and sells them for $100 each. SeeVu has a policy of keeping a 30-day supply of inventory on hand and requires customers to pay within 30 days.[1] For the months January through May, SeeVu has the following activity:

	(in millions)	
Month	*Number of Units Sold*	*Revenues*
January	1.0	$100
February	1.5	$150
March	2.0	$200
April	2.5	$250
May	3.0	$300
Total	10.0	$1,000

Each month, SeeVu produced what it predicted to be 30 days of screens. For example, in January it sold 1 million screens, but produced 1.5 million to meet the demand for February; in February it sold 1.5 million units and produced 2 million to meet the demand expected in March, and so on. Therefore, its inventory activity was:

	Number of Screens (in thousands)			
Month	*Beginning Balance*	*Add: Produced*	*Subtract: Sold*	*Ending Balance*
January	1,000	1,500	1,000	500
February	500	2,000	1,500	1,000
March	1,000	2,500	2,000	1,500
April	1,500	3,000	2,500	2,000
May	2,000	3,500	3,000	2,500

The cost of goods sold and ending balance of inventory, with each screen with a unit cost of $75, are:

	(in millions)	
Month	*Cost of Goods Sold*	*Ending Balance in Inventory*
January	$75.0	$37.5
February	112.5	$75.0
March	150.0	$112.5
April	187.5	$150.0
May	225.0	$187.5
Total	$750.0	

[1] This example is based on "How to Go Broke . . . While Making a Profit," *Business Week*, April 29, 1956, p. 46.

SeeVu's customers pay in 30 days, so SeeVu collects January's sales in February; February sales in March, and so on:

Accounts Receivable (in millions)

Month	Beginning Balance	Add: Sales on Credit	Subtract: Collections	Ending Balance
January	$100	$100	$100	$100
February	$100	$150	$100	$150
March	$150	$200	$150	$200
April	$200	$250	$200	$250
May	$250	$300	$250	$300

Companies produce four statements: the income statement, the balance sheet, the cash flow statement, and the statement of owners' equity. Of the three, financial analysts tend to focus on the cash flow statement because the other statements frequently have accounting adjustments that make it difficult to find the company's problems. We provide a simplified income and cash flow statement of the SeeVu Company as of June 1 that we show in Table 19-1. We have kept things simple so we can focus on the importance of working capital. Keeping things simple, SeeVu does not have any investment or financing cash flows, so therefore the change in cash is the same as the cash flow from operations.

We know from its income statement that SeeVu Company is a profitable company. When we add up the sales from January through May, we see that SeeVu had sales of $1,000 million. The screens had a $75 cost, so SeeVu had $750 million in cost of goods sold and therefore an operating profit was $250 million. So if SeeVu has a profit of $250 million, is SeeVu doing OK?

trade credit financing provided to customers for the purchase of a product or service

The problem is the change in SeeVu's working capital. SeeVu sells its screens to customers on credit, with customers paying with a 30-day lag. This is typical of **trade credit**, in which a customer orders SeeVu's screens, and the company ships them out, along with an invoice indicating the terms of payment, which in this case is 30 days. By June 1, SeeVu's accounts receivable has increased from $100 to $300 million, an increased investment in

TABLE 19-1   SeeVu Company Income Statement and Statement of Cash Flows

	January through June 1 (in millions)	
Income statement		
Sales	$1,000	
Cost of goods sold	750	
Net income		$250
Statement of cash flows		
Net income		$250
Increase in accounts receivable	$200	
Increase in inventory	150	
Less: Change in working capital		350
Cash flow from operations		–$100

receivables of $200 million. The reason for the increase is the increased sales level from $100 million in January to $300 million in May, meaning that SeeVu granted more credit to its customers, even though its credit policy had not changed.

Similarly, SeeVu has an inventory policy of keeping a 30-day supply on hand so that when customers place orders, SeeVu can box the order and send it out immediately. In January, SeeVu had 1 million screens on hand, with a cost of $75 million, and by June 1 it had 3 million thousand screens at $75 each, or $225 million. SeeVu had increased inventory by 2 million screens, or $15 million. Again, the reason for the increased inventory was the increase in sales level from $100 to $300 million. SeeVu requires a similar increase in inventory of $200,000-worth of screens because the company keeps one month's sales on hand. SeeVu has an increased inventory investment of $150 million.

SeeVu pays its bills immediately, so there are no accounts payable. The change in net working capital is the change in receivables plus inventory minus the change in payables: −$350 million. When the change in net working capital is added to the operating cash flow, we get *cash flow from operations* of −$100 million. Because SeeVu started with $100 million cash in the bank, by the end of May, the cash has been depleted, and SeeVu has run out of cash to finance its operations. At this point, SeeVu's checks would bounce. You can confirm this by tracing SeeVu's cash flows through this period:

		Flows (in millions)		
Month	*Beginning Cash Balance*	*Collections from Customers*	*Payments to Suppliers*	*Ending Cash Balance*
January	$100.0	$100	$112.5	$125.0
February	$125.0	$100	$150.0	$75.0
March	$75.0	$150	$187.5	$37.5
April	$37.5	$200	$225.0	$12.5
May	$12.5	$250	$262.5	$0.0

It is important to note that cash flow from operations is the correct measure of the cash-generating ability of the company. If SeeVu had a cash-only sales policy and did not extend credit, then with the same level of sales, the company would have $1,000 million in cash. However, the fact that SeeVu grants credit to its customers with a 30-day payment period means that as of June 1, SeeVu did not get any cash from the $300 million of sales in May. When companies sell on credit, they have to make sure that they are actually collecting the cash from those sales and consider the lag in receiving cash from its sales. Similarly, the income statement includes only the cost of producing items that the company sells. If production is unsold, it goes into inventory, but the company has still paid to produce it, so there is a cash outflow. The increase in receivables and inventory, net of payables, are the most important net working capital items.

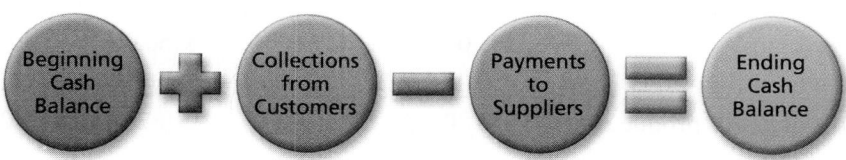

The Cash Budget

SeeVu has a cash flow problem, which is not apparent if the company focuses solely on profit. What is needed to help predict a cash flow problem is a cash flow statement for every month. Companies create a **cash budget**, which is essentially a cash flow statement projected for each month.

So let's think through SeeVu's problem. The sales level was $100 million in January, and SeeVu forecasted a $50 million increase every month in sales. We can start the sales at

cash budget cash flow statement for each period

$100 million for January and then increase by $50 million for every future month. SeeVu could forecast the cash inflow from these sales, which, for SeeVu with a 30-day credit policy, means that each month the company receives as an inflow the previous month's credit sales. In practice, things are slightly more complicated, as we will discuss later.

Remember that the only source of cash from operations is from sales; all the other items are uses of cash. SeeVu spends $75 producing every screen. SeeVu produces two types of screens: those that are sold and those that are held in inventory. For each month, SeeVu has a cash outflow for the cost of the screens produced and sold, which for month 1 (January) is $75 million, for February is $100 million, and so on. However, in February, in addition to production for sales, there is an additional $37.5 million outflow for the 0.5 million screens produced for inventory, because sales have increased by 0.5 million units and SeeVu has a one-month supply policy for inventory. In reality, for February at a sales level of $150 million, SeeVu is receiving only the $100 million from the previous month's sales, while it is paying $112.5 million to produce for the current month's sales and an additional $37.5 million to increase inventory, translating into a net cash outflow of $500.

The cash inflows and outflows record the change in the cash budget each month. SeeVu started with $100 million in cash, which increased to $125,000 after month 1 and then decreased to $75 million after month 2. If SeeVu needed 20 percent of sales in cash "just in case," then the excess cash in January was $105 million. But this excess cash could have been invested for a month. However, by February the drop in cash flow from operations means that the excess cash has dropped precipitously to $45 million. By March, the cash budget indicates that SeeVu has no excess cash and would now be below its desired holding of cash. This was two months *before* SeeVu actually ran out of cash and would have given SeeVu plenty of time to talk to the bank about arranging some short-term credit. We provide SeeVu's cash budget for the next four months in Table 19-2.

TABLE 19-2 SeeVu's Four-Month Cash Budget

	(in millions)	January	February	March	April
	Sales	$100.0	$150.0	$200.0	$250.0
	Cost of goods sold	$75.0	$112.5	$150.0	$187.5
	Number of units sold	1	1.5	2	2.5
	Addition to inventory	0	0.5	0.5	0.5
Start with	Cash inflow from collections	$100.00	$100.00	$150.00	$200.00
	Produced and sold inventory	$75.00	$112.50	$150.00	$187.50
	Produced and held in inventory	0.00	37.50	37.50	37.50
Less	Total outflow for cost of goods produced	$75.00	$150.00	$187.50	$225.00
Equals	Operating cash flow	$25.00	–$50.00	–$37.50	–$25.00
Begin with	Starting cash balance	$100.00	$125.00	$75.00	$37.50
Add	Operating cash	25.00	–50.00	–37.50	–25.00
Equals	Ending cash balance	$125.00	$75.00	$37.50	$12.50
Less	Required cash	20.00	30.00	40.00	50.00
Equals	Surplus or deficit	$105.00	$45.00	–$2.50	–$37.50

The important feature about the cash budget is that it allows the financial manager to forecast cash inflows and outflows over a forecast horizon and to see the cumulative effect on the company's cash balances. Typically, companies prepare a cash budget for at least the upcoming year on at least a monthly (and sometimes even a weekly or daily) basis. These cash budgets are important planning tools for the company. For example, they indicate when and for how long a company can expect to have excess cash balances that it can invest in marketable securities. For SeeVu, this was the first 2 months of the year. Cash budgets also show when and for how long a company may require some additional borrowing to cover any cash shortfalls, so it can arrange for some short-term borrowing.

Banks often require a cash budget as part of the documentation for a loan application because they need to see whether the loan is needed for a short period or is, in fact, permanent financing. If SeeVu had presented this cash flow forecast to the bank at the beginning of the year, the lending officer would have requested that management complete it for the whole year instead of just the first 6 months. We provide the 12-month budget in Table 19-3.

By completing the cash budget for the whole year, it becomes apparent that with the $500 increase in sales each month, SeeVu's cash flow problems peak in May and June and then correct themselves. By July, operating cash flow is positive at $125, and from then on, the operating cash flow increases every month. By October, SeeVu has surplus funds again and can start to invest the excess in marketable securities, as we show in Figure 19-1.

SeeVu would not have enhanced its reputation with the people at the bank if it had gone to see them in May, saying, "Please help me. I am out of cash." At the very least, it would have indicated very poor cash management, and the lending officer would have paid very close attention to any loans made to SeeVu. Instead, if SeeVu had completed the cash budget and explained that it needed to set up a facility whereby it could invest surplus funds at the start and end of the year, and that it needed some short-term borrowing in the middle months, the bank could have designed a borrowing and lending facility for SeeVu. Establishing a good reputation with the bank lending officer is critical, especially for small companies, and the tool for doing this is the cash budget because it enhances an understanding of the cash inflows and outflows through the company.

The key components of a cash budget are sales forecasts, estimated production schedules, and estimates of the size and timing of any other major inflows (e.g., from the sale of an asset) or outflows (e.g., capital expenditures, dividend payments) that the company expects.

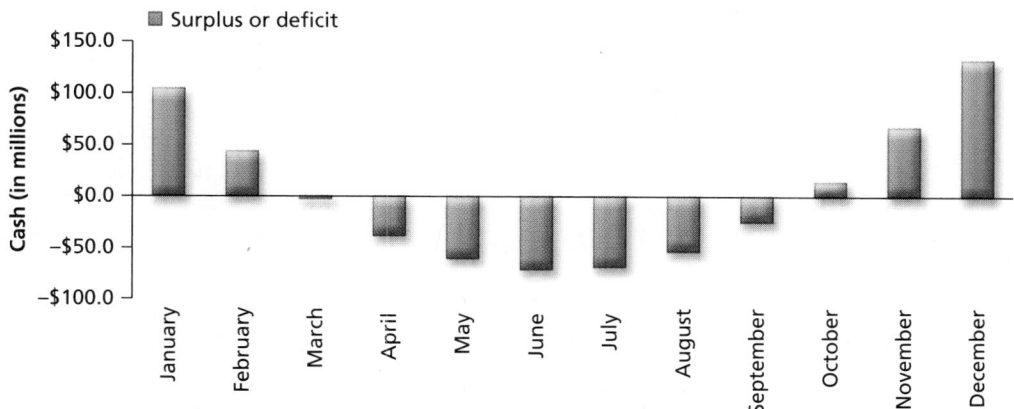

FIGURE 19-1 SeeVu's Cash Surplus or Deficit by Month

TABLE 19-3 SeeVu's 12-Month Cash Budget

(in millions)	January	February	March	April	May	June	July	August	September	October	November	December
Sales	$100.0	$150.0	$200.0	$250.0	$300.0	$350.0	$400.0	$450.0	$500.0	$550.0	$600.0	$650.0
Cost of goods sold	$75.0	$112.5	$150.0	$187.5	$225.0	$262.5	$300.0	$337.5	$375.0	$412.5	$450.0	$487.5
Number of units sold	1	1.5	2	2.5	3	3.5	4	4.5	5	5.5	6	6.5
Addition to inventory	0	0.5	0.5	0.5	0.5	0.5	0.5	0.5	0.5	0.5	0.5	0.5
Cash inflow from collections	$100.0	$100.0	$150.0	$200.0	$250.0	$300.0	$350.0	$400.0	$450.0	$500.0	$550.0	$600.0
Cash outflow for operations												
Produced and sold inventory	$75.0	$112.5	$150.0	$187.5	$225.0	$262.5	$300.0	$337.5	$375.0	$412.5	$450.0	$487.5
Produced and held in inventory	0.0	37.5	37.5	37.5	37.5	37.5	37.5	37.5	37.5	37.5	37.5	37.5
Total outflow for cost of goods produced	$75.0	$150.0	$187.5	$225.0	$262.5	$300.0	$337.5	$375.0	$412.5	$450.0	$487.5	$525.0
Operating cash flow	$25.0	–$50.0	–$37.5	–$25.0	–$12.5	$0.0	$12.5	$25.0	$37.5	$50.0	$62.5	$75.0
Starting cash balance	$100.0	$125.0	$75.0	$37.5	$12.5	$0.0	$0.0	$12.5	$37.5	$75.0	$125.0	$187.5
Operating cash flow	25.0	–50.0	–37.5	–25.0	–12.5	0.0	12.5	25.0	37.5	50.0	62.5	75.0
Ending cash balance	$125.0	$75.0	$37.5	$12.5	$0.0	$0.0	$12.5	$37.5	$75.0	$125.0	$187.5	$262.5
Required cash	20.0	30.0	40.0	50.0	60.0	70.0	80.0	90.0	100.0	110.0	120.0	130.0
Surplus or deficit	$105.0	$45.0	–$2.5	–$37.5	–$60.0	–$70.0	–$67.5	–$52.5	–$25.0	$15.0	$67.5	$132.5

PROBLEM

EXAMPLE 19.1

Cash Budget

A company has estimated its sales, purchases from suppliers, and wages and miscellaneous operating cash outlays for the first 4 months of next year as follows:

Month	Sales	Purchases	Wages and Miscellaneous
January	$10,000	$6,000	$3,000
February	$12,000	$7,500	$3,500
March	$15,000	$5,500	$4,000
April	$11,000	$5,000	$3,000

The company expects:

- 50 percent of its sales will be for cash and that it will collect 80 percent of its credit sales 1 month after the sale, with the remainder being collected in the following month.
- 50 percent of its purchases will be paid 30 days from the purchase date, and the remaining 50 percent will be paid in 60 days.
- Sales and purchases were the same in November and December as they are estimated to be in January.
- To pay dividends of $3,000 in March and to receive $1,500 in January from the sale of a used truck.

The beginning cash balance is $1,000, which is the minimum cash balance the company wants to maintain. Estimate the company's cash budget for the first 4 months of next year.

Solution

	January	February	March	April
Cash inflows				
Sales				
Current month sales	$5,000	$6,000	$7,500	$5,500
Previous month's sales	4,000	4,000	4,800	6,000
Sales from two months ago	1,000	1,000	1,000	1,200
Total sales receipts	$10,000	$11,000	$13,300	$12,700
Other cash inflows	1,500*			
Total cash inflows	$11,500	$11,000	$13,300	$12,700

	January	February	March	April
Cash outflows				
Purchases				
Previous month	$3,000	$3,000	$3,750	$2,750
Two months ago	3,000	3,000	3,000	3,750
Total purchase outflows	$6,000	$6,000	$6,750	$6,500
Wages and miscellaneous	3,000	3,500	4,000	3,000
Other cash outflows	0	0	3,000†	0
Total cash outflows	$9,000	$9,500	$13,750	$9,500
Net cash flow	$2,500	$1,500	–$450	$3,200
Beginning cash	1,000	3,500	5,000	4,550
Ending cash	$3,500	$5,000	$4,550	$7,750

* From sale of truck
† Dividend payment

The company's cash balance is expected to climb to $3,500 in January and not to go below that figure any time before April. Cash is expected to increase to $7,750 by the end of April. This implies that the company could invest as much as $2,500 for at least 3 months in marketable securities and still maintain its $1,000 minimum amount in cash. If the surplus cash position is expected to last longer, excess funds could be invested in other assets.

The cash budget is the basic tool for forecasting the cash inflows and outflows through a company. Although it helps financial managers identify key items, unfortunately, it does not explain the cause of the problem. Instead, we can look at the drivers of cash flow. These drivers include the company's:

credit policy decisions on how a company grants, monitors, and collects payment for outstanding accounts receivable

- **credit policy**, which is the terms under which the company grants credit to its customers;

payment policy decisions on how quickly the company pays its bills

- **payment policy**, which is how quickly the company pays off the credit it receives from other companies; and

inventory policy decisions on the levels of inventory to hold

- **inventory policy**, which is determining how much and of what type of inventory to have on hand.

Working Capital Ratios

quick (or acid test) ratio ratio of the most liquid of the current assets to current liabilities

Two common measures of company liquidity are the **current ratio** and the **quick (or acid test) ratio**:

$$\text{Current ratio} = \frac{\text{Current assets}}{\text{Current liabilities}} \tag{19-1}$$

$$\text{Quick ratio} = \frac{\text{Cash} + \text{Marketable securities} + \text{Accounts receivable}}{\text{Current liabilities}} \tag{19-2}$$

The current ratio measures a company's ability to repay current obligations from current assets, whereas the quick ratio is a more conservative estimate of liquidity that reflects the fact that inventory is generally not as liquid as other current assets, and prepaid expenses are virtually worthless in the event of company liquidation. There are no general rules of thumb as to what are "good" values for these ratios, and optimal ratios vary by industry. For both of these ratios, higher values indicate that a company has more liquidity. However, this does not necessarily mean that the company is practicing effective working capital management. In fact, it could indicate quite the opposite—that is, perhaps the company is being too conservative and maintaining excessive liquidity, or perhaps it has high ratios because its credit policy is too lenient, which has left it with high levels of receivables outstanding.[2]

Although the current and quick ratios are useful summary statistics, they do not tell the whole story of working capital management. To gain better insight into a company's strengths and weaknesses, we need to look at how it arrived at these levels of current assets and current liabilities. Several efficiency ratios are specifically related to working capital items. We begin by looking at two ratios related to accounts receivables, assuming that all sales are on credit:

$$\text{Accounts receivable turnover} = \frac{\text{Revenues}}{\text{Accounts receivable}} \tag{19-3}$$

$$\text{Days sales outstanding} = \frac{\text{Accounts receivable}}{\text{Average daily sales}} = \frac{365}{\text{Accounts receivable turnover}} \tag{19-4}$$

---

[2] The same could be said with respect to the current ratio if the company maintains excess inventory. This would not affect the quick ratio.

which is equivalent to:

$$\text{Days sales outstanding} = \frac{365}{\text{Accounts receivable turnover}}$$

The receivables turnover ratio is a measure of the sales generated for each dollar in receivables, whereas the **days sales outstanding (DSO)** is a measure of how long it takes the average customer to pay his or her account. The DSO is 365 divided by the receivables turnover—that is, if accounts receivable turn over 10 times per year, the DSO is 36.5 days ($365 \div 10$). Technically, we should use credit sales, not total sales, for both of these ratios; however, because most companies do not break out sales into cash and credit sales, it is common to use the total sales figures.

Efficiency ratios related to inventory include the inventory turnover ratio:

$$\text{Inventory turnover} = \frac{\text{Cost of goods sold}}{\text{Inventory}} \qquad (19\text{-}5)$$

The numerator of this ratio is the cost of goods sold because when the company sells inventory, it expenses this cost through this account.[3]

Similar to our derivation of the DSO, we can divide 365 days by the inventory turnover ratio to find the **days sales in inventory (DSI)**:

$$\text{Days sales in inventory} = \frac{\text{Inventory}}{\text{Average days cost of goods sold}} \qquad (19\text{-}6)$$

which is equivalent to:

$$\text{Days sales in inventory} = \frac{365}{\text{Inventory turnover}}$$

Notice that higher receivables turnover and higher inventory turnover generally indicate more efficient management of these current assets. However, they would cause a company's current ratio (and its quick ratio, in the case of receivables turnover) to decline, all else being equal. This in itself demonstrates why current and quick ratios, when viewed in isolation, are insufficient measures of working capital management.

Finally, we focus on the current liability side of the working capital management issue by introducing the following two ratios that pertain to a company's management of its accounts payable, the accounts payable turnover and the days payables outstanding. The accounts payable turnover is the number of times in a year, on average, the company has a complete cycle of generating payable accounts and paying on these accounts:

$$\text{Accounts payables turnover} = \frac{\text{Purchases}}{\text{Accounts payable}} \qquad (19\text{-}7)$$

The **days payables outstanding (DPO)** is the length of time, in days, it takes for the company to pay its suppliers:[4]

$$\text{Days payables outstanding} = \frac{\text{Accounts payable}}{\text{Average days' purchases}} \qquad (19\text{-}8)$$

---

[3] In practice, because of accounting differences, the cost of goods sold figure is neither always reliable nor always comparable across companies. Financial analysts must first adjust the companies' accounts to the same basis before any comparison. Because of the accounting principles, the easiest method is to convert the accounts to a first in, first out (FIFO) basis.

[4] Remember from accounting that beginning inventory, plus purchases, is equal to cost of goods sold plus ending inventory. Therefore, purchases = cost of goods sold + ending inventory − beginning inventory. Some use cost of goods sold in place of purchases; this, however, assumes that inventory does not change over the period.

which is also equal to:

$$\text{Days payables outstanding} = \frac{365}{\text{Accounts payable turnover}}$$

We interpret the accounts payables turnover ratio as how many times a year a company pays off its suppliers, on average. The days payables outstanding ratio represents how long, on average, a company defers payments to its suppliers.

Operating and Cash Conversion Cycles

Two additional summary measures of working capital management deal specifically with the amount of time a company must wait for cash to be generated from its sales and how much financing it will require. The **operating cycle**, also known as the **days working capital, DWC**, is the average time it takes the company to acquire inventory, sell it, and collect the sale proceeds. As such, we estimate the operating cycle as the sum of the average days of sales in inventory (DSI) and the average collection period (DSO):

$$\text{Operating cycle} = \text{DSI} + \text{DSO} \tag{19-9}$$

Using the operating cycle, we measure the average number of days a company holds items in inventory before they are sold, plus the average time it takes to collect on sales. A long operating cycle indicates that a company has a long operating cycle that requires large average investments in receivables or inventory. However, to estimate the amount of financing a company requires, we must also consider how long it is able to delay making payments to suppliers. We measure this by using the company's days of payables outstanding. Recall that this measures how long the company defers paying receivables on average.

The **cash conversion cycle (CCC)** is a measure of the average time between when a company pays cash for its inventory purchases and when it receives cash for its sales. In essence, the CCC represents the average number of days of sales that a company must finance outside the use of trade credit. As such, it is an important ratio that companies and their creditors consider when arranging financing. It can be broken into two components: the operating cycle and the DPO:

cash conversion cycle (CCC) estimate of the average time between when a company pays cash for its inventory purchases and when it receives cash for its sales

$$\text{CCC} = \text{DSI} + \text{DSO} - \text{DPO} \tag{19-10}$$

We now return to our discussion of SeeVu Company. SeeVu had a policy of keeping one month's sales in inventory, allowing 30 days of credit, and paying bills immediately. Therefore, SeeVu's DSI was 30 days, as was its DSO, whereas its DPO was zero. This translates into an operating cycle and a cash conversion cycle of 60 days. If SeeVu immediately pays its bills for its screens, it then has to finance them for 30 days while they sit in inventory and for another 30 days before the company receives payment for them when the screen are sold. In other words, SeeVu has to finance 60 days' worth of sales.

The cash conversion cycle is related to a company's need for cash. If the company speeds up its collection policy, it gets its cash earlier, and the number of days in receivables goes down. Similarly, if it increases its inventory turnover ratio, then it needs less inventory, and the number of days sales it ties up in inventory goes down. Finally, if it delays paying its bills, then it has larger accounts payable. As a result of undertaking any of these actions, the company can grow at a faster rate without needing cash, and the cash conversion cycle gets shorter.

An Example

Consider Archer-Daniels-Midland (ADM), an agricultural processing company. The basic information that we need to calculate the measures of working capital management comes from the balance sheet and the income statement.

PROBLEM

The 2010 Working Capital Scoreboard reports the median for the following:[5]

	Aerospace and Defense	Food Products	Semiconductors
Days sales outstanding	62	24	50
Days sales in inventory	48	40	44
Days payables outstanding	25	21	33

1. What is the operating cycle of each industry?
2. What is the cash conversion cycle of each industry?

Solution

	Aerospace and Defense	Food Products	Semiconductors
Operating cycle	110	64	94
Cash conversion cycle	85	43	61

EXAMPLE 19.2

The Operating Cycle

From the income statement, we need sales and cost of goods sold:

(in millions)	Fiscal Year End June 30, 2009
Sales	$69,207
Cost of goods sold	$65,118

From the balance sheet we need the balances in receivables, inventories, and accounts payables:

(in millions)	June 30, 2009	June 30, 2008
Accounts receivable	$7,311	$11,483
Inventories	$7,782	$10,160
Accounts payable	$5,786	$6,544

The only other data item we need is to calculate purchases for the fiscal year end June 30, 2009, which are $62,740 million.[6]

The days sales outstanding, DSO, with account values in millions, is:

$$DSO = \frac{\$7,311}{\$69,207/365} = 38.558$$

The days sales in inventory, DSI, with account values in millions, is:

$$DSI = \frac{\$7,782}{\$65,118/365} = 43.620$$

[5] "Working It Out: The 2010 Working Capital Scoreboard," CFO, June 1, 2010.

[6] This is from the relation: Beginning inventory + Purchases = Cost of goods sold + Ending inventory. Using the information on inventory from the two fiscal years' balance sheet, along with the cost of goods sold for fiscal year June 30, 2009, we can calculate purchases for the year.

TABLE 19-4 Working Capital Scoreboard Results for 2010

Based on a survey of 1,000 largest U.S. firms

Sample Averages, in Days	Year			
	2006	2007	2008	2009
Days sales outstanding	37.3	39.3	34.2	37.7
Days sales in inventory	48.5	48.0	42.5	47.1
Days purchases outstanding	47.5	48.6	40.6	46.3
Operating cycle	85.8	87.3	76.7	84.8
Cash conversion cycle	38.3	38.7	36.1	38.5
Net working capital as a percentage of sales	10.4%	10.7%	9.7%	10.5%

Source of data: *CFO.com, 2010 Working Capital Scoreboard*

And finally, the days payables outstanding, DPO, with account values in millions, is:

$$DPO = \frac{\$5,786}{\$62,740/365} = 33.661$$

From this information, we know that ADM's operating cycle is 82.178 days, and its cash conversion cycle is 48.517 days. Are these good or bad? We would need more information to evaluate these cycles, including the cycles of competitors, the trends in ADM's cycles, and ADM's profitability.

Variations Among Industries

Each year, *CFO* magazine reports a Working Capital Scorecard for companies that details several metrics for working capital management.[7] The findings provide information on days sales outstanding, days of sales in inventory, and days purchases outstanding, among other working capital metrics.

According to the REL/CFO survey results we show in Table 19-4, companies reduced their investment in working capital in 2008 and returned to the prerecession levels by 2009. From this same survey, we see that the working capital situation varies among industries. For example, in 2009 the DSO for airlines was 14 days, but 63 days in the software industry. Also, in 2009, the days of inventory ranged from 3 days in the media industry, to 68 days for household durables. The variation in working capital needs and practices among industries means that comparisons across industries with respect to working capital management may not be meaningful.

ETHICS | Bristol-Myers Squibb Company

The actions of Bristol-Myers back in 2000 and 2001 are a good illustration of a company using working capital accounts to manage its earnings.

The Securities and Exchange Commission today announced that it filed an enforcement action against Bristol-Myers Squibb Company, a New York-based company whose largest division, the U.S. Medicines Group, is based in New Jersey. The Commission's complaint, filed today in the United States District Court for the District of New Jersey, alleges that Bristol-Myers perpetrated a fraudulent earnings management scheme by, among other things, selling excessive amounts of pharmaceutical products to

---

[7] In addition to the ratios we discuss, these metrics include weighted working capital and days working capital.

its wholesalers ahead of demand, improperly recognizing revenue from $1.5 billion of such sales to its two largest wholesalers and using "cookie jar" reserves to meet its internal sales and earnings targets and analysts' earnings estimates.

In settling the Commission's action, Bristol-Myers agreed to an order requiring it to pay $150 million dollars and perform numerous remedial undertakings, including the appointment of an independent adviser to review and monitor its accounting practices, financial reporting and internal controls.

Stephen M. Cutler, Director of the SEC's Division of Enforcement, said, "Bristol-Myers' earnings management scheme distorted the true performance of the company and its medicines business on a massive scale and caused significant harm to the company's shareholders. The company's conduct warrants a stiff civil sanction. As our investigation continues, we will be focusing on, among other things, those individuals responsible for the company's failures."

Timothy L. Warren, Associate Regional Director of the SEC's Midwest Regional Office, added, "For two years Bristol-Myers deceived the market into believing that it was meeting its financial projections and market expectations, when, in fact, the company was making its numbers primarily through channel-stuffing and manipulative accounting devices. Severe sanctions are necessary to hold Bristol-Myers accountable for its violative conduct, and deter Bristol-Myers and other public companies from engaging in similar schemes."

Specifically, the Commission's complaint alleges, among other things, that:

From the first quarter of 2000 through the fourth quarter of 2001, Bristol-Myers engaged in a fraudulent scheme to inflate its sales and earnings in order to create the false appearance that the company had met or exceeded its internal sales and earnings targets and Wall Street analysts' earnings estimates.

Bristol-Myers inflated its results primarily by (1) stuffing its distribution channels with excess inventory near the end of every quarter in amounts sufficient to meet its targets by making pharmaceutical sales to its wholesalers ahead of demand; and (2) improperly recognizing $1.5 billion in revenue from such pharmaceutical sales to its two biggest wholesalers. In connection with the $1.5 billion in revenue, Bristol-Myers covered these wholesalers' carrying costs and guaranteed them a return on investment until they sold the products. When Bristol-Myers recognized the $1.5 billion in revenue upon shipment, it did so contrary to generally accepted accounting principles.

When Bristol-Myers' results still fell short of the Street's earnings estimates, the company tapped improperly created divestiture reserves and reversed portions of those reserves into income to further inflate its earnings.

At no time during 2000 or 2001 did Bristol-Myers disclose that (1) it was artificially inflating its results through channel stuffing and improper accounting; (2) channel-stuffing was contributing to a build-up in excess wholesaler inventory levels; or (3) excess wholesaler inventory posed a material risk to the company's future sales and earnings.

In addition, as a result of its channel-stuffing, Bristol-Myers materially understated its accruals for rebates due to Medicaid and certain of its prime vendors, customers of its wholesalers that purchased large quantities of pharmaceutical products from those wholesalers.

Bristol-Myers has agreed, without admitting or denying the allegations in the Commission's complaint, to the following relief: a permanent injunction against future violations of certain antifraud, reporting, books and records and internal controls provisions of the federal securities laws; disgorgement of $1; a civil penalty of $100 million; an additional $50 million payment into a fund for the benefit of shareholders; various remedial undertakings, including the appointment of an independent adviser to review, assess and monitor Bristol-Myers' accounting practices, financial reporting and disclosure processes and internal control systems.

Source: Securities and Exchange Commission press release, August 4, 2004. http://www.sec.gov/news/press/2004-105.htm.

Concept Review Questions

1. Why should all companies prepare a cash budget?

2. What are the limitations of the current ratio and the quick ratio as measures of working capital management?

3. What are the operating cycle and the cash conversion cycle, and how are they related to working capital policy?

19.2   MANAGING CASH AND CASH EQUIVALENTS

Most companies have a cash and cash equivalents line on their balance sheet. The cash is in the form of currency and deposits at financial institutions, whereas cash equivalents are marketable securities with maturities less than 3 months, such as 30-day Treasury bills.[8] Cash and cash equivalents are the most liquid assets of a business entity and serve to meet the day-to-day operations of the business.

Reasons for Holding Cash

Why do companies hold cash? Basically, they hold cash for the same reasons we do: to handle day-to-day spending requirements (e.g., to buy the morning coffee and newspaper); to take care of emergencies; to finance any major outlays, such as tax installments; and sometimes to buy a bargain that requires cash. We can break down the company's motives for holding cash into the following categories:

transactions motive holding cash to pay for normal operations, such as bills

precautionary motive holding cash to take care of unanticipated required outlays of cash, such as unexpected repairs on equipment

finance motive holding cash in anticipation of major outlays, such as lump-sum loan repayments and dividend payments

speculative motive holding cash to take advantage of "bargains," such as the opportunity to purchase raw materials very cheaply

1. **Transactions motive:** This refers to the cash that is required for a company's normal operations. For some companies, such as manufacturing companies, the actual "cash" portion required will be minimal, but they will require money in their checking account (which is called a *current account* for companies) to handle bill payments, and so on. Other companies, such as retail stores or restaurants, will need to have actual cash on hand, as well as money in their current account to handle checks.
2. **Precautionary motive:** This refers to the cash that companies keep on hand to take care of unanticipated required outlays of cash, such as unexpected repairs on equipment.
3. **Finance motive:** This refers to the cash that companies will accumulate in anticipation of any major outlays, such as lump-sum loan repayments, dividend payments, and so on.
4. **Speculative motive:** Companies may keep extra cash available to take advantage of unexpected "bargains," such as the opportunity to purchase raw materials very cheaply.

This review of the motives for holding cash highlights the fact that when we speak of "cash," we really mean "cash on hand," money in the company's current account and money in short-term marketable securities. This is because when we refer to "cash" in the definitions given, what we are really talking about is the need to have cash available almost instantaneously. Such items as investments in short-term marketable securities are often referred to as "near-cash" or cash equivalents and include all items that can be quickly and inexpensively converted into cash. These items are typically short-term marketable securities like Treasury bills, bankers' acceptances, commercial paper, and so on.

How much a company holds in cash and cash equivalents is also partly determined by its ability to borrow on an operating line of credit or to run an overdraft. In fact, most companies will hold more liquidity in borrowing facilities than they will in cash and equivalents because the cost of standby lending facilities is relatively cheap compared with the opportunity cost of raising capital from the company's shareholders to invest in marketable securities. In particular, motives 2 through 4 can all be satisfied by using near-cash items, such as investments in marketable securities, and by maintaining additional short-term borrowing capacity.

As individuals, we are certainly familiar with the concept of the importance of "near-cash" as a substitute for cash in our pockets. We can purchase almost anything by using debit or credit cards, which have greatly reduced the need to carry actual cash. In addition,

---

[8] Financial Accounting Standard 95, published by the Financial Accounting Standards Board, specifies that to be considered equivalent to cash, any security must have a maturity less than or equal to 3 months.

writing checks is becoming outdated, as most of us pay our bills via automatic debit from our accounts, or by using the Internet or automated banking machines (ABMs). From now on, for exposition purposes, when we refer to cash, we are talking about both cash and near-cash, unless we make the distinction clear.

Determining the Optimal Cash Balance

Now we turn to the question of how to determine the optimal amount of cash to maintain on hand. Like most decisions in finance, it comes down to a classic trade-off between risk and expected return. In general, cash and near-cash provide very low returns relative to investments in other assets; however, by definition, they provide the ultimate in liquidity and usually have minimal additional risks (i.e., usually cash and near-cash items are virtually default free). So, it is appropriate to assume that cash is low-risk, low-expected return.

A company can always take a conservative approach and choose to maintain a large amount of its assets in cash and near-cash. It will minimize the risk of not being able to satisfy its liquidity requirements. Unfortunately, this approach sacrifices potential returns, which may not be optimal.[9] Another company may choose to take an aggressive approach to cash management and maintain minimal balances. This approach may lead to higher returns; however, it also increases the company's risk of becoming illiquid and its risk of having to generate liquidity in a hurry. Creating liquidity quickly is often very expensive because the company may have to negotiate short-term loans with higher borrowing rates. In more extreme situations, the company may be forced to sell less liquid assets, such as inventory or even fixed assets, at discounted prices.

Given our earlier discussion, it is reasonable to conclude that the **optimal cash balance** is the one that balances the risks of illiquidity against the sacrifice in expected return that is associated with maintaining cash. Therefore, the optimal cash balance, as a percentage of total assets, for example, will differ substantially across companies; some companies have lower and more predictable cash requirements than others—these companies will require proportionately lower amounts of cash. Other companies with higher cash requirements for transactions purposes, or with less predictable cash flows (and therefore a greater need for precautionary liquidity), will hold higher levels of cash.

optimal cash balance amount of cash that balances the risks of illiquidity against the sacrifice in expected return that is associated with maintaining cash

Near-cash items provide a method for alleviating the problem of the low returns associated with holding cash without sacrificing too much in the way of liquidity. For example, a company can create excess borrowing capacity in the form of an operating line of credit. However, the lenders often charge fees on the unused portion of the line, which may offset the advantage of requiring the company to hold less in cash. In addition, companies often maintain a large portion of their liquidity requirements in money market instruments, which provide a higher return than does cash held in a traditional bank account. The level of investment in marketable securities is dictated to a large extent by the company's liquidity urgency and by how accurately it is able to forecast its future cash requirements. The latter will be a function partly of the volatility of the company's cash flows and partly of how well designed a company's cash budgeting system is. Companies that have well-developed cash management systems, and more predictable cash flows, will be able to maintain a higher portion of their liquidity in marketable securities and less in cash.

Cash Management Techniques

The general approach to good cash management is to speed up inflows as much as possible and delay outflows as much as possible. Qualifier "as much as possible" is important because companies always face constraints that will delay inflows and prevent them from

[9] In addition, it may make the company an attractive takeover candidate because the acquiring company can use some of this cash to pay down its takeover financing.

delaying outflows too much. For example, a company can speed up its inflows from sales by refusing to give credit to customers—of course, this will likely have a large impact on its sales, so this may not be a viable strategy. Similarly, a company may delay making payments to suppliers; however, if the company is perpetually late in making payments, it will develop a poor relationship with the suppliers. In the extreme, suppliers may end up selling to the company on a cash only basis, which would, in fact, speed up cash outflows, rather than delay them.

An important part of speeding up inflows is the establishment of an efficient credit policy, which specifies the policies for collecting receivables from customers—we discuss this in detail later in this chapter. Once the financial manager specifies the payment procedures for customers, it is important that companies process the payments as efficiently as possible. We refer to the funds that are due the company yet not received as the **float**. Float consists of a balance that is simultaneously on the accounts for both the sender and the receiver. For example, if Company A pays a bill owed Company B, during the time it takes for the mailing and processing of this payment, the amount remains on Company A's books until the payment is cleared through the banking system and is still a receivable on Company B's books until the funds are cleared and received.[10] One objective at this stage should be to minimize **float time**, which is the time that elapses between the time the paying company initiates payment, for example, mails the check, and when the funds are available for use by the receiving company. During this float period, the receiving company does not have the funds available for use.

There are three major sources of float:

1. the time it takes the check to reach the company after it is mailed by the customer;
2. the time it takes the receiving company to process the check and deposit it in an account; and
3. the time it takes the check to clear through the banking system so that the funds are available to the company.

Historically, the first source of float time has been the longest, but that is changing. Over the past decade in particular, companies have made great strides in eliminating float time by making payment options available to (or mandatory for) customers that eliminate the need to mail checks. Today, most retailers accept debit cards, which automatically debit the customer's accounts. This eliminates the problems associated with accepting checks (i.e., checking for identification, risking the account not having sufficient funds, taking the time to process and deposit the check). Many companies also make use of preauthorized payments, whereby customer accounts are automatically debited by the bank on the payment date. Other companies use more advanced electronic collection systems, such as electronic funds transfer (EFT) and electronic data interchange (EDI) systems.

Although there have been advancements in collecting funds, many companies still do things the "old-fashioned way": They bill their customers, and their customers pay by check. However, even these companies can take steps to speed up the process and reduce float time. Many companies establish centralized or concentrated banking arrangements. Under these arrangements, local offices receive customer payments and deposit them into a local bank account, which is combined with similar local accounts into one central account. This minimizes mail float. A similar strategy that can be used concurrently with the concentrated bank account option is to establish lock-box banking arrangements. A **lock-box system** is an arrangement of local post office boxes for customers to mail their payments to and authorizing the local bank to empty these boxes and deposit the checks into the company's account.

Although float works to a company's disadvantage with respect to collections, it works to the company's benefit with respect to disbursements. It is reasonable to assume that many of the company's suppliers will employ the strategies discussed to minimize

float funds due a company that are not yet received due to mail and processing delays

float time length of time that elapses between the time the paying company initiates payment, and the time the funds are available for use by the receiving company

lock-box system arrangement of local post office boxes for customers to mail their payments to and authorizing the local bank to empty these boxes and deposit the checks into the company's account

---

[10] You might remember from macroeconomics that the float in the banking system is attributed to check processing and distorts the measurement of the money supply because funds are counted twice.

their float, which implies there is little benefit in trying to maximize disbursement float. In addition, as discussed earlier, trying to delay making payments may cause poor relations with suppliers. However, companies can still take steps to improve the efficiency of their cash outflows and minimize the cash they need to maintain on hand for required disbursements. Just as it makes sense for companies to have a centralized system to monitor collections, it also does for payments. This will ensure that payments are made on time, but not early (or late), to the greatest extent possible. In addition, most companies establish zero-balance accounts, which are centralized accounts that combine the cash balances of many individual accounts into one central account. Under this system, funds are transferred from this account to cover checks written against the individual accounts as required. This system reduces the need for cash at the aggregate company level because it effectively transfers funds from individual accounts that have excess cash to those that need it. In addition, companies usually tie their operating loans to this central account, reducing the total amount of borrowing required by the company.

Companies can use these methods to speed up cash inflows and slow down outflows to the greatest extent possible. However, another critical component in any cash management system is the actual tracking of the cash requirements through time. This can be especially important for planning and for assessing short-term financing requirements. An important tool that companies use to forecast cash balances and borrowing requirements is, as we have noted, the cash budget. Recall that cash budgets tell companies when and for how long they can expect to have excess cash balances that can be invested in marketable securities. They also show companies how much they may require in excess borrowing capacity to cover any shortfalls, and the companies can arrange their short-term lending facilities accordingly. In fact, banks often require cash budgets as a part of any loan application package.

1. What is float, and why is it important to the company?

2. What methods can a company use to speed up collections on accounts?

Concept Review Questions

19.3 MANAGING ACCOUNTS RECEIVABLE

As soon as a company decides to extend credit to its customers, it has consciously made a decision to allow some of its funds to be tied up in accounts receivable. Companies base this decision on a cost-benefit analysis, just as the decision to have funds tied up in cash, or any other asset for that matter, should be. The expected benefits of extending credit are expanded sales and perhaps even improved relationships with customers. The costs may include losses because of an increase in nonpayment by customers, as well as the costs of financing the receivables. The financing costs are those associated with the time the company has to do without the cash payment for goods that have already been sold and whose production costs have already been paid (or at least partially paid, depending on its own ability to delay paying its suppliers and employees).

Although it is technically true that all companies face the decision of whether or not to provide credit for their customers, as a practical matter, many companies do not have much of a choice. For example, it is hard to imagine a furniture retailer or car dealer that could remain competitive within its industry if it did not provide customers with financing options. These types of companies typically provide financing for their customers through a finance subsidiary of the parent company or through arrangements made with one or more banks or financial institutions. Many companies extend credit to their customers by providing them with additional time to make payment on purchases. For these companies, the first decision they need to make is whether or not to extend credit at all. The second decision is to decide which customers will be granted credit. Next, the companies must determine the credit terms to be offered to customers (which may vary across customers). Finally, they must decide on the details of the collection process.

The Credit Decision

For most companies, the decision of whether or not to extend credit is largely determined by the nature of the product they sell, the industry they are in, and the prevailing policy used by competitors. Assuming the company decides to extend credit, it must then determine which of its customers will qualify for it. This decision is often based on a formal **credit analysis** process, which is designed to assess the risk of nonpayment by potential customers. The process involves collecting information about potential customers with respect to their credit history, their ability to make payments as reflected in their expected cash flows (which is closely related to income), and their overall financial stability (as reflected in their net worth and their level of existing debt obligations).

Before considering how companies make these decisions, it is important to note that the company's decision to extend trade credit is subtly different from that of a bank making a loan. Suppose, for example, a company is considering a $10,000 order for screens, for which the customer promises to pay in 60 days. If the cost of trade credit is 12 percent per year, the company might sell the screens for $10,200 due in 60 days. We will talk about trade credit terms later, but this is similar to a bank lending the customer $10,000 to buy the screens for cash and then charging 2 percent interest on the loan so that it is paid $10,200 in 60 days. In both cases, the purchaser owes $10,200, either to the company or to the bank. The bank's profit from the loan is limited to the interest rate, and if the customer defaults, the bank could be out the full $10,000 loan.[11] The company is in a slightly different position.

First, the company's cost is not the $10,000 it charges for the screens because it has to factor a profit margin into the calculation. If the company's profit margin is 10 percent and it can't sell the screens to other customers, then its decision involves a potential loss of $9,000 if the customer does not pay, rather than the $10,000 the bank would lose. If the customer does pay, it becomes an established customer that may make further purchases, generating further profit margins for the company. The fact that the company thinks in terms of future profit margins from developing a good customer and loses only its production cost in the case of default means that trade credit is granted to customers who could not secure credit from a bank on the same terms.

In making these decisions, companies can use a number of sources of information to assess the creditworthiness of a particular customer. Usually, companies begin by turning to professional credit agencies, such as Dun & Bradstreet (D&B), which provide credit ratings and comprehensive credit reports on companies. These reports are based on available financial data, the company's competitive position, and also the company's credit history. In many cases, this report will provide sufficient information to make a credit decision; however, for larger accounts or for arrangements that are expected to last for a long time, the company may decide to do some additional investigation. An important source of information can be the company's financial statements. Companies may also ask the company to provide a letter from its main banker. Finally, companies can always look for information regarding a company's past credit relationships from a variety of sources, such as trade associations, other companies that have had prior dealings with the company, and so on.

The evaluation of the credit information that has been gathered can vary significantly from one company to the next. Some companies will have very detailed and mechanical

credit analysis process designed to assess the risk of nonpayment by potential customers

---

[11] More likely in this situation, the bank would let the company advance the trade credit to the customer and then buy the receivable for $9,803.92 and make its 2 percent interest when the customer pays off the $10,000 debt. This is called factoring.

evaluation systems, whereas others will rely more on judgment. In either case, the key thing that potential creditors are assessing is the likelihood of the customer paying the bills as they come due. There are two sides to this coin.

The first side is the potential customer's ability to pay. We refer to this as the **capacity** of the company to pay. Two of the most important things affecting a company's ability to meet future obligations are the amount of cash flow it expects to generate, and how many other obligations it has to satisfy. Thus, it is important to examine a company's expected future profitability, as well as the level of debt and the amount of debt payments it has accumulated. In addition, because most, if not all, trade credit is of a short-term nature, potential creditors are particularly interested in a potential customer's liquidity. As a last resort, creditors can always turn to the assets pledged as security for a loan. In this way, the company's ability to offer collateral enhances its ability to secure credit. In many cases, items are sold on an **open account basis**, which means that the collateral is simply the assets that it sold to the customer. In such situations, the creditor must be wary because some assets do not hold their value. In addition, creditors may have difficulty getting the assets from the customer if it defaults on its obligation.

This leads us to the other side of the coin referred to earlier—how willing the company is to pay. We refer to this as the **character** of the borrower. In other words, how reliable and trustworthy is the company? This is an important question because even if a company is able to make the required payments, this makes little difference if it chooses not to. Creditors look for clues as to the character of the customer's management team by examining, among other things, its payment history and details about the customer's past dealings.

We often refer to capacity and character as two of the Cs of credit, with **collateral** or **capital** representing the third C. Collateral or capital in this context refers to the real estate, investments, and other property of the borrower. In addition, the state of the economy often affects both capacity and character. In a recession, the company's capacity to pay is often tested as cash flow dries up and finances are under pressure. So economic **conditions** affect the credit decision, and analysts include it as part of the **4 Cs of credit**: capacity, character, collateral, and conditions. All four are interrelated. Because the process of checking creditworthiness can be lengthy and costly, companies tend to prioritize the amount of time and effort devoted to the analysis. For example, all else being equal, larger orders require more scrutiny than do smaller ones.

capacity customer's ability to pay

open account basis credit in which the collateral is the assets sold to the customer

character how willing the company is to pay and how reliable and trustworthy the company is

conditions state of the economy

4 Cs of credit factors that affect credit: capacity, character, collateral, and conditions

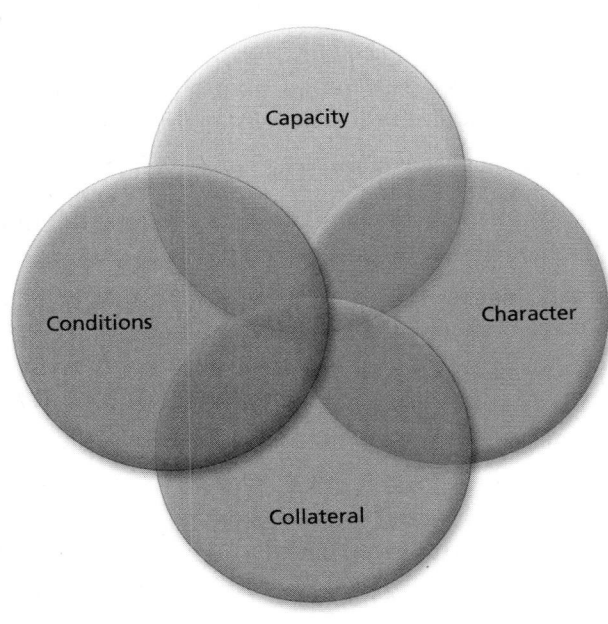

Credit Policies

Once a company has decided to grant credit, it then chooses the **terms of credit** to offer its customers, such as the due date, and the discount date and discount amount, where applicable. In practice, the terms a company offers can vary from one customer to the next, based on credit analysis and on the importance of the account. In other words, key accounts with an impeccable credit rating will likely demand, and receive, better credit terms than smaller accounts or those with weaker credit ratings. For ease of exposition in our discussion, we will assume that most customers receive the same credit terms.

The cost of trade credit is based on the traditional term in the form of a discount, discount period, and net day. For example, the terms 2/10, net 30 indicate that there is a 2 percent discount if paid within 10 days, otherwise the full amount is due at the end of 30 days. Breaking this down further, this means that the credit period is the amount of time beyond 10 days, the cash price is 100 percent less 2 percent, or 98 percent, and the rate of interest is 2 percent on the cash price. Therefore, the effective annual cost of trade credit, using notation, is:

$$i = \left(1 + \frac{d}{c}\right)^{365/n} - 1 \tag{19-11}$$

where

  d is the discount, as a percentage of the sales price
  c is the cash price, as a percentage of the sales price, and
  n is the number of days payment is made beyond the discount period.

Therefore, if the terms are 2/10, net 30 and you pay 12 days after the discount period (that is, you pay on day 22 after the sale),

$$i = \left(1 + \frac{0.02}{0.98}\right)^{365/12} - 1 = 84.873\%$$

If, instead, you pay on day 30, 20 days after the discount period, the cost is less:

$$i = \left(1 + \frac{0.02}{0.98}\right)^{365/20} - 1 = 44.585\%$$

In other words, if you miss the discount period, you should wait to pay as long as possible.

EXAMPLE 19.3

Trade Credit and Discounts

PROBLEM

A company is considering the purchase of one of its inputs from supplier A. The selling price = $1,200 and the credit terms are 2/10 net 40.

a. What is the effective annual cost of forgoing the discount?

b. Another supplier (B) offers the same product for a price of $1,205 on credit terms of net 60. What is the effective annual cost of this option?

c. If the company can finance these purchases by using a loan that has an effective annual cost of 8 percent, should it take the credit terms or the loan?

Solution

a. We need to recognize that forgoing the discount costs 2% of the $1,200 purchase price, or $24.

In essence, the "true" price = $1,200 − $24 = $1,176, and the $24 is the 30-day financing cost. So, we can estimate the cost of forgoing the discount

$$i = \left(1 + \frac{d}{c}\right)^{365/n} - 1 = (1.02040816)^{12.166667} - 1 = 0.2786 = 27.86\%$$

We could also solve this by replacing the discount percentage 2/98 for the actual dollar amounts of 24/1,176 because the two ratios must be equal. In other words,

$$i = \left(1 + \frac{24}{\$1,176}\right)^{365/30} - 1 = 0.2786 = 27.86\%$$

Forgoing the cash discount is an expensive decision.

b. Because we know from part a that the "true" cost is $1,176, we can see that company B is charging $29 (i.e., $1,205 − $1,176) in financing charges for 60 days of financing. We can estimate the effective annual cost of this option as

$$i = \left(1 + \frac{\$2}{\$1,176}\right)^{365/60} - 1 = 0.1597 = 15.97\%$$

This option is less expensive than forgoing the discount, but is still not cheap.

c. We know what the company should not do—that is, it should not choose supplier A and forgo the discount, because this costs 27.86 percent.

This leaves us with two purchase/financing options: (1) buy through supplier A and pay on day 10 using the 8 percent loan to take advantage of the discount, or (2) buy through supplier B.

We have already calculated that the cost of using supplier B would be 15.97 percent.

The cost of going with supplier A and paying the amount due on day 10 to take advantage of the discount is 8 percent because the company can use a loan with a cost of 8% to finance the purchase. Therefore, the preferred option is to buy through supplier A and pay on day 10 to take advantage of the discount by using a loan at 8 percent.

Generally, when a company decides to extend more lenient credit terms, it expects revenues to increase because the number of units sold will likely increase, and possibly, the company can charge higher prices. The costs include the increase in financing costs and the increased risk of nonpayment by customers. Conversely, when a company adopts a more restrictive policy, it likely results in accelerated collections, at the possible expense of sales. Companies can evaluate such decisions by using the now-familiar net present value (NPV) framework: The net present value is the present value of the future cash flows, less the initial cash outlays.

The future cash flows will generally be positive when companies loosen their credit terms and negative when they tighten them. The initial cash outlay will represent an outlay when the credit terms are loosened because that requires an additional investment in receivables, and it will represent an inflow when the terms are tightened because that will reduce the level of receivables. The after-tax cost of short-term debt is usually the appropriate discount rate to use because receivables are low risk and are generally financed by using short-term debt (and the operating line of credit, in particular).

Suppose a company that currently does not grant credit is considering adopting a credit policy that permits its customers to pay the full price for purchases (with no penalties) within 40 days of the purchase (i.e., the credit terms are net 40). The company estimates that it can increase the price of the product by $1 per unit with the new policy, which results in a new price per unit of $111. The company expects that unit sales will increase by 1,000 units per year (to 11,000 units) and that variable costs will remain at $99 per unit. It also estimates that bad debt losses will amount to $6,000 per year. The company will finance the additional investment in receivables by using its line of credit, which charges 6 percent interest. The company's tax rate is 40 percent. Should the company begin extending credit under the terms described?

Because the company did not previously have any receivables, the initial investment (CF_0) is the amount of additional funds tied up in receivables, which equals the number of days that the company finances sales, multiplied by the estimated sales per day:

$$\text{Additional investment} = 40 \text{ days} \times \text{Sales per day}$$

$$\text{Additional investment} = 40 \times [(\$111 \times 11{,}000 \text{ units}) \div 365 \text{ days}]$$

$$\text{Additional investment} = 40 \text{ days} \times \$3{,}345.21 \text{ per day} = \$133{,}808.$$

Now, we need to estimate the present value of future cash flows, which equals the present value of the incremental after-tax cash flows generated by extending credit.

Item	Calculation	Cash Flow
Profit per unit sold, current price	1,000 extra units sold × $12	$12,000
Profit from price increase	10,000 units × $1	10,000
Bad debt expense		6,000
Incremental before-tax annual cash flow		$16,000

The appropriate after-tax discount rate $= 6\% \times (1 - 0.40) = 3.6\%$. If we assume the company reaps the benefits of this change in policy indefinitely, we can find the present value of the future benefits by viewing the incremental after-tax annual cash flows as a perpetuity:

$$\text{Present value of future cash flow} = \frac{\text{After-tax incremental cash flows}}{\text{Discount rate}}$$

$$\text{Present value of future cash flow} = \frac{\$16{,}000 \times (1 - 0.40)}{0.036} = \$266{,}667$$

Therefore, the net present value is associated with expanding credit terms is positive:

$$\text{NPV} = \$266{,}667 - \$133{,}808 = +\$132{,}859$$

Thus, the company should begin extending credit under the terms described because this adds value. Alternatively, a company can choose to adopt a more stringent credit policy. In this case, the company will free up cash by reducing the amount of receivables it has outstanding, and the cost will be the forgone additional future cash flows that may result if the company loses sales or has to reduce its selling price.

Suppose the company adopts the net 40 credit policy, but 1 year later it considers changing the terms to net 30. The company estimates that it can maintain the same price for the product (i.e., $111 per unit) but that unit sales will decline by 500 units per year (to 10,500 units). Variable costs will remain at $99 per unit. The company estimates that bad debt losses will be reduced by $2,000 per year (to $4,000) as a result of the new policy. Should the company switch to the new policy?

The initial investment in this case can be viewed as the reduction in the accounts receivable that must be financed. The accounts receivable under the old and new policies are:

Accounts Receivable	Calculation	Result
...under the new policy	30 days × [($111 × 10,500 units) ÷ 365 days]	$95,795
...under the old policy	40 days × [($111 × 11,000 units) ÷ 365 days]	133,808
Change in accounts receivable		−$38,013

Now, we need to estimate the present value of the cash flows, which is the present value of the incremental after-tax cash flows generated by changing the credit policy. In this case, it will be negative because the company *loses* future cash flows when tightening its credit policy.

Item	Calculation	Cash Flow
Profit per unit sold, current price	500 fewer units sold × $12	–$6,000
Bad debt expense		2,000
Incremental before-tax annual cash flow		–$4,000

If we assume the company reaps the benefits of this change in policy indefinitely, we can find the present value of the future cash flows (forgone cash flows, in this case), by viewing the incremental after-tax annual cash flows as a perpetuity:

$$\text{Present value of future cash flow} = \frac{-\$4,000(1 - 0.40)}{0.036} = -\$66,667$$

$$\text{NPV} = -\$66,667 + 38,013 = -\$28,654.$$

Because the net present value (NPV) is negative, the company should not switch from its existing credit policy to the new one.

When a company offers discounts to its customers, two things may happen: (1) the company loses profits when customers take advantage of the discounts, and (2) the company receives payment sooner, so less money is tied up in receivables. The decision to offer discounts (or eliminate them) can be evaluated by using the NPV framework.

Suppose the same company is maintaining the net 40 credit policy. It is now considering adopting a new policy that would involve a discount. In particular, it is considering adopting a 2/10 net 40 policy. The company estimates that 60 percent of customers will take advantage of the discount, and the remaining 40 percent will pay on day 40. The company expects that it can maintain the same price for the product (i.e., $111 per unit), that unit sales will remain at 11,000 per year, that variable costs will remain at $99 per unit, and that bad debt losses will not changed. Should the company switch to the new policy?

The initial investment (CF_0) in this case can be viewed as the reduction in the amount of accounts receivable that need to be financed:

- The average collection period under the new policy will be reduced to $[(0.60 \times 10 \text{ days}) + (0.40 \times 40 \text{ days})] = 22$ days.
- The old average collection period was assumed to be the net date (i.e., 40 days).

The reduction in receivables is therefore:

$$\text{Change in accounts receivable} = (22 - 40) \times [(\$111 \times 11,000 \text{ units}) \div 365 \text{ days}]$$

$$\text{Change in accounts receivable} = -18 \text{ days} \times \$3,345.21 \text{ per day}$$

$$\text{Change in accounts receivable} = -\$60,214$$

Next, we estimate the present value of the future cash flows, which equals the present value of the incremental after-tax cash flows generated by changing the credit terms. In this case, it will be negative because the company *loses* future cash flows because of customers taking advantage of the discount.

The lost revenues from discounts is $0.6 \times 11,000 \times 0.02 \times \$111 = -\$14,652$. On an after-tax basis the incremental tax cash flow is $-\$14,652 \times (1 - 0.4) = -\$8,791$. The present value of these incremental cash flows is –$244,200:

$$\text{Present value of future cash flow} = \frac{-\$8,791}{0.036} = -\$244,200$$

Therefore, the net present value is –$244,200 + $60,214 = –$183,986. Thus, the company should not offer the discount.

The Collection Process

Companies have many options when deciding how their customers will pay for their purchases. As discussed, several electronic methods are available, such as automatic debit of their bank accounts or the use of electronic funds transfer (EFT). These approaches not only reduce payment processing time but also reduce (or eliminate) the risk of late payment. These obviously represent attractive collection systems for many companies. However, some companies still invoice their customers at the time of sale and then collect and deposit checks as they are received.

When companies wait for payments from customers, several issues arise. First, they must closely monitor their collections and receivables to avoid having many late payments or, worse yet, nonpayments. Second, they must determine what to do when late payments occur. Usually, companies establish a systematic process to deal with such accounts.

Sometimes a company avoids the collection process by entering into a **factoring arrangement**, whereby they sell their receivables at a discount to a financial company, a **factor**, which specializes in collections. Alternatively, many factors do not actually purchase the receivables but agree to handle the collections, for a fee of course.

It can be difficult to assess how well a company manages its accounts receivable. In addition to the ratios that we discussed previously, a tool that is useful for this purpose is the aged accounts receivable report, which categorizes the balances in receivables according to how long they have been outstanding. For example, a company might provide a list that shows how much of its receivables are outstanding before the due date, after the due date, a month after the due date, and so on. Generally, receivables that have not been outstanding that long are regarded as higher quality than those that have been outstanding well beyond their due date. In fact, banks often require that borrowing companies provide them with this list on a monthly basis to support any financing the banks provide in support of receivables. However, this report also has its limitations. For example, it would be preferable to have many receivables due from high-quality customers (such as government agencies) that are 30 days late than it would be to have many 10-day-old receivables from low-credit-quality customers. In fact, to accurately assess the quality of a company's receivables, it would help to have a list of the customers underlying the receivables and perhaps even a credit analysis of these customers, at least for the larger accounts.

factoring arrangement sale of a company's receivables, at a discount, to a financial company specializing in collections; outsourcing of the collections to a factor

factor financial company that buys receivables and collects on these accounts

---

Concept Review Questions

1. Why is trade credit different from bank credit?

2. What are the 4 Cs of credit?

3. What does 2/10 net 30 mean, and what is the implicit interest cost?

19.4 MANAGING INVENTORY

Companies tend to determine the level of inventory to hold as a trade-off between benefits and costs, similar to the decisions about investments in cash, marketable securities, and accounts receivable. One reason companies hold large amounts of inventory is that they may have received discounts on large-volume purchases. However, the more important benefits of holding inventory are that holding sufficient levels of raw materials minimizes disruptions in the production process, whereas maintaining adequate levels of finished goods on hand helps minimize lost sales (and lost customer goodwill) because of shortages.

The benefits of holding inventory do not come without significant costs. Aside from the obvious cost of financing the funds tied up in inventory, a number of other costs are important, including storage, handling, insurance, spoilage, and the risk of obsolescence. Thus, inventory decisions are critical to the company's performance.[12] We provide a brief discussion of some of the more common approaches to inventory management, but we do not elaborate on the technical details.

Inventory Management Approaches

Most inventory control systems used by large companies employ highly automated computerized systems that can easily track all kinds of inventory items as they flow into and out of the company. These systems control inventory levels by relating them to the production process, which in turn is related to the company's projected sales levels.

Any approach to inventory management must balance the benefits of holding inventory and the costs, as discussed earlier. We briefly describe four of these approaches:

1. The **ABC approach to inventory**: This approach divides inventory into several categories based on the value of the inventory items, their overall level of importance to the company's operations, and their profitability. The higher the priority of the inventory item, the more time and effort devoted to its management.

2. The **Economic Order Quantity (EOQ) Model**: The EOQ model defines (and determines) the optimal inventory level as the one that minimizes the total of shortage *costs* and carrying *costs*. As such, it determines the inventory level that balances out the benefits (i.e., reduced shortage costs) against the carrying costs (i.e., financing, storage, insurance, spoilage, obsolescence). The model shows that under certain assumptions, the minimum total cost occurs at the point at which carrying costs equal shortage costs. One of the key assumptions of the EOQ model is that items are sold relatively evenly throughout the year, so it works well for inventories that follow this pattern and not as well when they don't.

3. **Materials Requirement Planning (MRP)**: MRP is a detailed computerized system that orders inventory in conjunction with production schedules. The central idea is to determine the exact level of raw materials and work-in-process that must be on hand to meet finished goods demand. With this capability and good sales forecasts, a company can run on extremely low levels of inventory.

4. **Just-in-time (JIT) inventory system**: JIT systems fine-tune the receipt of raw materials so that they arrive exactly when they are required in the production process. The objective is to reduce inventory to its lowest possible level. JIT systems require close relationships with suppliers to work properly, and disruptions, such as the one caused by the 2011 Japanese Tōhoku earthquake and tsunami, can be quite costly.[13]

We will use the economic order quantity model to illustrate how inventory models work. Assume, for simplicity, that the company has one type of inventory, which we will refer to as screens. Suppose that the company uses 1 million screens during a fiscal year. Every time the company orders screens from its supplier, the supplier charges $10,000 in shipping and handling. The cost of keeping screens on hand, in terms of storage and maintenance costs, is $0.50 per screen. The question then arises: When the company orders screens, what quantity should they order?

The EOQ model specifies that the optimal order quantity is

$$EOQ = \sqrt{\frac{2 \times \text{annual usage, in units} \times \text{order cost}}{\text{Annual carrying cost per unit}}} \qquad (19\text{-}12)$$

ABC approach division of inventory into several categories based on the value of the inventory items, their overall level of importance to the company's operations, and their profitability, to determine the time and effort devoted to their management

Economic Order Quantity (EOQ) Model approach that defines and determines the optimal inventory level as the level that minimizes the total of shortage costs and carrying costs

Materials Requirement Planning (MRP) detailed computerized system that orders inventory in conjunction with production schedules to determine the level of raw materials and work-in-process that must be on hand to meet finished goods demand

just-in-time (JIT) inventory system inventory management approach that fine-tunes the receipt of raw materials so that they arrive exactly when they are required in the production process and thereby reduce inventory to its lowest possible level

[12] In fact, the field of operations management devotes a great deal of attention to modeling efficient inventory control systems.
[13] The 2011 earthquake and tsunami interrupted the supply chain in the automotive industry, interrupting not only auto production facilities in Japan, but also parts needed for automotive manufacturers in the U.S. and Europe.

Therefore, in our example, the EOQ is:

$$EOQ = \sqrt{\frac{2 \times 1,000,000 \times \$10,000}{\$0.50}} = 200,000$$

If the company orders 200,000 screens each time it orders, it will have on hand, on average, 100,000 units if sales are uniform during the period. The cost of carrying these units is $\$0.5 \times 100,000 = \$50,000$. If the company uses 1 million screens, it will make five orders during the year, for a total cost of $50,000. As you can see in this example, the EOQ model balances the cost of carrying inventory with the cost of ordering the inventory.

Evaluating Inventory Management

Although effective inventory management is critical to the success of most companies, just as accounts receivable management is, inventory management is difficult to evaluate. Generally, high inventory turnover is recognized as a good sign, whereas lower or declining turnover is a warning sign. In particular, a declining inventory turnover ratio indicates that sales are declining, inventory levels are accumulating, or both. The greater the inventory buildup, the greater the financing, storage, spoilage, and insurance costs, and the greater the risk of obsolescence.

Although the inventory turnover ratio is a useful indicator, it is far from comprehensive. For example, it does not measure shortage costs nor does it explicitly measure financing costs, and so on. As discussed earlier, these are critical considerations in the implementation (and evaluation) of any inventory management system. In addition, we cannot compare turnover ratios across companies that use different methods of accounting for inventory (i.e., LIFO, FIFO, average cost) unless we first adjust for the different methods of accounting. Finally, inventory turnover says nothing about the breakdown of inventory in terms of raw materials, work-in-process inventory, and finished goods, which can make a big difference in establishing the market value of inventory.

19.5   SHORT-TERM FINANCING CONSIDERATIONS

A common trait among investments in current assets, such as cash, accounts receivable, and inventory, is that they all tend to increase automatically as sales increase. The same cannot be said for short-term financing, with the exception of trade credit. Therefore, it is critical that companies forecast their short-term financing requirements as accurately as possible and ensure they have adequate financing in place.

Because there are many potential sources of short-term financing, companies need to assess the cost effectiveness of alternative financing mechanisms. For each financing alternative, we must estimate the annual effective rate cost.

Companies also need to consider any additional benefits or risks associated with these alternatives. We will discuss the most common short-term financing options available to companies.

Trade Credit

Trade credit is usually one of a company's most important sources of short-term financing. Many companies finance their purchases through the credit terms offered to them by their suppliers, which permits them to delay payments to the supplier. In essence, a company is borrowing from its suppliers when it purchases materials on account. This is the only form of short-term financing that automatically increases with sales, and as such, we often refer to it as a spontaneous source of funds.[14]

Trade credit provides companies with many advantages: It is generally readily available, convenient, and flexible, and it usually does not entail any restrictive covenants or pledges of security. In addition, it is usually inexpensive. It can, however, be expensive to forgo discounts, as we have demonstrated earlier.

Bank Loans

Several short-term loan arrangements are available through financial institutions. Generally, they are variable rate (or prime-based) loans tied to the prime lending rate (which is the rate offered to the bank's best customers). The most common arrangement for businesses is to establish operating loans (or lines of credit). As discussed previously, these loans are usually linked to the company's current account (i.e., their checking account), and they enable the business to borrow up to a predetermined amount to finance temporary cash deficits.

Operating loans are generally set up so that the company makes "interest only" payments. The amount of borrowing can be reduced at the company's discretion, and many companies will have the bank automatically "revolve" the loan for them (for a fee). This involves paying down the amount of the loan whenever there is sufficient cash in the current account or increasing the borrowing level when there is insufficient cash. Having the bank revolve the loan reduces unnecessary interest costs because the loan is paid down whenever the company has sufficient funds available.

Financial managers use cash budgets to estimate the amount of borrowing that should be arranged. This is important because companies do not want to have to go back to the bank to arrange additional financing when the need for funds is urgent. Therefore, companies will try to arrange to have the necessary amount of funds available and maintain a little extra cushion. However, companies will want to avoid arranging unnecessary borrowing capacity because banks normally charge a commitment fee against the unused portion of credit.

Operating loans are typically secured by accounts receivable and inventory because these are the assets they are usually intended to finance. The "standard" is for banks to offer an operating line for an amount that does not exceed 70 to 75 percent of the company's good accounts receivable under 90 days plus up to 50 percent of the company's inventory value. Operating loans provide companies with an opportunity to develop a solid banking relationship, which can be important. They also offer a fair degree of flexibility and the costs are usually quite low.

Typical bank loan

Consider the cost of a bank loan. Suppose a bank offers a company a 1-year variable rate loan at a rate of prime plus 1 percent at a time when the bank's prime lending rate is 5.25 percent. The company must repay the loan in monthly installments. Assuming there are no other fees associated with this loan, what is the effective annual cost of this loan?

The annual quoted rate = 5.25% + 1% = 6.25%. Now, we need to estimate the effective annual rate associated with this arrangement:

$$i = \left(1 + \frac{Quoted\ rate}{n}\right)^n - 1 = \left(1 + \frac{0.0625}{12}\right)^{12} - 1 = 0.0643 = 6.43\%$$

---

[14] Although it is true that the amount borrowed on an operating line of credit will increase with the borrowing requirement (which tends to rise with sales), the credit limits on these lending facilities do not automatically increase with sales—they have to be renegotiated. Therefore, they do not represent a truly spontaneous source of funds.

Line of credit

Now let's consider another form of financing, the **line of credit**. Suppose the company arranges a 1-year $800,000 operating line of credit, which carries an 8 percent quoted interest rate and a 0.5 percent commitment fee on the unused portion of the line. The loan calls for monthly payments. The company uses the line to borrow $600,000 in the first 7 months of the year, and then reduces the loan amount to $400,000 for the remainder of the year. What is the effective annual cost (rate) of this loan arrangement?

First, we determine the effective monthly rate, which is $0.08 \div 12 = 0.0066667 = 0.66667\%$. Now we can determine the total interest paid over the first 7 months and over the remaining 5 months.

$$\text{Interest (months } 1-7) = \$600,000 \times 0.0066667 = \$4,000.02$$

$$\text{Interest (months } 8-12) = \$400,000 \times 0.0066667 = \$2,666.68$$

We then need to estimate the commitment fees throughout the year:

$$\text{Commitment fee (months } 1-7) = (\$800,000 - \$600,000) \times 0.0050 = \$1,000$$

$$\text{Commitment fee (months } 8-12) = (\$800,000 - \$400,000) \times 0.0050 = \$2,000$$

Finally, we estimate the average monthly cost of financing using the internal rate of return method based on the loan's cash flows:

Month	Loan Amount	Loan Payments	Interest	Commitment Fee	Loan Cash Flow
Today		−$600,000.00			−$600,000.00
1	$600,000.00	$0.00	$4,000.02	$1,000.00	$5,000.02
2	$600,000.00	$0.00	$4,000.02	$1,000.00	$5,000.02
3	$600,000.00	$0.00	$4,000.02	$1,000.00	$5,000.02
4	$600,000.00	$0.00	$4,000.02	$1,000.00	$5,000.02
5	$600,000.00	$0.00	$4,000.02	$1,000.00	$5,000.02
6	$600,000.00	$0.00	$4,000.02	$1,000.00	$5,000.02
7	$600,000.00	$200,000.00	$4,000.02	$1,000.00	$205,000.02
8	$400,000.00	$0.00	$2,666.68	$2,000.00	$4,666.68
9	$400,000.00	$0.00	$2,666.68	$2,000.00	$4,666.68
10	$400,000.00	$0.00	$2,666.68	$2,000.00	$4,666.68
11	$400,000.00	$0.00	$2,666.68	$2,000.00	$4,666.68
12	$400,000.00	$400,000.00	$2,666.68	$2,000.00	$404,666.68

The monthly rate (i.e., the internal rate of return of the loan cash flows) is 0.9368 percent. Calculating the effective annual rate,[15]

$$i = (1 + 0.009368)^{12} - 1 = 0.1184 = 11.84\%$$

Factor Arrangements

As described earlier, a factor is an independent company that acts as an outside credit department for its clients. It checks the credit of new customers, authorizes credit, handles collections and bookkeeping, and sometimes will purchase a company's receivables (at a discount). In practice, various arrangements are possible, with factors providing various

---

[15] An approximation, which uses the averages of the loan amount ($516.666.67) and the sum of interest and fees, is $i = \left(1 + \dfrac{58,333}{516,667}\right)^1 - 1 = 0.1129 = 11.29\%$.

combinations of the services listed here. Factors provide the ultimate in convenience; however, as with most things, there is a cost, and the costs are typically quite high.

Let's estimate the cost of a factor arrangement. Suppose a company has daily credit sales of $40,000 and an average collection period of 45 days. A factor offers a 45-day accounts receivable loan equal to 75 percent of accounts receivable. The quoted interest rate is 10 percent, and there is a commission fee of 1 percent of accounts receivable. The company estimates that it will save $2,000 in collection costs and will experience a 0.5 percent reduction in bad debt losses (as a percentage of sales) as a result of the factoring arrangement. What is the effective annual cost of the arrangement?

First, we estimate the accounts receivable that the company can factor:

$$\text{Accounts receivable} = \text{DSO} \times \text{Daily credit sales} = 45 \times \$40,000 = \$1,800,000$$

Second, we calculate the amount of the loan, which is 75 percent of the accounts receivable:

$$\text{Loan amount} = 0.75 \times \text{Accounts receivable} = 0.75 \times \$1,800,000 = \$1.35 \text{ million}$$

Third, we calculate the commission and interest on this arrangement:

$$\text{Commission} = 0.01 \times \text{Accounts receivable} = 0.01 \times \$1.8 \text{ million} = \$18,000$$
$$\text{Interest} = 0.10 \times (45 \div 365) \times 1.35 \text{ million} = \$16,644$$

Fourth, we calculate the savings on the arrangement:

$$\text{Savings} = \$2,000 + (0.005 \times 45 \text{ days} \times \$40,000/\text{day}) = 2,000 + 9,000 = \$11,000$$

Assembling all the pieces, minus the cost and the savings, we have, on net, a cost of $23,644:

$$\text{Net cost} = \$18,000 + 16,644 - 11,000 = \$23,644$$

Translating this into an effective cost, which allows the company to compare this financing arrangement with other arrangements, we find that the cost is 15.12% per year:

$$i = \left(1 + \frac{\$23,644}{\$1,350,000}\right)^{\frac{365}{45}} - 1 = 15.12\%$$

Money Market Instruments

Larger companies with good credit ratings that require large amounts of short-term financing may be able to issue money market instruments. A **money market instrument** is a security with less than 1 year in maturity that trades in markets or can be privately placed. These securities provide the company with a cost advantage over other short-term financing options; however, the conditions may be somewhat restrictive. Companies generally have two major types of money market instruments available to them: commercial paper and bankers' acceptances.

money market instrument security with less than 1 year in maturity that trades in markets or can be privately placed

Commercial paper is essentially a short-term promissory note issued by companies, which is rated by external debt agencies in a similar fashion as bonds. Only large companies with very good credit ratings can issue commercial paper. Companies usually issue commercial paper at a discount from face value, providing purchasers with an implicit yield. Commercial paper is issued in large amounts (usually more than $100,000), and the most common maturity dates are 30, 60, and 90 days. Often, the issuer backs up its commercial paper with a bank line of credit.

A **bankers' acceptance** is similar to commercial paper in many regards—they are issued at a discount from face value in large denominations, with common maturity dates of 30, 60, and 90 days. They differ from commercial paper because they are "stamped" by a bank as accepted in return for a fee that is usually 0.25 percent to 1 percent of the face value of the bankers' acceptances. In return, the bank guarantees the payments associated with these instruments. Therefore, bankers' acceptances carry the credit risk of the bank that stamps them and not the company that borrows by using them. Most of the companies that issue bankers' acceptances are large, well-known companies with excellent credit ratings. However, because of the bank guarantee, some companies that are not able to issue commercial paper may be able to borrow by using bankers' acceptances—provided they can find a bank that is willing to guarantee their payments.

The yield on commercial paper and bankers' acceptances is most often based on the bond equivalent yield, i_{bey}, which is the annualized rate per period:

$$i_{bey} = \frac{FV - PV}{PV} \times \frac{365}{m} \tag{19-13}$$

If a company is comparing alternative financing arrangements, it would want to estimate the effective annual cost to the company, as we did for the other financing options, where the discount amount represents the major part of the financing cost.

EXAMPLE 19.4

Commercial Paper

PROBLEM

a. Estimate the effective annual cost to a company of issuing $10 million face value of 90-day commercial paper for net proceeds of $9.85 million. The company must maintain a $10 million credit line, on which it must pay a standby fee of 0.1 percent.

b. Determine the quoted yield for this commercial paper.

Solution

a. Discount = $10 million − $9.85 million = $0.15 million

Standby fee = 0.001 × $10 million = $50,000 = $0.01 million

Total financing cost = $0.15 million + $0.01 million = $0.16 million

$$i = \left(1 + \frac{d}{c}\right)^{365/n} - 1 = \left(1 + \frac{0.16 \text{ million}}{9.85 \text{ million}}\right)^{365/90} - 1 = 6.75\%$$

b. Approximate annual (quoted) yield

$$i_{bey} = \frac{\text{Discount}}{\text{market price}} \times \frac{365}{\text{Days to maturity}}$$

$$i_{bey} = \frac{\$0.15 \text{ million}}{\$9.85 \text{ million}} \times \frac{365}{90} = 0.0618 \text{ or } 6.18\%$$

EXAMPLE 19.5

Bankers' Acceptances

PROBLEM

Estimate the effective annual cost to a company that issues $100 million (face value) of 90-day bankers' acceptances at a quoted rate of 6.25 percent, if the bank charges a 0.30 percent stamping fee.

Solution

We estimate the selling price of the BAs, by rearranging Equation 19-13:

$$6.25\% = \frac{\text{Discount}}{\text{Market price}} \times \frac{365}{\text{Days to maturity}} = \frac{\text{Face} - \text{Price}}{\text{Price}} \times \frac{365}{90}$$

$$0.0625 \times (90 \div 365) = (\$100 \text{ million} - \text{Price}) \div \text{Price}$$

Solving for the price,

$$0.015411 = (\$100 \text{ million} - \text{Price}) \div \text{Price}$$

$$0.015411 \times \text{Price} = \$100 \text{ million} - \text{Price}$$

$$1.015411 \times \text{Price} = \$100 \text{ million}$$

$$\text{Price} = \$100 \text{ million} \div 1.015411 = \$98.482289 \text{ million}$$

Therefore, the discount is: Discount = $100 million − $98.482289 million = $1.517711 million

The stamping fee is a percentage of the face value: Stamping fee = 0.003 × $100 million = $300,000 = $0.3 million. Therefore, the total financing cost in dollars is $1.517711 million + $0.3 million = $1.817711 million.

The effective annual cost of this financing is:

$$i = \left(1 + \frac{\$1.817711 \text{ million}}{\$98.482289 \text{ million}}\right)^{365/90} - 1 = 7.70\%$$

Jittery Companies Stash Cash | FINANCE in the News

The financial crisis of 2007–2008 pointed out a flaw in some companies' planning: Credit is not always available, at any price. The reaction to the financial crisis, and to the low interest rates that followed, has been to hoard cash. This hoarding extends beyond this article. For example, PepsiCo, which is mentioned, had $5.943 billion in cash and cash equivalents at the end of fiscal year 2010, or 8.7 percent of its assets.

After Crisis, Big Businesses Hoard Most Bucks in 40 Years; Google's $22 Billion Cache

Stung by the financial crisis, companies are holding more cash—and a greater percentage of assets in cash—than at any time in the past 40 years.

In the second quarter, the 500 largest nonfinancial U.S. firms, by total assets, held about $994 billion in cash and short-term investments, or 9.8% of their assets, according to a Wall Street Journal analysis of corporate filings. That is up from $846 billion, or 7.9% of assets, a year earlier.

The trend appears to have continued in the third quarter, despite an improving economy. Of those 500 companies, 248 have reported third-quarter results. Their cash increased to 11.1% of assets, from 10.1% in the second quarter. Companies as diverse as Alcoa Inc., Google Inc., PepsiCo Inc. and Texas Instruments Inc. all reported big third-quarter increases in cash holdings.

"Everyone is hoarding cash," says Carsten Stendevad, head of Citigroup Inc.'s financial-strategy group. He and others call that a hangover from the financial crisis a year ago, when companies couldn't raise money or had to pay much higher rates than usual.

Large cash balances are both a curse for the economy and a potential blessing. Hoarding means companies are spending and investing less, damping economic growth. But that leaves them with more cash to deploy as the economy improves, giving them a freer hand to acquire, and to restart hiring and capital spending.

Large cash balances are "great news for the macroeconomy," says Mr. Stendevad. "A lot of firms now are in a position . . . to start reinvesting again, and that ultimately is what is going to drive employment."

In response to last year's financial crisis, executives have bolstered rainy-day funds to ensure they can cover day-to-day operations. Aggressive cost cutting and a recent boom in debt issuance also have swelled cash balances.

Many companies have no plans for the cash, beyond peace of mind. "They'd have to beat me over my head to get it out of my hands," says Charles McLane, Alcoa's chief financial officer.

The aluminum maker reported holding $1.1 billion in cash and cash-equivalents on Sept. 30, up 28% from a year earlier. As revenue slumped this year, Alcoa cut its dividend, its spending and more than 15,000 jobs to save cash. Alcoa posted a profit in the third quarter, but Mr. McLane remains cautious. "We're just going to be extremely prudent" about managing cash, he says.

Some companies are considering targeted spending or acquisitions. Semiconductor maker Texas Instruments this year has acquired two small companies, plus equipment from a bankrupt competitor. TI reported $2.8 billion in cash and short-term investments as of Sept. 30, up 42% from a year earlier, despite a 26% decline in revenue in the nine months ended Sept. 30, from the year-earlier period.

Chief Financial Officer Kevin March says executives decided a year ago to amass cash so they could seize opportunities to buy cheap manufacturing capacity, technology and other assets. Now, he says, TI can "move very quickly" on deals while maintaining strong reserves.

The cash stockpiling has accelerated a trend that dates back about two decades. In the second quarter of 1991, the 500 largest nonfinancial companies held 3.9% of their assets in cash, according to the Journal's analysis of data from corporate filings compiled by Capital IQ, a Standard & Poor's business. That number rose steadily to 9.2% in mid-2004.

Rene Stulz, a finance professor at Ohio State University's business school, says companies increased cash holdings as globalization and technological change exposed them to more risk. "Firms are riskier than they used to be, so they need a bigger security blanket," he says. They are holding more of their assets in cash than at anytime since the 1960s, when payment automation reduced the need to hold cash for daily operations, he says.

Kathleen Kahle, a professor at the University of Georgia's business school, offers another reason: the growth of high-tech companies, which tend to hold lots of cash. Younger, riskier firms have more difficulty raising money when credit is tight, so they keep more cash on hand, she says. "At the same time, they have a lot of growth opportunities and want to make sure that they have the funds necessary to invest in good projects," she adds.

At the end of the second quarter, the 54 biggest information-technology firms held $280 billion—or 27% of their assets—in cash, according to the Journal's analysis, a higher percentage than any other industry group. Cash balances grew further in the third quarter for the 34 companies in that group that have reported results.

Consider Google. The search giant's cash and short-term investments rose 53% to $22 billion in the third quarter from a year earlier, accounting for 58% of its total assets.

The cash provides "operating and strategic flexibility," Google Chief Executive Eric Schmidt told analysts last month. "We're very happy to have it sit in our bank account and earn a modest interest rate."

The cash-hoarding trend reversed for a few years earlier this decade, as activist investors and hedge funds pressured companies to put cash to use. Private-equity firms turned cash-flush companies into takeover targets, using the cash to repay acquisition debt. By the first quarter of 2008, the percentage of assets held in cash had fallen to 7.9%.

Then came the credit crisis. Unable to raise money in the bond markets or even issue short-term debt known as commercial paper, companies began slashing expenses and stockpiling cash. "Cash suddenly became very strategic," says Citigroup's Mr. Stendevad.

In the fourth quarter of 2008, cash holdings of the 500 largest companies jumped by $46 billon, or 5%, to $886 billion. Their cash balances increased by another 12% in the first half of this year, to $994 billion.

As investors regained an appetite for corporate debt last spring, companies rushed to take advantage. Through Friday, companies in the S&P 500 have issued $548 billion in corporate bonds this year, up from $403 billion in the year-earlier period, according to data provider Dealogic.

Some of that cash is now sitting idle on balance sheets. Baxter International Inc. sold $500 million in 10-year notes in August, helping to increase its cash and short-term investments by $769 million, or 43%, between the second and third quarters. A spokeswoman says Baxter plans to use the cash over time for working capital, capital spending, dividend payments, share repurchases and business development.

Pepsi plans to issue debt to cover roughly half of the $7.8 billion cost of acquiring its two largest bottlers without touching the company's $3.5 billion in cash and short-term investments. The cash total is up from $1.9 billion a year ago. The money will be reinvested over time with an eye toward growth, says a company spokeswoman.

Today investors are rewarding companies with big cash hoards, says Citigroup's Mr. Stendevad. But some firms have more than they need, he says, and investors are starting to pressure executives to reinvest the money or return it to shareholders through stock repurchases or dividends.

"During the crisis, no amount of cash was sufficient," he says. "Now it's about growth again."

Source: Tom McGinty and Cari Tuna, "Jittery Companies Stash Cash," *Wall Street Journal*, November 2, 2009.

Securitizations

A more recent innovation in financing trade credit is the use of a **special purpose vehicle (SPV)**, also known as a **special purpose entity (SPE)**. SPVs are conduits, usually formed as limited partnerships or limited companies, for packaging portfolios of receivables and selling them to investors in the money market. In this way, the purchaser relies on the credit of the SPV, rather than that of the company selling the receivables. It can do this by using any of the previously mentioned instruments. It can take out a bank loan or issue commercial paper or bankers' acceptances, and then use the proceeds to finance car loans. For many companies that offer financing for purchases, such as automobile companies, the volume of financing would quickly alter the company's balance sheet, making it look more like that of a financial institution with large amounts of short-term borrowing financing short-term loans. To avoid this, these companies sell the loans directly to the capital market through an SPV so that neither the loans nor the financing appear on its balance sheet. This process is called **securitization**.

The essence of securitization is that the credit risk of the seller of the receivables or loans is not directly involved. For example, when Harley-Davidson Financial Services packages its motorcycle loans, the buyers of these loans look primarily to the loans held in the SPV and evaluate their credit, rather than that of Harley-Davidson, which is what would happen if Harley-Davidson had issued commercial paper to finance its loans.[16]

The money market is very credit conscious because investments are very short term, and in practice any money market instrument has to be very good investment grade. This poses a problem because, as we have seen, many companies will extend credit in situations where a bank would not. This occurs because the company makes a profit on the sale and is anticipating a long-term relationship involving future sales and future profits. If a portfolio of receivables or loans is simply sold to investors, in all likelihood the credit quality would not be high enough to get an investment-grade rating. As a result, investors demand a **credit enhancement**, such as requiring collateral, insurance, or other agreements, to reduce credit risk.

A credit rating is required to access the money market. In generating their credit ratings, rating services look to the seller, the collateral, and the structure of the securitization. Although the primary credit concern is for the pool of receivables or loans, the financial health of the seller is still important for several reasons. The most obvious one is that the seller may sell poor-quality loans into the SPV so that over time the quality of the SPV deteriorates. Also, the seller still services the loans; when the creditor makes payments on the loan, or someone pays off the receivable, it is the seller who has to service those payments and pass them to the SPV to be distributed to investors.

The collateral in the SPV depends on the particular issue. In the case of Harley-Davidson, the underlying asset is motorcycle loans. Other securitizations have been made by Deere & Company (John Deere) and Bombardier, Inc., with equipment loans. In each case, credit rating services look at the historical default rates on the loans and the history of **prepayments** because frequently loans are paid off early. By pooling a large number of loans in an SPV, these financial characteristics are fairly stable, but the credit rating services will perform **stress tests** to gauge the effect of changing economic conditions to see how it affects the ability of the SPV to pay off on its securities.

prepayment payment of a debt before its due date

stress tests "what-if" examinations of the value of an asset under challenging conditions, such as an increase in interest rates or declining economic conditions

The most important aspects of the SPV are usually the credit enhancements because, as mentioned earlier, the SPV may need to enhance the credit quality of the underlying asset's need to get an AAA credit rating. For the sale of the loans to be taken off the seller's balance sheet, accounting standards require that the SPV can go back to the seller for no more than 10 percent of the assets. As a result, there are usually external as well as seller credit enhancements. These credit enhancements often take several forms; for example:

- Having 5 percent of the losses absorbed by the seller—this is often referred to as overcollateralization.
- Having the next 10 percent of losses on trade receivables absorbed by a third party, such as a major bank like the UBS.
- Issuing subordinated debt to absorb further defaults on termination of the SPV.
- Creating or issuing different classes of securities so that the prepayment risks are allocated to different securities, as is often the case with mortgage SPVs.

Securitization grew rapidly around the world as a means of generating cash flows from noncash assets. In practice, companies use some combination of the short-term financing options mentioned to provide them with the desired mix of flexibility and cost effectiveness. Trade credit and bank loans are the predominant sources of short-term financing, especially for smaller companies that do not have the option of accessing the money market.

[16] Harley-Davidson's financing subsidiary is Harley-Davidson Financial Services, Inc., which offers loans for motorcycle purchases, loans to dealers, and insurance through its various subsidiaries.

LESSONS LEARNED | No New Rules for Securitization

The Dodd–Frank Wall Street Reform and Consumer Protection Act of July 2010 left the rule-making regarding securitization up to different regulatory agencies.[17] Some of the changes as of the end of 2011:

- At least 5 percent of credit risk much be retained by the sponsors (that is, securitizers or originators) of asset-backed securities. This ensures that the entities that originate the loans have "skin in the game."[18]
- Enhanced disclosures of securitized transactions, including credit agencies disclosing information

in their rating of an asset-backed security, though much remains in the regulation of disclosure of securitization and compensation of parties.

- Disclosure of potential conflicts of interest, such as the sponsor of a securitized transaction having a financial interest in the asset-backed security.

Changes related to credit agencies and credit enhancements of asset-backed securities remained unresolved more than a year after the law passed.

Concept Review Questions

1. What is the difference between a bank operating line of credit and a traditional loan?
2. What additional services does a factor provide over a bank?
3. Why do securitizations require credit enhancements?

SUMMARY

- Cash budgets are useful in working capital management because these budgets are a means for companies to forecast their cash requirements.

- We can use some common ratios to assess a company's overall approach to working capital management.

- The optimal level of investment in cash, receivables, and inventory occurs when the benefits balance the costs. In the case of cash, the benefit is the reduced risk of insolvency, whereas the cost is the opportunity costs of having funds tied up in assets that provide a relatively low return.

- Managing receivables requires considering the benefits of extending credit (increased sales), whereas the costs include the financing costs and the increased risk of nonpayment by customers.

- When managing inventory, the benefits may be improved production processes or reduced risk of stock-outs, which result in forgone revenue and can also damage customer goodwill. The costs include financing, storage, spoilage, obsolescence, and insurance.

- Common short-term financing options available to companies include trade credit, bank loans, factoring arrangements, and money market instruments. Each method has advantages and disadvantages. Key to managing short-term financing is to estimate the effective annual cost of each alternative.

---

[17] Public Law 111-203, H.R. 4173, signed into law July 21, 2010.

[18] There are some exemptions for some types of loans, such as residential mortgages that meet certain requirements.

FORMULAS/EQUATIONS

(19-1) Current ratio $= \dfrac{\text{Current assets}}{\text{Current liabilities}}$

(19-2) Quick ratio $= \dfrac{\text{Cash} + \text{Marketable securities} + \text{Accounts receivable}}{\text{Current liabilities}}$

(19-3) Accounts receivable turnover $= \dfrac{\text{Sales}}{\text{Accounts receivable}}$

(19-4) Days sales outstanding $= \dfrac{\text{Accounts receivable}}{\text{Average daily sales}}$

(19-5) Inventory turnover $= \dfrac{\text{Cost of goods sold}}{\text{Inventory}}$

(19-6) Days sales in inventory $= \dfrac{\text{Inventory}}{\text{Average days cost of goods sold}}$

(19-7) Accounts payables turnover $= \dfrac{\text{Purchases}}{\text{Accounts payable}}$

(19-8) Days payables outstanding $= \dfrac{\text{Accounts payable}}{\text{Average days' purchases}}$

(19-9) Operating cycle $= \text{DSI} + \text{DSO}$

(19-10) $\text{CCC} = \text{DSI} + \text{DSO} - \text{DPO}$

(19-11) $i = (1 + \frac{d}{c})^{365/n} - 1$

(19-12) $\text{EOQ} = \sqrt{\dfrac{2 \times \text{Annual usage, in units} \times \text{Order cost}}{\text{Annual carrying cost per unit}}}$

(19-13) $i_{bey} = \dfrac{FV - PV}{PV} \times \dfrac{365}{m}$

QUESTIONS AND PROBLEMS

Multiple Choice

1. Which of the following usually does *not* increase as sales increase?
    A. Cash
    B. Trade credit
    C. Short-term debt
    D. Accounts receivable

Use the following information to answer Questions 2 to 4.

Cash	$500,000
Marketable securities	$800,500
Accounts receivable	$600,000
Inventory	$1,203,000
Short-term loans	$200,000
Accounts payable	$700,000
Sales	$1,287,555
Cost of goods sold	$550,000

2. The current ratio and quick ratio, respectively, are *closest* to:
    A. 2.8; 3.4.   B. 3.4; 2.8.   C. 3.4; 2.1.   D. 2.1; 3.4.

3. The average collection period is *closest* to:
    A. 145 days.   B. 150 days.   C. 170 days.   D. 175 days.

4. The operating cycle is *closest* to:
    A. 170 days.   B. 511 days.   C. 750 days.   D. 968 days.

5. The period between the purchase of raw materials and the sale of the finished goods produced from the raw materials is best described as the:
    A. operating cycle.   B. inventory period.   C. collection period.   D. net financing period.

6. The period of time between the sale of finished goods on credit and the collection of the cash is *best* described as the:
    A. operating cycle.   B. inventory period.   C. collection period.   D. net financing period.

7. Which of the following is not considered a short-term instrument?
    A. T-bills   B. Long-term debt   C. Commercial paper   D. Bankers' acceptances

8. Which of the following statements about float time is *false*?
    A. An efficient credit policy speeds up inflows.
    B. Check-processing time is one source of float.
    C. Using preauthorized payment is one way to shorten float time.

9. If the current credit policy is 3/30 net 45, which of the following *tightens* the credit policy?
    A. net 45   B. 3/30 net 40   C. 3/35 net 50   D. 3/40 net 50

10. Consider two companies; Company A has a current ratio of 0.75, and Company B has a current ratio of 1.5. If both companies borrow short-term to increase their cash balance, which of the following is most likely to occur?
    A. The current ratio of both companies will increase.
    B. The current ratio of both companies will decline.
    C. The current ratio of Company A will increase and that of Company B will decline.
    D. The current ratio of Company B will increase and that of Company A will decline.

Practice Questions and Problems

19.1   Analyzing Working Capital

11. How is net working capital calculated?

12. Why is the efficient use of net working capital important?

13. What is the connection between cash budgets and projected financial statements?

14. Boise Company provided the following accounting information:

Net operating income	$40,000
Depreciation on equipment and building	10,000
Sale of land	25,000
Purchase of equipment	15,000
Retirement of long-term debt	30,000
Dividends declared	15,000
Long-term investments	10,000

A. Which of the preceding are sources of funds?

B. Which of the preceding are uses of funds?

C. What is the overall increase or decrease in net working capital for this period?

15. Calculate the ending cash balance of the current month using the following information:

Beginning cash	$10,000
Prior month sales	$50,000
Current month sales	$80,000
Current purchase	$35,000
Prior month purchase	$20,000
Sale of old equipment	$70,000
Dividend payment	$60,000
Wages and others	$35,000

16. A company has estimated its sales, purchases from suppliers, and wages and miscellaneous operating cash outlays for the first 4 months of next year as follows:

Month	Sales	Purchases	Wages & Miscellaneous
January	$100,000	$60,000	$25,000
February	$102,000	$70,000	$28,000
March	$105,000	$55,000	$40,000
April	$110,000	$50,000	$35,000

The company's managers estimate that 40 percent of these sales will be for cash and that it will receive the remaining portion in two equal proportions at the end of the subsequent 2 months. It plans to pay for all of its purchases 2 months after the purchase date.

The company is scheduled to pay dividends of $30,000 in January and to pay $20,000 for new equipment in February. Its beginning cash balance is $16,000, and $10,000 is the company's minimum cash balance it wishes to maintain. Estimate the company's cash budget for the first 4 months of next year. Assume that the sales and purchases were the same in November and December as they are estimated to be in January.

17. Consider additional data for Archer-Daniels-Midland for fiscal years ending June 30, 2010 and 2011, in millions:

(in millions)	Fiscal Year End	
	June 30, 2011	June 30, 2010
Sales	$80,676	$61,682
Cost of goods sold	$76,376	$57,839

(in millions)	Fiscal Year End	
	June 30, 2011	June 30, 2010
Accounts receivable	$9,816	$6,122
Inventories	$12,055	$7,871
Accounts payable	$11,165	$8,115

A. Calculate the DSO, DIO, and DPO for fiscal years ending June 30, 2010, and 2011.

B. How do the operating and cash conversion cycles compare for 2010 and 2011 with fiscal years ending in 2008 and 2009? What has changed and why?

18. Christmas Inc. is a wholesaler of Christmas decorations and wrapping paper. It is a seasonal business, and due to the timing of cash inflows and outflows, it frequently experiences a cash shortfall in the fourth quarter of the year before it can liquidate its current assets. Christmas Inc. has a cash balance as of October 1 of $40,000. Cash receipts for October, November, and December are expected to be $20,000, $30,000, and $60,000, respectively. Fixed-cash operating expenses are $45,000 per month, and variable-cash operating expenses are generally 10 percent of the cash receipts for that month. If the line of credit is paid off the month following when it is used, there is no interest charged. Using a spreadsheet, prepare a cash budget for Christmas Inc., and determine whether Christmas Inc. will need to make use of its $10,000 credit line.

19.2   Managing Cash and Cash Equivalents

19. Briefly state four main motives companies have to hold cash.

20. What is float, and how does this affect a business entity? Explain.

21. What are three major sources of float? What are some common methods that address float?

22. Briefly explain the transactions motive for holding cash.

23. A company presently receives an average of $10,000 in checks per day from its customers. It presently takes the company an average of 5 days to receive and deposit these checks. It is considering a lock-box arrangement that would reduce its collection float time by 3 days and cost the company $50 per month. If its opportunity cost of funds tied up in float is 8 percent, should it adopt the new system? Explain.

19.3   Managing Accounts Receivable

24. What is the purpose of credit analysis, and how is it accomplished?

25. When deciding whether or not to extend credit to an applicant, what two things need to be established about the applicant?

26. What are captive finance companies?

27. Suppose Sio Inc. has 60 days of accounts receivable of $900,000 on its books. A factor offers a 60-day accounts receivable loan equal to 80 percent of accounts receivable. The quoted interest rate is 8 percent, and there is a commission fee of 0.5 percent. The factoring will result in a reduction of $8,000 in bad debt losses. What is the effective annual cost?

28. Consider the sale of an item for $600 with credit terms of 3/15 net 50.
    A. Calculate the effective annual cost of forgoing the discount, paying instead on day 50.
    B. Another supplier offers $612 on credit terms of net 60. If you could finance the purchase by using loans at an effective annual cost of 10 percent for Part A, which option should you choose?

29. Greenbay Inc. currently grants credit terms of net 25. It is considering a new policy that involves a more stringent credit policy: net 20. As a result, the price of its product will stay the same at $45. The expected sales will decrease by 2,000 per year to 10,000 units. Variable costs will remain at $37 per unit, and bad debt losses can be reduced by $1,000 per year to $2,000. Greenbay Inc. will finance the additional investment in receivables by using its line of credit, which charges 6.5 percent interest after tax, and its tax rate is 40 percent. Should Greenbay Inc. switch to the new policy?

30. Lakeland Inc. has a DSO of 60 days and has daily credit sales of $55,000. A factor offers a 60-day accounts receivable loan equal to 80 percent of accounts receivable. The quoted interest rate is 10 percent, and the commission fee is 1.5 percent of accounts receivable. As result, the company will save $3,000 and have 0.65 percent reduction in bad debt losses, which are $500,000. What is the effective annual cost of the factor arrangement?

19.4   Inventory

31. Briefly describe the four inventory management approaches.

32. What are some of the advantages of carrying inventories?

33. What are some of the disadvantages of carrying inventories?

34. Complete the following table:

	Annual Use, in Units	Cost of Ordering	Carrying Cost of a Unit	Economic Order Quantity
A.	1 million	$1,000	$1	
B.	10,000	$100	$0.5	
C.	10 million	$1,000	$2	
D.	63,000	$30	$1	
E.	1,000	$5	$0.10	

35. Consider a food processor that that uses 12 million pounds of sugar in a year in the production of its food products. The cost of ordering the sugar is $500 for each order. If the cost of carrying a pound of sugar is $0.01, what is the economic order quantity for this food processor?

19.5 Short-Term Financing Considerations

36. What are special purpose vehicles (SPVs)? What is the main advantage of SPVs?

37. List a few forms of credit enhancement for securitizations.

38. What distinguishes a bankers' acceptance from a bank loan? What is the effective annual cost if a company issues $1,500,000 face value of 90-day commercial paper for net proceeds of $1,450,000? The company pays a standby fee of 0.2 percent on the face value.

39. Calculate the effective annual cost of issuing 180-day bankers' acceptances at a quoted rate of 7.5 percent with a face value of $10,000,000. The bank charges a 0.4 percent stamping fee.

40. There are two suppliers of one input for a factory. Supplier A offers a selling price of $500 with terms of 2/10 net 30, and Supplier B offers $520 with net 60. Which supplier offers the lower effective annual cost?

41. A company engaged a 1-year monthly pay $100,000 line of credit at 7.5 percent plus a 0.5 percent commitment fee on the unused portion of the line. The company used 60 percent of the line for the first half year and reduced the loan amount to 30 percent for the rest of the year. What is the effective annual rate of the loan?

42. Calculate the effective annual cost of a 1-year $1,000,000 operating line of credit. The company borrowed $600,000 for the first 5 months of the year and reduced the loan amount to $500,000 for the rest of the year. The quoted interest rate is 7.5 percent, and there is a 0.8 percent commitment fee on the unused portion.

43. What is the effective annual cost if a company issues $10,000,000 of 90-day bankers' acceptances issued at a quoted rate of 6.5 percent, and the bank charges a 0.5 percent stamping fee? Compare the effective annual cost to a 90-day commercial paper issued at $10,000,000 face value for a price of $9,758,000, while the company must maintain a $10,000,000 credit line and pay a standby fee of 0.2 percent.

 44. Calculate the payment and the effective annual rate of interest for a purchase of $100,000 with the terms of 2/10, net 30, and graph the effective annual rate of interest if a payment is made on each of the days 14 through 30. Explain what you found regarding the effective annual rate for these terms.

Case

Case 19.1 Mikopo and Trade Credit

Mikopo Inc. currently grants no credit, but it is considering offering new credit terms: net 30. As a result, the price of its product will increase by $1.50 per unit. The original price per unit is $50. Expected sales will increase by 1,000 units per year, from the current 10,000 units, if discounts are offered. Variable costs will remain at $26 per unit, and bad debt losses will amount to $3,000 per year. The company will finance the additional investment in receivables by using a line of credit, which charges 5 percent interest. The company's tax rate is 40 percent.

A. Should the company begin extending credit? Why?

B. No matter the credit policy, the company's management believes that the price will remain the same at $51.50 per unit, unit sales will remain at 11,000 per year, and variable costs will remain at $26 per unit. Further, management estimates that bad debt losses will not be affected by the terms of credit. The credit manager at Mikopo has done some research and estimates that:

Policy 1   A switch to 1/10 net 30 will result in 50 percent of customers taking advantage of the discount, and the remaining 50 percent will pay on day 30.

Policy 2   A switch to 2/10 net 30 will result in 80 percent of customers taking advantage of the discount, and the remaining 20 percent will pay on day 30.

Policy 3   A switch to 3/10 net 30 will result in 90 percent of customers taking advantage of the discount, and the remaining 10 percent will pay on day 30.

Which policy should Mikopo consider? Why?

CHAPTER 20

LEASING

© Andrew Kolb/Masterfile

Leasing and accounting   The accounting for leases is a "hot button" issue as U.S. generally accepted accounting standards (GAAP) and International Financial Reporting Standards converge. The reason? The proposed accounting for leases would require more companies to report their obligations for leases on their balance sheets, which would result in many companies reporting leases that have been left off the balance sheet.*

At present, U.S. GAAP requires companies to account for leases as either capital leases or operating leases, depending on the characteristics of the lease. In some cases, the present U.S. accounting results in significant assets and obligations off-balance sheet; for example, if you look at airlines' balance sheets, you would think that some of the airlines do not have any planes.

When the original accounting for leases was released, many companies began to lease, rather than buy, because if the lease qualified as an operating lease, they could avoid reporting financial obligations on the balance sheet. If lease accounting moves most or all operating leases to a company's balance sheet, this may result in more companies buying rather than leasing, which will affect leasing companies.**

Learning Outcomes

After reading this chapter, you should be able to:

LO 20.1 Describe the basic characteristics of leases and differentiate between operating and financial (or capital) leases.

LO 20.2 Explain the accounting treatment of both operating and financial leases and how the accounting affects reported financial results.

LO 20.3 Evaluate a lease decision using discounted cash flow valuation methods.

Chapter Preview In this chapter, we discuss leasing arrangements, which may represent attractive alternatives for companies to finance both short- and long-term investments. The focus of this chapter is on the basic financial issues confronting anyone who faces a decision of whether to buy or lease an asset, whether this is a railroad company considering whether to lease or buy railroad cars, or an individual who is considering whether to lease or buy a car.

---

* Financial Accounting Standards Board, Project Update, Leases—Joint Project of the IASB and FASB.

** Scott Stafford, "Accounting Rules Could Affect Your Rental Operations," *Associated Equipment Distributors*, February 1, 2009.

20.1   LEASING ARRANGEMENTS

asset-based lending financing that is tied directly to a particular asset

secured financing financing that is based on an underlying asset that serves as collateral in the event of a default

In earlier chapters we have considered the purchase of a piece of equipment separate from its financing. However, these two decisions are often combined into one decision, which is generically referred to as **asset-based lending**. This definition flows from the fact that the financing is tied directly to a particular asset. It is thus an example of **secured financing**, where the financing is based on an underlying asset that serves as collateral in the event of a default. Examples of asset-based lending are secured loans, conditional sales contracts, and leases. We discuss the differences between these types of asset-based financing, but the focus of this chapter is on leases. Leasing is a type of capital budgeting decision that involves discounting cash flows that are related not only to the asset itself, but also to the financing of the asset.

First, let us step back and discuss the institutional framework for asset-based financing. The Equipment Leasing and Finance Association (ELFA) is the professional body that acts as the umbrella group for asset-based lenders, including captive finance companies, commercial banks, and manufacturers. A **captive finance company (CFC)** is a subsidiary of a company that provides financing for the customers of the parent company. Examples of captive finance companies include Ford Motor Credit Company and Mitsubishi Motors Credit of America.[1]

captive finance company (CFC) company that finances other companies that are divisions of major manufacturers to provide loans to purchase or lease their products

Asset-based financing is always tied directly to some underlying asset. The major assets financed in this way are broadly split among the different types of financial companies. The independents are mainly involved in machinery and equipment financing, where approximately 20 to 25 percent of all machinery and equipment is leased, with 60 percent of their customers classified as a **small and medium-sized enterprise (SME)**, which is a business with fewer than 50 employees. Approximately 40 percent of the assets financed are either transportation equipment, such as buses, trucks, and trailers, or office equipment. This financing tends to be flexible and is often tailor-made to meet the needs of the original manufacturers, and ranges across the whole spectrum of asset-based financing. Often an SME will approach a manufacturer for a piece of equipment and will be offered on-the-spot financing as a prearranged package with the asset-based financier.

small and medium-sized enterprise (SME) business that generally has fewer than 50 employees

In contrast, captive finance companies are subsidiaries of major manufacturing companies and finance the purchase of the equipment they sell. For example, Harley-Davidson Financial Services, Inc. (HDFS) is a captive finance company of Harley-Davidson, the motorcycle manufacturer and distributor; HDFS finances customers' purchases of motorcycles. The final group, the banking institutions, deal with both asset-based lending and leasing. For example, Wells Fargo & Company provides both asset-based lending and equipment leasing through its Wholesale Banking segment, which comprises approximately 25 percent of its revenues.[2]

operating lease rental agreement in which some of the benefits of ownership do not transfer to the lessee, remaining with the lessor

So what is a lease and how is it distinct from other asset-based forms of financing? A lease contract is an agreement in which the owner of the asset (the **lessor**) conveys to the user (the **lessee**) the right to use an asset in return for a number of specified payments over an agreed period. Leasing, therefore, is an alternative to purchasing an asset. Hence, when we evaluate a leasing arrangement, we often compare this with the outright purchase of the asset.

financial lease (or capital lease or full payout lease) lease agreement in which essentially all the benefits of ownership transfer to the lessee

As we indicated, there are different types of asset-based financing, and unfortunately the definitions differ among accountants, lawyers, and tax authorities. As a result, some forms of asset-based financing are specifically structured to get one interpretation for accounting and a different one for tax purposes. However, broadly speaking, we can differentiate between an **operating lease** and a **financial lease**, which are commonly referred to as a **full-payout lease** or a **capital lease**. In an operating lease, the benefits

---

[1] General Motors Acceptance Corporation (GMAC) was once a captive finance subsidiary of General Motors Company, known as GMAC. GMAC became a bank in December 2008 and subsequently changed its name to Ally Bank.

[2] Based on 10-K filings, Operating Segment footnote, for fiscal years 2008 through 2010.

of ownership do not transfer to the lessee; the lease is, essentially, a rental agreement. In a capital lease, the benefits of ownership transfer to the lessee.

Types of Asset-Based Financing

The tax and accounting treatments for asset-based financing may not always be in agreement, but each treatment focuses on the terms of the financing and ownership.

Taxes and asset-based financing

The Internal Revenue Code classifies a lease as either a tax lease or a nontax lease. In a **tax lease**, often referred to as a **true lease**, the lessor is the owner of the asset and therefore receives the tax benefits of depreciation and any tax credits associated with the asset. The lessee in a tax lease pays rent or lease payments, which are income to the lessor and deductible business expenses for the lessee.

In a **nontax lease**, the Internal Revenue Service considers a lease to be a purchase for tax purposes, and therefore the lessee receives the benefits of ownership, including deductions for depreciation and interest, as well as any tax credits. In this type, the lessor retains legal ownership of the asset, but the lessor is not considered "at risk" at the end of the lease period because the lessee has a nominal purchase option at the end of the lease. Therefore, the lessee receives ownership benefits at the end of the lease.

Because lease agreements are complex, the IRS has specified conditions in which a lease is not considered a true lease:[3]

1. Any portion of the lease payment applies toward the lessee's equity interest in the asset.
2. The lessee acquires ownership of the asset after a specified number of payments.
3. The payments that the lessee makes over a short period are a large portion of the asset's value.
4. The agreed-upon payments exceed the asset's current market value.
5. The purchase option requires a payment significantly less than the value of the property at the time of the exercise of this option.
6. A portion of the periodic payment is designated as interest.

> **tax lease** or **true lease** contractual arrangement in which the owner of the asset receives the benefits of depreciation, and the party that rents or leases the asset incurs a tax deductible expense
>
> **nontax lease** contractual arrangement in which the lease is considered a purchase for tax purposes

Attribute	Tax Lease	Nontax Lease
Depreciation and tax credits	Lessor	Lessee
Legal ownership of asset	Lessor	Lessor

SUMMARIZING: TAX LEASE VERSUS NONTAX LEASE

Accounting and asset-based financing

The accounting profession has a slightly different interpretation of asset-backed financing: Businesses classify such financing as either an operating lease or a capital lease, but the definitions are very precise. A financing arrangement is a capital lease if the arrangement contains one of the following provisions:[4]

1. The title of the property transfers automatically to the lessee at the end of the lease period.
2. A bargain purchase option.

---

[3] Revenue Ruling 55–540. The "true lease" criteria are spelled out so that the entire lease payment can be deducted as a business expense. These criteria distinguish the arrangement from a secured loan or a conditional sale.

[4] Statement of Financial Accounting Standards No. 13, *Accounting for Leases*, November 1976, Financial Accounting Standards Board.

3. The lease term is equal to 75 percent or more of the economic life of the property.
4. The present value of the minimum lease payments at the beginning of the lease agreement is equal to or greater than 90 percent of the value of the leased asset, adjusted for any tax credits that the lessor has on this asset.

If at least one of these criteria is not satisfied in the lease agreement, the lease is considered an operating lease. Comparing the criteria for accounting and tax treatments, we can see that the criteria for a nontax lease and a capital lease are similar, but that the financial accounting criteria are more specific.

So why does this classification make a difference? Because of the effect on the financial statements of the lessor and the lessee. We summarize the accounting for an operating lease in Table 20-1. As you can see in this table, the accounting for the operating lease is simple from the perspectives of both the lessor and the lessee.

Capital leases are a bit more complex. We summarize the accounting in Table 20-2. From the perspective of the lessee, as shown in Panel A of this table, the capital lease is considered as the acquisition of an asset, with payments comprising both the interest and the principal repayment.

We can show this with an example. Consider a lease of an asset for 5 years, with payments of $20,000 at the end of each year. The asset has an estimated economic life of 7 years. If the lessee's borrowing rate is 7 percent, the present value of the lease payments is $82,003.95 [PMT = $20,000; N = 5; i = 7%]:[5]

$$\text{Present value of lease} = \sum_{t=1}^{5} \frac{\$20,000}{(1 + 0.07)^t} = \$82,003.95$$

The lessee records the leased asset in the assets section of the balance sheet at $82,003.95, as well as a lease liability of $82,000.95 in the liability section. The lessee will then use the borrowing rate of 7 percent to allocate each interest payment to interest and the reduction of the liability. The lessee will also amortize the asset over the life of the lease, deducting the amount of amortization in its income statement and reducing the carrying value of asset on the balance sheet for the same amount. We show these calculations in Table 20-3.

TABLE 20-1 Accounting for Operating Leases

Item	Lessor	Lessee
Lease payment	Rental income on the income statement	Rental expense on the income statement
	Depreciation expense on the income statement	
Asset cost	Original cost, less depreciation, on the balance sheet	Not applicable
Lease obligation	Not applicable	Not applicable
Footnotes	Not applicable	Minimum lease payments for the next 5 years

---

[5] If there was a guaranteed purchase by the lessee at the end of the lease, we would include this purchase price in this calculation.

TABLE 20-2 Accounting for Capital Leases

Panel A: Perspective of the Lessee

Item	Balance Sheet	Income Statement
Lease payment		Implied interest Implied reduction of the liability
Present value of lease payments	Asset, less accumulated amortized principal	
Present value of lease obligation	Liability, less accumulated liability reduction	

Panel B: Perspective of the Lessor

Type of Lease	Accounting Treatment
Sales-type lease	Lessor earns interest income and a profit from the lease arrangement.
Direct financing lease	The lessor earns only interest income from the lease arrangement.
Leverage lease	The lessor borrows some of the funds to acquire the leased asset, or the asset is completely financed by a third party.

Examining the calculations in Table 20-3, you can see that the carrying value of the asset, which the lessee reports on its balance sheet, declines each year by the same amount, in this case $16,400.79. The carrying value of the liability that the lessee reports, however, declines through time at a different amount each year, with each lease payment including more repayment of the obligation.[6] We show this in Figure 20-1.

The accounting for a capital lease from the perspective of the lessor is a bit more complex. It all depends on the type of lease, as we show in Panel B of Table 20-2.

TABLE 20-3 Accounting for a Capital Lease from the Lessee's Perspective

		Determines Interest Expense and Liability			Determines Amortized Expense and Asset's Value	
		7 percent of lease obligation carrying value	*Lease payment, less interest expense*	*Original capitalized value, less reduction in lease obligation*	*Based on straight-line depreciation of $72,003.95*	*Original capitalized value, less depreciation*
Period	Lease Payment	Interest Expense	Reduction in Lease Obligation	Lease Obligation	Amortization	Carrying Value of Leased Asset
0				$82,003.95		$82,003.95
1	$20,000.00	$5,740.28	$14,259.72	$67,744.23	$16,400.79	$65,603.16
2	$20,000.00	$4,742.10	$15,257.90	$52,486.32	$16,400.79	$49,202.37
3	$20,000.00	$3,674.04	$16,325.96	$36,160.36	$16,400.79	$32,801.58
4	$20,000.00	$2,531.23	$17,468.77	$18,691.59	$16,400.79	$16,400.79
5	$20,000.00	$1,308.41	$18,691.59	$0.00	$16,400.79	$0.00

[6] This is similar to the payment of a mortgage obligation, in which each payment has less interest than the previous payment, whereas each payment has more principal repayment than the previous payment.

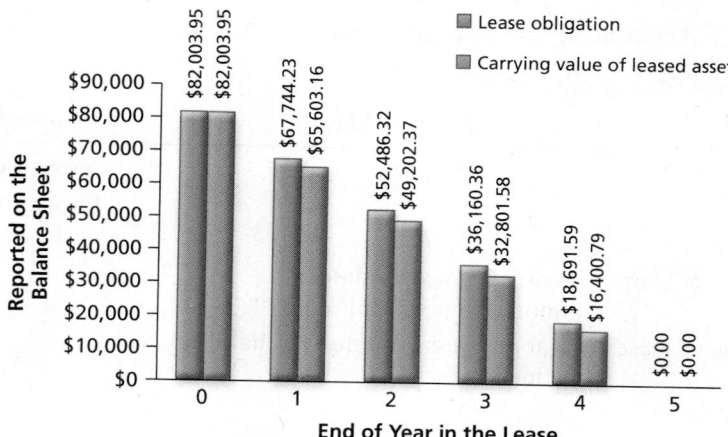

FIGURE 20-1 Balance Sheet Asset and Liability for the Lessee in a 5-Year Lease Requiring Payments of $20,000 Each Year

Direct financing lease

direct financing lease contractual agreement in which the party owning the asset records a lease receivable for the promised lease payments, as well as earning interest on the financing

If the lease is considered a **direct financing lease**, the lessor records a lease receivable for the sum of the contracted lease payments and then reduces its assets by the amount of the carrying value of the leased asset. Because the direct financing lease includes financing, the lessor also records unearned interest initially. As payments are made by the lessee, the lessor reduces the lease receivable, as well as unearned interest, and records the interest expense.

Consider the other side—the lessor's perspective—of the lease that we just looked at. Suppose the leased asset has an economic life of 5 years, and at the end of the 5-year lease term it has no residual value. To simplify this example, let's assume that the asset has a carrying value of $86,589.53 at the time the lease is made. These facts mean that the amount of the receivable is $20,000 × 5 = $100,000, and the unearned interest is $100,000 − 86,589.53 = $13,410.47.[7] The unearned interest rate is the rate that equates the receivable with the payments. We provide the details of these calculations in Table 20-4.

TABLE 20-4 Accounting for a Direct Lease from the Lessor's Perspective

Period	Lease Payment	5 percent of beginning value of lease obligation — Interest Expense	Unearned interest less accumulated interest expense — Carrying Value of Unearned Interest	Lease payment, less interest expense — Reduction in Lease Obligation	Original lease obligation, less accumulated reduction in the lease obligation — Lease Obligation	Original lease receivable, less accumulated lease payments — Lease Receivable
0			$13,410.47		$86,589.53	$100,000.00
1	$20,000	$4,329.48	$9,080.99	$15,670.52	$70,919.01	$80,000.00
2	$20,000	$3,545.95	$5,535.04	$16,454.05	$54,464.96	$60,000.00
3	$20,000	$2,723.25	$2,811.79	$17,276.75	$37,188.20	$40,000.00
4	$20,000	$1,859.41	$952.38	$18,140.59	$19,047.61	$20,000.00
5	$20,000	$952.38	$0.00	$19,047.62	$0.00	$0.00

[7] If the lessor and lessee had a contracted or a residual value at which the lessee would purchase the asset from the lessor, this residual value would be added to the lease obligation. Also, if there were initial costs to the transaction that are passed on to the lessee, these would be included in the original lease receivable.

Sale-type leaseback

Another type of leasing arrangement is a **sale-type lease**, also referred to as a **sale and leaseback (SLB) agreement** or simply as a **sale-leaseback agreement**. In an SLB, the owner of an asset sells it, usually to an insurance company or pension fund, and then signs an agreement to lease the asset back. Thus, the lessee retains the use of the asset and receives a large, one-time cash inflow at the time of the sale. This type of arrangement is particularly popular for organizations in very low tax brackets to become the lessee because they have little or no benefit from any depreciation tax deductions for the assets that they own. The low-tax company could sell an asset to someone who does pay taxes and can use the depreciation deduction. When the low-tax company leases the asset back, part of the tax savings that the new owner is enjoying could be passed back to the lessee in the form of lower lease payments.

What is a low-tax company? If could be a nonprofit entity, or it could be a company that is performing poorly and therefore not generating income for tax purposes. If a company is not generating taxable income, it cannot benefit immediately from the tax deductibility of depreciation.[8] In these cases, they could perform a sale-leaseback, in which the other party uses these deductions, and the selling company then leases back the asset with potentially some of the benefit from depreciation deductibility shared through lower lease payments.

sale-type lease or **sale and leaseback (SLB) agreement** or **sale-leaseback agreement** an agreement in which the owner of an asset sells it to another party and then leases the asset back

Leveraged lease

A **leveraged lease** is a popular financing vehicle in the United States. It is a three-way agreement among the lessee, the lessor, and one or more external lenders. As with other lease arrangements, the lessee uses the asset and makes regular lease payments, whereas the lessor purchases (or owns) the asset, delivers it to the lessee, and receives lease payments. However, the lessor puts up only a small portion (usually in the 20 to 50 percent range) of the purchase price of the asset, and lenders supply the remaining financing, in return for interest payments from the lessor. The lenders are protected against default because they have a first lien on the leased asset and because the lease payments go directly to the lenders in the event of a loan default by the lessor.

leveraged lease three-way agreement among the lessee, lessor, and a third-party lender in which the lessor buys the asset with only a small down payment, and the lender supplies the remaining financing

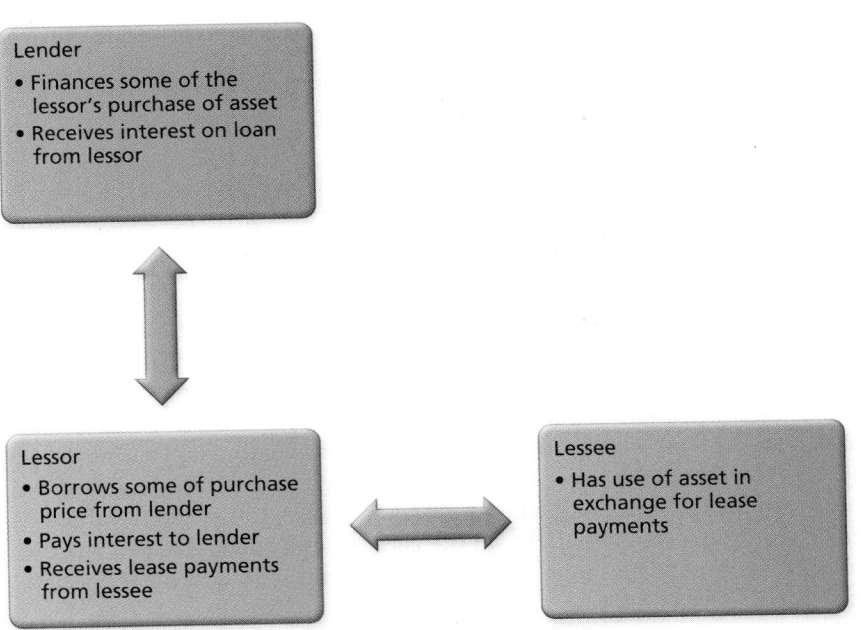

---

[8] A company without taxable income may be able to use tax loss carryovers to derive some benefit from the depreciation deduction, but in some cases there are no benefits from these carryovers for many years, if at all.

The attractiveness of leveraged leases is that the lessor puts up only a portion of the asset purchase price but receives all the tax benefits of ownership and has lease payments available to service the loan payments. In the United States, the lessee can benefit in the form of lower lease payments whenever the lessor's costs are reduced. This is not the case in all countries.[9]

FINANCE in the News | HSBC Sells Digs to Save Cash

Many companies are generating cash by selling their headquarters or other buildings and leasing them back. This example of HSBC's sale of their headquarters is typical of these transactions.

HSBC is putting more money aside for a rainy day. On Monday the British bank said it was selling its headquarters building in New York to Israeli investment holding company IDB Group for $330 million in cash as it looks to shield itself in the event of a second slump in the global economy.

Under the agreement with IDB, HSBC will lease back the offices in New York for 12 months and floors 0–11 for a decade, the bank said. The British company also said

the sale will the first of three similar deals as it looks to sell and then leaseback its offices in Hong Kong and London's Canary Wharf.

Analysts said HSBC's move is a reflection of its conservative approach to banking. "HSBC thinks all banks are going to require more capital so they are looking to do so now through the sales of their headquarters around the world and their listing in Shanghai," said Simon Curtice Maughan, an analyst with MF Global in London. "The sales don't move the dial up that much, but every little [bit] helps."

Source: Extracted from: Javier Espinoza, "HSBC Sells Digs to Save Cash," Forbes.com, October 5, 2009.

Concept Review Questions

1. What is the difference between an operating and a capital lease from the perspective of the lessee?

2. In the case of a direct financing lease, what method is used to reduce the receivable each period?

3. What is a sale and leaseback agreement?

20.2 ACCOUNTING ISSUES

off-balance-sheet financing financing arrangement that does not appear in a company's balance sheet, but only in the notes to the financial statements

Although analysts tend to use the broad definitions of operating and financial leases discussed earlier, accountants use a more stringent definition of financial leases. This is important because financial leases are included on the balance sheet of the lessee, whereas for operating leases the lease does not appear on the balance sheet of the lessee but does appear on the balance sheet of the lessor. Operating leases are an example of **off-balance-sheet financing** for the lessee and are included only in the notes to the financial statements. For a financial lease, the present value of all lease payments is entered along with debt on the right side of the lessee's balance sheet. The same amount is entered as the value of the asset that is leased on the left side of the balance sheet.

[9] Leveraged leases are not popular in Canada because Canadian Revenue Authority restricts the use of deductions to the party at risk, and the deductions cannot be carried over into other income.

In addition to the balance sheet differences noted earlier, the income statement is affected by the classification of a lease as operating or financial. For operating leases, the resulting expense for the lessee is the full amount of the lease payments made to the lessor, which is classified as rental expense for the lessee and as rental income for the lessor. Because the lessor retains the asset on its balance sheet, it charges depreciation expense against the asset. For financial leases, the lease payments is broken down into interest expense and principal repayment, the latter of which is not an expense but rather is reflected in the declining value of the liability reported on the balance sheet. As a result, for financial leases, the lessee's associated expenses will be in two forms: interest associated with the financing arrangement and depreciation expense associated with the asset. The lessor reports income in the form of a gain (or loss) on the asset at the time the lease arrangement (i.e., the sale) is initiated, and then it reports periodic interest income based on the interest portion of the lease payments it receives.

We summarize these accounting differences in Table 20-5. As you can see in this table, there are some potential benefits for companies that classify leases as operating, rather than financial, which we will elaborate on in the next section.

Financial Statement Effects of Lease Classification

Given our preceding discussion, it is not surprising that whether or not a lease is classified as operating or financial can have a significant impact on a company's financial statements. As a result, many of the financial ratios that analysts use to examine company performance can be affected, as will the company's cash flow statements.

We can see the difference by working through an example. Assume a company leases an asset with a present fair market value of $317,000. The lease arrangement requires four annual payments of $100,000. The appropriate interest rate is 10 percent. Assume that:

- the asset has a zero salvage value at the end of its useful life;
- its useful life is 4 years;
- the asset is depreciated using straight-line depreciation;[10] and
- the appropriate discount rate is 10 percent.

We can contrast the income statement and cash flow statement effects of classifying the lease as financial versus operating. Assume that the company's expected income and

TABLE 20-5 Operating Versus Financial Leases

Accounting	Operating Lease		Financial Lease	
	Lessee	Lessor	Lessee	Lessor
Asset reported on the balance sheet	No	Yes	Yes	No
Lease payments reported on the income statement	Yes, as rental payments	Yes, as rental income	Yes, as interest expense and principal repayment	Yes, interest as income
Depreciation expense (associated with leased asset)	No	Yes	Yes, as amortization	No

[10] We have simplified this example to allow focus on the accounting differences. However, a more realistic example would use straight-line for financial reporting purposes and MACRS for tax purposes. Our simplification in this example is to use straight-line for both purposes.

cash flow statements look like the following for the next 4 years, ignoring the effect of this lease arrangement:

Selected Financial Statement Information—Without Leasing

	Year 1	Year 2	Year 3	Year 4
Revenue	$10,000,000	$10,000,000	$10,000,000	$10,000,000
Net income (excluding lease)	$500,000	$500,000	$500,000	$500,000
Cash flow from operations	$600,000	$600,000	$600,000	$600,000
Cash flow from financing	$100,000	$100,000	$100,000	$100,000
Cash flow from investing	−$300,000	−$300,000	−$300,000	−$300,000
Net cash flows	$400,000	$400,000	$400,000	$400,000

If this lease is an operating lease the effects are:

Annual charge to the income statement = $100,000
Annual effect on cash flow from operations = $100,000
Annual effect on total cash flow = $100,000

The net effect on cash flows is to reduce the net income, and hence cash flow from operations, by $100,000:

Selected Financial Statement Information with an Operating Lease

	Year 1	Year 2	Year 3	Year 4
Net income	$400,000	$400,000	$400,000	$400,000
Cash flow from operations	$500,000	$500,000	$500,000	$500,000
Cash flow from financing	$100,000	$100,000	$100,000	$100,000
Cash flow from investing	−$300,000	−$300,000	−$300,000	−$300,000
Net cash flows	$300,000	$300,000	$300,000	$300,000

The effect of an operating lease is quite simple, especially when we compare these with the effects on the financial statements if this lease is a financial lease.

In the case of a financial lease, we must first calculate the interest expense for each period based on amortizing the asset:

Amortization of a Financial Lease

	Year 1	Year 2	Year 3	Year 4
Beginning of the year principal	$316,987	$248,700	$173,570	$90,927
Payment	$100,000	$100,000	$100,000	$100,000
Interest	$31,699	$24,870	$17,357	$9,093
Principal repayment	$68,301	$75,130	$82,643	$90,907
End of year principal	$248,700	$173,570	$90,927	$0

The depreciation expense, using straight-line, is $316,987 \div 4 = \$79,247$. Once we know the interest expense and the depreciation, we can calculate the effect on the income statement:

Expenses for the Financial Lease to Be Applied Against Net Income

	Year 1	Year 2	Year 3	Year 4
Interest	$31,699	$24,870	$17,357	$9,093
Depreciation	$79,247	$79,247	$79,247	$79,247
Total charges against net income	$110,945	$104,117	$96,604	$88,339

The cash flows for the financial lease are the interest expense and the principal repayment.

Net Effect of the Financial Lease on Total Cash Flows

	Year 1	Year 2	Year 3	Year 4
Interest expense	–$31,699	–$24,870	–$17,357	–$9,093
Principal repayment	–68,301	–75,130	–82,643	–90,907
Net effect on total cash flow	–$100,000	–$100,000	–$100,000	–$100,000

The financial lease will reduce the cash flows of the company by $100,000, as compared to before any lease:

Effect of the Financial Lease on Net Cash Flows

	Year 1	Year 2	Year 3	Year 4
Net income before leasing	$500,000	$500,000	$500,000	$500,000
Less: Charges to income with the financial lease	110,946	104,117	96,604	88,340
Net income with financial lease	$389,054	$395,883	$403,396	$411,660
Add: Lease payment	100,000	100,000	100,000	100,000
Add: Depreciation that was charged to income	79,247	79,247	79,247	79,247
Cash flow from operations with a financial lease	$568,301	$575,130	$582,643	$590,907
Cash flow from financing without leasing	$100,000	$100,000	$100,000	$100,000
Less: Principal repayment	68,301	75,130	82,643	90,907
Cash flow from financing with a financial lease	$31,699	$24,870	$17,357	$9,073
Cash flow from investing	–$300,000	–$300,000	–$300,000	–$300,000
Net cash flows	$300,000	$300,000	$300,000	$300,000

Comparing the effects of accounting for operating and financial leases, we see that there are differences in the income statement, the balance sheet, the statement of cash flows, and the statement of shareholders' equity. Net income will generally be higher for operating leases in the early years, and it will generally be lower in the later years. This is because the interest expense charged for financial leases declines as the liability (lease obligation) is amortized by the lease payments. This means that the expense associated with a financing lease will decrease through time because the depreciation expense usually is constant, whereas the lease expense for an operating lease remains constant through the years (i.e., it equals the amount of the lease payments).

The cash flow for operations will be lower when a lease is classified as operating because the full lease payment will be subtracted from cash flow from operations, unlike for financial leases, where only the interest portion of these payments is subtracted. On the other hand, its cash flow for/from financing will be higher because unlike financing leases, operating leases have no principal repayment component. Even more important to note is that the overall effect on total cash flow will be the same as for financial leases. It is merely the classification of the cash flows that is affected.

When leases are classified as financial leases versus operating leases, the company will report lower current ratios, higher debt and leverage ratios, lower asset turnover, and lower profitability ratios (at least in the early years). Because the classification of a lease has no impact on a company's total cash flows, its price should be unaffected; therefore, the P/E ratios should be higher to reflect the lower earnings per share (EPS). However, note that if the P/E ratio remained at 25, the share price would be lower, reflecting the lower EPS. This is inappropriate and should not happen in efficient markets.

The bottom line is that there will be a significant impact on a company's financial ratios depending on the classification of a lease as operating or financial. Thus we can see that managers have an incentive to have leases classified as operating rather than financial, from a financial ratio point of view. Therefore, we might suspect that a manager may try to make sure that her leases are categorized as operating leases in an attempt to "fool" the readers of her company's financial statements. However, whereas operating leases are not included on the balance sheet, companies are required to disclose information in the notes to the financial statements. Hence, the information is publicly available, and if markets are efficient, most investors and analysts would see through this type of manipulation.

Regarding the balance sheet effects, the company will appear larger and will have more debt if a lease is classified as financial, as compared to an operating lease. How does the company's balance sheet with a lease compare if the lease is classified as an operating lease or a financial lease? The starting point is the balance sheet without the lease:

Balance Sheet Without the Lease

Current assets	$2,000,000	Current liabilities	$1,000,000
Long-term assets	8,000,000	Long-term debt	6,000,000
		Equity	3,000,000
Total assets	$10,000,000	Total liabilities and equity	$10,000,000

With the operating lease, the balance sheet remains unchanged—it is exactly the same as the one just given. The only difference is that the company would have to disclose the lease in the footnotes to the financial statements.

With the financial lease, there are a number of differences. First, the new balance sheet would reflect the $317,000 on both sides of the balance sheet. The $317,000 on the liability side would be broken down into the current portion of the obligation (i.e., the first year's required principal repayment component of the lease payment), and the remaining part of the lease, which would be classified as long-term debt.

The addition to current liabilities is $68,301, the principal repayment. The addition to long-term debt is the difference between the $316,987 and the amount we designate as the short-term portion, $68,301, or $248,685. Therefore, the balance sheet at the initiation of the lease indicates more assets and higher liabilities than without the lease:

Balance Sheet at the Initiation of the Financial Lease

Current assets	$2,000,000	Current liabilities	$1,068,301
Long-term assets	$8,316,987	Long-term debt	$6,248,686
		Equity	$3,000,000
Total assets	$10,316,987	Total liabilities and equity	$10,316,987

EXAMPLE 20.1
Financial Ratio Effects

PROBLEM

For the example that we use for the operating and financial lease effects on the income statement, consider the financial statement of the company when it first enters into the lease agreement. Calculate and compare the financial ratios for accounting of the asset as an operating and as a financial lease:

a. Current ratio
b. Debt-to-equity

Solution

Ratio	Operating Lease	Financial Lease
a. Current ratio	$2,000,000 ÷ $1,000,000 = 2.0	$2,000,000 ÷ $1,068,300 = 1.87
b. Debt-to-equity	$7,000,000 ÷ $3,000,000 = 2.33	$7,316,987 ÷ $3,000,000 = 2.44

Off-Balance Sheet and Enron | LESSONS LEARNED

Although analysts and investors should recognize the liabilities associated with operating leases and other off-balance sheet items, in practice they often neglect or underestimate the associated risks. Such was the case for Enron, whose demise was caused to a large extent by the massive amount of off-balance sheet liabilities the company accrued through Special Purpose Entities (SPEs).[11] Although this information was publicly available, it was ignored to a large extent by analysts and investors in aggregate. Indeed many analysts had "buy" recommendations on Enron stock in the weeks preceding its collapse.[12]

The lesson to be learned is that proper analysis requires looking beyond the surface numbers, or significant risks can be overlooked or underestimated.

---

1. What are the implications for cash flow from operations of an operating versus a capital lease?

2. Which type of lease, operating or capital, results in a greater degree of financial leverage based on typical financial leverage ratios?

Concept Review Questions

---

[11] Ronald Fink, "Beyond Enron," *CFO*, February 1, 2002.

[12] Report of the Staff to the Senate Committee on Governmental Affairs, "Financial Oversight of Enron: The SEC and Private-Sector Watchdogs," October 8, 2002.

20.3 EVALUATING THE LEASE DECISION

Leasing provides an alternative to buying an asset. If a company needs an asset and has the opportunity to lease it, it must compare the cash flows from leasing with the cash flows from buying to determine which is better. The four main differences in the cash flows for a company that leases an asset instead of buying it are:

1. It does not have to pay for the asset up front.
2. It does not get to sell the asset when it is finished with it, if it is an operating lease, or if title is not transferred through a financial lease.[13, 14]
3. It makes regular lease payments. If the lease is an operating lease, then the full amount of the lease payments is tax deductible; if it is classified as a financial lease, then only the interest portion of the payments is deductible.
4. It does not get to depreciate the asset for tax purposes if it is an operating lease. If it is a financial lease, it does get to charge depreciation.

An Example

Suppose a company is considering obtaining a limousine for its executives. The limousine would cost $1 million to buy (it is very luxurious and also bulletproof). The limousine would be depreciated at a rate of $100,000 per year for tax purposes. Assume the limousine could be sold in 5 years for $500,000. The company could also sign a 5-year operating lease for a limousine with lease payments of $140,000 per year, with each payment due at the beginning of the year.[15] The company's effective tax rate is 40 percent. Should the company lease or buy the limo, assuming the company's before-tax cost of borrowing is 7 percent?

We need to consider the following cash flows:

1. The company saves $1 million in today's dollars by not buying the asset.
2. If the company buys the limousine, it will get $100,000 per year in depreciation. Each year this will result in a tax savings of (0.40 × $100,000) = $40,000, which can be assumed as an inflow at the end of the year (i.e., when the company pays its taxes). If the company leases, it forgoes this tax benefit.
3. The company must make regular tax-deductible lease payments at the beginning of each of 4 years. Using an effective tax rate of 40 percent, these payments translate into after-tax payments of $140,000 (1 − 0.40) = $84,000 per year.

We provide the cash flows associated with leasing rather than buying (in thousands of dollars) in Table 20-6.

Now that we have estimated the incremental cash flows that result from leasing instead of buying, the question is how to evaluate these cash flows. It is usually appropriate to consider leasing as a form of debt financing because it represents a legal obligation to make periodic payments to another party (i.e., the lessor). Viewing the preceding lease arrangement in this manner, we can say it is like a $1 million loan, and we can estimate the interest rate that the company is paying on this "loanlike arrangement," which we can then

---

[13] Technically it is not correct to adjust for tax savings to the "beginning" of year lease payments because the tax savings will result at year end. We do this for simplicity and demonstrate later that it does not make a substantial difference in our ending answer.

[14] Note that in many cases the salvage value would be discounted at a higher rate, reflecting the risk attached to the future value. For simplicity we abstract from this, but it is often an important component of the analysis.

[15] We realize that most lease payments are made monthly, and not annually; however, we assume annual payments for simplicity.

Table 20-6 **Incremental Cash Flows Associated with Leasing Versus Buying**

(amount in thousands)	Year					
	0	1	2	3	4	5
Initial cost	$1,000					
After-tax lease payment	−84	−$84	−$84	−$84	−$84	
Forgone tax shield	0	−40	−40	−40	−40	−$40
Forgone salvage value						−500
Incremental cash flows	$916	−$124	−$124	−$124	−$124	−$540

compare with the company's after-tax borrowing cost. To solve for this rate, we simply treat it like the following internal rate of return problem:

$$\$0 = \$916 - \frac{\$124}{1 + IRR} - \frac{\$124}{(1 + IRR)^2} - \frac{\$124}{(1 + IRR)^3} - \frac{\$124}{(1 + IRR)^4} - \frac{\$540}{(1 + IRR)^5}$$

CALCULATOR APPLICATION

HP 10B	BA II+	TI 83/84
916 +/− CF$_J$	CF	{124, 124, 124, 124, 540}
124 CF$_J$	916 +/− ENTER	STO L1
4 N$_j$	↑ *F01* 4 ENTER	APPS Finance 8:IRR
540 CF$_J$	↑ *C01* 124 ENTER	irr(−916, L1) ENTER
IRR	↑ ↑ *F02* 1 ENTER	
	↑ *C01* 540 ENTER	
	IRR CPT	

SPREADSHEET APPLICATION

Microsoft Excel

	A
1	−916
2	124
3	124
4	124
5	124
6	540
7	= IRR(A1:A6)

The IRR for this set of cash flows is 3.32 percent. Thus, leasing instead of buying involves receiving financing at an effective rate of 3.32 percent. This rate should be compared with the after-tax rate at which the company can normally borrow. For this example, the before-tax cost of borrowing is 7 percent, so:[16]

$$\text{After-tax cost of borrowing} = 7\% \times (1 - 0.40) = 4.20\%$$

Therefore, because 3.32% < 4.20%, the company should lease the limousine because leasing provides cheaper financing than normal borrowing.

An easier way to evaluate the lease is to simply use the after-tax borrowing rate as a discount rate and calculate the NPV (net present value) of leasing versus buying. For this example, we can estimate the NPV of leasing versus buying as follows (numbers in thousands):

$$NPV_{\text{Leasing}} = \$916 - \frac{\$124}{1.042} - \frac{\$124}{(1.042)^2} - \frac{\$124}{(1.042)^3} - \frac{\$124}{(1.042)^4} - \frac{\$540}{(1.042)^5} = -\$28.41$$

CALCULATOR APPLICATION

HP 10B		BA II+	TI 83/84
916 +/− CF$_J$		CF	{124, 124, 124, 124, 540}
124	CF$_J$	916 +/− ENTER	STO L1
4	N$_j$	↑ *F01* 4 ENTER	APPS Finance 7:NPV
540	CF$_J$	↑ *C01* 124 ENTER	npv(4.2, −916, L1) ENTER
4.2	I/YR	↑ ↑ *F02* 1 ENTER	
IRR		↑ *C01* 540 ENTER NPV	
		I = 4.2	
		CPT	

SPREADSHEET APPLICATION

Microsoft Excel

	A
1	−916
2	124
3	124
4	124
5	124
6	540
7	= NPV(.042,A2:A6) + A1

[16] This approach to estimating the after-tax cost of borrowing is correct if the borrowing is in the form of traditional bonds because they pay interest only, and the interest payments are completely tax deductible. It would not be strictly correct if the before-tax borrowing cost applied to a loan with blended payments of principal and interest because only the interest portion of these payments is tax deductible. However, for practical purposes, this estimate is close enough.

We could also estimate the NPV of leasing by finding the present value of the various kinds of cash flows, which can be expressed as follows:

Start with	CF_0, the purchase price savings	
Less	present value of forgone depreciation tax savings	
Less	present value of forgone salvage value	
Less	present value of after-tax lease payments	
Equals	$NPV_{Leasing}$	

The "parts" of this analysis are as follows:

- The present value of the forgone depreciation tax savings is the present value of a five-period ordinary annuity of $40,000 per year, discounted at 4.2 percent.
- The present value of salvage value is the present value of a lump sum; the $500,000 lump sum is discounted five periods at 4.2 percent.
- The present value of the after-tax lease payments is the present value of an annuity due of $84,000 for five periods, discounted at 4.2 percent.

Start with	CF_0, the purchase price savings	$1,000,000
Less	present value of forgone depreciation tax savings	177,077
Less	present value of forgone salvage value	407,035
Less	present value of after-tax lease payments	387,479
Equals	$NPV_{Leasing}$	$28,409

So, the NPV = $28,410, which is positive, so it is better to lease the limousine than buy it. Note that the positive NPV of leasing tells you that leasing is better than buying, but not whether you should acquire the asset in the first place. This question should be answered based on the total NPV of the project. To incorporate lease financing into an overall NPV problem, simply calculate the NPV of the project assuming that you buy the asset, then add on the NPV of leasing. This gives the NPV of the project including the advantage of financing the asset through leasing.

As mentioned previously, leases typically involve monthly, rather than annual, payments, with each payment due at the beginning of the month. In addition, the tax savings associated with these payments will be realized at year end when the company pays its taxes. We removed these complications in the preceding example to make things simpler. In most cases, it is reasonable to make the simplifying assumption of annual payments because the end result will be quite close. However, in situations where precision is critical, it will be worthwhile to use the more accurate approach.

We made one other simplification in our lease analysis: We assumed depreciation for tax purposes was a constant amount per year. In practice, we have learned that depreciation that may be charged for tax purposes is calculated using the declining balance method.

Consider a company that is evaluating whether to purchase or lease a machine that costs $100,000, and depreciation is a MACRS for a 3-year asset. The required lease payments are $25,000 per year for 4 years (with beginning of year payments as usual). The lessor has agreed to provide maintenance as part of the lease contract, and the company has estimated $10,000 per year in maintenance expense would be incurred if it decided to purchase the machine. It estimates the asset could be sold for $46,080 after

EXAMPLE 20.2

Leasing Versus Buying with Monthly Payments

PROBLEM

Suppose a company is considering obtaining a limousine for its executives. The limousine would cost $1 million to buy. The limousine would be depreciated at a rate of $100,000 per year for tax purposes. Assume the limousine could be sold in 5 years for $500,000. The company could also sign a 5-year operating lease for a limousine with lease payments of $11,667 per month, with each payment due at the beginning of the month. The company's effective tax rate is 40 percent. Should the company lease or buy the limo, assuming the company's before-tax cost of borrowing is 7 percent and that the tax benefits are received at the end of each year?

Solution

We estimate the NPV of leasing as we did in the example with annual lease payments except that we need to break out the present value of the before-tax lease payments and the present value of the tax savings from the present value of after-tax lease payments. We need to break these items out separately now because the company makes the lease payments monthly, yet the tax savings are annual. Instead of the $387,479 for the present value of the after-tax lease payments, we have:

- The present value of the before-tax lease payments, which is the present value of the monthly lease payment of $140,000 ÷ 12 = $11,667, discounted over the 60 months as an annuity due, using the monthly discount rate of $(1 + 0.042)^{1/12} - 1 = 0.34343379\%$. The present value is $633,798.

- The present value of the tax savings from the lease payments, which is the present value of an ordinary annuity of five payments of $56,000. This present value is $247,907.

The net effect of these two present values is $385,891, which is slightly different (due to the monthly payments instead of annual) from the $387,479 with annual lease payments.

Summarizing,

Start with	CF_0, the purchase price savings	$1,000,000
Less	present value of forgone depreciation tax savings	177,077
Less	present value of forgone salvage value	407,035
Less	present value of before-tax lease payments	633,798
Plus	present value of tax savings from lease payments	247,907
Equals	NPV$_{Leasing}$	$29,997

4 years. The company's before-tax borrowing rate is 10 percent, and its effective tax rate is 40 percent. Should it purchase or lease the machine, assuming the acquisition of the machine has a positive NPV and that the lease would qualify as an operating lease?

First, we estimate the present value of the different cash flows:

- The present value of maintenance costs are the present value of a four-payment ordinary annuity of $6,000, with a discount rate of 6 percent [PMT = $6,000; N = 4; i = 6%]. The present value of this cash flow series is $20,791.

- The present value of the salvage value of $46,080 is the present value of a lump-sum amount, discounted four periods at 6 percent [FV = $46,080; N = 4; i = 6%]. The present value of this lump sum is $36,500.

- The present value of the foregone depreciation tax shields requires first calculating the depreciation each year, then multiplying each depreciation expense by the tax rate to arrive at the depreciation tax shield. Once you have the tax shield for each year, you discount each of these to the present at 6 percent and then sum to arrive at $35,723:

Year	MACRS Rate	Depreciation	Depreciation Tax Shield	Present Value of Depreciation Tax Shield
1	33.33%	$33,330	$13,332.00	$12,577
2	44.45%	$44,450	$17,780.00	15,824
3	14.81%	$14,810	$5,924.00	4,974
4	7.41%	$7,410	$2,964.00	2,348
				$35,723

- The last piece of the puzzle is the present value of the after-tax lease payments, which is the present value of an annuity due consisting of four payments of $25,000(1 − 0.4) = $15,000 each, discounted 6 percent [PMT = $15,000; i = 6%; N = 4; Annuity due]. The present value of the after-tax lease payments is $55,095.

Summarizing, we have a net present value to leasing of −$6,527:

Start with	CF$_0$, the purchase price savings	$100,000
Plus	present value of maintenance costs savings	20,791
Less	present value of forgone salvage value	36,500
Less	present value of forgone depreciation tax savings	35,723
Less	present value of after-tax lease payments	55,095
Equals	NPV$_{Leasing}$	−$6,527

The net present value to leasing is negative. Therefore, it is better to buy than to lease.

How would the analysis change if the lease were a financial lease? The analysis would require three adjustments to what we have done so far:

- The lessee is able to claim the depreciation tax savings, so this is no longer a forgone cash flow.
- The lessee may also take ownership of the asset at the end of the lease term and, therefore, will be able to sell it for the estimated salvage value if it so chooses, so this cash flow is no longer forgone.
- The entire amount of the lease payment is not tax deductible, as is the case for operating leases. Rather, just the interest portion may be expensed. Note that this is exactly the same as it would be for a loan (i.e., only the interest portion of the loan payment is tax deductible). Therefore, the only real difference between a standard financial lease and a loan is that the lease payments are made at the beginning of the period, whereas the loan payments are made at the end of the period.[17]

As you can see, the lease versus buy decision requires looking at incremental cash flows and is usually performed from the perspective of leasing, using the buy decision as the base case. The lease versus buy decision can become quite complex when more realistic features of the lease are added, but the fundamental analysis does not change: What is the present value of the incremental cash flow?

Motives for Leasing

In the previous section, we showed how leases could, under some circumstances, provide "cheaper" financing than typical loan arrangements. The attraction of leases in such cases is obvious; however, leases provide other benefits to lessees. Next, we provide a description

---

[17] In reality, loans require some form of down payment, whereas leases may provide 100 percent financing.

of some of the most common reasons why companies enter into lease arrangements; some are better reasons than others.

1. *Cheaper financing*. This may occur for operating leases because the entire lease payment is tax deductible. In addition, the lessee may end up receiving attractive leasing rates if the lessor is better able to take advantage of the depreciation tax shields associated with ownership of the underlying asset, and market conditions induce him or her to pass these benefits on to the lessee.

2. *Reduce the risks of asset ownership*. Leasing allows companies to acquire needed equipment without assuming the risk of having to resell the asset or of having it become obsolete. This is particularly important for assets whose technological capabilities are constantly changing, which is one reason many companies lease computers rather than purchase them. Essentially this means that the equipment manufacturer or other lessor, rather than the user, bears the risk of the salvage value of the asset at the end of the lease.

3. *Implicit, fixed interest rates*. Leasing usually offers companies fixed rate financing over the life of the lease, whereas small companies in particular are often forced to use variable rate, prime-based lending when borrowing from banks.

4. *Maintenance*. Under a full-service lease arrangement, the lessor will provide maintenance. Often, the lessor will be a specialist in this type of equipment and is therefore better able to provide maintenance than the lessee.

5. *Convenience*. It is often more convenient to lease an asset than to purchase it, especially if it is only needed for a relatively short period and/or if it is a very specialized or illiquid asset that may be hard to sell in the future.

6. *Flexibility*. Leases often offer more flexibility. For example, they often include the option to cancel the lease, which may be important where obsolescence is a possibility.

7. *Circumvent capital budget restrictions*. Because leasing requires a very limited initial capital outlay (just the first lease payment plus any arrangement fees), managers may be able to circumvent capital budget constraints by leasing assets, rather than buying them. This is a dubious reason for leasing, because it allows division managers to circumvent broader-based company policies.

8. *Financial statement effects*. The use of operating leases versus debt or financial leases enhances the "appearance" of the company's financial statements because they provide off-balance-sheet financing. The use of operating leases can also lead companies to report higher net income, lower debt ratios, and higher liquidity ratios. This should not affect a company's value in efficient markets because it does not affect the level of its cash flows or the nature of the financial risks it faces. It merely changes the way these items are reported in the financial statements. Therefore, this is not a good reason for leasing.

Concept Review Questions

1. Explain how to evaluate a lease versus buy decision when the lease in question is an operating lease. How does the analysis change when the lease is a financial lease?

2. Why do you think that the major market for leasing is often smaller companies, rather than large corporations?

SUMMARY

- In a lease arrangement, the lessor retains ownership rights to an asset, but makes the asset available for use by the lessee, who in turn agrees to make periodic lease payments to the lessor.

- We distinguish between operating and financial leases because they are treated differently for tax and financial reporting purposes. As a result of these differences, with all else being equal, classifying a lease as operating rather than financial will result in a company reporting higher net income, lower debt ratios, and higher liquidity ratios.

- Companies can evaluate a potential lease decision using the discounted cash flow analysis framework.

- There are a number of motives that companies might have for entering into leasing arrangements, including the cost of financing, flexibility, and financial reporting.

- Lease contracts offer companies flexibility, and a close relationship often exists between manufacturers and equipment leasing companies.

QUESTIONS AND PROBLEMS

Multiple Choice

1. Which of the following statements about an operating lease is *false*?
   A. It's usually a full-service lease.
   B. It has a shorter term than a capital lease.
   C. The lessee cannot cancel the lease before the operating lease ends.
   D. Payments for one operating lease are usually not enough to fully cover the asset cost.

2. Capital leases are:
   A. short-term leases.
   B. cancellable before expiration without penalties.
   C. leases for which payments will cover the initial asset costs.
   D. leases for which the lessors are responsible for maintenance of the assets.

3. Which of the following statements about leveraged leases is *false*?
   A. The lender has the first lien on the leased asset.
   B. The lender receives interest payments from the lessee.
   C. There is an external lender, lessor, and lessee in the lease.
   D. The lessee could bargain for lower lease payments if the market is competitive.

4. Which of the following leases is classified as a financial lease?
   A. The lease term is 5 years, and the economic life of the asset is 6 years.
   B. The lease does not transfer the ownership of the asset to the lessee when the lease expires.
   C. The lessee could purchase the asset at $10,000 while the market value of the lease is $9,000 when the lease expires.
   D. In the lease inception, the fair market value of the assets is $60,000, and the present value of the lease payments is $50,000.

5. Which of the following organizations is *most likely* to enter into a sale and lease-back agreement?
   A. Factory
   B. University
   C. Investment company
   D. Real estate company

6. What is the asset/liability recognized on the lessee's balance sheet at the beginning of the lease, given the following operating lease information? Minimum annual lease payment at the beginning of each year = $12,000; lease term = 7 years; appropriate discount rate = 10 percent; salvage value = 0.
   A. $0   B. $58,000   C. $58,421   D. $61,000

7. Consider a financial lease of an asset that has a salvage value of $0, an annual minimum lease payment at the beginning of the year of $5,000, and a lease term of 5 years. If the appropriate discount rate is 8 percent, the present value of the lessee's depreciation expense is *closest* to:

   A. $19,964.   B. $20,099.   C. $21,561.   D. $23,506.

8. Which of the following is *higher* under operating leases?
   A. Net income and cash flow from operations
   B. Depreciation and net income
   C. Total cash flow and cash flow from operations
   D. Cash flow from financing and net income in the early years

9. Under financial leases, the following ratio is *higher*, compared with the operating lease:
   A. ROE
   B. NI margin
   C. Current ratio
   D. Leverage ratio

10. Which of the following financial figures is *unchanged*, regardless of the type of lease?
    A. P/E ratio
    B. Leverage ratio
    C. Asset turnover
    D. Total cash flow

Practice Questions and Problems

20.1 Leasing Arrangements

11. Describe the parties to a lease arrangement, being sure to identify which party owns the asset and which party uses the asset.

12. Diagram a sale-leaseback arrangement, labeling the direction of the initial and periodic cash flows associated with the arrangement.

13. Briefly describe three motivations for leasing an asset instead of buying it.

14. What is the role of taxes in the lease decision?

15. What is the role of accounting in the lease decision?

20.2 Accounting Issues

16. Why would a company's financial management be concerned about the accounting for leases?

17. Why would an analyst, viewing the company from the outside, be concerned about the accounting for leases?

18. Compare and contrast the effect of classifying a lease as an operating versus a financial lease for accounting purposes on the financial ratios of a company.

19. The convergence of International Financial Reporting Standards and U.S. GAAP may require U.S. companies to apply the principles currently applied to capital leases to what are now considered operating leases. If markets are efficient, why would companies not want there to be a change in the accounting for operating leases from the current method?

20.3 Evaluating the Lease Decision

20. Why would a nontaxable entity view the lease versus buy decision differently than a taxable entity?

21. The White River Manufacturing Company has just signed several leases, and it has hired the Macon Consulting Company to do the initial classification of the leases as operating and financial for accounting purposes. White River could have bought each asset for $1 million instead of leasing. The appropriate discount rate is 10 percent per year; all lease payments are annual and paid at the end of the year. For each of the following leases, classify them as operating or financial, and explain your reasoning:

Lease	Expected Economic Life of the Asset	Annual Lease Payments	Length of Lease	Purchase Price at End of Lease	Expected Market Value of Asset at End of Lease
A	10 years	$150,000	8 years	$10,000	$10,000
B	5 years	$100,000	2 years	$900,000	$700,000
C	10 years	$20,000	5 years	$500,000	$300,000
D	9 years	$185,000	8 years	$1,000	$50,000
E	25 years	$120,000	22 years	$8,000	$25,000
F	10 years	$200,000	5 years	$800,000	$500

22. Suppose you are going to enter into a 6-year, $22,000 financial lease that requires monthly payments based on an 8 percent lease rate. Alternatively, you could borrow $22,000 via a 6-year loan that requires monthly payments based on a 7 percent lending rate. Which option should you choose? Explain.

23. Minnie Appolis, the owner of a small moving company, has decided that economic conditions are perfect for her to expand her business. An expansion of her business will require her to buy five new moving trucks at a total cost of $200,000. Her company has $5,000 in cash and has a $30,000 line of credit at the bank. Being a small company, it does not have the option of issuing public debt, and Ms. Appolis is not comfortable with mortgaging her family home to buy the trucks. Describe two ways Ms. Appolis can acquire the trucks. Discuss the advantages and disadvantages of each.

24. Igor, an analyst with the Ace Consulting Company has provided his valuation of the Kitchen Gadget Company (KGC). He has identified two other companies (Kitchen Widgets and Kitchen Thingies) in exactly the same line of business as KGC and carried out his valuation using multiples. All three companies use 100 percent equity. Igor presents the following analysis:

	Kitchen Widgets	Kitchen Thingies	Average P/E
P/E ratio	15	20	$17.50

As the Kitchen Gadget Company has an EPS of $1, Igor has valued KGC at $17.50 per share. Igor's supervisor looks at Igor's work, tells him to do it again, and mumbles something about "notes." Igor is utterly confused and has come to you for help. You have quickly reviewed the analyst's work and noted that KGC has a policy of buying all its assets; in contrast Kitchen Widgets uses operating leases, and Kitchen Thingies uses financial or capital leases.

A. Explain to the analyst what the "notes" are and where to find them.

B. Explain how he should have done the valuation.

C. Is this likely to affect his valuation of KGC?

25. Madison Utility Corp. needs to increase its electricity production capacity. It is interested in a slightly used reactor located in Chicago. It has been offered two alternatives: buy the reactor for $10 billion (will have to hold it for 20 years) or lease it for 10 years at $1.3 billion per year. At the end of 10 years, Madison would have the option to either buy the reactor for $2 billion or renew the lease at annual payments of $1.8 billion. Madison has a cost of capital of 7 percent. Assume the economic life of the reactor is 20 years, the MACRS life of the asset is 20 years, and the marginal tax rate is 40 percent. At the end of 20 years, the reactor will have a salvage value of zero. Assume all lease payments are made at the beginning of the lease, all leases are

operating leases, and maintenance costs of $10 million per year will be covered by the lessor. The MACRS rates are as follows:

Year	MACRS Rate	Year	MACRS Rate
1	3.75%	12	4.46%
2	7.22%	13	4.46%
3	6.68%	14	4.46%
4	6.18%	15	4.46%
5	5.71%	16	4.46%
6	5.29%	17	4.46%
7	4.89%	18	4.46%
8	4.52%	19	4.46%
9	4.46%	20	4.46%
10	4.46%	21	2.23%

A. Diagram this problem for Madison, indicating the cash flows associated with each possible choice. What choices does it have to make, and when?

B. Ignoring the real options value, what is your recommended course of action to Madison's CEO?

 26. The Rental Company's lease term for forklifts is 4 years, whereas the economic life of the forklift is 5 years. The annual lease payment is $10,000 at the beginning of each year, and the appropriate discount rate is 8 percent. There is no salvage value at the lease end. The lessee uses the straight-line depreciation method.

A. Estimate and graph the *change* in net income, cash flow from operations (CFO), and cash flow from financing (CFF) at the end of the first year if The Rental Company decides to enter into a lease agreement.

B. Estimate and graph the *change* in net income, CFO, and CFF if the economic life of the asset is 6 years instead of 5 years.

C. What are the changes in current assets, long-term assets, current liabilities, and long-term liabilities for The Rental Company at the end of the first year?

 27. The Murietta Company plans to either lease a piece of equipment or purchase it. The purchase price up front is $500,000, and it is depreciated at $50,000 per year for tax purposes. The equipment could be sold in 9 years for $50,000. If the company leases the equipment under an operating lease, it pays annual lease payments of $25,000 at the beginning of each of 9 years. The company's effective tax rate is 40 percent. Create a spreadsheet to detail the difference in cash flows between the two choices for each relevant year, and determine whether or not Murietta should lease the equipment, assuming the before-tax cost of borrowing is 8 percent.

 28. The Elon Group, Inc., plans to either purchase or lease a machine that costs $250,000 and is considered a 20-year asset for MACRS purposes. The required lease payments are $30,000 at the beginning of each of 4 years. The lessor has agreed to provide maintenance as part of the lease contract, and the company has estimated $20,000 per year in maintenance expense would be incurred if it decided to purchase the machine. It estimates the asset could be sold for $115,200 after 4 years. Elon's before-tax borrowing rate is 8 percent, and its effective tax rate is 40 percent. Create a spreadsheet that supports your decision of whether the Elon Group should purchase or lease the machine, assuming the acquisition of the machine has a positive NPV and that the lease would qualify as an operating lease.

Case

Case 20.1 Malcolm as Tax Czar

Malcolm Middle has just been appointed the Tax Czar and is convinced that the leasing business is just a way for companies to avoid paying taxes. He has hired the Higher Consulting Firm to evaluate the cash flow effects to both the lessee and the lessor in financial leases. Mr. Middle wants to determine if there is any loss of tax revenue to the government.

The Higher Consulting Firm is using an example to analyze the taxes associated with a lease decision. The example has the following:

1. The cost of the asset is $1.25 million. The lessor will have to buy the asset to lease it to the lessee.

2. The cost of capital for both companies is 10 percent.

3. The annual cash flows (before tax) generated by the asset is $500,000, regardless of who uses the asset.

4. To acquire the asset, the company will make annual interest payments at the end of each year and repay the principal of $1.25 million at the end of the 5th year (just like a bond).

5. Maintenance and insurance costs = $0.

6. The economic life of the asset, which is equal to the term of the lease, is 5 years.

7. Depreciation of $250,000 is claimed at the end of each year (for convenience we are assuming straight line).

8. Annual lease payments made at the end of the year are $300,000.

9. The tax rate of both lessee and lessor is 40 percent, and both companies make sufficient income to claim any tax benefits.

A. Complete the following table assuming the company buys the asset instead of leasing it.

Company Buys Asset Instead of Leasing

	Year 1	Year 2	Year 3	Year 4	Year 5	Principal Repayment
Cash flow from asset						
Interest payments						
Lease payments						
Depreciation						
Tax payment						
After-tax cash flows						

B. Complete the following table assuming the company uses a financial lease instead of buying the asset. For simplicity, assume that the entire lease payment is treated as a financing charge (like interest).

Company Uses Financial Lease Instead of Buying (Lessee)

	Year 1	Year 2	Year 3	Year 4	Year 5	Principal Repayment
Cash flow from asset						
Interest payments						
Lease payments						
Depreciation						
Tax payment						
After-tax cash flows						

C. Complete the following table for the lessor in the financial lease. For simplicity, assume that the entire lease payment is treated as a financing charge (like interest).

Lessor in Financial Lease

	Year 1	Year 2	Year 3	Year 4	Year 5	Principal Repayment
Cash flow from asset						
Interest payments						
Lease payments						
Depreciation						
Tax payment						
After-tax cash flows						

D. Are Mr. Middle's suspicions about loss of tax revenue correct?

E. How could companies gain from leasing activities? In other words, why would a lessor lease the asset to the operating company rather than use the asset itself?

CHAPTER 21

MERGERS AND ACQUISITIONS

© Daniel Acker/Bloomberg/Getty Images, Inc.

Mashup: Spiderman meets Mickey Mouse On August 31, 2009, the Walt Disney Company announced that it was acquiring Marvel Entertainment in a transaction that exchanges Marvel Entertainment stock for Walt Disney Company stock, plus cash.[1] The total purchase price in this transaction is estimated to be $4 billion. This acquisition combines the characters of Walt Disney and Marvel Comics, in products, television, film, and print media.

This is a friendly merger, with boards of directors of both companies agreeing to terms. The merger was subject to approval by the shareholders of both companies. Prior to the announcement of the merger, the market capitalization of Disney was almost $50 billion and that of Marvel around $3 billion. Once the acquisition was announced, Marvel's stock price increased 26 percent, from $38 to $48 per share, and Disney's stock price fell 3 percent.

The key to success of this acquisition is for Disney to add value to the characters in the Marvel Entertainment library beyond what Marvel has itself been able to do.

Learning Outcomes

After reading this chapter, you should be able to:

LO 21.1 List and describe the different types of acquisitions.

LO 21.2 List and describe potential motives to merge or acquire another business entity.

LO 21.3 Explain different methods that may be used to value a merger or acquisition.

LO 21.4 Demonstrate the effect of mergers on financial statements and financial ratios, and explain how accounting may affect the acquisition decision.

Chapter Preview We usually think about companies expanding by making investments in long-lived assets, such as equipment and plants, as we saw in the previous chapters on capital budgeting. This is growth from within. However, companies can also grow by acquiring other companies, or by acquiring selected assets from other companies. Sometimes an entirely new entity is formed, and sometimes the "acquiring" company simply becomes larger and the "target" company ceases to exist. In this chapter, we illustrate how to evaluate decisions about mergers and acquisitions (M&A) on a financial basis using standard discounted cash flow valuation techniques.

---

[1] "Disney to Acquire Marvel Entertainment," Walt Disney Company Press release, August 31, 2009.

21.1 TYPES OF TAKEOVERS

Few topics generate more interest from the financial media than that of corporate **takeovers**, which refers to the transfer of control from one ownership group to another. Takeovers can occur in several ways, including an acquisition or a merger. Though the terms *acquisition* and *merger* are often used interchangeably, there is a distinction between the two in terms of the postcombination company.

An **acquisition** occurs when one company, the acquiring company, completely absorbs another company, the target company. Under this arrangement, the acquiring company retains its identity, and the acquired company ceases to exist. Such a situation is the acquisition of Foster's, an Australian brewer, by SAB Miller for 9.9 billion Australian dollars ($10.2 billion U.S. dollars) in December of 2011.[2] Immediately following approval of the acquisition by not only shareholders, but the state Supreme Court of Victoria, Foster's ceased trading. Thus the key idea in an acquisition is the disappearance of the purchased company, as all senior management functions reside with the acquirer.

In contrast, a **merger** is usually the combination of two companies into a new legal entity. Such a situation notionally occurred when, on May 7, 1998, Daimler-Benz and Chrysler announced that they were combining as a "merger of equals" worth almost $40 billion. The combination of the third-largest U.S. car company with the prestigious maker of Mercedes-Benz cars was obviously big news, and the fact that the new company's name was a hybrid of the merging companies' names—DaimlerChrysler AG—indicated that it was an integration of the two companies, with neither dominant. For a time it appeared as if nothing had changed, until 2003, when the *Detroit News* announced that the merger was in fact a takeover of Chrysler by Daimler. This sparked multiple lawsuits because it was clear that Chrysler was becoming a division within Daimler, and effective control and decision making would be in Germany.

We illustrate the structure of an acquisition and a merger in Figure 21-1. What this discussion indicates is the elasticity in the terms *merger*, *acquisition*, and *takeover*. The SAB Miller takeover of Foster's was clearly an acquisition right from the start, with Foster's ceasing to exist. The furor over the Chrysler acquisition by Daimler was that it was announced as a merger, with the implication that the new company would involve an integration of the two with shared responsibilities and management, when in fact it was an acquisition that left Daimler in charge. Shortly after, most of the senior Chrysler management left.[3]

takeover transfer of control from one ownership group to another

acquisition purchase of one company by another

merger combination of two companies into a new legal entity

FIGURE 21-1 Acquisition V. Merger

[2] The acquisition was subject to approval by the Australian government, which put conditions on the acquisition, especially for domestic production of domestically consumed beverages.

[3] This merged entity was not able to produce the expected benefits, and Chrysler was sold to a private equity group, Cerebus Capital Management, in 2007 and was renamed Chrysler Group LLC. Chrysler Group LLC filed for and emerged from bankruptcy in 2009. On coming out of bankruptcy, Chrysler was controlled by Fiat, as well as the workers' retirement health plan, and the U.S. and Canadian governments [United States Bankruptcy Court, Southern District of New York].

Because a merger creates a new company, both sets of shareholders have to agree to exchange their existing shares for shares in the new company. In this way, a genuine merger is a transaction that requires both sets of shareholders to approve the transaction.

One key consideration in classifying acquisitions and mergers is how the acquirer finances the deal. Most acquisitions are cash transactions, where the shareholders in the target company receive cash for their shares. When one company acquires another through a merger, the approval of the target company's shareholders is required because they have to agree to sell their shares. However, the shareholders of the acquiring company do not normally have to give their approval. Buying another company is regarded as the same as buying a new piece of equipment or any other purchase. Only if there is some specific provision in the company's charter do the shareholders of the acquiring company get to vote on whether or not the company should make the acquisition.

The alternative to a cash transaction is a share transaction, where the acquiring company offers shares or some combination of cash and shares to the target company's shareholders. In contrast to a cash transaction, a share transaction often requires the approval of the acquiring company's shareholders if it requires additional shares to be authorized by its shareholders.[4]

In addition to a pure cash or share transaction, acquisitions and mergers may involve both cash and stock, or an option of cash and stock. For example, the acquisition of Marvel Entertainment by Walt Disney Company in 2009 was a cash and stock deal, whereas the 2009 acquisition of Burlington Northern by Berkshire Hathaway was a cash or stock deal.

An acquisition can also become a tense situation after a company has partially completed a takeover. Sometimes the acquirer can end up with a majority of the shares, say 70 percent, so that it knows it can get the two-thirds majority for an acquisition, and yet there are still 30 percent of the shares outstanding held by dissident shareholders who have not agreed to sell their shares.

minority freeze-out acquisition of the remaining interest by a controlling shareholder

Regardless of how a public minority of shareholders is created, the issues and principles are the same. When a controlling shareholder seeks approval for acquiring the remaining shares, a transaction that we refer to as a **minority freeze-out**, special rules kick in. The reason for this is the presumption that the controlling shareholder knows much more accurately the true value of the shares and will abuse this position unless safeguards are in place.

Securities laws require that the majority shareholders provide extensive disclosures.[5] The Delaware courts take the position that a bid for the minority interest is subject to judicial review, and many states follow Delaware's lead regarding minority interests. If the controlling shareholder owns less than 89.5 percent of the target, the fairness standard applies. If the controlling shareholder owns more than 89.5 percent, this is a short-form merger.

fairness opinion appraisal by an independent party of the value of the shares

short-form merger merger that takes place without shareholder approval that follows an acquisition of over 89.5 percent of the target company's shares

going private transaction special form of acquisition where a publicly traded company is taken private

The fairness standard has two elements. The first is that there are fair dealings, which in this context means that a majority of the minority shareholders approves the special resolution to merge the two companies. The second element is that there is a **fairness opinion**, which is, essentially, an appraisal by an independent party of the value of the shares.

In a **short-form merger**, the acquiring party acquires more than 89.5 percent in a tender offer, and then a merger takes place without shareholder approval. This approach is common in transactions in which a company is a publicly traded company that is taken private in a **going private transaction**.

---

[4] If the company's authorized share capital is limited to, say, 3 million shares and it wants to offer shares that exceed this limit, shareholder approval is needed.

[5] Securities and Exchange Commission Rule 13e-3.

Securities Legislation

Securities legislation determines what can be done and when it can be done in a merger or takeover. Securities legislation is relevant because it governs an exchange of shares by the target company's shareholders and their right to receive full value for their shares. The relevant laws and regulations pertaining to mergers and acquisitions in the U.S. are the Securities Exchange Act of 1934, the state laws for the states in which the acquirer and the target are incorporated, and the rules and regulations of the Securities and Exchange Commission.

Securities laws require disclosures that include the offer, the prospectus, solicitation, and commencement of an offer pertaining to a merger or acquisition.[6] In general, all communications must be filed on or before they are distributed to the public or investors. If a company or other investor buys an interest in a publicly traded company that is more than 5 percent of that publicly traded company's stock, the purchaser of the interest is referred to as a beneficial owner and must file a Schedule 13D with the Securities and Exchange Commission (SEC) within 10 days of the purchase.[7] This allows the company to know who owns its shares and whether a significant block has been bought by an investor who is a potential acquirer. A holding of 5 percent is, basically, a toehold.

Unless the purchase is exempt from the Securities Act, any further acquisition of an interest follows strict rules. A company making an offer for shares of a publicly traded company specifies how these shares can be tendered; hence, we refer to this offer as a **tender offer**. A tender offer is made directly to the shareholders of the target company. If a tender offer will result in an ownership interest of more than 5 percent, the acquiring company must file a Schedule TO and Schedule 13D with the SEC. The tender offer, describing the bid, financing, and all relevant information, similar to a prospectus, must be sent to all shareholders for review. Shareholders of the target who wish to sell their shares to the acquiring company then **tender** their shares by signing the authorizations.

tender to sign an authorization accepting a takeover bid made to target company shareholders

The takeover bid does not have to be for 100 percent of the shares. If the bid is for, say, 60 percent, and more shares are tendered, the acquirer prorates the shares tendered so that everyone receives an equal proportion. That is, if 80 percent are tendered and 60 percent are bought by the bidder, everyone who has tendered gets to sell 75 percent (60 ÷ 80) of the shares tendered. While the tender offer is outstanding, the acquirer can buy additional shares through the facilities of the stock exchange as long as it announces that it intends to do so. Finally, the price that the acquirer pays for tendered shares is the highest consideration paid to any security holder for securities tendered in the tender offer.[8] This latter rule, which is referred to as the **best price rule**, is intended to ensure that all shareholders are treated fairly.

best price rule requirement that the bidder of a tender offer pay all security holders that tender shares the highest price paid in the tender offer

The best price rule, along with the protections in minority freeze-outs, is intended to make sure that an acquirer treats all the shareholders fairly and everyone gets the same price. Otherwise, there is an economic incentive to lock up shares early at a high price, so that an acquirer has control and can then offer a lower price, knowing that no one else can mount a competing bid. In this way, different classes of shareholders are treated differently, and the shares are sold below their true value. Once you have control, no one else can bid, and there is a temptation to try to buy the remaining shares cheaply without paying a premium price.

---

[6] The offer disclosure is required by Section 2(a)(3) of the Securities Act [15 U.S.C. 77b]; the prospectus is the advertisement of the offer, as specified under Section 2(a) [15 U.S.C 77b]. The solicitation is defined under Rule 14a-1 [17 CFT 240.14a-1], and the commencement communications are detailed in the Williams Act, Rule 14s-2(c) and (d) [17 CFR 240.14d-2(c) and (d)].

[7] Required under Section 12 of the Securities and Exchange Act of 1934.

[8] This rule, Rule 14d-10 under the Securities and Exchange Act of 1934, was amended by the SEC on October 18, 2006. The SEC interpreted the previous definition of best price, which included any share purchases around the tender offer, as too restrictive and that it discouraged tender offers.

As indicated before, all takeovers have to abide by these rules unless they are exempt from the Securities Exchange Act of 1934. Securities legislation is concerned with the involvement of the public, so takeovers of private companies are exempt. An acquirer can also buy shares from fewer than five shareholders as long as the premium over the market price is not more than 15 percent. This is to allow the sale of blocks of shares. Finally, and most important, a normal course tender offer can be made through a stock exchange as long as no more than 5 percent of the shares are purchased through the exchange over a 1-year period. This 5 percent rule allows for a **creeping takeover**, where a company acquires a target over a long period of time by slowly accumulating shares.

Friendly Versus Hostile Takeovers

We can classify mergers and acquisition in terms of the target company's approach to the offer, which may be friendly or hostile. The approach to the receipt of the offer affects the medium of exchange—that is, cash or stock—and the premium necessary to entice target shareholders to part with their shares.

Friendly takeovers

With knowledge of securities legislation, we can now consider whether an acquisition should be hostile or friendly and discuss how a deal is hammered out. To understand this, consider first the difficulty of valuing a company when an external party has access only to public sources of information. How do you value a small biotech company, for example, when you have no direct information on whether recent lab tests were positive or negative? Similarly, for an oil and gas company or mining company, it may not be obvious how much potential is left in an oil and gas field or mineral reserve. The obvious thing to do, when faced with this uncertainty, is to go to the target company and ask whether it is interested in being acquired. In this way the acquirer hopes for a **friendly acquisition**.

Friendly acquisitions also start out when the target voluntarily puts itself into play. This can occur for many reasons, but often occurs when the founder is no longer playing a part in the business and it is time for the company to leave the controlling family and be sold to other interests.

If a company decides to sell itself, it normally consults an investment bank to put together an **offering memorandum** describing the most important features of the company to potential buyers. This offering memorandum is much like an abbreviated prospectus. Regardless of whether it is the company that decides to sell itself or an acquirer that approaches it, the company that is willing to be sold has to provide more information so that its fair value can be estimated.

The target company can disclose more information by setting up a **data room** where it can keep confidential information. These data rooms may be physical locations, or virtual, online locations. When serious acquirers express interest, they can access the data room by signing a **confidentiality agreement**. Not all acquirers will want to sign a confidentiality agreement because normally this restricts the acquirer's freedom of action. Typically the acquirer is prohibited from using the information to damage the target, such as by hiring away key employees or approaching key customers. These restrictions usually also have a time limit. Clearly the objective of the confidentiality agreement is to restrict access to important information to serious potential acquirers. This process of evaluating the target is called **due diligence** and is an important part of the acquisition process.

Once the confidential data have been evaluated, if the acquirer goes forward, it normally signs a **letter of intent**. This letter provides details on the terms of an agreement and allows the acquirer to do the third stage of the due diligence process, where its legal

creeping takeover acquisition of a target company over time by the gradual accumulation of its shares

friendly acquisition acquisition of a target company that is willing to be taken over

data room place where a target company keeps confidential information about itself for serious potential buyers to consult

confidentiality agreement document signed by a potential buyer guaranteeing it will keep confidential any information it sees in the data room about a target company

due diligence process of evaluating a target company by a potential buyer

letter of intent letter signed by an acquiring company scoping out the terms of agreement of its acquisition, including legal terms

team checks the title for property, terms of contracts, and so on.[9] The letter of intent usually contains a **no-shop clause**, where the target agrees not to try to find another buyer. In this way, the target shows that it is committed to making the transaction work. There is also usually a **termination fee** or **break-up fee** (or **break fee**), generally stated as a percentage of the value of the transaction. There are also reverse termination fees, in which an acquirer pays the target firm if the merger or acquisition does not go through. For example, the $8.5 billion takeover offer by Microsoft for Skype in 2011 included a $260 million no-shop termination fee. As another example, consider that Google agreed to pay Motorola $2.5 billion in a reverse termination fee if the $12.5 billion 2011 acquisition offer does not go through.[10]

Break fees have become very controversial. The justification for the break fee is that once companies get into the final round of due diligence, the expectation is that a deal will be completed. However, despite a no-shop clause, sometimes a competing bid does come in. Faced with two alternative offers, the board of directors has a fiduciary duty to act in the best interests of the shareholders and seek the best possible price. It may then be that the company that started the process and has committed significant resources to negotiating an agreement finds itself the loser. The break fee is designed to compensate the original acquirer for these costs as well as to reward it for generating a competing bid and getting the target shareholders a better price.

Once the final due diligence phase is complete and everything has worked out to the satisfaction of the acquirer, the final sale agreement is reached and ratified or agreed to by both parties. It is then taken to the shareholders for approval. If it is a private company, that is the end of the story, but for a company with public shareholders, the deal then goes to the shareholders for approval. We illustrate the typical process in Figure 21-2.

A friendly transaction allows a lot of scope for structuring the acquisition to the mutual benefit of both parties. The key areas usually involve careful tax planning, legal structuring to avoid certain liabilities, providing milestones for incentive agreements, and the possibility of acquiring not all assets, but only the more valuable ones.

Careful tax planning is important in any transaction. When an acquisition is made for cash it is always taxable in the hands of the target company shareholders. If the share price has run up significantly, this could mean forcing the shareholders to pay capital gains tax on the appreciation in the value of their shares. On the other hand, a share swap is usually nontaxable. This is why in many smaller acquisitions the target company's shares are swapped for preferred shares in the acquiring company. The target's shareholders, usually the founders, get a steady income from the preferred shares and are relieved from day-to-day concerns about their company. The acquiring company can then integrate the target into its existing operations.

Tax concerns also often motivate the sale of the target company's assets to the acquirer instead of the shares. In an **asset purchase**, the target company receives the proceeds from the sale and uses these proceeds to pay off its debts. The target company then has the option of "reinventing itself" or liquidating itself and paying out the proceeds

no-shop clause clause in a letter of intent stating that the target agrees not to look for another buyer, demonstrating its commitment to close the transaction

termination fee or **break-up fee** or **break fee** fee paid to an acquirer or target should the other party terminate the acquisition, often stated as a percent of the value of the transaction

asset purchase purchase of the company's assets rather than the company itself

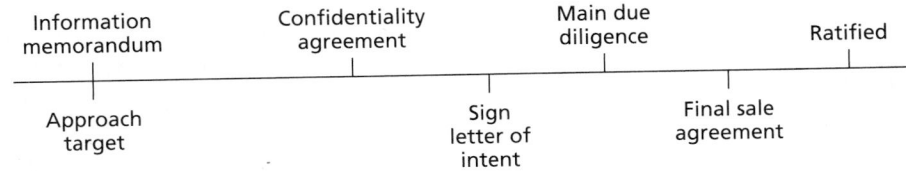

FIGURE 21-2 A Timeline for a Friendly Acquisition

---

[9] The first phase is the examination of public information that is usually included in the offering memorandum, the second phase is the provision of confidential documents in the data room, and the final phase is the serious verification process.

[10] Therefore, if the Federal Trade Commission blocks the merger for antitrust reasons, Google still pays the fee to Motorola.

to the company's shareholders. This approach may be attractive to the acquiring company because it can depreciate the assets at the value that it has paid for them, so there are usually tax advantages from having a depreciable value. In contrast, the target may be able to shield any potential tax payments with other losses.

Sometimes the target company has contingent liabilities that the acquirer does not wish to assume. For example, there may be potential warranty claims, which create a huge uncertainty surrounding the company. There is little potential, however, for sidestepping most contingent liabilities: Environmental claims, for instance, generally follow the assets so you can't dodge an environmental lawsuit from a polluting factory by selling the factory to someone else. In this case, the contingent liability stays with the asset, not the shareholders. Otherwise legitimate claims could be avoided simply by reorganizing the company.[11]

Deals often flounder based on fundamental disagreements concerning the target's value. What often happens is that the target's managers or founders are optimistic about the future prospects of the company and value it based on an optimistic scenario, where everything goes right. In contrast, the acquirer has often made many acquisitions, and approaches it on a more sanguine basis. Earn outs are often used to bridge the valuation gap when the acquisition is small. In this case, there will be an upfront price and then future conditional payments depending on the performance of the target after it has been acquired. These milestones are usually based on divisional sales or other reasonably objective data that both parties agree on. Of course not all friendly acquisitions follow this process. Some legal experts tell their clients not to sign a letter of intent because this is essentially a preliminary sale agreement, and the acquirer could be held liable if they back out of the deal.

Hostile offers

hostile takeover takeover in which the target has no desire to be acquired and actively rebuffs the acquirer and refuses to provide any confidential information

In practice, many deals do not begin as friendly, but instead are hostile. A **hostile takeover** is where the target has no desire to be acquired and actively rebuffs the acquirer and refuses to provide any confidential information.

An example of a hostile bid is the offer made by Microsoft to acquire Yahoo! On February 1, 2008, Microsoft made an offer to acquire Yahoo! shares at $31 per share, for a total acquisition value of $44.6 billion. This price was 62 percent higher than Yahoo!'s stock price prior to the offer. Despite the offer price at a substantial premium over market value, Yahoo!'s board of directors fought the acquisition, but not without a substantial cost: Yahoo! spent $79 million to fight off the acquisition, and shares of Yahoo! dropped to $13 after fighting off the bid.[12]

In hostile bids there is usually a **tender offer**, whereby the acquiring company makes a public offer to purchase shares of the target company from its existing shareholders. Typically, the bidder includes the provision that the offer is only good subject to its being able to obtain a certain minimum percentage of the outstanding voting shares. The advantage of this approach to the bidder is that a formal vote by the target shareholders is not required because they merely decide on their own whether or not they want to sell their shares to the acquiring company.

When a hostile tender offer is launched, external parties always look for certain clues. The most obvious is what happens to the market price relative to the offer price. If the market price immediately jumps above the offer price, then the market is saying that a competing offer is likely or that the bid is too low, and the bidder will have to increase the offer price. Alternatively, if the market price stays close to the offer price, it indicates that the price is fair, and the deal is likely to go through. What professionals then look for is the amount of trading in the target's shares.

---

[11] Deliberately selling assets to defraud legitimate claims on the company could also open up both sets of shareholders to lawsuits based on fraudulent conveyance.

[12] 10-K filing with the Securities and Exchange Commission, February 27, 2009. Some of the $79 million was paid to fight off a proxy fight by shareholder Carl Icahn.

If there is very little trading, this is usually a bad sign for the acquirer because shareholders are sitting on the shares and are reluctant to sell. On the other hand, a large amount of trading indicates that shares are cycling from regular investors into specialists' hands: people who specialize in predicting what happens in takeovers. We refer to such a specialist as an **arb**, which is short for **arbitrageur**.[13] This is good for the acquirer because arbs are only interested in selling as long as the price is right. However, the arbs buy the shares after the announcement, so they pay a premium, and they then expect to get a bigger premium when they sell, so their motivation is to extract the highest possible price.

One defensive tactic is to implement a **shareholder rights plan**, also known as a **poison pill**. This is a plan passed by a vote of the board of directors that indicates that in the event of a takeover, the nonacquiring company shareholders get the right to buy more shares (e.g., 50 percent more) at a discount price. Clearly this increase in the number of shares makes it much more expensive to make the acquisition and, all else constant, forces the acquirer to negotiate with the target company and make a friendly offer, because the board of directors can then remove the poison pill through a vote.

> **arbitrageur** or **arb** specialist who predicts what happens in takeovers and buys and sells shares in target companies
>
> **shareholder rights plan** or **poison pill** plan by a target company that allows its shareholders to buy more shares at a discount price in the event of a takeover, to make it less attractive

Alpharma Reaches for a Pill | FINANCE in the News

It aims to fend off hostile King Pharmaceuticals bid with a rights plan.

Specialty drug-maker Alpharma Inc.—faced with an unsolicited $1.4 billion takeover bid from King Pharmaceuticals Inc.—adopted a shareholder rights plan designed to thwart the offer that the target called "inadequate and not in the best interests of Alpharma shareholders."

The decision to implement the poison pill came in response to King's Aug. 27 filing with the Federal Trade Commission that it intends to acquire a majority of Alpharma's common stock and seek clearance under the Hart-Scott-Rodino Antitrust Improvements Act of 1976, according to Alpharma. Its $33-a-share offer was at a 37-percent premium, it said.

Alpharma's actions are somewhat unusual, given a move away from the poison-pill defense in recent years, although it has appeared to be making something of a comeback in recent months.

"Our board of directors has adopted this short-term shareholder rights plan in order to guard against a potential takeover by King Pharmaceuticals at an inadequate price that is not in the best interests of shareholders," said Dean Mitchell, Alpharma president and CEO. The board "is committed to enhancing value for and protecting the interests of all of Alpharma's shareholders and believes there are many avenues to that goal," he said, arguing that the poison pill will provide Alpharma time to "enhance the interests of Alpharma's shareholders."

The rights plan, he said, is not intended to prevent a takeover of the company "on terms that are fair to and in the best interests of all Alpharma shareholders."

Under the plan, rights will become exercisable if a person acquires 15 percent or more of the common stock of Alpharma or begins a tender offer that could result in that person owning 15 percent or more of the stock. The plan will not apply to existing shareholders unless they acquire beneficial ownership of additional shares. The one-year plan is set to expire next Sept. 1.

Meanwhile, Alpharma also said it responded to King's moves by amending the existing change-in-control plan "to preserve for its shareholders the benefits of retaining the company's recognized business leaders and valuable employees and motivate such employees to remain focused on the operation of the business during a period of some uncertainty." Under the revisions, a change of control will trigger executives at the vice president or director level receiving bonuses or other cash incentives at 100 percent of his or her annual target rate, with an assumed 100 percent funding of any bonus pool.

Source: Stephen Taub, "Alpharma Reaches for a Pill," CFO.com, September 2, 2008.

---

[13] "Arbs" is short for "arbitrageurs," but technically these specialists are taking significant risks, and their positions are not arbitrage (riskless) positions, which involve buying and selling the same security at different prices.

selling the crown jewels sale of a target company's key assets that the acquiring company is most interested in to make it less attractive for takeover

white knight entity that rescues a target company from a hostile takeover by making a counterbid

Other tactics involve making the target unattractive to the acquirer, and there are many ways of doing this. One way is to sell whatever the acquirer is really interested in. This tactic is called **selling the crown jewels**. For example, in 1979, Edper Equities made a hostile bid for Brascan. Brascan's major asset was $500 million in cash that it had just received from selling its major asset, a Brazilian power plant, so Edper made a partial bid for Brascan. It was a partial bid because Edper only needed 50.1 percent to control 100 percent of the cash. Regardless, the day after Edper approached Brascan, Brascan responded by making a hostile bid for Woolworths, knowing that Edper wanted the cash, not Woolworths.

The other major defense is to try to find a **white knight** to rescue the company and make a counterbid. In December 2000, Indigo made a hostile $13 a share offer for its main rival in selling books, Chapters, in an attempt to consolidate the Canadian bookselling industry in the face of potential U.S. competition. Chapters fiercely resisted the hostile offer and first tried selling the crown jewels. Chapters offered to buy back the minority interest in its Chapters' Online Internet bookstore for $3.40 a share; it had closed trading the previous day at $2.00. This got rid of cash and increased Chapters' ownership in something Indigo did not want. As Gerry Schwartz, who was bankrolling the Indigo bid, said, "Chapters has become virtually the only company in North America to offer cash to bail out the shareholders of a failing e-tailer."[14] When this failed, Chapters paid Future Shop a break-fee to get it to offer $16.80 a share as a white knight. This forced Indigo to finally raise its offer to $17, which was eventually successful.

Indigo was successful in its hostile bid for Chapters for several reasons. First, the business was straightforward and known to the acquirer, so little due diligence was needed; that is, there was no great uncertainty about the value of Chapters to Indigo. Second, there was no other strategic buyer that could generate similar value by acquiring Chapters. In this respect a combination of a bookstore (Chapters) and an electronics seller (Future Shop) offered little retail logic—it was simply a mechanism to get Indigo to bid more. Finally, Indigo could afford a long, drawn-out takeover battle because the value of Chapters was unaffected by the struggle. In contrast, sometimes the value of a target is dissipated as a result of lost contracts or key people leaving the company.

Concept Review Questions

1. What is the difference between an acquisition and a merger?

2. What goes into a confidentiality agreement, and why do people sign them?

3. What is due diligence?

4. What is a shareholder rights plan?

5. What are some standard takeover defenses?

21.2 MOTIVES FOR MERGERS AND ACQUISITIONS

Why do companies acquire other companies? Why do companies merge? The bottom line is that they do this to create value. But creating value is not an easy task, and many well-intended mergers do not end up creating value. Many motives are cited for mergers and acquisitions in press releases, but we will focus on those most likely to create value, the different sources of synergies. To better understand synergies, it is best to first understand the different types of mergers that are possible.

[14] "Chapters Plots to Fend Off Indigo Takeover," CBC News Online, www.cbc.ca, December 8, 2000.

Classifications of Mergers and Acquisitions

Acquisitions are made because the acquirer's management believes that the acquisition enhances the company's long-run value. The source of this value depends on the type of acquisition and structural changes occurring in the economy at various times. Three broad classifications of mergers and acquisitions are horizontal, vertical, and conglomerate.

Horizontal mergers

A **horizontal merger** or acquisition occurs when two companies in the same industry combine. For example, Google has been acquiring other Internet-based technology companies, such as YouTube (video sharing), DoubleClick (online advertising), and Panoramio (photo sharing). Other examples of horizontal mergers and acquisitions are the Schering-Plough and Merck merger in 2009 and Inbev's acquisition of Anheuser-Busch in 2008.

Companies seeking mergers or acquisitions in the U.S. must file a "Notification and Report Form" with the Federal Trade Commission (FTC) and the Antitrust Division of the Department of Justice (DOJ), as required by the Hart-Scott-Rodino Antitrust Improvement Act.[15] We provide a graph of the mergers reported under the Hart-Scott-Rodino Act in Figure 21-3. As you can see in this graph, the filings tend to move along with the economy, with fewer filings during periods of economic stress.

The DOJ and the FTC have 30 days to request further information from the parties and may then choose to review and contest the merger.[16] In the case of a review, the FTC and the DOJ apply standards that evaluate the merger on the basis of its effect on competition. If the DOJ determines that the merger may have an adverse effect on competition, as assessed by market power of the postmerger company, the DOJ can choose to block the merger.[17] However, of the filings, the DOJ and FTC make a request for information on a small percentage, as we show in Figure 21-4. An even smaller percentage result in "Fix-it-first" findings (that is, reduce business activity in specified markets), and very few result in any type of enforcement action. For example, in 2008, the government agencies requested additional information in only 43 of the 1,726 filings and blocked only 21 of these proposed mergers or acquisitions.

> **horizontal merger**
> merger in which two companies in the same industry combine

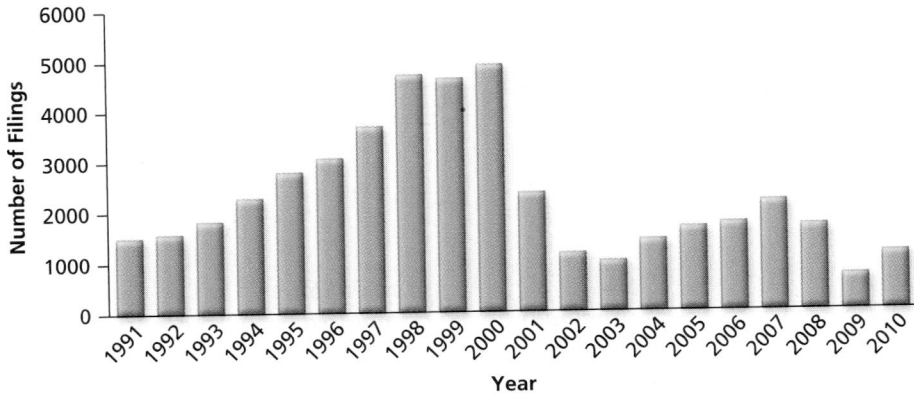

FIGURE 21-3 Hart-Scott-Rodino Merger Filings, 1999–2010
Source of data: *Federal Trade Commission, Bureau of Competition, Annual Competition Enforcement Reports, various years.*

---

[15] Hart-Scott-Rodino Antitrust Improvements Act of 1976 (Public Law 94-435).

[16] This waiting period is 15 days in the case of an all-cash deal.

[17] One of the criteria is the effect of the merger on the industry's Herfindahl-Hirschman index (HHI), which is a measure of the degree of concentration in a market that is based on market shares of the companies in an industry. See Horizontal Merger Guidelines, U.S. Department of Justice and the Federal Trade Commission, August 19, 2010.

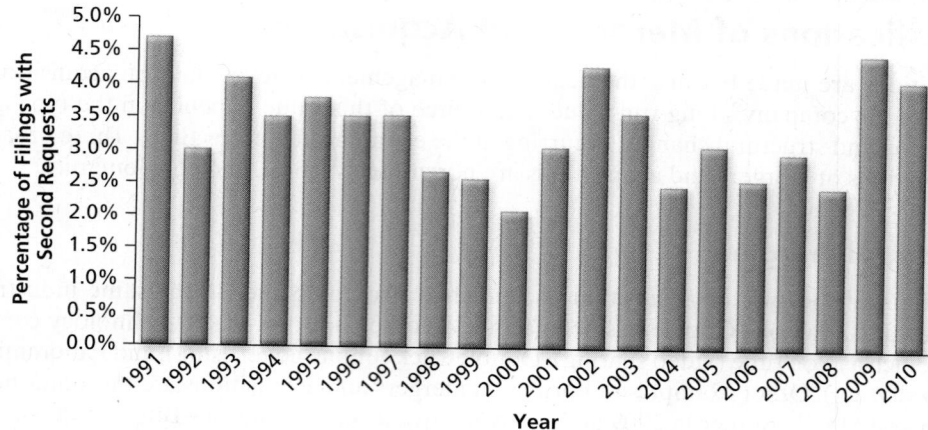

FIGURE 21-4 **Department of Justice and Federal Trade Commission Requests for Information, 1991 Through 2010**
Source of data: *Federal Trade Commission, Bureau of Competition, Annual Competition Enforcement Reports, various years.*

In the European Union, the European Commission evaluates potential mergers under the EU Merger Regulation and evaluates how these mergers affect competition in the European Economic Area (EEA). This review by the Commission is not only for companies based in the European Union, but also companies that do business within the European Union. For example, when Google was acquiring DoubleClick in 2008, the Commission ruled on this merger, concluding that it would not affect competition.[18]

Both the U.S. and European Union use the Herfindahl-Hirschman Index (HHI) in evaluating the potential effects of a merger on competition. The HHI is the sum of the squared market shares of the companies in the industry. For example, if there are five companies with the following market shares:

Company	Market Share
A	30%
B	25%
C	20%
D	15%
E	10%

The HHI for this industry is:[19]

Company	Market Share Squared
A	900
B	625
C	400
D	225
E	100
Sum	2,250

[18] The ruling was March 11, 2008, and the original case was filed with the Commission November 13, 2007 [Case IP/07/1688].

[19] The percentages are treated as whole numbers for this calculation. Therefore, a market share of 30 percent is considered 30 and $30^2 = 900$.

The increase in the HHI from the merger of two parties is quantified as twice the product of the companies' market shares. Therefore, if Company A and Company B propose a merger, the increase in the HHI is $2 \times 30 \times 25 = 1500$.

The U.S. Department of Justice and the Federal Trade Commission classify mergers using the following:

HHI Range	Conclusion
HHI < 1500	Unconcentrated market
1500 > HHI < 2500	Moderately concentrated
HHI > 2500	Highly concentrated

The EU also uses HHI to determine which mergers to analyze, considering both the HHI premerger and the expected change. For example, if the HHI is less than 1000, or if the HHI is less than 2000 and the change in HHI with the merger is less than 250, the EU concludes that the merger does not require further study.[20]

Vertical merger

A **vertical merger** occurs when a company expands by acquiring a company that is non-competing, yet is related to its existing customers ("going forward"), or its supplier that provides inputs into its production process ("going backward"). Vertical mergers are not often challenged for antitrust issues, but some may be ruled as anticompetitive. If a vertical merger were to make it difficult for companies to enter the industry, for example by buying or controlling the companies that provide the raw materials needed in an industry, a company could harm competition in the industry.

vertical merger combination of two or more companies in which one company acquires a supplier or another company that is closer to its existing customers

Consider the acquisition of Time Warner by AOL in 2000—probably the most storied failed merger in history—which was an attempt by AOL to go backward by accessing both media content and a cable distribution system to create an integrated media company. Referred to at the time as an "unprecedented powerhouse," it was later referred to as a "catastrophic merger."[21] Time Warner spun off the AOL division in November of 2009 as a separate company by distributing AOL stock to Time Warner–AOL shareholders.[22] AOL then merged with the Huffington Post in 2011.

Another example of a vertical merger is Comcast's acquisition of a majority position in NBC Universal from General Electric, creating what has been referred to as a "media powerhouse."[23] Because this acquisition involved companies regulated by the U.S. Federal Communications Commission (FCC), the FCC, along with the U.S. Department of Justice, reviewed this acquisition. The FCC approved this acquisition, but with strings attached to encourage competition.[24]

Conglomerate merger

A **conglomerate merger** occurs when two companies in unrelated businesses combine. The motivation to create a conglomerate is that the different businesses face different risks, which tend to cancel each other out, lowering the overall risk of the combined company. One classic example was in November 1981 when U.S. Steel bought control of Marathon Oil Company. In this case, U.S. Steel was the white knight, bidding in response to a

conglomerate merger merger in which two companies in unrelated businesses combine

[20] Vincent Verouden, European Commission, DG Competition, "Concentration Indices and Market Shares in the EU Horizontal Merger Guidelines," February 17–19, 2004.

[21] Adam Liptak, "The Making and Taking of AOL Time Warner," *New York Times*, January 18, 2004.

[22] Shira Ovide and Emily Stell, "It's Now Official: AOL, Time Warner to Split," *Wall Street Journal*, May 29, 2009, and Time Warner Investor Relations.

[23] Brian Stelter and Tim Arango, "Comcast-NBC Deal Wins Federal Approval," *New York Times*, January 18, 2011.

[24] These strings include provisions that Comcast share NBC content with its competitors and provide low-cost options for low-income customers.

hostile bid for Marathon by Mobil Oil. However, the result was an oil company and a steel company with few economic reasons for the combination.

Another example of a conglomerate merger or acquisition is the acquisition of Burlington Northern by Berkshire Hathaway in 2009. Burlington Northern is a railroad company, whereas Berkshire Hathaway is a company comprised of insurance, real estate sales, and restaurants, among other lines. In this deal, Berkshire Hathaway paid $26 billion, which is a 31.5 percent premium over Burlington Northern's premerger value.

Other classifications

We can also classify acquisitions as domestic or cross-border (international) mergers and acquisitions. Many U.S. companies have been involved, as both acquiring companies and as target companies, in high-profile cross-border mergers throughout the years. Most of the mergers reflect a trend toward industry consolidation (i.e., a large number of horizontal mergers), and many involve companies from outside the country, representing a trend of globalization.

The 2010 Kraft Foods (a U.S. company) acquisition of Cadbury (a British company), in a cash and stock deal valued at $18.9 to 19.5 billion, is an example of a cross-border acquisition.[25] To obtain approval by the EU Commission, Kraft was required to divest itself of Cadbury's Polish and Romanian confectionary businesses.

Potential Synergies

synergy value created from economies of integrating a target and acquiring company; the amount by which the value of the combined company exceeds the sum value of the two individual companies

Theoretically, the primary motive for a merger or acquisition should be the creation of **synergy**, which causes the value of the combined company to exceed the sum value of the two individual companies. Synergy is created due to economies of integration that are expected to occur for one reason or another. Basically, synergy exists if the value of the combined company is more than the sum of the parts (in other words, $1 + 1 > 2$).

If the target and acquirer have initial values of $50 million and $100 million, respectively, and the combined company is worth $200 million, there are synergy values of $50 million. Of course in this case, the key questions are: Where do these synergies come from, and who gets them? If the acquirer pays $100 million for the target, then all the synergy value flows through to the target shareholders and none to the acquirer. On the other hand, at any value less than $100 million, the synergy gains are split between the acquiring and target company shareholders. In this case the acquisition has created value of $50 million.

Most M&A announcements go to great lengths to espouse the synergies, or total positive gains, associated with the proposed transaction. Sometimes these gains materialize, and sometimes they don't. We list a variety of these value creation motives that are often used to justify a merger or acquisition decision. Some of these reasons hold greater merit than others, as we discuss next.

Operating synergies

1. Economies of Scale

These economies arise whenever bigger is indeed better. Some potential benefits include those that may arise in terms of:

- **Reducing capacity**. It may be, for example, that an industry has grown too big, and there are now too many companies operating in it. For instance, in 2003, Alcan, the major Canadian aluminum producer, purchased the French producer Pechiney, while the U.S. bank J.P. Morgan purchased another American bank, Chase.
- **Spreading fixed costs**. Often, significant costs in a business are fixed, independent of scale, so that by increasing size, these costs are spread over greater volumes, and the

---

[25] Kelsey Swanekamp, "Kraft Swallows Cadbury," Forbes.com, January 19, 2010.

company is more efficient. This was the ostensible motivation for the proposed AT&T and T-Mobile USA merger, which was stopped by the U.S. Justice Department in September 2011. The regulators concluded that the benefits from efficiency were not outweighed by the costs to consumers through reduced competition.[26]

- **Geographic synergies**. Often an industry is fragmented and ripe for consolidation. A geographic synergy may arise when a national company is created out of a series of regional companies. The original Standard Oil in the United States was created when John D. Rockefeller consolidated the U.S. oil industry, which allowed common marketing and managerial overhead. Retailing has similarly been consolidated with the creation of national chains from regional ones to gain economies in purchasing and an improvement in the distribution channel. For example, Federated Department Stores merged with or acquired a number of regional retailers, including Macy's, May Department Stores, and Marshall Fields, creating a national brand that was renamed Macy's in 2005.

2. Economies of Scope

An economy of scope occurs when the combination of two activities reduces costs. It typically results when the products share similarities in their production process, which can be exploited. A classic example is a distribution system that can be used to sell two lines of product instead of one. On this basis, Seagram (think whisky) purchased Martell (think fine cognac) in 1988. The basic rationale was that Seagram could sell Martell's cognac through its U.S. distribution system as easily as its own whisky and thereby generate expanded sales at little extra cost. Another example is when Coca-Cola bought Gatorade to gain entry into the sport drinks market, and Quaker Oats bought Snapple Beverage Corporation.

3. Complementary Strengths

These occur if one company is more efficient in one or more areas of operations than another and vice versa. For example, a marketing-oriented company may acquire a production-oriented company if it feels that the product line is not being sold efficiently. A classic example here is Remington, the razor company. It was acquired by Victor Kiam, who immediately cut engineering and product development and marketed a smaller range of razors. He did this to great effect by advertising himself, saying, *"I liked the razor so much I bought the company."*

Another example of complementary strengths is when certain organizational cultures are good at doing certain things, and in combination there are some synergies from the extension of the company's expertise. The research part of R&D, for example, usually requires a creative organizational culture that encourages risk taking. The development part, on the other hand, often requires extensive managerial and production skills. As a result, big pharmaceutical companies, like Merck and Pfizer, often buy small drug companies after they come up with a potential new drug because often only the big companies can take the drug through the clinical trials needed to be certified for use by consumers. As still another example, the Stanley–Black & Decker merger in 2010 combined a company with strong management (Stanley) with a company with strong brand names (Black & Decker).[27]

Similarly, many mineral finds have been made by small companies often consisting of a few geologists, but after a deposit is found, they sell the company to the major international companies that have the skills and resources to develop it. An example in Canada was the Voisey's Bay nickel deposits in Labrador, found by Diamond Field Resources in 1994. The deposits were the most significant in Canada in 40 years and sparked a furious bidding war that was eventually won by Inco Ltd. for the rights to develop the mineral deposits. In this case, the M&A occurs because the exploration and development functions, as opposed to the R&D functions, are best carried out by separate entities.

---

[26] "Statement of Commissioner Mignon L. Clyburn on the U.S. Department of Justice's Complaint against the AT&T/T-Mobile Merger," *News*, Federal Communications Commission, August 31, 2011, and "Justice Department Files Antitrust Lawsuit to Block AT&T's Acquisition of T-Mobile," Department of Justice, August 31, 2011.

[27] Tom Brennan, "A Coming Catalyst for Stanley Black & Decker," *CNBC.com*, December 17, 2010.

Efficiency increases

These gains materialize whenever one or both of the companies involved have excess capacity (i.e., they possess factors that are currently being underused). This is a common motivation for mergers, and unfortunately for employees, some of the synergy that arises involves the elimination of jobs. Efficiency gains do not always have to result in job losses; the excess capacity could exist in one or more of many factors such as shipping, storage, and information technology. Another important source of better efficiency could be improved company management (i.e., the acquiring company believes that its management team will operate more efficiently than that of the target company's management team). It is in this sense that people often refer to the *market for corporate control* as a viable corporate governance mechanism because inefficient management will pay the ultimate price.

Financing synergy

Financing synergies may arise for a number of reasons. The primary argument in these synergies is that larger is better in accessing capital markets. One reason is reduced cash flow variability. Cash flow volatility tends to be lower for larger entities, especially if the cash flows from the two underlying businesses are not highly correlated. This may enable the company to reduce its need for external financing because future financing needs can be forecast with greater certainty. Another potential source of synergy is increased debt capacity. This may arise due to the increase in size and/or reduction in cash flow volatility of the new company. Riskier companies generally cannot carry as much debt as larger companies, and the use of additional debt provides the company with greater tax savings, as we discuss in more detail later.

Some argue that there is synergy from the reduction in average issuing costs. Because most security issues occur in large increments, the average cost of floating new debt or equity will decrease as the company issues larger amounts. In addition, larger companies can access more sources of capital than smaller ones, resulting in cost savings. Still another source of financing synergy is fewer information problems. Larger companies usually attract more external security analysts and have greater exposure in the media. The result is that they attract big institutional investors, which lowers their financing costs.

Tax benefits

Tax benefits occur when one company has substantial operating loss credit that it cannot take advantage of because it is not operating profitably. These losses are valuable because they can be carried forward and used against future profits to reduce taxes. Yet, if the company is unlikely to become profitable in the near term, such losses may expire worthless. On the other hand, if the company combines with another profitable one in the same basic line of business, these losses can be used to offset the other company's profits to reduce taxes if the transaction is structured properly. This is the case of the Kmart–Sears merger of 2004. At the time of the merger, Kmart had $509 million in tax loss carryovers that were due to expire in 2021–2023 tax years, which Kmart had little chance of using without combining with a profitable company.[28] By combining with a profitable company, specifically with Kmart as the acquirer, the net operating loss carryover could then be used as offsets against future taxable income, hence reducing taxes of the combined company.[29]

Additional tax benefits may also arise due to the depreciation of capital assets (current cost accounting tax shields) that can be charged by the combined entity, and the increased use of debt financing with more interest tax shields, as discussed earlier.

---

[28] Kmart Holding Corporation 2004 fiscal year 10-K filing with the Securities and Exchange Commission, p. 49.

[29] Sears Holdings, the parent company after the acquisition, announced store closings at the end of 2011 because of a poor holiday earnings, a sign that the company continues to struggle. If Sears Holdings does not generate taxable earnings to apply against those net operating losses, these losses will expire worthless.

Strategic realignments

Mergers and acquisitions may enable the new entity to pursue strategies that were previously not feasible, as a result of the acquisition of enhanced managerial skills and new product/service line growth opportunities.

Managerial Motivations for M&A

Creating value for shareholders may be the basic motivation for running a business but as we discussed previously, it is the managers that control the company. So sometimes we get managerial motives for M&A that are distinct from the shareholder motivation. Two of the more common motivations are the following:

- **Increased company size**. This may or may not be a good thing, depending on whether any economic synergies are created. Unfortunately, in the past, some M&As have been advocated by managers who were equally concerned with the additional personal compensation and power they would accrue as a result of the transaction. The classic example here is the 1998 attempted merger between Glaxo Wellcome and Smith Klein, two big British pharmaceutical companies. In February 1998, the proposed merger was called off because the two CEOs couldn't decide on the management team of the new company. With the announcement of the cancellation of the merger, £13 billion was wiped out from the combined companies' market value. In this case, the personal egos of the senior managers destroyed value, whereas normally the value is destroyed by making bad acquisitions rather than cancelling potentially good ones.[30]

- **Reduced company risk through diversification**. M&As may also be used to diversify a company geographically, across industries, or across products through conglomerate mergers, as discussed earlier. Unfortunately, the evidence suggests that diversification is in general a poor motive for a merger because it often results in additional managerial complications and a lack of focus by managers running disparate businesses. The markets recognize this and are not willing to pay a premium for diversification because it is easy to diversify a portfolio across the same industries and geographic borders. In fact, the evidence suggests quite the opposite: Investors tend to pay a premium for "pure play" companies that are focused on one strategic plan.

Are There Really Gains from M&A?

So what does the evidence on M&A tell us about the gains? Numerous empirical studies examine the gains from mergers. The evidence suggests that the target company shareholders gain the most, with premiums over the prior stock market price in the 15 to 20 percent range for stock-financed takeovers and from 25 to 30 percent for cash-financed takeovers. These gains consist of a one-third run-up in the stock price prior to the announcement plus about a two-thirds gain after the announcement. There is considerable disagreement about the source of the run-up prior to the announcement.

On the one hand, some people believe that information about an impending merger is leaked, resulting in insider trading, which of course is illegal. On the other hand, many believe that informed industry specialists can make reasonable predictions about takeover activity based on transactions elsewhere. For example, on February 12, 2007, *The*

---

[30] Note that the deal eventually did go through, as even managerial egos could not stand in the way of $30 billion. The two companies merged in 2000 to form GlaxoSmithKline.

Times of London reported that BHP and Rio Tinto, two large British–Australian mining companies, had drawn up plans for a $40 billion bid for New York-based aluminum producer Alcoa. In response, rival Alcan's stock price jumped $4 on speculation that if it didn't buy Alcoa, someone might buy Alcan.

Regardless of the source, it always pays for the shareholders of the target company to be taken over. Short-term gains of 20 to 40 percent are the reasons why the M&A specialists, the arbs, exist.

Takeover gains to the target can be even higher, especially if bidding wars develop, and they tend to be higher still when the deals are 100 percent cash because the target shareholders usually have to pay capital gains tax. In contrast, the acquiring company's shareholders on average see no change in their stock price. In fact, usually the stock price dips marginally on the news. This implies that acquiring companies pay too much for target companies, acquire them for the wrong reasons, and/or overestimate the benefits resulting from the merger. In fact, numerous studies concerning postmerger value indicate there is little or no increase in value; there are no synergistic gains to the acquirer, which is the supposed rationale for mergers.

An interesting analysis of M&A deals was published by the U.S. periodical *Business Week* on October 12, 2002. The magazine hired the Boston Consulting Group's (BCG) M&A team to do the work. They analyzed 302 deals worth more than $500 million done between 1995 and 2001. On average the acquirer bought a company 47 percent its size, so these were big deals. Of these deals, 61 percent lost value over the next year. BCG estimated this by looking at the subsequent stock market performance relative to the companies' peers. The losers lost about 25 percent of relative value, and overall the average loss was 6.3 percent. The next year didn't get any better. The biggest losers were those deals that were financed with shares, which lost an average 8 percent, whereas those financed with cash only lost 0.3 percent. It seems that acquirers are freer with their shares than they are with their cash, and there is good reason for this.

Consider a $2 billion company that wants to take over a company with a $1 billion value because it thinks there are $0.5 billion in synergies. If it gets into a bidding war and pays $1.5 billion in cash for the company and then finds that there are no synergies, it has lost the $0.5 billion premium it paid. In this case, it has $0.5 ÷ $2 = 25 percent of its market value at risk in the acquisition. In contrast, if it did a share swap at $1.5 billion, the original shareholders own only $2 ÷ $3.5 = 57 percent of the new company. They will only lose this fraction of the lost $0.5 billion, or $285 million. The rest has been lost by the shareholders of the target that accepted shares in the new company, only to see them to go down in value.[31] This analysis is **shareholder value at risk (SVAR)**.

shareholder value at risk (SVAR) measure of the value that is at risk for a party to a merger or acquisition

Using SVAR analysis helps illustrate the basic point that when using cash, the acquirer bears all the risk, whereas when using share swaps, the risk is borne by the shareholders in both companies. SVAR supports the argument that when companies make deals using cash, they are a lot more careful about the acquisition price than when they use their shares. One reason for this is that the managers have less interest in the financing of the deal than in getting it done in the first place.

Concept Review Questions

1. What is the difference between a vertical and horizontal merger?

2. What financial synergies are possible in an M&A transaction?

3. What tax benefits can occur in an M&A?

4. What is SVAR, and why do managers prefer to finance with shares rather than cash?

---

[31] A. Rappaport and M. Sirower, "Stock or Cash: The Trade-offs for Buyers and Sellers in Mergers and Acquisitions," *Harvard Business Review*, 77, no. 6 (November–December 1999): 147–158, 217.

21.3 VALUATION ISSUES

So far we have discussed the process of an acquisition, different types of acquisitions, and the securities laws surrounding acquisitions. In fact, we have discussed almost everything about acquisitions except the critical question of how to value them. Because companies are always buying something, especially in a merger, where they have to determine the share exchange ratio, they have to know the basics on valuation. In principle this involves the same issues as valuing a project, as discussed in earlier chapters, and valuing securities like bonds and shares. However, determining value in an acquisition is considerably more complex for a variety of reasons.

A quote from William Cameron fits the valuation challenge in mergers and acquisitions: "Everything that can be counted does not necessarily count; everything that counts cannot necessarily be counted."[32] An acquirer may consider only some of the assets of the target company to be of value, and there may be intangibles that do not appear on the target's financial statements.

Further, value generally means a willingness to sell or to buy; that is, we are talking about supply and demand curves. The price, on the other hand, is the value at which a deal is consummated. When we look at most commodities bought and sold, many people in the market are buying and selling, so the price is clearly derived. In this sense it is an equilibrium price. For companies, on the other hand, although the shares may trade between many buyers and sellers, there is a limited market for the company as a whole, so we are dealing with only a few points on the demand and supply curves. This naturally leads to a wide range of possible deal prices.

This is also the underlying motivation for the definition of **fair market value (FMV)**, which is the "price at which the property would change hands between a willing buyer and a willing seller, neither being under any compulsion to buy or to sell and both having reasonable knowledge of relevant facts."[33] A similar definition is the "highest price, expressed in dollars, that a property would bring in an open and unrestricted market between a willing buyer and a willing seller who are both knowledgeable, informed, and prudent, and who are acting independently of each other."[34] We often need to know what the value of something is for tax and other legal purposes, so FMV reflects this specific valuation, which is not necessarily a transaction price.

> **fair market value (FMV)** highest price obtainable in an open and unrestricted market by parties who are informed and trading freely, without coercion

Fair Market Value

If we look at the various definitions of FMV, mentioned previously and otherwise, there are several common elements:

- *Open and unrestricted market*: There are no barriers, and anyone can buy or sell.
- *Knowledgeable, informed, and prudent parties*: All the information is in the market and the value determined by people who know what they are doing.
- *Arm's length*: The value is determined by parties who do not know each other.
- *Neither party under any compulsion to transact*: It is not a panic sale causing distressed valuations.

The Internal Revenue Service adopts fair market value as the standard definition because otherwise a party wishing to avoid capital gains tax could sell an asset to a related party at a knockdown price. This is why the arm's-length provision is there. In fact, if you look carefully at the four components, you will realize that this is a description of an ideal or perfect market, where everyone is rational and arrives at values in an objective,

[32] William Bruce Cameron, *Informal Sociology: A Casual Introduction to Sociological Thinking*, Random House, 1963, p. 13.

[33] 26 C.F.R. sec. 20.2031-1(b)

[34] Canada Revenue Agency Dictionary. Retrieved January 6, 2011, at www.cra-arc.gc.ca/tx/chrts/dnrs/dctnry/menu-eng.html#fmv

rational way. It is also why the courts have frequently thrown out actual transaction values because these conditions were not met.

The relevance of FMV is that it comes up all the time in valuing transactions, but the requirements for it highlight why transaction values frequently depart from FMV. In a hostile takeover, for example, the acquirer does not have access to a data room or confidential information and often overbids for a company. Similarly, companies selling a division or putting the whole company up for sale on the death of the founder frequently are under a compulsion to act and are dealing in a restricted market.

management buyout (MBO) or leveraged buyout (LBO) a purchase of a company in which the purchasers are a company's managers; usually involves high levels of debt financing

To put these comments in perspective, we can think of purchasers as belonging to different groups: passive investors, strategic investors, financials, and managers. We compare these groups in Figure 21-5. The different types of purchases would have different perspectives. For example, the financials would look at a company, consider the "breakup" value of a company, and consider selling pieces. Managers would want to control the reorganization of the company, taking on a significant amount of debt, which is why we often refer to such an acquisition as a **management buyout (MBO)** or a **leveraged buyout (LBO)**.

Alternative Methods of Valuation

Market pricing will reflect different buyers at different stages of the business cycle. Regardless of which group is dominant, the same basic valuation methods are used all the time. The basic reactive methods are multiples, liquidation, and discounted cash flow:

1. **Multiples or relative valuation.** In this approach we apply ratios, such as price-earnings (P/E), market-to-book (M/B), price-to-sales (P/S), and price-to-cash flow (P/CF), to the projected financial statements of the combined company.[35] We can estimate the multiples based on historical trading values, "rules of thumb," and using comparables such as industry averages.[36] A multiples valuation provides a starting point for the valuation process by establishing the value in relation to historical values, rules of thumb, and similar companies.

2. **Liquidation values.** This approach involves estimating the liquidation value of the company's assets at present market prices. For example, we know that cash is worth 100 percent and might estimate accounts receivable at 85 percent, inventory at 75 percent, and property, plant, and equipment at 50 percent of their book values. This can be an especially important consideration if the acquiring company plans on selling some of the target company's assets to pay off some of the debt financing associated with the purchase.

Passive investors	Strategic investors	Financials	Managers
• Value the resulting company based on estimated cash flows as they are at present, with only minor adjustments. • Passive investors would be mutual funds and any small investor that cannot change what the company is doing.	• Value the company based on estimated synergies and change that may arise due to the integration of the company's operation with their own. • Overcapacity, extension, and roll-up mergers would all fall into this category.	• Value the company based on how it can reorganize its operations by "juggling" the pieces and refinancing them. • This was common in the 1970s and 1980s as conglomerates were purchased and then reorganized.	• Value the company based on their own job potential and their ability to motivate their staff and reorganize the company's operations. • The transactions usually involve significant amounts of debt financing.

FIGURE 21-5 Different Types of Purchasers

[35] They are called multiples because we are arriving at a market value by using some multiple of an item in the companies' forecast financial statements.

[36] We saw this form of analysis in the earlier chapter on equity valuation.

3. **Discounted cash flow (DCF) models**. This approach involves estimating the future cash flows associated with the new combined entity and discounting them back to the present to determine the fair market value. Sound familiar? This is exactly how we evaluated the traditional investment decisions and individual securities. This simply reflects the fact that DCF valuation is the workhorse of finance.

Multiples valuation

We now use an example to illustrate how multiples may be used to evaluate a company and to highlight the difficulties that may arise from using this approach. Suppose we have the following information about a target company (Vendedor, Inc.) that an acquiring company (Comprador Co.) is considering buying. We provide the basic financial information on Vendedor in Panel A of Table 21-1. We also provide the multiples for Vendedor and those of the industry in Panel B of Table 21-1.

TABLE 21-1 Financial Data for Vendedor

Panel A   Financial information Vendedor

Sales and Income Statement Items

		(in millions)
	Sales	$10.0
Less	Variable costs	5.0
Less	Fixed cash costs	1.7
	EBITDA	$3.3
Less	Depreciation	0.8
	EBIT	$2.5
Less	Interest	0.8
	EBT	$1.7
Less	Income tax	0.7
	Net income	$1.0
	Dividends	$0.5
	Number of shares outstanding	0.5

Invested Capital (Book Values)

	(in millions)
Equity	$5.0
Debt	$5.0
Market value of equity	$15.0

Note: Sales = 1 million units × Price per unit $10

Panel B   Ratios for Vendedor and the industry

Valuation Ratios	Vendedor	Vendedor 5-year Average	Industry Average
Price-earnings (P/E) (trailing)	15.00	14.5	16.5
Value/EBIT	8.00	5.5	7.5
Value/EBITDA	6.06	4.8	6.0
Price/Sales	1.50	1.35	1.6
Price/Book value	3.00	3.00	3.2
Price per unit of output	$15	14.5	16.0
Return on equity	20.00%	16.5%	17.5%

Recall that EBIT (earnings before interest and taxes) and EBITDA (earnings before interest, taxes, depreciation, and amortization) belong to all the providers of capital, not just the shareholders, so these multiples are based on the total market value of the company, that is, the value of the equity plus the debt. In this case, to get the equity value, we then have to subtract the market value of the debt.[37]

Of course, the actual value ratios for Vendedor are based on the current market price of Vendedor's common shares, and we cannot use them to value Vendedor because they just give us back the current value. To use the multiples approach to estimate the true value of Vendedor, we would need to estimate "justifiable" P/E ratios drawn from comparables or a bottom-up analysis.

Let's estimate the value of Vendedor's equity using different approaches:

1. Industry averages for the five valuation ratios.
2. The 5-year averages for Vendedor for the five valuation ratios.
3. The forward P/E ratio based on the assumptions that 9 percent is a reasonable cost of equity for Vendedor, that Vendedor maintains its present dividend payout ratio, and that Vendedor's dividends and earnings grow at an annual rate of 6 percent indefinitely.

First, we apply the industry average to each multiple, as we show in Panel A of Table 21-2. The industry average multiples indicate that Vendedor's equity may be currently "undervalued" at $15 million, and it should be valued somewhere around $16 million, depending on which multiple is used. The company's historical (5-year) average multiples indicate that Vendedor's equity should be valued somewhere between $8.75 million and $15.84 million, depending on which multiple we use.

TABLE 21-2 Valuation of Vendedor

Panel A — Valuation using industry averages

Multiple	Formula	Calculation (Dollar amounts in millions)	Estimated Value (in millions)
P/E	P/E × Net income	16.5 × $1	$16.50
V/EBIT	(V/EBIT × EBIT) – Debt	(7.5 × $2.5) – $5	$13.75
V/EBITDA	(V/EBITDA × EBITDA) – Debt	(6.0 × $3.3) – $5	$14.80
P/S	P/Sales × Sales	1.6 × $10	$16.00
P/B	P/B × Book value	(3.2 × $5)	$16.00

Panel B — Valuation using Vendedor 5-year averages

Multiple	Formula	Calculation (Dollar amounts in millions)	Estimated Value (in millions)
P/E	P/E × Net income	14.5 × $1	$14.50
V/EBIT	(V/EBIT × EBIT) – Debt	(5.5 × $2.5) – $5	$8.75
V/EBITDA	(V/EBITDA × EBITDA) – Debt	(4.8 × $3.3) – $5	$15.84
P/S	P/Sales × Sales	1.35 × $10	$13.50
P/B	P/B × Book value	(3 × $5)	$15.00

[37] Often the price-to-sales ratio used may be the total company market value-to-sales ratio.

We base the justifiable forward P/E ratio for Vendedor on the assumption of a growth rate of 6 percent and a dividend payout consistent with the present:[38]

$$P/E(\text{forward}) = \text{Dividend payout ratio} \div (r_e - g)$$
$$= (\$0.5 \text{ million} \div \$1.0 \text{ million}) \div (0.09 - 0.06)$$
$$= 0.5 \div 0.03 = 16.67$$

Next year's earnings based on a 6 percent growth rate, or $1 million × 1.06, or $1.06 million.

$$\text{Value of Vendedor's equity} = P/E \times E_1 = 16.67 \times \$1.06 \text{ million} = \$17.67 \text{ million}$$

As you can see, various valuation models may be used to estimate justifiable multiples, which can then be used to evaluate a target company. However, in practice, we cannot just "passively" use these ratios, for several reasons. For one thing, the use of different accounting methods can affect many of the items used in the multiples approach. We can make adjustments to the financial statements of companies to put them on the same accounting basis. For example, if the subject company uses FIFO (first-in-first-out) accounting for inventory and the comparable company or companies use LIFO (last-in-first-out), we would adjust the financial statements of the comparable or comparables to put inventory on a FIFO basis.

Another problem with multiples is that some multiples may not be useful in some cases. For example, a P/E ratio is not meaningful if the company has losses, and a P/B ratio is not meaningful if the company has negative equity. Care must be taken to make sure that the particular multiples are appropriate to use in the situation.

Still another problem with multiples is comparing companies that have different capital structures. Comparing a company's P/E with another company that has more or less financial leverage may be misleading because of the effect of leverage on net income. EBITDA and EBIT multiples would be preferred in this situation because they remove the problem with capital structure, focus higher up the income statement, and avoid some of the accounting problems that result from companies focusing on the bottom line (i.e., net income).

Liquidation valuation

Estimating liquidation value requires first estimating the liquidation value of current assets based on their "realizable value." For example, if a company's accounts receivables are with good credit-quality companies and most of them are current, it might be reasonable to value them at 80 percent of their book value. This percentage could be lower for companies whose customers were of lower average credit quality, or if they had a large percentage of overdue receivables. Similarly, inventory could be valued according to its marketability.

Second, we estimate the present market value of tangible assets such as machinery, buildings, and land. Then we subtract the value of the company's liabilities from the total estimated liquidation value of all the company's assets. This represents the liquidation value of the company.

The liquidation value approach is useful, but it can involve several estimates, which may be imprecise at best, especially when a company has a lot of assets. More important, it values companies based on existing assets and is not forward looking. Therefore, we devote most of our time to the use of the discounted cash flow valuation approach, which we discuss next, although it must also overcome several challenges, as we shall see.

Discounted cash flow analysis

Let's apply the discounted cash flow analysis to the valuation of a company. The first step in this process is to estimate the future after-tax cash flows associated with a company.

---

[38] Remember that if $P_0 = D_1 \div (r_e - g)$, then $P_0/E_1 = (D_1/E_1) \div (r_e - g)$.

This step is fraught with difficulties, as alluded to in the following quote, which is referred to as *Professor Finagle's Three Laws of Information*:[39]

> The information we have is not what we want.
> The information we want is not what we need.
> The information we need is not available!

Let's examine these three "laws" one at a time, except we will modify the last statement, so that we have a viable way of approaching the issue.

1. *The information we have is not what we want.*

What we *have* (i.e., what we can find from the company's financial statements) is accounting earnings, which represents the bottom line, and which is affected by accounting choices, and that can be managed.

What we *want* is cash flow; so the typical solution is to add back noncash items such as depreciation, amortization, and deferred taxes, which leaves us with the traditional cash flow.

2. *The information we want is not what we need.*

What we *want*, or what analysts typically try to estimate, is cash flow from operations (CFO). Using CFO helps eliminate the issues involved with accounting differences such as the use of LIFO/FIFO and different revenue recognition policies. However, CFO does not truly reflect what we *need*, which we discuss next.

3. *The information we need, we can have, if only we look.*

What we really need is an estimate of the cash that can be withdrawn from a business after the company has made all required investments to sustain its future growth. This is best described as the free cash flow of a company and can be estimated as: Free cash flow = CFO – "Normal" capital expenditure requirements – Net borrowing. This cash flow estimate not only adjusts for the accounting problems discussed in items 1 and 2, but also ensures the company grows in the long run and does not "run down" its assets to sustain profitability in the short run.

ETHICS | Accounting Tricks 101: Off-Balance-Sheet Financing

Chesapeake Energy, a natural gas company, made a number of deals with large banks in which in exchange for cash, Chesapeake Energy promised to repay this debt in oil and natural gas every month until 2022.[40] Therefore, the value of what is paid on the debt depends on oil and gas prices, which are quite uncertain; hence, it is difficult to judge the cost of this capital.

Though this cash was received in exchange for this promise of oil and gas, which amounts to a debt obligation of uncertain cost, it was not reported on Chesapeake Energy's financial statements because it was accounted for as an off-balance-sheet obligation. What is uncertain is just how much this cash today will cost Chesapeake in the future.

To summarize, the cash flows we will use in the DCF valuation approach will be the company's free cash flows. These free cash flows, which are defined in Equation 21-1, are the free cash flows to equity holders because these cash flows represents what is left over after all obligations, including interest payments, have been paid.[41]

[39] Pearson Hunt, "Funds Position: Keystone in Financial Planning," *Harvard Business Review*, Vol. 52 (May/June 1975), pp. 106–115.

[40] Russell Gold, "Costly Liabilities Lurk for Gas Giant," *Wall Street Journal*, May 10, 2012.

[41] It also assumes the company does not issue any new debt, which would be added to the free cash flow amount. We ignore this component of free cash flow to equity for valuing takeover targets because the new financing would presumably come from the acquiring company going forward. The free cash flow to the company (both equity and debt holders) would simply be the free cash flow to equity plus the after-tax amount of the interest payments (less any new debt issued that was added to determine free cash flow to equity).

Free cash flow to equity (FCFE) = Cash flow from operations − Capital expenditures
+ Net borrowing   (21-1)

The next step is to discount all the future cash flow estimates back to the present, as we depict in Equation 21-2. This equation is the generalized version of the dividend discount model; the only difference is that we use cash flows in the numerator instead of dividends. Because we are using free cash flow to equity, the appropriate discount rate is the risk-adjusted cost of equity for the target company, r_e.[42]

Similar to the constant-growth version of the dividend discount model, we can simplify the valuation if we assume that these cash flows grow at some constant annual rate (g) to infinity.

$$V_0 = \frac{FCFE_1}{r_e - g} \qquad (21\text{-}2)$$

In practice, it is common to refine this process so that we can focus on estimating cash flows that will arise in the short to medium term and then make some simplifying assumption about cash flows beyond some terminal date (T):

$$V_0 = \frac{FCFE_1}{(1 + r_e)^1} + \frac{FCFE_2}{(1 + r_e)^2} + \dots + \frac{FCFE_\infty}{(1 + r_e)^\infty} = \sum_{t=1}^{\infty} \frac{FCFE_t}{(1 + r_e)^t}$$

$$= \left(\sum_{t=1}^{T} \frac{FCFE_t}{(1 + r_e)^t} \right) + \frac{V_T}{(1 + r_e)^T} \qquad (21\text{-}3)$$

The final term in this equation is the terminal value (V_T). This value is the present value of all future cash flows from time Z to infinity, and we estimate this assuming a reasonable sustainable annual growth rate in cash flows from some time T forward.

Let's see how this works for an acquisition. We are given the following information about a potential takeover candidate company, Tomar Company, for next year, based on what it is expected to contribute after it is acquired (i.e., with any arising synergies included):

Financial Item	Expected Value
EBIT	$2,000,000
Interest payments	$200,000
Depreciation and amortization expense	$100,000
Deferred taxes	$50,000
Tax rate	42 percent
Increase in net working capital	$200,000
Capital expenditures	$150,000

We calculate Tomar's free cash flow to equity next year using the expected net income, adjustments to net income to arrive at cash flows from operations, and capital expenditures. To keep it simple, let's assume that there is no borrowing or payoff of debt obligations. Net income is $986,000:

	EBIT	$2,000,000
Less	Interest payments	200,000
Less	Depreciation and amortization expense	100,000
Equals	Taxable income	$1,700,000
Less	Taxes	714,000
Equals	Net income	$986,000

[42] If we instead had decided to use free cash flow to the company, we would need to use the target company's weighted average cost of capital as the appropriate discount rate. Our discussion in Chapter 20 shows us that this discount rate reflects all financing costs, and therefore we should not include interest payments in our cash flow estimates. By using free cash flow to the company, we have already made this adjustment because we added back the after-tax interest amount to the free cash flow to equity estimates.

And cash flow from operations is therefore $936,000:

	Net income		$986,000
Plus	Depreciation and amortization expense		100,000
Less	Increase in net working capital		200,000
Plus	Deferred taxes		50,000
Equals	Cash flow from operations		$936,000

The free cash flow to equity is therefore $786,000:

	Cash flow from operations	$936,000
Less	Capital expenditures	150,000
Equals	Free cash flows to equity	$786,000

What is the value of Tomar's equity in total, and on a per share basis, assuming:

- that next year's free cash flow increases annually at a 5 percent rate indefinitely;
- the company has 500,000 shares outstanding;
- its stock has a beta of 1.2;
- the expected return on the market is 10 percent, and the risk-free rate is 4 percent; and
- a constant growth in cash flows to infinity.

Using the CAPM to estimate the cost of equity, r_e, we estimate that the cost of equity is 11.2 percent:

$$r_e = r_f + \beta(r_M - r_f) = 0.04 + 1.2(0.10 - 0.04) = 11.20 \text{ percent}$$

If the growth rate is 5 percent and the perpetual cash flows is $786,000, then the value of the equity is $12,677,419:

$$V_0 = \frac{FCFE_1}{r_e - g} = \frac{\$786,000}{0.112 - 0.05} = \$12,677,419$$

Therefore, the per share value is $12,677,419 ÷ 50,000 = $25.355.

Now let's see what happens when we value a company that has nonconstant growth of cash flows. Suppose we are given the following information about a potential takeover candidate company for the next 3 years.

	Year 0	Year 1	Year 2	Year 3
Net income	$1,450	$1,500	$1,550	$1,600
Depreciation	100	100	100	100
Deferred taxes	50	50	50	55
Accounts receivable	200	230	250	260
Inventory	150	160	180	190
Accounts payable	210	230	240	250
Capital expenditures	80	70	80	90
Dividends	150	150	160	160

After 3 years, analysts expect Tomar's free cash flow to grow at 6 percent per year indefinitely. We can estimate the value of Tomar's equity using DCF analysis. Let's assume that the appropriate discount rate is 12 percent.

		Year 1	Year 2	Year 3
	Net income	$1,500	$1,550	$1,600
Add	Depreciation	100	100	100
Add	Deferred taxes	150	150	155
Subtract	Increase in accounts receivable	230	220	210
Subtract	Increase in inventory	210	220	210
Add	Increase in accounts payable	120	110	110
Subtract	Capital expenditures	270	280	290
Equals	Free cash flow to equity	$1,560	$1,590	$1,655

Because we are assuming constant growth after 3 years:

$$V_0 = \left(\sum_{t=1}^{3} \frac{FCFE_t}{(1 + r_e)^t} \right) + \frac{V_3}{(1 + r_e)^3}$$

Now, we need to estimate the terminal value after three years, which can be determined using the constant growth version of the discounted cash flow formula, because g is 6 percent per year from year 3 to infinity.

$$V_3 = \frac{FCFE_{3+1}}{r_e - g} = \frac{\$1,655 \times 1.06}{0.12 - 0.06} = \$29,238.33$$

Now, we can estimate the value of the Tomar Company today:

$$V_0 = 1,392.86 + 1,267.54 + 1,178.00 + \frac{\$29,238.33}{1.12^3} = \$24,649.66$$

The Acquisition Decision

Determining the value of a takeover candidate is a critical part of the takeover decision process because an acquisition will only make sense if the target company can be acquired for a price that is less than its value to the acquiring company. For example, an acquisition of the Tomar Company in the last example would add value if it can be acquired at a cost less than or equal to $24,650.

Suppose the Grande Company estimates that it can purchase the Tomar Company in one of two ways: (1) by paying $24.00 per share in cash; or (2) by giving the Tomar Company's shareholders two shares in the new combined Company G-T for each share of the Tomar Company. Prior to the merger, the Tomar Company had 1,000 shares outstanding, which are trading at $20 per share, and the Grande Company had 3,000 shares outstanding, trading at $12 per share. Assuming that the Grande Company is properly priced prior to the acquisition, should the Grande Company acquire the Tomar Company? If so, which method should it use to acquire the Tomar Company?

To answer these questions, we need to first estimate the cost under each method.

Cash

The cost is $24 × 1,000 = $24,000, which means that purchasing the Tomar Company by cash would generate an NPV of $24,650 − $24,000 = $650.

Stock

Because the Grande Company is giving the Tomar Company's shareholders two of its shares (worth $12 each) for every share of the Tomar Company, and because the Tomar Company has 1,000 shares outstanding, the cost appears to be 2,000 shares × $12 = $24,000; however, this is not correct because what the Grande Company is really giving to the

Tomar Company's shareholders is 2,000 shares in the new company, Company G-T, which is created from the merger. To estimate the cost, we must therefore estimate the value of the new Company G-T after the merger:

$$\text{Postmerger value of G-T} = \frac{\text{Value of the}}{\text{Grande Company}} + \frac{\text{Value of the Tomar Company}}{\text{to the Grande Company}}$$

$$= (3,000 \times \$12) + 24,650$$

$$= \$60,650$$

Because there will be $3,000 + 2,000$ (new shares issued) $= 5,000$ shares outstanding in the new company, each share will be worth $\$60,650 \div 5,000 = \$12.13$.

So, the actual cost of giving the Tomar Company's shareholders 2,000 shares is:

$$\text{Cost} = 2,000 \text{ shares} \times \$12.13 \text{ per share} = \$24,260.$$

Thus, the NPV under this scenario would be $\$24,650 - \$24,260 = \$390$.

This example highlights the analysis: Using cash lets the original shareholders keep the expected NPV, whereas using a share swap lets the target company shareholders share in the NPV. Clearly if the company is very confident in the NPV, it should use cash, but if the NPV is highly uncertain, then a share swap reduces the risk to the original shareholders.

Concept Review Questions

1. What is fair market value?

2. What key multiples can we use in valuing companies?

3. Why do differing capital structures cause problems with using P/E multiples?

4. When does EPS increase when using a share swap?

21.4 ACCOUNTING FOR ACQUISITIONS

purchase method method of accounting for business combinations where one company assumes the fair market value of all of the assets and liabilities of the other (target) company and all operating results included from the date of acquisition going forward

Companies use the **purchase method** for accounting for acquisitions.[43] The purchase method requires valuing the assets and liabilities of the acquired firm and then adding these to these to those of the acquiring firm. We illustrate this process in Figure 21-6.

Under the purchase method, one company (the acquirer) basically assumes all the assets and liabilities of the other company (the target) and all operating results included from the date of acquisition going forward. No restatement of prior periods' results is necessary. At the time of the acquisition, all the assets and liabilities of the target company are restated to reflect its fair market value (FMV) as of the acquisition date. Because we know that equity is defined as assets minus liabilities, this implies the difference between the FMV of the target company's assets and liabilities is the FMV of its equity. If the purchase price exceeds the FMV of the target company's equity, the excess amount is

[43] Historically, companies could use one of two methods to account for business combinations: the purchase method or the pooling-of-interests method. However, the Financial Accounting Standards Board (FASB) of the United States eliminated the pooling-of-interests method of accounting for business combinations as of June 30, 2001, and the International Accounting Standards Board (IASB) also no longer permits the use of the pooling method. The accounting for business combinations is detailed in the International Financial Reporting Standards 3, effective in 2004, and amended in 2010.

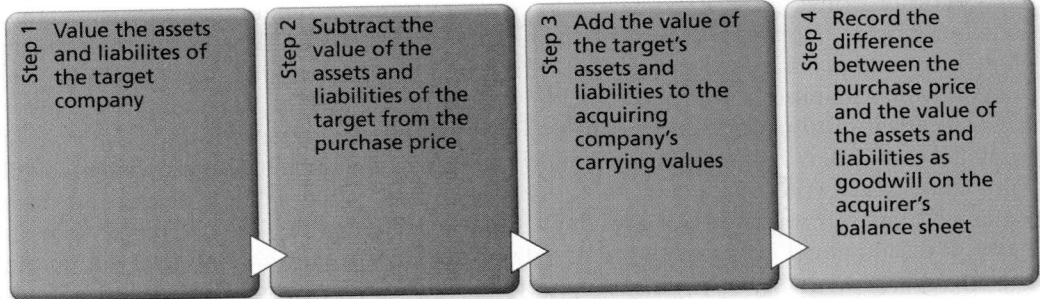

FIGURE 21-6 **The Purchase Method of Accounting for Business Combinations**

referred to as **goodwill**, which is reported on the asset side of the balance sheet for the new entity.

Assume Company B acquires Company C for $1,250 in cash on June 30, 2010. The balance sheets for B and C on that date, as well as the estimated market values for Company C's assets and liabilities, are:

	Company B	Company C Book Value	Company C Fair Market Value
Current assets	$10,000	$1,200	$1,300
Long-term assets	6,000	800	900
Total	$16,000	$2,000	$2,200
Current liabilities	$8,000	$800	$800
Long-term debt	2,000	200	250
Common stock	2,000	400	1,250
Retained earnings	4,000	600	
Total	$16,000	$2,000	$2,300

How do we construct Company B's balance sheet after the acquisition using the purchase method? We combine the two companies by adding the book values of Company B to the fair market values of Company C. Because Company B is acquiring the stock of Company C, Company C's equity ceases to exist in terms of the combined company's equity. When we add the values of Company B and C, we come up $100 short in terms of balancing assets with liabilities and equity. This $100 becomes the goodwill:

	Company B (Premerger)	Company B (Postmerger)
Current assets	$10,000	$11,300
Long-term assets	6,000	6,900
Goodwill	0	100
Total	$16,000	$18,300
Current liabilities	$8,000	$8,800
Long-term debt	2,000	2,250
Common stock	2,000	3,250
Retained earnings	4,000	4,000
Total	$16,000	$18,300

In other words, goodwill is the excess of what Company B paid for Company C that could not be accounted for in terms of acquired assets, less liabilities—or, in other words, how much the purchase price exceeds the acquired company's fair value. A cynical view of goodwill is that it is how much a company has overpaid to acquire another company.

Goodwill resulting from an acquisition may not be amortized.[44] Rather, the market value of goodwill must be assessed annually, and the company may write down goodwill and charge this write-off directly to earnings per share if the value is deemed to have been permanently impaired. As a result of this new treatment of goodwill, its fair value is subject to an annual impairment test. As discussed earlier, the value of goodwill on the balance sheet is what is left over after properly valuing everything else. As a result, companies are required to employ common valuation techniques, such as detailed discounted cash flow analysis, to determine fair value. The challenge for companies valuing goodwill is that it is what could not be attributed to a particular asset.

The Effect of an Acquisition on Earnings Per Share

Earnings per share (EPS) growth became a motive for several mergers and acquisitions during the 1960s. An acquiring company can increase its EPS if it acquires a company that has a P/E ratio lower than its own P/E ratio, even if no synergies arise from the merger. How does this happen? We can illustrate this with an example. Suppose that Company M acquires Company N for cash at Company N's present market value, and no synergies arise. Consider the following premerger information:

	Company M	Company N
Total earnings	$10,000	$3,000
Number of common shares outstanding	4,000	2,000
EPS	$2.50	$1.50
Market price per share (P_0)	$20	$9.00
P/E ratio	8 times	6 times
Total market value of equity	$80,000	$18,000

For the new company M + N:

Earnings = $10,000 + $3,000 = $13,000

Shares outstanding = 4,000 (i.e., the number of shares Company M had outstanding)

Postmerger EPS = $13,000 ÷ 4,000 = $3.25

Notice that if the market was inefficient and the P/E ratio for Company M remained at 8, the value of M + N would equal EPS × P/E ratio = $3.25 × 8 = $26.00. Therefore, the market value of M + N would equal $26.00 × 4,000 = $104,000.

This is well above what it should be in an efficient market because we know the combined market value should equal the market value of M plus the market value of N because we assumed no synergies were created. In other words, the combined market value of M + N should equal 80,000 + 18,000 = $98,000, and the total market value of M (after paying cash for N) is $80,000. This implies that the P/E ratio should be: $98,000 ÷ $13,000 = 7.54, and the share price for M + N should equal $3.25 × 7.54 = $24.50, not $26.00.

In an efficient market, the market value of the combined company should be $98,000 in the example, and not $104,000. Given full disclosure, analysts are aware of the earnings multiplier game and see through such accounting gimmicks. This would mean that the accounting motivation for M&A is not significant. However, many companies do not seem to disclose the full extent of their acquisitions.[45]

[44] Under accounting rules prior to 2002, goodwill was amortized.

[45] For example, Tyco, the large U.S. conglomerate, was the target of much criticism for its disclosure of its M&A activity, with some suspicion that its earnings were in part from accounting and not organic growth.

Losses in Good-Will Values Compound Bank Troubles

LESSONS LEARNED

When times were flush, businesses bought up rivals and absorbed smaller companies to grow as big as possible as fast as possible. But now, those purchases are starting to look a lot like housing bought at the peak of the bubble—overpriced and losing value fast.

Companies are taking billions of dollars in losses as they write down the value of assets known as good will—the amount they overpaid for a business compared with the sum of its parts. As the economy sinks lower and businesses struggle, that good will is going bad.

The losses from these write-downs have already been in the tens of billions of dollars, and analysts say they are likely to continue as companies reassess the value of old deals in the light of faltering stock markets, declines in real estate and weak corporate revenues.

"It's not the end of the tragedy," said Feng Gu, an assistant professor at the State University of New York at Buffalo and an author of a paper on good-will impairments with Baruch Lev, a professor at New York University. "Things continue to get worse."

For the nation's banks, which are already bracing for another spate of big losses from commercial real estate loans and credit card businesses, the rapid declines in good will represent another potential source of losses.

Banks wrote down more than $25 billion in good will in 2008, up sharply from $790 million a year earlier, according to data compiled by Frank Schiraldi of Sandler O'Neill & Partners. By the end of the year, banks still had $291 billion worth of good will on their books. An incomplete tally of write-downs from the first quarter showed that banks had taken a $3.5 billion hit to good-will values.

For some companies, the losses will be staggering.

Before it was scooped up in a merger with Wells Fargo last year, the Wachovia Corporation cut the value of its good will by $18.7 billion, largely from its purchase of the troubled mortgage lender Golden West Financial and other acquisitions that took on water as housing markets sank and the economy hurtled lower.

Macy's took a good-will charge of $5.4 billion in 2008. In February 2008, the cellular carrier Sprint Nextel wrote down $30 billion from Sprint's purchase of Nextel.

Companies characterize the hits as nothing more than accounting losses, a revaluing of assets that were not tangible to begin with. And they say the write-downs do not threaten their credit, their cash flow or their long-term health.

"It was just a paper entry sitting on your balance sheet," said Rex S. Schuette, chief financial officer of United Community Banks, which wrote down $70 million of good will in the first quarter.

But the losses take a real bite out of corporate earnings, like a first-quarter good-will charge of $2.6 billion

at Huntington Bancshares that contributed to its $2.4 billion first-quarter loss. And they could lead to more declines in company share prices as many are grappling with declining market value, crumbling real estate portfolios and lower revenues.

"Investors will have to be wary of these things," said J. Edward Ketz, an associate professor of accounting at the Pennsylvania State University, who has studied good will. "You never know when an intangible asset is going to be written off."

If nothing else, the decline in the value of good will shows that corporations across the spectrum spent far too much during the merger mania of the last decade, analysts said. As the markets roared higher, companies looked at their rising share prices like lottery money, and deployed their stock to go on a buying binge, eager to show shareholders growth and expanding sources of revenue.

If the mergers were lavish wedding ceremonies, the slumping value of the good will has been the rocky marriages that followed.

"If they overpaid for it and they have to take a write-down, that definitely is an indicator that they overpaid, and that the corporate acquisition group is not doing its job that well," said William Hughes, managing director of the Valuation Research Corporation.

The value of good will represents intangible qualities like the value of a company's brand name, its customer base and reputation. Every year, companies that list good will as a leftover asset from mergers have to test its value to see whether it has held up.

SunTrust Banks, based in Atlanta, had been monitoring its $7 billion in good will every quarter since the end of 2007, and cut its value by $715 million this spring. The bank said it had made the write-down because economic declines had continued to hammer its mortgage and commercial real estate assets.

"There's been some erosion in financial performance, but the uncertainty and sentiment in the marketplace has also had a meaningful effect," said the bank's controller, Thomas E. Panther.

For the quarter, SunTrust reported a net loss of $815 million but said the good-will charge had no effect on its levels of capital required by government regulators. It also said that some signs of improvement in deposits and mortgage lending were emerging and that it thought it had revalued its good will to match current conditions.

Although SunTrust played down the significance of the write-down, the analysis of good-will losses by Mr. Gu and Mr. Lev found that they often presaged rough waters ahead. If the write-downs mount, they can lead businesses to cut jobs, reduce capital investments, slash budgets and close plants.

Still, the losses don't mean that businesses have less money to pay off their debts, or that they are on the brink of insolvency. And with investors already bracing for the worst, some analysts said the good-will write-downs did not provide much additional shock.

"You're pushed down so low anyhow," Mr. Hughes said. "What's more bad news on top of bad news?"

Source: Jack Healy, "Losses in Good-Will Values Compound Bank Troubles," *New York Times*, April 26, 2009.

Concept Review Questions

1. Explain how the purchase method may result in goodwill.

2. How is goodwill treated for accounting purposes?

SUMMARY

- There are various forms of business combinations, including mergers and acquisitions. We can classify mergers and acquisitions on the basis of the response of the target company's board of directors (friendly versus hostile) and on the basis of the lines of business of the companies involved (horizontal, vertical, or conglomerate).

- The motives to merge or acquire another company are related to the expected benefits or synergies from the combination, which include operating synergies, gains from efficiencies, expanded capacity to take on debt, and tax benefits.

- We can evaluate a potential takeover candidate using the multiples approach and using discounted cash flow analysis.

- An acquisition can affect a company's financial statements, earnings per share, and other measures of performance.

FORMULAS/EQUATIONS

(21-1) Free cash flow to equity (FCFE) = Cash flow from operations − Capital expenditures + Net borrowing

(21-2) $V_0 = \dfrac{FCFE_1}{r_e - g}$

(21-3) $V_0 = \dfrac{FCFE_1}{(1 + r_e)^1} + \dfrac{FCFE_2}{(1 + r_e)^2} + \cdots + \dfrac{FCFE_\infty}{(1 + r_e)^\infty} = \sum_{t=1}^{\infty} \dfrac{FCFE_t}{(1 + r_e)^t} = \left(\sum_{t=1}^{T} \dfrac{FCFE_t}{(1 + r_e)^t} \right) + \dfrac{V_T}{(1 + r_e)^T}$

QUESTIONS AND PROBLEMS

Multiple Choice

1. Which of the following statements about takeovers is *false*?
   A. An acquisition of assets is one of the types of takeover.
   B. Mergers create a new company, whereas acquisitions do not.
   C. Both mergers and acquisitions require two-thirds votes from both companies.
   D. In the tender offer, the acquiring company makes a public offer to purchase shares of the target company.

2. Which of the following is *not* a type of merger or acquisition?
   A. Vertical   B. Horizontal   C. Proxy contest   D. Conglomerate

3. Which of the following is a poor motive for mergers and acquisitions as suggested by evidence?

   A. Diversification
   B. Economies of scale
   C. Economies of scope
   D. Complementary strengths

4. Which of the following is an example of a horizontal merger?

   A. An electric utility acquiring a coal mining company.
   B. A candy company buying a sugar producer.
   C. A retail department store chain buying a chemical company.
   D. A nuts and bolts manufacturer buying another nuts and bolts manufacturer.

5. Which of the following is *not* a reason for financial synergies?

   A. Increased debt capacity
   B. Reduced cash flow volatility
   C. Reduced average issuing costs
   D. Increased need of external financing

6. What is the market value of the equity of a company that has a trailing P/E ratio of 4.5 and expected earnings (E_1) of $550,000? The company is expected to grow at 5 percent.

   A. $1,850,000
   B. $2,050,099
   C. $2,357,143
   D. $2,475,000

7. Which of the following companies will have the *lowest* reported earnings figure, assuming all other information is the same? (Assume increasing prices for inventory.)

   A. A company using LIFO to account for inventory and accelerated depreciation methods
   B. A company using FIFO to account for inventory and accelerated depreciation methods
   C. A company using LIFO to account for inventory and straight-line depreciation methods
   D. A company using FIFO to account for inventory and straight-line depreciation methods

8. Which of the following cash flow measures is most appropriate to use in evaluating an acquisition?

   A. Free cash flow
   B. Traditional cash flow
   C. Cash flow from investing (CFI)
   D. Cash flow from operations (CFO)

9. Which of the following statements of liquidation valuation is *false*?

   A. Liquidation valuation approach is not forward looking.
   B. Liquidation value equals liquidation value of current assets and market value of tangible assets.
   C. Overdue accounts receivable with bad credit companies should be realized at a relatively low percentage of book value.
   D. Current accounts receivable with good credit companies should be realized at a relatively high percentage of book value.

10. Which of the following company structures is least likely to be the target for a bidder?

    A. Many legal problems
    B. The stock is undervalued
    C. Simple corporate structure
    D. Common shares are widely held

Practice Questions and Problems

21.1   Types of Takeovers

11. List and briefly describe the different types of takeovers based on the lines of business of the parties to the takeover.

12. Briefly describe three common defensive tactics against a takeover.

13. The Buyum Private Equity group has just made a tender offer for at most 60 percent of the Sellum Company. Sellum has 1,000 shares outstanding. Mr. Smith is a shareholder of Sellum and has tendered his shareholdings. For each situation given, indicate how many of Mr. Smith's shares will be accepted by Buyum.

	Total Shares Tendered by Sellum Shareholders	Mr. Smith Tendered	Total Number of Shares Accepted by Buyum	Number of Mr. Smith's Shares Accepted by Buyum
A	1,000	400		
B	1,000	300		
C	500	400		
D	500	300		
E	500	100		

14. Consider the possible merger between Company M and Company N. The market shares of the companies in the industry are as follows:

Company	Market Share
Company L	40%
Company M	25%
Company N	20%
Company O	10%
Company P	5%

A. What is the Herfindahl-Hirschman index for this industry before the merger of M and N?

B. What is the expected change in the HHI if M and N merge?

C. Would this be considered a merger that would reduce competition? Explain your reasoning.

15. Consider the possible merger between Company V and Company Z. The market shares of the companies in the industry are as follows:

Company	Market Share
Company U	35%
Company V	25%
Company W	20%
Company X	10%
Company Y	5%
Company Z	5%

A. What is the Herfindahl-Hirschman index for this industry before the merger of V and Z?

B. What is the expected change in the HHI if V and Z merge?

C. Would this be considered a merger that would reduce competition? Explain.

16. ABC Inc. is planning to purchase DEF Inc. in one of two ways: (1) by paying $22 per share in cash; or (2) by giving DEF's shareholders two shares in the new combined company ABC-DEF for each share of DEF. Prior to the merger, DEF had 500,000 shares outstanding trading at $20 per share. ABC had 600,000 shares outstanding trading at $18 per share. Assume that ABC is properly priced prior to the acquisition. DEF is valued at $15,875,000 to ABC. Should ABC acquire DEF? If so, which method should it use to acquire DEF?

21.2 Motives for Mergers and Acquisitions

17. Consider a merger between two companies: a food processor and a grocery store chain. Identify the possible synergies from this merger.

18. For each of the following, classify the merger as horizontal, vertical, or conglomerate:

	Acquirer	Target	Type of Merger
A.	Electric utility	Coal company	
B.	Retail discount store	Warehouse store	
C.	Oil refinery	Gasoline additives	
D.	Gasoline company	Ethanol producer	

19. You are a risk arbitrageur and you observe the following information about a deal: The current price of the target is $20 per share, and the current price of the bidder is $15 per share. The bidder is offering two bidder shares per target share, and you expect the deal to be completed in 1 year. Neither company is expected to pay dividends over the next year. Assume you can freely short sell and there are no margin requirements. You do not use any leverage.

   A. Calculate the offer premium.
   B. Clearly describe the transaction you will undertake to capture the premium.
   C. Show how your transaction will make money.
   D. Is it possible that your actual return will not equal the expected return? Describe two situations that can cause the risk in risk arbitrage.

21.3 Valuation Issues

20. Consider a company with the following financial information:

Sales	$1,550,000
CGS	350,000
Depreciation	400,000
Interest	150,000
Income tax	260,000
Dividends	300,000
Common shares outstanding	500,000
P/EBITDA	10X

   A. Calculate the market price of the company's common shares using a relative valuation approach.
   B. Calculate the trailing and forward P/E ratio. Assume a 6 percent earnings growth.
   C. Calculate the trailing and forward P/E ratio using the following assumptions: The risk-free rate of interest is 5 percent; β is 0.65; the market risk premium is 5 percent; dividends and earnings grow at 6 percent indefinitely; and the company maintains its current dividend payout ratio.

21. Before the market opened on Monday, Bunns and Bagels (B&B) announced that it had received a merger offer from Franks' Fine Franks. By the end of trading on Monday, B&B has earned a return of –2 percent (negative 2 percent). The return on the market that day was 4 percent, and the daily risk-free rate was close to zero. The beta for B&B is 2, with a standard deviation of the regression of 2 percent.

   A. What is the abnormal return for B&B on Monday?
   B. Given the empirical evidence on mergers and acquisitions, is the market's reaction unusual? Why or why not?

21.4 Accounting for Acquisitions

22. Consider the following additional information for a company:
   - cost of equity is 8.25%;
   - free cash flow to equity grows at 6 percent indefinitely;

- total debt outstanding of $1,000,000;
- increase in current assets of $400,000;
- increase in current liabilities of $300,000; and
- capital expenditures of $100,000.

A. Calculate the market value of the company.

B. If the free cash flow to equity grows at 8 percent for the first 2 years and then grows at 5 percent indefinitely, what is the market value of the company now?

23. Complete the following balance sheet for the postmerger company B-T. The bidder acquired the target for $2,000 *in cash*.

	Bidder	Target Book Value	Target Fair Market Value	B-T (Postmerger)
Current assets	$25,000	$3,500	$2,900	
Long-term assets	$10,000	$1,000	1,300	
Goodwill				
Total assets	$35,000	$4,500	4,200	
Current liabilities	$11,000	$1,500	$1,500	
Long-term debt	5,000	800	1,000	
Common stock	15,000	1,800	2,000	
Retained earnings	4,000	400		
Total	$35,000	$4,500	$4,500	

24. Calculate the postmerger EPS and market value of equity, assuming no synergies arise in this acquisition settled in cash. Analyze the difference, if there is any. Further, calculate the *new* P/E ratio and share price for postmerger B-T. Additional information is given as follows:

	Bidder	Target
Total earnings	$25,000	$7,000
Number of common shares outstanding	8,000	3,500
EPS	$3.13	$2.00
Market price per share	$29.50	$12.00
P/E ratio	9 times	6 times
Total market value of equity	$236,000	$42,000

Cases

Case 21.1 The Merger of Alpha and Beta

The Alpha Company is considering a bid for the Beta Company. The balance sheets of Alpha and Beta are as follows:

Alpha Company
Balance sheet as of 12/31/2012

Tangible assets	$50,000		
Accumulated depreciation	32,000	Total debt	$15,000
Net tangible assets	$18,000		
Goodwill	3,000	Equity	6,000
Total assets	$21,000	Total capital	$21,000

Beta Company
Balance sheet as of 12/31/2012

Tangible assets	$31,000		
Accumulated depreciation	10,000	Total debt	$19,000
Net tangible assets	$21,000		
Goodwill	0	Equity	2,000
Total assets	$21,000	Total capital	$21,000

The tax rate for both companies is 25 percent. The acquisition will be accounted for using the purchase method.

Prior to the acquisition, Alpha Company had 10,000 shares outstanding, with a share price of $20. Beta Company had 5,000 shares outstanding, with a market price of $10. Alpha acquired Beta by offering 0.80 bidder shares per target share. After analyzing the target, Alpha has decided that the market value of the Beta's assets is $65,000 and the market value of its own assets $45,000.

   A. How many shares will be outstanding for the combined company?
   B. What fraction of the combined company will be owned by Alpha's original shareholders?
   C. How much goodwill was created by this transaction?
   D. Show the consolidated balance sheets for the combined company (fill in the templates provided).

Pro Forma Balance Sheet of the Combined Company
As of 12/31/2012

Net tangible assets		Total debt	
Goodwill		Equity	
Total assets		Total capital	

Case 21.2 Stanford Sausage Company

Stan Ford is the CEO of Stanford Sausage Company (SSC), a publicly traded company, and believes that the best way for the company to grow is through acquisitions. He has identified a likely target, Princeton Pork Producers (PPP), a publicly traded company specializing in sausages and other pork products. SSC had revenues of $4 billion in fiscal year 2011, whereas PPP had revenues of $500 million in 2011.

   A. Describe two different possible types of motives for this acquisition.
   B. Stan is very uncertain about the value of PPP. Describe how he can structure the deal to reduce the risk to Stanford Sausage.
   C. Stan made an offer directly to the board of PPP, but his offer was rejected. Now Stan is contemplating making an offer directly to the shareholders of PPP. Is a takeover of PPP more likely to be friendly or hostile? Why?
   D. Is SSC more likely to use a tender offer or a merger offer? Why?
   E. Describe three ways PPP could try to defend itself from SSC.

ANSWERS TO MULTIPLE CHOICE QUESTIONS

CHAPTER 1
1 B
2 D
3 A
4 C
5 B
6 B
7 C
8 C
9 B
10 A

CHAPTER 2
1 A
2 C
3 A
4 A
5 B
6 C
7 B
8 C
9 B
10 B

CHAPTER 3
1 B
2 B
3 A
4 D
5 B
6 B
7 B
8 D Depreciation first year = $300,000 × 0.20
    = $60,000
9 B
10 D

CHAPTER 4
1 A Debt ratio = 2,000,000 ÷ $5,630,000 = 35.524%
2 B Debt-equity ratio = $2,000,000 ÷ $2,890,000
    = 69.2042%
    Times interest earned
    = ($360,000 + 150,000) ÷ $150,000 = 3.4

3 D Gross profit margin
    = ($1,090,000 − 380,000) ÷ $1,090,000
    = 65.1376%
    Operating margin
    = ($1,090,000 − 380,000 − 200,000) ÷ $1,090,000
    = 46.789%
4 A DSI = $250,000 ÷ ($380,000 ÷ 365) = 240 days
5 C Working capital ratio
    = ($400,000 + 500,000 + 250,000) ÷ $5,630,000
    = 20.426%
6 C Invested capital = $2,000,000 + 2,890,000
    = $4,890,000
7 B ROE = 0.05 × ($100 ÷ 50) = 10%
8 B
9 D ROA = 10% × 5 = 50%
10 D

CHAPTER 5
1 D $FV = \$1,000\,(1 + 0.05)^{10} = \$1,628.89$
2 D A: €1,800; B: €1,600; C: €1,838.46; D: €1,850.93
3 A Interest on interest = $12,166.53 − 12,000
    = $166.53
4 B $PV = ¥10\text{ million} ÷ (1 + 0.15)^{45}$
    = ¥0.185608 million or ¥18,561
5 C $i = \sqrt[8]{\text{£17,000}/\text{£10,000}} - 1 = 6.8578\%$
6 B $n = \dfrac{\ln 3 - \ln 1}{\ln(1 + 0.09)} = 12.7482$
7 C N = 20; PMT = $2,000; i
    = 10% ⇒ Solve for FV ⇒ FV = $114,550
8 B A: 10.2397%; B: 10.3618%; C: 10.1860%;
    D: 10.2934%
9 B PV = €1,500 ÷ 0.12 = €12,500
10 B 2nd payment: $199,800.9 × (0.06 ÷ 12)
    = $999.00 interest, $1,199.10 − 999
    = $200.10 principal

CHAPTER 6
1 A
2 A
3 A N = 10; i = 4%; PMT = 3.5 ⇒ PV = 95.9445
4 B N = 10; i = 4%; PMT = 2.5 ⇒ PV = 87.8337
5 D
6 C PV = 99.3; N = 12; PMT = 3.5 ⇒ i
    = 3.57275% ⇒ YTM = 7.1455%

7 A

8 B

9 B $5.5\% = [(\$10,000 - P) \div P] \times [365 \div 182];$
$P = \$9,733.07$

10 C

CHAPTER 7

1 C

2 B

3 C Required rate of return $= 0.04 + 0.065 = 10.5\%$

4 C Required rate of return
$$= 0.03 + 0.065 = 0.095 \Rightarrow P = \frac{\$2(1 + 0.045)}{0.095 - 0.045}$$
$$= \frac{\$2.09}{0.05} = \$41.8$$

5 C Required rate of return
$$= \frac{\$1.5(1 + 0.04)}{\$26} + 0.04 = 0.10 \text{ or } 10\%$$

6 D ROE $= \$9 \div \$36 = 25\%$ | Retention ratio
$= \$7.50 \div \$9.00 = 83.33\%$
Sustainable growth $= 83.33\% \times 25\% = 20.83\%$

7 A

8 C

9 D Value $= 15 \times \$3$ million $= \$15$ million

10 B $\dfrac{P_0}{EPS_1} = \dfrac{D_1 / EPS_1}{r_e - g} \quad \dfrac{P_0}{EPS_1}$

$\doteq \dfrac{\$2/\$5}{0.08 - 0.05} \quad \dfrac{P_0}{EPS_1} = \dfrac{0.40}{0.03} = 13.33$

CHAPTER 8

1 B Capital gain or loss $= \dfrac{\$24 - 25}{25} = -0.04 \text{ or } 4\%$

2 D Total return $= \dfrac{\$24 - 25 + 4}{25} = 0.12 \text{ or } 12\%$

3 B The geometric mean is less than the arithmetic mean

4 C Expected return
$= (0.3 \times 0.30) + (0.2 \times 0.4) + (0.5 \times 0.15)$
$= 0.09 + 0.08 + 0.075 = 24.5\%$

5 A

Probability	Possible return	Probability x return	Probability weighted squared deviations
30%	30%	0.090	0.0009075
20%	40%	0.080	0.0048050
50%	15%	0.075	0.0045125
		0.245	0.010225
		Standard deviation	**10.11%**

6 D

7 B

8 A

9 B Expected return on the portfolio
$= (0.25 \times 0.05) + (0.75 \times 0.1)$
$= 0.0125 + 0.075 = 8.75\%$

10 C

CHAPTER 9

1 D

2 B More return for the level of risk as predicted by the CAPM; therefore it is undervalued (when the price corrects, there will be an abnormally higher return)

3 C Expected return $= (0.2 \times 0.08) + (0.8 \times 0.2)$
$= 0.016 + 0.16 = 0.176 \text{ or } 17.6\%$
Standard deviation
$= \sqrt{(0.2^2 \times 0^2) + (0.8^2 \times 0.25^2) + 0}$
$= \sqrt{0.04} = 20\%$

4 A

5 D

6 C

7 C

8 B

9 C

10 B

CHAPTER 10

1 A PI $= (\$10 + 6) \div \$10 = 1.6$

2 D

3 A

Period	End of period cash flow
0	−$17,000
1	$0
2	$8,000
3	$8,000
4	$8,000
5	$8,000
6	$8,000
NPV	$2,937.41

Note: Cash flows are at the beginning of each period from 3 on, so this is equivalent to end of period cash flows from 2 on.

4 A

5 A

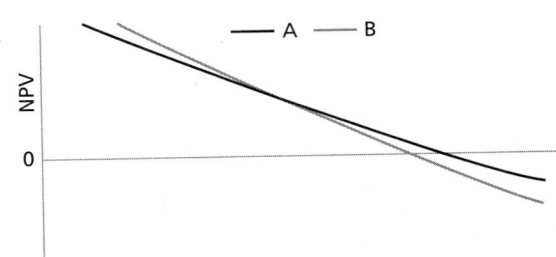

6   C $NPV_X = \$283$; $NPV_Y = \$351$

7   C   IRR = 35.87%. Note: the discount rate is not relevant for the calculation of the IRR.

8   B   The discount rate will be understated for high-risk projects.

9   C

10   A   This would be equivalent to a negative NPV project.

CHAPTER 11

1   A

2   A   Depreciation tax shield = $0.3 \times \$30,000 = \$9,000$

3   B   Change in annual cash flow
= $(\$50,000 - 18,000) \times (1-0.4) = \$19,200$

4   A   Depreciation tax shield
= $(\$300,000 \times 0.20) \times 0.40 = \$24,000$

5   B

6   C

7   A

8   B   Cash flow = $\$20,000 - (\$20,000 \times 0.35)$
= $\$13,000$

9   A   Investment cash flow
= $-\$400,050 - 90,000 + 15,000 - 5000 = \$480,050$

10   C   Investment cash flow
= $-\$120,000 + 75,000 - [0.4 \times (\$75,000 - 65,000)]$
= $-\$49,000$

CHAPTER 12

1   D

2   B   After-tax cost of debt = $0.08 \times (1 - 0.4) = 48\%$

3   B

4   C

5   D

6   D

7   B

8   D   Conversion value of the bond = $30 \times \$40$
= $\$1,200$

9   B   Bond equivalent yield
= $[(\$100 - 98) \div \$98] \times (360 \div 270) = 2.721\%$

10   C   After-tax cost of debt = $0.06 \times (1 - 0.38)$
= 3.72%

CHAPTER 13

1   A

2   B

3   D

4   A

5   A

6   C

7   D   Book value of equity = $\$1,000 + 50 + 100$
= $\$1,150$

8   A   Book value per share
= $\$500$ million $\div$ 100 million shares = $\$5$

9   A   Dividend yield = $\$1 \div \$30 = 3.33\%$

10   B

CHAPTER 14

1   B   Value of stock = $\$5.50 \div 0.15 = \$36.67$ per share

2   B   Earnings yield = $\$40,000 \div (\$10 \times 10,000)$
= 40%

3   B   Required return in dollar terms
= $0.125 \times \$69,000 = \$8,625$

4   C

5   C

6   C

7   D

8   A

9   A   Debt capital = $\$2$ million $+ 3$ million
= $\$5$ million

10   D   WACC = $[0.07 \times (1 - 0.40) \times 0.40]$
$+ [(((\$1.5 \times 1.04) \div \$20) + 0.04) \times 0.60]$
= $0.0168 + 0.0708 = 8.76\%$

CHAPTER 15

1   A   BE = $\$20,000 \div \$4 = 5,000$ units

2   B   DOL = $(\$30,000 - 20,000)$
$\div (\$30,000 - 20,000 - 1,000) = 1.1$

3   C   DTL = $1.5 \times 2 = 3.0$

4   D

5   A

6   D

7   B

8   D

9   C

10   C

CHAPTER 16

1   A

2   C

3   C

4   B

5   B   Share price = $\$20 \times (1 + g) \Rightarrow$ Solve for g: $\$20 = \$2 \div (0.10 - g) \Rightarrow g = 0\%$

6   C

7   C

8   C   DPO = $\$0.6$ million $\div \$3$ million = 20%

9   A   Dividend yield = $\$2 \div \$20 = 10\%$

10   D

CHAPTER 17

1   C

2   B

3   B

4   D

5   C

6   B   Sustainable growth = $0.20 \times (1 - 0.3) = 14\%$

7   C

8   C

9   D

10   A

CHAPTER 18
1 C
2 A Time value = $20 – 12.50 = $7.50
3 D
4 A
5 B
6 C
7 C
8 D
9 A
10 D

CHAPTER 19
1 C
2 C Current ratio = $3,103,000 ÷ $900,000
= 3.448 times
Quick ratio = $1,900,500 ÷ 900,000
= 2.1117 times
3 C DSO = $600,000 ÷ ($1,287,555 ÷ 365)
= 170.0898 days
4 D DSI = $1,203,000 ÷ ($550,000 ÷ 365) = 798.3545
Operating cycle = 180.0898 + 798.3545
= 968.444 days
5 B
6 C
7 B
8 A

9 B
10 C

CHAPTER 20
1 C
2 C
3 B
4 A
5 B
6 A
7 C N = 5; PMT = $5,000; i
= 8%; Annuity due ⇒ $21,560.63
8 D
9 D
10 D

CHAPTER 21
1 C
2 C
3 A
4 D
5 D
6 D Market value of equity = $550,000 × 4.5
= $2,475,000
7 A
8 A
9 B
10 A

4 Cs of credit factors that affect credit: capacity, character, collateral, and conditions

ABC approach division of inventory into several categories based on the value of the inventory items, their overall level of importance to the company's operations, and their profitability, to determine the time and effort devoted to their management

abnormal profit profit in excess of those expected for the asset's level of risk

absolute priority rule rule that any assets of the company in liquidation are distributed to creditors, in order of seniority, and, if anything remains, to shareholders

acid test ratio See *quick ratio*

acceptance fee See *stamping fee*

account manager financial professional who manages a bank's relationships with companies, extending credit, helping to manage receivables and cash, and directing them to the bank's more specialized services

accounting identity relationship resulting from double-entry bookkeeping such that assets are equal to the sum of liabilities and equity

accounts receivable turnover See *receivables turnover*

accounts payable amounts owed the suppliers of the business

accrual basis reporting convention in which revenues and expenses are recorded when a transaction occurs, regardless of when cash changes hands

accrued expenses amounts owed from transactions that have occurred but for which payment is not due

accumulated comprehensive income or loss income or loss that bypasses the income statement, going directly to equity

acquisition purchase of one company by another

active trading strategy trading based on timing the market, trends, or other criteria

activity ratios See *productivity ratios*

adjustable rate convertible subordinated security (ARCS) security that has fixed principal and maturity, and interest that normally comprises a fixed interest rate and some function of the dividend paid in the previous six months; typically convertible into common shares

adjustable rate preferred stock (ARPS) equity security issue for which the dividend yield is pegged to a specific interest rate

adverse opinion audit opinion when the financial statements do not represent fairly the financial position, results of operation, or the change in financial position in accordance with generally accepted accounting principles

affirmative covenant promise that the issuer makes regarding the debt obligation, such as the timely payment of interest

after-tax cost of debt net cost of the company using debt, calculated as the before-tax interest cost of the company's debt multiplied by one minus the corporate tax rate

agency costs costs associated with agency problems that arise from the inherent conflicts of interest between managers, owners, and creditors

agency problem issue or conflict that arises due to potential divergence of interest between managers, shareholders, and creditors

agency relationship relationship that occurs when managers work on behalf of the shareholders

Altman Z score predictive measure of the likelihood of a company filing for bankruptcy, based on a company's financial ratios

American option option that can be exercised at any time up to and including the expiration date

amortization expense deduction from income that reflects the reduction in the value of tangible assets over a period of time

amortization process of determining how much of each payment is interest and principal repayment; reduction in value of a long-lived intangible asset over a specified period of time

amortization schedule breakdown of each payment of an amortized loan into interest and principal components

amortize determine the repayment of a loan in which regular payments consist of both interest and principal

analyst entry-level job in a financial institution

anchoring tendency to use inappropriate or irrelevant factors in decision making

annual percentage rate (APR) stated rate of interest, calculated as the product of the interest rate per compounding period and the number of compounding periods

annuity due annuity for which the payments are made at the beginning of each period

annuity regular payments from an investment that are for the same amount and are paid at regular intervals of time

anomaly mispricing of an asset such that the pricing of the asset is not consistent with efficient markets

arb See *arbitrageur*

arbitrage pricing theory (APT) pricing model that uses multiple factors to relate expected returns to risk by assuming that asset returns are linearly related to a set of indexes, which are proxy risk factors that influence asset returns

arbitrage process of taking advantage of different pricing for the same item in different markets

arbitrageur specialist who predicts what happens in takeovers and buys and sells shares in target companies

arithmetic mean or **arithmetic average** sum of all observations divided by the total number of observations

articles of incorporation rules of the governance of the corporation that are filed with the state of incorporation

assessment bond security backed by the property taxes of a government entity

asset purchase purchase of the company's assets rather than the company itself

asset turnover See *total asset turnover ratio*

asset utilization ratios See *productivity ratios*

asset-backed commercial paper (ABCP) short-term debt instrument backed by the cash flows of specific securities, generally held in a special purpose vehicle

asset-backed note or **asset-backed bond** debt obligation that has a specific asset, a group of assets, or a set of future cash flows as collateral

asset-based lending financing that is tied directly to a particular asset

associate second-level job in a financial institution; it requires an MBA or a professional designation (e.g., CFA)

at the money situation in which the value of the underlying asset of an option is equal to the option's strike price

attainable portfolio collection of investments that may be constructed by combining the underlying assets and lies along the minimum variance frontier

auction market See *exchange market*

available-for-sale method of accounting for marketable securities is one in which unrealized gains or losses are reported as part of accumulated other comprehensive income

average collection period See *days sales outstanding*

balance sheet snapshot of the financial position of a company, listing assets on the left and liabilities and owner's equity on the right

balloon payment payment that represents repayment of some amount of the principal of loan above and beyond what is paid as part of the amortized loan payments

balloon principal See *bullet payment*

bank discount method convention for specifying the interest on a security that compares the amount of the discount with the face value of the security

bank discount yield method of stating interest rates that compares the discount with the face value of the security, annualized by 360 divided by the maturity of the security

bankers' acceptance (BA) short-term paper sold by an issuer to a bank, which guarantees or accepts it, obligating the bank to pay off the debt instrument at maturity if the issuer defaults

banking associate financial professional who generates reports on companies, prepares industry reports, and performs background checks on credit applicants

bankruptcy legal status of a company that permits the company to deal with debt problems

basic earnings per share (basic EPS) earnings per share of common stock based on the weighted average of the number of shares outstanding during the fiscal period

basis point one one-hundredths of 1 percent

behavioral finance study of how human behavior affects economic decision making

best price rule requirement that the bidder of a tender offer pay all security holders that tender shares the highest price paid in the tender offer

beta (ß$_i$) measure of market risk, or performance volatility, that relates the extent to which the return on an asset moves with that on the overall market; the covariance between an investment and the market divided by variance of the market

beta coefficient measure of a company's systematic or market risk

bill short-term debt instruments with an initial maturity of less than 1 year

bird in the hand argument notion that a cash dividend is worth more than an equivalent capital gain

bond equivalent method convention that specifies the yield on a security by comparing the discount to the C value of the security, and then annualizing

bond equivalent yield (BEY) yield for a short-term, discount security that is based on comparing the discount with the present value of the security, then annualizing

bond indenture legal document that specifies the payment requirements and all other salient matters relating to a particular bond issue, held and administered by a trust company

bond long-term debt instrument in which the borrower promises repayment, usually with interest, with an initial maturity longer than 7 years

bondholder party that lends funds by buying a bond issued by another party

book value per share shareholders' equity divided by the number of shares outstanding

bottom-up analysis investment strategy in which capital investment decisions are considered in isolation, without regard for whether the company should continue in this business or for general industry and economic trends

break fee See *termination fee*

break-up fee See *termination fee*

broker a market intermediary, who facilitates exchanges in a market.

bullet payment payment (partial or full) paid at maturity of a loan

business finance financing decision making within a business entity

business risk uncertainty regarding the operating earnings, which is influenced by both the sales risk and the operating risk of a company

buy-side analyst person whose job it is to evaluate the publicly available information for institutions in the capital market that invest in securities

C corporation business taxed as a corporation according to Subsection C of the Internal Revenue Code

call option right but not the obligation to buy an underlying asset at a fixed price within or at a specified time

call price price at which an issuer can buy back a bond from an investor of a callable bond

call protection provision that prohibits the issuer to call a bond for a specific length of time

call schedule series of call prices and applicable dates

callable bond debt obligation that give the issuer the option to repurchase outstanding bonds at predetermined prices at specified times

cannibalization competition of a new product with an existing product of the same company, resulting in diminished sales of the existing product

capacity customer's ability to pay

capital asset pricing model (CAPM) pricing model that describes the expected return on an asset as the sum of the risk-free rate of interest and compensation or a premium for bearing market risk

capital budgeting framework for analyzing investment or asset decisions; process through which a company makes capital expenditure decisions by identifying investment alternatives, evaluating these alternatives, implementing the chosen investment decisions, and monitoring and evaluating the implemented decisions

capital cost cost incurred to make an investment operational, such as machinery installation expenses, land-clearing costs, and so on

capital expenditure investment in long-lived assets, which may be tangible or intangible

capital expenditure analysis See *capital budgeting*

capital gain appreciation in the price of an asset from some starting point in time; in determining taxes, the taxable gain incurred when an asset is sold at a price greater than its original cost

capital gains yield return in the form of the appreciation or depreciation in the value of an asset

capital leases long-term rental agreements that are considered liabilities

capital loss depreciation in the price of an asset from some starting point in time; in determining taxes, the tax deductible loss generated when a nondepreciable asset is sold at a price lower than its original cost

capital market line (CML) line depicting the highest attainable expected return for any given risk level that includes only efficient portfolios

capital market security debt security with a maturity of greater than one year

capital rationing allotting investment capital among available investment projects

capital structure how a company finances its invested capital, consisting of debt capital and equity capital; mix of debt and equity used to finance an enterprise

capital yield See *capital gains yield*

capital sum of the interest-bearing debt and the equity of a company

captive finance company (CFC) company that finances companies that are divisions of major manufacturers to provide loans to purchase or lease their products

carrying value book value of an asset, which for a depreciable asset is the cost less accumulated depreciation

cash budget cash flow statement for each period

cash conversion cycle (CCC) estimate of the average time between when a company pays cash for its inventory purchases and when it receives cash for its sales

cash dividend payments to owners in the form of cash

cash flow bond debt obligation that has the same objectives as do income bonds

cash flow for/from financing (CFF) cash flow, on net, from financing activities

cash flow for/from investing (CFI) cash flow, on net, from investing activities

cash flow for/from operations (CFO) cash flow from the day-to-day operations of the business; the result of subtracting the increase in net working capital from traditional cash flow

cash flow statement See *statement of cash flows*

cash flow to debt ratio how long it takes to pay off a company's debt from its cash flow from operations; cash flow from operations divided by debt

cash flows actual cash generated from an investment

cash management bills short-term obligations of the U.S. government issued to meet temporary cash needs of the government

cash price the actual price paid for a debt obligation that considers the amount of accrued interest on the security

character how willing the company is to pay and how reliable and trustworthy the company is

characteristic line line of best fit through the returns on an individual asset, plotted on the vertical axis, relative to the returns for the market, plotted along the horizontal axis

chief financial officer (CFO) top financial manager in a company

clean price bond quote that does not consider the accrued interest

clearinghouse company that has the responsibility for reducing the credit risk and making sure that delivery takes place for futures contracts and option contracts

cognitive bias mistake in decision making that results from one's own preferences and beliefs

collateral the real estate, investments, and other property of the borrower; assets that are pledged to support a loan; assets that can serve as security for the bond in case of default

collateral trust bond bond secured by a pledge of other financial assets, such as common shares, bonds, or treasury bills

commercial paper (CP) short-term debt instruments, usually unsecured, issued by companies

commodity bond bond whose interest or principal is tied to the price of an underlying commodity, such as gold

commodity swap exchange of a fixed price for the floating price of a commodity

common life approach method of comparing mutually exclusive projects with different useful lives, assuming a finite number of replacements for each project, consistent with the projects' common life

common life revised useful life of projects considering a finite number of replacements such that the projects being compared have the same useful life

common share certificate of ownership in a corporation

common stock equity security that represents part ownership in a company and usually gives voting rights on major decisions affecting the company; residual ownership of a corporation

comparative advantage innate advantage that a company has over other companies due to access to resources, inputs, or markets

competitive advantage any strategy or feature that reduces the competition that the company experiences

compound factor amount that reflects the interest rate and the number of periods, which, when multiplied by a current or present value, results in the equivalent future value

compound interest arrangement in which interest is earned on the principal amount invested *and* on any accrued interest

compounding increase in value over time due to interest on both the principal amount and any interest earned up to that point in time

conditions state of the economy

confidentiality agreement document signed by a potential buyer guaranteeing it will keep confidential any information it sees in the data room about a target company

conglomerate merger merger in which two companies in unrelated businesses combine

constant growth DDM version of the dividend discount model for valuing common shares that assumes that dividends grow at a constant rate indefinitely

consultant See *corporate finance associate*

contingent interest interest on a debt security that is paid based on cash flows or earnings

contingent projects projects for which the acceptance of one requires the acceptance of another, either beforehand or simultaneously

continuously compounded interest or **continuous compounding** interest is instantaneous, compounded an infinite number of times

contribution margin portion of each dollar of sales that is available to cover fixed costs, after first satisfying variable costs; difference between the sales price per unit and the variable cost per unit

controller one of the two main finance jobs in a nonfinancial company; focuses on the accounting side: compliance, tax management, systems/MIS, internal audit, accounting, and budgeting

conversion premium difference between the value of a convertible security and the market value of the security into which it is convertible

conversion ratio number of common shares of the other security for which a convertible preferred share may be exchanged

conversion value value of the security the investor receives if he or she converts the security

convertible bond debt instrument that can be exchanged for a specified number of units of another security at a predetermined conversion price at the investor's option

convertible preferred stock preferred stock that can be exchanged for a specified number of units of another security

corporate finance associate finance professional who advises on restructuring, small-scale M&A, and corporate financing

corporate finance financial management of assets and financing decisions in a corporate enterprise

corporate governance set of processes and procedures established to manage the organization in the best interests of its owners

corporation business organized as a separate legal entity under corporation law, with ownership divided into transferable shares

correlation coefficient statistical measure that identifies how asset returns move in relation to one another; denoted by ρ

cost of capital the return the investor requires

costs of financial distress direct costs, opportunity costs, and losses to a company prior to declaring bankruptcy

counterparty party on the other side of a forward contract

counterparty risk See *credit risk*

coupon interest payment from a note or bond

coupon equivalent method See *bond equivalent method*

coupon rate percentage of a bond or note's face value that is paid in interest each year

covariance statistical measure of the the degree to which two or more series move together, or covary

covenant promise or restriction in a contract

credit analysis process designed to assess the risk of non-payment by potential customers

credit crunch lack of available loans for businesses

credit default swap (CDS) exchange of a payment or series of payments for a payoff in the event that the specified, underlying credit instrument (e.g., a bond) defaults; contract in which one party pays another party to assume a specified risk

credit enhancement action taken to reduce credit risk, such as requiring collateral, insurance, or other agreements

credit policy decisions on how a company grants, monitors, and collects payment for outstanding accounts receivable

credit risk uncertainty that a borrower will not repay what is owed or does not have the required payment

credit squeeze See *credit crunch*

credit watch status applied to a company by a rating agency when it is monitoring the company

creditor a party lending funds through a loan arrangement

creeping takeover acquisition of a target company over time by the gradual accumulation of its shares

crossover rate discount rate at which the net present value profiles of two projects cross

cumulative provision stipulation that no dividends can be paid on common shares until preferred share dividends, both current and arrears, are paid in full

currency future See *foreign currency future*

currency swap exchange of one currency for another to mitigate risk associated with specific assets or liabilities

current assets assets (cash and equivalents, short-term investments, accounts receivable, inventories, prepaid expenses) that are expected to be converted into cash within a year

current cost what it would cost to replace the asset or settle the liability

current liabilities short-term obligations

current ratio or **bankers' ratio** current assets divided by current liabilities

current yield (CY) the ratio of the annual coupon interest divided by the current market price

daily resettlement marking to market and adjusting investors' equity positions

data room place where a target company keeps confidential information about itself for serious potential buyers to consult

date of record See *record date*

day trader someone who buys and sells based on intraday price movements

days payables outstanding (DPO) number of days of purchases represented by the balance in accounts payable

days sales in inventory (DSI) average length of time between acquiring and selling inventory; number of days of sales represented by the amount in inventory

days sales outstanding (DSO) number of days, on average, that accounts receivable accounts are outstanding; number of days of sales represented by accounts receivable

dealer market secondary market that does not have a physical location and consists of a network of dealers who trade directly with one another

debenture debt instrument secured by a general claim on the issuer's unencumbered assets; debt obligation secured by the general credit of the issuer

debt capital interest-bearing obligations of an enterprise

debt contract between a lender and a borrower that stipulates the terms of repayment of a loan; promise by the borrower to repay the amount borrowed, plus interest

debt instrument legal obligation to repay borrowed funds at a specified maturity date and to provide interim interest payments

debt rating evaluation by professional debt-rating services after detailed analyses of bond issuers to determine their ability to make the required interest and principal payments

debt ratio total debt divided by total assets

debt-equity (D/E) ratio debt to shareholders' equity

debtor-in-possession (DIP) financing financing specifically for companies in financial distress that provides creditors more seniority than most existing claims of the distressed company

declaration date date on which the board of directors decides that the company will pay a dividend.

declining balance depreciation allocation of an asset's cost, less salvage value, over the life of the asset, with a rate applied against the declining carrying value of the asset

default free no risk of nonpayment

default risk uncertainty associated with the bond issuer and its ability to pay

default spread difference in yields attributed to the difference in default risk of the securities

deferred annuity annuity that begins two or more periods from the present

deferred income tax taxes that are anticipated to be paid in future years

deferred tax liability taxes that the company reasonably expects to pay in the future

degree of financial leverage (DFL) sensitivity of net income to changes in operating earnings, influenced by the use debt, relative to equity, as a source of capital

degree of operating leverage (DOL) measure of the sensitivity of the operating earnings to changes in the number of units produced and sold

degree of total leverage (DTL) sensitivity of net income to changes in unit sales, affected by the company's operating and financial leverage

demand line of credit See *operating*

depreciation expense deduction from income that reflects the reduction in the value of tangible assets over a period of time

depreciation recapture amount by which the salvage value (sale price) of an asset exceeds the asset's book or carrying value

depreciation reduction in value of a long-lived, tangible asset over a specified period of time

depreciation tax shield tax savings associated with the depreciation deduction for tax purposes, which is the amount of the depreciation expense multiplied by the marginal tax rate

derivative contract whose value depends on or is derived from a specified asset or variable

detachable warrant warrant that can be sold to investors apart from the security with which it was originally issued

diluted earnings per share (diluted EPS) net income divided by the total possible number of common shares that could be outstanding if all potentially dilutive securities outstanding were converted into common shares

direct financing lease contractual agreement in which the party owning the asset records a lease receivable for the promised lease payments, as well as earning interest on the financing

dirty price See *cash price*

disclaimer of opinion audit opinion in which the auditors cannot form an opinion on the business entity's financial statements

disclosure revelation of all material facts so that everyone in the market is buying and selling based on the same material facts about the firm

discount amount by which a bond's value is below its face value

discount factor value that, when multiplied by the future value, results in the present value of this future value

discount yield (DY) method See *bank discount method*

discounted cash flow (DCF) determining a value today by estimating future cash flows and comparing their discounted values with the cash outlay today

discounted payback period number of years required to fully recover the initial cash outlay associated with a capital expenditure, in terms of discounted cash flows

discounting calculating the present value of a future value, considering the time value of money

discrete compounding compound interest in which interest that is paid at specified intervals of time, such as quarterly or annually

disposition effect behavior of individuals in which they avoid realizing any paper losses, but tend to realize paper gains

diversifiable risk See *unique risk*

diversification reduction of risk by investing funds across several assets

dividend coverage ratio ratio of earnings to dividends for a fiscal period

dividend discount model (DDM) model for valuing common shares that assumes common shares are valued according to the present value of their expected future dividends

dividend payout ratio or **dividend payout** portion of earnings paid out in dividends to owners

dividend per share amount of a cash dividend paid by a company

dividend reinvestment plan (DRIP or DRP) plan allowing the use of cash dividends to be reinvested to buy new shares

dividend yield return on a stock in the form of cash dividends; the ratio of the dividend per share to the value of the stock

dividends received deduction amount of the dividends a corporation receives from another corporation that may be deducted from income for tax purposes

double declining balance method allocation of an asset's cost, less salvage value, over the life of the asset, with a rate applied against the declining carrying value of the asset at twice the straight-line rate

due diligence process of evaluating a target company by a potential buyer

DuPont System method of analyzing return ratios by breaking down these ratios into their components

duration measure of interest rate risk that incorporates several factors

Dutch auction bidding process that accepts the bids necessary to sell the intended amount; in the auction of interest-bearing securities, the rate on the securities is set at the rate that is necessary to sell the desired quantity of securities

Dutch auction tender offer method of repurchasing shares that requests shareholders to submit bids for the price they are willing to sell their shares, and then the company will pay the minimum price necessary to acquire the stated number of shares

earnings before interest and taxes (EBIT) earnings before interest and before taxes for nonoperating income and expenses

earnings before interest, taxes, depreciation, and amortization (EBITDA) operating earnings before depreciation and amortization

economic order quantity (EOQ) model approach that defines and determines the optimal inventory level as the level that minimizes the total of shortage costs and carrying costs

economic profit difference between revenue and expenses, after considering the opportunity cost of funds; return on an investment *in excess* of the normal profit

EE/E Savings bond debt obligation of the U.S. Treasury with a maturity of 20 or 30 years, with a fixed interest rate and accrued interest and paid at maturity

effective annual rate (EAR) rate at which a dollar invested grows over a given period; usually stated in percentage terms based on an annual period

efficiency ratio measure of how efficiently a dollar of sales is turned into profits

efficient frontier set of portfolios that offers the highest expected return for their given level of risk

efficient market hypothesis (EMH) theory that markets are efficient and therefore, in its strictest sense, implies that prices accurately reflect all available information at any given time

efficient market market in which prices reacts quickly and relatively accurately to new information

efficient portfolio collection of investments that offers the highest expected return for a given level of risk, or offers the lowest risk for a given expected return

enterprise risk management (ERM) process of identifying and managing risks throughout a business enterprise

enterprise value market value of an entity's debt and equity, less cash and cash equivalents

enterprise value to EBIT ratio total market value of the company, less cash and cash equivalents, divided by earnings before interest and taxes

enterprise value to EBITDA ratio total market value of the company, less cash and cash equivalents, divided by earnings before interest, taxes, and depreciation and amortization

EPS indifference point the EBIT level at which two financing alternatives generate the same EPS

equity trader See *fixed income*

equipment trust certificate type of debt instrument secured by equipment, such as the rolling stock of a railway

equity capital ownership interest of an enterprise

equity instrument or **equity security** ownership stake in a company

equity multiplier financial leverage ratio that is the ratio of total assets to shareholders' equity

equity security ownership interest in an underlying entity, usually a corporation or a partnership

equity swap exchange of a fixed cash flow stream for one based on the return on a stock portfolio

equivalent annual annuity amount of the annuity that is equivalent to the net present value of a project

equivalent annual annuity approach method of comparing mutually exclusive projects that have different useful lives, assuming reinvestment in each in perpetuity

European option option that can be exercised only at maturity

event study statistical examination of stock returns to determine the effect of a particular event on stock prices

ex ante return future or expected return

ex ante standard deviation weighted standard deviation, with the likelihood of each occurrences used as the weights applied to the squared deviations from the expected value; a forward-looking measure of risk

ex post return past or historical, return

ex post standard deviation measure of risk for a set of observations

exchange market secondary market that involves a bidding process that takes place in a specific location

ex-dividend date date on which shares trade without the right to receive a dividend

exercise price the price at which an investor can buy the underlying asset

exercise use the rights of options by buying (in the case of a call option) or selling (in the case of a put option)

expansion projects projects that add something extra to the company in terms of sales or cost savings; their new cash flows are incremental cash flows

expected return estimated future return

expiration date the last date on which options can be converted or exercised

extendible bond debt obligation that allows the bondholder to extend the bonds' maturity dates

external financing requirements (EFR) funds that a company must raise using borrowing or selling equity interests

externalities consequences that result from an investment that may benefit or harm unrelated third parties

face value promised fixed amount in a note or bond agreement

factor financial company that buys receivables and collects on these accounts

factoring arrangement sale of a company's receivables, at a discount, to a financial company specializing in collections; outsourcing of the collections to a factor

fair market value (FMV) highest price obtainable in an open and unrestricted market by parties who are informed and trading freely, without coercion

fair value amount reasonably expected to be received for an asset, or settled in the case of a liability, between knowledgeable, willing parties to the transaction, which may be based on present value or market valuations

fairness opinion appraisal by an independent party of the value of the shares

Fama–French model pricing model that uses three factors (a market factor, the market value of a firm's common equity, and the ratio of a firm's book equity value to its market value of equity) to relate expected returns to risk

Federal Insurance Office (FIO) federal agency responsible for monitoring and advising regulators about insurance companies' risk and solvency

Federal Open Market Committee (FOMC) twelve-member committee that affects the monetary policy of the U.S.

Federal Reserve System (the Fed) central bank of the U.S., consisting of the Board of Governors and twelve district banks

finance motive holding cash in anticipation of major outlays, such as lump-sum loan repayments and dividend payments

finance study of how and under what terms funds are allocated between those with excess funds and those who need funds

Financial Accounting Standards Board (FASB) organization that establishes the accounting principles for U.S. financial reporting

financial analyst finance professional who performs research, conducts detailed analyses of individual investments, and makes recommendations on overall financial strategy

financial break-even point return on investment or quantity produced or sold at which a company's ROE is zero

financial derivative investment whose value is based on some other investment

financial distress state of business failing where bankruptcy seems imminent if dramatic action is not taken

Financial Industry Regulatory Authority (FINRA) self-regulatory organization that monitors and regulates brokerage firms, brokers, and market intermediaries

financial institution entity that serves as an intermediary in the financial system, and includes banks, credit unions, and financing companies

financial instrument legal agreement that represents an ownership interest, a debt obligation, or other claim on assets or income

financial intermediary entity that transforms the nature of securities in a market

financial lease lease agreement in which essentially all the benefits of ownership transfer to the lessee

financial leverage use of debt, rather than equity, to finance a company

financial management management of the financial resources of a business or government entity, where financial resources include both the investments of the entity, but also how the entity finances these assets

financial planning dynamic system that includes forecasting revenues, forecasting expenses, planning capital expenditures, managing funding needs, and managing risk

financial risk uncertainty regarding the earnings to owners, influenced by the degree to which assets are financed by debt (relative to equity)

financial structure liabilities and equity of a company

financial system environment in which households provide funds to businesses and government

financing sources of money for a company, including using debt or equity, retaining earnings or issuing equity, going public, using bank debt or bonds, and using the short-term money market or borrowing from a bank

five forces based on the work of Michael Porter, the five critical factors that determine the profitability and, hence, attractiveness of investing an industry: entry barriers, the threat of substitutes, the bargaining power of buyers, the bargaining power of suppliers, and rivalry among existing competitors

fixed asset turnover revenues divided by net fixed assets

fixed contractual commitment requirement that the parties involved adhere to specific requirements, such as a specified payment made on a specified date

fixed income finance professional who implements investment strategies and either buys or sells the securities of companies

float funds due a company that are not yet received due to mail and processing delays

float time length of time that elapses between the time the paying company initiates payment, and the time the funds are available for use by the receiving company

flotation costs See *issuing costs*

floating interest rate interest rate that changes regularly

floating rate preferred stock equity security that has a long maturity date and every 3 or 6 months has its dividend reset by an auction mechanism so that the dividend yield is in line with market interest rates

floating-rate bond (floater) debt obligation that has adjustable coupons that are usually tied to some variable short-term rate

flow-through taxation income flows directly to the owners as taxable income and is not taxed at the business entity level

foreign currency future contract to exchange two specified currencies at a specified rate at a specified point of time in the future

forward contract or **forward** agreement in which parties to contract today for an exchange to take place sometime in the future

forward P/E ratio share price divided by the expected earnings per share

forward-rate agreement (FRA) a contract for an exchange based on the interest calculated on a notional amount based on the difference between specified fixed and floating interest rates

fourth market trading of securities directly between investors without the involvement of brokers or dealers

framing manner in which something is presented, which may influence how someone feels about this something

free cash flow (FCF) funds available to the business, calculated as operating cash flows less capital expenditures

free cash flow of equity (FCFE) funds available to owners, calculated as cash flow from operations, less capital expenditures, plus net borrowing

friendly acquisition acquisition of a target company that is willing to be taken over

full payout lease See *financial lease*

future value annuity factor sum of the individual periods' future value compound factors that, when multiplied by the amount of an annuity, provides the future value of the annuity

future value interest factor See *compound factor*

futures contracts or **futures** standardized forward contract

general obligation bond debt security backed by the general credit of the issuer

general partnership form of business in which all partners share in the management and the profits of the business, and the income and losses from the business are reflected on the individual owners' tax returns

generally accepted accounting principles (GAAP) set of basic principles and conventions that are applied in the preparation of financial statements

geometric mean average or compound growth rate over multiple time periods

going private transaction special form of acquisition where a publicly traded company is taken private

goodwill excess amount of a target company's purchase price over the fair market value of its equity; intangible asset that is the difference between what is paid for another business entity and the value of the acquired business entity's assets

Gordon model model of the value of a share of stock that assumes that dividends are a growing perpetuity

government-sponsored entity (GSEs) financial service corporations that are created by the government to perform a service, such as buying mortgages

gross profit margin revenues minus the cost of goods sold, divided by revenues

gross property, plant, and equipment sum of book values of all physical long-lived assets

growing perpetuity stream of cash flows that grows at a constant rate, forever

growth rate rate of increase in an amount or value

half-year convention use of half of a year's depreciation in the first year of depreciating an asset

hedge position formulated to reduce or eliminate an exposure to risk, generally by taking a position opposite a position that the investor has already assumed; transaction designed to reduce the chance of a loss

hedging offsetting an investment position to reduce risk

held-to-maturity method of accounting is used when marketable debt securities are reported at cost

hierarchy principle theory based on the fact that rating agencies rate debt issues and not companies; rating agencies rate each class of debt lower than the previous class, unless there is very little of the higher-ranked debt outstanding

high-yield debt See *speculative debt*

historical cost amount paid for an asset when it is purchased

holder of record person who officially owns a share or shares on a given date

horizontal merger merger in which two companies in the same industry combine

hostile takeover takeover in which the target has no desire to be acquired and actively rebuffs the acquirer and refuses to provide any confidential information

hurdle rate minimum acceptable return on an investment project; return on an investment required to create value; below this rate, an investment would destroy value

hybrid security security that is part debt and part equity

I Savings bond debt obligation of the U.S. Treasury that protects the investor against inflation

implied volatility estimate of the price volatility of the underlying asset based on observed option prices

in the money option would generate a positive payoff if generated today

income bond debt obligation issued after a reorganization with the interest tied to some cash flow level for the company and with quite long maturity dates

income statement or **statement of earnings** summary of the company's performance over a period of time, typically a fiscal quarter or a fiscal year

income yield return earned by investors as a periodic cash flow

indenture agreement legal agreement that binds the issuer of a security to specified requirements, minimum financial conditions, or prohibitions

independent director member of the company's board of directors who is not employed by the company

independent projects projects that have no relationship with one another; accepting one project has no impact on the decision to accept another project

indifference point the quantity produced and sold or return on investment at which two financing strategies provide the same return on equity

indenture agreement See *bond indenture*

initial cash flow See *investment cash flow*

initial cash outlay See *investment cash flow*

initial margin relatively small deposit made with the clearinghouse, usually between 2 and 10 percent of the value of the contract

initial public offering (IPO) first sale of equity interests to the public

insurance contract between two parties in which one party assumes the risk of the other party and receives compensation in the form of an insurance premium

insurance premium payment made to transfer risk from one party to another

intangible asset asset that does not have a physical presence

interest compensation for the time value of money

interest payment or **coupon** amount paid on a bond at regular intervals

interest rate risk sensitivity of bond prices to changes in interest rates

interest rate swap exchange of interest payments on a principal amount in which borrowers switch loan rates

interest-bearing debt obligations that require the payment of interest

interest-on-interest interest earned on previously accumulated interest

intermediate-term bond debt obligation with a maturity between 4 and 10 years

intermediation transfer of funds from lenders to borrowers

internal rate of return (IRR) discount rate that makes the present value of all project cash flows equal to zero; return implicit in a set of cash flows, assuming reinvestment of cash flows in a similar-yielding investment

International Accounting Standards Board (IASB) organization that establishes the accounting principles for business entities in the European Economic Community

International Financial Reporting Standards (IFRS) accounting standards promulgated by the International Accounting Standards Board (IASB)

intrinsic value value of an option at expiration; it is positive when the option is in the money and zero when it is out of the money

inventory policy decisions on the levels of inventory to hold

inventory turnover cost of goods sold divided by inventory

invested capital sum of owners' equity and short- and long-term interest-bearing debt

investment analyst See *financial analyst*

investment cash flow total cash outlay required to initiate an investment project, including the change in net working capital and associated opportunity costs

investment grade bond rating that means the issuer is likely to meet payment obligations

investment opportunity schedule (IOS) internal rate of return expected on each potential investment opportunity, ranked in descending order

investment yield method See *bond equivalent method*

investment-grade debt debt obligation with a credit rating of AAA, AA, A or BBB (or Aaa, Aa, A, Baa)

investments deals with financial markets and securities, including stocks, bonds, and options.

issuer party that receives funds in exchange for a security, such as a bond

issue-specific premium additional yield, relative to straight, option-free bonds, required by investors when bonds have features that cause them to be more or less attractive to investors

issuing costs costs incurred by a company when it issues new securities

junior debt debt that ranks behind other securities in terms of the issuer's capitalization

junk bond speculative bonds with ratings below investment grade; often called high-yield bonds

justified P/E multiple that is considered sustainable over the long-term

just-in-time (JIT) inventory system inventory management approach that fine-tunes the receipt of raw materials so that they arrive exactly when they are required in the production process and thereby reduce inventory to its lowest possible level

lessee person or company that leases an item, paying a periodic amount in exchange for the use of the item

lessor owner of the asset; conveys the right to use in return for payment

letter of intent letter signed by an acquiring company scoping out the terms of agreement of its acquisition, including legal terms

leveraged buyout (LBO) See *management buyout (MBO)*

leveraged lease three-way agreement among the lessee, lessor, and a third-party lender in which the lessor buys the asset with only a small down payment, and the lender supplies the remaining financing

limited liability company (LLC) business organized as a separate legal entity in which owners have limited liability, but the income is passed through to the owners for tax purposes

limited liability limit on the financial responsibility of owners of a business entity to the amount of their investment

limited partnership or **limited liability partnership (LLP)** form of business in which there are both general and limited partners, with general partners making management decisions and having unlimited liability, and the limited partners being passive investors with limited liability

line of credit borrowing arrangement that permits a company to borrow up to a predetermined amount at a specified rate of interest

liquidity how quickly something can be converted into cash

liquidity premium additional yield offered on bonds that are less liquid than others

liquidity support ensuring money is available to pay off a debt, often in the form of a dedicated backup line of credit from a bank that ensures companies have money to pay off commercial paper if the companies cannot roll it over by selling to new investors

loan contract in which the borrower uses the funds of the lender, and, in exchange, repays the amount borrowed plus compensation for the use of the funds

loan-to-value ratio ratio of the amount of a loan to the value of the collateral used as security on the loan

lock-box system arrangement of local post office boxes for customers to mail their payments to and authorizing the local bank to empty these boxes and deposit the checks into the company's account

London Interbank Offering Rate (LIBOR) average of the lending rates of selected European banks to their best customers

long call position investment in the right to buy an asset

long hedge commitment to buy a commodity by buying a futures contract

loss aversion willingness to avoid losses that is disproportionate to the willingness to seek similar-sized gains

low-grade debt See *speculative debt*

maintenance margin minimum amount that must be maintained in a margin account

management buyout (MBO) a purchase of a company in which the purchasers are a company's managers; usually involves high levels of debt financing

mandatory convertible preferred stock preferred equity security that must be converted to common shares at or before a specified date

mandatory redeemable preferred stock or **mandatorily redeemable preferred stock** security that an issuer is obligated to repurchase at a specified price at a specified point in time or event

margin call requirement to add money and increase an equity position to a minimum level

margin good faith deposit with the clearinghouse by both the buyer and the seller to ensure they complete the transaction

marginal cost of capital cost of raising one more dollar of capital

marginal or **incremental cash flow** the additional cash flow that result from a capital budgeting decision, generated by a new project

marked to market position valuation that considers all unrealized profits and losses

market capitalization total value of the company's shares outstanding, calculated as the product the market price per share of stock and the number of shares of stock outstanding.

market conversion price value of a share of stock that, considering the conversion ratio of the convertible bond, is equivalent to the value of the bond

market intermediary entity that facilitates the working of markets and helps provide direct intermediation but does not change the nature of the transaction; also called a *broker*

market portfolio portfolio that contains all risky securities in the market

market price of risk incremental expected return divided by the incremental risk; indicates the additional expected return that the market demands for an increase in risk

market rate of interest See *yield to maturity (YTM)*

market risk systematic part of total risk that cannot be eliminated by diversification

market risk premium compensation, in the form of expected return, for assuming the risk of the market portfolio; conditions; expected return on the market minus the risk-free rate

market-to-book value ratio or **market-to-book ratio (M/B)** market price per share divided by the book value per share; alternatively, the market capitalization divided by the book value of shareholders' equity

mark-to-market writing the value of an asset up or down, depending on its current market value

master limited partnership form of business in which there are general and limited partners, with limited partner interests traded in the public market

materials requirement planning (MRP) detailed computerized system that orders inventory in conjunction with production schedules to determine the level of raw materials and work-in-process that must be on hand to meet finished goods demand

maturity point in time at which the borrower repays the amount borrowed

maturity value See *face value*

medium of exchange something that provides a way to buy goods and services but has no value in and of itself

medium-term note (MTN) debt obligation that matures in 1 to 30 years

mental accounting process of investors separating money into different accounts in their thought process

merger combination of two companies into a new legal entity

method of multiples approach to valuing an entity or the equity of an entity by applying the market multiples of comparable companies

minimum variance frontier curve in return–standard deviation space, produced when determining the expected return-risk combinations available to investors from a given set of assets by allowing the portfolio weights to vary

minimum variance portfolio (MVP) portfolio that lies on the efficient frontier and has the minimum amount of portfolio risk available from any possible combination of available assets

minority freeze-out acquisition of the remaining interest by a controlling shareholder

minority interest represents the interest in a company that is not owned by the controlling parent company

modern portfolio theory set of theories that explain how rational investors, who are risk averse, can select a set of investments that maximize the expected return for a given level of risk

Modified Accelerated Cost Recovery System (MACRS) system of depreciation prescribed in the U.S. tax code that requires first identifying the asset's MACRS life and then applying the appropriate rate of cost recovery

Molodovsky effect trailing P/E ratios of cyclical companies are overstated during low points of the economic cycle

money market instrument security with less than 1 year in maturity that trades in markets or can be privately placed

money market security short-term debt instrument

moneyness status of whether the option is in, at, or out of the money

mortgage bond debt obligation that is secured, or backed, by specified real estate as collateral

mortgage loan, usually for real estate, that involves level, periodic payments consisting of interest and principal repayment over a specified payment period

mortgage-backed securities claims on the cash flows of a pool of mortgages

multi-stage growth dividend discount model version of the dividend discount model that accounts for different levels of growth in earnings and dividends

mutually exclusive projects projects for which the acceptance of one precludes the acceptance of one or more of the alternative projects

naïve diversification See *random diversification*

naked warrant warrant that is issued without being attached to another security issue of the issuer

Nationally Recognized Statistical Rating Organizations (NRSROs) credit rating firms that are registered with the U.S. Securities and Exchange Commission

negative covenant provision in the indenture agreement that prohibits issuers from taking certain actions

net operating cycle length of time it takes to convert the investment of cash in inventory back into cash, considering that purchases are acquired using trade credit

net operating loss (NOL) loss generated when a company's tax deductions are greater than its taxable income

net payment payment representing the difference between the fixed and floating rates, multiplied by the notional amount of the contract

net present value (NPV) added value from a capital project; sum of the present value of all future cash flows generated by an initial cash outlay, less the present value of the investment outlays

net present value profile or **NPV profile** graph of a project's net present value against the discount rate

net profit margin net income divided by revenues

net property, plant, and equipment difference between the gross property, plant, and equipment and accumulated depreciation

net realizable value amount the company would reasonably get for the asset if it had to dispose of it in an orderly sale, or the settlement value for a liability

net working capital (NWC) difference between a company's current assets and its current liabilities

new efficient frontier or **super-efficient frontier** portfolios composed of the risk-free rate and the tangent portfolio that offer the highest expected rate of return for any given level of risk

no-arbitrage principle rule that two otherwise identical assets cannot sell at different prices

nominal interest rate rate charged for lending today's dollars in return for getting dollars back in the future, without taking into account the purchasing power of those future dollars

nominal rate See *annual percentage rate (APR)*

nondiversifiable risk See *market risk*

nonsystematic risk See *unique risk*

nontax lease contractual arrangement in which the lease is considered a purchase for tax purposes

nonvoting shares common shares that have no voting rights

normal profit return on an investment that compensates the investor with the explicit and implicit costs, where implicit costs include the opportunity cost of the investor's capital

no-shop clause clause in a letter of intent stating that the target agrees not to look for another buyer, demonstrating its commitment to close the transaction

note debt instrument that takes the form of a security, generally with a maturity between one and ten years

notional amount or **notional value** base amount used to determine a position in a futures or options contract

number of days of inventory See *days sales in inventory (DPO)*

NYSE Euronext world's largest stock market

off-balance-sheet financing financing arrangement that does not appear in a company's balance sheet, but only in the notes to the financial statements

offering memorandum description of a security's terms, used for private placements of securities; document describing a target company's important features to potential buyers

offsetting cancelling a futures position by making an equivalent but opposite transaction

open account basis credit in which the collateral is the assets sold to the customer

open interest number of contracts outstanding; the true amount of futures market activity

open market repurchase method of repurchasing shares in the market through brokers

operating assets short-lived assets that support the company's long-term investments

operating break-even level of sales at which the company covers all its variable and fixed operating costs

operating cash flows cash flows that are estimated to occur as a result of the investment decision, comprising the associated expected incremental increase in after-tax operating cash flow

operating cycle or **days working capital (DWC)** average time that is required for a company to acquire inventory, sell it, and collect the proceeds; length of time it takes for the company's investment of cash in inventory to be converted into cash in the form of collected accounts

operating income or **operating profit** earnings before interest and before taxes for nonoperating income and expenses

operating lease rental agreement in which some of the benefits of ownership do not transfer to the lessee, remaining with the lessor

operating leverage volatility in operating income from changes in units produced and sold as a result of the relation between fixed and variable operating costs

operating margin operating income divided by revenues

operating or **demand line of credit** lending facility that is made available by the bank for the company's operating purposes and that generally cannot be used to back up a commercial paper program; these demand loans can be cancelled at any time

operating profit margin See *operating margin*

operating risk uncertainty regarding operating earnings based on the mix of fixed and variable operating costs

operational liabilities obligations of a company that arise from normal operations

opportunity costs cash flow that must be forgone as a result of an investment decision

optimal cash balance amount of cash that balances the risks of illiquidity against the sacrifice in expected return that is associated with maintaining cash

option buyer party who buys an option

option premium value of the option

option right, but not the obligation, to buy or sell a specific asset at a specific price, within a specified period of time or on a specific date

option writer party who sells an option

ordinary annuity equal payments from an investment over a fixed number of years, with the payments made at the end of each period

over-the-counter (OTC) market See *dealer market*

out of the money option would generate a negative payoff if exercised today

paper See *bill*

paper loss capital loss that people do not accept as losses until they actually sell and realize them

par value or **face value** or **maturity value** amount paid at maturity for traditional bonds

participating preferred stock equity issue in which a fixed dividend is supplemented with an additional dividend if the issuer's common stock dividend exceeds a specified threshold

partnership business owned and operated by two or more people

passive investment strategy buy-and-hold strategies and the purchase of such products as index mutual funds or exchange-traded funds (ETFs) that replicate the performance of a market index

payback period number of years required to fully recover the initial cash outlay associated with a capital expenditure

payment date or **payable date** actual date the dividend is paid to shareholders

payment policy decisions on how quickly the company pays its bills

payoff proceeds that would be generated from the option if today was the expiration date

pecking order order in which companies prefer to raise financing, starting with internal cash flow and then debt, and finally issuing common equity

percentage of sales method approach to forecasting balance sheet and income statement accounts that uses a fixed percentage of sales from the previous period to determine amounts in a future period

perpetuity annuity that provides periodic payments forever

plain vanilla swap "fixed for floating" interest rate swap; the simplest and most commonly used type of swap

plowback ratio proportion of earnings reinvested in a company

poison pill See *shareholder rights plan*

portfolio collection of assets, such as stocks and bonds, that are combined and considered a single asset

portfolio manager professional in charge of the overall management of a portfolio

positive covenant clause in a bond indenture that requires specific actions by the issuer

precautionary motive holding cash to take care of unanticipated required outlays of cash, such as unexpected repairs on equipment

pre-emptive right right of shareholders to maintain proportional ownership in a company when new shares are issued

preferred share certificate of ownership of a fixed claim on the equity of a corporation

preferred stock equity security that usually entitles the owner to fixed dividend payments that must be made before any dividends are paid to common shareholders; ownership of a corporation that has preference over common stock

premium amount by which a bond's value is above its face value

prepayment the payment of a debt before its due date

present value annuity factor sum of the discount factors that, when multiplied by the amount of an annuity payment, results in the present value of the annuity

present value of existing opportunities (PVEO) value today of the company's current operations assuming no new investment

present value of growth opportunities (PVGO) amount of the value of an asset that is attributable to the expected growth opportunities of the asset's cash flows; value today of the company's future investments

present value sum of the discounted expected future cash flows arising from the asset or expected to be paid in the case of a liability

price earnings (P/E) ratio share price divided by the earnings per share

price-to-cash-flow (P/CF) ratio: market price per share divided by per share cash flow

price-to-sales (P/S) ratio market price per share divided by sales per share

primary market market that involves the issue of new securities by the borrower in return for cash from investors (or lenders)

prime lending rate standard cost of the operating line; the interest rate banks use to calculate their other interest rates

principal amount loaned or the amount of the investment

productivity ratios measurements of how productive the company is in generating revenues from its assets

profitability index (PI) discounted cash flow approach used to evaluate capital expenditure decisions; the ratio of a project's discounted net incremental cash inflows over the discounted cash outflows

profitability ratio See *efficiency ratio*

project cost of capital discount rate that reflects the return suppliers of capital require considering the project's risk

promised yield quoted interest rate received if the issuer does not default and the investor is paid off on time, as promised

promissory note written promise to pay back a loan

prospect theory is the area of study of how individuals make choices given information about probabilities and outcomes

prospectus detailed document that describes the security offering, which is required by the Securities and Exchange Commission for all public offerings

protective covenant clause in a bond indenture that restrict the actions of the issuer; covenants can be positive or negative

purchase fund provisions requirements that the repurchase of a certain amount of debt can occur only if it can be repurchased at or below a given price

purchase method method of accounting for business combinations where one company assumes the fair market value of all of the assets and liabilities of the other (target) company and all operating results included from the date of acquisition going forward

pure play approach estimating betas and the risk associated with an investment by estimating the weighted average cost of capital of single line of business companies with a line of business similar to the project being evaluated

put option right, but not the obligation, to sell an underlying asset at a fixed price within or at a specified time

putable bond debt obligation that allows the bondholder to sell the bonds back to the issuer at predetermined prices at specified times earlier than the maturity date

qualified dividend cash dividends from a stock held more than 60 days during the 121-day period beginning before the ex-dividend date

qualified opinion audit opinion in which the auditors find that the financial statements are presented fairly in accordance with generally accepted accounting principles except for a matter of qualification

quick ratio or **acid test ratio** cash, plus marketable securities and accounts receivable, divided by current liabilities

random diversification randomly buying assets without regard to relevant investment characteristics

random walk hypothesis theory that prices follow a random walk, with price changes over time being independent of one another

range measure of dispersion calculated as the difference between the maximum and minimum values

real option opportunity to take an action that changes a capital project, such as expansion, abandonment, contraction, and delaying of a project, in which this option adds value to the project

real option valuation (ROV) valuation of a capital investment considering the value of all the options that the investment provides, such as the option to expand, abandon, or wait

receivables turnover or **accounts receivable turnover** revenues divided by accounts receivables

record date or **date of record** date that determines the holder of record; the date that determines who receives the forthcoming dividend, as declared by the board of directors

redeemable preferred stock See *retractable preferred stock*

relative valuation valuing a company relative to other comparable companies

replacement projects projects that involve the replacement of an existing asset with a new one

representativeness tendency for people to judge something, such as an investment, by the degree to which this something resembles something else in the person's experience

required rate of return or **discount rate** market interest rate or the investor's opportunity cost; minimum return that investors expect to earn on the investment in the stock; rate of return investors need to tempt them to invest in an asset

residual owner equity owner who receive any remaining cash flows or property (on the dissolution of the business) after all other commitments have been satisfied

residual theory of dividends theory that the dividends paid out should be the residual cash flow that remains after the company has taken care of all of its investment requirements

retail broker and **private banker** financial professional who helps clients, usually people who have small to medium-sized accounts, manage their personal wealth

retention ratio proportion of earnings reinvested in the company; the complement of the dividend payout ratio

retractable bond See *putable bond*

retractable preferred stock equity interest that gives the investor the right to sell it back to the issuer, thus creating an early maturity date

return on assets (ROA) net income divided by total assets

return on equity (ROE) net income divided by shareholders' equity; net income divided by the book value of equity

return on invested capital (ROI or ROIC) ratio of operating income to invested capital

revenue bond debt obligation backed by a specific revenue stream

reverse stock split reduction in shares outstanding by exchanging fewer shares for existing outstanding shares

revolving line of credit See *term line of credit*

reward-to-risk ratio See *Sharpe ratio*

reward-to-variablility ratio See *Sharpe ratio*

rights offering issuance of the opportunity to purchase new shares of stock of a company

risk appetite specification of how much risk a company will tolerate

risk averse to dislike risk, and require compensation to assume additional risk

risk chance that future outcomes may not turn out as expected

risk premium difference in yield that compensates the investor for the assumption of additional risks; expected payoff to get into a risky situation; compensation for bearing risk

risk-adjusted discount rate discount rate that reflects the overall riskiness of the projects

risk-based models models that estimate costs based on the associated risks

risk-free rate (r_f) compensation for the time value of money

risk-free rate of return compensation, in the form of a return, for the time value of money

sales and trading activity that involves executing trades on behalf of the clients and conducting proprietary trading for the dealer itself by using the bank's own capital

sales risk uncertainty regarding the price and quantity of goods and services sold

sale-type lease or **sale and leaseback (SLB) agreement** or **sale-leaseback agreement** an agreement in which the owner of an asset sells it to another party and then leases the asset back

salvage value estimated sale price of an asset at the end of its useful life

Sarbanes-Oxley Act (SOX) law passed in 2002 in response to accounting scandals intended to restore confidence in corporate governance and public accounting

scenario analysis examination of how an investment's cash flows change in response to varying more than one input variable at a time estimates at the same time, such as sales or costs

seasoned bond issues actively traded bond issues that have been outstanding for some time

secondary market trading (or market) environment that permits investors to buy and sell existing securities

secured debt debt obligation backed with collateral

secured financing financing that is based on an underlying asset that serves as collateral in the event of a default

Securities and Exchange Commission (SEC) U.S. agency responsible for ensuring that financial markets are fair, orderly, and efficient

securities law body of law that ensures, through capital market regulations, that all investors have equal access to, and an equal opportunity to react to, new and relevant information and that governs the buying and selling of assets

securitization process of packaging loans and/or receivables together to create new securities that have rights to specific cash flows from this pool

security analyst financial professional who monitors the valuations of the companies and makes recommendations to buy and sell a company's shares

security market line (SML) relationship between market risk and the required rate of return for any risky security, whether an individual asset or a portfolio

security negotiable financial instrument that is evidence of indebtedness or ownership

self-regulatory organization (SRO) organization that oversees and monitors its members and member organizations

selling the crown jewels sale of a target company's key assets that the acquiring company is most interested in to make it less attractive for takeover

sell-side analyst person whose job it is to monitor companies and regularly report on their value through earnings forecasts and buy/sell/hold recommendations; employed by the investment banks that underwrite and sell securities to the public

semi-strong-form efficient characteristic of a market in which that all publicly known and available information is reflected in security prices

senior debt debt that has preference over other debt obligations in terms of the issuer's capitalization

senior vice-president of finance in some companies functions as the CFO

sensitivity analysis examination of how an investment's NPV changes as the value of one input at a time is changed

separation theorem theory that the investment decision (how to construct the portfolio of risky assets) is separate from the financing decision (how much should be invested or borrowed in the risk-free asset)

settlement price price used to settle futures contracts; usually the daily closing price

share or **share of stock** security that represents a portion of the stock of a company

shareholder or **stockholder** owner of an equity security of a company

shareholder rights plan plan by a target company that allows its shareholders to buy more shares at a discount price in the event of a takeover, to make it less attractive

shareholder value at risk (SVAR) measure of the value that is at risk for a party to a merger or acquisition

shareholders' equity ownership interest of the corporation, as represented on the balance sheet

Sharpe ratio measure of portfolio performance that describes how well an asset's return compensates investors for the risk taken

short hedge commitment to sell a commodity by selling a futures contract

short position negative position in an investment; the position taken by the option writer

short-form merger merger that takes place without shareholder approval that follows an acquisition of over 89.5 percent of the target company's shares

simple cash flow net income plus depreciation, amortization, and depletion

simple interest interest paid or received on only the initial investment

sinking fund call repurchase of bonds that have a sinking fund provision permitting the issuer to buy back the bonds

sinking fund provision requirement that the issuer set aside funds each year to be used to pay off the debt at maturity

small and medium-sized enterprise (SME) business that generally has fewer than 50 employees

soft-retractable preferred shares equity interest that gives the issuer the choice of redeeming the stock for cash or in its common shares

sole proprietorship business owned and operated by one person

sovereign debt obligation of a national government that is denominated in a currency other than that of the issuing government

special dividend cash dividend paid in addition to the regular dividend

special purpose vehicle (SPV) or **special purpose entity (SPE)** entity created to issue securities and hold assets, often the assets provided by the parent company creating the entity

speculative debt debt that is not investment grade; debt rated below BBB or Baa

speculative motive holding cash to take advantage of "bargains," such as the opportunity to purchase raw materials very cheaply

spontaneous liabilities accruals and payables that arise during the normal course of business

spot contract agreement for the immediate purchase of an asset

spot price price that is established today for immediate delivery

spread difference in yields, generally expressed in basis points

stable rating philosophy ratings based on structural and not on cyclical factors; changes in ratings are made not based on temporary changes in the economy but on clear structural changes in a company's credit

stakeholder any party affected by the decisions and actions of an entity

stamping fee fee paid to the financial institution accepting a bankers' acceptance

standard deviation measure of risk; measure of dispersion

stated rate See *annual percentage rate (APR)*

statement of cash flows summary of a company's cash receipts and disbursements over a specified period

statement of financial condition See *balance sheet*

static trade-off theory theory where a company uses debt to maximize its tax advantages up to the point where these benefits are outweighed by the associated estimated costs of financial distress and bankruptcy

stock dividend dividend paid in additional shares rather than cash

stock ownership interest in a company

stock split proportionate distribution of shares outstanding, typically involving an increase in shares outstanding of more than 25 percent

straight bond or **straight coupon bond** debt obligation that commits the issuer to pay a fixed amount of interest periodically, and then repay the principal amount at maturity

straight preferred share preferred share that has no maturity date and pays a fixed dividend at regular intervals, usually quarterly

straight preferred stock preferred stock with no embedded option, for which the issuer promises to pay a fixed, periodic dividend

straight value value of a convertible bond without considering the conversion feature of the bond

straight-line depreciation allocation of an asset's cost, less salvage value, over the life of the asset, with an equal portion allocated to each period

strategy is the direction that the entity intends on moving in the long-term

stress test scenario-based evaluation of a company's solvency, where the scenario is the worst-case scenario

stress testing evaluation of outcomes based on economic downturns or particular stresses, generally with extreme risk exposures

stress tests "what-if" examinations of the value of an asset or business entity under challenging conditions, such as an increase in interest rates or a decline in economic conditions

strike price See *exercise price*

strong-form efficient characteristic of a market in which stock prices fully reflect all information, which includes both public and private information

Sub S corporation corporation that elects to be taxed as a partnership

subordinated debt unsecured debt that ranks behind other debt of the issuer

subprime mortgage home loan to a borrower with poor credit who would not otherwise qualify for a conventional mortgage

sunk costs costs that have already been incurred, cannot be recovered, and should not influence current capital budgeting decisions

sustainable growth expected growth rate of a business entity considering the entity's return on equity and its earnings retention

sustainable growth rate (SGR) earnings retention ratio multiplied by return on equity; growth rate that the business entity is expected to sustain into the future

swap contract or **swap** an agreement between two parties to exchange cash flows in the future

synergy value created from economies of integrating a target and acquiring company; the amount by which the value of the combined company exceeds the sum value of the two individual companies

systemic risk uncertainty that affects the larger economy

takeover transfer of control from one ownership group to another

tangent portfolio risky portfolio on the efficient frontier whose tangent line cuts the vertical axis at the risk-free rate

tax clienteles different preferences for receiving dividend income as a result of investors having different tax situations

tax lease contractual arrangement in which the owner of the asset receives the benefits of depreciation, and the party that rents or leases the asset incurs a tax deductible expense

taxes payable amounts that are owed to federal, state, or local governments

technical analysis study of historical trading information to identify patterns in trading data that can be used to invest successfully

tender offer offer made directly to shareholders to purchase shares of stock

tender to sign an authorization accepting a takeover bid made to target company shareholders

Term Asset-Backed Securities Loan Facility (TALF) U.S. government program to inject capital in the financial system by lending funds to investors of specific high-quality asset-backed securities

term line of credit line of credit extended by a bank to a company for a specific amount that automatically adjusts as payments are made or received

term loan borrowing to finance longer-term requirements, such as equipment purchases, which have a fixed maturity and require repayment to be made on a fixed schedule

term preferred share See *retractable preferred stock*

term structure of interest rates relationship between interest rates and the term to maturity on underlying debt instruments

term to maturity time remaining to the maturity date

terminal (or ending) cash flow total cash flow expected to be generated in the terminal year of a project, aside from that year's operating cash flow

termination fee fee paid to an acquirer or target should the other party terminate the acquisition, often stated as a percent of the value of the transaction

terms of credit due date, discount date, and discount amount, where applicable, offered to customers

third market trading of securities that are listed on organized exchanges in the OTC market

time to expiration or **time to expiry** time remaining for an option before it expires

time value difference between the option premium and the intrinsic value

time value of money idea that money invested today has more value than the same amount invested later

times interest earned (TIE) or **interest coverage ratio** earnings before interest and taxes divided by interest expense

top-down analysis investment strategy that focuses on strategic decisions, such as which industries or products the company should be involved in, looking at the overall economic picture

total asset turnover ratio (or **total asset turnover**) sales or revenues divided by total assets

total return income yield plus the capital gain (or loss) yield

trade credit financing provided to customers for the purchase of a product or service

trade payables See *accounts payable*

trading securities method of accounting for marketable securities occurs when unrealized gains or losses are reported in net income

traditional cash flow cash flow measure that is equal to net income plus noncash expenses such as depreciation and deferred taxes

trailing P/E ratio share price divided by the most recent year's earnings per share

transactions motive holding cash to pay for normal operations, such as bills

treasurer one of the two main finance jobs in a nonfinancial company; focuses on the finance side: forecasting, pension management, capital budgeting, cash management, credit management, financing, risk management

Treasury bill (T-bill) obligation of the federal government with maturities up to one year that are sold at a discount from face value

Treasury Inflation-Protected Securities (TIPS) bonds issued by the U.S. government that provide investors with protection against inflation

Treasury security obligation of a national government

treasury shares shares of stock bought back by the issuer

Troubled Asset Relief Program (TARP) U.S. government program to infuse capital in the financial system by purchasing assets and equity from troubled financial institutions

true lease See *tax lease*

trust preferred security preferred equity security issued by a trust created by a company; the company backs the obligations of the preferred security

two-stage growth rate model valuation model for equity in which there are two stages, each with a different growth rate

U.S. Treasury bond obligation of the U.S. government that has a maturity of 30 years and that pays interest semi-annually

U.S. Treasury note obligation of the U.S. government that has a maturity of 2, 3, 5, 7, or 10 years and pays interest semi-annually

underlying or **underlying asset** variable or asset on which derivative is based

unique risk company-specific part of total risk that is eliminated by diversification

unlimited liability responsibility for obligations of a business that extends beyond the original investment, including personal assets

unqualified opinion audit opinion in which the auditors find that the financial statements are presented fairly in accordance with generally accepted accounting principles

unsubordinated debt unsecured debt that ranks first with the company; no other unsecured debt ranks ahead of it

value at risk (VaR) tool for evaluating the risk of a loss over a specified period of time

variance standard deviation squared; denoted as σ^2 and expressed in units of squared units

vertical merger combination of two or more companies in which one company acquires a supplier or another company that is closer to its existing customers

wages payable amounts that are owed the employees of the business

warrant securities that provide the investor with the option to convert or exchange the warrant into another security, such as a common stock

weak-form efficient characteristic of a market in which asset prices fully reflect all market data, which refers to all past price and volume trading information

weighted average cost of capital (WACC) marginal cost of raising an additional dollar of capital

white knight entity that rescues a target company from a hostile takeover by making a counterbid

working capital assets used in the day-to-day operation of a business; current, operating assets of a company; also known as operating assets

working capital management manner in which a company manages both its current assets (cash and marketable securities, accounts receivable, and inventories) and its current liabilities (accounts payable, notes payables, and short term borrowing arrangements)

working capital ratio current assets divided by total assets

yield curve graphical representation of the term structure of interest rates, based on debt instruments that are from the same issuer

yield spread difference between the yield on one debt instrument and the yield on another

yield to call (YTC) return on a callable bond, assuming that the bond is called away before maturity

yield to maturity (YTM) discount rate used to value the cash flows of a debt obligation

zero-coupon bond or **zero-coupon note** (or **zero**) debt obligation issued at a discount from its face value, pays no coupons, and repays the face value at the maturity date

GLOBAL PERSPECTIVE

Equity Markets

Forms of Business

The Structure of the Balance Sheet

Tax Burden for Companies, 2010

Are U.S. GAAP and IFRS Financial Ratios Comparable?

Islamic Law and Interest

Issuing Debt in Different Currencies

The Linkage Between U.S. and the European Union Economies

Is There Still a Benefit from International Diversification?

Market Efficiency Around the World

Factoring in Political Risk

Using Tax Credits to Compete

The Preference for Preferred Shares

What About Companies That Do Business Globally?

What's the Difference Between Insurance and an Option Strategy?

What's the LIBOR Fuss All About?

LESSONS LEARNED

The Benefit of Being Nimble

Economic Value Added

Marking to the Market

Sirius XM, Inc.

P/E Ratios and the Economic Environment

Behold the Miracle of Compounding

I-O Mortgages

Poison Puts

The Yield to Maturity as an Internal Yield

Credit Spreads and the Economy

Irrational Exuberance I, II, and III

Low Price-Earnings Ratio

The Financial Crisis and Risk Models

Debunking Beta

Wacky Indicators

The Trouble with IRR

Tax Breaks Don't Boost Investment: Study

Funding Facility to the Rescue

A Losing Formula

Record Bankruptcies Despite De-Leveraging

Transparency in Dividends

This Is What You've Trained for All Your Life

No New Rules for Securitization

Off-Balance Sheet and Enron

Losses in Good-Will Values Compound Bank Troubles